T

Valuing a Business

The Analysis and Appraisal
of Closely Held Companies

Fifth Edition

Shannon P. Pratt, CFA, FASA, MCBA, MCBC, CM & AA
Chairman and CEO
Shannon Pratt Valuations, Inc.

Alina V. Niculita, CFA, MBA
President and COO
Shannon Pratt Valuations, Inc.

McGraw Hill

New York • Chicago • San Francisco • Lisbon • London
Madrid • Mexico City • Milan • New Delhi • San Juan
Seoul • Singapore • Sydney • Toronto

1 2 3 4 5 6 7 8 9 0   CCW/CCW   0 9 8 7

ISBN 978-0-07-144180-3
MHID 0-07-144180-8

This publication is designed to provide accurate and authoritative information in regard to the subject matter covered. It is sold with the understanding that the publisher is not engaged in rendering legal, accounting, or other professional service. If legal advice or other expert assistance is required, the services of a competent professional person should be sought.

—*From a declaration of principles jointly adopted by a committee of the American Bar Association and a committee of publishers.*

McGraw-Hill books are available at special quantity discounts to use as premiums and sales promotions, or for use in corporate training programs. For more information, please write to the Director of Special Sales, Professional Publishing, McGraw-Hill, Two Penn Plaza, New York, NY 10121-2298. Or contact your local bookstore.

To

The Staff at Shannon Pratt Valuations

*A very bright and dedicated
group of professionals*

Thank you very much for all your support

Contents

Nonoperating Items. Management Compensation and Perquisites.
Transactions Involving Company Insiders. Contingent Assets and Liabilities.
Adjustments to Asset Valuations. *Marketable Securities. Other Assets.*
Computation of Earnings per Share. *Weighted Average Basis. Basic versus
Diluted Earnings.* Computation of Book Value per Share. An Example of the
Effect of Alternative Accounting Methods. Adjusting the Balance Sheet to
Current Values. Summary. Bibliography.

Economic Income Model Produce? Common Errors. *Mismatching the Discount Rate with the Economic Income Measure. Confusing Discount Rates with Capitalization Rates. Projecting Growth Beyond What the Capital Being Valued Will Support. Projecting That Extrapolation of the Recent Past Represents the Best Estimate of Future Results. Discounting a Terminal Value for an Incorrect Number of Periods. Internally Inconsistent Capital Structure Projection. Assumptions That Produce a Standard or Premise of Value Other Than That Called for in the Valuation Engagement.* Summary. Bibliography.

Dividend-Paying Capacity. Multiples of Revenue. Multiple of Stock Value to Asset Value. Treating Nonoperating Assets, Excess Assets, and Asset Deficiencies. *Nonoperating Assets. Marginal Operating Real Estate. Excess Assets or Asset Deficiencies. Beware of Recent Acquisitions* . Multiline Companies. *Procedures for Valuation. "Portfolio Effect."* Typical Adjustments to Reach a Value Conclusion. Valuation Multiples Using Market Value of Invested Capital. Common Errors. *Failure to Conduct an Adequate Search for Guideline Company Data. Failure to Make Appropriate Financial Statement Adjustments to Guideline Companies. Multiples that Mismatch Numerator and Denominator. Simple Reliance on Average of Guideline Company Multiples without Comparative Analysis.* Summary. Bibliography.

Interests. *Illiquidity Factors Affecting Controlling Ownership Interests. Benchmark for the Illiquidity Discount for Controlling Ownership Interests. Differences between Private and Public Company Acquisition Price/ Earnings Multiples.* Factors That Affect the Discounts for Illiquidity and Lack of Marketability. *"Put" Rights. Dividend Payments. Potential Buyers. Size of Interest. Prospect of Public Offering or Sale of the Business. Information Access and Reliability. Restrictive Transfer Provisions. Company Characteristics: Size, Performance, and Risk.* Court Decisions on Discounts for Illiquidity and Lack of Marketability. *Mandelbaum v. Commissioner Reviews Lack of Marketability Factors. Estate of Barge v. Commissioner Considers Lack of Marketability Factors. Okerlund v. United States Approves Pre-IPO Studies. McCord v. Commissioner Lacks Rebuttal. Howard v. Shay Upholds 50 Percent DLOM.* Summary. Bibliography.

Nonparticipating. Convertible versus Nonconvertible. Method of Valuation. *Assessing Dividend and Liquidation Payment Risk. Comparison with Publicly Traded Preferred Stocks. Capitalizing the Income Stream.* Marketability Aspects of Closely Held Preferred Stock. Revenue Ruling 83-120. Summary. Bibliography.

Discounts. Key Person Discount. Contingent Liability Discounts.
Combined Discounts. Premiums. Trapped-In Capital Gains Taxes.
S Corporations. Family Limited Partnerships. *FLP Valuation Issues.*
Validity Issues. Focus on Willing Seller as Well as on Willing Buyer.
Inadequacy of the Valuation. Must Use Empirical Data to Quantify
Variables. Sufficiency of Data. Summary. References.

List of Exhibits

About the Authors

Shannon P. Pratt, CFA, FASA, MCBA, MCBC, CM&AA, is a well-known authority in the field of business valuation and has written numerous books that articulate many of the concepts used in modern business valuation around the world.

Shannon Pratt is Chairman and CEO of Shannon Pratt Valuations, Inc., a business valuation firm headquartered in Portland, Oregon. He is also a member of the board of directors of Paulson Capital Corporation, an investment banking firm that specializes in small-cap IPOs.

Over the last 35 years, he has performed valuation engagements for mergers and acquisitions, employee stock ownership plans (ESOPs), fairness opinions, gift and estate taxes, incentive stock options, buy-sell agreements, corporate and partnership dissolutions, dissenting stockholder actions, damages, marital dissolutions, and many other business valuation purposes. He has testified in a wide variety of federal and state courts across the country and frequently participates in arbitration and mediation proceedings.

He holds an undergraduate degree in business administration from the University of Washington and a doctorate in business administration, majoring in finance, from Indiana University. He is a Fellow of the American Society of Appraisers, a Master Certified Business Appraiser, a Chartered Financial Analyst, a Master Certified Business Counselor, and is certified in mergers and acquisitions.

Dr. Pratt's professional recognitions include being designated a life member of the Business Valuation Committee of the American Society of Appraisers, a life member of the American Society of Appraisers, past chairman and a life member of the ESOP Association Advisory Committee on Valuation, a life member of the Institute of Business Appraisers, the Magna Cum Laude in Business Appraisal award from the National Association of Certified Valuation Analysts, and the distinguished service award of the Portland Society of Financial Analysts. He recently completed two three-year terms as trustee-at-large of the Appraisal Foundation.

Dr. Pratt is the coauthor of *Valuing Small Businesses and Professional Practices*, 3rd edition, published by McGraw-Hill. He is the coauthor with Roger Grabowski of the forthcoming *Cost of Capital: Applications and Examples*, available in 2008, the coauthor with Jay Fishman and William Morrison of *Standards of Value*, author of *The Market Approach to Valuing Businesses*, 2nd edition, *Business Valuation Body of Knowledge*, *Business Valuation Discounts and Premiums*, and coauthor with the Honorable David Laro of *Business Valuation and Taxes: Procedure, Law and Perspective*, all published by John Wiley & Sons, and *The Lawyer's Business Valuation Handbook*, published by the American Bar

Association. He is also coauthor of *Guide to Business Valuations*, 17th edition, published by Practitioners Publishing Company.

He is publisher emeritus of a monthly newsletter, *Business Valuation Update* (primarily for the professional appraisal community).

Dr. Pratt develops and teaches business valuation courses for the American Society of Appraisers and the American Institute of Certified Public Accountants, and frequently speaks on business valuation at national legal, professional, and trade association meetings. He also developed and often teaches a full-day seminar (sometimes divided into two partial days) on business valuation for judges and lawyers.

Alina V. Niculita, CFA, MBA, is president and COO of Shannon Pratt Valuations, Inc. She is a Chartered Financial Analyst and a candidate for the ASA designation in business valuation. She is also a member of the CFA Institute, the American Society of Appraisers, and the Licensing Executives Society.

At Shannon Pratt Valuations, Ms. Niculita works on all aspects of case management including the fundamental aspects of business valuation and economic analysis and report writing. Ms. Niculita has been involved in business valuation engagements for various purposes such as transactions in company stock, estate and gift taxes, and litigation support. Ms. Niculita has also worked on valuations of intangible assets and fairness and solvency opinions. Ms. Niculita is a coauthor of *Business Valuation Body of Knowledge Workbook,* 2nd edition, and the *Cost of Capital Workbook.*

Before joining Shannon Pratt Valuations, Ms. Niculita was a financial editor of publications and resources for valuation professionals for Business Valuation Resources including being the managing editor of *Shannon Pratt's Business Valuation Update©, BVLibrary™,* and the *Economic Outlook Update™.*

Ms. Niculita received a dual MBA in finance from the Joseph M. Katz Graduate School of Business, University of Pittsburgh, and from the Czech Management Center, Czech Republic. She also received a B.S. in economics with a concentration in banking and finance from the Academy of Economic Studies, Bucharest, Romania.

About the Contributing Authors

Noah J. Gordon, Esq., in addition to serving as project manager for this edition, updated the court cases chapters in Part VII, "Valuations for Specific Purposes." He is legal counsel for Shannon Pratt Valuations, Inc., where he is regularly involved with business valuations. He was the associate editor of *Shannon Pratt's Business Valuation Update,® Economic Outlook Update,™* and *BV Q&A Update™* for Business Valuation Resources. Mr. Gordon also was an executive editor with Wolters Kluwer/Aspen Publishers and a managing editor with Prentice-Hall in those publishers' legal publications divisions. He has served as a contributing author and editor of several legal treatises and publications, and regularly contributes to various business valuation publications. Most recently, he has contributed to *Guide to Business Valuations,* 17th edition (2007), *Standards of Value* (2006), and the second edition of *The Market Approach to Valuing a Business* (2005). He also maintains a freelance editorial business. Mr. Gordon is admitted to the bars of Oregon, New York, New Jersey, the District of Columbia, and the United States Supreme Court. He holds a Bachelor of Arts in Political Science and a Bachelor of Arts in French Literature from Haverford College, and a Juris Doctor from the Benjamin N. Cardozo School of Law.

Curtis R. Kimball, CFA, ASA, updated the chapter "Valuations for Gift and Estate Tax Purposes." Mr. Kimball is a managing director of Willamette Management Associates, a nationally prominent valuation and financial advisory firm, and director of WMA's Atlanta regional office. He is a Chartered Financial Analyst (CFA) of the CFA Institute, an Accredited Senior Appraiser (ASA) of the American Society of Appraisers in business valuation, and a member of the Institute of Business Appraisers. He has been valuing companies and interests in companies, intangible assets, and other property for a variety of purposes for over 30 years and was formerly with Wachovia Bank and, later, the Citizens & Southern Trust Company (now Bank of America) prior to joining WMA in 1988. He holds a B.A. in Economics from Duke University and an M.B.A. from Emory University. He is a contributing author to several standard reference works on private business valuation including *Valuing Small Businesses and Professional Practices, Financial Valuation: Businesses and Business Interests* (1997 update), *Business Valuation Discounts and Premiums,* and *The Business Valuation Handbook,* 2nd edition. He also acts as WMA's national director for wealth management valuations including estate, gift, buy-sell agreement, trust, fiduciary liability, marital, and charitable issues. Mr. Kimball has appeared as an expert witness on valuation issues in U.S. District Court, U.S. Tax Court, U.S. Bankruptcy Court, and other venues. His most recent appearances include the U. S. Tax Court cases *Estate of Georgina T. Gimbel* (Reliance Steel and Aluminum Company), *Estate of H. A. True, Jr., and Jean D. True et al. v. Commissioner* (True Ranches and True Oil Company), and *Estate of Harriet Mellinger v. Commissioner* (Frederick's of Hollywood).

M. Mark Lee, CFA, updated the chapter "Introduction to Valuing Stock Options." He is a principal of Eisner LLP with over 37 years of experience in business valuation, corporate finance, and fairness opinions. Mr. Lee was a Senior Managing Director of Sutter Securities Incorporated and ran its New York office. In addition, his responsibilities have included serving as Principal-in-Charge of the Valuation Services Practice of KPMG LLP's Northeastern Region, establishing KPMG LLP's fairness opinion practice, and serving as Vice-Chairman of Bear, Stearns & Co. Inc.'s Valuation Committee, which was responsible for reviewing the firm's fairness opinions and valuations. He has participated in tax and acquisition negotiations, as well as provided testimony and trial support. He has authored numerous articles on business valuation and has made many presentations before attorneys, trade associations, educational groups, and associations of business valuation experts. He is an adjunct assistant professor teaching business valuation at the New York University School of Continuing and Professional Studies.

Angelina McKedy updated the chapters "Researching Economic and Industry Information," "Analyzing Financial Statements," and "Financial Statement Ratio Analysis." She is a senior analyst for Shannon Pratt Valuations, Inc. She has assisted in performing valuation assignments for litigation support and dispute resolution (including dissenting stockholder suits and marital dissolution cases), solvency opinions, and fairness opinions. In addition to her business valuations work, she also provides stock portfolio management. Ms. McKedy worked as a financial research analyst for Business Valuation Resources, where she was the project manager for the *BVPapers®* database, compiled statistical data for the *Economic Outlook Update®*, and wrote numerous abstracts on current and relevant business valuation books and articles for *Shannon Pratt's Business Valuation Update.®* She has contributed to many of Shannon Pratt's books, and regularly contributes to *Guide to Business Valuations.* She holds a Bachelor of Science, Business Administration with an emphasis in Finance, Portland State University, and is a Candidate Member of the American Society of Appraisers.

Chad P. Phillips, CFA, updated the chapters "Market Approach: Guideline Merged and Acquired Company Method" and "Sample Report." He is a member of the Valuation Services Group and Dealer Services Group of Moss Adams LLP. Mr. Phillips provides valuation consulting for business succession; gift, transfer and estate reporting; purchase or sale; buy/sell agreement requirements; shareholder dispute; purchase price allocation; joint ventures; marital dissolution; and corporate planning. Valuation projects include operating companies, family limited partnership, limited liability companies, and intangible assets. Mr. Phillips is a Chartered Financial Analyst (CFA), and has presented on a number of valuation related topics to industry groups, organizations, and service providers alike.

Kimberly Short, in addition to assisting with research, editing, and obtaining the reprint permissions for this edition, updated Appendix A. She is a financial analyst with Shannon Pratt Valuations, Inc. She has assisted Shannon Pratt and Roger Grabowski in researching and editing *Cost of Capital,* 3rd edition. She holds a Bachelor of Science in Business Administration, with an emphasis in Finance, from Portland State University.

Doug Twitchell updated the chapter "Gathering Company Data." He is the publisher at Business Valuation Resources, LLC, where he has worked for over a decade. He is the cofounder of the *Pratt's Stats™* database and has contributed to the *Business Valuation Update™* newsletter and several of Shannon Pratt's books. He holds a Bachelor of Science in Mechanical and Industrial Engineering from Clarkson University, a Masters degree in Business Administration from Portland State University, and an advanced graduate certificate in Computational Finance from the Oregon Health & Science University's Oregon Graduate Institute School of Science & Engineering.

Foreword

When I decided to get serious about the field of business valuation, the original book I bought was the first edition of *Valuing a Business* by Dr. Shannon Pratt. I spent my weekends that summer reading it cover to cover, sitting on the beach (if you can imagine) with my highlighter in hand, eagerly soaking up the valuable lessons along with the sun and the sand. For years, I used the first edition as my "go-to" source, as it held all my notes and highlighted text that I wanted to be able to quickly reference. That dog-eared edition still sits in our now fully stocked valuation library, right next to the second, third, and fourth editions. As each edition came out, it was a little thicker than the edition before, and each one offered a little more depth, complexity, and subject matter for valuation analysts and users of valuation reports alike to benefit from.

Since Dr. Pratt's first edition of *Valuing a Business* was published in 1981, he has educated the valuation profession, attorneys, and the courts. He has been a leader in the formulation not only of the literature that many of us turn to for guidance, but also in participating in the collection of data that is the very foundation upon which appraisers rely. This leadership continues with the fifth edition of *Valuing a Business*, offering the reader a comprehensive view of the current state of business valuation, from the perspective of one of the profession's most prolific and well-known experts.

The book is as useful to appraisers beginning their appraisal career, as I used it many years ago, as it is to seasoned appraisal professionals. Written in plain English, it is also useful to nontechnical readers and users of valuation reports who may need guidance in understanding the report they are reading. It is also helpful to owners of businesses who wish to gain an understanding of the valuation process.

Beginning with the basics, *Valuing a Business* takes the reader through the important elements that are necessary to arrive at an opinion of value. Valuation methodology, including some of the latest thinking from thought-leaders in the field of valuation, are discussed in detail.

Certain chapters have been significantly updated and expanded, including the chapters "Discounted Future Economic Income Method," "Estate and Gift Tax," and "Valuing Stock Options." There are greatly enhanced discussions relating to levels of value and noncontrol and other discounts, and discounts for trapped-in gains. There is an extremely valuable guide to the definition of fair value by state. Other new sections have been added, including a section on S corporation valuation and a chapter on buy-sell agreements. The new USPAP standards are discussed, and updated discussions on the standards and credentials of the various valuation organizations are provided.

A significant number of new and important court cases have been added since the fourth edition. Many tax court cases have come out that practitioners need to be aware of in the areas of Chapter 14, trapped-in capital gains, and S corporations.

In addition, several new cases on reasonable compensation have been added. As this is an identified area of focus with the I.R.S., there is considerable guidance offered by these additional cases that the professional practicing in this area should take note of. The chapters on divorce and dissent and oppression have been supplemented as well with recent decisions.

Without a doubt, one of the most notable things about the book is its impressive bibliography following most chapters. These bibliographies have grown enormously since the first edition, providing the profession with perhaps the most comprehensive body of knowledge, organized by topic, that is available anywhere. This in itself is an extremely valuable resource that should not be overlooked. I speak from personal experience on this point: In my initial years of valuation (and before so much information was available online), I spent countless hours in the University of Maine library searching for articles, using the bibliographies at the end of each chapter of Dr. Pratt's first edition of *Valuing a Business*. I found many of these articles, and it was from these readings that I augmented my early "advanced business valuation training." Today, these updated bibliographies include references to the latest economic, industry, financial, and valuation research sites available on the Web. As our body of knowledge has expanded, so too have the many resources available to us. The fifth edition provides a comprehensive guide not only to where to find it, but what you'll find.

Like every edition before it, this fifth edition of *Valuing a Business* will be acquired for our valuation library, used on a daily basis, read by staff, referred to often, and used to help teach. We owe a debt of gratitude to Dr. Pratt for this additional contribution to our growing body of knowledge.

Nancy Fannon, ASA, CPA•ABV, MCBA
Fannon Valuation Group
Portland, Maine

Preface

The book is designed to serve three purposes:

1. A comprehensive and updated reference for currently active business appraisers
2. An introductory text on business valuation for both academic and accreditation courses and beginning practitioners
3. A reference for nonappraisers who use and/or evaluate business appraisals

Evolution and State of the Profession

Since the first edition was published in 1981, the profession of business appraisal has matured immensely. There are now widely accepted business valuation standards, where there were none in 1981. Since the last edition of this book, the IRS has finally come out with business valuation guidelines, and the AICPA has finally published their business valuation standards. While each organization's standards or guidelines are slightly different from the others, there is unanimous agreement on the central concepts of business valuation.

The authors have endeavored to present the current state of the art, thinking, and practice of the business valuation profession, which has progressed significantly since the fourth edition in 2000. Where clear consensus on positions exist, such consensus is presented. Where there are differing opinions, we try to present the issues clearly and fairly, reflecting extensive peer review (see Acknowledgments). We also present considerable documentation of various courts' positions on controversial issues.

Emphasis on Valuations That Withstand Challenge

Virtually every business valuation is potentially subject to challenge from one party or another—one or more buying or selling parties, taxing authorities, ESOP beneficiaries, a spouse in a divorce, or any of a variety of interested parties. The section on valuations for specific purposes has been greatly expanded and enhanced with new sections and hundreds of court cases detailing which aspects of valuation in various contexts the courts have provided guidance on. These valuation contexts, with extensive discussion of legal challenges and the courts' positions include, especially:

- Gift and estate taxes
- Income taxes
- Employee stock ownership plans
- Marital dissolutions
- Dissenting stockholder and minority oppression actions

It is very enlightening to see just what methods, procedures, and data have held up under challenge and what methods, procedures, and data (or omissions in any of these categories) have caused appraisers to be admonished or rebuked by the courts. These insights should help analysts to avoid pitfalls, and should help attorneys, clients, and other users of valuations to critically evaluate valuation work products in light of the legal contexts that may govern the acceptability of these valuations.

Highlights of What's New in This Edition

This edition reflects the substantial advances in the tools and sophistication in business valuation, as well as new appraisal standards and regulations that have evolved since 2000. These advances fall broadly into three categories:

1. Major advances in the quantity, quality, and accessibility of empirical data available to support business valuation conclusions.
2. Growing consensus within the business valuation professional community on standards, methodology, and terminology.
3. New appraisal rules, regulations, and standards issued by governmental, or quasigovernmental, and professional bodies.

While there has been a growing consensus regarding business valuation issues, there also has been a growing volume of litigation over business valuations. This edition summarizes the important opinions in gift, estate, and income tax; shareholder disputes (dissenting stockholder and minority oppression actions); marital dissolutions; ESOPs; and ad valorem (property tax) cases. While there have not been any court cases yet because the area is so new, much attention has been focused lately on fair value for financial reporting and FAS 157.

Along with the growing body of litigation, there has been a proliferation of business valuation tools in the nature of empirical databases of actual transactions. *Pratt's Stats* has now expanded to over 4,000 sales of privately held businesses; *Mergerstat/Shannon Pratt's Control Premium Study* now has over 5,000 transactions of public companies bought out; the *Valuation Advisors' Discount for Lack of Marketability Study* now has about 3,000 transactions. Regarding the cost of capital, the *Duff & Phelps Risk Premium Study* is gaining wide usage. The latest on these and other databases are thoroughly described in this edition.

There have also been several Tax Court decisions on the valuation of minority and controlling positions in corporations, some of which have been widely criticized by the business valuation community. These stirred a spate of research on the valuation of S corporations and interests in them. We discuss the criticisms of the court decisions and the ensuing research.

Key additions reflecting these developments include:

- Extensive court case analysis and citations, as noted in the previous section.
- An added chapter on fair value for financial reporting.
- Greatly expanded treatment of the challenges to the conventional use of Ibbotson data to estimate cost of capital and details of the *Duff & Phelps Risk Premium Report*, which has come into wide usage for estimating cost of capital in recent years.
- Examples of the practical application of the Duff & Phelps data and discussion of the measure of size, including the accounting measure of size, in the Duff & Phelps studies.

- Significantly expanded section on the company-specific risk premium and discussion of how the Duff & Phelps studies can be applied to estimating this premium.
- New transactional databases, such as *LiquiStat,* and the expansion and refinement of many that existed as of the last edition.
- New restricted stock studies, including the Johnson study and the Columbia Financial Adviser's Study.
- A new Levels of Value chart.
- New market evidence regarding control and acquisition premiums, including the *Mergerstat/Shannon Pratt's Control Premium Study* and the Robinson, Rumsey, and White Study.
- New online databases that can be used for finding comparables when using the guideline publicly traded company method.
- New penalties for business appraisers, and the potential for blacklisting, in the Internal Revenue Code.
- A completely updated sample report (see Chapter 21).
- The latest court guidance on discounts for trapped-in capital gains and tax-affecting of pass-through entities.
- Updated section on avoiding common errors made in the income approach.
- The impact of IRC Section 409A on determining the fair market value of non-qualified deferred compensation plans, including stock option plans.
- Empirical research on the sales of controlling interests in S corporation versus C corporations, including the Erickson-Wang Study.
- Up-to-date credentialing standards of all major professional associations, including ASA, AICPA, IBA, and NACVA.
- New section on premises of value, and updated state-by-state treatment of fair value in dissenting shareholder appraisal actions.
- New section on "double-dipping" in marital dissolution appraisals.
- New section on the IRS's Business Valuation Guidelines, finalized in 2003.
- New section on using option pricing to value the built-in gains tax liability.
- Expanded treatment of the Black-Scholes and binomial models for valuing stock options.
- New section on Family Limited Partnerships (FLPs) and their treatment by the IRS and the courts.
- New sections on goodwill in the courts.
- The *International Glossary of Business Valuation Terms* supplemented with terms used by the American Society of Appraisers (see Appendix A).
- Hundreds of updated data sources and bibliographical references.
- A significantly expanded and much more user-friendly index.

Audiences for Which the Book Is Designed

The book is designed to be useful not only to business appraisers, but also to others dealing with business appraisal issues such as:

- Attorneys dealing with business valuation litigation and/or sales or mergers of business enterprises
- CPAs
- Financial planners

- Bank trust officers dealing with closely held businesses
- Investment bankers
- Business owners, CFOs, and corporate directors

Business Valuation Continues to Be Dynamic

The momentum of business valuation developments of the last eight years is sure to continue. Very importantly, the positions of various courts on many business valuation issues continue to evolve. We will reflect these developments in future editions. Please address your comments, observations, and suggestions to us at the addresses below.

In the meantime, Shannon Pratt and Alina Niculita are available to provide business valuation services, report reviews, consultation, and expert testimony.

Shannon P. Pratt, CFA, FASA, MCBA, MCBC, CM&AA
CEO
Shannon Pratt Valuations, Inc.
6443 S.W. Beaverton Hillsdale Highway, Suite 432
Portland, Oregon 97221
(503) 459-4700
(503) 459-4710 (fax)
e-mail: shannon@shannonpratt.com
Web site: www.shannonpratt.com

Alina V. Niculita, CFA, MBA
President and COO
Shannon Pratt Valuations, Inc.
6443 S.W. Beaverton Hillsdale Highway, Suite 432
Portland, Oregon 97221
(503) 459-4700
(503) 459-4710 (fax)
e-mail: alina@shannonpratt.com
Web site: www.shannonpratt.com

Acknowledgments

As with previous editions, this fifth edition has benefited immeasurably from peer review by a dedicated group of professionals who provided valuable input and assistance.

We wish to thank the following individuals who have reviewed significant portions or all of the manuscript and provided commentary and suggestions for this edition. We believe this volume truly represents a consensus of a broad cross section of the practitioners from all facets of the business valuation community.

Stephen J. Bravo
Apogee Business Valuations, Inc.

David W. King
Mesirow Financial Consulting

Nancy J. Fannon
Fannon Valuation Group

Gilbert E. Matthews
Sutter Securities Incorporated

Roger J. Grabowski
Duff & Phelps, LLC

Gary R. Trugman
Trugman Valuation Associates, Inc.

James R. Hitchner
The Financial Valuation Group

Richard M. Wise
Wise, Blackman LLP

Portions of the manuscript were reviewed by the following individuals:

Jeffrey M. Cheyne
Samuels Yoelin Kantor Seymour &
    Spinrad LLP

James Harrington
Ibbotson Associates

James S. Rigby, Jr.
The Financial Valuation Group

Jay E. Fishman
Financial Research Associates

Espen Robak
Pluris Valuation Advisors LLC

There are many others who assisted with this edition. Franz H. Ross of GAR Associates, Inc., assisted with sections on gross profits. Adam Manson and Paul Heidt of Business Valuation Resources, LLC, reviewed and provided materials and exhibits for transactional databases.

Several members of the staff of Shannon Pratt Valuations, Inc., provided assistance with this edition. Paul Anthony assisted with logistic support, typing, and assisting Dr. Pratt. Catherine Roessmann Peroni provided clerical support, and Deanna Patrick provided general assistance.

Noah Gordon, legal counsel for Shannon Pratt Valuations, Inc., served as the project manager for this undertaking. This included acting as a liaison and coordinating with the authors, contributing authors, the publisher, and the outside reviewers. He also edited and proofread the manuscript. This book would simply not have been completed without Noah's dedication and project management.

Kimberly Short, a financial analyst with Shannon Pratt Valuations, Inc., assisted with obtaining permission to use material reprinted in this book from other sources. Others who assisted with this endeavor were Alina Niculita, Angelina McKedy, Noah Gordon, and Deanna Patrick.

Stuart Weiss, CPA/ABV, created the index for this edition. Thanks to his dedication and professionalism, the index is more comprehensive and user friendly than in any prior edition.

Robert Schweihs and Robert Reilly were coauthors with Shannon Pratt on the third and fourth editions of this book. Much of the material from those editions is carried forward in this edition. Because they were coauthors and shared both writing and editing functions and much was carried forward from the first and second editions, it is not possible to single out which particular chapters or sections they were primarily responsible for. Therefore, we make a general acknowledgment of their contributions to the third and fourth editions.

We also wish to thank Jeanne Glasser, our editorial director at McGraw-Hill, for her assistance and patience with this project, and Pattie Amoroso, our senior editing supervisor at McGraw-Hill, for shepherding this edition through editing and production always with a positive attitude and sharp eye.

We express our gratitude to all of the people singled out above as well as to all those who have written letters and had discussions with us about many conceptual and technical points since the last edition. As always, final responsibility for all content and judgment rests with the authors.

Shannon Pratt   **Alina Niculita**
Portland, Oregon   Portland, Oregon

Notation System Used in This Book

A source of confusion for those trying to understand financial theory and methods is the fact that financial writers have not adopted a standard system of notation. For this edition, we have studied dozens of financial texts and have developed a system of notation that reflects either the most commonly used conventions or ones that seem intuitively easy to understand. If other financial writers adopt this standardized system of notation, we believe it will go a long way toward removing ambiguity, clarifying communication, and making it easier for readers to absorb financial articles and texts.

Value at a Point in Time

PV = Present value
FV = Future value
$MVIC$ = Market value of invested capital

Cost of Capital and Rate of Return Variables

k = Discount rate (generalized)

k_e = Discount rate for common equity capital (cost of common equity capital). Unless otherwise stated, it generally is assumed that this discount rate is applicable to common equity

k_p = Discount rate for preferred equity capital

k_d = Discount rate for debt (Note: For complex capital structures, there could be more than one class of capital in any of the above categories, requiring expanded subscripts)

$k_{d(pt)}$ = Cost of debt prior to tax effect

k_{ni} = Discount rate for equity capital when net income rather than net cash flow is the measure of economic income being discounted

c = Capitalization rate

c_e = Capitalization rate for common equity capital (cost of common equity capital). Unless otherwise stated, it generally is assumed that this capitalization rate is applicable to net cash flow available to common equity

c_{ni} = Capitalization rate for net income

c_p = Capitalization rate for preferred equity capital

c_d = Capitalization rate for debt (Note: For Complex capital stuctures, there could be more than one class of capital in any of the above categories, requiring expanded subscripts)

t = Tax rate (expressed as a percentage of pretax income)

R = Rate of return

$$R_f \;=\; \text{Rate of return on a risk-free security}$$

$E(R) =$ Expected rate of return

$E(R_m) =$ Expected rate of return on the "market" (usually used in the context of a market for equity securities, such as the NYSE or S&P 500)

$E(R_i) =$ Expected rate of return on security I

$B =$ Beta (a coefficient, usually used to modify a rate of return variable)

$B_L =$ Levered beta

$B_U =$ Unlevered beta

$RP =$ Risk premium

$RP_m =$ Risk premium for the "market" (usually used in the context of a market for equity securities, such as the NYSE or S&P 500)

$RP_s =$ Risk premium for "small" stocks (average size of lowest quartile of NYSE as measured by market value of common equity) over and above RP_m

$RP_u =$ Risk premium for unsystematic risk attribuable to the specific company

$RP_i =$ Risk premium for the ith security

$K_1 \ldots K_n =$ Risk premium associated with risk factor 1 through n for the average asset in the market (used in conjunction with Arbitrage Pricing Theory)

$WACC =$ Weighted average cost of capital

Income Variables

$E =$ Expected economic income (in a generalized sense; i.e, could be dividends, any of several possible definitions of cash flows, net income, and so on)

$NI =$ Net income (after entity-level taxes)

$NCF_e =$ Net cash flow to equity

$NCF_f =$ Net cash flow to the firm (to overall invested capital, or entire capital structure, including all equity and long-term debt)

$PMT =$ Payment (interest and principal payment on debt security)

$D =$ Dividends

$GCF =$ Gross cash flow (usually net income plus noncash charges)

$EBIT =$ Earnings before interest and taxes

$EBITDA =$ Earnings before interest, and taxes, depreciation, and amortization

Periods or Variables in a Series

$i =$ The ith period or the ith variable in a series (may be extended to the jth variable, the kth variable, and so on)

$n =$ The number of periods or variables in the series, or the last number in the series

$\infty =$ Infinity

$_o =$ Period$_o$, the base period, usually the latest year immediately preceding the valuation date

Weightings

W = Weight
W_e = Weight of common equity in capital structure
W_p = Weight of preferred equity in capital structure
W_d = Weight of debt in capital structure

NOTE: For purposes of computing a weighted average cost of capital (WACC), it is assumed that above weightings are at market value.

Growth

g = Rate of growth

Mathematical Functions

Σ = Sum of (add up all the variables that follow)
π = Product of (multiply together all the variables that follow)
$\times$ = Mean average (the sum of the values of the variables divided by the number of variables)
G = Geometric mean (the product of the values of the variables taken to the root of the number of variables)

Valuing a Business

Part I

State of the Profession,
the Engagement, and
the Basic Theory

Chapter 1

Business Valuation Standards and Credentials

Growing Consensus on Business Valuation Standards

The consensus regarding business appraisal professional standards that we commented on in the fourth edition has continued to grow. This has been accompanied by a proliferation of business valuation professional education.

It is important that all those either providing or using business valuation services be aware of these standards. The days when there was virtually no generally accepted guidance and almost anything could pass as a business valuation are gone forever. Owners, investors, attorneys, government agencies, and the courts all demand that business valuation work live up to these higher standards.

This chapter provides the reader a road map to business valuation professional standards as they exist as of this writing. It also gives the reader the sources to get complete copies of current standards and to keep up to date as they evolve. The chapter also catalogs the current state of business valuation professional credentials.

Both the standards and the credentials are still evolving. Readers can keep up to date on the changes through the monthly newsletters *Business Valuation Update*, *Business Valuation Review*, *CPA Experts*, *Financial Valuation and Litigation Expert*, and other industry journals.

The Appraisal Foundation

Background and Organization

The Appraisal Foundation was established in 1987 by nine appraisal organizations constituting the North American Council of Appraisal Organizations (NACAO) and six nonappraiser members including the American Bankers Association and the U.S. League of Savings Institutions. Eight of the nine appraisal organizations were composed entirely of real estate appraisers. One, the American Society of Appraisers (ASA), is multidisciplinary. The American Society of Appraisers awards certification in real estate appraisal, machinery and equipment appraisal, personal property appraisal, business valuation, and technical valuation.

The board of trustees of The Appraisal Foundation consists of representatives of the sponsor organizations plus trustees-at-large. The board of trustees appoints two independent boards:

1. The **Appraisal Standards Board** (ASB) promulgates the *Uniform Standards of Professional Appraisal Practice* (USPAP) (see next section).
2. The **Appraisal Qualifications Board** promulgates appraiser qualifications. So far, it has done so only for real estate appraisers and personal property appraisers. As of this writing, the Appraisal Qualifications Board has left the issue of business appraiser qualifications to the various professional credentialling organizations, discussed in a subsequent section.

Uniform Standards of Professional Appraisal Practice

The Financial Institution Reform, Recovery, and Enforcement Act (FIRREA) of 1989 makes compliance with USPAP mandatory for all federally related real estate transactions. Although not mandatory for federally related transactions involving personal property and business appraisals, USPAP has been adopted by major appraisal organizations in North America and has become widely recognized as the generally accepted standards of appraisal practice.[1] Although The Appraisal Foundation's ASB writes, amends, and interprets USPAP, the Board does not enforce USPAP. Through FIRREA, the federal government has mandated that the states enforce USPAP compliance using real property appraisers. Standards are included for real estate, personal property, business, and mass appraisals. State appraiser certification and licensing boards; federal, state, and local agencies; appraisal services; and appraisal trade associations require compliance with USPAP.

The content of USPAP is summarized in Exhibit 1–1. The 2006 edition of USPAP was adopted with an effective date of July 1, 2006, and the ASB anticipates that the 2006 edition will be effective until December 31, 2007 (a period of 18 months). Effective with the 2008 edition, the ASB plans to issue USPAP on a two-year publication cycle.

Standards Published by Business Valuation Professional Organizations

Four U.S. professional associations that offer education and accreditation in the discipline of business valuation also publish business valuation standards. These are:

1. American Society of Appraisers
2. Institute of Business Appraisers (IBA)
3. National Association of Certified Valuation Analysts (NACVA)
4. American Institute of Certified Public Accountants (AICPA)[2]

In all cases, the standards published by the above organizations are considerably more detailed than USPAP, but none of them is in direct conflict with USPAP.

The latest editions of the standards of all of the above organizations are available without charge from their respective headquarters. Contact information for each is shown in the bibliography for this chapter.

Other Organizations That Have Offered Guidance on Business Valuation Issues

Internal Revenue Service

Congress directs the U.S. Treasury Department to issue legislative and interpretive regulations to provide structure for the tax laws it passes. Interpretive regulations (e.g., revenue rulings) do not have the force of law, but present the position of the Internal Revenue Service (IRS) on various tax matters, including the valuation of businesses, business interests, and related intangible assets. Regulations are actually formulated by the IRS, but they are approved by the Secretary of the Treasury or his or her delegate. As an example, the regulations for Chapter 14 of the estate

---

[1] For example please refer to *Kohler et al. v. Commissioner of Internal Revenue*, 2006 Tax Ct. Memo LEXIS 156. (July 25, 2006).
[2] The AICPA issued its *Statement on Standards for Valuation Services No. 1*, Valuation of a Business, Business Ownership Interest, Security, or Intangible Asset, in June 2007. This standard is effective for valuations performed on or after January 1, 2008.

Exhibit 1–1

Uniform Standards of Professional Appraisal Practice
Table of Contents

Definitions
Preamble
Ethics Rule
Competency Rule
Departure Rule
Jurisdictional Exception Rule
Supplemental Standards Rule

Standards and Standards Rules

Standard 1	Real Property Appraisal, Development
Standard 2	Real Property Appraisal, Reporting
Standard 3	Appraisal Review, Development, and Reporting
Standard 4	Real Property Appraisal Consulting, Development
Standard 5	Real Property Appraisal Consulting, Reporting
Standard 6	Mass Appraisal, Development and Reporting
Standard 7	Personal Property Appraisal, Development
Standard 8	Personal Property Appraisal, Reporting
Standard 9	Business Appraisal, Development
Standard 10	Business Appraisal, Reporting

Statements on Appraisal Standards

SMT-1	Appraisal Review Clarification of Comment on Standards Rule 3-1(g) (Retired)
SMT-2	Discounted Cash Flow Analysis (RP)
SMT-3	Retrospective Value Opinions (RP, PP)
SMT-4	Prospective Value Opinions (RP, PP)
SMT-5	Confidentiality Section of the Ethics Rule (Retired)
SMT-6	Reasonable Exposure Time in Real Property and Personal Property Market Value Opinions (RP, PP)
SMT-8	Electronic Transmission of Reports (Retired)
SMT-9	Identification of the Client's Intended Use in Developing and Reporting Appraisal, Appraisal Review, or Appraisal Consulting Assignment Opinions and Conclusions (ALL)
SMT-10	Assignments for Use by a Federally Insured Depository Institution in a Federally Related Transaction (RP)

Advisory Opinions

AO-1	Sales History (RP)
AO-2	Inspection of Subject Property Real Estate (RP)
AO-3	Update of a Prior Assignment (ALL)
AO-4	Standards Rule 1-5(b) (RP)
AO-5	Assistance in the Preparation of an Appraisal (ALL)
AO-6	The Appraisal Review Function (ALL)
AO-7	Marketing Time Opinions (RP, PP)
AO-8	Market Value vs. Fair Value in Real Property Appraisals (RP)
AO-9	The Appraisal of Real Property That May Be Impacted by Environmental Contamination (RP)
AO-10	The Appraiser–Client Relationship (RP)
AO-11	Content of the Appraisal Report Options of Standards Rules 2-2 and 8-2 (RP, PP)
AO-12	Use of the Appraisal Report Options of Standards Rules 2-2 and 8-2 (RP, PP)
AO-13	Performing Evaluations of Real Property Collateral to Conform with USPAP (RP)
AO-14	Appraisals for Subsidized Housing (RP)
AO-15	Using the DEPARTURE RULE in Developing a Limited Appraisal (ALL)
AO-16	Fair Housing Laws and Appraisal Report Content (RP)
AO-17	Appraisals of Real Property with Proposed Improvements (RP)
AO-18	Use of an Automated Valuation Model (AVM) (ALL)
AO-19	Unacceptable Assignment Conditions in Real Property Appraisal Assignments (RP)
AO-20	An Appraisal Review Assignment That Includes the Reviewer's Own Opinion of Value (ALL)
AO-21	USPAP Compliance (ALL)
AO-22	Scope of Work in Market Value Appraisal Assignments, Real Property (RP)
AO-23	Identifying the Relevant Characteristics of the Subject Property of a Real Property Appraisal Assignment (RP)
AO-24	Normal Course of Business (RP, PP)
AO-25	Clarification of the Client in a Federally Related Transaction (RP)
AO-26	Readdressing (Transferring) a Report to Another Party (ALL)
AO-27	Appraising the Same Property for a New Client (ALL)

Glossary
Index

NOTE: AOs do not hold the same weight as standards or statements.
SOURCE: *Uniform Standards of Professional Appraisal Practice* (Washington, DC: The Appraisal Foundation, 2006). Reprinted with permission.
Note: ALL = Add disciplines, PP = personal property, RP = real property.

and gift tax laws require appraisers to use a special valuation methodology in certain circumstances with regard to family-owned businesses.

The IRS also issues pronouncements representing administrative (as opposed to legislative) tax authority. The pronouncements include: revenue rulings, revenue procedures, private letter rulings (PLRs), technical advice memorandums (TAMs), and general counsel memorandums. These pronouncements illustrate the treatment of certain issues not clearly addressed in the regulations. Over time, many of the positions espoused by the IRS through regulations and revenue rulings come up in court disputes. The resolution of these issues by the courts establishes case law precedent. Much, but by no means all, of the case law has been supportive of positions taken in the regulations and revenue rulings. The most important of the revenue rulings that relate to business valuation are:

59-60	Valuing closely held stock.
65-193	Deletes the final §4.02(f) of Revenue Ruling 59-60 dealing with the valuation of intangibles.
68-609	Discusses "formula method" for determining fair market value of intangible assets of a business. Supersedes ARM 34. Theory in Revenue Ruling 59-60 applies to income and other taxes as well as to estate and gift taxes, and to business interests of any type, including partnerships and proprietorships, and to intangible assets for all tax purposes.
77-287	Recognizes relevance of restricted stock studies (see Chapter 17) in determining discounts for lack of marketability.
83-120	Discusses valuing preferred stock (see Chapter 24).
93-12	Allows the application of minority interest discounts to partial interest transfers even when a family owns overall control of a closely held business. Supersedes and reverses Revenue Ruling 81-253, which disallowed such discounts, but was overturned by case law.

Representing less authority than revenue rulings, the PLRs, TAMs, and general counsel memorandums issued by the IRS are responses to specific inquiries from taxpayers (and/or from IRS field offices) and may not be cited as precedent. Nevertheless, these can be helpful in understanding the IRS's likely position on emerging issues for tax-related appraisals.

IRS internal publications and other official materials also provide useful insights. The February 1998 *IRS Valuation Training for Appeals Officers* is available through Commerce Clearing House or online (see bibliography).

Since the fourth edition of this book, the IRS has issued business valuation guidelines (see bibliography). They are very close to the business valuation standards found in USPAP.

Revenue rulings and other IRS pronouncements are often cited for valuation guidance for purposes other than taxes. This can be useful to the extent that the material contains general valuation guidance. However, as discussed extensively in this book, valuation methods may differ for different purposes, and all aspects of revenue rulings may not be appropriate for nontax purposes.

Department of Labor

Like the IRS revenue rulings, regulations issued by the Department of Labor (DOL) do not have the force of law. They represent the department's position with respect to interpretation of the law as it applies to certain issues.

In May of 1988, the DOL issued a proposed draft of a Regulation Relating to the Definition of Adequate Consideration (for employee stock ownership plan [ESOP] stock). Hearings have been held and written comments have been received. The complete text of the 1988 proposed regulation is included as Exhibit 1–8 of this chapter. On May 8, 1995, the DOL announced that it had withdrawn the proposed regulations, effective February 1, 1995. Many appraisers still abide by these regulations.

Association for Investment Management and Research

The Association for Investment Management and Research (AIMR) publishes educational materials, conducts seminars, and confers the professional designation CFA, chartered financial analyst, which is discussed later in the chapter.

AIMR materials and the CFA exams are oriented primarily to the analysis of publicly traded securities and the management of investment portfolios. As the interaction between publicly traded and closely held companies (mergers, acquisitions, leveraged buyouts, spinoffs, and so on) has accelerated in recent years, the AIMR has given increasing attention to the analysis and appraisal of closely held companies. In 1990, the Institute of Chartered Financial Analysts (formerly the AIMR) published a monograph titled *Valuation of Closely Held Companies and Inactively Traded Securities* (see bibliography) based on a seminar by the same name.

The ESOP Association

The ESOP Association is an organization of companies that have ESOPs and companies that provide professional advisory services to ESOP companies. One of the association's committees is the Advisory Committee on Valuation, composed of about 25 professional practitioner members of leading companies regularly performing ESOP valuations.

The ESOP Association Advisory Committee on Valuation meets twice a year to discuss issues concerning the valuation of ESOP shares, primarily those in closely held companies. The ESOP Association neither certifies nor endorses business appraisers or any other specialists, nor does it issue standards as such. However, it publishes a very useful book, *Valuing ESOP Shares*, reflecting the deliberations and views of the Advisory Committee on Valuation on many issues affecting the valuation of ESOP shares. The address to obtain this book and other ESOP Association information is presented in the bibliography at the end of this chapter.

Recognition of Professional Standards by Courts

Most business valuations that are performed have the potential for a legal challenge. Courts like to have professionally accepted standards to rely on for guidance in deciding disputed issues. Courts may suspect poor appraisal work, but it helps them tremendously to be able to cite authority for rejection of work that fails to meet professional standards. The authors, and many other valuation analysts, have brought the authority of the standards and other professional guidance discussed in this chapter to bear very fruitfully in court on numerous occasions.

One result of previous editions of this book, and the development of the standards and other professional guidance discussed in this chapter, is an increased consensus and consistency in the resolution of business valuation issues, both in the courts and elsewhere. There have been numerous references to this book in reported decisions quoting testimony that ultimately assisted the court in reaching its decision. We believe this has contributed to the consistency of judicial decisions. The standards and other guidance discussed in this chapter continue to build consensus and consistency on business valuation issues. As these materials are more widely disseminated and recognized, undoubtedly they will significantly impact court decisions in the future.

International Acceptance of U.S. Standards and Practices

The United States is by far the world leader in both markets for and analysis of securities, companies, and business interests. This is true for both publicly traded securities and closely held businesses and business interests.

Two factors have combined to accelerate the spread of U.S. technology in financial appraisals and markets throughout the world:

1. Rapidly increasing international flow of capital
2. Growing privatization of formerly socially owned businesses in almost every country of the world

The standards and guidance in this chapter and throughout this book are becoming increasingly applicable to international as well as to domestic transactions as the world financial markets become more homogeneous.

Parts or all of earlier editions of this book have already been translated into several foreign languages. Several governments have adopted USPAP and the ASA business valuation standards as mandatory criteria for business valuations for transactions involving privatization. The authors, and other ASA members, have taught material from this book, USPAP, and ASA business valuation standards in many countries throughout the world.[3] Such presentations have been made under the varied auspices of private business organizations, local professional appraisal societies, local governments, academic institutions, the United Nations, and the World Bank.

Most meetings of the professional organizations listed in this chapter are attended by representatives of many foreign countries. The worldwide appetite for translations and teachers of U.S. business appraisal standards and practices is challenging our professionals' ability to fill such demand. We believe this growing global homogeneity of business appraisal standards and practices will contribute positively to successful privatization, worldwide capital flows, and economic growth.

The 2007 edition of *International Valuation Standards* contains business valuation standards that closely follow USPAP (see bibliography).

---

[3] For example, ASA business valuation courses have been taught in Brazil, Hong Kong, Kuwait, Mexico, Russia, Slovenia, Taiwan, and Yugoslavia.

Professional Organizations Offering Accreditation in Business Valuation

Four organizations in the United States and one in Canada offer various professional accreditations in business valuation. These are:

- ASA
- IBA
- NACVA
- AICPA
- CICBV

A summary of the professional designations offered by each and the requirements for each designation are presented in Exhibit 1–2. Additional information about each of these organizations and their activities is shown in Exhibits 1–3 through 1–7.

The above organizations are undertaking certain cooperative efforts in an attempt to make business valuation practice more consistent. The five organizations have a joint Business Valuation Glossary Committee, which has prepared a jointly approved glossary of business valuation terms. This glossary is presented in the appendix at the end of this book. Also, the four U.S. organizations have formed a Joint Business Valuation Task Force for the purpose of making recommendations to the Appraisal Standards Board of The Appraisal Foundation for revisions to USPAP.

In addition to the above organizations, the CFA Institute confers the professional designation of Chartered Financial Analyst® (CFA®). Candidates must pass three rigorous all-day examinations, given in June and December each year.

The emphasis in the CFA program is on analysis and portfolio management of publicly traded securities. However, the required readings and exams include material on valuing closely held companies (including portions of this book). The AIMR Directory indicates that several hundred of the organization's 30,000+ members specialize in valuing closely held companies.

American Society of Appraisers

The ASA, formed in 1936, is a long-standing, multidisciplinary organization that offers education and professional accreditation in many appraisal disciplines, including real property, machinery and equipment, personal property, and a number of technical valuation specialties, as well as in business valuation. From 1984 through 2005, the business valuation discipline was the ASA's fastest growing area of accreditation.

For details of professional designations and accreditation requirements, publications, and other activities, see Exhibits 1–2 and 1–3.

Institute of Business Appraisers

The IBA, founded in 1978, offers seminars on business appraisal topics and several professional designations in the field of business appraisal. It also offers a variety of member support services.

Exhibit 1–2

Professional Accreditation Criteria

Organization	Certification	Prerequisites	Course/Exam	Reports	Experience/Other
American Institute of Certified Public Accountants (AICPA)	ABV—Accredited in Business Valuation	AICPA certificate or member with current CPA license.	Pass an 8-hour comprehensive multiple-choice exam.		Substantial involvement in at least 6 business valuation engagements, or provide evidence of 150 hours that demonstrate substantial experience and
American Society of Appraisers (ASA)	AM—Accredited Member	Obtain four-year college degree or equivalent.	Complete four courses of three days each and pass one half-day exam following each course, or complete one all-day challenge exam and USPAP exam.	Submit two actual reports from within the last two years to satisfaction of board examiners.	Two years full-time or equivalent (e.g., five years of 400 hours business appraisal work per year equals one year full-time equivalent). One full year of requirement is granted to anyone who has a CPA, CFA, or CBT designation with five years of practice held.
	ASA—Accredited Senior Appraiser	Meet AM requirements.			Five years of full-time or equivalent experience including two years for AM.
	FASA—Fellow of American Society of Appraisers	Meet ASA requirements, plus be voted into College of Fellows on the basis of technical leadership and contribution to the profession or the Society.			
Institute of Business Appraisers (IBA)	AIBA—Accredited by IBA	Complete four-year college degree or equivalent; possess business appraisal designation from AICPA, ASA, or NACVA, or complete IBA eight-day Appraisal Workshop.	Complete comprehensive written exam.	Submit one report for peer review.	Provide four references of character and fitness.
	CBA—Certified Business Appraiser	Complete four-year college degree or equivalent. Complete IBA's 16-hour course 1010 (Report Writing).	Pass six-hour exam. Applicants may be exempt from the exam if they hold the ASA, ABV, CVA, or AVA designation	Submit two business-appraisal reports showing professional competence.	Successfully complete 90 hours of upper-level business valuation course work (at least 24 hours from IBA) or five years full-time active experience as a business appraiser. Provide four references (two personal, two professional).
	BVAL—Business Valuator Accredited for Litigation	Obtain business appraisal designation from IBA, AICPA, ASA, NACVA, or CVA candidate who has passed the exam.	Five-day Expert Witness Skills Workshop and four-hour exam.		Provide letters of reference from two attorneys or complete 16 hours of education in the area of law in which the appraiser will testify.

continued

11

Exhibit 1–2

Professional Accreditation Criteria (continued)

Organization	Certification	Prerequisites	Course/Exam	Reports	Experience/Other
	MCBA—Master Certified Business Appraiser	Obtain four-year college degree and two-year postgraduate degree or equivalent; hold CBA designation for at least five years and hold one other designation (ASA, CVA, or ABV)			Ten years full-time practice. Provide three references from MCBAs with personal knowledge of applicant's work.
	FIBA—Fellow of the Institute of Business Appraisers	Meet all CBA requirements, plus be voted into College of Fellows on basis of technical leadership and contribution to the profession and the Institute.			
National Association of Certified Valuation Analysis (NACVA)	AVA—Accredited Valuation Analyst, includes prior GVA designation	Obtain business degree and/or an MBA or higher; member in good standing of NACVA.	Complete five-day course; four-hour exam; additional eight-hour exam for applicants without accounting fundamentals background.	Provide case study for exam.	Two years full-time or equivalent business valuation or related experience, or ten or more business valuations. Provide three personal references, three business references, and a minimum of one letter of recommendation from an employer or another CPA.
	CVA—Certified Valuation Analyst	Have college degree, unrevoked CPA license, and be a member in good standing of NACVA.	Complete five-day course; pass two-part exam: four-hour proctored exam plus take-home exam with case study.	Pass case study for exam.	Two years experience as a CPA. Provide three personal references and three business references.
	CFFA—Certified Financial Forensic Analyst	Possess one of the following designations: CVA, AVA, AM, ASA, CBA, CBV, CFA, CMA, CPA, or CA; hold advanced degree in economics, accounting, or finance, or undergraduate degree and MBA.	Complete two-week course and eight days of training at NACVA's Forensic Institute; pass two-part exam: four-hour proctored exam plus take-home exam with case study.	Submit case study report under Fed. Rule 26, or report admitted into evidence within the last three years.	Provide one business and two legal references. Substantial experience in ten litigation matters, including five in which a deposition or testimony was given.
Canadian Institute of Chartered Business Valuators (CICBV)	CBV—Chartered Business Valuator	Have college degree or equivalent: accounting or finance encouraged.	Successfully complete six courses, including assignments and exams for each course plus the required experience, followed by the writing of the		Have two years full-time experience or the equivalent of part-time obtained over a five-year period, attested to by a sponsoring CICBV member.

Exhibit 1–2

Professional Accreditation Criteria (continued)

Organization	Certification	Prerequisites	Course/Exam	Reports	Experience/Other
			Membership Entrance Exam. Writing of exam can be challenged without successful completion of courses if applicant has at least five years full-time experience in business valuations.		
	CA-CBV	Hold CA (Chartered Accountant) designation; complete CICBV Program of Studies or five years of full-time business valuation experience may allow for exemption.	Obtain at least 60% in the CICBV's Membership Entrance Exam comprising two three-and-one-half-hour examinations.		Submit a letter from a CBV that sponsors and confirms applicant's two full years of full-time business valuation experience and recommends applicant for membership; agree to uphold CICBV's Code of Ethics and Practice Standards.
	FCBV—Fellow of the Canadian Institute of Chartered Business Valuators	Be a member; have rendered outstanding service to the business valuation profession; or have earned distinction and brought honor through achievements in professional life or in the community.			Two years full-time experience or the equivalent of part-time obtained over a five-year period, attested to by a sponsoring CICBV member.

AIBA   Accredited IBA (Institute of Business Appraisers)
AM   Accredited Member (American Society of Appraisers)
ASA   Accredited Senior Appraiser (American Society of Appraisers)
AVA   Accredited Valuation Analyst (National Association of Certified Valuation Analysts)
BVAL   Business Valuator Accredited for Litigation (Institute of Business Appraisers)
CA-CBV   Chartered Accountant–Chartered Business Valuator (The Canadian Institute of Chartered Business Valuators)
CBA   Certified Business Appraiser (Institute of Business Appraisers)
CBV   Chartered Business Valuator (The Canadian Institute of Chartered Business Valuators)
CFA   Chartered Financial Analyst (CFA institute, formerly Association for Investment Management and Research)
CFFA   Certified Financial Forensic Analyst (National Association of Certified Valuation Analysts)
CPA/ABV   Certified Public Accountant Accredited in Business Valuation (American Institute of Certified Public Accountants)
CVA   Certified Valuation Analyst (National Association of Certified Valuation Analysts)
FASA   Fellow of the American Society of Appraisers
FCBV   Fellow of the Canadian Institute of Chartered Business Valuators
FIBA   Fellow of the Institute of Business Appraisers
MCBA   Master Certified Business Appraiser (Institute of Business Appraisers)

Exhibit 1–3

American Society of Appraisers (ASA)

555 Herndon Parkway, Suite 125, Herndon, VA 20170, (703) 478-2228, www.appraisers.org

Date formed:	1936	Ownership:	Owned by members

Description: Multidisciplinary professional organization offering courses and exams leading to designations in the appraisal of real estate, machinery and equipment, personal property, gems and jewelry, businesses and business interests (including intangible assets), and certain technical specialties.

Designations offered:

AM—Accredited Member:

Educational requirement: College degree or equivalent.

Courses/exams: Completion of four courses of three days each, with successful completion of one half-day exam following each of the four courses, OR successful completion of one all-day challenge exam. In addition, successful completion of an ethics exam and a USPAP exam is required.

Reports: Submission of two actual appraisal reports to satisfaction of Board of Examiners.

Experience requirement: Two years full-time or full-time equivalent (e.g., five years of 400 hours business appraisal work per year equals one year full-time equivalent).

Related experience offset: One full year of the experience requirement is granted to anyone who has any of the following three designations with five years of practice in that respective field: Certified Public Accountant (CPA), Chartered Financial Analyst (CFA), or Certified Business Intermediary (CBI).

ASA—Accredited Senior Appraiser:

has met all requirements above plus an additional three years of full-time or full-time equivalent experience.

FASA—Fellow of the American Society of Appraisers:

has met all requirements above plus is voted into the College of Fellows on the basis of technical leadership and contribution to the profession and the society.

Courses: Each of the core courses (BV201–204) are three days; BV201 through 204 are followed by a half-day exam

BV201: Introduction to business valuation
BV202: The income approach
BV203: The market approach
BV204: Business valuation case study

Seminars and conferences: Seminars on specialized topics lasting from two hours to two days and sponsored by various groups within the ASA.

Annual interdisciplinary meeting with two and a half days of technical presentations on each of the society's appraisal disciplines.

Annual Advanced Business Valuation Conference with two or two and a half days of advanced business valuation papers, presentations, and discussion.

Publications: *Business Valuation Review*, quarterly professional journal with articles accepted based on peer review. Published at P.O Box 24222, Denver, Colorado 80224, (303) 975-8895. The other valuation disciplines also have their professional journal, similar to *Business Valuation Review.*

Valuation, published on an irregular basis, contains articles on all of the disciplines of valuation within the ASA. Published at ASA headquarters (see title of exhibit for address).

Local chapters: Chapters with regular monthly meetings in 87 cities throughout the United States and Canada.

Exhibit 1–4

Institute of Business Appraisers (IBA)
P.O. Box 17410, Plantation, Florida 33318, (954) 584-1144, www.instbusapp.org

Date formed:	1978	Ownership: Florida not-for-profit corporation (privately owned)

Description: Offers programs of interest to members whose business valuation activities are less than full time and/or whose practice includes valuation of small to midsize businesses.

Certification offered:

AIBA—Accredited by IBA:

Educational requirement:	Must have business appraisal designation from AICPA, ASA, or NACVA or have completed IBA 8001 workshop. Four-year degree or equivalent.
Courses/exams:	Four-hour exam.
Reports:	Submission of one report for peer review.
Experience requirement:	Provide references; submit 24 hours CPE in business valuation every two years or another report for peer review every two years or demonstrate completion of 10 business appraisal assignments in two years or pass CBA exam and enter that process

CBA—Certified Business Appraiser:

Educational requirement:	Four years of college or equivalent, and 10,000 hours full-time BV experience or 90 hours BV education with 24 IBA hours and 1010 report writing workshop
Courses/exams:	Four-hour exam.
Reports:	Submission of two business appraisal reports demonstrating professional level of competence.
Experience requirement:	Have performed at least two valuation assignments.

MCBA—Master Certified Business Appraiser:

has met all requirements above plus has 10 years' practice experience or has received credit for published writing or lecturing; needs four work product references from other CBAs.

FIBA—Fellow of the Institute of Business Appraisers:

has met all requirements above plus is voted into the College of Fellows on the basis of technical leadership and contribution to the profession and to the Institute.

BVAL—Business Valuator Accredited for Litigation:

has met all requirements above and completes a seven-day workshop and four-hour exam; must submit four letters of reference from attorneys or complete 16 hours of education in law through continuing legal education (CLE)

Courses: Eight-day workshop, offered two to four times a year, in various locations
Two-day course on valuing small businesses using IBA market database
Seven-day workshop on litigation support and expert testimony
See www.go-iba.org/education.asp for course listings

Seminars and conferences: One-day seminars on business valuation held at various locations around the United States.
Annual conference held in different cities.

Publication: *Business Appraisal Practice,* semiannual professional journal with peer-reviewed articles on practical aspects of business valuation and litigation support.

Local chapters: A few at present, including Mid-Atlantic, North Central, Northeast, Northwest, South Central, Southeast, and Southwest.

Exhibit 1–5

National Association of Certified Valuation Analysts (NACVA)
1111 East Brickyard Road, Suite 200, Salt Lake City, Utah 84106, (801) 486-0600, www.nacva.com

Date formed:	1991	Ownership:	Group of shareholders

Description:	NACVA is an association of CPAs, government valuers, and other professionals that perform valuation services. Its purpose is to promulgate the members' status, credentials, and esteem in the field of performing valuations of closely held businesses.
Certification offered:	*AVA—Accredited Valuation Analyst:*

Educational requirement:	Business degree and/or MBA or higher and member in good standing of NACVA.
Courses/exams:	Eight-hour prequalification exam on accounting and comprehensive exam including 30–50-hour take-home case study. Five-day course and four-hour exam.
Reports:	Only case study for exam.
Experience requirement:	Two years' full-time or equivalent business valuation or related experience or have performed 10 or more business valuations or demonstrate evidence of substantial knowledge. Three personal, three business, and employer or CPA references.

CVA—Certified Valuation Analyst:

Educational requirement:	CPA
Courses/exams:	Five-day course and half-day proctored exam that includes one case study and report writing requirement (prior to 1999 there was a 60-hour, take-home exam).
Reports:	Only for sample case on exam.
Experience requirement:	Two years' experience required for certification as CPA. Three personal and three business references.

CFFA—Certified Financial Forensic Analyst:

Educational requirement:	Possess CVA, AVA, AM, ASA, CBA, CBV, CFA, CMA, CPA, or CA; degree in economics, accounting, or finance, or undergraduate degree and MBA.
Courses/exams:	Two-week course; eight-day training at Forensic Institute; four-hour proctored exam and take-home exam with case study.
Reports:	Only for sample case on exam.
Experience requirement:	One business and two legal references. Substantial experience in 10 litigation matters, including five in which a deposition or testimony was given.

Courses:	Five days of training consisting of the following:

Days 1–2:	Fundamentals, Techniques, and Theory
Day 3:	Case Analysis No. 1 and Report Writing
Day 4:	Using Valuation Master 4.0 Software
Day 5:	Working Effectively in the Litigation Environment

Seminars and conferences:	Two conferences held annually. Semi-annual one-and-a-half day seminars on business valuation topics. Also one- and two-day seminars on key valuation topics, including symposiums.
Publication:	*The Valuation Examiner*, a bimonthly magazine.
Local chapters:	State chapters presently in 38 states and one in Mexico City.

Exhibit 1–6

American Institute of Certified Public Accountants (AICPA)

201 Plaza Three, Jersey City, New Jersey 07311-3881, (201) 938-3000, www.aicpa.org

Date formed:	1887	Ownership:	Organization-sponsored

Description: Recognizes business valuation as a CPA service niche and confers an accreditation credential reflecting this recognition for those in public practice, industry, government, and education.

Certification offered: *ABV — Accredited in Business Valuation*

Prerequisite:	AICPA member with current CPA license
Courses/exams:	Half-day exam (ABV 1) for those holding CVA, CBA, or CFA credentials. Full-day exam (ABV 1 and 11) for those not certified by a recognized organization. No exam for CPAs with an ASA credential.
Reports:	None
Experience requirement:	Involvement in at least six business valuation engagement projects or 150 hours that demonstrate substantial experience and competence.

Courses/exams: *Business Valuation Essentials* six-day courses are based on *Financial Valuation: Applications and Models* and *Financial Valuation Workbook*, both published by John Wiley & Sons, Inc. The exam is offered each year in November through December. In addition, AICPA offers a variety of one-day advanced courses in business valuation.

Seminars and conferences: Annual National Business Valuation Conference; many professional education programs

Publications: *CPA Expert*, a quarterly newsletter

The AICPA also publishes an extensive list of consulting service publications, generally referred to as "practice aids" or "special reports," including practice aids related to consulting with specific industry engagements.

Details of the IBA's professional designations, publications, and some of its activities are shown in Exhibits 1–2 and 1–4.

National Association of Certified Valuation Analysts

The NACVA was formed in 1993 by a group of CPAs to provide certification and member support services specifically for certified public accountants and others performing business valuation services. Details of their certification criteria and activities are shown in Exhibits 1–2 and 1–5.

American Institute of Certified Public Accountants

The newest entrant in the field of business valuation accreditation is the AICPA, which started a business valuation specialty accreditation in 1997.

Information on the CPA specialty accreditation in business valuation and other AICPA business valuation activities is shown in Exhibits 1–2 and 1–6.

The Canadian Institute of Chartered Business Valuators

The CICBV, founded in 1971, provides educational meetings and the professional designation CBV, chartered business valuator.

Exhibit 1–7

The Canadian Institute of Chartered Business Valuators

277 Wellington St. West, Toronto, Ontario, Canada M5V 3H2, (416) 204-3396, www.cicbv.ca

Date formed:	1971 Ownership: Nonprofit federally incorporated corporation owned by members
Description:	The CICBV is the largest professional valuation organization in Canada. It was established to promote high standards in business and securities valuations. Members are entitled to use the professional designation CBV (Chartered Business Valuator) following completion of rigorous study and practical experience requirements. The Institute's members and students provide a broad range of business valuation services to Canada's business, legal, investment, banking, and governmental communities.
Designation Offered:	CBV (Chartered Business Valuator) FCBV (Fellow of the CICBV)
Educational Requirement:	Recommended college degree or equivalent.
Courses/examinations:	The Program of Studies, consisting of six courses, is offered by distance education (home study). The successful completion of the Program of Studies and 1,500 hours of suitable practical experience are requirements to write the Membership Entrance Examination (MEE). The MEE is the final step in the process of becoming a CICBV Member and obtaining a CBV designation.
Experience requirement:	1,500 hours of suitable practical experience obtained over a five-year period attested to by a sponsoring CICBV Member.
Courses:	The Program of Studies, consisting of six courses, is offered by distance education (home study) and includes mandatory assignments with proctored examinations. All courses are offered in both semesters. The courses offered are: Introductory Business and Securities Valuations, Intermediate Business and Securities Valuations, Advanced Business and Securities Valuations, Law and Tax in Business Valuation, Litigation Support I, Litigation Support II, Advanced Open Market Transactions, Corporate Finance, Private Company Finance (online course), and Restructuring (online course).
Subscription:	Subscription service is available for a yearly fee, which entitles the subscriber to receive all publications issued by the institute and to be maintained on a mailing list to receive other mailings.
Seminars and conferences:	Seminars and workshops offered in major cities across Canada Biennial National Conferences (two full days) Regional Conferences (one-and-one-half days)
Publications:	The *Valuation Law Review* is published once a year in each of the three topics: corporate securities law, family law, and taxation. *Business Valuation Digest* is published twice yearly and consists of articles on business valuations. *The Journal of Business Valuation* contains the proceedings of the Institute's Biennial Conferences. *The Business Valuator* is a quarterly publication dealing with the activities of the Institute.

The CICBV publishes the proceedings of its biennial professional meetings in *The Journal of Business Valuation*. It also publishes a Code of Ethics and CICBV Practice Bulletins. The CICBV accreditation requirements and other information are presented in Exhibits 1–2 and 1–7.

Summary

The first few years of the 2000s marked the culmination of long-time efforts to develop business valuation standards on which the professional business valuation community could achieve general consensus. This consensus has spread and is gaining momentum as this edition goes to press. These standards are rapidly being

Exhibit 1–8

53 FR 17632
DEPARTMENT OF LABOR
Pension and Welfare Benefits Administration

AGENCY: Pension and Welfare Benefits Administration, Department of Labor

29 CFR Part 2510

Proposed Regulation Relating to the Definition of Adequate Consideration

53 FR 17632

May 17, 1988

ACTION: Notice of proposed rule making

SUMMARY: This document contains a notice of a proposed regulation under the Employee Retirement Income Security Act of 1974 (the Act or ERISA) and the Federal Employees' Retirement System Act of 1986 (FERSA). The proposal clarifies the definition of the term "adequate consideration" provided in section 3(18)(B) of the Act and section 8477(a)(2)(B) of FERSA for assets other than securities for which there is a generally recognized market. Section 3(18)(B) and section 8477(a)(2)(B) provide that the term "adequate consideration" for such assets means the fair market value of the asset as determined in good faith by the trustee or named fiduciary (or, in the case of FERSA, a fiduciary) pursuant to the terms of the plan and in accordance with regulations promulgated by the Secretary of Labor. Because valuation questions of this nature arise in a variety of contexts, the Department is proposing this regulation in order to provide the certainty necessary for plan fiduciaries to fulfill their statutory duties. If adopted, the regulation would affect plans investing in assets other than securities for which there is a generally recognized market.

DATES: Written comments on the proposed regulation must be received by July 18, 1988. If adopted, the regulation will be effective for transactions taking place after the date 30 days following publication of the regulation in final form.

ADDRESS: Written comments on the proposed regulation (preferably three copies) should be submitted to: Office of Regulations and Interpretations, Pension and Welfare Benefits Administration, Room N–5671, U.S. Department of Labor, 200 Constitution Avenue NW., Washington, DC 20216, Attention: Adequate Consideration Proposal. All written comments will be available for public inspection at the Public Disclosure Room, Pension and Welfare Benefits Administration, U.S. Department of Labor, Room N-5507, 200 Constitution Avenue NW., Washington, DC.

FOR FURTHER INFORMATION CONTACT: Daniel J. Maguire, Esq., Plan Benefits Security Division, Office of the Solicitor, U.S. Department of Labor, Washington, DC 20210, (202) 523-9596 (not a toll-free number) or Mark A. Greenstein, Office of Regulations and Interpretations, Pension and Welfare Benefits Administration, (202) 523-7901 (not a toll-free number).

SUPPLEMENTARY INFORMATION:

A. Background

Notice is hereby given of a proposed regulation under section 3(18)(B) of the Act and section 8477(a)(2)(B) of FERSA. Section 3(18) of the Act provides the definition for the term "adequate consideration," and states:

The term "adequate consideration" when used in part 4 of subtitle B means (A) in the case of a security for which there is a generally recognized market, either (i) the price of the security prevailing on a national securities exchange which is registered under section 6 of the Securities Exchange Act of 1934, or (ii) if the security is not traded on such a national securities exchange, a price not less favorable to the plan than the offering price for the security as established by the current bid and asked prices quoted by persons independent of the issuer and of any party in interest; and (B) in the case of an asset other than a security for which there is a generally recognized market, the fair market value of the asset as determined in good faith by the trustee or named fiduciary pursuant to the terms of the plan and in accordance with regulations promulgated by the Secretary.

The term "adequate consideration" appears four times in part 4 of subtitle B of Title I of the Act, and each time represents a central requirement for a statutory exemption from the prohibited transaction restrictions of the Act. Under section 408(b)(5), a plan may purchase insurance contracts from certain parties in interest if, among other conditions, the plan pays no more than adequate consideration. Section 408(b)(7) provides that the prohibited transaction provisions of section 406 shall not apply to the exercise of a privilege to convert securities, to the extent provided in regulations of the Secretary of Labor, only if the plan receives no less than adequate consideration pursuant to such conversion. Section 408(e) of the Act provides that the prohibitions in sections 406 and 407(a) of the Act shall not apply to the acquisition or sale by a plan of qualifying employer securities, or the acquisition, sale or lease by a plan of qualifying employer real property if, among other conditions, the acquisition, sale or lease is for adequate consideration. Section 414(c)(5) of the Act states that sections 406 and 407(a) of the Act shall not apply to the sale, exchange, or other disposition of property which is owned by a plan on June 30, 1974, and all times thereafter, to a party in interest, if such plan is required to dis-

continued

pose of the property in order to comply with the provisions of section 407(a) (relating to the prohibition against holding excess employer securities and employer real property), and if the plan receives not less than adequate consideration.

Public utilization of these statutory exemptions requires a determination of "adequate consideration" in accordance with the definition contained in section 3(18) of the Act. Guidance is especially important in this area because many of the transactions covered by these statutory exemptions involve plan dealings with the plan sponsor. A fiduciary's determination of the adequacy of consideration paid under such circumstances represents a major safeguard for plans against the potential for abuse inherent in such transactions.

The Federal Employees' Retirement System Act of 1986 (FERSA) established the Federal Retirement Thrift Investment Board whose members act as fiduciaries with regard to the assets of the Thrift Savings Fund. In general, FERSA contains fiduciary obligation and prohibited transaction provisions similar to ERISA. However, unlike ERISA, FERSA prohibits party in interest transactions similar to those described in section 406(a) of ERISA only in those circumstances where adequate consideration is not exchanged between the Fund and the party in interest. Specifically, section 8477(c)(1) of FERSA provides that, except in exchange for adequate consideration, a fiduciary shall not permit the Thrift Savings Fund to engage in: transfers of its assets to, acquisition of property from or sales of property to, or transfers or exchanges of services with any person the fiduciary knows or should know to be a party in interest. Section 8477(a)(2) provides the FERSA definition for the term "adequate consideration," which is virtually identical to that contained in section 3(18) of ERISA. Thus, the proposal would apply to both section 3(18) of ERISA and section 8477(a)(2) of FERSA.

When the asset being valued is a security for which there is a generally recognized market, the plan fiduciary must determine "adequate consideration" by reference to the provisions of section 3(18)(A) of the Act (or with regard to FERSA, section 8477(a)(2)(A)). Section 3(18)(A) and section 8477(a)(2)(A) provide detailed reference points for the valuation of securities within its coverage, and in effect provides that adequate consideration for such securities is the prevailing market price. It is not the Department's intention to analyze the requirements of section 3(18)(A) or 8477(a)(2)(A) in this proposal. Fiduciaries must, however, determine whether a security is subject to the specific provisions of section 3(18)(A) (or section 8477(a)(2)(A) of FERSA) or the more general requirements of section 3(18)(B) (or section 8477(a)(2)(B)) as interpreted in this proposal. The question of whether a security is one for which there is a generally recognized market requires a factual determination in light of the character of the security and the nature and extent of market activity with regard to the security. Generally, the Department will examine whether a security is being actively traded so as to provide the benchmarks Congress intended. Isolated trading activity, or trades between related parties, generally will not be sufficient to show the existence of a generally recognized market for the purposes of section 3(18)(A) or section 8477(a)(2)(A).

In the case of all assets other than securities for which there is a generally recognized market, fiduciaries must determine adequate consideration pursuant to section 3(18)(B) of the Act (or, in the case of FERSA, section 8477(a)(2)(B)). Because it is designed to deal with all but a narrow class of assets, section 3(18)(B) and section 8477(a)(2)(B) are by their nature more general than section 3(18)(A) or section 8477(a)(2)(A). Although the Department has indicated that it will not issue advisory opinions stating whether certain stated consideration is "adequate consideration" for the purposes of section 3(18), ERISA Procedure 76-1, § 5.02(a) (41 FR 36281, 36282, August 27, 1976), the Department recognizes that plan fiduciaries have a need for guidance in valuing assets, and that standards to guide fiduciaries in this area may be particularly elusive with respect to assets other than securities for which there is a generally recognized market. See, for example, *Donovan v. Cunningham*, 716 F.2d 1455 (5th Cir. 1983) (court encourages the Department to adopt regulations under section 3(18)(B)). The Department has therefore determined to propose a regulation only under section 3(18)(B) and section 8477(a)(2)(B). This proposal is described more fully below.

It should be noted that it is not the Department's intention by this proposed regulation to relieve fiduciaries of the responsibility for making the required determinations of "adequate consideration" where applicable under the Act or FERSA. Nothing in the proposal should be construed as justifying a fiduciary's failure to take into account all relevant facts and circumstances in determining adequate consideration. Rather, the proposal is designed to provide a framework within which fiduciaries can fulfill their statutory duties. Further, fiduciaries should be aware that, even where a determination of adequate consideration comports with the requirements of section 3(18)(B) (or section 8477(a)(2)(B) of FERSA) and any regulation adopted thereunder, the investment of plan assets made pursuant to such determination will still be subject to the fiduciary requirements of Part 4 of Subtitle B of Title I of the Act, including the provisions of sections 403 and 404 of the Act, or the fiduciary responsibility provisions of FERSA.

B. Description of the Proposal

Proposed regulation 29 CFR 2510.3-18(b) is divided into four major parts. Proposed § 2510.3-18(b)(1) states the general rule and delineates the scope of the regulation. Proposed § 2510.3-18(b)(2) addresses the concept of fair market value as it relates to a determination of "adequate consideration" under section 3(18)(B) of the Act. Proposed § 2510.3-18(b)(3) deals with the requirement in section 3(18)(B) that valuing fiduciary act in good faith, and specifically discusses the use of an independent appraisal in connection with the determination of good faith. Proposed § 2510.3-18(b)(4) sets forth the content requirements for written valuations used as the basis for a determination of fair market value, with a special rule for the valuation of securities other than securities for which there is a generally recognized market. Each subsection is discussed in detail below.

1. General Rule and Scope

Proposed § 2510.3-18(b)(1)(i) essentially follows the language of section 3(18)(B) of the Act and section 8477(a)(2)(B) of FERSA and states that, in the case of a plan asset other than a security for which there is a generally recognized market, the term "adequate consideration" means the fair market value of the asset as determined in good faith by the trustee or named fiduciary (or, in the case of FERSA, a fiduciary) pursuant to the terms of the plan and in accordance with regulations promulgated by the Secretary of Labor. Proposed § 2510.3-18(b)(1)(ii) delineates the scope of this regulation by establishing two criteria, both of which must be met for a valid determination of adequate consideration. First, the value assigned to an asset must reflect its fair market value as determined pursuant to proposed § 2510.3-18(b)(2). Second, the value assigned to an asset must be the product of a determination made by the

continued

fiduciary in good faith as defined in proposed § 2510.3-18(b)(3). The Department will consider that a fiduciary has determined adequate consideration in accordance with section 3(18)(B) of the Act or section 8477(a)(2)(B) of FERSA only if both of these requirements are satisfied.

The Department has proposed this two-part test for several reasons. First, Congress incorporated the concept of fair market value into the definition of adequate consideration. As explained more fully below, fair market value is an often used concept having an established meaning in the field of asset valuation. By reference to this term, it would appear that Congress did not intend to allow parties to a transaction to set an arbitrary value for the assets involved. Therefore, a valuation determination which fails to reflect the market forces embodied in the concept of fair market value would also fail to meet the requirements of section 3(18)(B) of the Act or section 8477(a)(2)(B) of FERSA.

Second, it would appear that Congress intended to allow a fiduciary a limited degree of latitude so long as that fiduciary acted in good faith. However, a fiduciary would clearly fail to fulfill the fiduciary duties delineated in Part 4 of Subtitle B of Title I of the Act if that fiduciary acted solely on the basis of naive or uninformed good intentions. See *Donovan v. Cunningham*, supra, 716 F.2d at 1467 ("[A] pure heart and an empty head are not enough.") The Department has therefore proposed standards for a determination of a fiduciary's good faith which must be satisfied in order to meet the requirements of section 3(18)(B) or section 8477(a)(2)(B) of FERSA.

Third, even if a fiduciary were to meet the good faith standards contained in this proposed regulation, there may be circumstances in which good faith alone fails to insure an equitable result. For example, errors in calculation or honest failure to consider certain information could produce valuation figures outside of the range of acceptable valuations of a given asset. Because the determination of adequate consideration is a central requirement of the statutory exemptions discussed above, the Department believes it must assure that such exemptions are made available only for those transactions possessing all the external safeguards envisioned by Congress. To achieve this end, the Department's proposed regulation links the fair market value and good faith requirements to assure that the resulting valuation reflects market considerations and is the product of a valuation process conducted in good faith.

2. Fair Market Value

The first part of the Department's proposed two-part test under section 3(18)(B) and section 8477(a)(2)(B) requires that a determination of adequate consideration reflect the asset's fair market value. The term "fair market value" is defined in proposed § 2510.3-18(b)(2)(i) as the price at which an asset would change hands between a willing buyer and a willing seller when the former is not under any compulsion to buy and the latter is not under any compulsion to sell, and both parties are able, as well as willing, to trade and are well-informed about the asset and the market for that asset. This proposed definition essentially reflects the well-established meaning of this term in the area of asset valuation. See, for example, 26 CFR 20.2031-1 (estate tax regulations); Rev. Rul. 59-60, 1959-1 Cum. Bull. 237; *United States v. Cartwright*, 411 U.S. 546, 551 (1973); *Estate of Bright v. United States*, 658 F.2d 999, 1005 (5th Cir. 1981). It should specifically be noted that comparable valuations reflecting transactions resulting from other than free and equal negotiations (e.g., a distress sale) will fail to establish fair market value. See *Hooker Industries, Inc. v. Commissioner*, 3 EBC 1849, 1854-55 (T.C. June 24, 1982). Similarly, the extent to which the Department will view a valuation as reflecting fair market value will be affected by an assessment of the level of expertise demonstrated by the parties making the valuation. See *Donovan v. Cunningham*, supra, 716 F.2d at 1468 (failure to apply sound business principles of evaluation, for whatever reason, may result in a valuation that does not reflect fair market value).[1]

The Department is aware that the fair market value of an asset will ordinarily be identified by a range of valuations rather than a specific, set figure. It is not the Department's intention that only one valuation figure will be acceptable as the fair market value of a specified asset. Rather, this proposal would require that the valuation assigned to an asset must reflect a figure within an acceptable range of valuations for that asset.

In addition to this general formulation of the definition of fair market value, the Department is proposing two specific requirements for the determination of fair market value for the purposes of section 3(18)(B) and section 8477(a)(2)(B). First, proposed § 2510.3-18(b)(2)(ii) requires that fair market value must be determined as of the date of the transaction involving that asset. This requirement is designed to prevent situations such as arose in *Donovan v. Cunningham*, supra. In that case, the plan fiduciaries relied on a 1975 appraisal to set the value of employer securities purchased by an ESOP during 1976 and thereafter, and failed to take into account significant changes in the company's business condition in the interim. The court found that this reliance was unwarranted, and therefore the fiduciaries' valuation failed to reflect adequate consideration under section 3(18)(B). Id. at 1468-69.

Second, proposed § 2510.3-18(b)(2)(iii) states that the determination of fair market value must be reflected in written documentation of valuation[2] meeting the content requirements set forth in § 2510.3-18(b)(4). (The valuation content requirements are discussed below.) The Department has proposed this requirement in light of the role the adequate consideration requirement plays in a number

---

[1] Whether in any particular transaction a plan fiduciary is in fact well-informed about the asset in question and the market for that asset, including any specific circumstances which may affect the value of the asset, will be determined on a facts and circumstances basis. If, however, the fiduciary negotiating on behalf of the plan has or should have specific knowledge concerning either the particular asset or the market for that asset, it is the view of the Department that the fiduciary must take into account that specific knowledge in negotiating the price of the asset in order to meet the fair market value standard of this regulation. For example, a sale of plan-owned real estate at a negotiated price consistent with valuations of comparable property will not be a sale for adequate consideration if the negotiating fiduciary does not take into account any special knowledge which he has or should have about the asset or its market, e.g., that the property's value should reflect a premium due to a certain developer's specific land development plans.

[2] It should be noted that the written valuation required by this section of the proposal need not be a written report of an independent appraiser. Rather, it should be documentation sufficient to allow the Department to determine whether the content requirements of § 2510.3-18(b)(4) have been satisfied. The use of an independent appraiser may be relevant to a determination of good faith, as discussed with regard to proposed § 2510.3-18(b)(3), infra, but it is not required to satisfy the fair market value criterion in § 2510.3-18(b)(2)(i).

continued

of statutory exemptions from the prohibited transaction provisions of the Act. In determining whether a statutory exemption applies to a particular transaction, the burden of proof is upon the party seeking to make use of the statutory exemption to show that all the requirements of the provision are met. *Donovan v. Cunningham*, supra, 716 F.2d at 1467 n.27. In the Department's view, written documentation relating to the valuation is necessary for a determination of how, and on what basis, an asset was valued, and therefore whether that valuation reflected an asset's fair market value. In addition, the Department believes that it would be contrary to prudent business practices for a fiduciary to act in the absence of such written documentation of fair market value.

3. Good Faith

The second part of the Department's proposed two-part test under section 3(18)(B) and section 8477(a)(2)(B) requires that an assessment of adequate consideration be the product of a determination made in good faith by the plan trustee or named fiduciary (or under FERSA, a fiduciary). Proposed § 2510.3-18(b)(3)(i) states that as a general matter this good faith requirement establishes an objective standard of conduct, rather than mandating an inquiry into the intent or state of mind of the plan trustee or named fiduciary. In this regard, the proposal is consistent with the opinion in *Donovan v. Cunningham*, supra, where the court stated that the good faith requirement in section 3(18)(B):

is not a search for subjective good faith * * * The statutory reference to good faith in Section 3(18) must be read in light of the overriding duties of Section 404.

716 F.2d at 1467. The inquiry into good faith under the proposal therefore focuses on the fiduciary's conduct in determining fair market value. An examination of all relevant facts and circumstances is necessary for a determination of whether a fiduciary has met this objective good faith standard.

Proposed § 2510.3-18(b)(3)(ii) focuses on two factors which must be present in order for the Department to be satisfied that the fiduciary has acted in good faith. First, this section would require a fiduciary to apply sound business principles of evaluation and to conduct a prudent investigation of the circumstances prevailing at the time of the valuation. This requirement reflects the Cunningham court's emphasis on the use of prudent business practices in valuing plan assets.

Second, this section states that either the fiduciary making the valuation must itself be independent of all the parties to the transaction (other than the plan), or the fiduciary must rely on the report of an appraiser who is independent of all the parties to the transaction (other than the plan). (The criteria for determining independence are discussed below.) As noted above, under ERISA, the determination of adequate consideration is a central safeguard in many statutory exemptions applicable to plan transactions with the plan sponsor. The close relationship between the plan and the plan sponsor in such situations raises a significant potential for conflicts of interest as the fiduciary values assets which are the subject of transactions between the plan and the plan sponsor. In light of this possibility, the Department believes that good faith may only be demonstrated when the valuation is made by persons independent of the parties to the transaction (other than the plan), i.e., a valuation made by an independent fiduciary or by a fiduciary acting pursuant to the report of an independent appraiser.

The Department emphasizes that the two requirements of proposed § 2510.3-18(b)(3)(ii) are designed to work in concert. For example, a plan fiduciary charged with valuation may be independent of all the parties to a transaction and may, in light of the requirement of proposed § 2510.3-18(b)(3)(ii)(B), decide to undertake the valuation process itself. However, if the independent fiduciary has neither the experience, facilities nor expertise to make the type of valuation under consideration, the decision by that fiduciary to make the valuation would fail to meet the prudent investigation and sound business principles requirement of proposed § 2510.3-18(b)(3)(ii)(A).

Proposed § 2510.3-18(b)(3)(iii) defines the circumstances under which a fiduciary or an appraiser will be deemed to be independent for the purposes of subparagraph (3)(ii)(B), above. The proposal notes that the fiduciary or the appraiser must in fact be independent of all parties participating in the transaction other than the plan. The proposal also notes that a determination of independence must be made in light of all relevant facts and circumstances, and then delineates certain circumstances under which this independence will be lacking. These circumstances reflect the definitions of the terms "affiliate" and "control" in Departmental regulation 29 CFR 2510.3-21(e) (defining the circumstances under which an investment adviser is a fiduciary). It should be noted that, under these proposed provisions, an appraiser will be considered independent of all parties to a transaction (other than the plan) only if a plan fiduciary has chosen the appraiser and has the right to terminate that appointment, and the plan is thereby established as the appraiser's client.[3] Absent such circumstances, the appraiser may be unable to be completely neutral in the exercise of his function.[4]

4. Valuation Content—General

Proposed § 2510.3-18(b)(4)(i) sets the content requirements for the written documentation of valuation required for a determination of fair market value under proposed § 2510.3-18(b)(2)(iii). The proposal follows to a large extent the requirements of Rev. Proc. 66-49, 1966-2 C.B. 1257, which sets forth the format required by the IRS for the valuation of donated property. The Department believes that this format is a familiar one, and will therefore facilitate compliance. Several additions to the IRS requirements merit brief explanation.

---

[3] The independence of an appraiser will not be affected solely because the plan sponsor pays the appraiser's fee.

[4] With regard to this independence requirement the Department notes that new section 401(a)(28) of the Code (added by section 1175(a) of the Tax Reform Act of 1986) requires that, in the case of an employee stock ownership plan, employer securities which are not readily tradable on established securities markets must be valued by an independent appraiser. New section 401(a)(28)(C) states that the term "independent appraiser" means an appraiser meeting requirements similar to the requirements of regulations under section 170(a)(1) of the Code (relating to IRS verification of the value assigned for deduction purposes to assets donated to charitable organizations). The Department notes that the requirements of proposed regulation § 2510.3-18(b)(3)(iii) are not the same as the requirements of the regulations issued by the IRS under section 170(a)(1) of the Code. The IRS has not yet promulgated rules under Code section 401(a)(28).

continued

First, proposed paragraph (b)(4)(i)(E) requires a statement of the purpose for which the valuation was made. A valuation undertaken, for example, for a yearly financial report may prove an inadequate basis for any sale of the asset in question. This requirement is intended to facilitate review of the valuation in the correct context.

Second, proposed paragraph (b)(4)(i)(F) requires a statement as to the relative weight accorded to relevant valuation methodologies. The Department's experience in this area indicates that there are a number of different methodologies used within the appraisal industry. By varying the treatment given and emphasis accorded relevant information, these methodologies directly affect the result of the appraiser's analysis. It is the Department's understanding that appraisers will often use different methodologies to cross-check their results. A statement of the method or methods used would allow for a more accurate assessment of the validity of the valuation.

Finally, proposed subparagraph (b)(4)(i)(G) requires a statement of the valuation's effective date. This reflects the requirement in proposed § 2510.3-18(b)(ii) that fair market value must be determined as of the date of the transaction in question.

5. Valuation Content—Special Rule

Proposed § 2510.3-18(b)(4)(ii) establishes additional content requirements for written documentation of valuation when the asset being appraised is a security other than a security for which there is a generally recognized market. In other words, the requirements of the proposed special rule supplement, rather than supplant, the requirements of paragraph (b)(4)(i). The proposed special rule establishes a nonexclusive list of factors to be considered when the asset being valued is a security not covered by section 3(18)(A) of the Act or section 8477(a)(2)(A) of FERSA. Such securities pose special valuation problems because they are not traded or are so thinly traded that it is difficult to assess the effect on such securities of the market forces usually considered in determining fair market value. The Internal Revenue Service has had occasion to address the valuation problems posed by one type of such securities—securities issued by closely held corporations. Rev. Rul. 59-60, 1959-1 Cum. Bull. 237, lists a variety of factors to be considered when valuing securities of closely held corporations for tax purposes.[5] The Department's experience indicates that Rev. Rul. 59-60 is familiar to plan fiduciaries, plan sponsors and the corporate community in general. The Department has, therefore, modeled this proposed special rule after Rev. Rul. 59-60 with certain additions and changes discussed below. It should be emphasized, however, that this is a non-exclusive list of factors to be considered. Certain of the factors listed may not be relevant to every valuation inquiry, although the fiduciary will bear the burden of demonstrating such irrelevance. Similarly, reliance on this list will not relieve fiduciaries from the duty to consider all relevant facts and circumstances when valuing such securities. The purpose of the proposed list is to guide fiduciaries in the course of their inquiry.

Several of the factors listed in proposed § 2510.3-18(b)(4)(ii) merit special comment and explanation. Proposed subparagraph (G) states that the fair market value of securities other than those for which there is a generally recognized market may be established by reference to the market price of similar securities of corporations engaged in the same or a similar line of business whose securities are actively traded in a free and open market, either on an exchange or over the counter. The Department intends that the degree of comparability must be assessed in order to approximate as closely as possible the market forces at work with regard to the corporation issuing the securities in question.

Proposed subparagraph (H) requires an assessment of the effect of the securities' marketability or lack thereof. Rev. Rul. 59-60 does not explicitly require such an assessment, but the Department believes that the marketability of these types of securities will directly affect their price. In this regard, the Department is aware that, especially in situations involving employee stock ownership plans (ESOPs),[6] the employer securities held by the ESOP will provide a "put" option whereby individual participants may upon retirement sell their shares back to the employer.[7] It has been argued that some kinds of "put" options may diminish the need to discount the value of the securities due to lack of marketability. The Department believes that the existence of the "put" option should be considered for valuation purposes only to the extent it is enforceable and the employer has and may reasonably be expected to continue to have, adequate resources to meet its obligations. Thus, the Department proposes to require that the plan fiduciary assess whether these "put" rights are actually enforceable, and whether the employer will be able to pay for the securities when and if the "put" is exercised.

Finally, proposed subparagraph (I) deals with the role of control premiums in valuing securities other than those for which there is a generally recognized market. The Department proposes that a plan purchasing control may pay a control premium, and a plan selling control should receive a control premium. Specifically, the Department proposes that a plan may pay such a premium only to the extent a third party would pay a control premium. In this regard, the Department's position is that the payment of a control premium is unwarranted unless the plan obtains both voting control and control in fact. The Department will therefore carefully scrutinize situations to ascertain whether the transaction involving payment of such a premium actually results in the passing of control to the plan. For example, it may be difficult to determine that a plan paying a control premium has received control in fact where it is reasonable to assume at the time of acquisition that distribution of shares to plan participants will cause the plan's control of the company to be dissipated within a short period of time subsequent to acquisition.[8] In the Department's view, however, a plan would not fail to receive

---

[5] Rev. Rul. 59-60 was modified by Rev. Rul. 65-193 (1965-2 C.B. 370) regarding the valuation of tangible and intangible corporate assets. The provisions of Rev. Rul. 59-60, as modified, were extended to the valuation of corporate securities for income and other tax purposes by Rev. Rul. 68-609 (1968-2 C.B. 327). In addition, Rev. Rul. 77-287 (1977-2 C.B. 319). amplified. Rev. Rul. 59-60 by indicating the ways in which the factors listed in Rev. Rul. 59-60 should be applied when valuing restricted securities.

[6] The definition of the term "adequate consideration" under ERISA is of particular importance to the establishment and maintenance of ESOPs because, pursuant to section 408(e) of the Act, an ESOP may acquire employer securities from a party in interest only under certain conditions, including that the plan pay no more than adequate consideration for the securities.

[7] Regulation 29 CFR 2550.408b-(j) requires such a put option in order for a loan from a party in interest to the ESOP to qualify for the statutory exemption in section 408(b)(3) of ERISA from the prohibited transactions provisions of ERISA.

[8] However, the Department notes that the mere pass-through of voting rights to participants would not in itself affect a determination that a plan has received control in fact, notwithstanding the existence of participant voting rights, if the plan fiduciaries having control over plan assets ordinarily may resell the shares to a third party and command a control premium, without the need to secure the approval of the plan participants.

continued

control merely because individuals who were previously officers, directors or shareholders of the corporation continue as plan fiduciaries or corporate officials after the plan has acquired the securities. Nonetheless, the retention of management and the utilization of corporate officials as plan fiduciaries, when viewed in conjunction with other facts, may indicate that actual control has not passed to the plan within the meaning of paragraph (b)(4)(ii)(I) of the proposed regulation. Similarly, if the plan purchases employer securities in small increments pursuant to an understanding with the employer that the employer will eventually sell a controlling portion of shares to the plan, a control premium would be warranted only to the extent that the understanding with the employer was actually a binding agreement obligating the employer to pass control within a reasonable time. See *Donovan v. Cunningham*, supra, 716 F.2d at 1472-74 (mere intention to transfer control not sufficient).

6. Service Arrangements Subject to FERSA

Section 8477(c)(1)(C) of FERSA permits the exchange of services between the Thrift Savings Fund and a party in interest only in exchange for adequate consideration. In this context, the proposal defines the term "adequate consideration" as "reasonable compensation," as that term is described in sections 408(b)(2) and 408(c)(2) of ERISA and the regulations promulgated thereunder. By so doing, the proposal would establish a consistent standard of exemptive relief for both ERISA and FERSA with regard to what otherwise would be prohibited service arrangements.

Regulatory Flexibility Act

The Department has determined that this regulation would not have a significant economic effect on small plans. In conducting the analysis required under the Regulatory Flexibility Act, it was estimated that approximately 6,250 small plans may be affected by the regulation. The total additional cost to these plans, over and above the costs already being incurred under established valuation practices, are estimated not to exceed $875,000 per year, or $140 per plan for small plans choosing to engage in otherwise prohibited transactions that are exempted under the statute conditioned on a finding of adequate consideration.

Executive Order 12291

The Department has determined that the proposed regulatory action would not constitute a "major rule" as that term is used in Executive Order 12291 because the action would not result in: an annual effect on the economy of $100 million; a major increase in costs of prices for consumers, individual industries, government agencies, or geographical regions; or significant adverse effects on competition, employment, investment, productivity, innovation, or on the ability of United States based enterprises to compete with foreign based enterprises in domestic or export markets.

Paperwork Reduction Act

This proposed regulation contains several paperwork requirements. The regulation has been forwarded for approval to the Office of Management and Budget under the provisions of the Paperwork Reduction Act of 1980 (Pub. L. 96-511). A control number has not yet been assigned.

Statutory Authority

This regulation is proposed under section 3(18) and 505 of the Act (29 U.S.C. 1003(18) and 1135); Secretary of Labor's Order No. 1-87; and sections 8477(a)(2)(B) and 8477(f) of FERSA.

List of Subjects in 29 CFR Part 2510

Employee benefit plans, Employee Retirement Income Security Act, Pensions, Pension and Welfare Benefit Administration.

Proposed Regulation

For the reasons set out in the preamble, the Department proposes to amend Part 2510 of Chapter XXV of Title 29 of the Code of Federal Regulations as follows:

PART 2510—[AMENDED]

   1. The authority for Part 2510 is revised to read as follows:

      Authority: Sec. 3(2), 111(c), 505, Pub. L. 93-406, 88 Stat. 852, 894, (29 U.S.C. 1002(2), 1031, 1135); Secretary of Labor's Order No. 27-74, 1-86, 1-87, and Labor Management Services Administration Order No. 2-6.

      Section 2510.3-18 is also issued under sec. 3(18) of the Act (29 U.S.C. 1003(18)) and secs. 8477(a)(2)(B) and (f) of FERSA (5 U.S.C. 8477)

      Section 2510.3-101 is also issued under sec. 102 of Reorganization Plan No. 4 of 1978 (43 FR 47713, October 17, 1978), effective December 31, 1978 (44 FR 1065, January 3, 1978); 3 CFR 1978 Comp. 332, and sec. 11018(d) of Pub. L. 99-272, 100 Stat. 82.

      Section 2510.3-102 is also issued under sec. 102 of Reorganization Plan No. 4 of 1978 (43 FR 47713, October 17, 1978), effective December 31, 1978 (44 FR 1065, January 3, 1978), and 3 CFR 1978 Comp. 332.

   2. Section 2510.3-18 is added to read as follows:

     § 2510.3-18 Adequate Consideration

     (a) [Reserved]

     (b)(1)(i) General. (A) Section 3(18)(B) of the Employee Retirement Income Security Act of 1974 (the Act) provides that, in the case of a plan asset other than a security for which there is a generally recognized market, the term "adequate consideration"

continued

when used in Part 4 of Subtitle B of Title I of the Act means the fair market value of the asset as determined in good faith by the trustee or named fiduciary pursuant to the terms of the plan and in accordance with regulations promulgated by the Secretary of Labor.

(B) Section 8477(a)(2)(B) of the Federal Employees' Retirement System Act of 1986 (FERSA) provides that, in the case of an asset other than a security for which there is a generally recognized market, the term "adequate consideration" means the fair market value of the asset as determined in good faith by a fiduciary or fiduciaries in accordance with regulations prescribed by the Secretary of Labor.

(ii) Scope. The requirements of section 3(18)(B) of the Act and section 8477(a)(2)(B) of FERSA will not be met unless the value assigned to a plan asset both reflects the asset's fair market value as defined in paragraph (b)(2) of this section and results from a determination made by the plan trustee or named fiduciary (or, in the case of FERSA, a fiduciary) in good faith as described in paragraph (b)(3) of this section. Paragraph (b)(5) of this section contains a special rule for service contracts subject to FERSA.

(2) Fair Market Value. (i) Except as otherwise specified in this section, the term "fair market value" as used in section 3(18)(B) of the Act and section 8477(a)(2)(B) of FERSA means the price at which an asset would change hands between a willing buyer and a willing seller when the former is not under any compulsion to buy and the latter is not under any compulsion to sell, and both parties are able, as well as willing, to trade and are well informed about the asset and the market for such asset.

(ii) The fair market value of an asset for the purposes of section 3(18)(B) of the Act and section 8477(a)(2)(B) of FERSA must be determined as of the date of the transaction involving that asset.

(iii) The fair market value of an asset for the purposes of section 3(18)(B) of the Act and section 8477(a)(2)(B) of FERSA must be reflected in written documentation of valuation meeting the requirements set forth in paragraph (b)(4), of this section.

(3) Good Faith—(i) General Rule. The requirement in section 3(18)(B) of the Act and section 8477(a)(2)(B) of FERSA that the fiduciary must determine fair market value in good faith establishes an objective, rather than a subjective, standard of conduct. Subject to the conditions in paragraphs (b)(3) (ii) and (iii) of this section, an assessment of whether the fiduciary has acted in good faith will be made in light of all relevant facts and circumstances.

(ii) In considering all relevant facts and circumstances, the Department will not view a fiduciary as having acted in good faith unless

(A) The fiduciary has arrived at a determination of fair market value by way of a prudent investigation of circumstances prevailing at the time of the valuation, and the application of sound business principles of evaluation; and

(B) The fiduciary making the valuation either,

(1) Is independent of all parties to the transaction (other than the plan), or

(2) Relies on the report of an appraiser who is independent of all parties to the transaction (other than the plan).

(iii) In order to satisfy the independence requirement of paragraph (b)(3)(ii)(B), of this section, a person must in fact be independent of all parties (other than the plan) participating in the transaction. For the purposes of this section, an assessment of independence will be made in light of all relevant facts and circumstances. However, a person will not be considered to be independent of all parties to the transaction if that person—

(1) Is directly or indirectly, through one or more intermediaries, controlling, controlled by, or under common control with any of the parties to the transaction (other than the plan);

(2) Is an officer, director, partner, employee, employer or relative (as defined in section 3(15) of the Act, and including siblings) of any such parties (other than the plan);

(3) Is a corporation or partnership of which any such party (other than the plan) is an officer, director or partner.

For the purposes of this subparagraph, the term "control," in connection with a person other than an individual, means the power to exercise a controlling influence over the management or policies of that person.

(4) Valuation Content. (i) In order to comply with the requirement in paragraph (b)(2)(iii), of this section, that the determination of fair market value be reflected in written documentation of valuation, such written documentation must contain, at a minimum, the following information:

(A) A summary of the qualifications to evaluate assets of the type being valued of the person or persons making the valuation;

(B) A statement of the asset's value, a statement of the methods used in determining that value, and the reasons for the valuation in light of those methods;

(C) A full description of the asset being valued;

(D) The factors taken into account in making the valuation, including any restrictions, understandings, agreements or obligations limiting the use or disposition of the property;

(E) The purpose for which the valuation was made;

(F) The relevance or significance accorded to the valuation methodologies taken into account;

(G) The effective date of the valuation; and

(H) In cases where a valuation report has been prepared, the signature of the person making the valuation and the date the report was signed.

(ii) Special Rule. When the asset being valued is a security other than a security covered by section 3(18)(A) of the Act or section 8477(a)(2)(A) of FERSA, the written valuation required by paragraph (b)(2)(iii) of this section, must contain the information

continued

required in paragraph (b)(4)(i) of this section, and must include, in addition to an assessment of all other relevant factors, an assessment of the factors listed below:

(A) The nature of the business and the history of the enterprise from its inception;

(B) The economic outlook in general, and the condition and outlook of the specific industry in particular;

(C) The book value of the securities and the financial condition of the business;

(D) The earning capacity of the company;

(E) The dividend-paying capacity of the company;

(F) Whether or not the enterprise has goodwill or other intangible value;

(G) The market price of securities of corporations engaged in the same or a similar line of business, which are actively traded in a free and open market, either on an exchange or over-the-counter;

(H) The marketability, or lack thereof, of the securities. Where the plan is the purchaser of securities that are subject to "put" rights and such rights are taken into account in reducing the discount for lack of marketability, such assessment shall include consideration of the extent to which such rights are enforceable, as well as the company's ability to meet its obligations with respect to the "put" rights (taking into account the company's financial strength and liquidity);

(I) Whether or not the seller would be able to obtain a control premium from an unrelated third party with regard to the block of securities being valued, provided that in cases where a control premium is taken into account:

(1) Actual control (both in form and in substance) is passed to the purchaser with the sale, or will be passed to the purchaser within a reasonable time pursuant to a binding agreement in effect at the time of the sale, and

(2) It is reasonable to assume that the purchaser's control will not be dissipated within a short period of time subsequent to acquisition.

(5) Service Arrangements Subject to FERSA. For purposes of determinations pursuant to section 8477(c)(1)(C) of FERSA (relating to the provision of services) the term "adequate consideration" under section 8477(a)(2)(B) of FERSA means "reasonable compensation" as defined in sections 408(b)(2) and 408(c)(2) of the Act and § 2550.408b-2(d) and 2550.408c-2 of this chapter.

(6) Effective Date. This section will be effective for transactions taking place after the date 30 days following publication of the final regulation in the Federal Register.

Signed in Washington, DC, this 11th day of May 1988.

David M. Walker,

Assistant Secretary, Pension and Welfare Benefits Administration, U.S.

Department of Labor.

---

disseminated and recognized, not only throughout the professional business appraisal community and the courts in the United States, but also worldwide.

We believe these developments have already had some positive impact on the average quality of business valuation work. Business valuation practitioners are becoming more knowledgeable and rigorous in their practices. The standards also provide attorneys, CPAs, business owners, courts, and others who rely on business appraisals some widely accepted criteria by which to judge the quality of a business valuation. Chapter 22 of this book, "Reviewing a Business Valuation Report," will be helpful in evaluating a business valuation report against the background of these standards.

The standards will continue to undergo refinement, but a solid foundation is certainly in place.

The accreditations in business valuation are also achieving increased recognition, both by the courts in written opinions and by the legal community in selecting business appraisers (see Exhibit 1–8).

Bibliography

American Institute of Certified Public Accountants, Main Office, 1211 Avenue of the Americas, New York, NY 10036 (212) 596-6200, (800) 862-4272, www.aicpa.org

- Trugman, Gary R. *Conducting a Valuation of a Closely Held Business.* Jersey City, NJ: AICPA, Management Consulting Services Division, 1993. A consulting service practice aid available from the AICPA.
- Trugman, Gary R. and American Institute of Certified Public Accountants. *A CPA's Guide to Valuing a Closely Held Business.* New York: American Institute of Certified Public Accountants, 2001.
- *The CPA Expert*, a quarterly journal.

American Society of Appraisers, 555 Herndon Parkway, Suite 125, Herndon, VA 20170 (703) 478-2228, www.appraisers.org

- Principles of Appraisal Practice and Code of Ethics—available free of charge from the ASA.
- Standards for Business Valuation—single copies available free of charge from the publisher of *Business Valuation Review.*
- *ASA Professional*, a quarterly publication.

The Appraisal Foundation, 1155 15th Street NW, Suite 1111, Washington, DC 20005 (202) 347-7722, www.appraisalfoundation.org

- *Uniform Standards of Professional Appraisal Practice* (USPAP), updated on a periodic basis.
- Information Service. The Information Service is designed to provide summary-oriented information to appraisers, users of appraisal services, and others who have an interest in remaining current on the activities of the Appraisal Foundation, the Appraisal Standards Board (ASB), and the Appraiser Qualifications Board (AQB).
- Subscription Service. The Subscription Service is the complete source of information for appraisers, users of appraisal services, and others on the activities of the Appraisal Foundation, the Appraisal Standards Board (ASB), and the Appraiser Qualifications Board (AQB).

Business Valuation Resources, 1000 SW Broadway, Suite 1200, Portland, OR 972-205-3035, (888) BUS-VALU (888-287-8258), www.BVLibrary.com

- *Business Valuation Update*, monthly newsletter for business appraisers, intermediaries, buyers, sellers, and financial sources; "Association News" and "Legal and Court Case" departments report changes in professional standards and credentials, regulations, and laws affecting business valuation.
- *BVPapers*, online database containing hundreds of pages of research papers, conference presentations, and the most published restricted stock study.
- *BV Data, Publications & Internet Directory*, database of vendors and publishers of business valuation products.
- *BV Q&A Update and Database*, database of current answers to your most pressing business valuation questions.
- *Business Valuation Videocourse*, moderated by Shannon P. Pratt (New York: American Society of Certified Public Accountants, 1993, workbook updated in 1996). The objective of this videocourse is to provide practitioners with an overview of the essentials of business valuation. Joining Dr. Pratt in the two-and-one-half-hour video presentation are Robert F. Reilly, Robert P. Schweihs, and Jay E. Fishman.

The Canadian Institute of Chartered Business Valuators, 277 Wellington Street W., Toronto, Ontario, Canada M5V 3H2, (416) 204-3396, www.cicbv.ca

- *CICBV Practice Standards*
- *Business Valuation Digest*
- *The Journal of Business Valuation*
- *The Business Valuator*
- *The Valuation Law Review*

CFA Institute (formerly Association for Investment Management and Research), PO Box 3668, 560 Ray C. Hunt Drive, Charlottesville, VA 22903 (800) 247-8132 or (434) 951-5499, www.cfainstitute.org

- *Financial Analysts Journal*, published bimonthly.
- *CFA Magazine*, published bimonthly.
- *CFA Digest*, published quarterly.
- *CFA Institute conference proceedings*.
- *CFA Advantage*, a newsletter about the CFA Program. Posted online four times a year.
- *Valuation of Closely Held Companies and Inactively Traded Securities*, edited by E. Theodore Veit, 1990 (monograph).

The ESOP Association, 1100 17th Street NW, Suite 210, Washington, DC 20036, (202) 293-2971, www.esopassociation.org

- *Valuing ESOP Shares*, 1994
- *Report on Valuation Consideration for Leveraged ESOPs*, 1998

Institute of Business Appraisers, PO Box 17410, Plantation, FL 33318, (954) 584-1144, www.yo-iba.org

- *Business Valuation Practice*, a semiannual journal oriented to practical applications in business valuation.

Internal Revenue Service, 1111 Constitution Avenue NW, Washington, DC 20224, (202) 566-5000, www.irs.gov

- *IRS Valuation Training for Appeals Officers*, 1998. Available through Commerce Clearing House Publishers, (800) 248-3248. (This publication is also available through *Business Valuation Update Online*, www.BVLibrary.com.)
- *IRS Business Valuation Guidelines* (latest edition available free online at www.BVLibrary.com.)

International Valuation Standards Committee, International Bureau, 12 Great George Street, London, UK SW1P 3AD, Phone: +44 207 222 7000, Fax: +44 207 222 9480, ivsc@ivsc.org.

- *International Valuation Standards*, 2007

National Association of Certified Valuation Analysts, 1111 Brickyard Road, Suite 200, Salt Lake City, UT 84106, (800) 677-2009 or (801) 486-0600, www.nacva.com

- *The Value Examiner*, bimonthly magazine with information on NACVA activities and business valuation articles.

Valuation Products & Services, LC, 3340 Peachtree Rd. NE, Suite 1785 Tower PL, Atlanta, GA 30326, (404) 814-3731, www.valuationproducts.com.

- *Financial valuation and litigation expert*, James R. Hitchner, a bimonthly journal that contains views and tools in financial valuation, fraud, forensics, and litigation services.

Chapter 2

Defining the Assignment

It is impossible to intelligently discuss methods of valuation without reference to some assumed definition of value . . .[1]

Many people hold the mistaken notion that there can be only one "value." As is shown in this chapter, there are many definitions of value, and the purpose of the valuation usually determines the appropriate definition of value.

This chapter is designed to help the valuation analyst and the client (or the client's legal and other advisers) to focus together on all the elements that need to be specified in the valuation assignment, so that appropriate methodology will be employed to accomplish the objective of the specific engagement.

Identifying and clearly defining the purpose and objective of the business valuation assignment go a long way toward eliminating many of the problems that occur with the conclusions of business valuation projects. While it seems simple, and should be simple to understand, failure to clearly define the elements of the valuation assignment *at the outset of the business valuation* is one of the greatest sources of errors, delays, excess costs, and misunderstandings between client and appraiser in a business valuation.

Defining the valuation assignment is the logical beginning of the valuation process, providing focus for all the valuation considerations and efforts to be undertaken. Inadequate specification of the valuation assignment often results in misdirected efforts and invalid conclusions.

It may seem obvious that the first step is to define the task. However, when asked to participate in finding a solution to a client's problem, the client often does not know how to define the valuation assignment, and communication to agree on and mutually understand the assignment is often the most critical step. In fact, valuation engagements that turn out poorly are often due to a failure to carefully define the assignment at the outset.

The reason for this failure may be that the client lacks sufficient experience to realize all the details that should be included in the valuation assignment or has not thought through the implications of some aspects of the appraisal. People who do not engage in business valuations on a regular basis are unlikely to consider all of the key elements of a valuation assignment. The professional appraiser should help the client (and/or the client's attorney) with these details. However, appraisers are not lawyers and do not practice law. When legal issues are involved, it is the ultimate responsibility of the attorney, not the appraiser, to frame those issues.

Regardless of why the shortcomings occur, time spent at the outset in being thorough and explicit in defining the valuation assignment is time well spent.

Basic Elements of the Valuation Assignment

The basic elements of the valuation assignment are:

1. Name of the client and of the appraiser
2. Definition of the legal interest or interests to be appraised
3. Valuation date(s) (the date as of which the appraiser's opinion of value applies)

---

[1] James C. Bonbright, *Valuation of Property*, Vol. I (Charlottesville, VA: The Michie Company, 1965 [reprint of 1937 ed.]), p. 128.

4. Purpose or purposes of the appraisal (the use to which the valuation exercise is expected to be put)
5. Applicable standard (or definition) of value
6. Going-concern versus liquidation premise of value
7. Description of the specific ownership characteristics:

   a. Size of interest relative to total
   b. Degree of marketability (e.g., public, private, and related matters)

8. Form and extent of written and/or oral report
9. Special requirements, contingent or limiting conditions, or special instructions for the professional appraiser

Often it is impossible to define at the outset all of the relevant details of the valuation assignment. In such cases, it may be helpful for the appraiser to list the elements that are understood and the elements remaining to be understood. The appraiser can then follow up to try to resolve such questions. Exhibit 2–1 presents a general checklist for defining the valuation assignment.

Writing valuation objectives and requirements forces those responsible for the valuation to think carefully through all of its essential elements. It also helps prevent misdirecting the valuation process and helps the various parties involved, such as the principals, brokers, attorneys, and professional appraisers, avoid misunderstandings that otherwise might arise.

As the appraisal assignment develops, the file containing information on it will grow. As the missing details from the original appraisal assignment are changed or filled in, the appraiser notes them by memorandums to the file with copies to the client and/or to the client's attorney as they are discovered.

Exhibit 2–1

VALUATION ENGAGEMENT QUESTIONNAIRE AND CHECKLIST

Prospective Client: _____

Completed by: _____   Date: _____

> **Instructions:**   This form should be completed for a prospective new client or a prospective engagement for an existing client. The person completing this checklist need only complete those parts of the form that apply to the proposed engagement.

I. PROSPECTIVE CLIENT DATA

[The following data should be obtained for the prospective client (the person or company that will be engaging the consultant). That client may not be the actual entity being valued. Accordingly, a separate section of the form is designed for documenting information about the entity being valued.]

Prospective Client's Name: _____   Phone No.: _____

                                                                             Fax No.:_____

Business Address: _____

_____

Referral Source (how the consultant became aware of the potential engagement): _____

_____

_____

URL (Internet) Address: _____

Is the prospective client the same entity that is to be valued?

_____ Yes   Proceed to section II of this form (Entity to Be Valued). The remaining portion of section I does not need to be completed.

_____ No   Complete the remaining portion of section I before proceeding to section II.

Briefly explain the prospective client's relationship to the entity to be valued (the client's ownership interest in the entity, if any; whether the entity is a proposed acquisition candidate of the entity; etc.). _____

_____

_____

Professional references of the prospective client. (This is optional information. Some consultants may desire to obtain the names of the proposed client's attorney, CPA, and other business references.)

Reference Name: _____   Occupation: _____

Address: _____   Phone No.: _____

                _____

Reference Name: _____   Occupation: _____

Address: _____   Phone No.: _____

                _____

Reference Name: _____   Occupation: _____

Address: _____   Phone No.: _____

                _____

II. ENTITY TO BE VALUED

(If the prospective client and the entity to be valued are the same, it is not necessary to repeat the data obtained in the preceding section of this form.)

Name of Entity to Be Valued: _____

Type of Legal Entity (corp., S corp., partnership, proprietorship, etc.): _____

Business Address: _____

_____

Phone No.: _____   Fax No.: _____

Contacts at the entity with whom we would work (state name and title):

_____

_____

Brief description of the entity's business: _____

_____

_____

SIC Code: _____

NAICS Code: _____

Entity's Accounting Firm: _____

    Address: _____

    Phone No.: _____ Contact: _____

Entity's Primary Attorney: _____

    Address: _____

    Phone No.: _____ Contact: _____

Other References (optional): _____

    Address: _____ Phone No. _____

III. SCOPE OF THE ENGAGEMENT

Briefly describe the purpose of the engagement (determination of a party's interest in a divorce proceeding, valuation of a company for a proposed sale or acquisition, determination of a value for an estate tax return, etc.).

_____

_____

_____

Describe the interest to be valued (i.e., the ownership percentage being valued and whether it is a controlling or minority interest).

_____

_____

_____

Valuation Date(s): _____ Proposed Deadline: _____

Describe any obvious difficulties that may be associated with the valuation date (e.g., the date may be at an interim period when no year-end financials are available). _____

_____

_____

Does there appear to be enough historical financial statements and tax returns to assess the financial background and trends of the company? _____ Yes _____ No

If the answer to the preceding question is "No," explain how this absence will affect the scope of the engagement.

_____

_____

How are the valuation conclusions to be communicated? (check one)

_____ oral report _____ written report

What is the intended distribution of a written report? (check one)

_____ It will be restricted to internal use or to use solely by a court of law.

_____ It will be distributed to third parties.

Will historical or prospective financial statements be included in a written report? (check one) _____ Yes _____ No

Based on your knowledge of the company to be valued, what valuation methods appear to be appropriate for the engagement?

_____

_____

_____

_____

Will an asset appraiser be needed?

_____ Yes _____ No

Is it likely that we will be asked to provide expert witness testimony?

_____ Yes _____ No

What will our role be on this proposed engagement? (check one)

_____ We will be objective, third-party valuation consultants.

_____ We will be client advisors and, accordingly, will not be able to render an independent valuation conclusion or act as expert witnesses.

IV. ACCEPTANCE CONSIDERATIONS

	Yes	No
1. Are we aware of any independence problems or conflicts of interest?	_____	_____
2. Are we aware of any potential fee collection problems?	_____	_____
3. Is the professional competence (expertise) necessary to perform the engagement beyond our capabilities?	_____	_____
4. Is the staffing commitment required by the engagement beyond our capabilities?	_____	_____
5. Do the terms of the proposed engagement, including fee arrangements, violate applicable professional standards?	_____	_____
6. Is the fee arrangement unacceptable given the scope of the engagement?	_____	_____
7. Is there anything about the engagement that subjects us to undue legal risk or causes us to be uncomfortable about being associated with the engagement?	_____	_____

COMMENTS—A "Yes" answer does not necessarily indicate that the prospective engagement should be rejected. However, for any "Yes" answers, explain the steps that we plan to take to mitigate the situation (e.g., closer supervision, a substantial fee deposit before work can start, renegotiation of the fee, or use of specialists).

_____

_____

_____

_____

V. CONCLUSION

We should accept _____ not accept _____ the engagement.

Completed by: _____ Date: _____

Approved by:[a] _____ Date: _____

Note:
[a] If required by firm policy.

SOURCE: Jay E. Fishman, Shannon P. Pratt, J. Clifford Griffith, *Guide to Business Valuations*, 17th ed. (Fort Worth, TX: Practitioner's Publishing Company, 2007), Appendix 3A, copyright © 2007. All rights reserved. Reprinted with permission of Practitioner's Publishing Company. Copies of this *Guide* can be ordered by calling PPC at (800) 323-8724 or log onto *www.ppc.thomson.com.*

Definition of Who Offered and Who Accepted the Assignment

The most obvious reason for clearly defining the client and the appraiser is to know who is responsible for providing the services and who is responsible for paying for the services.

Another reason is that the appraiser has a responsibility to release confidential information about the appraisal only to the client. Others receive confidential information about the appraisal only with the client's permission, or if required by law.

If the case involves pending or potential litigation, the attorney may prefer to have his or her law firm retain the appraiser, rather than have the client retain the appraiser directly. This relationship may protect the appraiser's work and files from subpoena by the opposing attorney, although the effectiveness of such protection varies greatly from one situation to another.

Even when a business transaction is likely to be the ultimate outcome, it is important to specify by whom the appraiser is engaged. The appraiser may be engaged by the board of directors of the buying or selling company, a special committee of the board, the employee stock ownership plan trustee, or one or more individual shareholders of the buying or selling company, for example. The appraiser's relationship to the parties involved should be clear.

When specifying who is to provide the valuation services, the important distinction is whether the client is retaining the appraisal firm itself or the individual appraiser employed by the firm. The common practice is to retain the firm rather than the individual appraiser, even though expert witnesses testify based upon their individual expertise and opinions. This practice protects the client, since the firm is responsible for completing the assignment regardless of impairments to the individual's capability to perform the work. This practice also tends to provide continuity in retention of the working papers and related records, making them accessible if they are needed months—or even years—later, as they frequently are.

Description of the Legal Interest or Interests to Be Appraised

To determine the applicable valuation approaches and procedures to be performed, *exactly* what is to be appraised must be made clear. Much of the confusion and disagreement among appraisers and appraisal writings arises simply because it is not clear exactly what asset, property, or business interest is to be valued.

Description of the Business Entity

If the entity at issue is incorporated, both the official name and the state of incorporation are necessary to define the entity. The state of incorporation is necessary because two or more corporations that are incorporated in different states may have identical names. Furthermore, the laws of the state of incorporation may have a bearing on the value of a particular business interest.

If, on the other hand, the business is not a corporation but some other structure, the form as well as the name must be specified. Some of the most common forms of business organization are sole proprietorships, general and limited partnerships, and cooperatives. By the same token, if the entity's structure gives rise to special legal or tax considerations, that structure should be specified. Some of these forms include S corporations, limited liability corporations (LLCs), limited liability partnerships (LLPs), family limited partnerships (FLPs), professional corporations, real estate investment trusts (REITs), investment companies registered under the Investment Company Act of 1940, and personal holding companies. For FLPs and LLCs, the state is especially important, because each state's partnership or LLC laws may have different implications on the interest being valued.

Description of the Specific Business Interest

The definition of the specific business interest can be broken into two broad questions:

1. Is the valuation to be a valuation of assets or a valuation of securities?
2. In either case, exactly *what* assets or *what* securities are subject to valuation?

By *securities* in the above context, we mean ownership interests such as stock, debt, and partnership interests, as opposed to direct ownership of underlying assets of the subject business entity.

Assets versus Securities. An equity interest represents an indirect ownership interest in whatever bundle of assets and liabilities (actual and contingent) exists in the business. Stock or partnership ownership is quite different from direct ownership of assets and direct obligation for liabilities. If stock or a partnership interest is to be valued, it must be identified in the appraisal assignment. If assets are to be valued, those assets (and any liabilities to be assumed) must be specified. For example, the assignment might include language such as ". . . engaged to estimate the fair market value of the fixed assets, inventory, and goodwill, on a going-concern basis, of . . ." In the analysis of the stock or a partnership interest in a business as compared with the assets of a business, noteworthy tax, legal, and financial characteristics come into play. These may have a significant impact on the valuation.[2]

Partial Interests. If a partial interest in an entity is to be valued, the proportionate relationship of the partial interest to the whole is obviously important. If there is more than one class of stock, such as preferred and common, or voting and nonvoting common, the appraisal assignment should indicate which class of stock is being appraised. If the business to be appraised is only a portion of the entire entity, such as a division or branch, it is necessary to state explicitly which aspects are included in the project.

Equity or Invested Capital. The *value of the business* is an ambiguous term until it is clear exactly what elements of equity and debt are to be included in that value.

Equity means the ownership interest. In a corporation, equity is represented by stock. If there is more than one class of stock, the term *equity* by itself usually means the combined value of all classes of stock. If it is intended that the value represents only one class of stock in a multiclass capital structure, there should be a statement as to which class of equity the value purports to represent.

In a partnership, equity is represented by partners' capital. If it is a multiclass partnership (such as a limited partnership), there should be a statement as to which class or classes of partnership interests the value purports to represent.

---

[2] See, for example, *Edwin A. Gallun v. Comm.*, 33 T.C.M. 284 (1974).

In a sole proprietorship, equity is the owner's interest.

Invested capital is not always as clearly defined. Therefore, if the term is used, it should be supplemented by a definition of exactly what it means in the given valuation context.

Usually, invested capital means all equity and interest-bearing debt, whether short term or long term. Alternatively, some analysts understand *invested capital* to mean all equity and only long-term debt. Investment bankers often do not include the company's cash among the assets when assessing the value of "invested capital." There are so many variations that it is essential to pin down *exactly* what is and is not to be included on the left and right sides of the valuation balance sheet.

Enterprise Value. Unfortunately, the term *enterprise value* is used, at best, very ambiguously and, at worst, very carelessly. It means different things to different people, each of whom may believe that his or her definition is the right definition.

It is generally used to represent some sort of aggregate value of the company and is often used as a synonym for market value of invested capital (MVIC). However, enterprise value could mean aggregate value of minority stock, value of either all common equity or all equity on a control basis, value of all invested capital, value of some portion (or all) of the assets, or something else.

Both the *Uniform Standards of Professional Appraisal Practice* (USPAP) and the American Society of Appraisers (ASA) define a *business enterprise* as "a commercial, industrial, or service organization pursuing an economic activity." However, neither USPAP nor ASA offers a definition of *enterprise value*. The ASA Business Valuation Standards Subcommittee has discussed this term since 1985, and thus far has failed to find a consensus as to its definition.

If one encounters the term *enterprise value*, it is best not to assume any definition, but to make an attempt to identify the definition intended in its use. If one uses the term, it is important to spell out the intended definition, or the reader might infer an unintended definition. Because of the ambiguity, we generally avoid using the term in this book.

Interests Other than Direct Fee Simple Ownership

If the ownership is something other than direct fee simple ownership of the stock, partnership interest, or other interest, the ownership interest needs to be specified. For example, the interest being appraised could be a life or term estate, or a reversionary or remainder estate.

Ownership is, in effect, a bundle of rights. If the bundle of rights is anything less than a direct, unencumbered, simple ownership, the exact specification of the bundle of rights being appraised may have a significant bearing on value.

Description of the Specific Ownership Interest Characteristics

The description of the specific ownership interest subject to appraisal—and the particular investment attributes with regard to that ownership interest—can have a material impact on the appropriate valuation methodology and ultimate conclusion.

The primary ownership interest characteristics that need to be addressed in almost every business valuation are the following:

1. Control or minority valuation basis (not necessarily a black-and-white issue—there may be elements of control without absolute control).
2. Degree of marketability.

As such, the descriptions of the specific ownership interest characteristics are often in the nature of modifiers (adjectives) to the standard of value, such as "fair market value on a nonmarketable, noncontrolling ownership interest basis."

Sometimes the characteristics of the specific ownership interest subject to appraisal can be imposed artificially in a particular legal context. To give an example, under California Corporations Code Section 2000 (the California corporate dissolution statute), the case law is generally interpreted to mean that a minority ownership interest is valued *as if* it were a proportional share of the value of 100 percent of the company taken as a whole.[3]

To the extent that ownership interest characteristics are legally mandated or have been agreed on between the parties, they should be specified in the valuation assignment, with documentation as to their source. In many cases, the appraiser must consult with counsel to determine which ownership interest characteristics are appropriate. Also, the ownership interest characteristics may not be totally black-or-white issues, but in some cases may be matters of degree. *The descriptions of ownership interests often are major issues in disputed business valuation cases.* Consultation with the attorney involved and careful consideration of the implications of the purpose of the valuation can help to clarify issues related to choosing the appropriate description of the ownership interest for the situation.

Control versus Minority

As discussed in considerable detail in Part IV, the rights of control usually add value to shares of stock, typically making them worth more than noncontrolling shares.

The degree of control represented by the interest being valued often is not necessarily a clear-cut issue. The degree of control or lack of it may fall anywhere across a broad spectrum, depending on the percentage ownership, the distribution of other ownership interests, and state laws governing rights of various percentage ownership interests in circumstances pertinent to the valuation situation at hand.

In most valuation situations, the understanding as to the degree of control can be stated clearly and unequivocally at the outset. In some cases, however, the degree of control represented in the interest being valued is a matter of controversy. The impact of the degree of minority or control ownership on value is discussed at length in Chapters 15 and 16.

---

[3] See, for example, *Ronald v. 4-Cs Electronic Packaging*, 168 Cal. App. 3d 290 (1985) and *Brown v. Allied Corrugated Box Co.*, 91 Cal. App. 3d 477 (1979).

Degree of Marketability

For the purpose of this book, we define *marketability* as the ability to convert the asset to cash very quickly, at minimal cost, and with a high degree of certainty of realizing the anticipated amount of proceeds.[4]

The benchmark usually used to represent full marketability is an actively traded stock of a public company, which the owner can sell at or very near the last reported transaction price, at an insignificant transaction cost, merely by a phone call to a broker or by trading online, receiving cash within three business days. The premise as to the extent to which the entity or business interest being valued is or is not marketable is usually considered in relation to this benchmark.

All other things being equal, investors prefer to own something that they can liquidate immediately without any depressing effect on value rather than something that is difficult, time-consuming, and/or costly to liquidate. As will be seen in Chapter 17 on this subject, the degree of marketability or lack of it has a much greater impact on value than most people realize. It is not uncommon for discounts to run as high as 50 percent and, in many instances, higher!

The impact of the issue of marketability may be legally mandated or may be agreed upon between or among the parties. More often than not, however, this issue is an important subject of the appraiser's analysis. To the extent that matters affecting marketability are known (e.g., rights or restrictions regarding transfer of the ownership interest), it generally is desirable to note them in the engagement letter.

Valuation Date

The date, or dates, on which the business is being valued is critically important because circumstances can cause values to vary materially from one date to another, and the valuation date directly influences data available for the valuation. Every day, observers of the public stock markets see sudden and substantial changes in the value of a particular company's stock. In many court cases, especially those involving tax litigation, significant changes in value over very short time spans have been justified because of changes in relevant circumstances.[5]

Many internal and external factors can cause changes in the value of an interest in a company. Obviously, a sudden change in a company's earnings, especially if unanticipated, can have a substantial effect on value. Also, the value of a business interest varies with the cost of capital, a factor over which individual businesses have little control. Major events, such as the signing or termination of a major customer contract, can also have a dramatic, immediate impact on value.

In most business valuations, the opinion of value will be based at least partly on other, similar transactions, such as the prices at which stocks in the same or a related industry are trading in the public market relative to their earnings, assets,

---

[4] Some writings make a fine distinction between *marketability* and *liquidity*, with marketability focusing on finding the appropriate market, preparing the property for sale, and executing the trade, and liquidity focusing on realizing cash proceeds.

[5] See, for example, *Morris M. Messing*, 48 T.C. 502 (1967), *acq.* 1968-1 C.B. 2. Even though the company made a public offering at over $36 shortly after a gift of stock, the court upheld a value of $13 for gift tax purposes as of the date of the gift.

dividends, or other relevant variables, if such data are available. It is important to know the valuation date when using guideline companies in the valuation so that the guideline transaction data can be compiled as of the valuation date, or as near to it as is practically possible.

Sometimes there is more than one valuation date. For example, in a marital dissolution, the parties may be concerned with the change in value that occurred during the marriage. In estate tax cases, the trustee, executor, or personal representative will consider adopting the "alternative valuation date" (i.e., six months after the date of death) to determine which is more advantageous and thus would be interested in the value of the estate's property on two dates six months apart.

In some litigated cases, the valuation date itself is an issue to be resolved by the court. In such situations, the appraiser must be prepared to address the valuation as of several dates, sometimes without knowing which date the court determined to be relevant until after the judgment is rendered. Since the choice of valuation date in such cases is a legal matter, the attorney for whom the expert appraiser testifies should take the responsibility, as part of defining the assignment, of considering all the potentially applicable valuation dates and instructing the appraiser to be prepared to address the value as of each date. Sometimes a court will give an advance ruling on the valuation date to avoid the expense of appraisers doing valuations as of dates that the court will not deem relevant.

Purpose of the Appraisal

No single valuation method is universally applicable to all appraisal purposes. The context in which the appraisal is to be used is a critical factor.

Different statutory, regulatory, and case precedent standards govern valuations of businesses and business interests under various jurisdictions for diverse purposes. *Many business appraisals fail to reach a number representing the appropriate definition of value because the appraiser failed to match the valuation methods to the purpose for which it was being performed. The result of a particular appraisal can also be inappropriate if the client attempts to use the valuation conclusion for some purpose other than the intended one.*

Valuation reports should contain a set of limiting conditions, and one of the typical limiting conditions is as follows:

> This valuation is valid only for the valuation date or dates specified herein and only for the valuation purpose or purposes specified herein. No other purpose is intended or should be inferred.

Litigation over business valuation is commonplace. Much of this litigation arises because the parties have failed to match the valuation methods to the appraisal's intended purpose.

The purpose of the valuation encompasses the use to which the valuation exercise is expected to be put. Subsequent chapters of this book explore how valuation methods are impacted by special and specific purposes to which the valuation analysis may be put (Part VII). Valuations for each of these different purposes are often affected by a mass of complex federal and state statutes and legal precedents.

A valuation conclusion prepared for one purpose may not be the appropriate valuation conclusion for another purpose. The purpose of the valuation often determines the applicable standard of value—that is, the definition of value being sought—and almost always influences it. Standards of value are discussed in the next section, and an exhibit following that section illustrates the matching of certain valuation purposes with applicable standards of value.

Standards of Value

The word *value* means different things to different people. Even to the same person, value means different things in different contexts, as we discussed in the previous section.

Without carefully defining the term *value*, the conclusions reached in the valuation report have no meaning.

Is the objective of the valuation to estimate fair market value, market value, fair value, true value, investment value, intrinsic value, fundamental value, insurance value, book value, use value, collateral value, ad valorem value, or some other value?

Clients rarely give it much thought. Many don't have enough technical background in business valuation to raise the right questions. One of the professional appraiser's most important tasks is to work carefully and thoroughly with the client and/or attorney to arrive at a definition of value that is appropriate to the specific purpose of the valuation engagement.

In this book, a *standard of value* is a definition of the type of value being sought. A *premise of value* is an assumption as to the set of actual or hypothetical transactional circumstances applicable to the subject valuation (e.g., going-concern or liquidation).

For many situations, the standard of value is legally mandated, whether by law or by binding legal documents or contracts. In other cases, it is a function of the wishes of the parties involved. The standard of value usually reflects an assumption as to who will be the buyer and who will be the seller in the hypothetical or actual sales transaction regarding the subject assets, properties, or business interests. It defines or specifies the parties to the actual or hypothetical transaction. In other words, the standard of value addresses the questions: "value to whom?" and "under what circumstances?" The standard of value, either directly by statute or (more often) as interpreted in case law, often addresses what valuation methods are appropriate and what factors should or should not be considered.

Fair Market Value

In the United States, the most widely recognized and accepted standard of value related to business valuations is *fair market value*. With regard to business valuations, it is the standard that applies to virtually all federal and state tax matters, such as estate taxes, gift taxes, inheritance taxes, income taxes, and ad valorem taxes. It is also the legal standard of value in many other—though not all—valuation situations.

Fair market value is defined by the ASA as "the amount at which property would change hands between a willing seller and a willing buyer when neither is acting under compulsion and when both have reasonable knowledge of the relevant facts."[6] This definition comports to that found in the Internal Revenue Code and Revenue Ruling 59-60.

In most interpretations of fair market value, the willing buyer and willing seller are hypothetical persons dealing at arm's length, rather than any particular buyer or seller. In other words, a price would not be considered representative of fair market value if influenced by special motivations not characteristic of a typical buyer or seller.

There is also general agreement that the definition implies that the parties have the ability as well as the willingness to buy or to sell. The *market* in this definition can be thought of as all the potential buyers and sellers of like businesses or practices.

The concept of fair market value also assumes prevalent economic and market conditions at the date of the particular valuation. You have probably heard someone say, "I couldn't get anywhere near the value of my house if I put it on the market today," or, "The value of XYZ Company stock is really much more (or less) than the price it's selling for on the New York Stock Exchange today." The standard of value that those people have in mind is some standard *other than* fair market value, since the concept of fair market value means the price at which a transaction could be expected to take place under *conditions existing at the valuation date.*

The terms *market value* and *cash value* are frequently used interchangeably with the term *fair market value.* The use of these essentially synonymous standard of value terms is often influenced by the type of asset, property, or business interest subject to valuation.

In the United States, the most widely recognized and accepted standard of value related to real estate appraisals is *market value.* The Appraisal Foundation defines *market value* as follows:

> MARKET VALUE: Market value is the major focus of most real property appraisal assignments. Both economic and legal definitions of market value have been developed and refined. A current economic definition agreed upon by agencies that regulate federal financial institutions in the United States of America is:
>
> > The most probable price which a property should bring in a competitive and open market under all conditions requisite to a fair sale, the buyer and seller each acting prudently and knowledgeably, and assuming the price is not affected by undue stimulus. Implicit in this definition is the consummation of a sale as of a specified date and the passing of title from seller to buyer under conditions whereby:
> >
> > 1. buyer and seller are typically motivated;
> > 2. both parties are well informed or well advised, and acting in what they consider their best interests;
> > 3. a reasonable time is allowed for exposure in the open market;
> > 4. payment is made in terms of cash in United States dollars or in terms of financial arrangements comparable thereto; and

---

[6] American Society of Appraisers, Business Valuation Standards—Definitions.

5. the price represents the normal consideration for the property sold unaffected by special or creative financing or sales concessions granted by anyone associated with the sale.

Substitution of another currency for United States dollars in the fourth condition is appropriate in other countries or in reports addressed to clients from other countries.

Persons performing appraisal services that may be subject to litigation are cautioned to seek the exact legal definition of market value in the jurisdiction in which the services are being performed.[7]

The most salient change in the above definition of market value compared with definitions widely accepted a few years ago is the phrase "the most probable price" in substitution for "the highest price."

Investment Value

In real estate terminology, investment value is defined as "the specific value of an investment to a particular investor or class of investors based on individual investment requirements; distinguished from market value, which is impersonal and detached."[8] Fortunately, business appraisal terminology embraces the same distinction in most contexts.

One of the leading real estate appraisal texts makes the following comments regarding the distinction between market value and investment value:

Investment value reflects the subjective relationship between a particular investor and a given investment. It differs in concept from market value, although investment value and market value indications sometimes may be similar. If the investor's requirements are typical of the market, investment value will be the same as market value.[9]

The distinctions noted in the above quote can be carried over to business appraisal. There can be many valid reasons for the *investment value* to one particular owner or prospective owner to differ from the fair market value. Among these reasons are:

1. Differences in estimates of future earning power
2. Differences in perception of the degree of risk and the required rate of return
3. Differences in financing costs and tax status
4. Synergies with other operations owned or controlled

The discounted economic income valuation method can easily be oriented toward developing an investment value. Whether or not the value thus developed also represents fair market value depends on whether the assumptions used would be accepted by a consensus of market participants.

---

[7] *Uniform Standards of Professional Appraisal Practice* (Washington, DC: The Appraisal Foundation, 2006).
[8] *The Dictionary of Real Estate Appraisal*, 4th ed. (Chicago: Appraisal Institute, 2002), p. 152.
[9] *The Appraisal of Real Estate*, 12th ed. (Chicago: Appraisal Institute, 2001).

If sound analysis leads to a valid conclusion that the investment value to the current owner exceeded market value at a given time, the rational economic decision for that owner would be to not sell until a particular buyer is found who is willing to pay the investment value that is higher than the consensus of value among a broader group of typical buyers.

Of course, the concept of investment value as described above is not completely divorced from the concept of fair market value, since it is the actions of many specific investors, acting in the manner just described, that eventually lead to a balancing of supply and demand through the establishment of an equilibrium market price that represents the consensus value of the collective investors.

Intrinsic or Fundamental Value

Intrinsic value (sometimes called *fundamental value*) differs from *investment value* in that it represents an analytical judgment of value based on the perceived characteristics inherent in the investment, not tempered by characteristics peculiar to any one investor, but rather tempered by how these perceived characteristics are interpreted by one analyst versus another.

In the analysis of stocks, *intrinsic value* is generally considered the appropriate price for a stock according to a security analyst who has completed a *fundamental analysis* of the company's assets, earning power, and other factors.

> *Intrinsic value.* The amount that an investor considers, on the basis of an evaluation of available facts, to be the "true" or "real" worth of an item, usually an *equity security*. The value that will become the market value when other investors reach the same conclusions. The various approaches to determining intrinsic value of the *finance* literature are based on expectations and discounted cash flows. See *expected value; fundamental analysis; discounted cash flow method.*[10]
>
> *Fundamental analysis.* An approach in security analysis which assumes that a security has an "intrinsic value" that can be determined through a rigorous evaluation of relevant variables. Expected earnings is usually the most important variable in this analysis, but many other variables, such as dividends, capital structure, management quality, and so on, may also be studied. An analyst estimates the "intrinsic value" of a security on the basis of those fundamental variables and compares this value with the current market price of this security to arrive at an investment decision.[11]
>
> The purpose of security analysis is to detect differences between the value of a security as determined by the market and a security's "intrinsic value"—that is, the value that the security *ought* to have and will have when other investors have the same insight and knowledge as the analyst.[12]

If the market value is below what the analyst concludes is the intrinsic value, the analyst considers the stock a "buy." If the market value is above the assumed

---

[10] W.W. Cooper and Yuri Ijiri, eds., *Kohler's Dictionary for Accountants*, 6th ed. (Englewood Cliffs, NJ: Prentice Hall, 1983), p. 285. Reprinted by permission of Prentice Hall, Inc., Upper Saddle River, New Jersey.

[11] Ibid., p. 228.

[12] James H. Lorie and Mary T. Hamilton, *The Stock Market: Theories and Evidence* (Burr Ridge, IL: Irwin, 1973), p. 114.

intrinsic value, the analyst suggests selling the stock. (Some analysts also factor market expectations into their fundamental analysis.)

It is important to note that the concept of intrinsic value cannot be entirely divorced from the concept of fair market value, since the actions of buyers and sellers based on their *specific* perceptions of intrinsic value eventually lead to the general consensus market value and to the constant and dynamic changes in market value over time.

Case law often refers to the term *intrinsic value*. However, almost universally such references do not define the term other than by reference to the language in the context in which it appears. Such references to *intrinsic value* can be found both in cases where there is no statutory standard of value and in cases where the statutory standard of value is specified as *fair value* or even *fair market value*. When references to *intrinsic value* appear in the relevant case law, the analyst should heed the notions ascribed to that term as discussed in this section.

Fair Value under State Statutes

To understand what the expression *fair value* means, you have to know the context of its use. For certain bookkeeping applications, fair value is defined in the relevant accounting literature. In business valuation, the term *fair value* is usually a legally created standard of value that applies to certain specific transactions.

In most states, fair value is the statutory standard of value applicable in cases of dissenting stockholders' appraisal rights. It is also commonly used in valuations in state minority oppression cases, which have been on the rise. In these states, if a corporation merges, sells out, or takes certain other major actions, and the owner of a minority interest believes that he or she is being forced to receive less than adequate consideration for his or her stock, the owner has the right to have his or her shares appraised and to receive fair value in cash. In states that have adopted the Uniform Business Corporation Act, the definition of fair value is as follows:

> "Fair value," with respect to a dissenter's shares, means the value of the shares immediately before the effectuation of the corporate action to which the dissenter objects, excluding any appreciation or depreciation in anticipation of the corporate action unless exclusion would be inequitable.[13]

Even in states that have adopted this definition, there is no clearly recognized consensus about the interpretation of fair value in this context, but published precedents established in various state courts have not equated it directly to fair market value. When a situation arises of actual or potential stockholder dissent or dissolution action, it is necessary to carefully research the legal precedents applicable to each case. The appraiser should solicit the view of counsel as to the interpretation of fair value and, in most cases, should not assume that there is a definition that is clear and concise.

The term *fair value* is also found in the dissolution statutes of those states in which minority stockholders can trigger a corporate dissolution under certain circumstances (e.g., California Code Section 2000). Even within the same state, however, a study of case law precedents does not necessarily lead one to the same definition of fair value under a dissolution statute as under that state's dissenting stockholder statute.

---

[13] Oregon Revised Statutes, Section. 60.551(4).

Several countries undergoing privatization have adopted the term *fair value* to apply to certain transactions, often involving specific classes of buyers, such as employees. Such statutes vary widely in their definitions of fair value.

Fair Value for Financial Reporting

Unfortunately, the standard "fair value" is an ambiguity. It means one thing (as described in the previous section) in the context of state statutes for dissenting and oppressed stockholder actions, and something altogether different (as described in this section) for financial reporting as required by generally accepted accounting principles (GAAP) and the Securities and Exchange Commission (SEC).

The financial accounting standards board (FASB) issued Statement No. 157 on September 15, 2006, and is effective for financial statements issued for fiscal years beginning after November 15, 2007. This statement gave a single definition of fair value.

> Fair value is the price in an orderly transaction between market participants to sell the asset or transfer the liability in the market in which the reporting entity would transact for the asset or liability, that is, the principal or most advantageous market for the asset or liability.[14]

The statement gives guidance on the measurement of fair value as a market-based measurement. A hierarchy for considering market participant assumptions outlined and distinguishes between sources independent of the reporting entity and the reporting entities' own assumptions.

The statement also expands on the difference between fair value and fair market value as follows:

> The Board agreed that the measurement objective encompassed in the definition of fair value used for financial reporting purposes is generally consistent with similar definitions of fair market value used for valuation purposes. For example, the definition of fair market value in Internal Revenue Service Revenue Ruling 59-60 (the legal standard of value in many valuation situations) refers to "the price at which property would change hands between a willing buyer and a willing seller when the former is not under any compulsion to buy and the latter is not under any compulsion to sell, both parties having reasonable knowledge of relevant facts." However, the Board observed that the definition of fair market value relates principally to assets (property). Further, the definition has a significant body of interpretive case law, developed in the context of tax regulation. Because such interpretive case law, in the context of financial reporting, may not be relevant, the Board chose not to adopt the definition of fair market value, and its interpretive case law, for financial reporting purposes.[15]

One noticeable difference between fair value and fair market value (as pointed out in Chapter 25 on Valuing Stock Options) is that Statement of Financial Accounting Standards (SFAS) 123R governing the application of the fair value

---

[14] SFAS No. 157—Fair Value Measurements, paragraph 5.
[15] SFAS No. 157—Fair Value Measurements, paragraph C50.

Exhibit 2–2

Examples of Matching the Purpose of the Valuation with the Standard of Value

Purpose of Valuation	Applicable Standard of Value
Gift, estate, and inheritance taxes and charitable contributions	Fair market value.
Purchase or sale	Generally fair market value, but in many instances investment value, reflecting unique circumstances or motivations of a particular buyer or seller.
Marital dissolution	No statutory standards of value. Courts have wide discretion to achieve equitable distribution. Requires careful study of relevant case law.
Buy-sell agreements	Parties can do anything they want. Very important that all parties to the agreement understand the valuation implications of the wording in the agreement.
Dissenting stockholder actions	Fair value in almost all states. Consider relevant statute and case law to determine how interpreted in the particular state.
Minority oppression action	Generally, fair value in those states that address it at all. Not always interpreted the same as fair value for dissenting stockholder actions.
Employee stock ownership plans (ESOPs)	Fair market value.
Ad valorem (property) taxes	Generally, fair market value with varied nuances of interpretation. In many states, intangible portion of value excluded by statute.
Going private	Fair value in most states; governed by state statutes.
Corporate or partnership dissolutions	Fair value under minority oppression statutes.
Antitrust cases	Damages based on federal case law precedent; varies from circuit to circuit.
Other damage cases	Mostly governed by state statute and case law precedent; varies by type of case from state to state.
Financial reporting	Fair value, as defined by FASB

standard in employee incentive options allows no discount for illiquidity in the valuation of nonmarketable incentive stock options.

Exhibit 2–2 gives some examples of matching certain valuation purposes with applicable standards of value.

Going-Concern versus Liquidation Premise of Value

Virtually all businesses or interests in businesses may be appraised under each of these following four alternative premises of value:

1. *Value as a going concern*—Value in continued use, as a mass assemblage of income-producing assets, and as a going-concern business enterprise.
2. *Value as an assemblage of assets*—Value in place, as part of a mass assemblage of assets, but not in current use in the production of income, and not as a going-concern business enterprise.
3. *Value as an orderly disposition*—Value in exchange, on a piecemeal basis (not part of a mass assemblage of assets), as part of an orderly disposition; this premise contemplates that all of the assets of the business enterprise will be

sold individually, and that they will enjoy normal exposure to their appropriate secondary market.

4. *Value as a forced liquidation*—Value in exchange, on a piecemeal basis (not part of a mass assemblage of assets), as part of a forced liquidation; this premise contemplates that the assets of the business enterprise will be sold individually and that they will experience less than normal exposure to their appropriate secondary market.

Of these four premises, the last three are liquidation approaches under alternative assumptions about how the underlying assets will be disposed.

While virtually any business enterprise may be appraised under each of these four alternative fundamental premises, the value conclusions reached under each premise, for the same business, may be dramatically different.

Each of these alternative premises of value may apply under the same standard, or definition, of value. For example, the fair market value standard calls for a "willing buyer" and a "willing seller." Yet, these willing buyers and sellers have to make an informed economic decision as to how they will transact with each other with regard to the subject business. In other words, is the subject business worth more to the buyer and the seller as a going concern that will continue to operate as such, or as a collection of individual assets to be put to separate uses? In either case, the buyer and seller are still "willing." And, in both cases, they have concluded a set of transactional circumstances that will maximize the value of the collective assets of the subject business enterprise.

The selection of the appropriate premise of value is an important step in defining the appraisal assignment. Typically, in a controlling interest valuation, the selection of the appropriate premise of value is a function of the highest and best use of the collective assets of the subject business enterprise. The decision regarding the appropriate premise of value is usually made by the appraiser, based upon experience, judgment, and analysis.

Sometimes, however, the decision regarding the appropriate premise of value is made "for" the appraiser. This occurs when the appraiser knows—or is told—that the subject business enterprise will, in fact, be continued as a going concern or will be sold in a certain set of transactional circumstances. For example, if the business assets are, in fact, going to be sold on a value in exchange basis, it is not relevant for the appraiser to consider the value in continued use—or going concern—premise of value. Of course, if valuing a minority ownership interest, one would normally adopt the premise of "business as usual" unless given reason to do otherwise.

In some circumstances, it may be relevant—and, in fact, critical—to appraise the subject business enterprise under several alternative premises of value. For example, it may be extremely important to conclude the value of the same business enterprise under several alternative premises of value in appraisals performed for bankruptcy and reorganization or for financing securitization and collateralization purposes.

Sources of Guidance as to Applicable Standards and Premises of Value

The experience and expertise of the professional appraiser include the skill to seek out and interpret guidance as to the standard and premises of value that are relevant to the assignment at hand. Some of the most important sources of guidance as to the applicable standard and premises of value for the given situation are the following:

- Statutory law (state and federal)
- Case law (cases decided under the controlling statutory or common law)
- Administrative rulings (e.g., IRS revenue rulings)[16]
- Company documents (e.g., articles of incorporation or partnership, bylaws, meeting minutes, agreements)
- Contracts between the parties (e.g., buy-sell agreements, arbitration agreements)
- Precedent established by prior transactions
- Directives issued by the court (in some litigated cases where the standards or premises are not clear, the appraiser may take the initiative (usually through the attorney) to seek direction from the court regarding the relevant definition of value)
- Discussions with an attorney involved in the valuation matter or experienced in similar matters
- Legal case documents (e.g., complaint, response, and so forth)
- The appraiser's experience and judgment

Form of the Work Product

In many cases, the purpose of the report largely determines the form of the report. The appraiser's report to the client can be oral, written, or a combination.

An oral report can be anything from a quick phone call to lengthy meetings with the principals, attorneys, brokers, and/or other parties involved. The form and extent of a written report can range from a single-page letter to a detailed, hundred-page-plus volume.

An oral report is common in estate planning engagements, especially when the purpose of the exercise is to help the client get an approximate idea of the business's value in order to decide what action to take. A preliminary oral report is often the first deliverable product when the business valuation is being conducted in a litigation context, since the client attorney is concerned with the expert's opinion before the legal strategy is finalized because, if put into writing, it could be discovered and utilized by the opponents. Even oral reports, however, may be covered by USPAP. Although some departures from full reports are permitted, there must be a supportable basis for opinions expressed.

When the purpose of the assignment is to prepare a feasibility analysis for a potential employee stock ownership plan (ESOP), the client, or client's attorney, will usually require a brief opinion letter which can be utilized for further planning. Once the business's value is approximated, the rest of the ESOP team is engaged, the size of the ESOP can be determined, and the amount and cost of bank financing can be identified.

In most cases, especially those involving taxes or tax implications, such as gift or estate tax valuations, the appraiser will be required to prepare a formal written opinion report.

---

[16] Note that administrative rulings do not have the force of law, but represent the position of the agency administering the law as to their interpretation of the law and rules for applying it.

The valuation opinion report will typically include the following sections:

1. A valuation opinion letter summarizing the valuation procedures and conclusions.
2. Several sections summarizing the relevant valuation theory, methodology, procedures, analyses, and conclusions.
3. A valuation synthesis and conclusion.
4. An exhibit section presenting a summary of the quantitative and qualitative valuation analyses. (Exhibits can either be contained within the text of the report or presented as an appendix.)
5. A listing of the data and documents relied upon by the appraiser.
6. A statement of valuation contingent and limiting conditions.
7. An appraisal certification.
8. The professional qualifications of the principal appraisers.

Whether or not the report needs to conform to USPAP is either a matter of law or agreement with the client. Starting in 1999, USPAP stated:

> Compliance with these standards is required when either the service or the appraiser is obligated by law or regulation, or by an agreement with the client or intended users, to comply.[17]

Scheduling

One of the most important tools for conducting a business valuation thoroughly and on a timely basis is a proper schedule. Most first-time, or infrequent, business valuation clients (and their attorneys) tend to underestimate the amount of lead-time necessary for the appraiser to prepare a thorough and professional opinion. Scheduling problems often arise because the client delays in committing to the project, hoping that the valuation problem will go away. When it doesn't, there is little time left for anything but a crash assignment. Another common source of scheduling conflicts is a major change in some aspect of the assignment midway through the project—another good reason for the client and the appraiser to carefully think through and agree on the details of the valuation assignment as thoroughly as possible at the outset.

The valuation assignment should describe when the work is expected to be completed. But it should also make clear that the appraiser's ability to meet the proposed schedule depends upon receipt of the necessary information on a timely basis, and that changes midway through the assignment will likely cause changes in the schedule. To expedite getting necessary data to the appraiser on a timely basis, we recommend that anyone engaging an appraiser refer to Exhibit 4–1, "Preliminary Documents and Information Checklist for Business Valuation of Typical Corporation" (the exhibit can be readily modified for noncorporate forms of organization), and make sure the information is readily available.

---

[17] *Uniform Standards of Professional Appraisal Practice* (Washington, DC: The Appraisal Foundation. 2000), p. 2.

One tactic often used, especially during the month of December when clients make gifts of property or are conducting other estate planning activities, is to ask the appraiser to arrive at an oral opinion of value and later provide a formal, written, documented report.

Fee Arrangements

The valuation budget may be a fixed price, a range of estimated fees, or it may be based on an hourly or daily rate. The more clearly and thoroughly defined the scope of the assignment is, the more likely it is that the appraiser will be able to quote a total fixed fee or a narrow range.

If third-party independence of judgment is required of the appraiser—as in cases involving expert testimony in pending or potential litigation—the appraiser's fees must be fixed, hourly, or set in some manner totally independent of the outcome of any litigation, or the appraiser's independent third-party status will be jeopardized. For those appraisal assignments requiring independence, the independent professional appraiser is legally and ethically prohibited from entering into an arrangement making the appraiser's fee contingent on a certain settlement amount or the outcome of a court decision.

The fee arrangements should include the terms of payment as well as the basis for establishing the fee.

Summary

This chapter has provided guidance to both the appraiser and the client (or the client's attorney) as to matters that should be considered when entering into the valuation engagement. Most of these matters should be incorporated into the engagement letter; some will be resolved after execution of the engagement letter or left to the appraiser's judgment. Even for those matters discussed in this chapter that ultimately are left to the appraiser's judgment, it often is helpful for the appraiser and the client (or the client's attorney) to discuss them at the onset of the engagement.

The basic elements of the appraisal assignment are:

1. Name of the client and of the appraiser
2. Definition of the legal interest or interests to be valued
3. Effective valuation date(s) (the date as of which the appraiser's opinion of value applies)
4. Purpose or purposes of the appraisal (the use to which the valuation exercise is expected to be put)
5. Applicable standard and premise of value
6. Form and extent of written and/or verbal report
7. Schedule and fee arrangements

At some point, whether in the engagement letter or some other transmittal, additional topics typically are addressed, such as contingent and limiting conditions, limited use of the appraisal (only for the purpose intended and the effective date of valuation), confidentiality, and compliance with USPAP and/or other recognized professional business valuation standards.

Exhibit 2–3 is a sample engagement letter that covers the elements discussed in this chapter, as well as a few other important points such as indemnification of the appraiser. The appraiser should solicit the help of legal counsel in crafting a thorough engagement letter that best protects the interests of the appraiser. Valuation has a high rate of claims relative to other financial areas, and a strong engagement agreement is an absolute necessity. There are many resources that the practitioner's attorney can draw on to assist in creating an appropriate engagement letter. For example, many liability couriers have sample letters. The AICPA has a Practice Aid available to its members.

Exhibit 2–3

Sample Professional Services Agreement

Amanda Appraiser & Associates and Estate of Charles C. Client agree as follows:

1. **Description of services.** We agree to perform certain professional services for you, described briefly as follows as to purpose and objective, with the understanding that any modification to the assignment as stated below will be by a letter agreement signed by both parties.

    Estimate the fair market value in continued use of a 35 percent interest in Charles Client Crane Company, a New York corporation, held by the estate of Charles C. Client, as of September 30, 2007, for estate tax purposes.

2. **Date(s) services due.** We will begin performance upon receipt of all information requested of you, and will complete our assignment, unless delayed or prevented by matters beyond our control, according to the following schedule:

    Full, formal appraisal report due within 90 days of receipt of signed agreement and all requested documents.

3. **Fees.** Our fees for such professional services will be calculated on standard hourly rates in effect at the time services are rendered for staff members assigned to this project, plus out-of-pocket expenses. The fee is estimated at a range of $_____ to $_____, exclusive of expenses such as travel, long-distance telephone, purchases of data, copying and printing costs, and clerical time. The fee will not exceed such estimate by more than 25% without prior notification to you.

4. **Retainer.** $_____ is due as a retainer upon execution of this Agreement. Retainer paid by you will be applied to the final billings.

5. **Payment terms.** You will receive regular twice-monthly invoices, including fees and expenses incurred, for which payments will be due at our offices within 15 days of dates of invoices. Balances which remain unpaid 30 days from dates of invoices will be assessed a finance charge of 1.5% monthly (18% annual percentage rate).

    If we are to provide expert witness testimony as part of our assignment, you agree that payment of all fees and expenses invoiced and/or incurred to date will be received at our offices before we provide expert witness testimony, or if travel for testimony is necessary, payment will be received before travel is incurred.

    You agree that the fees and expenses invoiced by us must be paid current per the terms of this Agreement before we provide any report or analysis conclusions.

6. You understand that we will need prompt access to documents. materials, facilities, and/or company personnel in order to perform our services in a timely and professional manner, and you agree to fulfill all such requests in a timely manner and to cooperate fully with us. You further understand and agree that delays in providing data or information may result in a delay of the completion date of the project.

7. We agree to perform our services in a professional and objective manner. You understand that we do not guarantee the results of any analysis which we may undertake, but only agree that any report or analysis shall represent our professional opinion based on the data given to us or compiled by us. We will attempt to obtain and compile our data from reliable sources, but we cannot guarantee its accuracy or completeness.

8. You warrant that the information and data you supply to us will be complete and accurate in every respect to the best of your knowledge; that any reports, analysis, or other documents prepared by us will be used only in compliance with all applicable laws and regulations; and that you will hold us harmless for any breach of this warranty.

continued

9. You agree to indemnify and hold us harmless against any and all liability, claim, loss, cost, and expense, whatever kind or nature, which we may incur, or be subject to, as a party, expert witness, witness or participant in connection with any dispute or litigation involving you unless such liability, claim, loss, cost, and expense, whatever kind or nature, is due to our gross negligence and such gross negligence is not caused by, related to, or the result of information provided to us by you. This indemnity includes all out-of-pocket expenses (including travel costs and attorney fees) and payment for all our staff members' time at standard hourly rates in effect at the time rendered to the extent we attend, prepare for, or participate in meetings, hearings, depositions, trials, and all other proceedings, including travel time. If we must bring legal action to enforce this indemnity, you agree to pay all costs of such action, including any sum as the Court may fix as reasonable attorney fees.

10. If this Agreement, or any moneys due under the terms hereof, is placed in the hands of an attorney for collection of the account, you promise and agree to pay our attorney fees and collection costs, plus interest at the then legal rate, whether or not any legal action is filed. If any suit or action is brought to enforce, interpret, or collect damages for the breach of this agreement, you agree to pay our reasonable attorney fees and costs of such suit or action, including any appeal as fixed by the applicable Court or Courts.

Dated this 20th day of December, 2007, at New York, New York.

Estate of Charles C. Client

By: _____

Name: Charlotte Client, Executor

Address: 11 North 25th Street, Yonkers, New York 11111
Telephone: (914) 555-4455
Fax: (914) 555-4456

Amanda Appraiser & Associates

By: _____

Name: Amanda Appraiser, CFA, ASA

Chapter 3

Business Valuation Theory and Principles

One of the frequent sources of legal confusion between cost and value is the tendency of courts, in common with other persons, to think of value as something inherent in the thing valued, rather than as an attitude of persons toward that thing in view of its estimated capacity to perform a service . . . Certainly, for the purpose of a monetary valuation, property has no value unless there is a prospect that it can be exploited by human beings.[1]

There continues to be much controversy about the appropriate criteria by which to measure the value of a business or business interest. The previous chapter reconciled the issues surrounding the choices that determine the standard of value and the premise of value. In many cases, criticism of business valuation conclusions is more properly criticism of the definition of the valuation assignment. Once the context in which the value will be considered has been established (i.e., value to whom and in which market), the basic principles of business valuation are considered. While there are controversies here too, they tend to be more related to matters of professional judgment.

Generally Accepted Theory

In the simplest sense, the theory surrounding the value of an interest in a business depends on the future benefits that will accrue to its owner. The value of the business interest, then, depends upon an estimate of the future benefits and the required rate of return at which those future benefits are discounted back to present value as of the valuation date.

Thus, the theoretically correct approach is to project some category or categories of the future benefits of ownership (usually some measure of economic income, such as cash flow, earnings, or dividends) and estimate the present value of those future benefits by discounting them based upon the time value of money and the risks associated with ownership. Direct implementation of this theoretically correct approach is discussed in Chapter 9, "Income Approach: Discounted Future Economic Income Method." That chapter focuses heavily on net cash flow as a measure of economic income, both for conceptual reasons and also because it is the focus of most merger and acquisition income value analysis.

While there is general acceptance of a theoretical framework for business valuation, translating it into practice in an uncertain world poses one of the most complex challenges of economic and financial theory and practice. The reasonableness of the business valuation conclusions usually depends upon whether the projections and assumptions used to estimate future economic income benefits are acceptable to the decision maker for whom the business valuation is being prepared (e.g., the buyer, the seller, the opponent, the IRS, the judge).

Getting two or more parties with different economic and business expectations to agree on projected future benefits and the risks associated with achieving those projections is, perhaps, the most difficult task for the business appraiser. Therefore, business valuation practitioners have developed various approaches that use historically-based data rather than projected data to arrive at a valuation.

---

[1] James C. Bonbright, *The Valuation of Property*, Vol. I (Charlottesville, VA: The Michie Company, 1965 [reprint of 1937 ed.]), p. 21.

In general, approaches using current or historical data, if properly carried out, should yield a result that is reasonably reconcilable with what a well-implemented discounted economic income method would derive. This is an absolutely critical point that I see many "number crunchers" miss. This is because historical data, properly adjusted, represents an alternative method of predicting future income. This is important for the appraiser relying on historical income to realize, because an investor always bases his investment decision on the expectation of future returns, regardless of whether he relied on an estimate of future income to determine value, or used historical periods as a representative proxy for future expectations.

Reliance on Projected versus Historical Benefits

In virtually any business valuation, there is more than one point of view. Business appraisers are rarely engaged to conduct an assignment unless the client anticipates that the conclusions of the assignment may be scrutinized and/or challenged by someone with an adverse interest. Very often, the challenges surround the predictability of future benefits as they compare with the historical record.

In court, the parties to an action and the judge rely on *evidence* to support a particular position. Historical facts are often considered more credible evidence in the eyes of the court than future projections of what somebody thinks will happen. Therefore, when legal evidence is required, the focus tends to be on the historical record of financial performance; future benefits and their predictability as of the valuation date can be more difficult to establish, unless backed up with solid foundational research. The courts generally prefer provable historical results to unprovable expectations of future results, but some courts are becoming more amenable to accepting projections prepared in the ordinary course of business. The extent to which a court will accept projections as evidence in a valuation case is probably a function of the degree of confidence the court has in the validity of those projections based upon information available as of the valuation date, as well as the credibility of the evidence and the witness. While courts continue to apply judicial scrutiny to the reasonableness of specific projections, it is noteworthy that in recent years courts have become much more accepting of the application of the discounted cash flow method as a valuation methodology.

Businesspeople are trained to make and evaluate business and economic projections and to use them as a basis for daily decision making. Businesspeople can (and should) use their knowledge and experience in allocating resources entrusted to them for the purpose of taking business risks, and accept calculated risks inherent in decision making based on predictions of an uncertain future. In some mergers and acquisitions, a discounted future economic income model is used to identify the price. In developing investment recommendations, analysts often make estimates of the future benefits of ownership, and, if the analyst is credible, investors will act on their projections.

When preparing a business valuation for reorganization proceedings under bankruptcy statutes, the parties will frequently rely on capitalization of anticipated future cash flow. This makes sense because, unless there is a reasonable expectation that the future will be more rewarding than the recent past, the reorganization would appear to be a fruitless exercise.

Other categories in which projections are usually necessary are antitrust; lost business opportunity; breach of contract; infringement of patents, copyrights, or trademarks; and certain other types of damage calculations that need to address the amount of value lost as a result of a wrongful act. Eminent domain, a legal taking of property often subject to compensation for lost value, may also give rise to projections of lost future economic income.

As a practical matter, because of the lack of a set of projections and assumptions acceptable to all parties, many business valuations rely on historical data, which are evaluated and often adjusted in order to reflect reasonable expectations about foreseeable future results. In the end, it will be the most well-supported and reasoned income stream that is available to an investor in the future, whether it is based on projected or adjusted historical data that will carry the day.

In summary, this difference in focus between projections of the future and the historical record is dictated by what the respective decision makers find as most supportable. There may be a big difference in this respect between an investment decision in the market, where future performance of the business interest is critical, and a judicial decision in a court, where evidence rules the day, and projections unmet would mistreat one party; alternatively to rely on historical data when evidence supports a different forecast would mistreat the other party. To be practically useful, professionals must strongly support whichever method they choose. There has been a trend toward more court recognition of modern financial theory, which is based on discounting expected economic income at a discount rate that reflects the risk of achieving the expectations.

In the 1930s, Bonbright recognized the valuation controversy surrounding the reliance on historical earnings and projected earnings:

Realized Earnings versus Prophesied Earnings. In the valuation of entire business enterprises or of shareholdings in these enterprises, one of the most sharply contested questions has concerned the relative weight to be given to the adjusted or normalized earnings actually realized, as shown by the companies' financial statements after proper auditing, and the future earnings as estimated by the witnesses for the two parties to the controversy. Sometimes, indeed, the controversy arises from a denial by one of the parties that prophesied earnings should even be admitted as competent evidence. It is alleged that these prophecies are necessarily too highly speculative to merit consideration; that they are based on guesses as to future business conditions and as to managerial efficiency, the validity of which cannot adequately be checked by cross-examination or by the countervailing testimony of opposing experts. Hence, it is argued, only the realized earnings, whose amount can be approximately established by a careful audit, should be brought to the attention of the tribunal for such weight as it sees fit to give this type of data. Lawyers who take this position generally concede that facts having a general bearing on the immediate prospects of the business may be brought to the attention of the court. They object, however, to the false appearance of precision which is given by any estimate, in monetary amounts, of future net earnings. Their objection is likely to be even more strenuous if the case is being tried by a jury or by any other unsophisticated tribunal. Such bodies are in danger of taking the prophecies at their face value, without applying those drastic discounts for risk of nonoccurrence which cautious appraisal experts would apply.

The body of knowledge required to estimate the value of a business or business interest is more akin to that required by the securities profession than by the real estate profession. That fact is reflected by the material in this book and the typical academic and professional backgrounds of those practicing in the field of business valuation.

However, real estate appraisers dominate the generalized field of "appraisal" (defined by The Appraisal Foundation as "the act or process of estimating value"[7]). Among individual members of professional member organizations composing The Appraisal Foundation, real estate appraisers outnumber business appraisers more than 65 to 1. The field of real estate appraisal is far more familiar to both the public and the courts than is the field of business appraisal.

Consequently, the American Society of Appraisers Business Valuation Standards recognize an "income approach," a "market approach" (sales comparison approach), and an "asset-based approach" (somewhat similar to real estate's "cost" approach), thus following the three-pronged structure familiar to real estate appraisers. The term "method" is often used to refer to more specific ways to implement a business valuation within one of the three broad approaches. For example, *discounted cash flow* and *capitalization of cash flow* may be considered methods within the broader category of the income approach, and the *guideline public company method* and the *transaction merger and acquisition method* would fall within the market approach.

The presentation of business valuation methodology in this book parallels the real estate appraisers' traditional three-pronged structure, as well as the structure of the American Society of Appraisers Business Valuation Standards. Thus, the reader will find:

Chapter 9:   Income Approach: Discounted Future Economic Income Method
Chapter 10:   Income Approach: Capitalized Future Economic Income Method
Chapter 11:   Market Approach: Guideline Publicly Traded Company Method
Chapter 12:   Market Approach: Guideline Merged and Acquired Company Method
Chapter 13:   Asset-Based Approach: Capitalized Excess Earnings Method
Chapter 14:   Asset-Based Approach: Asset Accumulation Method

Interrelationship of the Three Broad Approaches

It is important to note that the three broad approaches are not independent of each other but are interrelated.

Income approach. Within the income approach, the business appraisal profession recognizes the discounted future economic income method and the capitalization of future economic income method. The two methods within the income approach require different rates at which to discount or capitalize the income stream. (See Chapters 9 and 10 for an explanation of the relationship between discount and capitalization rates in the context of business appraisal.)

In most cases, estimating the future benefits of owning an operating business are typically complex matters to assess and quantify: As such the business appraiser needs a broad understanding of relevant economic and industry factors, capital market conditions, business management, and accounting.

[7] *Uniform Standards of Professional Appraisal Practice* (Washington, DC: The Appraisal Foundation, 2006), p. 10.

These practical objections to the admission of prophesied gross and net earnings are well taken. Indeed, the courts have shown a wholesome tendency to belittle the significance of the prophecies, and even on occasion to refuse to admit them into the record. But the language by which they have justified their treatment of this type of evidence has not always been acceptable to appraisal theory and has sometimes been very confusing. At times the courts have come close to stating that, as a matter of principle, the present value of a business property depends on present earnings, and that future earnings are irrelevant because they will determine merely future value. More frequently they have stated that present value depends on both present and future earnings, but with the implication that the present earnings have the more direct bearing on the worth of the property as it exists today.

In fact, neither of these two statements correctly expresses the relevance of realized earnings and of prospective earnings. *The truth is that, when earnings have once been "realized," so that they can be expressed with some approach to accuracy in the company's accounts, they are already water under the mill and have no direct bearing on what the property in question is now worth. Value, under any plausible theory of capitalized earning power, is necessarily forward looking. It is an expression of the advantage that an owner of the property may expect to secure from the ownership in the future. The past earnings are therefore beside the point, save as a possible index of future earnings.*[2]

In a litigated appraisal, a more convincing argument for the capitalization of realized earnings, rather than of prophesied earnings, can be found in the possibility . . . of capitalizing the realized earnings at a rate objectively determined by rates established on the marketplace. Assume, for example, that the case at bar requires the valuation of a railroad enterprise, the net earnings of which have averaged $10 million per year. Assume also that the securities issued by this particular railroad have no established market value, since they are closely held. If the various securities of other, comparable railroad companies are quoted at prices which average twenty times current annual net earnings, a rate of 5 percent suggests itself as the appropriate rate at which the current earnings of the instant railroad company may fairly be capitalized. Of course, any such conclusion involves a number of highly shaky assumptions—assumptions, not only as to the comparability of the various railroad enterprises, but also as to the relevance of quoted security prices as bearing on the value of an entire enterprise. But the errors implicit in this method of arriving at a proper rate of capitalization are probably far less serious than are the errors implicit in any other method available to an inexpert tribunal.[3]

The above quotation, written more than 60 years ago, continues to offer wisdom regarding the same issues today.

[2] James C. Bonbright, *Valuation of Property*, pp. 249–250 (emphasis supplied).
[3] Ibid, p. 263.

Basic Variables Affecting Value

Whether using projections or relying on historical data as a proxy for reasonable future expectations, there are certain key variables on which the business valuation focuses. The relative importance of the key variables varies in different types of situations. For generations, theorists will continue to argue about which variables deserve the most attention and should be given the most weight in various valuation situations.

There are internal valuation factors that are a function of the performance of the business and there are external valuation factors that are a function of the environment in which the business operates.

One way or another, the financial benefits of ownership of an interest in a business enterprise must come from the following sources:

1. Dividends, distributions, or other type of cash flow
   a. from operations, or
   b. from investments (e.g., interest)
2. Liquidation or hypothecation of assets
3. Sale of the interest

Therefore, any valuation approach—at least from a financial point of view—must focus on quantifying the ability of the business interest to provide financial benefits to its owner from one or some combination of the above sources. The Delaware court of Chancery has used weighting in some recent cases. In *Andoloro v. PFPC Worldwide, Inc.*,[4] the court weighted DCF at 75 percent and comparable companies at 25 percent. In *In re United States Cellular Operating Company*[5], the weighting was 70 percent DCF and 30 percent comparable acquisitions. In *Montgomery Cellular Holding Co., Inc. v Dobler*[6], the court gave a 30 percent weight to DCF, 5 percent to comparable companies, and 65 percent to comparable acquisitions.

In many instances, value conclusions are tempered by other internal variables, often variables relative to the specific shareholding as opposed to the company as a whole, such as:

1. Size of the subject interest (reflecting not only magnitude but control issues)
2. The right to vote and to impact the direction of the business
3. Restrictive provisions affecting ownership rights
4. The marketability of the ownership position
5. Special ownership or management perquisites

There is no universal answer concerning which variable among the future benefit statistics deserves the greatest attention. Generally, earning power is the important internal variable affecting the going-concern value of the business. Earning power may be expressed in terms of the ability to realize cash flows, dividends, net income, or any of several other measures.

---

[4] 2005 WL 2045640 (Del. Ch. 2005).
[5] 2005 WL 43994 (Del. Ch. 2004).
[6] 2004 WL 2271592 (Del. Ch. 2004) and affirmed 2005 WL 1936157 (Del. 2005).

The external variables that affect a business's value are collectively referre as "the market." The market determines the amount of expected return tha required to attract investment—the *cost of capital*. The cost of capital depend: the general level of interest rates and the amount of premium for risk (above return available on a safe, fixed income investment) that the market demand: well as the risks attributable to the subject business. Sometimes, a change ir value of a business interest is entirely attributable to external market condit and the investors benefit more for being at the right place at the right time tha an improvement in the fundamental financial performance of the business.

Impact of Risk on Value

The analyst should consider the expected economic income in two dimension magnitude of the expected economic income and the risk that this ecor income will or will not be realized. For the purpose of discussion in this boc define *risk* as *the degree of uncertainty as to the realization of expected futur nomic income*. For a given level of expected future *economic income*, the n will pay more for a company's stock to the extent that a realization of that ecor income is more certain or less to the extent that a realization is less certa other words, for a given level of expected future economic income (e.g., cash dividends), the lower the risk, the higher the present value or, conversely, the the risk, the lower the present value.

Risk generally is reflected in the valuation through the discount or capi tion rates applied to the financial variables. The market determines a basi free required rate of return and the amount of premium required for assumir ious levels of risk. Of course, one thing the owners can do to lower their capital—and thus increase the value of their enterprise—is to lower the deg risk associated with it. All else being equal, the lower valuation analysts pe the risk to be, the lower will be the cost of capital considered applicable in t uation and, thus, the higher will be the resulting value.

Specific assessment and treatment of the all-important factor of risk cussed in detail in the chapters on implementing the various valuation appro

Accepted Business Valuation Approaches and Methods

Background and Structure

Business valuation as it is practiced today reflects a blending of two str academic and professional background:

1. The securities profession, which deals with financial analysis of bonds, and other financial instruments, and with business acqui divestitures, and mergers
2. The real estate profession, which deals with the analysis of transactions and real property improvements

While the valuation procedures are similar, in most cases, estimating the future benefits of owning an operating business is more difficult than estimating the future benefits of owning an apartment building, an office building, or a similar income-producing real estate property. Because it may be comprised of both tangible and intangible assets and liabilities, the risks of owning an operating business are typically more complex to assess and quantify than are the risks of owning operating real estate, and the resulting cash flows tend to be more volatile. Hence, the development of appropriate discount and capitalization rates is more difficult in the context of the business valuation. The business appraiser needs a broad understanding of relevant economic and industry factors, capital market conditions, business management, and accounting.

Pretax income streams from direct investment in real estate tend to be capitalized at lower required rates of return than comparably defined pretax income streams from investments in non–real estate oriented businesses. One reason for this is the lower perceived risk in the typical real estate investment. Another is that real estate investments often enjoy income tax deductions and credits that are not available to the comparable income stream earned by a business.

Real estate investors may accept a lower rate of return from their cash flow stream than they would accept from other assets because they expect extra return in the form of capital appreciation on the property. This is in sharp contrast to a business investment that includes machinery and equipment that will eventually lose value through wear and tear and/or obsolescence, or an investment that includes intangible assets that will become obsolete.

Market Approach. As for the market or sales comparison approach (covered in more detail in Chapters 11 and 12), the real estate appraiser will seek data on sales of comparable properties, and the business appraiser will seek data on transactions of comparable businesses. The business appraiser will interpret the transaction data for guidance in determining applicable valuation parameters—such as capitalization rates for earnings or cash flow—and ratios of the entity's market value to asset value measures, such as book value or adjusted book value.

There is a tendency for the market for businesses to change more rapidly than the market for real estate. After all, a business can be thought of as a collection of tangible and intangible assets, each with its own price volatility and risks of ownership. Effects of these risks can be observed in the volatility of stock prices every day.

Asset-Based Approach. The asset-based approach provides an indication of the value of the business enterprise by developing a fair market value balance sheet. All of the assets of the business are identified and listed on the balance sheet (note: this balance sheet is not the cost-based balance sheet that is prepared in accordance with generally accepted accounting principles), and all of the business's liabilities are brought to current value as of the valuation date.[8] The difference between the fair market value of the assets and the current value of the liabilities is an indication of the business enterprise equity value under the asset-based approach.

---

[8] For example, if the company had a 6 percent bond outstanding due in 10 years, and the current market rate for a comparative bond was 8 percent, the bond would be revalued downward on the liability side of the balance sheet to a value equivalent of an 8 percent, yield to maturity bond, unless it was contemplated that the bond would be paid before maturity.

The use of the asset-based approach should not be confused with the selection of the appropriate premise of value for the subject business valuation. Some analysts mistakenly confuse the use of the asset-based approach with a liquidation premise of value (or with a liquidation valuation). Rather, the asset-based approach can be used with all premises of value—including (1) value in use as a going-concern business enterprise and (2) value in exchange as part of a forced or orderly liquidation. The asset-based approach focuses on the value of the enterprise's component assets, properties, and business units. The use of the asset-based approach does not dictate the premise of value that should be adopted for the enterprise's component assets, properties, and business units.

Businesses Typically Owned through Securities. As discussed more fully elsewhere in the book, the fact that businesses typically are owned through corporate stock, partnership interests, or limited liability company membership units introduces an element of complexity not present in direct ownership of assets. These securities represent bundles of rights determined by articles of incorporation or partnership, limited liability company membership agreements, bylaws, and many contractual and legal rights and restrictions not relevant to direct ownership of physical assets. Valuation of stock, a partnership interest, or a membership interest requires an understanding of the bundle of rights and restrictions encompassed therein.

Also, the tax consequences of ownership and/or transfer of stock or partnership interests usually are quite different from those of ownership and/or transfer of direct investment in underlying assets. These tax implications often have a significant bearing on value.

The U.S. Supreme Court firmly established the principle that ownership of stock was not tantamount to ownership of a company's assets clear back in 1925:

> The capital stock of a corporation, its net assets, and its shares of stock are entirely different things. . . . The value of one bears no fixed or necessary relation to the value of the other."[9]

As George Lasry explains it:

> A share of common stock does not represent a share in the ownership of the assets of a business.[10]

> Only the corporation itself holds title to all its assets and liabilities. . . . A thirsty shareholder of a brewery cannot walk into "his" company and demand that a case of beer be charged to his equity account.[11]

Dozens of court cases have elaborated on the distinction between ownership of stock or partnership interests and direct ownership of assets.[12]

Fractional Interests. Stocks and partnership units are designed to be readily divisible into fractional interests in an enterprise, while fractional interests in direct investment in real estate or other assets are far less common and generally more cumbersome to transfer. To implement the market approach when valuing

---

[9] *Ray Consol. Copper Co. v. United States*, 45 S. Ct. 526 (1925).
[10] George Lasry, *Valuing Common Stock* (New York: AMACOM, 1979), p. 1.
[11] Ibid., p. 15.
[12] See, for example, *Charles S. Foltz, et al. v. U.S. News & World Report, et al.*, 865 F.2d 364 (D.C. Cir. 1989); *Sommers Drug Stores v. Corrigan Enterprises, Inc.*, 793 F.2d 1456 (5th Cir. 1986); and *Estate of Edwin A. Gallun*, 33 T.C.M. 1316 (1974).

noncontrolling interests, market data on fractional interest transactions in direct investment in real estate are meager, at best, while noncontrolling interest public stock transactions abound.

Generally, noncontrolling holders of stocks, and partnership interests, or membership interests enjoy fewer rights if they are dissatisfied with management than do direct fractional interest holders in income-producing real estate because of anticipated distributions or the right to seek partition in the latter type of investment. As a consequence, discounts from a pro rata portion of the control value of 100 percent of the business or property taken as a whole can be greater for noncontrolling stocks and partnership interests than they are for direct fractional interests in income-producing real estate.

Impact of Controlling versus Noncontrolling Ownership Interest

The owner of a controlling interest in an enterprise enjoys some valuable rights that the owner of a noncontrolling interest may not enjoy. Consequently, if ownership control is an issue in the valuation, the analyst should assess the extent to which the various elements of control do or do not exist in the particular situation and consider the impact of each element on the value of control. (The most important elements of control are discussed in Chapter 15, "Control and Acquisition Premiums.") A noncontrolling ownership interest holder may still enjoy some of the elements of ownership control. For instance, a noncontrolling ownership interest holder may be in a position to cast a crucial swing vote and, to some degree, influence important business policies.

The distribution of ownership can affect the value of a particular business interest. If each of three stockholders or partners owns a one-third interest, no one has complete control. However, no one is in a relatively inferior position unless only two of the three have close ties with each other. In this situation, the analyst could recognize that the discount from pro rata value for each equal interest normally will be lower than that for a minority interest that has no control whatsoever. In fact, it is possible that the owner of a one-third minority interest may extract a special-purpose price premium (such as a swing vote price premium) in a competitive bid from the other two one-third stockholders.

Many typical control rights may be denied to a company through relations with other stakeholders in the company, such as its banker. Indenture provisions in conjunction with debt obligations or senior classes of stock frequently prevent the company from taking such actions as dividend payments, increases in management compensation, liquidation of assets, acquisitions, or changes in the direction of the business, for example. Shareholder agreements, partnership agreements, and limited liability company membership agreements also may contain several restrictions.

Government regulation of operations may preempt the usual prerogatives of control; for example, liquidation of insurance companies and utilities can be lengthy and sometimes difficult. Government regulations may prevent certain acquisitions and, similarly, prevent a company from selling out to certain other companies or investors.

State statutes can affect the respective rights of controlling and noncontrolling stockholders. In about half the states, a simple majority can approve major actions such as a merger, sale, liquidation, or recapitalization of the company. Other states require a two-thirds or greater majority to approve such actions, which means that a minority of just over one-third (or even less in some states) has the power to block such actions. Under California and some other states' statutes, minority stockholders enjoy certain rights (e.g., demanding liquidation) under specific circumstances. The variations in state law concerning which rights are given to what proportion of ownership can have an important bearing on the valuation of certain percentage interests in some cases.

Voting rights constitute one of the most difficult variables to quantify in terms of impact on value. For extremely small minority ownership interests, the market accords very little value to voting rights. However, where swing votes or majority ownership interests are involved, the impact on value can be significant. In fact, a majority block of nonvoting stock may actually be worth less per share than a small block of voting stock, since there are fewer potential buyers for the large block without the right to vote on corporate matters.

In most cases, a noncontolling ownership interest is worth less than a pro rata proportion of the value of the entire business enterprise. The analysis and quantification of minority ownership values versus control ownership values are addressed in considerable detail in Chapters 15 and 16 on control and acquisition price premiums and lack of control discounts.

Impact of Marketability

Ready marketability adds value to a security. Conversely, lack of marketability reduces the security's value as compared with a security that is identical in all respects but is otherwise marketable. In other words, the market pays a premium for liquidity, or exacts a discount for the lack of liquidity.

Since interests in closely held businesses do not, by definition, enjoy the ready market of a publicly traded stock, a share in a privately held company usually is worth less than an otherwise comparable share in a publicly traded one. Many factors affect the relative marketability of different business interests. Sometimes size of the interest is a factor; a smaller block may be easier to market than a larger block, and in other cases the reverse is true. In most cases, the lack of marketability factor harshly impacts minority interests. However, even controlling interests in closely held businesses obviously are not as readily marketable as shares of publicly traded stock.

Restrictions in shareholder agreements, partnership agreements, and limited liability company agreements often severely affect the transferability of ownership interests. Some buy-sell agreements require that the shareholders be employed by the company and be a resident of a certain state. Others determine the price at which, and the circumstances under which, the shares are to be voluntarily or involuntarily transferred, put and call provisions, and who may be entitled to a right of first refusal on transactions. The presence of practically any type of restrictive agreement tends to reduce the estimated market value of a closely held business ownership interests.[13]

---

[13] See, for example, W. Terrance Schreier and O. Maurice Joy, "Judicial Valuation of 'Close' Corporation Stock: *Alice in Wonderland* Revisited," *Oklahoma Law Review* 31 (1978), p. 865.

Chapter 17, "Discounts for Illiquidity and Lack of Marketability," presents extensive empirical evidence on the quantification of discounts for lack of marketability.

Distinction between Discount for Lack of Control and Discount for Lack of Marketability

Confusion can result when clients, analysts, and the users of the analysis (e.g., the court) fail to distinguish between a discount for lack of ownership control and a discount for lack of marketability. These are two separate concepts, although they are somewhat interrelated. Frequently people overlook the fact that discounts are meaningless until the bases from which they are to be taken have been defined.

The base from which the discount for lack of control is subtracted is its proportionate share of the value of the total equity (or at least the common equity), taken as a whole, including all rights of ownership control. The base from which the discount for lack of marketability is subtracted is the value of an entity or interest, usually minority interest, that is otherwise comparable but enjoys higher liquidity (that is, can more readily be sold and converted to cash).

Lack of control is reflected in the projected cash flows; that is, whether or not control adjustments have been made to the cash flows. Marketability, or lack thereof, is the ability to sell the interest and obtain the cash quickly without loss of value.

Controlling ownership interests in closely held businesses can also suffer to some extent from a lack of ready marketability. Even 100 percent ownership interests in businesses are not liquid. And, majority but less than 100 percent control position may take longer to sell than a 100 percent ownership interest. Such an increased selling (or "market exposure") period reduces the present value of the proceeds from the sale of the majority ownership interest by the time value of money, for example.

In some cases, the value of control just may offset the disadvantage of lack of marketability. However, this should only be the result after careful consideration of the specific circumstances surrounding those factors and not the result of only an uninformed assumption.

In many published court decisions, especially older ones involving valuations for gift and estate tax purposes, a single lump sum discount to reflect lack of control, lack of marketability, and sometimes other factors is taken. However, conceptual thinking in the valuation process, supported by the use of empirical data, usually allows one to isolate and separately quantify the various valuation factors, especially the more important ones. In recent years, valuation practitioners and courts have been giving separate recognition to the impact of noncontrolling ownership interest and lack of marketability factors. A 1982 estate tax decision articulated the distinction between the lack of control and lack of marketability discounts very clearly:

> In their arguments, neither petitioner nor respondent clearly focuses on the fact that two conceptually distinct discounts are involved here, one for lack of marketability and the other for lack of control. The minority shareholder discount is designed to reflect the decreased value of shares that do

not convey control of a closely held corporation. The lack of marketability discount, on the other hand, is designed to reflect the fact that there is no ready market for shares in a closely held corporation. Although there may be some overlap between these two discounts in that lack of control may reduce marketability, it should be borne in mind that even controlling shares in a nonpublic corporation suffer from lack of marketability because of the absence of a ready private placement market and the fact that flotation costs would have to be incurred if the corporation were to publicly offer its stock.[14]

Many subsequent court decisions have distinguished between the concepts of lack of control and lack of marketability. And, many subsequent court decisions have separately quantified their conclusions regarding the impact of the respective factors. Several of these decisions are cited in later chapters. In addition, some court decisions have failed to recognize the multiplicative (rather than the additive) impact of valuation adjustments.

Other Qualitative Factors Affecting Value

Qualitative factors bear on value. However, such qualitative factors often defy quantification on the basis of empirical data within the valuation factors discussed up to this point. In some cases, such factors may influence the analyst's judgment and be reflected in a specific adjustment in arriving at the value conclusion. The analyst may incorporate these factors into the analysis when choosing valuation pricing multiples or capitalization rates. In some cases, the qualitative factors may be important enough to warrant a separate, specific (and therefore quantified) adjustment to value.

An important qualitative factor in many closely held companies is reliance on one or a few key management personnel. Also, limited product diversity can restrict the categories of potential customers, the number of potential customers within a category, and increase the risks arising from shortages of critical supplies or competitive product information. Lack of vertical integration can leave a closely held business vulnerable to vagaries in sources of supply or to a particular customer relationship—an example being the original equipment component manufacturer who is vulnerable should the customer decide to manufacture in-house. Lastly, lack of an efficient accounting system can affect the value of an entity as well. These factors, along with many other important qualitative considerations, are discussed in Chapter 18, "Other Valuation Adjustments."

Additional factors to consider in various cases include the company's research and development efforts, industry position, quantity and quality of asset base relative to competitors, and the quality and relationship with its workforce.

---

[14] *Estate of Woodbury G. Andrews*, 79 T.C. 938 (1982).

Matching the Valuation Methodology with the Standard and Premises of Value

Perhaps the single, most prevalent broad reason many valuation work products miss the mark is failure to use valuation approaches and methods that are consistent with the definition of value being adopted.

In the previous chapter, we discussed standards and premises of value and ownership characteristics, and presented a chart giving examples of how the purpose of the valuation can affect the appropriate definition of value. In this chapter, we have, at least broadly, introduced the topic of approaches to value and elaborated a bit further on two of the most important ownership characteristics to consider: controlling versus noncontrolling ownership interests and degree of marketability. *All these matters must be taken into consideration together in deciding exactly which valuation methods to use and what assumptions and data will go into the implementation of those methods.*

This art of matching the methodology to the valuation context will become clearer as the reader moves through Part III on business valuation approaches and Methods and Part VII on valuations for specific purposes. When either preparing or reviewing a business valuation report, always be alert to consider whether each step of the procedure is consistent with the standard and premise of value—and with the ownership characteristics—applicable to the specific valuation context.

Sum of Parts Not Necessarily Equal to Whole

Since partial interests in a business enterprise are impacted by discounts and premiums differently from controlling ownership interests, the sum of the individual ownership positions may be less than the overall business enterprise value. In most cases, when dealing with minority shares of a private company, the sum of the values of the partial interests taken individually is less than what might be received if a single buyer purchased the entire entity. The company in its entirety has a different value because it conveys different rights and interests than the sum of all the interests taken on a minority ownership interest basis. This economic fact, of course, is a catalyst for both merger and acquisition activity and dissenting shareholder lawsuits.

It is also important for attorneys and other advisers to alert clients entering into buy-sell agreements at "fair market value" that this term usually means something less than a pro rata proportion of the total enterprise value, unless other provisions are specified.

Since estate tax planning is seriously impacted by the fact that the sum of the parts do not always equal the whole, Chapter 14, the special valuation provision of the Internal Revenue Code, was added by the Revenue Reconciliation Act of 1990. These provisions mandate certain departures from strict fair market value in valuations for certain family company recapitalizations. However, there still are many opportunities in estate planning to benefit from the market reality fact that the sum of the values of parts often is considerably less than the value of the whole. These issues and opportunities are discussed at some length in Chapter 27, "Valuations for Estate and Gift Tax Purposes."

Summary of Business Valuation Principles

The specific methods and procedures for valuing a business or a business interest vary from one situation to another. However, several basic principles are fundamental to the business valuation discipline:

1. From a financial point of view, the value of a business or business interest is the sum of the expected future benefits to its owner, each discounted back to a present value at an appropriate discount rate.

2. The market for capital usually determines the appropriate discount rate. The discount rate is the expected rate of return that would be required to attract capital to the investment, which takes into account the rate of return available from other investments of comparable risk.

3. Projecting future benefits and determining an appropriate discount rate is difficult, especially when trying to bring two participants to either a transaction or a dispute to an agreement. There are accepted methods of estimating value by using current or historical—rather than projected—financial data. However, valuation methods that use current or historical financial data require adjustments to the historical data, if appropriate, to reflect the impact of future expectations. In addition, consideration should be given to expected growth rates, industry trends, and other microeconomic factors. Values estimated from such procedures should be reconcilable with estimates of value from a discounted future economic income method.

4. When relying on specific comparative market transactions for guidance in estimating the value of a subject business or interest, investors' specific expectations regarding future returns and risk that are incorporated into capitalization rates, multipliers, and other valuation parameters are not known. This makes it imperative that financial variables utilized in the valuation be defined on a consistent basis between the guideline and subject companies and that measurements for estimating variables be taken as of the same point in time or over the same time period relative to the valuation date for the guideline companies and the subject company.

5. Shareholders have no direct claim on a corporation's assets because a corporate or partnership entity intervenes between the assets and the shareholder or partner. Therefore, the value of a share of stock or a partnership interest can be more than or less than a proportionate share of the underlying net asset value and sometimes bears little relationship to the underlying net asset value.

6. Lack of control and lack of marketability are distinct concepts, yet they are related. Both controlling and minority ownership interests may suffer somewhat from lack of marketability, defined as the ability to convert the asset to cash very quickly, at minimal costs, with a high degree of certainty of realizing the anticipated amount of proceeds. The impact of both minority and marketability factors are influenced by internal and external facts and circumstances as of the valuation date.

7. Noncontrolling owners lack control over various decisions affecting the business enterprise, depending on the degree of control. Minority ownership interests may be worth considerably less than a pro rata portion of the business value if it were valued as a single, 100 percent ownership interest.

8. The market pays a premium for liquidity as compared with an illiquid asset, or, conversely, demands a discount for lack of liquidity as compared with a liquid asset. Business interests that lack ready marketability generally are worth less than otherwise comparable business interests that are readily marketable.

9. The sum of the values of individual fractional interests in a business is not necessarily, or even usually, equal to the value of a 100 percent ownership interest in the business.

Within the scope of these business valuation principles, different standards and premises of value and different ownership characteristics apply for different valuation purposes and within different legal contexts. These can affect both the valuation procedures to be utilized and the final determination of value. The appraiser should understand the applicable purpose and objective for the assignment and the implications of each.

These principles, though broad, provide a framework for consistency in the practice of the business valuation discipline. Many errors and unreasonable valuation conclusions can be avoided if the principles are understood and implemented. These principles provide the business valuation user with a basic perspective from which to review and evaluate a business valuation work product.

Bibliography

Booth, Laurence. "The Capital Asset Pricing Model: Equity Risk Premiums and the Privately-Held Business." *The Journal of Business Valuation* (Proceedings of the 4th Joint Business Valuation Conference of the Charted Business Valuators and the American Society of Appraisers). Toronto: The Canadian Institute of Charted Business Valuators, 1999, pp. 87–114.

"Bulls, Bears and Ivory Towers." *The Economist*, May 15, 1999, pp. 81–82.

Copeland, Tom, Tim Koller, and Jack Murrin. *Valuation: Measuring and Managing the Value of Companies*, Textbook and Workbook, 3rd ed. New York: John Wiley & Sons, 2000.

Copeland, Tom, Tim Koller, and Jack Murrin. *Valuation: Measuring and Managing the Value of Companies*, Web-delivered Spreadsheet, 3rd ed. New York: John Wiley & Sons, 2002.

Damodaran, Aswath. *Investment Valuation: Tools and Techniques for Determining the Value of Any Asset*, 2nd ed. New York: John Wiley & Sons, 2002.

Damodaran, Aswath. "Value and Risk: Beyond Betas," *Financial Analyst Journal*, March/April 2005.

Grabowski, Roger, Doug Lamdin, Alina Niculita, and Shannon Pratt. "Beta As an Essential Part of the Capital Asset Pricing Model." *Business Valuation Q&A*.

Hawkins, George B., and Michael A. Paschall. *CCH Business Valuation Guide*, 5th ed. Chicago: CCH Incorporated, 2002.

Mercer, Z. Christopher, and Terry S. Brown. "Fair Market Value vs. the Real World." *Valuation Strategies*, March/April 1999, pp. 6–15.

Miles, Raymond C. *Basic Business Appraisal*. New York: John Wiley & Sons, 1984.

Pratt, Shannon P. *Business Valuation Body of Knowledge: Exam Review and Professional Reference*, 2nd ed., New York: John Wiley & Sons, 2004.

Pratt, Shannon P. *Business Valuation Body of Knowledge Workbook*, 2nd ed., New York: John Wiley & Sons, 2004.

Pratt, Shannon P., Robert F. Reilly, and Robert P. Schweihs. *Valuing Small Businesses and Professional Practices*, 3rd ed. New York: McGraw-Hill, 1998.

Reilly, Robert F., and Robert P. Schweihs. *The Handbook of Business Valuation and Intellectual Property Analysis*. New York: McGraw-Hill, 2004.

Trugman, Gary R. *Understanding Business Valuation: A Practical Guide to Valuing Small to Medium-Sized Businesses*, 2nd ed. New York: American Institute of Certified Public Accountants, Inc., 2002.

West, Thomas L., and Jeffrey D. Jones. *Handbook of Business Valuation*, 2nd ed. New York: John Wiley & Sons, 1999.

Part II

Gathering and Analyzing Data

Chapter 4

Gathering Company Data

Generalized Company Information Checklist
Financial Statements
    Relevant Time Period
    Levels of Financial Statement Preparation
    Impact of Enterprise Legal Structure
Federal Tax Returns
Interim Statements
Other Financial Schedules
    Current Assets and Liabilities
    Plant and Equipment
    Officers' and Directors' Compensation Schedule
    Distribution of Ownership
    Dividend or Partnership Withdrawal Schedule
    Schedule of Key Person Life Insurance
Off-Balance Sheet Assets or Liabilities
Related Party Transaction Information
Operating Information
    Company History
    Brochures, Catalogs, Web Sites, and Price Lists
    Key Personnel
    Customer and Supplier Base
    Contractual Agreements and Obligations
    Industry and Trade Association Information
List of Past Transactions in the Stock or Offers to Buy
Budgets and Forecasts
Capital Requirements
    Capital Expenditures
    Deferred Maintenance
    Working Capital Requirements
Company Documents Relating to the Rights of Owners
    Corporate or Partnership Records
    Buy-Sell and Employee Stock Ownership Plan Agreements
    Employment and Noncompete Agreements
Summary

The first step in the valuation process, after carefully defining the assignment, is to gather the data necessary to conduct the assignment. These data can be categorized into three groups:

1. Company-specific data
2. Data about the company's industry and economic environment
3. Data about the subject property's market (market for ownership interests in the subject company)

The company-specific data are gathered from the subject company in written form and during site visits and interviews with people knowledgeable about the company. The gathering of this information is the subject of this and the next chapter.

Industry and economic data often can be provided by the subject company and can also be gathered from publicly available sources. This is the subject of Chapter 5. Data about the market for ownership interests in the subject company include information about changes in ownership of competitors, guideline company transactions, and premiums and discounts that might apply to the subject property. These two categories of information gathering are covered in subsequent chapters in Part III.

The manner and sequence in which the data are gathered are important only to the extent that the process is complete and efficiently carried out. For example, supporting analysts may be collecting industry, economic, rate of return, and guideline transaction information at the same time that the case manager is working directly with the management of the subject company. In any case, it is important to convey a sufficient overview of the company and of the assignment to all of the valuation team members at an early meeting so that all of the analysts will be in a position to recognize important data as they proceed on the project.

If time allows, information gathered should be reviewed and analyzed before the visit to the company so as to focus the interviewing process on the most essential factors that affect the value of the company, thereby minimizing the inconvenience to the company that might be associated with the management interviews, and also maximizing the productivity of the site visit.

Some of the information necessary to conduct the business valuation will need to be obtained through interviews with company management. Sometimes, however, the analyst merely inspects voluminous or highly sensitive documents and only gets copies of the information necessary for the performance of the assignment. In either case, the analyst should be sure that he or she has obtained all the information necessary to complete the assignment.

Generalized Company Information Checklist

Written company-specific information that is generally used in business valuations is presented in Exhibit 4–1. This list is generic. Not every item on the list will be required for every appraisal, and in many circumstances, documents not listed must be reviewed. Working with this list, nevertheless, will assist the analyst in developing a subject company-specific information request list. It will also be helpful to company officials and attorneys in the planning stages of a potential valuation engagement.

Exhibit 4-1

Preliminary Documents and Information Checklist
for Business Valuation of Typical Corporation

Financial Statements for Typical Corporation

Balance sheets, income statements, statements of changes in cash flow, and statements of stockholders' equity for the last five fiscal years or economic cycle

Income tax returns for the same years

Latest interim statements and interim statements for comparable period(s) of previous year

Other Financial Data

Summary property, plant, and equipment list, depreciation schedule, and capital budget

Aged accounts receivable summary

Aged accounts payable summary

List of marketable securities and prepaid expenses

Inventory summary, with any necessary information on inventory accounting policies

Synopsis of leases for facilities or equipment

Any other existing contracts (employment agreements, covenants not to compete, supplier agreements, customer agreements, royalty agreements, equipment lease or rental contracts, loan agreements, labor contracts, employee benefit plans, and so on)

List of stockholders, with number of shares owned by each

Schedule of insurance in force (key person life, property and casualty, liability)

Budgets or projections, for a minimum of five years, business or strategic plan, if available

List of subsidiaries and/or financial interests in other companies

Key personnel compensation schedule, including benefits and personal expenses

Details of any transactions with related parties

Company Documents

Articles of incorporation, bylaws, and any amendments to either

Any existing buy-sell agreements, options to purchase stock, or rights of first refusal

Franchise or operating agreements, if any

Other Information

Brief history, including how long in business and details of any changes in ownership and/or any bona fide offers recently received

Brief description of the business, including position relative to competition and any factors that make the business unique

Marketing literature (catalogs, brochures, advertisements, and so on)

List of locations where company operates, with size and recent appraisals

List of competitors, with location, relative size, and any relevant factors

Organization chart

Résumés of key personnel, with age, position, compensation, length of service, education, and prior experience

Personnel profile: number of employees by functional groupings, such as production, sales, engineering/R&D, personnel and accounting, customer service/field support, and so forth

Trade associations to which the company belongs or would be eligible for membership

Relevant trade or government publications (especially market forecasts)

Any existing indicators of asset values, including latest property tax assessments and any appraisals that have been performed

List of customer relationships, supplier relationships, contracts, patents, copyrights, trademarks, and other intangible assets

Any contingent or off-balance sheet liabilities (pending lawsuits, compliance requirements, warranty or other product liabilities, estimate of medical benefits for retirees, and so on)

Any filings or correspondence with regulatory agencies

Information on prior transactions in the stock or any related party transactions

Financial Statements

According to the American Institute of Certified Public Accountants (AICPA), "the term *financial statements* refers to a presentation of financial data, including accompanying notes, derived from accounting records and intended to communicate an entity's economic resources or obligations at a point in time or the changes therein for a period of time in conformity with a comprehensive basis of accounting."[1]

There are four traditional statements, along with the footnotes, which together comprise the financial statements of a business entity. These are:

1. Balance sheet (statement of financial position)
2. Income statement (statement of income, statement of operations, or statement of earnings)
3. Statement of cash flows (formerly, statement of changes in financial position)
4. Statement of stockholders' equity (or statement of partners' capital)

The amounts of a company's assets, liabilities, and equity, as determined by generally accepted accounting principles (not necessarily the fair market value of those accounts) as of a given point in time, is the statement of financial position, more commonly referred to as the company's balance sheet. In contrast, the statement of results of operations, or the income statement, presents a financial summary of a company's operating results for a certain period of time. The third statement, the statement of cash flows, is designed to provide information about the important changes in financial position that took place during the accounting period. This statement is useful if net cash flow is an important measure of economic income in the valuation (as it is in many cases) because the statement of cash flows is a source of information on capital expenditures and changes in working capital.

However, analysts should note that the statement of cash flows presents changes in balance sheet accounts as of two points in time. These changes may be unusual or temporary. In such cases, the statement of cash flows may not fully reflect the continuing cash-flow-generating capacity of the subject business.

Even within the scope of generally accepted accounting principles (GAAP), there are many decisions that management makes with respect to the accounting treatment of various company transactions. These include, for example, such things as choices of capitalizing or not capitalizing certain items, inventory accounting methods, and depreciation methods. The footnotes to financial statements and supporting schedules usually are helpful in understanding the company's treatment of such items.

The analyst's function is not to audit, but to express an opinion of value on the basis of available financial information. In some situations, nevertheless, the accountants' work papers and/or company books may provide additional insight that is relevant to the valuation, and the analyst may request to see such information.

---

[1] *AICPA Professional Standards*, Vol. 1 (Jersey City, NJ: American Institute of Certified Public Accountants, 2007). § 623.02

Relevant Time Period

When asking for historical financial statements on the subject property, one should endeavor to study statements during a *relevant period*. The most commonly used period is five years, but this should not be used as a rote number of years. Conceptually, the relevant period covers the most recent period of time immediately prior to the valuation date during which the statements represent the company's general operations.

If the company significantly changed its operations a few years before the valuation date, only those previous years may represent the relevant period. On the other hand, if the business has a long history and some or all recent years were abnormal in some way (such as during a cyclical peak or trough in the company's industry), statements for the past seven, ten, or more years may constitute a relevant period for valuation purposes.

Levels of Financial Statement Preparation

In the United States, we sometimes take for granted the degree of standardization of the financial statement presentation to which we have become accustomed. One only needs to work with financial statements from other countries to truly appreciate our financial reporting standards, as complicated and as curious as they are.

Valuation analysts prefer to work with audited financial statements because of their completeness and reliability, but the large majority of closely held businesses do not go to the trouble and expense of having their statements examined by an independent auditor. There are various levels of scrutiny represented by audited, reviewed, and compiled financial statements. The same company might have different levels of scrutiny performed for different years.

Audited Statements. In *audited statements*, the independent auditor expresses an opinion, or if circumstances require, disclaims an opinion, regarding the fairness with which the financial statements present the financial position, the results of operations, and the changes in financial position, in accordance with generally accepted accounting principles.

Reviewed Statements. The accountant expresses limited assurance in *reviewed statements* that there are no material modifications that should be made to the statements in order for them to be in conformity with generally accepted accounting principles. A review does not provide assurance that the accountant will become aware of all significant matters that would be disclosed in an audit.

Compiled Statements. Finally, the *compiled statements* are management's representations presented in the form of financial statements, but the accountant has not undertaken any efforts to express assurance on the statements.

Sometimes, statements are prepared internally by management without the services of an outside accountant.

As the level of outside review of the financial statements declines, the analysts should request additional information as they deem necessary and use their judgment as to the quality of the information available. Further, they should provide appropriate disclosure to the user of the appraised report.

Impact of Enterprise Legal Structure

When the legal structure of the company differs from the traditional corporation, the analyst should be cognizant of the potential impact on the analysis. Several of these legal organizations, and the valuation implications of the choice of legal structure, are discussed in later chapters.

It is important to point out that a different legal status of the business can have an impact on the valuation conclusions, especially when it comes to partnerships and limited liability companies. For example, in the case of partnerships where partners do not share the earnings (or losses) in the same proportion as their partnership share is entitled to upon liquidation, the legal rights and privileges of one equity owner could be substantially different from that of another owner. And, this could result in a substantially different value conclusion. The analyst valuing a partnership interest subject to any such complications will need to read the partnership or limited liability company membership agreement or to be sure that the partners' rights of the subject interests are understood.

S corporations and other pass-through entities also present special valuation issues that the analyst should be aware of. LLCs typically have provisions in their operating agreements that affect valuation as well.

Federal Tax Returns

There are common reasons for discrepancies between the amounts and items reported on financial statements and those reported on federal income tax returns. Many of the differences simply result from timing differences, such as different methods of revenue recognition and cost recovery of capital expenditures.

For corporations filing Form 1120, U.S. Corporate Income Tax Return, a summary of differences between tax return reporting and financial statement reporting is found in Schedule M-1, Reconciliation of Income per Books with Income per Return.

If such differences exist, the analyst must use his or her professional judgment to determine which figures will provide the most appropriate basis for appraisal purposes. A general rule is that the analyst should select the statements that most closely conform to industry practices and would most fairly represent the company's financial position and earning power. Most of the differences between book and tax reporting found on schedule M-1 are timing differences and temporary in nature. Normally, financial data and ratios derived from tax return data of the subject company would not be comparable to the financial data and ratios derived from the audited financial statements of publicly traded guideline companies.

It is not unusual to find small companies without any formally prepared financial statements. In this case, the analyst has only the tax returns as a basis for financial statements. In this situation, the analyst may format financial statements in the conventional manner by recasting information from the tax returns.

There are many federal income tax forms that may contain relevant data for a particular valuation assignment. A discussion of the various forms and their use would be too detailed to fit within the scope of this book. *Package X* is a two-volume set of the most frequently requested tax forms and their instructions and is available from the IRS. The IRS Web site provides most forms along with information and instructions. The Web address is www.irs.gov.

Interim Statements

Interim statements are those prepared as of a date other than the last day of the fiscal year. Analysis of interim statements can give a more timely indication of the financial performance of the subject company and can provide a better understanding of businesses with highly seasonal operations whose trends the analyst may want to track on a monthly or quarterly basis.

Some privately held companies prepare interim statements monthly. It is important, however, that the analyst have an idea of these statements' usefulness before demanding the effort required to develop this information. Because many businesses now use some form of a computerized accounting program, these interim reports are easier to create.

Several factors influence the usefulness of interim statements, particularly:

1. The proximity of the valuation date to the fiscal year-end
2. The quality of the interim statements
3. The importance of seasonality to the subject company
4. The extent to which information in interim statements is likely to affect the conclusion

Oftentimes, information regarding the latest 12 months (LTM) of operations can provide a worthwhile perspective about the company's condition. When LTM analysis is conducted, the interim statements for the subject period of time plus the interim statements for the corresponding period during the prior fiscal year are needed.

Interim statements usually do not contain certain adjustments for a variety of accrual items typically made when closing the books at year-end, such as a physical inventory inspection, prepaid expenses, and reserve for bad debt accounts.

Therefore, to interpret interim statements and to use them as if they were comparable to year-end statements, the analyst may need additional information with which to approximate such year-end adjustments.

Other Financial Schedules

The purposes of requesting financial information regarding equipment lists, aged receivables, aged payables, and prepaid expenses are (1) to give the analyst familiarity with the accounting policies of the company and (2) to alert the analyst to special situations that could affect the valuation. This information may assist the analyst in distinguishing excess assets from normal operating assets so the excess assets can be separately valued. Also, when applying the asset accumulation approach to business valuation (see Chapter 14), the information from these schedules can assist in the underlying assets valuation process. Chapter 7, "Analyzing Financial Statements," discusses when and how some of this information may be used.

Current Assets and Liabilities

Depending on the situation, any or all of the following schedules may be relevant:

- Aged receivables list
- Aged payables list
- Marketable securities list
- Prepaid expense list
- Inventory list

Among other things, an understanding of a company's current assets and liabilities gives insight into the company's working capital needs.

Aged Receivables and Payables Lists. The *aged receivables list* can yield insight into the company's profitability, liquidity, and even viability. However, many relatively small companies do not prepare them. Because the aged list gives the analyst a useful means for recognizing situations that could affect the company's value, the analyst should have either the client's accounting department or a member of his or her own staff prepare one, if appropriate.

The *aged payables list* may be particularly relevant if it appears that a company's working capital may be deficient.

Marketable Securities List. For companies that carry marketable securities, knowing what they are helps with understanding how they should best be treated in the valuation process.

Prepaid Expense List. Adjustments to prepaid expenses may be appropriate in some cases, and a listing will help to make this determination as well as provide insight into working capital needs.

Inventory List. The amount of detail desired in the inventory list varies from one appraisal to another. Depending upon the inventory's importance to the valuation conclusion and to the extent to which inventory accounting methods vary within the particular industry, the amount of inventory data to be gathered will vary. In any case, the total should be reconcilable with the inventory as shown on the financial statements, using whatever adjustments conform to the company's method of inventory valuation. The company's write-down policy may also call for a market value adjustment.

Plant and Equipment

Property Lists. Lists of property owned should include the acquisition date, a description adequate for identifying each piece or group, the original cost, the depreciation method and life used, and the net depreciated value. The totals of such schedules should reconcile with line items in the financial statements. For real estate, the schedule should show the size (acres of land and dimensions and square feet of floor space of buildings), with a brief description of the construction and any special features. It should also indicate the dates and costs of additions and remodeling.

Evidence of Real and Personal Property Values. Indicators of current real estate and equipment asset values can be helpful and necessary in valuations that utilize the adjusted net asset value method. A valuation of the assets can even be important in capital-intensive companies in which a weighted average cost of capital method is used if the analyst uses the asset base as a determinant of the amount of debt that the company can support. An independent appraisal by a qualified practitioner should be obtained if the asset base is a material consideration. Tax assessments are usually readily available but may represent a standard of value that is different from the one required for the business valuation. Insurance appraisals have a tendency to use the replacement value standard instead of the market value standard and thereby overvalue used property. This different standard is often used for insurance appraisal purposes in an attempt to ensure that the insurance will be adequate to cover potential losses.

Officers' and Directors' Compensation Schedule

An officers' and directors' compensation and benefits schedule for the same number of years as the financial statements should be prepared, when appropriate. The income statement could conceivably be adjusted in order to identify the company's earning capacity (see Chapter 7). The benefits of ownership should be identified separately from compensation for performing a specific role for the company.

Employees related to the owners should be included on the list. The analyst should be mindful that the IRS sometimes attempts to depict compensation paid to C corporation owners as excessive, so as to reclassify a portion of the C corporation owner's compensation as a stockholder dividend. The analyst should be careful when describing any adjustments made to compensation in order to avoid unintentionally triggering unfavorable tax consequences for the client. These benefits of ownership may include:

- Base salary
- Bonuses or commissions
- Pension contributions
- Profit sharing plans
- Other employee benefit funds
- Life insurance policies
- Noncash contributions:
    - Stock options
    - Related party transactions
    - Company cars
    - Country club memberships
    - Other company property used (plane, boat, condominium, etc.)
    - Expenses paid or reimbursed to the employee

Broad-based and vocation-specific compensation surveys are available from several sources. The most prominent of these include:

- ExecuComp, www.standardandpoors.com, 800-523-4534
- Executive Compensation Report, www.aspenpublishers.com, 800-638-8437
- Executive Compensation Reports, www.ecomponline.com, 212-441-2047
- Management Compensation Survey, www.mgma.com, 877-275-6462
- Physician Compensation and Production Survey, www.mgma.com, 877-275-6462
- Principals, Partners, and Owners Survey (for architects, consulting engineers, and environmental consulting firms), www.zweigwhite.com, 800-466-6275

- Salary Survey of North Central Engineering Firms, www.zweigwhite.com, 800-466-6275
- Salary Survey of Northeast Engineering Firms, www.zweigwhite.com, 800-466-6275
- Compensation Benchmarking Surveys (industry reports, chemical, general market, health, industrial, retail, utilities), www.haygroup.com, 800-716-4429
- ERI — Economic Research Institute, www.erieri.com, 800-627-3697
- SalaryExpert.com, www.salaryexpert.com, 877-799-3427

Distribution of Ownership

The list of equity owners should include each owner's name and number of shares, partnership, or membership units held as of the valuation date. The ownership list should describe and quantify individual and other entity ownership, especially if there is more than one class of equity. Family members and other relationships among the equity owners should be identified.

Dividend or Partnership Withdrawal Schedule

The *dividend schedule* normally should cover the same period of time as the financial statements. It should show the date of each dividend payment and the per share amount for each class of stock, per unit amount for each class of partnership unit, or amount for each limited liability membership unit.

Schedule of Key Person Life Insurance

In many companies, the loss of a single key employee can have a significant impact on the company's operations. It is always desirable to know how much of this risk is covered by life insurance. A schedule of *key person life insurance* will help identify how much key employee risk affects the value of the business.

Off-Balance Sheet Assets or Liabilities

There are many financial items that can significantly affect the business's value that do not appear as line items on the balance sheet, often because they are of a contingent nature. Such items may or may not be referenced in footnotes.

A common off-balance sheet asset or liability is a prospective award or payment arising from a lawsuit. The analyst should inquire about any pending or potential suits and note the details.

This category could also include the potential cost of compliance with environmental, Occupational Safety and Health Administration, or other government requirements. The adequacy of reserves for claims or other product liability should also be explored. Overfunded pension plans are another potential hidden asset, or, conversely, underfunded plans a hidden liability. Leasing is an important form of financing for many businesses. While some leases are capitalized and appear on the balance sheet, many others are classified as operating leases and the related liability is described only in a footnote disclosure. Information gathered on leases should include the nature of the assets under lease, lease terms including renewal options, and any options to buy at the end of the lease term.

Information regarding intangible assets, both those shown on the balance sheet and off-balance sheet intangibles, such as patents, copyrights, and trademarks, should include a description of the property protected by this legal right and the expiration date of the right. The list of intangibles should include a brief description and enough information to understand these items. The importance to the business's value of these legal rights and degree of detail required varies from one situation to the next. The importance of intangible assets is covered elsewhere in this book along with some of the documentation necessary to reflect their impact on the business's value.

Related Party Transaction Information

When it comes to related party transactions, it is important that the analyst gather as much information as is available in order to determine the nature of the transactions and their propriety.

As the Financial Accounting Standards Board (FASB) states in its *Statement No. 57* regarding *related party transactions*:

Related party[2] transactions may be controlled by one of the parties so that those transactions may be affected significantly by considerations other than those in arm's-length transactions with unrelated parties.[3]

Without disclosure to the contrary, there is a general presumption that the transactions reflected in the financial statements have been consummated on an arm's-length basis between independent parties . . . Because it is possible for related party transactions to be arranged to obtain certain results desired by the related parties, the resulting accounting measures may not represent . . . what they usually would be expected to represent.[4]

Related party transactions may be controlled entirely by one of the parties so that those transactions may be affected significantly by considerations other than those in arm's-length transactions with unrelated parties.

In the absence of audited or reviewed financial statements, which include related party information in their accompanying notes, the analyst should have a list prepared that describes the terms of the transactions. These types of related party transactions could include loans to and from related parties, leases, or purchases from or sales to related parties, guarantees to—or for—related parties, and so on.

---

[2] *Defined in Financial Accounting Standards Board (FASB) Statement No. 57*, Appendix B(f).
[3] *FASB No. 57*, Appendix A, para. 13 (1982).
[4] Ibid., para. 15.

Operating Information

Company History

The history of the company should put the business in the proper context for the user of the valuation analysis. A relatively brief history will suffice in most cases. The history should indicate how long the company has been in business and some chronology of major changes, such as form of organization, controlling ownership, location of operations, and lines of business. Sometimes predecessor companies are a relevant part of the background. A detailed explanation of the history may be required in some instances, and sometimes certain transactions that fundamentally contributed to the company's composition, as of the valuation date, should be included.

Brochures, Catalogs, Web Sites, and Price Lists

The company should furnish the analyst with a set of its sales materials, such as brochures, catalogs, Web site addresses, and price lists. These items will enable the analyst to become familiar with the company's products, services, and pricing and to evaluate the written sales materials. As with many of the written items furnished, these will help the analyst get an overview of the company and prepare relevant questions for the visit to the company's facilities and inquiries of company personnel.

Key Personnel

Hiring, motivating, and retaining human resources is often the closely held business owner's biggest challenge. Key personnel include directors and officers, heads of departments or divisions, and anyone else who plays an important part in the company's operation. Data on key personnel should include the person's age, position, tenure with the company and in the industry, educational and professional credentials, and compensation. An organization chart may help the analyst identify key personnel.

Customer and Supplier Base

Customer Base. An analysis of the customer (or client) base is especially important for businesses that rely on only a few customers for a significant portion of their revenue and/or profit. Many businesses fall under the "80/20 Rule" where 80 percent of their revenue is attributable to 20 percent of their customers. The information to analyze the impact on value attributable to customer base includes a list, in order of size of revenue (or profit), of the largest customers. The list should include revenue by customer for the most recent fiscal period and the dollar amounts of revenue for several prior periods. The columns for the prior periods should also show customers who accounted for a significant proportion of the revenue in the prior period, even if they are not on the current period's largest customer list. Sometimes a budgeted figure for each customer for the forthcoming period is available.

Order Backlog. If the company's order backlog (customer orders yet to be filled) is a significant factor in the business, the analyst should compare the backlog on the valuation date with that on previous dates. Such comparison, especially with the backlog one year prior to the valuation date, is one indication of the company's future prospects.

Supplier Base. Like the customer base, the supplier base can be an important factor affecting the value of a business, especially if the future availability of supplies is uncertain enough to increase the company's risk or if the company is reliant on a sole supplier. The supplier list could take the same format as the customer base.

Contractual Agreements and Obligations

There are a variety of other contractual commitments (e.g., leases, loans, franchise agreements, distributor agreements, customer contacts, etc.) that can have a significant impact on the value of a particular business interest. The list of potential contractual commitments is nearly infinite. The analyst should draw on personal experience to inquire about contracts that typically occur in certain lines of business and ask management whether any significant contracts exist. Some of the factors that should be analyzed are the time period of specific rights of ownership, restrictive covenants, transferability of commitments, favorable or unfavorable rates relative to rates available as of the valuation date, renewal options, personal guarantees, and the penalties that the company could suffer for lack of performance under these commitments.

Industry and Trade Association Information

Industry information can be provided by the subject company, in many cases, more readily than relying on independent research. A description of the industry, its trends, and its competitive environment is usually accessible from the company. It is also helpful if the company can furnish a list of trade associations to which it belongs, or is eligible to belong, along with the name and address of the executive director of each. The subject company can often readily supply copies of relevant publications from trade associations, governmental agencies, and other industry sources.

List of Past Transactions in the Stock or Offers to Buy

To the extent that past transactions in ownership interests were at arm's length, they provide objective evidence of value. Even if not accepted, a bona fide offer, particularly if submitted in writing, can at least corroborate the value. In such cases, it is important to verify whether the bona fide written offer was a funded offer. If financing was not in place for the written offer, it may provide less evidence to the analyst than if it was a funded offer. In preparing the record of past transactions or offers, it is important to list any relationships among the parties in order to determine whether each transaction was at arm's length. The transaction record usually should go as far back as the number of years of financial statements used. On this basis, past transaction prices can be compared with prevailing book values, earnings, or other relevant variables.

If the company has made an acquisition, details of the acquisition may be an extremely relevant past transaction. This is an important category of past transactions that often is overlooked.

Budgets and Forecasts

Budgets or forecasts prepared by closely held companies vary widely from no written budget at all ("It's all in my head. It doesn't need to be written down.") to fairly detailed and accurate ones. Since the value of a business interest ultimately depends on what the business will accomplish in the future, reasonable estimates of future expectations should help in arriving at a value. A good way to test the quality of a company's budgeting process is to compare past budgets with actual results.

Budgets and forecasts are heavily relied upon in valuations for mergers and acquisitions. On the other hand, some courts are reluctant to accept budgets because the future is inherently unprovable and (in the case of divorce) because they may incorporate fruits of a spouse's future efforts. In most cases, however, a company that produces convincing budgets will command a higher value than one that does not.

Capital Requirements

The business's capital requirements play a part in the valuation because they are an integral part of estimating net cash flow and dividend-paying capacity. Capital requirements include such items as:

1. Capital expenditures
2. Remedying deferred maintenance
3. Increasing working capital

The proper amount paid to the seller would be the total value of a properly financed business, less the amount of the required cash infusion. When cash infusions are known or reasonably expected to be required in the foreseeable future to support the expected earnings, they must be reflected as a cash outflow, the present value of which should represent a decrease in the value of the business as otherwise determined.

Capital Expenditures

Capital expenditures include replacements of worn-out or obsolete existing plant and equipment plus any additions to plant and equipment necessary to produce any revenues contemplated in the valuation. The latter category would include items needed to remain competitive and maintain the company's position, plus anything needed to support whatever level of growth is contemplated in the valuation methodology and parameters used. As capital expenditures made for increasing capacity tend to be lumpy, it is important to understand the current capacity and increments to capacity that will be added from future additions to plant and equipment.

Capital expenditures are a specific component in the discounted or capitalized net cash flow methods. When using a market comparison approach to valuation, capital expenditure requirements may influence valuation multiples chosen if the subject company's capital expenditure requirements are significantly different relative to guideline companies. Alternatively, abnormal capital expenditure conditions may be treated as a direct decrement or increment to value determined through income or market valuation methods.

Deferred Maintenance

Some businesses have not maintained plant and equipment to a competitive level of efficiency and productivity. While expenditures to remedy this may be expensed for accounting and tax purposes, they nevertheless require an outlay of funds, which detracts from value. The treatment as to how they impact value can be handled essentially the same as capital expenditures.

Working Capital Requirements

A company's working capital requirements can be estimated based on analysis of its past operations, industry data, guideline company data, and discussions with management. It is common to find companies with either excessive or inadequate working capital. Excesses or inadequacies in the valuation data can be treated in the valuation much as other capital requirements can be treated.

If growth is anticipated, growth in working capital generally must also be anticipated. The analysis of changes in net working capital is a specific component in the discounted or capitalized net cash flow method. When using a market approach to valuation, working capital requirements that differ significantly from guideline companies may be reflected in valuation multiples.

Company Documents Relating to the Rights of Owners

Corporate or Partnership Records

The official documents of a corporation or partnership often hold facts that significantly affect the valuation of the entity or of certain specific interests in the entity. The articles of incorporation, the partnership agreement or limited liability company agreement, along with any amendments, and documents specifying rights attached to each class of outstanding equity provide information that is particularly important for businesses with more than one class of equity. Other information in the articles or bylaws may be relevant to the value. Partnership and limited liability company agreements should describe the rights and privileges of each of the interest owners.

Board of directors' meeting and shareholders' meeting minutes may be important, especially regarding transactions with related parties.

Buy-Sell and Employee Stock Ownership Plan Agreements

Buy-sell or repurchase agreements among owners or between owners and the company may contain provisions that can strongly affect the value of the shares to which they apply. These agreements often restrict the marketability of the subject interests and they can, correspondingly, affect the value of other classes of equity as well. Provisions in such agreements may address the question of value directly or may impose a restriction on transferability, which may bear on the value of the affected interests. On the other hand, in certain litigation scenarios, the restrictive provisions of a buy-sell agreement may not be applicable to the standard of value being sought and, at the instruction of counsel, are to be ignored. However, the analyst should understand the circumstances under which he or she is being asked to ignore certain provisions, and if appropriate, make appropriate disclosures or limitations in his or her opinion and report. Chapter 29 discusses buy-sell agreements and their impact on value.

If the company has an employee stock ownership plan (ESOP), the terms of the buyback provisions can have a major bearing on the marketability of the shares involved and, thus, must be considered when valuing ESOP shares. In some cases, the existence of an ESOP may provide a limited market for non-ESOP shares. Chapters 32 and 33 discuss these issues in further detail.

Employment and Noncompete Agreements

Employment agreements with key personnel may affect the company's value, as may agreements not to compete. These agreements could have either a positive or negative effect on value depending on the relationship between the cost and the value to the company.

Summary

Gathering and analyzing the foregoing information will give the analyst the groundwork on which to base the company interview and pinpoint still-needed details that are relevant to the valuation assignment. The specific material needed will vary with the particular valuation assignment and is a matter of the analyst's judgment. Following the suggestions in this chapter will help the analyst to avoid the all-too-common pitfall of overlooking certain company data that may have a significant bearing on the value of the business or interest being valued. The chapter should also help company officers and/or their attorneys to be well prepared for an efficient and productive data gathering process.

Chapter 5

Site Visits and Interviews

This chapter provides a guide for the valuation analyst to conduct an efficient site visit that will contribute in a meaningful way to the valuation process. It should also be a helpful tool for company officials and any attorney involved to know what to expect and to prepare for the visit in order to make it as productive as possible.

In many cases, the analyst's understanding and impressions of the business can be dramatically improved by seeing the operations firsthand and participating in face-to-face interviews. The historical financial statements and other written material and their implications can become more meaningful to the analyst as a result of the site visit. Current and potential changes that might cause the company's future to differ from that indicated by a mere extrapolation of the historical data can be identified. The field trip and interviews should focus on establishing the relationship between the data gathered and the existing and prospective company situation and economic environment.

The need for the valuation analyst to visit the company facilities and have personal contact with the company personnel and other related people varies greatly from one valuation to another. The extent of the necessary fieldwork depends on many things, including the purpose of the valuation, the nature of the operation, and the size and complexity of the case. Another determining factor is the degree to which the analyst was able to gather and interpret the written material described in the previous chapter.

The title of the person to be interviewed is not as important as the categories of topics to be probed. To cover the topics described in this chapter, the analyst may need to interview the company's president, chief operating officer, marketing or sales manager, and chief financial officer. In some companies, these job titles are all the responsibility of one person. In some companies, these responsibilities are carried out by people who are not even employees of the subject company. The analyst can work with the client to determine exactly who should be interviewed in order to gain an understanding of the important information that affects the value of the business.

This chapter presents a generalized discussion of interview topics. The actual topics and sequence of coverage will vary considerably from one situation to the next. The top-to-bottom comprehension of the business that the analyst is pursuing may not be provided in top-to-bottom order.

The limitless number of inquiries has broad potential implications for the valuation and will vary from one company to another. Accordingly, only the most general discussion of these topics is possible within the scope of this chapter. The analyst should attempt to understand all of the major factors that affect the value of the subject company.

Gaining a broader perspective of the business and its operations is the primary objective of the site visit and interviews. In addition, details missing from an analysis of the written material can be filled in. Developing some level of comfort with people at the company is also an important objective of the fieldwork, so that if additional information is required after the fieldwork is complete, it can be more readily obtained.

Generally, it is advisable to prepare a thorough list of questions in advance of the site visit. By studying the financial statements and other basic information, the analyst can gain an overview of the company and prepare a list of specific questions that will make the fieldwork more meaningful and productive. Also, after seeing the operation and talking with management, the analyst will be able to read and analyze the written material with greater insight.

It is usually best to visit company facilities and interview management fairly early in the valuation process—after obtaining and reviewing enough preliminary information to get a general overview of the company. This way, other necessary steps can be planned or some previously planned steps can be dismissed as irrelevant. Other sources of information (e.g., trade associations, periodicals, governmental agencies, customers, suppliers, and competitors) can be identified.

History

An appropriate beginning of the fieldwork is often a discussion of the company's history. This will give the analyst a perspective on how the business evolved and can often put the valuation assignment in focus.

The history of the company should cover when the business, or any of its predecessors, was founded, any acquisitions or divestitures along the way, any changes in the basic form of organization, any major changes in lines of business, and any changes in the geographical areas served. It should cover major changes in ownership and how they came about.

Although the business's total history should be sketched briefly, the parts most relevant to the valuation analysis usually will be the most recent past. A chronology of major events will help the analyst decide how many years of the company's financial data are relevant to the current valuation assignment and identify any major changes in the business or special circumstances to consider in analyzing the financial statements.

Description of the Business

The analyst should try to gain an understanding of how the company perceives itself:

- What does the company do?
- Why does it need to be done?
- What makes this company particularly well qualified to do it?
- What is the company's perception of the economic niche into which it fits?
- How does it try to do the best job of fitting in its niche?
- What are the company's major strengths and weaknesses?
- What are the key factors that enable it to operate profitably?
- What is the company doing that will cause the future to differ from recent history?

The analyst should try to gain an understanding of how the company perceives the industry and the particular aspect within which it operates:

- What are the nature and rate of technological changes affecting the industry?
- What developments or trends are expected in the industry in the foreseeable future?
- What special industry factors have a bearing on this particular company?
- To what extent are its fortunes subject to outside forces over which it has no control?
- What is the progress and prognosis for new products or services, locations, channels of distribution, etc.?

- What other aspects of the operation and of the industry are in a developmental or transitional stage?
- How will all these forces impact the future compared with the recent history?

The analyst will want to know the company's program for corporate development, including further development of existing and/or new products and markets. The company's program for capital expenditures, acquisitions, divestitures, and research and development should be uncovered. These inquiries should cover capacity constraints, how much is being spent for what, and how much of it is being financed.

If future growth is to be financed by issuing additional stock, the analyst should assess the effect of the potential dilution. If the future growth is to be financed using debt, the analyst should consider both the direct expense and the risk of the additional financial leverage.

The present management's policies toward the future direction of the company are more important for the analyst to understand if a noncontrolling ownership interest—versus a controlling ownership interest—is the valuation subject. This is because a controlling stockholder can change management policies. Nevertheless, even in the case of a controlling ownership interest valuation, the perspective of the existing management team on the major opportunities and problems facing the company and how it plans to deal with them is an important area of inquiry.

The strength of the company's intangible assets, whether or not they are carried on the company's books, is an increasingly critical area of inquiry. Often, sometimes without necessarily realizing it, when responding to questions about what makes this company unique, management lists intangible assets. The analyst should be curious about the proprietary products and services, especially about the unique characteristics that generate a comparative advantage over their competition. Can management help quantify the benefit attributable to brand names, trademarks, copyrights, or patents? Does the company enjoy economic benefits from a favorable location, favorable supplier contracts, sustainable customer relationships?

Management and Management Compensation

Another critical factor is the assessment of management's competency, breadth, and depth. Many closely held companies are somewhat lacking when it comes to providing for management succession.

The analyst should inquire about management members' age, health, education and professional credentials, experience, background, and history with the company. Each key person's compensation package and level of compensation should be considered. This includes participation in all employee benefit plans, fringe benefits, expense allowances, and other perquisites. Part of the purpose of this inquiry is to help the analyst judge whether key people are being compensated well enough to discourage them from leaving the company, and part of the purpose is to judge whether there may be excess compensation that the company could reduce if it fell on hard times, by direct reductions or by replacement of certain personnel with others who could do a comparable job at a lower cost.

The time and effort devoted to the business by each key person should be discussed. Many closely held companies employ people—usually family members—at full salary even though they have only a figurehead role and work only occasionally. On the other hand, some senior people who devote only limited hours may make a significant contribution because of experience and acumen.

The matter of excess compensation should be considered after taking into account the manager's hours devoted to the company and the job responsibilities of the manager. Some managers in closely held companies are paid at what some consider to be excessive compensation levels.

In many cases, the management of the closely held business are also the owners. By taking income in the form of compensation for services rendered instead of in the form of dividends, owners of C corporations avoid a layer of income tax at the corporate level. A hypothetical buyer of the entire business would want to be able to separate the existing owner's take-home pay between the amount that the buyer would have to spend to pay a substitute employee to perform the same duties and the amount that is attributable to a return on the buyer's investment.

When the valuation subject is a controlling ownership interest in the company, the existing total compensation less a normal level of compensation may be considered excess compensation. Such excess compensation is adjusted out of the expense category and into income in order to better reflect the expected economic performance of the company on a go-forward basis. This is because new controlling owners are in a position to eliminate this excess compensation.

If the valuation subject is a noncontrolling interest where no control over compensation levels is part of the equity position being valued (such as in the case of a gift of a 10 percent interest in the equity of a business, for example), the excess compensation of the owner is generally not added back to the income statement. This is because ownership of the noncontrolling position does not possess the rights necessary to correct the imbalance.

In order to make the appropriate adjustments regarding executive compensation of the closely held business, the appraiser identifies the total compensation from all sources being paid to the existing executive and compares that to the total compensation required to attract an executive of similar skills. If public company executives are the appropriate basis for comparison, then total compensation from all sources paid to the public company executive (including stock options, bonus plans, pension plans, perquisites, etc.) should be evaluated along with the contribution to the company provided by the executive.

Operations

The objective when discussing operations of the company is to learn what operations the company carries out, how efficiently and effectively it does so, and the prospects for either improvement or deterioration.

Materials and Supplies

Supplies are vital to the operations of any business enterprise. To what extent does the company fabricate versus assemble, and how much flexibility does it have in this respect? How much is the make-or-buy decision within the company's control?

Access and pricing are the two key factors the analyst should pursue in questioning the company's supply situation. The extreme—which is less rare than one might think—is the existence of a single source for a critical supply that, if cut off, could shut down the company's operations. Most distributorships, for example, can be terminated on 30 days' notice. For many manufacturing companies, one or more raw materials with limited sources of supply are essential to the operation. For some companies, a reliable source for energy is a critical component of the subject company's prospects.

The analyst should identify key suppliers and alternates, including names of individuals with whom the company deals. It may be appropriate for the analyst to contact suppliers directly, whether for additional information about the present or potential supply situation or for references concerning the company's credit, reputation, or other attributes.

Labor and Government Relations

The availability and cost of labor can be another critical factor in the successful operation of the business. When on the facilities tour, the analyst should be alert to clues about labor morale and efficiency. What labor contracts exist? When do they expire, and what are the prospects for satisfactory renewal in terms of both acceptable costs and risk of work stoppage? How do company compensation policies compare with other companies in the industry and in this locale? What is the company's experience with personnel turnover, and how does this compare with industry norms?

Government relations may impinge on the company's operations. To what extent is the company subject to industry regulations, such as food quality standards or the rate of return limitations imposed on some utilities? Does the company face costs associated with environmental protection or with the Occupational Safety and Health Administration (OSHA)? Does the company have problems meeting these requirements? What is the impact of these regulations on the company's earning capacity, flexibility, and future prospects?

Plant and Equipment

When touring the company's facilities, the analyst should gain an understanding of the adequacy of the plant and equipment. The business valuation analyst can make a general evaluation and can get the assistance of appraisers specializing in real estate, machinery, or personal property when needed. It may be desirable to take a set of pictures, especially if the analyst will need to communicate some description of the facilities to someone not able to visit the facilities, such as a judge in a court case. It may be useful to note the size and the type of construction, too. Is the equipment well maintained, new, highly utilized? Is there unused capacity and room for expansion? In general, will the plant be a source of future cost savings or a source of increasing costs?

Inventory

Inventory consists of raw material, work in progress, and finished goods. The analyst is interested in getting some assistance in interpreting how much inventory is obsolete, damaged, excessive, or inadequate. The facilities tour is a good time to inquire about inventory turnover and quality. Since it can have a significant effect on reported earnings and net worth in some types of companies, the analyst should take into consideration near worthless inventory that is carried on the books at original cost or valuable inventory that has been written off.

Markets and Marketing

The objective of the marketing interview is for the analyst to identify and describe the company's markets and its program for reaching them. Who are its customers? Why do customers buy from this company instead of from the competition? Is its target market growing or shrinking? Overall, what are the company's prospects for the future?

What are the forces that determine the demand and changes in demand for the company's products or services? To what extent can the company rely on repeat business and customer continuity? Does the market have identifiable seasonal, cyclical, or secular characteristics?

Are there technological changes in progress or in prospect that will alter its share of the market? What is this business planning to do in order to remain competitive? What does the company do to anticipate and cope with market changes, and how effective are its efforts?

It is common for the marketing manager to understate the company's competition and overstate the defined market's potential. Asking questions on a similar topic from a slightly different perspective or at a different point in the interview will help the analyst verify the responses without challenging the respondent.

One of the most important aspects of the marketing interview is determining how the company competes. The analyst should endeavor to list the identified competitors for each product or service and in each target market segment. This leads to market share estimates and market share trends. What is the economic outlook for these markets, and what are the competitors' likely actions? Many companies, especially smaller ones, are blind-sided by competition that has not yet been identified.

The company's policies about pricing, warranty, providing quality services, on-time or in-stock delivery, and terms and conditions of sale are typical areas of inquiry.

The interview should also cover personnel. Does the company have its own direct sales force, or do they rely on dealers or distributors? What is the degree of turnover? How are new sales and marketing people identified, and where do terminated employees go? What are the structure and level of compensation for marketing people, and how do they compare with the competition?

With respect to the order backlog, how does this year's compare with last year's and next year's expectations? What is the customer turnover rate? To what extent is the company dependent on one or a few key customers? What are the customers' motivations in choosing to do business with this company or its competitors, and how is the company addressing those motivations?

What changes are anticipated for the marketing program? How does the company plan to capitalize on future opportunities? If competitive forces or other problems are building up, what is the company doing to protect itself?

At the conclusion of the marketing discussion, the analyst should have a good grasp of the future prospects of the company and potential constraints.

Finance

As an aid in financial analysis, the analyst may conduct interviews with the chief financial officer, controller, outside accountant, or attorney. Analyzing financial statements is covered in Chapter 7, and many of the most important lines of interrogation are discussed there.

Interviews can contribute a great deal toward genuine understanding of a company's financial position beyond simply what the financial statements show.

Current Assets

It may be important, given the scope of the assignment, to verify the cash and equivalents account and the company's cash management techniques. The accounts receivable account may be examined to understand the extent to which the figure represents an amount that is genuinely collectible and how long it will take to collect it. What is the prognosis for collection of any notes or other receivables? The company's policy for accounting for the inventory may be an important factor affecting value. The physical flow and the accounting flow are likely to be different in a manufacturing operation and may be treated differently between the subject company and its competitors. What is the write-off policy? To what extent does the inventory figure represent the value of the inventory in a going-concern context?

Fixed Assets

The subject company's real estate and equipment are presented on the balance sheet according to historical cost less depreciation, and may not represent the fair market value of those assets. The method for capitalizing assets and the depreciation method adopted by the subject company may also differ from the methods chosen by others in the industry and could affect the valuation conclusion. If a liquidation premise is to be considered, the analyst should discuss the probable time and cost of liquidating all or any part of the assets, as well as their potential net realizable value.

Intangible Assets

Management's perception of the factors that make the subject company different from its competitors usually introduces a discussion of the intangible assets of the company such as a trademark, patent, or copyright. It may be proprietary technology, a trained and assembled workforce, special know-how, customer relationships, supplier relationships, or other intangible assets that make the company a viable competitor and give it earning power. Some closely held business owners call these intangibles *blue sky* or *goodwill*. The accounting practices for these assets and the legal protection of these assets should be explored.[1]

---

[1] For a detailed discussion of the valuation of intangible assets, see Robert F. Reilly and Robert P. Schweihs, *Valuing Intangible Assets* (New York: McGraw-Hill, 1999).

Current Liabilities

The company's banking relationship may be an important factor to consider when assessing the company's current liabilities. If the company has a line of credit, what are the costs and terms? Is it under pressure to pay down the line or is there unused credit? How is the line used during the operating cycle? What are the relationships with suppliers, and what are the terms of payment? What are the terms, conditions, and expectations regarding other current liability items?

Capital Structure

If there is long-term debt maturing in the foreseeable future, what are the company's options and intentions about rolling it over? What is the company's debt capacity, and is it assumable by a hypothetical buyer? Are personal guarantees on the company loans necessary? Convertible notes, puts, calls, warrants, or options could mean the current shareholders will be facing dilution. What changes to the capital structure might be anticipated? In virtually every valuation case, the analyst will want to discuss who owns the shares currently outstanding and what the shareholders' relationships are with each other.

Off-Balance Sheet Items

Potential asset items and potential liability claims against the company should be investigated. If the company is involved in pending litigation, what is its substance, and are there any pending judgments that might be favorable or unfavorable? Are leases of real or personal property favorable or unfavorable? The pension liability may be underfunded or overfunded. Is there any potential tax liability or refund? Lack of compliance with environmental protection, OSHA, or other governmental regulations may mean that an unstated liability would be imposed on a hypothetical buyer of the company. Product liability claims or a generous warranty policy could represent a significant unstated liability.

The site visit may also be used to investigate off-balance sheet items that are physically present at the time of the field inspection. Such off-balance sheet items may include inventory, tools and equipment, and so forth.

Profitability and Budgeting

A review of past and current budgets can be a good starting point from which to gain greater insight into the company's profit history and potential. Budgeting is an important area of inquiry. How far into the future does the company budget its operations, and how often is the budget reviewed? In some industries, an evaluation of the company's sales outlook should include an analysis that distinguishes between changes in unit sales and price changes. The most profitable products or product lines, including the outlook for maintaining profitability, should also be considered. An analysis of fixed and variable expenses will help the analyst understand the extent to which increased or decreased volume will affect operating margins. What can be done to make the company more profitable and what are the associated costs?

Insurance

An uninsured catastrophe could wipe out a business. The questions about insurance should investigate the adequacy of the company's coverage for key person life insurance, product and other liability insurance, and casualty insurance, including fire, theft, and business interruption. If no insurance is carried, the analyst should assess adequacy of reserves.

Dividends

The analyst should try to obtain a complete record of past dividend payments. Beyond that, the analyst should assess both the company's dividend-paying capacity and intentions with regard to dividends if dividend-paying capacity exists.

Prior Arm's-Length Transactions or Offers

Verification of the completeness of the list of prior transactions or offers—and the circumstances surrounding them—is a good idea. Overlooking or overemphasizing prior transactions is a common area of controversy in business valuations. What price was paid for the stock? Was it really an arm's-length transaction? Was it a "clean" transaction for the stock or were various strings attached?

If there were one or more offers to buy stock but a transaction was not consummated, the offer may still provide an indication of value. If it was a bona fide, arm's-length offer, it may provide particularly good evidence of value. This is particularly true if the offer was funded (i.e., the financing was already in place to pay for the offer). The analyst should seek anything in writing about such an offer.

Prior transactions of significance may include acquisitions by the company as well as transactions in its own stock, so the analyst should inquire about acquisitions. If the company made a meaningful acquisition, it may be a useful comparative transaction to use in the valuation.

Catch-All Question

If the person performing the fieldwork for a valuation follows this chapter as an outline, the result should be a reasonably comprehensive facility visit and set of interviews. This will be especially true if the person is an experienced interviewer, because many interview subjects will call for more in-depth interrogation than shown here, and personal style and technique alone can uncover critical information. Depending on the analyst's assignment, the ramifications of certain topics may call for a different depth of questioning, beyond the scope of reasonable explanation in a single book, much less in one chapter.

Nevertheless, even the most experienced interviewer may fail to ask just the right questions to elicit responses on every aspect bearing on the valuation. Therefore, somewhere near the end of each interview, the analyst might ask each interviewee a catch-all question. This can be something like: "Is there any information that you know that hasn't been covered and that could have a bearing on the valuation of the company?" This helps protect the analyst against material omissions in the questioning process and places the burden on company management if they are deliberately withholding material information.

Interviews of Outsiders

It is usually a good idea to get the names of outsiders who are involved with the company because, although it may not be necessary to interview these people, an interview may be desirable. Sometimes interviews with the company's outsiders are helpful not only for specific technical information but for independent viewpoints on certain aspects of the company. However, for many valuation assignments, where the purpose of the assignment is confidential and sensitive, it is inappropriate to contact outsiders, especially without the client's permission and introduction.

Professionals Related to the Company

Attorney. There are times when the analyst may work very closely with the company's attorney. The wording of the legal documents when structuring a recapitalization, buy-sell agreement, or an employee stock ownership plan, for example, may have a considerable bearing on the valuation. In these circumstances, the attorney may solicit the analyst's opinion about the impact on the valuation due to certain prospective provisions. On the other hand, the analyst may need a legal interpretation of a company document or contract or need an assessment of a pending lawsuit or potential litigation.

Independent Accountant. To get an explanation or interpretation of something on the financial statements, or to consult working papers for details that augment the financial statements, it may be necessary to interview the company's outside independent accountant. This is most often the case when the financial statements are not audited, not completely footnoted, or contain some kind of qualified opinion by the independent accountant.

Banker. If the company's banking relationship is important, or in jeopardy, it is a good idea to hear first-hand how the banker perceives it. The banker may also be a good source of general information about the company and the industry.

Other Possible Outside Interviews

Customers. The company's customers can be a good source of information about the subject company's products, strengths, and weaknesses. Customers can help provide an indication of the longer-term outlook of the subject company and help the analyst evaluate the continuing demand for products and services. Customers may also provide a viewpoint about the competition and the customer's perceptions of the differences in product design, quality, service, pricing, and the various intangible assets (e.g., trade name) among competitors. Under some circumstances, former customers could be contacted to find out why they no longer patronize the company.

Suppliers. Particularly if the subject company deals in a technological area, the suppliers may be able to explain technology changes in the industry and, in some cases, make some evaluation of the subject company's expertise.

Competitors. When it is appropriate to contact competitors, it is usually necessary to avoid violating confidentiality. The analyst may ask the competitor many of the same questions asked of the subject company regarding demand, supply, and pricing factors, technological changes in the industry, and relative merits of the products and services of the various companies in the industry, including, of course, the subject company.

Former Employees. Sometimes former employees may be useful as information sources—about why they left and other aspects of the company as seen in hindsight and from a different viewpoint.

Summary

A good analyst can gain a great deal of insight into a company through the field trip and management interview process. The preceding queries should provide the analyst with a perspective on the company being valued and yield a multitude of details relevant to the valuation assignment. What the analyst gets from the process will depend partly on the thoroughness of preparation and partly on the degree of cooperation provided by the subject company and those being interviewed.

It may be helpful for relevant company officials to review this chapter prior to the site visit in order to be prepared to make the visit as efficient and meaningful as possible. Also, it often is helpful for the attorney involved in the matter for which the valuation is being done to review this chapter prior to the visit.

Chapter 6

Researching Economic and Industry Information

It is difficult to overemphasize the importance of thorough and relevant economic and industry research for a well-prepared business valuation. First, Revenue Ruling 59-60 requires consideration of "the economic outlook in general and the condition and outlook of the specific industry in particular." Second, an understanding of the economic and industry outlook is fundamental to developing reasonable expectations about the subject company's prospects. This chapter introduces some of the most useful sources of economic and industry information that can bear on a company valuation.

This chapter is organized in a top-down fashion. Because the general economic outlook influences all industries and all companies, this chapter starts with a discussion of general economic research, highlighting useful sources for researching both the national and regional economies. The chapter then turns to the topic of industry research for both general industry information and composite company statistics. Since the potential sources are so numerous, the chapter concludes with references to several indexes of economic and industry data sources.

The economic and industry outlooks included in valuation reports should be clearly related to the company being valued. It is particularly important to point out how the outlooks will affect the subject company and to focus on those issues most relevant to a thorough understanding of the company's competitive position in its market. As a corollary to this issue, it is important to understand the subject company's relationship to the structure of the industry. Each segment of an industry or an economy may be affected differently by a particular trend or development. Therefore, it is important to focus on the logical impact of each relevant factor on the subject company, whether positive or negative. Applying economic and industry research to the valuation of the subject company is too often neglected.

National Economic Information

Generally, economic outlooks should include a discussion of each of the most important leading economic indicators. For example, it typically is appropriate for valuation reports to discuss such variables as economic growth—usually measured by gross domestic product (GDP) on a national level or real gross state product (GSP) on a state level—inflation, employment, consumer spending, business investment, construction, interest rates, and population trends. The following sections outline some of the most useful sources of economic information for both national and regional economic research.

The Federal Statistical System

The United States collects, analyzes, and disseminates more economic data than any other country. While most countries have central statistical offices, this has never been the case in the United States. The remarkable range and extent of the government's statistical efforts developed piecemeal, according to the dictates of legislation and in response to emerging needs. Thus evolved the far-flung, highly decentralized federal statistical system. Only about a half dozen federal agencies exist solely to create statistics, but over 100 other governmental units also participate in the statistical process.[1] Four of the most widely used publications are the *Federal Reserve Bulletin, Survey of Current Business, Statistical Abstract of the United States,* and the *Economic Report of the President.*

- *Federal Reserve Bulletin* (Washington, DC: Board of Governors of the Federal Reserve System). Published monthly, the *Federal Reserve Bulletin* includes such data as employment, industrial production, housing and construction, consumer and producer prices, GDP, personal income and savings, and key interest rates. Three years of annual historical data are usually presented for each set of statistics, and data for the current year are provided in monthly or quarterly units. It is usually available at public and university libraries and is partially available online at www.federalreserve.gov/pubs/bulletin/default.htm.
- *Survey of Current Business* (Washington, DC: U.S. Department of Commerce). This monthly publication has two sections. The first deals with basic business trends and starts with an article, "The Business Situation," that reviews business developments. The second section contains an extensive compilation of basic statistics on all phases of the economy. It is usually available at public and university libraries and is available online at www.bea.gov/bea/pubs.htm.
- *Statistical Abstract of the United States* (Washington, DC: U.S. Department of Commerce). This annual publication contains statistics on all phases of U.S. life—economic, social, political, industrial—and some comparative international statistics. It is well-indexed and easy to use, and is available at most public libraries or at www.census.gov/compendia/statab/.
- *Economic Report of the President* (Washington, DC: U.S. Council of Economic Advisers). This annual publication is another valuable source of summary data on the U.S. economy. Released each year in January or February, the document is essentially a report from the executive branch to Congress on the state of the economy. An important feature of the narrative section is a five-year outlook for the U.S. economy, including projections for GDP and other key indicators. It is available at most public and university libraries and at www.gpoaccess.gov/eop/.

Banks

Bank letters are excellent sources for statistics, analysis, and projections of regional, national, and international economic and financial conditions. Several private and many government-owned banks, both in the United States and abroad, publish these periodicals and often distribute them free of charge.

The letters cover such areas as government policies, inflation rates, trade balances, employment, manufacturing, and investment for the reporting period (e.g., monthly or quarterly). Some bank letters end such summaries with predictions of trends in the economy, including changes in interest rates, wages and prices, and government monetary policies. A second part of these bank letters consists of a

---

[1] Michael R. Lavin, *Business Information: How to Find It, How to Use It*, 2nd ed. (Phoenix, AZ: Oryx Press, 1992), pp. 326–27.

statistical summary of major economic indicators for the reporting period. Several banks will include a section of international economic statistics to compare their economic situations with other countries.

Most bank letters concentrate on their state, region, or country of origin. For example, several of the banks in the Federal Reserve System publish data only on the states within their districts (e.g., New England or the Southeast). Although bank letters may vary in size, three excellent bank letters are *U.S. Economic Projections* (Bank of America), *Economic Trends* (Federal Reserve Bank of Cleveland), and *U.S. Financial Data* (Federal Reserve Bank of St. Louis).

- *U.S. Economic Projections* (New York: Bank of America). Issues are published weekly and feature an analysis of current economic and market conditions and an outlook for the week ahead. Details are provided regarding the bond and the stock market. It is available at www.bankofamerica.com/index.cfm?page=about.
- *Economic Trends* (Cleveland: Federal Reserve Bank of Cleveland). This monthly publication is an excellent source of economic variables, ranging from GDP and its components to money supply aggregates. The figures for such indicators as consumer income, business fixed investment, housing starts, producer and consumer prices, and so on, are usually given quarterly and monthly. Most major libraries have *Economic Trends* on hand, along with publications of the other 11 Federal Reserve Bank Districts, which also contain economic information. It is also available at www.clevelandfed.org.pubs.cfm.
- *U.S. Financial Data* (St. Louis: Federal Reserve Bank of St. Louis). This letter is published weekly and is an especially good compilation of statistics on the money supply, commercial paper and business loans, interest rates, and securities yields. It is available at www.stls.frb.org/publications/index.html.

Business Periodicals and Statistical Services

Business periodicals, such as *Barron's, Business Week, Forbes, Fortune*, the *New York Times*, and the *Wall Street Journal*, are good sources of timely information on the national economy, as well as other types of information. In every issue, both *Business Week* and *Fortune* include forecasts for certain segments of the economy and articles on recent economic developments. They and other magazines also publish extensive economic forecasts in their January issues. The *New York Times* and the *Wall Street Journal* are particularly valuable sources for the most current national economic information, since they are published daily. In addition to frequent articles on the most recent economic developments, the *Wall Street Journal*, in particular, includes a great deal of information on the financial markets.

Standard & Poor's Statistical Service, which is updated monthly, is one of the best sources of summary economic data. It contains economic statistics with special emphasis on banking and finance, production and labor, commodities prices, and the levels of activity in such industries as building and building materials, metals, and chemicals.

The *American Statistics Index* is a comprehensive tool to locate statistical information in the United States. This annual publication is in two volumes with monthly updates. The first volume is an index that refers to one or more abstracts in the second volume, which also contains full citations to the source publication. It is published by LexisNexis, a division of Reed Elsevier Inc.

Regional Economic Information

In addition to data on the national economic outlook, it is often appropriate to gather data on the outlook for the region or regions in which the subject company operates. The regional economic outlook is more relevant in some valuation analyses than in others. More often than not, however, the outlook for a specific city, county, or group of counties, cities, or states is relevant to the valuation of a particular company. It is crucial to recognize the importance of properly defining the region to be researched for a particular valuation. Even within the same state, the economic outlook can differ dramatically in different locales.

The primary sources for regional economic data are bank economics departments, public utilities, chambers of commerce, and various state agencies, such as departments of economic development and bureaus of labor statistics. Much of this information can now be found online, although the quantity and quality of the data vary from state to state and from city to city.

Most major local banks publish statistical tabulations of economic indicators, although their availability is limited. The best way to obtain regional bank publications is to visit their Web site or write or call the particular bank's economic department.

Some universities publish regional and local economic data that are sometimes focused on industries important to the region. Most states and multistate regions now have regular business magazines and newspapers that give economic statistics on business developments and offer economic analysis. The newspaper(s) for the major city in a particular state or region may also contain information on the state or local economy. Most newspapers have Web sites, but the ability to search the archives by keyword varies greatly from one paper to another.

Additional sources of information on regional and local economies are listed below.

- *The Complete Economic and Demographic Data Source* (Washington, DC: Woods & Poole Economics, annual). Available in print or on CD-ROM, this is an excellent source for statistical profiles of metropolitan areas, counties, and states. Historical as well as projected data are included in this source. Other publications from Woods & Poole include *State Profiles* and *MSA Profiles*, which currently include statistical economic data and forecasts through the year 2020.
- *Survey of Buying Power* (San Diego: Claritas, Inc., annual. 1-800-641-2030 www.salesandmarketing.com). Published annually by *Sales & Marketing Management* magazine, it breaks down demographic and income data by state, metropolitan area, and county or parish.
- *Federal Reserve Bank Districts*. Each of the 12 Federal Reserve districts publishes valuable information regarding outlooks and trends for its specific region. To find a complete list of the 12 districts and areas within each district, visit the Federal Reserve Web site at www.federalreserve.gov.

Industry Information

This section is divided into three parts. The first focuses on researching the industry outlook and briefly discusses some of the most useful sources for industry research. The second covers the various sources of composite financial statistics that can be used for comparison with the subject company. The third overviews sources of information on management compensation.

After reviewing the standard industry sources and while gathering more detailed information on the industry, the researcher should begin developing an outline of the relevant factors and events influencing the industry outlook. It is also advisable to keep a thorough bibliography of all information gathered, including the full name of the source and the date of the publication or meeting. The researcher should also comb through sources for additional references. Many articles cite individuals or other sources that will provide more informative and authoritative data.

In addition, the researcher should analyze the information in order to evaluate how the subject company is—and will be—affected by the various industry trends. For example, how will it be affected by price increases for key commodities? How will it be affected by shifts in demand, changes in technology, or shifts in the competitiveness of the industry? The industry section of the report should include the analyst's conclusion as to the impact of the industry outlook on the valuation of the subject company. And, it should also provide an overview of the industry outlook at the time of the valuation. These factors should be considered by the analyst in the selection of discount rates, direct capitalization rates, valuation pricing multiples, and other valuation variables.

General Industry Information

The first step in conducting industry research is to develop a general overview of the industry. This will allow the analyst to get a firm grasp on where the subject company fits into the industry and which industry factors or events are most relevant to the subject company. This general overview will also provide enough information about the overall industry to assist the researcher in finding additional information and analyzing the relevance of new information as it is gathered.

Standard & Poor's Industry Surveys. This is a useful starting point in researching an industry. It is organized into 52 broad industry groups and indexed for reference into 500 subgroups. It gives each industry group a reasonably comprehensive background analysis approximately twice a year. *Industry Surveys* generally includes discussion of the industry's structure, trends and outlook, and a section with financial statistics on publicly traded companies in the industry.

Industry Profiles. (First Research, 1-888-BUS-VALU, www.bvmarketdata.com or http://firstresearch.com/profiles) The industry profiles cover over 175 industries and are updated every 90 days. Each profile contains an overview of the industry, a quarterly update, business challenges, trends, opportunities, financial information, and industry forecasts. Most reports provide a free summary before initial purchase.

Trade Associations and Trade Magazines. Perhaps the most valuable source of authoritative information on a particular industry is that industry's trade association(s). Trade associations often collect financial statements from their members and compile composite financial data. Trade associations also publish general industry information, and they may include annual industry reports or articles in their trade magazines. In the data gathering and site visit stages of the valuation, the analyst may inquire of company management as to what are the appropriate trade associations and trade magazines to research.

The *Encyclopedia of Associations*, published annually by Thomson Gale, and *National Trade and Professional Associations of the United States*, published annually by Columbia Books, are two good sources to identify the association or associations that represent a particular industry or business sector. Many of these associations have regular publications that provide a wealth of data on their respective industries. They often provide periodic reviews and forecasts as well as statistical data.

After identifying the appropriate periodicals, the researcher can usually obtain them directly from the publishers, from a local business library, or on the Internet. If the periodical is not available or indexed on the Internet, it is worthwhile to phone the publisher and ask if any articles on the industry were published over a time period relevant to the valuation date.

Government Agencies and Government Publications. Federal and state agencies compile astronomical amounts of data, most of which are indexed in some form or another. The *Statistical Abstract of the United States* (discussed in more detail previously) can help direct the researcher to various federal agencies, state agencies, and other sources of industry information. Regulatory agencies are often good sources of data on industries that are—or used to be—regulated, such as communications, trucking, airlines, food, and drugs.

Business Press. A wide variety of business publications cover companies and industries on an intermittent basis. The *Wall Street Journal, Barron's, Business Week, Forbes*, and *Fortune* are but a few of the publications that frequently include industry articles. The best way to find these articles is (1) to perform an online search through an electronic database (e.g., ABI/INFORM, Business & Industry, Newsletter Database, Prompt, or Trade & Industry), or (2) to search Web-based services such as Northern Lights, Powerize, or Dow Jones Interactive. Often, articles in the business press provide valuable leads to authoritative sources or important industry observers.

Brokerage Houses. Brokerage houses provide current information in published report form on publicly traded companies. Such reports are an important source of information in order to gain insight into the functioning of an industry. In addition to providing information on publicly traded companies, brokerage houses often provide stock prices, financial data on companies, estimated earnings on those companies, information on interest rates, and historical graphs. Many brokerage houses publish weekly and monthly reports. Using analyst report services is an efficient method of obtaining reports (e.g., Investext, Multext, Northern Lights, and Profound's Brokerline) rather than directly from the brokerage house.

Composite Company Data

Business Source Books. The Business Source Books, prepared annually by the Statistics of Income Division, IRS, are by far the most comprehensive set of composite company statistics. However, they generally are about three to four years out of date. They include the *Corporation Source Book, Partnership Source Book*, and *Sole Proprietorship Source Book.*

Almanac of Business and Industrial Financial Ratios. The data used in the *Almanac* are compiled from corporate tax returns by the U.S. Treasury, IRS. They are disaggregated into 195 industries.

Exhibit 6–1 is a typical data presentation from the *Almanac*, in this case for meat products. Each industry group is presented in two tables. One table includes corporations that reported a profit as well as those that did not; the second table includes only those that reported a profit.

Each group for which there are sufficient data is presented in 13 asset size categories, compared with six in the *RMA Annual Statement Studies* data. The *Almanac* gives more income statement line items than does *RMA*, while *RMA* gives more balance sheet line items and more ratios.

The various ratios used are defined in the front part of the *Almanac*. Computations of some of the ratios differ from computations used by *RMA*.

The biggest drawback to the *Almanac* is the degree to which the information is outdated. The 2006 edition covers tax returns for fiscal years ended July 2002 through June 2003, the most recent year for which authoritative figures derived from tax return data of the IRS are available. Nevertheless, operating figures for most industries have at least some degree of stability over time, and the *Almanac* offers some income statement items not found elsewhere.

RMA Annual Statement Studies. Probably the most popular source of composite company data, including privately owned company data, is the *RMA Annual Statement Studies*, which is a product of a national association of bank loan and credit officers. The 2005–2006 edition was based on more than 190,000 financial statements submitted by representatives of their member banks. One reason for the broad appeal of the *Annual Statement Studies* is the over 700 different industries it covers. *Annual Statement Studies* is also available in computerized form from several sources.

Exhibit 6–2 is a typical page from *RMA Annual Statement Studies*, in this case "Manufacturing—Poultry Processing." Note that each industry group is presented in six size categories, based on sales. Also, data are shown in the aggregate for three years, so that year-to-year comparisons can be made.

Each of the ratios presented is defined in a section several pages long at the beginning of each annual volume. Note that "all ratios computed by *RMA* are based on year-end statement data only." For example, the cost of sales/inventory (inventory turnover ratio) is computed by dividing the cost of goods sold for the year by the ending inventory. A truer picture of inventory would be derived by dividing cost of goods sold by average inventory, but the data on which the *RMA* ratios are based are not sufficient to make that computation.

Analysts should be aware that sometimes a very small number of respondents are reported in the *RMA* categories. For example, in Exhibit 6–2, there are only 11 respondents in the $5 million to $10 million sale size category. Accordingly, analysts should be aware that a small number of respondents may produce data that are not truly representative of industry conditions.

Standard & Poor's Analyst's Handbook. One of the primary sources of composite financial information on the larger publicly traded companies is the *Standard & Poor's Analyst's Handbook*. The handbook is published annually, with income statement and balance sheet items and related ratios grouped by industry. Approximately 90 industry groups are included, with data going back 30 years.

Integra Information. Integra provides extensive information through data that is derived from 32 different proprietary and government data sources. Integra covers more than 900 industries with data from over 4.5 million privately held businesses. The reports cover detailed balance sheets, income statements, cash flows, and more than 70 ratios.

Exhibit 6–1

Sample Page from *Almanac of Business and Industrial Financial Ratios*

Table II		**MANUFACTURING**
Corporations with Net Income		**2010**

MEAT PRODUCTS

MONEY AMOUNTS AND SIZE OF ASSETS IN THOUSANDS OF DOLLARS

Item Description for Accounting Period 7/96 Through 6/97	Total	Zero Assets	Under 100	100 to 250	251 to 500	501 to 1,000	1,001 to 5,000	5,001 to 10,000	10,001 to 25,000	25,001 to 50,000	50,001 to 100,000	100,001 to 250,000	250,001 and over
Number of Enterprises 1	1700	11	414	214	32	313	442	100	103	36	15	10	9
Revenues ($ in Thousands)													
Net Sales 2	63884613	133708	80378	238024	93266	931962	3254175	4497258	6821329	6312467	3430646	5240773	32850627
Portfolio Income 3	217152	3548	·	116	129	6824	6535	2706	9379	15401	5927	7239	159347
Other Revenues 4	526152	2184	·	·	25778	44001	59514	11059	42690	8360	24918	52571	255077
Total Revenues 5	64627917	139440	80378	238140	119173	982787	3320224	4511023	6873398	6336228	3461491	5300583	33265051
Average Total Revenues 6	38016	12676	194	1113	3724	3140	7512	45110	66732	176006	230766	530058	3696117
Operating Costs/Operating Income (%)													
Cost of Operations 7	86.0	81.6	49.4	71.1	86.6	77.0	72.3	84.1	84.2	88.8	82.9	87.0	88.0
Salaries and Wages 8	2.5	1.0	18.5	6.0	·	3.2	6.7	4.8	2.7	1.9	3.4	3.2	1.6
Taxes Paid 9	1.0	3.0	2.6	2.6	0.8	1.7	1.8	0.9	1.0	0.6	0.7	0.7	1.1
Interest Paid 10	0.8	0.1	·	·	0.3	0.6	0.8	0.6	0.7	0.5	0.7	0.5	0.9
Depreciation, Depletion, Amortization 11	1.2	0.5	1.1	3.1	1.2	0.8	1.5	1.0	1.3	1.0	1.7	1.8	1.1
Pensions and Other Benefits 12	0.7	0.4	·	1.7	·	0.3	1.2	0.6	1.0	0.6	0.8	0.7	0.7
Other 13	6.2	3.7	18.7	14.1	5.9	10.2	9.6	6.4	6.1	4.4	6.6	5.9	6.0
Officers Compensation 14	0.7	·	5.6	·	9.6	7.2	4.9	0.4	0.8	0.4	0.5	0.2	0.2
Operating Margin 15	1.0	9.7	4.0	1.5	·	·	1.3	1.3	2.4	2.1	2.8	·	0.4
Oper. Margin Before Officers Compensation 16	1.7	9.8	9.6	1.5	5.2	6.2	6.2	1.7	3.1	2.4	3.3	0.3	0.6
Selected Average Balance Sheet ($ in Thousands)													
Net Receivables 17	2080	·	1	34	·	120	514	2231	3974	10078	16989	24801	196153
Inventories 18	2145	·	5	15	226	76	544	1970	3305	5552	12940	24766	243511
Net Property, Plant and Equipment 19	4315	·	20	66	89	189	695	2062	5794	14872	30695	61706	503978
Total Assets 20	11920	·	33	160	315	650	2414	6892	15916	37802	73308	146328	1409306
Notes and Loans Payable 21	3610	·	17	·	·	76	903	2718	4418	11280	23054	44066	420875
All Other Liabilities 22	2554	·	7	50	21	56	500	1769	3533	9342	16429	32075	293821
Net Worth 23	5756	·	9	110	294	518	1011	2405	7965	17181	33825	70187	694610
Selected Financial Ratios (Times to 1)													
Current Ratio 24	1.8	·	1.5	1.9	10.6	2.8	2.0	1.5	1.8	1.7	1.6	1.5	1.9
Quick Ratio 25	1.0	·	1.0	1.6	0.0	2.2	1.0	0.8	1.0	1.1	0.9	0.8	0.9
Net Sales to Working Capital 26	16.6	·	45.9	24.8	14.2	12.7	11.4	29.9	16.7	22.7	17.2	26.3	14.6
Coverage Ratio 27	3.8	·	·	·	·	8.3	5.2	3.7	5.6	6.5	6.3	3.3	2.7
Total Asset Turnover 28	3.2	·	5.9	7.0	9.3	4.6	3.1	6.5	4.2	4.6	3.1	3.6	2.6
Inventory Turnover 29	·	·	·	·	·	·	9.2	·	·	·	·	·	·
Receivables Turnover 30	·	·	·	·	·	·	·	·	·	·	·	·	·
Total Liabilities to Net Worth 31	1.1	·	2.7	0.5	0.1	0.3	1.4	1.9	1.0	1.2	1.2	1.1	1.0
Selected Financial Factors (in Percentages)													
Debt Ratio 32	51.7	·	72.8	31.0	6.8	20.4	58.1	65.1	50.0	54.6	53.9	52.0	50.7
Return on Assets 33	9.1	·	24.0	10.8	·	23.0	12.6	14.2	15.7	13.7	13.5	6.1	6.6
Return on Equity 34	11.1	·	·	13.6	·	23.9	22.7	23.2	23.0	23.5	22.0	6.1	5.7
Return Before Interest on Equity 35	18.9	·	·	15.7	·	28.9	30.0	·	31.4	30.1	29.2	12.6	13.4
Profit Margin, Before Income Tax 36	2.1	14.0	4.0	1.6	23.4	4.4	3.3	1.6	3.1	2.5	3.6	1.2	1.6
Profit Margin, After Income Tax 37	1.7	12.0	4.0	1.4	23.4	4.2	3.1	1.3	2.8	2.3	3.3	0.8	1.1

Trends in Selected Ratios and Factors, 1991-2000										
	1991	1992	1993	1994	1995	1996	1997	1998	1999	2000
Cost of Operations (%) 38	86.5	88.1	88.3	88.0	88.0	86.6	86.3	85.0	84.7	86.0
Operating Margin (%) 39	1.0	1.2	0.9	0.8	1.4	1.6	1.5	2.3	1.6	1.0
Oper. Margin Before Officers Comp. (%) 40	1.6	1.8	1.4	1.2	1.9	2.2	2.0	2.9	2.2	1.7
Average Net Receivables ($) 41	1280	2009	2185	1714	1306	1970	1789	1671	4859	2080
Average Inventories ($) 42	876	1636	2077	1696	1281	1636	1864	1676	3376	2145
Average Net Worth ($) 43	2722	4484	4485	4369	3618	4484	4936	5023	9410	5756
Current Ratio (x1) 44	1.7	1.7	1.6	1.6	1.6	1.9	1.9	1.7	1.7	1.8
Quick Ratio (x1) 45	1.0	1.0	0.8	0.8	0.8	1.1	0.9	0.9	1.0	1.0
Coverage Ratio (x1) 46	4.5	4.9	3.3	3.8	4.4	5.2	4.7	5.3	4.4	3.8
Asset Turnover (x1) 47	4.2	4.0	3.4	3.5	3.9	3.5	3.4	3.3	2.4	3.2
Operating Leverage 48	0.8	1.2	0.7	0.9	1.9	1.1	0.9	1.5	0.7	0.6
Financial Leverage 49	1.1	1.1	0.9	1.1	1.1	1.0	1.0	1.0	1.0	1.0
Total Leverage 50	0.8	1.3	0.6	0.9	2.1	1.2	0.9	1.6	0.7	0.6

SOURCE: Leo Troy, *Almanac of Business and Industrial Financial Ratios*, 37th ed. (Chicago, IL: CCH Incorporated, 2005), p. 46. Reprinted with permission of CCH Incorporated.

Exhibit 6–2

Sample Page from *RMA Annual Statement Studies*

MANUFACTURING—Poultry Processing NAICS 311615 (SIC 2015)

	Comparative Historical Data			Current Data Sorted By Sales					
Type of Statement	4/1/02-3/31/03	4/1/03-3/31/04	4/1/04-3/31/05	0-1MM	1-3MM	3-5MM	5-10MM	10-25MM	25MM & OVER
	ALL	ALL	ALL						
Unqualified	23	29	18		1			1	16
Reviewed	7	7	7				2	2	3
Compiled	1	8	5				1	3	1
Tax Returns	2	1	2					1	1
Other	16	7	18		3			4	11
					12 (4/1-9/30/04)			38 (10/1/04-3/31/05)	
NUMBER OF STATEMENTS	49	52	50		4		3	11	32

	%	%	%	%	%	%	%	%	%
ASSETS									
Cash & Equivalents	5.1	6.0	6.9		D		D	9.1	5.4
Trade Receivables (net)	18.5	16.3	21.4		A		A	27.4	18.6
Inventory	21.7	23.4	20.5		T		T	15.7	23.7
All Other Current	4.7	5.4	1.0		A		A	.7	.7
Total Current	50.0	51.1	49.8		N		N	52.9	48.4
Fixed Assets (net)	41.3	39.2	42.7		O		O	35.6	45.2
Intangibles (net)	4.3	4.1	3.2		T		T	6.9	2.4
All Other Non-Current	4.4	5.6	4.3					4.6	2.0
Total	100.0	100.0	100.0					100.0	100.0
LIABILITIES									
Notes Payable-Short Term	7.7	7.8	7.0		A		A	11.8	6.0
Cur. Mat.-L/T/D	4.0	4.5	3.3		V		V	2.0	3.2
Trade Payables	14.2	12.3	17.7		A		A	26.7	16.1
Income Taxes Payable	.2	.4	.4		I		I	.1	.5
All Other Current	8.6	9.0	6.8		L		L	4.6	7.9
Total Current	34.6	33.9	35.0		A		A	45.1	33.7
Long-Term Debt	18.3	17.1	16.1		B		B	11.2	17.0
Deferred Taxes	1.2	1.5	1.2		L		L	.3	1.5
All Other Non-Current	2.9	3.6	5.8		E		E	10.8	4.8
Net Worth	43.1	43.9	41.9					32.5	43.1
Total Liabilities & Net Worth	100.0	100.0	100.0					100.0	100.0

continued

112

Exhibit 6–2

Sample Page from *RMA Annual Statement Studies* (continued)

Col 1	Col 2	Col 3		Col 4	Col 5
			INCOME DATA		
100.0	100.0	100.0	Net Sales	100.0	100.0
17.2	16.4	19.3	Gross Profit	19.6	16.8
14.6	13.2	14.2	Operating Expenses	15.2	11.5
2.6	3.2	5.1	Operating Profit	4.4	5.3
.4	.4	.4	All Other Expenses (net)	.5	.4
2.1	2.9	4.6	Profit Before Taxes	3.9	4.9
			RATIOS		
2.7	2.6	2.4	Current	2.9	2.3
1.5	1.5	1.5		1.4	1.4
1.0	1.0	1.1		.8	1.1
.9	1.2	1.3	Quick	1.8	1.0
.6	.5	.8		.9	.7
.4	.4	.6		.5	.5
15 23.7	15 23.6	18 20.0	Sales/Receivables	14 25.3	18 20.1
20 17.1	20 18.3	21 17.5		20 18.4	21 17.7
26 12.3	26 14.1	30 12.0		31 11.9	29 12.8
21 17.1	23 15.9	17 21.2	Cost of Sales/Inventory	6 57.3	24 15.0
37 9.9	35 10.5	30 12.3		19 19.3	36 10.1
70 5.2	47 7.7	43 8.4		26 14.2	44 8.2
10 37.4	10 35.0	14 26.7	Cost of Sales/Payables	12 26.7	14 26.1
16 22.7	15 24.2	18 20.1		22 16.7	17 21.6
27 13.4	24 15.0	23 15.8		39 9.3	22 16.3
8.9	8.3	10.3	Sales/Working Capital	10.8	10.7
19.1	16.0	22.3		29.1	25.0
NM	NM	66.0		-53.3	79.6
(44) 12.1	(48) 12.2	(45) 21.3	EBIT/Interest		(30) 21.0
4.8	4.4	10.4			11.3
1.5	1.7	2.7			3.3
(19) 7.0	(14) 4.3	(14) 8.1	Net Profit + Depr., Depr., Amort./Cur. Mat. L/T/D		
4.2	2.3	4.9			
1.2	1.3	2.8			
.7	.6	.7	Fixed/Worth	.6	.8
1.1	1.0	1.1		.7	1.2

continued

113

Exhibit 6–2

Sample Page from *RMA Annual Statement Studies* (continued)

Ratio	Col 1	Col 2	Col 3	Col 4	Col 5	Col 6	Col 7
(top, unlabeled)	2.0	2.0	1.7			50.4	1.7
Debt/Worth	.7	.6	.7			.5	.8
	1.4	1.5	1.3			1.1	1.4
	4.9	2.8	3.7			74.1	1.9
% Profit Before Taxes/Tangible Net Worth	35.5 (47)	40.4 (49)	40.8 (47)			(31)	39.6
	15.5	15.9	29.7				30.7
	5.5	8.1	10.2				19.4
% Profit Before Taxes/Total Assets	12.4	12.0	17.9			23.5	18.3
	5.7	6.0	9.6			2.5	11.8
	1.1	1.3	2.8			.4	4.7
Sales/Net Fixed Assets	12.6	10.0	11.0			31.1	8.3
	6.4	6.3	6.7			7.8	6.7
	3.7	4.5	4.8			4.8	4.4
Sales/Total Assets	3.5	3.1	4.0			5.0	3.4
	2.3	2.6	2.9			3.4	2.7
	1.9	2.1	2.5			2.8	2.5
% Depr., Dep., Amort./Sales	1.2 (43)	1.3 (43)	1.1 (42)			.5 (10)	1.3
	2.3	2.0	1.8			2.2	1.6
	3.6	3.3	2.9			3.2	2.5
% Officers', Directors', Owners' Comp/Sales			.5 (10)			(25)	
			2.8				
			3.7				
Net Sales ($)	5170629M	7048256M	6162916M	7865M	18286M	177926M	5958839M
Total Assets ($)	2381990M	2820574M	2289065M	2957M	7459M	49601M	2229048M

M = $ thousand   MM = $ million

© RMA 2005

114

Information on Management Compensation

As discussed later in this book, management compensation often must be adjusted when valuing a company on a control basis. Following is a brief overview of some of the sources of comparative information on management compensation.

RMA Annual Statement Studies, the *Corporation Source Book of Statistics of Income*, and the *Almanac of Business and Industrial Financial Ratios*, described earlier, provide information on management compensation as a percentage of revenues. However, neither the *Almanac of Business and Industrial Financial Ratios* nor the RMA *Annual Statement Studies* provide information on what positions the individuals held or how many individuals make up the composition ratio.

Executive Compensation Assessor is an easy-to-use program that analyzes competitive pay for over 5,000 jobs and reports "up to the present day" competitive wage, salary, and incentive survey data. Each job has been tracked over time (many since 1977). The Executive Research Institute's (ERI's) database includes U.S. Securities and Exchange Commission (SEC) proxy data and 10-K reports, as well as U.K. annual reports.

Executive Compensation. This resource, provided by Dolan Technologies, Corp., analyzes national and regional data by base pay, incentive pay, and total cash compensation for 39 executive and senior management positions. Reports give information broken out by industry group, company size, and revenue profile. Data is gathered on nearly 27,000 incumbents in 37 states.

Pratt's Stats® provides owner compensation data for each transaction that can be extremely useful, particularly when valuing small- to mid-sized businesses or hard-to-find companies and jobs.

The proxy statements of comparative publicly traded companies are another useful source, since they generally present detailed information on the compensation of companies' top executives. Trade associations are another frequent source of information on management compensation, depending on the industry. For particularly small businesses, *Financial Statement Studies of the Small Business*, published annually, is a useful source. Additional sources are listed in the bibliography at the end of this chapter.

Online Information

The World Wide Web has rapidly become the preferred means of accessing information for research purposes. Thousands of Web sites and databases are available, covering millions of pieces of information that include all the multifaceted aspects of businesses. Access to these Web sites and databases allows for research to be conducted at lightning speed and for information to be gathered on a global basis.

The basics for searching on the Internet are through online search engines like Google, Yahoo!, and MSN. These search engines also provide a multitude of data through sponsored financial Web sites like Yahoo! Finance and MSN Money. The Internet additionally hosts many business databases, which are typically fee based, such as Alacra, a Web-based resource center for business appraisers that pools research tools and facilitates Web searches. Many local libraries maintain subscriptions to many of these databases and allow their patrons to search them.

The advantages of searching online for information include:

- Faster and more efficient information retrieval than is usually possible in printed sources
- The timeliness of business news
- The ability to combine different facets of a subject in a single search statement
- The ease of searching several databases in sequence to produce a comprehensive survey of the available literature
- The increased number of access points for standard reference sources
- The growing amount of information accumulating in databases
- The ability to retrieve data and store them for later review, editing, and manipulating

Factiva, a Dow Jones & Reuters Web site, runs the gamut from company directories, financial services, and statistical files to news wires, periodical indexes, and full-text files of newspapers, journals, and newsletters.

LEXIS/NEXIS databases offer electronic editions of a growing number of publications, including law reviews and medical journals. LEXIS/NEXIS business offerings include corporate annual reports, state corporation filings, Wall Street brokerage reports, and the complete text of newsletters, trade journals, and local business newspapers.

Information on where to find these resources, plus many more, is included in the bibliography at the end of this chapter.

Indexes to Economic and Industry Information

Several books and indexes are available to assist in finding additional sources of economic and industry data. Some indexes were already mentioned, such as the *American Statistics Index*. Another is the *Wall Street Journal/Barron's Index*. Other indexes, such as the *Business Periodical Index*, the *Public Affairs Information Service* (PAIS), both of which tend to have more economic information, and *Predicasts*, generally are available in public libraries.

Predicasts PROMT provides a fully integrated approach to the research of companies and industries. This resource serves to combine a variety of information normally accessible only by consulting many different resources, including trade journals, industry newsletters, newspapers, market research studies, and investment and brokerage firm reports.

In addition to these indexes, several directories can provide additional sources of economic and industry information. Three particularly valuable resources are *Encyclopedia of Business Information Sources*,[2] *Business Information: How to Find It, How to Use It*,[3] and *Best Websites for Financial Professionals, Business Appraisers, and Accountants*.[4]

---

[2] James Woy, ed., *Encyclopedia of Business Information Sources*, 14th ed. (Detroit: Thomson Gale, 2000).

[3] Michael R. Lavin, *Business Information: How to Find It, How to Use It*, 3rd ed. (Phoneix, AZ: Oryx Press, 1999).

[4] Eva M. Lang and Jan Davis Tudor, *Best Websites for Financial Professionals, Business Appraisers, and Accountants*, 2nd ed. (Hoboken, NJ: John Wiley & Sons, 2003).

Summary

This chapter has briefly described some of the sources of economic and industry data that appraisers and economists find particularly useful. Since the variety of potential sources is virtually boundless, the final section lists several of the most useful indexing services for locating sources relevant to a particular topic or industry. Locations of the sources' publishers and other information appear in the following bibliography.

To get maximum benefit from economic and industry research, the analyst must focus on the implications of the data for the value of the subject company. This focus must be maintained while conducting the research, using it toward arriving at an opinion as to value, and including the research as an integral part of the ultimate appraisal report.

Bibliography

National Economic Information

Consensus Forecasts USA. London, UK: Consensus Economics, monthly.
Detailed forecasts for 20 economic and financial variables for the United States. www.consensuseconomics.com

Economic Outlook Update. Portland, OR: Business Valuation Resources quarterly.
Each *Economic Outlook Update* quarterly report presents the general economic climate that existed at the end of the respective quarter. Topics addressed include general economic conditions, consumer prices and inflation rates, interest rates, unemployment, consumer spending, the stock markets, construction, manufacturing, and economic outlook. The economic outlook section contains short- and long-term forecasts for major economic indicators such as GDP, inflation, interest rates, and major stock market indexes. The reports are available quarterly and are delivered via e-mail to subscribers as a PDF file and Word and Excel documents. www.bvlibrary.com

Economic Report of the President. Washington, DC: Government Printing Office, annual. www.gpoaccess.gov/eop

Federal Reserve Bulletin. Washington, DC: Board of Governors of the Federal Reserve System, on continuing basis.
The quarterly paper version of the *Bulletin* will no longer be published. However, an annual compendium will be printed. www.federalreserve.gov

- *Statistical Supplement to the Federal Reserve Bulletin* contains tables that appeared in the Financial and Business Statistics section of the *Bulletin* (1914–2003), monthly.

FRASER (Federal Reserve Archival System for Economic Research). St. Louis: Federal Reserve Bank of St. Louis.
On the FRASER Web site you can find scanned information that was previously only available in print. The items include historical economic statistical publications, releases, and documents that provide valuable economic information and statistics. http://fraser.stlouisfed.org/

FRED II (Federal Reserve Economic Data). St. Louis: Federal Reserve Bank of St. Louis.

FRED II is a database with over 2,900 economic time series. The data is downloadable in Microsoft Excel or text formats. research.stlouisfed.org/fred2/

Monthly Labor Review. U.S. Bureau of Labor Statistics, Department of Labor. Washington, DC: Government Printing Office, monthly, www.bls.gov/opub/ mlr/mlrhome.htm (*Monthly Labor Review Online* is based on its print periodical, *Monthly Labor Review*).

A compilation of economic and social statistics. Most are given as monthly figures for the current year and one prior year. Features articles on the labor force, wages, prices, productivity, economic growth, and occupational injuries illnesses. Regular features include a review of developments in industrial relations, book reviews, and current labor statistics.

National Economic Review. Memphis, TN: Mercer Capital, quarterly.

National Economic Review is an overview of the major factors affecting the economy and includes discussions of the current and expected performance of the national economy, interest rates, employment, inflation, the stock and bond markets, construction, housing, and real estate. It consists of four to eight pages of text and two pages of exhibits (annual/quarterly economic indicators and investment trends). www.mercercapital.com or www.bizval.com

Standard & Poor's Statistical Service. New York: Standard & Poor's DRI, monthly, with cumulations, www.dri.mcgraw-hill.com.

Standard & Poor's Trends and Projections. New York: Standard & Poor's DRI, monthly, www.dri.mcgraw-hill.com.

This popular newsletter from Standard & Poor's is available as part of the loose-leaf version of their *Industry Surveys* or as a separate subscription. The newsletter provides a two- to four-page narrative economic outlook, plus a table of key forecasts from S&P economists. The list of variables is extensive, including GDP and its major components, various measures of personal and corporate income, the personal savings rate, the CPI, several key interest rates, the Index of Industrial Production, housing starts, auto sales, and the unemployment rate. Projections are given for the coming two years (both quarterly and annually). Actual data for the latest current year are provided for comparative purposes.

Statistical Abstract of the United States. Washington, DC: Government Printing Office, annual, www.census.gov/prod/www/statistical-abstract-1995_2000.html.

Survey of Current Business. Washington, DC: Government Printing Office, monthly, www.bea.doc.gov/bea/pubs.htm.

U.S. Industry & Trade Outlook. New York: McGraw-Hill, annual, www.dri. mcgraw-hill.com.

U.S. Macroeconomic Report. Eddystone, PA: WEFA Group, monthly, www.wefa.com.

This online database is compiled by the WEFA Group, a respected econometric forecasting firm formed in 1987 through the merger of Wharton Econometric Forecasting Associates and Chase Econometrics. Although these databases cover a wide variety of economic time series, almost all historical data come from governmental sources. Data are not limited to broad economic indicators; many industry-specific series are also included. Among the latter are detailed price indexes from the CPI and PPI, industrial production indexes, employment by industry, and manufacturer's shipments and inventories.

Federal Reserve Bank Periodicals (a sampling)

Federal Reserve Bank of Atlanta. *Economic Review.*
Federal Reserve Bank of Atlanta. *Econ South.*
Federal Reserve Bank of Atlanta. *Extra Credit.*
Federal Reserve Bank of Atlanta. *Financial Update.*
Federal Reserve Bank of Boston. *Regional Review.*
Federal Reserve Bank of Boston. *New England Economic Indicators.*
Federal Reserve Bank of Boston. *New England Economic Review.*
Federal Reserve Bank of Chicago. *Ag Letter.*
Federal Reserve Bank of Chicago. *On Reserve.*
Federal Reserve Bank of Cleveland. *Economic Commentary.*
Federal Reserve Bank of Cleveland. *Fourth District Conditions.*
Federal Reserve Bank of Cleveland. *Economic Review.*
Federal Reserve Bank of Dallas. *Economic & Financial Review.*
Federal Reserve Bank of Dallas. *Southwest Economy.*
Federal Reserve Bank of Kansas City. *Economic Review.*
Federal Reserve Bank of Minneapolis. *Fedgazette.*
Federal Reserve Bank of Minneapolis. *Quarterly Review.*
Federal Reserve Bank of New York. *Economic Policy Review.*
Federal Reserve Bank of Philadelphia. *Business Review.*
Federal Reserve Bank of Richmond. *Economic Quarterly.*
Federal Reserve Bank of Richmond. *Region Focus.*
Federal Reserve Bank of St. Louis. *International Economic Conditions.*
Federal Reserve Bank of St. Louis. *National Economic Trends.*
Federal Reserve Bank of St. Louis. *The Regional Economist.*
Federal Reserve Bank of St. Louis. *Review.*
Federal Reserve Bank of St. Louis. *U.S. Financial Data.*
Federal Reserve Bank of San Francisco. *Economic Review.*
Federal Reserve Bank of San Francisco. *Fed In Print (Index).*
Federal Reserve Bank of San Francisco. *Economic Letter.*

Regional Economic Information

American Business Climate & Economic Profiles, 6th ed., Priscilla Cheng Geahigan, Washington, DC: Gale Research, 1999.

The Complete Economic and Demographic Data Source. Washington, DC: Woods and Poole Economics, Inc., annual, www.woodsandpoole.com/main.

County and City Data Book, 2000 ed., U.S. Bureau of the Census, Department of Commerce, Washington, DC: Government Printing Office, www.census.gov/statab/www/ccdb.html.

Economic Census. U.S. Bureau of the Census, Department of Commerce. Washington, DC: Government Printing Office, www.census.gov.
The *Economic Census* is produced as 12 separate titles grouped according to type of business: accommodation and food services; administrative, support, waste management, and remediation services; arts, entertainment, and recreation; construction; educational services; health care and social assistance; manufacturing; mining; professional, scientific, and technical services; real estate and rental and leasing; retail trade; and wholesale trade. Each title consists of three subseries: geographic data for each state, detailed industry data by SIC numbers, and a subject series for special topics, though for some titles

the industry and subject series are combined. It profiles the U.S. economy every five years from the national to local levels. It contains statistics on housing, population, construction activity, and many other economic indicators.

State and Metropolitan Area Data Book, 5th ed. U.S. Bureau of the Census, Department of Commerce, Washington, DC: Government Printing Office, www.census.gov/statab/www/smadb.html.

Survey of Buying Power. New York: Bill Communications, Inc., annual, www.clusterbigip2.claritas.com/MySBP/Default.jsp or www.salesandmarketing.com /smm/surveys_reports/index.jsp. This survey, published annually by *Sales & Marketing Management* magazine, breaks down demographic and income data by state, metropolitan area, and county or parish. Retail sales data are presented for store groups and merchandise lines. Also included are population and retail sales forecasts for local areas.

U.S. Bureau of Economic Analysis, Department of Commerce. Washington, DC, (202) 606-9900, www.bea.gov.

WEBEC, Finland: Lauri Saarinen.

This is an extensive online library that provides links to free economic data. Categories include economic data, regional economics, financial economics, labor and demographics, a list of economic journals, and business economics. netec.wustl.edu/WebEc/WebEc.html

Industry Information

Almanac of Business and Industrial Financial Ratios. Englewood Cliffs, NJ: Prentice Hall, annual.

Corporation Source Book: Statistics of Income; Partnership Source Book: Statistics of Income; and *Sole Proprietorship Source Book: Statistics of Income*. Internal Revenue Service. Washington, DC: Government Printing Office, annual, www.irs.gov/taxstats/bustaxstats/article/.

Economic Census. Washington, DC: Government Printing Office, www. census.gov.

Economic Forecast Reports and Industry Forecast Reports. West Chester, PA: Economy.com, Inc.

Economic Forecast Reports available by country, state, or metropolitan area. Includes five-year forecasts, written analyses, and key statistics on income, migration, top employers, business/living costs, and more. Subscriptions include current report and two updates. Samples are available for each report. *Industry Forecast Reports* include five-year forecasts for up to 50 financial variables, current and forecasted trends, risk factors, etc. Each report also includes data on macroeconomic conditions, trends, and outlooks. Reports are four pages and updated three times yearly. Subscriptions include current report and two updates. Samples are available for each report. www.economy.com/research

Encyclopedia of American Industries (2 volumes), 2nd ed., Kevin Hillstrom, ed. Detroit: Gale Research, 1998.

Provides information on many industries, broken down by SIC code. Information includes an industry "snapshot," organization and structure of the industry, current conditions, a discussion of industry leaders, information on the work force, foreign competition and trade information, and additional sources of information. This is a very useful book, although its infrequency of publication can make its information dated.

FED STATS. Washington, DC.

Provides access to statistical data from the federal government. Data is searchable by subject, agency, and geographical location. Topics of interest include economic and population trends, health care costs, foreign trade, employment statistics, and more. www.fedstats.gov

First Call Database. New York: Thomson Financial.

Research covering over 34,000 companies in over 130 countries. Current and historical data, public filings, and forecasted data available. Forecasts include: P/E ratios, growth rates, return on assets, earnings, cash flow, sales, and more. Thomson Financial has completed the full integration of I/B/E/S onto the First Call Web site. www.firstcall.com

Industry Norms and Key Business Ratios. New York: Dunn & Bradstreet, Inc., annual.

Balance sheet and profit and loss ratios based on a computerized financial statement file. The 14 key ratios are broken down into median figures, with upper and lower quartiles. Covers over 800 lines of business, broken down into three size ranges by net worth for each SIC.

Industry Profiles: First Research.

Over 140 industry profiles available. Information includes recent developments, industry challenges and overview, important questions, and new links. Financial data includes ratios, profitability trends, economic statistics, and benchmark statistics. Most reports provide a free summary before initial purchase. www.bvmarketdata.com or firstresearch.com/profiles

Industry Reports, The Center for Economic and Industry Research.

Industry studies that provide information for a particular area and length of time. Studies range anywhere from 15 to 20 pages. www.c-e-i-r.com

Industry Valuation Update. Portland, OR: Business Valuation Resources, LLC.

The *Industry Valuation Update* is a six-volume series on industry valuation topics. Each volume includes seven general business valuation chapters, two industry-specific chapters, including articles by valuation experts, and insights on the best valuation approaches for each industry. Each volume also includes rules of thumb, SIC and NAICS codes, industry analysis, court cases, and Pratt's Stats analysis. www.bvstore.com

Manufacturing & Distribution USA, 2nd ed. Farmington Hills, MI: Thomson Gale, 2000.

Presents statistics on more than 500 SIC and NAICS classifications in the manufacturing, wholesaling, and retail industries. Information is compiled from the most recent government publications and includes projections, maps, and graphics. Classification of leading public and private corporations in each industry is also included. www.gale.com

Market Research Reports. Cleveland, OH: The Freedonia Group, Inc., ten new titles published monthly.

Provides industry analysis, including product and market forecasts, industry trends, and competitive strategies. Studies can be searched by title, table of contents, or full text. Individual reports or parts of reports are available. www.freedoniagroup.com

Market Share Reporter. Farmington Hills, MI: Thomson Gale, annual.

Presents comparative business statistics in a clear, straightforward manner. Arranged by four-digit SIC code, contains data from more than 2,000 entries. Each entry includes a descriptive title, data and market description, a list of producers/products along with their assigned market share, and more. www.gale.com

Mergent's Industry Review. Charlotte, NC: Mergent.

Mergent's Industry Review contains comparative rankings by industry for items such as revenues, net income, profit margins, assets, return on investment, return on equity, and cash position. In addition to the comparative rankings, this publication offers comparative statistics such as key business ratios and special industry specific ratios. www.mergent.com

Moody's Industry Review continued by Mergent Industry Review. Charlotte, NC: Mergent.

This comprehensive statistical reference offers comparative figures and rankings of 6,000 companies in 137 industry groups. www.mergent.com

Online Industry and Benchmark Reports: Kennesaw, GA: Integra.

The type of reports available from Integra: *Five Year Reports, Industry Growth Outlook Reports, Industry Narrative Reports, Industry QuickTrends Reports, Integra's Comparative Profiler, Three Year Industry Reports.* www.integrainfo.com

Plunkett's Industry Almanacs. Houston, TX: Plunkett Research, Ltd.

Includes profiles of approximately 500 companies, financial trends, salary information, market and industry analysis, and more. Choose from a variety of industries, including energy, computers and Internet, entertainment and media, and retail. www.plunkettresearch.com

Predicasts Basebook. Cleveland, OH: Predicasts, Inc. (ceased 1995).

This loose-leaf reference provides historical data on U.S. business and economic activities. Arranged by a modified, seven-digit SIC number, the industry statistics include production, consumption, plant and equipment expenditures, payroll, and exports/imports. The figures cover approximately 15 years. The sources of statistic and annual growth are also provided.

Predicasts Forecasts. Cleveland, OH: Predicasts, Inc., quarterly with annual cumulations.

Nearly 50,000 short- and long-range projections for products and industries, along with leading economic indicators for U.S. business are available in this reference. Arranged by modified seven-digit SIC code, each forecast gives the subject, quantities for a base year, short- and long-term projections, unit of measure, source of data, and projected annual rate.

Predicasts PROMPT. Foster City, CA: Information Access Company, updated daily.

This multi-industry resource provides broad, international coverage of companies, products, markets, and applied technologies for all industries. Available through online services, PTS PROMPT is comprised of abstracts and full-text records from more than 1,000 of the world's important business publications, including trade journals, local newspapers and regional business publications, national and international business newspapers, trade and business newsletters, research studies, S1 SEC registration statements, investment analysts' reports, corporate news releases, and corporate annual reports.

RMA Annual Statement Studies. Philadelphia: Robert Morrow Associates, annual.

Consists of two publications: the original *Statement Studies Financial Ratio Benchmarks* and its companion publication *Industry Default Probabilities and Cash Flow Measures.*

University of Michigan Documents Center: Ann Arbor, MI.

This Web site from the University of Michigan Documents Center is one of the most comprehensive resources for statistical data. Categories of interest include: agriculture, business and industry, government finances, labor, finance and currency, foreign economics, and demographics. www.lib.umich.edu/govdocs/stats.html

Industry Information Directories

Encyclopedia of Associations: Regional, State and Local Organizations. Detroit: Gala Research, annual.

Available in print, electronic, and Web-based formats. This is the largest compilation of nonprofit associations and organizations available anywhere. Contains descriptions of professional associations, trade and business associations, labor unions, chambers of commerce, and groups of all types in virtually every field.

National Trade and Professional Associations of the United States. Washington, DC: Columbia Books, annual.

Excellent source book for trade and industry sources of industry information. Restricted to trade and professional associations and labor unions with national memberships.

Nelson's Directory of Wall Street Research. Rye, NY: W. R. Nelson & Company, annual.

The "Research Sources" section gives names, addresses, and telephone numbers, and specialty research personnel at over 2,600 firms.

Management Compensation Sources

Almanac of Business and Industrial Financial Ratios. Leo Troy, Ph.D., ed. Englewood Cliffs, NJ: Prentice-Hall, annual.

Executive Compensation Assessor. Redmond, WA: Economic Research Institute, quarterly, www.erieri.com.

ERI's Executive Compensation Assessor reports salaries and bonuses for 400 top management positions within multiple industries. Data may be adjusted for geographic area, organization size, and compensation valuation date. This source provides analysis of data compiled from virtually all publicly available executive compensation surveys, along with direct analysis of SEC Edgar proxy data. Other compensation products are also available.

Executive Compensation Survey. Compdata Surveys, Dolan Technologies Corp.

Survey contains base pay, annual incentive, and benefit information on a national and regional (east, south, central, and west) basis for executive and senior management positions by industry group, company size, and revenue profile.

Hay Group: Benefits and Total Compensation Statements. Philadelphia: Center for Management Research, annual.

This study details the practices of thousands of companies and compensation activity by industry, job level, and function. Includes sections on prevailing compensation levels, team-based compensation, average monthly premium costs, and CEO reward practices. www.haygroup.com

National Executive Compensation Survey Results. Illinois: The Management Association of Illinois, annual.

This survey reports annual salaries for 10,451 executives in 33 positions at 1,544 participating organizations throughout the country. www.ercnet.org

Officer Compensation Database. Integra Information.

Officer compensation expense expressed in both dollars and as a percentage of sales by industry and company size for over 900 industries. www.integrainfo.com

Officer Compensation Report. Aspen Publishers, Inc., search for "officer compensation." The report provides data on salaries, bonuses, pay increases, ownership levels, and incentives for small- to medium-sized companies in eight industry groups—basic materials, heavy equipment and transportation, electrical and electronics, nondurable goods, fabricated metal and wood products, technological services, business services, and high tech industry.

Source Book Statistics of Income. Washington, DC: Internal Revenue Service, annual.

Standard & Poor's Execucomp. New York: Standard & Poor's, quarterly.

Available online or on CD-ROM, Execucomp is a comprehensive database that covers S&P 500, S&P mid-cap 400, and S&P small-cap companies. The study includes over 80 different compensation, executive, director, and company items, including breakdowns of salary, bonuses, options, and director compensation information.

Watson, Wyatt Data Services Compensation Survey Reports. Rochelle Park, NJ: Watson Wyatt Data Services, annual, www.watsonwyatt.com

Watson Wyatt publishes several different compensation surveys annually. Some are industry specific and some are position specific. The companies surveyed range from emerging growth businesses to Fortune 1000 companies. The surveys together encompass more than one million employees.

Online Information

You may contact these vendors directly for more information about their services:

CompuServe
5000 Arlington Center Boulevard
Columbus, OH 43220
800-524-3388
webcenters.netscape.compuserve.com/menu/index.jsp

The Dialog Corporation
11000 Regency Parkway, Suite 10
Cary, NC 27512
1-800-3-DIALOG
www.dialog.com

Dow Jones & Company
1 World Financial Center
200 Liberty Street
New York, NY 10281
212-416-2000
www.dowjones.com

LexisNexis Group
PO Box 933
Dayton, OH 45401-0933
Local Phone Number: (937) 865-6800
Toll Free Phone Number: (800) 227-9597
www.lexisnexis.com

Wilsonline
The H. W. Wilson Company
950 University Avenue
Bronx, NY 10452
800-367-6770
www.hwwilson.com

Indexes and Guides to Business Information

American Statistics Index: A Comprehensive Guide and Index to the Statistical Publications of the U.S. Government. Washington, DC: Congressional Information Service, monthly, via annual cumulations.

Published by a reputable firm specializing in providing access to government publications, the ASI provides access to federal statistics. Each edition is two volumes, Index and Abstracts. Also included in the index volume are a title index, a guide to the Standard Industrial Classification code, the Standard Occupation Classification, and a list of standard metropolitan statistical areas (SMSAs).

The Basic Business Library: Core Resources, 4th ed. Rashelle S. Karp and Bernard S. Schlessinger, Greenwood Press, December 2002.

This new edition preserves the objectives of the 1983 and 1989 volumes but updates and revises the second edition (Professional Reading, LJ 4/15/89). Numerous new titles have been added as well as obsolete or out-of-print titles deleted. The 200 titles now included have a total cost of $38,000, so obviously librarians will still have to be selective. The review of business reference literature now covers the years 1976–1994, a time period that has seen the business section grow in importance to patrons. Online business services have multiplied and increased in usefulness; Sharon L. Criswell improved and updated that section. Another area of growth and importance is the chapter called "The Best Investment Sources" by Barbara A. Huett. The Investment Bookshelf list alone will endear librarians to investors, as passbook savings no longer provide even a hedge against inflation. Buy wherever possible and share with colleagues—no other collection depends so much on currency.

Business Periodicals Index (BPI). New York: H. W. Wilson, monthly, with quarterly and annual cumulations, www.hwwilson.com.

Subject index to approximately 400 periodicals in the business field. The periodicals indexed are English-based and come from trade and professional associations and government agencies. Articles are indexed under specific business subject headings, including names of executives and corporations. Available in print, on CD-ROM, and online. Over 57,000 subject terms for immediate access—search by subjects, key words, company names, and SIC codes.

Business Valuation Data Directory. Portland, OR: Business Valuation Resources, annual, www.bvlibrary.com.

Published annually as a supplement to Business Valuation Update, this resource lists hundreds of sources for compensation, industry, cost of capital, guideline company, and mergers and acquisitions data.

Encyclopedia of Business Information Sources, 17th ed. James Woy. Detroit: Gale Research, 2002.

A bibliographic guide to more than 33,000 citations covering over 1,100 subjects of interest to business personnel. Includes abstracting and indexing services, almanacs and yearbooks, bibliographies, biographical sources, directories, encyclopedias and dictionaries, financial ratios, handbooks and manuals, online databases, periodicals and newsletters, price sources, research centers and institutes, statistical sources, trade associations and professional societies, and other sources of information on each topic.

Government Information on the Internet, 6th ed. Greg R. Notess. Lanham, MD: Bernan Press, April 2003.

This resource covers all of the changes in formats and accessibility of the new generation of government information sources, including the Internet, CD-ROM products, online databases, diskettes, electronic bulletin boards, and telephone hot line numbers, as well as print sources. Now with more than 4,800 entries, including over

- 250 sites from international governmental organizations and other countries
- 150 U.S. state government sites
- 540 U.S. congressional member sites and e-mail addresses
- 1,400 individual government publications

Web sites and content descriptions are verified and updated for all entries.

International Business Information: How to Find it, How to Use It. 2nd ed. Ruth A. Pagell and Michael Haperin. AMACOM, February 2000.

Reference librarians who have found that queries about international business information leave them feeling slightly inadequate will appreciate this new book. Modeled after Michael Lavin's *Business Information: How to Find It, How to Use It* (Oryx, 1992. 2nd ed.), it describes key international publications and databases. In addition, background information for each chapter gives the researcher and librarian the necessary information to locate the correct and most useful source. The authors have been selective in the sources they have included, having examined all printed sources and searched the databases. A most useful element is the inclusion of sample entries from both printed and online sources, illustrating the information and providing researchers with a quick reference to see if the source has the information they are looking for. This is not a bibliography, though in many ways it is more useful. As more business enterprises become international, many libraries will find this book to be of tremendous value, especially given the affordable price.

PAIS Select Journal List. New York: Public Affairs Information Service, annual, www.pais.org.

A selected subject list of the latest books, pamphlets, government publications, reports of public and private agencies, and periodical articles relating to economic and social conditions, public administration, and international relations.

Predicasts F&S Index United States. Foster City, CA: Information Access Company, weekly, with cumulations.

Provides comprehensive reference indexes of business and economic information PTS & F&S Index covers worldwide company, product, and information. One- and two-line article summaries offer access to information on international companies, business and financial activities, demographics, government regulations, and economics. Detailed coverage of more than 750 trade journals, newspapers, (including the *Wall Street Journal*), government documents, and special studies.

Statistical Reference Index. Washington, DC: Congressional Information Service, monthly with annual cumulation, www.lexisnexis.com.

Since 1980, *Statistical Reference Index* has indexed and abstracted statistical reports from agencies other than the federal government. Nonprofit organizations, trade and professional associations, state government agencies, university research centers, and commercial publishers are just some of the sources of the statistical information included. Since 1983, CIS also has published *Index to International Statistics*, which includes statistical publications of over 50 international, intergovernmental agencies such as the United Nations and OECD.

Chapter 7

Analyzing Financial Statements

Normalizing versus Controlling Adjustments
Adequacy of Allowance and Reserve Accounts
    Allowance for Doubtful Accounts—Accounts Receivable
    Allowance for Doubtful Accounts—Notes Receivable
Inventory Accounting Methods
    FIFO, LIFO, and Other Methods
    Write-Down and Write-Off Policies
Depreciation Methods and Schedules
    Declining-Balance Method
    Sum-of-the-Years'-Digits Method
    ACRS and MACRS
    Analytical Implications
Depletion
Treatment of Intangibles
    Leasehold Interests
Other Intangible Assets
Capitalization versus Expensing of Various Costs
Timing of Recognition of Revenues and Expenses
    Contract Work
    Installment Sales
    Sales Involving Actual or Contingent Liabilities
    Prior-Period Adjustments
    Accounting for Leases
Net Operating Loss Carryforwards
Treatment of Interests in Affiliates
Extraordinary or Nonrecurring Items
    Ordinary versus Extraordinary Items
    Other Nonrecurring Items
    Discontinued Operations
Operating versus Nonoperating Items
Management Compensation and Perquisites
Transactions Involving Company Insiders
Contingent Assets and Liabilities
Adjustments to Asset Valuations
    Marketable Securities
    Other Assets

The financial analyst knows that there is some latitude permitted in the preparation of financial statements. Even within the broad confines of generally accepted accounting principles (GAAP), rarely do any two companies follow exactly the same set of accounting practices in keeping their books and preparing their financial statements. When it comes to the typical closely held company, most are not audited and many prepare financial statements that deviate from GAAP, to put it kindly. Therefore, the analyst must evaluate each item and adjust for differences in accounting practices, where appropriate, in order to compare two or more companies or to measure a company against some industry or other standard.

When there is a choice among accounting practices, private companies tend toward a more conservative selection in order to minimize taxes, while public companies may account more aggressively in order to report more income so as to please shareholders. Also, some public companies have been accused of "managing" their earnings in order to minimize earnings peaks and valleys by making more conservative accounting decisions in good years and more aggressive accounting decisions in bad ones. Furthermore, the smaller the private company, the more pronounced the difference between public companies and private companies tends to be.

All discussions of financial statement analysis in this book are subject to the caveat that GAAPs are constantly being reviewed and changed. Also, publicly traded companies are subject to certain disclosure requirements of the Securities and Exchange Commission (SEC), which continue to be challenged and interpreted by the courts.

There are complete books dedicated to the subject of financial statement analysis (see bibliography at the end of this chapter). The material presented in this chapter is only a refresher to those who are presented with the task of valuing a business or reviewing a business valuation made by others.

The purpose of analyzing income statements is to better understand and interpret the earning power of the subject company, since earning power is usually the most important element of the value of a business.

Asset values may also play an important role and, therefore, adjustments to the balance sheet may be necessary for analytical purposes. Some variables adjusted for in the income statement analysis may or may not require that adjustments also be made in the balance sheet analysis. And, some adjustments to the balance sheet require that adjustments also be made to the income statement.

This chapter discusses the most common categories of adjustments to the income statement and balance sheet in the business valuation. It begins with adjustments for different ways of measuring asset and liability items. Then it examines a number of items arising from the treatment of revenue and expense items. Finally, it looks at a number of miscellaneous items. The reader can explore more complete discussions of financial statements and the appropriate adjustments of various financial statement accounts by referring to other sources, including those referenced in the bibliography at the end of this chapter.

Normalizing versus Controlling Adjustments

It is important to consider the different types of adjustments that can be made to financial statements. These adjustments need to bear the consideration of the appraiser and the level of value that is being applied. The following is an excerpt from *Business Valuation and Taxes: Procedure, Law, and Perspective* by David Laro and Shannon Pratt; it discusses the types of adjustments that an appraiser may apply in a valuation:

NORMALIZING ADJUSTMENTS

The general idea of normalizing adjustments is to present data in conformance with GAAP and any industry accounting principles and to eliminate nonrecurring items. The goal is to present information on a basis comparable to that of other companies and to provide a foundation for developing future expectations about the subject company. Another objective is to present financial data on a consistent basis over time.

The following are some examples of normalizing adjustments:

- Adequacy of allowance and reserve accounts:
  - Allowance for doubtful accounts (correct to reasonable amount, in light of historical results and/or management interviews)
  - Pension liabilities
- Inventory accounting methods:
  - First in, first out (FIFO); last in, first out (LIFO); and other methods (adjust to methods usually used in the industry)
  - Write-down and write-off policies (adjust to normal industry practices)
- Depreciation methods and schedules
- Depletion methods and schedules (adjustments to industry reporting norms often appropriate)
- Treatment of intangible assets:
  - Leasehold interest (adjust to market value)
  - Other intangible assets
- Policies regarding capitalization or expensing of various costs (adjust to industry norms)
- Timing of recognition of revenues and expenses:
  - Contract work (including work in progress; e.g., percentage of completion or completed contract)
  - Installment sales
  - Sales involving actual or contingent liabilities (e.g., guarantees, warranties)
  - Prior period adjustments (e.g., for changes in accounting policy or items overlooked)
  - Expenses booked in one year applying to other years

- Net operating losses carried forward
- Treatment of interests in affiliates
- Adequacy or deficiency of assets:
  - Excess or deficient net working capital (adjust to industry average percent of sales)
  - Deferred maintenance (based on plant visit and management interviews)
- Adequacy or deficiency of liabilities:
  - Pension termination liabilities
  - Deferred income taxes
  - Unrecorded payables
- Unusual gains or losses on sale of assets
  Note: It does not have to be extraordinary in a GAAP sense to be nonrecurring in a financial analysis sense. This factor is a matter for the analyst's judgment (e.g., rental income).
- Nonrecurring gains or losses:
  - Fire, flood, or other casualty, both physical damage and business interruption to extent not covered by insurance
  - Strikes (unless common in the industry and considered probable to recur)
  - Litigation costs, payments, or recoveries
  - Gain or loss on sale of business assets
  - Discontinued operations

A valuer should consider all of these adjustments, whether they have been made, and, if not, why not.

CONTROLLING ADJUSTMENTS

A control owner or potential owner might make control adjustments, but a minority owner, generally, could not force the same changes. Therefore, control adjustments normally would be made only in the case of a controlling interest valuation, unless there was reason to believe that the changes were imminent and probable. These include:

- Excess or deficient compensation and perquisites
- Gains, losses, or cash realization from sale of excess assets
- Elimination of operations involving company insiders (e.g., employment, non-market-rate leases)
- Changes in capital structure

Note: There is a minority (but legitimate) school of thought that considers what we have just classified as control adjustments to be normalizing adjustments, even in a minority interest valuation where the minority holder cannot force the company policy to change. The reason for this is to put the subject company on a basis comparable to the guideline companies. The minority interest factor is then handled as a separate discount at the end of the valuation.[1]

---

[1] David Laro and Shannon Pratt, *Business Valuation and Taxes: Procedure, Law, and Perspective* (Hoboken, NJ: John Wiley & Sons, 2005).

Adequacy of Allowance and Reserve Accounts

It is common to find that a company is either under- or over-reserved for certain items. Some so-called reserve accounts should not be considered reserve accounts at all but merely portions of equity that management has chosen to earmark for some future expenditure or contingency. If under-reserved, the effect is an overstatement of earnings due to inadequate reserve charges to expenses, with an accompanying overstatement of net asset value. If over-reserved, the opposite occurs. The analyst may encounter a variety of reserve or allowance accounts from time to time and should question and analyze each on its own merits.

Allowance for Doubtful Accounts—Accounts Receivable

Most companies carry accounts receivable and deduct some allowance for potentially uncollectible accounts. The typical policy is to increase the allowance for doubtful accounts at the end of each month by a percentage of that month's credit sales. This shows up as a deduction from accounts receivable on the balance sheet. Then, as individual uncollectible accounts are finally written off, they are credited against accounts receivable and debited against the allowance for doubtful accounts, with no direct effect on either earnings or net asset value at the time of the write-off.

Since the expense charge actually represents an estimate of future write-offs, the analyst may wish to make some judgment as to that estimate's accuracy, at least if the effect might be material. One way is to compare the historical percentage of bad debt losses from past credit sales with the percentage of current credit sales being charged to bad debt expense to see if too little or too much is currently being charged. Another approach is to compare the aged accounts receivable schedule allowance relative to the amount of overdue accounts. Some companies tend to carry receivables on their books indefinitely, with little or no doubtful account allowance, resulting in overstatement of earnings and net asset value. Other companies follow a very aggressive write-off policy, removing from their books many accounts that eventually are collected; this tends to understate earnings and net asset value.

Allowance for Doubtful Accounts—Notes Receivable

Notes receivable may be taken to improve the company's chance of collecting a delinquent trade receivable, but their collectibility may be in question. Notes receivable from stockholders may really be more in the nature of long-term loans, deferred compensation, or even undeclared dividends, even though they may be carried on the balance sheet in the current asset section. A review of balance sheets from prior periods to see how long some "current" items have been carried may lead to questions for management regarding the probability of collection during the company's normal operating cycle. [In some cases, the analyst may even reclassify notes receivable from owners into equity.]

Inventory Accounting Methods

FIFO, LIFO, and Other Methods

The *FIFO*, or *first-in, first-out*, inventory accounting method assumes, for accounting purposes, that the oldest unit of an inventory item purchased is the next unit sold. The *LIFO*, or *last-in, first-out,* method assumes that the most recently purchased unit of an inventory item purchased is the next unit sold. The difference between FIFO and LIFO accounting shows up in the ending inventory on the balance sheet, affecting both the cost of goods sold and earnings. To the extent that prices go up, LIFO produces lower figures for earnings and inventory than does FIFO. Since LIFO accounting is acceptable for federal income tax purposes, many companies have adopted LIFO over FIFO inventory accounting in response to inflation.

However, it should be noted that if inventory has been accounted for using LIFO, and if the level of inventory *declines* over the course of the year—that is, withdrawals from inventory exceed purchases—an accounting phenomenon known as *LIFO liquidation* occurs. This reduces inventories to a point at which cost layers from prior years are matched to current inflated prices. If prices from the "old" inventory are much lower than current prices, a distortion of income occurs. Audited and reviewed financial statements should disclose whether LIFO liquidation has occurred and the extent of its effects. If a decline in inventory that is being accounted for using LIFO occurs, and the financial statements lack proper disclosures, the analyst should conduct further examination and inquiry in order to eliminate the distorting effects of LIFO liquidation.

When comparing two or more companies for valuation purposes, all of the companies' earnings and asset values should have been derived based on the same inventory accounting method if the difference is substantial enough to affect the valuation. If they do not all use the same accounting method, the analyst can adjust the earnings and asset values to the same basis using information in the financial statements.

As a simple example, imagine a company that started its accounting period with 30 widgets, purchased for $10 each. Later in the period, it purchased 60 more widgets at $15 each, and before its next fiscal year-end it sold 50 widgets, ending the period with 40 widgets in inventory. The cost of goods sold would be computed under the FIFO and LIFO methods as shown in Exhibit 7–1. In other words, LIFO accounting assumes that the original units in the inventory are the ones that are still there. In the above case, if sales were $1,000, the gross margin would be $400 under FIFO accounting and $250 under LIFO accounting.

For most companies that report on FIFO, the information the analyst needs in order to adjust earnings and inventory to the LIFO basis is not readily available. If a company reporting on LIFO has audited statements, however, the footnotes will provide a figure for the LIFO in inventory reserve that the analyst can use to adjust earnings and inventory values from LIFO to FIFO. If the statements are not audited, the company's accountant should be able to provide the analyst with the necessary information for adjusting to a FIFO basis. Therefore, because of the availability of this information, if one or more companies' inventory accounting needs to be adjusted for comparative purposes, the analyst usually should adjust the LIFO-reporting companies to a FIFO basis rather than vice versa.

The analyst should keep in mind that (1) if earnings are adjusted from LIFO to FIFO and (2) if after-tax income or after-tax cash flow are used as the appropriate

Exhibit 7–1

Cost of Goods Sold
FIFO and LIFO Methods

		FIFO		LIFO	
	Beginning inventory	30 Units @ $10 =	$300	30 Units @ $10 =	$300
Plus:	Purchases	60 Units @ $15 =	$900	60 Units @ $15 =	$900
Equals:	Goods available for sale		$1,200		$1,200
Less:	Ending inventory	40 Units @ $15 =	$600	30 Units @ $10 =	$300
				10 Units @ $15 =	$150
					$450
Equals:	Cost of goods sold		$600		$750

measure of economic income, then the adjustment should be net of the income tax effect (either additional taxes or benefit) associated with it. Choosing the correct income tax rate to use in making the adjustment may be more complicated than just using the effective or the marginal income tax rate. The analyst should carefully scrutinize the income tax characteristics of the company whose income is being adjusted to determine the most likely consequences of the additional income or losses, as adjusted, on income taxes.

Besides adjusting the income statement from a LIFO to a FIFO basis, it may be necessary to adjust the balance sheet, generally in three areas. First, the inventory level should be adjusted to the FIFO basis. Second, an income tax liability account should be adjusted to account for the additional income taxes that would have resulted from the adjustment to inventory. Third, retained earnings should be adjusted by the net difference between the inventory and income tax liability adjustments.

Continuing with our widget company example, let's assume that the company is using LIFO accounting and the appropriate tax rate for the adjustment is 30 percent. The company has a LIFO reserve of $150; therefore, to adjust the inventory to FIFO, the analyst adds $150 to the ending inventory level of $450 to reach an adjusted inventory level of $600. Then the analyst adds $45 ($150 × 30% tax rate) to an income tax liability account and $105 ($150 − $45) to retained earnings. Exhibit 7–2 illustrates the calculations.

In some lines of business, specific inventory items are clearly identifiable from the time of purchase through the time of sale and are accounted for and costed on this basis. Some companies also account for inventory on some type of *average cost basis*.[2] In particular, in some industries it is possible to adjust inventory from LIFO only to average cost, not to FIFO. The adjustment is calculated in the same way as the adjustment to FIFO.

Write-Down and Write-Off Policies

Regardless of whether the company uses FIFO, LIFO, specific identification, or average cost inventory accounting, most companies adhere to the *lower-of-cost-or-market* principle, which says that the carrying value should be reduced if the

---

[2] For a discussion of the average cost method, see Leopold A. Bernstein and John J. Wild, *Analysis of Financial Statements: Theory, Application, and Interpretation*, 6th ed. (New York: McGraw-Hill, 1997), pp. 168–69.

Exhibit 7–2

Adjusting LIFO to FIFO

Continuing with Exhibit 7–1:

Assume:	
Tax rate	30%
LIFO reserve	$150
Adjust ending inventory to FIFO:	
LIFO inventory	$450
Add LIFO reserve	150
Adjusted ending inventory	$600
Compute accrued income tax liability, and add to income tax liability account:	
LIFO reserve	$150
Multiply by tax rate	0.30
Addition to accrued income tax liability	$ 45
Add net effect to retained earnings:	
LIFO reserve	$150
Less related accrued income tax	45
Addition to retained earnings	$105

market value is less than cost. *Market value* for this purpose is defined as "current replacement cost except that market shall not be higher than net realizable value nor should it be less than net realizable value reduced by the normal profit margin."[3] Implementation of the lower-of-cost-or-market principle varies tremendously— one company may have stockrooms full of obsolete inventory and another an aggressive program of automatic write-downs and write-offs of inventory based on the number of months it has been in stock. If the company goes to one extreme or the other in its implementation of this principle, the analyst may need to adjust earnings and asset values.

Depreciation Methods and Schedules

The five most common methods of computing depreciation charges—all acceptable to the IRS for income tax purposes—are the straight-line, declining-balance, sum-of-the years'-digits, accelerated cost recovery systems (ACRS), and modified accelerated cost recovery system (MACRS) introduced by the Tax Reform Act of 1986. The method that produces the largest, quickest depreciation deductions is the one most often selected by closely held businesses, since they are most eager to minimize reported taxable income.

For income tax reporting purposes, the Internal Revenue Code defines the period and the amount per period over which the cost of most depreciable assets can be recovered.

The *straight-line method* simply charges depreciation on the asset in even increments over the asset's useful life. The declining-balance, sum-of-the-years'-digits,

---

[3] Ibid., p. 170.

ACRS, and MACRS methods are called *accelerated methods* because, unlike the straight-line method, they charge a higher proportion of the total depreciation in the early years of the asset's useful life than in later years.

Declining-Balance Method

The *declining-balance method* uses some multiple, such as two times or one and one-half times, of the straight-line depreciation rate. For example, if an asset had a useful life of 10 years, straight-line depreciation would be at the rate of 10 percent per year. Double-declining-balance depreciation would be at twice that rate, or 20 percent, but with the percentage always applied to the remaining book value. For example, in the first year, a $100,000 piece of equipment with a 10-year life would be depreciated at 20 percent of $100,000 or $20,000, leaving a depreciated balance of $80,000. In the second year, the asset would be depreciated at 20 percent of $80,000, or $16,000, leaving a depreciated balance of $64,000.

Sum-of-the-Years'-Digits Method

In the *sum-of-the-years'-digits method*, the depreciation charge is a fraction whose denominator is the sum of the years' digits of the asset's useful life and whose numerator is the number of years of remaining useful life. Thus, for a 10-year useful life, the denominator is 55 $(1 + 2 + 3 + 4 + 5 + 6 + 7 + 8 + 9 + 10 = 55)$, and the numerator the first year is 10. Therefore, the first year's depreciation charge is 10/55 of the asset's cost, in the second year 9/55, and so on.

For some assets, the company assumes a residual or salvage value at the end of the depreciable life. In these cases, the difference between the cost and salvage value is the depreciable amount. Salvage value may not be deducted from cost when applying the declining-balance method, however, because that method never results in the asset being depreciated to zero.

ACRS and MACRS[4]

The fourth widely used depreciation method is *ACRS*, which was enacted as part of the Economic Recovery Tax Act of 1981. It is used mainly for federal tax purposes. The Tax Reform Act of 1986 revised the use of ACRS for property placed in service after 1986, thus creating the MACRS. One can consult a periodic tax guide for a presentation of the original and revised provisions of ACRS.

Still another depreciation method sometimes used is *units of production* (also referred to as *units of utilization*). For example, if a $100,000 asset is expected to provide 10,000 hours of useful service, it might be depreciated on the basis of $10 for each hour it is used.

Exhibit 7–3 illustrates the depreciation computations under the straight-line, declining-balance, sum-of-the-years' digits, and ACRS methods assuming an asset with a cost of $50,000, no salvage value, and an estimated useful life of five years.

---

[4] The MACRS example is quite complex and beyond the scope of this book. The reader may wish to refer to the *U.S. Master Tax Guide* (Chicago: Commerce Clearing House, 2006) for a comprehensive discussion of MACRS.

Exhibit 7–3

Alternative Depreciation Methods

Data used for the following examples:

Piece of equipment, purchased at beginning of Year 1

Original cost of equipment	$50,000
Salvage value	0
Estimated useful life	5 years

Year	Computation			Annual Depreciation Charge	Balance Accumulated Depreciation	Book Value at Year-End
Straight-Line Method						
1	1/5 (20%)	×	$50,000	$10,000	$10,000	$40,000
2	20%	×	50,000	10,000	20,000	30,000
3	20%	×	50,000	10,000	30,000	20,000
4	20%	×	50,000	10,000	40,000	10,000
5	20%	×	50,000	10,000	50,000	0
200% Declining-Balance Method						
1	40%	×	$50,000[a]	$20,000	$20,000	$30,000
2	40%	×	30,000	12,000	32,000	18,000
3	40%	×	18,000	7,200	39,200	10,800
4	40%	×	10,800	4,320	43,520	6,480
5	40%	×	6,480	2,592	46,112	3,888
Sum-of-the-Years'-Digits Method						
1	5/15	×	$50,000[b]	$16,667	$16,667	$33,333
2	4/15	×	50,000	13,333	30,000	20,000
3	3/15	×	50,000	10,000	40,000	10,000
4	2/15	×	50,000	6,667	46,667	3,333
5	1/15	×	50,000	3,333	50,000	0
Modified Accelerated Cost Recovery System						
1	20.00%	×	$50,000[c]	$10,000	$10,000	$40,000
2	32.00%	×	50,000	16,000	26,000	24,000
3	19.20%	×	50,000	9,600	35,600	14,400
4	11.52%	×	50,000	5,760	41,360	8,640
5	11.52%	×	50,000	5,760	47,120	2,880
6	5.76%	×	50,000	2,880	50,000	0

a.   Based on double the straight-line rate of 20 percent, multiplied by the undepreciated book value.

b.   Numerator is the remaining estimated useful life. Denominator is the sum of the years (5 + 4 + 3 + 2 + 1 = 15).

c.   Statutory percentages for MACRS five-year property used for federal income tax purposes.

Note: The above are examples of the more popular depreciation methods now in use. An introductory accounting text can be consulted for a thorough presentation of potential depreciation methods. The modified accelerated cost recovery system (MACRS) was enacted as part of the Economic Recovery Tax Act of 1986 and is used for federal tax purposes. One of the periodic tax guides can be consulted for a thorough presentation of the provisions of MACRS.

Analytical Implications

The analyst should make some judgment of the appropriateness of the depreciation schedule, both as it stands alone and in relation to other companies, if such comparisons are to be made. For example, a company may use an eight-year useful life for equipment that it manufactures and leases to customers, but most other companies in the industry may use a six-year useful life for the same type of equipment, assuming that the machinery will be technologically obsolete in six years. In valuing the company using an eight-year depreciation schedule, the analyst might apply a downward adjustment to both the earnings base and the equipment's net remaining book value to reflect the relatively inadequate depreciation charges, if such an adjustment would be material. There can be a fairly wide range of normal practices within any industry, and the analyst must be prepared to do considerable research to reach an informed judgment of the reasonable depreciation life for some types of assets.

Let's say we are valuing a closely held company using a multiple of earnings method and that 10 times earnings is appropriate based on capital market multiples of publicly traded guideline companies. Suppose, however, that the publicly traded guideline companies are reporting straight-line depreciation for financial statement purposes while the subject company is reporting on an accelerated depreciation basis. If the difference is material, the analyst may want to adjust the closely held company's earnings to a straight-line basis (remembering to also adjust the related income taxes) before applying the publicly traded company multiple so that the earnings to be capitalized will be stated on a comparable basis. Usually a reasonable approximation suffices for this kind of adjustment. Using an EBITDA multiple can be a helpful alternative.

Depletion

Depletion is the process of charging the cost of a natural resource to expense over the time during which it is extracted. It applies to such natural resources as metals and hydrocarbons in the ground and to timber stands. The basic concept of depletion accounting is simple: If a natural resource costs $1 million and 5 percent of it is removed in a year, the depletion expense charge is 5 percent × $1,000,000 = $50,000. A like amount is credited to the allowance for depletion account on the balance sheet, reducing the net carrying value of the natural resource asset. The IRS also accepts this method of calculating depletion and refers to it as *cost depletion*.

An unrelated method, *percentage depletion*, also appears in the Internal Revenue Code and is defined so as to allow an excess tax deduction in prescribed circumstances. Percentage depletion, as defined by the IRS, has no conceptual basis and is allowed only for calculating a depletion deduction for tax purposes. The problems of applying depletion are basically ones of measurement. How much of the natural resource is there? What is included in the "cost" of a natural resource undergoing continuous development? If depletion is involved, the analyst should ask how it is measured and how thoroughly the company's depletion accounting practices conform to (or depart from) industry norms. Although depletion is relatively easy to define, it is very difficult to measure. Reasonable estimates can be subject to wide variations.

Treatment of Intangibles

It may be necessary to adjust the balance sheet and income statement for the diverse accounting treatments (or lack thereof) for intangible assets.

Leasehold Interests

If a company owns a leasehold at something other than fair market rent, the balance sheet may be adjusted by the analyst to show an asset or liability representing the present value of the difference between the leasehold (contract) rent and the current fair market rent. The formula for this calculation is as follows:

Formula 7–1

$$PV = \sum_{i=1}^{n} \frac{A}{(1+k)^i}$$

where:

PV = Present value
A = Amount of difference per period between leasehold rent and fair market rent
n = Number of periods remaining on the lease
k = Before-tax discount rate per period at which to capitalize the leasehold interest
i = ith period

For example, suppose a company has 25 months remaining on its lease at $5,000 per month and a new lease on comparable space today would cost $6,500 per month. (Alternatively, the company could sublet the space at $6,500 per month for the 25 months remaining on the lease.) The company's before tax cost of capital is 12 percent per annum. The present value of the company's leasehold interest is computed as follows:

Formula 7–2

$$PV = \sum_{i=1}^{25} \frac{\$6,500 - \$5,000}{\left(1 + \dfrac{0.12}{12}\right)^i}$$

$$= \sum_{i=1}^{25} \frac{\$1,500}{(1+0.01)^i}$$

An upward adjustment of $33,035 could be made by the analyst to the asset side of the balance sheet to recognize the value of the leasehold interest.

Other Intangible Assets

Effective for acquisitions after August 10, 1993, all "Section 197 intangibles" must be amortized over 15 years. Much like MACRS, §197 forces the taxpayer to use the 15-year period even if the useful life is actually more or less than 15 years. Section 197 intangibles include a number of items such as goodwill, going-concern value, covenants not to compete, information bases such as customer or subscription lists, know-how, customer-based intangibles, governmental licenses and permits (e.g., liquor licenses, taxicab medallions, landing or takeoff rights, regulated airline routes, television or radio licenses), franchises, trademarks, and trade names.[5]

The following are some other examples of intangible assets:

1. Patents
2. Copyrights
3. Employment contracts
4. "Intangible drilling costs" or similar natural resource development costs
5. Natural resource exploration rights

Financial accounting principles state that identifiable intangible assets with a finite life be amortized and identifiable intangible assets with an indefinite life should not be amortized. Intangibles that can be amortized are to be carried on the books at cost and then amortized over their useful economic lives. An intangible asset that is not amortized needs to be tested for impairment on an annual basis (or possibly more frequently, depending on circumstances). Goodwill is not to be amortized and needs to be tested for impairment. Impairment is the difference in value between the carrying amount of goodwill and the actual fair value of the goodwill. However, for federal income tax reporting purposes:

> The costs of developing, maintaining, or restoring intangibles which are unidentifiable, have indeterminate lives, or are inherent in a continuing enterprise should be expensed as incurred. By contrast, such intangible assets which are purchased must be carried at cost and amortized over their useful lives and cannot be written down or written off at date of acquisition.[6]

Thus, a company may have spent a great amount of money internally developing valuable intangible assets without showing their value on the balance sheet, while another company may show comparable intangible assets on the balance sheet and be charging amortization expenses as deductions from earnings because it purchased the intangibles instead of developing them internally. If a company's intangible assets have true economic value, that value is likely to be reflected in increased earnings. In comparing companies with very different accounting practices, one way for an analyst to adjust for intangible items on the financial statements is to eliminate (1) all intangible assets from the balance sheets and (2) all amortization expense from the income statements.

Capitalization versus Expensing of Various Costs

Many cost items fall into a "gray" area, in which the decision to expense or to capitalize the expenditure is subjective. One such decision is the dividing line between maintenance expenditures, which are expenses, and capital improvements, which are capitalized. For example, many seasonal operations, such as resorts and food processing plants, employ skeletal crews year-round. Their compensation

---

[5] James W. Pratt and William N. Kulsrud, eds., *Federal Taxation 1995* (New York: McGraw-Hill, 1994), pp. 9–35. Reprinted with permission.
[6] Ibid., p. 176.

generally is expensed, even though they make improvements during the slow period that probably would be capitalized if outside contractors were hired for the same job. Companies that want to report higher earnings will capitalize items that fall into this gray area, and companies that want to minimize income taxes will elect to expense rather than capitalize whenever possible. In analyzing the quality of the company's earnings and balance sheets, the appraiser should watch for opportunities to choose between capitalization and expensing and should ask management about the company's practice of accounting for these items.

Timing of Recognition of Revenues and Expenses

Certain types of companies have considerable latitude in their choice of accounting practices in the timing of recognition of some of their revenues and expenses.

Contract Work

Contract work can be accounted for either on a completed-contract or percentage-of-completion basis. To better match revenue with expenses, the latter is conceptually preferable, but it can be implemented only under strict guidelines established by the American Institute of Certified Public Accountants (AICPA).[7] Furthermore, the method is only as good as the estimates of the percentages completed. If the company being valued is in the contracting business, its accounting practices deserve careful scrutiny. This can be one of the most difficult areas for the outside analyst to evaluate critically. If it is a major issue in the valuation, it may necessitate considerable inquiry into the company's records as well as investigation of industry experience in comparable situations.

Installment Sales

When is a sale a sale? For years many companies booked huge profits by selling land on high-face-value contracts with 5 percent or 10 percent down and the balance over extended periods at a low floating interest rate. The down payments were not high enough to deter many buyers from defaulting, and even good contracts were worth nowhere near their face value because of the low cost of debt. In 1982, the Financial Accounting Standards Board (FASB) released *Statement of Financial Accounting Standards No. 66*[8] to help prevent such abuses, but there is still some latitude for differences in treatment from one company to another. If installment sales are a significant part of the company's business, the analyst should look into their accounting treatment.

Sales Involving Actual or Contingent Liabilities

Generally, sales involving actual future liabilities are those in which certain services are due to the customer in conjunction with the transaction. Such sales would

---

[7] *AICPA Statement of Position*, 81-1
[8] *FASB Statement of Financial Accounting Standards No. 66*, "Accounting for Sales of Real Estate."

include service contracts and subscriptions or products with future servicing warranted for some period. The unearned portion of the revenues is usually carried on the balance sheet as a liability item, commonly labeled deferred income, and then transferred to income as it is earned. Knowing when to recognize such income as revenues may require considerable judgment. Thus, the analyst should scrutinize the accounting treatment in companies that make sales involving future liabilities.

Sales involving contingent liabilities most commonly are those in which the customer has rebates, allowances, or certain rights to return products for a refund of revenue already recorded. If contingent liabilities exist, the analyst should assess the adequacy of their accounting treatment because they will affect the reported earnings and assets.

Prior-Period Adjustments

For a variety of reasons a company may find that its revenues or expenses, or both, were understated or overstated in certain prior accounting periods. The most common reasons are errors in accounting and underpayment or overpayment of income taxes. The company usually records such an adjustment in the accounting year in which it is discovered by charging the adjustment to the opening balance of retained earnings. Thus, the adjustment does not affect net income during the current period. In assessing the company's earnings history, the analyst should spread the effect of the adjustment back over the prior periods to which it applies. Sometimes the information needed for accurately allocating the adjustment to the appropriate prior periods is not available. Even if a rough estimate of the appropriate prior-period allocation is the best one can make, usually it is better, for analytical purposes, to spread the adjustment on the basis of such an estimate rather than leave it in the single period in which it was reported.

Accounting for Leases

The analyst may decide to make adjustments for analytical purposes to the company's accounting treatment for leases. According to the *Statement of Financial Accounting Standards No. 13* as amended and interpreted, leases that are of a financial nature (those that transfer essentially all of the benefits and risks incident to ownership of the property) must be capitalized as assets on the lessee's balance sheet. All other leases are accounted for as operating leases—that is, the lease payments are simply expensed as they are incurred. Since there is sometimes room for argument about which method of accounting is appropriate (and because unaudited closely held companies are less prone to strictly adhere to GAAP than are audited public companies), the analyst may want to examine leases.

Net Operating Loss Carryforwards

An item that frequently causes controversy in a business valuation is the value of a net operating loss carryforward. The amounts are presented in the footnotes to the financial statements rather than in the body of the balance sheet. This is because their value is contingent upon generating future profits against which to use them. The company's ability to generate such profits may be questionable, since the company has generated net operating losses as part of its operating history.

As far as the income statement is concerned, net operating loss carryforwards properly are classed as extraordinary credits in the periods in which they are used. They should usually be adjusted out of the earnings base in those periods for analytical purposes. It may be reasonable to spread back the tax loss carryforward credits that actually were used to offset the losses in the periods in which the tax loss carryforwards were generated to normalize the taxes in the historical loss periods.

In terms of the valuation of net operating loss carryforwards, it is noteworthy that it may take years for the buyer of the subject business to take advantage of the use of the loss carryforwards. In this regard, the analyst should be aware that there are time limits to the period in which net operating losses may be carried forward. In addition, there are serious restrictions as to (1) the seller's ability to transfer net operating losses and (2) the buyer's ability to use transferred net operating losses subsequent to a corporate acquisition.

Treatment of Interests in Affiliates

If a company owns 50 percent to 100 percent of another company's stock, it generally prepares consolidated statements. However, in some situations the parent company properly accounts for the subsidiary by the equity method, defined below. If a company owns 20 percent to 50 percent of another company's stock, it may account for it by either the equity method or the cost method, depending on whether the parent exerts "significant influence"[9] over the company in which it holds the ownership interest. If a company owns less than 20 percent of another company's stock, it almost always accounts for it by the cost method, although accounting principles leave the door open for using the equity method if a significant degree of control can be demonstrated.

Consolidated statements treat the parent and subsidiaries as if they were all one company, with minority interests in subsidiaries, if any, shown as deductions on the financial statements. When accounting is done by the equity method, the parent's share of the subsidiary's earnings or losses (net of intercorporate eliminations, if any) is shown on its income statement, and the carrying value of the interest in the subsidiary is adjusted accordingly on its balance sheet. When subsidiaries are accounted for by the cost method, the parent shows only dividends received on its income statement and continues to carry the investment on its balance sheets at cost. This is true except if the subsidiary has a permanent impairment in its value, in which case accounting principles state that the investment should be written down. Frequently an analyst would consider an adjustment appropriate on the basis of the evaluation, even though the account would not necessarily recognize permanent impairment.

The greatest distortions in the reporting of a parent company's overall results, of course, arise under the cost method, which does not reflect earnings or losses of the subsidiary interest in the parent's financial statement. If a subsidiary's earnings and losses are significant, the analyst may wish to make appropriate adjustments. On the other hand, presenting consolidated statements or accounting using the

---

[9] *APB Opinion No. 18*, 1971.

equity method implies that a dollar of the subsidiary's earnings is worth a dollar to the parent, which is not necessarily true. There may be restrictions on distributions of the subsidiary's earnings due to loan agreements, regulator authorities, or other reasons. Also, the analyst should ensure that the parent has allowed for any income taxes incident to potential transfer of funds from subsidiary to parent.

Extraordinary or Nonrecurring Items

In analyzing a company's historical earnings as a guide to estimating the company's earnings base, the analyst should make every reasonable effort to distinguish between past earnings that represent ongoing earning power and those that do not. The analyst should adjust the income statements to eliminate the effects of past items that would tend to distort the company's current and future earning power. Implementation of this analysis and adjustments requires much judgment.

Ordinary versus Extraordinary Items

Accounting Principles Board (APB) Opinion No. 30, issued in 1973, is very restrictive as to what may be reported as an "extraordinary" gain or loss. *APB Opinion No. 30* states that an item must be *both* unusual in nature and infrequent in occurrence to be categorized as extraordinary. It defines these two requirements as follows:

> *Unusual nature*—the underlying event or transaction should possess a high degree of abnormality and be of a type clearly unrelated to, or only incidentally related to, the ordinary and typical activities of the entity, taking into account the environment in which the entity operates.
>
> *Infrequency of occurrence*—the underlying event or transaction should be of a type that would not reasonably be expected to recur in the foreseeable future, taking into account the environment in which the entity operates.[10]

If an item meets these definitions, it almost certainly cannot be considered representative of ongoing earning power. That does not necessarily mean it should be totally ignored, however, since an extraordinary item could indicate a risk that the company may face again in the future.

Other Nonrecurring Items

Since the use of the *extraordinary* designation is so restrictive, obviously many items do not meet the strict definition for accounting purposes but nevertheless should be regarded as nonrecurring for analytical purposes. Some examples of such items would be:

1. Gains or losses on the sale of assets, especially when the company clearly lacks a continuing supply of assets available for sale
2. Gains or losses on disposition of a segment of the business

---

[10] *APB Opinion No. 30*, 1973

3. Insurance proceeds from life insurance on a key person or from some type of property and casualty claim
4. Proceeds from the settlement of lawsuits
5. Effects of a strike or of an extended period in which critical raw materials are unavailable
6. Effects of abnormal price fluctuations, especially those of a very short-term nature that are due to regulatory, industry, or other aberrations that are not likely to be repeated
7. Write-offs and other expenses related to an acquisition

It is possible, of course, for most of these unusual events to recur, resulting in a greater or smaller effect on the company's financial results. The analyst must carefully consider the likelihood of their recurrence and decide whether and how to adjust the financial statements to produce a best estimate of the company's continuing earning power.

Discontinued Operations

Apart from any one-time gain or loss associated with the disposal or discontinuation of an operating segment, the analyst must also determine how to treat the operating earnings or losses that were generated by that segment before its discontinuation. If the amounts can be distinguished from the results of the ongoing operations, the analyst may decide to adjust the earnings of the ongoing operations by removing the effect of the discontinued operations. The analyst must also consider the effect on the company's overall resources, however, because lost earnings from one source may be replaced by redeploying the resources in other efforts.

Operating versus Nonoperating Items

Depending on the method of valuation, it may be useful to distinguish between operating and nonoperating earnings even if the latter are recurring. The nonoperating item most commonly found on financial statements is income from investments. We suggest elsewhere in this book that it may be appropriate to value certain portions of a company, such as investments, with a market value approach and operating portions primarily on a capitalization of earnings approach. If the analyst values nonoperating assets separately, he or she should exclude any income generated or expenses incurred by the nonoperating assets from the earnings base capitalized in valuing the company's operations.

Management Compensation and Perquisites

In closely held companies, compensation and perquisites to owners and managers may be based on the owners' personal desires and the company's ability to pay rather than on the value of the services these individuals perform. How much to adjust the earnings base to reflect discrepancies between compensation paid and value of service performed depends on the valuation's purpose.

Owners of successful closely held businesses tend to take out what normally would be considered profits in the form of compensation and discretionary expenses. This practice, found primarily in corporations, may be an effort to avoid the double taxation that arises from paying a corporate income tax and then paying a personal income tax on what the closely held business pays to the owner in the form of dividends. It is not uncommon to find an owner/manager of a successful company with annual compensation greater than the amount an equivalent nonowner employee would earn as compensation.

If the above owner/manager wants to sell the business and retire, the difference between the compensation and the cost to replace the owner's services will become available as a part of pretax profits, and the company's earning power should be adjusted accordingly in establishing the business's selling price. If, on the other hand, the principal owner plans to continue working and maintain a similar compensation program for a long period after the valuation date, after establishing an employee stock ownership plan (ESOP) for example, the analyst may not adjust the earnings base since the level of compensation can be expected to continue.

It is also common for management to be undercompensated because the company lacks the ability to pay. Usually the analyst should assume that the underpayment will be corrected when adequate resources are available and should make an appropriate upward adjustment to the management compensation expense in estimating the company's earnings base.

In general, adjustments for compensation, if appropriate, will be made when valuing controlling interests, because it will be within the power of the controlling interest's owner to change such compensation. Adjustments for compensation may or may not be appropriate when valuing noncontrolling interests, because the noncontrolling stockholder may receive no benefit from such compensation and lacks the power to change it.

Transactions Involving Company Insiders

The analyst should carefully scrutinize and evaluate material transactions involving owners or management. One of the most common situations is one in which the business leases premises from a person associated with the company. In such cases, the analyst usually should evaluate whether the lease amounts are equivalent to what the company would pay on an arm's-length basis. If not, the appropriate adjustment will depend on the situation, especially the length of time over which the present lease arrangement can be expected to continue, and the ability of the stockholder whose stock is being valued to change the arrangement.

Another common occurrence in closely held businesses is loans to or from stockholders or officers. Here the analyst should examine the borrower's ability and intent to repay. If there is little or no likelihood of collecting a receivable from an insider, it should be removed from the balance sheet for analytical purposes. If interest is being accrued and is unlikely to be collected, it should be adjusted out of the earnings used to evaluate the earning power. It is also common to find a demand note payable in the current liability section of the balance sheet, even though there is no intent to pay the note any time soon or even ever. Interest may or may not be paid on it. For analytical purposes, it may be more appropriate to treat such an item as if it were long-term debt or even subordinated capital of a nature more like equity than debt.

Contingent Assets and Liabilities

One of the most difficult categories of items to treat analytically for valuation purposes is contingencies. The very fact that an item is a contingency defies precise quantification. Nevertheless, the valuation analyst must try to discover contingent assets and liabilities, whether or not they are on the financial statements in some form, and deal with them within the scope of the available information.

The most common categories of contingent assets and liabilities are those that arise from existing or potential litigation. If the outcomes were known, there would be no need for litigation. These situations are so varied that it is virtually impossible to generalize about how to treat them for valuation purposes. The analyst should at least be alert to opportunities to investigate and evaluate contingencies. When necessary, the analyst should seek legal opinions with regard to the likely occurrence of certain contingencies.

Adjustments to Asset Valuations

Marketable Securities

It is generally agreed that marketable securities should be adjusted to fair market value for most asset valuation purposes. However, there is not necessarily total agreement that such an adjustment should be accompanied by a partially offsetting adjustment for the related income tax effects, implied by the unrealized gain or loss to which the adjustment gives rise. The argument that the tax consequence of recognizing the fair market value of marketable securities should be ignored for analytical purposes is generally based on whether a tax strategy is available that delays or avoids recognition of the capital gain or loss.

Other Assets

The appropriateness of adjusting various other categories of balance sheet assets for financial analysis purposes is controversial and depends on the purpose of the assignment. Revenue Ruling 59–60 states that for gift and estate tax purposes, values of assets of an investment nature (as opposed to operating assets) should be adjusted. The theory apparently is that such assets could be liquidated without impairing the company's operations. Sometimes, however, that will not be true, such as if the assets must be maintained as loan collateral or are necessary for maintaining certain financial ratios that lenders or regulatory agencies require. Other portions of this book, especially Chapter 14, "Asset-Based Approach: Asset Accumulation Method," discuss the appropriateness of adjusting different categories of asset values under various circumstances.

Computation of Earnings per Share

Weighted Average Basis

Earnings per share should be computed on a weighted average basis, that is, the number of shares weighted by the length of time they have been outstanding. Let's say that a company had 100,000 shares outstanding at the beginning of the year and issued 30,000 more shares on May 1. The 100,000 shares would be outstanding for four months and the 130,000 shares for eight months, or two-thirds of the year. The weighted average number of shares outstanding for the year would be computed as follows:

$$1/3 \times 100,000 \qquad = \quad 33,333$$
$$2/3 \times 130,000 \qquad = \quad \underline{86,667}$$
$$\text{Weighted average shares outstanding} \quad = \quad 120,000$$

If the earnings were $300,000, earnings per share would be $300,000 ÷ 120,000 = $2.50.

Basic versus Diluted Earnings

In general, basic earnings per share are computed by dividing the earnings available to common equity by the weighted average number of common shares outstanding, plus "dilutive common stock equivalents." The definition and computations can be very technical, and the reader who needs this detail should turn to a technical, accounting-oriented manual, such as Bernstein's.[11]

For analytical purposes, it seems that the earnings per share are best stated on a diluted basis, that is, showing the maximum potential dilution that could have resulted had all likely conversions and exercises of options and warrants been exercised. Naturally, the effect of any interest or dividends paid on the convertible issues would have to be added back to the earnings base. Any conversions that would be antidilutive in their effect should not be included.

Computation of Book Value per Share

Book value per share is based on the number of shares outstanding at the end of the accounting period rather than the weighted average used in computing earnings per share. Also, book value normally is computed without considering possible dilutive effects of conversions, although the analyst may wish to make such a computation for analytical purposes. Thus, the computation of book value per share usually is a simple matter of dividing the total common equity by the number of shares outstanding. (Treasury stock—that is stock once issued and subsequently reacquired—is *not* included in the number of shares outstanding.) On most balance sheets, the

---

[11] Bernstein, *Financial Statement Analysis*, pp. 326–36.

common equity consists of the common stock account, any paid-in capital in excess of par or stated value, and the accumulated retained earnings or deficit. Of course, if there were any contingent payments on senior securities not shown on the balance sheet, such as preferred dividends in arrears, such amounts would have to be deducted from common equity in computing book value per share. Several investment services, including *S&P Corporation Records* (referenced elsewhere in this book), exclude intangibles in their computed book values per share.

An Example of the Effect of Alternative Accounting Methods

Exhibit 7–4 illustrates the impact on reported earnings of using different methods of accounting for a particular set of operations.

Adjusting the Balance Sheet to Current Values

If it is appropriate to rely heavily on an asset approach in the valuation, the analyst may prepare a pro forma balance sheet with some or all of the line items adjusted to current values. Depending on the valuation criteria to be used, the adjustments may affect only nonoperating assets or may affect all assets (see Chapter 14, "Asset-Based Approach: Asset Accumulation Method"). The treatment of the tax effect on impounded capital gains on the unrealized appreciation remains a matter of some controversy, as noted earlier. Consensus is building among financial analysts that the built-in capital gains tax should be recognized one way or another (at least with regard to the valuation of C corporations), either in the form of a balance sheet adjustment or some type of a discount.[12]

Summary

Adjustments to the financial statements require both analytical judgment and an understanding of accounting principles. This chapter presented the categories of financial statement adjustments that are most frequently encountered in the course of the business valuation process. The chapter presented both the accounting mechanics and also some discussion of the judgmental factors that the analyst should consider in analyzing the financial statements for appropriate adjustments. The analyst should be guided by common sense, experience, and an understanding of the company in determining what adjustments should be made to present the statements in the manner most appropriate for valuation purposes. In some cases, there may not be enough information to make certain adjustments, or the process may be too time-consuming relative to the results achieved. Which adjustments to make should be a matter of professional judgment as to their materiality in the context of the specific valuation objective.

---

[12] For example, see *Estate of Artemus D. Davis v. Commissioner*, 110 T.C. 35 (June 30, 1998).

Exhibit 7–4

Example of the Effect of the Variety of Accounting Principles on Reported Income

Rival Manufacturing Company
Consolidated Statement of Income
for Year Ended 20___

	Method A	Adjustments Debit	Adjustments Credit	Method B
Net sales	$365,800,000			$365,800,000
Cost of goods sold	(276,976,200)		[1] 1,730,000	
			[2] 88,000	
			[3] 384,200	
			[4] 346,000	
			[5] 78,000	(274,350,000)
Gross profit	88,823,800			91,450,000
Selling, general, & administrative expenses	(51,926,000)		[6] 9,226,000	(42,700,000)
Operating profit	36,897,800			48,750,000
Other income (expense):				
Interest expenses	(3,085,000)	10,000		(3,095,000)
Net income—subsidiaries	1,538,000	78,000		1,460,000
Amortization of goodwill	(390,000)		[7] 220,000	(170,000)
Miscellaneous expenses	(269,000)		40,000	(229,000)
Total other income (expense)	(2,206,000)			(2,034,000)
Income before taxes	34,691,800			46,716,000
Taxes:				
Income taxes—deferred	(556,000)	294,000		(850,000)
Income taxes—current	(13,906,500)	4,733,000		(18,639,500)
Net income	$20,229,300			$27,226,500
Earnings per share	$6.98			$9.39

Explanations:

[1] Inventories   Difference: $1,730,000
     A uses last-in, first-out
     B uses first-in, first-out

[2] Administrative costs   Difference: $88,000
     A includes some administrative costs as period costs
     B includes some administrative costs as inventory costs

[3] Depreciation   Difference: $384,200
     A uses sum-of-the-years'-digits method
     B uses straight-line method

[4] Useful lives of assets   Difference: $346,000
     A uses conservative assumption—8 years (average)
     B uses liberal assumption—14 years (average)

[5] Pension costs   Difference: $78,000
     A uses realistic assumptions regarding rates of return on assets and future inflation
     B uses less realistic assumptions regarding rates of return on assets and future inflation

[6] Executive compensation   Difference: $840,000
     A compensates executives with cash bonuses
     B compensates executives with stock options

[7] Goodwill from acquisition   Difference: $220,000
     A amortizes over 10 years
     B amortizes over 40 years

SOURCE: Leopold A. Bernstein, *Financial Statement Analysis: Theory, Application and Interpretation*, 6th ed. (New York: McGraw-Hill, 1997), p. 309. Reprinted with permission.

Bibliography

Articles

Brown, Terry S. "Assessing the Quality of Company Earnings." *CPA Litigation Service Counselor*, March 1999, pp. 8–9.

Clark, Lynne. "Demystifying Dilution." *CA Magazine*, May 1993, pp. 62–64.

Craig, Thomas, and Timothy Hoerr. "Recasting Income Statements in Valuations of Closely Held Businesses." *Business Valuation Review*, September 1993, pp. 134–39.

Evans, Frank C. "Analyzing a Financial Statement." *Management Review*, November 1993, pp. 52–53.

Lee, Cheng F., and Chunchi Wu. "Rational Expectations and Financial Ratio Smoothing." *Journal of Accounting, Auditing & Finance*, Spring 1994, pp. 283–306.

Mercer, Z. Christopher. "Normalizing Adjustments to the Income Statement." *Value Matters*, September 24, 2004, pp. 1–4.

Speece, Fred H. "Assessing the Quality of Earnings and Management." In *Equity Research and Valuation Techniques*. Charlottesville, VA: Association of Investment Management & Research, 1998, pp. 16–19.

Taub, Maxwell J. "Valuing a Minority Interest: Whether to Adjust Elements of a Financial Statement over Which the Minority Shareholder Has No Control." *Business Valuation Review*, March 1998, pp. 7–9.

Turner, Mark A. "Accounting for Inventory in a Reorganization or Liquidation." *Management Accounting*, February 1993, pp. 29–32.

Reference Books

Bandler, James. *How to Use Financial Statements: A Guide to Understanding the Numbers*. New York: McGraw-Hill, 1994.

Beasley, Mark S., and Joseph V. Carcello. *2006 Miller GAAS Guide*. Chicago: CCH, 2005.

Bernstein, Leopold A. *Analysis of Financial Statements*, 5th ed. New York: McGraw-Hill, 2000.

_____. *Financial Statement Analysis: Theory, Application, and Interpretation*, 8th ed. New York: McGraw-Hill, 2004.

Fraser, Lyn M., and Aileen Ormiston. *Understanding Financial Statements*, 7th ed. Englewood Cliffs, NJ: Prentice-Hall, 2004.

Fridson, Martin S. *Financial Statement Analysis: A Practitioner's Guide*, 3rd ed. New York: John Wiley & Sons, 2002.

Hitchner, James R., *Financial valuation application and models*, 2nd ed., Hoboken, NJ: John Wiley & Sons, 2006.

Mercer, Christopher Z. *Valuing Enterprise and Shareholder Cash Flows—The Integrated Theory of Business Valuation*. Memphis, TN: Peabody Publishing, 2004.

Stickney, Clyde P., Paul R. Brown, and James M. Wahlen. *Financial Reporting and Statement Analysis: A Strategic Perspective*. Stamford, CT: Thomson Learning, 2004.

Szurovy, Geza, and S. B. Costales. *Guide to Understanding Financial Statements*, 2nd ed. New York: McGraw-Hill, 1993.

White, Gerald I., Ashwinpaul C. Sondi, and Dov Fried. *The Analysis and Use of Financial Statements*, 3rd ed. Hoboken, NJ: John Wiley & Sons, 2002.

Williams, Jan R. *2006 Miller GAAP Guide*. New York: Harcourt Brace Professional Publishing, 2005.

Chapter 8

Financial Statement Ratio Analysis

Use and Interpretation of Ratio Analysis

When used properly, analysis of financial statement ratios can be a useful tool in a business valuation. In particular, it can help identify and quantify some of the company's strengths and weaknesses—both on an absolute basis and relative to other companies or industry norms. Accordingly, financial ratio analysis is an important process within the business valuation.

The implications gleaned from financial statement analysis may be considered in arriving at the value of the business or business interest in several ways. The point in the valuation process where the financial statements ratio analysis has the greatest impact is in the selection of various fundamental financial multiples (e.g., market value of invested capital [MVIC]/earnings before interest and taxes [EBIT] multiple) to apply to the subject company. To the extent that the ratios indicate sustainable growth, the business should be worth a higher multiple than it would if they did not indicate growth. The higher the degree of risk factors the ratios reveal, the lower the business's worth should be relative to earnings, book value, and other fundamental financial variables.

One use of ratio analysis is to compare a company's own figures over time, a method sometimes called *trend analysis*. In this way, aspects of the business that demonstrate any trends of improvement or deterioration can be identified. It can also indicate levels of the different variables that have been normal within the period studied, as well as ranges that reveal high and low points for each variable over time.

Another way to use ratio analysis is to compare the subject company with other companies, either specific companies or industry averages. Patterns of strength in the subject company relative to guideline companies would tend to support a multiple in the high end of the industry range. Conversely, poor performance ratios relative to similar companies would suggest lower multiples for the subject company.

In comparing ratios from one period to another or from company to company, the analyst should understand the extent to which comparative ratios are based on comparable accounting policies. The previous chapter noted that different choices among accounting methods can result in wide variations in reported figures. When making a comparative analysis of a company's financial statements over time, the analyst should allow for any changes in accounting policies that occurred during the period. When comparing a company with others in its industry, the analyst should allow for any differences in accounting policies between the subject company and industry norms.

Another consideration is whether to calculate the ratios before or after any adjustments in the balance sheet or income statement, such as for nonrecurring items or for inventory, or pro forma adjustments. In many cases, these adjustments can significantly affect the magnitude of the company's ratios.

Two factors should guide the analyst in making this decision. First, if the ratios are to be compared with those of similar publicly traded companies, the analyst should make the same adjustments to the statements of both the subject company and the guideline companies. Second, if the computed ratios are to be compared with industry norms, the analyst should make only those adjustments that are likely to put the subject company on a basis comparable to other companies in the industry. In most cases, however, ratios calculated on adjusted statements will reveal a more accurate picture of the company's financial health.

The relative significance of the various ratios will differ in each valuation. Certain ratios have greater significance for value in particular industries. A ratio may be especially significant in some situations because it departs markedly from industry norms. The analyst must apply judgment to each individual case in selecting and evaluating the significance of figures as they apply to the particular situation.

If the analyst does the ratio computations prior to making the field trip to interview company personnel, the ratio analysis will usually generate some questions about departures from industry norms. Of course, if the ratio work follows the field trip, the analyst can cover such questions in later telephone interviews.

This chapter discusses ratios that help evaluate the company's financial position. First, it looks at those that measure short-term liquidity, followed by the commonly used longer-term balance sheet leverage ratios. Then the chapter discusses a variety of operating ratios. Each ratio is illustrated with an example from our hypothetical company, Warm Chicken Company. A summary of Warm Chicken Company ratios appears in Exhibit 21–6 in Chapter 21, "Sample Report." All exhibits referred to in this chapter may be found at the end of Chapter 21.

Common-Size Statements

A common first step in ratio analysis of financial statements is to prepare what are sometimes called *common-size statements*. On these statements, each line item is expressed as a percentage of the total. On the balance sheet, each line item is shown as a percentage of total assets. On the income statement, each item is expressed as a percentage of sales.

Exhibit 21–3 shows five years of balance sheets and Exhibit 21–4 shows five years of income statements for Warm Chicken Company presented on a common-size basis.

Short-Term Liquidity Measures

Generally, *liquidity ratios* demonstrate the company's ability to meet its current obligations. Liquidity ratios can help resolve one of the common controversies in business valuations: whether the company has any assets in excess of those required for its operating needs or, conversely, whether its assets fall short of its needs.

Current Ratio

The most commonly used short-term liquidity ratio is the *current ratio*, which is defined as current assets divided by current liabilities. Its greatest significance is as an indicator of the company's ability to pay its short-term liabilities on time. A single rule of thumb—that, for example, a satisfactory current ratio is 2.0:1—is not widely followed because of vastly different conditions typical in various industries, such as accounts receivable collection periods and inventory turnover periods. As with most ratios, the adequacy of the current ratio for a given company can be better gauged by comparison with industry norms than by comparison with any absolute standard.

Using figures from Exhibit 21–3, the current ratio for Warm Chicken Company for 2004 is calculated as follows:

Formula 8–1

$$\frac{\text{Current assets}}{\text{Current liabilities}} = \frac{\$149,692,000}{\$81,565,000} = 1.84:1$$

Quick (Acid-Test) Ratio

The next most commonly used ratio is the quick ratio, which some analysts refer to as the *acid-test ratio*. It is defined as the sum of cash and cash equivalents plus receivables (usually all current assets listed above inventory) divided by current liabilities. For most companies, the only other significant current asset is inventory—usually the slowest of the current assets to be converted to cash. One old rule of thumb is that a satisfactory quick ratio is 1.0:1; but, as with the current ratio, comparison with industry norms is more meaningful in most cases than comparison with an absolute standard.

Using figures from Exhibit 21–3, the quick or acid-test ratio for 2004 is calculated as follows:

Formula 8–2

$$\frac{\begin{array}{c}\text{Cash} + \text{Cash equivalents} \\ + \text{Investments} \\ \text{(generally marketable securities)} \\ + \text{Receivables}\end{array}}{\text{Current liabilities}} = \frac{\begin{array}{c}\$298,000 + \$14,000 \\ +\$50,120,000\end{array}}{\$81,565,000} = 0.62:1$$

It is important to realize that both the current ratio and the quick ratio measure liquidity at a point in time and may not reflect a company's use of short-term credit to finance its short-term liquidity needs. To be most meaningful, the investments that qualify as current assets should be computed at market value.

Activity Ratios

Activity ratios generally measure how efficiently a company uses its assets.

Accounts Receivable Turnover

The *accounts receivable turnover* can be expressed either as the number of times per year the accounts turn over on average or as the average number of days required for collecting accounts. A slow accounts receivable turnover (long average collection period) not only puts a strain on a company's short-term liquidity, it can indicate excessive bad debt losses. On the other hand, a fast accounts receivable turnover (short average collection period) can indicate an overly stringent credit policy that may be limiting sales.

The accounts receivable turnover typically is computed by dividing net credit sales by average accounts receivable. If cash sales (as opposed to credit sales) are insignificant, or if the available figures do not distinguish between cash and credit sales, total sales may be used in the computation. Because of limitations on available data, average accounts receivable may have to be computed by averaging the receivables at the beginning and at the end of the period. The procedure of averaging receivables figures at the end of each quarter or each month gives a more accurate picture, especially if the business is subject to seasonal variations. In any case, if the ratio is for comparative purposes, the amount of data available for the guideline companies may limit the extent of fine-tuning that is possible in computing this ratio.

Using data from Exhibits 21–3 and 21–4, the accounts receivable turnover for Warm Chicken Company for 2004 is computed as follows:

Formula 8–3

$$\frac{\text{Fiscal 2004 Sales}}{\left(\begin{array}{l}\text{Accounts receivable FYE 2004} + \\ \text{Accounts receivable FYE 2003}\end{array}\right) \div 2} = \frac{\$743,999,000}{\left(\begin{array}{l}\$50,120,000 \\ +\$46,910,000\end{array}\right) \div 2} = 15.34 \text{ times}$$

The accounts receivable turnover is divided into 365 days to express this variable in terms of average collection period. For Warm Chicken Company, we divide 365 days by the turnover of 15.34 times a year for an average collection period of 23.8 days. Incidentally, some analysts use 360 days instead of 365 days—one of many inconsistencies in valuation practice.

The sales-to-receivables ratio reported in *RMA Annual Statement Studies*[1] is net sales for the year divided by accounts and trade notes receivable *as of the end of the year*. Therefore, if the analyst wishes to compare the subject company with RMA statistics, the ratio for the subject company should be computed in the same manner as the RMA ratio. For Warm Chicken Company, this simplifies the computation to the following:

Formula 8–4

$$\frac{\text{Fiscal 2004 Sales}}{\text{Accounts receivable FYE 2004}} = \frac{743,999,000}{50,120,000} = 14.84 \text{ times}$$

This level of accounts receivable turnover is equivalent to $(365 \div 14.84) = 24.6$ average days collection period.

Inventory Turnover

The *inventory turnover ratio* typically is computed by dividing the cost of goods sold by the average inventory. As is true of accounts receivable turnover, a slow inventory turnover (long average holding period) not only puts a strain on the company's liquidity, but can indicate obsolete or otherwise undesirable inventory. On the other hand, a fast inventory turnover may indicate that sales are being lost due to insufficient inventory on hand.

Also, as with accounts receivable turnover, the ratio is more meaningful if it can be computed using quarterly or monthly inventory data, especially for companies with seasonal aspects in their operation; however, data limitations more often than not make these computations impractical.

---

[1] *RMA Annual Statement Studies* (Philadelphia: Risk Management Association, 2005), published annually.

Using data from Exhibits 21–3 and 21–4, the inventory turnover for Warm Chicken Company for 2004 is computed as follows:

Formula 8–5

$$\frac{\text{Fiscal 2004 Cost of goods sold}}{\left(\begin{array}{l}\text{Inventory FYE 2004} \\ \text{+ Inventory FYE 2003}\end{array}\right) \div 2} = \frac{\$672,290,000}{\left(\begin{array}{l}\$92,805,000 \\ +\$111,437,000\end{array}\right) \div 2} = 6.58 \text{ times}$$

Like accounts receivable turnover, inventory turnover can be expressed as the average number of days in inventory. For Warm Chicken Company, average days in inventory is calculated by dividing 365 days by an inventory turnover of 6.58 times per year for an average of 55.5 days needed for selling inventory.

RMA Annual Statement Studies reports inventory turnover in the same manner as accounts receivable turnover—dividing cost of sales *by ending inventory*. For making comparisons with RMA data, this ratio should be computed by RMA's formula. For Warm Chicken Company, this ratio is computed as follows:

Formula 8–6

$$\frac{\text{Fiscal 2004 Cost of goods sold}}{\text{Inventory FYE 2004}} = \frac{\$672,290,000}{\$92,805,000} = 7.24 \text{ times}$$

From an inventory turnover of 7.24 times per year, we calculate an average of 50.4 days in inventory ($365 \div 7.24 = 50.4$).

Sales to Net Working Capital

Net working capital is defined as current assets minus current liabilities. If a company's current ratio, accounts receivable collection period, and inventory turnover remain constant as its sales go up, the working capital must rise, because the company will have to carry more receivables and inventory to support the increased sales level. A simple way to compute the sales-to-net-working-capital ratio is to divide sales for the fiscal year just ended by net working capital at the fiscal year-end. This ratio can be useful in comparing the company's own history with those of other companies in the industry.

Using the figures from Exhibits 21–3 and 21–4, the sales-to-net-working-capital ratio for Warm Chicken Company is calculated as follows:

Formula 8–7

$$\frac{\text{Sales}}{\begin{array}{l}\text{Current assets} \\ -\text{Current liabilities}\end{array}} = \frac{\$743,999,000}{\begin{array}{l}\$149,692,000 \\ -\$81,565,000\end{array}} = 10.9:1$$

A more reasonable way to compute the ratio would be to use average net working capital rather than ending net working capital as the denominator. Again, using the figures from Exhibits 21–3 and 21–4, sales to average net working capital is calculated as follows:

Formula 8–8

$$\frac{\text{Fiscal 2004 Sales}}{\left(\begin{array}{c}\text{Working capital FYE 2004} \\ +\text{Working capital FYE 2003}\end{array}\right)\div 2} = \frac{\$743,999,000}{\left[\left(\begin{array}{c}\$149,692,000 - \$81,565,000 \\ +\$166,919,000 - \$93,398,000\end{array}\right)\right]\div 2} = 10.5$$

A high ratio of sales to net working capital results from a favorable turnover of accounts receivable and inventory and indicates efficient use of current assets. However, a high sales-to-net-working-capital ratio can also indicate risk arising from possibly inadequate short-term liquidity. The economy and most industries are subject to some degree of cyclicality in economic activity and liquidity that do not necessarily run exactly in tandem. In order to assess the company's ability to meet peak needs, the analyst should consider the highest reasonable level of sales that might be anticipated, couple it with the largest accounts receivable and longest inventory turnover periods that might occur, and assess the adequacy of the working capital under that scenario.

Sales to Fixed Assets and Total Assets

Sales-to-fixed-assets and *sales-to-total-assets ratios*, sometimes called *asset utilization ratios*, measure how efficiently a company's assets are generating sales. They are calculated by dividing sales by either ending asset levels or by an average of the asset levels over the last two years. The results indicate the number of dollars of sales being generated by a dollar of assets. When observed over time, these ratios can indicate changing levels of asset productivity and reveal possible nonoperating assets relative to comparative companies.

Using the figures in Exhibits 21–3 and 21–4, the simplest way to calculate these ratios is as follows:

Formula 8–9

$$\frac{\text{Sales}}{\text{Fixed assets}} = \frac{\$743,999,000}{\$99,984,000} = 7.4:1$$

$$\frac{\text{Sales}}{\text{Total assets}} = \frac{\$743,999,000}{\$295,902,000} = 2.5:1$$

Another approach would be to use the average asset levels over the last two years. In this instance, monthly or quarterly figures are less important, since one would not expect to see seasonality in total assets or fixed assets levels in the same manner as current assets. Using the figures in Exhibits 21–3 and 21–4, the calculation of these ratios using this method is as follows:

Formula 8–10

$$\frac{\text{Fiscal 2004 Sales}}{\left(\begin{array}{c}\text{Fixed assets FYE 2004} \\ + \text{Fixed assets FYE 2003}\end{array}\right)\div 2} = \frac{\$743,999,000}{\left(\begin{array}{c}\$99,984,000 \\ +\$109,016,000\end{array}\right)\div 2} = 7.1:1$$

$$\frac{\text{Fiscal 2004 Sales}}{\left(\begin{array}{c}\text{Total assets FYE 2004} \\ + \text{Total assets FYE 2003}\end{array}\right)\div 2} = \frac{\$743,999,000}{\left(\begin{array}{c}+\$295,902,000 \\ +\$321,154,000\end{array}\right)\div 2} = 2.4:1$$

These ratios are subject to misinterpretation. The age and, thus, depreciated book value of the assets used in these calculations should be considered, particularly when comparing them to those of other, similar companies.

Risk Analysis

At this point it is appropriate to briefly investigate risk analysis, since it is closely related to the leverage ratios and coverage ratios discussed in the following sections. The purpose of risk analysis is to ascertain the uncertainty of the income flows to the company's various capital suppliers. Generally, there are two classes of capital suppliers—those that provide debt capital and receive a fixed return and those that provide equity capital and receive a variable return but can participate in the company's growth through increased future returns. The higher the risk to any category of capital suppliers to the company, the higher the cost of that class of capital.

The capital asset pricing model suggests using the factor called *beta* to measure risk. However, because of a lack of regularly quoted market prices for their stocks, betas for most closely held companies cannot be measured directly. One can make a good case for the fact that the nonsystematic portions of risk (those not reflected in beta) are more important for closely held companies than for publicly traded companies. Therefore, the risk analysis portion of financial statement analysis is a very important part of the valuation process.

It is possible to examine the uncertainty of income to the various suppliers of capital by investigating the uncertainty of income to the company. The greater the uncertainty of income to the company, the greater the uncertainty of income to the investor in the company. There are two general classes of risk of the company: business risk and financial risk.

Business Risk

Business risk is the uncertainty of income due largely to two factors: (1) fluctuation in sales and (2) the level of the company's fixed operating costs, which is a function of how the company operates. There are basically two ways to measure a company's business risk.

The first—and simpler—way is to measure the coefficient of variation of earnings, which is equal to the standard deviation of net income divided by the mean of net income:

Formula 8–11

$$\text{Business risk} = \frac{\text{Standard deviation of net income}}{\text{Mean of net income}}$$

For example, using the figures from Exhibit 21–4, the standard deviation of net income is $7,669,800 and the mean of net income is $5,178,600. (Note that all numbers are before effect of the accounting change.) Substituting into the above equation produces a measure of business risk:

Formula 8–12

$$\text{Business risk} = \frac{\$7,669,800}{\$5,178,600} = 1.48$$

For many companies, sales volatility is the most important determinant of the fluctuation of net income measured by the standard deviation. Although companies may have some control over annual sales volume, sales volatility is, to a considerable extent, a function of the economy's overall health and consumers' willingness to spend their disposable income.

The second method used to measure business risk is the calculation of the degree of operating leverage. *Operating leverage* reflects both the variability of sales and the level of the company's fixed operating costs. These fixed operating costs are a function of the manner in which the company produces its product. The operating earnings of companies with high variable operating costs fluctuate at about the same rate as sales do, whereas those of companies whose production processes entail high fixed operating costs fluctuate more widely than sales.

Operating leverage is measured by the percentage change in operating earnings relative to the percentage change in sales during any given period:

Formula 8–13

$$\text{Degree of operating leverage} = \frac{\text{Percentage change in operating earnings}}{\text{Percentage change in sales}}$$

Financial Risk

The second type of risk to investigate is financial risk. Whereas business risk, as measured by operating leverage, reflects the incidence of fixed operating costs and their effect on the income flows to capital suppliers, *financial risk* reflects the incidence of fixed financial costs, or interest, and their effect on the fluctuation of income flows to investors. A company's financial risk occurs in addition to business risk. If there were only business risk, the fluctuation of earnings available to stockholders would be the same as that of operating earnings. However, when fixed financial costs—that is, the interest associated with the use of financial leverage—are introduced, the fluctuation of earnings available to shareholders is greater than that of operating earnings. When the company uses debt to finance some of its activities, the payments to the holders of this debt come before any payments to shareholders. During good times, there is plenty left over for the shareholders. In bad times, however, the company's operating earnings are used to pay the interest on the debt and little may be left over for the shareholders, increasing the fluctuation in their earnings.

Financial risk is measured in two ways: (1) through calculating the degree of financial leverage and (2) through calculating various leverage ratios. The degree of financial leverage is similar to the degree of operating leverage in that both measure relative volatility. Financial leverage measures the fluctuation of earnings available to the common shareholders relative to the fluctuation of operating earnings (measured as EBIT):

Formula 8–14

$$\text{Degree of financial leverage} = \frac{\text{Percentage change in income to common stockholders}}{\text{Percentage change in EBIT}}$$

For example, using the figures from Exhibit 21–4, the degree of financial leverage for Warm Chicken Company for 2004 is:

Formula 8–15

$$\text{Degree of financial leverage} = \frac{(\$2,883,000 - \$1,864,000) \div \$1,864,000}{(\$10,883,000 - \$11,073,000) \div \$11,073,000} = -31.86$$

This result indicates that a 1.0 percent change in operating income is accompanied by approximately a negative 31.9 percent change in income available to common shareholders.

The higher the degree of financial leverage, the more risk exists for the company's equity investors, because there is a greater possibility that they will receive lower cash flows both today and in the future.

The balance sheet leverage ratios discussed in the next section are also used to measure financial leverage. They are used in conjunction with the degree of financial leverage to indicate the company's overall financial riskiness.

Balance Sheet Leverage Ratios

The general purpose of capital structure or *balance sheet leverage ratios* is to aid in making some quantifiable assessments of the long-term solvency of the business and its ability to deal with financial problems and opportunities as they arise. As with most ratios, such analysis generally is most meaningful when compared with other companies in the same industry. Comparisons within the same company over time also can be useful.

There are numerous variations of balance sheet leverage ratios, but the following are the ones most frequently used.

Total Debt to Total Assets

Of the various balance sheet ratios designed to measure the long-term adequacy of the company's capital structure, the *total-debt-to-total-assets ratio* probably is the most popular. It is defined as total debt divided by total assets and measures the total amount of the company's funding provided by all categories of creditors as a percentage of the company's total assets.

Using the figures from Exhibit 21–3, the total-debt-to-total-assets ratio for Warm Chicken Company at the fiscal year-end of 2004 is calculated as follows:

Formula 8–16

$$\frac{\text{Total liabilities}}{\text{Total assets}} = \frac{\$168,957,000}{\$295,902,000} = 0.57$$

Equity to Total Assets

The *equity-to-total-assets ratio*, or simply *equity ratio*, is computed by dividing the company's total equity by its total assets. It is equal to 1 minus the total-debt-to-total-assets ratio. Since these two ratios are merely alternative ways of stating the same thing, most analysts would include one or the other, but not both, in the presentation.

Using figures from Exhibit 21–3, the equity-to-total-assets ratio for Warm Chicken Company at the fiscal year-end of 2004 is calculated as follows:

Formula 8–17

$$\frac{\text{Total equity}}{\text{Total assets}} = \frac{\$126,945,000}{\$295,902,000} = 0.43$$

Long-Term Debt to Total Capital

Unfortunately, there is considerable ambiguity in the terminology of financial statement analysis, especially in ratio definitions. By debt ratio, some analysts mean "debt divided by total assets," the ratio just discussed, but others mean "long-term debt divided by total capital." Therefore, to avoid misinterpretation, it seems best to avoid the term *debt ratio* entirely and use the more specific term *long-term-debt-to-total-capital ratio*. Total capital is sometimes defined as total assets minus current liabilities (with the current liabilities balance excluding the current portion of long-term debt). However, many analysts include all interest-bearing debt as part of total capital.

Using figures from Exhibit 21–3, and using the first definition above, the long-term-debt-to-total-capital ratio for Warm Chicken Company is computed as follows:

Formula 8–18

$$\frac{\text{Long-term debt}}{\text{Total assets} - \text{Current liabilities}^{*}} = \frac{\$61,231,000}{\$295,902,000 - \$78,812,000} = 0.28$$

* excluding the current portion of long-term debt

The analyst should check to ensure that any ratios used for comparisons actually are computed by the same definitions, or the comparisons may be misleading. For example, some analysts include deferred taxes in the denominator as part of long-term capital, and others do not.

Equity to Total Capital

The *equity-to-total-capital ratio* is simply 1 minus the long-term-debt-to-total-capital ratio, so there usually is no need to compute both.

Using the figures from Exhibit 21–3, the equity-to-total-capital ratio for Warm Chicken Company at the fiscal year-end of 2004 is calculated as follows:

Formula 8–19

$$\frac{\text{Total equity}}{\text{Long-term debt} + \text{equity}} = \frac{\$126,945,000}{\$61,231,000 + \$126,945,000} = 0.67$$

Fixed Assets to Equity

One can get another view of the company's leverage by looking at the proportion of the fixed assets that are financed by equity as opposed to long-term debt. A larger value for the *fixed-assets-to-equity ratio* indicates that much of the company's productive capacity is being financed by borrowed funds rather than owners' funds.

Using the figures from Exhibit 21–3, the fixed-assets-to-equity ratio for Warm Chicken Company in 2004 is calculated as follows:

Formula 8–20

$$\frac{\text{Net fixed assets}}{\text{Total equity}} = \frac{\$99,984,000}{\$126,945,000} = 0.79$$

Debt to Equity

Sometimes the company's debt is expressed as a ratio to equity rather than to total assets. Again, some analysts prefer to focus on total debt and others just on long-term debt. *RMA Annual Statement Studies* uses total debt and only *tangible equity*. In other words, the RMA *debt-to-equity ratio* is computed as follows:

Formula 8–21

$$\frac{\text{Total liabilities}}{\text{Total equity} - \text{Intangible assets}}$$

This ratio is also sometimes expressed in reverse, that is, equity to total debt or equity to long-term debt.

Income Statement Coverage Ratios

In general, *income statement coverage ratios* are designed to measure the margin by which certain of the company's obligations are being met.

Times Interest Earned

The most popular income statement coverage ratio is times interest earned (referred to as the *interest coverage ratio*). It is designed to measure the company's ability to meet interest payments. The *times-interest-earned ratio* is defined as EBIT divided by interest expense.

Using figures from Exhibit 21–4, the times-interest-earned ratio for Warm Chicken Company for 2004 is:

Formula 8–22

$$\frac{\text{Earnings before interest and taxes}}{\text{Interest expense}} = \frac{\$4,804,000 + \$6,079,000}{\$6,079,000} = 1.8 \text{ times}$$

Note that the Warm Chicken Company statements are presented in the conventional manner, showing interest expense as a separate deduction after operating income. Since some closely held companies do not present the statements in this way, the EBIT figure may have to be computed rather than taken directly from a line item on the income statement.

Another way to look at interest coverage is to calculate the ratio based on earnings before depreciation, interest, and taxes (EBDIT) rather than EBIT. EBDIT is basically pretax, pre-interest cash flow that is available to pay the interest expense.

Using figures from Exhibit 21–4, the EBDIT interest coverage ratio for Warm Chicken Company for 2004 is computed as follows:

Formula 8–23

$$\frac{\substack{\text{Earnings before depreciation,} \\ \text{interest, and taxes}}}{\text{Interest expense}} = \frac{\substack{\$4,804,000 + \$20,949,000 \\ +\$6,079,000}}{\$6,079,000} = 5.2 \text{ times}$$

Coverage of Fixed Charges

The *coverage of fixed charges* is a more inclusive ratio than the times-interest-earned ratio in that it includes coverage of items in addition to interest. It is defined as the sum of earnings before interest and taxes and fixed charges divided by fixed charges. This definition leaves open an almost unlimited spectrum of possibilities for determining which items of fixed charges to include. The most common items are lease payments and required installments of principal payments toward debt retirement.

In the Warm Chicken Company example, the information shown in Exhibits 21–3 and 21–4 is inadequate for computing this ratio. Typically, the analyst must request some schedules or ask questions beyond the normal statement presentations in order to acquire the information necessary for computing this ratio. Audited financial statements normally contain such information in the footnotes.

Let's assume that the current portion of long-term debt (in this example, notes and mortgage payable, as shown in the current liability section of the balance sheet in Exhibit 21–3) is an annual required reduction of debt principal and that the operating expenses shown in Exhibit 21–4 include $4,000,000 per year lease payments on the premises the company occupies. The coverage of fixed charges for Warm Chicken Company, then, can be computed as:

Formula 8–24

$$\frac{\text{Earnings before interest and taxes} + \text{Lease payments}}{\text{Interest} + \text{Current portion of long-term debt} + \text{Lease payments}}$$

or

$$\frac{\$4,804,000 + \$6,079,000 + \$4,000,000}{\$6,079,000 + \$2,753,000 + \$4,000,000} = 1.16 \text{ times}$$

Income Statement Profitability Ratios

The four most commonly used measures of operating performance are *gross profit from sales, operating profit from sales, pretax income from sales*, and *net profit from sales*. Since all are percentages of sales, they may be read directly from the common-size income statements shown in Exhibit 21–4.

Return on Investment Ratios

Analysts will argue until doomsday whether return on equity, return on investment, or return on assets is the most meaningful measure of investment return. Proponents of return on equity say that the return on stockholder investment is what counts, and most adhere to this argument. Return on investment recognizes both the shareholders and the debtholders and can be quite important if the company is contemplating a change in the capital structure. However, proponents of return on assets say that management should be measured by the return on total assets utilized, without regard for the company's capital structure, which can have a considerable bearing on return on equity if return on assets is held constant. Each measure is useful for its own purpose.

Return on Equity

Return on equity usually means return on common equity capital. If a company has preferred stock outstanding, the analyst might consider computing return on total equity and return on common equity, since both can be useful measures. If comparing one or more ratios of return on equity for other companies with preferred stock outstanding, the analyst should ensure that the ratios are being computed on the same basis for the subject company as for the guideline companies.

Unless otherwise specified, return on equity means *after* taxes. Once in a while, someone—perhaps a broker trying to sell a business—quotes return on equity computed on a pretax basis. This definition can be very misleading, since *income taxes are a very real cost*, and the investor's return is what remains after corporate taxes. In fact, if the computation is being made for an S corporation, a partnership, or a sole proprietorship, many analysts recommend that the taxes the company would pay if it were a regular corporation be deducted from the net income before making the calculations. Sometimes there are legitimate reasons for comparing companies' returns on equity on a pretax basis, but when doing so it should be clearly specified—and recognized by the parties using the data—that it is a departure from the conventional meaning and computation of return on equity. Perhaps the best way to specify this is to use the expression *pretax return on equity* when that is what, in fact, is being shown.

One other issue to be resolved in the return on equity analysis is whether the selected equity base is the one at the beginning of the period, the end of the period, or the average for the period. There is consensus among analysts that the average equity provides the basis for the most meaningful analysis. However, an emerging group believes that beginning equity is the most important measure, since that is the equity base on which the earnings are generated. Still, the most commonly used method is to divide the earnings for the year by the average of the beginning and ending equity. If adequate information is available, return on equity can be further fine-tuned by averaging quarterly or monthly equity figures.

Since return on equity is a percentage, the result should be the same whether the computations are made on a total-company basis or on a per-share basis, at least if there is no dilution. If a weighted average number of shares has been used in the per-share earnings computation, the calculation will work out if the average equity base is weighted in the same manner.

Using the data from Exhibits 21–3 and 21–4, the return on equity for Warm Chicken Company for 2004 is calculated as follows:

Formula 8–25

$$\frac{\text{Net income}}{\begin{array}{c}\text{Average common}\\\text{stockholders' equity}\end{array}} = \frac{\$2{,}893{,}000}{\left(\begin{array}{c}\$126{,}945{,}000\\+\$124{,}291{,}000\end{array}\right) \div 2} = 2.3\%$$

Using beginning equity in this case yields the same percentage, as follows:

Formula 8–26

$$\frac{\text{Net income for 2004}}{\text{Stockholders' equity for 2003}} = \frac{\$2{,}883{,}000}{\$124{,}291{,}000} = 2.3\%$$

On a per-share basis with 1,577,420 shares outstanding for Warm Chicken Company, the computation is as follows:

Formula 8–27

$$\frac{\text{Earnings per share}}{\text{Average book value per share}} = \frac{\$1.83}{(\$80.48 + \$78.79) \div 2} = 2.3\%$$

Another way to look at the above ratio (i.e., net income divided by equity)—and perhaps to understand and appreciate it more fully—is in terms of the components that make up return on equity. These components of return on equity are:

Formula 8–28

$$\text{ROE} = \text{Profitability} \times \text{Turnover} \times \text{Leverage}$$

Stated more completely:

$$\frac{\text{Net income}}{\text{Equity}} = \frac{\text{Net income}}{\text{Sales}} \times \frac{\text{Sales}}{\text{Assets}} \times \frac{\text{Assets}}{\text{Equity}}$$

The formula above is commonly referred to as the *DuPont formula*, since the DuPont Company was widely known to use that formula as an integral part of its financial planning and control.

Return on Investment

The computations for *return on investment*, sometimes called *return on total capital*, are similar to those for return on equity. One key difference is that interest should be added back to net income to reflect the return to *both* equity *and* debt. Whether interest should be adjusted for taxes depends on the information to be conveyed in the ratio presentation. The analyst should adjust interest for income taxes by multiplying interest by 1 minus the tax rate—a product that is the equivalent of computing the ratio on an invested capital basis, as if all of the investment was in the form of equity. If, on the other hand, there is no adjustment for income taxes, the ratio will reflect the return under the company's existing capital structure. Again, the issue of average investment versus beginning investment should be recognized. In addition, the debt portion of the investment figure in the denominator could be long-term debt plus interest-bearing short-term debt, since the interest expense in the numerator is *total* interest expense.

Looking at it all four ways and using figures from Exhibits 21–3 and 21–4, the computation of return on investment for Warm Chicken Company for 2004 is as follows:

Formula 8–29

$$\frac{\text{Net income} + \text{Interest} (1 - \text{Tax rate})}{\left[\left(\begin{array}{c}\text{Beginning stockholders' equity} \\ + \text{Long-term debt}\end{array}\right) + \left(\begin{array}{c}\text{Ending stockholders' equity} \\ + \text{Long-term debt}\end{array}\right)\right] \div 2}$$

$$\frac{(\$2,883,000 + \$6,079,000\,(1 - 0.40)}{[(\$124,291,000 + \$75,797,000) + (\$126,945,000 + \$61,231,000) \div 2]} = 3.4\%$$

or

$$\frac{\text{Net income} + \text{Interest}}{\left[\left(\begin{array}{c}\text{Beginning stockholders' equity} \\ + \text{Long-term debt}\end{array}\right) + \left(\begin{array}{c}\text{Ending stockholders' equity} \\ + \text{Long-term debt}\end{array}\right)\right] \div 2}$$

$$\frac{\$2,883,000 + \$6,079,000}{[(\$124,291,000 + \$75,797,000) + (\$126,945,000 + \$61,231,000)] \div 2} = 4.6\%$$

Based on beginning investment, return on investment becomes:

Formula 8–30

$$\frac{\begin{array}{c}\text{Net income} \\ + \text{Interest} (1 - \text{Tax rate})\end{array}}{\begin{array}{c}\text{Beginning stockholders' equity} \\ + \text{Long-term debt}\end{array}} = \frac{\$2,883,000 + \$6,079,000\,(1 - 0.40)}{\$124,291,000 + \$75,797,000} = 3.3\%$$

or

$$\frac{\text{Net income + Interest}}{\text{Beginning stockholders' equity} \atop \text{+ Long-term debt}} = \frac{\$2,883,000 + \$6,079,000}{\$124,291,000 + \$75,797,000} = 4.5\%$$

Conceptually, the amount of interest expense that should be added back is only the interest expense that relates to the company's long-term debt, since that is the figure in the denominator. However, in practice, while one may be able to get this information for the subject company, the data for the guideline companies will rarely be available. Another alternative is to use total interest expense in the numerator and total interest-bearing debt in the denominator. The problem with this, however, is that often the fiscal year-end amount of short-term interest-bearing debt does not relate to the amount of interest expense that was paid during the year on the average amount of short-term interest-bearing debt utilized. To correct for this, one would have to find out what the average amount of short-term interest-bearing debt was over the course of the year, and that depth of analysis may not be justified.

Due to these complexities, for practical purposes it is acceptable to use the ratio as we have defined it. However, the analyst is well advised to research both the subject and guideline companies' use of short-term debt to determine whether to adjust this ratio to include all interest-bearing debt.

The analyst should be aware of two other potential problems with the above formula. First, the comparisons among rates of return may not be meaningful when comparing companies with dissimilar capital structures. Second, the rates of return can be misleading in the cases of many (especially smaller) companies that show on their balance sheet short-term liabilities that actually are being used as long-term financing.

Return on Total Assets

The computations for *return on total assets* are similar to those for return on investment, with the same issues of income tax adjustments and beginning or average assets. A realistic analysis of return on total assets should not be influenced by how the company chooses to use debt in its capital structure.

Again, using figures from Exhibits 21–3 and 21–4, the computation of return on assets for Warm Chicken Company for 2004 is as follows:

Formula 8–31

$$\frac{\text{Net income} \atop \text{+ Interest (1 – Tax rate)}}{\left(\text{Beginning total assets} \atop \text{+ Ending total assets} \right) \div 2} = \frac{\$2,883,000 + \$6,079,000\,(1 - 0.40)}{\left(\$321,154,000 \atop + \$295,902,000 \right) \div 2} = 2.1\%$$

or

$$\frac{\text{Net income + Interest}}{\left(\text{Beginning total assets} \atop \text{+ Ending total assets} \right) \div 2} = \frac{\$2,883,000 + \$6,079,000}{\left(\$321,154,000 \atop + \$295,902,000 \right) \div 2} = 2.9\%$$

Based on beginning assets, the ratio becomes:

Formula 8–32

$$\frac{\text{Net income} + \text{Interest}(1 - \text{Tax rate})}{\text{Beginning total assets}} = \frac{\$2,883,000 + \$6,079,000\,(1 - 0.40)}{\$321,154,000} = 2.0\%$$

or

$$\frac{\text{Net income} + \text{Interest}}{\text{Beginning total assets}} = \frac{\$2,883,000 + \$6,079,000}{\$321,154,000} = 2.8\%$$

Use care when comparing these ratios to published ratios to determine whether the bases are an average or beginning or year-end figures. The return-on-investment ratios shown in Exhibit 21–6 are calculated using both average and ending equity and both average and ending total assets.

Asset Utilization Ratios

Asset utilization ratios indicate how efficiently the company is employing its assets in its operations. These are almost always based on average asset levels, unless a study used for industry comparative ratio analysis calculates them using year-ending asset figures. This series of ratios relates sales to each of several assets or asset groups. Ratios sometimes computed include sales to cash, to accounts receivable, to inventories, to working capital, to fixed assets, to other assets, and to total assets (discussed under the "Activity Ratios" section earlier in this chapter).

Summary

Comparative ratio analysis helps identify and quantify some of the company's strengths and weaknesses, both on an absolute basis and relative to guideline companies or industry norms.

The analyst should allow for changes in the subject company's accounting policies during the period under analysis and differences in accounting policies between the subject company and the guideline companies or industry norms. The analyst should also be aware of off-balance sheet financing that may not be reflected in the ratio analysis.

Analysis of the various ratios will help the analyst to evaluate the subject company's financial position and to understand the risks it may be facing. The relative significance of the various ratios will differ in each valuation.

A further discussion of the valuation implications of these comparative ratios is included in Chapter 21, "Sample Report."

Part III

Business Valuation Approaches and Methods

Chapter 9

Income Approach: Discounted Future Economic Income Method

THEORY OF VALUATION

The value of an asset is the present value of its expected returns. Specifically, you expect an asset to provide a stream of returns during the period of time you own it. To convert this estimated stream of returns to a value for the security, you must discount this stream at your required rate of return. This process of valuation requires estimates of (1) the stream of expected returns and (2) the required rate of return on the investment.[1]

Value today always equals future cash flow discounted at the opportunity cost of capital.[2]

This chapter presents the most commonly accepted methods of discounting expected economic income. This is the very heart of valuation. The next chapter deals with capitalizing economic income. We present discounting first because, as shown in the next chapter, capitalizing is merely a shortcut version of discounting. We believe that the reader needs a basic understanding of discounting in order to

---

[1] Frank K. Reilly, *Investment Analysis and Portfolio Management*, 7th ed. (Mason, OH: South-Western, 2003), p. 374.
[2] Richard A. Brealey and Stewart C. Myers, *Principles of Corporate Finance*, 7th ed. (New York: McGraw-Hill, Inc., 2003), p. 75.

thoroughly understand the theory of capitalizing and to evaluate the reasonableness of any capitalization method that may be presented.

This chapter necessarily includes many algebraic formulas and quantitative examples. We have tried to present each formula clearly and precisely, with each variable defined in understandable terms, and with examples provided. In doing so, we hope to make a somewhat technical topic clear and understandable not only to appraisers, but also to accountants, attorneys, business owners, and other appraisal users who do not necessarily have a finance background.

Introduction: Theoretical and Practical Soundness of the Approach

When someone buys a company or an interest in a company, what is that person really buying? Management? Markets? Technological skills? Products? Although each of these factors may be involved in the investment decision, what is actually being bought is a stream of prospective economic income.

It may be worthwhile to define the term *economic income*, since we will use it in this discussion of the income approach to valuation. As the term implies, we define income according to the economists' definition and not the accountants' definition. In the landmark text *Economics*, Paul D. Samuelson and William D. Nordhaus define income as: "The flow of wages, interest, payments, dividends, and other receipts accruing to an individual or nation during a period of time (usually a year)."[3]

For purposes of this discussion of the income approach, we will use a similarly broad definition of economic income. We define economic income as any inflow into an economic unit in exchange for goods, services, or capital.

In this definition, the economic unit can be either a business entity (e.g., a corporation, partnership, or professional practice) or an individual (e.g., an individual investor). And, the inflow can be gross (before recognition of any outflows) or net (after recognition of certain outflows). So, from the perspective of a business entity, economic income could mean, among other things, gross revenues, gross profits, net operating profits, net income before tax, net income after tax, operating cash flow, net cash flow before tax, net cash flow after tax, or net cash flow available for distribution to owners (e.g., dividends). Any of these measures of economic income could be converted into a value indication through the use of a discount (or capitalization) rate appropriate to the measure of economic income. Of course, different discount (or capitalization) rates would be appropriate to the different measures of economic income.

In theory, the value of a business or an interest in a business depends on the future economic benefits that will accrue to that business, with the value of those future benefits being discounted back to a present value at some appropriate discount rate. In other words, the basic concept of the income approach is to project the future economic income associated with the investment and to discount this projected economic income stream to a present value at a discount rate appropriate for the expected risk of the prospective income stream.

The income approach is based upon the economic principle of anticipation (sometimes also called the principle of expectation). In this approach, the value of

---

[3] Paul A. Samuelson and William D. Nordhaus, *Economics*, 18th ed. (New York: McGraw-Hill, 2005), p. 741.

the subject investment (i.e., the subject business interest) is the present value of the economic income expected to be generated by the investment. As the name of this economic principle implies, the investor "anticipates" the economic income "expected" to be earned from the investment. This expectation of prospective economic income is converted to a present worth—that is, the indicated value of the subject business interest.

For valuation purposes, the measurement of economic income to be analyzed can be defined in several different ways, as discussed in various sections of the chapter. Different measurements of economic income that are commonly analyzed in this approach include the following:

1. Payouts (e.g., dividends, interest, security sale proceeds, or partnership withdrawals)
2. Cash flow (often measured as net cash flow)
3. Some measure of accounting earnings (often net income or net operating income)

In any event, it is essential that the economic income stream that is projected be clearly defined and that a discount rate appropriate for that definition of economic income be used in the analysis.

The discounted economic income method of the income approach to valuation is often used in the context of merger and acquisition analysis. In these instances, this method is not always used to estimate a fair market value. This is because the projections used in a merger and acquisition analysis may be specific to the individual acquirer. While the discount rate in a merger and acquisition analysis should reflect the risk of the investment and not the risk of the acquirer's existing business, the appropriate discount rate may not be the stand-alone discount rate of the target business; rather, it may reflect the risk of combining the target business with the acquirer's existing business. Accordingly, such an analysis would estimate investment value, use value, acquisition value, or some other buyer-specific standard of value.

However, the same type of discounted economic income analysis could be performed—but with market-derived projections of economic income and with a market-derived discount rate—in order to estimate the fair market value of the subject business interest.

The discounted economic income method may also be used to value a wide range of valuation subjects. For example, this method may be used in the valuation of both controlling and noncontrolling ownership interests, provided that (1) the prospective economic income stream is consistent with the business interest subject to valuation, and (2) the discount rate is appropriate for that measure of economic income and for that particular valuation subject.

Since the value of a business interest depends on the prospective economic income, the correct application of this method requires a projection of the economic income that is relevant to the valuation subject, be that dividends, cash flow, accounting earnings, or some other measure of economic income. The discounted economic income method is practical only to the extent that the projections used are reasonable to the decision maker for whom the valuation is being prepared. Without supportable projections, the discounted economic income method can convey an aura of precision that is not justified.

Such economic income projections may be difficult to make—and even more difficult to get two or more parties with different investment perspectives and transaction expectations to agree on. Therefore, valuation analysts have developed various other approaches to and methods of valuation, based on both historical and prospective economic data. These approaches are discussed in subsequent chapters.

However, the valuation analyst should keep in mind that the value of an investment is a function of what that investment will do for an owner in the future, not what it has done for an owner in the past. Therefore, regardless of the valuation approach being used, in order for the analysis to make rational economic sense from a financial point of view, the results should be compatible with what would result if a well-supported discounted economic income analysis were carried out. Of course, the discounted economic income analysis should include both (1) projected income from the operations of the investment for a discrete period of time and (2) an estimate of the value of cash flows beyond the discrete projection period (the terminal or expected sale or liquidation value).

The Basic Discounted Economic Income Framework

The basic arithmetic of the present value calculation is presented in Exhibit 9–1.

The basic formula for valuation using the discounted economic income method is as follows:

Formula 9–1

$$PV = \sum_{i=1}^{n} \frac{E_i}{(1+k)^i}$$

where:

PV = Present value
$\sum$ = Sum of
n = The last period for which economic income is expected; n may equal infinity (i.e., ∞) if the economic income is expected to continue in perpetuity
E_i = Expected economic income in the ith period in the future (paid at the end of the period)
k = Discount rate (the cost of capital, i.e., the expected rate of return available in the market for other investments that are comparable in terms of risk and other investment characteristics)
i = The period (usually stated as a number of years) in the future in which the prospective economic income is expected to be received

This basic formula can be expanded very simply as follows:

Formula 9–2

$$PV = \frac{E_1}{(1+k)} + \frac{E_2}{(1+k)^2} + \frac{E_3}{(1+k)^3} + \ldots + \frac{E_n}{(1+k)^n}$$

where:

$E_{1, 2, 3, \text{ etc.}}$ = Expected economic income in the 1st period, 2nd period, 3rd period, and so on
E_n = Expected economic income in the nth or last period in which an element of income is expected (An investment with an

Exhibit 9–1

Arithmetic of Discounting vs. Compounding

COMPOUNDING

The formula for estimating the future value of an amount invested at an annually compounded interest rate for a certain number of years is as follows:

$$FV = PV (1 + k)^i$$

where:

FV = Future value

PV = Present value

k = Rate of return

i = ith year (the number of years into the future when the principal plus the compound rate of return will be received)

Example

Assume that we invest $1,000 for three years at 10 percent interest. Substituting in the preceding formula gives us the following:

$$
\begin{aligned}
FV &= \$1,000 (1 + 0.10)^3 \\
&= \$1,000 (1.10 \times 1.10 \times 1.10) \\
&= \$1,000 (1.331) \\
&= \$1,331
\end{aligned}
$$

DISCOUNTING

Start with the formula for compounding:

$$FV = PV (1 + k)^i$$

As we learned in basic algebra, we can divide both sides of an equation by the same factor:

$$\frac{FV}{(1+k)^i} = \frac{PV(1+k)^i}{(1+k)^i}$$

Also, if the same factor appears in both the numerator and the denominator of an expression, we can cancel them out:

$$\frac{FV}{(1+k)^i} = \frac{PV(\cancel{1+k})^i}{(\cancel{1+k})^i}$$

We then have the formula for discounting from a future value to a present value. Since it is customary to put the dependent variable (the value we are solving for) on the left-hand side, the basic formula for discounting is written as follows:

$$PV = \frac{FV}{(1+k)^i}$$

Example

If we can earn 10 percent annually compounded interest, how much do we have to invest today to get a lump sum payment of $1,331 exactly three years from now? Substituting in the preceding formula gives us the following:

$$
\begin{aligned}
PV &= \frac{\$1,331}{(1+10)^3} \\
&= \frac{\$1,331}{1.331} \\
&= \$1,000
\end{aligned}
$$

DISCOUNTING A SERIES OF FUTURE ECONOMIC INCOME FLOWS

Discounting a series of future economic income flows simply involves discounting each individual future flow and adding up the present values of these flows to get a total present value for the series of flows. The formula for discounting a series of future economic income flows may be written as follows:

$$PV = \sum \frac{FV^i}{(1+k)^i}$$

continued

Exhibit 9–1

Arithmetic of Discounting vs. Compounding (continued)

The capital Greek letter sigma (Σ) stands for "sum of." It means to add up each of the components that follow, in this case the present values of each of the expected future amounts.

Example

Let's assume that a bond pays $100 interest at the end of each year for three years and pays $1,000 principal at the bond's maturity date at the end of three years. If the market requires a 10 percent total rate of return on bonds of this quality and maturity at this time, what is the present value of the bond? Substituting in the preceding formula gives us the following:

$$PV = \frac{\$100}{(1+0.10)} + \frac{\$100}{(1+0.10)^2} + \frac{\$100}{(1+0.10)^3} + \frac{\$1,000}{(1+0.10)^3}$$

$$= \frac{\$100}{1.10} + \frac{\$100}{(1.10 \times 1.10)} + \frac{\$100}{(1.10 \times 1.10 \times 1.10)} + \frac{\$1,000}{(1.10 \times 1.10 \times 1.10)}$$

$$= \$90.9 + \$82.64 + \$75.13 + \$751.31$$

$$= \$1,000$$

It can readily be seen from this calculation that if the discount rate (i.e., the rate of return required to attract capital to the investment) goes up, then the present value goes down, and vice versa.

Note: In all the examples in this book, unless otherwise indicated, it is assumed for simplicity that compounding is on an annual basis, and that all returns are received at the end of each year. With minor adjustments in the arithmetic, assumptions of semiannual, quarterly, monthly, daily, or even continuous compounding can be accommodated. It can also be assumed that proceeds are received at some time other than the end of the year. For example, proceeds received at the middle of the year, or more or less evenly throughout the year, may be accommodated by the midyear discounting convention.

---

expected perpetual life can be assumed to terminate at some point, since income in the remotely distant future will have only negligible impact when discounted to present value.)

k = Discount rate (The equation assumes that k is always the same.)

1, 2, 3, etc. = 1st period, 2nd period, 3rd period, and so on

This basic valuation model, which is central to the income approach to valuation, has only two variables:

1. The amount of the expected prospective economic income in each period
2. The required rate of return (or yield rate) by which the expected prospective economic income receipts should be discounted

Before attempting to quantify the numbers that go into this model, it is first necessary to define each of the variables more specifically.

The Numerator: Expected Prospective Economic Income

Income Associated with What? The answer to this question depends on the answer to one of the questions in Chapter 2, "What exactly are we valuing?" Usually the focus is on the amount of economic income available to one of the following categories of investments:

1. One class of common equity
2. All classes of common equity

3. All classes of equity
4. All equity and all long-term debt
5. All equity and all interest-bearing debt
6. All equity and all debt (i.e., total business assets)

When debt is included in what is being valued, the result is often referred to as either "the value of the business entity," "the business enterprise value," "the total capital value," or "market value of invested capital" (MVIC). For more discussion of defining the capital structure when debt is included, see the subsection on defining the capital structure under the section titled "Discounting Economic Income Available to Overall Capital."

Of course, we are sometimes interested in projecting the economic income associated with other types of investments, such as asset/property investments (e.g., income-producing real estate), security investments (e.g., minority interests in shares of stocks or in bonds), or intangible asset investments (e.g., patents, trademarks, or copyrights).

Obviously, the economic income to be measured should be that level of income that is associated with—and available to—whatever business or investment interest is being valued.

Definition of Economic Income Measured. Depending partly on the answer to the question, "Income associated with what?" there can be many ways of measuring the economic income used in the valuation. Some of the most common measurements of economic income include the following:

1. Dividends (or other payouts to security holders, such as partnership withdrawals)
2. Net cash flow to equity (NCF_e in the notation used in this book):

     Net income (after taxes)
   + Noncash charges (e.g., depreciation, amortization, deferred taxes)
   − Capital expenditures (the net changes in fixed and other noncurrent assets)[*]
   +/− Changes in net working capital[*]
   +/− Net changes in long-term debt[*]
   = Net cash flow to equity[†]

   [*] Assumes that the amounts are those necessary to support projected business operations.

   [†] If there are preferred dividends, they will have to be subtracted, of course, if the objective is to estimate net cash flow available to holders of common equity. If one wants to project net cash flow available to all equity and interest-bearing debt holders, then interest needs to be added to the income measurement, but changes in long-term debt need not be considered (see following point 3).

3. Net cash flow to overall invested capital (NCF_f in the notation used in this book):[4]

     Net income (after taxes) available to common shareholders
   + Noncash charges

---

[4] An alternative formula for net cash flow to overall invested capital is the following:

     Earnings before interest and taxes
   − Taxes on earnings before interest and taxes (EBIT) at the effective tax rate
   + Noncash charges
   − Capital expenditures
   +/− Changes in working capital
   = Net cash flow to overall invested capital

−   Capital expenditures*
+/−   Changes in working capital*
+   Interest expense, net of the tax effect (interest expense × [1 − tax rate])
+   Preferred dividends, if any
=   Net cash flow to overall invested capital
      * Assumes that the amounts are those necessary to support projected business operations.

4. Net income (after taxes)

It is noteworthy that the capital expenditures, net changes in working capital, and net changes in long-term debt components of net cash flow may be negative. In other words, if there are reductions (sales) of capital assets, decreases in net working capital, or decreases in long-term debt, these components would be represented by negative numbers. And, the subtraction of a negative number (e.g., a decrease in net working capital) would represent an increment—instead of a decrement—to net cash flow.

It is also noteworthy that the measures of net cash flow defined here (i.e., to equity and to overall invested capital) are different from the measures of cash flows reported in a Statement of Cash Flows prepared in accordance with generally accepted accounting principles.

Of course, many other variables representing some relevant measurement of economic income may be estimated. These might include, for example, pretax income, net operating income, or some other measure of accounting income. However, for many of these other economic income measures, it may be difficult, if not impossible, to develop an empirically supportable discount rate and to justify them as benefit streams that an investor is willing to anticipate and pay for.

The Denominator: The Discount Rate

Definition of a Discount Rate. In economic terms, a present value discount rate is an "opportunity cost," that is, the expected rate of return (or yield) that an investor would have to give up by investing in the subject investment instead of investing in available alternative investments that are comparable in terms of risk and other investment characteristics.

The discount rate is the cost of capital for that particular category of investment. It is determined by market conditions as of the valuation date and as they apply to the specific characteristics of the subject contemplated investment.[5]

Matching the Discount Rate with the Definition of the Prospective Economic Income. The choice of the discount rate is driven by the definition of economic income used in the numerator. The discount rate used in the analysis must be appropriate for the definition of the economic income in the numerator and for the class of capital (or other type of investment) to which it applies.

As a practical matter, the choice of economic income used in the numerator may be constrained by the ability, or lack of it, to develop an empirically supportable

---

[5] To the extent that a particular buyer or seller chooses to use a discounted economic income analysis based on a discount rate that deviates from the market consensus rate as of the valuation date, the resulting indicated value will depart from the strict standards of *fair market value* and, probably, approximate *investment value*, as defined in Chapter 2.

discount rate. For this reason, we sometimes find definitions of economic income used in market approach methods, where a market-derived capitalization rate is available, that are not used in discounting methods. In the next chapter, we explain the relationship between discount rates and capitalization rates.

In any case, we cannot overemphasize how important it is that *the discount rate developed must be matched conceptually and empirically to the definition of economic income being discounted*. Also, the discount rate must reflect the degree of risk of the investment, which is discussed in some detail later.

Constant or Variable Discount Rate? A question that sometimes arises is whether the discount rate should remain constant over the projection period or should vary with time. The argument for a variable discount rate is that the investment risk may be greater—or lower—later in the projection period than it is at the beginning of the projection period. This is a highly judgmental (and usually quite subjective) matter. Most commonly, analysts use a constant discount rate—reflecting the average amount of investment risk—throughout the projection period.

Estimating the Discount Rate

As noted in Chapter 3 on business valuation theory and principles and earlier in this chapter, in a valuation estimating fair market value, *the discount rate is a market-driven rate. It represents the expected yield rate—or rate of return—necessary to induce investors to commit available funds to the subject investment, given its level of risk.*

Return and Rate of Return Defined

When we speak of *return* and *rate of return*, we are referring to the *total yield to the investor*, reflecting all dividends, interest, or other cash or cash equivalents received, plus or minus any realized or unrealized appreciation or depreciation in the investment's value. The yield rate, or rate of return, on an investment for a given time period is as follows:

Formula 9–3

$$R = \frac{\text{Ending price} - \text{Beginning price} + \text{Cash distributions}}{\text{Beginning price}}$$

where:

R = Rate of return (for the period)

This formula simply says that the investment yield—or rate of return—is equal to the ending price of an investment minus the beginning price plus any cash flows received from holding that investment, with the result divided by the initial price. For example, if Paola Pizza Parlors stock started the year at $10 per share, paid $0.50 in cash dividends during the year, and ended the year at $11.50 per share, then the total investment yield or rate of return for the year would be computed as follows:

Formula 9–4

$$R = \frac{\$11.50 - \$10.00 + \$0.50}{\$10.00} = 0.20$$

Given a series of prices for a particular investment and the economic income received by the owner of that investment, it is possible to calculate the rate of return over any time period—or over any number of subperiods.

The *discount rate* is the expected total yield rate—or rate of return—that investors require for the particular class of investment.

Components of the Discount Rate

Broken down into its simplest components, the discount rate, or the rate of return that investors require, incorporates the following elements:

1. A "risk-free rate" (the amount that an investor feels certain of realizing over the holding period). This includes:
   a. A "rental rate" for forgoing the use of funds over the holding period
   b. The expected rate of inflation over the holding period[6]
2. A premium for risk. This includes:
   a. Systematic risk (that risk that relates to movements in returns on the investment market in general)
   b. Unsystematic risk (that risk that is specific to the subject investment)

Other important characteristics of an investment that sometimes are incorporated into the discount rate are (1) the degree of minority ownership versus control position represented by the investment and (2) the degree of ready marketability or lack of marketability.

Control is *most* often demonstrated through the level of cash flow used by the analyst; a further discount for lack of control (DLOC) may be either appropriately reflected as an increment to the discount rate or considered separately if the analyst has started with control cash flow. Although there are exceptions, valuation analysts often explicitly treat the important valuation issues of ownership control and lack of marketability separately rather than implicitly incorporating those issues in the estimation of the appropriate discount rate.[7]

The Risk-Free Rate

The "risk-free" rate generally used is the rate available on instruments that are considered to have virtually no possibility of default, such as U.S. Treasury obligations. As noted earlier, such instruments compensate the holders for renting out their money and for the expected loss of purchasing power (inflation) during the holding period.

---

[6] This assumes that the forecasted returns are in nominal terms, that is, that they include expected inflation over the forecast period. In economies that are characterized by hyperinflation, the practical procedure is to perform the discounted income analysis in "real" terms—that is, removing inflation from both the income forecast and also the discount rate. In any case, the forecast income and the discount rate must "match" in this respect—that is, either both the forecast income and the discount rate include inflation, or neither of them does.

[7] One notable exception is in the field of venture capital, where buyers of interests often incorporate the lack of marketability characteristic into their required rate of return in their discounted economic income analysis.

The ultimate risk-free security is considered to be the short-term U.S. Treasury bill. However, in estimating the cost of capital for equity investments, the short-term Treasury bill has an important shortcoming: its maturity does not match the anticipated investment horizon (or holding period) of most equity investors. The Treasury bill rate is much more volatile than longer-term Treasury rates, and the yield may not reflect longer-term inflation expectations. Therefore, most valuation analysts prefer to use the yield on a long-term Treasury bond—such as the 20-year U.S. Treasury bond—as the risk-free component for estimating the cost of equity capital.[8]

The Equity Risk Premium

Over and above the risk-free return, investors must expect some additional return to induce them to invest in non-Treasury bonds, in equities, or in similar securities—to compensate them for the additional risk incurred in such an investment. In the context of cost of capital, we define *risk* as *the degree of uncertainty as to the realization of the expected future returns*.

For a given level of expected future returns, the market will pay more to the extent that the realization of those returns is more certain and less to the extent that their realization is less certain. In other words, for a given level of expected prospective economic income (e.g., cash flow, dividends, accounting earnings, and the like), the lower the risk, the higher the present value, or conversely, the higher the risk, the lower the present value.

The mechanism by which the assessment of risk is translated into its effect on value is normally the discount rate.[9]

Since the cost of capital is one of the most important variables in the valuation of a business or a business interest, both academicians and practitioners have expended an enormous amount of theoretical and empirical research effort in an attempt to quantify the effect of risk on the cost of capital for equity investments. The state of the art in the twenty-first century involves incorporating one or all of the following elements into the discount rate to reflect risk:

1. A basic equity risk premium over the risk-free rate selected as the base
2. One or more coefficients modifying the basic equity risk premium based on industry or other characteristics that are expected to affect the degree of risk for the subject investment
3. An element reflecting the size effect
4. A final adjustment reflecting judgments about investment-specific risk for the subject investment that was not captured in the first three elements

Extensive empirical research that attempts to quantify the effect of the first three of these elements on the discount rate is available. Nonetheless, there are

---

[8] The reason for using 20-year rather than 30-year Treasury bonds is that Morningstar's (formerly Ibbotson Associates') *Stocks, Bonds, Bills, and Inflation (SBBI) Yearbook* includes equity risk premium data related to 20-year Treasury bond maturities, but no such equity risk premium data are available for 30-year maturities.

[9] Bierman and Smidt, two Cornell professors, make a convincing argument that the theoretically most correct way to handle the element of risk is to adjust the future expectations stream to what they call a *certainty adjusted equivalent*. They adjust the expectations downward by some factor that reflects the probability that the expectations will be achieved. They then apply the same cost of capital to the valuation of all alternative investment choices. They do quite a good job, in our opinion, of explaining the rationale for this approach (Harold Bierman, Jr., and Seymour Smidt, *The Capital Budgeting Decision*, 8th ed. [Englewood Cliffs, NJ: Prentice-Hall, 1992]). Notwithstanding Bierman and Smidt's fine presentation, however, the more commonly used approach to incorporating risk into the valuation of a business is to reflect it in the cost of capital.

choices to be made based on informed analysis of the evidence at each step. The fourth element, the unsystematic risk specific to the subject business or business interest, still remains largely a matter of the analyst's judgment, without a commonly accepted set of empirical support evidence. The analyst will base this judgment on factors discussed in Part II of this book, such as financial statement and comparative ratio analysis and the qualitative matters to be considered during the site visit and management interviews. However, after carefully analyzing these elements of investment-specific risk, there is no accepted model for quantifying their exact effect on the discount rate. The analyst must depend on experience and judgment in this final element of the discount rate development, but should explicitly describe the factors that affect this final element.

Exhibit 9–2 gives a schematic summary of the elements of a discount rate using the capital asset pricing model (CAPM) applicable when net cash flow to equity is the measure of economic income being discounted. The basic equity risk premium, modifications to it, and the effect of company size on the equity risk premium are discussed in some detail in subsequent sections.

Later in the chapter, a procedure is presented to convert a discount rate applicable to net cash flow to a discount rate applicable to net income, providing that certain fairly stringent assumptions are met.

The Capital Asset Pricing Model

The capital asset pricing model is part of a larger body of economic theory known as *capital market theory*. Capital market theory also includes *security analysis* and *portfolio management theory*, a *normative theory* that describes how investors *should* behave in selecting common stocks for their portfolios under a given set of assumptions. In contrast, the CAPM is a *positive* theory, meaning that it describes the market relationships that *will* result *if* investors behave in the manner prescribed by portfolio theory.

The CAPM is a conceptual cornerstone of modern capital market theory. Its relevance to business valuations is that businesses and business interests are a subset of the investment opportunities available in the total capital market; thus, the determination of the prices of businesses theoretically should be subject to the same economic forces and relationships that determine the prices of other investment assets.

Systematic and Unsystematic Risk

In the previous section, we defined risk conceptually as *the degree of uncertainty as to the realization of expected future returns*. Capital market theory divides risk into two components: systematic risk and unsystematic risk. Stated in nontechnical terms, *systematic risk* is the uncertainty of future returns resulting from the sensitivity of the return on the subject investment to movements in the return on the investment market as a whole. *Unsystematic risk* is a function of characteristics of the industry, the individual company, and the type of investment interest. Company characteristics could include, for example, management's ability to weather economic conditions, relations between labor and management, the possibility of

Exhibit 9–2

Schematic Diagram and Example of Elements of a Discount Rate Applicable to Expected Net Cash Flow Available to Common Equity

Risk-free rate	In the United States, usually 20-year, 5-year, or 30-day U.S. Treasury obligation yield available as of the valuation date. (Empirical equity risk premium data are available to match each of these three Treasury instrument maturities.)	4.81	20-year U.S. Treasury bond yield as of December 30, 2005. Source: *Federal Reserve Statistical Release*.
Equity risk premium (reflecting systematic risk)	Historical return data available from Ibbotson Associates based on S&P 500 stock returns over income yields of 20-year, 5-year, or 30-day U.S. Treasury instrument rates. May be modified by one or more coefficients, such as beta, based on the capital asset pricing model, and/or by other coefficients based on the arbitrage pricing theory model.	$7.17 \times 1.5 = 10.76$	Long-horizon expected equity risk premium times beta. Source for long-horizon historical equity risk premium: *SBBI Valuation Edition 2005 Yearbook*, p. 71. Source for beta: median of beta from Standard & Poor's Compustat for industry. (Note that this illustration uses Ibbotson's ERP. See the later discussion of why the authors think this is too high.)
Impact of size effect on risk	Incremental addition to the discount rate to reflect research showing additional returns to stocks of companies smaller than the S&P 500. In this case we add the Ibbotson estimate of return in excess of CAPM for the smallest 10 percent of companies on the NYSE.	6.41	Expected size premium. Source of historical size premiums: *SBBI Valuation Edition 2005 Yearbook*, p. 135.
Investment-specific risk (reflecting unsystematic risk)	Matter of analyst's judgment. May be based on ratio analysis of the subject company compared to industry averages or specific guideline companies and/or on qualitative factors such as depth and quality of management, competitive position, and so on. This element of the discount rate will be supported conceptually by the analysis done pursuant to Part II of this book. However, there is no widely accepted model or set of formulas to convert the results of these analyses into an exact quantified effect on the discount rate.	3.00	Based on analyst's judgment regarding results for the subject company compared with those for the guideline companies used.
Total discount rate Total discount rate (rounded)		24.78 25	Given the number of significant digits in the estimation of the investment-specific risk factor (and other cost of equity capital components), it is not uncommon to see the discount rate rounded to a full percentage point.

strikes, the success or failure of a particular marketing program, or any other factor specific to the company. Total risk, therefore, depends on both systematic and unsystematic factors.

The fundamental assumption of the CAPM is that the risk premium portion of the expected return on a security is a function of that security's systematic risk. Capital market theory assumes that investors hold or have the ability to hold common stocks in large, well-diversified portfolios. In fact, under the textbook version of the CAPM, all investors will hold the same portfolio of risky assets (the market portfolio), something that in fact does not occur. Under that assumption, the unsystematic risk associated with a particular company's stock is eliminated because of the portfolio's diversification. Therefore, the only risk that is pertinent to a study of capital asset pricing theory is systematic risk.

Beta: The Measure of Systematic Risk

In the capital asset pricing model, systematic risk is measured by a factor called *beta*. Beta in theory is a forward-looking risk measure. It is a function of the *excess* expected return on an individual security relative to the *excess* expected return on the market index. By "excess return," we mean the return over and above the return available on a risk-free investment (e.g., U.S. Treasuries). In fact, practitioners and many published data sources estimate this forward-looking risk measure (beta) by calculating the historical relationship observed between the return on an individual security and the return on the market as measured by a broad market index such as the Standard & Poor's 500 Stock Composite Index.

For the market index as a whole, the average beta, by definition, is 1.0. If a stock tends to have a positive excess return greater than that of the market when the market return is greater than the risk-free return, and a more negative excess return than that of the market when the market return is less than the risk-free return, then the stock's beta is greater than 1.0. If the difference between the stock's return and the risk-free return tends to be less than the difference between the market return and the risk-free return, then the stock's beta is less than 1.0.

In other words, beta measures the volatility of the excess return on an individual security relative to that of the market. Securities that have betas greater than 1.0 are characterized as aggressive securities and are riskier than the market. Securities that have betas of less than 1.0 are commonly characterized as defensive securities and have systematic risks lower than that of the market. These are generalities: risky companies can have low betas. (For example, gold mining companies are highly volatile but have low betas because the returns on such stocks are not highly correlated with market returns.)

It is possible (although not very common) for a security to have a negative beta (i.e., a beta less than zero). Such a beta would indicate that the returns of these securities are countercyclical to the returns of the broad investment market index. This is more likely to be the result of problems with the data than of a truly countercyclical stock price.

One common method for calculating beta is illustrated in Exhibit 9–3. (The computation may be performed by carrying out a regression of the excess stock returns against the excess market returns.)

Betas for small publicly traded companies are often unreliable and biased downward. A primary reason for this is that small companies trade less frequently

Exhibit 9–3

Illustrative Example of One Common Method for the Calculation of Beta

Month End, t [a]	Return on Security A [b]	Return on S&P Index [c]	Calculated Covariance [d]	Calculated Variance [e]
1/89	0.041	0.069	0.00211	0.00325
2/89	(0.007)	(0.029)	0.00045	0.00168
3/89	0.052	0.021	0.00043	0.00008
•				
•				
•				
10/98	0.113	0.077	0.00709	0.00423
11/98	0.033	0.057	0.00131	0.00203
12/98	(0.016)	0.055	(0.00086)	0.00185
Sum	0.500	1.488	0.21060	0.26240
Average	0.004	0.012	0.00176 [f]	0.00219 [g]

$$\text{Beta} = \frac{\text{Covariance (Security A, S\&P Index)}}{\text{Variance of S\&P Index}} = \frac{0.00176}{0.00219} = 0.80$$

a.   10 years or 120 months.
b.   Returns based on end-of-month prices and dividend payments.
c.   Returns based on end-of-month S&P Index.
d.   Values in this column are calculated as:

   (Observed return on Security A − Average return on Security A) × (Observed return on S&P Index − Average return on S&P Index)

   $0.00211 = [(0.041 − 0.004) × (0.069 − 0.012)]$
e.   Values in this column are calculated as:

   (Observed return on S&P Index − Average return on S&P Index)^2

   $0.00325 = (0.069 − 0.012)^2$
f.   The average of this column is the covariance between Security A and the S&P Index.
g.   The average of this column is the variance of return on the S&P Index.

than the large companies in the market index, and this leads to an apparent covariance between the company and the "market" that is lower than the reality. Academics have proposed various ways of correcting for this problem, the simplest being the "sum beta" measure, which incorporates lagged market effects in the beta statistic. This method is described in Morningstar's *SBBI Valuation Edition Yearbook*. Ibbotson Associates, now owned by Morningstar, used to publish "sum beta" estimates in its *Beta Book*, but it has since discontinued the practice, so at present there are no commercially available sources for this statistic. It is possible for analysts to estimate sum betas using an Excel spreadsheet. It should be noted that the small stock premium as measured in the *SBBI Yearbook* is sensitive to the method chosen for estimating beta. The *SBBI Yearbook* contains data on small stock premiums using alternative methods of estimating beta, and over the time horizon covered in its calculation, the sum beta approach indicates lower small stock premiums than other methods. It is also noteworthy that the Grabowski/King premiums over CAPM are estimated using the sum beta measure, and their research indicates higher size premiums than the *SBBI Yearbook* results using sum beta (though their period of measuring returns begins in 1963, whereas the *SBBI Yearbook* begins in 1926).[10]

Using Beta to Estimate Expected Rate of Return

The capital asset pricing model leads to the conclusion that the equity risk premium (the required excess rate of return for a security over and above the risk-free rate) is a linear function of the security's beta. This linear function is described in the following univariate linear regression formula:

Formula 9–5

$$E(R_i) = R_f + B(RP_m)$$

where:

$E(R_i)$ = Expected return on an individual security

R_f = Rate of return available on a risk-free security (as of the valuation date)

B = Beta for the individual security

RP_m = Equity risk premium for the market as a whole (or, by definition, the equity risk premium for a security with a beta of 1.0)

To illustrate the use of this formula as part of the process of estimating a company's cost of equity capital, consider stocks of average size; publicly traded companies *i, j,* and *k,* with betas of 0.8, 1.0, and 1.2, respectively; a risk-free rate in the market at the valuation date of 7 percent (0.07); and a market equity risk premium of 5 percent (0.05). The expected investment rate of return on common equity for stocks of these companies would be computed as follows:

Formula 9–6

$$
\begin{aligned}
E(R_i) &= 0.07 + 0.8(0.05) \\
&= 0.07 + 0.04 \\
&= 0.11 \\
E(R_j) &= 0.07 + 1.0(0.05) \\
&= 0.07 + 0.05 \\
&= 0.12 \\
E(R_k) &= 0.07 + 1.2(0.05) \\
&= 0.07 + 0.06 \\
&= 0.13
\end{aligned}
$$

Exhibit 9–2 and later sections of this chapter discuss sources for the market risk-free rate, the equity risk premium, and betas.

The linear relationship just discussed is presented schematically in Exhibit 9–4, which shows the security market line. According to capital asset pricing theory, if the combination of the expected rate of return on a given security and its risk, as measured by beta, places it below the security market line, such as security X in Exhibit 9–4, that security (e.g., common stock) is mispriced. It is mispriced

---

[10]See, for example, Roger Ibbotson, Paul Kapplan, and James Peterson, "Estimates of Small Stock Betas Are Much Too Low," *Journal of Portfolio Management,* Vol. 24, 1977, pp. 104–111; Morningstar's *SBBI Valuation Edition Yearbook*; Elroy Dimson, "Risk Measurement When Shares Are Subject to Infrequent Trading," *Journal of Financial Economics,* Vol. 7, 1979.

Exhibit 9–4

Security Market Line

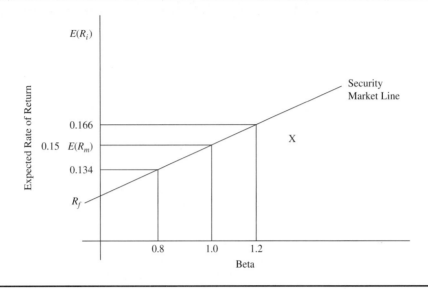

In this diagram:

$E(R_i)$ = Expected return on the individual security
$E(R_m)$ = Expected return on the market
R_f = Risk-free rate available as of the valuation date

In a market in perfect equilibrium, all securities would fall on the security market line. Thus, security X is mispriced, with a return less than it would be on the security market line.

in the sense that the return on that security is less than what it would be if the security were correctly priced, assuming fully efficient capital markets.

For the return on such a security to be appropriate for that security's risk, the price of the security must decline, allowing the rate of return to increase until it is just sufficient to compensate the investor for bearing the security's risk. In equilibrium, the prices of all common stocks in the market adjust until the rate of return on each is sufficient to compensate investors for holding that stock. In that situation, the systematic risk/expected rate of return characteristics of all those securities will place them on the security market line.

Levered and Unlevered Betas

Published betas for publicly traded stocks reflect the actual capital structure of each respective company. As a result, they can be referred to as *levered betas*, or betas reflecting the actual financial leverage of the company's capital structure. If the leverage of the company subject to valuation differs significantly from the leverage of the guideline companies selected for analysis, it may be desirable to adjust the guideline betas before using them in estimating the required rate of return on equity for the subject company in the context of the CAPM.

This adjustment is performed by first computing *unlevered betas* for the guideline companies. An *unlevered beta* is the beta that the company would have if it had no debt. The second step is to decide where the subject company's risk would fall on an unlevered basis relative to that of the guideline companies. The third and final step is to relever the beta for the subject company on the basis of one or more assumed capital structures. The result will be a market-derived beta that has been specifically adjusted for the degree of financial leverage of the subject company.[11]

To summarize, the steps are as follows:

1. Compute an unlevered beta for each of the guideline companies.
2. Decide where the risk would fall for the subject company relative to the guideline companies, assuming that all had 100 percent equity capital structures.
3. Relever the beta for the subject company based on one or more assumed capital structures.

Formulas and an example for carrying out this process are presented in Exhibit 9–5. Of course, this financial leverage adjustment procedure takes all of the assumptions of the capital asset pricing model as given.

Keep in mind that capital structures for both the guideline and the subject companies are assumed to be at market value in this process. If the relevered beta is used to estimate the *market value* of the company on a controlling ownership basis, and if it is anticipated that the actual capital structure will be adjusted to the proportions of debt and equity in the assumed capital structure, then only one assumed capital structure is necessary. However, if the amount of debt in the subject capital structure will *not* be adjusted, an iterative process may be required. The initial *assumed* capital structure for the subject will influence the cost of equity, which will, in turn, influence the relative proportions of debt and equity at market value. It may be necessary to try several assumed capital structures until one of them produces an estimate of equity value that actually results in the assumed capital structure.

This process of unlevering and relevering betas to an assumed capital structure is based upon the assumption that the business interest subject to valuation has the ability to change the capital structure of the subject company. In the case of the valuation of a noncontrolling ownership interest, for example, the valuation subject may not have that ability. Note, however, that for those valuations that start with the valuation of 100 percent of the subject company and then consider lack of control and lack of marketability discounts, the adjustment to an assumed capital structure would be appropriate.

Assumptions Underlying the Capital Asset Pricing Model

The assumptions underlying the capital asset pricing model are as follows:

1. Investors are risk averse.
2. Rational investors seek to hold efficient portfolios—that is, portfolios that are fully diversified.
3. All investors have identical investment time horizons (i.e., expected holding periods).

---

[11] Robert S. Hamada, "Portfolio Analysis, Market Equilibrium and Corporation Finance," *Journal of Finance*, Vol. 24, March 1969, pp. 19–30.

Exhibit 9–5

Computing Unlevered and Relevered Betas

The following is one commonly used formula for computing an unlevered beta (a beta assuming 100 percent equity in the capital structure).

$$B_U = \frac{B_L}{1 + (1 - t)(W_d / W_e)}$$

where:

B_U	=	Beta unlevered
B_L	=	Beta levered
t	=	Tax rate for the company
W_d	=	Percentage of debt in the capital structure
W_e	=	Percentage of equity in the capital structure

Example:

Assume the following for guideline company A:

Levered (published) beta: 1.2

Tax rate: 0.40

Capital structure: 30% debt, 70% equity

$$B_U = \frac{1.2}{1 + (1 - 0.40)(0.30 \div 0.70)}$$
$$= \frac{1.2}{1 + 0.60(0.429)}$$
$$= \frac{1.2}{1.257}$$
$$= 0.95$$

Assume that you made this calculation for all the guideline companies, the average unlevered beta was 0.90, and you believe that the riskiness of your subject company, on an unlevered basis, is about equal to the average for the guideline companies. The next step is to relever the beta for your subject company based on its tax rate and one or more assumed capital structures. The formula to adjust an unlevered beta to a levered beta is as follows:

$$B_L = B_U [1 + (1 - t) (W_d/W_e)]$$

where the definitions of the variables are the same as in the formula for computing unlevered betas except that they pertain to the subject private company.

Example:

Assume the following for the subject company:

Unlevered beta: 0.90

Tax rate: 0.30

Capital structure: 60% debt, 40% equity

B_L	=	$0.90 [1 + (1 - 0.30) (0.60 \div 0.40)]$
	=	$0.90 [1 + 0.70 (1.5)]$
	=	$0.90 (2.05)$
	=	1.85

These formulas are consistent with the theory that:

- The discount rate used to calculate the tax savings on interest expense equals the cost of debt capital (i.e., the tax savings on interest expense have the same risk as debt).
- Debt capital has negligible risk that interest payments and principal repayments will not be made when owed, which implies that tax deductions on the interest expense will be realized in the period in which the interest is paid.
- The value of tax deductions on interest expense is proportionate to the market value of debt capital (i.e., $= t \times W_d$).

But these formulas are correct only if one assumes constant debt. The formulas are not correct if the assumption is that debt capital remains at a constant percentage of equity capital (equivalent to debt increasing in proportion to net cash flow to the firm in every period).[*] The formulas are often wrongly assumed to hold in general.

---

[*] Enrique R. Arzac and Lawrence R. Glosten, "A Reconsideration of Tax Shield Valuation," *European Financial Management,* 2005, pp. 453–461. See Appendix 10.1. See Shannon Pratt and Roger Grabowski, *Cost of Capital: Estimation and Applications,* 3rd ed (Hoboken, NJ, John Wiley & Sons, 2007) for a complete discussion of alternative formulas.

4. All investors have identical expectations about such variables as expected rates of return and how capitalization rates are generated.

5. There are no transaction costs.

6. There are no investment-related taxes (i.e., there may be corporate income taxes).

7. The rate received from lending money is the same as the cost of borrowing money.

8. The market has perfect divisibility and liquidity (i.e., investors can readily buy or sell any desired fractional interest).

Obviously, the extent to which these assumptions are or are not met in the real world will have a bearing on the application of the CAPM for the valuation of closely held businesses. While these assumptions appear unrealistic on their face, a "modified CAPM" that includes adjustments for size and specific company risks is generally accepted.

The Size Premium

Several research studies of publicly traded companies provide convincing evidence that, on average, smaller companies have higher rates of return than larger companies.[12] The *total* risk, or standard deviation of annual returns, also increases with decreasing company size.[13]

The *SBBI Valuation Edition 2005 Yearbook* states:

> First, the greater risk of small stocks does not, in the context of the capital asset pricing model (CAPM), fully account for their higher returns over the long term. In the CAPM, only systematic or beta risk is rewarded; small company stocks have had returns in excess of those implied by their betas. [14]

(For an example from the *SBBI Valuation Edition Yearbook*, see Exhibit 9-11.)

The implication would seem to be that the market does not ignore unsystematic risk; indeed, it demands and achieves extra return for accepting it. The 2005 *SBBI* data showing higher returns to higher standard deviation stocks are consistent with Shannon Pratt's research as far back as 1926, which showed increasing returns to risk as measured by the standard deviation.[15]

We believe that the reflection of this unsystematic risk in the discount rate is especially important for the valuation of closely held stocks. Most owners of closely held businesses or interests in closely held businesses do not diversify their investment

---

[12] See, for example, Eugene Fama and Kenneth French, "The Cross Section of Expected Stock Returns," *Journal of Finance*, Vol. 47, 1992, pp. 427–465; Eugene Fama and Kenneth French, "Common Risk Factors in the Returns on Stocks and Bonds," University of Chicago Working Paper No. 360, November 1992; Eugene Fama and Kenneth French, "The Economic Fundamentals of Size and Book-to-Market Equity," University of Chicago Working Paper No. 361, September 1992; Christopher B. Barry and Stephen J. Brown, "Differential Information and the Small Firm Effect," *Journal of Financial Economics*, Vol. 13, 1984, pp. 283–294; and Rolf W. Banz, "The Relationship between Return and Market Value of Common Stocks," *Journal of Financial Economics*, Vol. 9, 1981, pp. 3–18. Also see Chapter 7 of *SBBI Valuation Edition 2005 Yearbook* (Chicago: Ibbotson Associates, 2005).

[13] *SBBI Valuation Edition 2005 Yearbook*, p. 129.

[14] Ibid., p. 132.

[15] Shannon P. Pratt, "Relationship between Variability of Past Returns and Levels of Future Returns for Common Stocks, 1926–1960" (abridged version, previously unpublished), in *Frontiers of Investment Analysis*, revised ed., E. Bruce Fredrikson, ed. (Scranton, NY: Intext Educational Publishers, 1971), pp. 338–353.

portfolios nearly to the extent to which investors diversify their holdings of publicly traded stocks. Thus, since the unsystematic portion of total risk is unlikely to be diversified away to the same extent as for a portfolio of publicly traded securities, it is worth considering reflecting at least some part of unsystematic risk—as well as systematic risk—in estimating an appropriate expected rate of return.

An explanation of the data quantifying the size premium is contained in a later section on sources of data.

A series of small stock premium studies have been developed by Roger Grabowski and David King.[16] They use eight different measures of size:

Measures of Equity Size

- *Market value of common equity* (common stock price times number of common shares outstanding)
- *Book value of common equity* (does not add back the deferred tax balance)
- *Five-year average net income* (net income before extraordinary items)

Measures of Company Size

- *Market value of invested capital* (market value of common equity plus carrying value of preferred stock, long-term debt [including current portion] and notes payable)
- *Total assets* (as reported on the balance sheet)
- *Five-year average EBITDA* (operating income before depreciation plus non-operating income)
- *Sales* (net)
- *Number of employees* (number of employees, either at year-end or yearly average, including part-time and seasonal workers and employees of consolidated subsidiaries; excludes contract workers and unconsolidated subsidiaries)

The data used in the studies consist of a cross section of company data drawn from the database of the Center for Research in Security Prices (CRSP) at the University of Chicago and the Standard & Poor's Compustat database. The starting point for the studies is 1963 because Standard & Poor's Compustat database covers public companies beginning in 1963. Excluded from the analysis are nonoperating companies and financial companies, as well as companies lacking five years of history, with sales of less than $1 million, or with a negative five-year average EBITDA. In addition to the 25 size-ranked portfolios, a portfolio was created to include high-leverage and financially distressed companies—the high-financial-risk portfolio. Dividing the companies on the NYSE into 25 groups and then inserting the companies from AMEX and Nasdaq into the appropriate portfolios created the 25 portfolios.

The size studies present historical rates of return and equity risk premiums for the 25 size-ranked portfolios using the eight measures of size. These studies were first published in a series of articles.[17] The studies are updated annually. The 2005 study covers historical data for the period 1963 through the end of 2004.

---

[16] In Duff & Phelps LLC *Risk Premium Report* (formerly known as Standard & Poor's Corporate Value Consulting *Risk Premium Report*), published annually and available at *http://corporate.morningstar.com/ib/html/home.htm* and *www.bvresources.com*.

[17] "New Evidence of Size Effect and Equity Returns," *Business Valuation Review*, September 1996 (covering the period 1963–1994); "Size Effect and Equity Returns: An Update," *Business Valuation Review*, March 1997.

Grabowski and King conclude from their research that there is a clear inverse relationship between size and the historical rates of return. Exhibit 9–6 presents the results of the 2005 study where the measure of size is the market value of equity (similar exhibits for the other seven measures of size are available in the study). From Exhibit 9–7, we notice that the smaller the average market value of the portfolio, the greater the arithmetic average return, the greater the arithmetic average equity risk premium, and the greater the premium over CAPM. Other observations from this exhibit are that the leverage does not vary much across portfolios and that the leverage of the high-risk portfolio is much higher compared to that of the other portfolios. The authors' suggestion is that changes in leverage do not explain why the returns vary across size-ranked portfolios.

The practical application of the data in Exhibit 9–6 is twofold:

1. Estimation of the discount rate for a company using the build-up model as the sum of the risk-free rate as of the valuation date and the smoothed equity risk premium for the portfolio closest in size to the subject company.

   For instance, assuming that the risk-free rate as of the valuation date was 4.5 percent, a simple build-up model for a company with a market value of equity of $50 million would result in:

$$E(R_i) = R_f + \text{Smoothed equity risk premium for portfolio 25}$$
$$E(R_i) = 4.5\% + 13.79\%$$
$$E(R_i) = 18.3\%$$

2. Extrapolation of the smoothed equity risk premium for a company.

   For instance, for a company with a market value of equity of $50 million, the regression equation in Exhibit 9–6 allows estimation of the smoothed equity risk premium as follows:

$$\begin{aligned} \text{Smoothed premium} &= 19.828\% - 3.566\% * (\log 50) \\ &= 19.828 - 3.566\% * (1.699) \\ &= 13.77\% \end{aligned}$$

The availability of the regression equation and the use of it in this manner become very useful when the size of the subject company is smaller than that of the smallest portfolio.

The practical application of the data in Exhibit 9–7 is twofold:

1. Estimation of a discount rate for a company using the size premium (premium over CAPM) for the portfolio closest in size to the subject company.

   For example, for a company with a market value of equity of $50 million, the data would result in a discount rate as follows:

$$E(R_i) = R_f + \text{Beta} * \text{Equity risk premium} + \text{Smoothed premium over CAPM}$$
$$E(R_i) = R_f + \text{Beta} * \text{Equity risk premium} + 7.19\%$$

2. Extrapolation of the smoothed premium over CAPM for a subject company using the regression equation. The availability of the regression becomes very useful when the size of the subject company is smaller than that of the smallest portfolio.

Exhibit 9–6

Companies Ranked by Market Value of Equity

Historical Equity Risk Premium: Average Since 1963
Data for year Ending December 31, 2004

Equity Risk Premium Study: Data through December 31, 2004
Data Smoothing with Regression Analysis
Dependent Variable: Average Premium
Independent Variable: Log of Average Market Value of Equity

Regression Output:	
Constant	19.828%
Std Err of Y Est	1.051%
R Squared	86%
No. of Observations	25
Degrees of Freedom	23
X Coefficient(s)	−3.566%
Std Err of Coef.	0.297%
t-Statistic	−11.99

*Smoothed Premium = 19.828% - 3.566% * Log (Operating Margin)*

Smoothed Premium vs. Unadjusted Average

Portfolio Rank by size	Average Mkt Value ($mills.)	Log of Average Mkt Value	Number as of 2004	Beta (sumBeta) Since '63	Standard Deviations of Return	Geometric Average Return	Arithmetic Average Return	Arithmetic Equity Risk Premium	Smoothed Average Equity Risk Premium	Average Debt/ MVIC
1	84,208	4.93	44	0.91	17.03%	10.78%	12.11%	4.83%	2.26%	16.44%
2	20,847	4.32	36	0.92	16.73%	10.88%	12.15%	4.87%	4.43%	22.87%
3	11,172	4.05	42	0.98	16.64%	9.83%	11.08%	3.80%	5.39%	25.14%
4	8,187	3.91	41	0.97	16.46%	11.88%	13.09%	5.81%	6.35%	25.94%
5	6,025	3.78	44	0.97	16.11%	11.84%	13.00%	5.72%	6.86%	27.05%
6	4,339	3.64	42	1.03	17.14%	13.25%	14.55%	7.27%	7.26%	27.02%
7	3,335	3.52	47	1.03	18.12%	13.35%	14.76%	7.48%	7.50%	27.38%
8	2,872	3.46	42	1.08	19.77%	12.56%	14.28%	7.00%	7.86%	26.42%
9	2,278	3.36	44	1.08	18.78%	14.13%	15.65%	8.37%	8.15%	25.36%
10	1,889	3.28	46	1.10	18.76%	12.29%	14.47%	7.19%	8.29%	25.16%
11	1,717	3.23	44	1.09	18.79%	13.77%	15.34%	8.06%	8.54%	25.16%
12	1,460	3.16	47	1.11	19.38%	13.55%	15.14%	7.86%	8.71%	26.72%
13	1,312	3.12	43	1.09	21.15%	12.00%	13.97%	6.69%	8.94%	26.66%
14	1,131	3.05	50	1.14	19.81%	14.63%	16.35%	9.07%	8.94%	27.33%
15	915	2.96	56	4.14	20.34%	13.89%	15.78%	8.50%	9.27%	26.70%
16	766	2.88	55	1.14	22.13%	15.69%	17.79%	10.51%	9.54%	25.99%
17	704	2.85	54	1.21	23.94%	15.23%	17.59%	10.31%	9.67%	26.79%
18	582	2.76	63	1.20	22.77%	14.73%	16.99%	9.71%	9.97%	27.03%
19	502	2.70	62	1.24	24.53%	14.39%	16.90%	9.62%	10.20%	26.54%
20	406	2.61	79	1.26	24.11%	15.71%	18.21%	10.93%	10.53%	27.40%
21	354	2.55	65	1.27	23.96%	15.85%	18.22%	10.94%	10.74%	27.61%
22	274	2.44	100	1.27	24.82%	15.89%	18.47%	11.19%	11.14%	27.89%
23	197	2.29	87	1.24	24.86%	15.35%	17.98%	10.70%	11.65%	28.33%
24	132	2.12	148	1.27	25.18%	17.21%	19.79%	12.51%	12.27%	29.13%
25	49	1.69	337	1.30	31.67%	19.64%	23.52%	16.24%	13.79%	31.27%
High Financial risk			665	1.62	38.48%	16.82%	22.15%	14.87%		47.95%
Large stocks (Ibbotson SBBI data)						10.89%	12.18%	4.09%		
Small stocks (Ibbotson SBBI data)						15.24%	17.96%	10.68%		
Long-Term Tresury Income (Ibbotson SBBI data)						7.26%	7.28%			

Exhibit 9-7

Companies Ranked by Market Value of Equity—Premium Over CAPM

Historical Equity Risk Premium: Average Since 1963
Data for year Ending December 31, 2004

Equity Risk Premium Study: Data through December 31, 2004
Data Smoothing with Regression Analysis
Dependent Variable: Premium over CAPM
Independent Variable: Log of Average Market Value of Equity

Regression Output:	
Constant	11.921%
Std Err of Y Est	1.029%
R Squared	80%
No. of Observations	25
Degrees of Freedom	23
X Coefficient(s)	-2.799%
Std Err of Coef.	0.291%
t-Statistic	-9.61

*Smoothed Premium = 11.921% - 2.799% * Log (Market Value)*

Smoothed Premium vs. Unadjusted Average

Portfolio Rank by size	Average Mkt Value ($mills.)	Log of Size	Beta (sumBeta) Since '63	Arithmetic Average Return	Arithmetic Equity Risk Premium	Indicated CAPM Premium	Premium over CAPM	Smoothed Premium over CAPM
1	84,208	4.93	0.91	12.11%	4.83%	4.44%	0.38%	-1.86%
2	20,847	4.32	0.92	12.15%	4.87%	4.53%	0.34%	-0.17%
3	11,172	4.05	0.98	11.08%	3.80%	4.78%	-0.97%	0.59%
4	8,187	3.91	0.97	13.09%	5.81%	4.77%	1.04%	0.97%
5	6,025	3.78	0.97	13.00%	5.72%	4.75%	0.97%	1.34%
6	4,339	3.64	1.03	14.55%	7.27%	5.06%	2.21%	1.74%
7	3,335	3.52	1.03	14.76%	7.48%	5.02%	2.45%	2.06%
8	2,872	3.46	1.08	14.28%	7.00%	5.31%	1.69%	2.24%
9	2,278	3.36	1.08	15.65%	8.37%	5.28%	3.09%	2.52%
10	1,889	3.28	1.10	14.47%	7.19%	5.38%	1.81%	2.75%
11	1,717	3.23	1.09	15.34%	8.06%	5.36%	2.70%	2.87%
12	1,460	3.16	1.11	15.14%	7.86%	5.42%	2.44%	3.06%
13	1,312	3.12	1.09	13.97%	6.69%	5.33%	1.36%	3.09%
14	1,131	3.05	1.14	16.35%	9.07%	5.60%	3.47%	3.38%
15	915	2.96	1.14	15.78%	8.50%	5.59%	2.91%	3.63%
16	766	2.88	1.14	17.79%	10.51%	5.57%	4.94%	3.85%
17	704	2.85	1.21	17.59%	10.31%	5.92%	4.39%	3.95%
18	582	2.76	1.20	16.99%	9.71%	5.88%	3.83%	4.18%
19	502	2.70	1.24	16.90%	9.62%	6.07%	3.56%	4.36%
20	406	2.61	1.26	18.21%	10.93%	6.19%	4.74%	4.62%
21	354	2.55	1.27	18.22%	10.94%	6.20%	4.74%	4.79%
22	274	2.44	1.27	18.47%	11.19%	6.21%	4.98%	5.10%
23	197	2.29	1.24	17.98%	10.70%	6.07%	4.63%	5.50%
24	132	2.12	1.27	19.79%	12.51%	6.23%	6.28%	5.99%
25	49	1.69	1.30	23.52%	16.24%	6.36%	9.88%	7.19%
High Financial risk			1.62	22.15%	14.87%	7.93%	6.94%	
Large stocks (Ibbotson SBBI data)				12.18%	4.90%			
Small stocks (Ibbotson SBBI data)				17.96%	10.68%			
Long-Term Tresury Income (Ibbotson SBBI data)				7.28%				

SOURCE: Copyright 2005 Duff & Phelps, LLC, *Risk Premium Report.* Distributed by Ibbotson Associates.

For example, for a company with a market value of equity of $25 million, the data would result in a discount rate as follows:

$$E(R_i) = R_f + \text{Beta} * \text{Equity risk premium} + \text{Smoothed premium over CAPM}$$

where

$$
\begin{aligned}
\text{Smoothed premium over CAPM} &= 11.921\% - 2.799\% * \text{Log}_{10} (\$25) \\
&= 11.921\% - 2.799\% * 1.3979 \\
&= 8.01\%
\end{aligned}
$$

From Exhibit 9–7, we notice that the smaller the average market value of the portfolio (column 2), the higher the arithmetic average return (column 5) and the higher the premium over CAPM (column 8). The practical applications of the data in Exhibit 9–7 are similar to those presented earlier for Exhibit 9–6, except that the smoothed premium over CAPM would be used in the context of the CAPM model, not in the build-up model, as follows:

$$
\begin{aligned}
\text{Required return} = \text{Riskless rate} + \text{Beta} * \text{Market risk premium} \\
+ \text{Smoothed premium over CAPM}
\end{aligned}
$$

This study tries to answer the question, "Does the evidence support the claim that smaller companies have greater risk?"[18] The authors conclude that as a company's size decreases, its risk increases, and so do its historical rates of return. This study also quantifies the relationship between rates of return and accounting risk measures. Exhibit 9–8 presents the research results for companies ranked into 25 portfolios using the median of the five-year average operating margin as the sorting risk measure. It makes the point that these studies further support the validity of the small stock premium. However, the premiums could also be viewed as indications of specific company risk.

Exhibit 9–8 indicates that the operating margins are directy correlated with company size and inversely correlated with company risk as indicated by the Smoothed Premium over CAPM.

Analyses of size differentials relating to cost of capital on the *Pratt's Stats, BIZCOMPS,* and *IBA Market Database* all show that the size effect continues to carry on down to smaller companies. For example, relative median valuation multiples for 12 industry groups from *BIZCOMPS* and *Pratt's Stats* are shown in Exhibit 9–9. It is very clear that the average transaction size is significantly lower and the valuation multiples are similarly significantly lower for the *BIZCOMPS* companies compared with the *Pratt's Stats* companies.

The Build-Up Model[19]

We have previously defined the discount rate or the cost of capital generally as the sum of a risk-free rate and a risk premium. The build-up model divides the risk premium into its three main subcomponents and estimates the cost of capital as the sum of the following:

---

[18] Duff & Phelps LLC, *Risk Premium Report,* 2005 (formerly known as Standard & Poor's Corporate Value Consulting *Risk Premium Report*), published annually and available at http://corporate.morningstar.com/ib/html/home.htm and www.bvresources.com.
[19] This section draws upon Chapter 7 in Shannon Pratt and Roger Grabowski, *Cost of Capital: Application and Examples*, 3rd ed. (Hoboken, NJ: John Wiley & Sons, 2008).

Exhibit 9–8

Companies Ranked by Operating Margin

Historical Equity Risk Premium: Average Since 1963
Data for year Ending December 31, 2004

Equity Risk Premium Study: Data through December 31, 2004
Data Smoothing with Regression Analysis
Dependent Variable: Average Premium
Independent Variable: Log of Median Operating Margin

	Regression Output:
Constant	2.381%
Std Err of Y Est	1.189%
R Squared	77%
No. of Observations	25
Degrees of Freedom	23
X Coefficient(s)	−7.526%
Std Err of Coef.	0.860%
t-Statistic	−8.75

$Smoothed\ Premium = 2.381\% - 7.526\% * Log\ (Operating\ Margin)$

Smoothed Premium vs. Unadjusted Average

Portfolio Rank by size	Median Operating Margin	Log of Median Op Margin	Number as of 2004	Beta (sumBeta) Since '63	Standard Deviations of Return	Geometric Average Return	Arithmetic Average Return	Arithmetic Equity Risk Premium	Smoothed Average Equity Risk Premium	Average Debt/MVIC
1	32.4%	−0.49	80	0.81	17.08%	13.22%	14.46%	7.18%	6.07%	31.05%
2	25.3%	−0.60	55	0.76	16.61%	11.16%	12.38%	5.10%	6.87%	34.95%
3	22.3%	−0.65	55	0.8	16.09%	12.95%	14.11%	6.83%	7.28%	32.95%
4	20.0%	−0.70	52	0.95	17.08%	12.50%	13.80%	6.52%	7.64%	27.19%
5	18.1%	−0.74	50	0.99	17.56%	13.53%	14.88%	7.60%	7.96%	22.78%
6	17.1%	−0.77	65	1.11	18.94%	13.46%	15.01%	7.73%	8.15%	19.24%
7	15.3%	−0.81	67	1.15	19.92%	14.36%	16.01%	8.73%	8.51%	18.33%
8	14.3%	−0.85	59	1.12	19.60%	13.05%	14.76%	7.48%	8.75%	20.20%
9	13.3%	−0.88	49	1.19	19.98%	16.11%	17.84%	10.56%	8.97%	20.97%
10	12.4%	−0.91	64	1.20	21.74%	14.29%	16.31%	9.03%	9.20%	21.67%
11	11.7%	−0.93	64	1.21	21.31%	12.65%	14.61%	7.33%	9.40%	22.71%
12	11.1%	−0.95	55	1.18	21.45%	14.27%	16.19%	8.91%	9.55%	23.10%
13	10.6%	−0.98	63	1.21	22.37%	15.34%	17.45%	10.17%	9.72%	22.90%
14	10.0%	−1.00	66	1.20	23.10%	15.46%	17.79%	10.51%	9.90%	23.97%
15	9.5%	−1.02	58	1.22	24.62%	14.92%	17.39%	10.11%	10.08%	24.87%
16	9.0%	−1.05	67	1.17	22.91%	16.14%	18.41%	11.13%	10.25%	26.72%
17	8.4%	−1.07	59	1.26	24.45%	16.39%	18.97%	11.69%	10.46%	27.24%
18	7.9%	−1.10	79	1.26	24.85%	16.33%	18.98%	11.70%	10.69%	28.02%
19	7.2%	−1.14	73	1.29	25.12%	17.44%	20.07%	12.79%	10.97%	29.40%
20	6.7%	−1.17	68	1.27	26.48%	16.30%	19.20%	11.92%	11.21%	31.50%
21	5.8%	−1.23	82	1.25	25.88%	16.96%	19.66%	12.38%	11.66%	31.76%
22	5.0%	−1.30	106	1.29	28.88%	16.43%	19.84%	12.56%	12.16%	32.37%
23	4.2%	−1.38	94	1.29	26.14%	17.42%	20.22%	12.94%	12.77	34.14%
24	3.3%	−1.48	89	1.31	28.64%	17.80%	21.10%	13.82%	13.50%	33.88%
25	2.0%	−1.69	89	1.29	27.87%	16.16%	19.41%	12.13%	15.12%	32.27%
High Financial risk			665	1.62	38.48%	16.82%	22.15%	14.87%		47.95%
Large stocks (Ibbotson SBBI data)						10.89%	12.18%	4.90%		
Small stocks (Ibbotson SBBI data)						15.24%	17.96%	10.68%		
Long-Term Tresury Income (Ibbotson SBBI data)						7.26%	7.28%			

SOURCE: Copyright 2005 Duff & Phelps, LLC, *Risk Premium Report*. Distributed by Ibbotson Associates.

Exhibit 9–9

Comparison of Median Valuation Multiples

	BIZCOMPS Data				Pratt's Stats Data			
	Median of Sale Price/Gross Sales	Median of Sale Price/SDE	Median Sale Price (in $000s)	Median Gross Sales (in $000s)	Median of MVIC/Net Sales	Median of MVIC/Disc. Earnings	Median MVIC Price (in $000s)	Median Net Sales (in $000s)
Publishing businesses	0.76	1.89	139	209	1.71	2.30	15,200	5,756
Printing businesses	0.53	2.21	187	386	0.58	2.55	495	773
Manufacturing: machine shops	0.60	2.40	350	649	0.84	3.08	7,512	6,628
Distributor: automotive	0.28	1.84	190	771	0.35	2.80	1,068	2,517
Distributor: industrial supplies	0.30	1.74	240	759	0.43	3.32	1,525	2,763
Distributor: food markets	0.28	1.69	140	399	0.34	1.93	300	1,034
Bakeries: retail	0.36	1.93	98	236	0.43	2.50	135	341
Restaurants	0.36	1.80	100	300	0.38	2.05	125	340
Grocery stores: retail	0.27	1.75	114	385	0.34	2.66	198	678
Florists: retail	0.36	1.66	83	240	0.38	1.69	93	236
Day care centers	0.45	1.88	110	257	0.49	2.38	140	317

SDE = Seller's discretionary earnings
MVIC = Market value of invested capital
SOURCE: BIZCOMPS year-end 2005 and Pratt's Stats year-end 2005.

1. A risk-free rate
2. A risk premium, including one or all of the following subcomponents:
   a. An equity risk premium
   b. A size premium
   c. A company-specific risk premium

   Each subcomponent of the risk premium represents the reward to an investor for taking on a specific risk. The risk-free rate is the rate of return available on a risk-free security as of the valuation date. The equity risk premium is the reward for investing in the stock market. The size premium is the reward for investing in smaller companies. The company-specific risk premium is the reward for investing in a specific company and industry, or the reward for unsystematic risk. Because the build-up model estimates the cost of capital as the sum of the risk-free rate and various risk premia, the model is called an additive model, and the model's components are referred to as "building blocks."

Formula for the Build-Up Model

The build-up model for estimating the cost of equity can be expressed as a formula as follows:

Formula 9–7

$$E(R_i) = R_f + RP_m + RP_s + RP_u$$

where:

$E(R_i)$	=	Required (expected) return on security i
R_f	=	Risk-free rate
RP_m	=	Equity risk premium (market risk)
RP_s	=	Size premium
RP_u	=	Unsystematic risk premium

Grabowski and King also provide data for the build-up model, combining the equity risk premium and size premium. For example, see Exhibit 9–6.

The practical application of the data in Exhibit 9–6 is twofold:

1. Estimation of a discount rate for a company using the smoothed equity risk premium (which includes the size premium) for the portfolio closest in size to the subject company.

    For example, for a company with a market value of equity of $50 million, the data would result in a discount rate using a simple build-up model of

    $$E(R_i) = R_f + \text{Smoothed equity risk premium for portfolio 25}$$
    $$E(R_i) = R_f + 13.79\%$$

2. Extrapolation of the smoothed equity risk premium (which includes the size premium) for the subject company using the regression equation. Again, the availability of the regression becomes very useful when the size of the subject company is smaller than that of the smallest portfolio.

    For example, for a company with a market value of equity of $25 million, the data would result in a discount rate as follows:

    $$E(R_i) = R_f + \text{Smoothed equity risk premium}$$

    where:

    $$\text{Smoothed equity risk premium} = 19.828\% - 3.566\% * \text{Log}_{10}(\$25)$$
    $$= 19.828\% - 3.566\% * 1.3979$$
    $$= 14.84\%$$

Ibbotson Associates introduced an alternative formula for the build-up model in the *SBBI Valuation Edition 2002 Yearbook*.

Formula 9–8

$$E(R_i) = R_f + RP_m + RP_s + /- RP_i + RP_u$$

where:

$$RP_i = \text{Industry risk premium}$$

All other components are defined as in Formula 9–7.

The first three components in the build-up model are the same as those discussed in the context of the CAPM: the risk-free rate, the equity risk premium, and the size premium. The same data points can be used for the CAPM and the build-up model for a given valuation date. Ibbotson's position is that the beta-adjusted size premium should be used for both the CAPM and the build-up model, as opposed to a non-beta-adjusted small stock premium.[20] The new components in the build-up model are the company-specific risk premium, or the unsystematic risk premium, and the industry risk premia, and they are discussed here.

Company-Specific Risk Premium

A company-specific risk premium may be applicable when the risk characteristics of the subject company are different from the risk characteristics of the companies that were used to derive the equity risk premium and the size premium used in the build-up model.

The application of a company-specific risk premium is commonly based on a quantitative analysis and a qualitative analysis. The quantitative analysis may involve a comparison of the subject company to its industry and to its group of guideline public or private peers in terms of financial and operating performance. The qualitative analysis is based on interviews of the subject company's management and site visits.

The direction and magnitude of the company-specific risk premium may be based on an analysis of the following factors:

1. Leverage—to the extent that it is not considered in cash flow
2. Size
3. Volatility of earnings or cash flow—to the extent that it is not reflected in the forecast
4. Industry risk
5. Other company-specific factors

Under other company-specific factors, a multitude of factors that affect the risk of company may be analyzed, as follows:[21]

- Management depth
- Management expertise
- Access to capital
- Customer concentration
- Customer pricing leverage
- Customer loyalty and stability
- Level of current competition
- Potential new competitors
- Supplier concentration
- Supplier pricing advantage
- Product or service diversification
- Life cycle of current products or services
- Geographical distribution
- Demographics
- Availability of labor
- Employee stability

---

[20] *SBBI Valuation Edition 2005 Yearbook*, pp. 38–39.
[21] James R. Hitchner and Katherine Morris, "Cost of Capital Controversies: It's Time to Look behind the Curtain" (Parts 1 and 2 of 3), *Shannon Pratt's Business Valuation Update*, October 2004 and January 2005; James R. Hitchner and Paul Vogt, "Cost of Capital Controversies: It's Time to Look behind the Curtain" (Part 3 of 3), *Shannon Pratt's Business Valuation Update,* May 2005.

- Internal and external culture
- Economic factors
- Industry and government regulations
- Political factors
- Fixed assets' age and condition
- Strength of intangible assets
- Distribution system
- IT systems
- Technology life cycle
- Location
- Legal/litigation issues
- Internal controls
- Currency risk

However, the analyst who chooses to use these data should take care to note what companies are included in the industry grouping, and determine whether they are truly comparable to the subject company.

Grabowski and King present research that quantifies the relationship between fundamental measures of risk and historical rates of return. These studies were first published in a 1999 article[22] and are updated annually.[23] The 2005 study covers historical data for the period 1963 through the end of 2004.

The three fundamental risk measures and their correlation coefficients with observed equity risk premiums are as follows:

- **Operating margin** (five-year mean of operating income net of depreciation divided by sales). The lower the operating margin, the higher the risk. This had the highest R-squared at 77 percent.
- **Coefficient of variation of operating margin** (standard deviation of operating margin over the prior five years divided by the mean operating income for the same years). This had an R-squared of 54 percent.
- **Coefficient of variation of return on book value of equity** (net income before extraordinary items minus preferred dividends divided by book value of common equity; the calculation then is the standard deviation of return on book value of equity for the prior five years divided by the mean return on book value of equity for the same years). This also had an R-squared of 54 percent.

The results for companies ranked into 25 portfolios using the median of the five-year average operating margin as the sorting risk measure are summarized in Exhibit 9–8. Exhibit 9–8 indicates that the operating margins are inversely related to the equity risk premium. The premiums can be viewed as indicators of specific company risk.

The practical usage of the data in Exhibit 9–8 is that they can be used to estimate the discount rate for a company using the company's operating margin (similar exhibits are available in the study for the application of the coefficient of the operating margin and the coefficient of variation of the return to equity). A simple build-up model would add to the risk-free rate on the valuation date the smoothed average equity risk premium for the portfolio having an average operating margin closest to that of the subject company. Also, one could use the regression equation to estimate the smoothed average equity risk premium as a function of the five-year average operating margin for the subject company. The smoothed average equity

---

[22] "New Evidence on Equity Returns and Company Risk," *Business Valuation Review*, September 1999 (revised March 2000).

[23] The study is updated annually and is available at www.morningstar.com and www.bvresources.com.

risk premium incorporates the equity risk premium, the size premium, and the specific company risk premium. It adjusts the size premium depending on the specific risk of the subject company (i.e., whether the subject company is more or less risky than the average company).

The studies also find that, on the average, operating margins are inversely correlated with company size. They make the point that these studies can be viewed as further support for the validity of the small stock premium.[24] The authors conclude that as the size of a company decreases, on the average its risk increases and on the average so does its historical rate of return. The study quantifies the relation between accounting risk measures and rates of return.

Industry Risk Premia

The *SBBI* industry risk premia are calculated using a full information beta estimation process that is described in Chapter 6 of the *SBBI Valuation Edition 2005 Yearbook*. Simply put, the full beta estimation process calculates a weighted-average beta for an industry from the betas of companies that contribute sales to the respective industry. The weighting for each company's beta is based on the sales of the industry as a whole.

The Discounted Cash Flow or the Implied Method of Estimating the Cost of Capital

To use the DCF or implied method for estimating the cost of equity capital for a closely held company, one must select a group of publicly traded companies with risk characteristics similar to those of the subject company. These usually are companies in the same industry, and may be the group of companies selected as guideline publicly traded companies in the market approach.

The implied method uses the discounted cash flow formula. Since the present value of the publicly traded companies' stock is known, the formula is merely rearranged to solve for the implied expected rate of return.

The expected dollar amounts of returns used as inputs to the formula usually are five years of analysts' earnings estimates from one of the estimates sources, such as I/B/E/S (Institutional Broker's Estimate System) or First Call. The next five years' projections usually are an industry projection for years six through ten. Beyond the tenth year, it is usually assumed that earnings will increase at the growth rate of real gross domestic product (GDP) plus the projected rate of inflation. There are also simpler versions, but the "three-stage model" just described tends to produce the most reliable results.

Because the inputs are earnings estimates, the variable to which the implied cost of capital applies is net income rather than net cash flow, as discussed elsewhere in this chapter. Many valuation analysts feel that this long-run cost of capital estimate for net income is not significantly different from the long-run cost of capital applicable to net cash flow. The validity of this assumption depends on the

---

[24] "New Evidence of Size Effect and Equity Returns," *Business Valuation Review*, September 1996 (covering the period 1963–1994); and "Size Effect and Equity Returns: An Update," *Business Valuation Review*, March 1997.

extent to which net income and net cash flow tend to even out for the industry in question over the long run.

Cost of capital estimates from applying the implied method are presented in Morningstar's *Cost of Capital Yearbook* (see example in Exhibit 9–14).[25]

Arbitrage Pricing Theory

The concept of the arbitrage pricing theory (APT) was introduced by academicians in 1976,[26] but it was not until 1988 that data in a commercially usable form became generally available to permit the application of the theory to the estimation of required rates of return in day-to-day practice.

As noted in the previous section, the CAPM is a univariate model—that is, it recognizes only one risk factor: systematic risk relative to a market measure. In a sense, APT is a multivariate extension of the CAPM in that it recognizes a variety of risk factors that may bear on an investment's required rate of return, one of these being systematic or "market timing" risk. However, in another sense, it may be argued that the CAPM and APT are not mutually exclusive, nor is either of them of greater or lesser scope than the other. It can be argued that the CAPM beta implicitly reflects the information included separately in each of the APT "factors." Under APT, the required rate of return for an investment varies according to that investment's sensitivity to each risk factor. The APT model takes the following form:

Formula 9–9

$$E(R_i) = R_f + (B_{i1}K_1) + (B_{i2}K_2) + (B_{in}K_n)$$

where:

$E(R_i)$	=	Expected rate of return on the subject security
R_f	=	Rate of return on a risk-free security
$K_1 \dots K_n$	=	Risk premium associated with factor K for the average asset in the market
$B_{i1} \dots B_{in}$	=	Sensitivity of security i to each risk factor relative to the market average sensitivity to that factor

The risk factors considered in current APT applications, in addition to market timing risk, include:

- Confidence risk
- Time horizon risk
- Inflation risk
- Business cycle risk

Each of these risk factors is discussed in Exhibit 9–10. Like the CAPM, APT ignores risk factors that are unique to a particular company, since investors theoretically could avoid such risks through diversification.

---

[25] An entire chapter is devoted to the implied or DCF method of estimating the cost of equity capital, including examples, in Shannon Pratt and Roger Grabowski, *Cost of Capital: Application and Examples*, 3rd ed. (Hoboken, NJ: John Wiley & Sons, 2007).

[26] Stephen A. Ross, "The Arbitrage Theory of Capital Asset Pricing," *Journal of Economic Theory*, December 1976, pp. 341–360; and Stephen A. Ross, "Return, Risk, and Arbitrage," in *Risk and Return in Finance*, Irwin I. Friend and J. Bisksler, eds. (Cambridge, MA: Ballinger, 1977), pp. 189–218. See also Stephen A. Ross, Randolph W. Westerfield, and Jeffrey F. Jaffe, *Corporate Finance*, 3rd ed. (New York: McGraw-Hill, 1993), Chapter 11, "An Alternative View of Risk and Return: The Arbitrage Pricing Theory," pp. 315–337.

Exhibit 9–10

Explanation of APT Risk Factors

Confidence Risk

Confidence risk is the unanticipated changes in investors' willingness to undertake relatively risky investments. It is measured as the difference between the rate of return on relatively risky corporate bonds and the rate of return on government bonds, both with 20-year maturities, adjusted so that the mean of the difference is zero over a long historical sample period. In any month when the return on corporate bonds exceeds the return on government bonds by more than the long-run average, this measure of confidence risk is positive. The intuition is that a positive return difference reflects increased investor confidence because *the required yield on risky corporate bonds has fallen relative to the yield on safe government bonds.* Stocks that are positively exposed to this risk will then rise in price. (Most equities *do* have a positive exposure to confidence risk, and small stocks generally have greater exposure than large stocks.)

Time Horizon Risk

Time horizon risk is the unanticipated changes in investors' desired time to payouts. It is measured as the difference between the return on 20-year government bonds and 30-day Treasury bills, again adjusted to have a mean of zero over a long historical sample period. A positive realization of time horizon risk means that the price of long-term bonds has risen relative to the 30-day Treasury bill price. This is a signal that investors require a lower compensation for holding investments with relatively longer times to payouts. The prices of stocks that are positively exposed to time horizon risk will rise to appropriately decrease their yields. (Growth stocks benefit more than income stocks when this occurs.)

Inflation Risk

Inflation risk is a combination of the unexpected components of short- and long-run inflation rates. Expected future inflation rates are computed at the beginning of each period from available information: historical inflation rates, interest rates, and other economic variables that influence inflation. For any month, inflation risk is the unexpected surprise that is computed at the end of the month, i.e., it is the difference between the actual inflation for that month and what had been expected at the beginning of the month. Since most stocks have negative exposures to inflation risk, a positive inflation surprise causes a negative contribution to return, whereas a negative inflation surprise (a deflation shock) contributes positively toward return.

Industries whose products tend to be "luxuries" are most sensitive to inflation risk. Consumer demand for luxuries plummets when real income is eroded through inflation, thus depressing profits for industries such as retailers, services, eating places, hotels and motels, and toys. In contrast, industries that are least sensitive to inflation risk tend to sell "necessities," the demands for which are relatively insensitive to declines in real income. Examples include foods, cosmetics, tire and rubber goods, and shoes. Also, companies that have large asset holdings such as real estate or oil reserves may benefit from increased inflation.

Business Cycle Risk

Business cycle risk represents unanticipated changes in the level of real business activity. The expected values of a business activity index are computed at both the beginning and the end of the month, using only information available at those times. Then, business cycle risk is calculated as the difference between the end-of-month value and the beginning-of-month value. A positive realization of business cycle risk indicates that the expected growth rate of the economy, measured in constant dollars, has increased. Under such circumstances, firms that are more positively exposed to business cycle risk—for example, retail stores that do well when business activity increases as the economy recovers from a recession—will outperform such firms as utility companies that do not respond much to increased levels of business activity.

Market Timing Risk

Market timing risk is computed as that part of the S&P 500 total return that is not explained by the first four macroeconomic risks and an intercept term. Many people find it useful to think of the APT as a generalization of the CAPM, and by including this market timing factor, the CAPM becomes a special case: if the risk exposures to all of the first four macroeconomic factors were exactly zero, then market timing risk would be proportional to the S&P 500 total return. Under these extremely unlikely conditions, a stock's exposure to market timing risk would be equal to its CAPM beta. Almost all stocks have a positive exposure to market timing risk, and hence positive market timing surprises increase returns, and vice versa.

A natural question, then, is, "Do confidence risk, time horizon risk, inflation risk, and business cycle risk help to explain stock returns better than I could do with just the S&P 500?" This question has been answered using rigorous statistical tests, and the answer is very clearly that they do.

SOURCE: Presented in a talk based on a paper, "A Practitioner's Guide to Arbitrage Pricing Theory," by Edwin Burmeister, Richard Roll, and Stephen A. Ross, written for the Research Foundation of the Institute of Chartered Financial Analysts. The exhibit is drawn from Notes for "Controlling Risks Using Arbitrage Pricing Techniques" by Edwin Burmeister.

Roger Ibbotson and Gary Brinson make the following observations regarding APT:

> In theory, a specific asset has some number of units of each risk; those units are each multiplied by the appropriate risk premium. Thus, APT shows that the equilibrium expected return is the risk-free rate plus the sum of a series of risk premiums.[27]

Arguably, APT is more realistic than CAPM because investors can consider other characteristics besides the beta of assets as they select their investment portfolios.

Research suggests that, on average, the cost of equity as estimated using APT tends to be slightly higher than the cost of equity as estimated using CAPM. Early research also suggests that the multivariate APT model explains expected rates of return better than the univariate CAPM.[28]

A source of data for required rates of return using APT is included later in this chapter.

Sources of Data to Estimate the Cost of Equity Capital

Risk-Free Rate

The risk-free rate should be the yield available to investors as of the valuation date. In the United States, the yield most often used is for 20-year, 5-year, or 30-day U.S. Treasury obligations because those are the maturities for which matching equity risk premium data are available.

The *SBBI* risk premium data are based on yields of U.S. government coupon bonds. Therefore, the coupon bond yield as of the valuation date is appropriate to use with the *SBBI* equity risk premium data.

Equity Risk Premium

SBBI contains three equity risk premium series annually, as presented in Exhibit 9–11. These are based on arithmetic (as opposed to geometric) means of the differences between historical stock market returns and risk-free security returns, for reasons explained in Exhibit 9–12. This is a widely (but not universally) accepted procedure for estimating the equity risk premium.[29] While the *SBBI Yearbook* contains historical premium data for every year since 1926, the most commonly cited data are the arithmetic means of differences between historical one-year stock

---

[27] Roger G. Ibbotson and Gary P. Brinson, *Investment Markets* (New York: McGraw-Hill, 1987), p. 52. For a more extensive discussion of APT, see Frank K. Reilly, *Investment Analysis and Portfolio Management*, 7th ed. (Mason, OH: South-Western, 2003), pp. 280–286.

[28] Tom Copeland, Tim Koller, and Jack Murrin, *Valuation: Measuring and Managing the Value of Companies*, 2nd ed. (New York: John Wiley & Sons, 1994), p. 267.

[29] For example, the Ibbotson view that the arithmetic mean is appropriate for estimating discount rates is supported in one of the leading corporate finance texts: Richard A. Brealey and Stewart C. Myers, *Principles of Corporate Finance*, 7th ed. (New York: McGraw-Hill, Inc., 2003), p. 157. However, for a contrary view (i.e., that the geometric mean differences more closely approximate the market's required return), see Tom Copeland et al.; *Valuation: Measuring and Managing the Value of Companies*, 2nd ed., pp. 261–263.

Exhibit 9–11

Key Variables in Estimating the Cost of Capital

	Value

Yields (Riskless Rates)[1]

Long-term (20-year) U.S. Treasury coupon bond yield — 4.8%

Equity Risk Premium[2]

Long-horizon expected equity risk premium (historical): large company stock total returns minus long-term government bond income returns — 7.2

Long-horizon expected equity risk premium (supply side): historical equity risk premium minus price-earnings ratio calculated using three-year average earnings — 6.1

Size Premium[3]

Decile	Market Capitalization of Smallest Company (in millions)		Market Capitalization of Largest Company (in millions)	Size Premium (Return in Excess of CAPM)
Mid-Cap, 3–5	$1,607.931	-	$6,241.953	0.95%
Low-Cap, 6–8	$506.410	-	$1,607.854	1.81
Micro-Cap, 9–10	$1.393	-	$505.437	4.02
Breakdown of Deciles 1–10				
1–Largest	$14,099.878	-	$342,087.219	-0.37
2	$6,258.530	-	$14,096.886	0.60
3	$3,473.335	-	$6,241.953	0.75
4	$2,234.146	-	$3,464.104	1.07
5	$1,607.931	-	$2,231.707	1.44
6	$1,098.284	-	$1,607.854	1.75
7	$746.249	-	$1,097.603	1.61
8	$506.410	-	$746.219	2.36
9	$262.974	-	$505.437	2.86
10–Smallest	$1.393	-	$262.725	6.41
Breakdown of the 10th Decile				
10a	$144.122	-	$262.725	4.54
10b	$1.393	-	$143.916	9.90

[1] As of December 31, 2004. Maturity is approximate.
[2] See Chapter 5 *SBBI Valuation Edition 2005 Yearbook* for complete methodology.
[3] See Chapter 7 *SBBI Valuation Edition 2005 Yearbook* for complete methodology.

SOURCE: *SBBI Valuation Edition 2005 Yearbook*, p. 258.

market returns and one-year risk-free security returns for the entire series of years (1926 to the most recent year).

In its 2004 *SBBI*, Ibbotson Associates introduced a new method for estimating the equity risk premium—the supply-side model. The supply-side model for estimating the equity risk premium is based on an article by Roger Ibbotson and Peng Chen.[30] It is based on the assumption that stock market returns are generated by the performance of companies in the real economy and that over the long run, equity returns should approximate the long-run supply estimate.[31] The model is based on four types of earnings: inflation, income return, growth in real earnings per share, and growth in the price/earnings (P/E) ratio. The first three types of

[30] Roger G. Ibbotson and Peng Chen, "Long-Run Stock Returns: Participating in the Real Economy," *Financial Analysts Journal*, Vol. 59, no. 1, January/February 2003, pp. 88–98.
[31] *SBBI Valuation Edition 2005 Yearbook*, p. 90.

Exhibit 9–12

SBBI Discussion of Arithmetic versus Geometric Mean for Calculating the Expected Equity Risk Premium for Estimating Cost of Capital (Discount Rate)

Arithmetic versus Geometric Means

The equity risk premium data presented in this book are arithmetic average risk premia as opposed to geometric average risk premia. The arithmetic average equity risk premium can be demonstrated to be most appropriate when discounting future cash flows. For use as the expected equity risk premium in either the CAPM or the building block approach, the arithmetic mean or the simple difference of the arithmetic means of stock market returns and riskless rates is the relevant number. This is because both the CAPM and the building block approach are additive models, in which the cost of capital is the sum of its parts. The geometric average is more appropriate for reporting past performance, since it represents the compound average return.

The argument for using the arithmetic average is quite straightforward. In looking at projected cash flows, the equity risk premium that should be employed is the equity risk premium that is expected to actually be incurred over the future time periods. The graph below shows the realized equity risk premium for each year based on the returns of the S&P 500 and the income return on long-term government bonds. (The actual, observed difference between the return on the stock market and the riskless rate is known as the realized equity risk premium.) There is considerable volatility in the year-by-year statistics. At times the realized equity risk premium is even negative.

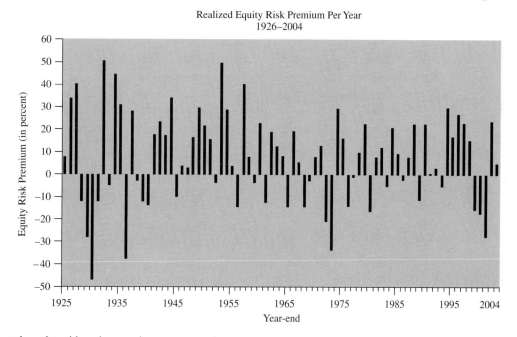

Realized Equity Risk Premium Per Year
1926–2004

To illustrate how the arithmetic mean is more appropriate than the geometric mean in discounting cash flows, suppose the expected return on a stock is 10 percent per year with a standard deviation of 20 percent. Also assume that only two outcomes are possible each year—+30 percent and –10 percent (i.e., the mean plus or minus one standard deviation). The probability of occurrence for each outcome is equal. The growth of wealth over a two-year period is illustrated in the graph.

The most common outcome of $1.17 is given by the geometric mean of 8.2 percent. Compounding the possible outcomes as follows derives the geometric mean:

$$[(1 + 0.30) \times (1 + 0.10)]^{1/2} - 1 = 0.082$$

However, the expected value is predicted by compounding the arithmetic, not the geometric, mean. To illustrate this, we need to look at the probability-weighted average of all possible outcomes:

$$(0.25 \times \$1.69) = \$0.4225$$
$$+(0.50 \times \$1.17) = \$0.5850$$
$$+(0.25 \times \$0.81) = \underline{\$0.2025}$$
$$\text{Total} \qquad \$1.2100$$

Therefore, $1.21 is the probability-weighted expected value. The rate that must be compounded to achieve the terminal value of $1.21 after two years is 10 percent, the arithmetic mean:

$$\$1 \times (1 + 0.10)^2 = \$1.21$$

The geometric mean, when compounded, results in the median of the distribution:

$$\$1 \times (1 + 0.0.82)^2 = \$1.17$$

The arithmetic mean equates the expected future value with the present value; it is therefore the appropriate discount rate.

SOURCE: *SBBI Valuation Edition 2005 Yearbook,* © Ibbotson Associates.

earnings are supplied by companies, while the fourth—the growth in P/E ratio—reflects investors' prediction of future growth[32] or risk.

Using the supply-side model, the 2004 *SBBI* reported an estimate of the equity risk premium that is approximately 1.25 percent lower than that derived using the historical model. The 2005 *SBBI* reported a historical equity risk premium of 7.2 percent and a supply-side equity risk premium of 6.1 percent—a 1.1 percent difference.[33] The supply-side equity risk premium data reported in the *SBBI Yearbook* are again based on the entire series of years (1926 to the most recent year).

William Goetzmann and Roger Ibbotson, commenting on the supply-side approach to estimating expected risk premiums, note:

> These forecasts tend to give somewhat lower forecasts than historical risk premiums, primarily because part of the total returns of the stock market have come from price-earnings ratio expansion. This expansion is not predicted to continue indefinitely, and should logically be removed from the expected risk premium.[34]

In contrast to the *SBBI* data, other recent research[35] indicates that the historical realized equity risk premium may overestimate the forward-looking equity risk premium or the expected equity risk premium. In a series of papers, Roger Grabowski and David King researched the equity risk premium issue and concluded that a reasonable forward-looking estimate of the equity risk premium as of 2005 should be in the range of 3.5 to 6 percent.[36]

Even if one were to rely on the mean historical realized equity risk premium as one's estimate of the equity risk premium, the mean historical realized equity risk premium for more recent periods, say 1963 to 2004, is 4.9 percent, significantly lower than the mean historical realized equity risk premium for the entire *SBBI Yearbook* series of years since 1926.

Beta

Since privately held companies by definition have no market quotes and thus no market fluctuations, they have no observable betas. The most common procedure when using the CAPM to develop a discount rate for a privately held company is to

---

[32] Ibid., p. 91.

[33] Ibid., p. 96.

[34] William N. Goetzmann and Roger G. Ibbotson, "History and the Equity Risk Premium," Yale ICF Working Paper No. 05-04, April 2005, p. 8.

[35] See Eugene Fama and Kenneth R. French, "The Equity Premium," *Journal of Finance,* Vol. 75, no. 2, April 2002, p. 637; Ellen R. McGrattan and Edward C. Prescott, "Is the Market Overvalued?" *Federal Reserve Bank of Minneapolis Quarterly Review,* Vol. 24, 2000 and "Taxes, Regulations and Asset Prices," Federal Reserve Bank of Minneapolis Working Paper 610, July 2001; Ivo Welch, "The Equity Premium Consensus Forecast Revisited," Cowles Foundation Discussion Paper No. 1325, September 2001; John Graham and Campbell Harvey, "Expectations of Equity Risk Premia, Volatility and Asymmetry from a Corporate Finance Perspective," National Bureau of Economic Research Working Paper, December 2001, updated quarterly by Duke CFO Outlook Survey (www.cfosurvey.org); Elroy Dimson, Paul Marsh, and Mike Staunton, "Global Evidence on the Equity Premium," *Journal of Applied Corporate Finance,* Vol. 15, no. 4, Summer 2003; and Elroy Dimson, "Global Evidence on the Equity Risk Premium," NACVA 12th Annual Consultant's Conference, June 2005. See also *The Global Investment Returns Yearbook 2005* (ABN-AMRO/London Business School, 2005); and William N. Goetzmann and Roger G. Ibbotson, "History and the Equity Risk Premium," Yale ICF Working Paper No. 05-04, April 2005, p. 8.

[36] Roger Grabowski and David King, Chapter 1, "Equity Risk Premium," in *The Handbook of Business Valuation and Intellectual Property Analysis*, (New York: McGraw-Hill, 2004); Roger Grabowski and David King, "Equity Risk Premium: What Valuation Consultants Need to Know about Current Research," *Valuation Strategies,* September/October 2003; Roger Grabowski and David King, "Equity Risk Premium: What Valuation Consultants Need to Know about Current Research, 2005 Update," *Valuation Strategies,* September/October 2005; Roger Grabowski, "Equity Risk Premium: What Is the Current Evidence?" *Shannon Pratt's Business Valuation Update,* November 2005; Roger Grabowski, "Equity Risk Premium: What Is the Current Evidence?" *Business Valuation Review,* Fall 2005; and Roger Grabowski, "Equity Risk Premium: What Is the Current Evidence?" *Business Valuation Digest,* Vol. 12, no. 1, February 2006, The Chartered Institute of Chartered Business Valuators.

derive an estimate of beta from the betas of publicly traded guideline companies, most often guideline companies in the same industry as the subject company.

Many different financial reporting services publish betas for publicly traded securities. These include Value Line Investment Survey, Bloomberg, Tradeline North America, and Morningstar (formerly Ibbotson Associates). See the bibliography at the end of the chapter for details on locating these sources.

One will find significant differences among betas for the same stock published by different financial reporting services. This is because of differences in computation methods. See Exhibit 9–13 for a discussion of the controversy over different details of computing betas, which can sometimes lead to widely

Exhibit 9–13

Beta Measurement Problems

A major weakness of using the CAPM for its original purpose of understanding the value of securities in a portfolio is the measurement of the various components of the CAPM equation. In particular, there is no single accepted source of data or method for measuring the beta coefficient component of the model.

Different financial reporting services provide different estimates of beta—for the same industry, and even for the same individual security. And, there are at least a dozen reputable financial reporting services that analysts may refer to in order to obtain a beta for a particular security.

One reason that betas differ is that they are calculated using different market indexes. Some financial reporting services use the Standard & Poor's 500 as their benchmark market index; some use the Value Line index; some use the Russell 1000, 2000, or 3000; and so on. Another reason is that different firms use different time frames for beta estimates, which can lead to different estimates of the subject beta. In order to compare the subject security prices to the guideline market index, some financial reporting services use weekly observations, some use monthly observations, some make their observations on the last trading day of each week or month, some make their observations on the last Friday of each month (or of each week), and so forth. These differences in data collection—particularly the differences between weekly observations and monthly observations—can have a material impact on the estimation of beta for the same security.

These first three beta measurement problems are illustrated by the data in the following table; this table presents the beta measurement characteristics of several commonly used financial reporting services.

Fourth, betas are typically measured infrequently; therefore, they can be "out of date" as of the particular valuation date. It is common for the most recent betas reported by reputable financial reporting services to have been estimated several months before the publication date of the financial service. And, most financial reporting services do not estimate individual betas on a real-time basis. Rather, they will estimate the beta for an individual security periodically—typically only a few times each year.

Fifth, betas are not available for many securities. For example, betas are not generally available for infrequently traded securities. And, there are literally thousands of publicly listed securities that are not followed by the financial reporting services. So, published betas are not readily available for those securities.

Therefore, with all of these beta measurement problems, the analyst is often uncertain as to the following:

1. What is the correct beta for the selected guideline companies used in the subject valuation analysis?

2. What is the correct beta for the subject company (whether or not a "published" beta is estimated directly or a beta based upon guideline companies is estimated indirectly)?

Beta Measurement Characteristics of Common Financial Reporting Services

Financial Reporting Service	Market Index	Measurement Interval	Measurement Time Period
Bloomberg Professional	S&P 500 and others	Daily, weekly, monthly, annually	Adjustable
Ibbotson Associates	S&P 500	Twice yearly	5 years
Merrill Lynch	S&P 500	Monthly	5 years
S&P Compustat	S&P 500	Monthly	5 years
Tradeline North America	S&P 500	Weekly	3 years
Value Line Investment Survey	NYSE Composite	Weekly	5 years

divergent results. One of the implications of this is that the betas for all of the guideline companies used in a valuation should come from the same source. If not all of the betas for the guideline companies are available from a single source, the best solution is probably to use the source that provides betas for the largest number of guideline companies, and to not use betas for the other guideline companies. Ultimately, the decision on which betas to use involves judgment on the part of the analyst.

Size Premium

As noted earlier, a substantial body of published research indicates that the size of the company is important in that stocks of smaller companies are riskier than those of larger ones and that small-company stocks command a higher expected rate of return in the market. The *SBBI Yearbook* quantifies this in the chapter "Firm Size and Return," as presented in Exhibit 9–11.

Starting with the *SBBI Valuation Edition 2001 Yearbook*, the size premium data were expanded to include a split of the 10th decile into two size groupings—the 10a decile and the 10b decile—based on the data from the University of Chicago Center for Research in Security Prices (CRSP). The 10th decile still includes the smallest 10 percent of the stocks on the combined NYSE/AMEX/Nasdaq markets as measured by market value of equity—in 2004 up to approximately $263 million.[37]

The two size premium categories added in the 2001 *Yearbook*—the 10a and 10b deciles—were introduced to help with the cost of capital estimation process for very small companies. In 2004, the market capitalization of the largest company in the 10a size grouping was about $263 million, while the market capitalization for the smallest company in the 10b grouping was about $84 million.[38]

Roger Grabowski has presented evidence that the historical size premium embedded in the 10b decile data may be biased high because *SBBI* measures "size" only by market value.[39] Evidence that makes the use of the size premium from the 10b decile problematic is:

- The beta of 10b is less than the beta of 10a even though users of the data believe that the companies making up 10b are more risky; this may indicate that there may be beta measurement issues.
- Troubled companies make up a large number of the companies included in 10b; their market values are trading as call options, causing the beta measurement problem.
- The size premium of 10b is 2.50 to 3.00 percent greater than the size premiums indicated in the Grabowski-King studies for their 25th portfolio (smallest companies); Grabowski and King eliminate troubled companies in their studies.

It is noteworthy that the size premium is *in addition* to the basic equity risk premium already modified by the effect of the beta, and betas for smaller stocks tend to be greater than those for larger stocks. The correct formula, reflecting *both* beta and the size premium, is the following:

---

[37] *SBBI Valuation Edition 2005 Yearbook*, p. 129.

[38] Ibid., p. 136.

[39] Roger Grabowski, "Cost of Capital: The 10th Decile," presentation to Business Valuation Conference of Foundation for Accounting Education, New York, May 2005; and Roger Grabowski, "Alternatives to Traditional CAPM," presentation to NACVA 12th Annual Consultants Conference, Philadelphia, June 2005.

Formula 9–10

$$E(R_i) = R_f + B(RP_m) + RP_s$$

where:

$E(R_i)$	=	Expected return on an individual security
R_f	=	Rate of return available on a risk-free security (as of the valuation date); when using the *SBBI* size premium data, the risk-free rate should be 30-day, 5-year, or 20-year government bond yields, used in conjunction with the corresponding equity risk premium
B	=	Beta of the individual security
(RP_m)	=	Equity risk premium for a security with a beta of 1.0
RP_s	=	Risk premium for size (size premium)

Industry Risk Premia

Starting with the 2000 *Yearbook*, the *SBBI Valuation Edition* has expanded to include a new set of data points that can potentially be useful in estimating the cost of equity by the build-up method—the industry risk premia estimates, if the analyst is aware of the underlying data. In 2000, industry risk premia estimates were available only for a limited number of broad two-digit Standard Industry Classification (SIC) codes, but the data set was expanded over time. As of the 2005 *Yearbook*, industry premia estimates were available for over 300 SIC codes. The SIC codes have been expanded to include four-digit SIC codes, allowing users to match the risk characteristics of a subject company with those of the industry group more closely. To help users of data to more closely match a subject company with the industry, in 2003 Ibbotson started offering a list of the companies used in the computation of the industry risk premium estimates as a supplement to the *SBBI*. The report can be downloaded from www.morningstar.com/irp.

It is important to note that the *SBBI* "Industry Risk Premium" is really a version of the CAPM method. It is estimated as [BETA * MRP minus MRP], which when added to the MRP will give you BETA * MRP, where BETA is Morningstar's (formerly Ibbotson Associates') estimate of the industry beta for the given industry group and MRP is the market risk premium. It is equivalent to using CAPM with all of the companies in the SIC code as guideline companies.

Investment-Specific Risk

The estimation of the effect of investment-specific (unsystematic) risk is often a matter for the analyst's professional judgment. The risk factors will be developed as part of the quantitative and qualitative analyses discussed in Part II of this book, and the significant positive and negative factors related to these analyses should be noted in the valuation report. These analyses will reveal many things that will affect the economic income projections, as well as the probability of achieving those projections. The analyst should be careful to distinguish between those factors that influence the *magnitude* of the projection (the numerator in the model) and those factors that affect the *degree of uncertainty* of achieving the mathematical expectation projection (that is, the *risk*, which determines the discount rate, the denominator in the model). The analyst must be especially careful to avoid undue double counting, such as reflecting a negative factor fully by a reduction in the economic income projection, and then magnifying the effect by an increase in the discount rate for the negative factor.

Care must be taken to assure that adjustments to the discount rate do not duplicate adjustments to value made elsewhere in the analysis. For instance, an analyst may believe that the shares of a privately held company should offer a higher rate of return than those of a publicly traded company, and may wish to adjust the discount rate accordingly. But it is common practice to adjust for the privately held status of a company by applying a discount for lack of marketability to the marketable value (see Chapter 17). Making both adjustments will lead to double counting of the effects of nonmarketability.

There is no specific model or formula for quantifying the exact effect of all the investment-specific risk factors on the discount rate. This ultimately is based on the analyst's experience and judgment. It is noteworthy that the analysis may lead to the conclusion that the subject company is *less risky* than industry or guideline company averages, in which case the investment-specific risk adjustment may *reduce* the discount rate.

Arbitrage Pricing Theory Factors

There is one major source for arbitrage pricing theory data. Birr Portfolio Analysis, Inc., publishes *BIRR Risks and Returns Analyzer*, a PC-based software tool. The contact information for this source can be found in the bibliography at the end of this chapter.

Rate of Return Allowed to Regulated Companies

Additional cost of capital data are available when estimating the appropriate discount rate for a regulated company.

Public utility commissioners in all 50 states allow regulated utilities to charge rates to their customers that provide what supposedly is a fair rate of return on investment (often called the *rate base*). These allowed rates of return generally are based on the respective commissions' perceptions of the cost of debt capital and the cost of equity capital based on studies by their staffs. Utility commissions' allowed rate of return orders usually also specify an allowed overall rate of return on invested capital, based on their conclusions as to the appropriate capital structure. Multimillions of dollars are involved in these rate-setting decisions, which come about through hard-fought negotiations and hearings that sometimes culminate in lawsuits and rate base decisions rendered in court.

Regulated companies usually are regulated because they have a captive market and are in a monopoly position to supply a needed service; thus, their cost of capital should be considerably lower than that for an average company. Therefore, allowed rates of return for regulated companies can be viewed as a reasonable benchmark for a minimum boundary of the overall cost of capital.

Cost of Capital Yearbook

Starting in 1995, Ibbotson Associates combined into one publication several of the previous data items plus other information relevant to estimating the cost of equity, and also information useful for valuation work. Exhibit 9–14 is an example of the

Exhibit 9–14

STATISTICS FOR SIC CODE 1381
Drilling Oil and Gas Wells
This Industry Comprises 10 Companies

Industry Description

Establishments primarily engaged in drilling wells for oil or gas field operations for others on a contract or fee basis. This industry includes contractors that specialize in spudding in, drilling in, redrilling, and directional drilling.

Sales (million$)

Total	7,368
Average	736.8
Three Largest Companies	
PRIDE INTERNATIONAL INC	1,712.2
DIAMOND OFFSHRE DRILLING INC	1,221.0
ENSCO INTERNATIONAL INC	1,046.9
Three Smallest Companies	
PIONEER DRILLING CO	185.2
ATWOOD OCEANICS	168.5
TRI-VALLEY CORP	4.4

Total Capital (million$)

Total	42,821
Average	4,282.1
Three Largest Companies	
DIAMOND OFFSHRE DRILLING INC	12,528.9
ENSCO INTERNATIONAL INC	8,391.4
PRIDE INTERNATIONAL INC	6,783.8
Three Smallest Companies	
PARKER DRILLING CO	1,380.4
PIONEER DRILLING CO	833.2
TRI-VALLEY CORP	180.0

SIC vs. S&P 500 for Last 10 Years (%)

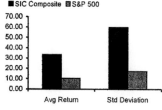

■ SIC Composite ▨ S&P 500

Number of Companies & Total Capital (billion$)

S&P Debt Rating	Large Cap	Mid Cap	Low Cap	Micro Cap	Totals	
AAA, AA, A	1	0	0	0	1	(companies)
	12.5	0.0	0.0	0.0	12.5	(capital)
BBB	1	0	0	0	1	
	8.4	0.0	0.0	0.0	8.4	
BB, B, CCC, CC, D	0	1	2	0	3	
	0.0	6.8	3.1	0.0	9.9	
Not Rated	0	2	2	1	5	
	0.0	9.4	2.5	0.2	12.0	
Totals	2	3	4	1	10	
	20.9	16.1	5.6	0.2	42.8	

Annualized Statistics for Last 10 Years (%)

	Avg Return	Std Deviation
S&P 500	10.29	17.20
SIC Composite	33.38	59.86
Large Composite	29.71	58.58
Small Composite	47.03	77.69

Compound Annual Equity Return (%)

	5 Years	10 Years
75th Percentile	19.98	32.29
Median	12.47	17.92
25th Percentile	7.87	14.88
SIC Composite	16.89	21.73
Large Composite	14.89	18.16
Small Composite	32.63	30.27

Sales, Income & Market Capitalization (billion$)

	Sales	Operating Income	Net Income	Equity Capital	Debt Capital
Current Yr.	7.4	2.7	1.0	38.7	4.2
Last Yr.	5.7	1.4	0.1	25.4	5.0
2 Yrs. Ago	4.6	1.2	0.0	15.9	4.7
3 Yrs. Ago	5.4	1.8	0.4	13.6	4.4
4 Yrs. Ago	4.8	1.8	0.7	16.4	3.9

Growth Over Last 5 Years (%)

	Net Sales	Operating Income	Net Income
Median	17.68	20.17	18.16
SIC Composite	16.98	21.98	44.50
Large Composite	17.04	24.26	40.53
Small Composite	18.31	6.59	9.08

Capital Structure Ratios (%)

	Debt/Total Capital Latest	Debt/Total Capital 5-Year Avg	Debt/MV Equity Latest	Debt/MV Equity 5-Year Avg
Median	5.66	16.84	6.00	20.38
SIC Composite	5.88	18.06	6.25	22.04
Large Composite	5.66	20.77	6.00	26.21
Small Composite	3.40	13.78	3.52	15.99

Distribution of Sales & Total Capital (million$)

	Distribution of Sales Latest	Distribution of Sales 5-Year Avg	Total Capital Latest	Total Capital 5-Year Avg
90th Percentile	1,270.1	925.7	8805.1	5,134.6
75th Percentile	1,035.4	794.0	6467.3	3,842.6
Median	748.9	539.3	2777.9	1,573.3
25th Percentile	271.9	219.6	1447.7	822.0
10th Percentile	152.1	88.7	767.9	274.7

Margins (%)

	Operating Margin Latest	Operating Margin 5-Year Avg	Net Margin Latest	Net Margin 5-Year Avg	Asset Turnover Latest	Asset Turnover 5-Year Avg	Return on Inv. Cap. Latest	Return on Inv. Cap. 5-Year Avg	Return on Assets Latest	Return on Assets 5-Year Avg	Return on Equity Latest	Return on Equity 5-Year Avg
Median	30.45	29.02	15.69	8.42	46.42	42.13	8.39	3.50	7.82	3.07	2.42	2.61
SIC Composite	36.01	31.94	14.25	7.84	45.65	38.95	6.93	3.29	6.50	3.05	2.95	2.53
Large Composite	39.53	34.33	14.03	8.25	35.63	30.97	6.46	2.78	5.00	2.56	2.44	2.31
Small Composite	25.73	27.24	9.95	6.92	49.84	45.31	3.65	3.19	4.96	3.13	1.52	2.13

Equity Valuation Ratios (Multiples)

	Price/Earnings Latest	Price/Earnings 5-Year Avg	Market/Book Latest	Market/Book 5-Year Avg	Price/Sales Latest	Price/Sales 5-Year Avg	Price/Cash Flow Latest	Price/Cash Flow 5-Year Avg	Price/Operating Income Latest	Price/Operating Income 5-Year Avg	Dividend Yield (% of Price) Latest	Dividend Yield (% of Price) 5-Year Avg
Median	41.40	38.37	3.87	2.02	4.66	2.98	54.79	NMF	14.26	10.07	0.00	0.00
SIC Composite	33.86	17.17	3.57	2.07	4.82	3.09	51.25	213.54	13.40	9.69	0.97	0.70
Large Composite	41.00	19.89	3.52	1.90	5.75	3.58	73.12	162.00	14.55	10.41	1.38	0.92
Small Composite	66.00	29.21	4.10	2.60	6.57	3.25	120.93	NMF	25.53	11.94	0.00	0.00

Growth Rates (%) / Cost of Equity Capital (%) / Weighted Average Cost of Capital (%) / Levered Betas / Unlevered Betas

	Analysts' Estimate	CAPM CAPM + Size Prem	3-Factor Fama-French	Discounted Cash Flow 1-Stage	Discounted Cash Flow 3-Stage	CAPM CAPM + Size Prem	3-Factor Fama-French	Discounted Cash Flow 1-Stage	Discounted Cash Flow 3-Stage	Levered Betas Raw Beta	Levered Betas Adjusted Beta	Unlevered Betas Adjusted Beta
Median	48.89	13.33	14.50	15.13	48.89	14.30	12.89	13.17	14.70	47.30	13.55	1.21	1.17	1.09
SIC Composite	48.89	11.78	12.80	14.81	49.19	18.50	11.34	12.27	14.10	45.40	17.46	1.12	0.95	0.89
Large Composite	48.15	12.04	12.04	15.23	49.48	17.80	11.44	11.44	14.28	44.82	16.57	1.17	0.98	0.91
Small Composite	62.44	12.61	14.42	16.62	48.89	12.40	12.39	14.13	16.23	47.19	12.18	1.35	1.07	1.04

SOURCE: Ibbotson Associates, *Cost of Capital 2006 Yearbook*, data through March 2006.

information offered in the *Cost of Capital Yearbook* for each of over 350 SIC code groups (see the bibliography at the end of this chapter).

This is a convenient and potentially powerful compilation of data for use in valuation work. We caution readers who use it, however, to study the definitions of all data items carefully before using the data in a valuation analysis. Some definitions are not completely implied by the short titles describing the data points in the tables. Other definitions are not what we may ideally desire, usually because of limitations on the availability of data. The definitions *are* explained in detail. Used carefully, this can be a very useful reference source for valuation analysis.

Discounting Economic Income Available to Overall Capital

Until now in this chapter, we have focused on discounting economic income that is available to common equity holders. In some situations (which will be described elsewhere in this book), it is desirable to value more than just the common equity—often all the equity and all the interest-bearing debt [sometimes referred to as the *entire capital structure,* the *value of the company,* the *enterprise value,* or *market value of invested capital* (MVIC)].

In these instances, the projected cash flow (or other economic income) must include that which is available to *all* the components of the capital structure being valued. The discount rate must be the weighted average of the costs of each of the components of the capital structure, *with the weighted average being based on the market value of each capital component.* This is called the *weighted-average cost of capital* (WACC). In other words, the cost of a company's overall capital is the weighted average of the costs of all of the financing sources in its capital structure.

Defining the Capital Structure

When people refer to "the value of the company" (as opposed to just the value of the equity), they usually mean the value of the company's capital structure. However, this still may leave ambiguity concerning exactly what is included in the "capital structure."

Treatment of Interest-Bearing Debt. The most commonly used conceptual definition of *capital structure* is all equity and all long-term debt (including current maturities of long-term debt). However, to value the capital structure defined in this way using the discounted economic income method, it is necessary to include the interest on the long-term debt in the income being discounted and to treat other interest (such as on a bank operating line of credit) as an expense. If getting the necessary information to separate the two elements of interest is not practical, a commonly used solution to the problem is to define the capital structure to include all interest-bearing debt. Interest-bearing debt may be defined to include the permanent portion of interest-bearing current liabilities. This would be the case if, for example, 90-day notes payable (otherwise classified as a current liability) are used as a permanent source of capital for the subject company. Using all interest-bearing debt eliminates a judgment call by the analyst as to the appropriate levels of long-term versus short-term debt.

Treatment of Non-Interest-Bearing Items. Another issue in some cases is whether or not to include certain non-interest-bearing long-term liabilities in the capital structure. This may include, for example, such items as deferred taxes and pension liabilities. If any such items are included, some portion of the capital structure will have zero cost of capital.

Conceptually, the most commonly accepted answer is that these items should be included if it is expected that they will be paid and excluded if payment is not expected. This, then, requires a judgment call. The analyst should also keep in mind that weightings of the components of the capital structure for the purpose of estimating a WACC are at *market value*. Therefore, if non-interest-bearing liabilities are to be included, an estimate of when they will be paid is required so that their face value can be discounted to a present market value to determine their weight. As a practical matter, non-interest-bearing liabilities usually are not included in calculations of a WACC, but there are times when they are important enough to consider.

In any case, when discounting the economic income available to the company, it is important to specify what is assumed to be included in the capital structure.

Weighted-Average Cost of Capital Formula

The basic formula for computing the after-tax WACC is as follows:

Formula 9–11

$$WACC = (k_e \times W_e) + [k_d (1-t) \times W_d]$$

where:

$WACC$	=	Weighted average cost of capital
k_e	=	Company's cost of common equity capital
k_d	=	Company's cost of debt capital
W_e	=	Percentage of equity capital in the capital structure
W_d	=	Percentage of debt capital in the capital structure
t	=	Company's effective income tax rate

Assume the following:

Cost of equity capital:	0.25
Cost of debt capital:	0.10
Proportion of equity in capital structure:	0.70
Proportion of debt in capital structure:	0.30
Income tax rate:	0.40

These data would be substituted into this formula as follows:

$$(0.25 \times 0.70) + [0.10(1-0.40) \times 0.30]$$
$$= 0.175 + (0.06 \times 0.30)$$
$$= 0.175 + 0.018$$
$$= \underline{\underline{0.193}}$$

So, the overall cost of capital in this example is 19.3 percent.

In many cases, there is a more complex capital structure, perhaps with preferred stock and more than one class of debt. This formula would simply be expanded to include a term for each class of capital.

Should an Actual or a Hypothetical Capital Structure Be Used?

If the company is to be valued *as it is* (under the strict fair market value standard, assuming that the capital structure will remain intact), then the amount of debt in the company's actual capital structure should be used. Certainly, if a minority ownership interest is to be valued directly by a procedure involving (first) valuing overall capital and (then) subtracting debt, using the actual amount of debt in the company's capital structure would seem appropriate. This is because it would be beyond the power of a noncontrolling stockholder to change the capital structure. However, if a minority interest is being valued by first valuing 100 percent of the company and then subtracting lack of control discounts, it may be more appropriate to use a hypothetical capital structure. This is because one of the things you might consider in selecting the amount of lack of control discount to apply might be the inability to affect the capital structure—therefore, if the analyst was to reflect a disadvantaged capital structure in the WACC *and* include it in the lack of control discount, it would be double-counted.

The analyst should keep in mind that the weightings in the capital structure are at market value. Therefore, if there is a fixed amount of debt and the WACC is used to estimate the market value of equity, computations may need to be iterated with different assumed capital structures until the estimated market value of equity results in the assumed market value capital structure weights.

Regardless of the rationale behind the choice of capital structure, it should be kept in mind that the weighted-average cost of capital assumes a ratio of debt to equity that is roughly consistent with the company's financial leverage over the long term. In other words, the current leverage is less important than the desired future leverage of the company. It is seldom the case, for instance, that a company wishes to sustain a proportion of debt greater than that of equity in its capital structure (with the exception of a few industries such as public utilities). Companies with very high leverage generally achieve such status *involuntarily*. For instance, a company may have lost equity value as a result of bad investments or deteriorating market conditions, leading to a high debt-to-equity ratio. Moreover, companies that *voluntarily* take on high leverage often hope to pay down their debt aggressively out of future operating cash flows. This is commonly the plan in the case of leveraged buyouts.

Financial theory has not yet developed a generally accepted theory for predicting a given company's capital structure. For this reason, analysts commonly look at the average capital structure of guideline companies as a benchmark for a company's normal capital structure.

In cases in which it is necessary to use an actual leverage that is unusually high or low relative to the normal long-term leverage of the company, the analyst should consider one of various approaches to value that incorporate changing leverage over time. The simplest of these approaches is the "adjusted present value" approach. This approach discounts unlevered cash flows using a debt-free cost of capital (an "unlevered equity" rate of return), adds the value of the tax savings created by the interest tax shield on debt financing, and may add other adjustments to value for "financial side effects" such as expected costs of financial distress in the case of a highly leveraged company).[40]

---

[40] For the adjusted present value method, see, for example, T. Luehrman, "Using APV: A Better Tool for Valuing Operations," *Harvard Business Review,* Vol. 75, 1997, pp. 145–154; S. Kaplan and R. Ruback, "The Valuation of Cash Flow Forecast: An Empirical Analysis," *Journal of Finance,* Vol. 50, 1995, pp. 1059–1093; and R. A. Brealey and S. C. Myers, *Principles of Corporate Finance,* 8th ed. (New York: McGraw–Hill, 2006).

If a controlling ownership interest is to be valued and the standard of value is fair market value, an argument can be made that an industry-average capital structure should be used. This is because a control buyer would have the power to change the capital structure and the industry average could represent the most likely result. However, in such a case, it would be important to understand how the industry-average capital structure is derived and whether or not it is reasonable to expect the subject company to achieve it, given (1) the current conditions of the company itself and (2) the current financial market conditions. Alternatively, it may be appropriate to consider a capital structure that the company could achieve under an asset-based loan scenario. By availing itself of extra funding, the company could take advantage of growth opportunities that the current ownership is simply not taking advantage of. If a controlling ownership interest is to be valued under the standard of investment value, then the buyer's or owner's capital structure could be used.

Specific Projection Period plus a Terminal Value

So far, we have presented the basic discounted economic income model, in which specific projections of economic income are made over the life of the investment. However, as a practical matter, there are very few investments for which reliable projections can be made over the entire life of the investment. Variations of the model reflect this limitation.

The most common multistage variation of the discounted economic income model is a two-stage model that projects economic income for a finite number of periods, usually one business cycle of somewhere between 3 and 10 years, and then assumes a *terminal value* at the end of the discrete projection period. Note that the only reason one would use a discounted cash flow method as opposed to a capitalized cash flow model is that the subject company predicts a period of variability in its earnings stream for some period of time into the future. The appropriate length of the forecast period should be until that variability stops; at the point in time that the company expects normalized or level growth, the terminal value is calculated. If no variability is expected, then there is no point in forecasting interim years' cash flow, as there are no variable interim years. In effect, the terminal year, next year, is the only year from which value is ever calculated, and growth is built into the rate of return instead of the cash flow. However, it is important to note that the capitalization model implies a steady rate of growth in perpetuity.

This terminal value is sometimes also called the *residual value*, the *reversionary value*, or the *future value*. The formula for this model can be generalized as follows:

Formula 9–12

$$PV = \frac{E_1}{(1+k)} + \frac{E_2}{(1+k)^2} + \ldots + \frac{E_n}{(1+k)^n} + \frac{FV}{(1+k)^n}$$

where:

$E_1 \ldots E_n =$ Expected amounts of economic income (often net cash flow) in each of periods E_1 through E_n

k =   Discount rate

n =   Number of periods in the discrete projection period

FV =   Future value or terminal value (the prospective value as of the end of the discrete projection period)

The immediately obvious characteristic of this formula is that it depends partly on a projection of the value of the subject company several periods in the future to estimate the value of the subject company today! It is not uncommon for the present value of the terminal value in this formulation to account for more than half of the total present value. Therefore, the matter of how the terminal value is estimated is an important part of the estimate of present value.

If one assumes that the business will continue indefinitely as a viable going concern after the number of years for which discrete projections were made, two procedures are commonly used to estimate the terminal value:

1. Capitalization of ongoing economic income
2. An estimated market multiple of the economic income projected for the last year of the discrete projection period

The capitalization method is the procedure favored by most business appraisers. It is discussed in some detail in the next chapter.

Many investment bankers are prone to use the market multiple method. If one is discounting returns to equity, this method involves a multiple of some measure of income available to equity, most typically a P/E multiple. If one is discounting returns available to overall capital, this method involves a multiple of some measure of income available to overall capital, most typically EBIT or EBITDA. From this result, debt must be subtracted.

The market multiple method introduces into the income approach the added dimension of projecting a market multiple as of the end of the projection period. As noted earlier, the terminal value often accounts for half or more of the value indicated by the DCF method. The market multiple brings a major element of the market approach into the income approach. Many valuation analysts prefer to keep the income approach and the market approach as distinct from each other as possible. Many believe that using the Gordon growth model capitalization procedure described in the next chapter does a better job of keeping the indications of value derived from the income approach and the market approach as independent of each other as possible.[41]

Under certain circumstances, the terminal value may be based on the premise that the company will be liquidated at the end of the discrete projection period. In this case, the terminal value requires an estimate of the liquidation value of the subject company assets as of that future date.

The "Midyear Discounting Convention"

In the formulas presented up to this point, we have implied (by using whole integer exponents) that the cash flows (or other economic income) are expected to be received at the *end* of each period. This may be a reasonable approximation if a

---

[41] Whether one is using a market multiple or the Gordon growth model to estimate the terminal value, the resulting implied growth rate and market multiple, respectively, should be checked for reasonableness.

closely held company waits until the end of its fiscal year to see how things are before assessing capital requirements and deciding on shareholder distributions, although it ignores the fact that cash can be reinvested pending distribution.

On the other hand, sometimes it seems more reasonable to assume that cash flows are received (or at least available) more or less evenly throughout the year. This projection can be reflected in the discounted economic income model by using the *midyear discounting convention*. This convention projects cash flows as being received at the middle rather than the end of each year, thus more or less approximating the valuation effect of even cash flows throughout the year.

The modification to Formula 9–12 to accommodate the midyear discounting convention results in the following:

Formula 9–13

$$PV = \frac{E_1}{(1+k)^{0.5}} + \frac{E_2}{(1+k)^{1.5}} + \ldots + \frac{E_n}{(1+k)^{n-0.5}} + \frac{FV}{(1+k)^n}$$

where the variables are defined the same as in Formula 9–12. Note, in particular, that in all calculations, the terminal value is calculated as of the beginning of the nth period. To calculate it at any other time would require an adjustment to the cash flows included in the interim periods.

The next chapter explains how the terminal value calculation can be modified for the midyear discounting convention (see Formula 10–12).

Of course, failure to use the midyear discounting convention slightly decreases the indicated present value. This is because the midyear discounting convention assumes that the cash flows will be received earlier on average than the year-end discounting model assumes.

The valuation model can be varied to accommodate any material assumptions about the timing of cash flows, such as monthly, quarterly, or irregularly. For example, a toy company may have predictably high seasonal cash flows in the fourth quarter, or an accounting firm may have a predictable bulge in cash flows during tax season. The calculations for any such variations can be done on any pocket financial calculator.

Example of Application of Discounted Economic Income Methods

In a series of exhibits, we present the use of several of the basic discounted economic income methods to value 100 percent of the equity of Global Consulting, Inc., as of December 31, 2005. The basic information, including the December 31, 2005, balance sheet, three years of projected balance sheets, income statements, cash flows to equity, cash flows to invested capital, and other information, is presented as Exhibit 9–15A.

The example projects stable growth for the entire projection period. This projection allows us to show how any of four methods can be used, all resulting in the same value:

1. Discounted net cash flow available to equity
2. Perpetual growth model using net cash flow available to equity

Exhibit 9–15A

Global Consulting, Inc.

Balance Sheets (in 000s)

End of Year	Actual 2005	2006	Projected 2007	2008
Current assets	$30,000	$31,500	$33,075	$34,728
Plant and equipment	90,000	101,000	112,550	124,677
Less: Accumulated depreciation	60,000	69,000	78,450	88,372
Net plant and equipment	30,000	32,000	34,100	36,305
Total assets	$60,000	$63,500	$67,175	$71,033
Current liabilities	$10,000	$10,500	$11,025	$11,576
Long-term debt	40,000	42,000	44,100	46,305
Equity	10,000	11,000	12,050	13,152
Total liabilities and equity	$60,000	$63,500	$67,175	$71,033

Income Statements (in 000s)

	2006	2007	2008
Sales	$200,000	$210,000	$220,500
Cost of sales	120,000	126,000	132,300
Gross margin	80,000	84,000	88,200
General operating expenses	52,000	54,600	57,330
Depreciation	9,000	9,450	9,922
Earnings before interest & taxes (EBIT)	19,000	19,950	20,948
Interest (10% of beginning LTD)	4,000	4,200	4,410
Taxable income (EBT)	15,000	15,750	16,538
Income taxes (40%)	6,000	6,300	6,615
Net income	$9,000	$9,450	$9,923

Other Information

Expected growth rate in perpetuity is 5 percent (applies to all income statement items, net working capital, capital expenditures, and long-term debt).

Capital expenditures year 2006: $11 million.

Market value of long-term debt = Book value of long-term debt.

All net cash flow to equity will be paid out in dividends.

Calculation of Net Cash Flow to Equity (in 000s)

	2006	2007	2008
Net income	$9,000	$9,450	$9,923
+ Depreciation	9,000	9,450	9,922
− Capital expenditures	11,000	11,550	12,127
− Increase in net working capital	1,000	1,050	1,102
+ Increase in long-term debt	2,000	2,100	2,205
= Net cash flow to equity	$8,000	$8,400	$8,820

Statements of Stockholders' Equity (in 000s)

	2006	2007	2008
Balance at beginning of year	$10,000	$11,000	$12,050
+ Net income	9,000	9,450	9,923
− Dividends paid	8,000	8,400	8,820
= Balance at end of year	$11,000	$12,050	$13,152

Calculation of Net Cash Flow to Invested Capital (in 000s)			
	2006	**2007**	**2008**
Net income	$9,000	$9,450	$9,923
+ Depreciation	9,000	9,450	9,922
− Capital expenditures	11,000	11,550	12,127
− Increase in net working capital	1,000	1,050	1,102
+ Interest expense (net of 40% income taxes)	2,400	2,520	2,646
= Net cash flow to invested capital	$8,400	$8,820	$9,261

3. Discounted net cash flow available to all invested capital (market value of invested capital less value of debt)
4. Perpetual growth model using net cash flow available to all invested capital (market value of invested capital less value of debt)

Note again, however, that although we present the DCF and CCF for illustrative purposes, if these were the actual facts, there would be no point in creating a discounted cash flow model (either equity or WACC) in the case of level growth (assuming further, in the case of WACC, that the debt-to-equity ratio will stay constant).

Estimating an Equity Discount Rate

Exhibit 9–15B illustrates the estimation of the cost of equity capital for the subject company using the capital asset pricing model. The sources of all components are footnoted in the exhibit, so that one can seek out the sources and replicate the work.

Discounting Net Cash Flow to Equity

Exhibit 9–15C illustrates discounting the cash flow to equity using the projected net cash flows to equity from Exhibit 9–15A and the discount rate developed in

Exhibit 9–15B

Illustrative Example of Discount Rate Applicable to Equity

	Risk-free rate (20-year U.S. Treasury bond) [a]		4.61%
+	Systematic risk:		
	Long-horizon expected equity risk premium [b]	7.17	
	× Beta [c]	1.5	
			10.76
+	Expected size premium [d]		6.41
+	Specific (unsystematic) risk [e]		3.00
=	Discount rate (indicated)		24.78
	Discount rate (rounded)		25.00

a. Rate available as of December 31, 2005, from *Federal Reserve Statistical Release*.
b. *Stocks, Bonds, Bills, and Inflation Valuation Edition 2005 Yearbook*, p. 71.
c. Median beta of guideline companies from Standard & Poor's Compustat.
d. *Stocks, Bonds, Bills, and Inflation Valuation Edition 2005 Yearbook*, p. 135.
e. Analyst's estimate.

Exhibit 9–15C

Estimation of Value of Equity (Discounted Cash Flow Method)

2006		2007		2008		Terminal Value
$\dfrac{\$8,000,000}{(1+0.25)}$	$+$	$\dfrac{\$8,400,000}{(1+0.25)^2}$	$+$	$\dfrac{\$8,820,000}{(1+0.25)^3}$	$+$	$\dfrac{\$46,305,000}{(1+0.25)^3}$
$= \dfrac{\$8,000,000}{(1.25)}$	$+$	$\dfrac{\$8,400,000}{(1.25)^2}$	$+$	$\dfrac{\$8,820,000}{(1.25)^3}$	$+$	$\dfrac{\$46,305,000}{(1.25)^3}$
$=$ \$6,400,000	$+$	\$5,376,000	$+$	\$4,515,800	$+$	\$23,708,200
$=$ \$40,000,000 Indicated value of equity						

Exhibit 9–15B. This example uses the perpetual growth model to estimate the terminal value.

With a very short specific projection period, the terminal value constitutes more than half of the total value. The shorter the specific projection period and the lower the discount rate, the greater the proportion of the total value that will be accounted for by the terminal value.

Estimating a Weighted-Average Cost of Capital

Exhibit 9–15D illustrates the estimation of the WACC using the information provided in Exhibit 9–15A and the equity discount rate developed in Exhibit 9–15B.

Discounting Net Cash Flow to Invested Capital

Exhibit 9–15E illustrates discounting the cash flow available to all invested capital using the projected cash flow to invested capital from Exhibit 9–15A and the WACC from Exhibit 9–15D.

In this example, with the short projection period and a WACC that is much lower than the equity discount rate, the terminal value accounts for more than three-quarters of the total market value of invested capital! Some market multiples that might be used as a check on the reasonableness of the terminal value are discussed in Chapter 12 on the guideline transaction method.

The market value of debt, as of the valuation date, is then subtracted from the MVIC to arrive at the market value of equity.

Note: The underlying assumption of using WACC to discount all income to all components of the capital structure is that the capital structure will remain constant in perpetuity.

Caveats in Using Discounted Economic Income Methods

The discounted economic income methods are extremely sensitive to changes in the input variables—that is, the projected cash flows and the discount rate. This is

Exhibit 9–15D

Estimation of Weighted Average Cost of Capital

Capital Component	Amount	Percent of Capital		Cost of Capital		Weighted Average Cost
Market value of debt	$400,000	0.50	×	0.06*	=	0.030
Market value of equity	$400,000	0.50	×	0.25	=	0.125
Weighted average cost of capital						0.155

* Cost of debt × (1 − income tax rate) = 0.10(1 − 0.40) = 0.06.

Exhibit 9–15E

Estimation of Market Value of Invested Capital (Discounted Cash Flow Method)

	2006		2007		2008		Terminal Value
	$\dfrac{\$8,400,000}{(1+0.155)}$	+	$\dfrac{\$8,820,000}{(1+0.155)^2}$	+	$\dfrac{\$9,261,000}{(1+0.155)^3}$	+	$\dfrac{\$92,610,000}{(1+0.155)^3}$
=	$\dfrac{\$8,400,000}{(1.155)}$	+	$\dfrac{\$8,820,000}{(1.155)^2}$	+	$\dfrac{\$9,261,000}{(1.155)^3}$	+	$\dfrac{\$92,610,000}{(1.155)^3}$
=	$7,272,700	+	$6,611,600	+	$6,010,500	+	$60,105,200
=	$80,000,000	Market value of invested capital					
Less	$40,000,000	Value of debt					
Equals	$40,000,000	Indicated value of equity					

especially true of the MVIC version, where one values the entire invested capital using a WACC discount rate and then subtracts the value of existing debt to get an estimate of the value of the equity. This issue is discussed further in the following chapter, where estimates of terminal values using a capitalization method are explored in detail.

Because relatively small changes in input variables may have large impacts on the result, it is often enlightening to perform some sensitivity analysis in conjunction with a discounted economic income method. This could take the form of a sensitivity table showing the impact of a range of discount rates, terminal value multiples, growth rates, and cash flow projections.

Converting a Discount Rate Applicable to Net Cash Flow to a Discount Rate Applicable to Net Income

If it can be assumed that the relationship (ratio) of net income to net cash flow is constant over time, then the formula for converting a discount rate applicable to net cash flow to a discount rate applicable to net income for use in the multiperiod discounted economic income model is as follows:[42]

---

[42] For a proof of the derivation of this formula, see Z. Christopher Mercer, *Valuing Financial Institutions* (New York: McGraw-Hill, 1992), pp. 262–264.

Formula 9–14

$$k_{ni} = \left[\frac{NI}{NCF_e}(k_e - g) \right] + g$$

where:

k_{ni} = Discount rate applicable to net income

$\dfrac{NI}{NCF_e}$ = Assumed constant ratio of net income to net cash flow to equity

k_e = Discount rate applicable to net cash flow

g = Annual compound growth rate in perpetuity for both net income and net cash flow

Note carefully the *critical assumptions* inherent in this formula:

1. Net income and net cash flow bear a constant relationship to each other over time.
2. Both grow at the same constant annual compound rate in perpetuity.

It should be noted that a similar formula can give discount rates appropriate for earnings streams other than net income, such as pretax income.

One way to assess whether these assumptions are realistic is to compute the ratio of net income to net cash flow for the subject company for several years in the past to see whether the ratio has been steady historically. One would still need to judge whether this stability would be expected to continue to hold true.

Another avenue is to research publicly traded companies in the industry to see the extent to which the ratio is reasonably consistent from company to company and over time. One would then have to analyze the extent to which the subject company could be expected to parallel the public companies in this respect.

If the subject company comes close enough to these assumptions to allow one to realistically use this formula, then it is useful to know the following characteristics about how it works out:

1. The higher the cash flow discount rate, the greater the difference between the cash flow discount rate and the net income discount rate.
2. The higher the ratio between net income and net cash flow, the greater the difference between the net cash flow discount rate and the net income discount rate. For any given combination of discount rate and growth rate, this relationship moves proportionately with changes in the percentages by which net income exceeds net cash flow.
3. The higher the growth rate, the less the difference between the net cash flow discount rate and the net income discount rate.

Examples of the application of this formula are presented in Exhibit 9–16. As can be seen, the greatest differences between net cash flow discount rates and net income discount rates are found in situations where there are high net cash flow discount rates, high ratios of net income to net cash flow, and low growth rates.

Net cash flow is generally lower than net income or any other economic income measures that the appraiser is likely to discount or capitalize. Therefore, the discount rate applicable to other measures is almost inevitably higher than the discount rate applicable to net cash flow.

Exhibit 9–16

Differences between Net Cash Flow Discount Rate and Net Income Discount Rate

Formula:

$$k_{ni} = \left[\frac{NI}{NCF_e} (k_e - g) \right] + g$$

	Constant Ratio of Net Income to Net Cash Flow					
	150%	140%	130%	120%	110%	100%
$k_e = 30\%$						
Growth Rate						
2%	14.0%	11.2%	8.4%	5.6%	2.8%	0.0%
4%	13.0%	10.4%	7.8%	5.2%	2.6%	0.0%
6%	12.0%	9.6%	7.2%	4.8%	2.4%	0.0%
8%	11.0%	8.8%	6.6%	4.4%	2.2%	0.0%
$k_e = 25\%$						
Growth Rate						
2%	11.5%	9.2%	6.9%	4.6%	2.3%	0.0%
4%	10.5%	8.4%	6.3%	4.2%	2.1%	0.0%
6%	9.5%	7.6%	5.7%	3.8%	1.9%	0.0%
8%	8.5%	6.8%	5.1%	3.4%	1.7%	0.0%
$k_e = 20\%$						
Growth Rate						
2%	9.0%	7.2%	5.4%	3.6%	1.8%	0.0%
4%	8.0%	6.4%	4.8%	3.2%	1.6%	0.0%
6%	7.0%	5.6%	4.2%	2.8%	1.4%	0.0%
8%	6.0%	4.8%	3.6%	2.4%	1.2%	0.0%

where:

k_{ni} = Discount rate applicable to net income

$\dfrac{NI}{NCF_e}$ = Assumed constant ratio of net income to net cash flow to equity

k_e = Discount rate applicable to net cash flow to equity

g = Annually compounded growth rate in perpetuity for both net income and net cash flow

CAUTION: The preceding critical assumptions for the conversion of a discount rate applicable to net cash flow to equity to a discount rate applicable to net income are rarely met in real-world situations. Therefore, we strongly recommend the use of net cash flow as the measure of economic income to utilize in the discounted economic income method.

It is also noteworthy that the discount rate conversion procedures described here are appropriate for the multiperiod (or yield capitalization) discounted economic income model. They are not necessarily appropriate for the single-period capitalization (direct capitalization) or capitalization of economic income model.

Does the Discounted Economic Income Model Produce a Control or a Minority Value?

As noted earlier in the chapter, the discounted economic income model can produce either a control value or a minority value, depending on the model inputs involving the valuation variables. Generally, if the inputs in the valuation model reflect changes that only a control owner would (or could) make (e.g., changed capital structure, reduced owner's compensation, and so on), then the model would be expected to produce a control value.

If the economic income projections merely reflect the continuation of present policies, then the model would be expected to produce a minority value. If every facet of the company is being so well optimized that a control owner could not improve on it, then there is little or no difference between a control value and a minority value. Further discussion of this notion will be found in Chapters 15 and 16 on control premiums and discounts for lack of control.

The argument is often made that, because discount rates typically are developed based on minority trades in publicly traded stocks, the discount rate is a minority interest discount rate, and therefore the value indicated by a discounted economic income model must be a minority value. There are at least two problems with this argument. First, *most, if not all, of the difference between a control value and a minority value in a discounted economic income model results from differences in the projected economic income (the numerator), not from differences in the discount rate.* Second, while the cost of equity capital is estimated from trades of minority ownership interests, the capital structure (i.e., the percentage of debt versus the percentage of equity) of the subject company is clearly influenced by the controlling stockholder. And, the capital structure mix is at least as important as the cost of equity capital in the estimation of a company's overall WACC—that is, the discount rate associated with net cash flow. In other words, the cost of equity capital may be the same, or nearly the same, whether a control or a minority interest is being calculated. However, the controlling owner (and, generally, not the minority owner) influences the projection of economic income (the numerator in the model) and the capital structure component of the WACC (the denominator in the model).

What Standard of Value Does a Discounted Economic Income Model Produce?

As with the control/minority ownership issue, the answer to this question depends to some extent on the individual valuation variable inputs that go into the model.

If the analyst is valuing a company on a stand-alone basis, the use of that company's own economic income projections and a market-derived cost of capital as the discount rate would be expected to estimate the *fair market value* of the subject business enterprise. If, on the other hand, a particular acquirer with a lower cost of capital would discount an economic income projection at that acquirer's lower cost of capital, then the result would be *investment value*, the value of the subject enterprise to that individual acquirer and only to that acquirer. Similarly, if a potential acquirer were to include synergistic benefits or other enhancements in the economic income projections, then the result would be *investment value* rather than *fair market value*.

Common Errors

While simple in basic concept, the application of the discounted economic income method provides virtually limitless opportunities for errors. The following are a few of the common errors that are made.

Mismatching the Discount Rate with the Economic Income Measure

The most common error in the application of the income approach is using a discount or capitalization rate that is not appropriate for the definition of economic income being discounted or capitalized. This general category of error has almost infinite variations. The following are only a few.

Using a "Safe" Rate to Discount or Capitalize a Risky Return. While not the most common error, this certainly is one of the most egregious. Some analysts have even erroneously discounted a highly risky series of projected economic income figures using the Treasury bill rate!

Applying a Discount Rate to an Income Variable Defined Differently from That to Which the Discount Rate Is Applicable. This general error in itself has many variations. As discussed earlier, most of the methods and sources for developing discount rates used in the practical application of contemporary financial theory and discussed in this book produce a discount rate that is applicable to net cash flow, as defined in an earlier section. The *SBBI Valuation Edition 2005 Yearbook* makes the following point: "It is implicit that the market return data represents returns after corporate taxes but before personal taxes."[43]

Applying a Discount Rate in Real Terms to an Economic Income Projection in Nominal (Current) Terms. Some analysts erroneously subtract the anticipated inflation rate from the discount rate and then apply the adjusted discount rate to an economic income projection that includes inflation (and vice versa). It is noteworthy that all the Ibbotson data are in nominal terms—that is, including inflation.

Applying a Levered Equity Discount Rate to a Debt-Free Earnings Stream, or Applying a WACC to an Equity Cash Flow Stream. As discussed previously in this chapter, net cash flow to equity (after interest) should be discounted at the cost of equity, and net cash flow to invested capital (debt-free) should be discounted at WACC. This error mismatches the cash flows and the discount rates.

Actual Debt Rate in WACC. A common error is to use a cost of debt that is incompatible with the capital structure assumed in the WACC. For instance, it may be that the subject company is highly levered, with very high borrowing costs. However, the analyst may be using a much lower leverage in the WACC weightings, either because the company is undergoing a reorganization of its balance sheet or because an industry-average leverage is appropriate for the purpose at hand. In such a case, the analyst should use a rate of interest appropriate for the lower leverage assumed in the analysis, rather than the company's actual "high yield" rate. This is analogous to the reasoning behind "relevering" beta to the assumed capital structure for determining the required return on equity using CAPM.

---

[43] *SBBI Valuation Edition 2005 Yearbook*, p. 97.

Confusing Discount Rates with Capitalization Rates

The *discount rate* is the cost of capital and applies to all prospective economic income. The *capitalization rate* (as discussed in the following chapter) is a divisor that is applied to some particular economic income (e.g., latest 12 months' earnings, cash flow, and so on). Only when the expected level of economic income is constant in perpetuity are these two rates equal, other than by sheer coincidence.

Nevertheless, some appraisers fall into the trap of using the discount rate (i.e., the cost of capital) as a capitalization rate. We also see the opposite from time to time: using a capitalization rate to discount prospective cash flow or other expected economic income to a present value. The relationship between discount rates and capitalization rates is explained in the next chapter.

Projecting Growth Beyond What the Capital Being Valued Will Support

As businesses grow, they typically need additional working capital and capital expenditures to support the increased level of operations. One of the many advantages of using net cash flow as the prospective economic income measure is that it forces the analyst to explicitly consider these needs. Nevertheless, they are often underestimated. They can be addressed, however, if the projections include a balance sheet along with the income statement.

Projecting That Extrapolation of the Recent Past Represents the Best Estimate of Future Results

All economic, finance, and regulatory literature makes it clear that valuation is a function of expected prospective economic income. The past history is relevant only to the extent that it may, in some cases, provide useful guidance in projecting future economic income. Nevertheless, it is not as uncommon as one might think to see "projections" that are nothing more than a statistical extrapolation of past results, with no analysis of the extent to which the forces generating future economic income will or will not duplicate the recent past. Usually, they will not.

Discounting a Terminal Value for an Incorrect Number of Periods

Referring back to Formula 9–12, it can be seen that the terminal value usually is assumed to be the value at the *beginning* of the period immediately following the discrete projection period. Therefore, it usually should be discounted back to a present value by the same number of years as the last term in the discrete projection period (n in the formula). A common error is to discount the terminal value for $n + 1$ periods, which would be appropriate only if the terminal value represented the estimated value one year following the end of the discrete projection period.

Internally Inconsistent Capital Structure Projection

"Debt-free" methods and methods using betas adjusted for leverage require projections concerning the subject company's capital structure. These projected capital structures are on the basis of *market value*. Often appraisers assume a capital structure in the process of estimating a market value of equity, and the resulting estimated market value of equity makes the capital structure, at the estimated market value, different from that which was assumed.

In such cases, the assumed capital structure needs to be adjusted and the process iterated until the estimated market value of equity results in a capital structure consistent with that which is projected in estimating the cost of capital.

Assumptions That Produce a Standard or Premise of Value Other Than That Called for in the Valuation Engagement

A common example of this type of error is making unsupported adjustments to projected economic income that only a control owner could cause to happen (e.g., lowering the control owner's salary) when valuing a minority ownership interest.

Another common error is projecting a capital structure other than the company's actual capital structure (thereby getting a WACC different from the company's actual WACC) when the standard of value is fair market value on a noncontrolling basis. If an acquirer were to use its own WACC, the implied result would be *investment value* to that acquirer instead of fair market value. Moreover, if the interest is a noncontrolling interest, the holder could not force a change in capital structure.

Summary

This chapter has presented the rationale for the discounted economic income method and step-by-step explanations of each important aspect of its implementation. The chapter has explained the conceptual elements of discount rates and sources of information for developing estimates of appropriate betas.

The discounted economic income method can be used in conjunction with almost any combination of standards of value and ownership characteristics, as long as the projections underlying the valuation variables used in the calculation are consistent with the definition of value being sought.

Bibliography

Adhikari, Mike. "WACC as Used in Capitalization Formula Causes Overvaluation." *Business Valuation Update*, October 2003, pp. 1–4.

Alamar, Benjamin C. "Monte Carlo Simulation in the Valuation of High Risk Businesses." *Business Valuation Review*, December 2002, pp. 186–189.

Budyak, James. "Getting a Grip on Foreign Discount Rates." *Shannon Pratt's Business Valuation Update*, January 2000, pp. 8–10.

Dailey, Michael, and E. Bryant Finison. "A SWOT Model for Quantifying the Company-Specific Risk Premium." *Shannon Pratt's Business Valuation Update*, July 2003.

Dimson, Elroy, Paul Marsh, and Mike Staunton. "Global Evidence on the Equity Premium." *Journal of Applied Corporate Finance*, Summer 2003, pp. 27–38.

Dobner, Michael. "Mid-Year Discounting and Seasonality Factors." *Business Valuation Review*, March 2002, pp. 16–18.

Dorrell, Darrell D. "Discount Rate Comparisons." *National Litigation Consultant's Review*, July 2002, pp. 8–11.

Duvall, Richard M. "Mid-Year or End-of-Year Discounting." *Business Valuation Review*, December 2000, pp. 208–212.

Evans, Frank C. "Debt and Equity Weightings in WACC." *CPA Expert*, Fall 1998, pp. 4–5.

Fama, Eugene, and Kenneth French. "The Equity Premium." *Journal of Finance*, April 2002, pp. 637–659.

Grabowski, Roger. "Equity Risk Premium: What Is the Current Evidence?" *Shannon Pratt's Business Valuation Update*, November 2005, pp. 1–7.

Hitchner, James, and Katherine Morris. "Cost of Capital Controversies: It's Time to Look behind the Curtain" (Parts 1 and 2 of 3). *Shannon Pratt's Business Valuation Update*, October 2004 and January 2005, pp. 18–21 and 1–5.

Hitchner, James, and Paul Vogt. "Cost of Capital Controversies: It's Time to Look behind the Curtain" (Part 3 of 3). *Shannon Pratt's Business Valuation Update*, May 2005, pp. 1, 3–5.

Ibbotson, Roger G., and Peng Chen. "Long-Run Stock Returns: Participating in Real Economy." *Financial Analysts Journal*, Vol. 59, no. 1, January/February 2003, pp. 88–98.

_____. "Stock Market Returns in the Long Run: Participating in the Real Economy." Yale ICF Working Paper No. 00-44, March 2002.

James-Earles, Melanie, and Edwin H. Duett. "Use of the Capital Asset Pricing Model for Valuing Closely Held Companies." *Valuation Strategies*, July/August 2002, pp. 12–17.

Kania, John J. "The Current Status of Adding a Small Firm Risk Premium to the Valuation Discount Rate." *Business Valuation Review*, September 2000, pp. 136–141.

_____. "The Small Firm Risk Premium—Is It a Myth or Is It a Reality?" *Business Valuation Review*, June 2001, pp. 46–47.

_____. "The Small Firm Risk Premium Remains Largely a Myth." *Shannon Pratt's Business Valuation Update*, November 2003.

Kaplan, Stephen N., and Richard S. Ruback. "The Valuation of Cash Flow Forecasts: An Empirical Analysis." *Journal of Finance*, 1995, pp. 1059–1094.

King, David. "Do Data Biases Cause the Small Stock Premium?" *Business Valuation Review,* June 2003, pp. 55–61.

Mandron, Alix. "DCF Valuation Should Be Improved." *Shannon Pratt's Business Valuation Update*, January 2001, pp. 1–4.

_____. "Improved Techniques for Valuing Large-Scale Projects: A Follow-Up." *Journal of Project Finance*, Vol. 6, no. 1, Spring 2000, pp. 33–45.

_____. "Project Valuation: Problem Areas, Theory and Practice." *The Current State of Business Disciplines*, vol. 3, S. B. Dahiya, ed. Rohtak, India: Spellbound Publications, 2000.

Margulis, Mark S., Jeremy Krasner, and Mark J. Melancon. "Size-Adjusting Beta." *Valuation Strategies*, March/April 2005, pp. 4–9, 47.

McNulty, James M., Tony D. Yeh, William S. Schulze, and Michael H. Lubatkin. "What's Your Real Cost of Capital?" *Harvard Business Review*, October 2002, p. 114.

Mellen, Chris M. "The Income Approach in Practice: Where Do We Stand?" *Business Appraisal Practice*, Fall 2002, pp. 33–39.

Pistor, Rubos, and Robert F. Stambaugh. "Cost of Equity Capital and Model Mispricing." *Journal of Finance*, February 1999, pp. 67–114.

Pratt, Shannon P. "Discount Rates Based on CAPM Don't Always Lead to Minority Value." *Shannon Pratt's Business Valuation Update*, March 2001, pp. 1–3.

_____. "More Evidence that Small Company Stocks Have Additional Risk." *Shannon Pratt's Business Valuation Update*, October 2001, p. 2.

_____. "New Measures of Risk That Really Work!" *Shannon Pratt's Business Valuation Update*, December 1999, pp. 1–4.

_____. "One Key Distinction between Market and Income Approach in Use of Net Cash Flow." *Shannon Pratt's Business Valuation Update*, May 2003, pp. 1–2.

_____. "Small Stock Risk Premium No Myth: Size Does Matter." *Shannon Pratt's Business Valuation Update*, September 2001, pp. 1–3.

_____. "Smaller Companies Have Much Higher Cost of Capital than Big Companies; *Pratt's Stats* Multiples Strikingly Different." *Shannon Pratt's Business Valuation Update*, May 2002.

_____. "What's New in Ibbotson Associates' *SBBI Valuation Edition 2002 Yearbook*." *Shannon Pratt's Business Valuation Update*, April 2002.

Reynolds, Kevin B. "Reconciling the Single Period Capitalization Method with the Discounted Future Earnings Method." *Business Appraisal Practice*, Spring 2000, pp. 16–27.

Russell, Robb. "Analysis of Nonfinancial Matters Adds Value to Appraisal." *Shannon Pratt's Business Valuation Update*, November 2004.

Seigneur, Ronald L. "Ibbotson's *SBBI 2001 Valuation Edition* Has Enhanced Features." *Shannon Pratt's Business Valuation Update*, April 2001.

Seigneur, Ronald L., and Tara McDowell. "Ibbotson Associates Launches New Cost of Capital Center at www.ibbotson.com." *Shannon Pratt's Business Valuation Update*, April 2001.

Tarbell, Jeffrey S. "The Small Company Risk Premium: Does It Really Exist?" American Society of Appraisers 18th Annual Advanced Business Valuation Conference, New Orleans, LA, October 29, 1999.

Trout, Robert. "Mid-Year Discounting without Bias." *Business Valuation Review*, December 2001, pp. 39–41.

Vander Linden, Eric. "Cost of Capital Derived from Ibbotson Data Equals Minority Value." *Business Valuation Review*, December 1998, pp. 123–127.

Wiggins, C. Donald. "Matching Cash Flows and Discount Rates in Discounted Cash Flow Appraisals." *Business Valuation Review*, March 1999, pp. 26–35.

Zyla, Mark. "Valuing Companies with Changing Debt Levels: Is the APV Method Better than the DCF?" *Shannon Pratt's Business Valuation Update*, June 2005, pp. 1–5.

Reference Texts

Bierman, Harold, Jr. and Seymour Smidt. *The Capital Budgeting Decision,* 8th ed. Englewood Cliffs, NJ: Prentice-Hall, 1992.

———. *Financial Management for Decision Making*. Frederick, MD: Beard Books, 2003.

Brealey, Richard A., and Stewart C. Myers. *Principles of Corporate Finance*, 8th ed. New York: McGraw-Hill, 2006.

Copeland, Tom, Tim Koller, and Jack Murrin. *Valuation: Measuring and Managing the Value of the Companies*, 3rd ed. Hoboken, NJ: John Wiley & Sons, 2000.

Cornell, Julius. *The Equity Risk Premium*. Hoboken, NJ: John Wiley & Sons, 1999.

Damodaran, Aswath. *Damodaran on Valuation: Security Analysis for Investment and Corporate Finance,* 2nd ed. Hoboken, NJ: John Wiley & Sons, 2006.

_____. *Investment Valuation*, 2nd ed. Hoboken, NJ: John Wiley & Sons, 2002.

Dewing, Arthur Stone. *The Financial Policy of Corporations*, 5th ed. New York: Ronald Press, 1953.

Ehrhardt, Michael C. *The Search for Value: Measuring the Company's Cost of Capital*. Boston: Harvard Business School Press, 1994.

Ibbotson Associates, *Stock, Bonds, Bills, and Inflation, Valuation Edition 2005 Yearbook*. Chicago: Ibbotson Associates, 2004.

Pratt, Shannon P., and Roger Grabowski. *Cost of Capital: Application and Examples*, 3rd ed. Hoboken, NJ: John Wiley & Sons, 2007.

Reilly, Frank K. *Investment Analysis and Portfolio Management,* 7th ed. Mason, OH: South-Western, 2003.

Reilly, Frank K., and Keith C. Brown. *Investment Analysis and Portfolio Management,* 8th ed. Fort Worth, TX: Dryden Press, 2005.

Reilly, Robert F., and Robert P. Schweihs, eds. *The Handbook of Business Valuation and Intellectual Property Analysis*. New York: McGraw-Hill, 2004.

Ross, Stephen A., Randolph W. Westerfield, and Jeffrey F. Jaffe. *Corporate Finance*. New York: McGraw-Hill, 2004.

Sharpe, John. *Texas Property Tax Manual for Discounting Oil and Gas Income*. Austin, TX: Texas Comptroller of Public Accounts, 1994.

Sharpe, William F., Gordon J. Alexander, and Jeffrey V. Bailey. *Fundamentals of Investments*, 3rd ed. Englewood Cliffs, NJ: Prentice-Hall, 2002.

Standard & Poor's. *Standard & Poor's Corporate Value Consulting Group Risk Premium Report 2005*. New York: Standard & Poor's Corporate Value Consulting, 2005.

Williams, John Burr. *The Theory of Investment Value*. Cambridge, MA: Harvard University Press, 1938. Reprint, Flint Hill, VA: Fraser Publishing, 1997.

Arbitrage Pricing Theory Data Sources
Birr Portfolio Analysis, Inc.
BIRR Risks and Returns Analyzer
Durham, NC 27705
(919) 687-7053
www.birr.com

Ibbotson Associates c/o Morningstar
The Beta Book
Cost of Capital Yearbook
225 West Wacker Drive
9th Floor
Chicago, IL 60606
(312) 696-6000
www.ibbotson.com

Sources of Beta
Bloomberg L.P.
499 Park Avenue
New York, NY 10022
(212) 318-2200
www.bloomberg.com

Merrill Lynch & Co., Inc.
4 World Financial Center
New York, NY 10080
(212) 449-9765
www.ml.com

MSN Money
http://moneycentral.msn.com

Tradeline North America
SunGard Market Data Services
112 West Park Drive
Mt. Laurel, NJ 08054
(856) 235-7300
www.marketdata.sungard.com
www.tradeline.com

Standard & Poor's Compustat and
Standard & Poor's Stock Reports
Standard & Poor's Corporation
55 Water St.
New York, NY 10041
(212) 438-1000
www.standardpoors.com
www.compustat.com

Value Line Investment Survey
220 East 42nd Street, 6th Floor
New York, NY 10017
(212) 907-1500
www.valueline.com
Yahoo Finance
http://finance.yahoo.com

Other Cost of Capital Data
Ibbotson Associates c/o Morningstar
Cost of Capital Yearbook
Duff & Phelps, LLC *Risk Premium Report*
Stocks, Bonds, Bills, and Inflation
Stocks, Bonds, Bills, and Inflation: Valuation Edition
225 West Wacker Drive
9th Floor
Chicago, IL 60606
(312) 696-6000
www.ibbotson.com

Chapter 10

Income Approach: Capitalized Economic Income Method

There are two variations of the capitalized future economic income method that are widely used in business valuation today:

1. The perpetual economic income stream model
2. The constant growth model (with a variation commonly referred to as the *Gordon growth model*)[1]

This chapter transitions the reader from the discounted future economic income method of valuation to the capitalized future economic income method, and presents the mechanics, applications, and caveats in utilizing the various versions of the capitalized income method that are used in practice.

Essential Difference between the Discounting Model and the Capitalization Model

A *discount rate* converts *all* of the expected future returns on investment (however defined) to an indicated present value.

In contrast to the more comprehensive method of discounting *all* of the expected returns, a *capitalization rate* converts *only a single expected economic return number* to an indicated present value.

Discount rate	A rate of return used to convert a monetary sum, payable or receivable in the future, into a present value
Capitalization rate	Any divisor (usually expressed as a percentage) that is used to convert anticipated economic benefits of a single period into value[2]
Capitalization of economic income method	A method within the income approach whereby economic benefits for a representative single period are converted to value through division by a capitalization rate[3]
Capitalization	A conversion of a single period of economic benefits into value[4]

In property appraisal terminology, the similar method is called *direct capitalization*, the basic subject matter of this chapter. It is distinguished from what property appraisers call *yield capitalization*, which is comparable to the business appraiser's *discounted economic income*, the subject of the previous chapter.

The capitalized economic income method means the application of one divisor (or multiple) to one economic income measure. The result is an indication of value derived from that single division or multiplication.

For example, let's assume that the next year's net cash flow is expected to be $200,000,000 and the appropriate direct capitalization rate is 25 percent. In this case, the indicated value of the business is $800,000,000:

$$\frac{\$200,000,000}{0.25} = \$800,000,000$$

---

[1] There can be other variations, such as capitalizing an income stream with a finite life. One who understands the details of the last chapter and this chapter should be able to construct capitalization rates for such variations.

[2] American Society of Appraisers, Business Valuation Standards, Definitions (Herndon, VA: American Society of Appraisers, 2005).

[3] Ibid.

[4] Ibid.

Note from the definition above that the method is based on anticipation. Like the discounted economic income method, it is a method to convert *anticipated* income to a present value.

The capitalized economic income method is used as frequently as the discounted economic income method, and probably even more frequently in the valuation of smaller businesses. So why does this text put the discounted economic income method first? Because, *the capitalized economic income method is simply an abridged version of the discounted economic income method.* The discounted economic income method is presented first because the valuation theory that is applied in the discounted economic income method is more comprehensive. And once the analyst has a grasp of the discounted economic income method, the valuation theory that is applied in the capitalized income method can be grasped more easily.

The Perpetual Economic Income Stream Model

Consider the case of a preferred stock that has no maturity and no call provision (i.e., no expected redemption), paying a fixed dividend in perpetuity. The basic discounted economic income formula would value this preferred stock as follows:

Formula 10–1

$$PV = \sum_{i=1}^{n} \frac{E_i}{(1 + k_p)^i}$$

where:

PV = Present value

Σ = Sum of

n = The last period for which economic income is expected; n may equal infinity (i.e., ∞) if the economic income is expected to continue in perpetuity

E_i = The expected amount of economic income in each ith period in the future

k_p = Rate of return on preferred stock

i = The period (usually stated as a number of years) in the future in which the prospective economic income is expected to be received

It can be shown mathematically that when the expected economic income is a constant amount in perpetuity, the above formula can be simplified to:

Formula 10–2

$$PV = \frac{E}{k}$$

where:

E = An expected amount of economic income in every period ahead in perpetuity

k = Discount rate (cost of capital for that level of economic income)

In this unique case, the result is that the expected level amount of economic income can be capitalized by dividing it by the discount rate, and the capitalization rate equals the discount rate. Thus, in this case:

Formula 10–3

$$c = k$$

where:

c = Capitalization rate

k = Discount rate (cost of capital for that level of economic income)

In other words, *in the unique case where the expected economic income is a net level amount in perpetuity, the discount rate is equal to the capitalization rate.*

In any other case, where expected future amounts of economic income differ from the amount used in the capitalization formula, the difference between expected prospective amounts and the amount being capitalized is reflected in the difference between the appropriate discount rate (i.e., total yield or total required rate of return) and the capitalization rate (the divisor by which a single period return is converted to an estimate of value).

The simplest example of this is a noncallable preferred stock that pays a fixed dividend in perpetuity. Assume the following valuation variables:

Annual dividend rate $5 per share
Required rate of return   10%

In this case, the stock would be valued as follows:

$$\frac{\$5}{0.10} = \$50 \text{ per share}$$

Converting a Discount Rate to a Capitalization Rate— The Constant Growth Model

Discounting, for which a *discount rate* is used, is a process applied to one or a series of specific expected income amounts, as of a specified time or times in the future, to convert those expected amounts to an estimate of present value. The discount rate is applied to all the expected future economic income. Therefore, any expected future growth in returns is captured in the numerator of the discounted economic income formula.

Capitalizing, for which a *capitalization rate* is used, is a process applied to an amount representing some measure of economic income, for some single period, to convert that economic income amount to an estimate of present value. Capitalization procedures can be used with expected, current, historical, or "normalized" (or "stabilized") measures of economic income. If growth is expected from the base level of economic income being capitalized, then that expected growth is reflected in the capitalization rate.

This leads to the logical answer as to the difference between the discount rate and the capitalization rate: *for an investment with perpetual life, the difference between the discount rate and the capitalization rate is the annually compounded percentage rate of growth or decline in perpetuity in the economic income variable being discounted or capitalized.*

If the level of economic income expected in the 12 months immediately following the valuation date is expected to increase after that time at a constant average annually compounded rate in perpetuity, then it can be demonstrated mathematically that the basic discounted economic income formula of:

Formula 10–4

$$PV = \sum_{i=1}^{n} \frac{E_i}{(1+k)^i}$$

can be simplified to:

Formula 10–5

$$PV = \frac{E_1}{k-g}$$

where:

PV = Present value

E_1 = Expected amount of economic income in the period immediately ahead

k = Discount rate (required total rate of return)

g = Expected average growth rate of E, annually compounded in perpetuity

In the above formula, the divisor $(k{-}g)$ represents the capitalization rate, a relationship that can be expressed as an algebraic formula as follows:

Formula 10–6

$$c = k - g$$

where:

c = Capitalization rate (a rate to be used as a divisor to convert a return flow variable, such as net cash flow, to an indication of value)

k = Discount rate

g = Annually compounded rate of growth in the economic income variable being capitalized over the life of the investment (if there is an expected rate of decline, g is negative, so the effect is that the rate of decline is *added* to the discount rate to conclude the capitalization rate)

This leads to the basic capitalization formula:

Formula 10–7

$$PV = \frac{E_1}{c}$$

where:

PV = Present value

E_1 = Expected economic income in the period immediately ahead

c = Capitalization rate

In this formula, the capitalization rate is the reciprocal of a valuation pricing multiple. For example, if next year's economic income is projected to be $1.00, and the stock is priced at $12.50, it is selling at 12.5 times next year's income. This equates to a capitalization rate of 8 percent—that is, $1 \div 12.5 = 0.08$.

A simple example of the perpetual growth model would be a stock for which we have an economic income estimate for the year immediately following the effective valuation date, and for which we expect a constant growth rate in that amount of income in the years to follow. Assume the following:

Next year's expected economic income (E_1) $10
Discount rate (k) (required total rate of return)   15%
Sustainable income growth rate (g) 5%

In this case, the share of stock would be valued as follows:

$$\frac{\$10}{0.15 - 0.05} = \frac{\$10}{0.10} = \$100$$

The Gordon Growth Model

As noted earlier, the direct capitalization model assumes that the base level of normalized economic income to be capitalized is the expected income in the period *immediately following* the effective valuation date (i.e., E_1 in our notation system).

If the normalized economic income for the period *immediately* preceding the effective valuation date is considered a reasonable base level from which to project sustainable growth, the *Gordon growth model* version of the capitalized economic income method is appropriate. Using net cash flow as the economic income measure, the formula for the Gordon growth model is as follows:

Formula 10–8

$$PV = \frac{E_o(1 + g)}{k - g}$$

where:

PV = Present value
E_o = Amount of economic income in the period immediately past
k = Discount rate (required yield rate or total rate of return)
g = Expected average growth rate of E, annually compounded in perpetuity

Formulas 10–5 and 10–8 are often referred to as the *Gordon growth model*, the *dividend growth model*, or the *constant growth model*.[5] They represent a technically correct simplification of the basic discounted economic income model, *provided that the critical assumption underlying this simplification is met—that is, the economic income variable is expected to have a constant average annually compounded rate of growth in perpetuity*.

[5] For a mathematical proof of this formula, see, for example, Richard A. Brealey and Stewart C. Myers, *Principles of Corporate Finance*, 7th ed. (New York: McGraw-Hill, 2003), pp. 37–38.

Since this assumption is rarely met in the real world, this growth model is often used only as the final stage of a multistage discounted economic income model. For example, it is common to make specific income forecasts for some period (often five years or until the company is expected to reach a reasonably stable state), and then use the constant growth model to reflect income expectations from that point forward. An example of this will be shown later in the chapter.

Assume the following:

Last year's economic income (E_o) $10
Discount rate (k) (required total rate of return)   15%
Sustainable income growth rate (g)   5%

In this case the investment would be valued as follows:

$$\frac{\$10\,(1+0.05)}{0.15-0.05} = \frac{\$10.50}{0.10} = \$105$$

Sensitivity to Growth Rate Assumptions

Changes in the growth rate projected, sometimes seemingly small, can result in striking changes. In the basic constant growth example, we had the following:

$$\frac{E_1}{k-g} = \frac{\$10}{0.15-0.05} = \frac{\$10}{0.10} = \$100$$

Now let's just increase the assumed growth rate by 1 percent. Now we have:

$$\frac{E_1}{k-g} = \frac{\$10}{0.15-0.06} = \frac{\$10}{0.09} = \$111.11$$

One percentage point change in the growth rate produced more than an 11 percent change in the indicated value!

Taking the example a step further, let's assume a 10 percent weighted average cost of capital, with $100 debt and a 5 percent growth rate:

$$PV_f = \frac{NCF_f}{k-g} = \frac{\$10}{0.10-0.05} = \frac{\$10}{0.05} = \$200$$

less debt   100
value of equity $100

Now let's increase the assumed growth rate by 1 percent. Now we have:

$$PV_f = \frac{NCF_f}{k-g} = \frac{\$10}{0.10-0.06} = \frac{\$10}{0.04} = \$250$$

less debt   100
value of equity $150

In this leveraged investment a one percentage point change in the growth rate resulted in a 25 percent increase in the indicated value of invested capital and a 50 percent increase in the indicated value of equity!

This example actually overstates the effect of higher growth relative to a more detailed analysis. As mentioned in Chapter 9, higher growth would require higher investment in fixed assets and working capital. Thus, the numerator (net cash flows) of the capitalization formula would logically get smaller with a higher expected growth assumption. Under certain industry conditions, the higher growth might add nothing to value if the required extra annual investments were sufficiently large.

Obviously, the closer the growth rate to the discount rate, the greater the sensitivity. When the projected growth rate reaches or exceeds the discount rate in the perpetual growth model, mathematically, the capitalization rate is zero or negative. This relationship leads to the generally unreasonable conclusion that the company is infinitely valuable.

Because such large impacts may result from relatively small changes in input variables, it is often enlightening to perform some sensitivity analysis in conjunction with a discounted or capitalized economic income method. This could take the form of a sensitivity table showing the impact of a range of discount rates, terminal value multiples, growth rates, and cash flow projections.

When to Use the Discounting versus the Capitalization Method

The obvious implication of all this, when one stops to think about it simplistically, is that *the difference between the discounting model and the capitalization model is how one treats anticipated changes in future income over time*:

1. In discounting, *changes over time in the expected economic income are treated specifically in the terms of the numerator of the present value equation.*
2. In capitalizing, *changes over time in the expected economic income are treated as a single average percentage change, and that annualized percentage is subtracted (assuming it is positive) from the cost of capital in the denominator.*

The important conceptual underpinning of the capitalized economic income valuation model is that there is either a constant annual income stream in perpetuity or a constant annualized rate of growth (or decline) in the economic income variable being capitalized in perpetuity. Obviously, this constant growth rate projection is rarely met in the real world.

Unlike the discounted economic income model, the capitalization model does not take into consideration the timing of future changes in expected economic income. The greater the differences in the anticipated changes over time, especially in the early years, the more the analyst is encouraged to apply the discounted economic income method rather than the capitalized income method.

This leads to some generalizations about the relative attractiveness of the two basic income approach valuation methods:

1. *Stable or evenly growing economic income flow.* If the economic income flow is either stable or growing (or declining) at a fairly even rate, the capitalized

economic income method should conclude as accurate a value indication as the discounted economic income method.

2. *Predictable but uneven changes.* If there are reasons to believe that changes will be significant but predictable, even though uneven, the discounted economic income model should produce a more accurate valuation.

3. *Short- or intermediate-term supergrowth.* If growth is expected to be quite high in the immediate future, the discounted economic income model should produce a more accurate valuation. One of the most common mistakes in the application of this method is to use a 10 percent growth for the first few years (even though it may not be sustainable over the long term) and then subtract that 10 percent from the present value discount rate. This mistake will result in a low capitalization rate and in an overvaluation of the subject company.

4. *Changes that are erratic and unpredictable as to timing.* If the company's economic income is unstable and also more or less random as to timing, the company's risk increases, and thus the present value discount rate increases. However, the discounted economic income method may not be able to produce any more accurate a value indication than the direct capitalization method.

Equivalence of the Discounting and Capitalization Methods

Exhibit 10–1 shows that, with the same set of assumptions, the discounted economic income method and the capitalized economic income method using the Gordon growth model with a 5 percent growth rate will produce an identical valuation indication. Therefore, an analyst using the capitalized economic income method should understand its parent method (the discounted economic income method) and think through, as a form of mental verification of reasonableness, "If I carried out the full discounting procedure, would I get approximately the same answer?" If not, the valuation variables used in the capitalization method should be reexamined, or perhaps the capitalization method should only be used for a terminal value in conjunction with the discounting method.

Implementing the Capitalized Economic Income Method

As we have seen, like the discounted economic income method, the essence of the capitalized income method is twofold:

1. *Projecting an anticipated economic income stream.* As opposed to projecting the amount and timing of each individual economic income flow the business is expected to produce for its owner, the direct capitalization method requires projecting a single, sustainable amount of future economic income (the *numerator* in the arithmetic formula).

2. *Capitalizing the expected economic income amount to produce a present value.* This second step involves dividing the expected economic income by a rate that reflects the risk (degree of certainty or uncertainty) of receiving that expected amount on a regular basis. In other words, the starting point is the *present value discount rate*, as discussed in the previous chapter. However, the numerator

Exhibit 10–1

Equivalence of Discounted Economic Income Method and Capitalized Economic Income Method under Constant Growth Rate Scenario

Projection scenario: $8,000,000 net cash flow to equity in Year 1, a 5 percent perpetual annual growth rate from Year 1 forward, and a 25 percent present value discount rate

Discounted Economic Income Method

Projection period:	Year 1		Year 2		Year 3		Terminal Value
Indicated value of business entity*	$= \dfrac{\$8,000,000}{(1+0.25)}$	$+$	$\dfrac{\$8,400,000}{(1+0.25)^2}$	$+$	$\dfrac{\$8,820,000}{(1+0.25)^3}$	$+$	$\dfrac{\dfrac{\$8,820,000\,(1.05)}{0.25-0.05}}{(1+0.25)^3}$
	$= \dfrac{\$8,000,000}{(1.25)}$	$+$	$\dfrac{\$8,400,000}{(1.25)^2}$	$+$	$\dfrac{\$8,820,000}{(1.25)^3}$	$+$	$\dfrac{\dfrac{\$8,820,000\,(1.05)}{0.20}}{(1.25)^3}$
	$= \$6,400,000$	$+$	$\$5,376,000$	$+$	$\$4,515,800$	$+$	$\dfrac{\$46,305,000}{(1.25)^3}$
	$= \$6,400,000$	$+$	$\$5,376,000$	$+$	$\$4,515,800$	$+$	$\$23,708,200$
Indicated value of business entity	$= \$40,000,000$						

Capitalized Economic Income Method

Projection period:	Year 1
Economic income to equity	$\$8,000,000$
Present value discount rate minus expected long-term growth rate	$0.25 - 0.05$
Indicated value of business entity	$\$40,000,000$

* using Formula 10–12

reflects only a *single period* of economic income, not any future changes. Therefore, if changes are expected, the present value discount rate should be modified by subtracting (or adding) the anticipated rate of growth (or decline) in the economic income flow to convert the present value discount rate into a direct capitalization rate (the *denominator* in the arithmetic formula).

Projecting the Basic Economic Income Level and the Growth Rate

The projections needed for the capitalized economic income method are twofold:

1. The normalized and sustainable expected base economic income
2. The expected sustainable long-term growth rate

These projections may be prepared by the company or by the valuation analyst, ideally with some involvement by both. The arithmetic of this valuation method could not be more simple. However, this fact implies the extreme importance of the realism and reasonableness of the expectations impounded in the base expected economic income estimate and the expected long-term growth rate.

Start with Sustainable Expected Economic Income

In order for the capitalized economic income method to produce a realistic value indication, the numerator should be a realistic sustainable base of expected economic income. The expected economic income should be either stable or expected to change at a somewhat constant average rate over a long period of time.

As with the discounted economic income method, this method requires carrying out the adjusted income statement procedures discussed in Chapter 7. Of course, if the operational economic income variable is net cash flow, the adjustments to reach that measure (as defined in the previous chapter) also should be made.

Again, the capitalized economic income method is a forward-looking analysis, just as the discounted economic income method is. The economic income measure capitalized should represent *expected* future economic income. A simple average—or a weighted average—of past operating results is not an adequate procedure, in and of itself, to develop this projection. The historical average should be used only if the analyst is able to justify the notion that this past average is indeed a reasonable proxy for future economic income expectations. Of course, the analyst may consider company budgets, plans, forecasts, and other forward-looking data in the estimation of the normalized (or sustainable) economic income measure.

The Projected Long-Term Growth Rate

Treating the Impact of Inflation. If the build-up procedure or the capital asset pricing model (CAPM) procedure is used to develop the present value discount rate from which the growth rate is to be subtracted in order to derive a direct capitalization rate, that discount rate incorporates the expected rate of inflation as part of the required rate of return. Since the nominal government bond interest rates used in developing these discount rates incorporate expected inflation over the duration of the bond, the implication is that the selected long-term growth rate should also reflect the impact of expected inflation on the economic income variable being capitalized.

For example, if the projection of the financial performance for the company assumes no real growth, but it is expected that the economic income will grow enough to keep up with the general level of expected inflation, the consensus long-term inflation rate should be subtracted from the present value discount rate in order to arrive at the appropriate direct capitalization rate. A good source for expected long-term inflation is the semiannual *Livingston Survey* published by the Federal Reserve Bank of Philadelphia. Another is the monthly newsletter *Blue Chip Economic Indicators*.

Sustainability. The economic income capitalization method has impounded in it the implied projection that the growth rate used to arrive at the direct capitalization rate is a long-term sustainable growth rate. In fact, technically, it is a growth rate expected *in perpetuity*.

As a practical matter, discount rates and capitalization rates for investments in small businesses and professional practices are relatively high compared with most other investments. Therefore, changes in the growth rate after 15 or 20 years would have almost no impact on the present value. However, misspecification of the projected growth rate during the first 10 years or so can have a major impact on the indicated value.

As suggested earlier, if significant changes in the growth rate are expected within the first 10 years, the discounted economic income model probably is preferable to the economic income capitalization model. The economic income capitalization model can be incorporated to estimate the terminal value in the discounted economic income calculations, as explained further in a subsequent section.

If some changes in the growth rate are expected but are either too minimal or too unpredictable as to timing to justify using the discounted economic income method, some subjective adjustment to the projected growth rate using the capitalized economic income method might be an acceptable compromise. To the extent that the higher growth is expected in the early years, the long-term average growth rate used might be raised slightly to reflect an average of higher short-term and lower long-term growth and vice versa.

A company's expected long-term growth rate will be little affected by near-term growth considerations if the rate is being estimated for a terminal value at the end of a forecast horizon in the discounted economic income model. Many analysts argue that the terminal growth rate should never be higher than the expected long-term nominal growth rate of the general economy, which includes both inflation and real growth. If the company is in an industry subject to vigorous competitive pressure, with little prospect for real growth without large capital expenditures, then perpetual growth at the rate of expected long-term inflation may be reasonable (i.e., zero real growth). The growth rate may be negative if the company's income comes from a wasting asset, such as petroleum reserves.

Defining the Components in the Capitalization Method

It is noteworthy that, as presented above, this is a *very generalized* formula. To actually use this valuation method, the analyst should be specific about the same points as in the discounted economic income method:

1. Is the analyst valuing *all invested capital* or just the *common equity* with these calculations?
2. What measure of economic income is being projected to be used as the numerator (e.g., net cash flow, net income, or some other economic income measure)?
3. The direct capitalization rate (c) represents the cost of what kind of capital (e.g., weighted average for net cash flow to invested capital, net cash flow available to equity, or something else)? In other words, the direct capitalization rate is a single figure representing the cost of a certain type of capital (the present value discount rate), modified by the projected annual percentage growth (or decline) in the economic income flow available to the capital

structure being valued. *The direct capitalization rate must be appropriate for the definition of economic income being capitalized.*

Valuing Equity versus Invested Capital

The same fundamental principles apply with regard to the valuation of equity versus invested capital as those that apply in the discounting method.

Whichever measure of capital is selected as the valuation subject—owners' equity or invested capital—all of the economic income accruing to that class of capital should be included in the numerator.

It is noteworthy, however, that the direct capitalization model is much more sensitive to the projected rate of growth when it is applied to all invested capital than when it is applied only to owners' equity. This is because the present value discount rate is the *weighted average cost of capital* for invested capital (blended debt rate and equity rate). And, that rate is lower than the cost of equity capital alone. If the same percentage growth rate is projected on economic income available to invested capital as to owners' equity, the growth rate will have a greater impact on the resulting value of the invested capital.

Selecting the Appropriate Measure of Economic Income

As with the discounted economic income method, most valuation professionals today prefer to use *net cash flow* whether valuing equity or invested capital, for the same reasons as discussed in the previous chapter.

If you are considering using *net income*, the entire discussion in the previous chapter applies and should be read and applied in conjunction with this chapter.

We believe that capitalization of other income variables (e.g., gross revenue; owner's discretionary earnings; gross cash flow; and earnings before interest, taxes, depreciation, and amortization (EBITDA) are better handled within the scope of the market approach. That is because capitalization rates for those economic income variables are better developed by direct observations of transactions in the market than by modifications to a build-up or CAPM present value discount rate.

Modification of the Capitalized Economic Income Method to Reflect the Midyear Discounting Convention

The basic capitalized economic income method, as presented so far, reflects the implicit assumption that the income becomes available to the owners of the subject business at the end of each period (usually assumed to be a year). This is a reasonable assumption for some businesses. This is because, at the end of the year, the owners assess the operating results and capital requirements, and distribute income in some form—such as dividends, partner withdrawals, or bonuses to owners.

If a more realistic scenario is that economic income will be available for distribution to the business owners more or less evenly throughout the year, a simple modification to the capitalized economic income formula can reflect this assumption:

Formula 10–9

$$PV = \frac{E_1(1+k)^{0.5}}{k-g}$$

where:

PV = Present value
E_1 = Expected economic income in the full period immediately following the effective valuation date
k = Present value discount rate (i.e., the cost of capital)
g = Expected long-term growth rate in E

Similarly, if the Gordon growth model version of the capitalized economic income method is used, the modified formula is as follows:

Formula 10–10

$$PV = \frac{E_0(1+g)(1+k)^{0.5}}{k-g}$$

where:

PV = Present value
E_0 = Expected economic income in the full period immediately preceding the effective valuation date
k = Present value discount rate (i.e., the cost of capital)
g = Expected long-term growth rate in E

This modified formula for the economic income capitalization method accomplishes the same result as the midyear discounting convention described in the previous chapter on the discounted economic income method.[6] Since this convention reflects earlier availability of economic income to the business owners, it slightly raises the indicated value of the business from what it would be using the end-of-the-year convention.

A simple example of the Gordon growth model would be a stock for which we know the economic income (or have estimated the normalized economic income) for the year immediately preceding the effective valuation date, and for which we expect a constant growth rate in that amount from last year's base amount. Assume the following:

Last year's economic income	$10
Discount rate (required total rate of return)	15%
Sustainable expected economic income growth rate	5%

For a simple example of the capitalized economic income model reflecting the midyear convention, use the stock in our previous example, but assume that the

[6] Proof of the accuracy of this method was presented in Todd A. Kaltman, "Capitalization Using a Mid-Year Convention," *Business Valuation Review*, December 1995, pp. 178–82.

cash flows are received evenly over each year rather than at the end of each year. In this case, the investment would be valued as follows:

$$\frac{\$10(1+0.05)(1+0.15)^{0.5}}{0.15-0.05}=\frac{\$10.50(1.15)^{0.5}}{0.10}=\frac{\$10.50(1.0723)}{0.10}=\frac{\$11.26}{0.10}=\$112.60$$

This example demonstrates the principle that in the capitalization method, as in the discounting method, the midyear convention produces a higher indicated value because of the assumption that the cash flows will be received earlier.

Using the Capitalized Economic Income Method to Develop a Terminal Value for the Discounted Economic Income Method

Why the Capitalized Economic Income Method Is Preferable

As noted in the previous chapter, the discounted economic income method often involves projecting cash flows for some discrete time period, followed by a *terminal value* as of the end of the discrete projection period. It is not uncommon for the present value of the terminal value to be 50 percent or more of the total value indicated by the discounted economic income method.

There are a variety of ways to develop a terminal value. The most common methods are (1) the capitalized economic income method or (2) a pricing multiple of some economic income variable, such as earnings before interest and taxes (EBIT) or EBITDA. Between these two methods, we recommend the capitalized economic income method.[7]

One reason for this recommendation is that multiples of EBIT, EBITDA, and other economic income variables used in estimating a terminal value should be market derived. That is, they should be dependent on pricing multiples observed in actual market transactions. (It should be noted that future pricing multiples may be lower than currently observed pricing multiples.) Terminal value multiples should not be estimated by modifying a discount rate or capitalization rate to be applicable to that economic income variable. Such pricing multiples are best developed through the use of the market approach, for which two chapters are included in this edition.

If the terminal value is estimated for the discounted economic income method using a market-derived pricing multiple of some economic income variable other than that used for the interim economic income flows, the analysis is not a pure income approach. Rather, the analysis is a mixture of a market approach and income approach. The greater the impact of the terminal value on the total present value, the more important this distinction becomes, and the more the method will be as a market versus income method.

---

[7] Whether using a market multiple or the Gordon growth model to estimate the terminal value, the resulting implied growth rate and market multiple, respectively, should be checked for reasonableness.

We have seen valuations where the present value of the interim cash flows was zero or even negative, and the terminal value was based on a market-derived multiple of EBIT or EBITDA. Such an analysis should in no way be classified as an income approach (as we've described it). Rather, such an analysis is driven entirely by what we have classified as a market approach.

A major problem with using a market-derived pricing multiple method to estimate the terminal value is estimating what that multiple will be 3 to 10 years from now. Unlike the current pricing multiples used in the market approach, that future multiple can't be directly observed in the marketplace. Rather, it must be estimated. The procedure most commonly used is to naively assume that the future multiple will be the same as the current multiple. However, current pricing multiples impound investors' expectations about future changes, especially expectations regarding growth (including acquisitions). Companies in some industries often sell at high multiples reflecting high short-term growth expectations. If the expected future growth will be less following the terminal value date (due to, for example, maturity of the company and/or its industry), using the current pricing multiple will reflect too high a growth expectation following the terminal value date. This will have the effect of overstating the terminal value. We suspect that using a market-derived pricing multiple for estimating the terminal value, on balance, has a tendency to upwardly bias the valuation indication.

One of the primary objectives of using market price methods is to weight and check the results of each multiple against each other for reasonableness. When using a multiple of only a single variable, any possible benefit of comparing the indicated results from using multiples of several variables is lost. For the reasons discussed, we believe that this differentiation of methods is best accomplished by using the economic income capitalization method rather than a market multiple method to estimate the terminal value within the discounted economic income method.

Implementation of the Capitalized Economic Income Method to Estimate the Terminal Value

The *terminal value* is the expected value of the entity *as of the end of the discrete projection period*.

Constant Income Scenario. If the economic income is expected to be constant following the discrete projection period, the formula for the terminal value is as follows:

Formula 10–11

$$PV = \frac{E_{(n+1)}}{c}$$

where:

PV	=	Present value
$E_{(n+1)}$	=	Expected economic income in the period immediately following the end of the discrete projections
c	=	Direct capitalization rate (which is equal to k, the present value discount rate, when the expected economic income is a constant amount in perpetuity)

Constant Growth Scenario. One of the most common ways to estimate the terminal value is to use the constant growth model presented earlier. This assumes that, after the discrete projection period, the economic income will grow at some constant compound rate in perpetuity. This version of the terminal value estimate merely continues the projection of prospective economic income with a simplifying assumption of a constant growth rate past the discrete projection period. The length of the discrete projection period should be until the last entry in the discrete projection period represents a normalized level of economic income. Using the constant growth model to estimate the terminal value results in the following formula:

Formula 10–12

$$PV = \frac{E_1}{(1+k)} + \frac{E_2}{(1+k)^2} + \ldots + \frac{E_n}{(1+k)^n} + \frac{\dfrac{E_n(1+g)}{k-g}}{(1+k)^n}$$

where:

PV	$=$	Present value
$E_1 \ldots E_n$	$=$	Expected amounts of the economic income (often net cash flow) in each of periods E_1 through E_n
k	$=$	Discount rate
n	$=$	Number of periods in the discrete projection period
g	$=$	Annually compounded growth rate in perpetuity for the prospective economic income, beyond the discrete projection period

With a very short discrete projection period, the terminal value often constitutes over half the total value. The shorter the discrete projection period and the lower the discount rate, the higher the proportion of the total value will be accounted for by the terminal value. When using the perpetual growth model to estimate the terminal value, it may be useful to check its reasonableness by computing implied pricing multiples and comparing the implied pricing multiples to pricing multiples currently observed in the market (see Chapters 11 and 12 on the market approach). This is not to suggest that market approach pricing multiples should be used to estimate the income approach terminal value. Rather, it suggests that the terminal value pricing multiples implied by the perpetual growth model can be checked for reasonableness by reference to observable market-derived pricing multiples.

Midyear Discounting Scenario. If the economic income for the discrete projection period was discounted using the midyear discounting convention, consistency would suggest using the direct capitalization formula modified to reflect the midyear convention. This procedure was presented in a prior section. Using the midyear convention for the terminal value makes the complete DCF formula as follows:

Formula 10–13

$$PV = \frac{E_1}{(1+k)^{0.5}} + \frac{E_2}{(1+k)^{1.5}} + \ldots + \frac{E_n}{(1+k)^{n-0.5}} + \frac{\dfrac{E_n(1+g)(1+k)^{0.5}}{k-g}}{(1+k)^n}$$

where:

PV	=	Present value
$E_1 \dots E_n$	=	Expected amounts of the economic income (often net cash flow) in each of periods E_1 through E_n
E_n	=	Expected economic income in the final (nth) increment of the discrete projection period
g	=	Long-term sustainable growth rate in E
k	=	Present value discount rate (i.e., the cost of capital)
n	=	Number of periods in the discrete projection period

Number of Periods by Which to Discount Terminal Value. In all of the above formulas, the terminal value is then discounted back to a present value at the present value discount rate (k) for n periods, the same number of periods for which the final increment of the discrete projection period was discounted. This is because the terminal value is the value *at the beginning* of the time immediately following the discrete projection period. This is exactly the same point in time as *the end* of the discrete projection period. (A common error is to discount the terminal value for $n + 1$ periods instead of n periods.)[8]

Does the Capitalized Economic Income Method Produce a Control Value or a Minority Value?

The answer to this question is the same as was presented for the discounted economic income method (the value indication can be either a control value or a minority value, depending primarily on the normalization adjustments made to the economic income flow being capitalized). If the adjustments include changes that only a control owner could make, such as normalization of compensation, then the value generally would represent a control ownership position. If such adjustments are not made, the value generally would represent a noncontrolling ownership position. If adjustments are not reasonably available for a control owner to make, it is possible that there may be little difference between a control value and a minority value—at least before consideration of marketability factors. (For example, the more the minority stockholder's access to the business's net cash flow is restricted, the greater the discount for lack of marketability. See Chapter 17 for further discussion of this topic.) There is also the risk that the control owner may make changes in the future that negatively affect the minority owner.

---

[8] If midyear discounting is used, a mathematical equivalent to using the modified (midyear) capitalization model is (1) to use the standard capitalization model (typically the Gordon growth version) and (2) to discount the indicated terminal value by $n - 0.5$ periods. While this procedure produces exactly the same answer, it seems that using the modified capitalization formula is a conceptually preferable presentation. This is because the modified formula, along with explanatory text, would make it easier for the valuation reader to understand the calculations.

What Standard of Value Does the Capitalized Economic Income Model Produce?

The answer to this question is also essentially the same as was presented for the discounted economic income method.

If the economic income capitalized and the direct capitalization rate used reflect the condition of the company as it is on a stand-alone basis, the value indication should be *fair market value*. If synergies or circumstances peculiar to a particular investor are reflected in the economic income stream or in the direct capitalization rate, the value indication would reflect those elements of *investment value*.

Since the capitalized economic income method can be used to develop either fair market value or investment value, and most family law courts lean toward one or the other of those two standards of value, the capitalized economic income method is often used in valuations for purposes of marital dissolution.[9]

Relationship between the Capitalized Economic Income Method and the Market Approach

In the capitalized economic income method, we divide an indication of income by a capitalization rate. We noted earlier in the chapter that the reciprocal of the capitalization rate is a multiplier. In the market approach, we use multipliers of income variables to derive indications of value. So what is the difference between the capitalized economic income method and the market approach using multiples of income variables?

There are two primary differences:

1. The way that capitalization rates are derived in the income approach versus the way that multiples are derived in the market approach
2. The economic income variables typically capitalized in the income approach versus the economic income variables for which multiples are applied in the market approach

Derivation of Income Approach Capitalization Rates versus Market Approach Multiples

As we have seen in this chapter, in the income approach, capitalization rates are derived from discount rates. To repeat, the capitalization rate is the discount rate minus the sustainable long-term growth rate.

---

[9] See, for example, *Bersin v. Golonka,* 2005 N.C. App. LEXIS 1032 (N.C. Ct. App. 2005); *Sampson v. Sampson,* 62 Mass. App. Ct. 366, 816 N.E.2d 999; 2004 Mass. App. LEXIS 1223 (Mass. Ct. App. 2004); *Schaeffer v. Schaeffer,* 2001 Conn. Super. LEXIS 3035 (Conn. Super. Ct. 2001); *Long v. Long,* 129 Md. App. 554; 743 A.2d 281; 2000 Md. App. LEXIS 1 (Md. Ct. App. 2000); *DeLucia v. DeLucia,* No. FA950249319s, 1997 WL 16832 (Conn. Super. Ct., Jan. 10, 1997); *Backhaus v. Backhaus,* No. A-94-1083, 1996 WL 737590 (Neb. App., Dec. 17, 1996); *Giuliani v. Giuliani,* No. CA 9305268865 Conn. Super. Ct., 1996 WL 409324 (June 19, 1997); *Neuman v. Neuman,* 842 P.2d 575 (Wyo. 1992); *Bidwell v. Bidwell,* 504 N.Y.S.2d 327 (N.Y. App. Div. 1986); *Thomas v. Thomas,* 407 N.W.2d 124 (Minn. Ct. App. 1987); *Siegel v. Siegel,* 523 N.Y.S.2d 517, 521 (N.Y. App. Div. 1987).

In the market approach, multiples of income variables are derived from direct observation of the multiples in the market, as we will see in the next chapter.

Economic Income Variables Used in the Income Approach versus the Market Approach

In the income approach, the economic income variable generally preferred is net cash flow, either to equity or to overall invested capital, as defined in the previous chapter. This is partly because net cash flow is the discretionary amount that owners can take out of the business on an ongoing, sustainable basis without disrupting continuing operations, the variable on which many investors and corporate finance people will ultimately focus. It is also partly because net cash flow is the income variable that most analysts consider most appropriate to match with Ibbotson Associates equity risk premium data, which uses stock market returns over government security returns. The only other income variable widely used in the income approach is net income, as discussed in the previous chapter.

As will be seen in the next chapter, the market approach uses all kinds of economic income variables *except* expected net cash flow. Remember, in the income approach, the amounts of capital expenditures and changes in net working capital used to derive net cash flow are "amounts necessary to support projected business operations." In the market approach, it is difficult to determine for any given company whether or not amounts of capital expenditures and/or changes in net working capital meet that criterion. Therefore, while other cash flow–related measures of economic income (e.g., EDITDA) are used, net cash flow is not often used in the market approach. Some analysts believe that the inverse of a P/E multiple, E/P, is equal to a cap rate. This is true; however, it results in an earnings cap rate, not a cash flow cap rate as derived by the traditional build-up or CAPM.

By observing these differences, and by using the perpetual income or the Gordon growth model rather than a market multiple for the terminal value, the income and market approaches are quite discrete from each other and, if there are good data for both, can provide good checks against one another.

Summary

There are three principal variables in the direct capitalization of economic income method:

1. The projected base-level economic income flow
2. The present value discount rate (i.e., the cost of capital)
3. The expected long-term growth rate that modifies the present value discount rate to derive the direct capitalization rate

The capitalized economic income method is essentially an abridged version of the discounted economic income method. The primary difference is in the treatment of future changes in the expected economic income. In the discounted economic income method, future changes in economic income are specifically reflected in the discrete income projections in the numerator of the arithmetic equation.

In the capitalized economic income method, future changes in economic income are combined into a single growth rate. This single growth rate is subtracted from the present value discount rate in the denominator of the arithmetic equation.

The economic income flow to be capitalized can be either the amount available to equity or the amount available to all invested capital (usually defined to include owners' equity plus long-term interest-bearing debt, although other definitions are sometimes used).

The economic income flow that is projected is usually net cash flow (at least that is the preference of a consensus of valuation professionals), although other definitions of economic income are sometimes used.

Like the discounted economic income method, the capitalized economic income method is a forward-looking exercise. Using some average of actual past economic income is only appropriate if that average does, in fact, represent the expected level of sustainable economic income in the future.

The projected base-level sustainable economic income flow is divided by a direct capitalization rate, which is typically calculated as the present value discount rate less an expected long-term growth rate in the economic income being capitalized. This expected long-term growth rate is projected to be constant in perpetuity.

The development of the present value discount rate is the same as for the discounted economic income method, as discussed in Chapter 9. If either a build-up procedure or the CAPM procedure is used to develop the discount rate, that rate includes expected inflation. Therefore, the growth rate used should also reflect inflation—to the extent that it impacts the economic income variable being capitalized.

The results are extremely sensitive to changes in the growth rate factor, especially when valuing invested capital. This is because the analysis of invested capital starts with a lower present value discount rate than for equity only.

It is essential that the direct capitalization rate be developed so that it is appropriate for the definition of the economic income flow being capitalized. One of the most common errors in implementing the capitalized economic income method is using a direct capitalization rate that is not appropriate for the particular definition of economic income that is being capitalized.

The capitalized economic income method is also an excellent method for developing the terminal value in the discounted economic income method.

Bibliography

Adhikari, Mike. "WACC As Used in Capitalization Formula Cases Overvaluation." *Shannon Pratt's Business Valuation Update*, October 2003.

Agiato, Joseph A., and Thomas L. Johnston. "The Relationship between the Earnings Yield and the Cash Flow Yield." *CPA Expert*, Winter 1996, pp. 6–9.

Alerding, James R. "Income Approach versus Asset Approach." *BV Q&A Newsletter*, August 2005.

Bakken, John E. "Capitalization of Earnings—an Income Approach." Chapter 17 in *Handbook of Business Valuation,* 2nd ed., Thomas L. West and Jeffrey D. Jones, eds. New York: John Wiley & Sons, 1999, pp. 192–200.

Collins, Michelle, and Julie King. "Valuation Formulas: The Income Method." *CanadaOne,* http://www.canadaone.com.

Dobner, Michael. "Mid Year Discounting and Seasonality Factors." *Business Valuation Review*, March 2002, pp. 16–18.

Dorrell, Darrel D. "Discount Rate Comparisons." *National Litigation Consultants' Review*, July 2002, pp. 8–11.

Duvall, Richard M. "Capitalization of Earnings with Temporary Rapid Growth." *Business Valuation Review*, June 2001, pp. 3–4.

_____. "Mid-Year or End-of-Year Discounting." *Business Valuation Review*, December 2000, pp. 208–12.

_____. "Tips for the Valuator." *Journal of Accountancy*, March 2000.

Evans, Frank C. "Recognizing the Key Factors in the Income Approach to Business Valuation." *Business Valuation Review*, June 1996, pp. 80–86.

Greer, Willis R. "The Growth Rate Term in the Capitalization Method." *Business Valuation Review*, June 1996, pp. 72–79.

Hawkins, George B. "Is the Capitalization Rate Reasonable?" *Fair$hare*, June 1997, pp. 2–7.

Kaltman, Todd A. "Capitalization Using a Mid-Year Convention." *Business Valuation Review*, December 1995, pp. 178–82.

Lippitt, Jeffrey W., and Nicholas J. Mastrachhio Jr. "Developing Capitalization Rates for Valuing a Business." *The CPA Journal*, November 1995, pp. 24–28.

Matthews, Gilbert, "CapX = Depreciation Is Unrealistic Assumption for Most Terminal Values; Frequent Error Causes Overvaluation." *Shannon Pratt's Business Valuation Update*, March 2002.

McNulty, James M., Tony D. Yeh, William S. Schulze, and Michael H. Lubatkin. "What's Your Real Cost of Capital?" *Harvard Business Review*, October 2002, p. 114.

Mellen, Chris M. "The Income Approach in Practice: Where Do We Stand?" *Business Appraisal Practice*, Fall 2002, pp. 33–39.

Mercer, Z. Christopher. "Adjusting Capitalization Rates for the Differences between Net Income and Net Free Cash Flow." *Business Valuation Review*, December 1992, pp. 201–7.

Posgate, Louis R. "The Single Period, Income Capitalization Approach to Valuing Mineral Royalties." *Business Valuation Review*, December 2001, pp. 42–43.

Pratt, Shannon P. "Discounting versus Capitalizing." Chapter 4 in *Cost of Capital: Estimation and Applications*, 2nd Ed. New York: John Wiley & Sons, 2002.

_____. "Drawing a Clear Distinction Between Income and Market Approaches and Methodology." *Shannon Pratt's Business Valuation Update*, June 2000.

_____. NACVA Advisory Board Member Challenges Methods Taught." *Shannon Pratt's Business Valuation Update*, February 1996, pp. 9–11.

_____. "One Key Distinction between Market and Income Approaches Is to Use Net Cash Flow. *Shannon Pratt's Business Valuation Update*, May 2003.

Presogna, Jeffrey J. "Capitalization and Discounted Returns Valuation Methods." Kansas City, Mo.: Business Technology Association, 2000.

Reynolds, Kevin B. "Reconciling the Single Period Capitalization Method with the Discounted Future Earnings Method." *Business Appraisal Practice*, Spring 2000, pp. 16–27.

_____. "Where Do Capitalization Rates Come From?" *CPA Litigation Service Counselor*, November 1999, pp. 9–11.

Rigby, James, and Michael J. Mattson. "Capitalization and Discount Rates: Mathematically Related, But Conceptually Different." *CPA Expert*, Fall 1996, pp. 1–3.

Schilt, James H. "Selection of Capitalization Rates—Revisited." *Business Valuation Review,* June 1991, pp. 51–52.

Sliwoski, Leonard. "Capitalization Rates Developed Using the Ibbotson Associates Data: Should They Be Applied to Pretax or After Tax Earnings?" *Business Valuation Review, March* 1994, pp. 8–10.

_____. "Capitalization Rates, Discount Rates, and P/E Ratios: One More Time." *Business Valuation Review,* September 1992, pp. 122–34.

Swad, Randy. "Discount and Capitalization Rates in Business Valuations." *CPA Journal,* October 1994, pp. 40–46.

Trout, Robert. "Mid-Year Discounting Without Bias." *Business Valuation Review,* December 2001, pp. 39–41.

Chapter 11

Market Approach: Guideline Publicly Traded Company Method

The use of comparable publicly held corporations as a guide to valuation, as a practical matter, may be the most important and appropriate technique for valuing a privately held operating business. Obviously finding a business exactly the same as the enterprise to be valued is an impossibility. The standard sought is usually one of reasonable and justifiable similarity. This degree of likeness is attainable in most cases.[1]

In the market determined price of a stock, thousands of investors act through Adam Smith's "invisible hand" to arrive at an equilibrium value.[2]

While the income approach discussed in the previous chapters is the core of valuation theory, actual market transaction data can provide compelling empirical evidence of value.

There is a large storehouse of reliable guideline transaction data from the day-to-day transactions in publicly traded companies. Approximately 12,550 companies are filing with the Securities and Exchange Commission (SEC). Additionally, approximately 15,000 companies are public but are not required to file with the SEC because they fall under various SEC thresholds.[3] I agree with the above quote that publicly traded corporation capital market data may provide relevant valuation guidance in many cases.

Exhibit 11–1 summarizes the several mechanisms available to effect a public offering. The size requirements for a public offering and public trading are far less than many people think. Many closely held companies that might be thought of as small actually are large enough to go public if they so desire. However, it is not necessary for a company to be eligible to go public in order to use valuation guidance from the public market. The capital markets provide general guidelines as to how securities in many industries are being priced.

---

[1] Frank M. Burke, Jr., *Valuation and Valuation Planning for Closely Held Businesses* (Englewood Cliffs, NJ: Prentice-Hall, Inc., 1981), p. 49.

[2] Kent Hickman and Glenn H. Petry, "A Comparison of Stock Price Predictions Using Court Accepted Formulas, Dividend Discount, and P/E Models," *Financial Management*, Summer 1990, p. 84.

[3] Shannon P. Pratt, *The Market Approach to Valuing Businesses* (Hoboken, NJ: John Wiley & Sons, 2005).

Exhibit 11–1

Mechanisms for Going Public in the United States

Registration Statements

Registration statements are of two principal types: (1) offering registrations filed under the Securities Act of 1933, and (2) trading registrations filed under the Securities Exchange Act of 1934.

Offering Registrations

Offering registrations are used to register securities before they are offered to investors. Part I of the registration, a preliminary prospectus or "red herring," contains preliminary information that will be in the final prospectus. Included in Part I (or incorporated by reference) in many registration statements are:

- Description of securities to be registered
- Use of proceeds
- Risk factors
- Determination of offering price
- Potential dilution
- Selling security holders
- Plan of distribution
- Interests of named experts and counsel
- Information with respect to the registrant (description of business, legal proceedings, market price and dividends on common equity, financial statements, management discussion and analysis, changes in and disagreements with accountants, directors and executive officers, security ownership of certain beneficial owners and management and certain relationships and related transactions)

Part II of the registration contains information not required in the prospectus. This includes:
- Expenses of issuance and distribution
- Indemnification of directors and officers
- Recent sales of unregistered securities, undertakings, exhibits, and financial statement schedules

Types of Offering Registrations

Offering registration statements vary in purpose and content according to the type of organization issuing stock.

S-1   Companies reporting under the 1934 Act for fewer than three years. Permits no incorporation by reference and requires complete disclosure in the prospectus.

S-2   Companies reporting under the 1934 Act for three or more years but not meeting the minimum voting stock requirement. Reference to the 1934 Act reports permits incorporation and presentation of financial information in the prospectus or in an annual report to shareholders delivered with the prospectus.

S-3   Companies reporting under the 1934 Act for three or more years and having at least $150 million of voting stock held by nonaffiliates, or as an alternative test, $100 million of voting stock coupled with an annual trading volume of 3 million shares. Allows minimal disclosure in the prospectus and maximum incorporation by reference of 1934 Act reports.

S-4   Registration used in certain business combinations or reorganizations.

S-6   Filed by unit investment trusts registered under the Investment Act of 1940 on Form N-8B-2.

S-8   Registration used to register securities to be offered to employees under stock option and various other employee benefit plans.

S-11   Filed by real estate companies, primarily limited partnerships and investment trusts.

SE   Nonelectronically filed exhibits made by registrants filing with the EDGAR Project.

N-1A   Filed by open-end management investment companies.

N-2   Filed by closed-end management investment companies.

N-5   Registration of small business investment companies.

N-14   Registration of the securities of management investment and business development companies to be issued in business combinations under the Investment Act of 1940.

F-1   Registration of securities by foreign private issuers eligible to use Form 20-F, for which no other form is prescribed.

F-2   Registration of securities by foreign private issuers meeting certain 1934 Act filing requirements.

F-3   Registration of securities by foreign private issuers offered pursuant to certain types of transactions, subject to the 1934 Act filing requirements for the preceding three years.

F-4   Registration of securities issued in business combinations involving foreign private registrants.

F-6   Registration of depository shares evidenced by the American Depository Receipts (ADRs).

F-7   Registration of certain Canadian issues offered for cash upon the exercise of rights granted to existing security holders.

F-8   Registration of certain Canadian issues to be issued in exchange offers or a business combination.

F-9   Registration of certain investment grade debit or investment grade preferred securities of certain Canadian issues.

F-10   Registration of certain Canadian issues.

SB-1   Registration for certain small businesses.

SB-2   Registration statement for small businesses. No aggregate offering value of securities.

Trading Registrations

Trading registrations are filed to permit trading among investors on a securities exchange or in the over-the-counter market. These registration statements do not include a prospectus. Registration statements that serve to register securities for trading fall into three categories:

1. Form 10 may be used by companies during the first two years they are subject to the 1934 Act filing requirements. It is a combination registration statement and annual report with information content similar to that of SEC required 10-Ks.

2. Form 8-A is used by 1934 Act registrants wishing to register additional securities or classes thereof.

3. Form 8-B is used by "successor issuers" (usually companies that have changed their name or state of incorporation) as notification that previously registered securities are to be traded under a new corporate identification.

Prospectus

When the sale of securities as proposed in an offering registration statement is approved by the SEC, any changes required by the SEC are incorporated into the prospectus. This document must be made available to investors before the sale of the security is initiated. It also contains the actual offering price, which may have been changed after the registration statement was approved.

SOURCE: *Guide to SEC Filings*, published by Thomson Research, a division of Thomson Financial (http://research.thomsonib.com/help/sec_guide04-03-02.htm). Reprinted with permission.

The public capital markets in the United States (as well as in other countries) reprice thousands of stocks every day, mostly through transactions among financial buyers and sellers who are well informed (because of stringent disclosure laws, at least in the United States) and have no special motivations or compulsions to buy or to sell. This constant repricing gives up-to-the-minute evidence of prices that buyers and sellers agree on for securities in all kinds of industries relative to the fundamental variables perceived to drive their values, such as dividends, cash flows, and earnings. Pricing multiples of these and other relevant financial variables are important investor valuation yardsticks.

Furthermore, companies that are already public are high on the list of potential acquirers for many private companies. And, valuation parameters of the potential acquirers' stock may influence the pricing of a potential acquiree. If the subject company *could* be a candidate to go public, this makes the comparison of the guideline publicly traded companies to the subject company more relevant.[4]

---

[4] It should be noted that noncontrolling stockholders cannot initiate or consummate a public offering. This fact typically is recognized by a discount for lack of marketability for private company shares when valued by reference to guideline publicly traded company shares. This valuation adjustment is discussed in detail in Chapter 17, "Discounts for Illiquidity and Lack of Marketability." Of course, it would depend on whether one starts with control or minority earnings.

Overview of the Guideline Publicly Traded Company Method

The purpose of compiling guideline company statistics is to develop valuation multiples based on prices at which stocks of similar companies are trading in a public market. The valuation multiples thus developed will be applied to the subject company's fundamental data and correlated to reach an estimate of value for the subject company or its shares or other interests.

A "valuation multiple" is usually a multiple computed by dividing the price of the guideline company's stock as of the valuation date by some relevant economic variable observed or calculated from the guideline company's financial statements. Some variables, such as projections of next year's earnings, may be estimated by security analysts. The reciprocal of the pricing multiple is the capitalization rate for that variable.

Income statement variables often used to develop pricing measures from guideline companies are the following:

- Net sales
- Gross cash flow (net income plus noncash charges)
- Gross cash flow before taxes (earnings before depreciation, other noncash charges, and taxes, sometimes called EBDT)
- Net cash flow (gross cash flow adjusted for capital expenditures, changes in working capital, and sometimes changes in debt)
- Net income before taxes
- Net income after taxes
- Dividends or dividend-paying capacity

In addition to business valuation multiples using only the value of the common stock to develop the pricing multiple, some measures address the value of *all* the invested capital. In this case, the numerator for the valuation multiple is often called *market value of invested capital* (MVIC). This measure is also sometimes called *adjusted market value of capital structure, aggregate market value of capital structure*, or *enterprise value*. This measure includes the market value of all classes of stock and all interest-bearing debt. Many analysts deduct cash and marketable securities in situations where they are analyzing the performance of operating assets. The denominator used to compute the pricing multiples should include the returns available to all classes of capital reflected in the numerator— for example, preferred dividends and interest.

Income statement variables often used to develop business valuation multiples for MVIC are:

- Revenues
- Earnings before interest and taxes (EBIT)
- Earnings before interest, taxes, depreciation, and amortization (EBITDA)
- Net cash flow available to invested capital
- Revenues

The above variables usually are computed on an operating basis, with nonoperating items treated separately. Any of the above income variables may be measured for any or all of a variety of time periods to create the denominator for a valuation multiple. The typical time periods used are:

- Latest 12 months (LTM)
- Latest fiscal year
- Estimates for the forthcoming year
- Simple average of some number of past years
- Weighted average of some number of past years

All of the above performance variables and time periods may have various other permutations, depending on availability and relevance of data.

In certain industries, valuation multiples may also be developed based on balance sheet data. Such measures normally are developed by dividing the price as of the valuation date by the balance sheet variables as of a date as close as possible preceding the valuation date for which both guideline company and subject company data are available. Balance sheet variables typically used are:

- Book value
- Tangible book value
- Adjusted book value
- Adjusted tangible book value

As with valuation multiples based on operating data, valuation multiples based on asset values may also be performed on a total capital value basis. In such cases, the market value of the senior equity and interest-bearing liabilities generally is added into both the numerator and the denominator in developing the valuation multiple.

Note that *unlike* operating variables, which are measured over one or more *periods* of time, asset value variables normally are measured only at the latest practical *point* in time.

The actual valuation multiple applied to the subject company may be anywhere within (or sometimes even outside) the range of valuation multiples developed from the market data. Where each valuation multiple should fall will depend on the quantitative and qualitative analysis of the subject company relative to the companies that comprise the market transaction data.

One occasionally sees multiples based on physical measures of the size of the business. We have encountered metrics such as number of customers for Internet service providers and megawatt capacity for electric power generators. Since these are measures of the operating assets of the company, they would be used for invested capital multiples rather than equity multiples. As with all metrics used to develop market multiples, the denominator must be logically related to the ability of the business to provide future benefits to investors. One must be cautious about the use of physical measures because companies with similar physical size or metrics may have very different profitability due to differing market conditions, operating costs, condition of the assets, or any variety of other factors.

When Is the Guideline Publicly Traded Company Method Most Useful?

The initial value derived from the guideline publicly traded company method, before adjustment for shareholder-level factors such as size of the block and degree of marketability or lack of it, is often called a *publicly traded equivalent value* or *as if freely traded value*—that is, the price at which the stock would be expected to trade if it were traded publicly. In other words, the value indication is appropriate for a marketable, minority ownership interest, using the premise of value in continued use, as a going-concern business. In some cases, where the public companies are selling at or near their control value, the value indication could be thought to be control value.

The method can be used in conjunction with a valuation for any standard of value, certainly most importantly for fair market value. Use of the method in conjunction with each of the standards of value is discussed next. That discussion is followed by an explanation of the adjustments that are necessary when the method is used to value a nonmarketable minority stock and to value controlling ownership interests.

Finally, we discuss the impact of the quantity and quality of available data on the use of the method.

Standard of Value

Fair Market Value. While the guideline company method can be used in conjunction with any standard of value, it generally is most useful when the standard of value is fair market value. By definition, the method is based on making comparisons between the subject stock and transactions in guideline publicly traded stocks.

Fair market value is the standard of value in most income tax–related transactions. (Revenue Ruling 59-60 references the public markets no less than seven times.) It is also the standard of value for all employee stock ownership plan (ESOP) valuations.

Fair Value. As noted in Chapter 2, fair value is a statutorily mandated standard of value. In the United States, it is applicable in almost all states to dissenting stockholder actions and, in the states that have corporate and partnership dissolution statutes, to such dissolutions. It is interpreted by judicial precedent in each state. As a generality, in most states it is a broader standard that incorporates market value along with values indicated by income and asset approaches. Therefore, we would say that a guideline publicly traded company method usually would be a part of the analysis when fair value is the standard.

Investment Value. This is the standard of value that could depart the most from the value developed by a strict application of the guideline publicly traded company method. The guideline publicly traded company method would be expected to develop a value based on a *consensus* of market participants, as evidenced by their transactions. Investment value, by definition, is the value to a *particular* buyer or seller. Therefore, the income approach gives more opportunity for a specific party to project income flows and use discount and capitalization rates that are appropriate to his or her individual investment criteria.

Even a party primarily interested in investment value, however, generally would want to have some notion of what a consensus value would be. Furthermore, the analyst interested in investment value can always adjust the financial variables on a pro forma basis reflecting anticipated changes in the subject company and use the guideline publicly traded company method to test the sensitivity of market value to various possible changes in the financial variables.

Ownership Characteristics

Marketable versus Nonmarketable. The guideline company method would be most ideal, of course, when valuing marketable shares by direct comparison with marketable shares.

Marketability, or lack of it, like most shareholder-level attributes of securities, is often an issue that is not totally black or white. For example, private placements of stocks that already have a public market generally will be restricted for a time and then will enjoy full marketability. Most ESOP stock by law enjoys the right of a "put," which guarantees a market at the appraised price at the occurrence of specified triggering events. There are many data and precedents for adjusting for the limited marketability in such situations.

The use of the guideline publicly traded company method to value stocks of closely held companies that have no market has been enhanced in the last 20 years by two important developments:

1. An increased number of small and medium-size available actively traded public companies to choose from, which may be more comparable in many respects to many closely held companies than those traded in public markets a decade ago.
2. Development of extensive new databases that provide empirical guidance not previously available to assist in quantifying the discount for lack of marketability between a publicly traded security equivalent value and an otherwise similar closely held security value. These data are described in detail in Chapter 17, "Discounts for Illiquidity and Lack of Marketability."

On the other hand, the number of public companies listed on the New York Stock Exchange, American Stock Exchange, and NASDAQ has been declining recently from a peak of over 9,000 in 1997 to less than 7,000 at the end of 2004.[5]

Control versus Minority. Since guideline public company shares are, by definition, noncontrolling ownership interests, their trading prices are most directly relevant for valuation of other noncontrolling ownership interests. However, as noted earlier, in some cases this method may also be relevant for valuing controlling interests.

In applying the guideline publicly traded company method, qualitative and quantitative differences between the guideline and subject companies are reflected in arriving at the publicly traded equivalent value of the subject stock, usually in the choice of multiples applied to the subject's fundamental data relative to the guideline companies' multiples. Adjustments may also be made for other factors such as relative excess assets or deficiencies in arriving at a publicly traded equivalent value. Thus, having arrived at a publicly traded equivalent value, the only remaining adjustment necessary for a minority interest value is the shareholder-level attribute of lack of marketability. As already noted, there are a plethora of empirical data on which to base this adjustment.

When valuing controlling interests, it may be preferable to apply the market approach by using only guideline controlling interest transactions, which is the subject of the next chapter. In the past, there were far more reliable guideline public company noncontrolling interest transaction data available than guideline merged and acquired controlling interest transaction data. In recent years, the

---

[5] Shannon Pratt, *The Market Approach to Valuing Businesses*, 2nd ed. (Hoboken, NJ: John Wiley & Sons, 2005), pp. 27–28 (hereafter "*Market Approach*").

number of public companies listed in the main exchanges has dropped while the number of both public and private companies bought and sold and captured by transaction databases has increased dramatically.[6] In spite of the increased number of guideline merged and acquired controlling interest transaction data, sometimes transactions of companies that are similar enough to the subject company may not be available. Even if available, the number of data points per transaction may not be enough to render an indication of value that is reliable. Therefore, it often is useful to apply the guideline publicly traded company method even when valuing controlling interests. (This method may require consideration of a premium to reflect the prerogatives of control.) This premium may be offset in part or even fully by a discount for lack of marketability. This is a complicated issue, which is briefly addressed toward the end of this chapter in the section on typical adjustments to reach the value conclusion and in considerable detail in Chapters 15 through 17.

Going-Concern versus Liquidation Value

In almost all cases, the public market is pricing stocks on the assumption that they will continue as a going concern. Unless there is evidence to the contrary, the guideline publicly traded company method would be expected to produce a value on the premise that the subject is expected to continue as a going concern. In contrast, the various forms of liquidation value are addressed in Chapter 14 in the context of the asset-based approach.

Quantity and Quality of Available Data

As with any valuation method, the quantity and quality of relevant data available to implement it will have an important bearing on the usefulness of the method. As noted earlier, there are more publicly traded companies, especially small ones, than most people realize, and it is important to search them out.

After discussing criteria for selection of companies, we address the question of how many guideline publicly traded companies would ideally be used in this method. In the final analysis, the quantity and quality of the guideline company data compared with the quantity and quality of data available for other methods will influence the weight accorded the method in correlating the results of various methods and reaching a value conclusion.

Criteria for Guideline Company Selection

One succinct quote summarizes the essence of the key characteristic that should be present in a guideline company: "Do the underlying economics driving this comparable company match those that drive our company?"[7] Of course, this quote does not suggest that the economics of the guideline companies be a perfect match

---

[6] *Market Approach*, Chapters 3 and 6.
[7] Daniel W. Bielinski, "The Comparable-Company Approach: Measuring the True Value of Privately Held Firms," *Corporate Cashflow Magazine*, October 1990, pp. 64–66.

to the economics of the subject company. Although this relationship is ideal, analysts rarely encounter it in the real world. Rather, this quote indicates that the microeconomic factors that drive the guideline companies should be sufficiently similar to the microeconomic factors that drive the subject company. Otherwise, the guideline companies will not provide meaningful pricing guidance to the analyst.

In Revenue Ruling 59-60, the IRS, one of the strongest proponents of the guideline publicly traded company method, makes the following observation:

> Although the only restrictive requirement as to comparable corporations specified in the statute is that their lines of business be the same or similar, yet it is obvious that consideration must be given to other relevant factors in order that the most valid comparison possible will be obtained.[8]

In analyzing (1) whether or not a particular publicly traded company should be considered an appropriate guideline or (2) which of the guideline publicly traded companies are most comparable to the subject company (and therefore deserve more weight in the valuation), the analyst should consider several important factors.

For example, at issue in *Caracci v. Commissioner*[9] was the value of a home health care agency and related entities that were transferred into S corporations. The IRS's expert used the market approach, considering two types of transfers: valuation of comparable publicly traded home health care agencies and valuation of merged or acquired companies. As a basis for valuations under the market approach, the expert estimated the subject company's MVIC, using a price/revenue multiple. The court favored this approach, saying, "We believe that the best evidence of the value of [the company] arises from the use of the comparable value method employed by both experts . . . use of the MVIC approach to compare the privately held [company] entities to similar publicly traded businesses is especially appropriate here. . . . "

In *Estate of Leichter v. Commissioner*,[10] both experts used comparables for an importer and wholesale-distributor. The IRS expert compared the subject company to five publicly traded firms and discounted the value of the subject to more accurately match the comparables. Although the court found that his conclusion was "within a reasonable range," it also found some weakness in his analysis, most notably his use of guideline companies that were not similar to the subject.

At issue in *Hess v. Commissioner*[11] was the value of the stock of a closely held corporation. In his guideline companies analysis, the IRS expert relied solely on price/earnings (P/E) ratios to compare the subject company to the guideline companies. The taxpayers argued that use of P/E ratios was erroneous, claiming that P/E ratios are a "crude measure" for calculating value and do not consider important differences in interest levels, tax levels, and depreciation levels between the subject company and the guideline companies. The court agreed that the IRS expert's guideline companies method would have been more complete and more persuasive if it had employed additional measures of comparison. However, the court also noted that it is clear that P/E ratios bear a well-recognized relationship in the valuation of companies, and that reliance on P/E ratios was not inherently

---

[8] Revenue Ruling 59-60 (1959-1 C.B. 237), Section 4(h).
[9] *Caracci v. Commissioner*, 118 T.C. 379, 118 T.C. No. 25, 2002 U.S. Tax Ct. LEXIS 25 (U.S. Tax Ct. May 22, 2002).
[10] *Estate of Leichter v. Commissioner*, T.C. Memo 2003-66, 2003 Tax Ct. Memo LEXIS 66 (U.S. Tax Ct. Mar. 6, 2003).
[11] *Hess v. Commissioner*, T.C. Memo 2003-251 (U.S. Tax Ct. Aug. 20, 2003).

flawed. The P/E ratios of publicly held companies do not compare to the P/E ratios of a closely held company if the companies themselves are not comparable. Whether the stock price of one company with a given earnings stream will be similar to that of another company with the same earnings depends upon a wide variety of factors, including management policy, management ability, past performance, and dividend policy. Although taxpayers suggested that the guideline companies did not compare to the subject company, the court pointed out that two of the four guideline companies used by the IRS expert in his analysis were companies used by the subject to "benchmark" its performance, and three of the four guideline companies were also used by the taxpayers' expert in his market comparable analysis. Accordingly, the court found that the guideline companies, when properly adjusted, were comparable to the subject company.

The court in *Estate of Hendrickson v. Commissioner*[12] accepted as guideline companies thrifts that were comparable in size to the subject one-branch bank, and rejected bank holding companies that were principally comparable on the basis of geography, rather than size, financial, or operating characteristics.

The comparability of guideline publicly traded companies used in a valuation frequently has become a central issue in litigated valuations, partly because of the difficulty of choosing truly comparable companies. In *Tallichet v. Commissioner*, the Tax Court emphasized that there are "guideposts in determining comparability."[13] According to the Court, the following factors are among those to consider in determining comparability:

1. Capital structure
2. Credit status
3. Depth of management
4. Personnel experience
5. Nature of competition
6. Maturity of the business

In *Estate of Victor P. Clarke*, the Tax Court reemphasized that it is "imperative that the characteristics of the subject company and the purportedly comparable company relevant to the question of value be isolated and examined so that a significant comparison can be made."[14] In that case, the Court cited the following as relevant factors:

1. Products
2. Markets
3. Management
4. Earnings
5. Dividend-paying capacity
6. Book value
7. Position of company in industry

Although these lists seem comprehensive, depending on the nature of the industry, the analyst may need to consider additional factors, such as number and size of retail outlets, sales volume, product or service mix, territory of operations, and customer mix. Clearly, even this additional list is not exhaustive, and we

---

[12] *Estate of Hendrickson v. Commissioner,* T.C. Memo 1999-278 (Aug. 23, 1999).
[13] *Tallichet v. Commissioner*, 33 T.C.M. 1133 (1974).
[14] *Estate of Victor P. Clarke*, 35 T.C.M. 1482 (1976).

cannot overemphasize the necessity of tailoring the list of factors to be considered to fit each valuation. Much of this information can be gathered in a thorough review of each public company's Form 10-K, but it may also be necessary to consult additional sources such as industry and trade publications (discussed in Chapter 6, "Researching Economic and Industry Information") or to call the company for additional information.

It is also useful to analyze the financial statements for both the subject company and the guideline companies to uncover similarities and differences to consider in the valuation. Bearing in mind the company being valued and the nature of the industry, we generally compare the performance of the subject company to the guideline companies by analyzing financial ratios that measure liquidity, leverage, activity, and profitability, as well as historical trends in revenues, expenses and profitability. This type of analysis is illustrated in Chapter 8, "Financial Statement Ratio Analysis." In particular, if this analysis indicates that the guideline companies' capital structures differ significantly from that of the subject (one of the examples cited by the IRS in Revenue Ruling 59-60 regarding factors relevant to comparability), this difference can sometimes be factored out or at least mitigated somewhat by using market value or invested capital procedures referred to earlier.

In many valuation situations, the subject company is so unique that it is difficult to find a set of good guideline companies. In these cases, the analyst may find a group of companies that can shed some light on the valuation question, but may consider one or a few more directly comparable to the subject company than the rest. In such cases, the analyst may tabulate data for the whole group but elect to accord more weight to the data for those guideline companies considered most comparable.

Sometimes, though, the subject company seems so unique that even an exhaustive search produces no companies for use as guideline companies. The appraiser should keep in mind that there are over 30,000 small public companies out there that have sold stock through public offerings at one time or another and are still operating. Also, if the valuation is for federal gift and estate taxes, Revenue Ruling 59-60 states that the companies may be in the same "or similar" industries. This phrase gives the analyst latitude to exercise reasonable judgment in selecting companies from related industries if unable to find guideline companies in the subject company's industry group or companies with adequate trading volume.

In considering "the same or similar lines of business," the analyst should keep in mind the comparability of the driving underlying investment risk and expected rate of return characteristics of the guideline companies and the subject company. Important investment risk and expected rate of return factors include the market(s) into which the company sells, its brand acceptance, or lack of it, and, sometimes, the raw material supply conditions. Three quick examples will help to illustrate the point.

Example 1: Industrial Equipment Manufacturer

We were retained to value a company whose line of business was the manufacture of electronic control equipment for the forest products industry. We found plenty of manufacturers of electronic control equipment, but none for whom the forest products industry was a significant part of their market. Therefore, for guideline companies, we selected manufacturers of other types of industrial equipment and supplies that sold to the forest products and related cyclical industries. We decided that the markets served were more of an economic driving force than the physical nature of the products produced.

Example 2: The Gallo Wine Company

At the valuation date in the *Estate of Mark Gallo*,[15] there was only one publicly traded wine company stock, a tiny midget compared with the huge Gallo and, for other reasons as well, not a good guideline company. Experts for both the taxpayer and the IRS recognized this and used as guideline companies distillers, brewers, soft drink bottlers, and food companies that enjoyed strong brand recognition and were subject to seasonal crop conditions and grower contracts.

Example 3: The Hallmark Greeting Card Co.

In the *Estate of Joyce Hall*,[16] there was only one good publicly traded greeting card guideline company as of the valuation date. The expert for the IRS used that company and also other companies that manufactured consumer consumable products and whose consumer brand names commanded the dominant market share for their respective products. The court commented very positively on this procedure.

However, the analyst who finds it difficult to find suitable guideline companies should also remember that in several cases, courts have decided that the comparability between the subject company and the guideline publicly traded companies was insufficient. In *Righter v. U.S.*, for example, the court decided that companies that manufactured toys or toys and games were not sufficiently comparable to a company that produced two types of games, partly because their products appealed to and were used by different age groups.[17] In *Estate of Joseph E. Salsbury*, the Tax Court rejected several companies that one of the experts had chosen as comparable because they "did not even have divisions engaged in the animal and poultry health industry" (which was the subject company's business). As a result, the Court concluded that the selection of these companies "fails to satisfy the 'same or similar line of business' requirement of the regulations."[18] In *Estate of Brookshire v. Commissioner*,[19] the subject company owned a chain of grocery stores and related businesses. The court determined that companies that had "significant sales in markets other than retail grocery" were not comparable. In *Rakow v. Commissioner*,[20] the court rejected the guideline company method despite its use by the experts for both sides. The court rejected the taxpayer's expert's reliance on this method because his calculations did not focus on the period of time close to the valuation date of the subject company, and rejected the IRS's expert's use of this method because the companies he chose were much larger than the subject company. Instead, the court relied on a discounted cash flow analysis.

A problem also arises if an appraiser establishes criteria that are too restrictive. By unnecessarily limiting the number of guideline companies considered, an appraiser may miss relevant market evidence that would have led to a different valuation. Several court cases have noted that experts were too selective,

---

[15] *Estate of Mark S. Gallo*, 50 T.C.M. 470 (1985).
[16] *Estate of Joyce C. Hall*, 92 T.C. No. 19 (1989).
[17] *Righter v. U.S.*, 439 F.2d 1244 (1971).
[18] *Estate of Salsbury v. Commissioner*, T.C. Memo 1975-333.
[19] *Estate of Brookshire v. Commissioner*, T.C. Memo 1998-365 (Oct. 8, 1998).
[20] *Rakow v. Commissioner*, T.C. Memo 1999-177 (May 27, 1999).

excluding companies that would have provided useful valuation guidance. In *Estate of Victor P. Clarke*, the Tax Court addressed this problem forcefully by stating that the definition of a guideline corporation cannot be "unduly restrictive, as it strips the inquiry into the valuation of closely held stock of the flexibility needed to make an informed judgment."[21] The U.S. Court of Claims stated its opinion on this issue quite succinctly in *Central Trust Company v. U.S.* In employing the guideline publicly traded company method, "every effort should be made to select as broad a base of comparative companies as is reasonably possible, as well as to give full consideration to every possible factor in order to make the comparison more meaningful."[22] In *Estate of Mark S. Gallo*, this point was again emphasized when the Tax Court commended one of the experts for making "careful and reasoned comparisons with each comparable instead of arbitrarily relying upon the outer limit of a range."[23] Clearly, the message of these cases is that the appraiser must choose guideline companies logically and be able to justify their selection.

How Many Guideline Companies?

The answer to this question depends on a number of factors:

1. Similarity to the subject—the more similar, the fewer needed
2. Trading activity—again, the more actively traded, the fewer needed
3. Dispersion of valuation multiple data points—the wider the range of relevant valuation multiple data points, the more companies it takes to identify a pattern relevant to the subject company

In the *Gallo* and *Hall* cases cited earlier, where companies in other industries but with related characteristics were used, the guideline company lists encompassed 10 to 16 companies. In *Hall*, the court rejected the reliance by one appraiser on the only other company in the greeting card industry, even though it was an excellent comparable, stating "one company does not a market make."

We have used as few as two or three guideline companies. However, in those cases we would be reluctant to rely on the guideline publicly traded company method exclusively. Our confidence rises sharply when we can find four to seven good guideline publicly traded companies. In those rare cases where it seems that there are a dozen or more good guideline companies in terms of line of business, we often narrow down the criteria in terms of size, earning pattern, and other factors to utilize what our analysis indicates to be the best ones.

In *Doft & Co. v. Travelocity.com, Inc.*,[24] a statutory appraisal case, the Delaware Court of Chancery rejected a discounted cash flow approach, ruling that the projections were not reasonably reliable. It adopted a guideline company analysis that relied on a single comparable company, Expedia, which had been used by both experts and in the prior fairness opinion. Because of quality differences, the Court discounted Expedia's multiples in its valuation of Travelocity.

---

[21] *Estate of Victor P. Clarke*, p. 1501.
[22] *Central Trust Company v. U.S.*, 305 F.2d 393 (Ct. Cl., 1962).
[23] *Estate of Mark S. Gallo*, 50 T.C.M. 470 (1985).
[24] 2004 Del. Ch. LEXIS 75, 2004 WL 1152338 and 2004 WL 1366994, May 20, 2004 (revised May 21; supplemented June 10, 2004).

Time Period to Consider

In the absence of a compelling reason to do otherwise, the time period most commonly used for analysis of operating data is three to five years. This conventional time period should not, however, be blindly and mechanistically adopted. The operative phrase is "relevant time period."

For a cyclical industry, a complete economic cycle for that industry is widely considered to be a good choice of time period from which to develop average operating results to be used as the basis for valuation multiples. This has led us on occasion to use averages of operating data for as long as 10 years.

Sometimes the relevant time period is constrained by major changes that affected either the subject company or the industry as a whole. Such events may render comparative financial data before such changes irrelevant for valuation purposes. In these cases it may only be relevant to use one or a few years' comparative data.

Once in a while, the historical data include an aberration that is so clearly nonrecurring for either the subject company or the industry that the best thing to do is just to omit that year when computing the valuation multiples. In such cases, however, the data normally are tabulated and presented and the reason for omitting that year from the valuation multiple calculations is given.

Typically, the same time period that is used for gathering and presenting data is also used for both income statement and balance sheet data. Valuation multiples based on income statement data typically are computed by dividing the valuation date price by the income variables or averages of variables for one or a number of prior periods, usually (but not necessarily) years. Valuation multiples based on balance sheet variables (e.g., price/book value) typically are computed by dividing the valuation date price by the most recent balance sheet variable. The reason for collecting and presenting several years of balance sheet information is to identify and interpret comparative trends among the guideline and subject companies, although the earlier years' balance sheet data usually are not used directly in the computation of valuation multiples.

Deciding Which Valuation Multiples to Use

As noted earlier in the chapter, there is a wide variety of financial variables for which capitalization rates for the guideline companies can be computed. For the income variables, there is also a wide choice of time periods and possible weighting schemes for each variable. The analyst's skill, experience, and judgment play an important role in making these choices and, ultimately, in deciding the appropriate weight to accord to each. This section discusses criteria to consider in order to make relevant choices in each case.

Influence of the Ownership Characteristics

Controlling Ownership Interest versus Noncontrolling Ownership Interest Value. When valuing a controlling ownership interest, emphasis is often placed heavily on measures of the MVIC rather than of the equity only, because the controlling interest holder would be able to make the financial decision to change the capital structure if so desired. Conversely, when valuing a noncontrolling ownership interest, focus logically is on measures that directly value the subject equity interest. Sometimes, however, measures of the MVIC are used to value noncontrolling ownership interests, subtracting the debt to reach an indication of the value of equity. This procedure is most often used when the subject and guideline companies have wide variations in capital structure, to even out the effects of the differences in leverage.

Marketable versus Nonmarketable. Public companies tend to focus more on net income than do private companies, while private companies tend to focus more on cash flows than do public companies. Therefore, when valuing a private company, one may choose to focus a bit more on cash flow variables than net income variables.

Going-Concern versus Liquidation Value

Going-concern value tends to be based largely—and sometimes entirely—on income and cash flow analyses. Liquidation value often involves an analysis of individual asset values, so the emphasis is on balance sheet items. As noted earlier, however, the guideline publicly traded company valuation method is often used in connection with a going-concern premise of value.

Type of Company

Operating versus Holding Companies. In the broadest general sense, valuation of operating companies tends to focus on earning power variables, while valuation of holding companies tends to focus on asset value variables. Therefore, for operating companies, focus tends to be on ratios of price to cash flows, earnings, and dividends. For holding companies, focus tends to be on ratios of price to book value or price to adjusted book value.

Stage of Company in Life Cycle. The more mature or stable the company, the more the focus may be on cash flow variables, whereas companies in a growth phase may focus more on net income. In fact, young companies in a very high growth phase may be expected to have negative net cash flow for years, so that net cash flow would be meaningful in a long-term discounted cash flow valuation method but meaningless for the same company in a market approach using current guideline publicly traded company data. This is not to imply diminished importance of ultimate ability to produce meaningful net cash flows, but only because multiples of negative current numbers are meaningless.

Line of Business. The more meaningful the assets are to the type of business, the more they should be considered in the valuation multiples computed. Usually, assets that are more liquid and not "special purpose" are more important. Furthermore, they are easier to deal with in valuation if their generally accepted accounting principles (GAAP) values are close to their market values. For example, for financial institutions, the financial assets and liabilities are extremely important, and price-to-book-value ratios are much more important than for most other types of operating companies. For distribution companies (especially wholesalers, but also retailers), inventories (and in some cases receivables) are a major part of their asset mix, usually making price to book value a relevant measure to consider. For manufacturing companies, plant and equipment can vary tremendously from one to another, both in age and condition and also in importance to their operations, so that price-to-asset-value multiples can be difficult to implement on a comparative basis and frequently are not very meaningful. For service companies, assets typically play a very minor role, if any, in valuation multiples.

Availability of Data

We often face the frustrating obstacle of lack (or limited availability) of data for the valuation multiples we would conceptually most prefer to use in the guideline publicly traded company method. The analyst should perform the most thorough search possible for the data he or she would *prefer* to use, and then make the best possible use of whatever is available.

Gross Cash Flow versus Net Cash Flow. A good example of this problem is the choice between gross cash flow and net cash flow as an economic income variable in a guideline company valuation multiple. In the discounted future economic income method, we generally prefer—and generally use—net cash flow. If one is willing to do the work, using the statement of cash flows along with the income statements and balance sheets, one can compute net cash flow for most public companies for each year. However, if data such as capital expenditures have been subject to wide variations, as they frequently are, these data generally are harder to adjust objectively for abnormal or nonrecurring items than most other data. Therefore, gross cash flow is more commonly used because it is straightforward, easier to compute, and simple to explain.

Multiples of Market Prices to Asset Values. When using multiples of market prices of stock or invested capital to underlying tangible asset values, it is more meaningful if the tangible asset values are adjusted to their respective fair market values. For example, publicly traded, closed-end investment companies are required to reprice their tangible assets at market value regularly, so the multiple of price to adjusted net tangible asset value is available for such companies.

Real estate investment trusts (REITs) and other real estate holding companies are not required to disclose market prices of their assets, but many choose to do so. Thus, if one is valuing a real estate holding company and has market values for the subject company tangible assets, one may limit guideline company selection to those that report market values of their holdings. Alternatively, one may use those that report market values for a price-to-adjusted-net-asset-value multiple and a broader list for income-related valuation multiples. (The availability of market prices of assets does not necessarily mean that assets are the primary value drivers.)

Data on values of timber holdings for many forest products companies are available from Wall Street analysts. Therefore, when valuing a company with timber holdings, a valuation multiple of price to net asset value adjusted for timber holdings can sometimes be developed.

For most other types of public companies, market values of asset holdings are not available. This leaves the analyst with no choice, if desiring to use a measure based on asset value in the guideline company method, but to use a simple price-to-book-value multiple. As noted earlier in the "Type of Company" section, the price-to-book-value multiple tends to have more relevance if assets are meaningful to the type of business, and if they are of such a nature that book values tend to be fairly close to market values.

Use of Only a Portion of the Guideline Companies for Some Valuation Multiples. It is not necessary to use every guideline company selected for every valuation multiple utilized. Not all public companies have earnings estimates, for example. Also, one of the guideline companies may have had deficit net income, so it can't be used for the P/E pricing multiple. However, that guideline company may still have had meaningful gross cash flow so that it could be used in developing a price-to-gross-cash-flow pricing multiple. Sometimes an industry group includes a good guideline company that went public recently, say only three years ago. That guideline company would not be available for the calculation of the price-to-five-year-average-income pricing multiple, but it would be available for calculation of the price-to-latest 12-months' income pricing multiple. Likewise, earnings projections may not be available for all of the guideline companies. The analyst should use caution and careful judgment, however, to make sure that the use of certain guideline companies for the calculation of some pricing multiples and not others does not introduce bias or distortion to the pricing multiple implications.

This section has touched on some of the more common general problems of availability of data to implement the guideline company method. Sometimes, we find that the guideline company data we have been able to develop are not as strongly and compellingly convincing of value as we would like. Generally, to the extent that they provide some general guidance with respect to value, we still would tend to present them rather than ignore them. And, the strength of the data leads to the judgment as to the weight ultimately accorded to them among the various valuation multiples within the guideline publicly traded company method, and accorded to the guideline publicly traded company method among other valuation methods.

Compiling Guideline Company Tables

The purpose of gathering data on guideline publicly traded companies is to derive some benchmarks by which to value the subject privately held company. For example, public companies in an industry selling at price-to-earnings multiples higher than the overall market average indicate that the public market is optimistic about the industry's future relative to its recent earnings, and this optimism should also be reflected in the private companies' P/E multiples. Similarly, the public market can provide benchmarks concerning the relation of stock prices to such variables as book values, adjusted underlying net asset values, dividends, and gross revenues. Any or all of these parameters can be relevant to a specific valuation situation, as discussed throughout this book.

Compiling a comprehensive list of guideline publicly traded companies is not simple. No single source provides an exhaustive list. It is much easier to find good guideline companies in some industries than in others. A complete search requires creativity, ingenuity, and experience. This chapter presents the most comprehensive general sources available. If not satisfied with the list developed through these sources, the analyst can consult trade association membership lists and regional investment publications or ask the management of the subject company and of the companies discovered through the conventional search for additional prospects.

Of all the criteria by which different companies may be judged as comparable for valuation purposes, the one that typically receives the most attention is the industry in which the subject company operates. In fact, Revenue Ruling 59-60 specifically states that of the factors that "are fundamental and require careful analysis in each case" for gift and estate tax valuations, one is "the market price of stocks of corporations engaged in the same or a similar line of business having their stocks actively traded on a free and open market, either on an exchange or over-the-counter."[25]

Therefore, the starting point in compiling a list of guideline companies is to form a list of the companies that operate in the subject company's industry group. Still, the most widely accepted categorization of industry groups is the U.S. government's *Standard Industrial Classification Manual*, which publishes and defines Standard Industry Classification (SIC) codes. (The SIC code is the statistical classification standard underlying all establishment-based federal economic statistics classified by industry.) In 1997, the North American Industry Classification System (NAICS)[26] replaced the 1987 U.S. SIC system and the classification systems of Canada and Mexico. NAICS was erected on a production-oriented conceptual framework. It is not a grouping of products but a grouping of producing units that allows for the collection of data on inputs and outputs on a comparable basis for production-oriented (not market-oriented) analysis. NAICS uses a six-digit coding system that resembles SIC codes. It is expected to eventually supersede the SIC system.

The search for guideline publicly traded companies should be as exhaustive as the scope of the particular valuation case permits. Frequently, the most obvious public companies in an industry are the largest ones and, for this and related reasons, may be less comparable to most closely held companies than some of the smaller, more obscure public companies. A comprehensive search for guideline companies also demonstrates that the analyst took into account all companies that might be considered reasonably comparable and selected for analysis the most comparative companies available. The analyst must establish and adhere to an objective set of selection criteria so that the final list will not tend to bias the valuation result either upward or downward.

Developing a List of Guideline Companies

The use of the SIC and NAICS codes as a means of identifying potential guideline publicly traded companies has already been discussed. The starting point in a search for developing similar guideline publicly traded enterprises is a search for the appropriate SIC or NAICS code that applies to the subject company. Data concerning publicly traded companies by SIC and/or NAICS group are found in a number of sources, including in printed material, on CD-ROMs, and in online databases.

U.S. Government Printing Office. *SEC Directory. The Directory of Companies Required to File Annual Reports with the Securities and Exchange Commission, under the Securities Act of 1943* is available from U.S. Government Printing Office, Superintendent of Documents, Washington, D.C. 20402, (202) 512-1800, www.gpo.gov. The directory lists the companies alphabetically and by industry groups according to the *Standard Industrial Classification Manual*. The

---

[25] Revenue Ruling 59-60 (1959-1 C.B. 327), Section 4.

[26] *The North American Industry Classification System: United States* is a publication available from the U.S. Government Printing Office, Superintendent of Documents, Washington, D.C. 20402, (202) 512-1800, www.gpo.gov. It includes 350 new industries, definitions for each industry, tables showing correspondence between the 1997 NAICS and the 1987 SIC codes and vice versa, and an alphabetical list of more than 18,000 businesses and their corresponding NAICS codes.

latest edition of the directory—as of September 1999—lists over 12,000 companies required to file annual reports with the SEC.

Other sources of information available from the U.S. Government Bookstore that are helpful in searching guideline public companies include:

Statistics of Income Bulletin (provides information from individual and corporation income tax returns in addition to nonfarm sole proprietorships and partnerships).

Statistics of Income: Corporation Income Tax Returns (provides data by industry on assets, liabilities, receipts, deductions, net income, income subject to tax, tax, and credits).

North American Industry Classification System: United States (description provided in a previous section).

Standard and Poor's. Standard and Poor's provides a variety of publications in variety of formats (print, electronic, CD-ROM, and over the Internet) that can be used in searching for guideline public companies. Publications that started and were available as print publications in the past are now available as databases distributed through a variety of channels and vendors. Some of these products include *Compustat, Standard and Poor's Corporation Records,* and *Standard and Poor's Register.*

Standard and Poor's Corporation Records provides information on publicly held U.S., Canadian, and international companies. Published continuously since 1917, the publication has evolved to meet investor demand for complete corporate data and is now available in print form, electronic form, CD-ROM, and over the Internet from various commercial vendors. The monthly print volumes contain comprehensive data on the business, finances, securities, and background of over 10,000 of the largest concerns, while the Daily News section—included in the *S&P Corporation Records* database—provides updated information such as management changes and annual and interim earnings for those companies.

Capital IQ (www.capitaliq.com) is an online, Internet-based product that offers abundant information on public and private companies, both in the U.S. and internationally. One can use Capital IQ to screen companies by industry group and obtain descriptions and financial data on a given set of companies.

The *Corporation Records* features: full income statements and balance sheets, corporate profiles, equity and fixed income descriptions, recent news, shareholder reports, SEC reports, newspaper articles, press releases, officers and directors, subsidiaries, and divisions.

In its print format, the analysts can locate companies by SIC code and by name. In its database format, advanced searching capabilities allow screening based on any item in the database. Custom report formatting capabilities allow for specification of the data items needed in a report and the format used to display the data. Companies in a report can be sorted according to any data item desired. *Standard and Poor's Corporation Records* is available electronically from DIALOG Information Services, Lexis-Nexis, and FactSet.

Standard & Poor's Register of Corporations, Directors and Executives is perhaps the most comprehensive directory of companies by SIC group. This two-volume subscription lists 75,000 public and private corporations and 290,000 officers, directors, and other principals, plus 68,000 biographical sketches of top-level managers. Corporate listings include a business description, annual sales, subsidiary listings, etc. This publication is also available on CD-ROM and online from various vendors (DIALOG Information Services, Lexis-Nexis).

Standard & Poor's Compustat North America. *Compustat North America* offers financial information on publicly traded U.S. and Canadian companies. After collecting data from diverse sources, *Standard & Poor's* standardizes it by financial statement and by specific data item definition, preparing information that is comparable across companies, industries, time periods, and sectors. This standardized presentation makes it easier to identify companies with similar characteristics, such as capital structure and operating performance. This online database is delivered by itself and as part of other more comprehensive Standard & Poor's products such as *Research Insight, Research Insight on the Web, Market Insight, Standard & Poor's Compustat Xpressfeed*, or select third-party providers.

Standard & Poor's Compustat Global. The *Compustat Global* database provides financial and market data on more than 16,000 non-U.S. and non-Canadian companies, in addition to over 5,600 U.S. and Canadian mid- and large-cap companies (active and inactive). The international database covers publicly traded companies in more than 80 countries, representing over 90% of the world's market capitalization. This online database is delivered by itself and as part of other more comprehensive Standard & Poor's products such as *Standard & Poor's Research Insight, Research Insight on the Web, Standard & Poor's Compustat Xpressfeed*, or select third-party providers.

Both the *Corporation Records* and the *Register of Companies* are also available as part of larger Standard and Poor's databases such as *Market Insight* and *NetAdvantage*. These are integrated information solutions for academic libraries, public libraries, corporate libraries, and information centers that are pulled from throughout the Standard and Poor's organization. *NetAdvantage* features powerful searching and screening tools to facilitate research; private company information (includes data on over 85,000 companies that are not publicly traded); NAICS code searching to identify potential guideline companies; biographies of thousands of corporate executives and directors; and export tools to enable researchers to download data into spreadsheet programs for further analysis.

As part of *Market Insight*, the *Register of Corporations* delivers data on over 90,000 private/affiliate and subsidiary companies, including company background, sales, employee count, and officers while The *Corporation Records* details bond descriptions, capitalization, management, stocks, and subsidiaries for over 12,000 public companies. *Market Insight* also utilizes the *Standard & Poor's Compustat* database, which provides fundamental data on approximately 10,000 actively traded and 11,000 inactive U.S. companies, as well as 12,000 global companies in 80 countries. Financial statements and ratio and valuation reports are available in Microsoft Excel.

For more information about Standard and Poor's products, visit one of Standard and Poor's Web sites: www2.standardandpoors.com, www.netadvantage. standardandpoors.com, www.compustat.com, call (800) 523-4534 or (303) 721-4802, or e-mail clientsupport@standardandpoors.com.

Mergent (Previously Moody's). *Mergent Manuals* (previously *Moody's Manuals*). This service consists of annual hardback volumes updated by loose-leaf reports with detailed financial information and bond ratings in separate sets according to type of business or government entity. The information included for companies in the manuals includes: history, business, properties, subsidiaries, officers, directors, long-term debt, capital stock, letter to shareholders, notes to financial statements, income statements, balance sheets, statements of cash flow, footnotes, auditors, general counsel, exchange and symbol, number of employees, number of shareholders, address, telephone and fax numbers, shareholder relations contact, stock price ranges, dividends, report of independent auditors, transfer agents, stock splits, annual meeting date, etc. As of the time of this writing, the following titles were available in this series (not a comprehensive list):

Mergent Industrial Manual and News Reports (information on 2,000 top industrial corporations)

Mergent OTC Industrial Manual and News Reports (information on more than 2,500 industrial corporations trading on NASDAQ's national market)

Mergent OTC Unlisted Manual and News Reports (information on over 2,200 companies not listed on national or regional exchanges)

Mergent Transportation Manual and News Reports (information on more than 650 active and historical major publicly held airline, railroad, trucking, freight, shipping, and oil pipeline companies)

Mergent Public Utility Manual and News Reports (information on publicly held U.S. public utilities)

Mergent Bank and Finance Manual and News Reports (information on over 3,000 banks, savings and loans, insurance companies, and real estate investment trusts, as well as the facts on more than 6,500 unit investment trusts)

Mergent Industry Review (includes comparative figures and rankings on 6,000 companies in 137 industry groups)

Mergent Handbook of Common Stocks (includes information on nearly 900 New York Stock Exchange companies in one-page profiles, updated quarterly)

Mergent Handbook of NASDAQ Stocks (includes information on NASDAQ companies, updated quarterly)

Mergent International Manual and News Reports (information on more than 13,000 non-U.S.-based public companies)

Mergent International Company Archives Manual (includes the final statistical record of more than 2,000 non-U.S. companies that have merged, were acquired, went bankrupt, or otherwise disappeared as public companies from 1995 forward)

Mergent U.S. Company Archives Manual (includes the final statistical record of U.S. companies that have merged, were acquired, went bankrupt, or otherwise disappeared as public companies from 1996 forward)

Mergent Dividend Record and Annual Dividend Record (includes current dividend data on more than 30,000 securities and a year-end summary of full-year dividends)

Microfiche. *Manuals on Microfiche.* This service includes all the Mergent and Moody's Manuals published since 1909:

Industrial Manual since 1920
OTC Industrial Manual since 1970
OTC Unlisted Manual since 1986
Bank & Finance Manual since 1928
Public Utility Manual since 1914
Transportation Manual since 1909
International Manual since 1981
Municipal & Government Manual since 1918

Online Databases. As of the time of this writing, the following online databases were available (not a comprehensive list):

Mergent Equity Portraits. This resource combines Mergent's database of fundamental company information with stock price, volume, performance ratios, and other data to offer detailed "portraits" of more than 10,000 firms.

Mergent Industry Reports. This online resource provides in-depth analysis of industries covering North America, Asia/Pacific, and Europe by country and region.

Mergent Online. The basic subscription to *Mergent Online* includes their U.S. company data, which is based on the *Moody's Manual of Industrial and Miscellaneous Securities.* This database includes over 15,000 U.S. public companies (both active and inactive) that are listed on the New York Stock Exchange, the American Stock Exchange, and the NASDAQ. The U.S. company data gives detailed information about each company's business descriptions, history, property, subsidiaries, officers and directors, long-term debt, and capital structure. The basic subscription also includes access to Wall Street consensus earnings estimates on companies that have at least one Wall Street analyst that follows it. EDGAR filings dating back to 1996 are also available through the basic subscription. Several modules may be added to the basic subscription. These modules include:

- U.S. Company Archives Data (a database of companies that have been acquired, went bankrupt, liquidated, or merged out of existence since 1996)
- U.S. Annual Reports (a collection of more than 40,000 U.S. company annual reports)
- Institutional Holdings Data (a listing of the 25 largest institutional investors per company)
- Insider Trading Data (a record of all insider stock transactions for the previous six months)
- U.S. FactSheets (one-page summary equity reports)
- Expanded Long-Term Debt (detailed information on over 10,000 companies with corporate bonds issued)
- Industry Reports
- And several international databases that follow the same format as the U.S. company databases

There are three search options available to the basic subscriber: a basic search, an advanced search, and an EDGAR search. The basic search enables the user to search by two broad categories: specific company information or classification information. The specific company search can be conducted by searching for a specific company name, ticker symbol, or Committee on Uniform Securities Identification Procedures (CUSIP) number. The classification information allows searches to be done by SIC code, NAICS code, and Market Identifier Code (MIC).

The advanced search is a tiered process. The first tier consists of choosing the information (or modules) you would like to search through. The second tier is the selection of categories to search by. This section allows searches to be done by financial information, industry codes, ratios, executives, corporate information, or just a textual search. Within a search for financial information, you may select from the following data points: cash flow from operations, current liabilities, EBITDA, income from continuous operations, long-term debt, net income, operating income, total assets, total liabilities, and total revenues. Each of these data points can be searched independently or in combination with one another. You may also choose the year in which to search through these data points. This would be extremely helpful in an appraisal with a valuation date a few years into the past; historical data is available back to 1990.

Equity pricing dating back 30 years is available. Company financials are accessible in annual or quarterly formats for up to 15 years or 15 quarters. Company financials can be viewed by a chosen denomination, meaning you may view the financials in actual dollar amounts (thousands or millions).

All financial information can be downloaded directly into Microsoft Excel. You may also utilize the "create reports" feature, which allows the user to customize a report or create comparison reports. Comparison reports allow for comparisons against the industry or against a customized group.[27]

These publications and more information are available from: Mergent, 60 Madison Avenue, 6th Floor, New York, New York 10010, Tel: (888) 411-0893 or (212) 413-7700, Fax: (212) 413-7670, e-mail: customerservice@mergent.com, Web site: www.mergent.com.

Thomson Financial. *Global Access Direct* (*gadirect.disclosure.com/gad/*). *Global Access Direct* is an online database and research tool that covers EDGAR as well as paper filings to provide financial information on U.S. and international companies. *Global Access Direct* documents are automatically preformatted and entire filings or subsets can be printed directly from the filings headlines, without having to open a document first. The EDGAR documents can be viewed in either HTML or rich text format. All filings are quick-tabbed to display their key sections, making the information needed easy to locate. Search capabilities include searching by old or new ticker symbol and by old or new company name, as well as keyword searches. This database is available at university libraries and for sale through commercial vendors. For more information, contact Thomson Financial, Sales (800) 607-4463, Customer Support (800) 347-7822, www.thomson.com/financial/financial.jsp.

Compact D-SEC (*www.thomson.com/financial/financial.jsp*). This Thomson product is a series of CD-ROMs containing historical information primarily taken from data filed with the SEC and presented in a standardized Excel format. It contains information on over 12,000 publicly owned companies including: company annual and quarterly financial statements, financial ratios, stock information, auditor's reports, and excerpts from company annual reports. The information is taken primarily from various company reports, proxy reports, and registrations. The subscription to this product needs to be renewed each year and needs to be complemented with an EdgarOnline subscription. At the time of this writing, the annual fee started at approximately $5,000. For more information, contact Thomson Financial at (800) 843-7747.

Thomson One Banker (*banker.thomsonib.com/*). This Thomson product is targeted at investment bankers but provides information useful to valuation analysts. Two modules are particularly relevant to valuation professionals: the Private Equity-Backed Company Information Module and the Private Equity Module. The Private Equity-Backed Company Information Module includes a detailed business description, a listing of the firms and funds investing in the company, specifics on

---

[27] This abstract is based on "Mergent Online is a one-stop resource for appraisers" in Shannon Pratt's *Business Valuation Update*, October 2005.

the investment rounds, and a compilation of executives and board members. Users can search for public and private companies separately or simultaneously. The Private Equity module offers comprehensive information on venture funds, private firms, executives, venture-backed companies, and limited partners. This tool also includes more than 100,000 private equity transactions as well as private equity news, press releases, and key industry statistics. With these private equity modules, users can now integrate private equity and venture capital information from Thomson Venture Economics and Thomson Macdonald. The annual fee at the time of this writing was $4,200 ($350 monthly fee) for core packages such as Thomson SDC, Thomson First Call, Thomson Extel, and several other add-on packages such as Thomson Research and Thomson Deals Module for an additional fee. For more information, contact Thomson Financial at (800) 843-7747.

Yahoo Finance *(biz.yahoo.com/research/indgrp)*. This is a free site that allows the analyst to select an industry to view companies ranked by analyst recommendations, market capitalization, and earnings growth.

MSN Money *(moneycentral.msn.com/investor/research/welcome.asp)*. This is a free site that allows the analyst to search public companies using a stock screener. The search can be done by company basics (industry, market cap, Dow Jones Index membership, S&P Index membership) and by key financial indicators (dividend yield, price/earnings ratio, average daily volume over last 2 weeks, net profit margin, 12-month relative strength, debt/equity ratio, revenue growth year vs. year).

OneSource *(www.onesource.com/)*. *OneSource* integrates content from over 30 very diverse providers and represents over 2,500 separate information sources. This online database and research tool is used in sales, marketing, finance, and management consulting; therefore, the available information is broad and not as in-depth in the financial area as other databases. The information provided covers public and private companies in the United States, Canada, the United Kingdom, Europe, and Asia Pacific. It offers company news, industry reports, corporate structures, executive profiles, and more. For one annual fee the customer can access *OneSource* (at the time of this writing quotes ran from $1,800 with an outsourcing fee of $10,000). For more information, contact OneSource sales at (978) 318-4300.

Factiva *(www.factiva.com/)*. Factiva is an archive of news and business information not available on the free Web. This tool provides up to 25 years of historical market data, interactive charting, financial statements and company reports from Reuters, Investext, and more. Subscribers can run one search across the entire collection using a standard search screen. For ongoing projects, users can create up to thirty 25-day holding areas for later use. *Factiva* utilizes more than 20,000 sources in 22 languages, including influential local, national, and international newspapers, leading business magazines, trade publications, media programs, and newswires. Pricing includes a standard fixed-fee annual payment and is offered on an enterprise-wide basis or on a per-user basis with the fee being determined primarily by the number of users, and secondarily by the usage requirements of the organization. For more information, contact Factiva sales at (800) 369-0166.

EDGAR (Electronic Data Gathering, Analysis, and Retrieval). With the EDGAR system, analysts can access "as reported" financial data from companies required to file with the SEC. The EDGAR database, conceptualized by SEC Chairman John Shad in 1983 and started in 1984, is an effort to improve the speed and collection of financial documents required by the various U.S. securities laws and regulations. Since 1996, all public companies subject to the Securities Act or the Exchange Act have been required to file specific documents electronically. Although EDGAR does not hold every single type of disclosure document, it does contain the disclosure documents most valuable to analysts, such as Forms 10-K, 10-Q, and 8-K.

The EDGAR database is accessible from the Internet, as well as from a variety of commercial vendors. With an Internet connection, analysts can access disclosure documents free of charge from the SEC (www.sec.gov/edgar.shtml). The formatting is not good, but there is freeware available to convert the documents to a more convenient format. Several companies provide EDGAR documents with value-added features, such as Boolean search capabilities or preformatted documents. These companies usually offer free access to SEC filings and charge a fee for data that is user-friendlier and more readily usable in a valuation assignment. An example of a value-added feature is the ability to perform sophisticated searches and obtain selected portions of documents in a short amount of time. In other words, when analysts access the EDGAR database from the SEC, they cannot limit the printout to specific portions of a 10-K, such as company name, ticker symbol, SIC Code, balance sheet, and statement of operations. With several of the sources discussed below, researchers can essentially perform a guideline publicly traded company search and download only the portions of the source documents of the selected guideline companies that are needed. However, the value-added features in these sources come with a price and analysts need to consider the costs associated with using such services. Such sources are discussed below.

Edgar® Online (www.edgar-online.com). The *Edgar® Online* database contains more than three million documents that more than 15,000 companies have filed through the SEC's EDGAR system since 1994. This site provides free access to Annual Reports through one of its Web sites—FreeEDGAR (freeedgar.com). It also provides value-added services through two online databases—*Edgar® Online Pro* (pro.edgar-online.com) and *Edgar® Online Access* (access.edgar-online.com). *Edgar® Online Pro* provides complete access to the data for $1,200 per year, while *Edgar® Online Access* provides limited access to subsections of the data for $60 a quarter. FreeEDGAR also provides two-day subscriptions for $9.95.

Some of the enhancement in data manipulation and usability offered by *Edgar® Online Pro* and *Edgar® Online Access* include:

- Financial statement downloads (export spreadsheets to Excel for analysis)
- Document formatting (view or output in HTML, RTF, XML, or PDF)
- Section printing (select specific sections for viewing/printing)
- Company profiles (snapshots of key business information)
- Full text search and people search (use specific words and phrases to locate information)
- Peer analyses (comparisons of current and historical financials on up to five companies)

For more information, contact EDGAR Online, Inc., 50 Washington Street, 9th Floor, Norwalk, CT 06854, Tel: (800) 416-6651 (toll free) or (203) 852-5666, Fax: (203) 852-5667, e-mail: edgarpro@edgar-online.com.

EdgarScan™ (edgarscan.pwcglobal.com/servlets/edgarscan). EdgarScan™ is an interface to the SEC's EDGAR filings that was developed by PricewaterhouseCoopers and is a free site. EdgarScan™ focuses on 10-K and 10-Q reports because they contain income statements and balance sheet information and offers the ability to search across filings using financial variables from these statements. Filings have hyperlinks that allow for easy locating of specific sections of the filing, including the financial statements, footnotes, extracted financial data, and computed ratios. A module called the "Benchmarking Assistant" performs graphical financial benchmarking of the subject company against its peers. Tables showing company comparisons can be downloaded as Excel charts and registered users can store company portfolios for future benchmarking. Also included on the site are links to listings of initial public offerings (sorted by industry, company, or date) and to the Standard Industrial Classification system. For more information, visit the Web site or e-mail ContactEdgar@us.pwcglobal.com.

LIVEDGAR® *(www.gsionline.com/livedgar)*. Created by Global Securities Information, *LIVEDGAR®* offers a comprehensive collection of content that ranges from a listing of SEC filings dating back to 1967 to over 144,000 annual reports to shareholders from 33,000 companies in 115 countries. *LIVEDGAR®* has a very powerful search engine that allows for precise searches by company/ticker, filing number, date, form type, and full-text searches (phrases, names, keywords). One search enhancement is to search inside the 10-K—the 10-K Section search feature—which allows users to focus searches on any particular part or item number on Form 10-K. This feature provides 24 check boxes, one for each part and item number on Form 10-K, as well as four further defined subsets for all financials, balance sheet, income statement, and notes to financial statements under item 8, financial statements and supplementary data. *LIVEDGAR®* provides online access for hard-to-find paper filings like no-action letters and the complete collection of System for Electronic Document Analysis and Retrieval (SEDAR®) filings from the Canadian Securities Administrators (CSA). In addition to various types of subscriptions, *LIVEDGAR®* has a pay-as-you-go account option. For more information, contact Global Securities Information, 419 Seventh St. NW, Suite 300, Washington, DC 20004, Phone: (202) 628-1155, Fax: (202) 628-1133, e-mail: info@gsionline.com.

SEC Info^sm *(www.secinfo.com)*. *SEC Info^sm* is a fee-based service and provides information from both the SEC EDGAR® database and CSA SEDAR® database. The filings can be searched by name, industry, business, SIC code, area code, topic, Central Index Key (CIK), accession number, file number, date, zip, and more. The databases include "all SEC EDGAR® filings, including those that the SEC and other services delete." Enhancements to data usability include indexed exhibits, linked table of contents for every filing and document, linked topics within each document and exhibit, intra- and inter-document links, and relationship links (such as between registrants, group members, owners, issuers, signatories, and agents).

10K Wizard *(www.tenkwizard.com)*. *10K Wizard* allows for searches for SEC filings by ticker, CIK, company name, word searches, form type, industry, date ranges, and more. *10K Wizard* offers a range of "pre-packaged" subscription options ranging from $185 per year to $2,395 per year, or a subscription can be tailored to a specific user. 10-K Financial Pro—the $999 per year option—allows access to financials for more than 10,000 U.S. public companies and the possibility to verify the numbers with direct links to the source filings. More than 400 data items are available and include: yearly and quarterly ratios, eight-year history, links to source filing, download to Excel, dynamic charting, fundamental financial data, and more. For more information, contact 10-K Wizard, 1950 Stemmons Freeway, Suite 3014, Dallas, TX 75207, Tel: (214) 800-4560, Toll Free: (800) 365-4608, e-mail: sales@10KWizard.com.

Financial Statement Adjustments to Guideline Companies

Generally, the same types of adjustments should be made to the financial statements of the guideline companies as are made to the financial statements of the subject company. Some main categories of adjustments are the following:

- Remove nonrecurring items (and any required tax effects) from income statements.
- Where applicable, put guideline and subject companies on a comparable accounting basis (e.g., adjust any companies accounting for inventory on last in–first out (LIFO) basis to first in–first out (FIFO) basis, use consistent depreciation methods and lives).
- Adjust for nonoperating items.
- Adjust for discontinued operations.

Adjusting for Operating Leases

In certain industries, companies commonly finance their operating assets using operating leases rather than debt (or capital leases). This creates a fixed obligation that is one of the most common forms of "off balance sheet" financing. Operating leases are likely to be important for companies that make heavy use of transportation equipment, retail space, and electronic equipment.

If the guideline companies and subject company have differing policies with respect to the use of operating leases, then the analyst should consider making adjustments to put all the companies on a similar footing. The rent expense for leased assets includes a financing component (comparable to interest expense) and a component related to consumption of the asset (comparable to depreciation). Other things being equal, a company that finances with operating leases will have lower EBITDA and EBIT than a company that finances using debt, since its operating expenses include rent on the leased property.

One can capitalize operating leases and add them to debt. There are two common methods for this. A traditional method is to multiply rent by a fixed ratio (often six to eight times the annual rent). An alternative method is to calculate the present value of the future minimum lease payments, discounted at an interest rate appropriate for financing the leased assets. For guideline publicly traded companies in the United States, information on historical rent and future minimum lease obligations are disclosed in footnotes to the financial statements.

If one is adjusting the numerator (adding operating leases to invested capital), then one must also adjust the denominator by removing the rental expenses from operating income. To adjust EBITDA, one simply adds rent to obtain EBITDAR (earnings before interest, taxes, depreciation, amortization, and rent). To adjust EBIT, one would adjust for (by adding) only the interest component of the rent expense. A simple method for estimating annual interest associated with operating leases is to multiply the capitalized value of leases by the interest rate used to capitalize the leases.

It should be noted that if the analyst is using only equity multiples, then the earning measure is net of all interest, depreciation, and rent expense, so there is no reason to make the above adjustments to the multiples. It may still be useful to capitalize leases even in this case for purposes of financial analysis, in that the adjustments to debt may help to standardize the calculation of leverage ratios.

Comparative Ratio Analysis

For purposes of comparative performance and other ratios between the subject company and the guideline companies, the comparisons will be more meaningful if the ratios are computed *after* the adjustments to the financial statements of the guideline companies as well as the subject company.

On the other hand, it is much faster and cheaper to use ratios for publicly traded companies from one of the many handy online or CD-ROM services, such as Dialog on Disk, Compustat, Compact D/SEC, or Media General -Plus. Whether to use ratios computed by a service or to compute them oneself depends on the analyst's judgment as to the extent to which the difference in results is likely to justify the cost, which is a case-by-case decision.

An example of comparative ratio analysis based on guideline companies is included in Exhibit 21–9E and 21–9F in Chapter 21, "Sample Report." This is a part of the analysis that helps guide the analyst's judgment as to where the various valuation multiples for the subject company should fall relative to the range of the respective valuation multiples for the guideline companies.

Typically, the comparative ratio analysis exercise is done only for the latest available comparative year, or the latest 12 months, even if valuation multiples are based on several years' average results. If the comparative ratio analysis is used to help decide where the subject's valuation multiples should be relative to the guideline companies' valuation multiples, the analyst should be careful to recognize any distortions or abnormalities in the year for which the ratios were calculated that would cause the ratios to be misleading for use in pinpointing a relevant valuation multiple. It may be helpful to calculate the ratios for past years, as well, to identify any possible distortions.

Obtaining the Guideline Companies' Market Value Data

If the valuation multiples to be used are only those that relate to common equity, then all that is needed is the price for each guideline company's stock as of the valuation date.

If valuation multiples based on the MVIC are to be used, then the market value of all the components of the invested capital needs to be estimated. Some of the guideline companies' senior securities (e.g., debt and/or preferred stock) may not be publicly traded. In that case, book value often is used as a proxy for market value. If, however, the analyst suspects that the book value may be far enough apart from market value to create a significant distortion in the valuation multiple computed, the senior securities should be revalued to market value. (Chapters 23 and 24, "Valuing Debt Securities" and "Valuing Preferred Stock," respectively, discuss how to do this.)

The analyst may consider using the fair value of financial instruments disclosure in the footnotes for the guideline companies, where the company gives an estimate of the value of its short- and long-term debt as of the fiscal year end.

Presenting Guideline Company Tables

Guideline company tables may be presented on a direct equity basis or on an invested capital basis. They usually show the names of the guideline companies, the market in which they are traded (e.g., New York Stock Exchange, American Stock Exchange, NASDAQ, and so on), the per-share market price as of the valuation date, the financial fundamentals (e.g., EBIT, EBITDA, earnings), and the resulting valuation multiple (the price divided by the financial fundamental). The table typically has a line at the bottom showing the comparable financial fundamental for the subject company.

For each valuation multiple presented, the table typically presents a low, high, mean, and median. The sample report in Chapter 21 shows guideline publicly traded company tables for a variety of financial fundamentals.

A question often arises as to what extent valuation multiples that were not ultimately used in reaching the value conclusion should be presented in the tables in the report. There is no clear-cut, right or wrong answer to this. We might suggest that there is not much point in presenting valuation multiples that were never seriously considered to be used. If, however, a valuation multiple was considered but discarded because of the nature of the data (perhaps a very wide dispersion of value multiples), it might be worthwhile to present it, so the reader can see the data that led to its being discarded in the final analysis.

Selecting and Weighting Multiples for the Subject Company Based on Guideline Companies

The result of the guideline company analysis is an array of pricing multiples for each of several valuation multiples. At this point, it is necessary to again visit the question of which multiples to use in reaching an indication of value and the relative weight to be accorded to each of those used.

For each valuation multiple used, it is also necessary to decide what the pricing multiple for the subject company should be relative to the observed multiples for the guideline companies.

Impact of Guideline Company Data Evaluation

The same general thought processes and decision criteria apply to both deciding on whether or not to rely on any particular valuation multiple at all, and also to deciding on the relative weight to be accorded each valuation multiple ultimately used in reaching the opinion of value.

The earlier discussion of the relative conceptual significance of different valuation multiples as more or less applicable to different types of companies and with different ownership characteristics applies here, of course. However, a study of the data developed may lead to greater or lesser reliance on certain valuation multiples than one might have expected before compiling the data.

Number of Data Points Available. If it turns out that very few data points are available for a particular valuation multiple, that problem may lead one to abandon that multiple or to put relatively little weight on it, even though it might be quite conceptually significant if there were more data. A common example is price to latest 12 months' earnings. If only two of seven guideline companies had meaningful positive earnings (and thus meaningful P/Es), the analyst has to decide whether the two convey enough information to be accorded weight in the final analysis. The analyst might, for example, decide instead to use a price-to-gross-cash-flow multiple or a price to some number of years average earnings. One must be careful, however, that this procedure does not give undue weight to companies with losses if the subject is a profitable company. One way to avoid this situation is to make profitability (or nonprofitability) part of the search criteria.

Comparability of Data Measurement. Another issue to consider is the extent to which the analyst is satisfied that the adjustments, if any, to the subject and guideline companies' financial fundamentals have resulted in stating the data on a comparable basis. The analyst's confidence regarding the comparability of fundamental data may influence his or her judgment regarding the use of, or weight accorded to, valuation multiples based on that particular fundamental variable.

Comparability of Data Patterns. Another factor in assessing comparability is the extent to which the data for the subject company "track" with the data for the guideline companies. For example, if the subject and six of the seven guideline companies had a generally upward earnings trend, but one guideline company had a downward trend, the analyst may omit or place less reliance on the aberrational company when deciding on appropriate pricing measures relative to earnings.

In the case of one annual valuation, the subject company's earnings always followed a pattern somewhat similar to a good group of guideline companies. Each year, we put considerable weight on the multiple of price to latest 12 months' earnings. Then, one year, the company had a banner year while the guideline group struggled. First we satisfied ourselves that this sudden divergence was an aberration. Then, in that year, we placed most of the weight on the price to five years' average earnings multiple instead of on the latest 12 months, pricing multiple, which would have resulted in an inflated valuation.

Apparent Market Reliance. The extent to which the valuation multiples are tightly clustered or widely dispersed tends to indicate the extent to which the market tends to focus on that particular multiple in pricing stocks in the particular industry. For this reason, when analyzing the guideline companies, the analyst may want to calculate not only measures of central tendency (such as mean and median), but also measures of dispersion (such as standard deviation and coefficient of variation).

Generally, the lower the dispersion of the valuation multiple, the greater the weight the analyst might consider according to that multiple. In some cases, the guideline company table may lead the analyst to conclude that the valuation multiples based on some particular financial fundamental are so widely dispersed that those multiples have no usefulness as guidance to value.

Measures of Central Tendency and Dispersion

Measures of Central Tendency. The *median* (the number in the middle of the array) usually, but not always, provides a better measure of central tendency for ratios than the *mean* (the arithmetic average).[28] This is because one or a few outliers

---

[28] A little knowledge of statistics is helpful here, but beyond the scope of this book. Relevant basic references would be, for example, Gerald I. White, Ashwinpaul C. Sondhi, and Dov Fried, *The Analysis & Use of Financial Statements*, 3rd ed. (New York: John Wiley and Sons, 2003), and Robert D. Mason and Douglas A. Lind, *Statistical Techniques in Business and Economics*, 11th ed. (New York: McGraw-Hill, 2002).

(extreme observations) may have more of a distorting effect on the mean than on the median.

Another problem with the arithmetic average is that when it is used to summarize ratios that have stock price or MVIC in the numerator (such as the P/E multiple), it weights each guideline company in proportion to that company's ratio. It does not give equal weight to each guideline company. For example, the arithmetic mean P/E multiple of two guideline companies' P/E multiples of 15 and 5 is 10. While it might appear that this mean is giving equal weight to each company, it actually gives three times as much weight to the first company because its P/E multiple is triple the second's. Assuming that we invest a total of $200 in both companies, the only way the resulting portfolio's P/E multiple is 10 is by investing $150 (for $10 of earnings) in the first company and $50 (for $10 of earnings) in the second.

The harmonic mean is used to give equal weight to each guideline company in summarizing ratios that have stock price or MVIC in the numerator.[29] It is the reciprocal of the average of the reciprocals of the guideline company multiples. In the example above, the reciprocal of the P/E multiple of 15 is 0.0667, the reciprocal of the P/E multiple of 5 is 0.200, the average of the two reciprocals is 0.1334, and the reciprocal of the average is 7.5. This P/E multiple of 7.5 is the same as the P/E multiple of a $200 portfolio with $100 invested (for $6.67 of earnings at a P/E multiple of 15) in the first company and $100 invested in the second company (for $20 of earnings at a P/E multiple of 5). With the $200 invested equally in each guideline company, the total earnings are $26.67 and the P/E multiple is 7.5 ($200/$26.67).

Measures of Dispersion. A simple but important measure of dispersion is the range—that is, the spread between the highest and lowest observation. Generally, the tighter the range of the data points, the less room for judgmental error in deciding on the appropriate multiple for the subject company relative to the guideline companies.

Occasionally, differences between the subject and guideline companies lead the analyst to conclude that a multiple for the subject should be outside the range for the guideline companies. When this occurs, it is important that the analyst explain carefully the reason for choosing a multiple outside the guideline company range.

The most familiar measure of dispersion is the *standard deviation*.[30] When using the standard deviation, it is generally helpful to focus primarily on the *coefficient of variation*, which is the standard deviation divided by the mean. By using the coefficient of variation, the relative dispersion of data for different valuation multiples with different mean values can be compared directly with each other.

Multiples of Economic Income Variables

Multiples of economic income variables (price/earnings multiples, price/EBITDA multiples, and so on) are the reciprocals of the capitalization rates applicable to those

---

[29] Gilbert E. Matthews, "When Averaging Multiples, use the Harmonic Mean," *Business Valuation Update*, June 2006.

[30] For the mathematical formula for the standard deviation, see one of the statistics books referenced in footnote 28. In any case, many financial calculators are programmed to compute standard deviations.

variables. For example, a pricing multiple of 8 is the inverse of a capitalization rate of 0.125 ($1 \div 8 = 0.125$). Therefore, valuation pricing multiples are influenced by the same forces that influence capitalization rates, the two most important of which are:

1. Risk
2. Expected growth in the operating variable being capitalized

Therefore, in order for the analyst to make an intelligent estimate of what multiple is appropriate for the subject company relative to the multiples observed for the guideline companies, the analyst must make some judgments as to the relative risk and growth prospects of the subject compared with the guideline companies.

Relative Risk. Since a closely held stock does not have a regular price trading history from which to compute a *beta* (as described in Chapter 9), other means must be used to assess relative risk. One such mean is a study of comparative financial ratios between the subject and guideline companies, as discussed in Chapter 8. Operating and financial leverage ratios are of the greatest importance in assessing relative risk. The analyst can then use judgment to adjust multiples up or down from those of the guideline companies to reflect relative risk as revealed by the comparative financial ratios.

Another way to assess relative risk is to compare historical earnings or cash flow volatility between the subject and the guideline companies. Any of several measures of dispersion, such as a standard deviation, may be used for this purpose. It then becomes a matter of analysts' judgment as to how much to adjust multiples from those observed for the guideline companies to reflect differences in risk evidenced by differences in earnings or cash flow volatility.

The size factor is also an important indicator of risk. We presented data in Chapter 9 that showed that companies of the size of the smallest decile of the New York Stock Exchange required a discount rate several points above the average for the New York Stock Exchange. This differential in the discount rate can translate directly into a difference in the capitalization rate.

Relative Growth. As discussed in Chapter 9, the expected growth rate in perpetuity for cash flow translates point for point into the capitalization rate for that variable. Therefore, if the subject company has very long-term growth prospects above or below those of the guideline companies, those growth rate differentials should be reflected in the capitalization rates chosen. Be careful, however, not to understate the proper capitalization rate by making a large adjustment for growth prospects that are only short or intermediate term.

An Example. We will continue with the example where the guideline company indicated price/cash flow ratio is 8, resulting in a capitalization rate for cash flow of 12.5. Let's assume that the comparative risk analysis leads us to conclude that the discount rate for the subject company would be five percentage points higher than for the guideline companies, which would bring the capitalization rate to 17.5 ($12.5 + 5.0 = 17.5$). On the other hand, let's assume that our smaller, riskier company had two percentage points higher infinitely sustainable long-term growth prospects than the guideline companies. This offsetting factor would bring the capitalization rate back down to 15.5 ($17.5 - 2.0 = 15.5$). This, then, equates to a valuation multiple of 6.5 ($1 \div 15.5 = 6.5$).

Capitalization of Dividends or Dividend-Paying Capacity

Dividends from operations ultimately are possible only as a result of earnings and adequate available cash flow. Therefore, capitalization of dividends or dividend-paying capacity may or may not be analyzed as a valuation method separate from capitalization of earnings and/or cash flow, depending on the circumstances and the valuation's purpose. Revenue Ruling 59-60 states that dividends or dividend-paying capacity should be one factor in the valuation of a business interest for federal estate or gift tax purposes. Most potential acquirers are not specifically interested in the acquiree's dividend-paying capacity, since the acquiree will not continue to operate as an independent entity.

If the valuation is of a controlling interest, dividend-paying capacity is more important than actual dividends paid, since the controlling stockholder has the discretion to pay or not pay dividends as long as the company has the capacity to do so. In valuing a noncontrolling interest, however, the actual dividends the company pays usually are more important than the dividend-paying capacity, since the noncontrolling stockholder generally cannot force the company to pay dividends even if it unquestionably has the capacity to do so.

When the capitalization of dividends method is used as an element in valuation, it usually is by reference to dividend yields on guideline publicly traded companies. For example, if guideline publicly traded companies were found to have an average dividend yield (annual dividends per share divided by market price per share) of 5 percent and the subject company paid dividends or was estimated to have a dividend-paying capacity of $1 per share, the capitalization of dividends method would be to simply divide the dividend-paying capacity per share by the appropriate capitalization rate or dividend yield—in this case, 0.05, which implies a $20 per share value by the capitalization of dividends method.

An estimate of dividend-paying capacity may be based in part on typical payout ratios of publicly traded companies in the subject company's industry. For example, if public companies in that industry typically pay out 30 percent of their earnings in dividends, 30 percent of earnings might be a good starting point from which to estimate the subject company's dividend-paying capacity. However, the typical closely held company is less well capitalized than its publicly traded counterpart and may have less dividend-paying capacity per dollar of earnings capacity than most of the publicly traded companies with which it might be compared. This factor must be considered in estimating the subject company's dividend-paying capacity.

Multiples of Revenue

Multiples of revenue tend to be most highly correlated with return on sales, but the strength of the correlation varies greatly from one industry to another. Therefore, when considering using a multiple of sales, it is useful to first see whether the guideline company multiples of revenue are well correlated with return on sales. This valuation multiple tends to be more useful for industries where such a correlation is high than for those where it is not. In a way, capitalization of revenues can be considered a shortcut to capitalization or earnings, since generally there is an implicit assumption that a certain level of revenues should be able to generate a specific earnings level in a given type of business.

Capitalization of revenues is applied most frequently to start-up companies and to service businesses, such as advertising agencies, insurance agencies, mortuaries, professional practices, and some types of publishing operations.

One can find guidance in arriving at an appropriate multiple of revenues for a particular business in both public stock market data and merger and acquisition data. There are quite a few publicly traded companies in most service business categories, such as insurance agencies, advertising and public relations firms, and securities brokers. If the subject company's true return on sales is known, an estimate of a reasonable price/sales multiple can be derived by simple regression analysis using guideline companies' price/sales ratios and returns on sales.

Exhibit 11–2 illustrates the relationship between return on sales and price to revenue multiples for publicly traded insurance agency companies as of December 31, 2005. The exhibit also presents the computation of a suggested price to revenue multiple for a subject insurance agency company realizing a 10 percent return on revenue at that time.

Valuations by multiples of revenue are particularly susceptible to distortion because of differences in capital structure between subject and guideline companies.

Exhibit 11–2

Correlation between Price/Revenues and Return on Revenues

Company	December 31, 2005 Return on Revenues	Price/Revenues
Marsh & McLennan Companies, Inc.	3.2%	1.47
Hilb, Rogal & Hobbs	8.3%	2.08
Healthextras, Inc.	3.3%	1.49
Arthur J. Gallagher & Co.	1.9%	2.00
Brown & Brown, Inc.	19.2%	5.42
$r^2 = 0.908$		

The regression formula to be solved is $y = a + bx$. The price/revenues multiple $= a + b$ (return on revenues), where:

a = price/revenues multiple (y) intercept

b = slope of the line

Using a calculator capable of linear regression analysis, the analyst can calculate the y intercept a and slope of the line b using return on revenues and price/revenues multiple data from the guideline companies.

Using the returns on revenues and price/revenues multiple data for 12/31/05, we calculate:

$a = 0.8994$

$b = 22.1951$

$y = 0.8994 + 22.1951(x)$

Substituting in the subject company's return on revenues (0.10), we compute an indicated price/revenues multiple:

$y = 0.8994 + 22.1951(0.10)$

$y = 0.90 + 2.22$

$y = 3.12$

Return on Revenues = Net income divided by net sales

Price/Revenues = stock price times shares outstanding divided by net sales

Therefore, this valuation pricing multiple should be calculated on a market value of invested capital basis, as discussed in a later section.

One step removed from a multiple of revenues is a multiple of some measure of unit volume or capacity. Examples would include nursing homes at so much per bed, forest products plants at so much per thousand board feet of production, service stations and fuel distributors at so much per gallon sold per month, cell phone and cable television companies at so much per subscriber, and so on. The implication of this method is that so much volume can be expected to translate into some anticipated amount of sales and economic income.

Multiple of Stock Value to Asset Value

When the analyst has determined that book value or some adjusted book value figure provides a useful representation of the company's underlying net asset values, the next step is to translate that figure into its implication for the value of the shares of stock or partnership interest being valued. This usually is accomplished by referring to the relationship of the prices of guideline companies' stocks to their respective underlying net asset values. The data for the guideline companies may be based on prices of stocks traded on the open market, prices paid in acquisitions, or both, depending on several factors, including the percentage ownership interest being valued.

As in any aspect of valuation based on comparisons with other companies, the analyst should use experience and expertise to ensure that the comparisons are as valid as possible within the limitations of data availability.

Price/Book Value Multiple. It may be possible to compute the multiple of market price to book value for a group of guideline companies that have stock trading in the public market and apply a multiple somewhere within the range of such multiples to the subject company's book value. If the book values of the subject and guideline companies were computed on comparable bases, and if the assets' composition is comparable, this procedure may provide a reasonably realistic figure for the value of the business interest.

If accounting methods for the subject and guideline companies differ significantly, the analyst should make appropriate adjustments before computing the market price/book value multiples and applying them to the valuation. There can be additional significant differences, such as in asset mix, that challenge the validity of using one company's price to book value multiple in valuing another's stock.

Often the valuation multiples are computed on only *tangible* book value. This may help to avoid distortions, since some companies may have created their own intangibles, and thus expensed them for accounting purposes, while others may have acquired their intangibles, and thus carry them on the balance sheet.

If the subject company's return on equity is high relative to the guideline companies', the appropriate price to asset value multiple probably should be in the upper end of the relevant range, and vice versa. As common sense would suggest, empirical tests indicate a significant degree of correlation between price/book value multiples and return on equity for both publicly traded stocks and acquisition prices in most industries. As a consequence, an analysis of the relationship between price/book value ratios and return on equity for the guideline companies often can provide objective guidance in deciding on an appropriate price/book

Exhibit 11–3

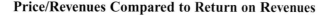

Price/Revenues Compared to Return on Revenues

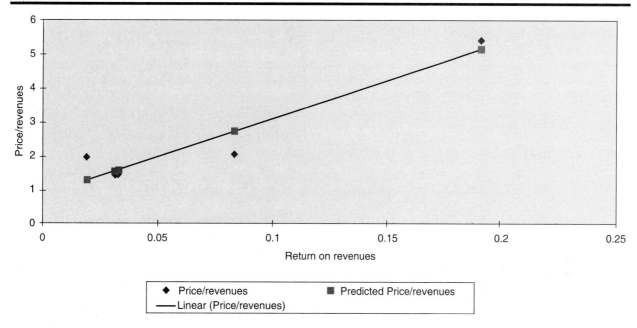

value multiple for the subject company. If the correlation between the price/book value multiples and return on equity for the guideline companies is reasonably good, the analyst may use a simple linear regression to compute an indicated price/book value multiple for the subject company based on market data. The mechanics of this analysis are the same as for the price/revenues analysis presented in Exhibit 11–3.

Price/Adjusted Net Asset Value. For a limited number of industries, data on market values of underlying assets are available. Where this is the case, it is possible to compute pricing multiples of the public stock's price to its adjusted net asset value.

In particular, market values for some real estate companies are provided in *Realty Stock Review*. Also, estimates of timber values for many forest products companies are available from brokerage house analysts. When using multiples of price to adjusted net asset value, it is important to make the same kinds of adjustments to the subject company as have been made to the asset values for the guideline companies. For example, some real estate company adjusted net asset values are reported net of impounded capital gains taxes and some are not.

The use of the various price/asset value pricing multiples are market approach valuation procedures. The use of these pricing multiples is independent of, and should not be confused with, the use of asset-based approach valuation methods (such as the asset accumulation method or the capitalized excess earnings method).

Treating Nonoperating Assets, Excess Assets, and Asset Deficiencies

If the subject company has significant nonoperating assets, excess assets, or asset deficiencies that distinguish it from the guideline companies, adjustments for those items may be appropriate. If some of the guideline companies also have such asset anomalies, it is important, of course, to make similar adjustments to them for consistency.

Nonoperating Assets

Many privately held companies own assets that are not part of their operations. Such assets may add some value to the closely held stock over and above the values indicated by the ratios of guideline company stock prices to their underlying financial fundamentals.

If nonoperating assets are to be given separate consideration, they should be separated from the operating company data (and, if possible, from the guideline companies). Any income they generate (or expenses incurred on behalf of their maintenance) should be removed from earnings or cash flows capitalized. If a price/asset value multiple is used based on guideline companies, the nonoperating assets should be removed from the asset value. These financial statement adjustments should be made before the ratio analysis of the financial statements, if such analysis is to be used to help decide on multiples relative to guideline company multiples.

The question then becomes, "How much extra value do these assets contribute to the stock?"

The theory of valuing nonoperating assets separately from operating assets rests on the assumption that the nonoperating assets could be liquidated without impairing operations. Thus, if the market value of nonoperating assets is higher than their book value and the analyst is going to mark the nonoperating assets up to the market value to perform the valuation, the analyst should also consider offsetting factors. These factors might include the capital gains or ordinary income tax, as the case might be, that the company would have to pay if it liquidated the assets, any costs of liquidation, and any discounts that might be appropriate in reflecting the estimated time required to liquidate and the risk that the actual amounts realized might be less than the estimated market values as of the valuation date.

From there, it often makes a significant difference whether one is valuing a noncontrolling interest or a controlling interest. It also is important to know, if possible, the likelihood of sale of the assets. The market attributes very little weight to non–income producing, nonoperating assets, unless they are likely to be sold, because their existence provides little, if any, benefit to the noncontrolling stockholder. Even when valuing a controlling interest, they could be discounted from their net realizable value, because most control buyers would rather buy a pure operating company and not have to deal with disposing of nonoperating assets.

Marginal Operating Real Estate

An issue that often is a gray area in stock valuations is whether certain real estate should be valued separately when using the guideline company valuation method.

One factor is the degree of comparability. If the subject company owns its real estate and the guideline companies do not, then it often is appropriate to value the real estate separately. This is more true for controlling ownership interests than for noncontrolling ownership interests—for the same reasons discussed in connection with nonoperating assets. Of course, if the real estate is valued separately, then the company's income statement should be adjusted to reflect a market rent and other related expenses.

Real estate used in operations but used far below its highest and best use is often controversial. This becomes a matter of the analyst's judgment. Certainly, the imminence—or lack of it—of prospective development or sale of the real estate will play a role in the judgment.

Excess Assets or Asset Deficiencies

An often controversial area for possible adjustment may arise when the subject company has significantly greater amounts of some assets relative to its operations than do the guideline companies. The most common assets giving rise to such a potential adjustment are cash and marketable securities.

If it appears that some assets may be held in excessive amounts, the analyst should ask the company officials if there is a rationale for why such apparent excesses may be necessary for operations. If they are not necessary, then some adjustment may be appropriate. The same reasoning regarding noncontrol and control valuation premises discussed earlier also applies here.

It is also common to find the reverse situation—that is, one in which it might be appropriate to value the company by a capitalization of earnings method but then to subtract an amount reflecting the inadequacy of operating assets. This can easily be the case if net working capital is inadequate to support the level of business, if an adverse legal judgment is predictable, or if certain plants and equipment are in imminent need of replacement or major repair. Evaluating such inadequacies may require more subjective judgment than would assessing excess or nonoperating assets, but the potential problem of measurement does not render recognition of the concept of asset inadequacy any less important.

The value of the guideline companies may be impacted by excess working capital, nonoperating assets, or certain liabilities. If these factors materially differ from the subject company, then they should be accounted for with appropriate adjustments to the guideline companies. Examples of assets and liabilities that should be considered include:

- Excess cash or marketable securities
- Excess net working capital
- Nonoperating assets
- Unfunded pension liabilities
- Environmental liabilities
- Other contingent liabilities
- Employee stock options and warrants

The general rule is that if an excess or nonoperating item enhances the value of a guideline company, then its value should be subtracted form the guideline company's value, and if it detracts from the value of the guideline company, then its value should be added back. (If material, the analyst should make adjustments for any earnings or expenses associated with these items.) The resulting multiple will be free and clear of these factors. Similar adjustments, but in the opposite direction, need to be made to the resulting indicated value of the subject company.

Beware of Recent Acquisitions

Analysts frequently overlook the impact of recent acquisitions on a guideline company's value and earnings. Suppose that a company makes a large acquisition near the end of its most recent fiscal year. The current market value of invested capital of the company will include the value of the acquired operation. However, under purchase accounting, the company's earnings for the year will only reflect earnings of the preacquisition company before the date of the acquisition. This will lead to a multiple of, say, MVIC-to-EBIT that is too high. One can correct this by using pro-forma financial results reflecting a full year of earnings for the combined entity. An alternative approach may be reasonable if the acquisition occurs sufficiently close to the end of the year: One can subtract the value of the acquired company from the invested capital of the guideline company.

Multiline Companies

There are a variety of ways to handle multiline companies within the application of the guideline company method.

Procedures for Valuation

Separate Valuations. When a company has two or more separate and different operations, and if the financial information can be adequately segregated between them, the valuation of the combined operations might be handled as if it were two or more separate and independent valuations, using the valuation multiples most applicable for each.

Blended Valuation Multiples. More often, it is not possible to separate revenues and expenses so that values of different operating groups can be estimated separately. In this case, valuation multiples from the respective guideline company industry groups may be weighted in accordance with the subject company fundamental weights, such as sales or gross margin dollars.

Use of Conglomerates. One alternative for multiline companies is to use valuation multiples from publicly traded conglomerates. We would recommend this procedure only if the industry lines of the subject company bear some reasonable resemblance to the industry lines of the guideline company conglomerates used.

"Portfolio Effect"

Multiline companies sometimes are valued at some discount from the sum of the indicated values of their various operations. This is because most buyers tend to seek a participation in a particular industry, and are less enthusiastic about a participation in somebody else's predetermined combination of some group of industries. This discount tends to apply whether valuing a noncontrolling or a controlling ownership interest. Guidance for quantifying this discount can sometimes be observed in the marketplace by comparing prices of conglomerate companies with the aggregate values of their parts, sometimes referred to as their breakup value.

Typical Adjustments to Reach a Value Conclusion

As discussed earlier, the guideline company method is based on minority interest, day-to-day transactions in publicly traded stocks. Therefore, if valuing a closely held noncontrolling ownership interest, it would not be appropriate to take a discount for lack of control, but it would be appropriate to take a discount for lack of marketability (discussed in Chapter 17, "Discounts for Illiquidity and Lack of Marketability").

If a controlling interest is being valued, it may or may not be appropriate to apply a premium for control. This is discussed in Chapter 15, "Control and Acquisition Premiums." Also, as discussed in Chapter 17, a control premium may be fully or partially offset by a discount for lack of marketability.

Valuation Multiples Using Market Value of Invested Capital

Sometimes it is desirable to address the value of the entire invested capital. As noted in the section on defining the capital structure in Chapter 9, "Income Approach: Discounted Future Economic Income Method," the most commonly used conceptual definition of *invested capital* is all equity and long-term debt (including current maturities of long-term debt).

Valuing the entire capital structure often is useful when valuing a controlling interest, since a control buyer is usually interested in the value of the entire company irrespective of its current capital structure, which a control buyer might change.

Valuing all of the invested capital based on guideline company values and then subtracting the value of the senior securities may also be useful for valuing noncontrolling interests where the capital structures differ significantly between the subject and guideline companies. This procedure can help even out distorting effects of widely differing capital structures.

As a practical matter, when using the guideline company method, it generally is necessary to include *all* interest-bearing debt. Unless repayment at face is imminent, it usually should be valued at market. It often is difficult or even impossible to separate out how much of each of the guideline companies' interest expenses is attributable to long-term versus short-term debt.

Therefore, the numerator for MVIC ratios in the guideline company method usually is the aggregate market value of all equity (with appropriate adjustment for options and warrants) and all interest-bearing debt. Some practitioners subtract cash, which then would be added on at the end of the valuation procedures.

As noted earlier in the chapter, the denominators for MVIC measures typically are the following:

- Gross or net sales
- EBIT

- EBITDA
- Net free cash flow available to invested capital

Exhibit 11–4 presents a simple illustration of a valuation exercise using MVIC for three guideline companies where the capital structures for the guideline companies differed significantly from the subject company. As can be seen in Exhibit 11–4, the range of indicated values for the subject company using MVIC for the guideline companies is tighter than the wide scatter using typical straight equity valuation multiples. In particular, the straight equity measures distort the price/book value multiple on the high side and the price/revenues multiple on the low side.

The analysis suggests that a control buyer might be willing to pay $27 to $32 a share for the equity on the assumption that the buyer could leverage the purchase with debt similar to the industry average. On the other hand, a minority buyer could not take advantage of the leverage opportunity, and probably would not be willing to pay nearly as much.

Common Errors

The guideline publicly traded company method can be a powerful and useful tool in the valuation of closely held business interests. Proper application of it, however, requires some expertise in the analysis of publicly traded securities. This section discusses a few of the most common categories of errors frequently encountered in the use of the guideline publicly traded company method.

Failure to Conduct an Adequate Search for Guideline Company Data

As noted early in the chapter, there are thousands of publicly traded stocks. Some services report only a fraction of them, usually the largest ones. It is common to see reports that say something to the effect that, "We searched for publicly traded companies in the industry, but there were none," when, in fact, a more thorough search might unearth several. A related error is to use only companies in some service such as *Value Line Investment Survey*, which generally covers larger companies, when smaller companies not included in *Value Line* may be more comparative to the subject company.

Failure to Make Appropriate Financial Statement Adjustments to Guideline Companies

We frequently see a good job done on adjustments to the subject company statements, but little or no consideration given to possible appropriate adjustments to the guideline companies' financials. It is important that the analyst peruse the financial statements of the guideline companies to determine whether adjustments may be appropriate for one or more of the companies to put them on a basis as comparative as possible to the subject.

Exhibit 11–4

Market Value of Invested Capital Valuation Using Guideline Publicly Traded Companies with Different Capital Structures than the Subject Company $000s

	Guideline Company A	Guideline Company B	Guideline Company C	Subject Company
Comparative Balance Sheets				
Current assets	$25,000	$15,000	$12,000	$10,000
Net plant and equipment	45,000	35,000	18,000	15,000
Total assets	$70,000	$50,000	$30,000	$25,000
Current liabilities	$15,000	$10,000	$10,000	$5,000
Long-term debt	30,000	20,000	10,000	-
Stockholders' equity	25,000	20,000	10,000	20,000
Total liabilities and equity	$70,000	$50,000	$30,000	$25,000
Book value of invested capital (equity + interest-bearing debt)	$55,000	$40,000	$20,000	$20,000
Comparative Income Statements				
Sales	$90,000	$60,000	$40,000	$30,000
Cost of sales	55,000	35,000	25,000	18,000
Gross margin	35,000	25,000	15,000	12,000
General and administrative	16,000	12,000	7,000	5,500
Earnings before interest, taxes, depreciation, and amortization (EBITDA)	19,000	13,000	8,000	6,500
Depreciation	7,000	5,000	3,000	2,500
Earnings before interest and taxes (EBIT)	12,000	8,000	5,000	4,000
Interest	3,000	2,000	1,000	—
Net income before taxes	9,000	6,000	4,000	4,000
Taxes	4,000	2,500	1,500	1,500
Net income	$5,000	$3,500	$2,500	$2,500
Market value per share	$6.00	$5.00	$25.00	
Shares outstanding	10,000	6,000	1,000	1,000
Aggregate market value of equity	$60,000	$30,000	$25,000	
Add: Market value of debt [a]	30,000	20,000	10,000	—
Market value of invested capital	$90,000	$50,000	$35,000	
Debt/equity ratio (at market)	0.33	0.40	0.290	0.00

	Guideline Company A	Guideline Company B	Guideline Company C	Average	Implied Value of Subject [b] ($000)	Implied Value Per Share
Valuation Multiples						
Price/book value	2.4	1.5	2.5	2.1	42,000	$42.00
Price/sales	0.7	0.5	0.6	0.6	18,000	18.00
Price/earnings	12.0	8.6	10.0	10.2	25,500	25.50
Price/gross cash flow (net income + depreciation)	5.0	3.5	4.5	4.3	21,500	21.50
MVIC/BVIC	1.6	1.3	1.8	1.6	32,400	32.40
MVIC/Sales	1.0	0.8	0.9	0.9	27,000	27.00
MVIC/EBIT	7.5	6.3	7.0	6.9	27,600	27.60
MVIC/EBITDA	4.7	3.8	4.4	4.3	27,950	27.95

a. Assumes market value of debt = book value of debt

b. Using averages of guideline company multiples in all cases, since fundamentals are similar except for capital structure

Along the same line, we generally like to use the guideline companies' original financial statements and SEC filings rather than secondary sources, especially if the guideline company method is to be the primary method relied on. Secondary sources often do not provide the detail of data needed for certain adjustments. Also, people sometimes are not careful to understand the definition a secondary source may use for certain data, and thus may get caught in a mismatch when using it to value the subject company.

Multiples that Mismatch Numerator and Denominator

There are many ways to mismatch the numerator in a valuation multiple (the multiple selected on the basis of guideline company market evidence) with the denominator (the fundamental data for the subject company to which the numerator is applied to get an indication of value). Two of the most common are mismatched time periods and mismatched definitions.

Mismatched Time Periods. It is not uncommon to find valuation multiples computed from guideline company data for some time period applied to subject company data for a different time period. This inconsistency can result in serious distortions, especially if industry conditions differed significantly between the time periods. At a market turning point for a cyclical industry, a single quarter's difference in the fundamental data used between the guideline companies and the subject company can result in seriously misleading valuation multiples.

In order to avoid such distortion, it is often necessary to work with interim (versus fiscal year-end) data for the guideline companies in order to match time periods as closely as possible with available subject company data closest to the effective date of the valuation. This usually requires more work on the part of the analyst but often is worth it to produce a more reliable result.

Mismatched Definitions of Variables. If a valuation multiple is computed based on guideline company data defined in a certain way, that multiple should be applied to fundamental data defined the same way for the subject company. Looking at the same point another way, if subject company data are defined in a certain way, the same definition should be used for guideline company data from which a valuation multiple is computed.

Elementary as this sounds, inexperienced analysts often make data mismatches. A few of the more common data mismatches are:

- Fully diluted data used for the guideline companies or the subject company, but not for both
- Subject company—but not guideline company—data adjusted for nonrecurring item
- After-tax pricing multiples for guideline companies applied to pretax data for subject company
- Income data after officers' compensation for guideline companies applied to subject company income data before owner/officer compensation

The above list provides a flavor of typical mismatches. Analysts should be on the lookout to avoid them.

Simple Reliance on Average of Guideline Company Multiples without Comparative Analysis

Unless the guideline and subject companies are extremely homogeneous in their financial characteristics, the mean or median of the guideline company pricing multiples may not be the most appropriate pricing multiples for the subject company. Yet analysts often use the mean or median guideline company pricing multiple with no explanation to justify the implied notion that the subject company's characteristics indicate that it should be valued right at the average of the guideline companies.

A section of this chapter was devoted to selecting the pricing multiple for the subject company relative to guideline company pricing multiples. Such analysis is little more than common sense, yet it is surprising how often it is ignored!

Summary

This chapter presented the procedures and sources for implementing the guideline public company method of valuing the equity ownership of a business. It is widely used and accepted, but it must be implemented very carefully.

Exhibit 11–5 summarizes the steps in carrying out the guideline public company method.

Exhibit 11–5

Steps in the Guideline Publicly Traded Company Method

1. Set criteria for selection of guideline publicly traded companies.
2. Search for and identify the companies that meet the criteria.
3. Decide on the relevant time period for comparative analysis of the subject company and the guideline companies.
4. Obtain the guideline companies' financial statements for the time period decided in Step 3.
5. Broaden or narrow the criteria, if necessary, to provide the best group of guideline companies, adding or deleting companies according to the revised criteria.
6. Analyze and adjust the subject and/or guideline company financial statements as appropriate (Chapter 7).
7. Compile comparative financial ratios for the subject and guideline companies (Chapter 8).
8. Decide which guideline company valuation multiples to use.
9. Obtain the market price of each guideline company's stock as of the valuation date. (If market value of invested capital is used in any of the valuation multiples, it is necessary to obtain the market value of all the guideline companies' securities that are included in their invested capital.)
10. Compile guideline company valuation multiple tables for the valuation multiples decided in Step 8.
11. Based on analysis of the valuation multiple tables in conjunction with the comparative financial analysis of the subject and guideline companies, decide on the appropriate multiple for the subject company for each valuation multiple to be used.
12. Multiply each valuation multiple to be used by the relevant financial variable for the subject company to get indications of value according to each valuation multiple.
13. Weight or otherwise correlate the indications of value from Step 11 to reach an estimate of "value as if publicly traded" (a marketable, minority ownership interest value).
14. Make adjustments to this value, if appropriate, for factors in the definition of value but not reflected in the value as if publicly traded, such as discount for lack of marketability and/or premium for control. Also, adjust any other elements of value, if appropriate, that were adjusted out of the guideline company analysis, such as nonoperating assets.

The guideline public company method commonly uses measures that indicate the value of the equity directly, such as price/earnings multiples. However, sometimes the market value of the total invested capital is estimated and the value of debt subtracted to reach an indicated value for the equity.

Because the guideline public company method usually uses publicly traded minority interest stock transactions, the value reached usually is minority interest value on a fully marketable basis. If the analyst is valuing a minority ownership interest in a private company, he or she should normally make an adjustment for lack of marketability. If the analyst is valuing a controlling ownership interest, a premium for control may or may not be appropriate, and such a premium may be fully or partially offset by a discount for the lack of liquidity of the privately held company controlling interest.

The chapter should be helpful both for those preparing a valuation utilizing the guideline public company method, and also for those reviewing and evaluating a valuation report that uses the method.

Bibliography

Articles

Crow, Matthew R. "Developing Valuation Multiples Using Guideline Companies." *CPA Litigation Service Counselor*, September 1999, pp. 8–9.

Fowler, Bradley, A. "How Do You Handle It?" *Business Valuation Review*, September 1996, pp. 136–37.

Goeldner, Richard W. "Adjusting Market Multiples of Guideline Companies." Presentation to the 18th Annual Advanced Business Valuation Conference of the American Society of Appraisers, October 29, 1999. Available on www.BVLibrary.com.

_____. "Bridging the Gap between Public and Private Market Multiples." *Business Valuation Review*, September 1998, pp. 97–101.

Hitchner, James R. *Financial Valuation: Applications and Models*, 2nd ed. (Hoboken, NJ: John Wiley & Sons, 2006).

Nath, Eric W. "How Public Guideline Companies Represent 'Control' Value for a Private Company." *Business Valuation Review*, December 1997, pp. 167–71.

Peters, Jerry O. "Adjusting Price/Earnings Ratios for Differences in Company Size. *Business Valuation Review*, June 1999, pp. 71–85.

Pratt, Shannon P. "Controversies Involving the Market Approach to Business Valuation; Raising the Issues, Soliciting Feedback." *Shannon Pratt's Business Valuation Update*, November 2000.

_____. *The Market Approach to Valuing Businesses,* 2nd ed. (Hoboken, NJ: John Wiley & Sons, 2005).

Pratt, Shannon P., and Alina V. Niculita. *The Market Approach to Valuing Businesses Workbook*, 2nd ed. (Hoboken, NJ: John Wiley & Sons, 2006).

Reilly, Robert, F. "Problems in Using Capital Market Data to Value Operating Business Assets." *Valuation Strategies*, January/February 1999, pp. 17–19, 44, 46.

Ross, Franz. "'Just One Thing': The Most Reliable Variable for Use in the Market Approach." *Shannon Pratt's Business Valuation Update*, August 2004.

Sheeler, Carl L. "The Market Approach: A Neglected and Misunderstood Aspect of Business Value." *Journal of Financial Planning*, May 2004, Article 7.

_____. "A Misunderstood Aspect of Business Value: The Market Approach." *The CPA Journal*, October 2004.

Slee, Robert T. "Is the Subject Company Similar?" *Valuation Strategies*, May/June 1998, pp. 4–7, 34.

Trugman, Gary. "Guideline Public Company Method—Control or Minority Value?" *Shannon Pratt's Business Valuation Update*, December 2003.

_____. "Guideline Public Company Method: Control or Minority? Control Position." *BVPapers,* February 2005. Available at www.BVLibrary.com.

Wise, Richard. "Application of the Market Approach in Valuing a Canadian Business." *BVPapers*, February 2005. Available at www.BVLibrary.com.

_____. "Caveats for Market Approach." *CA Magazine*, January-February 2004.

_____. "Multiple-of-Revenues as a Valuation Method." *Business Valuation Digest*, October 1996, pp. 1–4.

Sources of Guideline Publicly Traded Company Data

Compustat and other Standard and Poor's Products
Standard & Poor's Corporation
www.compustat.com
www.standardandpoors.com
(800) 523-4534

Directory of Companies Required to File Annual Reports with the Securities and Exchange Commission under the Securities Exchange Act of 1934
U.S. Government Printing Office
(202) 512-1800
www.gpo.gov

EDGAR Database
Securities and Exchange Commission
www.sec.gov/cgi-gin/srch-edgar
www.sec.gov/edgar/searchedgar/webusers.htm

Factiva
www.factiva.com
(800) 369-0166

Mergent (previously Moody's)
www.mergent.com
(888) 411-0893

OneSource (a division of *infoUSA*)
www.onesource.com
(978) 318-4300

Thomson Financial
www.thomson.com/solutions/financial
www.dialog.com
(800) 843-7747

Chapter 12

Market Approach: Guideline Merged and Acquired Company Method

This chapter was revised from the previous edition by Chad Phillips.

The most difficult decision an executive faces in negotiating an acquisition is the price to be paid. The decision is difficult because there are so many factors to consider—the process by which the target company is being sold, the expected competition, the future profitability of the target, expected synergies, complex tax rules, alternate legal forms of effecting a transaction and accounting considerations.[1]

The essential difference between this chapter and the previous chapter on the guideline publicly traded company method is the nature of the market data used as a starting point. In the previous chapter, we started with noncontrolling ownership interest transactions, mostly in the public stock market and thus fully marketable. In this chapter, we start with data on transfers of controlling ownership interests, usually (but not entirely) 100 percent ownership interests.

The business interest transferred often includes the entire capital structure, not necessarily just equity. The company being sold may have been either public or private before the transaction. The nature of the transaction and the nature and availability of data about it vary much more than public market guideline company transaction data.

The quote introducing this chapter helps explain why there may be different values under different valuation criteria and different circumstances. It also explains why we should examine merger and acquisition transactions as carefully as possible when using them as guidance in the market approach to valuing a company, and why we need to be very careful in interpreting and applying the results of our analysis.

Overview of the Merged and Acquired Company Method

The previous chapter dealt with data on day-to-day trading prices of securities. However one also can derive indications of value from the prices at which entire companies or operating units of companies have been sold or the prices at which significant interests in companies have changed hands. Such data are harder to find than daily stock trading data, since there is no centrally organized mechanism for collecting and making such price information available.

The general notion of merger and acquisition analysis is the same as guideline public company analysis—one relates the price at which the transaction took place to financial fundamentals that affect the value. As noted earlier, the financial variables used in the valuation of the entire company usually focus on the market value of the entire invested capital rather than on the equity alone. This is because the transaction often involves the entire capital structure, or if it does not, at least the acquiring control owner usually has the power to change the capital structure.

Also, it is common to consider transactions over a fairly long time. This might involve analyzing transactions in the subject company's industry or similar industries over several years. This is partly because there are fewer transactions and also

---

[1] Joseph H. Marren, *Mergers & Acquisitions: A Valuation Handbook* (New York: McGraw-Hill, 1993), p. v.

because acquisition pricing multiples generally fluctuate somewhat less over time than public stock market pricing multiples.

Generally, the criteria for selection of merged and acquired guideline company transactions are similar to those for selecting publicly traded stock guideline companies. However, in situations where limited transaction data are available, the criteria may have to be broadened.

When Is the Guideline Merged and Acquired Company Method Most Useful?

The initial value derived from the guideline merged and acquired company method, before adjustment for factors such as size of the subject block and degree of marketability, is an indication of transaction prices of major ownership interests, usually controlling ownership interests. The characteristics of each transaction need to be carefully analyzed to make judgments as to what adjustments may be necessary in order to use the transaction pricing multiples as guidance in a specific valuation assignment.

Standard of Value

Merger and acquisition transaction prices may be representative of *fair market value*, *investment value*, or somewhere in between. At one end of the spectrum, a sale to a pure financial buyer (one who is buying strictly for a return on investment from the company as a stand-alone entity) usually would be representative of fair market value, although even financial buyers may have some special motivations and advantages. Furthermore, they may have to compete with strategic buyers. At the other end of the spectrum, the more unique the synergies between the acquirer and the target, the more the transaction is representative of investment value rather than fair market value, because the pricing may reflect the synergistic benefits to a *particular* buyer rather than the price a *hypothetical* buyer would pay (as required in the definition of fair market value).

William D. Rifkin explains how investment value characteristics often influence merger and acquisition prices:

> The same acquisition target will have different values to different buyers, due both to perception and reality. Potential buyers will have different views on: (1) the expected financial performance of the target; (2) what can be done to enhance performance; and (3) the risk of deviation from expected results. Certain potential buyers, regardless of their perception of the future, may have a true economic advantage over others. This could be due to tax factors (such as ability to utilize net operating loss carry forwards), potential economies of scale, or opportunities to achieve synergies. Economic benefits which may result from the combination of two going concerns would not, for instance, be available to a so-called financial buyer, such as a leveraged buyout firm. Unless a company is purchased for immediate resale, as in a "bust-up" acquisition, the potential acquiror's first step must be a determination of what the target is worth

specifically to it, not others—and this requires a careful and honest assessment of what the acquiror can do with the combined company.[2]

The same distinction arises when using merger and acquisition data in the context of fair value. Most state statutes defining fair value specifically exclude the value of any benefits arising from the merger itself.

There is no formula to sort out the amount by which a price that was paid in a transaction reflected synergistic value over and above a strict, stand-alone fair market value price. This is a continuing source of contention when using merger and acquisition data to resolve disputed valuations.

Going-Concern versus Liquidation Value

Sometimes, but not often, it is possible to analyze a transaction to estimate the extent to which a price represents a going-concern value or a liquidation value. Often, a transaction price reflects some combination of the two, where some assets acquired will be liquidated while others will be operated as part of a going-concern business. This is a matter that varies on a case-by-case basis.

Quantity and Quality of Data Available

Some industries are characterized by lots of acquisition activity while others are not. Even one good transaction generally is better than nothing, if it is a reasonably good guideline transaction and the data are complete and reliable. We generally would want to see at least a few transactions, however, if we were to weight the guideline merged and acquired company method heavily in the final analysis.

If the target(s) were public, generally adequate data are available. On the other hand, if the target(s) were private, good, verifiable data may be limited. If the private company is acquired by a public company in a transaction, that might be material to the public company, the buyer discloses the transaction by filing Form 8-K. Reported purchase prices may not reflect considerations such as covenants not to compete or employment contracts. It is often difficult to determine exactly what assets were included in the purchase price or what liabilities were assumed. It is often difficult to get any reliable data on profitability. All of these problems must be factored into the decision whether to use private company acquisition data and, if so, the weight to be accorded to it in the final analysis.

Control Transaction (Acquisition) Valuation Multiples

When valuing a controlling ownership interest, the analyst often focuses on guidance from other controlling interest transactions (mergers and acquisitions). Control transaction valuation analysis typically focuses on market value of invested capital (MVIC, as defined in Chapter 11) or on *aggregate consideration*, defined

---

[2] William D. Rifkin, "Valuing and Pricing Mergers and Acquisitions I: Concepts and Mechanisms," Chapter 3 in *Mergers, Acquisitions, and Leveraged Buyouts*, Robert Lawrence Kuhn, ed. (New York: McGraw-Hill, 1990), p. 39. Reprinted with permission.

as *"purchase price of equity plus total debt less cash."*[3] This is common sense, since the control owner has the power to change the capital structure, and control buyers very frequently do.

This, of course, means that all the returns available to both equity and debt should be included in the denominator when computing the pricing multiple. Control transaction valuation multiples (often called *deal multiples or acquisition multiples*) often use the following measures of returns in the denominator:

- Revenues
- Operating income available to invested capital (earnings before interest and taxes [EBIT])
- Operating cash flow available to invested capital (EBIT plus depreciation, and amortization [EBITDA])
- Tangible book value
- Discretionary earnings (also called seller's discretionary cash flow, defined as EBIT plus *all* noncash charges plus all compensation and benefits for one owner operator, used primarily for smaller businesses with heavy owner/manager involvement)

Nonoperating income, expenses, and the assets and/or liabilities that produce them are treated separately if they are significant.

Exhibit 12–1 presents a typical example of the use of the merger and acquisition method to develop an indicated value range for an acquisition candidate. Note that five valuation multiples are computed, but only three of them are used in the valuation analysis applied to the subject company. The reason seems obvious: three valuation multiples fall into a fairly tight range while the other two are widely dispersed. Note that the preferred three involve aggregate consideration as the numerator (defined similarly to our definition of market value of invested capital, but not exactly the same). Had the tangible book value ratio also been computed on the basis of aggregate consideration instead of only price paid for equity securities, the range for that valuation multiple may have been applied.

Robert Kuhn recognizes that comparative transaction data are widely used in the merger market, but also cautions to carefully analyze differences between companies, time period differences, and market aberrations:

> In merger market valuation models, we compare prices among similar companies, much like comparison shopping for a consumer item among similar retail stores. Guideline transactions (i.e., similar industry, company size, financial structure, time frame, etc.) are identified for the purpose of conducting a comparative analysis to judge the relative worth of the target company. Investment bankers favor this technique, generating long lists of comparable transactions to advise clients on both buy and sell sides.
>
> In theory, the M&A market is the true reflection of current interaction between willing sellers and willing buyers. In the real world, however, this is rarely the case. Corporations are not yellow pencils, quickly stacked and easily matched; it is difficult to make true comparisons of complex situations—in one way or another virtually every M&A sale can be considered special or extraordinary. Furthermore, the M&A market often evinces aberrations—companies selling too low when suffering distressed conditions

---

[3] Marren, *Mergers & Acquisitions: A Valuation Handbook*, p. 188.

Exhibit 12–1

Example Application of Merger and Acquisition Method Analysis
of Selected Transactions Involving Building Material Retailers
(Figures in millions except ratios)

Target/Acquirer	AC PP	AC PP/Sales	AC PP/OCF	AC PP/EBIT	AC PP/Net Income	AC PP/TBV
Scotty's/GB Inno	$303.8	$574.4	$32.4	$19.4	$11.9	$174.6
BM SA	$243.9	0.53 ×	9.40 ×	15.70 ×	20.50 ×	1.40 ×
Payless	$1,189.3	$1,844.9	$131.0	$93.0	$52.4	$397.5
Cashways/PCI	$911.9	0.64 ×	9.10 ×	12.80 ×	17.40 ×	2.29 ×
Acquisition Corp.						
Pay 'N Pak	$292.3	$398.1	$29.6	$19.3	$5.7	$100.1
Stores/PNP	$212.6	0.73 ×	9.90 ×	15.10 ×	37.30 ×	2.12 ×
Prime Corp.						

Statistical Summary					
Low:	0.53	9.08	12.79	17.40	1.40
High:	0.73	9.87	15.66	37.30	2.29
Mean:	0.64	9.44	14.53	25.07	1.94
Median:	0.64	9.38	15.15	20.50	2.12
Sample:	3	3	3	3	3

PP = Purchase price for all equity securities including options and convertible debt

AC = Aggregate consideration (PP plus total debt less cash)

EBIT = Earnings before interest and taxes

OCF = Operating cash flow (EBIT plus depreciation and amortization)

TBV = Tangible book value (total book value less intangibles)

Comparable Transactions Valuation Analysis (Figures in millions except ratios)

	Comparable Transaction Multiples		Target Company LTM[a]	Valuation Range	
	Mean	Median	Results	Mean	Median
Aggregate consideration[b] sales	0.64	0.64	$1,050	$668	$677
Aggregate consideration[b] operating cash flow[c]	9.44	9.38	55	519	516
Aggregate consideration[b] EBIT	14.53	15.15	35	509	530
			Range	$509	$677

a. Aggregate consideration equals purchase price of equity plus total debt less cash.

b. Operating cash flow equals EBIT plus depreciation and amortization.

c. LTM means last 12 months.

SOURCE: Joseph H. Marren, *Mergers & Acquisitions: A Valuation Handbook* (New York: McGraw-Hill, 1993), pp. 188–189. Reprinted with permission.

and companies selling too high when faddish or foolish buyers are over-eager to acquire. The feeding frenzy of M&A in recent years—the search for synergy and hostile takeover battles—have bid up many M&A prices to unrealistic levels.[4]

Announcement versus Closing Date Value

There are two important dates involving price discovery in connection with an acquisition. The first is the announcement date. The second is the closing date. These dates can be months apart and there may be a difference between the indicated deal values on the two dates. For instance, if a publicly traded acquirer is paying for the deal with its own shares, the value of these shares may change between the two dates and the agreed exchange ratio may not adjust fully to account for the change.

Which price should be used for determining the deal value? Also, should we develop multiples based on trailing earnings as of the announcement date, or as of the closing date? It generally does not make a material difference which date is used. The most common approach is to develop multiples based on the announcement date, following the example of most M&A database services. This gives an indication of what the buyer and seller originally intended to pay or receive for the company, based on financial statements available at the time that the deal was originally analyzed and negotiated.

Caveat: Check the Deal Structure

Deal Terms

For guideline valuation purposes, and certainly if the standard of value is fair market value, it is necessary that the deal price used to develop a valuation multiple be a cash or cash equivalent price. In many acquisitions, the consideration paid is all or partly something other than cash, such as common or preferred stock (sometimes convertible), notes (also sometimes convertible), and so on. The cash value of such consideration often is less than its face value (rarely more). If using a guideline transaction in which the consideration paid was not all cash, the analyst should make the best possible effort to convert the consideration paid to a cash equivalent value.

Exactly What Was Transacted?

When using publicly traded guideline company stock transactions, we know that what was sold was stock. When entire companies are sold, however, the deal is often structured as an asset sale. In such instances, it is important to know exactly what

---

[4] Robert Kuhn, *Mergers, Acquisitions, and Leveraged Buyouts*, p. 61.

assets were sold and what liabilities assumed. In addition to the fact that not everything on the seller's balance sheet (or off-balance sheet assets or liabilities) may have been included in the transaction, the income tax ramifications of an asset sale usually are considerably different than for a stock sale.

Differences in the structure between the guideline transaction and the contemplated subject transaction should be noted and adjusted or accounted for appropriately in developing valuation multiples. This is of particular importance when the guideline transaction was an asset sale instead of a stock sale.

Noncompete and Employment or Consulting Agreements

Noncompete and employment or consulting agreements are often executed in conjunction with change of control transactions. If these are of significant importance, as for middle-market and smaller company transactions, and available, they should be carefully analyzed for each comparative transaction used.

The noncompete or employment agreement usually (although not always) is the property of the individual rather than the selling corporation or partnership. In marital dissolution, dissenting shareholder, and bankruptcy cases, the ownership of noncompete and employment agreements often is an issue.[5]

If a noncompete agreement is included in a transaction, the value allocated is included in the deal prices found in *Pratt's Stats*, *Bizcomps*, and the Institute of Business Appraisers database. Whereas *Bizcomps* and the Institute of Business Appraisers database also include the value allocated of an employment agreement, *Pratt's Stats* does not. If using multiples for comparative purposes, the multiples shown in the above sources often need to be adjusted if they are to be applied to a valuation where the agreements should not be considered a part of the entity value. This situation is especially a problem in valuations for marital dissolutions and is discussed more fully in Chapter 38.

Sources of Merger and Acquisition Data

Sources for Large Company Transactions

Generally, sources of price and underlying financial data on control transactions are more expensive and less consistent in content and reliability than public market stock transaction data. Public stock financial data are subject to very consistent reporting requirements by the Securities and Exchange Commission (SEC) and the accounting profession. Data on acquisitions of private companies are not subject to any such regulation, and data on mergers and acquisitions of public companies vary tremendously in scope and format.

The bibliography at the end of the chapter gives contact information for several merger and acquisition data sources.

---

[5] For a discussion of this issue with case references, see Shannon P. Pratt, "Ownership of Personal Intangibles: A Frequent Subject of Controversy," *Valuation Strategies*, May/June 1999, pp. 5–9.

Information about mergers is obtained from disclosure filings, the news media, and business intermediaries (business brokers and investment bankers). When publicly held companies are involved, the participants must submit disclosure documents such as SEC Form 8-K and others known collectively as William's Act reports. The major filings are Forms 14D-1, 13D, and 8-K. Companies attempting to purchase another company in the open market (called a tender offer) submit the Form 14D-1. Individuals purchasing 5 percent or more of a company's stock with the intent to obtain substantial voting control or otherwise influence the management of the company file Form 13D. There are also many other relevant required reports, depending on the transactions, such as 14D-9s, proxy statements, and prospectuses. News stories, including press releases from the participants, are the primary source of information on private transactions. The business media also can provide additional details on mergers involving public companies.

An amazing variety of reporting services, newsletters, and online databases utilize information from disclosure filings, company announcements, the media, and business intermediaries to provide extensive, organized analysis of merger transactions as they unfold. General business indexes and news databases can be useful in conducting merger research, but the following sources provide specific coverage of merger and acquisition activities. As with any secondary sources, errors and inconsistencies occur, so the original source documents are the only guarantees of absolute accuracy.

- *Mergerstat Review*
- The *Merger Yearbook*
- *Mergers & Acquisitions* magazine
- *Buyouts*, published every other week by Securities Data Publishing
- *Mergers & Acquisitions Report*

In addition to traditional print sources, online databases provide a variety of information sources for tracking merger and acquisition-related information.

- *SDC Platinum*
- *Mergerstat/Shannon Pratt's Control Premium Study*

Sources for Middle-Market and Smaller Company Transactions

Practical application of the guideline transaction method for companies valued under $100 million has been enhanced significantly due to the development of databases covering "middle-market" and smaller company transactions. These databases are less expensive than those devoted to large company acquisitions.

There are at least four databases devoted to middle-market and small company controlling ownership interest transactions:

1. *Pratt's Stats*
2. *Done Deals*
3. *Bizcomps*
4. *IBA Market Database*

The bibliography at the end of the chapter gives contact information for each of these databases.

Exhibit 12–2

Comparison of Private and Public Company Transaction Databases as of June 29, 2007

	Pratt's Stats®*	BIZCOMPS®*	IBA	Done Deals	Mergerstat®*
Type of transactions	Private companies	Private companies	Private companies	Private and public	Public companies
Number of transactions	9,933	9,885	30,000	~8,000	5,590
Since	1990	1993	~1980		1998
Median sale price	$1.3M	$160K			$128.2M
Range of sale prices	$3K–$16.6B deal size	$0–$35M	most < $500K revs.	$1M–$1B	$40K–$116B
Median revenues	$1.3M	$368K			$96M
SIC codes	704	445			657
Data points on each transaction	81	21	8(+)	21	56

*Available from BVResources at www.BVMarketData.com.

Exhibit 12–2 presents a side-by-side comparison of the foregoing private company sales databases as of June 29, 2007.

Past Subject Company Transactions

Past transactions involving the subject company may be fruitful subjects to analyze for guidance as to value.

Past Subject Company Changes of Control

If the subject company itself has changed control in the last few years, the transaction may be an excellent source of valuation multiples. The valuation multiples used would generally be the same as those discussed earlier. The valuation multiples indicated by the prior transaction may need some adjustment to reflect internal changes in the company or changes in the industry or market conditions.

Bona Fide Offers

Documentable, arm's-length, bona fide offers to buy or sell may also be useful evidence of value. Funded bona fide offers (i.e., offers for which the financing for the offer is already in place) should be given more weight and more consideration than unfunded bona fide offers. It is usually difficult, however, to obtain adequate documentation or to verify the arm's-length relationship of the potential buyer/seller.

Past Acquisitions by the Subject Company

If the company has made one or more acquisitions in the last several years, such transactions may prove to be excellent sources of valuation multiples. Again, adjustments may be necessary for changes between the dates of the acquisitions and the relevant valuation date.

It may be easy to overlook such acquisitions, because they may not come to light in any of the search procedures normally used to identify merger and acquisition transactions. The subject company may be the *only* source for such data, but typically is a very comprehensive and reliable source. Therefore, if considering using a merger and acquisition method, it often is a good idea to ask whether the company has made any acquisitions.

Formulas or Rules of Thumb

Some industries have rules of thumb (sometimes referred to as industry valuation formulas) about how companies in their industry are valued for transfer of controlling ownership interests. On the one hand, if such rules of thumb are widely disseminated and referenced in the industry, they probably should not be ignored. On the other hand, there usually is no credible evidence of how such rules were developed nor how well they actually comport to actual transaction data.

Rules of thumb usually are quite simplistic. As such, they obscure much important detail. They fail to differentiate either operating characteristics or assets from one company to another. They also fail to differentiate changes in conditions for companies in various industries from one time period to another.

Furthermore, it is common for companies in many industries to sell on terms other than for cash, so the "prices" generated by the rules of thumb often are not cash equivalent values. The terms may vary considerably from one transaction to another, but usually are worth less than cash equivalent value. Rules of thumb, therefore, may tend to overstate a cash equivalent value. Consequently, rules of thumb rarely, if ever, should be used without reference to other, more reliable valuation methods.

In an article targeted primarily to valuations for divorce, and still widely quoted after 20 years, Jay Fishman offers the following summary:

> There are no "quick fixes" to the valuation of closely held entities. It is essential to remember that industry formulas or rules of thumb are commonly not market derived representations of actual transactions. Since most industry formulas or rules of thumb are derived from textbooks, trade publications, verbal representations, or other similar sources of information, they are poor substitutes for the Direct Market Comparison Approach.[6]

---

[6] Jay E. Fishman, "The Problem with Rules of Thumb in the Valuation of Closely-Held Entities," *Fair$hare: The Matrimonial Law Monthly*, December 1984, p. 13.

Under a heading "Cautions about Using Formulas" in his book *Handbook of Small Business Valuation Formulas and Rules of Thumb*, Glenn Desmond makes the following observations:

Formulas Are General in Nature

Formulas are general in nature. Adjustments must be made to account for variations in revenue and cash-flow trends; location; lease; condition of the plant, fixtures, and equipment; reputation with customers, suppliers, bankers, and others; special skills required; difficulty in starting the business; and so forth.

There Is No Single, All-Purpose Formula

There is no single formula that will work for every business. Formula multipliers offer ease of calculation, but they also obscure details. This can be misleading. Net revenue multipliers are particularly troublesome because they are blind to the business's expense and profit history. It is easy to see how two businesses in any given industry group might have the same annual net revenue (ANR), yet show very different cash flows. A proper valuation will go beyond formulas and include a full financial analysis whenever possible.[7]

Nonoperating Assets, Excess Assets, and Asset Deficiencies

If the subject company has significant nonoperating assets, excess assets, or asset deficiencies that distinguish it from the guideline companies, adjustments for those items may be appropriate. The same principles apply as were discussed in the previous chapter on the guideline publicly traded company method.

Selecting and Weighting Multiples for the Subject Company Based on Guideline Transactions

The result of the guideline transaction analysis is an array of pricing multiples for each of several valuation multiples. At this point, it is necessary to again visit the questions of (1) which multiples to use in reaching an indication of value and (2) the relative weight to be accorded to each of the multiples used.

Earnings based multiples, such as price to net income, and price to pretax income, are generally considered to provide the best indication of business value. However, as with many valuation topics, there is no unanimity respecting the use and derivation of valuation multiples. Franz Ross in his September 2004 *Business Valuation Update* article, titled, "Just one thing: the most reliable variable for use in the market approach,"[8] makes a case for the use of gross profit multiples. In

---

[7] Glenn M. Desmond, ASA, MAI, *Handbook of Small Business Valuation Formulas and Rules of Thumb*, 3rd ed. (Camden, ME: Valuation Press, 1993), p. 12.

[8] Franz Ross, CBA, "Just one thing: the most reliable variable for use in the market approach," *Business Valuation Update*, September 2004.

particular, Mr. Ross notes that the use of pro forma earnings inputs in the market approach often compounds potential errors of omission or commission in developing such pro forma earnings and, as a result, tends to invalidate the use of the market approach as a check on the reasonableness of value indications produced using other approaches. Further, Ross argues that earnings are often subject to manipulation or management, particularly in small, privately held companies, and therefore may not be representative of the potential returns available to an investor in the subject company. Care must be taken by the analyst to ensure that the use of a given valuation multiple is appropriate given the nature of the subject company's operations, the reliability of the source data, and the apparent market reliance on such data. As a result of this research, *Pratt's Stats* added multiples of gross profits to the multiples presented for each transaction reported in the database for each company.

For each valuation multiple used, it is also necessary to decide what the pricing multiple for the subject company should be relative to the observed multiples for the guideline transaction companies.

Impact of Guideline Transactional Data Evaluation

The same general thought processes and decision criteria apply to both (1) deciding on whether or not to rely on any particular valuation multiple at all and (2) deciding on the relative weight to be accorded each valuation multiple ultimately used in reaching the opinion of value. A study of the transactional data may lead to greater or lesser reliance on certain valuation multiples than one might have expected prior to compiling the data.

Number of Data Points Available. If it turns out that very few data points are available for a particular valuation multiple, that problem may lead one to abandon that multiple or to put relatively little weight on it. This is true even though it might be quite conceptually significant if there were more data. For example, if only two of seven comparative transaction companies had meaningful positive earnings, and thus meaningful price to earnings multiples, the analyst must decide whether the two multiples convey enough information to be accorded weight in the final analysis. Instead, the analyst may, for example, decide instead to use a price to cash flow pricing multiple or a price to some number of years average earnings pricing multiple.

Comparability of Data Measurement. Another issue to consider is the extent to which the analyst is satisfied that the adjustments, if any, to the subject company and to the guideline companies' financial fundamental data for the purpose of presenting the data on a comparative basis. The analyst's confidence regarding the comparability of fundamental financial data may influence the analyst's judgment regarding the use of or weight accorded to valuation multiples based on that particular financial variable.

Comparability of Data Patterns. Another factor in assessing comparability is the extent to which the data for the subject company "track" with the data for the guideline merged and acquired companies. For example, if the subject company and six of the seven guideline merged and acquired companies had a generally upward earnings trend but one guideline company had a downward trend, the analyst may omit the aberrant company when deciding on appropriate pricing multiples relative to earnings.

Apparent Market Reliance. The extent to which the valuation multiples are tightly clustered or widely dispersed tends to indicate the extent to which the market focuses on that particular valuation multiple in pricing companies in the particular industry.

Multiple of Stock Value to Asset Value

When the analyst has determined that either book value or some adjusted book value figure provides a useful representation of the subject company's fair market value, the next step is to translate that figure into its implication for the value of the company or interest being valued. This translation usually is made by referring to the relationship of the transactional prices of the guideline companies to their respective underlying net asset values.

It may be possible to compute the multiple of market price to book value for a group of guideline transaction companies and to apply a multiple somewhere within in the range of such multiples to the subject company book value. If (1) the book values of the subject company and guideline transaction companies were computed on comparable bases, and (2) the asset composition is comparable, this procedure may provide a reasonably realistic estimate for the value of the subject business interest.

If using *Pratt's Stats*, the analyst may be able to derive a sufficient sample in order to determine a multiple of adjusted asset value, depending on the deals selected and data provided. This can be very useful for asset-intense businesses.

If accounting methods for the subject company and for the guideline companies differ significantly, the analyst should make appropriate adjustments before (1) computing the market price to book value multiples and (2) applying them in the subject valuation. There can be additional significant differences, such as in asset mix, that challenge the validity of using one company's price to book value multiple in valuing another company's stock.

Reaching the Value Conclusion

Relative weighting of valuation multiples is similar to that used in the guideline publicly traded company method, except that assets may get a little more weight in a control valuation, since the control owner has discretion over their use or disposition. The same observations apply to nonoperating assets, excess assets, and asset deficiencies. (See Chapter 11, "Market Approach: Guideline Publicly Traded Company Method," for a detailed discussion of these topics.)

One should recognize, of course, that an actual accomplished merger or acquisition observed in the market usually has been consummated at the highest possible value to the seller, not at some average of possible values. For every such transaction observed, many unsuccessful attempts at transactions were usually made. Furthermore, many transactions reflect some synergistic value, which would contain elements of investment value over and above pure fair market value. All these factors must be considered when deciding on what multiples to apply to the subject transaction, and the relative weight to be accorded to each.

Since merger and acquisition value analysis usually focuses on market value of invested capital, the value of the debt must be subtracted to reach the value of equity.

This debt would be valued at market if it is expected to remain outstanding, but usually at face if it is expected to be retired in conjunction with the transaction.

If a noncontrolling interest is being valued, both lack of control and lack of marketability discounts should be considered. Even in the case of a controlling interest, it may be appropriate to make some adjustment for lack of marketability (or "lack of liquidity") relative to the values indicated from actual consummated transactions. This is discussed in Chapter 17.

Summary

The merger and acquisition method is similar in concept to the guideline publicly traded company method, seeking valuation guidance from actual sale transactions in the market. Since the transaction data used usually are controlling interests, it is most directly applicable for valuing other controlling ownership interests, although it can be used for noncontrolling interest valuations with proper adjustments.

Merger and acquisition data come from diverse sources and are less consistent (and sometimes less reliable) than data on day-to-day public stock market transactions. Sometimes, past transactions involving the subject company are a good source of valuation multiples.

Since merger and acquisition transaction dates almost always differ from the subject company effective valuation date, adjustments often are needed to reflect differences in economic and industry conditions between the dates.

Merger and acquisition prices often, to some extent, reflect synergies and/or strategic advantages between acquirer and target. To the extent that this is true, a transaction may be more reflective of *investment value* (value to that particular buyer) than *fair market value* (the value to a hypothetical buyer). For this reason, the circumstances and details of the merger and acquisition transactions must be carefully analyzed, if available, which is often not the case.

Bibliography

Desmond, Glenn M. *Handbook of Small Business Valuation Formulas and Rules of Thumb.* 3rd ed. Camden, ME: Valuation Press, 1993.

Fannon, Nancy J., and Heidi Walker. "Uses and Abuses of Market Data: An In-Depth Look at the Tools of Our Trade," *Business Valuation Review*, Summer 2006.

Fishman, Jay E. "The Problem with Rules of Thumb in the Valuation of Closely-Held Entities." *Fair$hare: The Matrimonial Law Monthly*, December 1984, p. 13.

Kuhn, Robert Lawrence, ed. *Mergers, Acquisitions and Leveraged Buyouts.* New York: McGraw-Hill, 1990.

Marren, Joseph H. *Mergers & Acquisitions: A Valuation Handbook.* New York: McGraw-Hill, 1993.

Pratt, Shannon P. "Insights on Private Company Sale Pricing." *The Journal of Business Valuation* (Proceedings of the 4th Joint Business Valuation Conference of the Canadian Institute of Chartered Business Valuators and the American Society of Appraisers). Toronto: The Canadian Institute of Chartered Business Valuators, 1999, pp. 133–40. Also available at www.BVLibrary.com.

_____. *The Market Approach to Valuing Businesses*, 2nd ed. Hoboken, NJ: John Wiley & Sons, 2005.

Reilly, Robert F., and Robert P. Schweihs. *Handbook of Advanced Business Valuation*. New York: McGraw-Hill, 1999.

West, Thomas L., ed. *Business Reference Guide*, 16th ed. Concord, MA: Business Brokerage Press, 2006.

Sources of Transactions

Bizcomps
Jack R. Sanders
PO Box 97757
Las Vegas, Nevada 89193
(702) 454-0072
www.bizcomps.com

BIZCOMPS National Industrial Edition (annual)

BIZCOMPS National Industrial Edition is an annual study of over 1,250 actual businesses sold totaling over $1 billion. It includes only larger manufacturing, wholesale/distribution, and service businesses that have sold nationwide.

These sales have been divided into a number of different categories to provide even more useful information:

- Sales price to gross sales (also graphed—both averages and medians)
- Sales price to seller's discretionary earnings (also graphed—both averages and medians)
- Sales compared by geographical area
- Average sale over $1,000,000
- Terms versus all cash sales
- More profitable compared to less profitable businesses
- The value of furniture, fixtures, and equipment
- The value of inventory at time of sale

BIZCOMPS Western, Central, and Eastern Regional Studies (annual)

a) Western Study
BIZCOMPS Western Study is an annual study of over 2,950 actual businesses sold totaling over $912 million. The sold businesses are compared by:

- Sales price to gross sales (also graphed and with medians)
- Sales price to seller's discretionary earnings (also graphed and with medians)
- Actual down payment versus all cash
- Rent as a percent of gross sales
- The value of furniture, fixtures, and equipment
- The value of inventory at time of sale

b) Central Study
BIZCOMPS Central Study is an annual study of over 1,500 actual businesses sold totaling over $441 million. The sold businesses are compared by:

- Sales price to gross sales (also graphed and with medians)
- Sales price to seller's discretionary earnings (also graphed and with medians)

- Actual down payment versus all cash
- Rent as a percent of gross sales
- The value of furniture, fixtures, and equipment
- The value of inventory at time of sale

c) Eastern Study

BIZCOMPS Eastern Study is an annual study of over 3,060 actual businesses sold totaling over $787 million. These sales have been subdivided into a number of different categories to provide even more useful information. The sold businesses are compared by:

- Sales price to gross sales (also graphed and with medians)
- Sales price to seller's discretionary earnings (also graphed and with medians)
- Actual down payment versus all cash
- Rent as a percent of gross sales
- The value of furniture, fixtures, and equipment
- The value of inventory at time of sale

BIZCOMPS Special Food Service

This special food service edition includes restaurants, fast food, delicatessens, catering, coffee houses, and cocktail lounges. It is an annual study of over 1,500 actual food-service businesses sold totaling over $200 million. The sold businesses are compared by:

- Sales price to gross sales (also graphed and with medians)
- Sales price to seller's earnings (also graphed and with medians)
- Actual down payment versus all cash
- Rent as a percent of gross sales
- The value of furniture, fixtures, and equipment
- The value of inventory at time of sale

BIZCOMPS is also available through various valuation software packages, including www.BVMaretdata.com.

Business Valuation Resources

Business Valuation Resources
7412 S.W. Beaverton-Hillsdale Highway, Suite 106
Portland, Oregon 97225
(888) 287-8258
www.BVLibrary.com
www.BVMarketdata.com

Pratt's Stats™

Pratt's Stats™ is a private transaction database that contains data variously described as guideline company, guideline transaction, comparable sales data, business comparable, and/or market data. Specifically, *Pratt's Stats™* compiles and reports information on up to 80 data points, including 11 valuation multiples and eight financial ratios, highlighting the financial and transactional details of the sales of privately and closely held companies. Primarily, the data found in *Pratt's Stats™* is used to conduct the market approach to valuing a business in an effort to determine a business's fair market value or to perform financial research on the pricing of similar companies. Additionally, *Pratt's Stats*™ data is used in price discovery by entrepreneurs, investors, advisors, and business owners who are considering a business purchase or sale. A significant benefit of the data found in *Pratt's Stats*™ is its ability to remove marketplace uncertainty and provide the user with detailed, meaningful financial and transactional information about "real world" business sales.

As of May 2006, *Pratt's Stats*™ had compiled details on over 8,600 private and closely held business sales since 1990, ranging in deal price from under $1,000,000 to $7,300,000,000. The industries represented in *Pratt's Stats*™ are no less diverse, as evidenced by the roughly 680 unique Standard Industry Classification (SIC) codes and 820 unique North American Industry Classification System (NAICS) codes.

Public Stats™

Public Stats™ is a public transaction database. Specifically, *Public Stats*™ compiles and reports information on 62 data points, including 10 valuation multiples and eight financial ratios, highlighting the financial and transactional details of the sales of publicly held companies. Primarily, the data found in *Public Stats*™ is used to conduct the market approach to valuing a business in an effort to determine a business's fair market value or to perform financial research on the pricing of similar companies. A significant benefit of the data found in *Public Stats*™ is its ability to remove marketplace uncertainty and provide the user with detailed, meaningful financial and transactional information about "real world" business sales.

As of May 2006, *Public Stats*™ had compiled details on approximately 1,970 public company business sales since 1995, ranging in deal price from under $1,000,000 to $114,000,000,000. The industries represented in *Public Stats*™ are no less diverse, as evidenced by the roughly 380 unique SIC codes and 430 unique NAICS codes.

Mergerstat®/Shannon Pratt's Control Premium Study™

The *Mergerstat®/Shannon Pratt's Control Premium Study*™ is a Web-based tool used to quantify minority discounts and control premiums used in the business valuation, business appraisal, venture capital, and merger and acquisition (M&A) professions. Subscribers to the *Mergerstat®/Shannon Pratt's Control Premium Study*™ are granted access to all of the details in the database, including the control premium, five valuation multiples, and the available information to calculate the return on equity (ROE) (Net income / [book value per share $\times$ number of shares outstanding]).

Approximately 58% of the *Mergerstat®/Shannon Pratt's Control Premium Study*™ represents U.S.-based companies, with the remainder being international companies. Subscribers will instantly gain access to eight plus years of valuable back data (1998–present). The database has also been enhanced with the addition of the transaction purpose code, classifying each transaction into either a horizontal, vertical, conglomerate, or financial transaction.

As of May 2006, the *Mergerstat®/Shannon Pratt's Control Premium Study*™ contained 5,010 total transactions, with over 750 deals in business services, over 670 deals on depository institutions, and 191 deals in the communications industry. Fifty-two percent of the deals in the database have net sales of less than $100 million, with the remainder having net sales greater than $100 million.

Institute of Business Appraisers

Institute of Business Appraisers
PO Box 17410
Plantation, Florida 33318
(954) 584-1144
www.go-iba.org

IBA Market Database

IBA's *Market Database* is the largest database of guideline transactions for valuing midsized and smaller businesses. The database includes information on over 30,300 sales of closely held businesses in more than 725 SIC codes. Access to the database is free to IBA members.

FactSet Mergerstat

FactSet Mergerstat LLC
2150 Colorado Avenue, Suite 150
Santa Monica, California 90404
Phone: (310) 315-3100
Fax: (310) 829-4855
E-mail: info@mergerstat.com
www.mergerstat.com

Mergerstat Review (annual)

The *Mergerstat Review* analyzes mergers and acquisitions involving U.S. companies, including privately held, publicly traded, and foreign companies. It also analyzes unit divestitures, management buyouts, and certain asset sales. It includes industry analysis by size, premium, and transaction multiples. It also provides trend analysis by seller, type, deal size, and industry, as well as offering 25 years of summary M&A statistics, including average premium and price/earnings (P/E) ratio.

Flashwire Monthly (monthly)

Published electronically each month and delivered in PDF format via e-mail, the *Flashwire Monthly* covers the world of mergers and acquisitions. This unique publication contains analyses and graphics that quickly give readers an understanding of the latest trends in M&A. Each issue of the *Flashwire Monthly* is packed with the analysis of the M&A world and the most valuable aggregate statistics from their comprehensive *Factset Mergerstat* database.

- Key trend information for the overall and middle M&A markets, such as deal volume, deal value, mega-deals, leading buyers, leading industries, leading sectors, cross-border deals, U.S. regional deals, average P/E, average premiums, payment methods, and much more
- Industry reports on the Internet, telecommunications, health care, banking, and much more

- Special reports on technology, the public and private M&A markets, cancellation fees, individual industry activity, etc.
- Leading financial and legal advisor rankings

Online Transaction Roster

The *Online Transaction Roster* provides unlimited access to comparable transaction data (where available) for each transaction tracked by *Factset Mergerstat*:

- Seller and buyer SIC codes, location, and description
- Announced date, closed date, and base price
- P/E ratio and payment method
- An insightful synopsis of the transaction

An easy-to-use interface with quick and flexible custom search capability allows you to:

- Search deals by seller industry, broken down into 49 intelligent categories.
- Search by seller SIC code breakdowns.
- Search by seller and/or buyer name.
- Search a specific year, current year, or the entire database.

Flashwire Weekly (weekly)

Published electronically each week, and delivered in PDF format via e-mail, every issue contains:

- A list of M&A deals in the United States
- Charts and graphs showing valuable M&A trend information on middle market transactions
- A review of recent deals of the past week
- Plus, market and industry features and a regular dealmakers-in-the-news column

Delivery is immediate, arriving each Monday via e-mail as it's published.

Control Premium Study

This is an annual subscription published in four quarterly installments. The *Control Premium Study* tracks acquisition premiums for completed transactions involving publicly traded target companies where a controlling interest was acquired. Analysis compares acquisition prices to the trading prices one day, one week, one month, and two months prior to the announcement date of the transaction. In addition, an event study is performed for each transaction to ascertain the target company's common stock price per share unaffected by the acquisition announcement. The study indicates the percentage of shares held before and after the transaction as well as additional information.

M&A Decade Library (on CD-ROM)

Each *M&A Decade Library* contains 10 editions of the annual *Mergerstat Review*, spanning 10 consecutive years from 1990 to 2000. Each edition contains in-depth statistical, industry, geographic, and historical analysis of M&A activity, plus multiyear trend analysis.

NVST.com
NVST.com, Inc.
1100 Dexter Ave. North
Seattle, Washington 98109
(800) 910-NVST (6878) or
(203) 676-3802
www.nvst.com

Business Valuation by Industry (series)

This comprehensive series, now in its ninth edition, reports the details gathered from in-depth studies on the sale of thousands of small to midsize companies. Included are purchase price ratios, financial background on buyers and sellers, recent initial public offerings (IPOs), industry forecasts, and rule-of-thumb valuations for businesses of all sizes in any industry.

Corporate Growth Report (weekly)

The *Corporate Growth Report* contains the *Deal Retriever* online database, which contains thousands of leading M&A transactions. The *Deal Retriever's Online Database* provides access to transactional data, including:

- Purchase price ratios for transactions
- Takeover speculations
- Complete detailed summaries for each transaction
- Current and historical stock prices
- Industry valuations
- Financial statement data
- M&A news
- Transaction details

M&A Insight Online Transaction Database

M&A Insight is an online searchable database of over 13,900 mid-cap and large-cap M&A transactions. Transactions have been tracked since 1995 and are updated weekly.

Merger & Acquisition Sourcebook (annual)

Merger & Acquisition Sourcebook is a professional desktop reference book that summarizes the prior year's M&A activity. Purchase price details are reported on the year's biggest transactions, presented by industry and sorted by SIC number.

Features of the *Sourcebook*:

- Complete coverage of public and private M&A deals
- Financial data for three to five prior years
- Purchase price ratios
- In-depth industry valuations
- Complete descriptions of the most active buyers by industry
- Analysis of industries with high takeover activity
- List of takeover targets
- IPO valuations
- Termination announcements

Merger & Acquisition the Dealmaker's Journal (monthly)

Merger & Acquisition the Dealmaker's Journal is a monthly magazine published by Source Media covering the latest methods and influences impacting the buying and selling of businesses.

Thomson

Thomson PPC
Practitioners Publishing Company
PO Box 966
Fort Worth, Texas 76101-0966
(800) 323-8724
www.donedeals.com

Done Deals®

Done Deals®, with over 7,200 transactions, is a comprehensive source of unique midmarket transaction data, with approximately half the deals under $15 million and half over $15 million, and approximately 79 percent of the selling companies being privately owned.

The *Done Deals®* database provides access to corporate transaction details for private and public midmarket companies sold for purchase prices between $1 million and $1 billion.

Done Deals® has many significant features, including the following:

- It is the only transaction database that includes financial information subjected to analysis by the SEC in filings made by public companies after acquiring other entities.
- It includes over 7,200 transactions for private and public midmarket companies with up to 250 new transactions added each quarter. The median transaction size is $15 million.
- Over 79 percent of the companies sold were privately owned, and another 11 percent were subsidiaries of public companies.
- The reported price multiples include: P/E; price/EBITDA; price/cash flow from operations; price/revenue; price/assets; and price/stockholders' equity.
- Online access is available 24/7 with weekly updates.

Thomson Financial
195 Broadway
New York, New York 10007
(800) 782-5555
www.thomson.com/financial

SDC Platinum™ (previously Securities Data Corp.)

SDC Platinum™ is a financial transactions database that accounts for the entire global financial marketplace. The database provides detailed information on new issues, M&A, syndicated loans, private equity, project finance, poison pills, and more. *SDC Platinum™* satisfies the need for a global reach from a local perspective with an international team of expert analysts researching hundreds of sources daily. The database is now in version 2.3.

Chapter 13

The Capitalized Excess Earnings Method

As will be discussed in Chapter 14, the asset-based approach can be applied on either (1) a collective basis or (2) a discrete basis. When the asset-based approach is applied on a collective basis, all of the intangible value of the business—in excess of its tangible asset value—is estimated in the aggregate. When the asset-based approach is applied on a discrete basis, the individual intangible assets of the business are identified and quantified. The capitalized excess earnings method is a common method for estimating the collective intangible value of the business. This chapter describes the capitalized excess earnings method (or the collective basis application) of the asset-based valuation approach.

Some analysts consider the excess earnings method to be an income approach valuation method. In truth, the classification of any valuation method is purely a semantic matter. The classification of a particular valuation method in no way affects the applicability (or lack of applicability) of that method.

In this book, we classify the capitalized excess earnings method as an asset-based approach method. That is because the conclusion of the application of the capitalized excess earnings method is an indication of the value of an asset: the company's intangible value. And, the valuation of a business by reference to its component assets (both tangible and intangible)—whether the intangible assets are appraised on a collective basis or a discrete basis—is the very definition of an asset-based approach.

Some analysts disparage the capitalized excess earnings method. They allege that this method is obsolete and that it is formulaic and mechanical. It is true that the capitalized excess earnings method is sometimes referred to as "the formula method." This does not mean that the method is formulaic or mechanical. Rather, the application of the capitalized excess earnings method requires a great deal of analysis and judgment. In fact, one conclusion of this chapter is that the capitalized excess earnings method requires as much (or more) analysis and judgment on the part of the analyst than do other business valuation methods.

The capitalized excess earnings method—while often used—is often misused. It is sometimes applied by analysts who do not appreciate the subtle complexities of this method. The objective of this chapter is to educate readers about how to deal with these subtle complexities.

The History of the Capitalized Excess Earnings Method

The capitalized excess earnings method is sometimes called the *Treasury method*. This is because this valuation method originally appeared in a 1920 publication by the U.S. Treasury Department entitled Appeals and Review Memorandum Number 34 (ARM 34). It was adopted in order to estimate the intangible value of goodwill that breweries and distilleries lost because of the legal imposition of prohibition in the U.S. Treasury Department laws.

Since then, both taxpayers and the IRS have often used (and often misused) this valuation method in connection with business valuations for gift tax, estate tax, and other taxation purposes. Also, (1) perhaps partly because of its fairly wide dissemination and (2) partly because of its apparent simplistic nature, this valuation method is widely adopted in one form or another for other valuation purposes, such as marital dissolution.

In 1968, the IRS updated and restated the ARM 34 valuation method. This restatement was promulgated in IRS Revenue Ruling 68-609. This revenue ruling is reproduced as Exhibit 13–1. Revenue Ruling 68-609 is still in effect today.

The reader should keep in mind that the excess earnings method was originally created for the purpose of valuing the intangible value of a business, *not* for the purpose of valuing the company as a whole. Consequently, perhaps the most

Exhibit 13–1

Revenue Ruling 68-609

The "formula" approach may be used in determining the fair market value of intangible assets of a business only if there is no better basis available for making the determination; A.R.M. 34, A.R.M. 68, O.D. 937, and Revenue Ruling 65–192 superseded.

SECTION 1001.—DETERMINATION OF AMOUNT OF AND RECOGNITION OF GAIN OR LOSS

26 CFR 1.1001-1: Computation of gain or loss. Rev. Rul. 68-609* (Also section 167; 1.167(a)-3)

The purpose of this Revenue Ruling is to update and restate, under the current statute and regulations, the currently outstanding portions of A.R.M. 34, C.B. 2, 31 (1920), A.R.M. 68, C.B. 3, 43 (1920), and O.D. 937, C.B. 4, 43 (1921).

The question presented is whether the "formula" approach, the capitalization of earnings in excess of a fair rate of return on net tangible assets, may be used to determine the fair market value of the intangible assets of a business.

The "formula" approach may be stated as follows:

A percentage return on the average annual value of the tangible assets used in a business is determined, using a period of years (preferably not less than five) immediately prior to the valuation date. The amount of the percentage return on tangible assets, thus determined, is deducted from the average earnings of the business for such period and the remainder, if any, is considered to be the amount of the average annual earnings from the intangible assets of the business for the period. This amount (considered as the average annual earnings from intangibles), capitalized at a percentage of, say, 15 to 20 percent, is the value of the intangible assets of the business determined under the "formula" approach.

The percentage of return on the average annual value of the tangible assets used should be the percentage prevailing in the industry involved at the date of valuation, or (when the industry percentage is not available) a percentage of 8 to 10 percent may be used.

The 8 percent rate of return and the 15 percent rate of capitalization are applied to tangibles and intangibles, respectively, of businesses with a small risk factor and stable and regular earnings; the 10 percent rate of return and 20 percent rate of capitalization are applied to businesses in which the hazards of business are relatively high.

The above rates are used as examples and are not appropriate in all cases. In applying the "formula" approach, the average

earnings period and the capitalization rates are dependent upon the facts pertinent thereto in each case.

The past earnings to which the formula is applied should fairly reflect the probable future earnings. Ordinarily, the period should not be less than five years, and abnormal years, whether above or below the average, should be eliminated. If the business is a sole proprietorship or partnership, there should be deducted from the earnings of the business a reasonable amount for services performed by the owner or partners engaged in the business. See *Lloyd B. Sanderson Estate v Commissioner*, 42 F 2d 160 (1930). Further, only the tangible assets entering into net worth, including accounts and bills receivable in excess of accounts and bills payable, are used for determining earnings on the tangible assets. Factors that influence the capitalization rate include (1) the nature of the business, (2) the risk involved, and (3) the stability or irregularity of earnings.

The "formula" approach should not be used if there is better evidence available from which the value of intangibles can be determined. If the assets of a going business are sold upon the basis of a rate of capitalization that can be substantiated as being realistic, though it is not within the range of figures indicated here as the ones ordinarily to the adopted, the same rate of capitalization should be used in determining the value of intangibles.

Accordingly, the "formula" approach may be used for determining the fair market value of intangible assets of a business only if there is no better basis therefore available.

See also Revenue Ruling-59-60, C.B. 1959-1, 237, as modified by Revenue Ruling 65-193, C.B. 1965-2, 370, which sets forth the proper approach to use in the valuation of closely-held corporate stocks for estate and gift tax purposes. The general approach, methods, and factors, outlined in Revenue Ruling 59-60, as modified, are equally applicable to valuations of corporate stocks for income and other tax purposes as well as for estate and gif tax purposes. They apply also to problems involving the determination of the fair market value of business interests of any type, including partnerships and proprietorships, and intangible assets for all tax purposes.

A.R.M. 34, A.R.M. 68, and O.D. 937 are superseded, since the positions set forth therein are restated to the extent applicable under current law in this Revenue Ruling. Revenue Ruling 65-192, C.B. 1965-2, 259, which contained restatements of A.R.M. 34 and A.R.M. 68, is also superseded.

_____
* Prepared pursuant to Rev. Proc. 67-6. C.B. 1967-1, 576.

SOURCE: Rev. Rul. 68-609, 1968-2 C.B. 327.

appropriate application of the excess earnings method is for the purpose of *allocating* total value between tangible and intangible assets. Examples of such purposes include:

- Marital dissolution cases in jurisdictions where personal goodwill value is considered a personal rather than a marital asset and therefore needs to be separately valued from the rest of the business enterprise
- Conversions from C corporation status to S corporation status
- Eminent domain cases where the tangible asset values and intangible asset values have to be recognized separately
- Property tax cases where a company's tangible assets are subject to property taxation but its intangible assets are not
- Economic damage or deprivation cases, such as a breach of a contract or the infringement of a patent or trademark

The capitalized excess earnings method is most often used to value small- and medium-sized businesses; however, it may be used to value larger businesses, especially for the purposes listed above.

The Capitalized Excess Earnings Valuation Method

Practical Application of This Method

There are several variations in the application of this valuation method. The most typical procedures in the capitalized excess earnings method are summarized as follows:

1. Estimate the net tangible asset value for the subject business. The tangible assets should be appraised at a standard of value and a premise of value consistent with the standard of value appropriate to the business enterprise value. The various standards of value and premises of value related to tangible assets are discussed in Chapter 14, with regard to the asset accumulation method.

   This estimate of value relates to the net tangible assets of the company only. As we will see, net tangible assets may or may not include such discrete intangible assets as leasehold interests, patents, trademarks, and copyrights. However, if the intangibles such as patents, trademarks, and so on, are separately identified and valued, then the only intangible asset remaining might be goodwill.
2. Estimate a normalized level of economic earnings. There are many different definitions of economic earnings that may be used in this method. These various measures of economic earnings were discussed in Chapter 9 related to the income approach.
3. Quantify the amount of excess earnings. First, estimate an appropriate fair rate of return on the estimated net tangible asset value of the subject business. Next, multiply the estimated net tangible asset value (from step 1) by the estimated fair rate of return. This product estimates the amount of economic earnings that would be attributable to the company's net tangible assets. Next, subtract that fair return on net tangible assets amount from the normalized level of economic earnings estimated in step 2. The result of this procedure is

sometimes called the *excess earnings* or the *excess economic income*. This residual is the amount of economic earnings above a fair rate of return on the net tangible asset value of the subject company.

4. Estimate an appropriate direct capitalization rate to apply to the amount of excess economic earnings. These excess earnings are the economic earnings attributable to the intangible value of the subject business (as opposed to being attributable to the net tangible assets of the subject business).

5. Capitalize the excess economic earnings at that estimated direct capitalization rate.

6. Add the values from step 1 (i.e., the net tangible asset value) and step 5 (i.e., the intangible value). The sum of these two values indicates the value of the subject business.

7. Perform a sanity check by calculating the implied overall capitalization rate.

The Seeming Simplicity of This Method

In a subsequent section, we will consider the many analytical decisions and judgments encountered in each of the above valuation procedures. The discussion will indicate that the application of this valuation method is anything but simple. First, let's consider an illustration of an application of the capitalized excess earnings method.

An Illustration

In this illustration, let's assume that Client Corporation has a net tangible asset value of $2,000,000 as of December 31, 2005. Let's also assume that Client Corporation is expected to earn a normalized level of economic earnings (that we will define as net income in this illustration) of $800,000 per year. For the purpose of this example, we have estimated a fair rate of return of 15 percent on the Client Corporation net tangible assets. Also, for purposes of this illustration only, we have estimated that the appropriate direct capitalization rate for excess earnings to Client Corporation is 20 percent. (The issue of the estimation of direct capitalization rates is discussed later in the chapter.)

In this simplified application of the capitalized excess earnings method, the business enterprise value of Client Corporation is estimated in Exhibit 13–2.

Exhibit 13–2

Client Corporation Business Enterprise Value Capitalized Excess Earnings Method as of December 31, 2005

Net tangible asset value		$2,000,000
Normalized economic earnings	$800,000	
Less: Economic earnings attributable to net tangible assets ($2,000,000 × 15%)	($300,000)	
"Excess" economic earnings	$500,000	
Indicated intangible value of capitalized excess economic earnings ($500,000 ÷ 20%)		$2,500,000
Indicated Client Corporation business enterprise value		$4,500,000

In this simple illustration, the Client Corporation business enterprise value is $4,500,000. This value is the sum of (1) a $2,000,000 value of net tangible assets and (2) a $2,500,000 intangible value in the nature of goodwill.

Analysis of the Capitalized Excess Earnings Method

Even though the capitalized excess earnings method has been criticized by some analysts, it is commonly used for many business valuation purposes. Therefore, this section will consider the analytical strengths and weaknesses of this valuation method.

First, it is worth reiterating that the Treasury Department did not promulgate this valuation method to estimate the value of the total business enterprise. Rather, this valuation method was promulgated to value the goodwill, or the total intangible value (in excess of the net tangible asset value), of breweries and other companies affected by the Prohibition of the 1920s. Nonetheless, it is logical from an economics perspective that the intangible value identified by the capitalized excess earnings valuation method should be added to the net tangible asset value of a company in order to estimate the total business enterprise value.

Unfortunately for analysts, IRS Revenue Ruling 68-609 contains many ambiguities, undefined variables, and unanswered questions. Various valuation analysts have adopted a wide variety of interpretations to these ambiguities and undefined variables.

In the following section, we will discuss these ambiguities and undefined variables. We will consider these ambiguities and variables in the same order as they were presented in the "Practical Application of This Method" section above.

Estimation of the "Net Tangible Asset Value"

The first procedure in the capitalized excess earnings method is the estimation of the net tangible asset value for the subject business. Unfortunately, Revenue Ruling 68-609 does not specifically define what it means by *net tangible asset value*. For example, the Revenue Ruling does not provide substantive guidance with respect to the important question "net of what?"

Definition of Net Tangible Asset Value. Revenue Ruling 68-609 offers little procedural guidance to analysts with respect to either (1) the appropriate standard of value or (2) the appropriate premise of value that should be used when estimating *net tangible asset value*.

As with the application of other business valuation methods, the determination of standard of value and premise of value with respect to the capitalized excess earnings method should be concluded after the analyst's consideration of (1) the purpose and objective of the individual appraisal, (2) the quantity and quality of available data, and (3) the highest and best use of the subject business interest.

There is general agreement among analysts that the most common definition of *net tangible asset value* is the fair market value standard and the value in continued use premise. Typically, this standard of value and premise of value would be measured by one or more of the generally accepted asset appraisal approaches, which will be discussed in Chapter 14 related to the asset accumulation method.

IRS Private Letter Ruling 79-05013 takes the position that the appropriate standard of value for the net tangible assets should be fair market value:

> Rev. Rul. 68-609 addresses the determination of fair market value of intangible assets by the formula approach, and for this reason it is proper that all terms used in the formula be consistent. The formula uses value in terms of fair market value, so the term '... value of the tangible assets used in a business,' in the formula, should be in terms of fair market values, as defined in Rev. Rul. 59-60.[1]

As a practical matter, analysts do not always rely upon fair market value appraisals of all of the subject tangible assets in the capitalized excess earnings valuation of a large company. This is because it would be very time consuming and, often, prohibitively expensive to conduct real estate and personal property appraisals of all of the tangible assets of a substantial business.

Therefore, analysts often resort to using the book value of the subject tangible assets simply because it is too complicated and time consuming of a process to obtain appraisals of tangible asset fair market value. This use of book value for estimating the value of the subject net tangible assets is not preferred. However, tangible assets are often such a major component of the business value for some corporations that it would not be practical to use the capitalized excess earnings method if this simplifying assumption was not made.

Should Asset Value Adjustments Be Tax-Affected? Because the objective of the analysis is to estimate the value of subject net tangible assets on a continued use basis—on which a reasonable rate of return should be earned—the analyst normally does not make any adjustment to recognize the income tax effect of unrealized (built-in) gains or losses. This is because the business will not, in the normal course of business, sell its tangible assets at their appraised values. Therefore, in reality, no income tax liability will arise.

However, analysts should not just ignore income tax considerations. For example, there could be cases (e.g., a large inventory write-up where a tax payment on the sale of the inventory is imminent) where an income tax adjustment may be appropriate.

Are Intangible Assets Included or Excluded? Typically, as the phrase *net tangible asset value* implies, intangible asset values should be removed from the subject company balance sheet before performing the capitalized excess earnings analysis. However, some analysts leave on the balance sheet those intangible assets that are already capitalized on the subject company financial statements. Examples of intangible assets that may already be recognized on the company's financial statements would include purchased goodwill, purchased computer software, computer software internally developed in anticipation of resale, and so forth.

Treatment of nonoperating Assets. There is general agreement among analysts that it is preferable to remove nonoperating and/or excess assets from the balance sheet (and the related economic income from the income statement) and to treat such items separately in the capitalized excess earnings method.

Treatment of Leased Real Estate. In some closely held corporations (including substantial corporations), the real estate is owned separately by the business

---

[1] Priv. Ltr. Rul. 79-05013 (Oct. 24, 1979).

owners and leased to the company. In these cases, it is important for the analyst to ensure that the real estate rent is adjusted to market rent. And, if the real estate lease is a long-term lease, it is not uncommon for analysts to capitalize the lease—that is, to treat the real estate as if it was owned instead of leased.

Estimation of Net Tangible Asset Value. There is no universally accepted conclusion as to what accounts should be "netted out" in the estimation of net tangible asset value. For example, various analysts have interpreted net tangible assets to mean any one of the following:

1. Gross assets net of accumulated depreciation (i.e., current market value of the tangible assets net of economic depreciation)
2. Net current value of the financial assets and the tangible assets less current liabilities only
3. Net current value of the financial assets and the tangible assets minus all liabilities

The most common interpretation of the term *net tangible asset value* is alternative 2—that is, net current value of the financial assets and the tangible assets less current liabilities only. However, if properly applied, alternative interpretations, such as the "average" of net tangible assets employed during the year, may be equally relevant.

Estimation of the Value of Debt. The conceptual answer to the question of the amount of debt to be deducted in this method is that it depends on when the debt is likely to be paid. If payment at face value is imminent (e.g., if a payment is triggered by the very transaction for which the valuation is being conducted), then it is appropriate to value the subject debt at face value. If the debt may remain outstanding for a period of time, many practitioners would value the subject debt at its fair market value.

Estimation of the "Normalized Level of Earnings"

Step 2 in the capitalized excess earnings method is the estimation of a normalized level of earnings. This is also called a normalized level of economic income. This more generic description is particularly appropriate because Revenue Ruling 68-609 does not specifically define the term *earnings*. It does, however, make the key statement that the earnings "*should fairly reflect the probable future earnings*" (emphasis supplied).

When suggesting the use of past years' earnings as a basis for estimating future earnings, the Revenue Ruling notes that abnormal years should be eliminated from consideration. Analysts generally agree that nonrecurring income and/or expense items should be eliminated from any historical period that is used for the earnings base for projecting future normalized earnings.

Treatment of Nonoperating Income. Consistent with the removal of nonoperating assets from the net tangible asset base, related nonoperating income typically should be removed from the earnings base.

Treatment of Owners' Compensation. Revenue Ruling 68-609 states that "if the business is a sole proprietorship or partnership, there should be deducted from the earnings of the business a reasonable amount for services performed by the owner or partners engaged in the business." Analysts generally agree that owner/employee's abnormal compensation should be adjusted to a normal level of compensation in the valuation of a closely held business. This is true whether the owner/operator compensation is either above normal levels or below normal levels. The "normal level" of compensation is generally considered to be the expense of employing a nonowner/employee to perform the services currently performed by the owner/employee.

Treatment of Income Taxes. The measure of earnings—or economic income—to be capitalized should normally be net of federal and state income taxes paid by the subject business. Many closely held businesses operate as S corporations or other pass-through entities. It often is appropriate to tax-affect the economic income even where the subject business does not pay income taxes. The reason for this is, if the subject business were to be sold to a corporation that would have to pay income taxes on the subject's income, in estimating that buyer's investment value, the buyer almost surely would tax-affect the economic income. If that actual buyer were also the typical "willing buyer," the tax-affected earnings would also be the appropriate measure of economic income to use in estimating fair market value. Also, a significant (and not uncommon) problem arises when tax liability flows through to an owner but the earnings giving rise to the tax liability are not paid out. Tax-affecting the subject business earnings is one of several possible ways to treat this problem for purposes of valuation. (See Chapter 26, "Valuing S Corporation Stock and Interests in Other Pass-Through Entities.")

Again, with regard to the income tax issue, what is most important is consistency in application. That is, the measure of "earnings" or economic income that is selected—whether it is net income, net cash flow, or operating cash flow and whether it is before tax or after tax—should be consistent with (1) the measure of the fair rate of return and (2) the measure of the direct capitalization rate.

Definition of "Earnings." Revenue Ruling 68-609 does not provide a definition of the term *earnings*. Is it net income? Net cash flow? Or some other measure of economic income?

There is some agreement among analysts that the economic variable best suited to represent earnings in the context of the capitalized excess earnings method is cash flow. However, even within this general agreement, there is a difference in opinion about whether (1) net cash flow or (2) operating cash flow are the best measures of economic income. These different measures of economic income were discussed in Chapter 9, related to the income approach. The trend among analysts is to favor net cash flow. This is because that measure of income is the amount that the stakeholders can take out of the business without disrupting operations.

Appropriate Rate of Return on Tangible Assets

Several alternative procedures are used to quantify the appropriate rate of return on the subject company's net tangible assets. Most analysts agree that the required return is dependent largely on the asset mix. The riskier the assets, the higher the rate of return required to support them.

One common procedure is to use a weighted average of the company's cost of debt and cost of equity, with the weighting based on the proportions of the various asset classes that can be financed by debt. The following is an example of this appropriate rate of return procedure.

Asset Class	Percent Financible	Borrowing Capacity	Capacity
Receivables	$10,000,000	80%	$8,000,000
Inventory	20,000,000	60%	12,000,000
Fixtures and equipment	20,000,000	50%	10,000,000
	$50,000,000		$30,000,000

If the company's borrowing cost is 10 percent and its cost of equity is 20 percent, then the weighted average would be calculated as follows:

Debt   @ 10% × 0.6 (i.e., $30,000,000 ÷ $50,000,000)   =   6%
Equity @ 20% × 0.4 (i.e., $20,000,000 ÷ $50,000,000)   =   8%
Weighted average required rate of return on net tangible assets   = 14%

If the subject company is a C corporation that pays income taxes, the cost of debt would be tax-affected by multiplying the cost of debt by 1 minus the income tax rate. For example, if the company's income tax rate is 30 percent, the cost of debt would be $10\% \times (1 - 0.30) = 10\% \times 0.7 = 7\%$.

If the borrowing capacity of a closely held corporation is dependent on personal guarantees of the business owners, this is an additional debt cost factor. While no empirical support for the amount of this cost factor exists, it is reasonable to add to the cost of debt if personal guarantees are involved. Such guarantees carry risk to the guarantor and limit the guarantor's borrowing capacity for purposes unrelated to the subject closely held business.

Some analysts use historical industry average rates of return. The problem with this is that required rates of return, by definition, are based on the future expectations and alternative opportunity cost of the investor. The historical industry rate of return may not be representative of future expectations.

Appropriate Direct Capitalization Rate for Excess Earnings

Since the company's debt rate and the "safe part" of the company's equity rate are typically used in the estimation of the rate of return for net tangible assets, the direct capitalization rate applicable to excess earnings normally would have to be higher than the company's required equity rate.

Most analysts agree that one of the most important factors in the estimation of the direct capitalization rate for excess earnings is the perceived persistence of the excess earnings. The longer the time period and the greater the certainty of the expectation of the excess earnings, the lower the direct capitalization rate. Direct capitalization rates that are equal to the company's cost of equity capital assume a solid earnings base expected to continue well into the future. A low capitalization rate is usually applicable only for a very long and very predictable persistence of the excess earnings.

The selection of the excess earnings direct capitalization rate by these typical considerations is one of the more subjective judgments that are made within the various business valuation methods. However, ultimately, the weighted average of the capitalization rates for the net tangible assets and excess earnings (weighted by the amount of value ascribed to each of the two components) should be the same as the company's overall direct capitalization rate.

Commentary on the Estimation of Direct Capitalization Rates. Analyst David Bishop offers the following insights regarding what procedures *not* to use in the estimation of the appropriate direct capitalization rates:

Automatic reliance on industry rates such as the return on total assets, tangible net worth or equity (e.g., Risk Management Associates [RMA] rates) can neither assure a reasonable rate of return on tangible assets nor provide support for the development of the excess earnings capitalization rate (EECR). The inappropriateness of the automatic use of such rates is explained as follows:

1. Industry return rates are calculated on book values and the appraisal process requires fair market values.
2. Industry return rates attribute all earnings to those book valued assets. The objective in the excess earnings method (EEM) is to segregate the return stream appropriate to the fair market value (FMV) of the tangibles and attribute the excess earnings, if any, to the intangible assets.
3. Industries with poor performance will have low rates of return and industries with excellent performance will have higher rates of return. When an appraiser (or valuation software program) automatically uses these rates, the higher rates of the more successful industries produce lower values; conversely, the lower rates of poor industries indicate higher values.

These differences invalidate the use of such rates despite their surface appeal. The objective is to determine the *expected market rates* not simply the *achieved book rates*. Automatic use of industry rates implicitly assumes *achieved* rates are equal to *expected* rates. While expected rates may be found to be equal to *achieved* rates, this relationship must be determined, not assumed.[2]

Comprehensive Example

Exhibits 13–3 through 13–6 present a comprehensive example of the application of the capitalized excess earnings method in the valuation of a small closely held corporation.

Exhibit 13–3 presents the balance sheet at cost for the illustrative company, Small Close Corporation (hereinafter "Small"). Exhibit 13–4 presents an income statement. Exhibit 13–5 presents a calculation of net cash flow for Small.

The objective of this valuation is to estimate the fair market value of 100 percent of the owner's equity of Small, on a controlling ownership interest basis, as of December 31, 2005.

Assume for this example that the appraised fair market value of net tangible assets is $2,500,000.

Assume that the appropriate asset-specific rate of return on the tangible assets is 10 percent. This would be a rate of return specific to the risk and expected return of these tangible assets. For purposes of this illustration, let's assume that this 10 percent

---

[2] David M. Bishop, "Excess Earnings Cap Rate—Six Market Influences," *Business Appraisal Practice*, Winter 1999, p. 6.

Exhibit 13–3

Small Close Corporation Summary Balance Sheet (Historical Cost Basis) as of December 31, 2005

ASSETS		LIABILITIES AND OWNERS' EQUITY	
Current assets (cash, receivables, and inventory)	$1,000,000	Current liabilities (payables and accruals)	$1,000,000
Tangible assets (real estate and equipment—net of accumulated depreciation)	2,000,000	Long-term debt	1,000,000
		Owners' equity	1,000,000
TOTAL ASSETS	$3,000,000	TOTAL LIABILITIES AND OWNERS' EQUITY	$3,000,000

Exhibit 13–4

Small Close Corporation Summary Income Statement for the 12 Months Ended December 31, 2005

Net revenues	$5,000,000
Operating expenses	
Cash expenses	3,700,000
Depreciation expense	200,000
Interest expense	100,000
Total expenses	4,000,000
Profit before taxes	1,000,000
Income taxes	400,000
Profit after taxes	$600,000

Exhibit 13–5

Small Close Corporation Calculation of Net Cash Flow for the 12 Months Ended December 31, 2005

Net cash flow (invested capital basis):

	Profit after taxes	$600,000
Plus:	Tax-affected interest expense ($100,000 interest expense less $40,000 income tax expense)	60,000
Equals:	Profit after taxes—invested capital basis	$660,000
Plus:	Depreciation expense	200,000
Less:	Capital expenditures (during 2005)	200,000
Less:	Increase in net working capital (from 12/31/04 to 12/31/05)	100,000
Equals:	Net cash flow (invested capital basis)	$560,000

is the cost of financing for these tangible assets. In other words, let's assume that Small could borrow funds, using some equity, at a blended rate of 10 percent for the purposes of purchasing such tangible assets. Note that in the application of the asset-specific rate of return procedure, there could be several asset-specific rates of return: one for land, one for buildings, one for machinery and equipment, and so on.

At this point, we need to estimate an asset-specific direct capitalization rate for goodwill (based on the premise that we are subsuming all of the Small intangible value in the asset called "goodwill"). If we believe that a buyer would pay

Exhibit 13–6

Small Close Corporation Application of Capitalized Excess Earnings Method as of December 31, 2005

	Net cash flow (after-tax)		$560,000	(Exhibit 13–5)
	Fair market value of net tangible assets	$2,500,000		
Times:	Asset-specific required rate of return on net tangible assets	× 10%		
	Required level of economic income		250,000	
	Excess economic income (i.e., net cash flow less required level of economic income)		310,000	
Divided by:	Direct capitalization rate (based upon applying an asset-specific required rate of return on goodwill)		25%	
Equals:	Estimate of intangible asset value in the nature of goodwill		1,240,000	
Add:	Fair market value of net tangible assets		2,500,000	
	Implied value of Small invested capital (including existing equity and debt)		3,740,000	
Less:	Existing debt		1,000,000	
Indicated value of Small equity			2,740,000	

for four years of expected earnings from the company's goodwill (which assumes a reasonably reliable and persistent expected income stream from the goodwill), then the direct capitalization rate would be 25 percent ($1 \div 4 = 0.25$). The application of these asset-specific direct capitalization rates is presented in Exhibit 13–6.

Readers should note that the estimation of the direct capitalization rate applicable to excess earnings is the most subjective procedure in the excess earnings method. It is a matter of the analyst's informed judgment. There is no generally accepted procedure to estimate the direct capitalization rate without first valuing the overall business enterprise. And, there is little or no published market-derived empirical evidence with regard to the selection of the excess earnings direct capitalization rate.

Exhibit 13–6 applies these estimated direct capitalization rates to the excess earnings and adds this value to the value of net tangible assets in order to arrive at an indicated value by the excess earnings method.

We know that the blended, or overall, direct capitalization rate for the entire capital structure should be equal to the company's weighted average cost of capital, less the estimated long-term growth rate in the economic income variable being capitalized. When valuing a controlling ownership interest, analysts typically value the overall capital structure of the subject business as opposed to just the equity of the subject business.

Assume that we developed an overall direct capitalization rate for Small, using the procedures presented in Chapter 10, of 15 percent.

As a "reasonableness check" on the value indications from the excess earnings method in Exhibit 13–6, we can apply this direct capitalization rate to the Small net cash flow to invested capital, and then compare the results:

$$\frac{\$560,000}{0.15} = \$3,733,000$$

The value indication is reasonably close to the $3,740,000 indicated value of the Small invested capital as developed in Exhibit 13–6. If the results were not within a reasonable range of each other, it would be appropriate (1) to examine the assumptions of each method and (2) to make some revisions in order to make one or the other of the two methods more realistic.

The weights assigned to the capital structure components (generally debt and equity) usually should be the "target" weights for the subject company—that is, "the proportions of debt and equity that the firm targets for its capital structure over the long-term planning period."[3] This often is based on industry average capital structures.

In the comprehensive example, we did not illustrate the effect of the alternative growth rate projections on the excess economic income, on the direct capitalization rate, and (ultimately) on the estimation of goodwill. The effect of growth rate projections on the estimate of economic income and on the selected direct capitalization rate is discussed in detail in Chapter 10, related to the income approach.

The Treatment of Negative Goodwill

The capitalized excess earnings method is classified here as an asset-based valuation approach method. In a strict application of this method, all of the subject entity's assets—both tangible and intangible—are valued. However, the capitalization of excess economic income procedure itself values only one asset: the entity's intangible value in the nature of goodwill. This intangible value is the value of the company's economic income (if any) over and above a reasonable rate of return on the value of the company's net tangible assets. A significant conceptual and practical question is: What if the subject company's economic income is less than a reasonable rate of return on the net tangible assets?

The result of this phenomenon (i.e., the amount of economic income is less than a fair return on net tangible assets) is often referred to as *negative goodwill*. Negative goodwill indicates that the collective going-concern value of the total subject entity is less than the sum of the individual values of the entity's total tangible assets.

In such a situation, the subject company's economic income is insufficient to justify buying the business on the basis of the collective value of its individual tangible and intangible assets. In such an instance, the collective value of the company's assets (including tangible assets and any discrete intangible assets) would be reduced to the level of economic value indicated by the company's overall direct capitalization rate.

Should the adjusted net asset value indicated by the application of the company's negative goodwill fall below the liquidation value of the company's net assets, an analyst may conclude that the business would be worth more on a liquidation basis than on a going-concern basis. That is, a liquidation of the subject business would be a rational economic choice.

---

[3] Alfred Rappaport, *Creating Shareholder Value*, rev. ed. (New York: The Free Press, 1998), p. 37.

Common Errors in Applying the Capitalized Excess Earnings Method

As mentioned previously, the capitalized excess earnings method is often misused in business valuation. This may be due to the apparent simplicity of this valuation method. In any event, the most common errors in the application of this valuation method are discussed in the following sections.

Failure to Allow for Shareholder/Employee Salary

As noted in Revenue Ruling 68-609 (Exhibit 13–1), "If the business is a sole proprietorship or partnership, there should be deducted from the earnings of the business a reasonable amount for services performed by the owner or partners engaged in the business."

This guidance is equally valid with regard to the valuation of even the most substantial closely held corporations. And, this guidance is noteworthy whether the shareholder/employees are receiving compensation (and other perquisites) that are materially greater than or less than industry norms. For example, in established and financially successful corporations, shareholder/employees sometimes pay themselves executive compensation in amounts that are materially greater than nonshareholder/employees would earn for the same services. Also, in development stage or unprofitable corporations, shareholder/employees sometimes pay themselves less than what they would pay to nonshareholder/employees for the same services. This is because the shareholder/employees would rather maximize the value of their business as opposed to maximizing their current (taxable) individual incomes.

Nonetheless, analysts often perform valuations using the capitalized excess earnings method without including a reasonable (or industry normal) allowance for executive compensation to the shareholder/employees for the services that they perform.

Failure to Use Realistic Estimate of Future Normalized Earnings

To the extent that this valuation method is valid, it depends on a reasonable estimate of the subject business's normalized earnings. As noted in Revenue Ruling 68-609: "The past earnings to which the formula is applied should fairly reflect the probable future earnings."

However, this valuation method is sometimes applied naively either (1) to the latest year earnings of the subject business or (2) to some simple or weighted average of recent years' earnings of the subject business. This measure of normalized earnings is calculated without considering whether the earnings measure being used fairly reflects the probable future earnings.

Inconsiderate use of some historical earnings base usually results in either an undervaluation or an overvaluation of the subject business. As the guidance provided by Revenue Ruling 68-609 indicates, historical earnings should be used in the application of this method only to the extent that those historical earnings provide a reasonable indication of future normalized earnings.

Errors in Developing the Appropriate Direct Capitalization Rates

The development of the two direct capitalization rates is critical to the validity of the result of the capitalized excess earnings method. A conceptual approach to the development of the appropriate direct capitalization rates was discussed in an earlier section of this chapter. However, one clearly erroneous procedure for the development of the direct capitalization rates is to use the illustrative rates suggested in the ruling itself.

The revenue ruling, written in 1968, suggests capitalization rates of 8 to 10 percent on net tangible assets and capitalization rates of 15 to 20 percent to be applied to the excess earnings. However, the revenue ruling itself states that:

> The percentage of return . . . should be the percentage prevailing in the industry involved at the date of the valuation. . . . The above rates are used as examples and are not appropriate in all cases. . . . The capitalization rates are dependent upon the facts pertinent thereto in each case.[4]

Both the wording of the revenue ruling and common sense indicate that the specific capitalization rates mentioned in the ruling are illustrative only. The appropriate direct capitalization rates depend on the facts at the time of the valuation. These contemporaneous facts relate to (1) current economic indicators, (2) current capital market indicators, (3) current industry conditions, and (4) current company-specific conditions.

In spite of that, even in the year 2006, some analysts naively use the capitalization rates for the capitalized excess earnings method originally published in the ARM 34 example back in 1920, and repeated in Revenue Ruling 68-609 published in 1968.

Summary

The capitalized excess earnings method (also called the *formula method* or the *Treasury method*) dates back to the period of Prohibition. It was the U.S. Treasury Department's method of determining the amount to compensate distilleries for the loss of their intangible value in the nature of goodwill as a result of the effects of Prohibition.

The IRS's current position with regard to this business valuation method is embodied in Revenue Ruling 68-609 and in Private Letter Ruling 79-05013, both referenced in this chapter.

The capitalized excess earnings method is one of the most widely used (and sometimes misused) methods of business valuation—particularly in regard to valuations performed for marital dissolution purposes. This is because analysts often carelessly apply the mechanics of this "formula method" without considering the sophisticated nuances of this conceptually elegant methodology.

---

[4] Revenue Ruling 68-609, 1968-2 C.B. 327.

In addition, analysts often ignore the professional guidance regarding the proper implementation of this method promulgated in the above IRS references. Therefore, the result of a naive application of this method is a plethora of misapplications of a fundamentally sound (and potentially analytically rigorous) valuation method.

This chapter has developed the proper use of the capitalized excess earnings method. It has quoted the relevant guidance provided in each of the IRS references cited above. And, it has provided guidance on how to develop the four key variables in the capitalized excess earnings method:

1. Net tangible asset value
2. Earnings base to be capitalized
3. Reasonable rate of return on net tangible assets
4. Direct capitalization rate to be applied to the "excess earnings"

The chapter concluded with a discussion of several of the more common errors found in the inexperienced application of the capitalized excess earnings method. By following the guidance in this chapter, the analyst should be able to (1) properly apply the capitalized excess earnings method and (2) identify common errors resulting from a naive application of the capitalized excess earnings method.

Bibliography

Barson, Kalman A. "Is It Time to Bury Revenue Ruling 68-609?" *Fair$hare*, January 1998, pp. 7–8.

Bishop, David M. "Excess Earnings Cap Rate: Six Market Influences." *Business Appraisal Practice*, Winter 1999, pp. 4–9.

Fishman, Jay E. "The Business of Celebrity." *BV Papers*, February 2005. Available at www.BVLibrary.com.

Fishman, Jay E., and William J. Morrison. "Capitalization of Excess Earnings for Talent-Based Personal Service Business." *Fair$hare*, February 1996, p. 13.

George, Thomas. "Managing Capital Assignment in Banks to Optimize ROC." *Journal of Bank Cost & Management Accounting*, 2002.

Getz, Lowell V. "Valuing A/E Firms." *The Valuation Examiner*, May/June 2002, pp. 4–7.

Goodman & Company LLP. "Husband's Earlier Sale Valuation Damages His Later Divorce Valuation." *Valuation Outlook*, Fall 2005.

Hawkins, George B. "The Excess Earning Method—Should It Be Put Out to Pasture in Equitable Distribution Cases." *Fair Value*, 2003 (reprinted from *Fair Value,* Summer 1999), pp. 1–5.

Howe, Harry, Eric E. Lewis, and Jeffrey W. Lippitt. "Estimating Capitalization Rates for the Excess Earnings Method Using Publicly Traded Comparables." American Accounting Association, 1999.

Jenkins, David S. "The Benefits of Hybrid Valuation Models." *The CPA Journal*, January 2006.

Kruschke, Linda L. "Business Valuation Case Law Update" (presented during 2001 IBA National Conference), January 2000–March 2001. Available at www.BVLibrary.com.

Lev, Baruch, and Doron Nissim. "Taxable Income, Future Earnings and Equity Values." *The Accounting Review*, October 2004.

Lippitt, Jeffrey W. "A Comparison of the Earnings Capitalization and the Excess Earnings Method in the Valuation of Closely-Held Businesses." *Journal of Small Business Management*, January 1996.

Lippitt, Jeffrey W., and Nicholas J. Mastriacchio. "Developing Capitalization Rates for Valuing a Business." *The CPA Journal*, November 1995, pp. 24–28.

Luttrell, Mark, and Shannon P. Pratt. "Defining Methodologies." *BValuation Q&A Newsletter,* October 2005. Available at www.BVLibrary.com.

Mastriacchio, Nicholas J., and Jeffrey W. Lippitt. "A Comparison of the Earnings Capitalization and the Excess Earnings Models." *Journal of Small Business Management*, January 1996, pp. 1–12.

Paschall, Michael A. "Kick the Habit: The Excess Earnings Method Must Go." *Business Valuation Review*, vol. 21, no. 3, September 2001, pp. 1–5.

"Practitioners Disagree Strongly on Excess Methodology." *Shannon Pratt's Business Valuation Update*, April 1997, pp.1–13.

Pratt, Shannon P. "The Excess Earnings Method: How to Get a Defensible Result." *Shannon Pratt's Business Valuation Update*, October 1996, pp. 1, 20–21.

Raymond, Richard. "Valuation Expert Provides Insight on *Howell v. Howell*— Court Accepts Value to Owner versus Fair Market Value." *Shannon Pratt's Valuation Update*, June 1999.

Reilly, Robert F. "Identifying and Quantifying Obsolescence in Valuation of Industrial and Commercial Property." *Valuation Strategies*, March/April 2006.

Shayne, Mark. "A Re-examination of Revenue Ruling 68–609." *Fair$hare*, July 1992, pp. 5–8.

Summers, S. Chris. "The Excess Earnings Method," Chapter 15. In Thomas L. West and Jeffrey D. Jones, eds. *Handbook of Business Valuation*. New York: John Wiley & Sons, 1992, pp. 167–76

Walter, James. *Valuation Report,* August 16, 1996. Available at www.BVLibrary.com.

Chapter 14

Asset-Based Approach: Asset Accumulation Method

For the most part, business financial statements are prepared based on the *cost principle* of accounting. That is, assets are usually recorded at their historical purchase/acquisition cost.

There are some exceptions to the application of the cost principle. Companies in certain industries may report their financial statements in compliance with a statutory basis of accounting other than GAAP. And under GAAP, assets that have been permanently impaired have to be written down from their historic cost to their market value. Companies that acquire other companies or assets must restate their assets, both tangible and intangible, to fair value for financial reporting purposes and test for impairment. (SFAS 141, 142, 144, and 157). Also under GAAP, some companies report certain assets at the lower of their historical cost or market value. And, some companies in certain industries report their financial assets (such as investments in marketable securities) at their current market value. Accordingly, analysts who use any asset-based approach valuation method should be sure that they understand the accounting principles that were used to prepare the subject company financial statements.

Under GAAP, wasting assets, such as real estate (other than land) and tangible personal property, are depreciated over their expected useful lives. Therefore, at any point in time, the balance sheet presents the depreciated historical cost for these types of tangible assets. The depreciated historical cost of assets recorded on the balance sheet is often referred to as *book value*. The total depreciated historical cost of the recorded assets minus the total historical values of the recorded liabilities is often referred to as the *net book value* (or sometimes "book value") of the business owners' equity.

A fundamental *accounting* principle is: The book value of assets minus the book value of liabilities equals the book value of the business owners' equity.

A fundamental business *valuation* principle is: The current value of assets minus the current value of liabilities equals the current value of the business owners' equity.

In a business valuation, the relevant standard of value for both the business and the component business assets is the standard that is defined by the purpose and objective of the valuation. Chapter 2 presented several alternative standards of value, including fair market value, fair value, intrinsic or fundamental value, and investment value. Any of these standards of value may be used in a business valuation performed using asset-based approach methods.

Based on the purpose and objective of the valuation, the analyst will apply the appropriate standard of value to the subject equity interest. The standard of value for the individual assets and liabilities may be different from the standard of value for the subject equity interest. For example, the analyst may apply the fair market value standard to the individual assets and liabilities even though a different standard of value is determined for the subject equity interest.

In the asset accumulation method, the analyst restates all of the assets and liabilities of the subject company from their historical cost basis to the appropriate standard of value. For the purpose of this discussion, let's assume that the appropriate standard of value is fair market value. After the revaluation of all asset and liability accounts from their historical cost basis to fair market value, the analyst can then apply the axiomatic "assets minus liabilities" formula to indicate the value of the subject business enterprise.

At this point, the asset accumulation method will typically indicate the value of 100 percent of the subject company equity, on a controlling ownership interest basis. If the ownership interest valuation subject is some other level of value, then appropriate valuation discounts and/or premiums may be applied.

In some cases, a discount for lack of marketability and/or other valuation discounts or premiums may be appropriate even when valuing an overall business enterprise.

Fundamentals of the Asset Accumulation Method

If properly applied, asset-based approach methods are some of the more complex and rigorous valuation analyses. The costs and benefits of using asset-based approach valuation methods are described below. Before we consider these costs and benefits, or the various asset-based approach valuation methods, several fundamentals should be reiterated.

First, analysts use the company's cost-based balance sheet only as a point of departure from which to begin the valuation.

The value-basis balance sheet may be materially different from the cost-basis balance sheet in two ways: (1) the balances in the asset and liability accounts have been revalued and (2) several new asset and liability accounts may be added.

Second, all assets and liabilities should be restated to an appropriate standard of value. This standard of value should be consistent with (but not necessarily the same as) the standard of value selected for the business valuation. As described below, if certain asset and liability accounts are immaterial, or if the revaluation change is immaterial, the analyst may decide to leave those account balances at their cost basis.

Third, *all* of the company's assets and *all* of the company's liabilities should be considered for revaluation. In many cases, the analyst may need to rely on experts in real estate appraisal, in machinery and equipment appraisal, or in other asset appraisal disciplines.

Often, many of a company's most valuable assets may not be recorded on the company's cost-basis balance sheet. Intangible assets are typically not included on a cost-basis balance sheet (unless the intangible assets were acquired as part of a business acquisition that was accounted for under the purchase method of accounting).

Also, many of a company's more significant liabilities may not be recorded on the company's cost-basis balance sheet. This includes the whole category of the company's contingent liabilities. Accordingly, as part of the asset accumulation method, new asset and, possibly, new liability accounts may be recorded on the value-basis balance sheet.

Asset-Based Approach versus Book Value

It is important to distinguish between the application of any asset-based approach valuation method and simple reliance on accounting "book value" to conclude a value estimate. Under any standard of value, the true economic value of a business enterprise equals the company's accounting book value only by coincidence. More likely than not, the true economic value of a company will be either higher or lower than its accounting book value. There is no theoretical support, conceptual reasoning, or empirical data to suggest that the value of a business enterprise (under any standard of value) will necessarily equal the company's accounting book value.

From a valuation perspective, the terms *book value* or *net book value* are merely accounting jargon. Net book value (often called book value, in the vernacular) is synonymous with the amount of owners' equity recorded on the company's cost-basis balance sheet.

In fact, accounting book value is not a business valuation method at all, although it is popular in buy-sell agreement formulas. The values presented on the cost-based balance sheet are usually not representative of a current economic value for business valuation purposes. Also, there may be one or more intangible asset accounts or contingent liability accounts that should be considered in a business valuation—but that are not presented on the cost-basis balance sheet at all.

Asset Accumulation Method and Capitalized Excess Earnings Method

In the valuation literature, there are several names for the asset-based approach method that is based on the discrete revaluation of all of the company's individual assets and liabilities. This individual asset revaluation analysis is sometimes referred to as the *net asset value method*, the *adjusted net asset value method*, the *adjusted book value method*, the *asset build-up method*, or the asset accumulation method. As a convention, in this chapter (and in this book) we refer to this individual asset revaluation analysis as the *asset accumulation method*.

There are two general methods in the asset-based approach to business valuation:

1. The collective revaluation of all of the company's assets and liabilities. This analysis is usually conducted through the application of the capitalized excess earnings method, which was discussed previously in Chapter 13.
2. The individual revaluation of all of the company's assets and liabilities. We call this analysis the asset accumulation method. This method is the subject of the present chapter.

In order to illustrate the practical differences between these two asset-based approach methods, the following discussion will compare and contrast (1) the capitalized excess earnings method and (2) the asset accumulation method.

Asset Accumulation Method—Individual Revaluation

In the asset accumulation method, all of the subject's individual asset and liability account categories are analyzed and valued separately. This method involves a separate identification and individual revaluation of the company's:

1. Financial asset account categories (e.g., cash, accounts receivables, prepaid expenses, inventory)
2. Tangible personal property (e.g., machinery and equipment, furniture and fixtures, trucks and automobiles)

3. Real estate (e.g., land, land improvements, buildings, building improvements)
4. Intangible real property (e.g., leasehold interests, easements, mineral exploitation rights, air and water rights, development rights, and so on)
5. Intangible personal property (e.g., patents, trademarks, copyrights, computer software, trade secrets, customer relationships, going-concern value, goodwill, and so on)
6. Current liability account categories (e.g., accounts payable, taxes payable, salaries payable, accrued expenses, and so on)
7. Long-term liability account categories (e.g., bonds, notes, mortgages, and debentures payable, and so on)
8. Contingent liabilities (e.g., pending tax disputes, pending litigation, pending environmental concerns, and so on)
9. Special obligations (e.g., unfunded pensions, earned vacations or other leaves of absence, employee stock ownership plan [ESOP] repurchase liabilities, and so on)

In the asset accumulation method, the value of the individual assets (both tangible and intangible) less the value of the liabilities (both recorded and contingent) represents the subject business value. Theoretically, the business value concluded under the collective revaluation method (i.e., the capitalized excess earnings method) should equal the business value concluded under the individual revaluation method (i.e., the asset accumulation method).

The determination of which asset-based method to use in a given valuation engagement should be a function of:

1. The experience and judgment of the analyst
2. The quantity and quality of available data
3. The purpose and objective of the valuation
4. The scope, budget, and timing of the valuation assignment

Combining Elements of Asset Accumulation Method and Capitalized Excess Earnings Method

Sometimes it is only practical to revalue some—but not all—of the company's individual assets and liabilities. In these instances, it is possible to combine elements of the asset accumulation method and the capitalized excess earnings method.

The asset accumulation method may be used to quantify a portion of the business value, based on the asset/liability accounts that it is practical to revalue. The capitalized excess earnings method may then be used to "finish the job." That is, the capitalized excess earnings method may be used to quantify the remaining portion of the business value, based on an analysis of the remaining intangible value that was not already identified by the asset accumulation method.

In this combination of asset-based methods, those assets and liabilities that can be individually revalued are individually revalued. The value-basis balance sheet at this point would then have some accounts stated at current value and some accounts still stated at historical cost.

The capitalized excess earnings method is then applied at this point. The result of this capitalized excess earnings analysis is an indication of the remaining business enterprise value that has not already been captured in the revaluation of the individual asset/liability accounts. When using elements of both the asset accumulation method and the capitalized excess earnings method in the same valuation, the analyst should pay particular attention to the selection of (1) the required rates of return and (2) the capitalization rates used in the excess earnings component of the valuation. When selecting the required rates of return and the capitalization rates to apply to the company "excess earnings," the analyst should consider the extent to which the excess earnings are (1) the result of revalued assets and (2) the result of assets still recorded on the value-basis balance sheet at their historical cost.

This combination of the two asset-based methods is sometimes used when the analyst has current appraisals of some asset categories available—but not of all asset categories. For example, the subject company may have current appraisals of its real estate—but not of its machinery and equipment. This combination of the two methods is sometimes used when it is possible for the analyst to value some of the subject company's discrete intangible assets (e.g., computer software) but not other of the company's intangibles (e.g., trademarks or contractual relationships).

If this combination of both asset-based approach methods is properly applied, it should conclude the same business value indication as would be concluded from either (1) the asset accumulation method or (2) the capitalized excess earnings method.

Asset Accumulation Method Procedures

This section lists and briefly discusses the practical application of the asset accumulation method, as divided into the following six procedures:

1. Obtain or develop a cost-basis balance sheet.
2. Determine which assets and liabilities on the cost-basis balance sheet require a revaluation adjustment.
3. Identify off-balance sheet intangible assets or contingent assets that should be recognized and valued.
4. Identify off-balance sheet or contingent liabilities that should be recognized and valued.
5. Estimate the value of the various asset and liability accounts identified in steps 2 through 4.
6. Construct a value-basis balance sheet, based on the indicated values concluded during steps 1 through 5, and quantify the subject value.

Obtain or Develop a Cost-Basis Balance Sheet

Ideally, the cost-basis balance sheet will be prepared in accordance with GAAP. Also ideally, this balance sheet will be prepared as of the valuation date. If a cost-basis balance sheet is not available because the valuation is conducted as of an interim date, the analyst has three options:

1. The client (or an accountant retained by the client) may prepare a cost-basis balance sheet as of the valuation date and give it to the analyst.
2. The analyst may prepare a cost-basis balance sheet as of the valuation date from the company's trial balance or general ledger, assuming that the analyst has the requisite basic accounting expertise to prepare such a financial statement.

3. The analyst may rely on the most recent cost-basis balance sheet prepared at the fiscal period end prior to the valuation date. Typically, a recent fiscal period end balance sheet will require more revaluation adjustments than a valuation date balance sheet. However, using a recent fiscal period end balance sheet is usually better than not having a balance sheet to start with at all.

Identify Assets and Liabilities to Be Revalued

Second, the analyst will carefully analyze and understand each material asset account and liability account recorded on the subject company financial statements. The objective of this analysis is to determine which recorded assets and liabilities will need to be revalued—based on (1) materiality and (2) the selected standard of value appropriate for the subject business valuation.

As a convention throughout the remainder of this discussion, we will assume that fair market value is the appropriate standard of value for the subject business valuation.

Identify Off-Balance Sheet Assets

Third, the analyst will identify which unrecorded (sometimes called "off-balance sheet") assets need to be recognized on the value-basis balance sheet. For example, intangible assets are not normally recorded on financial statements prepared under GAAP. However, they often represent the largest component of overall business enterprise value in many industries.

Usually intangible assets are only recorded on the balance sheet if they are acquired in a purchase.

Some tangible assets may have been expensed rather than capitalized when they were acquired. Other tangible assets may be fully depreciated (and "written off") on the financial statements, even though they still have a remaining useful life and a considerable economic value (e.g., tools, dies, molds). For these reasons, the analyst should look for unrecorded tangible assets as well as for unrecorded intangible assets.

Identify Off-Balance Sheet and Contingent Liabilities

Fourth, the analyst will identify which unrecorded material contingent liabilities, if any, need to be recognized on the value-based balance sheet. If there are potential environmental liabilities, a specialized expert opinion may be needed.

Under current GAAP accounting, contingent liabilities are typically not recorded on a cost-basis balance sheet. However, in audited and reviewed financial statements material contingent liabilities are usually discussed in the explanatory footnotes to the financial statements.

Certainly, for those companies that have material pending litigation against them, income or property tax claims against them, environmental claims against them, and so forth, these contingent liabilities have a significant (and often quantifiable) effect on the risk of the business. Therefore, these material contingent liabilities may have a significant effect on the business enterprise value.

Value the Accounts Identified Above

Fifth, the analyst will begin the quantitative process of revaluing each of the asset accounts and, if necessary, each of the liability accounts.

The standard categories of assets for purposes of applying the asset accumulation method are: (1) financial assets, (2) tangible personal property, (3) real estate, (4) intangible real property, and (5) intangible personal property. For some of these asset categories, the analyst may need to rely on specialized asset appraisal experts.

The general valuation approaches, methods, and procedures for appraising these asset categories (and the individual tangible and intangible assets) will be summarized later in this chapter.

Construct a Value-Basis Balance Sheet

Sixth, the analyst will construct a value-basis balance sheet, as of the valuation date.

From this value-basis (as opposed to cost-basis) balance sheet, it is a simple procedure to subtract the value of the company's liabilities (recorded and contingent) from the value of the company's assets (tangible and intangible). The remainder of this subtraction procedure is the value of a 100 percent interest in the company owners' equity. This value indication is typically related to a controlling ownership level of value.

In addition, if the subject valuation assignment relates to something less than the overall business value (e.g., to a particular class of securities or to nonmarketable or noncontrolling ownership interest levels of value), then additional valuation discount analyses may be required.

Individual Asset Valuation Procedures

The conceptual cornerstone of the asset accumulation method is the identification and valuation of all of the company's assets. This includes the financial assets, the tangible assets (real and personal), and the intangible assets (real and personal).

In Chapter 7, the procedures related to adjusting the balance sheet were discussed. Those adjustment procedures should be considered when analyzing the company's balance sheet in preparation for the application of *any* business valuation approach or method. The procedures discussed below are individual asset valuation procedures, as compared with common balance sheet adjustment procedures.

Since this is not a text devoted to individual asset valuation, this discussion will be introductory in nature. Valuation analysts who desire a more detailed description of individual asset valuation procedures should consult the many specialized textbooks related to real estate appraisal, machinery and equipment appraisal, intangible asset appraisal, and so forth. A sampling of these books may be found in the bibliography at the end of this chapter.

Financial Assets

The most common assets included in this category include cash, accounts and notes receivable, and prepaid expenses.

With regard to cash, no revaluation procedures need to be performed, of course.

In the sale of a business, it is common for the seller to retain some or all of the cash balances on hand. This is true in a transaction involving the sale of stock as well as in a transaction involving the sale of assets. Accordingly, in a transactional valuation, the analyst should verify the amount of cash, if any, that will actually be transferred with the business enterprise.

With regard to accounts and notes receivable, the analyst may estimate the net realizable value of these receivables. The net realizable value is, essentially, the present value of the expected realization of (i.e., collection of) the receivables.

For businesses with audited or reviewed financial statements (or more sophisticated accounting systems), a reserve for uncollectible accounts is typically established as a contra-asset valuation account. Particularly if the valuation date is other than a fiscal period end, the analyst may assess the adequacy of this reserve for uncollectible accounts. For businesses that have not established reserves for uncollectible accounts, the analyst may assess the ultimate collectibility of the gross receivables. Based on this assessment of historical collection patterns, the analyst may revalue the gross accounts receivable in order to conclude an estimate of net cash collections. Finally, if the expected realization of the receivables is anticipated to occur over an extended period of time (i.e., longer than the normal collection cycle) the analyst also may apply a present value analysis to the longer-term receivables.

Normally, the business will realize the economic benefit of prepaid expenses within the normal course of one business cycle. Therefore, normally, no revaluation adjustment is required with respect to recorded prepaid expenses. However, if the analyst determines that the company will not enjoy an economic benefit from a prepaid expense during a normal business cycle, then a revaluation adjustment may be appropriate. For example, if the company has recorded prepaid rent expense on a facility it is no longer using, that asset will likely have little economic value. The expected realization of the prepaid expenses represents the net realizable value of this asset category.

Real Estate

Real estate includes such assets as owned land, land improvements, buildings, and building improvements.

Technically, in the appraisal literature, real estate represents the tangible element of real property ownership. Real estate is distinguished from intangible real property. Intangible real property represents the bundle of legal rights associated with real estate. For example, a real property interest would be a limited legal interest (i.e., less than a fee simple ownership interest)—such as a leasehold estate—in real estate.

There is a prodigious body of literature with respect to the valuation of real estate. And, both the appraisal regulatory agencies and the various professional appraisal organizations have promulgated professional standards with respect to its valuation.

All real estate is valued by reference to three generally accepted appraisal approaches: (1) the cost approach, (2) the income capitalization approach, and (3) the sales comparison approach. Each of these three approaches represents a general category of several discrete appraisal methods. Each of these approaches is described briefly below.

Cost Approach. The cost approach is based on the economic principle of substitution. That is, no one would pay more for an asset than the price required to obtain (by purchase or by construction) a substitute asset of comparable utility. This assumes, of course, that the subject asset is fungible. In other words, the cost approach assumes that substitute properties of comparable utility may be obtained. If, in fact, the subject asset is unique in one or more respects, the cost approach may not be a viable valuation approach.

Using the cost approach, the value of land is valued separately from the value of all appurtenances to land. The subject land is valued as if vacant and unimproved. The subject land is also valued at its highest and best use. The value of vacant land is typically estimated by reference to the sale of comparable land parcels in the reasonably proximate marketplace.

The subject buildings and improvements are valued by reference to the current cost to recreate their functional utility. There are several commonly used cost approach methods. One of the common methods is the depreciated reproduction cost method. This method is described as follows:

	Reproduction cost new of buildings and improvements
Less:	Allowances for incurable functional obsolescence
Equals:	Replacement cost
Less:	Allowance for physical deterioration
Equals:	Depreciated replacement cost
Less:	Allowance for external obsolescence
Less:	Allowances for curable functional obsolescence
Indicates:	Market value of buildings and improvements

To complete the cost approach, the value of the land is added to the value of the buildings and improvements. The sum of these two values indicates the market value of the subject real estate.

Income Capitalization Approach. The income capitalization approach is based on the economic principles of (1) risk and expected return investment analysis and (2) anticipation. Using this approach, the value of the real estate is the present value of the expected economic income that could be earned through the ownership of the property.

There are two categories of valuation methods under the income capitalization approach: (1) the direct capitalization method and (2) the yield capitalization method. From an investment analysis perspective, these two methods are conceptually similar. Therefore, from a theoretical perspective, both methods should conclude essentially the same value for the same real estate parcel.

Using the direct capitalization method, the analyst first estimates the normalized level of economic income that would be earned from the rental (whether hypothetical or actual) of the subject real estate. Economic income may be defined many ways (i.e., before tax, after tax, before interest expense, after interest expense, and so on). However it is important to note that the level of income that is included in the direct capitalization analysis is the income related to the ownership of the real estate only—and not the income related to the operation of the business that occupies the real estate. In other words, the level of income that should be included in the analysis is a hypothetical real estate lessor's income—not the business operating income of the actual property owner/operator.

The most common definition of economic income used in the direct capitalization method of real estate valuation is (before-tax) net operating income. This estimate of economic income is normalized to represent an average or typical period's rental income (including normal repairs, maintenance, etc.).

The normalized economic income is capitalized, typically, as an annuity in perpetuity. The capitalization rate used in this procedure should be (1) commensurate with the risk of investment and (2) consistent with the measurement of economic income. For example, if projected economic income is measured on an after-tax basis, the capitalization rate should be derived on an after-tax basis. If economic income is measured before tax, the capitalization rate should be derived before tax, and so forth.

Consistent with the definition of economic income as before-tax net operating income, the most common derivation of the direct capitalization rate is a blended debt and equity rate (or a weighted average cost of capital). The capitalization rate should be the blended cost of capital related to the subject property, and not the blended cost of capital related to the business that is the owner/operator of the property. The appropriate real estate valuation capitalization rate considers the mortgage interest in the property, the replacement rate of return to a real estate investor, and the loan-to-value ratio appropriate to a mortgage on the subject property. The capitalization rate should not consider the cost of debt, the cost of equity, or the capital structure of the business that is the owner/operator of the property.

The equity component of this blended rate represents the typical real estate investor's current income yield expectation for similar rental properties. It excludes the investor's derived long-term capital appreciation expectation for the subject property. The debt component of this blended rate represents the typical mortgage debt rate for similar rental properties. It includes a yield component for the amortization of mortgage principal as well as the payment of mortgage interest.

The debt component and the equity component are blended, or weighted together, based on the typical loan-to-value ratio for new mortgages offered on comparable real estate properties. The result of this analysis is the direct capitalization rate.

Using the direct capitalization method, the value of the real estate is presented algebraically, as follows:

$$\text{Value} = \frac{\text{Normalized economic income}}{\text{Direct capitalization rate}}$$

Using the yield capitalization method, the value of the subject real estate is the present value of the projected economic income to be derived from the property over a discrete period of time. While there is no universally correct projection period, discrete projection periods of from 5 to 10 years are common. These projection periods usually correspond to the typical investment holding period for institutional real estate investors.

The analyst projects the economic income to be derived from the rental of the subject property for each year in the discrete projection period. Again, before-tax net operating income is the most common measurement of economic income.

The analyst next derives a present value discount rate to calculate the present value of the discrete projection of economic income. This present value discount rate is often called the *going-in capitalization rate*. The analyst then estimates the normalized economic income to be generated by the property after the conclusion of the discrete projection period. This is sometimes called an estimate of the residual value (or reversionary period) income. This is the average or typical level of income to be generated by the property after the end of the projection period.

The analyst next derives a capitalization rate consistent with the estimate of residual value (or reversionary period) income. This rate is often called the *residual (or reversionary) capitalization rate*. It is sometimes called the *coming-out capitalization rate*. The coming-out capitalization rate is often different from the going-in capitalization rate due to the changing relative remaining life of the property and the different risk positions of the two investment periods.

The estimate of residual normalized economic income is capitalized by the residual capitalization rate. The result is the estimated value of the property at the end of the discrete projection period. This residual value is brought back to its present value, using the discrete projection period present value discount rate.

Finally, under the income capitalization approach, the value of the real estate is the sum of discrete projection period present value plus the residual value present value.

Sales Comparison Approach. The sales comparison approach is based on the economic principles of (1) efficient markets and (2) supply and demand. That is, when there is a relatively efficient and unrestricted secondary market for comparable properties and when that market accurately depicts the activities of a representative number of willing buyers and willing sellers, the market is most determinative of the value of the subject property.

Using the sales comparison approach, the analyst first collects data with regard to relatively recent sales of comparable real estate properties. Next, the analyst analyzes each of these sale transactions to determine if any quantitative adjustments are necessary due to the lack of comparability of the subject property when compared with the comparable properties.

The analyst considers these factors, among others, when determining if quantitative adjustments to the sales comparison data are necessary:

1. Age of each transaction (i.e., elapsed time from the valuation date)
2. Land-to-building ratio of each property
3. Absolute location and relative location of each property in relation to population centers, highways, and so forth
4. Age of each property
5. Physical condition of each property
6. Municipal and other services available to each property
7. Frontage and access of each property
8. Topography of land and soil type of each comparable property
9. Environmental aspects of each property
10. Special financing or other terms regarding each sales transaction

Accordingly, if necessary, the analyst adjusts the sales comparison data to make each transaction as comparable to the subject property as possible. Based on these adjusted sales comparison data, the analyst will conclude a market-derived pricing multiple. This pricing multiple is often expressed in terms of price per square foot of improved building space. Next, the analyst applies the market-derived pricing multiple to the size characteristics of the subject property. The resulting product is the estimate of value of the real estate according to the sales comparison approach.

Final Value Reconciliation. To reach a final valuation synthesis and conclusion regarding the real estate, the analyst will carefully consider the quantitative results of each of the valuation approaches used. In reaching the valuation conclusion, the analyst will consider the quantity and quality of available data used in each approach. The analyst will also assess the appropriate degree of confidence in the applicability and validity of each approach with respect to unique characteristics of the subject real estate. Based on these factors, the analyst will synthesize the results of each approach and conclude an overall value for the real estate.

Tangible Personal Property

The tangible personal property category of assets includes inventory, office furniture and fixtures, computer and office automation equipment, store racks and fixtures, manufacturing machinery and equipment, processing equipment, tools and dies, trucks and automobiles, and material handling and transportation equipment.

There is a considerable body of literature with regard to the appraisal of industrial and commercial tangible personal property. There is also literature regarding the appraisal of special-purpose and technical tangible personal property, such as scientific and laboratory equipment, medical and health care equipment, mining and extraction equipment, and so forth.

All of the various tangible personal property valuation methods and procedures can be grouped into three approaches: (1) the cost approach, (2) the income approach, and (3) the market approach.

Inventory. With regard to inventory, the analyst should distinguish between (1) the work-in-process inventory of a professional services firm (e.g., accounting firms, law firms, and so on) and (2) the merchandise inventory of a manufacturer/processor or of a wholesale/retail company.

The work-in-process inventory of a professional services firm is essentially the unbilled receivables of the firm. Therefore, the same net realizable value rules discussed with respect to accounts and notes receivable would apply to this asset as well. With regard to tangible merchandise inventory, there are three common valuation methods: (1) the cost of reproduction method, (2) the comparative sales method, and (3) the income method. These valuation methods apply equally to raw material, work-in-process, and finished goods inventory.

While these three inventory valuation methods are discussed elsewhere in the valuation literature, they are concisely summarized in IRS Revenue Procedure 77-12.[1]

Revenue Procedure 77-12 (presented in Exhibit 14–1) was originally issued with respect to the valuation of merchandise inventory for purchase price allocation purposes. Nonetheless, these valuation methods provide reasonable guidance for the appraisal of merchandise inventory as part of a business valuation as well.

The cost of reproduction method generally provides a good indication of fair market value if the inventory is readily replaceable in the volume and in the mix equal to the subject quantity on hand. In valuing inventory under this method, however, other factors may be relevant. For example, a well-balanced inventory

---

[1] Rev. Proc. 77-12, 1977-1 C.B. 569.

Exhibit 14–1

Revenue Procedure 77-12

26 CFR 601.105: Examination of returns and claims for refund, credit or abatement; determination of correct tax liability. (Also Part 1, Section 334; 1.334-1.)

Rev Proc. 77-12

Section 1. Purpose.

The purpose of this Revenue Procedure is to set forth guidelines for use by taxpayers and Service personnel in making fair market value determinations in situations where a corporation purchases the assets of a business containing inventory items for a lump sum or where a corporation acquires assets including inventory items by the liquidation of a subsidiary pursuant to the provisions of section 332 of the Internal Revenue Code of 1954 and the basis of the inventory received in liquidation is determined under section 334(b)(2). These guidelines are designed to assist taxpayers and Service personnel in assigning a fair market value to such assets.

Sec. 2. Background.

If the asets of a business are purchased for a lump sum, or if the stock of a corporation is purchased and that corporation is liquidated under section 332 of the Code and the basis is determined under section 334(b)(2), the purchase price must be allocated among the assets acquired to determine the basis of each of such assets. In making such determinations, it is necessary to determine the fair market value of any inventory items involved. This Revenue Procedure describes methods that may be used to determine the fair market value of inventory items.

In determining the fair market value of inventory under the situations set forth in this Revenue Procedure, the amount of inventory generally would be different from the amounts usually purchased. In addition, the goods in process and finished goods on hand must be considered in light of what a willing purchaser would pay and a willing seller would accept for the inventory at the various stages of completion, when the former is not under any compulsion to buy and the latter is not under any compulsion to sell, both parties having reasonable knowledge of relevant facts.

Sec. 3. Procedures for Determination of Fair Market Value.

Three basic methods an appraiser may use to determine the fair market value of inventory are the cost of reproduction method, the comparative sales method, and the income method. All methods of valuation are based on one or a combination of these three methods.

.01 The cost of reproduction method generally provides a good indication of fair market value if inventory is readily replaceable in a wholesale or retail business, but generally should not be used in establishing the fair market value of the finished goods of a manufacturing concern. In valuing a particular inventory under this method, however, other factors may be relevant. For example, a well balanced inventory available to fill customers' orders in the ordinary course of business may have a fair market value in excess of its cost of reproduction because it provides a continuity of business, whereas an inventory containing obsolete merchandise unsuitable for customers might have a fair market value of less than the cost of reproduction.

.02 The comparative sales method utilizes the actual or expected selling prices of finished goods to customers as a basis of determining fair market values of those finished goods. When the expected selling price is used as a basis for valuing finished goods inventory, consideration should be given to the time that would be required to dispose of this inventory, the expenses that would be expected to be incurred in such disposition, for example, all costs of disposition, applicable discounts (including those for quantity), sales commissions, and freight and shipping charges, and a profit commensurate with the amount of investment and degree of risk. It should also be recognized that the inventory to be valued may represent a larger quantity than the normal trading volume and the expected selling price can be a valid starting point only if customers' orders are filled in the ordinary course of business.

.03 The income method, when applied to fair market value determinations for finished goods, recognizes that finished goods must generally be valued in a profit motivated business. Since the amount of inventory may be large in relation to normal trading volume the highest and best use of the inventory will be to provide for a continuity of the marketing operation of the going business. Additionally, the finished goods inventory will usually provide the only source of revenue of an acquired business during the period it is being used to fill customers' orders. The historical financial data of an acquired company can be used to determine the amount that could be attributed to finished goods in order to pay all costs of disposition and provide a return on the investment during the period of disposition.

.04 The fair market value of work in process should be based on the same factors used to determine the fair market value of finished goods reduced by the expected costs of completion, including a reasonable profit allowance for the completion and selling effort of the acquiring corporation. In determining the fair market value of raw materials, the current costs of replacing the inventory in the quantities to be valued generally provides the most reliable standard.

Sec. 4 Conclusion.

Because valuing inventory is an inherently factual determination, no rigid formulas can be applied. Consequently, the methods outlined above can only serve as guidelines for determining the fair market value of inventories.

SOURCE: Rev. Proc. 77-12, 1977-1 C.B. 569.

available to fill customers' orders in the ordinary course of business may have a fair market value in excess of its cost of reproduction. This is because such an inventory provides a continuity of business. However, an inventory containing obsolete merchandise unsuitable for customers may have a fair market value of less than the cost of reproduction.

The comparative sales method uses the actual or expected selling prices of finished goods to customers as a basis of determining the fair market value of that inventory. When the expected selling price is used as a basis for valuing inventory, consideration should be given to the time that would be required to dispose of this inventory, the expenses that would be expected to be incurred in such disposition, applicable discounts (including those for quantity), sales commissions, and freight and shipping charges, and a profit commensurate with the amount of investment and degree of risk.

Whether the quantity of inventory to be valued is a larger than normal trading volume should also be recognized. Also, the expected selling price can be a valid starting point only if customers' orders are filled in the ordinary course of business.

The income method, when applied to the fair market value estimation of inventory, recognizes that inventory should generally be valued in a profit-motivated business. Since the amount of inventory may be large in relation to the normal trading volume, the highest and best use of the inventory will be to provide for a continuity of the marketing operation of the going-concern business.

Additionally, the inventory will usually provide the only source of revenue of the subject business during the period it is being used to fill customers' orders. The historical financial data of the company can be used to estimate the amount that could be attributed to inventory in order to pay all costs of disposition and provide a return on the investment during the period of disposition.

The analyst will apply one or more of these inventory valuation methods (1) based on the quantity and quality of available data and (2) based on the most likely ultimate disposition of the subject inventory. The analyst will estimate the value of the subject inventory based on the results of these inventory valuation methods.

Other Tangible Personal Property. The conceptual underpinnings of the cost approach for tangible personal property are essentially identical to those for real estate. As with real estate, there are several common cost approach methods. These methods include the depreciated reproduction cost method, the depreciated replacement cost method, the creation cost method, and the recreation cost method.

For special-purpose tangible personal property (which may experience a considerable amount of incurable obsolescence), the depreciated reproduction cost method is a common valuation method. However, for most general-purpose tangible personal property, the depreciated replacement cost method is the more common valuation method.

The depreciated replacement cost method for tangible personal property is presented algebraically below:

	Replacement cost new
Less:	Allowance for physical deterioration
Equals:	Depreciated replacement cost
Less:	Allowance for external obsolescence
Less:	Allowance for curable functional and technological obsolescence
Indicates:	Fair market value

If the subject asset is no longer produced, the replacement cost of the most comparable available substitute asset is used as the starting point in the cost approach (and, specifically, in the depreciated replacement cost method).

Using the income approach, the value of the tangible personal property is often quantified as the present value of the rental income from the hypothetical rental of the subject property over its remaining useful life.

First the analyst estimates the remaining useful life of the subject asset. This is typically the shortest of the asset's remaining physical, functional, technological, or economic lives.

Second, the analyst estimates a fair rental rate for the subject asset. This gross rental income is reduced by insurance, maintenance, and other expenses that are the responsibility of the lessor. The result is a projection of the net rental income (real or hypothetical) to be derived from the subject asset over the asset's expected remaining life.

Next, the analyst derives an appropriate present value discount rate. This discount rate is intended to provide for a fair, risk-adjusted rate of return to the property lessor over the term of the lease. The present value of the projected rental income over the expected remaining life of the property represents the value of the subject asset, per the income approach. (Since tangible personal property has a finite life, analysts typically do not have to consider a residual value to tangible personal property—as would be appropriate with regard to real estate.)

Using the market approach, the value of the subject asset is the price that it would command in its appropriate secondary market. This approach is based on the economic principle of efficient markets. It assumes that an efficient secondary market exists with regard to the exchange of the subject asset. It also assumes that reliable information is available regarding this tangible personal property exchange market.

Using this approach, the analyst first obtains data regarding secondary transactions with respect to comparable assets. Next, the analyst analyzes these data with regard to a set of reasonable comparability criteria. The market transactional data are adjusted, if necessary, to enhance their comparability and applicability to the subject asset. Based on the adjusted transactional database, the analyst selects comparable sales most indicative of a hypothetical transaction involving the subject asset. These adjusted sales data are used to indicate the value of the subject asset.

Finally, the analyst concludes an overall value of the subject asset based on a synthesis of the results of the various appraisal approaches used. Based on the analyst's perceived reliability of, and confidence in, the various approaches, the analyst will reach a final value estimate for the subject tangible personal property.

Intangible Real Property

Intangible real property assets represent intangible legal claims on tangible real estate. The type of assets encompassed by this category of assets includes leasehold interests (and various other leasehold estates), possessory interests (associated with franchise ordinances or other permits), exploration rights, air rights, water rights, land rights, mineral exploitation rights, use rights, development rights, easements (including scenic easements), and other intangible rights and privileges related to the use or exploitation of real estate. As intangible claims on real estate, the value of these assets is generally a subset of, or a derivative of, the value of the associated real estate.

As with real estate, there are many individual methods and techniques to appraise intangible real property. All of these methods can be grouped into the same three approaches: (1) the cost approach, (2) the income capitalization approach, and (3) the sales comparison approach. Each of these approaches (and some associated methods) was discussed above with respect to the value of real estate. Those general discussions will not be repeated here.

Intangible real property typically represents a legal claim on the use of, exploitation of, development of, or forbearance of real estate. Accordingly, the cost of the underlying real estate is generally irrelevant to the intangible property right holder.

The income approach is typically the most widely used approach with respect to the valuation of intangible real estate interests.

The sales comparison approach also is used to value certain intangible real estate interests. For example, there is a reasonable sales transaction secondary market for certain intangible real estate interests—such as the unexpired portion of assignable, below-market industrial and commercial leases (i.e., leasehold interests).

Intangible Personal Property

This discussion of the identification, valuation, and remaining life analysis of intangible assets will be somewhat cursory. There are two reasons for this. First, the topic of this book is business valuation and not intangible asset valuation. From this perspective the valuation of intangible assets is one procedure within one method (the asset accumulation method) within one approach (the asset-based approach) to business valuation. Second, there is already a substantial body of literature available on the topic of intangible asset valuation. Analysts who want to research this topic in greater detail are referred to the book, *Valuing Intangible Assets* by Robert F. Reilly and Robert P. Schweihs,[2] *Financial Valuation Application and Models* edited by James R. Hitchner,[3] or *Valuation for Financial Reporting: Intangible Assets, Goodwill and Impairment* by Michael J. Mard, James R. Hitchner, and Steven D. Hyden.[4]

Analysts experienced with intangible asset valuation could create a list of a hundred intangibles commonly found in the industrial and commercial environment. For an intangible asset to exist from an economic valuation perspective, it should possess certain attributes such as:

- It should be subject to specific identification and recognizable description.
- It should be subject to legal existence and protection.
- It should be subject to the right of private ownership, and this private ownership must be legally transferable.
- There should be some tangible evidence or manifestation of the existence of the intangible asset (e.g., a contract, a license, a document, or a registration document).

---

[2] Robert F. Reilly and Robert P. Schweihs, *Valuing Intangible Assets* (New York: McGraw-Hill, 1999).

[3] James R. Hitchner, ed., *Financial Valuation Application and Models*, 2nd ed. (Hoboken, NJ: John Wiley, 2006).

[4] Michael J. Mard, James R. Hitchner, and Steven D. Hyden, *Valuation for Financial Reporting: Intangible Assets, Goodwill and Impairment*, 2nd ed. (Hoboken, NJ: John Wiley, 2007).

- It should have been created or have come into existence at an identifiable time or as the result of an identifiable event.
- It should be subject to being destroyed or to a termination of existence at an identifiable time or as the result of an identifiable event.

There should be a specific bundle of legal rights (and/or other natural properties) associated with the existence of an intangible asset. For an intangible asset to have a quantifiable value, it should possess certain additional attributes such as:

- It should generate some measurable amount of economic income to its owner. This economic benefit could be in the form of an income increment or a cost decrement. This economic income may be measured in any of several ways, including present value of net income, net operating income, net cash flow, and so on.
- It should enhance the value of other assets with which it is associated; the other assets may include tangible personal property, real estate, or other intangible assets.

Categorization of Intangible Assets

Individual intangible assets are often grouped into distinct categories. Intangible assets in each category are generally similar in nature and function. Intangible assets are grouped in the same category when similar valuation and economic analysis methods apply to that group of assets. A common categorization of intangible assets follows:

- *Technology-related* (e.g., engineering drawings and technical documentation)
- *Customer-related* (e.g., customer lists and customer relationships)
- *Contract-related* (e.g., favorable supplier or other product/service contracts)
- *Data processing-related* (e.g., computer software, automated databases)
- *Human capital-related* (e.g., employment agreements, a trained and assembled workforce)
- *Marketing-related* (e.g., trademarks and trade names)
- *Location-related* (e.g., leasehold interests, certificates of need)
- *Goodwill-related* (e.g., going-concern value)
- *Engineering-related* (e.g., patents, trade secrets)
- *Literary-related* (e.g., literary copyrights, musical composition copyrights)

There is a specialized classification of intangible assets called *intellectual properties*. Intellectual properties manifest all of the legal existence and economic value attributes of other intangibles. Because of their special status, intellectual properties enjoy special legal recognition and protection.

Intellectual properties are generally registered under, and protected by, specific federal and state statutes.

Like other intangibles, intellectual properties may be grouped into like categories. The intellectual properties in each category are generally similar in nature, feature, method of creation, and legal protection. Similar valuation methods would apply to the intellectual properties in each category. A common categorization of intellectual properties follows:

- Creative (e.g., copyrights)
- Innovative (e.g., patents)

Valuation of Intangible Assets

The three previously discussed valuation approaches apply equally to tangible assets and to intangible assets. However, within each approach, different methods and procedures may be appropriate to value individual intangible assets.

Market Approach. The market approach provides a systematic framework for estimating the value of an intangible asset based on an analysis of actual sale and/or license transactions of intangibles that are comparable to the object. This approach requires comparing the subject intangible to intangibles that have been listed for sale/license or have been sold/licensed in their appropriate primary or secondary markets. Correlations between actual sale/license transaction prices are also examined.

Generally, it is difficult for analysts to use the market approach to value intangible assets. This is true for several reasons. First, discrete intangible assets are not often sold separately from other business assets. In other words, they are often (but not always) sold as part of a going-concern business. In these cases, the analyst faces the problem of allocating a lump-sum transaction price among all of the assets transferred—including the subject intangible asset. Second, more than in the case of transactions involving the sale of real estate or tangible personal property, buyers and sellers of intangible assets tend to keep actual transactional data private. So analysts face difficulty in obtaining, verifying, and confirming transactional data on the actual terms of arm's-length sales/licenses of intangible assets.

It is true that when they can be used, market approach methods are often the best methods to estimate intangible asset value. It is equally true for intangible assets as for tangible assets that an actual and active secondary market provides the best indicator of value for any asset, property, or business interest. An active secondary transfer market exists for the sale/license of many intangible assets. In these cases, the analyst may obtain verifiable transaction pricing data regarding the actual asset/license transfers of comparative intangible assets.

Some intangibles do lend themselves to the market approach. These would include situations where there are often "naked sales" of intangibles within an industry. A naked sale occurs when the subject intangible asset is sold "naked"—or separately and independently from any other tangible or intangible assets. For example, in the financial institution industry, bank "core deposit" accounts, loan portfolios, credit card portfolios, mortgage servicing rights, and trust customer accounts are often—in negotiated arm's-length transactions—sold separately and independently from the rest of the financial institution.

In the real estate industry, leasehold interests, possessory interests, air rights, water rights, mineral rights, other development rights, easements, and other real estate-related intangible assets are often—in an active secondary marketplace—bought and sold separately from the actual underlying real estate (and separately from any other intangible assets).

In the aviation industry, airport landing rights (sometimes called "slots" at controlled airports), airline routes, airline reservation systems, Federal Aviation Administration licenses, aircraft parking or "tiedown" rights, and airport gate positions are frequently—in negotiated arm's-length transactions—bought and sold independently from the rest of the assets of the going-concern airline business.

In fact, many licenses and permits are sold separately from other business assets. This may include Federal Communication Commission licenses, liquor licenses, franchise agreements, territory development agreements, certificates of need, and so forth.

Income Approach. The income approach provides a systematic framework for estimating the value of an intangible asset based on economic income capitalization or on the present value of future "economic income" to be derived from the use, forbearance, license, or rental of that intangible.

Under the income approach, *economic income* can be defined in many ways, including:

- Net income before tax
- Net income after tax
- Net operating income
- Gross or net rental income
- Gross or net royalty or license income
- Operating cash flow
- Net cash flow

The income capitalization procedure can also be accomplished in several ways, including:

- Capitalizing current year's economic income
- Capitalizing an average of several years' economic income
- Capitalizing a normalized or stabilized period's economic income
- Projecting prospective economic income over a discrete time period and estimating a present value

Quantifying the appropriate direct capitalization rate or present value discount rate is an essential element of the income approach. The appropriate direct capitalization rate or present value discount rate should reflect a fair return on the stakeholders' investment in the subject intangible. In selecting the rate, the analyst should consider the following:

- The opportunity cost of capital (i.e., expected return on alternative investments)
- The time value of money (including consideration of a real rate of return and the expected inflation rate over the investment time horizon)
- The term of the investment (including consideration of the expected remaining useful life of the subject intangible asset)
- The risk of the investment

The most important factor with regard to estimating the appropriate direct capitalization rate or present value discount rate is that the selected rate must be consistent with the measurement of economic income used. For example, a before-tax capitalization rate should be applied to a before-tax measurement of economic income. An after-tax capitalization rate should be applied to an after-tax measurement of economic income. An economic income stream representing a return to stockholders only should be capitalized by a rate based on a cost of equity capital only. An economic income stream representing a return to all stakeholders (i.e., both debt holders and equity holders) should be capitalized by a rate based upon a blended—or weighted average—cost of debt and equity capital.

With regard to intangible assets, economic income can be derived from two categories of sources: (1) increments to revenue or (2) decrements to cost. From a valuation perspective, either source of economic income is a valid contributor to the value of the subject intangible.

With regard to incremental revenue, certain intangibles may allow the asset owner or licenser to sell more products (than otherwise), sell products at a higher average selling price, gain a larger market share, enjoy a monopolistic market position, ensure a relatively sure source of recurring customers, ensure a relatively sure source of future business, generate add-on or renewal business, develop new markets, introduce new products, and so on.

With regard to decremental costs, certain intangibles may allow the asset owner or licenser to incur lower labor costs, incur lower material costs, incur lower scrap (or other waste) costs, enjoy lower rent expense, enjoy lower utilities expense, enjoy lower advertising or promotional expenses, defer the costs to recruit and train employees, avoid start-up costs, avoid construction period interest, avoid interest in an otherwise greater level of receivables or inventory, avoid or defer design or development costs, supply a low-cost and dependable source of financing, avoid or defer software development or ongoing data processing costs, and so on.

Some intangibles lend themselves very well to the application of the income approach. Such contract-related or customer-related intangible assets as favorable leases, favorable supply contracts, favorable labor agreements, customer lists, and customer contracts are likely candidates for an application of the income approach. Other technology-related, engineering-related, and marketing-related intangible assets are also likely candidates for an application of the income approach. These intangible assets may include patents, proprietary technology or processes, trademarks and trade names, copyrights, and so forth.

When using an income approach method, the expected remaining useful life of the subject intangible is important. The economic income projection associated with the subject intangible should not extend beyond the term of the expected remaining useful life for that intangible.

Also, "double-counting" the economic income associated with the subject intangible is a common error. The analyst should ensure that the same stream of economic income (whether it represents a revenue increment or a cost decrement) is not assigned to more than one asset. For example, the same stream of excess earnings for a particular business should not be assigned both to the company's patent and to the company's trademark. However, streams of income may be divided between two assets. Clearly, only one of these intangible assets deserves to be associated with that specific stream of economic income. The other intangible in this example, though it has legal existence, may have little or no incremental economic value.

Only that stream of economic income that associates with the subject intangible asset should be considered. A fair return on the tangible assets used or used up in the production of income related to the subject intangible should be assigned. This fair return on associated tangible assets should be subtracted from the economic income stream assigned to the subject intangible in order to avoid the "double-counting" of asset values.

Cost Approach. The cost approach provides a systematic framework for estimating the value of an intangible asset based on the economic principle of substitution. A prudent investor would pay no more for a fungible intangible than the cost that would be incurred to replace the subject with a substitute of comparable utility or functionality.

Replacement cost new typically establishes the maximum amount that a prudent investor would pay for a fungible intangible. To the extent that an intangible is less useful than an ideal replacement asset, the value of the subject should be adjusted accordingly. The subject's replacement cost new is adjusted for:

- Physical deterioration (which is unusual in the case of intangible assets)
- Functional obsolescence
- Technological obsolescence (a specific form of functional obsolescence)
- External obsolescence (economic obsolescence is a specific form of external obsolescence)

Physical deterioration is the reduction in value due to physical wear and tear resulting from continued use. Physical deterioration is quite rare with respect to most intangibles.

Functional obsolescence is the reduction in value due to the intangible's inability to perform the function (or yield the periodic utility) for which it was originally designed.

Technological obsolescence is a decrease in value due to improvements in technology that make the intangible less than the ideal replacement for itself. Technological obsolescence occurs when, due to improvements in design or engineering technology, a new replacement produces a greater standardized measure of utility production than the subject intangible.

External obsolescence is a reduction in value due to the effects, events, or conditions that are external to—and not controlled by—the current use or condition of the intangible. The impact of external obsolescence is typically beyond the control of the asset's owner. Therefore, external obsolescence is typically considered incurable.

In estimating the amounts (if any) of functional obsolescence, technological obsolescence, and external obsolescence related to the subject intangible asset, the consideration of the asset's actual age—and its expected remaining useful life—is important.

A common cost approach formula for quantifying an intangible's value is as follows:

	Reproduction cost new
Less:	Incurable functional and technological obsolescence
Equals:	Replacement cost new
Less:	External obsolescence
Less:	Curable functional and technological obsolescence
Indicates:	Fair market value

An intangible's deficiencies are considered curable when the prospective economic benefit of enhancing or modifying it exceeds the current cost (in terms of material, labor, and time) to change it. An intangible's deficiencies are considered incurable when the current costs of enhancing or modifying it (in terms of material, labor, and time) exceed the expected future economic benefits of improving it.

Reproduction cost is the cost to construct, at current prices, an exact duplicate or replica of the subject. This duplicate would be created using the same materials, standards, design, layout, and quality of workmanship used to create the original intangible. An intangible's reproduction cost encompasses all of the deficiencies, "superadequacies," and obsolescence that exist in the subject intangible asset. Many of these conditions or characteristics are inherent in the subject and are, therefore, incurable.

The replacement cost of an intangible is the cost to create, at current prices, an asset having equal utility to the subject. However, the replacement asset would be created with modern methods and constructed according to current standards, state-of-the-art design and layout, and the same quality of workmanship.

The difference between reproduction cost and its replacement cost is typically the quantification of incurable functional and technological obsolescence. That is, in an ideal replacement intangible, all elements of incurable functional and technological obsolescence are removed or "reengineered" from the subject.

With respect to both reproduction cost and replacement cost, four elements of cost should be considered in the analyses:

1. *Direct costs* (including material, labor, and overhead)
2. *Indirect costs* (including associated legal, registration, engineering, administrative, etc.)
3. *Developer's profit* (a fair return on the intangible asset creator's time and effort)
4. *Entrepreneurial incentive* (the economic benefit required to motivate the intangible asset development process)

Some intangibles lend themselves to the cost approach. Examples of this include computer software and automated databases, technical drawings and documentation, blueprints and engineering drawings, laboratory notebooks, technical libraries, chemical formulations, food and other product recipes, and so forth.

Remaining Useful Life Analysis of Intangible Assets

One factor that has been mentioned in all three approaches is the estimation of remaining useful life. This estimation (sometimes called *lifting* the intangible asset) is obviously important in the market approach. This is because the analyst should select comparative sale/license transactions where the sold/licensed intangible has a similar remaining useful life to the subject. This estimation is important in the income approach. The analyst should estimate the time period or duration over which to project (and capitalize) the economic income. This estimation is also important in the cost approach. The analyst should make an assessment of the remaining functionality or utility of the subject intangible in order to quantify elements of functional obsolescence, technological obsolescence, and external obsolescence.

Analysts should consider each of these measures when estimating the remaining useful life of intangible assets.

1. *Remaining legal (or legal protection) life* (e.g., remaining term of trademark protection)
2. *Remaining contractual life* (e.g., remaining term on a lease)
3. *Statutory or judicial life* (e.g., some courts have allowed a "standardized" life of five years for computer software)
4. *Remaining physical life* (e.g., some intangible assets just wear out from continued use, such as blueprints or technical libraries)
5. *Remaining functional life* (e.g., some intangible assets just become dysfunctional with the passage of time, like chemical formulations that need to be continuously updated)
6. *Remaining technological life* (e.g., period until the current technology becomes obsolete, for patents, proprietary processes, etc.)

7. *Remaining economic life* (e.g., period after which the intangible asset will no longer generate income, such as a legally valid copyright on a book that is out of print)
8. *Actuarial/analytical life* (e.g., estimating the remaining life of group intangible assets, such as customer accounts, by reference to the historical turnover— or mortality—of such accounts)

Typically, the shortest resulting measurement of remaining useful life will be appropriate for the valuation.

Example

To illustrate the application of the asset accumulation method, let's consider the hypothetical Seller Company, Inc. ("Seller"). Seller is a successful closely held manufacturing company. The owners of Seller are contemplating the sale of the business.

Therefore, the objective of the valuation is to estimate the fair market value of the entire business enterprise as of December 31, 2006. In other words, the appropriate level of value is a controlling ownership interest. The purpose of the valuation is to provide an independent opinion to the current owners as to the most likely transaction price regarding the sale of the company.

Exhibit 14–2 presents the statement of financial position (i.e., balance sheet) of Seller as of the December 31, 2006, valuation date. This statement of financial position is prepared in accordance with GAAP. In other words, Exhibit 14–2 is prepared on a historical-cost basis. This balance sheet will be the beginning point in the asset accumulation method analysis.

Exhibit 14–3 presents the final summary of the Seller asset accumulation method valuation. Exhibit 14–3 presents both the cost-basis values for all Seller recorded asset and liability accounts (slightly rearranged from the cost-basis balance sheet presentation) and the fair market values for all of the asset (both tangible and intangible) and liability accounts of the company.

Let's review each of the asset and liability fair market value conclusions in Exhibit 14–3. The following paragraphs describe an illustrative valuation analysis for each individual asset and liability account.

The cash balance remains at its historical cost value.

The accounts and notes receivable remain at their historical cost value. This conclusion was reached based on the analyst's assessment of the timing and collectibility of the receivables.

Prepaid expenses remain at their historical cost value. This conclusion was reached based on the analyst's assessment of the economic value of the prepaid expenses to the going-concern business.

Inventory is revalued upward. This revaluation is based on the sales comparison method described in IRS Revenue Procedure 77-12.

Long-term notes receivable are valued at their historical cost. This conclusion is based on (1) an analysis of the stated interest rate versus current interest rates for similar risk notes and (2) the historical and likely prospective payment pattern regarding the notes.

The note receivable from a supplier is revalued to zero. Some years ago, Seller extended a loan to one of its key suppliers. This decremental revaluation was based

Exhibit 14–2

Seller Company, Inc.
Statement of Financial Position
as of December 31, 2006
(in 000s)

ASSETS		LIABILITIES AND OWNERS' EQUITY	
Current assets:		Current liabilities:	
Cash	$2,000	Accounts payable	$6,000
Accounts and notes receivable	6,000	Wages payable	1,000
Prepaid expenses	2,000	Taxes payable	1,000
Inventory	8,000	Accrued liabilities	2,000
Total current assets	18,000	Total current liabilities	10,000
Noncurrent assets:		Noncurrent liabilities:	
Land	2,000	Bonds payable	2,000
Buildings and improvements	12,000	Notes payable	4,000
Office furniture and fixtures	2,000	Mortgages payable	6,000
Machinery and equipment	8,000	Debentures payable	2,000
Tools and dies	3,000	Total noncurrent liabilities	14,000
Total plant, property, and equipment	27,000		
Less: Accumulated depreciation	12,000	Owners' equity:	
Net plant, property, and equipment	15,000	Capital stock	1,000
Other noncurrent assets:		Additional paid-in capital	4,000
Long-term notes receivable	2,000	Retained earnings	7,000
Note receivable from supplier	1,000	Total owners' equity	12,000
Total other noncurrent assets	3,000		
TOTAL ASSETS	**$36,000**	**TOTAL LIABILITIES AND OWNERS' EQUITY**	**$36,000**

on the following facts: (1) the supplier has made no payments on the note for the last several years, (2) there is no security related to the note, (3) the documentation of the debt is not particularly good, so (4) it is unlikely that Seller could enforce collection of the note even if it attempted to do so.

Land is revalued upward. This incremental revaluation is based on a contemporaneously prepared market value appraisal of the land, as if vacant and unimproved, at its highest and best use, using the sales comparison approach.

Buildings and improvements are revalued incrementally, as market value exceeds the (depreciated) historical cost of these properties. This revaluation is also based on a contemporaneously prepared market value appraisal of the Seller facilities. This appraisal was based on the depreciated replacement cost of the subject facilities.

Office furniture and fixtures, machinery and equipment, and tools and dies are revalued incrementally. That is, the market value conclusions for each asset category exceed their (depreciated) historical cost. The depreciated replacement cost method would be a typical valuation method for the valuation of this category of assets.

A leasehold interest is identified and capitalized on the value-basis balance sheet. In this example, Seller enjoys a favorable rental advantage (i.e., below-market

Exhibit 14–3

Seller Company, Inc.
Business Enterprise Valuation/Asset-Based Approach/Asset Accumulation Method
as of December 31, 2006 (in 000s)

	At Historical Cost	At Fair Market Value
ASSETS		
Financial assets:		
Cash	$2,000	$2,000
Accounts and notes receivable	6,000	6,000
Prepaid expenses	2,000	2,000
Inventory	8,000	10,000
Long-term notes receivable	2,000	2,000
Note receivable from supplier	1,000	–
Total financial assets	21,000	22,000
Real estate:		
Land	2,000	4,000
Buildings and improvements	12,000	10,000
Less: Accumulated depreciation	6,000	–
Net real estate	8,000	14,000
Tangible personal property:		
Office furniture and fixtures	2,000	2,000
Machinery and equipment	8,000	6,000
Tools and dies	3,000	3,000
Less: Accumulated depreciation	6,000	–
Net tangible personal property	7,000	11,000
Intangible real property:		
Leasehold interests	–	2,000
Net intangible real property	–	2,000
Intangible personal property:		
Trademarks and trade names	–	2,000
Computer software	–	3,000
Patents and patent applications	–	2,000
Favorable supplier contracts	–	2,000
Goodwill	–	1,000
Net intangible personal property	–	10,000
TOTAL ASSETS	**$36,000**	**$51,000**
LIABILITIES AND OWNERS' EQUITY		
Current liabilities:		
Accounts payable	$6,000	$6,000
Wages payable	1,000	1,000
Taxes payable	1,000	1,000
Accrued liabilities	2,000	2,000
Total current liabilities	10,000	10,000
Noncurrent liabilities:		
Bonds payable	2,000	2,000
Notes payable	4,000	4,000
Mortgages payable	6,000	5,000
Debentures payable	2,000	2,000
Total noncurrent liabilities	14,000	13,000
Contingent liabilities:		
Contingent claims	–	2,000
Total contingent liabilities	–	2,000
Total liabilities	24,000	25,000
TOTAL LIABILITIES AND OWNERS' EQUITY	**$36,000**	**$51,000**
TOTAL OWNERS' EQUITY	**$12,000**	**$26,000**

rental rates) on some warehouse space that it leases. The analyst used the income capitalization approach to project and capitalize this favorable (below-market) lease rate advantage and to conclude the market value of the leasehold interest. This leasehold interest intangible asset was not previously recorded on the Seller cost-basis balance sheet.

The entire category of intangible personal property typically would not be recorded on a cost-basis balance sheet. However, individual intangible assets will be identified and valued as part of this business enterprise valuation.

Trademarks and trade names are an important intangible asset for Seller. Company management spends a great deal of time and money promoting and protecting the company's name. They advertise, send promotional announcements, sponsor booths at trade shows, and so forth. They have actively defended the company name and market against any possible infringement. The analyst used the recreation cost method to quantify the value of this intangible asset. The analyst estimated the current cost required for the company to recreate its current level of customer awareness, brand recognition, and consumer loyalty. The estimated cost to recreate this level of name awareness is capitalized as the value of this intangible.

Computer software also is an important intangible asset for Seller. This computer software was internally developed and maintained by an in-house data processing department. The value of such computer software typically would not be recorded on a cost-basis balance sheet.

The systems analysts at Seller have developed and implemented an automated materials requirement planning (MRP) system. This system is extremely useful to the company with regard to material purchasing, labor scheduling, and production planning.

The analyst used the market approach to estimate the value of this intangible asset, as there is a relatively similar (in terms of functionality) MRP system available on the market from a commercial software value of a comparable commercial system, and after including the costs of customization, installation, testing, and training, the analyst estimated the value in continued use of the Seller computer software.

Seller holds a number of patents and patent applications. The Seller products have certain unique and proprietary technological feature advancements compared with the products manufactured by Seller's competitors. And, other manufacturers cannot reverse-engineer and copy the Seller product advanced features because these products are protected by the company patents.

Because of the advanced features (protected by the several patents), Seller management estimates that (1) Seller sells more widgets than it otherwise would, (2) Seller has a greater market share than it otherwise would, and (3) Seller's average selling price per unit is higher than its competitors' prices. Accordingly, the analyst used the income approach to estimate the value of the Seller patents and patent applications.

Seller also has a favorable supply contract with a key supplier. The materials buyer for Seller is a skilled negotiator. Using these superior negotiating skills, the materials buyer convinced the key supplier to agree to supply an essential raw material to Seller at 20 percent below the prices that the supplier normally charges to its other, similar-sized customers. This long-term agreement is documented in a written five-year-term supply contract. The analyst used the income approach to estimate the economic value of the Seller favorable supply contract.

Goodwill is sometimes considered the accumulation of all the other elements of economic value of a business enterprise not specifically with (or allocated to) individual tangible and intangible assets. The analysis and qualification of goodwill (or the lack of goodwill) is an important component in the application of the asset accumulation method to a company like Seller.

With respect to the subject company, the analyst used the capitalized excess earnings method to value the Seller goodwill. First, the analyst identified and valued all of the other individual Seller assets—both tangible and intangible. Second, the analyst assigned a fair rate of return against each Seller asset category—both tangible and intangible. Third, the analyst compared the total calculated fair return on the total tangible and intangible assets with the total economic income actually earned by the company. Fourth, any excess economic income (above a fair return on all identified tangible and intangible assets) was capitalized as an annuity in perpetuity. The capitalized excess earnings method is described in Chapter 13.

The conclusion of the capitalized excess earnings analysis is the indicated value of the Seller intangible value in the nature of goodwill.

The current liabilities of Seller also were analyzed. Given the short-term nature of these monetary liabilities, the analyst estimated their fair market value at their historical cost carrying amounts.

The noncurrent liabilities also were analyzed. The analyst considered the terms and conditions of these liabilities and concluded that the stated interest rates approximated current market rates for comparative debt instruments. Accordingly, the analyst estimated the fair market value of the bonds, notes, and debentures at their historical cost carrying amounts.

The mortgage payable, however, has a substantial remaining term and a fixed interest rate which is considerably below current market rates. The analyst confirmed with the mortgage bank that they would allow Seller to pay off the mortgage at a discount compared to the principal balance. The analyst estimated this discount by reference to the difference in the imbedded interest rate and the market interest rate over the remaining term of the mortgage. The analyst reduced the liability by the present value of the imbedded interest rate advantage and then estimated the fair market value of the mortgage payable.

There is an outstanding lawsuit against Seller. The plaintiff, a former distributor, alleges that Seller violated the distributor's exclusive marketing territory agreement. Although there were extenuating circumstances, Seller management recognizes that it did violate the agreement and that it owes damages to the former distributor.

While the trial is not yet scheduled, and no one can predict the court's decision regarding either liability or damages, both Seller management and Seller legal counsel believe that an offer of $2,000,000 will be adequate to settle the case and to satisfy all future liability to the plaintiff.

The analyst reviewed this estimate and used it to recognize a contingent liability on the Seller value-basis balance sheet.

In the final step, the analyst summed the estimated fair market values for all of the Seller tangible and intangible assets, and summed the estimated fair market values for all of the Seller recorded and continent liabilities. The analyst subtracted the total liability value from the total asset value. The remainder is an indication of the fair market value of the Seller total owners' equity, as of December 31, 2006, as indicated by the asset accumulation method.

Advantages of the Asset Accumulation Method

As should be apparent from the discussion of the theoretical concepts and the practical applications of this method, there are a number of analytical advantages of the asset accumulation method.

First, the results of the asset accumulation method are presented in a traditional balance sheet format. This format should be familiar to anyone who has ever worked with basic financial statements. Therefore, business buyers and sellers, commercial and investment bankers, judges and lawyers, and individual and institutional investors should all be familiar with the basic balance sheet presentation of the results of this valuation method.

Second, this method compartmentalizes all of the subject business value. In the example above, the valuation conclusion was slightly greater than two times accounting book value for Seller. Other business valuation methods would, presumably, reach the same valuation conclusion. But those methods would not explain why the subject company is worth more than two times accounting book value. The asset accumulation method identifies (1) exactly which assets (tangible and intangible) are contributing economic value to the company and (2) exactly how much economic value each asset is contributing.

Third, this method is useful when structuring the sale of a business. This method can quickly quantify the effects on business value of many common seller structural considerations, such as these:

1. What if the seller retains the company's cash on hand or accounts receivable?
2. What if the seller retains (or leases back to the company) the operating real estate facilities?
3. What if the seller personally retains title to the patents or to some other intangible asset owned by the company?
4. What if the seller personally retains any or all of the debt instruments (or other liabilities) of the company?

Fourth, this method is useful to the seller when negotiating the sale of the company. If the buyer offers a lower price than the asset accumulation method indicates, the seller can ask, "Since you're not willing to pay for all of the assets of the business, which of these assets don't you want to include as part of the transaction?"

Fifth, this method is useful to the buyer when negotiating the purchase of the company. If the seller wants a higher price than the value indicated by the asset accumulation method, the buyer can ask, "What other assets will be included in the transaction—in addition to the assets included on this value-based balance sheet—to justify the price you are asking?"

Sixth, after the sale transaction is consummated, this business valuation method allows for a ready and reasonable allocation of the lump-sum purchase price among the assets acquired. This purchase price allocation is often required for both financial accounting purposes and tax accounting purposes. This is important because the tangible assets are subject to depreciation cost recovery—and the intangible assets are subject to amortization cost recovery—for both financial accounting and federal income tax purposes.

Seventh, this method is useful with regard to financing the subject transaction. Typically, all categories of lenders (secured, unsecured, mezzanine, etc.) will want to know the value of all of the company's individual assets—both tangible and intangible—before they will commit to financing the business purchase deal. This valuation method generally provides the acquisition lenders with the information they need.

Eighth, this method is particularly useful in litigation and other controversial matters. Since it identifies the individual value components of the individual assets of the company, it allows for the easy measurement of the impact of certain alleged actions (or lack of actions) on the overall business enterprise value. Also, this method can be used to allocate assets (as well as—or instead of—stock) in a stockholder/partner dissolution dispute or in a marital dissolution dispute.

Disadvantages of the Asset Accumulation Method

The primary disadvantage of the asset accumulation method is that, if taken to an extreme, it can be very expensive and time consuming. It also may necessitate the involvement of appraisal specialists in several asset valuation disciplines. The costs and efforts of these appraisal specialists may be prohibitive with regard to the valuation of larger or complex businesses.

Also, as described in this chapter, this method requires the valuation of all of the company assets—the intangible assets as well as tangible assets. Many intangible asset values depend, in good measure, on the income valuation approach. Therefore, the value indication of the asset accumulation method may ultimately depend as much on the economic income capitalization variables as it does on the values of tangible assets. This is especially true for larger and more complex businesses. Of course, ultimately, the value of all assets, properties, or business interests depends on their economic income-generating capacity.

Also, the aggregate value of all assets, both tangible and intangible, are captured in the income and market approaches. As such the asset accumulation method may not be necessary.

Summary

The asset accumulation method is a common asset-based approach. The theoretical underpinning of this method is simple: the value of the business enterprise is the value of the business assets (both tangible and intangible) less the value of the business liabilities (both recorded and contingent). Basically, this method recognizes that all of the economic value of a business has to come from—and can be identified with—the productive assets of the business.

The asset accumulation method involves the separate identification and individual valuation of all business asset categories. In addition, this method involves the identification and valuation of all business liability categories. In these individual asset and liability valuations, it is important for the analyst to apply both (1) a standard of value and (2) a premise of value that are consistent with the purpose and objective of the business enterprise valuation.

It is conceptually incorrect to automatically conclude that the value of a business is based only on the value of its tangible assets. Likewise, it is also conceptually incorrect to conclude that the value of a business is equal to its accounting book value—without the use of generally accepted valuation procedures and rigorous fundamental analyses to support that conclusion.

The intangible assets of the company often contribute substantial economic value. In some cases, a company's intangible assets may even contribute negative economic value, which is recognized as external obsolescence. External obsolescence is recognized as a decrease in the value of the tangible assets of the company. Again, the application of the asset accumulation method requires a structured, rigorous, and comprehensive valuation analysis of all the company's assets.

There are numerous advantages to the asset accumulation method. These advantages include application to transaction pricing and structuring, deal negotiation, acquisition financing, purchase accounting, and dispute resolution.

However, there are costs associated with the application of the asset accumulation method. This method requires more time and effort on the part of the analyst than many other business valuation methods. It requires more access to company facilities and to company management than many other valuation methods. It requires more access to company data, particularly operational data, than many other valuation methods. And, it requires more time and effort on the part of company management and more involvement of company management in the valuation process.

Finally, the asset accumulation method requires that the analyst have expertise in the identification and valuation of both tangible assets and intangible assets. Certainly, this method is only recommended for analysts who have adequate experience and expertise in the valuation of individual business assets. The use of other experts with the requisite experience and qualifications may fill the void for a particular asset type for which the analyst lacks technical expertise.

Bibliography

AICPA NBV4: The Income Approach and the Asset Based Approach to Valuation.

Aldering, James. "Income Approach versus Asset Approach." *BV Q&A Newsletter*, August 2005. Available at www.BVLibrary.com.

Alico, John, ed. *Appraising Machinery and Equipment.* Herndon, VA: American Society of Appraisers, 1989.

Altman, Edward I. "Mark-to-Market and Present Value Disclosure: An Opportunity or a Costly Annoyance?" *Financial Analysts Journal*, March–April 1993, pp. 14–16.

Anonymous. "Whether to Mark up Assets; Whether to Tax Affect Gains." *Shannon Pratt's Business Valuation Update*, April 2002.

The Appraisal of Real Estate, 11th ed. Chicago: Appraisal Institute, 1996.

Baxter, William. "Asset and Liability Values (Complexities of Current Value Accounting)." *Accountancy*, April 1994, pp. 135–37.

Cheung, Joseph K., and Mandy Li. "Income Tax Effects on Asset Valuation and Managerial Analysis." *Abacus*, March 1992, pp. 98–106.

Churchill, Michael. "Asset Valuation." *Australian Accountant*, April 1992, pp. 35–39.

Crawford, Robert G., and Gary C. Cornia. "The Problem of Appraising Specialized Assets." *Appraisal Journal*, January 1994, pp. 75–85.

Dandekar, Manoj P., and Pamela Garland. "Tangible Personal Property Remaining Useful Life Estimation Analysis." *Willamette Management Associates Insights*, Winter 1996, pp. 13–20.

Dandekar, Manoj P., and Robert F. Reilly. "Tangible Personal Property Valuation Approaches, Methods, and Procedures." *Willamette Management Associates Insights*, Winter 1996, pp. 1–12.

DeThomas, Arthur R., and Robert R. Neyland. "Asset Valuation: A Practical Approach for Decision Making." *CPA Journal*, September 1991, pp. 82–83.

Hitchmer, James R., ed. *Financial Valuation Application and Models*. 2nd ed. Hoboken, NJ: John Wiley & Sons, 2006.

Jacoby, Henry D., and David G. Laughton. "Project Evaluation: A Practical Asset Pricing Method." *Energy Journal*, 1992, pp. 19–47.

King, Alfred M. *Valuation: What Assets Are Really Worth*. New York: John Wiley & Sons, 2002.

Lynn, Daniel M., and Robert R. Neyland. "Asset Valuation: Softening the Bankruptcy Blow." *Bank Management*, April 1992, pp. 48–49.

Mard, Michael J., James R. Hitchmer, and Steven D. Hyden. *Valuation for Financial Reporting: Intangible Assets, Goodwill and Impairment*. Hoboken, NJ: John Wiley & Sons, 2002.

Reilly, Robert F., and Robert P. Schweihs. *Valuing Intangible Assets*. New York: McGraw-Hill, 1999.

_____. "Valuation of Trademarks and Trade Names." *Valuation Strategies*, November/December 1999, pp. 7–13, 45–46.

Rosado, Robert J., Susannah Sabnekar, and Donna Beck Smith. "Valuing a Start-Up Company That Has Little or No History or Earnings." *BV Q&A Newsletter*, February 2005. Available at www.BVLibrary.com.

Schmidt, Richard M. "Valuing the Assets of a Manufacturing Company." *The Appraisal Journal*, April 1997, pp. 120–23.

Part IV

Discounts, Premiums, and the Value Conclusion

Chapter 15

Control and Acquisition Premiums

Control premiums and discounts for lack of control are mirror images of each other. This chapter discusses control premiums, and the following chapter discusses discounts for lack of control. These chapters appear before the chapter on discounts for lack of marketability because the appropriate level of value, i.e., either control or minority marketable, should be established before applying a discount, if any, for lack of marketability.

Levels of Value

Exhibit 15–1 is a schematic "levels of value" chart. Note that there is one line on the chart even higher than control value, which is synergistic or strategic value. Note also that the base from which the control premium is measured is, the "publicly-traded equivalent value"—in other words, minority marketable value.

While there is a great deal of empirical evidence available to quantify the discount for lack of marketability, the empirical evidence to quantify the control premium or, conversely, the minority discount is, indeed, scant. The only body of

Exhibit 15–1

"Levels of Value" in Terms of Characteristics of Ownership

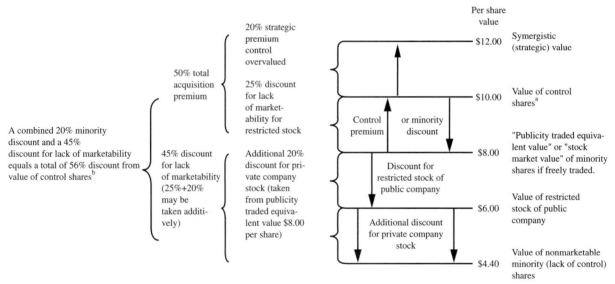

Notes:

[a] Control shares in a privately held company may also be subject to some discount for lack of marketability, but usually not nearly as much as minority shares.

[b] Minority and marketability discounts normally are multiplicative rather than additive. That is, they are taken in sequence:

$	10.00	Control value
–	2.00	Less minority interest discount (.20 × $10.00)
$	8.00	Marketable minority value
–	3.60	Less lack of marketability discount (.45 × $8.00)
$	4.40	Per share value of nonmarketable minority shares

SOURCE: Jay E. Fishman, Shannon P. Pratt, and J. Clifford Griffith, *Guide to Business Valuations*, 17th ed. (Fort Worth, TX: Practitioners Publishing Co.), Exhibit 8–8. Copies of this *Guide* can be ordered by calling PPC at 800-323-8724 or log onto www.ppc.thomson.com.

empirical evidence that is available is from the public market. Of the several hundred public companies that are taken over each year, most (about 85 percent) are at prices that represent a premium over the previous public trading price.

However, it is difficult, if not impossible, to sort out how much of this premium is for elements of control, and how much is for synergies between the seller and the buyer. Therefore, the levels of value chart (Exhibit 15–1) is schematic. That is, although it contains dollar values and percentages, they are only illustrative of how to apply the concepts.

Elements of Control

Control shares are normally more valuable than minority shares because they contain a bundle of rights that minority shares do not enjoy. The following is a partial list of some of the rights that go with control shares that minority shares do not have:

1. Appoint or change operational management.
2. Appoint or change members of the board of directors.
3. Determine management compensation and perquisites.
4. Set operational and strategic policy and change the course of the business.
5. Acquire, lease, or liquidate business assets, including plant, property, and equipment.
6. Select suppliers, vendors, and subcontractors with whom to do business and award contracts.
7. Negotiate and consummate mergers and acquisitions.
8. Liquidate, dissolve, sell out, or recapitalize the company.
9. Sell or acquire Treasury shares.
10. Register the company's equity securities for an initial or secondary public offering.
11. Register the company's debt securities for an initial or secondary public offering.
12. Declare and pay cash and/or stock dividends.
13. Change the articles of incorporation or bylaws.
14. Set one's own compensation (and perquisites) and the compensation (and perquisites) of related-party employees.
15. Select joint venturers and enter into joint venture and partnership agreements.
16. Decide what products and/or services to offer and how to price those products/services.
17. Decide what markets and locations to serve, to enter into, and to discontinue serving.
18. Decide which customer categories to market to and which not to market to.
19. Enter into inbound and outbound license or sharing agreements regarding intellectual properties.
20. Block any or all of the above actions.

Control or Lack of Control Covers a Spectrum

Control or minority is not a black and white concept with a bright dividing line. Control, or lack of it, covers a broad spectrum. Therefore, in some instances, it is more appropriate to use the phrase "discount for lack of control" rather than "minority discount." Even some blocks of control shares may lack absolute control, and even some minority shares may enjoy some elements of control.

The following is a partial listing of possible scenarios:

100 percent control. From the standpoint of estimating a control premium, this purely 100 percent scenario is the ultimate.

More than a majority or supermajority, but less than 100 percent. Most acquirers prefer to get 100 percent of the stock. One or a few minority stockholders could be a nuisance.

More than 50 percent but less than a supermajority, where state statutes or articles of incorporation require a supermajority. About half the states have statutes that require a supermajority (usually two-thirds) to effect certain corporate actions, such as a merger or liquidation. Some companies' articles of incorporation also require a supermajority for certain corporate actions.

50 percent. This is neither control nor minority. It is not enough to take actions, but is enough to block actions. In many cases, this leads to deadlock.

Less than 50 percent but "effective control." Where one stockholder has close to 50 percent and the balance of the shares are widely distributed, the plurality owner usually has effective control over operations.

Minority shares that control by a voting block. Some companies have both voting and nonvoting classes of shares. When a holder has a majority of the voting shares, no matter how small the block, that holder has control. Empirical evidence is presented later in the chapter regarding the value of that control.

How the Standard of Value Affects the Control Premium

The applicable standard of value can often determine, or at least impact, whether a control premium is applicable.

Fair Market Value

If starting with a control value, one would not normally add a control premium, because that would be redundant, that is, double counting the value of control.

If starting with a marketable minority interest value, one needs to make a choice. Publicly traded shares are, by definition, minority interests. However, according to the Nath hypothesis, they represent control values.[1] Otherwise, he says, there would be more takeovers in the public markets.

But there are some takeovers in the public markets, about 85% of which are at premiums to the previous public trading price. Empirical evidence on this is presented in a later section of this chapter.

Can evidence from the takeovers be used to estimate a control premium when reaching an opinion as to fair market value for control shares? Exhibit 15–1 shows a line above the control value line representing acquisition or synergistic value. Exhibit 15–2 is a schematic in which Chris Mercer raises the question, "which value is fair market value for 100 percent?"

---

[1] Eric W. Nath, "Control Premiums and Minority Interest Discounts in Private Companies." *Business Valuation Review*, September 1994, pp. 107–12.

Exhibit 15–2

Which Value Is Fair Market Value for 100 Percent?

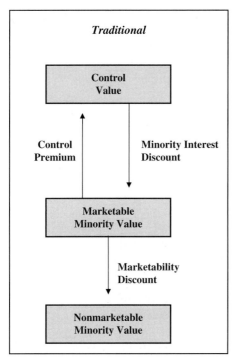
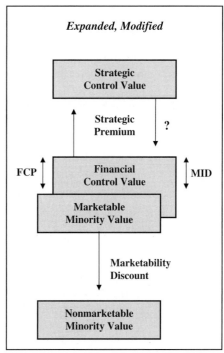

SOURCE: Z. Christopher Mercer, "Understanding and Quantifying Control Premiums: The Value of Control vs. Synergies of Strategic Advantages, Part II," *The Journal of Business Valuation* (Proceedings of the Fourth Joint Business Valuation Conference of The Canadian Institute of Chartered Business Valuators and the American Society of Appraisers, September 24 and 25, 1998). Toronto: The Canadian Institute of Chartered Business Valuators, 1999, p. 51.

In the U.S. Treasury definition, fair market value is defined as "the most probable price," and the buyer as a "hypothetical buyer" rather than any particular buyer. Consequently, the Tax Court has generally interpreted this to mean the value excluding synergy with a particular buyer. However, in an industry undergoing consolidation, where there is a pool of potential synergistic buyers, the multiples drawn from acquisition prices, including whatever synergies there may be, have been used to estimate fair market value.

In Canada, on the other hand, the definition of fair market value includes the phrase "the *highest* price" (emphasis supplied), and the appraiser is expected to seek out synergistic buyers, if any, and to include the value of synergies in fair market value.

Fair Value

In the context of dissenters' rights and minority oppression, discussed in detail in Chapters 35 and 36, the trend among courts is to interpret the fair value standard as a proportionate share of the enterprise value, without any discount for lack of control, even though the shares at issue usually are minority shares. For example, when starting with a publicly traded equivalent value, the Delaware Court of Chancery consistently adds a control premium. The case law varies from state to state, however, and the analyst should study the most recent relevant case law in the state in which the case is being tried.

Fair Value for Financial Reporting

As discussed more thoroughly in Chapters 2 and 39, fair value for financial reporting, although not yet totally settled, generally resembles fair market value.

Investment Value

Investment value, the value to some *particular* owner or potential owner, is found most often in the contexts of mergers and acquisitions and in family law disputes.

As noted earlier, some states and some companies have "coattail provisions," which mean that if a buyer buys the control shares, that buyer must offer the same amount for the minority shares. In a situation like that, the analyst must make a judgment as to the likelihood of a takeover in describing whether a control premium is applicable and, if so, how much. However, there are many cases in which control shares are bought and either no offer is made for the minority shares or a lower price per share is offered to the minority shareholders.

In the context of marital dissolutions, the practice varies widely, and the analyst must study the relevant case law very carefully. In some cases, a control premium may be applied if the holder is an officer or director of the company. In other cases, a control premium may be applied because of "family attribution" (other members of the family own the controlling shares), a practice specifically prohibited under the fair market value standard since Revenue Ruling 93-12.

Market Evidence Regarding Control and Acquisition Premiums

As noted earlier, there is a great deal of evidence regarding acquisition premiums, but there is no evidence to indicate what part of the premium paid is for synergies and what part is merely for the elements of control.

There are two convenient and inexpensive sources of control premium data: the *Mergerstat Review* and the *Mergerstat/Shannon Pratt's Control Premium Study.* As noted earlier, premiums and discounts are meaningless until the base to which they are applied is specifically identified. The only publicly available base from which to apply control premiums is stock market prices. Therefore, both sets of control premium data relate acquisition prices of public companies to their previous public trading prices. As the names of the two sources imply, they are compiled from the same data by Factset Mergerstat, but are presented differently, and contain very little overlap.

The Mergerstat Review

The *Mergerstat Review* has been printed annually in hardcover format since 1981. It publishes a wide variety of statistics on acquisition activity in the United States and abroad.

Exhibit 15–3

Price to Earnings* Multiples and Percent Offered over S&P 500, 1993–2005

	S&P 500 P/E**	Average P/E Offered	Average P/E Offered Relative to S&P 500 P/E
1993	23.4	24.4	4.3%
1994	19.9	24.5	23.1%
1995	16.6	23.8	43.4%
1996	19.2	26.2	36.5%
1997	22.4	27.4	22.3%
1998	26.9	25.1	−6.7%
1999	32.6	24.3	−25.5%
2000	25.4	23.8	−6.3%
2001	48.3	21.6	−55.3%
2002	28.2	22.9	−18.8%
2003	28.0	23.5	−16.1%
2004	26.8	25.3	−5.4%
2005	19.5	25.7	32.0%

* Excludes negative P/E multiples and P/E multiples larger than 100.

** Based upon an average of weekly prices and quarterly earnings.

SOURCE: Mergerstat® Review, 2006 (Santa Monica: FactSet Mergerstat LLC, 2006). www.mergerstat.com.

With respect to control premiums, it publishes annual average control premiums for about 50 broad industry groups. These are averages (means, not medians) and negative premiums (takeovers at discounts from previous public trading prices) are excluded.

The *Mergerstat Review* data indicate a strong inverse relationship between (1) the general level of the stock market (as measured by price/earnings [P/E] multiples) and (2) the price premiums paid over the market average P/E multiple in acquisition transactions. When the general stock market is low, the P/E multiples offered relative to the general stock market P/E multiple are high, and vice versa. Exhibit 15–3 presents this relationship. Many times, individual stocks, and even entire industries, may be overpriced. In those instances, it would not be prudent for acquirers to make takeover bids high enough in order to be successful. In such instances, a public market, noncontrolling interest stock price may be equal to—or even greater than—a controlling interest stock price.

The Mergerstat/Shannon Pratt's Control Premium Study

The *Mergerstat/Shannon Pratt's Control Premium Study* is an online database consisting of all takeovers of public companies resulting in over 50 percent ownership since 1998. As of the beginning of 2006, it contained 4,711 transactions and is updated quarterly. The transactions are all completed deals and are presented as of the closing date rather than the announcement date. Although presented here in the chapter on control premiums, the database is also useful for valuations because it has 51 data points for each transaction, including five valuation multiples.

Exhibit 15–4

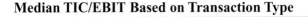

Median TIC/EBIT Based on Transaction Type

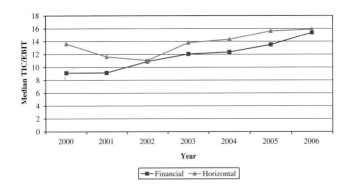

The control premium is based on the "Mergerstat unaffected trading price," which may vary from the actual price the day before the close of the deal.

A unique feature of the *Mergerstat/Shannon Pratt's Control Premium Study* is a transaction code by type of transaction:

F – Financial
H – Horizontal integration
V – Vertical integration
C – Conglomerate

This may be of some use to the analyst in assessing the degree of synergism reflected in the control premium. For example, Exhibit 15–4 shows that median total invested capital (TIC)/earnings before interest and taxes (EBIT) multiples were consistently lower for financial transactions than for horizontal integration transactions.

Negative Control Premiums

From time to time, the acquisition price premium data presented in the *Mergerstat Review* and the *Control Premium Study* report control event merger and acquisition transactions that have been consummated at a below-market price.

Valuation analysts who use the guideline public company valuation method, and then automatically tack on a percentage "control premium" based on *Mergerstat Review* control premium averages, should reconsider their methodology.

In fact, over the period since 1998, it surprises most people to know that about 15 percent of all takeovers of public companies occurred below the public trading prices. In fact, as shown in Exhibit 15–5, in the third quarter of 1998, about one-third of all takeovers were at discounts from their public trading prices.

Means, Medians, and Effect of Negative Premiums

Means (arithmetic averages) can be skewed by one or a few outliers. That is why most valuation analysts prefer medians as measures of central tendency.

Exhibit 15–5

Control Transactions at Discounts from Public Price
Third Quarter 1998

Target Name	Purchase Price Per Share	HLHZ Unaffected Price	HLHZ Control Premium	Price 1 Day Before	Premium 1 Day Before
Award Software International, Inc.	7.89	14.25	−44.6%	14.25	−44.6%
BankAmerica Corp.	62.87	76.44	−17.8%	76.44	−17.8%
Bristol Hotel Co.	23.08	27.63	−16.5%	27.63	−16.5%
Cameo International Inc.	52.22	71.88	−27.4%	62.25	−16.1%
CBT Corp.	32.81	33.25	−1.3%	33.25	−1.3%
Dime Financial Corp.	31.84	33.00	−11.6%	36.00	−3.5%
Domain Energy Corp.	9.69	12.50	−22.5%	12.50	−22.5%
Dresser Industries Inc.	29.44	37.69	−21.9%	37.69	−21.9%
FTP Software, Inc.	0.91	2.00	−54.5%	2.00	−54.5%
Hyperion Software Corp.	30.40	38.13	−20.3%	38.13	−20.3%
IBS Financial Corp.	15.75	20.00	−21.3%	20.00	−21.3%
John Alden Financial Corp.	22.50	28.44	−20.9%	22.63	−0.6%
Oncormed Inc.	1.93	3.31	−41.8%	3.31	−41.8%
Retirement Care Associates Inc.	7.39	8.63	−14.4%	9.00	−17.9%
Saks Holdings Inc.	28.06	43.38	−35.3%	40.69	−31.0%
Teleport Communications Group	55.29	60.13	−8.0%	57.75	−4.3%
US Rentals Inc.	20.57	30.19	−31.9%	30.19	−31.9%
Western Atlas Inc.	64.48	79.75	−19.2%	79.95	−19.2%
Whitehall Corp.	18.67	22.00	−15.1%	22.00	−15.1%
Zero Corp.	28.48	28.88	−1.4%	28.88	−1.4%

SOURCE: Shannon P. Pratt, "Control Premiums? Maybe, Maybe Not—34% of 3rd Quarter Buyouts at Discounts," Shannon Pratt's Business Valuation Update, January 1999, p. 1. Business Valuation Resources, LLC. © 1999. All rights reserved. Used with permission.

The upward skewness of using means versus medians as measures of central tendency for control premiums is demonstrated in Exhibit 15–6.

The effect of excluding versus including negatives in the calculations is also shown in Exhibit 15–6. Aren't the negatives a real part of the data set, and shouldn't a measure of central tendency reflect them? The difference between the typical control premium (actually, an acquisition premium) as measured by means without negatives and medians including negatives is rather striking!

One of the reviewers of this book, Gil Matthews, makes the following comment:

Use of the average acquisition premium in other transactions is a flawed approach. Since the average premium includes the prices paid for companies that buyers viewed as attractive undervalued targets and excludes companies that acquirers considered overpriced or fairly priced in the marketplace, the average premium paid in acquisitions is biased upward. Only a small portion of publicly traded companies are acquired in any particular year.

In addition, a fluctuation in market price affects the premium. A company's market price may increase when a similar company is acquired. A premium depends on the specific factors, most importantly the value placed on the target by the acquiror. Therefore, relative multiples must be considered in determining an

Exhibit 15–6

Percent Mean and Median Premium Paid

Year of buyout	Mean Premium Paid (%) (without negatives)[*]	Median Premium Paid (%) (without negatives)[*]	Mean Premium Paid (%) (with negatives)[*]	Median Premium Paid (%) (with negatives)[*]
1998	35.9	29.3	23.6	22.7
1999	46.5	32.4	40.0	28.7
2000	48.7	37.1	35.3	28.9
2001	52.1	35.9	34.0	25.9
2002	49.1	34.0	33.1	24.6
2003	53.9	37.7	46.2	33.3
2004	36.4	26.2	28.6	22.5
2005	33.1	24.3	23.1	16.7
2006	29.0	20.5	23.5	17.2

[*] *Without negatives* does not include public company sale transactions at *discounts* from their previous trading prices. *With negatives* does include such discount transactions.

SOURCE: Complied from *Mergerstat®/Shannon Pratt's Control Premium Study*.™ Santa Monica: FactSet Mergerstat LLC, 2006.

acquisition premium for purposes of a valuation. If multiples of guideline acquisitions are higher than multiples for guideline companies, the difference in multiples can be used to determine a reasonable acquisition premium.[2]

Robinson, Rumsey, and White Study

Chris Robinson, John Rumsey, and Alan White studied firms having voting and nonvoting classes of stock listed on the Toronto Stock Exchange (TSE) from 1981 through 1990. A valuable quality of the data is the large number of dual-class shares traded on the TSE. The total number of different firms in the sample was 93. The number of firms in the sample varied from a low of 47 in 1981 to a high of 77 in 1986. About half the sample had "coattail" protection for the nonvoting stock, which the authors explain as follows:

> An unusual characteristic of the data makes this estimation procedure more revealing. About half of the companies in our sample have takeover protection for the B shareholders, spelled out in the Articles of Incorporation. This protection, called a "coattail," has not been reported for any country other than Canada. It is triggered by a takeover offer to the A shareholders which is not made identically to the B shareholders.

---

[2] See, for example, Richard A. Booth, "Minority Discounts and Control Premiums in Appraisal Proceedings," *Business Lawyer*, November 2001, p. 127; Philip J. Clements and Philip W. Wisler, *The Standard & Poor's Guide to Fairness Opinions* (New York: McGraw Hill, 2005), p. 94; Bradford Cornell, *Corporate Valuation* (New York: McGraw Hill, 1993), p. 243; M. Mark Lee and Gilbert E. Matthews, "Fairness Opinions," in *The Handbook of Advanced Business Valuation*, Robert F. Reilly and Robert P. Schweihs, eds. (New York: McGraw Hill, 2000), p. 327; Gilbert E. Matthews, "Fairness Opinions: Common Errors and Omissions," in *The Handbook of Business Valuation and Intellectual Property Analysis*, Robert F. Reilly and Robert P. Schweihs, eds. (New York: McGraw Hill, 2004), pp. 214–216; Gilbert E. Matthews, "A Review of Valuations in Delaware Appraisal Cases, 2004–2005," *Business Valuation Review*, Summer 2006.

The two basic mechanisms used are: (1) the B shares acquire the same voting rights as the A shares; or (2) the B shares become convertible into the A shares for the purpose of tendering to the bid. Since the B shares outnumber the A shares in almost all cases, the B shareholders can defeat any takeover proposal, or make its acceptance very unlikely. Since August 1987 in Canada all new issues of dual class equity must include a coattail agreement for the B Shares, so that the proportion of firms with two classes of shares without coattails is diminishing.

The authors conclude:

> A takeover model became a significant explanatory variable for firms that had no coattail. A voting power model was a significant explanatory variable for firms that had a coattail provision.
>
> The empirical results suggest that if the observed premium is a result of an expected windfall takeover (a relatively rare event in which substantial gains may be reaped by the buyer), the expected gain to the A [voting] shareholders in the event of the takeover is between 8% and 18% of the total equity value.[3]

Summary

Control shareholders have legal rights which make the shares more valuable than minority shares. However, absent some oppressive actions toward minority shareholders, many analysts tend to overstate the value of these rights.

In general, the only measure of a control premium is in the public market, when a public company is taken over. But this measurement includes the value of synergies as well as the value of control. Most analysts tend to draw conclusions from these data that exaggerate the value of control, as analyzed in this chapter.

Bibliography

Annin, Michael. "Understanding and Quantifying Control Premiums: The Value of Control vs. Synergies or Strategic Advantages, Part I." *The Journal of Business Valuation* (Proceedings of the 4th Joint Business Valuation Conference of The Canadian Institute of Chartered Business Valuators and the American Society of Appraisers). Toronto: The Canadian Institute of Chartered Business Valuators, 1999, pp. 31–35.

Cimasi, Robert, and Charles Wilhoite. "Fair Market Value." *BV Q&A Newsletter,* October 2005. Available at www.BVLibrary.com.

---

[3] Chris Robinson, John Rumsey, and Alan White, "The Value of a Vote in the Market for Corporate Control," paper published by York University Faculty of Administrative Studies, February 1996. Used with permission from authors, Alan White (Peter L. Mitchelson/Sit Investment Associates Foundation Professor of Investment Strategy, Joseph L. Rotman School of Management, University of Toronto), John Rumsey, and Dr. Chris Robinson, whose work appears in *Convergence and Diversity of Corporate Governance Regimes and Capital Markets*, J. McCahery, P. Moerland, T. Raaijmakers, and L. Renneboog, eds., Oxford University Press, 2002.

Curtiss, Rand M. "A Practical Methodology for Determining Premiums and Discounts." *Business Valuation Review*, vol. 16, no. 4, December 1997, pp. 172–79.

Dickson, Lisa, M. Mark Lee, and Shannon P. Pratt. "Implications of Fair Market Value." *BV Q&A Newsletter,* August 2004. Available at www.BVLibrary.com.

Dickson, Lisa, Shannon P. Pratt, and Gary Trugman. "Fair Market Value on a Control Basis." *BV Q&A Newsletter,* August 2004. Available at www.BVLibrary.com.

Estabrook, Joseph. "Blockage Discounts: What Are They and How Do They Affect the Fair Market Value of Publicly Traded Stocks, Real Estate, and Other Assets." *BV Papers* (Presented at 2001 ASA conference). Available at www.BVLibrary.com.

Fishman, Jay E., and Shannon P. Pratt. "Differences between Fair Value and Fair Market Value." *BV Q&A Newsletter,* August 2004. Available at www.BVLibrary.com.

Fishman, Jay E., Shannon P. Pratt, J. Clifford Griffith, and D. Keith Wilson. "Premiums and Discounts in Business Valuations." Parts I and II. *Fair$hare*, May and June 1992, pp. 11–17, 14–16.

Fishman, Jay E., Shannon P. Pratt, and Don Schiller. "Fair Market Value." *BV Q&A Newsletter,* October 2005. Available at www.BVLibrary.com.

Frazier, William, Eric Nath, and Shannon P. Pratt. "Effect on Fair Market Value Is a Gain Times the Tax Rate." *BV Q&A Newsletter,* June 2005. Available at www.BVLibrary.com.

Freeman, Jeff, James Hitchner, and Chris Treharne. "Investment Value Approach Instead of Fair Market Value." *BV Q&A Newsletter,* May 2005. Available at www.BVLibrary.com.

Garber, Steven D. "Control Premiums vs. Acquisition Premiums – Is There a Difference?" Presentation to the International Conference of the American Society of Appraisers, June 1998. Available on www.BVLibrary.com.

Hitchner, James R., and Gary Roland. "Marketability and Control Govern Value of Family Businesses." *Taxation for Accountants*, January 1994, pp. 24–28.

Julius, J. Michael. "Using Control Premium Statistics." *CPA Litigation Service Counselor*, July 1999, pp. 8–10.

Lease, Ronald C., John J. McConnell, and Wayne H. Mikkelson. "The Market Value of Control in Publicly-Traded Corporations. *Journal of Financial Economics 11* (1983), pp. 439–71.

Mercer, Z. Christopher. "A Brief Review of Control Premiums and Minority Interest Discounts." *The Journal of Business Valuation* (Proceedings of the 12th Biennial Business Valuation Conference of The Canadian Institute of Chartered Business Valuators). Toronto: The Canadian Institute of Chartered Business Valuators, 1997, pp. 365–87.

_____. "Understanding and Quantifying Control Premiums: The Value of Control vs. Synergies or Strategic Advantages, Part II." *The Journal of Business Valuation* (Proceedings of the 4th Joint Business Valuation Conference of The Canadian Institute of Chartered Business Valuators and the American Society of Appraisers). Toronto: The Canadian Institute of Chartered Business Valuators, 1999, pp. 36–54. Also available at www.BVLibrary.com.

Nath, Eric W. "Control Premiums and Minority Interest Discounts in Private Companies." *Business Valuation Review*, vol. 13, no. 3, September 1994, pp. 107–12.

Pratt, Shannon P. "Control Premiums? Maybe, Maybe Not—34% of 3rd Quarter Buyouts at Discounts." *Shannon Pratt's Business Valuation Update*, vol. 5, no. 1, January 1999, pp. 1–2.

Pratt, Shannon P., and Candice Robertson. "Calculating Fair Market Value of Corporation Shares." *BV Q&A Newsletter*, March 2005. Available at www.BVLibrary.com.

Roach, George P. "Control Premiums and Strategic Mergers." *Business Valuation Review*, vol. 17, no. 2, June 1998, pp. 42–49.

Robinson, Chris, John Rumsey, and Alan White, "The Value of a Vote in the Market for Corporate Control," paper published by York University Faculty of Administrative Studies, February 1996. Used with permission from authors, Alan White (Peter L. Mitchelson/Sit Investment Associates Foundation Professor of Investment Strategy, Joseph L. Rotman School of Management, University of Toronto), John Rumsey and Dr. Chris Robinson, whose work appears in *Convergence and Diversity of Corporate Governance Regimes and Capital Markets*, J. McCahery, P. Moerland, T. Raaijmakers and L. Renneboog, eds., Oxford University Press, 2002.

Schubert, Walt, and Les Barenbaum. "Control Premiums and the Value of the Closely-Held Firm." *Journal of Small Business Finance*, vol. 1, no. 2 (1991), pp. 155–59.

Tiernan, Peter B. "How 50% Ownership Affects Estate Planning for Closely Held Stock." *Journal of Taxation*, October 1999, pp. 232–40.

Chapter 16

Discount for Lack of Control

This chapter discusses the valuation of noncontrolling ownership interests in businesses. This type of ownership interest is often referred to in the valuation literature and in court cases as a *minority interest* or *minority ownership interest*. This type of ownership interest should be more properly referred to as a noncontrolling ownership interest. The value of a noncontrolling interest can sometimes be calculated by applying a discount to the value of a controlling interest.

This nomenclature is more consistent with the concepts of marketability and lack of marketability. A marketable ownership interest is one that is reasonably liquid. In other words, it can be sold and converted into cash quickly and at a low transaction cost. A business interest or security that does not enjoy this economic attribute is said to be nonmarketable. In the valuation process, that nonmarketable security may be valued by the application of a lack of marketability discount, or a "discount for lack of marketability," which is the subject of the next chapter.

As we pointed out in the previous chapter, a discount for lack of control is the mirror image of a control premium. Therefore, much of what was said in the last chapter is applicable to this chapter, and they should be read in conjunction with each other. The application of any discounts should always be taken in the context of:

1. The level of value that it is taken from
2. The legal documents that control the rights and restrictions of the interest holder, and
3. The ultimate rate of return produced for the interest.

Too often, analysts fail to consider these three critical elements, often resulting in vast overstatements (or understatements) of the magnitude of the differential between the controlling and the noncontrolling interest. Many nuances affect these three issues. However, the analyst should always keep in mind that, like a controlling interest investor, a noncontrolling interest investor must determine what amount of cash he or she will have access to, and what rate of return will induce him or her to invest in it. Often times, the best way to evaluate this is the same way that minority investors actually do in the marketplace—that is, by assessing cash returns, and by assessing a rate of return. For analysts, this is best represented by working the assumptions of the minority investor into the income approach. At the very least, the analyst should consider the reasonableness of the internal rate of return produced by the use of discount procedures discussed in this chapter.

Lack of Control Covers a Spectrum

We said in the previous chapter that control and lack of control do not have a bright line dividing point—they encompass a spectrum. Even minority shares can have some elements of control. These elements of control may reduce, but rarely eliminate, the discount for lack of control.

The following are three such scenarios:

Blocking power: About half the states and many individual companies have statutes or articles that require a supermajority to effect certain corporate actions. If the minority block is of sufficient size to block such actions, there may be cause to reduce the discount for lack of control. In most cases, this would only be grounds for a slight reduction in the discount.

Swing vote: If a minority block can be combined with another block to create a controlling interest (say the stock was distributed 40, 40, and 20 percent, or even 49, 49, and 2 percent), the small minority block obviously has some elements of control. If starting with a controlling interest value, this could be grounds for a substantial reduction in the minority interest discount, unless there was reason to believe the two larger block holders would vote in unison. If starting with a minority value, this could be reason to add a partial control premium.

Takeover, or "coattail" protection: Some companies' articles of incorporation have provisions that if majority shares are sold in a change of control transaction, the minority shareholders must be offered the same price. Empirical evidence of how this effectively reduces the control premium (thus reducing the lack of control discount) was presented in the previous chapter.

Factors That Influence the Lack of Control Discount

The matter of a controlling ownership position versus a noncontrolling ownership position is not an either/or proposition. Relevant state statutes, the subject company's articles of incorporation and bylaws, and the way the overall ownership of the subject company is distributed have an important bearing on the relative rights of the noncontrolling and of the controlling stockholders.

Effect of State Statutes

Statutes affecting the relative rights of controlling versus noncontrolling stockholders vary from state to state.

Supermajority Vote Requirements. In some states, a simple majority vote can approve major actions, such as a merger, sale of all of the assets, or liquidation of the company. Other states require a two-thirds—or even greater—majority vote in order to approve such corporate actions. In these instances a stockholder with just over a one-third ownership interest in the company (or, in a few states, even less) has the power to block such actions. This is true even if there is a stockholder with a clear majority (i.e., over 50 percent) ownership position. In that case, the "majority" stockholder may enjoy relative—but not absolute—control of the business.

State Dissolution Statutes. Under the statutes of a majority of the states, non-controlling stockholders enjoy certain legal rights under some circumstances that noncontrolling stockholders in some other states generally do not enjoy. For example, under certain circumstances, usually if the noncontrolling stockholders can show that there is a deadlock or that they are somehow oppressed, noncontrolling stockholders can bring suit to dissolve the corporation. If the suit is successful, and if the controlling stockholders wish to avoid dissolution, the remedy is to pay the noncontrolling stockholders the "fair value" for their stock. For this reason, the variations in state law concerning legal rights; attributable to various equity ownership percentage interests have an important bearing on the valuation of a noncontrolling ownership interest.

Articles of Incorporation and Bylaws

A myriad of possible provisions in companies' articles of incorporation and bylaws can impact the relative degree of control, or lack of it, for any particular block of stock or partnership interest. For example, even in a state that requires only a simple majority for any corporate action, many companies write requirements for supermajorities for certain actions into their articles of incorporation.

The analyst should understand any provisions in company documents (or other shareholder agreements) that may impact the degree of control when quantifying a lack of control discount (or a control premium) for a specific ownership interest.

Potential Dilution

Another factor that can affect the degree of control—or lack of control—is a change in the relative distribution of ownership as a result of either issuance of shares or redemption of outstanding shares. Many companies have stock options outstanding, the exercise of which could affect the balance of control. An employee stock ownership plan (ESOP) could have control at one point in time, but lose that control position as a result of retiring participants exercising options to "put" their stock to the company. Even if an ESOP has a right of first refusal, it may not always have the resources available to exercise the right.

Preemptive Rights

Some companies give their stockholders *preemptive rights*. The *Encyclopedia of Banking & Finance* defines this right as follows:

> **PREEMPTIVE RIGHT** Stockholders' privilege to subscribe to new issues of voting stock, usually the common stock or securities convertible into voting stock, before such offerings are made to nonstockholders. A preemptive right is often referred to as a privileged subscription right. The preemptive right has been eroded in recent years.[1]

Such rights are designed to protect stockholders from dilution. However, they can make it awkward for a company to issue new shares, first having to offer stock to existing stockholders in accordance with the preemptive right provisions. For this reason, the trend in recent years has been toward elimination of preemptive rights.

Even if preemptive rights exist on paper, they may not be of equal efficacy to each respective holder of such rights, because one owner may have adequate resources to exercise such rights, while another owner may not.

Cumulative versus Noncumulative Voting

Either state statutes or a company's articles of incorporation may allow for cumulative voting. Under noncumulative voting, a simple majority of the stock can elect *all* the directors. Under cumulative voting, votes may be "cumulated" for a single

---

[1] Charles J. Woelfel, *Encyclopedia of Banking & Finance*, 10th ed. (Burr Ridge, IL: Probus Publishing Company, 1994), p. 912. Reprinted with permission.

director. For example, if five directors are to be elected, the owner of a share of stock could cast five votes for a single director, thus enabling minority shareholders with a sufficient number of shares to elect one or more directors.

The *Encyclopedia of Banking & Finance* offers the following formula for determining how many shares are required to elect one or more directors with cumulative voting:

$$\frac{\text{Total number of shares voting} \times \text{Number of directors desired}}{\text{Total number of directors} + 1} + 1$$

To illustrate, if there are five directors to be elected, and 500 shares are outstanding and voting for the election of directors, the minimum number of shares necessary to elect one director would be 84 shares. Proof: 84 shares times five directors to be elected equals 420 votes, all cast for one director. Assuming the rest of the stock (416 shares) votes en bloc as the majority, such total of 2,080 votes distributed among five directors would be 416 votes each. Therefore, the individual representing the minority and receiving its 420 votes is sure to get one of the places on the board, the majority getting the other four places. The minority in this example must be sure to vote all of its 420 votes for one director; if it distributed the 420 votes among two, it obviously would not win any places on the board.

Cumulative voting, therefore, does *not* automatically assure the minority of representation on the board; the minority must have the minimum shares necessary for election of the directors desired and, second, must concentrate its cumulative votes properly. A good general rule to remember is Dr. Harry G. Guthmann's generalization: The minority for election of at least one director fraction of the total board must own the next lower fraction plus one share; e.g., on a board of five directors, the minority must have one-sixth of the stock plus one share; six directors, one-seventh of the stock plus one share, etc. Cumulative voting, moreover, requires a majority of the stock to be able to elect a majority of the board; in the above example, to elect three of the five directors, 251 shares are necessary, or a majority of the 500 shares total.[2]

Contractual Restrictions

Many ownership control rights may be denied to a company (or to the controlling owner) due to contractual restrictions. For example, indenture provisions in conjunction with debt obligations frequently prevent dividend payments, increased management compensation, liquidation of assets, acquisitions, or changes in the direction of the business.

Financial Condition of Business

Many of the rights associated with ownership control are rendered economically empty—or of little economic value—simply because of the company's financial condition. These could include the right to decide on management compensation, dividends, stock or asset purchases, or acquisition of other companies. Alternatively, companies that are generating a superior rate of return may not

[2] Ibid., p. 276.

deserve a substantial control premium if most advantages of control are already being enjoyed by the shareholders.

Highly Regulated Industries

With respect to companies in highly regulated industries, a lack of control discount may apply even if the subject is a 100 percent equity ownership interest. This is because the controlling stockholders of a highly regulated business do not have all of the perquisites of control that owners of less regulated businesses have. In some industries, governmental authority is needed to buy, sell, or merge a company. In some industries, government authority is needed to liquidate or otherwise shut down a company (or a part of a company)—even when company operations have turned unprofitable. And in some industries, government authority is needed to open a new branch (or sell a new product or provide a new service).

For these highly regulated companies, a lack of control discount may be applicable to the overall business value. This is because the government—not the 100 per cent stockholder—enjoys many of the prerogatives of ownership control. In such instances, there may be a greater discount for lack of control applicable to a noncontrolling block of stock than to a controlling block of stock. But the difference in the two levels of lack of control discounts would not be as great as in a less regulated industry. This is because, in a highly regulated industry, neither the noncontrolling stockholder nor the controlling stockholder enjoys absolute control.

Buy-Sell and Other Shareholder Agreements

In some companies, all shareholders have entered into buy-sell agreements or into other shareholder agreements. The provisions of such agreements usually dictate the valuation of the company stock for purposes of transactions (1) between the company and shareholders and (2) among shareholders.

If the language of the relevant agreements indicates that minority blocks of stock will be valued on a controlling ownership interest level of value, a full lack of control discount will not apply to the transactions to which the provision is applicable. For example, the agreement may say that the subject shares will be valued "on an enterprise basis" or as "a per share portion of the overall company value." In such instances, the company stockholders have agreed to deal with each other on a controlling ownership interest basis—according to the terms of the agreements.

Fiduciary Duties

Sometimes, controlling stockholders cannot or do not exercise all of the prerogatives of ownership control. This may occur when the controlling stockholder has a fiduciary or other special duty to the noncontrolling stockholders. In such cases, controlling stockholders and noncontrolling stockholders could be treated equally with regard to economic benefits of equity ownership.

In such instances, the lack of control discount may not be so great as it otherwise would be. This is because the base to which the discount would apply—that is, the overall business enterprise value—may not be inflated due to the influences of ownership control. And this is because all stockholders—noncontrolling and controlling—would expect to share equally in the economic fruit of the company's commercial success. However, there are very few situations in which a fiduciary obligation would require treating a noncontrolling stockholder on a basis equivalent to a controlling stockholder. Under most state laws, a controlling stockholder can even sell the control stock without requiring that any offer be made to purchase noncontrolling stock.

Private Company with Public Securities

Some privately owned companies have publicly traded securities that are subject to the Securities and Exchange Commission (SEC) registration process. This situation generally occurs when all of the company's common stock is closely held but some of the company's bonds are publicly traded. In this circumstance, the company is generally subject to all of the periodic disclosure requirements of other public companies.

In such instances, the discount for lack of control may be less than it would otherwise be. Due to the SEC public reporting requirements, the controlling stockholder would have to disclose information not normally available to noncontrolling stockholders, such as detailed financial statements, officers' compensation, transactions between the company and shareholders, and so forth. Therefore, some of the benefits of ownership control are lost due to these public disclosure requirements. Also, the controlling stockholder would always be aware of the applicable regulatory authority of the SEC. Accordingly, the controlling stockholder may not always act like a controlling stockholder would in a company not subject to SEC scrutiny.

Private Company That Operates Like a Public Company

Even if they don't have public debt outstanding, some closely held companies operate very much like publicly owned companies. They follow the business, accounting, and legal formalities of public companies. They have independent directors on their boards of directors. And, they believe in full disclosure to all stockholders.

In such an instance, the lack of control discount is usually less than it would otherwise be. One reason is that in such a case the controlling stockholder is (presumably on a voluntary basis) not exercising all of the prerogatives of control.

Control Has Already Been Dissipated

Earlier, we mentioned the case of three equal shareholders. Let's consider slightly more extreme cases. What happens if there are 10 or 20 equal (or relatively equal) stockholders? Such a scenario may not be uncommon at all in family-owned businesses or in professional practices. For example, consider a consultancy corporation with 20 shareholder/consultants. In such instances, ownership control may have already been dissipated.

In such circumstances, the lack of control discount is often less than it would otherwise be. That is because when all owners are sharing (relatively) equally in the wealth of the business, the overall business enterprise value may not be affected by the actions of a controlling owner. Consequently, the base to which the lack of control discount is applied is lower than it would otherwise be. And with all owners sharing (relatively) equally in the wealth of the business, there is no significant disparity between the economic benefits available to noncontrolling owners and to majority owners.

Nonoperating Assets

Nonoperating or excess assets are of little value to a minority stockholder unless there is a prospect of doing something productive with them, such as selling them and paying out the proceeds in dividends or redeploying the proceeds into profitable operating assets. The values of such nonoperating assets could be part of the basis for a minority discount.

Empirical Evidence to Quantify Lack of Control Discounts

As noted in the previous chapter, minority discounts are the mirror image of control premiums. So, much of the evidence to quantify control premiums can be used in reverse to quantify discounts for lack of control. Exhibit 16–1 is an expanded version of Exhibit 15–6, with four additional columns showing the implied minority discount for the control premium selected for each year.

Exhibit 16–1

Percent Mean and Median Premium Paid and Implied Minority Discount

Year of buyout	Mean Premium Paid (%) (without negatives)[a]	Implied Minority Discount (%)[b]	Median Premium Paid (%) (without negatives)[a]	Implied Minority Discount (%)[b]	Mean Premium Paid (%) (with negatives)[a]	Implied Minority Discount (%)[b]	Median Premium Paid (%) (with negatives)[a]	Implied Minority Discount (%)[b]
1998	35.9	26.4	29.3	22.7	23.6	19.1	22.7	18.5
1999	46.5	31.7	32.4	24.5	40.0	28.6	28.7	22.3
2000	48.7	32.8	37.1	27.1	35.3	26.1	28.9	22.4
2001	52.1	34.3	35.9	26.4	34.0	25.4	25.9	20.6
2002	49.1	32.9	34.0	25.4	33.1	24.9	24.6	19.7
2003	53.9	35.0	37.7	27.4	46.2	31.6	33.3	25.0
2004	36.4	26.7	26.2	20.8	28.6	22.2	22.5	18.4
2005	33.1	24.9	24.3	19.5	23.1	18.8	16.7	14.3
2006	29.0	22.5	20.5	17.0	23.5	19.0	17.2	14.7

Notes:

[a] *Without negatives* does not include public company sale transactions at *discounts* from their previous trading prices. *With negatives* does not include such discount transactions.

[b] Formula: $1 - [1 \div (1 + \text{Median Premium Paid})]$.

SOURCE: Complied from *Mergerstat®/Shannon Pratt's Control Premium Study.*™ Santa Monica: FactSet Mergerstat LLC, 2006.

The formula for converting a control premium to an implied minority discount is:

Formula 16–1

$$1 - \frac{1}{1 + \text{premium}}$$

For example, if we choose the median premium including negatives (22.5 percent), the implied minority discount would be:

Formula 16–2

$$1 - \frac{1}{1 + .225} = 18.4$$

The number 18.4 appears in the "Implied Minority Discount" column, following the chosen control premium column. See the previous chapter for comments about mean versus median premiums.

Also, it is important to emphasize that what is called a "control premium" in this book is in reality an "acquisition premium," including the premium paid for synergies as well as for the elements of control. Therefore, when using these data to estimate minority interest discounts, it is worthwhile to look at the actual transactions and estimate what portion of the premium actually represented synergies; they could be significant.

Discounts from Net Asset Value

As noted several times in this book, net asset value (or adjusted net asset value) is not equal to the true economic value of a company's stock unless a complete asset revaluation analysis—recognizing all intangible assets and all forms of obsolescence—has been conducted.

Holding Companies

Adjusted net asset values are available for most publicly traded closed-end investment companies (including both real estate investment trusts [REITs] and operating real estate companies), for some real estate holding companies, and for some companies with significant timber holdings. If one were to assume the company could be liquidated for its adjusted net asset value (and, therefore, that value represented a control level of value), then the price at which minority shares traded may be an indication of a lack of control discount. There could, however, also be other factors affecting this adjusted net asset value to price difference. For example, the amount of income taxes on the built-in gains related to unrealized appreciation of asset values could affect these security prices.

Limited Partnerships

Most market transactions in limited partnership interests in recent years have been at substantial price discounts from underlying net asset values. Unlike stocks, most limited partnerships sold in public offerings never develop a secondary public trading market. A few limited partnerships are exchanged in a limited market made by a few brokerage houses. Their number is diminishing in recent years due to liquidation and lack of new public limited partnership offerings. Those that are still outstanding with some trading are tracked by a publication called *Direct Investments Spectrum*,[3] which publishes trading prices relative to estimates of underlying asset values. Therefore, unlike most stocks, where one body of empirical data helps to quantify lack of control discounts and another discount for lack of marketability, the discounts from net asset value for limited partnership transactions encompass aspects of both (1) the lack of control discount and (2) the lack of marketability discount. The authors believe that most of the discount is due to lack of control.

Built-In Gains Discount

If valuing a company by the asset approach, the analyst should check to see whether capital gains taxes would be incurred on the liquidation of the assets. If so, it is possible that a discount should be taken for the capital gains tax liability. For more on this topic, see Chapter 18, "Other Valuation Discounts."

Trust and Estate Sales Study

H. Calvin Coolidge, a 'bank trust officer responsible for administering trusts and estates that owned all or portions of closely held businesses, performed two studies several years ago in which he compiled data on actual sales prices of closely held businesses. As an introduction, Coolidge offers the following generalities:

> A number of years of experience has demonstrated that it is extremely difficult to find any market for minority interests ..., despite efforts to do so. ... On the relatively rare occasions when an offer is made to buy a minority interest, it is almost always for an amount far less than the fiduciary and the beneficiary expect to get.[4]

In his first study, Coolidge compiled data on 30 actual sales of noncontrolling ownership interests. He found that the average transaction price was 36 percent below book value, and he concluded with the following observations:

> Only 20 percent of the sales were made at discounts less than 20 percent. A little more than half the sales ($53\frac{1}{3}$ percent) were made at discounts that ranged from 22 percent to 48 percent, and $23\frac{1}{3}$ percent of the sales were made at discounts of from 54.4 percent to 78 percent.
>
> It would be dangerous to draw too many generalizations from the survey, but those sales where the discounts were below 20 percent involved, with one exception, purchases from close relatives where friendly relations existed. The exception was the sale by a holder of swing shares who used his leverage well, but still took a 4.3 percent discount. At the other end of the spectrum was the settlement of a three-year bitter dispute between two families; the majority family raised its token offer only after

---

[3] *Direct Investments Spectrum*, published bimonthly by Partnership Profiles, Inc., P.O. Box 7938, Dallas, TX 75209-0938. 800-634-4614.

[4] H. Calvin Coolidge, "Fixing Value of Minority Interest in Business: Actual Sales Suggest Discount as High as 70%," reprinted with permission from *Estate Planning*, ©Spring 1975, p. 141 Warren, Gorham & Lamont, 31 St. James Avenue, Boston, MA 02116, (800) 950-1216.

threat of a lawsuit, but the price the minority interest took nonetheless represented a 78 percent discount.[5]

It is noteworthy that the discounts in the foregoing surveys were from accounting book value and not from the market value of the subject business enterprise. Accounting book value, of course, recognizes no appreciation in asset values above their depreciated original cost. Although, in a very few cases in the above survey, the price discounts were computed from an adjusted book value, reflecting appreciation in real estate values. One would expect that the subject business enterprise value would be above the book value in most cases. If that expectation is correct, then the discounts from the owners' proportionate shares of the total enterprise value would be even greater than the discounts as presented in the survey (which were from accounting book value).

An update published in 1983 indicated a trend toward even higher discounts when disposing of noncontrolling ownership interests in closely held corporations. That study concluded a much higher concentration of discounts from accounting book value at the high end of the range, and the average discount for the two studies combined was approximately 40 percent. The updated study concludes as follows:

> Each of the sales used in the survey involved a combination of factors that made it somewhat unique. To use any of the data, or any classification of the data, as definitive proof of the discount to be applied in a prospective valuation would be dangerous. This should not, however, obscure the true significance of the data, which is that in the actual marketplace, the typical discount is not of token size, but of substantial magnitude.[6]

Although the study is over two decades old, and has not been updated since, we imagine that if it were updated today, similar results would ensue.

Discounts for Direct Undivided Ownership Interests in Real Estate

Empirical market data on sales of fractional ownership interests in real estate are scarce. However, the available data do support the concept that fractional ownership interests in real estate, when they are sold, generally are priced at less than a pro rata portion of the market value of the total real estate parcel.

One study covered 54 undivided interests, with the undivided ownership interest price discounts ranging from zero to 82 percent, with a median price discount of 35 percent.[7] Another study covered 21 undivided ownership interests, with the undivided ownership interest price discounts ranging from 5 to 94 percent, with a median price discount of 30 percent.[8]

Real estate undivided ownership interest discounts tend to be considerably smaller than lack of control discounts for stocks or partnership interests. This probably is explained in large part by differences in the respective rights of the ownership interests. An owner of an individual ownership interest in real estate may sue for partition—that is, to have the property divided and to give each owner

[5] Ibid., p. 141.

[6] H. Calvin Coolidge, "Survey Shows Trend Toward Larger Minority Discounts," *Estate Planning*, September 1983, p. 282.

[7] Peter J. Patchin, "Market Discounts for Undivided Minority Interest in Real Estate," *Real Estate issues*, Fall/Winter 1988, pp. 14–16.

[8] Don L. Harris, Philip A. McCormick, and W.D. Davis Sr., "The Valuation of Partial Interests in Real Estate," *ASA Valuation*, December 1983, pp. 62–73.

his or her pro rata share. If the court finds that the property is not divisible, then it may order the property to be sold. Owners of noncontrolling stock and partnership ownership interests have no such rights.

It is interesting to note that the U.S. Tax Court has distinguished between (1) lack of control (i.e., minority interest) and (2) lack of marketability discounts for an undivided interest in real estate. The court stated:

> "A minority interest discount for an interest in real property may be allowed on account of the lack of control which accompanies co-ownership." The minority interest discount should consider "the cost, uncertainty, and delays attendant upon partition proceedings… The marketability discount, by contrast, measures the diminution in value attributable to the lack of a ready market for the property." This two-step process is similar to prior Tax Court decisions regarding corporate and partnership interests.[9]

Procedures for the Valuation of Noncontrolling Ownership Interests

There are three basic ways of approaching the valuation of noncontrolling ownership interests:

1. The discount approach—based on a proportionate share of the overall business enterprise value, less a specific valuation lack of control discount applied to the enterprise value.
2. The direct comparison approach—based on a direct comparison of the subject ownership interest with the values of other noncontrolling ownership interests.
3. The bottom-up approach (income approach)—based on the estimation of the economic benefits that the noncontrolling ownership interest holder expects to realize over the expected holding period of the subject investment, discounted at an appropriate rate of return.

Conceptually, there is some analogy of the above-mentioned approaches to the three generally accepted approaches to individual asset appraisal: the cost approach, the market approach, and the income approach. The discount approach considers the "cost" of lack of control to the security holder in terms of a specific value decrement. The direct comparison approach relies on market-derived data regarding the sales of guideline or comparable noncontrolling securities (e.g., sales of other blocks of noncontrolling stock in the same closely held corporation). And, the bottom-up approach values the subject noncontrolling security by reference to the present value of all components of economic income that will be derived from the ownership of that noncontrolling security.

The Discount Approach

A common way to approach the valuation of a noncontrolling ownership interest is to apply the following four-step process:

---

[9] *Samuel J. LeFrak v. Commissioner*, 66 T.C.M. 1297 (1993).

1. Estimate the overall value of the subject business enterprise.
2. Calculate the noncontrolling owner's pro rata allocation of the business enterprise value.
3. Estimate the amount of the valuation adjustment—that is, the lack of control discount applicable to the pro rata allocation of the overall business enterprise value in order to properly reflect economic disadvantage of the noncontrolling owner vis-à-vis the controlling owner.
4. Subtract the lack of control discount from the controlling owner pro rata allocation of the overall business enterprise value. (In most cases, one would then also subtract a lack of marketability discount.)

The value of the overall business enterprise should be estimated on a controlling ownership level of value as discussed previously in this book. The proportionate value is normally a straightforward calculation. However, occasionally there may be complications due to special rights of different classes of partners or stockholders.

The amount of the valuation adjustment—or discount—to reflect the noncontrolling ownership interest should be a matter of rigorous analysis. The degree of ownership control, or the lack of it, has a bearing on the magnitude of the applicable valuation discount. However, there is no single formula to quantify this valuation adjustment.

Also, the valuation discount is generally lower for stocks that pay cash dividends or partnerships that distribute considerable cash flow, than for those that do not. However, there is no simple formula to quantify that factor either. Some guidance with regard to typical discounts—and to typical ranges of discounts—related to noncontrolling ownership interests is presented in later sections of this chapter.

The Direct Comparison Approach

If data are available on actual sales of comparative noncontrolling ownership interests, the analyst may be able to reach a conclusion of value by direct comparison to such transactions. This analysis can be performed without ever going through the step of estimating a value for the total business enterprise. The analyst can value the subject noncontrolling ownership interest using market valuation approach procedures similar to those used for valuing a total company. Such procedures include, for example, the capitalization of earnings, the capitalization of cash flow, the capitalization of dividends (or partnership withdrawals), the application of a market-derived multiple of price to book value, the application of a market-derived price to adjusted net asset value, and so on.

Guidance with regard to the quantification of the market-derived pricing multiples comes from an analysis of comparative noncontrolling ownership interest transactional data.

Sources of Comparative Data. One obvious source of comparative data would be prior arm's-length transactions involving noncontrolling ownership interests in the subject company.

There is no generally available source of data on any broad group of noncontrolling ownership interest transactions in closely held companies. There is, of course, a readily available database on daily transactions in minority equity interests in literally thousands of publicly traded companies. Subject to several limitations discussed earlier in the book, guidance with respect to market-derived pricing multiples for the valuation of noncontrolling ownership interests may be drawn from the prices of comparative publicly traded stocks. When public capital market minority share transactional data are used, ordinarily this data will indicate the marketable, noncontrolling ownership interest level of value. However, some analysts believe that, at least in some cases, the guideline public company method produces a stand-alone (nonsynergistic) control value.

However, many analysts believe that the guideline public company method produces a level of value that would be consistent with the level of income used in the calculation of value. That is, if a normalized level of earnings (including control adjustments) were used, it would produce a control value. If the analyst used earnings that had not been normalized, then it could produce noncontrol value. This is consistent with current thinking with the income approach, in which the level of value is determined in the numerator of the value calculation. That is, the income stream, and not the denominator. Both the income approach and the guideline public company method derive a rate of return from the public stock markets; if the income (numerator) is controlling as to level of value in one, then it makes intuitive sense that it would be controlling in the other.

Adjustments for Risk and for Lack of Marketability. As discussed earlier in the book, if the comparison with public stock prices procedure is performed, adjustments need to be made for differences in (1) risk, (2) liquidity, and (3) other factors. The most important of these factors is the lack of marketability of the noncontrolling ownership interest in the closely held company, compared with the virtually instant marketability of publicly traded stock.

This difference in marketability is a more important factor with respect to valuation than many people realize. The fair market values of noncontrolling ownership interests in closely held companies typically cluster between 35 percent to 50 percent less than prices of comparative noncontrolling equity interests in liquid, publicly traded companies, all other things being equal. This topic is discussed in great detail in the following chapter on discounts for lack of marketability.

The Bottom-Up Approach (Income Approach)

In the two above-described approaches, the noncontrolling ownership interest valuation started with an estimated value. In the discount approach, the methodology applied a valuation discount (or two) in order to estimate the value of the noncontrolling ownership interest. In the direct comparison approach, the analysis started with the known values of comparable security sale transactions. In the bottom-up approach, the methodology starts with a *tabula rasa* (empty slate) and estimates what the noncontrolling equity interest owner may realize on the basis of a fundamental economic analysis.

In most cases, the economic benefits that the noncontrolling ownership interest holder may realize fall into two categories:

1. Dividends or partnership withdrawals (i.e., current economic income).
2. Proceeds from the ultimate sale of the ownership interest or liquidation of the subject business (i.e., including any long-term appreciation in the value of the security interest itself).

This approach, for a minority investor, is really analogous to an application of the discounted economic income method of the income approach to business valuation.

The income approach is discussed in Chapter 9. The general procedures in the bottom-up approach to noncontrolling ownership interest valuation are as follows:

1. Project the expected income distributions (i.e., dividends, property distributions, or partnership withdrawals).
2. Project an investment holding period and a price at which the subject ownership interest can be expected to be sold. The projected holding period is often the amount of time before a "control event" (such as an initial public offering [IPO] sale of the company, liquidation of the company, etc.) is expected to occur.
3. Estimate an appropriate present value discount rate, using the methods and information discussed in Chapter 9.
4. Discount the projected periodic income distributions and the projected ultimate security sale price to a present value, using the present value formula presented in Chapter 9.

Adjustments to Income Statement

We have previously suggested that, when developing the company's earnings capacity as part of the business enterprise valuation process, the analyst may remove from expenses such discretionary items as the controlling shareholder's excess compensation and the cost of the controlling shareholder's discretionary expenditures. That previous discussion was relevant to the valuation of the entire company. These discretionary expense adjustments assume that it is within the controlling owner's discretion to remove such expenses with no significant impairment to company revenues. The noncontrolling stockholder, however, has no such power to eliminate these discretionary expenses. Therefore, these adjustments may not be relevant in estimating an earnings base for the valuation of noncontrolling ownership interests. This is true unless there is reason to believe that the discretionary expense changes are actually going to be made.

Some analysts take the position that reasonable compensation adjustments and other adjustments should be made to the income statement in order to put the company on a basis comparable to public companies. In such cases, if there are discrepancies in reasonable compensation between the guideline and subject companies, this discrepancy would be added to the amount of the minority interest discount.

Summary

The types and amounts of appropriate discounts and/or premiums are often major matters of dispute in the resolution of business valuation controversies. The primary discounts are for lack of control and lack of marketability.

When dealing with discounts and/or premiums, it is essential to be very precise as to the base of value to which the discount or premium applies. (This also means the basic valuation work product should be precise in its identification of the level of value it has estimated.) It is essential that the level of discounts and/or premiums be appropriately matched to the level of value estimated.

Many of the same indicators of market value (price/earnings multiples, capitalization of dividends, discounted economic income, price/book value multiples, and so on) used in valuing controlling ownership interests can also be used to value noncontrolling ownership interests. However, in valuing noncontrolling ownership interests, the focus of value normally is on the business as a going concern, rather than in either total or partial liquidation. And, relatively more emphasis is directed to the analysis of operating variables, such as earnings and dividends, and relatively less emphasis is directed to the analysis of asset values than when valuing a controlling interest. Also, the assumptions underlying the noncontrolling ownership interest ownership valuation usually reflect business as usual, rather than any changes that an outside control buyer would introduce.

If existing or potential litigation is involved, it is important to understand if there are any required standards of value and premises of value that should be estimated. The range of court case outcomes in disputes regarding valuations of noncontrolling ownership interest is extremely wide, even under comparable statutory law. Therefore, in controversy situations, an understanding of the facts and circumstances of the particular interest is essential, along with strong supporting data and careful reasoning that lead to an objective conclusion that is consistent with applicable statutes and legal precedent.

This chapter discussed the concepts, factors influencing, and empirical data sources to help quantify the lack of control discount. The next chapter presents and analyzes empirical data regarding the discount for lack of marketability.

Bibliography

Abrams, Jay. *Quantitative Business Valuation: A Mathematical Approach for Today's Professionals*. New York: McGraw-Hill Professional Publishing, 2001.

Aucutt, Ronald Esq. "FLP Trilogy a Victory for Taxpayers." *Shannon Pratt's Business Valuation Update*, January 2001.

Bendixen, Christian. "A Practical Approach to Estimating Discounts for Real Estate Partnerships." *Business Valuation Review*, vol. 19, no. 1, March 2000.

Bishop, David Bishop, and John White. "Multiple Period Discounting Method." *Presentations and Reviewed Articles*, BV Papers. July 2001.

Bolotsky, Michael J. "Adjustments for Differences in Ownership Rights, Liquidity, Information Access, and Information Reliability: An Assessment of 'Prevailing Wisdom' Versus the 'Nath Hypotheses.'" *Business Valuation Review*, September 1991, pp. 94–110.

Brown, Gregory K. "A Legal Perspective on Using Control Premiums in ESOP Transactions." Willamette Management Associates, *Insights*, Spring 2001, pp. 28–30.

Burkert, Rodney P. "Valuing the Minority Interest: To Adjust or Not to Adjust?" *Business Valuation Alert*, December 1999, pp. 4, 13–14.

Coolidge, H. Calvin. "Fixing Value of Minority Interest in Business: Actual Sales Suggest Discounts as High as 70%." *Estate Planning,* Spring 1975, pp. 138–41.

Davidoff, Howard. "Understanding Buy-Sell Agreements." New York State Society of CPAs. *CPA Journal*, April 2006.

Ferguson, Patrice Leigh and John E. Camp. "Valuation Basics and Beyond: Tackling Areas of Controversy." *Family Law Quarterly*, vol. 35, no. 2, Summer 2001.

Fraizer, William H. "Its Turtles All the Way Down." Presented at the 23rd Annual Advanced Business Valuation Conference, October, 2004. Also available at www.bvlibrary.com *BVPapers*.

Glazar, Russell T. "Nondistributing Partnerships Show 46% Discount from NAV." *Shannon Pratt's Business Valuation Update*, August 1999.

Hitchner, James R. "50% +50% ≠ 100%." *CPA Expert,* Winter 1998, pp. 13–15.

———. *Financial Valuation: Application and Models*. New York: John Wiley and Sons, 2nd ed., 2006.

Hitchner, James, Shannon Pratt, Chris Treharne, and Dan Van Vleet. "S Corporation Minority Equity Value Could Exceed the Pro Rata Portion of a Controlled Interest." *Business Valuation Q&A. BV Papers,* May 2005.

Houren, Jay. "Family Limited Partnerships (Houren)." *Presentation and Reviewed Articles. BV Papers*, February 2005.

Jankowske, Wayne C. "Valuing Minority Interests in Relation to Guideline Firms." *Business Valuation Review,* December 1991, pp. 139–43.

Maher, J. Michael. "An Objective Measure for a Discount for a Minority Interest and Premium for a Controlling Interest." *Taxes,* July 1979, pp. 449–54.

Mercer, Z. Christopher. "A Brief Review of Control Premiums and Minority Interest Discounts." *Journal of Business Valuation* (Proceedings of the 12th Biennial Business Valuation Conference of the Canadian Institute of Chartered Business Valuators). Toronto: The Canadian Institute of Chartered Business Valuators, 1997, pp. 365–87.

———. "Understanding and Quantifying Control Premiums: The Value of Control vs. Synergies or Strategic Advantages, Part II." *Journal of Business Valuation* (Proceedings of the 4th Joint Business Valuation of the Canadian Institute of Chartered Business Valuators and the American Society of Appraisers). Toronto: The Canadian Institute of Chartered Business Valuators, 1999, pp. 36–54.

Murdoch, Charles W. "The Evolution of Effective Remedies for Minority Shareholders and its Impact upon Valuation of Minority Shares." *Notre Dame Law Review,* vol. 65 (1990), pp. 425–89.

Nath, Eric W. "Control Premiums and Minority Interest Discounts in Private Companies." *Business Valuation Review,* June 1990, pp. 39–46.

———. "Tale of Two Markets." *Business Valuation Review,* September 1994, pp. 107–12.

"Partnership Re-Sale Discounts Justified." *The Partnership Spectrum*, January/February 2002, pp. 1–7.

Paschall, Michael. "Pass-Through Entity Discounts for Built-In Capital Gains Taxes." *Shannon Pratt's Business Valuation Update*, May 2004.

Phillips, John, and Neil Freeman. "What Is Marketability Discount for Controlling Interests?" *Business Valuation Review*, vol. 18, no. 1, March 1999.

Polacek, Timothy C., and Richard A. Lehn. "Tax Court Allows Sizable Fractional Interest Discounts." *Trusts & Estates,* September 1994, pp. 29–40.

Pratt, Shannon P. *Business Valuation Discounts and Premiums*. New York: John Wiley & Sons, October 2001.

Reilly, Robert F., and Robert Schweihs. *The Handbook of Business Valuation and Intellectual Property Analysis.* New York: McGraw-Hill, 2004.

Reto, James. "A Simplified Method to Value an S Corp Minority Interest." *Shannon Pratt's Business Valuation Update*, July 2004.

Shishido, Zenichi. "The Fair Value of Minority Stock in Closely Held Corporations." *Fordham Law Review,* October 1993, pp. 65–110.

Sonneman, Donald. "Business Valuation Controversies and Choices: Understand Them and Their Impact on Value." *Business Valuation Review,* vol. 19, no. 2, June 2000.

Stockdale Jr., John. "Business Valuation Cases in Brief." *Business Valuation Review,* vol. 20, no. 1, March 2001.

Tiernan, Peter B. "How 50% Ownership Affects Estate Planning for Closely Held Stock." *Journal of Taxation,* October 1999, pp. 232–40.

Trugman, Gary. "Guideline Public Company Method—Control or Minority Value?" *Shannon Pratt's Business Valuation Update*, December 2003.

Zipp, Alan. "Business Valuation Standards in Divorce." *Business Valuation Review,* vol. 19, no. 3, September 2000.

Chapter 17

Discounts for Illiquidity and Lack of Marketability

All other things being equal, an ownership interest in a business is worth more if it is readily marketable. An ownership interest in a business is worth less if it is not readily marketable. This is because business owners—and all investors—prefer liquidity to illiquidity. Ownership interests in closely held businesses—even substantial closely held businesses—are illiquid relative to many other types of investments. This phenomenon may be further compounded by restrictions on the transfer of ownership interests often found in close corporation buy-sell agreements or shareholder agreements. Therefore, analysts have to identify and quantify the valuation adjustment associated with (1) the illiquidity of the subject business enterprise and (2) the lack of marketability in the subject business ownership interest.

For purposes of this chapter, we will use the term *illiquidity* to mean the inability of the owner of an entire business enterprise to convert his or her investment into cash quickly and at a reasonably low and predictable cost. We will use the term *lack of marketability* to mean the inability of the owner of a noncontrolling equity interest to convert his or her investment into cash quickly and at a reasonably low and predictable cost.

These two concepts of illiquidity and lack of marketability are related but distinctly different. As with all valuation adjustments, it is important to identify the base of comparison to which the adjustment relates.

The measurement base for the discount for illiquidity relates to "control event" transfers (i.e., asset sales, stock sales, or mergers) of controlling ownership interests or entire business enterprises. This discount quantifies the inherent liquidity differences between the subject business enterprise and the selection of guideline merged and acquired companies that are used as a benchmark for estimating the subject business enterprise value.

The measurement base for the discount for lack of marketability relates to noncontrol event transfers (i.e., sales of small blocks of securities on organized stock exchanges). This discount quantifies the inherent liquidity differences between the subject noncontrolling equity interest and the selection of guideline publicly traded company securities that are used as a benchmark for estimating the value of the subject securities.

First, this chapter will discuss the theoretical concepts of illiquidity and lack of marketability. Second, this chapter will present the most recent empirical studies that are frequently used by analysts to quantify these valuation adjustments.

Concept and Importance of Marketability

The concept of *marketability* deals with the liquidation of the subject business ownership interest. That is, how quickly can the business ownership interest be converted to cash at the investor's discretion?

In this text, we will define *marketability* as the ability to convert the business ownership interest (at whatever ownership level) to cash quickly, with minimum transaction and administrative costs in so doing and with a high degree of certainty of realizing the expected amount of net proceeds.

Our definition is consistent with the definition offered by the *Encyclopedia of Banking & Finance*, which focuses on securities for which *some* public market already exists:

> **Marketability.** The relative ease and promptness with which a security or commodity may be sold when desired, at a representative current price, without material concession in price merely because of the necessity of sale. Marketability connotes the existence of current buying interest as well as selling interest and is usually indicated by the volume of current transactions and the spread between the bid and asked price for a security —the closer the spread, the closer are the buying and selling interests to agreement on price resulting in actual transactions. To look at it from the standpoint of a dealer maintaining the MARKET, the closer his [or her] bid to current transactions and the smaller his [or her] markup is to asking prices, the larger the volume will be. By contrast, inactive securities that rarely trade or for which buyers have to be located or sales negotiated are characterized by large spreads between the bid and asked prices.[1]

With respect to the ownership characteristics of operating assets (such as operating real estate and tangible personal property), the terms *marketability* and *liquidity* are sometimes interchangeable. The *Encyclopedia of Banking & Finance* offers the following:

> **Liquidity.** The amount of time required to convert an asset into cash or pay a liability. For noncurrent assets, liquidity generally refers to marketability....
>
> In economics, liquidity is the desire to hold assets in the form of cash. Common elements often included in the concept of liquidity include marketability, realizability, reversibility (as to the difference between buying and selling prices), divisibility of the asset, predictability or capital certainty, and plasticity (ease of maneuvering into and out of various yields after the asset has been acquired). Firms and individuals often prefer to hold money for the sake of holding money. Liquidity may be desired for the following reasons: (1) the transactions motive, (2) the precautionary motive, and (3) the speculative motive. Money is desired to carry out future monetary transactions, to save for a rainy day, or to take advantage of movements in the price level.[2]

---

[1] Charles J. Woelfel, *Encyclopedia of Banking & Finance*, 10th ed. (Burr Ridge, IL: Probus Publishing Company, 1994), p. 729. Reprinted with permission.
[2] Ibid., p. 703.

Barron's Dictionary of Business Terms defines marketability and liquidity as follows:

> **Marketability.** Speed and ease with which a particular product or investment may be bought and sold. In common use, *marketability* is interchangeable with *liquidity*, but *liquidity* implies the preservation of value when a security is bought or sold.[3]

The North American Business Valuation Standards Council, including ASA, is proposing the following definitions by way of an exposure draft on an international glossary.

> **Liquidity**. The degree to which an asset, business, business ownership interest, or security can readily be converted into cash without significant loss of principal.
>
> **Marketability**. The capability and ease of transfer or salability of an asset, business, business ownership interest, or security.

The market for securities in the United States is generally considered to be the most liquid market for any kind of property anywhere in the world. This is one of the reasons that companies are able to raise investment capital from both institutional and individual investors: the ability to liquidate the investment immediately, at little cost, and with virtual certainty as to realization of the widely publicized market price. Empirical evidence suggests that investors are willing to pay a price premium for this level of liquidity. Conversely, investors extract a price discount relative to actively traded securities for stocks or other investment interests that lack this high degree of liquidity.

Adjustment for Lack of Marketability for Noncontrolling Ownership Interests

For a valuation "adjustment" to have a precise meaning, there should be a precise definition of the level of value to which the adjustment is made. When noncontrolling business ownership interests are valued by reference to the prices paid for guideline actively traded securities, the benchmark for the lack of marketability of the noncontrolling ownership interests is the active public securities markets. This publicly traded counterpart value is often called the *publicly traded equivalent value* or the *freely traded value*.

In the U.S. capital markets, a security holder is able to sell a security over the telephone or the Internet in seconds, usually at or within a small fraction of a percent of the last price at which the security traded, with a relatively small commission cost, and to receive the cash proceeds within three working days.

By contrast, the universe of potential buyers for most noncontrolling business ownership interests is an infinitesimal fraction of the universe of potential buyers for publicly traded securities.

Besides the problem of actually trying to sell the subject ownership interest, the liquidity of noncontrolling business ownership interests is further impaired by the relative unwillingness of banks and other lending institutions to accept them as loan collateral the same way they would accept public stock.

---

[3] Jack P. Friedman, ed., *Barron's Dictionary of Business Terms*, 2nd ed. (Hauppauge, NY: Barron's, 1994), p. 363.

Because of these extreme contrasts between the ability to sell or hypothecate noncontrolling business ownership interests as compared with publicly traded stock, empirical evidence suggests that significant valuation discounts for lack of marketability are appropriate. These lack of marketability discounts for noncontrolling business ownership interests tend to cluster in the range of 30 percent to 50 percent from their publicly traded counterparts. Naturally, each valuation should be analyzed on the basis of the individual facts and circumstances. Accordingly, each individual noncontrolling equity interest valuation may justify a discount for lack of marketability above or below this typical range.

Evidence for the Quantification of Discount for Lack of Marketability

There are two general types of empirical studies designed to quantify the valuation adjustments associated with the lack of marketability of noncontrolling ownership interests in closely held businesses:

1. Discounts on the sale of restricted shares of publicly traded companies.
2. Discounts on the sale of closely held company shares—compared with prices of subsequent initial public offerings of the same company's shares.

As noted earlier, the above empirical studies indicate that the base from which to take the indicated lack of marketability discount is the actual (or estimated) price at which the shares would sell if registered and freely tradable in a public stock market.

The immediately following sections of this chapter summarize the findings of these two extensive lines of empirical evidence. The second line of empirical studies is more recent. More importantly, the transactions are more similar to noncontrolling privately held business ownership interest transactions. This is because that is what they are, even though the subject company may have contemplated a public offering at the time of the transaction.

The data presented in this chapter relate to the quantification of the discount for lack of marketability only. As mentioned previously, the discount for lack of marketability is separate and distinct from the discount for lack of control. The discount for lack of control is discussed in the previous chapter.

The body of empirical evidence from which to quantify illiquidity discounts for controlling business ownership interests is much less extensive and of a different nature. This subject will be covered later in the chapter.

Marketability Discounts Extracted from Prices of Restricted Stocks

One body of empirical evidence specifically isolates the pricing implications of marketability from all other valuation-related factors: the body of data on transactions in letter stocks. A *letter stock* is identical in all respects to the freely traded stock of a public company except for the fact that it is restricted from trading on the open stock market for a certain period. The duration of the restrictions may vary from one security to another. Since marketability is the only difference between the letter stock and its freely tradable counterpart, the analyst may quantify differences in the price at which letter stock transactions take place compared with open market transactions in the same stock on the same date. This difference will provide some evidence of the price spread between (1) a readily marketable security and (2) one that is otherwise identical but subject to certain restrictions on its marketability.

Publicly traded corporations frequently issue letter stock when making acquisitions or when raising private capital. This is because the time and cost of registering the new stock with the Securities Exchange Commission (SEC) would make registration at the time of the transaction impractical. Also, company founders or other insiders may own portions of a publicly traded company stock that has never been registered for public trading. Even though such stock cannot be sold to the public on the stock market, it may be sold in private transactions under certain circumstances. Such transactions usually must be reported to the SEC. Therefore, these private transactions become a matter of public record. Accordingly, empirical data on the prices of private transactions in restricted securities—or letter stocks—can be used for comparison with prices of the same but unrestricted securities eligible for trading on the open market.

Since these data represent hundreds of actual arm's-length transactions, anyone who is considering a deal involving such securities (for example, receiving letter stock in connection with selling out to a public company) would be well advised to become familiar with the information. Furthermore, courts have often referenced the data on letter stock price discounts when estimating the discount for lack of marketability appropriate to noncontrolling ownership interests in closely held companies.

The restrictions on the transfer of letter stock eventually lapse, usually within 24 months up to 1997, and generally within a year since that time except for the "dribble out" provisions, subject to volume limitations. At that point, the holder can sell the shares into the existing market, subject to whatever volume and other restrictions may be imposed. Consequently, all other things being equal, shares of closely held stock—which may never have the benefit of a public market—would be expected to require a higher discount for lack of marketability than that applicable to stock that would trade on an organized exchange but is restricted from doing so. In fact, the market does impose a higher discount on closely held noncontrolling ownership interests than on restricted stock of a public company, as we will see in a later section.

SEC Institutional Investor Study

In a major SEC study of institutional investor actions, one topic was the amount of discount at which transactions in restricted stock (or letter stock) occurred compared with the prices of identical but unrestricted stock on the open market.[4] The most pertinent summary tables from that study are reproduced in Exhibits 17–1 and 17–2.

---

[4] "Discounts Involved in Purchases of Common Stock," in U.S. 92nd Congress, 1st Session, House, *Institutional Investor Study Report of the Securities and Exchange Commission* (Washington, DC: Government Printing Office, March 10, 1971, 5:2444B2456, Document No. 92-64, Part5).

Exhibit 17–1

Table XIV–45 of SEC *Institutional Investor Study*: Discount by Trading Market

| | Discount | | | | | | | | | | | | | | |
| | −15.0% to 0.0% | | 0.1% to 10.0% | | 10.1% to 20.0% | | 20.1% to 30.0% | | 30.1% to 40.0% | | 40.1% to 50.0% | | 50.1% to 80.0% | | Total | |
Trading Market	No. of Trans-actions	Value of Purchases	No. of Trans-actions	Value of Purchases	No. of Trans-actions	Value of Purchases	No. of Trans-actions	Value of Purchases	No. of Trans-actions	Value of Purchases	No. of Trans-actions	Value of Purchases	No. of Trans-actions	Value of Purchases	No. of Trans-actions	Value of Purchases
Unknown	1	$1,500,000	2	$2,496,583	1	$205,000	0	$0	2	$3,332,000	0	$0	1	$1,259,995	7	$8,793,578
New York Stock Exchange	7	3,760,663	13	15,111,798	13	24,503,988	10	17,954,085	3	11,102,501	1	1,400,000	4	5,005,068	51	78,838,103
American Stock Exchange	2	7,263,060	4	15,850,000	11	14,548,750	20	46,200,677	7	21,074,298	1	44,250	4	4,802,404	49	109,783,439
Over-the-Counter (reporting companies)	11	13,828,757	39	13,613,676	35	38,585,259	30	35,479,946	30	58,689,328	13	9,284,047	21	8,996,406	179	178,477,419
Over-the-Counter (nonreporting companies)	5	8,329,369	9	5,265,925	18	25,122,024	17	11,229,155	25	29,423,584	20	11,377,431	18	13,505,545	112	104,253,033
Total	26	$34,681,849	67	$52,337,982	78	$102,965,021	77	$110,863,863	67	$123,621,711	35	$22,105,728	48	$33,569,418	398	$480,145,572

Exhibit 17–2

Table XIV–47 of SEC *Institutional Investor Study*: Discount by Size of Transaction and Sales of Issuer

| | Discount | | | | | | | | | | | | | | |
| | 50.1% or More | | 40.1% to 50.0% | | 30.1% to 40.0% | | 20.1% to 30.0% | | 10.1% to 20.0% | | 0.1% to 10.0% | | Total | |
Trading Market	No. of Trans-actions	Size of Transactions	No. of Trans-actions	Size of Transactions	No. of Trans-actions	Size of Transactions	No. of Trans-actions	Size of Transactions	No. of Trans-actions	Size of Transactions	No. of Trans-actions	Size of Transactions	No. of Trans-actions	Size of Transactions
Less than 100	11	$2,894,999	7	$2,554,000	17	$19,642,364	16	$12,197,394	6	$12,267,292	9	$12,566,000	66	$62,122,049
100–999	7	474,040	2	1,221,000	0	0	1	500,000	1	1,018,500	2	3,877,500	13	7,091,040
1,000–4,999	8	4,605,505	13	8,170,747	12	10,675,150	15	9,865,951	10	9,351,738	3	2,295,200	61	44,964,291
5,000–19,999	6	1,620,015	4	1,147,305	13	25,986,008	25	27,238,210	24	21,441,347	47	12,750,481	119	90,183,366
20,000–99,999	3	605,689	3	4,372,676	6	11,499,250	8	11,817,954	18	22,231,737	17	36,481,954	55	87,009,260
100,000 or More	2	1,805,068	0	0	2	2,049,998	3	7,903,586	10	24,959,483	7	10,832,925	24	47,551,060
Total	37	$12,005,316	29	$17,465,728	50	$69,852,770	68	$69,523,095	69	$91,270,097	85	$78,804,060	338	$338,921,066

SOURCE: *Institutional Investor Study Report of the Securities and Exchange Commission,* Chapter XIV Section F.8., "Discounts Involved in Purchases of Common Stock," H.R. Doc. No. 64, Part 5, 92d Cong., 1st Sess. (1971), pp. 2444–56.

Exhibit 17–1 presents the price discount from stock market prices on letter stock transactions disaggregated by the market in which the unrestricted stock trades. The four categories are the New York Stock Exchange (NYSE), American Stock Exchange (AMEX), over-the-counter (OTC) reporting companies, and OTC nonreporting companies. A *reporting company* is a publicly traded company that must file Forms 10-K, 10-Q, and other information with the SEC. A *nonreporting company* is one whose stock is publicly traded OTC but is not subject to the same reporting requirements. A company whose stock is traded OTC can avoid becoming a SEC reporting company either by maintaining its total assets under $1 million or by keeping its number of stockholders under 500.

Because most closely held businesses (even substantial close corporations) are much smaller than typical well-known public companies, the smaller nonreporting public companies may have characteristics that are more comparable with the subject closely held business. However, since these nonreporting public companies need not report to the SEC, the analyst may have trouble obtaining annual and interim reports for them.

Exhibit 17–1 indicates that, compared with their free-trading counterparts, the price discounts on the letter stocks were the least for NYSE-listed stocks and increased, in order, for AMEX-listed stocks, OTC reporting companies, and OTC nonreporting companies. For OTC nonreporting companies, the largest number of observations fell in the 30 to 40 percent price discount range. Slightly over 56 percent of the OTC nonreporting companies had price discounts greater than 30 percent on the sale of their restricted stock—compared with the stock market price of their free-trading stock. A little over 30 percent of the OTC reporting companies were discounted over 30 percent, and over half had price discounts over 20 percent.

Using midpoints of the price discount range groups from Exhibit 17–1—and even including those that sold at price premiums for one reason or another—the overall mean average price discount was 25.8 percent and the median price discount was about the same. The study also noted, "Average discounts rose over the period January 1, 1966, through June 30, 1969," and average discounts were "27.9 percent in the first half of 1969."[5] For nonreporting OTC companies (which are more comparative with smaller businesses), the average price discount was 32.6 percent, and the median price discount again was about the same.

Since the time of the SEC study, the efficiency of the OTC market has improved considerably. This has been aided by the development of inexpensive and virtually instantaneous electronic communications and the advent of the Nasdaq system. Since the market in which restricted OTC shares will eventually trade once the restrictions expire (or are removed) is now somewhat more efficient, one would expect the differential in price discounts for restricted listed versus OTC stocks to be less pronounced. This generally has been the case.

Exhibit 17–2 presents the discounts from open market prices on letter stock transactions, disaggregated by the subject companies' annual sales volumes into six groups. Companies with the largest sales volumes tend to receive the smallest discounts, and companies with the smallest sales volumes tend to receive the largest discounts. Well over half the companies with sales under $5 million (i.e., the three smallest of the six size categories used) had price discounts of over 30 percent. However, this may not be a size effect but just further evidence of the influence of the trading market. This is because most of the largest companies were listed on the NYSE, by far the most liquid market at that time.

---

[5] Ibid., p. 2452.

Exhibit 17–3

Gelman Study
Distribution of Price Discounts

Size of Discount	No. of Common Stocks	% of Total
Less than 15.0%	5	6
15.0–19.9	9	10
20.0–24.9	13	15
25.0–29.9	9	10
30.0–34.9	12	13
35.0–39.9	9	10
40.0 and Over	32	36
Total	89	100

SOURCE: Milton Gelman, "An Economist-Financial Analyst's Approach to Valuing Stock of a Closely Held Company," *Journal of Taxation*, June 1972, p. 354.

Gelman Study

In 1972, Milton Gelman published the results of his study of prices paid for restricted securities by four closed-end investment companies specializing in restricted securities investments.[6] From 89 transactions between 1968 and 1970, Gelman found that (1) both the arithmetic average and median price discounts were 33 percent and that (2) almost 60 percent of the purchases were at price discounts of 30 percent and higher. The distribution of price discounts found in the Gelman study is presented in Exhibit 17–3.

Trout Study

In a study of letter stocks purchased by mutual funds from 1968 to 1972, Robert Trout attempted to construct a financial model that would provide an estimate of the price discount appropriate for a private company's stock.[7] His multiple regression model involved 60 purchases and found an average price discount of 33.45 percent for restricted stock from freely traded stock. As the SEC study previously indicated, Trout also found that companies with stock listed on national exchanges had lower discounts on their restricted stock transactions than did companies with stock traded OTC.

Moroney Study

In an article published in the March 1973 issue of *Taxes*, Robert E. Moroney presented the results of a study of the prices paid for restricted securities by 10 registered

---

[6] Milton Gelman, "An Economist-Financial Analyst's Approach to Valuing Stock of a Closely Held Company," *Journal of Taxation*, June 1972, pp. 353–54. Copyright © 1972 by Warren Gorham & Lamont, 31 St. James Avenue, Boston, MA 02116, (800) 950-1216.

[7] Robert R. Trout, "Estimation of the Discount Associated with the Transfer of Restricted Securities," *Taxes*, June 1977, pp. 381–85.

investment companies.[8] The study reflected 146 purchases. The average price discount for the 146 transactions was 35.6 percent, and the median price discount was 33.0 percent.

Moroney points out:

> It goes without saying that each cash purchase of a block of restricted equity securities fully satisfied the requirements that the purchase price be one, "at which the property would change hands between a willing buyer and a willing sellcr, neither being under any compulsion to buy or to sell and both having reasonable knowledge of relevant facts." Reg. Sec. 20.2031-1(b)[9]

Moroney contrasts the evidence of the actual cash deals with the lower average price discounts for lack of marketability adjudicated in most prior court decisions on gift and estate tax cases. He points out, however, that the empirical evidence on the prices of restricted stocks was not available as a benchmark for quantifying lack of marketability discounts at the time of the prior cases. And, he suggests that higher price discounts for lack of marketability be allowed subsequently based on relevant data available.

Maher Study

Another well-documented study on lack of marketability discounts for closely held business ownership interests was performed by J. Michael Maher and published in *Taxes*.[10] Maher's analytical method was similar to Moroney's in that it compared prices paid for restricted stocks with the market prices of their unrestricted counterparts. Maher found that mutual funds were not purchasing restricted securities during 1974 and 1975, which were very depressed years for the stock market. Therefore, the data actually used covered the five-year period from 1969 through 1973. The study showed, "The mean discount for lack of marketability for the years 1969–1973 amounted to 35.43 percent."[11] Maher further eliminated the top and bottom 10 percent of purchases in an effort to remove especially high- and low-risk situations. The result was almost identical with the outliers removed, with a mean price discount of 34.73 percent.

Standard Research Consultants Study

In 1983, Standard Research Consultants (SRC) analyzed recent private placements of common stock to test the current applicability of the SEC study.[12] SRC studied 28 private placements of restricted common stock from October 1978 through June 1982. Price discounts ranged from 7 to 91 percent, with a median of 45 percent.

---

[8] Robert E. Moroney, "Most Courts Overvalue Closely Held Stocks," *Taxes*, March 1973, pp. 144–54.

[9] Ibid., p. 151.

[10] J. Michael Maher, "Discounts for Lack of Marketability for Closely-Held Business Interests," *Taxes*, September 1976, pp. 562–71.

[11] Ibid., p. 571.

[12] William F. Pittock and Charles H. Stryker, "Revenue Ruling 77-287 Revisited," *SRC Quarterly Reports*, Spring 1983, pp. 1–3.

Willamette Management Associates Study

Willamette Management Associates analyzed private placements of restricted stocks for the period January 1, 1981, through May 31, 1984. The early part of this study overlapped the last part of the SRC study, but few transactions took place during the period of overlap. Most of the transactions in the Willamette Management Associates study occurred in 1983.

Willamette Management Associates identified 33 transactions during that period (1) that could reasonably be classified as arm's length and (2) for which the price of the restricted shares could be compared directly with the price of trades in identical but unrestricted shares of the same company at the same time. The median price discount for the 33 restricted stock transactions compared with the prices of their freely tradable counterparts was 31.2 percent.

The slightly lower average percentage price discounts for private placements during this time may be attributable to the somewhat depressed pricing in the public stock market. This, in turn, reflected the recessionary economic conditions prevalent during most of the period of the study.

Silber Study

In a 1991 article in the *Financial Analysts Journal*, William L. Silber presented the results of his analysis of 69 private placements of common stock of publicly traded companies between 1981 and 1988.[13] He found that the average price discount was 33.75 percent, which is very consistent with earlier studies.

Silber also found that the size of the price discount tended to be higher for private placements that were larger as a percentage of the shares outstanding. He found a small effect on the price discount on the basis of the size of the company as measured by revenues.

FMV Opinions, Inc. Study

An article in the January/February 1994 issue of *Estate Planning* referenced a study by FMV Opinions, Inc., that "examined over 100 restricted stock transactions from 1979 through April 1992."[14] The FMV study found a mean price discount of only 23 percent.

Management Planning, Inc. Study

A detailed study of restricted public securities was conducted by the valuation firm Management Planning, Inc. This study is titled "Analysis of Private Sales of Unregistered Common Stock, January 1, 1980–December 31, 1996." The results of this study are reported in *The Handbook of Advanced Business Valuation*.[15]

There was clear size effect in the Management Planning Study, with smaller companies tending to have larger discounts, as shown in Exhibit 17–4.

---

[13] William L. Silber, "Discounts on Restricted Stock: The Impact of Illiquidity on Stock Prices," *Financial Analysts Journal*, July–August 1991, pp. 60–64.

[14] Lance S. Hall and Timothy C. Polacek, "Strategies for Obtaining the Largest Valuation Discounts," *Estate Planning*, January/February 1994, pp. 38–44.

[15] Robert Oliver and Roy Meyers, "Discounts Seen in Private Placements of Restricted Stock: The Management Planning, Inc., Long-Term Study (1980–1996)" (Chapter 5) in Robert F. Reilly and Robert P. Schweihs, eds. *The Handbook of Advanced Business Valuation*, (New York: McGraw-Hill, 2000).

Exhibit 17–4

Analysis of Restricted Stock Discounts by Revenue Size
Based upon Data from the Management Planning, Inc. Study

Revenues	Percent of Sample	Average Revenues ($ Millions)	Average Discounts	Standard Deviations	Range of Discounts	
					Low	High
Under $10 million	28.6%	6.6	32.9%	15.6%	2.8%	57.6%
$10-$30 million	22.4%	22.5	30.8%	11.2%	15.3%	49.8%
$30-$50 million	20.4%	35.5	25.2%	15.1%	5.2%	46.3%
$50-$100 million	16.3%	63.5	19.4%	7.3%	11.6%	29.3%
Over $100 million (adjusted)*	8.2%	224.9	14.9%	10.5%	0.0%	24.1%
Overall sample averages	95.9%	47.5	27.7%	14.1%	0.0%	57.6%
*Over $100 million (actual calculation)	4.1%	187.1	25.1%	17.9%	0.0%	46.5%

NOTE: Excludes Sudbury Holdings, Inc., whose private placement consisted of 125 percent of the pre-transaction shares outstanding. Excludes Starrett Housing Corp. which is one of the five most thinly traded companies in the sample.

The purpose of the Management Planning restricted stock study was to compare (1) the per share prices paid in private placements of restricted stock with (2) the same company's freely traded, stock market price. The Management Planning study shows that in the vast majority of cases, restricted shares are privately placed at a lower price than the concurrent publicly traded price of the same stock. The difference in price, or discount, stems from the burden of the holding period, and resultant lack of liquidity, placed on the restricted stock. The restricted shares, it should be remembered, can be expected to have marketability after the initial two- to three-year holding period (a one- to two-year holding period for shares privately placed after April 29, 1997) and the various other Rule 144 requirements are met. In contrast, there is little likelihood that the typical privately held security will ever have the ready liquidity of a public stock or access to the infrastructure that supports our efficient public stock markets. Nonetheless, research and understanding of the discounts in private placements of restricted stock provide a good starting point for estimating the size of discounts for lack of marketability.

The private placement of restricted stock is a means by which corporations raise capital. This alternative is selected when, for reasons related to control issues, costs, or timing, it is not advantageous or practical to raise new equity capital in the already established market for a company's stock. Management Planning found three publications to be excellent sources of private placement transactions. All are now published by Securities Data Publishing (SDP), located in New York. (They were formerly published by Dealer's Digest, Inc.) Up until 1989, Management Planning reviewed *Investment Dealers Digest*. When *Investment Dealers Digest* reduced its coverage of private placements in 1989, Management Planning first switched to *Private Placement Letter* and, later, to *Private Equity Week*. Using these three publications as a source, Management Planning reviewed all the private placements that were reported from January 1, 1980, to December 31, 1996. In selecting the transactions for further analysis, they established the following initial tests, or screening.

- The company selling stock in a private placement should make its financial statements available to the public.

- The company should have a publicly held and actively traded common stock "counterpart" equal in all other respects to the unregistered stock.
- Sufficient data on the private transaction should be readily available.
- The publicly traded common stock counterpart should be selling at a price of at least $2 per share.
- The company should be a domestic corporation.
- The company should not be characterized as being in the "developmental" stage at the time of the transaction.

In order to obtain the most meaningful group of private placement transactions that would have the most relevance to business valuation analysts, Management Planning established three additional tests that had to be met by each transaction.

- If the company issuing the restricted shares lost money in the year prior to the transaction, it was excluded.
- All start-up companies were excluded. Companies with less than $3 million in sales volume were also excluded.
- If the transaction involved restricted shares and the terms of the transaction conferred on the holder the right to register the shares for public trading, the transaction was excluded.

Management Planning reached the following conclusions about the final 53 transactions included in their study:

- The average lack of marketability discount was about 27 percent.
- The median lack of marketability discount was about 25 percent.
- These median and average lack of marketability discounts are slightly lower than the median (28 percent) and the average (29 percent) discounts of the entire prescreen group of 231 transactions.
- Only one of the 53 transactions occurred at a price equal to the market price.
- The remaining 52 transactions all occurred at lack of marketability discounts ranging from a low of 3 percent to a high of 58 percent.

Johnson Study

Bruce Johnson, of the firm Munroe, Park, & Johnson, studied 72 private placement transactions that occurred from 1991 through 1995.[16] This was the first half-decade after the Rule 144 restrictions were relaxed. The range was a 10 percent premium to a 60 percent discount, with an average discount for these 72 transactions of 20 percent.

The study analyzed four factors that might influence the size of the discount: (1) positive net income, (2) sales volume, (3) transaction value, and (4) net income strength. The results of his study are shown in Exhibit 17–5.

Columbia Financial Advisors Study

As of this writing, the only restricted stock study undertaken since the Rule 144 holding period was reduced to one year in 1997 is the one headed by Kathryn Aschwald at Columbia Financial Advisors, Inc. (CFA).[17]

---

[16] Bruce Johnson, "Restricted Stock Discounts, 1991-95," *Shannon Pratt's Business Valuation Update*, March 1999, pp. 1–5.

[17] Kathryn F. Aschwald, "Restricted Stock Discounts Decline as Result of 1-Year Holding Period," Shannon Pratt's Business Valuation Update, May 2000, pp. 1–5.

Exhibit 17–5

Johnson Study

Total Net Income	Avg Discount
Negative	22.5%
$0 to $1M	26.0%
$1M to $10M	18.1%
+ $10M	6.3%

Total Sales	Avg Discount
$0 to $10M	23.5%
$10M to $50M	19.4%
$50M to $200M	17.7%
+ $200M	13.0%

Transaction Size	Avg Discount
$0 to $5M	26.7%
$5M to $10M	20.9%
$10M to $25M	17.0%
+ $25M	10.8%

Net Income Margin	Avg Discount
Negative	22.5%
0% to 5%	23.7%
5% to 10%	15.2%
+10%	11.6%

SOURCE: Bruce A. Johnson, "Quantitative Support for Discounts for Lack of Marketability," *Business Valuation Review*, December 1999, pp. 152–55.

Their study was divided into two parts: January 1, 1996, through April 30, 1997 (before the reduction in the Rule 144 holding period), and May 1, 1997, through December 31, 1998 (after the one-year holding period became effective, April 29, 1997).

They identified 23 transactions for the 1996 to April 1997 period, with discounts ranging from .8 to 67.5 percent, with a mean of 21 percent. For the May 1997 to December 1998 period, they identified 15 transactions, with a range of 0 to 30 percent, and a mean of 13 percent, and a median of 9 percent.

As explained by Kathryn Aschwald, author of the CFA study:

Many "rumblings" in the appraisal community have centered around the fact that discounts for restricted stock have been declining, and many appear to be concerned about what this might mean in valuing privately held securities. It makes perfect sense that the discounts for restricted securities have generally declined since 1990 as the market (and liquidity) for theses [sic] securities has increased due to Rule 144A and the shortening of restricted stock holding periods beginning April 29, 1997. Thus, while the newer studies are specifically relevant for determining the appropriate discounts for restricted securities, the studies conducted after

1990 are not relevant for purposes of determining discounts for lack of marketability for privately held stock, because they reflect the increased liquidity in the market for restricted securities. Such increased liquidity is not present in privately held securities.[18]

LiquiStat Database

As of this writing, the latest restricted stock study to be published is the LiquiStat database, a study by Espen Robak at Pluris Valuation Advisors LLC. The LiquiStat database is a continuously updated database of transactions in the secondary market for illiquid securities.[19] This sets LiquiStat apart from the rest of the restricted stock studies reviewed in this chapter. Of the three categories of empirical studies reviewed herein (restricted stock studies, pre-IPO studies, and studies of acquisition multiples for public vs. private companies), LiquiStat almost fits into a separate category. This is because all the other restricted stock studies measure the discounts taken in private placements: mostly very large corporate transactions where a (sometimes cash-strapped) company sells a significant portion of its shares to an investor or, most frequently, a group of investors. LiquiStat, on the other hand, analyzes discounts taken when investors not affiliated with the issuing company sell restricted stock in private transactions to other investors.

The average holding period remaining for the shares sold in the secondary market was 138 days, which is shorter than the holding periods in restricted stock private placement studies have been assumed to be. Surprisingly, therefore, the LiquiStat data shows significantly higher discounts than in other recent studies. Based on 61 transactions in plain-vanilla common equity from April 2005 to January 2007, their study found an average and median discount of 32.8 percent and 34.6 percent, respectively.[20] As explained by Espen Robak, author of the study:

> The expected illiquidity period for the shares sold in the private placement studies may be significantly and systematically understated. (...) PIPE investments have become highly popular partly because issuers often register the stock shortly after the private placement. When investing, PIPE buyers have fairly strong visibility over how long they will have to wait for the shares to be registered. However, those details are not always available to the authors of private placement studies. Thus, whether or not stock is issued with registration rights, or even a promise of registration very shortly after the placement, may be unknown. This, if true, would tend to overstate the actual expected period of illiquidity for the shares in the studies.[21]

Furthermore, the data shows that the discounts are higher for larger blocks, relative to market trading volume, shares with a greater number of days of illiquidity remaining, shares with lower share price, and riskier shares.

---

[18] *Ibid.*, pp. 4–5.

[19] The transactions in the LiquiStat database are made on the Restricted Securities Trading Network (RSTN), an online trading platform managed by Restricted Stock Partners of New York, NY. More information on this trading market for restricted securities is available at www.restrictedsecurities.net.

[20] Robak, Espen "Restricted Securities and Illiquidity Discounts," *Trusts & Estates*, February 2007.

[21] Robak, Espen "Lemons or Lemonade? A fresh look at restricted stock discounts," *Valuation Strategies*, January/February 2007.

Exhibit 17–6

LiquiStat™ Discounts for Restricted Stocks

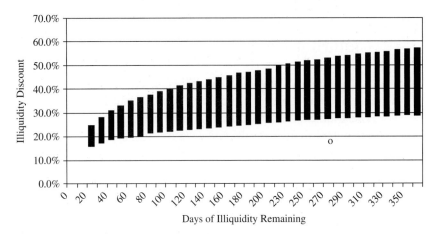

Source: Espen Robak, Discounts for Illiquid Shares and Warrants: The LiquiStat™ Database of Transactions on the Restricted Securities Trading Network." *Pluris Valuation Advisors White Paper* (January 2007): 30. All rights reserved. Used with permission. Available at www.plurisvaluation.com/pressroom/index.htm.

The LiquiStat database also provides the first-ever sample of real-world transaction data on sales of warrants.[22] The discounts for these restricted securities, which are directly comparable with the nonqualified stock options, issued by thousands of companies, are significantly higher than for restricted stock. Based on 76 transactions in illiquid warrants from April 2005 to January 2007, their study found an average and median discount of 41.5 percent and 44.0 percent, respectively. Discounts are higher for more volatile stocks, for longer times to expiration, and for options that are out-of-the-money. See Exhibit 17–6 for the LiquiStat discounts for restricted stock.

Summary of Empirical Studies on Restricted Stock Transactions

The 12 empirical studies cover several hundred restricted stock transactions spanning the late 1960s through 1998. Considering the number of independent researchers and the very long time span encompassing a wide variety of market conditions, the results are remarkably consistent, as summarized in Exhibit 17–7.

In many of the cases of restricted stock transactions tabulated in Exhibit 17–7, the purchaser of the stock had the right to register the stock for sale in the existing public market. Sometimes investors get a commitment from the issuer to register the securities at a certain future date. Sometimes investors have "demand" rights, where they can force the issuer to register the securities at a time of their choosing. Sometimes investors get "piggyback" rights where there is no obligation other than to include the securities on any future registration that the issuer undertakes. And, sometimes the purchaser has to rely on SEC Rule 144, where he or she can

---

[22] Robak, *supra*, note 2.

Exhibit 17–7

Summary of Restricted Stock Studies

Empirical Study	Years Covered in Study	Average Price Discount (%)
SEC overall average [a]	1966–1969	25.8
SEC nonreporting OTC companies [a]	1966–1969	32.6
Gelman [b]	1968–1970	33.0
Trout [c]	1968–1972	33.5
Moroney [d]	[k]	35.6
Maher [e]	1969–1973	35.4
Standard Research Consultants [f]	1978–1982	45.0 [1]
Willamette Management Associates [g]	1981–1984	31.2 [1]
Silber [h]	1981–1988	33.8
FMV Opinions, Inc. [i]	April 1992	23.0
Management Planning, Inc. [j]	1980–1996	27.1
Johnson (m)	1991-1995	20.0
Columbia Financial Advisors	1996–April 1997 (n)	21.0
Columbia Financial Advisors	May 1997–1998 (n)	13.0

a. "Discounts Involved in Purchases of Common Stock (1966–1969)," *Institutional Investor Study Report of the Securities and Exchange Commission*, H.R. Doc. No. 64, Part 5, 92nd Congress, 1st Session, 1971, pp. 2444–56.

b. Gelman, Milton, "An Economist-Financial Analyst's Approach to Valuing Stock in a Closely Held Company," *Journal of Taxation*, June 1972, p. 353.

c. Trout, Robert R., "Estimation of the Discount Associated with the Transfer of Restricted Securities," *Taxes*, June 1977, pp. 381–85.

d. Moroney, Robert E., "Most Courts Overvalue Closely Held Stocks," *Taxes*, March 1973, pp. 144–55.

e. Maher, J. Michael, "Discounts for Lack of Marketability for Closely Held Business Interests," *Taxes*, September 1976, pp. 562–71.

f. Pittock, William F., and Charles H. Stryker, "Revenue Ruling 77-276 Revisited," *SRC Quarterly Reports*, Spring 1983, pp. 1–3.

g. Willamette Management Associates study (unpublished).

h. Silber, William L., "Discounts on Restricted Stock: The Impact of Illiquidity on Stock Prices," *Financial Analysts Journal*, July–August 1991, pp. 60–64.

i. Hall, Lance S., and Timothy C. Polacek, "Strategies for Obtaining the Largest Valuation Discounts," *Estate Planning*, January/February 1994, pp. 38–44.

j. Oliver, Robert P., and Roy H. Meyers, "Discounts Seen in Private Placements of Restricted Stock: The Management Planning, Inc., Long-Term Study (1980–1996)" (Chapter 5) in Robert F. Reilly and Robert P. Schweihs, eds. *The Handbook of Advanced Business Valuation* (New York: McGraw-Hill, 2000).

k. Although the years covered in this study the likely to be 1969–1972, no specific years were given in the published account.

l. Median discounts.

m. Johnson, Bruce, "Restricted Stock Discounts, 1991–95," *Shannon Pratt's Business Valuation Update*, March 1999, p. 1–3; "Quantitative Support for Discounts for Lack of Marketability," *Business Valuation Review*, December 1999, pp. 152–155.

n. Aschwald, Kathryn, F., "Restricted Stock Discounts Decline as Result of 1-Year Holding Period," *Shannon Pratt's Business Valuation Update*, May 2000, p. 1–5.

sell after one year if other parts of the rule are followed. In recent years, more transactions have occurred under SEC Rule 144(a), which relaxes some of the restrictions on such transactions, thus making the restricted securities more marketable. In any case, investors generally expect to be able to resell the stock in the public market in the foreseeable future.

The Internal Revenue Service specifically recognized the relevance of restricted stock transaction data as evidence for quantification of the discount for lack of marketability in Revenue Ruling 77-287. Revenue Ruling 77-287 is presented in Exhibit 17–8.

Exhibit 17–8

Revenue Ruling 77-287

Section 1. Purpose.

The purpose of this Revenue Ruling is to amplify Rev. Rul. 59-60, 1959-1 C.B. 237, as modified by Rev. Rul. 65-193, 1965-2 C.B. 370, and to provide information and guidance to taxpayers, Internal Revenue Service personnel, and others concerned with the valuation, for Federal tax purposes, of securities that cannot be immediately resold because they are restricted from resale pursuant to Federal securities laws. This guidance is applicable only in cases where it is not inconsistent with valuation requirements of the Internal Revenue Code of 1954 or the regulations thereunder. Further, this ruling does not establish the time at which property shall be valued.

Sec. 2 Nature of the Problem.

It frequently becomes necessary to establish the fair market value of stock that has not been registered for public trading when the issuing company has stock of the same class that is actively traded in one or more securities markets. The problem is to determine the difference in fair market value between the registered shares that are actively traded and the unregistered shares. This problem is often encountered in estate and gift tax cases. However, it is sometimes encountered when unregistered shares are issued in exchange for assets or the stock of an acquired company.

Sec. 3. Background and Definitions.

.01 The Service outlined and reviewed in general the approach, methods, and factors to be considered in valuing shares of closely held corporate stock for estate and gift tax purposes in Rev. Rul. 59-60, as modified by Rev. Rul. 65-193. The provisions of Rev. Rul. 59-60, as modified, were extended to the valuation of corporate securities for income and other tax purposes by Rev. Rul. 68-609, 1968-2 C.B. 327.

.02 There are several terms currently in use in the securities industry that denote restrictions imposed on the resale and transfer of certain securities. The term frequently used to describe these securities is "restricted securities," but they are sometimes referred to as "unregistered securities," "investment letter stock," "control stock," or "private placement stock." Frequently these terms are used interchangeably. They all indicate that these particular securities cannot lawfully be distributed to the general public until a registration statement relating to the corporation underlying the securities has been filed, and has also become effective under the rules promulgated and enforced by the United States Securities & Exchange Commission (SEC) pursuant to the Federal securities laws. The following represents a more refined definition of each of the following terms along with two other terms—"exempted securities" and "exempted transactions."

(a) The term "restricted securities" is defined in Rule 144 adopted by the SEC as "securities acquired directly or indirectly from the issuer thereof, or from an affiliate of such issuer, in a transaction or chain of transactions not involving any public offering."

(b) The term "unregistered securities," refers to those securities with respect to which a registration statement, providing full disclosure by the issuing corporation, has not been filed with the SEC pursuant to the Securities Act of 1933. The registration statement is a condition precedent to a public distribution of securities in interstate commerce and is aimed at providing the prospective investor with a factual basis for sound judgment in making investment decisions.

(c) The terms "investment letter stock" and "letter stock" denote shares of stock that have been issued by a corporation without the benefit of filing a registration statement with the SEC. Such stock is subject to resale and transfer restrictions set forth in a letter agreement requested by the issuer and signed by the buyer of the stock when the stock is delivered. Such stock may be found in the hands of either individual investors or institutional investors.

(d) The term "control stock" indicates that the shares of stock have been held or are being held by an officer, director, or other person close to the management of the corporation. These persons are subject to certain requirements pursuant to SEC rules upon resale of shares they own in such corporations.

(e) The term "private placement stock" indicates that the stock has been placed with an institution or other investor who will presumably hold it for a long period and ultimately arrange to have the stock registered if it is to be offered to the general public. Such stock may or may not be subject to a letter agreement. Private placements of stock are exempted from the registration and prospectus provisions of the Securities Act of 1933.

(f) The term "exempted securities" refers to those classes of securities that are expressly excluded from the registration provisions of the Securities Act of 1933 and the distribution provisions of the Securities Exchange Act of 1934.

(g) The term "exempted transactions" refers to certain sales or distributions of securities that do not involve a public offering and are excluded from the registration and prospectus provisions of the Securities Act of 1933 and distribution provisions of the Securities Exchange Act of 1934. The exempted status makes it unnecessary for issuers of securities to go through the registration process.

Sec. 4. Securities Industry Practice in Valuing Restricted Securities.

.01 *Investment Company Valuation Practices*. The Investment Company Act of 1940 requires open-end investment companies to publish the valuation of their portfolio securities daily. Some of these companies have portfolios containing restricted securities, but also have unrestricted securities of the same class traded on a securities exchange. In recent years the number of restricted securities in such portfolios have increased. The following methods have been used by investment companies in the valuation of such restricted securities:

(a) Current market price of the unrestricted stock less a constant percentage discount based on purchase discount;

(b) Current market price of unrestricted stock less a constant percentage discount different from purchase discount;

(c) Current market price of the unrestricted stock less a discount amortized over a fixed period;

(d) Current market price of the unrestricted stock; and

(e) Cost of the restricted stock until it is registered.

The SEC ruled in its Investment Company Act Release No. 5847, dated October 21, 1969, that there can be no automatic formula by which an investment company can value the restricted securities in its portfolios. Rather, the SEC has determined that it is the responsibility of the board of directors of the particular investment company to determine the "fair value" of each issue of restricted securities in good faith.

.02 *Institutional Investors Study*. Pursuant to Congressional direction, the SEC undertook an analysis of the purchases, sales, and holding of securities by financial institutions, in order to determine the effect of institutional activity upon the securities market. The study report was published in eight volumes in March 1971. The fifth volume provides an analysis of restricted securities and deals with such items as the characteristics of the restricted securities purchasers and issuers, the size of transactions (dollars and shares), the marketability discounts on different trading markets, and the resale provisions. This research project provides some guidance for measuring the discount in that it contains information, based on the actual experience of the marketplace, showing that, during the period surveyed (January 1, 1966, through June 30, 1969), the amount of discount allowed for restricted securities from the trading price of the unrestricted securities was generally related to the following four factors.

(a) *Earnings*. Earnings and sales consistently have a significant influence on the size of restricted securities discounts according to the study. Earnings played the major part in establishing the ultimate discounts at which these stocks were sold from the current market price. Apparently earnings patterns, rather than sales patterns, determine the degree of risk of an investment.

(b) *Sales*. The dollar amount of sales of issuers' securities also has a major influence on the amount of discount at which restricted securities sell from the current market price. The results of the study generally indicate that the companies with the lowest dollar amount of sales during the test period accounted for most of the transactions involving the highest discount rates, while they accounted for only a small portion of all transactions involving the lowest discount rates.

(c) *Trading Market*. The market in which publicly held securities are traded also reflects variances in the amount of discount that is applied to restricted securities purchases. According to the study, discount rates were greatest on restricted stocks with unrestricted counterparts traded over-the-counter, followed by those with unrestricted counterparts listed on the American Stock

continued on next page

Exhibit 17–8

Revenue Ruling 77-287 (continued)

Exchange, while the discount rates for those stocks with unrestricted counterparts listed on the New York Stock Exchange were the smallest.

(d) *Resale Agreement Provisions.* Resale agreement provisions often affect the size of the discount. The discount from the market price provides the main incentive for a potential buyer to acquire restricted securities. In judging the opportunity cost of freezing funds, the purchaser is analyzing two separate factors. The first factor is the risk that underlying value of the stock will change in a way that, absent the restrictive provisions, would have prompted a decision to sell. The second factor is the risk that the contemplated means of legally disposing of the stock may not materialize. From the seller's point view, a discount is justified where the seller is relieved of the expenses of registration and public distribution, as well as of the risk that the market will adversely change before the offering is completed. The ultimate agreement between buyer and seller is a reflection of these and other considerations. Relative bargaining strengths of the parties to the agreement are major considerations that influence the resale terms and consequently the size of discounts in restricted securities transactions. Certain provisions are often found in agreements between buyers and sellers that affect the size of discounts at which restricted stocks are sold. Several such provisions follow, all of which, other than number (3), would tend to reduce the size of the discount:

(1) A provision giving the buyer an option to "piggyback," that is, to register restricted stock with the next registration statement, if any, filed by the issuer with the SEC;

(2) A provision giving the buyer an option to require registration at the seller's expense;

(3) A provision giving the buyer an option to require registration, but only at the buyer's own expense;

(4) A provision giving the buyer a right to receive continuous disclosure of information about the issuer from the seller;

(5) A provision giving the buyer a right to select one or more directors of the issuer;

(6) A provision giving the buyer an option to purchase additional shares of the issuer's stock; and

(7) A provision giving the buyer the right to have a greater voice in operations of the issuer, if the issuer does not meet previously agreed upon operating standards.

Institutional buyers can and often do obtain many of these rights and options from the sellers of restricted securities, and naturally, the more rights the buyer can acquire, the lower the buyer's risk is going to be, thereby reducing the buyer's discount as well. Small buyers may not be able to negotiate the large discounts or the rights and options that volume buyers are able to negotiate.

.03 *Summary.* A variety of methods have been used by the securities industry to value restricted securities. The SEC rejects all automatic or mechanical solutions to the valuation of restricted securities, and prefers, in the case of the valuation of investment company portfolio stocks, to rely upon good faith valuations by the board of directors of each company. The study made by the SEC found that restricted securities generally are issued at a discount from the market value of freely tradable securities.

Sec. 5 Facts and Circumstances Material to Valuation of Restricted Securities.

.01 Frequently, a company has a class of stock that cannot be traded publicly. The reason such stock cannot be traded may arise from the securities statutes, as in the case of an "investment letter" restriction; it may arise from a corporate charter restriction, or perhaps from a trust agreement restriction. In such cases, certain documents and facts should be obtained for analysis.

0.2 The following documents and facts, when used in conjunction with those discussed in Section 4 of Rev. Rul. 59-60, will be useful in the valuation of restricted securities:

(a) A copy of any declaration of trust, trust agreement, and any other agreements relating to the shares of restricted stock;

(b) A copy of any document showing any offers to buy or sell or indications of interest in buying or selling the restricted shares;

(c) The latest prospectus of the company;

(d) Annual reports of the company for 3 to 5 years preceding the valuation date;

(e) The trading prices and trading volume of the related class of traded securities 1 month preceding the valuation date, if they are traded on a stock exchange (if traded over-the-counter, prices may be obtained from the National Quotations Bureau, the National Association of Securities Dealers Automated Quotations (NASDAQ), or sometimes from broker-dealers making markets in the shares);

(f) The relationship of the parties to the agreements concerning the restricted stock, such as whether they are members of the immediate family or perhaps whether they are officers or directors of the company; and

(g) Whether the interest being valued or represents a majority ownership.

Sec. 6 Weighing Facts and Circumstances Material to Restricted Stock Valuation.

All relevant facts and circumstances that bear upon the worth of restricted stock, including those set forth above in the preceding Sections 4 and 5, and those set forth in Section 4 of Rev. Rul. 59-60, must be taken into account in arriving at the fair market value of such securities. Depending on the circumstances of each case, certain factors may carry more weight than others. To illustrate:

.01 Earnings, net assets, and net sales must be given primary consideration in arriving at appropriate discount for restricted securities from the freely traded shares. These are the elements of value that are always used by investors in making investment decisions. In some cases, one element may be more important than in other cases. In the case of manufacturing, producing, or distributing companies, primary weight must be accorded earnings and net sales; but in the case of investment or holding companies, primary weight must be given to the net assets of the company underlying the stock. In the former type of companies, value is more closely linked to past, present, and future earnings while in the latter type of companies, value is more closely linked to the existing net assets of the company. See the discussion in Section 5 of Rev. Rul. 59-60.

.02 Resale provisions found in the restriction agreements must be scrutinized and weighted to determine the amount of discount to apply the preliminary fair market value of the company. The two elements of time and expense bear upon this discount; the longer the buyer of the shares must wait to liquidate the shares, the greater the discount. Moreover, if the provisions make it necessary for the buyer to bear the expense of registration, the greater the discount. However, if the provisions of the restricted stock agreement make it possible for the buyer to "piggyback" shares at the next offering, the discount would be smaller.

.03 The relative negotiation strengths of the buyer and seller of restricted stock may have a profound effect on the amount of discount. For example, a tight money situation may cause the buyer to have the greater balance of negotiation strength in a transaction. However, in some cases the relative strengths may tend to cancel each other out.

.04 The market experience of freely tradable securities of the same class as the restricted securities is also significant in determining the amount of discount. Whether the shares are privately held or publicly traded affects the worth of the shares to the holder. Securities traded on a public market generally are worth more to investors than those that are not traded on a public market. Moreover, the type of public market in which the unrestricted securities are traded is to be given consideration.

Sec. 7. Effect on Other Documents.

Rev. Rul. 59-60, as modified by Rev. Rul. 65-193, is amplified.

SOURCE: Rev Rul. 77-287. 1977 2 C.B. 319.

Studies of Private Transactions before Initial Public Offerings

Before the 1980s, virtually all the empirical research directed at quantifying the value impact of marketability (or the discount for lack of marketability) focused on comparisons between the prices (1) of freely tradable shares of stock and (2) of restricted but otherwise identical shares of stock. There is a general consensus among analysts that price discounts for lack of marketability for ownership interests of closely held companies were greater than those for restricted shares of publicly held companies. This is because the closely held ownership interests had no established market in which they could eventually sell following the removal of certain trading restrictions. However, data for quantifying how much greater this price discount should be had not yet been collected and analyzed.

During the 1980s, an investment banking firm and a valuation consulting firm independently undertook the assemblage of data with which to address this question. The research proceeded along basically parallel lines, although each firm was unaware of the other's efforts until their respective research was far along and each had enough data to reach some conclusions.

Both firms used data from *registration statements*, forms that companies must file with the SEC when they sell securities to the public. Each of the series of studies reported in the following sections used data from these forms in order to analyze prices of the private transactions relative to the public offering prices and market prices following initial public offerings.

Robert W. Baird & Company Studies

Eight studies were conducted under the direction of John D. Emory, first vice president of appraisal services at Robert W. Baird & Company, a regional investment banking firm headquartered in Milwaukee.[23] The studies covered various time periods from 1981 through 2000.

The basic methodology for the eight studies was identical. The population of companies in each study consisted of initial public offerings during the respective period in which Baird & Company either participated or received prospectuses. The prospectuses of these over 2,200 offerings were analyzed to determine the relationship between (1) the price at which the stock was initially offered to the public and (2) the price at which the latest private transaction occurred up to five months prior to the initial public offering.

---

[23] John D. Emory, "The Value of Marketability as Illustrated in Initial Public Offerings of Common Stock—January 1980 through June 1981," *Business Valuation News*, September 1985, pp. 21–24, also in *ASA Valuation*, June 1986, pp. 62–66; "The Value of Marketability as Illustrated in Initial Public Offerings of Common Stock, January 1985 through June 1986," *Business Valuation Review*, December 1986, pp. 12–15; "The Value of Marketability as Illustrated in Initial Public Offerings of Common Stock (August 1987–January 1989)," *Business Valuation Review*, June 1989, pp. 55–57; "The Value of Marketability as Illustrated in Initial Public Offerings of Common Stock, February 1989–July 1990," *Business Valuation Review*, December 1990, pp. 114–16; "The Value of Marketability as Illustrated in Initial Public Offerings of Common Stock, August 1990 through January 1992," *Business Valuation Review*, December 1992, pp. 208–12; "The Value of Marketability as Illustrated in Initial Public Offerings of Common Stock, February 1992 through July 1993," *Business Valuation Review*, March 1994, pp. 3–5; "The Value of Marketability as Illustrated in Initial Public Offerings of Common Stock, January 1994 through June 1995," *Business Valuation Review*, December 1995, pp. 155–60; "The Value of Marketability as Illustrated in Initial Public Offerings of Common Stock, November 1995 through April 1997," *Business Valuation Review*, September 1997, pp. 123–31.

Emory gives the following explanation regarding the studies:

In order to provide a reasonable comparison of prices before and at the IPO, I felt it necessary both for the company to have been reasonably sound, and for the private transaction to have occurred within a period of five months prior to the offering date.

The transactions primarily took one of two forms: (1) the granting of stock options with an exercise price equal to the stock's then fair market value; or (2) the sale of stock.... In most cases, the transactions were stated to have been, or could reasonably be expected to have been, at fair market value. All ultimately would have had to be able to withstand SEC, IRS or judicial review, particularly in light of the subsequent public offering.[24]

Following the above guidelines, and after eliminating development-stage companies (i.e., companies with a history of operating losses) and companies with no transactions within the five months before the initial public offering, 310 qualifying transactions remained in the eight studies.

The mean price discount for the 543 transactions was 46 percent, and the median price discount was 47 percent. The fact that these averages are a little more than 10 percentage points greater than those shown in restricted stock studies is about what one might reasonably expect. This is because the transactions occurred when there was not yet any established market for the stocks at all.

A summary of the results of each of the eight Emory studies is presented as Exhibit 17–9.

Exhibit 17–9

The Value of Marketability as Illustrated in Initial Public Offerings of Common Stock

Study	Number of IPO Prospectuses Reviewed	Number of Qualifying Transactions	Discount Mean	Discount Median
1997-2000	1847	266	50	52
1995-97	732	84	43	41
1994-95	318	45	45	47
1991-93	443	49	45	13
1990-92	266	30	34	33
1989-90	157	17	46	40
1987-89	98	21	38	43
1985-86	130	19	43	43
1980-81	97	12	59	68
All 8 studies	2,241	543	46%	47%

SOURCE: John D. Emory, Sr., ASA, John D. Emory, Jr., and F.R. Dengel, III. *Business Valuation Review*, December 2002. See Emory & Co., LLC's Web site, www.EmoryCo.com, for a free downloadable spreadsheet of the underlying data.

---

[24] John D. Emory, "The Value of Marketability as Illustrated in Initial Public Offerings of Common Stock, November 1995 through April 1997," *Business Valuation Review*, September 1997, p. 124.

Willamette Management Associates Studies

Over many years, Willamette Management Associates has conducted a series of studies on the prices of private stock transactions relative to those of subsequent public offerings of stock of the same companies. The studies covered the years 1975 through 2002.

The Willamette Management Associates studies differed from the Emory studies in several respects. One important difference was that the source documents for the Willamette Management Associates studies were complete SEC registration statements primarily on Form S-1 and Form S-18. By contrast, the source documents for the Emory studies were prospectuses. Although the prospectus constitutes a portion of the registration statement, it is required to disclose only transactions with affiliated parties. Form S-1 and Form S-18 registration statements require disclosure of *all* private transactions in the stock within the three years before the public offering, in a section of the registration statement separate from the prospectus portion.

The Willamette Management Associates studies attempted to include only transactions that were on an arm's-length basis. The data analyzed included sales of stock in private placements and repurchases of treasury stock by the companies. All stock option transactions and sales of stock to corporate insiders were eliminated, unless there was reason to believe they were bona fide transactions for full value. Many registrant companies were contacted by telephone to validate the arm's-length nature of the transaction.

The Willamette Management Associates studies considered all public offerings in the files of the *IPO Reporter*. According to the *IPO Reporter*, they included all public offerings during the respective period except for offerings of closed-end fund companies. Eliminated from each of the studies were financial institutions, natural resource companies, offerings priced at $1 or less per share, and offerings that included units or warrants since such offerings might be thought to have unique characteristics. The private transactions analyzed took place from 1 to 36 months before the initial public offering. If a company had more than one transaction that met the study's criteria, all such transactions were included.

For each transaction for which meaningful earnings data were available in the registration statement as of both the private transaction and public offering dates, the price/earnings multiple of each private transaction was compared with the subsequent public offering price/earnings multiple. Companies that had no meaningful earnings as of the private transaction date and/or the public offering date were eliminated.

Because the private transactions occurred over a period of up to three years prior to the public offering, Willamette Management Associates made adjustments to reflect differences in market conditions for stocks of the respective industries between the time of each private transaction and the time of each subsequent public offering. Price/earnings multiples were adjusted for differences in the industry average price/earnings multiple between the time of the private transaction and that of the public offering.

The formula used to derive the discount for the private transaction price from the public offering price was as follows:

$$\frac{P/E_o - P/E_p \left(\dfrac{IP/E_o}{IP/E_p} \right)}{P/E_o}$$

where:

P/E_o = Price per share of the public offering
P/E_p = Price per share of the private transaction
IP/E_o = Industry price index at time of offering
IP/E_p = Industry price index at time of private transaction

Between 1975 and 1997, the Willamette Management Associates' studies indicated mean discounts that ranged from 28.9 percent (1991) to 56.8 percent (1979), and median discounts that ranged from 31.8 percent (1991) to 73.1 percent (1984). Willamette Management Associates' 1998 pre-IPO study indicated a mean discount for lack of marketability (DLOM) of 35 percent and a median of 49.4 percent.

The DLOM conclusions in Willamette Management Associates' 1999 and 2000 studies were lower than the long-term trends and conclusions of other analysts. For example, the Emory studies for those years showed a mean discount of 50 percent and a median discount of 52 percent, whereas the Willamette Management Associates' study returned only a mean discount of 26.4 percent and median discount of 27.7 percent in 1999 and a mean discount of 18.0 percent and median discount of 31.9 percent in 2000.

Willamette Management Associates has indicated that it believes the low conclusions could be the result of three factors. First, few IPO companies and private sale transactions qualified for inclusion in Willamette Management Associates' study. Second, the height of the dot.com "bubble" occurred during this two-year period. Lastly, the average first-day returns for pre-IPO stocks were extraordinarily high in 1999 and 2000.[25]

The Willamette Management Associates' DLOM conclusions for 2001 and 2002 were also inconsistent with their previously published pre-IPO studies. The 2001 DLOM conclusions had a mean and median of negative 195.8 percent. The mean DLOM conclusion for 2002 was 55.8 percent, which was abnormally high when compared with the mean DLOM conclusions of the decade prior to 1999. These results can be explained by the fact that there were too few private market stock sale transactions in 2001 and 2002 that met the Willamette Management Associates' criteria for the study results to be statistically meaningful—there were only two private market sale transactions in 2001, and only seven in 2002 that qualified.

Criticisms of Willamette Management Associates Studies

Over the years that Willamette Management Associates has used pre-IPO studies in support of the estimation of the lack of marketability discount, the work has been the subject of certain criticisms. In the following discussion, we will attempt to respond to some of these criticisms.

1. *The results are impossible to verify because Willamette Management Associates will not provide the underlying data or calculation.* The analyses are performed in response to individual client situations at great expense and

---

[25] Robert F. Reilly, "Willamette Management Associates' Discount for Lack of Marketability Study for Marital Dissolution Valuations," *American Journal of Family Law*, Spring 2005, pp. 44-51.

are proprietary. However, (1) they are based entirely on publicly available data, and (2) all the calculations can be replicated when needed, as the methodology is set forth in detail in several books and articles published by Willamette Management Associates professional staff.

2. *There is a self-selection bias in the determination of "qualifying transactions," resulting in an overestimation of the discount for lack of marketability by excluding "troubled" companies.* The Willamette Management Associates studies exclude, by definition, companies that fail, or fail to go public. This is obvious because only companies that go public create a benchmark of liquidity for minority ownership interest shares. Conversely, companies that do not go public are useless for the purpose of deriving a marketable stock price. In order to estimate the lack of marketability discount, one should have a benchmark for comparison (i.e., a marketable price to compare with the nonmarketable price).

   If there was a bias based upon the fact that the Willamette Management Associates studies include only "successful" companies, it would understate the size of the lack of marketability discount. One would expect a "troubled" company to be less liquid than a "successful" company, with fewer options for liquidity resulting in a greater lack of marketability discount.

   An argument has been made that the less successful company may trade at a price below the price realized in an earlier transaction (presumably resulting in a premium, or negative lack of marketability discount). This may be true at first glance. However, since we adjust the pricing for changes in the price/earnings multiple, the resulting lack of marketability discount is more reliable. In other words, the exclusion of "troubled" companies, while necessary and logical, does not necessarily lead to an overestimation of the lack of marketability discount.

3. *Many of the transactions are not arm's-length transactions.* A comprehensive effort is made to eliminate non-arm's-length transactions. Each of the transactions included in the database has also passed the scrutiny of the SEC. Although the level of effort that Willamette puts forth to verify the validity of the arm's-length nature of the pre-IPO transaction is subject to challenge, the small number of non-arm's-length transactions that may have been inadvertently included would not skew the results.

Valuation Advisors Studies

Studies published using the Valuation Advisors' database break down the number of transactions by length of time that the private transaction occurred prior to the IPO: 1–90 days prior, 91–180 days prior, 181–270 days prior, 271–365 days prior, and 1–2 years prior. Results for years 1999–2004 are shown in Exhibit 17–10.

Summary of Conclusions from Private Transaction Studies

The evidence from the Emory, Willamette Management Associates, and Valuation Advisors studies, taken together, is compelling. The studies covered hundreds of transaction over more than 30 years. Average differentials between private transaction prices and public market prices varied under different market conditions, ranging from about 40 percent to 72 percent, after eliminating the outliers.

This is very strong support for the hypothesis that the fair market values of noncontrolling ownership interests in privately held businesses usually are greatly discounted from their publicly traded counterparts.

Other Analysis of Discounts for Lack of Marketability for Minority Ownership Interests

Ultimately, of course, the value of the nonmarketable, minority ownership interest is the present value of the benefits it will produce for its owner. This fact is recognized in the *Quantitative Marketability Discount Model* (QMDM).[26] The model simply estimates a time horizon at which the interest will be liquidated, a liquidating price based on annual percentage growth in value from the valuation date, and interim cash flows to the holder.

These estimated values are discounted back to a present value in the QMDM at a discount rate that is higher than the normal discount rate for cash flows for the subject company to reflect the illiquidity and extra uncertainty of being "locked up" for an indeterminate time. There are several factors to consider, and approximate percentage points for each factor add to the discount rate.

The model is sound, but the inputs require substantial subjective estimation. It is useful for identifying situations where the discount should be significantly above or below the averages shown by the restricted stock or pre-IPO studies.

The book *Quantifying Marketability Discounts* also analyzes some of the studies discussed in this chapter in detail.

Discounts for Lack of Marketability for Controlling Ownership Interests

It is often necessary to agree on the cash equivalent value as of a valuation date for a controlling business ownership interest. This is true whether or not the business will actually be sold. Examples of situations where this cash equivalency analysis is necessary include *federal estate tax cases* (in the case of a death of the controlling business owner) and many *marital property cases* (in the case of a marital dissolution).

Federal estate taxes, by law, require a cash equivalency value as of a date certain. The estate taxes themselves are paid in cash, not in kind by tendering shares of stock. Therefore, many analysts make an adjustment from the estimated (but uncertain) sale value of the subject controlling business interest at some undetermined time in the future to a cash equivalency value as of the valuation date, reflecting the time, costs, and risks attendant to achieving such a sale. And, of these three factors, the risk of actually being able to consummate the business sale is typically much more significant than the timing and the costs of the business sale.

This valuation adjustment, or discount, is the discount for illiquidity (i.e., the discount for lack of marketability of the controlling business ownership interest).

---

[26] Z. Christopher Mercer, *Valuing Shareholder Cash Flows: Quantifying Marketability Discounts*, E-Book (Memphis: Peabody Publishing, 2005).

Exhibit 17–10

Valuation Advisors' Lack of Marketability Discount Study™
Transaction Summary Results by Year from 1999–2006

Time of Transaction Before IPO	1–90 Days	91–180 Days	181–270 Days	271–365 Days	1–2 Years
1999 Results					
Number of Transactions	148	174	103	91	174
Median Discount	30.8%	53.9%	75.0%	76.9%	82.0%
2000 Results					
Number of Transactions	129	176	116	91	141
Median Discount	28.7%	45.1%	61.5%	68.9%	76.6%
2001 Results					
Number of Transactions	15	17	18	17	48
Median Discount	14.7%	33.2%	33.4%	52.1%	51.6%
2002 Results					
Number of Transactions	9	13	7	16	36
Median Discount	6.2%	17.3%	21.9%	39.5%	55.0%
2003 Results					
Number of Transactions	12	22	24	21	44
Median Discount	28.8%	22.3%	38.4%	39.7%	61.4%
2004 Results					
Number of Transactions	37	74	63	59	101
Median Discount	16.7%	22.7%	40.0%	56.3%	57.9%
2005 Results					
Number of Transactions	18	59	58	62	99
Median Discount	14.8%	26.1%	41.7%	46.1%	45.5%
2006 Results					
Number of Transactions	25	76	69	72	106
Median Discount	20.7%	20.8%	40.2%	46.9%	57.2%
1999–2006 Transaction Results					
Number of Transactions	393	611	458	429	749
Median Discount	27.3%	37.5%	51.9%	61.7%	68.0%

SOURCE: The Valuation Advisors' *Discount for Lack of Marketability Database*. Database access is available at www.bvmarketdata.com. Used with permission. All rights reserved.

In many reported decisions, the U.S. Tax Court has recognized that discounts for lack of marketability for controlling ownership interests in closely held companies are appropriate. The courts have used language such as the following:

> Even controlling shares in a nonpublic corporation suffer from lack of marketability because of the absence of a ready private placement market and the fact that flotation costs would have to be incurred if the corporation were to publicly offer its stock.[27]

Similarly, in the marital dissolution situation, the spouse most actively involved in the closely held business usually gets the controlling ownership interest in the business. And the nonoperating spouse usually gets much more liquid assets, such as cash, marketable securities, and real estate.

---

[27] *Estate of Woodbury G. Andrews*, 79 T.C. 938 (1982).

A rational argument can be made that the same factors discussed above should be reflected in the value of the illiquid controlling business ownership interest for marital dissolution valuation purposes.

Illiquidity Factors Affecting Controlling Ownership Interests

Unlike the owner of publicly traded securities, the owner of a controlling owner-ship interest in a closely held business cannot (1) call a securities broker, (2) sell that controlling ownership interest in seconds at a predetermined price and with a nominal transaction commission, and (3) realize the cash proceeds of the sale in three business days. Rather, selling a controlling business ownership interest is a lengthy, expensive, and uncertain undertaking. This assertion is equally true even if the subject investment is a 100 percent (i.e., absolute controlling) ownership interest in a closely held business enterprise.

The typical means of liquidating a controlling business ownership interest are as follows:

1. Consummate a public offering of the controlling block of stock.
2. Ina private transaction:
   a. Sell the overall business enterprise (and equitably allocate the sale pro-ceeds to all of the business owners).
   b. Sell the controlling ownership interest only (to the other minority owner-ship stockholders or to an independent third-party buyer).

Under various conditions in the public capital markets for stocks and the merger/acquisition markets for companies, one or more of the above transactional alternatives may be clearly more or less attractive—at any given point. The values realizable from these transactional alternatives usually have some relationship to each other. This is because potential acquirers of a closely held business may be public companies.

The controlling owner of a closely held business who wishes to liquidate his or her controlling ownership interest generally faces the following transactional considerations:

1. Uncertain time horizon to complete the offering or sale.
2. Cost to prepare for and execute the offering or sale.
3. Risk concerning eventual sale price.
4. Noncash and deferred transaction proceeds.
5. Inability to hypothecate.

Time Horizon. It may take many months, and in some cases years, to com-plete either an offering or a sale of a closely held business. To some extent, the time factor may be offset by cash flows available to the owner awaiting sale, if they are equal to or greater than the company's cost of capital on a stand-alone basis.

Costs. There will be many costs attendant to the sale:

1. Auditing and accounting fees, to provide potential buyers the financial infor-mation and assurances they demand.
2. Legal costs, at a minimum to draft all the necessary documents and often to clear away potential perceived contingent liabilities and/or to negotiate warranties.

3. Administrative costs on the part of business owners to deal with the accountants, lawyers, potential buyers, and/or their representatives.

Risk. There is a high degree of risk concerning the amount of the actual sale
price that will be realized relative to the estimated sale price. This is (1) partly
because business valuations are only estimates and (2) partly because internal and/or
external factors may influence the business value during the sale negotiation period.

Furthermore, in many cases, there is substantial risk concerning whether the
business can be sold at all. There is always considerable risk as to whether a transaction or an initial public offering can actually be completed at any given stock
price. The capital markets are more or less receptive to stocks of companies in different industries at different points. And, some closely held companies will not be
accepted by the public markets at all.

Form of the Proceeds. Even when a sale is complete, the business sale proceeds
may not be all in cash. Often, the seller may receive part of the business sale proceeds in a note or contingent compensation, or in stock of the acquiring company
(and usually restricted stock if the acquiring company is a publicly traded company).

From 1975 to 1980, almost half the reported business acquisitions were for all
cash. In 1999, about 46 percent of the business acquisitions were all cash, 30 percent were all stock, and 24 percent were some combination of cash, debt, and
stock.[28] In most of these cases, the stock received is restricted stock. Accordingly,
the cash equivalency value of a closely held business sale transaction may be substantially lower than the announced deal price.

For closely held company sales through business brokers, seller financing
through a note is involved in the vast majority of transactional cases. Usually, these
seller paper notes are at interest rates below market rates for notes of comparable
risk. Furthermore, many close corporation "deal prices" have a portion of the payments contingent on given levels of revenues or earnings, further reducing the cash
equivalency value.

In the initial public offering transaction scenario, normally it is not possible to
sell 100 percent of the company's stock at one time. Underwriters generally are not
willing to sell an offering in which insiders are bailing out of all their stock. Thus,
the closely held business seller usually is left with some unregistered (restricted)
stock. This stock would still be subject to the discount for lack of marketability for
restricted stocks as discussed in an earlier section.

Inability to Hypothecate. Ownership interests in closely held businesses, even
controlling ownership interests, generally do not make satisfactory bank collateral.
If, while awaiting a sale, an owner of a controlling ownership interest wants cash
for an emergency or an opportunity or whatever, it will be time-consuming—and
may be impossible—to borrow against the estimated value of the business interest.

Benchmark for the Illiquidity Discount for Controlling Ownership Interests

If the appropriate standard of value is fair market value, the price ultimately
expected to be reached between "a willing buyer and a willing seller"—before the
costs and risks listed above are considered—is a benchmark from which the

---

[28] *Mergerstat Review 2000* (Los Angeles: Applied Financial Information, LP, 2000), p. 15.

illiquidity discount could be taken. Other possibilities concerning the appropriate base from which an illiquidity discount on a controlling business ownership interest basis should be taken are:

1. The price one might receive in an initial or secondary public stock offering (i.e., the publicly traded equivalent value).
2. The price achievable in the private sale of the entire closely held business enterprise.
3. A control transaction of a publicly-funded company.

In addition to the underwriting commissions and the direct expenses, underwriters frequently receive stock warrants, especially in connection with smaller initial public offerings. Although this is not an immediate cash expense, it is a very real cost of the transaction if the company is successful, possibly amounting to several percentage points of dilution.

There are also other indirect transaction costs, such as a large commitment of top management's time to negotiate and to carry out a successful stock offering. If the illiquidity discount is a critical issue in the subject business valuation, it may be appropriate to obtain the most current data with regard to the cost of a public flotation.

Many of the same or similar costs are involved in preparing a company for a private sale. In addition, the cost of an intermediary to effect the sale may need to be considered. Also, if the benchmark for the estimated sale price is valuation multiples observed in acquisitions of public companies, data indicate that valuation multiples for acquisitions of private companies tend to be lower. This pricing phenomenon is discussed in the following section.

Differences between Private and Public Company Acquisition Price/Earnings Multiples

Every year, *Mergerstat Review* publishes a table presenting the average price/earnings multiples for the acquisitions of private companies for which they have data—compared with the average price/earnings multiples for the acquisitions of companies that had been publicly traded. Almost every year, the average price/earnings multiple for the acquisitions of private companies is significantly lower than the average price/earnings multiple for the acquisitions of public companies.

The public versus private acquisition price/earnings multiple table from the *2000 Mergerstat Review* is presented in Exhibit 17–11.

Observers have hypothesized a number of reasons for this consistent and significant acquisition pricing differential. The most common reasons for this phenomenon are as follows:

1. Exposure to the market.
2. The quality of financial accounting and other information.
3. The size effect.

Exposure to the Market. The names and stock prices of publicly traded companies are published in hundreds of newspapers throughout the world every day. Publicly traded companies also issue many press releases every year with quarterly earnings and other information; these press releases are also published in hundreds of newspapers. Financial information on thousands of publicly traded companies is accessible online.

Exhibit 17–11

Median P/E* Offered Public versus Private 1990–2005

Year	Acquisitions of Public Companies		Acquisitions of Private Companies	
1990	17.1	(117)	13.2	(36)
1991	15.9	(93)	8.5	(23)
1992	18.1	(89)	17.6	(15)
1993	19.7	(113)	22.0	(14)
1994	19.8	(184)	22.0	(18)
1995	19.4	(239)	15.5	(16)
1996	21.7	(288)	17.7	(31)
1997	25.0	(389)	17.0	(83)
1998	24.0	(362)	16.0	(207)
1999	21.7	(434)	18.4	(174)
2000	18.0	(379)	16.0	(130)
2001	16.7	(261)	15.3	(80)
2002	19.7	(161)	16.6	(83)
2003	21.2	(198)	19.4	(107)
2004	22.6	(188)	19.0	(108)
2005	24.4	(230)	16.9	(127)

( ) Denotes number of transactions reporting P/E.
*Excludes negative P/E multiples and P/E multiples larger than 100.

SOURCE: Mergerstat® Review 2006 (Santa Monica: FactSet Mergerstat, LLC, 2006). www.mergerstat.com. Used with permission. All rights reserved.

Publicly traded companies are required to file Forms 10-K, 10-Q, and 8-K, as well as other detailed financial information, with the SEC. Any company, or financial intermediary, interested in an acquisition in any industry has this list of publicly traded companies and the detailed financial information on them at its fingertips.

By contrast, there is no such comprehensive and reliable listing of closely held businesses. And privately owned businesses normally do not disclose financial data. Many privately owned businesses do not even disclose gross revenues. Therefore, acquisition seekers do not have privately owned businesses constantly exposed to them.

Business buyers have difficulty making a comprehensive list of available closely held businesses even if they attempt to do so. Generally, business buyers cannot get financial information regarding closely held businesses—short of a direct approach to the subject business, which they are often reluctant to take and which is often rebuffed. Often, private company sales are initiated by the seller, which may put downward pressure on the price paid for the private company.

Quality of Financial Accounting and Other Information. The SEC requirements for accounting information and other disclosures are far more stringent and extensive than what is required for an unqualified audit opinion under normal generally accepted accounting practices (GAAP) rules. Many analysts believe that this difference in the quantity and reliability of financial data has an impact on the differential in average price/earnings multiples paid for the acquisition of public companies versus the acquisition of private companies.

Size Effect. Empirical studies have proven that larger companies tend to be less risky than smaller companies. This phenomenon would generally result in a lower present value discount rate and a higher price for larger companies. On average, the privately owned companies reported in *Mergerstat Review* are smaller in size than the publicly traded companies reported in *Mergerstat Review*.

This appears to be a contributing factor to the price/earnings multiple differential between privately owned and publicly traded company acquisitions reported in the *Mergerstat Review*. However, it is highly questionable whether this difference in average acquisition size is significant enough to account for the large magnitude of difference between privately owned and publicly traded company acquisition price/earnings multiples.

It is not possible, with the data currently available, to completely explain the relative impact of the various influences that cause privately owned business acquisitions to trade at much lower price/earnings multiples than publicly traded company acquisitions. In any case, the data are clear that privately owned businesses realize lower acquisition price/earnings multiples, on average, when compared with publicly traded companies. Additional research on this point is clearly warranted. Nonetheless, the three factors listed above (i.e., exposure to market, quality of financial accounting, and size effect) generally explain this phenomenon.

If the analysis of the value of a controlling ownership interest in a privately owned business is based on market prices for the acquisitions of publicly traded companies, these data suggest that some amount of valuation adjustment is applicable. For convenience, we may refer to this valuation phenomenon as a part of the illiquidity discount of a controlling business ownership interest.

Empirical data clearly suggest that a valuation discount is appropriate for controlling ownership interests (and, for that matter, for 100 percent ownership interests) in closely held businesses. This illiquidity discount applies—although to varying degrees—regardless of whether the subject business is valued by reference to discounted or capitalized economic income analyses, to guideline publicly traded companies, to consummated guideline acquisitions, or to an asset-based valuation method.

There is some empirical research supporting the notion that private companies sell for discounts relative to public companies.

Fuller, Netter, and Stegemoller studied the stock market returns of firms that acquired public and private targets over the period 1990 through 2000. They interpreted their results as supporting the idea of a liquidity discount for acquisitions of private companies, though they did not quantify the magnitude of the discount.

Koeplin, Sarin, and Shapiro compared controlling transaction multiples paid for privately held companies with a matching sample of publicly traded companies over the period 1984 through 1998. They examined multiples of enterprise value to EBIT, EBITDA, sales, and "book value" (book debt plus book equity). They calculated enterprise value as the offering price of equity plus book value of debt and preferred stock, less marketable securities. They found that median private deal multiples for domestic U.S. transactions were 0 percent to 31 percent smaller than median public multiples, depending on the multiple chosen for comparison. The median enterprise value/EBITDA ratio paid for private domestic companies in their samples was 18 percent lower than the median public company. For foreign transactions, the difference in median multiples ranged from 6 percent to 23 percent.[29]

---

[29] John Koeplin, Atulya Sarin, and Alan C. Shapiro, "The Private Company Discount," *Journal of Applied Corporate Finance* 12 (4) (2000), pp. 94–101. doi: 10.1111/j.1745-6622.2000.tb00022.x, Kathleen Fuller, Jeffry Netter, and Mike Stegemoller, "What Do Returns to Acquiring Firms Tell Us? Evidence from Firms That Make Many Acquisitions," *Journal of Finance*, August 2002 (Vol. 57:4)

Factors That Affect the Discounts for Illiquidity and Lack of Marketability

It is important to recognize that the discounts for illiquidity and lack of marketability are not a black-and-white issue. That is, an ownership interest is not necessarily simply "marketable," freely tradable in a public market, or "nonmarketable," not freely tradable. There are degrees of marketability. These *degrees* of marketability depend on the circumstances in each case.

The following are some of the factors that affect the degree of marketability. Although there is no empirically supported formula to assess the impact of each, consideration of these factors should guide the analyst's judgment about where the subject ownership interest should fall within the reasonable range of discounts for illiquidity and lack of marketability.

"Put" Rights

Generally, the most powerful factor that could reduce or eliminate a discount for lack of marketability would be the existence of a "put" right. A put is a contractual right that entitles the holder, at his or her option, to sell the ownership interest to a specified party at some time or under some specified circumstances, at the price (or mechanism for determining the price) specified in the contract. In other words, a put *guarantees* a market under specified circumstances. Put rights are most commonly found in connection with employee stock ownership plan (ESOP)-owned stock.

Dividend Payments

Stocks with no or low dividends suffer more from lack of marketability than stocks with high dividends. Besides being empirically demonstrable, this makes common sense. If the stock pays no dividend, the holder is dependent *entirely* on some future ability to sell the stock to realize any return. The higher the dividend, the greater the return the holder realizes without regard for sale of the stock. For this reason, dividend-paying preferred stocks would typically be subject to a lower discount for lack of marketability than non-dividend-paying common stocks.

Potential Buyers

The existence of a reasonable number of potential buyers or even one strong potential buyer (often as demonstrated by past activity in the company's stock) could dampen the discounts for lack of marketability. For example, if an ESOP regularly purchases shares, the possibility of sometime selling shares to the ESOP may cause the discount for lack of marketability to be less than if the ESOP did not exist.

Size of Interest

Strictly from a marketability perspective, the empirical evidence cited in earlier sections suggests that larger blocks may tend to have larger discounts for lack of marketability than do smaller blocks. There may be fewer potential buyers for a large block, and a large block transaction may be more difficult to finance.

One may logically conclude that a larger ownership interest may have higher value because of possible elements of ownership control, such as a swing vote position or a seat on the board of directors. However, this is a discount factor different from lack of marketability, as discussed in the previous chapter.

Ashok Abbott has developed a quantitative measure of the discount for lack of liquidity by studying the time it takes for different sizes of blocks of stock to become liquid. This method, while derived from observations of blocks of publicly traded stock, can be adapted to interests in privately held companies by estimating the discount for lack of liquidity for a similar size block using data for the corresponding time period for a peer group of publicly traded firms. Some of the conclusions reached by applying this method are that blocks of all sizes of publicly held stock are not equally liquid and that liquidity can differ significantly even within each market, depending on the attributes of the block and prevailing market conditions. Applying this method, Abbott concludes that as markets become more volatile and the liquidation periods get longer, the discounts for lack of liquidity become larger. Also, he concludes that discounts are not symmetric across the markets, but peak at different times.[30]

Prospect of Public Offering or Sale of the Business

An imminent public offering or sale of the business could decrease the discount for lack of marketability. However, such prospects are almost never certain, and the degree of offset to the discount for lack of marketability is problematic since much of the empirical evidence that illustrates the discount is taken from companies that subsequently went public. In some cases, even if such an event were to occur, all noncontrolling shareholders may not necessarily have the right to participate.

Conversely, a business being absolutely committed to remaining private and in the hands of current control owners for the foreseeable future would tend to increase the discount for lack of marketability.

Information Access and Reliability

The degree to which information is made available to noncontrolling equity owners and the reliability of that information affects the discount for lack of marketability. For example, a recent article on partnership interest valuations states, "An important basis for illiquidity discounts is the difficulty faced by prospective purchasers in obtaining information."[31]

---

[30] Ashok Abbott, "A Quantitative Measure of Discount for Lack of Liquidity," *Business Valuation Review,* Spring 2007, pp. 2–7.

[31] Mark S. Thompson and Eric S. Spunt, "The Widespread Overvaluation of Fractional Ownership Positions," *Trusts & Estates*, June 1993, pp. 62–66. See also Michael J. Bolotsky, "Adjustments for Differences in Ownership Rights, Liquidity, Information Access, and Information Reliability: An Assessment of 'Prevailing Wisdom' versus the 'Nash Hypotheses,'" *Business Valuation Review*, September 1991, pp. 94–110. Bolotsky's position is that, conceptually, this is a factor separate from marketability, but he recognizes the reality that we have no good way to measure this factor separately.

Restrictive Transfer Provisions

Many closely held stocks are subject to provisions that severely restrict the rights of the holder to transfer stock. Any provision that limits the right of the holder to transfer the stock would tend to increase the amount of the discount for lack of marketability.

In some cases, the restrictive provision may fix the value or put a ceiling on it. The impact of such restrictions is a matter of judgment that should be analyzed in light of the provisions in each case, in some cases with the advice of legal counsel regarding enforceability.

Company Characteristics: Size, Performance, and Risk

Empirical evidence shows that private placement discounts are related to the financial condition of the company. Companies with a history of losses or high leverage tend to issues shares at higher discounts than companies with more solid financial conditions. Discounts tend to be higher for companies with other risk characteristics, including high stock price volatility, unstable earnings, or reliance on a speculative or unproven product line. Perhaps related to the above, larger companies tend to command smaller discounts.

Court Decisions on Discounts for Illiquidity and Lack of Marketability

There is a substantial body of judicial precedent with regard to the identification and quantification of the discounts for illiquidity and lack of marketability. Each of these judicial decisions depends on the facts and circumstances of the particular case in point. Therefore, it is inappropriate to rely on discount data from judicial precedent.

However, it may be useful for analysts to review published judicial precedent with regard to lack of marketability discounts. This review should *not* be used to extract a particular discount percentage. Rather, it may be used to better understand the various factors that the courts have considered in their estimates of the lack of marketability discounts.

There is a substantial amount of precedent related to lack of marketability discounts with respect to federal gift taxes, estate taxes, and income taxes. These cases are summarized in the *Federal Tax Valuation Digest*, published annually.[32] *Quantifying Marketability Discounts* also offers an overview of marketability discounts in the tax court and detailed analysis of four cases.[33]

The topics of illiquidity and lack of marketability arise in many other litigation contexts, including shareholder disputes, marital dissolution cases, and damages matters. One report, *BVR's Guide to DLOM Case Law 2008 Edition* covers (in addition to gift and estate tax cases) other federal and state cases where discounts were an issue in marital dissolutions, corporate disagreements, ESOPs, bankruptcy cases, income tax cases, dissenting stockholder cases, and other litigation.[34]

---

[32] Idelle A. Howitt, ed., *Federal Tax Valuation Digest* (New York: Warren, Gorham & Lamont, 1999).

[33] Mercer, *Quantifying Marketability Discounts*.

[34] *BVR's Guide to DLOM Case Law 2008 Edition*. Portland, OR: Business Valuation Resources, 2008.

Mandelbaum v. Commissioner Reviews Lack of Marketability Factors

In *Bernard Mandelbaum, et al. v. Commissioner.*[35] The Tax Court listed numerous factors that it considers in its quantification of an appropriate lack of marketability discount.

> Valuers beware! The tax courts continue to emphasize the importance of detailed analysis of the closely held company being valued when using the many discount studies that practitioners often rely on to support their conclusions. In *Bernard Mandelbaum, et al. v. Commissioner* … the Court cites nine factors to be considered when selecting a discount for lack of marketability, one of the most controversial areas in business valuations. This valuation of minority blocks of Big M, Inc., a closely held chain of women's apparel retail stores, was for gift tax purposes.
>
> With these benchmarks established, the Court presented the following nine factors [among others] that should be considered in determining discounts for lack of marketability:
>
> 1. *Financial Statement Analysis*
> 2. *Company's Dividend Policy*
> 3. *The Nature of the Company, Its History, Its Position in the Industry, and its Economic Outlook*
> 4. *Company's Management*
> 5. *Amount of Control in Transferred shares*
> 6. *Restrictions on Transferability of Stock*
> 7. *Holding Period for Stock*
> 8. *Company's Redemption Policy*
> 9. Costs Associated with Making a Public Offering
>
> The Court deserves praise for its willingness to address this important issue, as well as the depth of its analysis, even though some of its conclusions are arguable. The conclusions reached in this case continue a clear trend in the Tax Courts concerning discounts. They no longer seem satisfied by a blind application of discount studies. They want a much more detailed comparison of the particular characteristics of the ownership interest being valued with the characteristics of the companies that make up the studies, whether individually or in the aggregate.[36]

Estate of Barge v. Commissioner Considers Lack of Marketability Factors

In the *Estate of Barge v. Commissioner,*[37] the Tax Court also provided a very specific list of the factors that it considered in its estimation of the lack of marketability discount in this case.

> In a more recent case, *Barge,* the Court used a quantitative model quite similar to the "quantitative model" generally used by appraisers and analyzed

---

[35] *Bernard Mandelbaum, et al. v. Commissioner*, T.C. Memo 1995-255 (June 12, 1995).

[36] James R. Hitchner, "Tax Court Reviews Nine Factors for Selecting Marketability Discounts," *CPA Expert*, Winter 1996, pp. 11–13.

[37] *Estate of Barge v. Commissioner*, TC Memo 1997-188, (April 23, 1997).

by the Court in *Mandelbaum*. The basic difference in *Barge*, however, is that *all of the basic factors of a quantitative model were specified.*

The discount for an undivided interest can be compared, by analogy, to the marketability discount applicable to minority interests in private businesses, since it deals specifically with the restrictions on sale and impediments to ultimate liquidity of the interest during a reasonably definable investment horizon. The factors considered by the Court included:

- *Base Value*
- *Expected Holding Period*
- *Expected Growth Rate of Value*
- *Expected Dividends or Distributions*
- *Required Holding Period Return*

The Tax Court continues to follow the line of reasoning found in *Mandelbaum* and furthered in *Barge*, and tends to accept the value opinions of business appraisers who develop improved methodologies to quantify marketability discounts in the appraisal of non-marketable minority interests of private businesses *and* in estimating the appropriate discounts when valuing undivided interests in real property.[38]

Okerlund v. United States Approves Pre-IPO Studies

For example, in *Okerlund v. United States*,[39] a Court of Federal Claims case, to support discounts for lack of marketability on two valuation dates, both parties' experts used data that relied on restricted stock studies and pre-IPO studies. Although the data were similar, there was a 15 percent gap between the respective experts' DLOM conclusions for both dates—30 percent for the IRS, 45 percent for the taxpayer. The court found, however, that the taxpayer expert's analysis was far more detailed and persuasive than the IRS expert's, and commended the taxpayer's expert (Shannon Pratt, the author of this book) for emphasizing the pre-IPO studies, which, the court determined, were more comparable to the subject company. The court said:

> Dr. Pratt's expert reports contain a far more detailed analysis of the empirical studies of trading prices of restricted shares and pre-initial public offering transactions than the AVG Report.... According to Dr. Pratt, the discounts observed in restricted stock studies reflect the existence of a public market for the stock once the temporary restrictions lapse. For a variety of reasons, ... purchasers of restricted stock 'generally expect to be able to resell the stock in the public market in the foreseeable future.' Pre-IPO discounts, on the other hand, are based on purely private transactions before a company enters the public market, a situation more comparable to closely held companies.

The court thus concluded a 40 percent DLOM for one date and 45 percent for the other.

Okerlund demonstrates the importance of a thorough analysis and explanation of both the restricted stock and pre-IPO studies when supporting a discount for lack of

---

[38] Z. Christopher Mercer, "Are Qualifying Marketability Discounts New Or Not?," *Trusts & Estates*, February 1998, pp. 44–45.

[39] *Okerlund v. United States,* 53 Fed. Cl. 341 (Fed. Ct. 2002), *motion for new trial denied,* 2003 U.S. Claims LEXIS 42 (Fed Cl. 2003), *aff'd,* 365 F.3d 1044 (Fed. Cir. 2004). See also Chapter 28 for a discussion of this case.

marketability. Other cases, while not relying on the restricted stock and pre-IPO studies, have said as much.

McCord v. Commissioner Lacks Rebuttal

In *McCord v. Commissioner*,[40] the taxpayer's expert opined that a 35 percent marketability discount was appropriate based on his analysis of the restricted stock studies, including the SEC study, the Silber study, the Standard Research Consultants (SRC) study, and the Hertzel & Smith study. He also testified that pre-IPO studies, including the Willamette Management Associates study and the Emory studies, supported this discount. The IRS expert determined a 7 percent discount based on the expert's own study of 88 private placements (the "Bajaj study"). The Tax Court found that of the 88 private placements, only the 29 middle placements were useful. Using these, the court concluded a 20 percent DLOM. There was no rebuttal to the IRS DLOM evidence in this case. Although the court rejected the pre-IPO studies, the court did review the taxpayer's expert's restricted stock study analysis, and found a number of flaws in his reasoning and methodology. Expressly because of these errors, the court rejected his restricted stock analysis. Nonetheless, the court did not completely reject the restricted stock studies as a source of marketability discount data, but concluded that the expert had not adequately analyzed the data from the studies in reaching his 35 percent discount.

Howard v. Shay Upholds 50 Percent DLOM

In *Howard v. Shay*,[41] the appraiser (also Shannon Pratt, the author of this book) applied a 50 percent discount for lack of marketability on the sale of a block of ESOP stock constituting about 38 percent of the outstanding stock. This discount reflected the facts that (1) the company's stock was not publicly traded and (2) the ESOP plan participants did not have the right to "put" the stock to the company. In successfully defending the suit brought by beneficiaries for alleged undervaluation, the appraiser used the Willamette pre-IPO database, isolating transactions constituting 25 to 49.9 percent of the outstanding stock. This case, which is discussed more thoroughly in Chapter 33, resulted in the largest discount for lack of marketability that a court has ever accepted.

Summary

This chapter presented a substantial amount of evidence to assist in estimating appropriate discounts (1) for lack of marketability related to noncontrolling business ownership interests and (2) for illiquidity related to controlling business ownership interests. In the final analysis, however, as with many other valuation issues, this estimation should be made in light of a studied examination of the facts

---

[40] *McCord v. Commissioner*, 120 T.C. No. 13, 2003 U.S. Tax Ct. LEXIS 16 (U.S. Tax Ct. May 14, 2003). See also Chapter 28 for a discussion of this case.
[41] *Howard v. Shay*, 1993 U.S. Dist. LEXIS 20153 (C.D. Cal. Sept. 15, 1993), *rev'd and rem'd*, 100 F.3d 1484 (9th Cir. 1996), *retried*, 1998 U.S. Dist. LEXIS 23146 (C.D. Cal. June 12, 1998).

and circumstances of each valuation assignment. The specific data that the analyst collects and relies on for each valuation should relate as closely as possible in time and other characteristics to the valuation subject.

Ownership interests in closely held businesses, most of which will never be freely tradable, suffer much more from lack of marketability than do restricted shares of publicly traded companies. In general, they also have fewer prospects of being marketable than do shares of companies that are considering (or are already in the process of attempting) an initial public offering.

Some recent decisions have failed to reflect the full impact of lack of marketability, due primarily to weak evidence presented. The levels of discounts allowed in most judicial decisions still seem to be below what the empirical evidence related to arm's-length transactions tends to suggest.

We hope that business owners, their legal and accounting advisers, and valuation analysts, will use the types of data presented in this chapter, along with continuing related research, to reduce the disparity between the (often low) discounts concluded in judicial decisions and the illiquidity and lack of marketability discounts empirically evidenced in actual market transactions.

Bibliography

Abbott, Ashok. "Discount for Lack of Marketability: An Empirical Analysis." *Business Valuation Review*, vol. 22, no. 4, December 2003.

Abrams, Jay B. "Discount for Lack of Marketability: A Theoretical Model." *Business Valuation Review*, September 1994, pp. 132–39.

_____. "Problems in the QMDM and Comparison to Economic Components Model: A Response to Chris Mercer." *Business Valuation Review*, vol. 21, no. 2, June 2002.

Aschwald, Kathryn. "Restricted Stock Discounts Decline as a Result of 1-Year Holding Period." *Shannon Pratt's Business Valuation Update*, May 2000, pp. 1–3.

Barenbaum, Les, and Walter Shubert. "Modern Financial Engineering and Discounts: The Collar Message." *Business Valuation Review*, vol. 23, no. 2, June 2004.

Barron, Michael S. "When Will the Tax Court Allow a Discount for Lack of Marketability?" *Journal of Taxation*, January 1997, pp. 46–50.

Bogdanski, John A. "Dissecting the Discount for Lack of Marketability." *Estate Planning*, February 1996, pp. 91–95.

Bowers, Helen, and Tara Stephenson. "*Determinants of the Discount for Lack-of-Marketability*." The Woodward Group, 2004.

Budyak, James T. "Estate Freeze Rules Affect Partnership Valuation Discounts." *Taxation for Accountants*, December 1996, pp. 340–47.

BVR's Guide to DLOM Case Law 2008 Edition. Portland, OR: *Business Valuation Resources*, 2008.

Casey, Christopher. "Marketability Discounts for Controlling Interests Revisited." *Business Valuation Review*, March 2000, pp. 10–15.

Cavanaugh, James C. "Valuation Discounts Are Available in an Estate Plan." *Taxation for Accountants*, July 1995, pp. 31–37.

Chaffe, David B.H. III. "Option Pricing as a Proxy for Discount for Lack of Marketability in Private Company Valuations." *Business Valuation Review*, December 1993, pp. 182–88.

Chipalkatti, Narinjan. "Estimating the Discount for Lack of Marketability Using Proportional Bid-Ask Spreads." *Business Valuation Review*, vol. 20, no. 1, March 2001.

Curtiss, Rand M. "A Practical Methodology for Determining Premiums and Discounts." *Business Valuation Review*, December 1997, pp. 172–79.

Davidoff, Howard. "Understanding Buy-Sell Agreements." *CPA Journal*, April 2006.

Davis, Greig, Jay E. Fishman, Frank Pankow, and Shannon P. Pratt. "Marketability Discounts." *BV Q&A Newsletter*, August 2004. Available at www.bvlibrary.com.

"Discounts for Lack of Marketability: Uses & Misuses of Databases." Business Valuation Resources, LLC. Telephone Conference, May 13, 2003.

"Discounts Involved in Purchases of Common Stock (1966-1969)." *Institutional Investor Study Report of the Securities Exchange Commission*, H.R. Doc. N.64, part 5, 92nd Cong., 1st Session, 1971, 2444–2456. Available at www.bvlibrary.com.

Eckstein, David. "Black-Scholes and Marketability: Another View." *Valuation Strategies*, January/February 1999, p. 41.

Eckstein, David, and Philip Schwab. "Layered Discounts in FLPs." *BV Q&A Newsletter*, November 2005. Available at www.bvlibrary.com.

Emory Sr., John D. "Discounts for Lack of Marketability Emory Pre-IPO Discount Studies 1980–2000 as Adjusted October 10, 2002." *Business Valuation Review*, vol. 21, no. 4, December 2002.

Emory Sr., John D. "Expanded Study of the Value of Marketability as Illustrated in Initial Public Offerings at Common Stock—May 1997 through December 2000." *Business Valuation Review*, vol. 20, no. 4, December 2001.

Emory Sr., John D. "Preview of the Value of Marketability as Illustrated in Initial Public Offerings of Dot-Com Companies—May 1997 through March 2000." *Business Valuation Review*, vol. 19, no. 2, June 2000.

Emory Sr., John D. "The Value of Marketability as Illustrated in Initial Public Offerings of Common Stock—May 1997 through December 2000." *Business Valuation Review*, vol. 20, no. 3, September 2001.

Emory Sr., John D. "The Value of Marketability as Illustrated in Initial Public Offerings of Dot-Com Companies—May 1997 through December 2000." *Business Valuation Review*, vol. 19, no. 3, September 2000.

Emory Sr., John D., and John D. Emory Jr. Emory Business Valuation, LLC. *"Emory Studies: 2002 Revision."* Presented to the IBA 25th Annual National Conference, Orlando, Florida, June 3, 2003.

Emory Sr., John D., F.R. Dengel III, and John D. Emory Jr. "Emory Responds to Dr. Bajaj: Miniscule Adjustments Warranted." *Shannon Pratt's Business Valuation Update*, May 2002, pp. 1, 3.

Emory Sr., John D., J.R. Hochwalt, and James Lurie. "Lack of Control Discount for the Managing and Non-Managing Member." *BV Q&A Newsletter*, March 2005. Available at www.bvlibrary.com.

Emory Sr., John D., Philip Schwab, and L. Deane Wilson. "Best Source for Determining Discounts of Lack of Marketability of FLPs with Only Real Estate?" *BV Q&A Newsletter*, May 2005. Available at www.bvlibrary.com.

Feldman, Stanley Jay. "A Note on Using Regression Models to Predict the Marketability Discount." *Business Valuation Review*, vol. 21, no. 3, September 2002.

Fiore, Owen, Jay Fishman, and Kevin Hines. "Discounts for Minority Interest and Lack of Marketability." *BV Q&A Newsletter*, June 2004. Available at www.bvlibrary.com.

Fowler, Bradley A. "How Do You Handle It?" *Business Valuation Review*, September 1995, pp. 130–33.

Fraizier, William, M. Mark Lee, Eric Nath, and Shannon Pratt. "Subchapter S election." *BV Q&A Newsletter*, June 2005. Available at www.bvlibrary.com.

Garber, Steven. "A Proposed Methodology for Estimating the Lack of Marketability Discount Related to ESOP Repurchase Liability." *Business Valuation Review*, December 1993, pp. 172–81.

Gelman, Milton. "An Economist-Financial Analyst's Approach to Valuing Stock of a Closely-Held Company." *Journal of Taxation*, June 1972, pp. 353–54.

Grabowski, Roger J. Standard & Poor's Corporate Value Consulting. "The Bubbling Pot in Marketability Discounts." Presented to the Foundation for Accounting Education, New York, NY, June 17, 2002.

Hall, Lance. "The Discount Alchemy of QMDM." *Business Valuation Review*, vol. 21, no. 4, December 2002.

_____. "The Discount for Lack of Marketability: An Examination of Dr. Bajaj's Approach." *Shannon Pratt's Business Valuation Update*, February 2004, pp. 1–4.

Hall, Lance S., and Timothy C. Polacek. "Strategies for Obtaining the Largest Valuation Discounts." *Estate Planning*, January/February 1994, pp. 38–44.

Hall, Lance, Z. Christopher Mercer, and Shannon P. Pratt. "Using the Term Marketability and Liquidity Interchangeably." *BV Q&A Newsletter*, October 2004. Available at www.bvlibrary.com.

Hall, Lance, Z. Christopher Mercer, Robert Oliver, and Shannon P. Pratt. "Applying the Discounted Cash Flow without Accounting for Dilution. "*BV Q&A Newsletter*, October 2004. Available at www.bvlibrary.com.

Hatch, John. "Restricted Stock Studies and Discounts for Lack of Marketability." *Business Valuation Review*, vol. 23, no. 2, June 2004.

_____. "Discount for Lack of Marketability: Do IPO Studies Tell Us Anything?" *Business Valuation Review*, vol. 23, no. 1, March 2004.

Hayes, John W., and Scott D. Miller. "Marketability Issues in the Valuation of ESOPs." *CPA Expert*, Summer 1996, pp. 7–11.

Hempstead & Co. "Tax Court Sets FLP Discounts for Lack of Marketability and Minority Interest." *The Hempstead Letter*, vol. 23, no. 5, 2005.

Hertzel, Michael, and Richard L. Smith. "Market Discounts and Shareholder Gains for Placing Equity Privately." *Journal of Finance*, June 1993, pp. 459–85.

Hitchner, James R. "Tax Court Reviews Nine Factors for Selecting Marketability Discounts." *CPA Expert*, Winter 1996, pp. 11–13.

Hitchner, James R., and Gary Roland. "Marketability and Control Govern Value of Family Businesses." *Taxation for Accountants*, January 1994, pp. 24–28.

Hitchner, James R., and Kevin J. Rudd. "The Use of Discounts in Estate and Gift Tax Valuations." *Trusts & Estates*, August 1992, pp. 49–56, 60.

Holmer, William E. "How to Use Put Options to Determine Discounts for Lack of Marketability." Presented at 23rd Annual Advanced Business Valuation Conference, October, 2004. Also available at www.bvlibrary.com.

Howitt, Idelle A. "Estate of Joseph R. Cloutier." *Valuation Strategies*, November/December 1997, pp. 40–41.

Johnson, Bruce. "Quantitative Support for Discounts for Lack of Marketability." *Business Valuation Review*, vol. 18, no. 4, December 1999, pp. 152–55.

_____. "Restricted Stock Discounts, 1991-95." *Shannon Pratt's Business Valuation Update*, March 1999, pp. 1–3.

Kania, John. "Evaluation of the Discount for Lack of Marketability." *Business Valuation Review*, vol. 20, no. 1, March 2001.

_____. "Has Restricted Stock Data Become Irrelevant for Determining Marketability Discounts?" *Business Valuation Review*, vol. 20, no. 2, June 2001.

_____. "Predicting Lack of Marketability Discounts by Use of an Economic (Statistical Regression) Model." *Business Valuation Review*, vol. 21, no. 4, December 2002.

Kubersky, Andrew S. "Marketability Discounting Issues for ESOP Acquisitions of Minority Shares." *Business Valuation Review*, September 1999, pp. 100–03.

_____. "Marketability Discounts and ESOP Acquisitions of Minority Share Interests." *Journal of Employee Ownership Law & Finance*, Fall 1998, pp. 97–103.

LaPray, Joseph. "Hypothecation Impairment as a Component of a Discount for Lack of Marketability." *Business Valuation Review*, vol. 21. no. 3, September 2002.

Lerch, Mary Anne. "The Economic Values of Restricted Stock Discounts Measured on Secondary Offerings from April 1998 through July 2001." *Business Valuation Review*, vol. 22, no. 4, December 2003.

Lerch, Mary Anne. "Measuring Lack of Marketability Discounts from IPO Pricing—the Graphic Approach IPO Data: November 1995 – April 1997." *Business Valuation Review*, vol. 19, no. 2, June 2000.

Luft, Carl F., Lawrence M. Levine, and Jon Howe, "Illiquidity Considerations in Valuing Stock Options." *Valuation Strategies*, May/June 1998, pp. 14–21, 46, 48.

Maher, J. Michael. "Discounts for Lack of Marketability for Closely Held Business Interests." *Taxes*, September 1976, pp. 562–71.

Mercer, Z. Christopher. "Are Marketability Discounts Applicable to Controlling Interests in Private Companies?" *Valuation Strategies*, November/December 1997, pp. 31–36.

_____. "Are Qualifying Marketability Discounts New or Not?" *Trusts & Estates*, February 1998, pp. 39–46.

_____. *Quantifying Marketability Discounts*. Memphis: Peabody Publishing, 1997.

_____. "Revisiting the Quantitative Marketability Discount Model." *Valuation Strategies*, March/April 2000, pp. 12–21.

_____. "Should 'Marketability Discounts' Be Applied to Controlling Interests of Private Companies?" *Business Valuation Review*, June 1994, pp. 55–65.

Mercer, Z. Christopher, and Matthew R. Crow. "Black-Scholes Rather Than the Quantitative Marketability Discount Model?" *Valuation Strategies*, September/October 1998, pp. 5–13, 44.

Mercer, Z. Christopher, and Travis Harms. "Marketability Discount Analysis at a Fork in the Road." *Business Valuation Review*, vol. 20, no. 4, December 2001.

Moroney, Robert E. "Most Courts Overvalue Closely Held Stocks." *Taxes—The Tax Magazine*, March 1973, pp. 144–56.

_____. "Why 25 Percent Discount for Nonmarketability in One Valuation, 100 Percent in Another?" *Taxes*, May 1977, pp. 316–20.

Oliver, Robert P., and Roy H. Meyers. "Discounts Seen in Private Placements of Restricted Stock: The Management Planning, Inc. Long-Term Study (1980–1996)." Chapter 5 in *Handbook of Advanced Business Valuation*, Robert F. Reilly and Robert P. Schweihs, eds. New York: McGraw-Hill, 2000.

Patton, Kenneth W. *"The Marketability Discount: Academic Research in Perspective—The Hertzel/Smith Study."* E-Law Business Valuation Perspective, Vol. 2003-02, June 5, 2003, pp. 1–8.

Paulsen, Jon. "Marketability Discount Concerns." *Business Valuation Review*, vol. 20, no. 1, March 2001.

_____. "More Evidence on IPO Marketability Discounts," *Business Valuation Review*, March 1998, pp. 10–12.

Pavri, Zareer. "Letter to the Editor: Discounts for Lack of Marketability: An Empirical Analysis." *Business Valuation Review*, vol. 23, no. 1, March 2004.

Pearson, Brian K. "1999 Marketability Discounts as Reflected in Initial Public Offerings." *CPA Expert*, Spring 2000, pp. 1–6.

_____. "Y2K Marketability Discounts as Reflected in IPOs." *CPA Expert*, Summer 2001, pp. 1–5.

Peters, Jerry O. "Lack of Marketability Discounts for Controlling Interests: An Analysis of Public vs. Private Transactions." *Business Valuation Review*, June 1995, pp. 59–61.

Phillips, John R., and Neill W. Freeman. "What Is the Marketability Discount for Controlling Interests?" *Business Valuation Review*, March 1999, pp. 3–11.

Pittock, William F., and Charles H. Stryker. "Revenue Ruling 77-287 Revisited." *SRC Quarterly Reports*, vol. 10, no. 1, Spring 1983, pp. 1–3.

Pratt, Shannon P. *Business Valuation Discounts and Premiums.* Hoboken, NJ: John Wiley & Sons, 2001.

_____. "Lack of Marketability Discounts Suffer More Controversial Attacks." *Shannon Pratt's Business Valuation Update*, February 2002, pp. 1–3.

_____. "Marketability Discounts Frequently a Big Money Appraisal Controversy." Editor's Column, *BV Update (Judges and Lawyers)*, April 2001.

_____. "Using Pre-IPO and Restricted Stock Data to Estimate Discounts for Lack of Marketability." *Business Valuation Review*, vol. 23, no. 2, June 2004.

Ressegieu, Matthew. "Valuation Discounts: What Is Required?" *Taxation for Lawyers*, March/April 1995, pp. 283–88.

Robak, Espen. "Liquidity and Levels of Value: A New Theoretical Framework." *Shannon Pratt's Business Valuation Update*, October 2004.

Robinson, Debra A., and Edward J. Rappaport. "Impact of Valuation Discounts on Estate and Income Tax Basis." *Estate Planning*, June 1997, pp. 223–30.

Saliba, R. Gary, and Jason K. Chung. "When Linking Post-IPO Return Data with Pre-IPO Marketability Discount Data Should Initial Public Offering (IPO) Discounts Be Considered When Estimating Value at the Shareholder Level?" *Business Valuation Review*, December 1998, pp. 128–35.

Saunders, Phillip. "Marketability Discounts and Risk in Transactions Prior to Initial Public Offerings." *Business Valuation Review*, vol. 19, no. 4, December 2000.

Seaman, Ronald. "Minimum Marketability Discounts." 2nd ed., *Business Valuation Review*, vol. 24, no. 2, June 2005.

Shenkman, Martin M., and Cal R. Feingold. "Minority, Marketability Discounts Affect Valuation of Partnership Interest." *Real Estate Finance Journal*, Summer 1993, pp. 18–25.

Shiffrin, Daniel. "Tax Court Disregards Stock Repurchase Agreement, Applies 40% Discount." *CPA Litigation Service Counselor*, December 1998, p. 3.

Silber, William L. "Discounts on Restricted Stock: The Impact of Illiquidity on Stock Prices." *Financial Analysts Journal*, July–August 1991, pp. 60–64.

Sliwoski, Leonard J. "Built-in Gains Tax, Discounts for Lack of Marketability, and Eisenberg v. Commissioner." *Business Valuation Review*, March 1998, pp. 3–6.

"Stock Marketability Restrictions That Apply to Decedent, but Not Estate, Will Affect Its Valuation." *The Tax Adviser*, September 1998, pp. 644, 646.

Sziklay, Barry S. "Discounts & Premiums Core." Presented at AICPA National Business Valuation Conference, November 2004. Also available at www.bvlibrary.com.

Tabak, David. "Liquidity or minority discount applied to a private company." *BV Q&A Newsletter*, April 2005. Available at www.bvlibrary.com.

Trout, Robert. "Estimation of the Discount Associated with the Transfer of Restricted Securities." *Taxes—The Tax Magazine*, June 1977, pp. 381–85.

_____. "Minimum Marketability Discounts." *Business Valuation Review*, vol. 22, no. 3 September 2003, pp. 124–26.

Wallgren, Don. "Jointly Owned Property May Not Be Subject to Valuation Discounts." *The Tax Adviser*, April 1999, pp. 218–20.

Chapter 18

Other Valuation Discounts

In the two previous chapters, we have discussed two valuation discounts that are common to the valuation of many closely held businesses and business interests: (1) the discount for lack of control, and (2) the discount for lack of marketability. In this chapter, we will consider several additional valuation discounts.

In practice, these miscellaneous valuation discounts are encountered less frequently than the discounts for lack of control and lack of marketability. Experienced analysts could list dozens of miscellaneous valuation discounts. However, upon reflection, each of these individual discounts can be grouped into the following two categories:

1. Entity level discounts
2. Shareholder level discounts

Entity Level Discounts[1]

Typically, entity level discounts are not a function of the valuation assignment. Rather, they are a function of the valuation subject. These valuation discounts relate to the facts and circumstances of the subject business interest. Regardless of what level of value is determined by the valuation assignment, certain valuation discounts are appropriate if the appraisal subject has attributes or features that call for such a discount.

Entity level discounts affect *all* shareholders. They may be reflected in the discount rates in the income approach or the valuation multiples used in the market approach, or they may warrant a separate adjustment to the value otherwise indicated by these approaches. The four categories of entity level discounts most commonly seen are presented in the following sections.

Key Person Discounts[2]

Key person dependence indicates the subject company's unusually concentrated dependence on one executive or on a small group of executives. The key person could be "key" in any number of business operation functions: general management, finance, production, new product development, sales and marketing, and so on. It is not uncommon for a business to have more than one key person.

The key person does not need to be the founder or the principal owner of the business. In fact, the key person may not own any equity in the subject business at all. A nonowner commissioned salesperson who brings in over half of all of the company orders could easily be a key person.

The IRS recognizes the key person discount factor in Revenue Ruling 59-60:

Rev. Rul. 59-60

Section 4.02

...The loss of the manager of a so-called "one-man" business may have a depressing effect upon the value of the stock of such business, particularly

---

[1] Entity Level Discounts is the subject of Chapter 12 in Laro and Pratt, *Business Valuation and Taxes*, op cit.
[2] Key Person Discounts is the subject of Chapter 13, pages 224–36, in Shannon Pratt, *Business Valuation Discounts and Premiums*, New York: John Wiley & Sons, Inc., 2001.

Exhibit 18–1

Tax Court Cases Accepting Key Person Discount

Cases Involving Decedent's Estate

Estate of Mitchell v. Commissioner[1]	10%
Estate of Feldmar v. Commissioner[2]	25%
Estate of Rodriguez v. Commissioner[3]	
Estate's expert adjusted earnings	
Estate of Yeager v. Commissioner[4]	10%
Estate of Huntsman v. Commissioner[5]	
Court applied discount of unspecified amount as the final adjustment to value	

Case Where Key Person Still Active

Furman v. Commissioner[6]	10%

[1] *Estate of Mitchell v. Commissioner*, T.C. Memo 1997-461, 74 T.C.M. (CCH) 872 (1997).
[2] *Estate of Feldmar v. Commissioner*, T.C. Memo 1988-429, 56 T.C.M. (CCH) 118 (1988).
[3] *Estate of Rodriguez v. Commissioner*, T.C. Memo 1989-13, 56 T.C.M. (CCH) 1033 (1989).
[4] *Estate of Yeager v. Commissioner*, T.C. Memo 1986-448, 52 T.C.M. (CCH) 524 (1986).
[5] *Estate of Huntsman v. Commissioner*, 66 T.C. 861 (1976).
[6] *Estate of Furman v. Commissioner*, T.C. Memo 1998-157 (1998).

if there is a lack of trained personnel capable of succeeding to the management of the enterprise. In valuing the stock of this type of business, therefore, the effect of the loss of the manager on the future expectancy of the business, and the absence of management-succession potentialities are pertinent factors to be taken into consideration. On the other hand, there may be factors, which offset, in whole or in part, the loss of the manager's services. For instance, the nature of the business and of its assets may be such that they will not be impaired by the loss of the manager. Furthermore, the loss may be adequately covered by life insurance, or competent management might be employed on the basis of the consideration paid for the former manager's services. These, or other offsetting factors, if found to exist, should be carefully weighed against the loss of the manager's services in valuing the stock of the enterprise.

The most common situation in which to apply a key person discount is to estate stock when the decedent was the key person. However, the key person discount may be applied when the person is still living and active in the business. Exhibit 18–1 lists some of the Tax Court cases where the key man discount was accepted.

Discounts for Trapped-In Capital Gains Taxes[3]

Prior to 1986, a rule of law known as the "*General Utilities* Doctrine" (named after a U.S. Supreme Court case, *General Utilities & Operating Co. v. Commissioner*), was in effect. This law allowed corporations to elect to liquidate, sell all their

---

[3] Discounts for Trapped-in Capital Gains Taxes is the subject of Chapter 14, pages 237-49, in Pratt, *Business Valuation Discounts and Premiums*, op cit.

assets, and distribute the proceeds to shareholders without paying corporate capi-tal gains taxes. The Tax Reform Act of 1986 eliminated this option, thus leaving no reasonable method of avoiding the "double tax" effect of the corporate capital gains tax liability on the sale of appreciated assets.

For all the years up to the repeal of *General Utilities*, and many years after, the IRS held steadfastly to the position that there could be no discount for trapped-in capital gains (sometimes referred to as built-in gains, giving rise to the term "BIG discount").

In 1998, the U.S. Tax Court first recognized a discount for trapped-in capital gains in *Estate of Davis v. Commissioner*.[4] The amount of the discount allowed in *Davis* was between one third and one half of the trapped-in capital gains tax lia-bility. The court held:

> [E]ven though no liquidation of [the company] or sale of its assets was planned or contemplated on the valuation date, a hypothetical willing seller and a hypothetical willing buyer would not have agreed on that date on a price…that took no account of [the company's] built-in capital gains tax. We are also persuaded…that such a willing seller and such a willing buyer…would have agreed on a price…that was less than the price that they would have agreed upon if there had been no…built-in capital gains tax…

At the time of the *Davis* decision, *Eisenberg v. Commissioner*,[5] in which the Tax Court had denied a discount for trapped-in capital gains, was on appeal in the Second Circuit Court of Appeals. The Second Circuit, citing *Davis* favorably, reversed and remanded the case with instructions to recognize a discount for trapped-in capital gains.

After that, the IRS capitulated on its position. Referring to the *Eisenberg* case, the IRS posted the following notice on its Web site:

> The Second Circuit reversed the Tax Court and held that, in valuing closely-held stock, a discount for the built in capital gains tax liabilities could apply depending on the facts presented. The court noted that the Tax Court itself had recently reached a similar conclusion in *Estate of Davis v. Commissioner* 110 T.C. 530 (1998).
>
> We acquiesce in this opinion to the extent that it holds that there is no legal prohibition against such a discount. The applicability of such a dis-count, as well as its amount, will hereafter be treated as factual matters to be determined by competent expert testimony based upon the circum-stances of each case and generally applicable valuation principles. Recommendation: Acquiescence.

The Notice indicated that it was approved by Stuart L. Brown, Chief Counsel, and Judith C. Dunn, Associate Chief Counsel. Of course, it contained that standard caveat: "This document is not to be relied upon or otherwise cited as precedent by taxpayers."

Subsequent tax cases regularly recognized the trapped-in capital gains dis-count for C corporations in which a double tax would potentially apply to the liq-uidation of assets at the corporate level and also to distribution of proceeds at the shareholder level.

---

[4] *Estate of Davis v. Commissioner*, 110 T.C. 530 (1998).
[5] *Eisenberg v. Commissioner*, 155 F.3d 50 (2nd Cir. 1998).

Estate of Dunn was appealed to the Fifth Circuit Court of Appeals, which held "as a matter of law" that a dollar-for-dollar discount for trapped-in capital gains must be applied to the results of the asset-based approach.[6]

In *Estate of Simplot v. Commissioner*, the company being valued owned a large block of highly appreciated stock in a publicly traded company, Micron Technology. Experts for both the taxpayer and the Service deducted 100 percent of the trapped-in capital gains tax in valuing this nonoperating company, and the Tax Court accepted this conclusion. The decision was appealed and reversed on other grounds, but the holding regarding trapped-in capital gains tax was not challenged.[7]

In *Estate of Welch*,[8] the company was eligible for a Code Section 1033 rollover on sale proceeds from real estate, which it exercised. The Tax Court denied the discount, but the Sixth Circuit reversed, writing that the availability of the election does not automatically foreclose the application of a capital gains discount.[9]

Although family law courts do have a tendency to follow Tax Court positions, most decisions in family laws courts to date have not allowed a discount for trapped-in capital gains unless a sale was imminent. A Washington case, *In re the Marriage of Hay*,[10] is typical. The trial court adjusted the gross value of the parties' interest in a real estate partnership from $119,049 to $101,000 to reflect the capital gains tax that would be paid if it were sold. The court of appeals reversed. The appellate court noted, "There is no Washington case specifically addressing whether capital gains tax consequences should be a factor in determining the value of marital assets." Thus, the court looked to other states for precedent, citing cases in seven other states. The court then concluded:

> Courts have generally found that consideration of tax consequences is either required or at least appropriate where the consequences are immediate and specific and/or arise directly from the court's decree, but find they are not an appropriate consideration where speculation as to a party's future dealings with property awarded to him or her would be required. We agree with the rule adopted by most jurisdictions…Mr. Hay testified at trial that he had no plans to sell his partnership interest… [We] remand to enable the trial court to consider the property division without regard to the capital gains tax consequences of a hypothetical sale of H&L Investments.

There are, however, cases where the potential tax consequences on sale have been deducted in valuing the marital estate, even when no immediate sale was contemplated. For example, in *Liddle v. Liddle* (Wisconsin), the court concluded that it was proper to deduct the amount of capital gains tax that the husband would have to pay on the anticipated sale of limited partnership interests.[11] The wife objected to reducing the value by the impounded taxes, claiming that they were "hypothetical, speculative, imaginary, unfair, and arbitrary." Evidence was introduced to show that the partnership was a tax shelter that would lose its desirability in five to seven years and would probably be sold. The court concluded that the date of sale was neither imaginary nor hypothetical.

---

[6] *Dunn v. Commissioner*, 2002 U.S. App., LEXIS 15453 (5th Cir. 2002).

[7] *Estate of Simplot v. Commissioner*, 112 T.C. 130 (1999), *rev'd.* 2001 U.S. App. LEXIS 9220 (9th Cir. 2001).

[8] *Estate of Welch v. Commissioner*, T.C. Memo 1998-167, 75 T.C.M. (CCH) 2252.

[9] Ibid.

[10] *In re the Marriage of Hay*, 80 Wash. App. 202, 907 P.2d 334 (Wash. Ct. App. 1995).

[11] *Liddle v. Liddle*, 140 Wis.2d 132, 410 N.W.2d 196 (Wis. Ct. App. 1987).

The court then offered an interesting broader statement that *"partnerships ought to be reduced by future capital gains taxes"* where the partnerships were investments that *"were only valuable as long as other investments were not more desirable,"* and the husband *"was more likely to sell his interest in the partnerships than die owning them,"* and would, therefore, incur a capital gains tax from the sale of the partnerships (emphasis added). From the viewpoint of a financial analyst, it is reasonable to think that this reasoning should apply to *any* investment asset.

Another interesting decision upholding subtraction of capital gains tax involved a commercial building. In *Hogan v. Hogan* (Missouri), the appellate court held that the trial court did not abuse its discretion in subtracting the capital gains tax that would be incurred on sale, even though there was no evidence that the property was going to be sold.[12] The court found that experts for both parties attested to the property's fair market value and that the concept of fair market value assumes the sale of the property to an interested buyer. Thus, the court was reluctant to find any error by the trial court in presuming a sale of the real estate with its attendant tax consequences in order to value that marital asset.

In *Zoldan v. Zoldan* (Ohio), the trial court accepted the valuation of the husband's expert, which was net of tax consequences (and also net of both minority and marketability discounts).[13] The trial court stated that it found the husband's expert more credible. The wife's expert "did not consider all the facts and procedures the court considered applicable." The court of appeals upheld, stating that "there was sufficient credible evidence considering the totality of the circumstances, from which the trial court could have accepted the valuations given by [the wife's] expert witness."

"Portfolio" (Nonhomogeneous Assets) Discount

A *portfolio discount* is applied when a company owns such dissimilar assets that it would not be attractive to the typical buyer. Investors tend to prefer "pure plays," that is, companies that operate in one or a connected group of industries. In the public market, conglomerates tend to sell at a discount from their breakup value.

This discount was accepted in *Estate of Maxcy v. Commissioner*[14] and *Estate of Piper v. Commissioner.*[15]

Discount for Contingent Liabilities[16]

Contingent liabilities are difficult to quantify at a typical valuation date because they depend on uncertain future events. These may include, for example, environmental liabilities, product warranty liabilities, or outcomes of future lawsuits.

In a transactional context, contingencies are usually handled by setting up an escrow account to be settled when the contingency is satisfied. When a point estimate of the value of a stock is required as of a point in time, as in most litigated valuation contexts, estimates must be made.

---

[12] *Hogan v. Hogan*, 796 S.W.2d 400 (Mo. Ct. App. 1990).
[13] *Zoldan v. Zoldan*, 1999 Ohio App. LEXIS 2644 (Ohio Ct. App. 1999).
[14] *Estate of Maxcy v. Commissioner*, T.C. Memo 1969-158, 28 T.C.M. (CCH) 783.
[15] *Estate of Piper v. Commissioner*, 72 T.C. 1062 (1979).
[16] This is the subject of Chapter 17, pp. 269–72, in Pratt, *Business Valuation Discounts and Premiums*, op cit.

In one case where I was retained to estimate a point value, the company did not carry product liability insurance in an industry where product liability suits were common, and most of the guideline companies that I used in the market approach did carry such insurance. In that case, even though the company had never had a product liability suit, for both the market and income approaches, I deducted the cost of insurance premiums from the cash flows.

There was a case in which I was retained by the IRS to value a company which operated three waterfront creosoting plants, all of which had known contamination that could put the company out of business at any time. Even though the problem had been known and studied for 10 years, the company was still operating the plants. I proposed an arbitrary 50 percent discount to the values otherwise indicated by conventional methods, and the parties accepted this discount.

U.S. Tax Court cases in which a discount for contingent liabilities was accepted include *Estate of Klauss v. Commissioner,*[17] *Payne v. Commissioner,*[18] and *Estate of Desmond v. Commissioner.*[19]

Other Shareholder Level Discounts[20]

Shareholder level discounts are those that affect only one shareholder or group of shareholders. Other than discounts for lack of marketability and lack of control, the most common shareholder discounts are for nonvoting vs. voting stock and blockage.

Nonvoting versus Voting Stock[21]

There are generally two scenarios where there are classes of voting stock and classes of nonvoting stock:

1. Where there are substantial numbers of shares in both classes, or
2. Where a small block holds voting control.

When there are a substantial number of both voting and nonvoting shares outstanding, studies on the public markets have shown that the difference in the value of voting versus nonvoting shares is very small, generally in the range of 0 percent to 7 percent, because the vote is not likely to have much influence, if any. The results of these studies are shown in Exhibit 18–2.

On the other hand, when voting power is concentrated in a small block of shares, that block may have considerable value compared to the nonvoting stock, unless the nonvoting shares have "coattail" protection (the right to receive what the voting block receives if it is sold). If faced with a situation where there is a small block of voting stock which dominates, the analyst should check the articles of incorporation to see whether the nonvoting stock has coattail protection.

---

[17] *Estate of Klauss v. Commissioner,* T.C. Memo 2000-191, 79 T.C.M. (CCH) 21777 (2000).
[18] *Payne v. Commissioner,* T.C. Memo 1998-227, 75 T.C.M. 2548 (CCH) (1998).
[19] *Estate of Desmond v. Commissioner,* T.C. Memo 1999-76, 77 T.C.M. 1529 (CCH) (1999).
[20] "Other Shareholder Level Discounts" is the subject of Chapter 19, pp. 311–323 in Laro and Pratt, *Business Valuation and Taxes,* op. cit.
[21] "Voting versus Nonvoting stock" is the subject of Chapter 12, pp. 208–223 in Pratt, *Business Valuation Discounts and Premiums,* op. cit.

Exhibit 18–2

Studies of Voting versus Nonvoting Stock

Study	Premium for voting shares
Lease, McConnell, and Mikkleson[1]	5.44%
O'Shea and Siwicki[2]	3.5%
Houlihan, Lokey, Howard, and Zukin[3]	2.05–3.20%
Financial Valuation Group (Tampa) mean	44–9.08%
median[4]	0–3.54%*

[1] Ronald C. Lease, John J. McConnell, and Wayne H. Mikkelson, "The Market Value of Control in Publicly Traded Corporations," *Journal of Financial Economics* (1983): 439–471, at 469.

[2] Kevin C. O'Shea and Robert M. Siwicki, "Stock Price Premiums for Voting Rights Attributable to Minority Interests," *Business Valuation Review* (December 1991): 165–171.

[3] Paul J. Much and Timothy J. Fagan, "The Value of Voting Rights," in *Financial Valuation: Business and Business Interests*, 1996. Update, James H. Zukin, ed. (New York: Warren Gorham & Lament, 1996).

[4] James R. Hitchner, *Financial Valuation: Applications and Models*, 2nd ed. (Wiley 2006) pp. 432–450.

Blockage[22]

Blockage is a function of limited marketability; specifically, it applies when the block of property is so large that placing it on the market would cause a depression in the price of the property. The concept is often found in real estate, when the quantity being appraised could only be sold at a discount from prevailing prices of smaller parcels or else it would take the market a long time to absorb it. The phenomenon also applies to other types of property, such as art and antiques.

In the market for equities in businesses, blockage applies primarily in the context of publicly traded stocks. In some cases, the detrimental effects of both restricted stock and blockage are lumped together and taken as a single discount. More often, they are separated. Moreover, blockage discounts are more common for freely tradable stock than for restricted stock.

A study by Robinson, Rumsey, and White on the Toronto Stock Exchange concluded that the value of a small voting block for companies with no coattail provisions could be between 3.5 percent to 18 percent of the total equity value, depending on the likelihood of takeover.[23]

Discounts for blockage are specifically recognized in the estate and gift tax regulations:

> In certain exceptional cases, the size of the block of stock to be valued in relation to the number of shares changing hands in sales may be relevant in determining whether selling prices reflect the fair market value of the block of stock to be valued. If the executor can show that the block of stock to be valued is so large in relation to the actual sales on the existing market that it could not be liquidated in a reasonable time without depressing the market, the price at which the block could be sold as such outside the usual market, as through an underwriter, may be a more accurate indication of value than market quotations. Complete data in support of any allowance

[22] "Blockage Discounts" is the subject of Chapter 15, pp. 250–259 in Pratt, *Business Valuation Discounts and Premiums*, op cit.

[23] Chris Robinson, John Rumsey, and Alan White, "The Value of a Vote in the Market for Corporate Control" paper published by York University Faculty of Administrative Studies, February 1996.

claimed due to the size of the block of stock shall be submitted with the return (Form 706 Estate Tax Return or Form 709 Gift Tax Return). On the other hand, if the block of stock to be valued represents a controlling interest, either actual or effective, in a going business, the price at which other lots change hands may have little relation to its true value.[24]

When quantifying a discount for blockage, the analyst must consider the various ways that the block could be sold. Possibilities are:

- A private placement
- Dribbling the stock onto the open market in small lots that would not be expected to affect the market
- The sale to an underwriting syndicate for resale to the public—secondary distribution
- A special offering by which a broker may buy the entire block and resell it
- Exchange distributions, in which one member acting as a principal or agent sells a block to other members of the exchange who have solicited purchases.[25]

When quantifying discounts for blockage, the analyst should consider the following factors:

- Size of the block relative to trading volume
- The market in which the stock is traded
- Price volatility
- Other block trades, if any
- Recent price trends in the stock (Upward trend lowers the discount and downward trend increases the discount; although, if stocks actually follow a random walk, this factor shouldn't make any difference.)

Exhibit 18–3 is a summary of Tax Court cases where a discount for blockage was an issue. In addition to the cases on the table, *Estate of Branson v. Commissioner*[26] was unique in that there was no organized market for the stock, but the company (a bank) maintained a list of interested buyers. Decedent's block size equaled several years' worth of historical transactions, but the court also considered transactions of about a tenth to a quarter of decedent's block size shortly before death and within a year after death in deciding that the blockage discount should be 10 percent. The opinion also cites and quotes several earlier blockage discount cases.

Summary

The discounts discussed in this chapter fall into two categories:

1. Entity-level discounts, which affect the enterprise value, and thus apply to the company as a whole, and
2. Shareholder level discounts, which affect the values of the interest of one or a specified group of shareholders.

---

[24] Estate Tax Reg. Sec. 2031-2(b)(1). Gift Tax Reg. Sec. 25.2512-2(e) contains the same language.

[25] Joseph S. Estabrook, "Blockage Discounts," Chapter 7 in *Handbook of Advanced Business Valuation*, Robert F. Reilly and Robert P. Schweihs, eds. (New York: McGraw-Hill, 2000), pp. 139–153.

[26] *Estate of Branson v. Commissioner*, T.C. Memo 1999-231, 78 T.C.M. 78 (1999).

Exhibit 18–3

Summary of Selected Tax Cases Involving Blockage Discounts

Year	Case Citation	Blockage Discount	Comments
2006	*Estate of Gimbel* v. Commissioner, T.C. Memo. 2006-270	Overall 14.2% (combining 80% estate shares and 20% repurchased shares)	The discount was around the midpoint between the IRS's original 8% discount and the taxpayer's 20.72% discount.
2000	*Estate of Brocato v. Commissioner*, T.C. Memo 1999-424	11% (on 7 of 8 real properties)	Petitioner asserted a 12.5% blockage discount for all eight real properties while the IRS argued that a discount of 1.92% should be applied to only seven properties.
1999	*Estate of Mellinger v. Commissioner*, 112 T.C. 26	25%	Both parties presented expert testimony for a blockage discount ranging from 15–35%; the court made adjustments to petitioner's methods.
1999	*Estate of Foote v. Commissioner*, T.C. Memo 1999-37	3.3%	Court accepted IRS expert opinion of a 3.3% blockage discount based on 16 factors; rejected taxpayer's expert's reliance on past cases and a 22.5% blockage discount.
1998	*Estate of Davis v. Commissioner*, 110 T.C. 530	Zero	Court disallowed a blockage discount because Estate failed to carry burden of establishing that a blockage or SEC Rule 144 discount should apply.
1998	*Estate of McClatchy v. Commissioner*, 147 F.3d 1089 (9th Cir.)	15%	IRS conceded a 15% blockage discount opined by petitioner. Issue on appeal related to federal securities law restrictions.
1997	*Estate of Wright v. Commissioner*, T.C. Memo 1997-53	10%	Starting with the over-the-counter price of $50 per share, taxpayer's experts applied a 24% discount for blockage and other factors; IRS expert applied a control premium but no blockage discount.
1987	*Adair v. Commissioner*, T.C. Memo 1987-494	5%	For valuation of petitioner Adair's stock, a blockage discount was inappropriate. For valuation of petitioner Borgeson's stock, IRS expert opined to no blockage discount and petitioner's expert opined to a 15% blockage discount.
1985	*Robinson v. Commissioner*, T.C. Memo 1985-275	18%	Respondent opined to a 6% blockage discount; petitioner Robinson opined to a 40% combined discount for federal securities restrictions and blockage.
1983	*Steinberg v. Commissioner*, T.C. Memo 1983-534	27.5%	Petitioner argued for a 30% blockage discount; IRS argued for a 12.5% blockage discount.
1974	*Rushton v. Commissioner*, 498 F. 2d 88 (5th Cir.)	Zero	Commissioner disallowed a blockage discount for sale of 4 blocks of stock.

Source: Pratt, *Business Valuation Discounts and Premiums*, New York: John Wiley & Sons, 2001, p. 257.

The entity-level discounts generally can be classified into four groups:

1. Key person discounts
2. Discount for trapped-in capital gains (built-in-gains or BIG discounts)
3. "Portfolio" (Nonhomogeneous assets) discounts
4. Contingent liabilities discounts

Besides lack of marketability and lack of control, two other discounts that sometimes apply to the shareholder level are:

1. Nonvoting versus voting stock
2. Blockage

ount for Locked-In Capital Gains Tax Justified after
Journal of Taxation, April 1992, pp. 218–23.

Restricted Securities." *Securities Regulation Law*
90.

curities, Part 2." *Securities Regulation Law*
207.

"Should a Blockage Discount Apply?
Willing Buyer and a Hypothetical Willing
arch 2000, pp. 3–9.

Limited Partnerships Holding Only
n *Service Counselor*, May 1999, pp.

no Discount for Closely Held Investment Holding
n *Strategies*, January/February 1999, pp. 26–37.

R. "Is a Discount for Built-In Capital Gain Tax Justified?"
aluation Review, June 1993, pp. 76–79.

Hawkins, George B. "Selling Out to a Public Company Buyer: Blockage,
Restricted Shares, and Value—The Stated Price versus Reality." *Fair Value*,
Spring/Summer 1997, pp. 1–2.

Hitchner, James R. "Large Discounts Allowed in Real Estate Partnership." *CPA
Expert*, Spring 1997, pp. 10–11.

———. *Financial Valuation, Application and Models,* 2nd ed. Hoboken, NJ: John
Wiley and Sons, 2006, pp. 432–450.

Larson, James A., and Jeffrey P. Wright. "Key Person Discount in Small Firms: An
Update." *Business Valuation Review*, September 1998, pp. 85–94.

Mulligan, Michael D., and Angela Fick Braly. "Family Limited Partnerships Can
Create Discounts." *Estate Planning*, July/August 1994, pp. 195–204.

Osteryoung, Jerome S., and Derek Newman. "Key Person Valuation Issues for
Private Businesses." *Business Valuation Review*, September 1994, pp. 115–19.

Shiffrin, Daniel. "Recent Developments in the Treatment of Built-in Gains: Davis,
Jameson, and Eisenberg." *CPA Litigation Service Counselor*, May 1999,
pp. 3–4.

———. "Tax Court: No Discount for Built-in Gains Tax." *CPA Litigation Service
Counselor*, March 1998, pp. 1–2.

———. "Tax Court Reduces Blockage Discount: Estate of Foote." *CPA Litigation
Service Counselor*, March 1999, p. 4.

———. "Value Adjusted to Reflect Built-in Gains." *CPA Litigation Service
Counselor*, August 1998, pp. 3–4.

Silwoski, Leonard. "Built-in Gains Tax, Discounts for Lack of Marketability, and
Eisenberg v. Commissioner." *Business Valuation Review*, March 1998, pp.
3–6.

Sonneman, Donald. "The Single Customer Business—Valuation of a Captive
Business." *Business Valuation Review*, March 2000, pp. 44–48.

Chapter 19

Valuation Synthesis and Conclusion

When all the relevant valuation factors have been individually analyzed and assessed, they should be brought together to arrive at a final estimate that represents the valuation conclusion. Sometimes it may be obvious that the analyst should rely on the indications of a single valuation method or approach. This could be due to (1) the nature of the company or (2) the nature of the business interest subject to valuation. In other cases, two or more valuation approaches may produce such similar value indications that it is not mathematically significant how much weight each approach receives. However, in many cases, business valuation approaches and methods generate apparently inconsistent value indications. When the different valuation approaches result in materially different value indications, and the objective of the subject analysis is a point value estimate, the indications should be reconciled into a single value estimate.

This chapter describes this reconciliation process, a process that encompasses both quantitative and qualitative analyses and judgments.

The Reconciliation Process

During the reconciliation process, it is important for the analyst to review all of the procedures conducted during the valuation. Sometimes the reconciliation process is undertaken with a "cold" review by an independent analyst who challenges the most important valuation factors. The first step in this reconciliation process is for the analyst to review the valuation assignment itself. At this point, the analyst should address these three questions:

1. Did I value the right thing?
2. Did I value it the right way?
3. Did I conclude the right value?

The first question covers the issue of the valuation subject. Did the valuation assignment encompass the total assets of the business, the invested capital of the business, the shareholders' equity of the business, the common stock only, one class of common stock only, and so on? This question also considers the level of value—that is, controlling ownership interest versus noncontrolling ownership interest, marketable securities versus nonmarketable securities, and so on.

The second question addresses the issue of the appropriateness of the valuation methods that were used. Were equity methods used to value assets, or vice versa? Were methods applicable to the valuation of an overall business enterprise used to value a small block of securities, or vice versa?

The third question considers the reasonableness of the value indications. Are they mutually supportive or mutually contradictory? Do the value indications pass a basic "smell test" or reasonableness threshold for a business interest of the size and nature of the valuation subject?

A review of the valuation assignment should help the analyst answer the three questions listed above. This review should consider:

1. The purpose and objective of the valuation
2. The business ownership interest to be valued
3. The bundle of legal rights to be valued
4. The ownership characteristics of the business interest to be valued
5. The date of the valuation

6. The standard (or definition) of value to be estimated
7. The premise of value to be used (based upon the highest and best use of the subject business interest)

The valuation is performed to answer a specific question regarding the value of a business or business interest. Even within the same valuation approach, different methods will typically result in different value indications. For example, it is not uncommon for different indicated values to result from the application of two different market approach methods [e.g., from a publicly traded guideline securities method versus a guideline transaction (merger and acquisition) method.]

The process of reconciliation is the analysis of the alternative valuation indications in order to arrive at a final value estimate. Before reaching a final value estimate, the analyst should review the entire business valuation for appropriateness and accuracy. The review of the business valuation work product is the subject of Chapter 22. The definition of value estimated and its relationship to each procedure in the valuation process should be reviewed during the reconciliation process.

Criteria for the Selection of Valuation Approaches and Methods

Of the recommended valuation approaches discussed in this text, each approach will be more or less applicable based on the facts and circumstances of the particular analysis.

There is also no precise guideline or quantitative formula for selecting which approach or approaches are most applicable in a given situation. However, the following list presents the common factors to be considered by the analyst when selecting among alternative valuation approaches.

1. The quantity and quality of the available financial and operational data
2. The degree of the analyst's access to the available financial and operational data
3. The supply of industry private sale transactional data
4. The supply of industry publicly traded company data
5. The type of business, nature of business assets, and type of industry subject to valuation
6. The nature of the business interest subject to valuation
7. Statutory, judicial, and administrative considerations
8. The informational needs of the valuation audience
9. The purpose and objective of the valuation
10. The professional judgment and expertise of the analyst

Quantity and Quality of Available Data

Practically, this may be the most important of the valuation approach selection criteria. The analyst usually cannot perform a valuation approach (no matter how conceptually robust it is or how applicable it is based on industry observations) if the requisite financial, operational, or empirically market-derived data are not available.

Degree of Access to Available Data. In valuations performed, for example, for litigation support, dispute resolution, or other controversy purposes, the analyst may not have unrestricted access to company data, company management, company facilities, and so forth. In these cases, all the desired historical and prospective data may exist. However, the analyst may not be granted reasonable access to the existing data. Accordingly, in selecting among the valuation approaches, the analyst may have to consider not only what data exist, but also what data will be made available in analysis.

In most litigation cases, however, the client retaining the analyst has a legitimate financial interest in the business. In most such cases, if the management tries to stonewall the analyst for legitimate discovery requests, the attorney can obtain a court order compelling the company's compliance with the legitimate discovery. To avoid the company's defense that the requests are overly broad and burdensome, the analyst should try to ensure that the requests are reasonable.

Supply of Industry Transactional Data and Public Company Data. Some industries have a large quantity of publicly available data regarding business purchase and sale transactions. When the supply of such reliable industry private sale transactional data is substantial, then the analyst will more likely select and rely on transaction-based, market approach methods. Also, some industries have a large quantity of publicly traded companies that provide useful valuation pricing guidance. Other industries have few or no pure play publicly traded companies. And, some industries have publicly traded companies that are infrequently traded or have other characteristics that made them inapplicable for providing meaningful valuation pricing guidance.

Type of Business, Nature of Business Assets, and Type of Industry Subject to Valuation

Certain industries have rules of thumb that industry participants may use as quick estimates regarding the value of businesses. While these industry rules of thumb, guidelines, or conventions should not be considered as rigorous as a business valuation analysis, they should not be ignored altogether. Depending on the nature of the subject business (e.g., whether it is capital asset–intensive or intangible asset–intensive), different valuation approaches may be more or less applicable.

Nature of the Business Interest Subject to Valuation

Obviously, the valuation of a controlling ownership interest in a business enterprise is a different assignment from the valuation of a nonmarketable, noncontrolling ownership interest in the restricted, nonvoting common stock of the same business enterprise. In selecting the most appropriate valuation approach, the analyst should consider that some valuation approaches are more appropriate for overall business enterprise valuations, while other approaches are more appropriate for the analysis of ownership interests representing less than 100 percent of the business.

Statutory, Judicial, and Administrative Considerations

For those valuations performed for certain taxation employee stock ownership plans (ESOP) and other regulatory purposes, the analyst should consider whether certain valuation approaches are required—and whether associated valuation approaches are prohibited—by the appropriate regulatory authority. For example, the IRS has published valuation procedures and guidelines for appraisals performed for federal gift and estate tax purposes, such as the specific Chapter 14 guidelines that apply to business valuations performed for estate freeze purposes. And, some states (often as a matter of either statutory authority or judicial precedent) require some valuation approaches—and prohibit other valuation approaches—for valuations performed for appraisal rights pursuant to minority squeeze-out mergers, other shareholder appraisal rights cases, marital dissolution cases, and so forth. The analyst should be generally aware of specific statutory requirements, administrative guidance, or judicial precedent that may affect the subject valuation. Of course most valuation analysts are not practicing attorneys and therefore should not practice law. In some cases, legal counsel should be consulted regarding the applicability of statutory, judicial, or administrative considerations.

Informational Needs of the Valuation Audience

The ultimate audience for the valuation may affect the selection of valuation approaches. These considerations include the level of sophistication of the audience and the degree of familiarity of the audience with the subject company. The ultimate purpose of the valuation—as either notional or transactional—may also affect which valuation approach (and how many valuation approaches) will be selected.

Purpose and Objective of the Analysis

Overall, the purpose and objective of the business valuation may influence the selection of the valuation approaches. The factors encompassed in the valuation objective include the description of the subject business ownership interest, the description of the ownership characteristics (e.g., the bundle of ownership legal rights) of the subject business interest, the definition (or standard) of value applied, the premise of value applied (including consideration of the highest and best use of the subject business interests), the level of value applied, and the valuation date. The factors encompassed in the valuation purpose include (1) the audience for the valuation and (2) the decision (or decisions) that will be made based on the value conclusion.

Professional Judgment and Expertise of the Analyst

Ultimately, the most important factors that affect the selection of the appropriate valuation approach or approaches are the professional judgment, technical expertise, and experienced common sense of the analyst.

Reconciling Divergent Indications among Valuation Methods

Ideally, the analyst will use two or more approaches in the subject valuation, and these approaches will yield virtually identical value indications. In practice, of course, this rarely happens.

Exhibit 19–1

Illustrative Business Enterprise, Inc.
Fair Market Value of Total Equity
Valuation Synthesis and Conclusion
Example of Outlier Phenomenon
As of December 31, 2000

Valuation Approach	Valuation Method	Value Indication
Market approach	Guideline publicly traded company method	$38,000,000
Income approach	Discounted economic income method	$40,000,000
Asset-based approach	Capitalized excess earnings method	$42,000,000
Asset-based approach	Asset accumulation method	$20,000,000
	Valuation synthesis and conclusion	$40,000,000

Experienced analysts expect to derive a range of value indications when alternative valuation approaches are used. Sometimes several valuation approaches all conclude a reasonably narrow dispersion of value indications. These alternative indications, then, imply the reasonable range of values for the subject business. They also provide mutually supportive evidence as to the final value estimate.

Occasionally, two or three valuation methods produce value indications within a reasonable range—and then one valuation method produces an obvious value estimate outlier.

An illustrative example of this value indication outlier phenomenon is presented in Exhibit 19–1.

In this example, the value indication of the asset accumulation method is an obvious outlier compared with the three other indications. Accordingly, this valuation reconciliation would initiate further analysis and consideration before a final value estimate is concluded.

The question is: What is the analyst to do regarding such an outlier value indication? There are three alternatives.

First, the analyst could discard the valuation method that yields the outlier value indication. This action is based on the rationale that the outlier valuation method simply does not apply to the specific subject set of facts and circumstances.

Second, the analyst could include the outlier valuation method in the valuation reconciliation but assign a very low weight to the outlier value indication. This action is based on the rationale that if the method is fundamentally sound, even a comparatively unreasonable value indication should be given some weight in the final value estimate.

Third, the analyst could thoroughly investigate why the particular valuation method is producing outlier value indications. The analyst could attempt to reconcile all the value indications. The analyst could search for an answer, or at least an explanation, to this apparent anomaly. As part of this reconciliation process, the analyst should recheck all the quantitative analyses and rethink all the qualitative conclusions. The analyst may find that an error was made in the analysis and application of the outlier method. For example, this reconciliation could reveal that one or more intangible assets were inadvertently not included in the asset accumulation method.

If an analytical or data error is discovered, it can be corrected. Then, the outlier method may produce a more reasonable, and more consistent, value indication.

Of course, this third alternative to handling the phenomenon of an outlier value indication (which involves additional analyses and reconciliation procedures) is the preferred procedure. Only with such analyses can a discrepancy be adequately explained and reconciled with the other value indications.

If, after careful review, one of the valuation methods that appears to have merit still produces an outlier, then it becomes a matter of the analyst's professional judgment as to the extent to which the factors reflected in the valuation method actually contribute to the estimate of value of the subject business or business interest. And, the analyst will weight that outlier method accordingly in the final value estimate.

Weighting of Valuation Method Results

As with the selection of which valuation methods to use, there are no scientific formulas or specific rules to use with regard to the weighting of the results of two or more valuation methods. In fact, the same factors or guidelines that affect the selection of the valuation methods will influence the analyst with regard to weighting the conclusions of these valuation methods.

This section is really only a brief summary of the relative applicability of different methods in different circumstances. The chapters on the various approaches and methods contain more extensive discussion of the circumstances under which each approach is more or less useful. The reader is encouraged to review those sections for guidance in the weighting of approaches and methods.

The different valuation approaches are not totally independent. Rather, they often have some degree of conceptual and practical overlap. For example, within the market approach, heavy emphasis may be appropriately placed on a pricing multiple of a certain economic income measure, such as a price/earnings multiple. Some analysts say this is a shortcut form of an income approach, thus lessening the need for a separate weight to be assigned to the income approach per se.[1] However, net cash flow is the preferred measure of economic income by most analysts in the income approach, but is seldom used in the market approach. The use of net cash flow in the income approach helps to make the approaches more discrete from each other. Similarly, income approach methods are dependent on empirical data regarding market-derived conditions in order to estimate appropriate discount and capitalization rates. Thus, the better the job the income approach does of capturing and documenting market-derived discount and/or capitalization rate data, the less the need for a separate weight to be assigned to the market approach per se.

The analyst should ask, "What attributes of the ownership of the subject business or business interest create the economic value associated with its ownership?" If the income available for distribution to the business owner is the primary value driver, then it may be appropriate that one or more methods within the income approach dominate the value conclusion. Of course, a capitalization (1) of dividends (for a noncontrolling ownership interest) or (2) of dividend-paying capacity (for a controlling ownership interest) within the market approach could very well also capture this income-related value.

---

[1] However, net cash flow is the preferred measure of economic income by most analysts in the income approach, but is seldom used in the market approach. The use of net cash flow in the income approach helps to make the approaches more discrete from each other.

If the ability to sell the subject business or business interest is the primary value driver, then it may be appropriate that one or more methods within the market approach dominate the value conclusion.

If the economic value derives primarily from the ownership or use of the business assets, then one or more methods within the asset-based approach may dominate the value conclusion. A market approach using a pricing multiple of stock price to underlying net asset value may also be a satisfactory way to capture this asset-driven economic value. As a general rule, the asset-based approach tends to be more appropriate when valuing a controlling ownership interest than a noncontrolling ownership interest. However, the asset-based approach is sometimes used for minority interests, in which case discounts for lack of control and/or lack of marketability are usually applied. This is because one of the important factors that the controlling owner controls—and a minority owner does not—is the commercialization (e.g., license, lease, sale, or use) of the subject business assets.

Through all of this, the analyst should keep in mind (1) the applicable standard of value, (2) the applicable premise of value, and (3) the applicable level of value. For example, family law courts in some states adhere to a strict definition of *fair market value* on the premise of value in exchange. In such cases, the personal goodwill of the business owner that could not be easily transferred with the business sale may not be considered a marital asset. This may be the case even though that personal goodwill may give rise to considerable economic value to the business owner and it would be considered if *investment value* was the applicable standard of value.

The final value estimate should typically be a number within the range of value indications derived from the various methods used in the valuation analysis. The final value estimate may be a number indicated by one of the valuation methods. Or, it may be heavily weighted to the result of the valuation method relied on most. Or, it may be another number from within the indicated range of values.

Occasionally, an arithmetic average to arrive at a final value estimate is appropriate. Using the arithmetic average implies that all of the valuation methods have equal validity and equal weight. While this may occur in certain instances, this is usually not the case. When this is the case, it should be based on a conscious decision on the part of the analyst—and not on a naive averaging of all value indications.

The final value opinion regarding the subject business enterprise or business interest should be derived from the analyst's reasoning and judgment of all the factors considered and from the impartial weighting of all of the market-derived valuation evidence.

At What Point Are Valuation Discounts and Premiums Applied?

The appropriate point in the analysis at which to apply valuation discounts and premiums depends on the level of value indicated by each method used. As discussed in earlier chapters, the most important discounts or premiums are usually related to the degree of ownership control or lack of ownership control of the subject business interest and the degree of marketability or lack of marketability of the subject business interest. Therefore, it is necessary to examine, for each valuation method included in the reconciliation process, the extent to which that valuation method indicates: (1) a controlling or noncontrolling ownership interest and (2) a readily marketable or a less than readily marketable ownership.

If all the methods used indicate values at the same level of value (e.g., a marketable, noncontrolling ownership interest value), then any applicable premiums and/or discounts may be applied at the conclusion of the analysis, after the relative weightings are applied to the various methods. If, on the other hand, the various valuation methods used indicate values at different levels of value, then premiums and/or discounts normally would be applied separately to each individual method before the relative weightings of the methods.

For example, let's assume a guideline publicly traded company method and a discounted economic income (cash flow) method were used. Let's assume that no adjustments were made to the subject company economic income to reflect the influence of ownership control. Let's also assume that valuation pricing multiples and the present value discount rates were derived from public capital market minority share transactional data. In this case, both the methods used would indicate the marketable, noncontrolling ownership interest level of value.[2] However, especially when control adjustments have been made to the financial statement, some analysts believe that, at least in some cases, the guideline public company method produces a control value. If the business interest being valued is a noncontrolling ownership interest in a closely held company, the results of the two methods could be synthesized. Then, a discount for lack of marketability could be applied to the combined value indication in order to estimate a nonmarketable, noncontrolling ownership interest level of value.

Let's assume now that, in addition to the two above-mentioned methods, a market approach using guideline merged and acquired company transaction data also was used. The valuation pricing multiples derived from merger and acquisition transactional data frequently reflect ownership control and/or acquisition price premiums. If that is true in the instant case, it would be appropriate to apply a minority ownership interest discount to the value indications of the guideline merged and acquired company method before weighting these indications in with the indication of the other two valuation methods.

A common error that inexperienced analysts make is to apply valuations of a single premium or discount to a value indication developed from two or more valuation methods that indicate different levels of value. This error can result in a serious distortion to the value estimate. Such a value conclusion that mixes two or more different levels of value is truly a meaningless valuation conclusion.

Accordingly, it is important for analysts to ensure in each situation that any discount or premium applied is appropriate to adjust from the level of value indicated in the valuation method to the level of value to be estimated in the valuation assignment.

Concluding the Value Estimate

Explicit Weighting

An intuitively appealing method of concluding the value estimate is for the analyst (1) to use subjective but informed judgment and decide on a percentage weight to assign to the indications of each meaningful valuation approach or method and (2) to base the final value estimate on a weighted average of the indications of the

---

[2] However, especially when control adjustments have been made to the financial statements, some analysts believe that, at least in some cases, the guideline public company method produces a control value.

Exhibit 19–2

Illustrative Business Enterprise, Inc.
Fair Market Value of Total Equity
Valuation Synthesis and Conclusion
Example of Explicit Weighting
As of December 31, 2000

	Indicated Value per Share	Assigned Weight	Value Indication
Price to earnings multiple:			
$2.00 per share × 5.0	$10.00	0.6	$6.00
Direct capitalization of dividends multiple:			
$0.60 per share ÷ 0.05	$12.00	0.1	$1.20
Price to net asset value multiple:			
$20.00 book value × 0.8	$16.00	0.3	$4.80
			$12.00
Less: Discount for lack of marketability (at assumed 35%)			
35% × 12.00			$4.20
Value conclusion per share			$7.80

various methods. Let's assume that the analyst is valuing a noncontrolling ownership interest in a closely held manufacturing company. The analyst ultimately relies on three value measures developed through the guideline publicly traded company method. The subject is an operating company. However, it has a substantial asset base, and the analyst concludes that the appropriate price-to-earnings pricing multiple should be accorded 60 percent of the total weight, the direct capitalization of dividends method a 10 percent weight, and the price-to-net-asset value pricing multiple a 30 percent weight. Let's assume, in this case, that the company has been unable to generate an adequate rate of return on its net asset base. Accordingly, the value estimate would be synthesized as presented in Exhibit 19–2.

In the case presented in Exhibit 19–2, let's assume that companies in the subject industry generally are selling at below net book value. However, the subject company is valued at a greater discount from net book value than the average company in the subject industry. This is because of the subject company's inadequate earnings. However, the net asset base is accorded some weight, and the company is valued at a lower discount from net book value than it would be if it were valued strictly on a price-to-earnings multiple basis. In this case, the effect of the direct capitalization of dividends on the final value estimate valuation method is neutral.

Regarding the above-described valuation synthesis procedure, it is noteworthy that no specific mathematical model is available for use in deriving the weights to assign to the indications of each valuation method. The relative weight to assign to each method depends on the analyst's judgment. However, one benefit of the explicit weighting valuation synthesis is that it forces the analyst to present his or her thinking in clearly quantified terms. The valuation synthesis narrative description, coupled with the explicit weighting, provides important information as to the analyst's thought process. The explicit weighting synthesis procedure also has the appeal of being relatively simple for the valuation audience to understand. If someone reviewing the valuation disagrees with some aspect of the analyst's judgment, the point of departure can be easily identified and quantified—by adjusting the valuation synthesis explicit weighting schema. It is important that the analyst not "double-count" the effect of issues that arose in the valuation process in the weights assigned. For example, if an analyst lowered the transaction multiples used due to concerns regarding the guideline companies' superior performance, and then weighted the transaction method less than other methods due to the same concerns, that could have the effect of "double-counting" the impact of that factor in the valuation.

Numerous court cases in which business and security values have been estimated under dissenting stockholders' appraisal rights have relied on this explicit weighting procedure. However, Revenue Ruling 59-60 does not appear to enthusiastically embrace the explicit weighting synthesis procedure:

> Because the valuations cannot be made on the basis of a prescribed formula, there is no means whereby the various applicable factors in a particular case can be assigned mathematical weights in deriving the fair market value. For this reason, no useful purpose is served by taking an average of several factors (for example, book value, capitalized earnings, and capitalized dividends) and basing the valuation on the result. Such a process excludes active consideration of other pertinent factors, and the end result cannot be supported by a realistic application of the significant facts in the case except by mere chance.[3]

However, a balanced reading of this revenue ruling indicates that the IRS is not prohibiting the use of the explicit weighting procedure. Rather, it is discouraging a naive application of a weighted average procedure that is not based on reasoned judgment. Analysts can certainly comply with this guidance by thoughtfully considering each factor delineated in Revenue Ruling 59-60 in their selection of the specific weights to assign to each value indication.

Also, despite the above language from this revenue ruling, the explicit weighting procedure has been used successfully in many federal gift and estate tax cases, both in audit negotiations with the IRS and in cases decided in court. The wording of Revenue Ruling 59-60 indicates concern that the averaging or weighted average method allows for the omission of pertinent factors. Of course, it is possible to use the basic weighted average of factors procedure and still, at one stage or another, incorporate active consideration of all the pertinent factors mentioned in Revenue Ruling 59-60. Accordingly, it is important to demonstrate in each taxation-oriented valuation that all other pertinent factors were actively considered and reflected in the final value estimate.

Implicit Weighting

Some analysts use an implicit weighting scheme in the valuation reconciliation process. These analysts present the value indications for each method performed, and then they present the final value estimate without an explicit quantitative weighting. The implicit weighting procedure does not quantitatively justify the valuation synthesis process. It does so in a qualitative manner.

An example of this implicit weighting scheme is provided in Exhibit 19–3.

This valuation synthesis and conclusion presents the final value estimate. However, it does not explicitly or quantitatively explain the reconciliation process. Nonetheless, this implicit weighting procedure is still informative to the valuation

---

[3] Rev. Rul. 59-60 (1959-1 C.B. 237).

Exhibit 19–3

Illustrative Business Enterprise, Inc.
Fair Market Value of Total Equity
Valuation Synthesis and Conclusion
Example of Implicit Weighting
As of December 31, 2000

Valuation Approach	Valuation Method	Value Indication
Market approach	Guideline publicly traded company method	$38,000,000
Income approach	Discounted economic income method	$40,000,000
Asset-based approach	Asset accumulation method	$44,000,000
	Valuation synthesis and conclusion	$42,000,000

audience if the analyst adequately explains the reconciliation process in the narrative section of the valuation report. The narrative explanation can cover both (1) the conceptual preferability among the methods used and (2) the degree of the analyst's confidence in each method used—based on the relative quantity and quality of available data.

Final Value Estimate

Any of the following types of final value estimates may be appropriate, given the purpose and objective of the valuation:

1. A point estimate—usually the business valuation final value estimate is stated as a single figure or point estimate.
2. A range of value—in this conclusion, the business valuation value estimate is said to fall somewhere within a stated range of values. This may be reported solely, as the conclusion of value, or in conjunction with a single point estimate.
3. A relationship value—in this conclusion, the value estimate is expressed as a relationship to a stated value. For example, the value estimate is indicated to be "no less than $X million" or "no more than $Y million."

Summary

The final value estimate is ultimately based on an analysis and assessment of the accumulated market-derived pricing evidence by the reasoned professional judgment of the analyst. The valuation process should be presented in such a way as to lead the valuation audience to the same final value estimate concluded by the analyst. Accordingly, the relevant qualitative and quantitative data and analyses should be summarized in the valuation. And, the analyst's significant judgments and thought processes should be summarized in the valuation. In this way, the audience of the valuation should understand—and be able to re-create—how the analyst concluded the final value estimate.

Part V

Writing and Reviewing Business Valuation Reports

Chapter 20

Writing the Business Valuation Report

This chapter discusses the following topics related to the preparation and issuance of business valuation reports:

1. An overview of the valuation reporting process
2. *Uniform Standards of Professional Appraisal Practice* (USPAP) business valuation reporting standards
3. The form, format, and content of various common types of reports, as categorized by USPAP
4. The valuation work paper documentation and retention requirements of USPAP
5. The confidentiality requirements of USPAP
6. Other valuation industry standards with regard to reports

In addition, this chapter presents some general suggestions with regard to effective writing of business valuation reports.

Overview of the Business Valuation Report

According to the 2006 edition of the USPAP, the definition of an appraisal is: "the act or process of developing an opinion of value; an opinion of value ..."[1] The USPAP definition of an appraisal report is: "any communication, written or oral, of an appraisal, appraisal review, or consulting service that is transmitted to the client upon completion of an assignment."[2] And, the USPAP definition of an assignment is: "a valuation service provided as a consequence of an agreement between an appraiser and a client."[3] The term "valuation services" is defined as: "services pertaining to aspects of property value."[4] See Chapter 1 for the background, history, and purpose of USPAP.

As we will discuss below, USPAP does provide standards with regard to "business appraisal reporting." However, USPAP does not define either a "business appraisal" or a "business appraisal report." And, while there are USPAP reporting standards with regard to the form and format of real estate appraisal reports, USPAP does not provide specific guidance with regard to the form or format of business valuation reports.

Accordingly, the length, type, and (to a certain extent) content of a business valuation report may be influenced by:

1. The valuation client
2. Any applicable regulatory requirements
3. Any applicable statutory authority
4. The courts, through published judicial precedent
5. The type of business ownership interest being valued
6. The nature of the business valuation problem

---

[1] *Uniform Standards of Professional Appraisal Practice*, 2006 edition, (Washington, DC: The Appraisal Foundation, 2006) Available at www.appraisal-foundation.org.
[2] Ibid.
[3] Ibid.
[4] Ibid.

USPAP Reporting Standards

The USPAP describes minimum standards to be applied in many types of appraisal reports. USPAP states that each written or oral "business appraisal report" must:

1. Clearly and accurately set forth the appraisal in a manner that will not be misleading
2. Contain sufficient information to enable those who receive or rely on the report to understand it properly
3. Clearly and accurately disclose any extraordinary assumption or limiting condition that directly affects the appraisal, and indicate its impact on the concluded value

The professional standards related to reporting the results of a business are presented in USPAP Standard 10. Since this standard provides clear and cogent professional guidance to analysts who prepare valuation opinion reports, whether or not those reports have to be prepared in accordance with USPAP standards, it is presented in its entirety in Exhibit 20–1.

Written Business Valuation Reporting Standards

As it relates to business valuation, USPAP provides the guideline that each written "business appraisal report" comply with the following disclosure requirements:

1. Identify and describe the business or the business ownership interest that is the subject of the valuation.
2. State the purpose of the valuation and the client's intended use of the valuation opinions and conclusions.
3. Define the standard of value to be estimated.
4. Indicate the effective or "as of" date of the valuation and the date of the valuation opinion report.
5. Describe the extent of the valuation process.
6. Set forth all assumptions and limiting conditions that affect the analyses, opinions, and conclusions.
7. Set forth the information considered, the analytical procedures followed, and the reasoning that supports the valuation opinions and conclusions.
8. Explain the analyst's rationale for the valuation methods used and the valuation procedures considered.
9. Set forth any additional information that may be appropriate to demonstrate compliance with, or clearly identify and explain permitted departure from, the requirements of the USPAP "business appraisal development" standards.
10. Include a signed certification in compliance with USPAP Standards Rule 10-3 (which is included in Exhibit 20–1).

Oral Business Valuation Reporting Standards

USPAP Standards Rule 10-4 provides professional guidance with regard to oral business valuation reports. Oral reports are often presented within the context of expert witness testimony, either in deposition or in trial.

Exhibit 20–1

USPAP STANDARD 10—BUSINESS APPRAISAL, REPORTING

In reporting the results of an appraisal of an interest in a business enterprise or intangible asset, an appraiser must communicate each analysis, opinion, and conclusion in a manner that is not misleading.

<u>Comment:</u> STANDARD 10 addresses the content and level of information required in a report that communicates the results of an appraisal of an interest in a business enterprise or intangible asset developed under STANDARD 9.

STANDARD 10 does not dictate the form, format, or style of business or intangible asset appraisal reports, which are functions of the needs of intended users and appraisers. The substantive content of a report determines its compliance.

Standards Rule 10-1

Each written or oral appraisal report for an interest in a business enterprise or intangible asset must:
(a) clearly and accurately set forth the appraisal in a manner that will not be misleading;
(b) contain sufficient information to enable the intended user(s) to understand the report; and
(c) clearly and accurately disclose all assumptions, extraordinary assumptions, hypothetical conditions, and limiting conditions used in the assignment.

Standards Rule 10-2

Each written appraisal report for an interest in a business enterprise or intangible asset must be prepared in accordance with one of the following options and prominently state which option is used: Appraisal Report or Restricted Use Appraisal Report.

<u>Comment:</u> When the intended users include parties other than the client, an Appraisal Report must be provided. When the intended users do not include parties other than the client, a Restricted Use Appraisal Report may be provided.

The essential difference between these options is in the content and level of information provided. The appropriate reporting option and the level of information necessary in the report are dependent on the intended use and intended users.

An appraiser must use care when characterizing the type of report and level of information communicated upon completion of an assignment. An appraiser may use any other label in addition to, but not in place of, the label set forth in this Standard for the type of report provided.

The report content and level of information requirements set forth in this Standard are minimums for both types of report.

A party receiving a copy of an Appraisal Report or Restricted Use Appraisal Report does not become an intended user of the appraisal unless the appraiser identifies such party as an intended user as part of the assignment.

(a)   The content of an Appraisal Report must be consistent with the intended use of the appraisal and, at a minimum:
    (i)   state the identity of the client and any other intended users, by name or type;[1]
        <u>Comment:</u> An appraiser must use care when identifying the client to ensure a clear understanding and to avoid violations of the Confidentiality section of the ETHICS RULE. In those rare instances when the client wishes to remain anonymous, an appraiser must still document the identity of the client in the workfile but may omit the client's identity in the report.
    (ii)   state the intended use of the appraisal;[2]
    (iii) summarize information sufficient to identify the business or intangible asset and the interest appraised;
        <u>Comment:</u> The identification information must include property characteristics relevant to the type and definition of value and intended use of the appraisal.
    (iv)   state the extent to which the interest appraised contains elements of ownership control, including the basis for that determination;
    (v)   state the extent to which the interest appraised lacks elements of marketability and/or liquidity, including the basis for that determination;
    (vi)   state the standard (type) and definition of value and the premise of value and cite the source of the definition;
        <u>Comment:</u> Stating the definition of value also requires any comments needed to clearly indicate to the intended users how the definition is being applied.
    (vii) state the effective date of the appraisal and the date of the report;
        <u>Comment:</u> The effective date of the appraisal establishes the context for the value opinion, while the date of the report indicates whether the perspective of the appraiser on the market or property as of the effective date of the appraisal was prospective, current, or retrospective.
    (viii) summarize the scope of work used to develop the appraisal;[3]
        <u>Comment:</u> Because the intended user's reliance on an appraisal may be affected by the scope of work, the report must enable them to be properly informed and not misled. Sufficient information includes disclosure of research and analyses performed and might also include disclosure of research and analyses not performed.
        When any portion of the work involves significant business and/or intangible asset appraisal assistance, the appraiser must summarize the extent of that assistance. The signing appraiser must also state the name(s) of those providing the significant business and/or intangible asset appraisal assistance in the certification, in accordance with SR 10-3.

(Continued on next page)

Exhibit 20–1

USPAP STANDARD 10—BUSINESS APPRAISAL, REPORTING (Continued)

   (ix)   **summarize the information analyzed, the appraisal procedures followed, and the reasoning that supports the analyses, opinions, and conclusions; exclusion of the market approach, asset-based (cost) approach, or income approach must be explained;**

       Comment: An Appraisal Report must include sufficient information to indicate that the appraiser complied with the requirements of STANDARD 9. The amount of detail required will vary with the significance of the information to the appraisal.

       The appraiser must provide sufficient information to enable the client and intended users to understand the rationale for the opinions and conclusions, including reconciliation in accordance with Standards Rule 9-5.

   (x)   **clearly and conspicuously:**

- **state all extraordinary assumptions and hypothetical conditions; and**
- **state that their use might have affected the assignment results; and**

   (xi)   **include a signed certification in accordance with Standards Rule 10-3.**

(b)   **The content of a Restricted Use Appraisal Report must be consistent with the intended use of the appraisal and, at a minimum:**

   (i)   **state the identity of the client, by name or type;[4] and state a prominent use restriction that limits use of the report to the client and warns that the appraiser's opinions and conclusions set forth in the report may not be understood properly without additional information in the appraiser's workfile;**

       Comment: An appraiser must use care when identifying the client to ensure a clear understanding and to avoid violations of the Confidentiality section of the ETHICS RULE. In those rare instances when the client wishes to remain anonymous, an appraiser must still document the identity of the client in the workfile but may omit the client's identity in the report.

       The Restricted Use Appraisal Report is for client use only. Before entering into an agreement, the appraiser should establish with the client the situations where this type of report is to be used and should ensure that the client understands the restricted utility of the Restricted Use Appraisal Report.

   (ii)   **state the intended use of the appraisal;[5]**

       Comment: The intended use of the appraisal must be consistent with the limitation on use of the Restricted Use Appraisal Report option in this Standards Rule (i.e. client use only).

   (iii)   **state information sufficient to identify the business or intangible asset and the interest appraised;**

       Comment: The identification information must include property characteristics relevant to the type and definition of value and intended use of the appraisal.

   (iv)   **state the extent to which the interest appraised contains elements of ownership control, including the basis for that determination;**

   (v)   **state the extent to which the interest appraised lacks elements of marketability and/or liquidity, including the basis for that determination;**

   (vi)   **state the standard (type) of value and the premise of value, and cite the source of its definition;**

   (vii)   **state the effective date of the appraisal and the date of the report;**

       Comment: The effective date of the appraisal establishes the context for the value opinion, while the date of the report indicates whether the perspective of the appraiser on the market or property as of the effective date of the appraisal was prospective, current, or retrospective.

   (viii)   **state the scope of work used to develop the appraisal;[6]**

       Comment: Because the client's reliance on an appraisal may be affected by the scope of work, the report must enable them to be properly informed and not misled. Sufficient information includes disclosure of research and analyses performed and might also include disclosure of research and analyses not performed.

       When any portion of the work involves significant business and/or intangible asset appraisal assistance, the appraiser must state the extent of that assistance. The signing appraiser must also state the name(s) of those providing the significant business and/or intangible asset appraisal assistance in the certification, in accordance with SR 10-3.

   (ix)   **state the appraisal procedures followed, state the value opinion(s) and conclusion(s) reached, and reference the workfile; exclusion of the market approach, asset-based (cost) approach, or income approach must be explained;**

       Comment: An appraiser must maintain a specific, coherent workfile in support of a Restricted Use Appraisal Report. The contents of the workfile must include sufficient information to indicate that the appraiser complied with the requirements of STANDARD 9 and for the appraiser to produce an Appraisal Report. The file must be available for inspection by the client (or the client's representatives, such as those engaged to complete an appraisal review), such third parties as may be authorized by due process of law, and a duly authorized professional peer review committee except when such disclosure to a committee would violate applicable law or regulation.

(Continued on next page)

Exhibit 20–1

USPAP STANDARD 10—BUSINESS APPRAISAL, REPORTING (Continued)

(x)   clearly and conspicuously:
   - state all extraordinary assumptions and hypothetical conditions; and
   - state that their use might have affected the assignment results; and

(xi)   include a signed certification in accordance with Standards Rule 10-3.

Standards Rule 10-3

Each written appraisal report for an interest in a business enterprise or intangible asset must contain a signed certification that is similar in content to the following form:

   I certify that, to the best of my knowledge and belief:

   –   the statements of fact contained in this report are true and correct.

   –   the reported analyses, opinions, and conclusions are limited only by the reported assumptions and limiting conditions and are my personal, impartial, and unbiased professional analyses, opinions, and conclusions.

   –   I have no (or the specified) present or prospective interest in the property that is the subject of this report, and I have no (or the specified) personal interest with respect to the parties involved.

   –   I have no bias with respect to the property that is the subject of this report or to the parties involved with this assignment.

   –   my engagement in this assignment was not contingent upon developing or reporting predetermined results.

   –   my compensation for completing this assignment is not contingent upon the development or reporting of a predetermined value or direction in value that favors the cause of the client, the amount of the value opinion, the attainment of a stipulated result, or the occurrence of a subsequent event directly related to the intended use of this appraisal.

   –   my analyses, opinions, and conclusions were developed, and this report has been prepared, in conformity with the *Uniform Standards of Professional Appraisal Practice*.

   –   no one provided significant business and/or intangible asset appraisal assistance to the person signing this certification. (If there are exceptions, the name of each individual providing significant business and/or intangible asset appraisal assistance must be stated.)

Comment: A signed certification is an integral part of the appraisal report. An appraiser who signs any part of the appraisal report, including a letter of transmittal, must also sign this certification.

In an assignment that includes only assignment results developed by the business and/or intangible asset appraiser(s), any appraiser(s) who signs a certification accepts full responsibility for all elements of the certification, for the assignment results, and for the contents of the appraisal report. In an assignment that includes real property or personal property assignment results not developed by the business and/or intangible asset appraiser(s), any business and/or intangible asset appraiser(s) who signs a certification accepts full responsibility for the business and/or intangible asset elements of the certification, for the business and/or intangible asset assignment results, and for the business and/or intangible asset contents of the appraisal report. When a signing appraiser(s) has relied on work done by others who do not sign the certification, the signing appraiser is responsible for the decision to rely on their work. The signing appraiser(s) is required to have a reasonable basis for believing that those individuals performing the work are competent.[7]

The names of individuals providing significant business and/or intangible asset appraisal assistance who do not sign a certification must be stated in the certification. It is not required that the description of their assistance be contained in the certification, but disclosure of their assistance is required in accordance with SR 10-2(a) or (b)(vii), as applicable.

Standards Rule 10-4

To the extent that it is both possible and appropriate, an oral appraisal report for an interest in a business enterprise or intangible asset must address the substantive matters set forth in Standards Rule10-2(a).

Comment: See the Record Keeping section of the ETHICS RULE for corresponding requirements.

---

[1] See Statement on Appraisal Standards No. 9, *Identification of Intended Use and Intended Users*.

[2] Ibid.

[3] See Advisory Opinion 28, *Scope of Work Decision, Performance, and Disclosure*, and Advisory Opinion 29, *An Acceptable Scope of Work*. References to Advisory Opinions are for guidance only and do not incorporate Advisory Opinions into USPAP.

[4] See Statement on Appraisal Standards No. 9, *Identification of Intended Use and Intended Users*.

[5] Ibid.

[6] See Advisory Opinion 28, *Scope of Work Decision, Performance, and Disclosure* and Advisory Opinion 29, *An Acceptable Scope of Work*. References to Advisory Opinions are for guidance only and do not incorporate Advisory Opinions into USPAP.

[7] See Advisory Opinion 5, *Assistance in the Preparation of an Appraisal*. References to Advisory Opinions are for guidance only and do not incorporate Advisory Opinions into USPAP.

Effectively, USPAP does not distinguish between oral reports and written reports, at least with regard to professional standards. That is, USPAP Standards Rule 10-4 indicates that an oral report "must, at a minimum, address the substantive matters set forth in Standards Rule 10-2(a)" (i.e., the Standards Rule that describes the content of written business valuation reports).

USPAP Ethics Provisions

The USPAP Ethics Rule applies to all valuations (or other professional services) prepared in compliance with USPAP. Accordingly, these ethics provisions encompass business valuations, as well as other types of valuation.

Many analysts do not have an administrative or judicial requirement to comply with USPAP. However, the USPAP ethics provisions relate to basic professional conduct issues. Accordingly, all analysts may benefit from the useful professional guidance provided by the USPAP Ethics Rule.

The USPAP Ethics Rule is divided into four sections: (1) conduct, (2) management, (3) confidentiality, and (4) record keeping. The following sections will summarize the professional guidance provided by USPAP in the areas of record keeping/retention and client confidentiality.

Retention of Valuation Reports and Work Paper Files

The record keeping section of the USPAP ethics provision provides the following professional guidance:

> An appraiser must prepare a workfile for each assignment. The workfile must include the name of the client and the identity, by name or type, of any other intended users; true copies of any written reports, documented on any type of media; summaries of any oral reports or testimony, or a transcript of testimony, including the appraiser's signed and dated certification; all other data, information, and documentation necessary to support the appraiser's opinions and conclusions and to show compliance with this rule and all other applicable standards, or references to the location(s) of such other documentation.
>
> An appraiser must retain the workfile for a period of at least five (5) years after preparation or at least two (2) years after final disposition of any judicial proceeding in which testimony was given, whichever period expires last, and have custody of his or her workfile, or make appropriate workfile retention, access, and retrieval arrangements with the party having custody of the workfile.[5]

Confidentiality Provision

The confidentiality section of the USPAP ethics provision addresses the confidential nature of the valuation analyst–valuation client relationship. The confidentiality provisions of USPAP provide the following professional guidance:

> An appraiser must protect the confidential nature of the appraiser-client relationship.

---

[5] Ibid.

An appraiser must not disclose confidential information or assignment results prepared for a client to anyone other than the client and persons specifically authorized by the client; state enforcement agencies and such third parties as may be authorized by due process of law; and a duly authorized professional peer review committee except when such disclosure to a committee would violate applicable law or regulation. It is unethical for a member of a duly authorized professional peer review committee to disclose confidential information presented to the committee.[6]

Internal Revenue Service Business Valuation Guidelines

In 2003, the IRS finalized Business Valuation Guidelines. Exhibit 20–2 is the Reporting Guidelines section of the overall IRS guidelines. It is worth noting that the IRS guidelines are fully compatible with USPAP.

The IRS Business Valuation Guidelines are subject to updating. The latest version can be found on the IRS Web site, www.irs.gov.

Exhibit 20–2

IRS Business Valuation Reporting Guidelines

4.1. Overview

4.1.1. The primary objective of a valuation report is to provide convincing and compelling support for the conclusions reached.

4.1.2. Valuation reports should contain all the information necessary to ensure a clear understanding of the valuation analyses and demonstrate how the conclusions were reached.

4.2. Report Contents

4.2.1. The extent and content of the report prepared depends on the needs of each case.

4.2.2. Valuation reports should clearly communicate the results and identify the information relied upon in the valuation process. The valuation report should effectively communicate the methodology and reasoning, as well as identify the supporting documentation.

4.2.3. Subject to the type of report being written, valuation reports should generally contain sufficient information relating to the items in Sections 2.2 and 2.3, above, to ensure consistency and quality of valuation reports issued by IRS Valuators.

4.2.4. Reports written with respect to Section 2.5.2.8, above, shall contain, at a minimum, those items in Sections 2.2 and 2.3 necessary to support the revised assumptions, analyses, and/or conclusions of the Valuator.

4.3. Statement

4.3.1. Each written valuation report should contain a signed statement that is similar in content to the following:

To the best of my knowledge and belief:

- The reported analyses, opinions, and conclusions are limited only by the reported assumptions and limiting conditions.
- I have no present or prospective interest in the property that is the subject of this report, and I have no personal interest with respect to the parties involved.
- I have no bias with respect to the property that is the subject of this report or to the parties involved with this assignment.
- My compensation is not contingent on an action or event resulting from the analyses, opinions, or conclusions in, or the use of, this report.
- My analyses, opinions, and conclusions were developed, and this report has been prepared in conformity with, the applicable Internal Revenue Service Valuation Guidelines.

---

[6] Ibid.

Valuation Industry Reporting Standards

Numerous valuation industry professional membership organizations also have addressed the issue of business valuation reporting standards. These professional association standards do not have the same legislative authority as USPAP. Nonetheless, these standards are usually binding on each organization's respective membership. And, these standards collectively do provide useful guidance to analysts as to what is the standard practice in the industry with regard to business valuation reports.

Valuation analyst and author Jay Fishman compared various professional organization valuation reporting standards in an article. This discussion summarizes that article as amended to reflect current developments.[7]

American Society of Appraisers

The Fishman article first summarizes the American Society of Appraisers (ASA) business valuation standards (BVS) with regard to report writing. In particular, the chapter focuses on the requirements of ASA BVS-VIII. All ASA business valuation standards, including BVS-VIII, are presented in Appendix B. We recommend that the reader review the actual language of BVS-III.

The Canadian Institute of Chartered Business Valuators

In its discussion of the CICBV business valuation reporting standards, the Fishman article mentions the following:

> The Canadian Institute of Chartered Business Valuators (CICBV) specifically addresses the format and content of appraisal reports in their Standard 110. The CICBV differentiates between Valuation Reports, Advisory Reports, and Expert Reports. A Valuation Report is defined as:
>
> > Any written communication on letterhead and/or where the author(s) is identified, containing a conclusion as to the value of shares, assets, or an interest in a business, prepared by a Valuator acting independently and that is not clearly marked as being in draft form.

Advisory Reports deal with reporting requirements when a valuator is not acting independently, and Expert Reports deal with the reporting requirements offering an independent opinion "containing a conclusion as to the damages or the quantum of financial gain or loss."

At a minimum, a Valuation Report must contain the standard elements that are seen in most appraisal reports. These include valuation date, description of the valuation, and definition of the term value. Appendix A of this standard is a summary of the CICBV valuation reporting requirements for these typed of reports. Appendix A indicates the following:

> While it is not required that sufficient information be provided to enable the reader to perform his or her own independent valuation, a Valuation

---

[7] Jay E. Fishman, "Appraisal Reports: The Long and Short of It," *The Journal of Business Valuation* (Proceedings of the Fourth Joint Business Valuation Conference of The Canadian Institute of Chartered Business Valuators and the American Society of Appraisers) (Toronto: The Canadian Institute of Chartered Business Valuators, 1999).

Report should contain sufficient narrative and schedules to support the opinion and calculations for the purposes at hand. The source of any fact, which is material to the formal valuation, must be clearly stated, including sufficient details so that the significance of the fact can be reasonably assessed by the reader of the Report. Adequate disclosure will usually include a comparison of valuation calculations and conclusions arrived at through different methods, a discussion of the rationale for accepting or rejecting each methodology, and the relative importance or weighting of relevant methodologies in arriving at a final valuation conclusion.[8]

National Association of Certified Valuation Analysts

Mr. Fishman discusses the NACVA business valuation reporting standards as follows:

The most recent version of National Association of Certified Valuation Analysts' (NACVA) Professional Standards is as of May 31, 2002. Reporting standards are covered in Section 4. In Section 4.3(b), NACVA indicates the following:

Any reporting of a Conclusion of Value must be in writing and set forth the following information concerning the valuation engagement and its results:

- identification of the subject being valued;
- description of the interest being valued;
- valuation date;
- report date;
- purpose and use of the valuation;
- definition of the standard of value;
- identification of the premise of value;
- identification of the assumptions, limiting conditions, and scope limitations;
- conclusion of value;
- limitations on use of the report—all valuation cases vary as to specific assumptions, limiting conditions, and scope, therefore, the member must identify material matters considered
- responsible member signature—the member who has primary responsibility for the conclusion of value must sign or be identified in the report
- a statement of independence;
- ownership size, nature, restrictions, and agreements;
- a description of the fundamental analysis;
- valuation approaches and method(s);
- historical financial statement summaries, when applicable;
- adjustments to historical financial statements, when applicable;
- adjusted financial statement summaries, when applicable; and
- projected/forecasted financial statements including the underlying assumptions, when applicable.[9]

---

[8] Ibid., pp. 192–93. Also available at www.cicbv.ca.
[9] Ibid., pp. 193–94. Also available at www.nacva.com.

Institute of Business Appraisers

As part of the discussion of the IBA business valuation reporting standards, the Fishman article provides the following guidance:

> Perhaps more than any other appraisal society, the Institute of Business Appraisers (IBA) has more written concerning reporting requirements. According to the IBA, there are: oral reports, expert testimony, letter reports, formal reports and lastly, preliminary reports. Standard 1 of the IBA deals with professional conduct and ethics. This standard refers to communicating appraisal results in a general way. It indicates that:
>
> > It is essential that a business appraiser communicate the research and thought processes which lead to his [or her] opinions and conclusions in a manner that is clear, meaningful and not misleading. Said communication, whether oral or written, shall not be rendered in a careless or negligent manner.[10]

American Institute of Certified Public Accountants

The AICPA recently released standards that include report writing standards. Also, the AICPA also has ethical standards relating to consulting (which includes business valuation). These standards cover many of the same issues as the USPAP ethical standards.

The above sections summarized relevant business valuation reporting standards as promulgated (1) by the USPAP, and (2) by recognized valuation industry professional membership organizations. The next sections do not report published professional standards. Rather, the following discussions will provide general suggestions to analysts for the preparation of clear, concise, and convincing business valuation reports.

Guidelines for Effective Report Writing

Obviously, it is important for the analyst to comply with applicable professional standards with regard to the conduct and the reporting of the business valuation. Nonetheless, compliance with applicable professional standards will not ensure an effective valuation report presentation. Unfortunately, many technically correct valuations fail to convince their intended audience to make the appropriate investment, transaction, regulatory, or judicial decision. This is because the valuation opinion report did not effectively communicate the analyses and conclusion to the report reader.

Previous chapters have focused on the quantitative and qualitative rigor of business valuation approaches and methods. The previous sections of this chapter have focused on technical compliance with professional standards related to valuation reporting (and work paper documentation and client confidentiality). This section will provide practical recommendations with regard to improving the content and style of valuation opinion reports.

---

[10] Ibid., p. 195.

What Causes Ineffective Report Writing?

In recent years, many commentators have lamented the fact that valuation reports often ineffectively communicate the intended valuation conclusion. These commentators are usually representative of the audience for valuation opinions, such as investors, lawyers, and judges. Most of these criticisms are the result of the analyst's failure to follow the fundamental "golden rule" of effective valuation report writing:

1. Say what you did, and
2. Do what you said.

While this "golden rule" may seem simplistic, compliance with it would satisfy many valuation report criticisms. Active consideration of this simple rule will assist the analyst in more effective communication of the valuation analyses and conclusion. Also, active consideration of this simple rule will assist the analyst in the general compliance of many valuation reporting professional standards.

Investment manager and valuation analyst Robert Willis wrote an article in which he effectively described many of the common mistakes that analysts make in ineffectively communicating their valuation opinions:

> Three broad criticisms explain why most appraisal reports and testimony are ineffective and unpersuasive. First, the court is dismissive of superficial reports lacking thoroughness and depth. Second, the court gives little weight to reports that fail to connect the particular facts and circumstances of the case to the proffered studies and the methodologies applied ("connectivity"). Third, the court is increasingly irritated with reports and testimony that fail to adequately consider the position of the hypothetical seller.[11]

In particular, Willis comments on what is arguably the most common criticism of valuation opinion reports: that they do not effectively support the stated valuation conclusion. In many cases, the valuation report presents the appropriate supporting data and analyses. However, the report fails to communicate how the analyst reached the value conclusion from the stated data and analyses.

> The second area of deficiency is the lack of connectivity in valuation reports. By this, I mean there is little connection made between the facts of the subject company and the empirical data proffered or the studies cited; and governing legal documents and state law are not connected to valuation issues (e.g., a connection is not shown between a family limited partnership [FLP] agreement and state statutes). There seems to be a general belief that all one has to do is cite the standard lack of marketability studies and, voila, a 35% discount appears! I have noted this tendency in many reports that cross my desk. The court increasingly is challenging such a rote approach of appraisers who do not make the effort to connect the facts and circumstances of the subject company to relevant legal documents, state law, empirical data, and discount studies.[12]

In the same article, Willis explains that the inability of the analyst to effectively organize and present the valuation report causes the reader to doubt the very credibility of the valuation analyses. In the following passage, Willis provides suggestions

---

[11] Robert T. Willis Jr., "Preparing Valuation Reports to Withstand Judicial Challenge," *Estate Planning*, December 1998, p. 455.
[12] Ibid., p. 457.

for enhancing the credibility of the valuation analyses by improving the quality of the valuation report.

In this regard, the credibility of a valuation report is enhanced by commenting on the impact and outcome of using a range of assumptions (e.g., varying growth and discount rates). By exploring the valuation effect of several different assumptions (instead of just one set of assumptions), the appraiser illustrates a higher level of analysis and investigation, and the report takes on a higher level of credibility and objectivity by appearing less "results driven."[13]

Make the Report "Incisive"

Webster defines "incisiveness" as follows:

1. Having a cutting edge or piercing point; facilitating cutting or piercing, as sharp
2. Marked by sharpness and penetration, especially in keen, clear, unmistakable resolution of matter at issue or in pointed decision effectiveness of preparation
3. Clear genius that states in a flash the exact point at issue
4. Keen penetration and sharp presentation that is decisive or effective; rapier quality of highly tempered steel
5. Unmistakably clear outlining, analysis, and presentation that defies disbelief or question[14]

We would all like to write reports that meet the above criteria.

Summary

This chapter presented the professional standards related to reporting the results of the business valuation. In particular, the standards rules related to USPAP Standard 10 were discussed. USPAP provides valuable professional guidance for analysts, even in the instances when the valuation report does not technically have to comply with USPAP. Accordingly, we recommend that analysts generally consider the guidance provided by USPAP with regard to most business valuation reports.

This chapter summarized the valuation reporting standards of several prominent valuation industry professional membership organizations. Of course, only members of each professional organization are bound to follow their individual reporting standards. Nonetheless, a summary of these professional standards provides the analyst with a good indication of what is the current standard of practice with respect to business valuation reports. Accordingly, we recommend that even analysts not associated with these organizations be generally familiar with their professional guidance with regard to business valuation reports.

Many competent analysts cannot effectively communicate their valuation analyses and conclusions. Effective valuation opinion reports are clear, convincing, and cogent.

---

[13] Ibid., p. 456.

[14] *Webster's 3rd New International Dictionary of the English Language, Unabridged*, Philip Babcock Cove, Editor-in-Chief, Springfield, MA: G&C Merriam Co., 1966.

These reporting principles do not rise to the level of professional standards. Rather, they are recommendations intended to assist the analyst to more effectively (and convincingly) present an otherwise competent valuation.

Well-researched and well-documented valuation opinion reports, presented in a complete, logical, and readable manner, can be instrumental (1) in expediting sound transactions and (2) in reducing the risks of litigation subsequent to the subject transactions. Conversely, poorly written valuation opinion reports may delay or prevent a transaction and may invite litigation—even if the transaction itself was basically sound.

This chapter is intended to assist analysts in the presentation of sound valuation opinion reports that will be readable by—and be acceptable to—the valuation audience, business buyers, business sellers, financier's beneficiaries, fiduciaries, governmental or other regulators, judges, juries, or other parties who will rely upon the subject business valuation.

Bibliography

Articles

Curtiss, Rand M. "Improving Your Appraisal Reports: Some Constructive Suggestions." *Business Appraisal Practice*, Winter 1999, pp. 42–49.

Dankoff, Timothy. "Ten of the Most Common Errors in Business Valuation Reports." *The Litigation Newsletter*.

The Financial Group. "Non-Appraisers Guide to Reviewing Business Valuation Reports." Available at www.FVGI.com. Also available at www.BVLibrary.com.

Fishman, Jay E. "Appraisal Reports: The Long and Short of It." *Journal of Business Valuation* (Proceedings of the 4th Joint Business Valuation Conference of The Canadian Institute of Chartered Business Valuators and the American Society of Appraisers). Toronto: The Canadian Institute of Chartered Business Valuators, 1999, pp. 189–214.

Fishman, Jay E., Shannon P. Pratt, et al. "Valuation Reports" (Chapter 9). In *Guide to Business Valuations*, 16th ed. Fort Worth, TX: Practitioner's Publishing Company, 2006.

Glass, Carla. "Keys to Successful Reporting Writing." Presentation to the International Appraisal Conference of the American Society of Appraisers, June 1996. Available from *Business Valuation Review*, P.O. Box 19237, Denver, CO 80219, (303) 975-8895.

Hawkins, George B. "Identifying and Excluding Faulty Valuation Report Content and Testimony." *Fair Value*, vol. 10, no. 2, Summer 2001.

Hawkins, George B., and Michael A. Paschall. "Valuation Report Contents in Jointly Retained Valuation Assignments." *Fair Value*, vol. 10, no. 2, Winter 2001.

Pratt, Shannon P. "Checklists and Useful Tools for Lawyers to Review Reports." *Judges and Lawyers Business Valuation Update*, November 2001. Also available at www.BVLibrary.com.

_____. *The Lawyer's Business Valuation Handbook: Understanding Financial Statements, Appraisal Reports and Expert Testimony*. Chicago: American Bar Association, 2000.

_____. "Quality Report Writing Eludes Many Appraisers." *Shannon Pratt's Business Valuation Update*, August 1996, pp. 1, 3.

Reilly, Robert F. "Ten Guidelines: Business and Property Appraisals." *Valuation Strategies*, May/June 1998, pp. 9–13.

Trugman, Gary R. "The Appraisal Report" and "Sample Appraisal Reports" (Chapters 12 and 13). In *Understanding Business Valuation*. Jersey City, NJ: American Institute of Certified Public Accountants, 1998.

Wietzke, Robert R. "Common Errors in Business Valuation Reports Revisited." *CPA Litigation Service Counselor*, June 1999, pp. 1–2, 11–12.

Willis, Robert T. Jr. "Preparing Valuation Reports to Withstand Judicial Challenge." *Estate Planning*, December 1998, pp. 455–62.

Yeanoplos, Kevin R. "The Creation of an Effective Valuation Report." Presentation to the AICPA National Business Valuation Conference, December 1999. Available on www.BVLibrary.com.

Technical Report Writing

Himstreet, Wiliam C. *Communicating the Appraisal: The Narrative Report*. Chicago: Appraisal Institute, 1991.

Houp, Kenneth W., Elizabeth Tebeaux, and Thomas E. Pearsall. *Reporting Technical Information*, 9th ed. New York: John Wiley & Sons, 1998.

English Style and Usage

The Chicago Manual of Style, 15th ed. Chicago: University of Chicago Press, 2003.

The Chicago Manual of Style has long been the standard reference text for writers in many fields. Its precise rules leave little room for doubt about style matters.

Hodges, John C., Winifred Bryan Horner, et al. *Harbrace College Handbook*, rev. 13th ed. San Diego: Harcourt Brace Jovanovich, 1998.

The staying power of the *Harbrace College Handbook* can be attributed to its straightforward instruction in grammar, mechanics, and punctuation. It provides a wide variety of excellent examples and leads the reader through the information in a logical and concise manner. It includes the Modern Language Association documentation guide.

Strunk, William Jr., and E. B. White. *Elements of Style*, 4th ed. New York: Longman, 2000.

This is one of the standards in the composition field, and for a very good reason: in fewer than 100 pages, Strunk effectively communicates the most important aspects of good writing.

Chapter 21

Sample Report

Fair Market Value of a Noncontrolling Ownership Interest in the Common Stock of Warm Chicken Company as of December 31, 2004

Introduction
  Description of the Assignment
  Summary Description of the Company
  Capitalization and Ownership
  Sources of Information
Analysis of the U.S. Economy
  Overview
  Outlook
Analysis of the Poultry Processing Industry
  Overview
  The Current Market
  Exports
Identification of Guideline Companies
  Overview
  Descriptions of Selected Guideline Companies
Financial Statement Analysis
  Overview
  Balance Sheets
Income Statements
  Cash Flow Statements
  Adjustments
  Financial and Operating Ratios
Valuation of Common Stock
  Overview
  The Guideline Publicly Traded Company Method
  The Discounted Cash Flow Method
Overall Valuation Conclusion
  Discount for Lack of Marketability
  Summary and Conclusion of Empirical Research
  Selection of the Applicable Lack of Marketability Discount for a Warm
      Chicken Noncontrolling Ownership Interest

This report was revised from the previous edition by Chad Phillips.

Warm Chicken Company is a sample case contrived to illustrate the application of many of the principles and procedures presented in several chapters of this book.

This is a hypothetical company and is not intended to be patterned after any real-world company. The reader should not be concerned whether or not any of the assumptions bear resemblance to the reader's perception of reality in the poultry industry. The point of the case is to demonstrate an example of a valuation report and to illustrate, by example, the application of some of the procedures commonly used in valuation reports.

Introduction

Description of the Assignment

We were retained by Warm Chicken Company ("Warm Chicken" or "the Company") to provide our opinion of the fair market value of Warm Chicken's common stock on a nonmarketable, noncontrolling ownership interest basis, as of December 31, 2004 (the "valuation date"), to assist with a contemplated 5.45 percent ownership interest gift of common stock. A summary of our valuation is presented as Exhibit 21–1. All exhibits in this report are presented at the end of this chapter.

Standard and Definition of Value. The appropriate standard of value for federal gift tax purposes is fair market value. The Treasury Regulations define fair market value as follows:

> The price at which such property would change hands between a willing buyer and a willing seller, neither being under any compulsion to buy or to sell, and both having reasonable knowledge of relevant facts.[1]

Court decisions frequently state in addition that the hypothetical buyer and seller are assumed to be able, as well as willing, to trade and to be well informed about the property and the market for such property.

Our valuation analysis takes into consideration Revenue Ruling 59–60, which outlines and reviews the general factors to be considered in the valuation of the capital stock of closely held companies and thinly traded public corporations, as follows:

1. The nature of the business and the history of the enterprise from its inception
2. The economic outlook in general and the conditions and outlook of the specific industry in particular
3. The book value of the stock and the financial condition of the business
4. The earning capacity of the company
5. The dividend-paying capacity
6. Whether or not the enterprise has goodwill or other intangible value
7. Sales of the stock and the size of the block of stock to be valued
8. The market prices of stocks of corporations engaged in the same or a similar line of business, having their stocks actively traded in a free and open market, either on an exchange or over the counter[2]

---

[1] Gift Tax Reg. §25.2512-1.
[2] Rev. Rul. 59–60, 1959-1 C.B. 237.

Summary Description of the Company

Warm Chicken was founded by Simon P. Warm in 1920 as a table egg poultry farm in Galena, Illinois. Today Warm Chicken is a fully integrated producer, processor, marketer, and distributor of fresh and processed poultry products.

The Company's focus on providing a quality products is reflected by the fact that it averages two to three times more quality control checks than required by the USDA and provides a money-back guarantee to consumers.

As of December 31, 2004, the Company was headquartered in Chicago, Illinois, and operated out of five production facilities throughout the Midwest. Product sales are currently concentrated throughout the Midwest. The Company's goal is to supply food services nationwide.

Capitalization and Ownership

Warm Chicken is a closely held company capitalized with one class of common stock that has a par value of $0.10.

The Company's common stock is owned 93.0 percent by the Warm family and 7.0 percent by various members of the Company management and directors. Exhibit 21–2 presents a detailed list of the Company's shareholders, along with their respective ownership percentages.

As of the valuation date, there were 5,000,000 shares of common stock authorized and 1,577,420 shares issued and outstanding.

Shareholders	Number of Common Shares Outstanding	% of Total Shares Outstanding
Simon P. Warm	733,500	46.5
Jake Warm	366,750	23.3
Sydney Warm	183,375	11.6
Gayle Warm	183,375	11.6
Paige Poulet	44,168	2.8
Alan Abacus	44,168	2.8
Fred Fryer	22,084	1.4
Total	1,577,420	100.0

Sources of Information

We used the following information and documents in the valuation analysis:

1. Company audited financial statements for the fiscal years ended March 31, 2000 through 2004.
2. Company unaudited financial statements for the nine-month periods ended December 31, 2003 and 2004.
3. Management's financial projections for the fiscal years ending March 31, 2005 through 2009.
4. Company's summary operating plan, overhead budget, and capital budget for fiscal year 2005.

5. Summary of product and divisional financial information for the 12 months ended December 31, 2004.
6. Schedule of ownership of common stock outstanding as of December 31, 2004.
7. In our analysis of the U.S. economy, we relied on information from *Forecast 2003-2004*, First Interstate Bancorp; *Business Week; The Wall Street Journal; Outlook and Trends & Projections*, Standard & Poor's Corporation; *U.S. Financial Data*, Federal Reserve Bank of St. Louis; *Economic Trends*, Federal Reserve Bank of Cleveland; *Barron's; Reuters; Nation's Business; United & Babson Investment Report*; and *The Outlook for Interest Rates and the Economy in 2004*, Sheshunoff Information Services, Inc.
8. In our analysis of the poultry industry, we relied on information from *Watt Poultry Yearbook 2004, Industry Surveys*, Standard & Poor's, *Livestock, Poultry, and Dairy Situation and Outlook*, Economic Research Service of the U.S. Department of Agriculture; *Feedstuffs; Journal of Commerce & Commercial*; and Warm Chicken management.
9. For financial and descriptive information on publicly traded guideline companies, we relied upon information from Securities and Exchange Commission Forms 10-K and 10-Q, annual reports to shareholders, Standard & Poor's *Compustat* and *Dialog-on-Disc*, and Disclosure's *Compact D/SEC*.

In addition, we conducted interviews with Warm Chicken's management at the Company's headquarters in Chicago, Illinois.

Analysis of the U.S. Economy

In the valuation of any business interest, the general economic outlook as of the valuation date should be considered, since the national economic outlook influences how investors perceive alternative investment opportunities at any given time. In our analysis, we considered the general economic climate that prevailed at the end of 2004.

Overview

The U.S. economy expanded faster than expected in the last quarter of 2004. Gross domestic product (GDP) surged ahead at a 5.6 percent rate for the quarter, the fastest pace in two and one-half years, while inflation was near a 40-year low. GDP growth for all of 2004 matched 2003's advance. The United States, however, was an island of prosperity amid global chaos in Asia, Latin America, and Russia. U.S. consumers accounted for much of the economic growth in 2004, spurred by low inflation, low interest rates, and low unemployment. There were worker shortages in some industries. Despite increases in GDP, manufacturing activity weakened during most of the year.

On November 17, 2004, the Federal Reserve Board reduced interest rates for the third time in seven weeks to cushion the U.S. financial system against the spillover from financial turmoil in Russia. After each of the Federal Reserve Bank's interest rate cuts, major banks cut their prime rate.

The U.S. Labor Department reported that energy prices decreased in 2004. Food prices increased moderately, and prescription drug and education costs both jumped significantly. New car prices were unchanged and clothing costs were down slightly for the year. Computer prices fell substantially in 2004.

Nonfarm payroll employment increased moderately in December 2004. More service jobs were created than manufacturing jobs destroyed by the Asian crisis. The year 2004 had the strongest job market in 41 years. Unemployment in December 2004 decreased slightly.

The employment cost index, which measures wages, salaries, and fringe benefits, increased modestly in the fourth quarter of 2004. Wages and salaries increased moderately in 2004, as did employee benefit costs and personal income.

Consumer spending increased moderately in 2004's fourth quarter. Likewise, spending on durable goods also increased, albeit at a rate higher than consumer spending. For the entire year, consumer spending was ahead moderately.

The Dow Jones Industrial Average closed out 2004 by gaining 16.0 percent for the entire year. The Standard & Poor's 500 index gained 26.7 percent, and the Nasdaq Composite index gained 39.6 percent. It was the fourth consecutive year with gains of more than 20.0 percent in the S&P 500 and the Nasdaq Composite.

During 2004, a global slump decreased foreign demand for many American-made goods, but domestic demand remained strong. For all of 2004, new orders for durable goods had the smallest gain since 1991. In December 2004, durable goods orders increased slightly.

After decreasing during the third quarter of 2004, capital goods spending by businesses increased in the last quarter of 2004. Companies faced a tighter labor market and scrambled to improve labor productivity and keep costs in control.

Outlook

Estimating economic growth for 2005 was more difficult than usual for economists because of a myriad of global uncertainties. The consensus estimate of the 54 economists polled by *The Wall Street Journal* at the end of 2004, however, called for continued growth in 2005, albeit at a slower pace than in 2004. One reason given for the slowdown in economic growth was that companies were experiencing a profit squeeze, which could produce a slowdown in capital spending. Many of the surveyed economists believed that inflation would increase slightly in 2005, and a majority thought there was a chance the stock market would enter a bear market during the year. More crises abroad could crimp growth in the U.S. economy in 2005. The Company is not overly worried about a negative impact on the poultry industry, since poultry consumption has not been shown to vary significantly with changes in U.S. prosperity.

Analysis of the Poultry Processing Industry

As an integrated poultry processing company, Warm Chicken's performance is directly related to the poultry processing industry. As part of our analysis, we researched the poultry processing industry in order to determine the current state of the industry as well as to identify any trends that may affect the industry in the future.

Overview

Beginning in the early 1930s, the poultry industry was dominated by many small growers and processors. The U.S. poultry business evolved into a vertically integrated industry in the mid-1930s, in which a few top companies accounted for most of the country's broiler and turkey production. Vertical integration combined the previously independent and fragmented operation of feedmills, hatcheries, farms, slaughterers, and processors into giant conglomerates that managed all stages of production.

Broilers, which are chickens raised specifically for table consumption, represented by far the largest segment of the industry, with the value of production exceeding $11.8 billion in 2004, compared with $3 billion for turkey. Other poultry, such as ducks and geese, accounted for only about $300 million in industry sales. Broiler production is mainly concentrated in 17 southeastern states on the eastern seaboard and along the Gulf of Mexico. This so-called "broiler belt" is the source of 90 percent of production.

Profitability in the poultry industry is related to consumer demand and feed grain prices. Feed grain accounts for approximately 50 percent of the cost of poultry production. An agricultural business such as Warm Chicken, which purchases and sells perishable commodities, is cyclical and very sensitive to market supply and demand pressures. Supply and demand are affected by such factors as weather conditions, pricing and supply of alternative products, changes in export markets, government policy, and current industry production capacity.

Demand for consumer food products is affected significantly by population growth. The U.S. population is expanding by less than 1 percent annually, and immigrants constitute about one-fourth of this increase. The population is continuing to age as the size of the average U.S. household shrinks. A shift in demographics is expected as the population age groups above 40 years of age constitute a larger total percentage of the population. The diet concerns of an aging population combined with the recent focus on health concerns has already affected U.S. food consumption. Consumers are eating more poultry and fish, and less red meat, as a result of those concerns.

The increased demand for poultry products has encouraged the introduction of several value-added products such as ground turkey, chicken nuggets, and other convenience-type poultry products. The favorable reception of rotisserie chicken in fast-food outlets has also increased demand. This could result in slightly higher margins on average.

The Current Market

The U.S. poultry industry is dominated by several large, vertically integrated companies, with approximately 65 percent of total production concentrated among the top 10 firms.

Exports

After experiencing a near decade of double-digit export growth, U.S. poultry exports faltered in 2004 as bind flu affected the market for poultry. Despite a last-minute rally by U.S. broiler exports in December 2004, poultry meat exports came in 2 percent below those of 2003—the first export decline since 1984.

The 2005 outlook for U.S. poultry meat shipments remains lackluster. Slowing international demand for poultry meat, aggravated by concern about the bird flu, is expected to exert downward pressure on poultry exports, by an additional 5 percent in 2005.

Lower prices, and a slight recovery in consumer demand in Hong Kong/China, induced recovery in shipments to Hong Kong (up 13 percent); exports to Mexico, and Japan followed suit (both up 11 percent). Price responsiveness was revealed in some of the smaller markets in Latin America, the Caribbean, and the Middle East also, with shipments to those regions increasing 42 percent in 2004.

Uncertainty characterizes the 2005 outlook for U.S. broiler meat with import demand hinging on the economic environment in Russia and China and the ability of the U.S. industry to adhere to Mexico's Avian Influenza (AI) regulations. In addition, the devaluation of the Brazilian real will test the United States' ability to compete effectively in the Japanese market.

Against these competing factors, U.S. poultry exports in 2005 are forecast to drop 5 percent to 2.4 million tons. As broiler meat shipments slide (forecast at 2 million tons), exports will account for 15 percent of domestic output, down from the peak of 17 percent in 2003.

Constrained export prospects for U.S. poultry meat in 2005 contrasts with the overall favorable outlook for the entire U.S. broiler industry. Despite low leg-quarter prices, domestic broiler meat prices have remained robust and, combined with low feed prices, are generating favorable net returns for the industry. Consequently U.S. production is predicted to increase by 5 percent to 15.8 million tons.

Sluggish demand for the overall U.S. poultry export market is occurring against a backdrop of increasing broiler meat output in 2005. U.S. broiler production in 2004, beset by hatchery supply flock problems and higher heat-induced bird mortality, experienced the slowest output growth since 1982.

Constrained production gains and strong domestic demand from the fast-food sector allowed the U.S. industry, despite record U.S. meat supplies and declining export prices, to maintain relatively high broiler prices in 2004. These robust prices, combined with the lowest feed costs since 1987, supported producer net returns in 2004 that were considerably higher than five-year averages.

Favorable producer returns are prompting a rise in anticipated U.S. broiler production of 5 to 6 percent in 2005. Indicators reveal that the industry's planned expansion includes (1) large increases in the broiler-type chick hatch, (2) a 3 to 5 percent increase in egg sets in incubators for broiler production, and (3) a steady increase in average unit weight gain as the industry moves to produce heavy broilers for cut-ups.

Identification of Guideline Companies

Overview

In order to gain market-derived pricing guidance from the guideline publicly traded company valuation method, the valuation analyst should identify a group of publicly traded companies that are similar to the subject company from an investment perspective. The first step in finding such guideline companies is to identify the most appropriate Standard Industrial Classification (SIC) code. Warm Chicken most closely resembles companies in the following SIC codes:

SIC 0251:   Broiler, Fryer & Roaster Chickens
SIC 0252:   Chicken Eggs
SIC 0259:   Poultry and Eggs, Not Elsewhere Classified
SIC 2015:   Poultry Slaughtering & Processing

We performed a search for publicly traded companies with SIC codes of 0251, 0252, 0259, and 2015. Standard & Poor's *Dialog-on-Disc* provides detailed information on more than 12,000 publicly traded companies. Detailed descriptions of the general operations, plant locations, subsidiaries, financial structure, and securities of these public companies are available. Disclosure's *Compact D/SEC* provides detailed information on more than 15,000 public companies. All information in these databases is updated monthly from various documents filed with the SEC.

From these databases, we obtained information on numerous potential guideline companies. Our next step was to identify companies that satisfied the following criteria:

- Industry and specific business lines that are comparable to Warm Chicken
- Relative asset size and revenues that are comparable to Warm Chicken
- Absolute and relative values of earnings and cash flow that are comparable to Warm Chicken
- Information on each guideline company was available for the entire relevant time period

Some of the most common reasons for rejection at this point were:

- Company serves unrelated business or geographic markets
- Company is too diversified
- Company is in poor financial condition
- Company has a pending merger/acquisition

After giving consideration to the above selection criteria, it was determined that five companies were most comparable to Warm Chicken. A description of each of the five comparable companies follows.

Descriptions of Selected Guideline Companies

Cagle's, Inc. Cagle's, Inc. ("Cagle's") operates an integrated poultry enterprise, including the breeding, hatching, raising, and feeding of chickens, and the processing and marketing of fresh and frozen poultry products.

Cagle's products are sold to national and regional independent and chain supermarkets, food distributors, food processing companies, national fast-food chains, and institutional users, such as restaurants, schools, and distributors.

Pilgrim's Pride Corporation. Pilgrim's Pride Corporation ("Pilgrim") produces chicken products and controls the breeding, hatching, and growing of chickens and the processing, preparation, and packaging of its product lines. Pilgrim also produces table eggs, animal feeds, and ingredients.

Pilgrim is one of the largest producers of prepared and fresh chicken products in North America and has one of the best known brand names in the chicken industry.

Pilgrim is the fourth largest producer of chicken in the United States and one of the two largest in Mexico.

Products consist mainly of prepared foods, including portion-controlled breast fillets, tenderloins and strips, formed nuggets, patties, and bone-in chicken parts, which are sold frozen and may be either fully cooked or raw; fresh chicken, including refrigerated (nonfrozen) whole or cut-up chicken, sold to the food service industry either premarinated or nonmarinated, and prepackaged chicken, including various combinations of freshly refrigerated, whole chickens and chicken parts in trays, bags, or other consumer packs, labeled and priced, ready for the retail grocer's fresh meat counter; and bulk packaged chicken, including parts and whole chicken, either refrigerated or frozen for U.S. export or domestic use.

Pilgrim also sells fresh eggs under the Pilgrim's Pride brand name as well as under private labels in various sizes of cartons and flats to domestic retail grocery and institutional food service customers located mainly in Texas. Pilgrim has a housing capacity for about 2.3 million commercial egg laying hens that can produce about 41 million dozen eggs annually.

Sanderson Farms, Inc. Sanderson Farms, Inc. ("Sanderson") produces, processes, markets, and distributes fresh and frozen chicken, and processes, markets, and distributes processed and prepared food items.

Sanderson sells its chicken products under the Sanderson Farms brand name to retailers, distributors, and fast-food operators in the southeastern, southwestern, and western United States. Through its foods division, Sanderson also sells over 200 processed and prepared frozen entrees and other specialty food products to distributors, food service establishments, and retailers.

Seaboard Corporation. Seaboard Corporation ("Seaboard"), a diversified international agribusiness and transportation company, processes poultry and pork; operates an ocean liner service for containerized cargo; operates bakeries in Puerto Rico; trades commodities; produces and processes fruits, vegetables, shrimp, and pen-raised salmon; produces polypropylene bags; operates power generation facilities; and mills flour.

Seaboard produces and processes poultry in the United States and sells processed chicken and chicken parts, both directly and through commercial distributors, to retail, food service, and institutional markets, primarily in the eastern half of the United States. Seaboard also produces hogs and processes pork in the United States and sells fresh pork to domestic and foreign markets. Ocean liner service is operated between Florida and ports in Central and South America and the Caribbean Basin. Seaboard also operates bulk carriers primarily in the Atlantic Basin. In Puerto Rico, Seaboard mills four and produces and distributes a full line of baked goods. These goods are distributed directly within Puerto Rico and neighboring islands to food-service and retail outlets. Commodities traded, primarily in the Eastern Mediterranean and the Atlantic Basin, include bulk grains and oil seeds.

Tyson Foods. Tyson Foods, Inc. ("Tyson") produces, distributes, and markets chicken, beef, pork, prepared foods and related allied products.

Tyson's operations consist of breeding and raising chickens as well as the processing, further processing, and marketing of related products, including animal and pet food ingredients.

Wal-Mart Stores accounted for approximately 13 percent of Tyson's consolidated sales during the fiscal year ended October 1, 2004 (fiscal 2004). Tyson exported to more than 80 foreign countries in fiscal 2004.

Financial Statement Analysis

Overview

An important step in the valuation of any company is an analysis of its financial performance over time. Past sales and earnings growth can provide an indication of future growth and can put a company's earnings in a historical context. Other things being equal, a company with rapidly rising sales and earnings is worth more than one with little or no growth.

The following section examines significant trends in Warm Chicken's balance sheets, income statements, statements of cash flow, and pertinent financial ratios over the past five years. In addition, the Company's financial performance is compared to its peers in the poultry industry as a means of measuring the Company's relative historical performance.

Balance Sheets

Exhibit 21–3 presents Warm Chicken's balance sheets as of March 31, 2000, through December 31, 2004.

Over this period, total assets increased $126.2 million, from $191.7 million at March 31, 2000, to $317.9 million as of December 31, 2004. As of December 31, 2004, net property, plant, and equipment accounted for the largest percentage of total assets at 35.2 percent. Other assets increased from $4.3 million at March 31, 2000, to $48.2 million at March 31, 2001. Most of the increase in other assets may be attributed to an increase in intangible assets.

Total liabilities increased $88.9 million, from $81.5 million at March 31, 2000, to $170.4 million at December 31, 2004. Most of this increase may be attributed to an increase in interest-bearing debt. Over the past five years, interest-bearing debt increased from $14.5 million (representing 7.6 percent of total liabilities and stockholders' equity) to $67.2 million (representing 21.1 percent of total liabilities and stockholders' equity).

Stockholders' equity increased $37.4 million, from $110.2 million at March 31, 2000, to a five-year high of $147.6 million at December 31, 2004.

Income Statements

Exhibit 21–4 represents Warm Chicken's income statements for fiscal years ended March 31, 2000 through 2004, and the latest 12-month (LTM) period ended December 31, 2004.

The table below presents the Company's annual revenues over the past five fiscal years and the LTM period.

	LTM Ended	Fiscal Years Ended March 31,				
	12/04 $000	2004 $000	2003 $000	2002 $000	2001 $000	2000 $000
Net Sales	754,600	743,999	725,015	635,970	501,378	450,311
Growth (%)	1.4	2.6	14.0	26.8	11.3	15.0

As presented, the Company reported increases in sales in each of the past five years. However, sales growth has declined from a five-year high of 26.8 percent in fiscal 2002 to a five-year low of 1.4 percent in the LTM period. Net sales increased $304.3 million, or 11.5 percent compounded annually, between fiscal 2000 and the LTM period. Warm Chicken's 11.5 percent revenue growth over the past five years exceeded the guideline companies' median growth rate of 8.8 percent over the five-year period reviewed.

Cost of products sold increased $257.3 million, from $389.4 million in fiscal 2000 to $646.7 million in the LTM period. More importantly, cost of products sold as a percentage of revenues increased from 86.5 percent in fiscal 2000 to a five-year high of 90.4 percent in fiscal 2004. This increase was mainly the result of an increase in average grain prices.

The poultry industry is extremely dependent on the cost of key inputs. Consequently, the Company's profitability has been volatile. For instance, the Company's pretax profit margin increased from 3.4 percent in fiscal 2000 to a five-year average high of 5.4 percent in fiscal 2001. Pretax margins declined sharply in 2002, improving thereafter to 4.7 percent in the LTM period, up from 0.6 percent in 2004.

Cash Flow Statements

Exhibit 21–5 presents the company's historical cash flow statement.

Adjustments

In estimating an indication of value for a company, it is sometimes necessary to make adjustments to the company's historical balance sheets and income statements in order to eliminate items such as nonoperating assets and nonrecurring or unusual income or expense. Exhibit 21–8 presents the adjustments we made to Warm Chicken's earnings.

Financial and Operating Ratios

Exhibit 21–6 presents pertinent financial and operating ratios for Warm Chicken for the fiscal years ended March 31, 2000 through 2004, and for the LTM period ended December 31, 2004. Exhibit 21–7 presents comparative ratios for Warm Chicken and the five guideline publicly traded companies.

The current and quick ratios provide a rough indication of a company's liquidity (i.e., the degree to which current liabilities are covered by the most liquid assets). For Warm Chicken, these measures of liquidity decreased from 2.5 and 0.9, respectively, at March 31, 2000, to 1.8 and 0.7, respectively, at December 31, 2004.

Working capital, another measure of liquidity, reflects a company's ability to finance current operations. Warm Chicken's working capital increased from $60.4 million at March 31, 2000, to $69.9 million at December 31, 2004.

Activity ratios indicate how efficiently a company utilizes its assets. Warm Chicken's activity ratios indicate fairly consistent performance during the five-year period. Inventory turnover decreased from 6.9 at March 31, 2000, to 6.5 at December 31, 2004. The Company's operating cycle increased from 70 days at March 31, 2000, to 77 days at December 31, 2004.

Coverage ratios and debt ratios provide an indication of how heavily leveraged a company is. Highly leveraged companies are more vulnerable to business downturns than those with lower interest-bearing debt positions. Warm Chicken's interest expense ratios have improved since fiscal 2002, but were, nevertheless, below pre-2002 levels. The Company's debt/equity ratio has decreased since fiscal 2002 as a result of a decrease in interest-bearing debt.

In addition to indicating profits and returns over a period, profitability ratios assist in evaluating management performance. As previously mentioned, the cyclicality of the poultry industry has a strong influence on the Company's profitability. As shown in Exhibit 21–6, all of Warm Chicken's profitability ratios have increased since fiscal 2002. Consequently, return on investment increased from a negative 1.8 in fiscal 2002 to 10.2 in the LTM period. This financial strength leads us to believe that the Company is not significantly more risky in operating characteristics than the guideline publicly traded companies.

Valuation of Common Stock

Overview

In general, the factors outlined in Revenue Ruling 59-60 can be categorized into three general approaches for valuing the common stock of closely held companies. Valuation analysts use one or more of these three approaches to estimate the value of closely held company common stock. Of course, the objective of using more than one approach is to develop mutually supporting evidence as to the conclusion of value.

While the specific titles of these three approaches may vary, the generic names are as follows:

1. Market approach
2. Income approach
3. Asset-based approach

After giving consideration to each of these approaches, we concluded that two approaches are the most relevant for our analysis of Warm Chicken's common stock: (1) the market approach, particularly the guideline publicly traded company method, and (2) the income approach, particularly the discounted cash flow method.

We considered the asset-based approach, but we did not rely upon this approach. This is because a noncontrolling equity owner in Warm Chicken does not have access to the value of the underlying assets.

The Guideline Publicly Traded Company Method

It has been stated that values are best determined and tested in the marketplace. One of the fundamental approaches to estimating the value of a closely held company is to look to the public market for evidence of the prices investors are willing to pay for similarly situated companies. Such a comparison to "guideline" publicly traded companies is the basis of the guideline publicly traded company method.

The following section outlines the theory, procedures, and conclusions of our analysis using the guideline publicly traded company method.

Valuation Theory and Procedures. There are four primary steps involved in the guideline publicly traded company method:

1. Identification of guideline publicly traded companies
2. Calculation of market-derived pricing multiples based upon the guideline companies' trading prices and financial fundamentals
3. Selection of appropriate market-derived pricing multiples to be applied to Warm Chicken's financial fundamentals
4. Calculation of indicated values for Warm Chicken based upon the application of the selected market pricing multiples

Qualitative Adjustment. In order to make an accurate comparison between Warm Chicken and the guideline publicly traded companies, we applied a qualitative adjustment to the market-derived pricing multiples selected in our analysis. This adjustment is necessary to reflect the modest additional risk factors inherent in an investment in Warm Chicken compared with an investment in the guideline companies. Such factors include:

1. **Geographical diversification.** Several of the guideline companies have significantly wider market territories than does Warm Chicken. Warm Chicken's operations are concentrated in the Midwest. As a result, the Company has greater exposure to regional economic fluctuations.
2. **Product-line diversification.** Several of the guideline companies have significantly broader product lines than Warm Chicken. Warm Chicken offers primarily chicken products while several of the guideline companies offer chicken, turkey, beef, pork, and even seafood products. As a result, Warm Chicken has greater exposure to fluctuating consumer tastes and demands.

Within the guideline publicly traded company method, we used an invested capital valuation method. The following section discusses the invested capital valuation method.

Invested Capital Valuation Method. An invested capital valuation method is commonly used in the valuation of closely held companies in order to minimize the differences between the subject company and the guideline companies, which may have significantly different capital structures. Certain adjustments are made to the financial fundamentals of both the subject and the guideline companies in order to minimize the effects of leverage on the companies' capital structures. These adjustments consist primarily of adding back interest expense to the relevant earnings measure.

Since the effects of leverage are minimized, the invested capital valuation method results in a value indication for a company's total capital (including both interest-bearing debt and equity). For purposes of our analysis, we refer to this indication of value as the *market value of invested capital* (MVIC), which we define as follows:

	Market value of short-term interest-bearing debt
+	Market value of long-term interest-bearing debt, including capitalized leases
+	Market value of preferred stock outstanding
+	Market value of common stock outstanding
=	Market value of invested capital

Since MVIC consists of the market-derived pricing value of both debt and equity, the value of Warm Chicken's interest-bearing debt should be subtracted from its MVIC in order to arrive at a value indication for its total stockholders' equity.

We calculated the following market-derived pricing multiples in the invested capital valuation method of our guideline publicly traded method analysis:

1. MVIC/earnings before interest and taxes (EBIT)
2. MVIC/earnings before interest, taxes, depreciation, and amortization (EBITDA)
3. MVIC/revenues

We calculated these market-derived pricing multiples on both an LTM and five-year average basis.

The invested capital valuation method relies upon the five publicly traded companies described above in the section on identification of guideline companies. The calculations of invested capital market pricing multiples are presented in Exhibit 21–9A.

MVIC/EBIT. Exhibit 21–9B presents the five guideline companies' EBIT performance in comparison to each other and Warm Chicken for the past five years. Warm Chicken's EBIT increased at a compound annual growth rate of 18.1 percent during the past five years as compared to median and low compound growth rates of 34.4 and 27.0 percent, respectively, for the selected guideline companies.

Last 12 Months. The MVIC/EBIT multiple for the guideline companies ranged from 5.1 to 10.4 with a mean of 6.6 and a median of 5.5.

Based on Warm Chicken's below average EBIT growth rate and below average EBIT return on revenues (see Exhibit 21–9E) it is our opinion that Warm Chicken would command an MVIC/EBIT multiple lower than the low end of the range exhibited by the guideline companies, i.e., 5.1.

Applying the selected pricing multiple of 3.4 to the LTM EBIT of $36,355,000 results in a market value of invested capital of $123,610,000.

Five-Year Average. Five-year average EBIT multiples ranged from a low of 12.0 to a high of 14.9, with a mean of 13.6 and a median of 13.8.

Warm Chicken's five-year average EBIT profit margin of 3.0 percent is below average relative to the guideline company average of 4.6 percent, and excluding Seaboard, which reported an EBIT deficit, was below average relative to all other selected guideline companies. Consequently, it is our opinion that Warm Chicken would command an MVIC/EBIT multiple lower than the low end of the range exhibited by the guideline companies, i.e., 12.0.

Applying the selected pricing multiple of 8.0 to Warm Chicken's five-year average EBIT of $19,199,000 results in a market value of invested capital of $153,591,000.

MVIC/EBITDA. Exhibit 21–9C presents the five guideline companies' EBITDA performance in comparison to each other and Warm Chicken for the past five years. Warm Chicken's EBITDA increased at a compound annual growth rate of 13.8 percent during the past five years as compared to median and low compound growth rates of 29.6 and 22.7 percent, respectively, for the selected guideline companies.

Depreciation and amortization are noncash items used by companies to decrease their operating earnings to result in lower taxable income. Eliminating the effects of depreciation and amortization in a company provides a more realistic earnings level for that company. The more capital-intensive a company is, the greater the difference will be between EBIT and EBITDA. The poultry industry is extremely capital intensive. For example, four out of five guideline companies, as well as the subject company, have an EBITDA fundamental that is significantly greater than their respective EBIT fundamental.

	LTM Financial Fundamentals	
	EBIT **$000**	**EBITDA** **$000**
Cagle's	61,430	NA
Pilgrim's Pride	150,837	177,163
Sanderson Farms	256,942	321,562
Seaboard	17,993	21,856
Tyson Foods	886,000	1,359,000
Warm Chicken Company	36,355	56,719

Last 12 Months. The MVIC/EBITDA pricing multiple for the guideline companies ranged from 4.2 to 6.8 with a mean of 5.0 and a median of 4.5.

Based on Warm Chicken's below average EBITDA growth rate and below average EBITDA return on revenues (see Exhibit 21–9E), it is our opinion that Warm Chicken would command an MVIC/EBITDA multiple lower than the low end of the range exhibited by the guideline companies, i.e., 4.2.

Applying the selected pricing multiple of 2.8 to the LTM EBITDA of $56,719,000 for Warm Chicken results in a market value of invested capital of $158,810,000.

Five-Year Average. Five-year average EBITDA multiples were also examined. These multiples ranged from a low of 8.7 to a high of 29.3, with a mean of 13.0 and a median of 8.9.

Warm Chicken's five-year average EBITDA profit margin of 6.1 percent was below average relative to the guideline company average of 7.5 percent. Accordingly, it is our opinion that Warm Chicken would command an MVIC/EBITDA multiple lower than the low end of the range exhibited by the guideline companies, i.e., 8.7.

Applying the selected pricing multiple of 5.8 to Warm Chicken's five-year average EBITDA of $38,579,000 results in a market value of invested capital of $223,756,000.

MVIC/Revenues. Exhibit 21–9D presents the historical revenues reported by the guideline companies and Warm Chicken and Exhibit 21–9E presents various returns on revenues for both the LTM and five-year average.

A revenue-based valuation method can be considered a derivative of an earnings-based valuation method, since generally there is an implicit assumption that a certain level of revenues should be able to generate a certain level of earnings in a given type of business.

In selecting a multiple of revenues to apply to the revenues of Warm Chicken, we reviewed returns on revenues investors are willing to pay. The following table presents the EBITDA returns and the MVIC/revenues pricing multiples for the guideline companies.

	LTM EBITDA Return on Revenues	MVIC/LTM Revenues
Cagle's	22.8	0.81
Pilgrim's Pride	16.8	0.78
Sanderson Farms	12.0	0.53
Seaboard	(4.4)	0.37
Tyson Foods	5.2	0.35
Warm Chicken Company	7.5	NM

Applying the selected pricing multiple of 0.23 to Warm Chicken's LTM revenues of $754,600,000 results in a market value of invested capital of $173,560,000.

A similar pattern exists when looking at the five-year average for both the guideline companies and Warm Chicken. Based on the foregoing, it is our opinion that an MVIC/five-year average revenue multiple of 0.19 is appropriate for Warm Chicken.

Applying the selected pricing multiple of 0.19 to Warm Chicken's five-year average revenues of $635,212,000 results in a market value of invested capital of $120,690,000.

Summary of Indicated Values. The indicated values for the guideline publicly traded company method are summarized in Exhibit 21–10.

As presented in Exhibit 21–10, this method resulted in a range of indicated values—from a low of $120,690,000 to a high of $223,756,000. Since we are estimating an indication of value of the Company on a going-concern basis, we placed primary emphasis on the Company's earnings capacity. We also gave equal weighting to the LTM period and the five-year average. As a result, this method resulted in an indicated MVIC of approximately $159,000,000.

The Discounted Cash Flow Method

Overview. The second method that we relied on was the discounted cash flow (DCF) method of the income approach. This method is intuitively appealing since it reflects the tradeoff between risk and expected return that is critical to the investment process. Generally, common stocks are purchased in light of anticipated stock price appreciation, which, in turn, is strongly influenced by expectations about a company's cash flow capacity.

The discounted cash flow method estimates value on the basis of future return flows over an investment horizon using empirical market data, macroeconomic and industry evidence, and the underlying fundamental trends for the subject company. The DCF method then applies a present value discount rate, known as the required rate of return on investment, to the projected future cash flows, which results in an estimation of the net present value of a series of cash flows. Exhibit 21–11 presents the pro forma consolidated income statements that are the basic for the valuation by the DCF method.

We conducted the DCF method on an after-tax, invested capital basis, and we selected net cash flow as the measure of economic income. We used an invested capital method to eliminate the impact of the Company's leverage on the value of the Company's common stock.

The DCF method estimates the value of a company by projecting the cash flows that the Company is expected to produce and discounting those cash flows back to the valuation date using a discount rate that reflects the related risk and the time value of money. This method requires an in-depth analysis of the Company's revenues, fixed and variable expenses, and capital structure.

The DCF method can result in an indication of value on either a controlling ownership interest or a noncontrolling ownership interest basis, depending on (1) the nature of the cash flows, and (2) the discount rate that have been incorporated in the analysis. In this case, we did not incorporate any adjustments to the Company's results of operations or to its capital structure that would be considered of a controlling ownership interest nature. Therefore, our DCF analysis results in an indication of value on a noncontrolling ownership interest basis.

Valuation Calculations. The variables and calculations essential to our analysis using the DCF method are outlined below.

Present Value Discount Rate. In a rational investment environment, an investor faces various alternatives for investing current funds, all of which may earn future returns to compensate for: (1) the time the invested funds are committed, (2) the expected rate of inflation or loss of purchasing power experienced over the investment time horizon, and (3) the relative uncertainty of the future returns. The expected return on investment is therefore a function of the investment risk inherent in the future returns.

We estimated the appropriate present value discount rate for Warm Chicken's projected cash flows by analyzing the Company's weighted average cost of capital (WACC). The WACC incorporates the present cost of the Company's debt capital and equity capital as determined from market-derived empirical evidence. These capital costs, expressed as required rates of return, are then weighted according to the Company's capital structure (calculated on an estimated market value basis).

We estimated the cost of Warm Chicken's debt capital by analyzing the current rates on its various debt issues. Since corporate interest expense is tax deductible, we estimated the Company's after-tax cost of debt to be approximately 4.80 percent $(0.08 \times [1 - 0.40])$, using management's projected income tax rate of 40.0 percent.

We estimated the cost of Warm Chicken's equity capital using the capital asset pricing model (CAPM) which incorporates certain market rates of return and risk premiums, including: (1) a risk-free rate, (2) a long-term equity risk premium, (3) an industry beta, (4) a size premium, and (5) a company-specific risk premium. Each of these factors is discussed below.

Since our DCF analysis is based upon a long-term investment horizon, the appropriate risk-free rate is represented by a long-term government security. The most appropriate proxy for this rate is the yield to maturity of long-term (20-year) U.S. Treasury bonds. These bonds yielded approximately 4.9 percent as of the valuation date.

Historical equity risk premiums are quantified annually by Ibbotson Associates[3]. Ibbotson calculates the long-term equity risk premium as the total annual rates of return from common stocks less the long-term rates of return on 20-year U.S. Treasury bonds. According to the Ibbotson data, the arithmetic mean risk premium for the period 1926 to 2004 was approximately 7.2 percent. Chapter 9, "Income Approach: Discounted Future Economic Income Method," discusses alternative sources for the equity risk premium and also presents research that shows that the historical ERP may overstate the forward looking ERP.

Beta is a measure of the systematic risk inherent in a company's investment returns. We calculated betas for the five guideline publicly traded companies used in our guideline publicly traded company analysis. We unlevered and relevered the guideline companies' betas—as well as the selected beta for Warm Chicken—in order to eliminate any significant differences in capital structure. We used this beta

---

[3] *Stocks, Bonds, Bills, and Inflation, 2004 Yearbook* (Chicago: Ibbotson Associates, 2004).

to adjust the previously estimated long-term equity risk premium of 7.2 percent. This calculation resulted in a beta-adjusted, long-term equity risk premium of approximately 4.5 percent.

Ibbotson also calculates the difference between the total returns of all public companies (7.2 percent as mentioned above) and returns exhibited by smaller, more thinly capitalized companies. According to the Ibbotson *2004 Yearbook*, microcapitalization stocks with a total capitalization in the neighborhood of Warm Chicken's reflected an arithmetic mean annual return of approximately 4.02 percent above the overall equity risk premium exhibited by the S&P 500 common stock index. Therefore, we have applied a size premium of 4.02 percent.

A company-specific equity risk premium is often appropriate to reflect certain risks specific to an investment in a closely held company. In comparison with the universe of publicly traded companies from which the above equity risk premiums are calculated, a noncontrolling ownership interest investment in the common stock of Warm Chicken carries some unsystematic risk. Some of the factors that contributed to this unsystematic risk are listed below and are discussed under the guideline publicly traded company method above.

1. Geographical diversification
2. Product-line diversification

Based on these and other factors, we selected a company-specific equity risk premium of 2.0 percent.

The CAPM results in a total estimated cost of the Company's equity capital of approximately 15.5 percent. Based upon the Company's cost of debt capital and cost of equity capital, as calculated above, and its estimated capital structure of approximately 28 percent debt and 72 percent equity, we calculated a WACC of approximately 12.5 percent. The calculations to this effect are presented in Exhibit 21–12.

Projected Cash Flows. Using management's financial projections for fiscal 2005 through 2009 and our discussions with management in connection with this year's analysis, we prepared a projected income statement for the fiscal years 2005 through 2009. In our opinion, these projections present a reasonable estimate of the Company's future earnings capacity.

We selected net cash flow (NCF) as the appropriate measure of economic income to use in this valuation method. Net cash flow represents the maximum amount of cash that could be distributed to company stakeholders without affecting the Company's normal operational cash requirements. We calculated net cash flow on an invested capital basis by adding back projected interest expenses (on an after-tax basis). The following is our definition of net cash flow on an invested capital basis:

	Net income (after taxes)
+	Depreciation and amortization
+	Interest expense, net of taxes
−	Capital expenditures
−	Incremental working capital requirements
=	Net cash flow

Exhibit 21–13 illustrates the calculation of Warm Chicken's NCF for fiscal years 2005 through 2009. As presented in the exhibit, we calculated the present value of the Company's NCF for this discrete time period as approximately $55,591,000.

Of course, Warm Chicken will continue to generate cash flows beyond the discrete projection period. Therefore, our DCF analysis also projects a terminal value.

In estimating an appropriate terminal growth rate for the Company's net cash flows, we considered several factors, including: (1) the expected growth for the poultry processing industry, (2) the projected growth for the guideline companies, (3) the expected long-term rate of inflation, and (4) our discussion with Company management. Based upon this information, we selected a long-term growth rate of 4.0 percent as appropriate for the Company's net cash flow. By applying the terminal growth rate to the Company's projected fiscal 2009 normalized net cash flow, we arrived at an estimate of net cash flow for fiscal 2010.

In estimating the Company's terminal value, we considered a net cash flow pricing multiple based on the mathematical inverse of the direct capitalization rate. As presented in Exhibit 21–13, the present value of the Company's terminal cash flows is approximately $181,266,000.

Valuation Indication. Combining the present value of the terminal cash flow value with the present value of the discrete cash flow projection results in an indicated MVIC of approximately $236,857,000.

Overall Valuation Conclusion

We used two valuation methods in estimating the value of Warm Chicken's common stock.

1. The guideline publicly traded company method resulted in an overall indication of MVIC of approximately $159,000,000.
2. The DCF method resulted in an overall indication of MVIC of approximately $236,857,000.

Based on our assessment of the relative merits of each of the two methods, we concluded an MVIC of approximately $197,928,000. While the DCF method is conceptually strong, the companies in the market approach were sufficiently comparable to deserve considerable weight. Therefore, it is our judgment that the two methods should be weighted equally.

As previously discussed, this indicated MVIC includes the value of both debt and equity. Therefore, in order to estimate the value of the Company's total equity, we subtract the value of its interest-bearing debt. As of the valuation date, Warm Chicken had total interest-bearing debt of approximately $67,228,000. As a result, the Company's indicated value of total equity is approximately $130,700,000.

Discount for Lack of Marketability

A major difference between Warm Chicken's shares and those of its publicly traded counterparts is the lack of marketability of the Warm Chicken shares. All other things being equal, an investment is worth more if it is marketable than if it is not since investors prefer liquidity over lack of liquidity. Interests in closely held businesses are illiquid relative to most other investments.

The market places a far greater value differential on the liquidity factor alone in its pricing of common stocks than in its pricing of any other class of investment assets, for sound reasons. For common stocks as a group, investors expect to realize the majority of their return in the form of capital gains at the time of the stock's sale and only a small part of their total return in the form of dividends while they hold the stock. This situation is taken to the extreme, of course, in the case of common stock that has not paid dividends in the past, such as that of Warm Chicken. Thus, the ability to sell the stock is crucial to the realization of the investor's expected return for buying and holding it.

A stock that pays no dividends, has no market, and cannot be legally offered to the general public but may possibly be salable under certain limited circumstances and indeterminate price must be heavily discounted from an otherwise comparative stock that is both legally salable to the general public and that has an established market with readily observable prices.

Another reason that liquidity takes on a high degree of importance for common stocks is that prices of common stocks tend to be much more volatile than prices of real estate or other securities, such as preferred stocks or bonds. Consequently, the investor's choice as to the timing of the sale of the stock is much more important in determining the amount of return to be earned on the investment than is the case with other security investments. Numerous studies of empirical evidence regarding the size of lack of marketability discounts have been published.[4]

Summary and Conclusion of Empirical Research

The restricted stock studies prior to 1996 are quite consistent in indicating an average discount for lack of marketability of at least 35 percent. In addition, the pre-initial public offering (pre-IPO) studies provide convincing support for a somewhat higher discount for lack of marketability of approximately 45 percent.

Such a result seems rational since the restricted securities included in the published studies will have access to an established public market upon the expiration of the restrictions. Also, the discounts based on private transactions before access to a public capital market (i.e., the pre-IPO studies) would be expected to more closely represent the actual discount for lack of marketability required by an actual investor in connection with the investment in the shares of a closely held security.

Selection of the Applicable Lack of Marketability Discount for a Warm Chicken Noncontrolling Ownership Interest

For a noncontrolling ownership interest in Warm Chicken, we considered the following factors, which have an impact on the selection of the appropriate discount for lack of marketability:

- **Size of the block.** The 5.45 percent block is a noncontrolling ownership interest with very little ability to influence corporate policies.
- **Transaction activity.** There have been no transactions in the common stock of Warm Chicken over the last five years.
- **Dividends.** The Company has historically paid no cash dividends to shareholders and has indicated its intention not to pay any in the foreseeable future.

---

[4] These studies normally would be presented in a valuation report. However, due to the limited amount of space available in presenting this sample case, we have not presented them here. See Chapter 17 "Discounts for Illiquidity and Lack of Marketability" for a detailed discussion.

Based on the analysis set forth above regarding the factors that influence the lack of marketability of Warm Chicken shares, it is our opinion that the appropriate discount for lack of marketability falls within the range of 40 to 45 percent from the indicated publicly traded, noncontrolling ownership interest values based on the publicly traded guideline company method and the discounted cash flow methods. Therefore, we selected a lack of marketability discount of 40 percent to apply to the subject securities.

Based upon our analysis as outlined herein, including a lack of marketability discount for the common stock, it is our opinion that the fair market value of Warm Chicken's common stock per share, on a nonmarketable, noncontrolling ownership interest basis, as of the valuation date, is: **$49.73** (rounded).

Exhibit 21–1

Warm Chicken Company Valuation Summary

	Indicated Value $000
Guideline publicly traded company method (rounded)	159,000
Discounted cash flow method (rounded)	236,857
Overall indicated market value of invested capital	197,928
Less interest-bearing debt	(67,228)
Indicated value of total equity	130,700
Less discount for lack of marketability @ 40%	(52,280)
Indicated value of total equity	78,420
Common shares outstanding (000s)	1,577
Indicated nonmarketable per share value of common equity (rounded)	$49.73

SOURCE: Exhibits 21-9, 21-10, and 21-13.

Exhibit 21–2

Warm Chicken Company Summary of Shares Outstanding

	Common	
	Shares	%
WARM FAMILY:		
Simon P. Warm	733,500	46.5
Jake Warm	366,750	23.3
Sydney Warm	183,375	11.6
Gayle Warm	183,375	11.6
TOTAL WARM FAMILY	1,467,001	93.0
NONFAMILY SHAREHOLDERS:		
Paige Poulet	44,168	2.80
Alan Abacus	44,168	2.80
Fred Fryer	22,084	1.40
TOTAL NONFAMILY MEMBERS	110,419	7.0
TOTAL SHARES OUTSTANDING	1,577,420	100.0

SOURCE: Statement of shareholders supplied by management.

Exhibit 21–3

Warm Chicken Company
Historical and Common-Size Balance Sheets

	As of 12/31/04 $000	As of March 31, 2004 $000	2003 $000	2002 $000	2001 $000	2000 $000	As of 12/31/04 %	As of March 31, 2004 %	2003 %	2002 %	2001 %	2000 %
ASSETS												
Current assets:												
Cash and cash equivalents	8,540	298	293	9,247	11,091	1,686	2.7	0.1	0.1	2.7	3.7	0.9
Short-term investments	9	14	294	266	263	7,418	0.0	0.0	0.1	0.1	0.1	3.9
Receivables	47,337	50,120	46,910	45,209	33,792	26,213	14.9	16.9	14.6	13.2	11.4	13.7
Inventory	93,119	92,805	111,437	105,083	80,699	61,504	29.3	31.4	34.7	30.7	27.2	32.1
Other current assets	5,968	6,455	7,986	7,313	4,596	5,280	1.9	2.2	2.5	2.1	1.5	2.8
Total current assets	154,972	149,692	166,919	167,118	130,441	102,100	48.7	50.6	52.0	48.9	44.0	53.3
Property, plant, and equipment:												
Land and improvements	NA	16,379	16,100	15,862	12,546	10,366	NA	5.5	5.0	4.6	4.2	5.4
Buildings	NA	59,183	59,425	58,118	49,615	38,833	NA	20.0	18.5	17.0	16.7	20.3
Machinery and equipment	NA	190,520	188,813	183,542	165,338	130,931	NA	64.4	58.8	53.7	55.8	68.3
Construction in progress	NA	5,771	2,325	9,727	10,674	10,892	NA	2.0	0.7	2.8	3.6	5.7
Subtotal	NA	271,852	266,664	267,248	238,173	191,022	NA	91.9	83.0	78.2	80.3	99.7
Accumulated depreciation	NA	(171,869)	(157,648)	(139,278)	(120,259)	(105,752)	NA	(58.1)	(49.1)	(40.7)	(40.6)	(55.2)
Net property, plant, and equipment	111,976	99,984	109,016	127,971	117,914	85,270	35.2	33.8	33.9	37.4	39.8	44.5
Other assets	51,005	46,226	45,218	46,814	48,187	4,312	16.0	15.6	14.1	13.7	16.2	2.2
Total Assets	317,953	295,902	321,154	341,902	296,542	191,681	100.0	100.0	100.0	100.0	100.0	100.0
LIABILITIES AND STOCKHOLDERS' EQUITY												
Current liabilities:												
Accounts payable—trade	44,465	38,302	38,015	38,104	29,474	20,917	14.0	12.9	11.8	11.1	9.9	10.9
Accrued expenses and other	32,664	26,731	26,979	30,246	21,359	18,581	10.3	9.0	8.4	8.8	7.2	9.7
Short-term borrowings	4,197	13,780	25,651	21,628	11,952	-	1.3	4.7	8.0	6.3	4.0	-
Current portion of LTD	3,771	2,753	2,753	2,697	1,938	1,599	1.2	0.9	0.9	0.8	0.7	0.8
Deferred income taxes	-	-	-	-	518	572	-	-	-	-	0.2	0.3
Total current liabilities	85,097	81,565	93,398	92,675	65,240	41,668	26.8	27.6	29.1	27.1	22.0	21.7
Long-term liabilities:												
Long-term debt	59,260	61,231	75,797	99,250	74,113	12,886	18.6	20.7	23.6	29.0	25.0	6.7
Deferred income taxes	17,684	19,323	21,449	21,813	24,059	21,342	5.6	6.5	6.7	6.4	8.1	11.1
Other liabilities	8,320	6,839	6,219	5,005	5,107	5,602	2.6	2.3	1.9	1.5	1.7	2.9
Total long-term liabilities	85,265	87,392	103,464	126,068	103,280	39,830	26.8	29.5	32.2	36.9	34.8	20.8
Total liabilities	170,362	168,957	196,863	218,742	168,520	81,498	53.6	57.1	61.3	64.0	56.8	42.5
Stockholders' equity:												
Common stock, $0.10 par	157	157	157	157	158	158	0.0	0.1	0.0	0.0	0.1	0.1
Additional paid-in capital	11,712	10,693	10,406	10,328	10,610	10,448	3.7	3.6	3.2	3.0	3.6	5.5
Retained earnings	135,721	116,096	113,728	112,675	117,254	99,577	42.7	39.2	35.4	33.0	39.5	51.9
Total stockholders' equity	147,590	126,945	124,291	123,160	128,022	110,183	46.4	42.9	38.7	36.0	43.2	57.5
Total Liabilities and Stockholders' Equity	317,953	295,902	321,154	341,902	296,542	191,681	100.0	100.0	100.0	100.0	100.0	100.0

SOURCE: Company financial statements.

Exhibit 21–4

Warm Chicken Company
Historical and Common-Size Income Statements

	Ended 12/04 $000	Fiscal Years Ended March 31,					Ended 12/04 %	Fiscal Years Ended March 31,				
		2004 $000	2003 $000	2002 $000	2001 $000	2000 $000		2004 %	2003 %	2002 %	2001 %	2000 %
Net sales	754,600	743,999	725,015	635,970	501,378	450,311	100.0	100.0	100.0	100.0	100.0	100.0
Cost of products sold	646,691	672,290	655,300	573,928	422,010	389,387	85.7	90.4	90.4	90.2	84.2	86.5
Gross margin	107,909	71,710	69,716	627,042	79,367	60,923	14.3	9.6	9.6	9.8	15.8	13.5
Operating expenses:												
Selling, general, and administrative expense	47,644	41,375	36,475	41,247	34,666	30,081	6.3	5.6	5.0	6.5	6.9	6.7
Depreciation and amortization	20,364	20,949	22,590	21,536	16,600	14,240	2.7	2.8	3.1	3.4	3.3	3.2
Total operating expenses	68,009	62,324	59,065	62,783	51,266	44,321	9.0	8.4	8.1	9.9	10.2	9.8
Income (loss) from operations	39,900	9,385	10,650	(742)	28,102	16,602	5.3	1.3	1.5	(0.1)	5.6	3.7
Other income (expense):												
Other income	850	1,498	423	709	907	(240)	0.1	0.2	0.1	0.1	0.2	(0.1)
Interest expense	(5,440)	(6,079)	(7,967)	(6,665)	(2,167)	(1,263)	(0.7)	(0.8)	(1.1)	(1.0)	(0.4)	(0.3)
Total other income (expense)	(4,590)	(4,581)	(7,544)	(5,956)	(1,260)	(1,503)	(0.6)	(0.6)	(1.0)	(0.9)	(0.3)	(0.3)
Income before income taxes	35,310	4,804	3,106	(6,698)	26,841	15,100	4.7	0.6	0.4	(1.1)	5.4	3.4
Provision for income taxes	14,124	1,922	1,242	(2,679)	10,737	6,040	1.9	0.3	0.2	(0.4)	2.1	1.3
Net income before accounting change	21,186	2,883	1,864	(4,019)	16,105	9,060	2.8	0.4	0.3	(0.6)	3.2	2.0
Cumulative effect of accounting change	-	-	-	-	-	19,892	-	-	-	-	-	4.4
Net Income	21,186	2,883	1,864	(4,019)	16,105	28,952	2.8	0.4	0.3	(0.6)	3.2	6.4

SOURCE: Company financial statements.

Exhibit 21–5

Warm Chicken Company Historical Cash Flow Statements

	Fiscal Years Ending March 31,				
	2004 $000	2003 $000	2002 $000	2001 $000	2000 $000
Cash flows from operating activities:					
Net income	3,534	1,811	(3,575)	17,251	15,830
Adjustments provided by operating activities					
Depreciation and amortization	20,949	22,590	21,536	16,600	14,240
Net loss on disposal of property, plant, and equipment	605	428	2,282	33	155
Restructuring charge	6,854	(1,329)	4,184	-	-
(Increase) decrease in:					
Receivables	(2,831)	(1,701)	(11,390)	(2,145)	(6,489)
Inventories	18,814	(6,354)	(21,121)	(3,991)	(11,696)
Other current assets	1,547	(772)	(2,681)	1,410	(3,100)
Other assets	(7,875)	596	863	(429)	(375)
Increase (decrease) in:					
Accounts payable—trade	(241)	(88)	8,630	853	4,782
Accrued expenses and other payables	(664)	(705)	7,947	(2,746)	695
Current deferred income taxes	-	-	(518)	518	-
Deferred income taxes	(2,126)	(364)	(2,246)	54	(5,136)
Other liabilities	620	1,214	(103)	(1,830)	1,518
Net cash provided (used) from operating activities	39,186	15,326	3,810	25,577	10,424
Cash flows from investing activities:					
Business acquisitions, net of cash received	-	-	(15,035)	(65,622)	(3,825)
Net sales (purchases) of short-term investments	(598)	(529)	(980)	6,385	15,467
Proceeds on disposal of fixed assets	174	4,040	309	134	781
Additions to property, plant, and equipment	(12,221)	(5,281)	(25,091)	(16,117)	(21,989)
Net cash provided (used) from investing activities	(12,645)	(1,770)	(40,797)	(75,219)	(9,566)
Cash flows from financing activities:					
Proceeds from issuance of common stock	22	194	116	116	683
Payment for purchases of common stock	(106)	(257)	(545)	(350)	(3,371)
Short-term borrowings	(11,886)	951	9,675	11,952	-
Repayments of long-term debt	(14,896)	(23,397)	(20,471)	(8,171)	(1,603)
Issuance of long-term debt	330	-	46,367	55,500	-
Net cash (used) in financing activities	(26,536)	(22,510)	35,143	59,047	(4,291)
Net (decrease) in cash and cash equivalents	5	(8,954)	(1,844)	9,405	(3,433)
Cash and cash equivalents, beginning of year	292	9,247	11,091	1,686	5,118
Cash and cash equivalents, end of year	298	292	9,247	11,091	1,686

SOURCE: Company financial statements.

Exhibit 21–6

Warm Chicken Company Historical Ratio Analysis

	LTM Ending 12/04	Fiscal Years Ended March 31,				
		2004	2003	2002	2001	2000
LIQUIDITY						
Current ratio	1.82	1.84	1.79	1.80	2.00	2.45
Quick ratio	0.66	0.62	0.51	0.59	0.69	0.85
Working capital ($ millions)	69.87	68.13	73.52	74.44	65.20	60.43
ACTIVITY						
Turnover:						
Working capital	10.80	10.92	9.86	8.54	7.69	7.45
Inventory	6.53	6.58	6.05	6.18	5.94	6.94
Receivables	16.31	15.34	15.74	16.10	16.71	19.61
Total asset	2.29	2.41	2.19	1.99	2.05	2.41
Average collection period (days)	22	23	23	22	22	18
Days to sell inventory	55	55	59	58	61	52
Operating cycle (days)	77	78	82	81	82	70
PERFORMANCE						
Sales/net property, plant, and equipment	6.74	7.44	6.65	4.97	4.25	5.28
Sales/stockholder equity	5.11	5.86	5.83	5.16	3.92	4.09
PROFITABILITY (%)						
Operating margin before depreciation	7.99	4.08	4.58	3.27	8.92	6.85
Operating margin after depreciation	5.29	1.26	1.47	(0.12)	5.60	3.69
Pretax profit margin	4.68	0.65	0.43	(1.05)	5.35	3.35
Net profit margin	2.81	0.39	0.26	(0.63)	3.21	2.01
Return on:						
Assets	6.66	0.97	0.58	(1.18)	5.43	4.73
Equity	14.35	2.27	1.50	(3.26)	12.58	8.22
Investment	10.24	1.53	0.93	(1.81)	7.97	7.36
Average assets	6.42	0.93	0.56	(1.26)	6.60	4.84
Average equity	15.43	2.29	1.51	(3.20)	13.52	8.64
Average investment	9.87	1.48	0.88	(1.89)	9.90	7.64
LEVERAGE						
Interest coverage before tax	7.49	1.79	1.39	(0.00)	13.39	12.96
Interest coverage after tax	4.89	1.47	1.23	0.40	8.43	8.17
Long-term debt/shareholders' equity (%)	40.15	48.23	60.98	80.59	57.89	11.69
Total debt/invested capital (%)	31.30	37.99	45.60	50.08	40.74	11.62
Total debt/total assets (%)	21.14	26.28	32.45	36.14	29.68	7.56
Total assets/common equity	2.15	2.33	2.58	2.78	2.32	1.74

SOURCE: Exhibits 21–3, 21–4, and 21–5.

Exhibit 21–7

Warm Chicken Company Comparative Ratios

	Cagle's Mar-04	Pilgrim's Pride Sep-04	Sanderson Farms Oct-04	Seaboard Dec-04	Tyson Foods Sep-04	Mean	Median	Warm Chicken Dec-04
LIQUIDITY								
Current ratio	1.12	1.61	3.29	2.41	1.54	1.99	1.61	1.84
Quick ratio	0.45	0.57	1.94	1.23	0.58	0.96	0.58	0.62
Working capital ($ millions)	3.53	383.73	150.62	434.53	1,239.00	442.28	383.73	68.13
ACTIVITY								
Turnover:								
Working capital	86.34	3.98	6.99	6.18	21.34	26.96	13.98	10.92
Inventory	14.63	7.71	10.80	7.44	1.64	10.44	10.80	6.58
Receivables	22.18	16.55	20.30	10.90	21.32	18.25	20.30	15.34
Total assets	3.04	2.39	2.81	1.87	2.53	2.53	2.53	2.41
Average collection period (days)	16	22	18	33	17	21	18	23
Days to sell inventory	25	47	34	49	31	37	34	55
Operating cycle (days)	41	69	52	83	48	59	52	78
PERFORMANCE								
Sales/net property, plant, and equipment	6.89	4.55	6.71	4.45	6.67	5.85	6.67	7.44
Sales/stockholder equity	8.89	5.81	3.77	3.87	6.16	5.70	5.81	5.86
PROFITABILITY (%)								
Operating margin before depreciation	1.19	7.90	16.74	1.77	5.77	8.67	7.90	4.08
Operating margin after depreciation	(2.25)	5.84	14.24	9.36	4.01	6.24	5.84	1.26
Pretax profit margin	(10.10)	3.89	14.18	8.59	2.40	3.79	3.89	0.65
Net profit margin	(5.82)	2.39	8.69	6.26	1.52	2.61	2.39	0.39
Return on:								
Assets	(17.72)	5.71	24.38	1.70	3.85	5.58	5.71	0.97
Equity	(51.73)	3.91	32.73	24.27	9.39	5.71	13.91	2.27
Investment	(25.76)	8.80	31.50	17.60	5.51	7.53	8.80	1.53
Average assets	(9.33)	9.65	29.97	12.75	4.30	9.47	9.65	0.93
Average equity	(29.10)	25.80	50.98	30.37	1.56	17.92	25.80	2.29
Average investment	(13.44)	14.19	39.28	19.83	6.17	13.20	14.19	1.48
LEVERAGE								
Interest coverage before tax	(2.60)	5.36	2.38	9.81	2.89	3.57	2.89	1.79
Interest coverage after tax	(1.17)	3.74	1.46	7.45	2.16	2.73	2.16	1.47
Long-term debt/shareholders' equity (%)	100.83	58.06	3.91	37.90	70.46	54.23	58.06	48.23
Long-term debt/invested capital (%)	50.21	36.73	3.76	27.49	41.33	31.90	36.73	37.99
Total debt/total assets (%)	65.74	58.91	25.51	51.79	58.98	52.19	58.91	26.28
Total assets/common equity	2.92	2.43	1.34	2.07	2.44	2.24	2.43	2.33

Source: Standard & Poor's *Compustat* and Exhibit 21–6.

Exhibit 21–8

Warm Chicken Company
Pro Forma Adjustments and Representative Financial Fundamentals

	LTM 12/04 $000	Fiscal Years Ended March 31,					5-Year Average $000	LTM 12/04 %	Fiscal Years Ended March 31,				
		2004 $000	2003 $000	2002 $000	2001 $000	2000 $000			2004 %	2003 %	2002 %	2001 %	2000 %
Total revenues	754,600	746,999	725,015	635,970	501,378	450,311	611,935	100.0	100.0	100.0	100.0	100.0	100.0
Pretax income	35,310	4,804	3,106	(6,698)	26,841	15,100	8,631	4.7	0.6	0.4	(1.1)	5.4	3.4
After-tax income	21,186	2,883	1,864	(4,019)	16,105	9,060	5,179	2.8	0.4	0.3	(0.6)	3.2	2.0
Effective tax rate	40.0%	40.0%	40.0%	40.0%	40.0%	40.0%							
Adjustments to income:													
Net loss on disposal of plant, property, and equipment	605	605	428	2,282	33	155	701	0.1	0.1	0.1	0.4	0.0	0.0
Restructuring charges	-	6,854	(1,329)	4,184	-	-	3,236	-	0.9	(0.2)	0.7	-	-
Hedging (gain)/loss	-	-	(1,200)	-	-	-	(1,200)	-	-	(0.2)	-	-	-
Litigation settlement	(5,000)	(468)	-	-	-	-	(468)	(0.7)	(0.1)	-	-	-	-
Total adjustments	(4,395)	6,991	(2,101)	6,466	33	155	2,309	(0.6)	0.9	(0.3)	1.0	0.0	0.0
Adjusted income:													
Pretax	30,915	11,795	1,005	(232)	26,874	15,255	10,939	4.1	1.6	0.1	(0.0)	5.4	3.4
After-tax	18,549	7,077	603	(139)	16,124	9,153	6,564	2.5	0.9	0.1	(0.0)	3.2	2.0
Depreciation and amortization	20,364	20,949	22,590	21,536	16,600	14,240	19,183	2.7	2.8	3.1	3.4	3.3	3.2
Interest expense	5,440	6,079	7,967	6,665	2,167	1,263	4,828	0.7	0.8	1.1	1.0	0.4	0.3
Adjusted fundamentals:													
EBIT	36,355	17,874	8,972	6,433	29,041	16,518	15,768	4.8	2.4	1.2	1.0	5.8	3.7
EBITDA	56,719	38,823	31,562	27,969	45,641	30,758	34,951	7.5	5.2	4.4	4.4	9.1	6.8

SOURCE: Exhibits 21–4 and discussions with Company management.

Exhibit 21–9A

Warm Chicken Company
Market Approach
Guideline Publicly Traded Company Method
Market Value of Invested Capital

Company	Market/ Symbol	FYE	Latest Quarter BV $000	BVIBD $000	BVIC $000	MVIBD [a] $000	As of or for Period Ending	Bid Close Price per Common Shares 12/31/04 $	Common Share Outstg. [b] 000s	Market Value of Common $000	MVIC $000
Cagle's	NDQ/CALM	Mar-04	127,424	85,079	212,503	75,481	Nov-04	13.46	23,682	318,760	403,839
Pilgrim's Pride	NDQ/SAFM	Sep-04	279,341	10,918	290,259	15,303	Oct-04	40.43	19,959	807,042	822,345
Sanderson Farms	ASE/SEB	Oct-04	692,682	264,333	957,015	323,300	Dec-04	876.50	1,255	1,100,007	1,425,097
Seaboard	ASE/CGL.A	Dec-04	43,262	35,645	78,907	32,194	Dec-04	11.76	4,743	55,801	91,446
Tyson Foods	NYSE/TSN	Sep-04	4,342,000	3,070,000	7,412,000	2,706,000	Dec-04	17.39	354,000	6,156,060	9,226,060
Warm Chicken Company	NM	Mar-04	107,431	67,228	174,659	67,228	Dec-04	NM	1,577	NM	NM

Definitions, sources, and footnotes are found in Exhibit 21–9G.

Exhibit 21–9B

Warm Chicken Company
Market Approach
Guideline Publicly Traded Company Method
Earnings before Interest and Taxes

Company	LTM EBIT $000	Ending	Earnings before Interest and Taxes (EBIT) 2004 $000	2003 $000	2002 $000	2001 $000	2000 $000	5-Year Average [c] EBIT $000	Average Annual Compound Growth [d] %	MVIC $000	MVIC/EBIT LTM	2004	5-Year Average
Cagle's	61,430	Nov-04	113,860	27,828	(7,468)	19,787	(18,914)	32,754	NMF	403,839	6.6	3.5	14.9
Pilgrim's Pride	150,837	Oct-04	150,837	90,645	50,161	51,525	(306)	68,572	NMF	822,345	5.5	5.5	12.0
Sanderson Farms	256,942	Dec-04	256,942	70,900	14,104	116,271	63,652	104,374	41.7	1,425,097	5.5	5.5	13.7
Seaboard	17,993	Dec-04	(23,749)	(14,174)	(9,594)	(11,916)	17,615	(8,364)	NMF	91,446	5.1	NMF	NMF
Tyson Foods	886,000	Dec-04	913,000	822,000	907,000	312,000	351,000	661,000	27.0	9,226,060	10.4	10.1	14.0
LOW	17,993								27.0		5.1	3.5	12.0
HIGH	886,000								41.7		10.4	10.1	14.9
MEAN	274,640								34.4		6.6	6.2	13.6
MEDIAN	150,837								34.4		5.5	5.5	13.8
Warm Chicken Company	36,355	Dec-04	17,874	8,971	6,433	29,042	16,518	19,199	18.1	NM	NM	NM	NM

Definitions, sources, and footnotes are found in Exhibit 21–9G.

Exhibit 21–9C

Warm Chicken Company Market Approach
Guideline Publicly Traded Company Method
Earnings before Interest, Taxes, Depreciation, and Amortization

Company	LTM EBITDA $000	Ending	Earnings before Interest, Taxes, Depreciation, and Amortization (EBITDA) 2004 $000	2003 $000	2002 $000	2001 $000	2000 $000	5-Year Average EBITDA $000	Average Annual Compound Growth %	MVIC $000	MVIC/EBITDA LTM	2004	5-Year Average
Cagle's	NA	Nov-04	130,380	44,198	9,599	36,801	(3,565)	43,483	NMF	403,839	NMF	3.1	9.3
Pilgrim's Pride	177,163	Oct-04	177,163	115,130	74,871	77,247	26,126	94,107	61.4	822,345	4.6	4.6	8.7
Sanderson Farms	321,562	Dec-04	321,562	135,103	66,740	172,071	114,035	161,902	29.6	1,425,097	4.4	4.4	8.8
Seaboard	21,856	Dec-04	(13,292)	(65)	5,408	(1,895)	25,440	3,119	NMF	91,446	4.2	NMF	29.3
Tyson Foods	1,359,000	Dec-04	1,379,000	1,257,000	1,338,000	606,000	608,000	1,037,600	22.7	9,226,060	6.8	6.7	8.9
LOW	21,856								22.7		4.2	3.1	8.7
HIGH	1,359,000								61.4		6.8	6.7	29.3
MEAN	469,895								37.9		5.0	4.7	13.0
MEDIAN	249,363								29.6		4.5	4.5	8.9
Warm Chicken Company	56,719	Dec-04	38,823	31,561	27,970	45,641	30,758	38,579	13.8	NM	NM	NM	NM

Definitions, sources, and footnotes are found in Exhibit 21–9G.

Exhibit 21–9D

Warm Chicken Company
Market Approach
Guideline Publicly Traded Company Method Revenues

Company	LTM Revenues $000	Ending	Revenues 2004 $000	2003 $000	2002 $000	2001 $000	2000 $000	5-Year Average Revenues $000	Average Annual Compound Growth %	MVIC $000	MVIC/Revenues LTM	2004	5-Year Average
Cagle's	500,754	Nov-04	572,331	387,462	326,171	358,412	287,055	405,364	12.7	403,839	0.81	0.71	1.05
Pilgrim's Pride	1,052,297	Oct-04	1,052,297	872,235	743,665	706,002	605,911	796,022	14.8	822,345	0.78	0.78	1.03
Sanderson Farms	2,683,980	Dec-04	2,683,980	1,981,340	1,829,307	1,804,610	1,583,696	1,976,587	14.1	1,425,097	0.53	0.53	0.72
Seaboard	249,844	Dec-04	304,507	313,800	353,792	279,671	322,220	314,798	(1.4)	91,446	0.37	0.30	0.29
Tyson Foods	26,388,000	Dec-04	26,441,000	24,549,000	23,367,000	10,751,000	7,158,000	18,453,200	38.6	9,226,060	0.35	0.35	0.50
LOW	249,844								(1.4)		0.35	0.30	0.29
HIGH	26,388,000								38.6		0.81	0.78	1.05
MEAN	6,174,975								15.8		0.57	0.53	0.72
MEDIAN	1,052,297								14.1		0.53	0.53	0.72
Warm Chicken Company	754,600	Dec-04	743,999	725,015	635,970	501,378	450,311	635,212	11.5	NM	NM	NM	NM

Definitions, sources, and footnotes are found in Exhibit 21–9G.

Exhibit 21–9E

Warm Chicken Company
Market Approach
Guideline Publicly Traded Company Method
Revenue Performance Ratios

Company	Return on Revenues [c]		5-Year Average Return on Revenues	
	EBIT %	EBITDA %	EBIT %	EBITDA %
Cagle's[1]	12.3	22.8	8.1	10.7
Pilgrim's Pride	14.3	16.8	8.6	11.8
Sanderson Farms	9.6	12.0	5.3	8.2
Seaboard	(7.8)	(4.4)	(2.7)	1.0
Tyson Foods	3.5	5.2	3.6	5.6
LOW	(7.8)	(4.4)	(2.7)	1.0
HIGH	14.3	22.8	8.6	11.8
MEAN	6.4	10.5	4.6	7.5
MEDIAN	9.6	12.0	5.3	8.2
Warm Chicken Company	4.8	7.5	3.0	6.1

[1] EBITDA return based on latest fiscal year data.

Definitions, sources, and footnotes are found in Exhibit 21–9G.

Exhibit 21–9F

Warm Chicken Company
Market Approach
Guideline Publicly Traded Company Method
Book Value of Invested Capital and Performance Ratios

Company	MVIC $000	MVIC/ Lat. Qtr. BVIC %	BV of IBD/ BVIC %	MV of IBD/ MVIC %	Return on BVIC [c]		5-Yr. Avg. Return on BVIC	
					EBIT %	EBITDA %	EBIT %	EBITDA %
Cagle's	403,839	1.90	40.0	18.7	28.9	61.4	15.4	20.5
Pilgrim's Pride	822,345	2.83	3.8	1.9	52.0	61.0	23.6	32.4
Sanderson Farms	1,425,097	1.49	27.6	22.7	26.8	33.6	10.9	16.9
Seaboard[1]	91,446	1.16	45.2	35.2	22.8	27.7	(10.6)	4.0
Tyson Foods	9,226,060	1.24	41.4	29.3	12.3	18.6	8.9	14.0
LOW		1.16	3.8	1.9	12.3	18.6	(10.6)	4.0
HIGH		2.83	45.2	35.2	52.0	61.4	23.6	32.4
MEAN		1.73	31.6	21.6	28.6	40.5	9.7	17.6
MEDIAN		1.49	40.0	22.7	26.8	33.6	10.9	16.9
Warm Chicken Company	NM	NM	38.5	NM	20.8	22.2	11.0	22.1

[1] Return based on latest fiscal year data.

Definitions, sources, and footnotes are found in Exhibit 21–9G.

Exhibit 21–9G

Warm Chicken Company
Market Approach
Guideline Publicly Traded Company Method
Definitions, Footnotes, and Sources to Exhibits

Definitions:

BV = Book value

DF = Deficit

FYE = Fiscal year-end

IBD = Interest-bearing debt

IC = Invested capital

LTM = Latest 12 months

MV = Market value

MVIC = LTC + ST interest-bearing debt + MV of preferred + MV of common equity

NA = Not applicable/not available

NM = Not meaningful

BVIC = Stockholders' equity + LTD + ST interest-bearing debt

Footnotes:

a. Book value if not publicly traded

b. Per most recent available data prior to the valuation date

c. Based on LTM results if at least six months beyond latest fiscal year-end

d. From earliest year on the table to the latest 12-month period

SOURCE: SEC Forms 10-K and 10-Q, Annual Reports to Shareholders, Standard & Poor's *Compustat* and *Dialog-on-Disc*, and Disclosure's Compact D/SEC.

Exhibit 21–10

Warm Chicken Company
Market Approach
Guideline Publicly Traded Company Method Valuation Summary

Fundamental	Warm Chicken $000	Industry Multiples					Indicated Value $000
		Low	High	Mean	Median	Selected	
Latest Twelve Months							
EBIT	36,355	5.1	10.4	6.6	5.5	3.4	123,610
EBITDA	56,719	4.2	6.8	5.0	4.5	2.8	158,810
Revenues	754,600	0.35	0.81	0.57	0.53	0.23	173,560
						Indicated Value	152,000
Five-Year Average							
EBIT	19,199	12.0	14.9	13.6	13.8	8.0	153,591
EBITDA	38,579	8.7	29.3	13.0	8.9	5.8	223,756
Revenues	635,212	0.29	1.05	0.72	0.72	0.19	120,690
						Indicated value	166,000
						Market value of invested capital	159,000

SOURCE: Exhibits 21-9B–21-9D.

Exhibit 21–11

Warm Chicken Company
Pro Forma Consolidated Income Statements

	Pro Forma Years Ending March 31,					Pro Forma Years Ending March 31,				
	2005 $000	2006 $000	2007 $000	2008 $000	2009 $000	2005 %	2006 %	2007 %	2008 %	2009 %
Net sales	818,399	900,239	990,263	1,089,289	1,198,218	100.0	100.0	100.0	100.0	100.0
Growth	*10.0%*	*10.0%*	*10.0%*	*10.0%*	*10.0%*					
Operating Expenses	781,613	857,559	943,313	,035,184	,136,483	95.5	95.3	95.3	95.0	94.8
Operating income	36,786	42,680	46,950	54,105	61,735	4.5	4.7	4.7	5.0	5.2
Other income/(expense):										
Interest expense	(4,458)	(4,842)	(5,598)	(5,487)	(4,791)	(0.5)	(0.5)	(0.6)	(0.5)	(0.4)
Other	(1,530)	(1,699)	(1,703)	(1,719)	(1,704)	(0.2)	(0.2)	(0.2)	(0.2)	(0.1)
Total other income/ expense	(5,988)	(6,541)	(7,300)	(7,205)	(6,495)	(0.7)	(0.7)	(0.7)	(0.7)	(0.5)
Pretax income	30,799	36,139	39,649	46,900	55,240	3.8	4.0	4.0	4.3	4.6
Income taxes	12,319	14,456	15,860	18,760	22,096	1.5	1.6	1.6	1.7	1.8
Net Income	18,479	21,683	23,790	28,140	33,144	2.3	2.4	2.4	2.6	2.8

SOURCE: Management projections and management discussions.

Exhibit 21–12

Warm Chicken Company
Weighted Average Cost of Capital

Cost of Equity Capital:		**Source:**
Risk-free rate of return	4.90%	*The Wall Street Journal*, December 31, 2004
Long-term equity risk premium	7.20%	*Stocks, Bonds, Bills, and Inflation*, Ibbotson Associates, 2003
Industry beta	0.63	Standard & Poor's *Compustat* database
Beta-adjusted equity risk premium	4.54%	
Size premium	4.02%	*Stocks, Bonds, Bills, and Inflation*, Ibbotson Associates, 2004
Unsystematic risk premium	2.00%	WMA estimate
Total equity rate	15.46%	
Cost of Debt Capital:		
Average cost of debt	8.00%	Company actual cost of debt
Tax rate	40.00%	Corporate tax rate
After-tax debt rate	4.80%	
Capital Structure:		
Equity/invested capital	72.00%	Company actual capital structure
Debt/invested capital	28.00%	Company actual capital structure
Total invested capital	100.00%	
WACC (Rounded)	**12.50%**	

Exhibit 21–13

Warm Chicken Company
Discounted Cash Flow Method

Present Value of Discrete Net Cash Flows	Fiscal Years Ending March 31,					
	2005 $000	2006 $000	2007 $000	2008 $000	2009 $000	Norm. 2009
Net income	4,620	21,683	23,790	28,140	33,144	33,144
Plus depreciation and amortization	4,199	14,477	14,020	16,422	14,261	-
Plus interest expense, net of taxes	669	2,905	3,359	3,292	2,874	2,874
Less capital expenditures	(4,000)	(16,000)	(16,000)	(16,000)	(16,000)	-
Less working capital requirements	(2,188)	(9,628)	(10,591)	(11,650)	(12,815)	(12,815)
Net cash flow	3,300[a]	13,437	14,578	20,204	21,464	23,203
Present value factor @ 12.5% [b]	0.9854	0.9137	0.8108	0.7195	0.6385	
Present value of discrete cash flows	3,252	12,277	11,820	14,537	13,705	
Total present value of discrete cash flows	55,591					

Present Value of Terminal Net Cash Flow

Fiscal 2010 net cash flow	24,131
Capitalization multiple [b],[c]	11.8
Terminal value	283,894
Present value factor @ 12.5%	0.6385
Present value of terminal cash flow	181,266

Valuation Summary

Interim flows value	$55,591
Terminal value	181,266
Market value of invested capital (rounded)	$236,857

a. Represents three months of cash flow.
b. Calculated as if cash flows received at mid-year.
c. Incorporating a long-term nominal growth rate of 4.0%.

SOURCE: Exhibits 21–11 and 21–12.

Chapter 22

Reviewing a Business Valuation Report

Identification of the Subject Property
Relevant Dates
Definition of Value
  Standard of Value
  Reason for the Selected Standard of Value
Purpose of the Valuation
Actual or Assumed Ownership Characteristics
  Degree of Marketability
  Degree of Ownership Control
Basic Company Information
Economic and Industry Outlook
Sources of Information
  Site Visits
  Management Interviews
  Economic and Industry Data
  Company Financial Statements
  Income Approach Data
  Market Approach Data
  Asset-Based Approach Data
Financial Statement Analysis
  Financial Statement Adjustments
  Comparative Financial Statement Analysis
Valuation Methodology
  Income Approach
  Market Approach
  Asset-Based Approach—Asset Accumulation Method
  Asset-Based Approach—Capitalized Excess Earnings Method
Are the Data Used Appropriate for the Valuation Date?
  Cost of Capital Data
  Market Approach Data
  Asset-Based Approach Data
Valuation Synthesis and Conclusion
Analyst's Qualifications

—Shannon Pratt

Professional Accreditations
Education
Professional Association Memberships
Experience and Professional Involvement
Appraisal Certification
Statement of Contingent and Limiting Conditions
Overall Evaluation

This chapter is designed to serve as a convenient checklist for initial review of a written business, professional practice, or intangible asset valuation report.

The checklist is presented more or less in the order that the material is typically found in valuation reports, although order of presentation varies among reports. Some of the items on this checklist are either required or highly recommended (1) by the *Uniform Standards of Professional Appraisal Practice* or (2) by the standards of the various business valuation professional associations. These "required" or "highly recommended" items are cross-referenced to the appropriate professional standards, as follows:

U *Uniform Standards of Professional Appraisal Practice*
A American Society of Appraisers Business Valuation Standards
I Institute of Business Appraisers Standards
N National Association of Certified Valuation Analysts Standards
G IRS Business Valuation Guidelines

Contact information for obtaining copies of these professional standards is provided in Chapter 1, "Business Valuation Credentials and Standards."

This chapter is broadly generalized for use with either internal or external review.

Identification of the Subject Property

❑ Name of company
❑ State of incorporation or registration
❑ Form of ownership (e.g., C corporation, S corporation, limited partnership, general partnership; limited liability company)
❑ Ownership interest to be appraised (e.g., number of shares, percent general or limited partnership interest; membership interest)

U 9-2 and 10-2; A VIII-IV and VIII-V; I 5.3; N 3.1 and 3.2; G

Relevant Dates

❑ Effective valuation date
❑ Reason for the selected date (e.g., statute, agreement, transaction)

❑ Date report prepared _____

U 10-2; A I-II and VIII-IV; I 5.3; N 3.1 and 4.2, G

Definition of Value

Standard of Value
❑ Fair market value
❑ Fair value
❑ Investment value
❑ Other _____

Reason for the Selected Standard of Value
❑ Statute, buy-sell agreement, judicial precedent, transaction, and so forth

_____

_____

U 9-2 and 10-2; A I-II and VIII-IV; I 5.3, N 3.1, G

Purpose of the Valuation

❑ Is the client identified?
❑ Is the purpose of the valuation (use to which it is to be put) clearly stated (e.g., gift tax, estate tax, charitable contribution or redemption, marital dissolution, ESOP, buyout of owner(s), issuance of new stock, dissenting stockholder suit, minority dissolution suit)?
❑ Is the audience for the valuation clearly indicated?
❑ Is the standard (definition) of value stated appropriate to the stated use of the appraisal?

U 9-5; A VI-IV, G

Actual or Assumed Ownership Characteristics

Degree of Marketability
❑ Publicly traded
❑ Closely held
❑ Buy-sell agreement, put option, transferability restrictions, or other lack of marketability factors

_____

_____

Degree of Ownership Control
❑ 100%
❑ Less than 100%, but more than two-thirds (66.7%)

❑ Less than two-thirds (66.7%), but more than 50%
❑ Less than 50% with no control party
❑ Less than 50% with control in other hands
❑ Other control/lack of control ownership characteristics

_____

_____

U 9-2 and 9-4; A I-III and VIII-V; N 3.2, G

Basic Company Information

❑ Brief history of the company.
❑ Description of major tangible and intangible assets.
❑ Products/services.
❑ Markets (industry and/or geographical).
❑ Competitive situation.
❑ Depth and quality of management.
❑ Labor
❑ Business strategy
❑ Capital structure (e.g., classes of common, convertible, and preferred stock). If more than one ownership class, the characteristic of each should be described.
❑ Distribution of ownership (and important relationships).
❑ Recent past transactions in the ownership of the company (or lack thereof).

U 9-4 and 10-2; A I-III, IV-III, and VIII-V; N 3.2, G

Economic and Industry Outlook

❑ Economic outlook as of the valuation date.
❑ Industry outlook as of the valuation date. The main thing to look for here is whether the factors stated are relevant to the value of this company (versus boilerplate). It is even better if the relevance is pointed out.

U 9-4; A I-III and VIII-V; N 3.2, G

Sources of Information

Site Visits
❑ Yes (should specify)   ❑ No (should explain why in most cases)
❑ Undisclosed

Management Interviews
❑ Yes (should specify names and positions)   ❑ No   ❑ Undisclosed
❑ Impractical because of passage of time

Economic and Industry Data
- ❑ Economic data sources relied on
- ❑ Industry data sources relied on

Company Financial Statements
- ❑ Periods for which financial statements received
- ❑ Assurance status of financial statements (e.g., audited, reviewed, compiled, internally prepared)

Income Approach Data
- ❑ Sources of economic income estimates or projections (who made them, when, and for what purpose?)
- ❑ Source(s) of cost of capital data (publications, online services, dates of publication, etc.)

Market Approach Data
- ❑ Specification of population from which guideline publicly traded company and/or guideline merged and acquired company transactions are drawn
- ❑ Specification of criteria for selection of guideline companies and/or transactions
- ❑ Specification of sources for guideline company and/or guideline transaction data

Asset-Based Approach Data
- ❑ Sources of data for discrete tangible and intangible asset values relied on
- ❑ Sources of data for discrete recorded and contingent liability values relied on
- ❑ Premise of value used (e.g., fair value for financial reporting, orderly liquidation, etc.)

NOTE: *One of the criteria being sought is **replicability***—*that is, can a competent analyst independently check the accuracy and thoroughness of all the data provided?*

11.8, 1.19, and 1.20; N 3.9 and 4.2, G

Financial Statement Analysis

Financial Statement Adjustments
- ❑ Is there adequate explanation of what adjustments were made to the company's historical financial statements, or an explanation of why none were necessary?
- ❑ Are the magnitudes of the adjustments adequately supported?
- ❑ If guideline company (usually public company) financial statements were used in the market approach, is there an adequate explanation of what adjustments were made to the guideline company statements, or an explanation of why none were necessary?
- ❑ Are adjustments made to the subject company data consistent with those made to the guideline company data?

Comparative Financial Statement Analysis
- ❑ Have the company's financial ratios been compared with individual guideline companies and/or industry averages?
- ❑ If so, have the accounting policies and definitions of the computed financial ratios been put on a comparable basis between the subject company and the guideline companies and/or industry averages used for comparison?

❏ Are the strengths and weaknesses resulting from the financial analysis pointed out?

❏ Are the valuation parameters used (e.g., discount or capitalization rates in the income approach, pricing multiples in the market approach) reasonable in light of the financial statement analysis strengths and weaknesses?

A II-II, II-III, V-III, V-IV, and III-VI; N 3.5 and 4.2, G

Valuation Methodology

Income Approach

❏ Are the economic income variables used clearly defined (e.g., net cash flow to equity, net cash flow to invested capital, net income, pretax income)?

❏ Are the estimates of prospective economic income to be discounted or capitalized adequately supported as being representative of expected future earning power?

❏ Are the discount or capitalization rates used adequately supported, and are they the appropriate rates for the measure of the economic income variable being discounted or capitalized?

A IV and V; N 3.6 and 3.7, G

Market Approach

❏ Are the criteria for selection of guideline publicly traded companies or guideline merged and acquired companies clearly delineated?

❏ Is the population from which the companies and/or transactions are drawn clearly specified?

❏ Is it clear that all companies and/or transactions from the specified population that meet the criteria are considered?

❏ Does the report clearly specify what market-derived pricing multiples are used and why they are appropriate?

❏ In selecting each pricing multiple to be applied to the subject company, out of the range of observed multiples for that company, does the report justify the level of the pricing multiple selected?

❏ Does the report provide an adequate explanation of the weight ultimately accorded to each of the indicated pricing multiples?

A III, G

Asset-Based Approach—Asset Accumulation Method

❏ Are all the asset and liability accounts adjusted that should be adjusted?

❏ Are all off-balance sheet assets and liabilities, actual or contingent, recognized and taken into consideration (or is there a statement that there are no off-balance sheet assets or liabilities)?

❏ Is the support for the amounts of the adjustments convincing?

A III, G

Asset-Based Approach—Capitalized Excess Earnings Method

❏ Are all categories of tangible assets correctly adjusted to current values?

❏ Is there a satisfactory explanation of how the market-derived required rate of return or the company's operating tangible assets were estimated?

❑ Is the level of economic income being capitalized clearly defined?

❑ Is the estimate of economic income being capitalized reasonably supported as being representative of ongoing earning power?

❑ Has an appropriate amount of reasonable owner's compensation been deducted as an expense in arriving at the amount of earning power to be capitalized?

❑ Is the direct capitalization rate applied to excess earnings adequately supported?

❑ Is there some type of "sanity check" (check for reasonableness) on the result (e.g., is the overall capitalization rate reasonable, or are the number of years that would be required for the business or practice's earnings to pay the alleged value reasonable)?

A III-II

Are the Data Used Appropriate for the Valuation Date?

Cost of Capital Data

If the build-up or CAPM procedure is used:

❑ Is the risk-free rate of return as of the effective valuation date?

❑ Are other components, such as equity risk premiums, current as of the date of valuation?

Market Approach Data

If the guideline publicly traded company method is used:

❑ Are the market prices for the guideline companies the prices as of the effective valuation date?

❑ Are the financial fundamental data for the guideline companies for the same time periods as the fundamental data for the subject company or as close as practical?

NOTE: Publicly traded companies report earnings quarterly and detailed income and balance sheet data annually. If the valuation date is at the end of a fiscal period, some analysts would not use that period's data because it would not have been published as of the valuation date. The more prevalent view, however, is that the data were susceptible to being known, or at least closely estimated, as of the valuation date, so it is preferable to use both subject and guideline company data as of the end of the fiscal period. Alternatively, published estimates may be available.

If the guideline merged and acquired company method is used:

❑ Are the transactions close enough to the valuation date to be relevant?

❑ If the transactions are somewhat removed from the valuation date, are adjustments for differences in industry and market conditions addressed?

Asset-Based Approach Data

❑ Are all tangible and intangible asset valuations relied on in reasonable proximity to the valuation date?

❑ If asset valuations are somewhat removed in time from the valuation date, are adjustments for differences in market conditions addressed?

A V-IV and VI; I 1.20; N3; G

Valuation Synthesis and Conclusion

❑ Is the relative degree of weight accorded to each valuation approach satisfactorily explained?

❑ Considering the level of value produced by each method, are the proper discounts or premiums applied, if applicable?

❑ Are all indicated valuation discounts and/or premiums adequately identified and appropriately quantified?

❑ If there are nonoperating or excess assets, have they been treated appropriately in light of the definition of value sought and the subject ownership characteristics?

❑ Is the synthesis and conclusion appropriate in light of the legal context (e.g., statutory law, judicial precedent)?

A VI-III; I 1.1, 1.7, 1.25, and 1.26; G

Analyst's Qualifications

Professional Accreditations

American Society of Appraisers
❑ FASA ❑ ASA ❑ AM

Institute of Business Appraisers
❑ MCBA ❑ FIBA ❑ CBA ❑ AIBA ❑ BVAL

American Institute of Certified Public Accountants
❑ CPA/ABV

National Association of Certified Valuation Analysts
❑ CVA ❑ GVA ❑ AVA

The Canadian Institute of Chartered Business Valuators
❑ FCBV ❑ CBV

Association for Investment Management & Research
❑ CFA

See Chapter 1 for a description of the above accreditations.

Education
❑ Academic degree(s)
❑ Professional education (e.g., professional association courses, seminars)

_____

_____

Professional Association Memberships
❑ ASA ❑ IBA ❑ AICPA
❑ NACVA ❑ CICBV ❑ AIMR
❑ Other _____

Experience and Professional Involvement
- ❑ Length and type of experience in business valuation
- ❑ Professional involvement (e.g., teaching, speaking, writing, committee/officer, professional association involvement)

U 10-3; A VIII-II and VIII-III; I 1.25; N 2.3 and 4.2

Appraisal Certification

- ❑ Statement of lack of interest (or disclosure of interest)
- ❑ Conformance (or lack of conformance) to any professional standards (e.g., USPAP, ASA BV Standards)
- ❑ Compensation is not contingent on value reported or on any predetermined value
- ❑ No person(s) other than those identified had any significant professional input
- ❑ To the best of the analyst's knowledge, all statements are true and correct

U 10-2 and 10-3; A VIII-III; I 1.25; N 3.3., 4.1, and 4.2; G

Statement of Contingent and Limiting Conditions

- ❑ The opinion of value is valid only for the stated effective valuation date and only for the stated valuation purpose.
- ❑ Reliance on data supplied by others without independent verification.

NOTE: The typical valuation report will have a fairly lengthy list of assumptions and limiting conditions of which the reviewer should be aware.

U 10-1; A VIII-III; I 1.9; N 4.2

Overall Evaluation

- ❑ Is the report *understandable* to the reader?
- ❑ Did the analyst clearly appraise the property that was identified to be appraised?
- ❑ Is the valuation methodology appropriate for the purpose of the valuation, the relevant standard of value, the ownership characteristics (e.g., a noncontrolling, nonmarketable interest) and any judicial precedent?
- ❑ Is the report *internally consistent* (i.e., nothing in one place that seems to contradict something somewhere else)?
- ❑ Is the *methodology appropriate* for the stated definition of value and controlling statutes and judicial precedent?
- ❑ Is the report *comprehensive* (e.g., does it do everything it promises to do; are all the topics and information included that seem necessary to support the conclusion(s) reached)? (To some extent, this question addresses questions of omission rather than commission.)

❑ Does the report logically lead to convincing support for the conclusion(s) reached?

❑ Are the approaches, methods, and procedures employed those generally accepted in the appraisal community and grounded in strong economic theory and application (i.e., would the report withstand a "Daubert" type challenge)?

U 9-4 and 9-5; A I-II, I-IV, VI-III, and VIII-VIII; I 1.6, 1.9, 1.16, and 4.3; N 3.4 and 4.2; G

Part VI

Valuing Specific Securities and Interests

Chapter 23

Valuing Debt Securities

> *Lender:* *"At least you could pay me the interest on it."*
> *Debtor:* *"It is not my interest to pay the principal, nor my principle to pay the interest."*

Although debt securities play an important role in the analysis and appraisal of closely held companies, their valuation can in no way be thoroughly discussed in a single chapter. Therefore, this chapter confines discussion to general areas of reference that the analyst may want to consider when valuing debt securities. References to more extensive discussions of the areas of interest to the reader, including complete books on fixed-income analysis and valuation, are included in the bibliography at the end of this chapter.[1]

Corporate securities can be classified many different ways. As long as investors find them attractive, traditional features of corporate securities will be replaced with newly created ones. The word "debt" sounds straightforward, but financial arrangements that look suspiciously like debt are often accounted for differently. For example, instead of borrowing money to buy equipment, many companies lease or rent the equipment on a long-term basis. Such arrangements are economically equivalent to secured long-term debt. Also, preferred stock typically offers a fixed dividend that resembles interest payments on debt and yet preferred stock is legally an equity security whose dividend payment is not tax-deductible.

Extensive financial innovation has regularly introduced new varieties of debt securities: domestic and eurobonds; coupons and zeros; secured and unsecured; fixed-rate and floating-rate; senior and junior; callable, extendible, retractable; and so on. The use of derivatives has become a routine tool of corporate finance, allowing firms to protect themselves from adverse changes in external factors, such as interest rates, exchange rates, or commodity prices.

This chapter first discusses common situations that require the valuation of debt securities; it then moves to the general method of valuing them. The chapter also discusses the discount for lack of marketability, if any, and then examines the impact on value of special characteristics that many debt securities have.

Common Situations Requiring Valuation of Debt Securities

The most frequently encountered reasons for needing to value debt securities are the following:

1. Purchase or sale for cash
2. Exchange of equity for debt, or vice versa
3. Gift and estate taxes
4. Allocating total enterprise value among classes of securities in a leveraged buyout, recapitalization (including tax-free reorganizations), or bankruptcy reorganization
5. Adjusting a balance sheet for debt securities owned or owed

Purchase or Sale for Cash

From time to time, a company may have occasion to purchase or sell debt securities for cash. If they are existing securities, it is necessary to estimate their cash

---

[1] See, for example, Frank J. Fabozzi, *Handbook of Fixed-Income Securities*, 6th ed. (New York: McGraw-Hill, 2000).

equivalent value. If they are to be newly issued securities, it is necessary to structure the provisions so that the value will be equal to the price paid or received.

Exchange of Equity for Debt

If debt securities are to be exchanged for some consideration other than cash, such as stock or other property, it usually is most expedient to estimate the cash-equivalent values of both the debt securities and the stock (or other consideration) to be exchanged.

Most typically, a company, or some or all of its stock, is to be sold and a debt security received as all or part of the consideration. The seller needs to know the cash-equivalent value of the consideration being received in return for the company or stock being given up. It is not uncommon for notes or other debt securities issued in connection with the acquisition of a company to have a cash-equivalent value of 20 percent or more below the securities' face value.[2]

Gift and Estate Taxes

Debt securities may be gifted or may reside in an asset in an estate. As in all gift and estate tax situations, the standard of value is fair market value. Quite often, debt securities transferred as a gift or included in an estate have a fair market value considerably below the face value. Depending on the fair market value of a decedent's debt securities, a variety of planning opportunities are available for the estate's personal representative to consider.[3]

Allocation of Total Enterprise Value among Classes of Securities

A leveraged buyout, by its nature, results in the creation of new classes of securities, almost always including at least one class of debt. Therefore, in dealing with the valuation for a leveraged buyout, it usually is necessary not only to value the entire enterprise but to allocate this total value among the various classes of participants.

Recapitalizations involving debt securities may be undertaken for a variety of reasons. One common reason is a leveraged recapitalization—issuing high-yield debt for the purpose of redeeming a substantial portion of outstanding equity to create a more optimal capital structure. Popular during the 1980s, high-yield debt is still used in transactions where several layers of capital are appropriate.

Bankruptcy recapitalizations, by their nature, involve debt securities, sometimes both before and after the recapitalization. Creative structuring of debt and other securities to meet the varying objectives of the parties at interest can be an essential tool in achieving a successful bankruptcy reorganization.

---

[2] While this may be true in a business of any size, it is particularly prevalent in the sale of small businesses. For an extended discussion of this, see Chapter 27, "Trade-Off between Cash and Terms," in Shannon P. Pratt, Robert F Reilly, and Robert P. Schweihs, *Valuing Small Businesses and Professional Practices*, 3rd ed. (New York: McGraw-Hill, 1998).

[3] M. Read Moore and D. Alan Hungate, "Valuation Discounts for Private Debt in Estate Administration," *Estate Planning*, June 1998, pp. 195–203.

Adjusting a Balance Sheet for Debt Securities Owned or Owed

For various reasons, the balance sheet may be analyzed to adjust each line item to its fair market value. In many cases, debt may need to be adjusted to market on both the asset and liabilities sides of the balance sheet. An example would be the use of market value of invested capital valuation methods to value the common stock, as discussed in Chapter 11.

The extent of analysis undertaken for the valuation of debt securities will vary with the assignment and the accuracy required. For example, generally more analysis will be undertaken in the valuation of a debt security when that security is to be gifted (and thus subject to gift tax consequences) than when the assignment is to value the common stock of a closely held company by a market value of invested capital valuation method. Even if the analyst does not contemplate going through all the steps in the analysis of debt securities, it is important to understand them in order to have a general idea of the potential impact of an adjustment in the value of a debt security to market value.

Lease Financing

Lease financing is a substitute for secured debt financing. Just as with secured debt financing, the consequences for failure to make timely lease payments is the same as the failure to make debt payments: The lessor becomes a creditor and can force the lessee into bankruptcy. Therefore, for financial analysis purposes, the company's lease payment obligations are considered in the same category as the company's interest and principal repayment obligations. The disadvantages to the lessee of leasing as compared with conventional debt financing are that (1) the lessee gives up depreciation tax advantages of asset ownership and (2) the asset and the value of the asset are surrendered at the conclusion of the term or the lease.

The advantages of leasing to the lessee are that (1) the financing terms of the lease usually take into consideration the lessor's ability to more efficiently use the tax advantages of asset ownership; (2) most leases are short-term operating leases, and that reduces the transaction costs (i.e., identifying qualified buyers and complications associated with equipment obsolescence) at the end of the anticipated period of use; and (3) there is less of a capital commitment so that equity and borrowing power are freed for other financing. The financial terms of a lease will typically also reflect the fact that special provisions of bankruptcy law give the lessor greater flexibility to seize the asset because the lessor owns the asset. For many smaller or less creditworthy companies, utilizing the asset under the terms of a lease is an attractive alternative to conventional debt financing.

The Internal Revenue Service has established guidelines to distinguish operating leases from capital leases, installment sales agreements, and secured loans. If the terms of the lease satisfy the guidelines, the taxpayer can deduct for tax purposes the full amount of each lease payment.

For financial analysis purposes, long-term debt is usually defined to include conventional long-term debt plus capitalized lease obligations.

Method of Valuation

Valuation theory states that the fair market value of an investment is equal to the present value of the future payments, discounted back to the current time at an appropriate discount rate. The higher the risk or uncertainty associated with the payments, the higher the appropriate discount rate will be. This is precisely how the value of a debt security is estimated. The value of this type of security can be estimated by the following present value formula:

$$\text{Present value} = \sum_{i=1}^{n} \frac{PMT_i}{(1+r)^i}$$

where:

PMT_i = Payment in the ith period in the future
i = Period when payments are generated
r = Interest rate at which payments are to be discounted back to the present
n = Maturity of the debt, in periods

There are extensive public trading markets for many debt securities, including corporate bonds and notes, U.S. government and agency bonds and notes, some municipal government bonds and notes, and various short-term money market instruments. If the debt security being valued can be bought and sold in one of the public trading markets, its observed market price at any given time will reflect the present value of the future payments as determined by the market. The rate of interest that, when applied to the expected future payments on a debt security, produces a present value of the payments equal to the debt security's observed market price is called the *yield to maturity* of that security.

If the debt security cannot be purchased or sold in a public market (a closely held debt security), its value must be estimated by using the above formula. The information needed for estimating the value of a closely held debt security from the above formula is the following: (1) the amount of future payments generated by the debt security; (2) the timing of the future payments generated by the security; and (3) the appropriate rate of interest or yield to maturity to apply to the future payments to estimate the present value. The timing and amounts of the contractual payments can be determined from the debt instruments themselves. The third item, an appropriate interest rate or yield to maturity to apply to the future payments, requires both quantitative and qualitative analysis and the appraiser's judgment.

The rate of interest for straight debt is primarily a function of two factors:

1. The timing of the payments, with longer-term bonds having a different (usually higher) interest rate than shorter-term bonds.
2. The risk of the security, with higher risk securities having a higher interest rate than lower risk securities.

Amount and Timing of Future Payments

The amount of future payments generally is set by the contract establishing the debt security. Interest payments are specified at a certain amount and frequency and, as determined by the contract, the principal will be repaid at some specific future time. Certain characteristics of some debt securities may alter the amount and timing of the future payments. Some of these characteristics include call provisions and sinking fund provisions, the debt's income taxation status, and whether the debt is a "zero coupon" debt issue or has conversion privileges. The nature of each of these characteristics is discussed later in the chapter.

Estimation of Yield to Maturity

The critical step in the final determination of the value of a debt security is to choose an appropriate interest rate or yield to maturity to apply to the future payments. Many quantitative and qualitative factors help to estimate this figure at any point in time.

The yield to maturity for a debt security may differ from the security's coupon rate of interest (the rate expressed as a percentage of face value) at any point in time. If the market-determined yield to maturity for a debt security is equal to the security's coupon interest rate, the security's fair market value is equal to its face or par value. If the coupon interest rate is greater than the market-required yield to maturity, as indicated by the market yields of comparable bonds, the debt security's market value is greater than its face or par value. Conversely, if the coupon interest rate for a debt security is less than the market-required yield to maturity as indicated by the market, the security's market value is less than its face or par value. The coupon rate of interest determines the amount of the payments that can be expected from holding a debt security, but the yield to maturity required by the market establishes the market value of the payments generated by the debt security at any particular point in time.

Guideline Analysis. In order to estimate the yield to maturity to apply to a closely held debt security, it is necessary to examine several characteristics related to the security's issuer. By comparing the various characteristics of the closely held debt issuer with comparable characteristics of issuers of publicly traded debt securities that already have a market-determined yield to maturity, the analyst can gain insight into the proper yield to maturity to apply to the closely held debt security.

The first step in the guideline analysis is the quantitative analysis of the debt security issuer's operating performance and financial position. This analysis is very similar to that described in Chapter 8, "Comparative Ratios," and generally includes analysis of the debt issuer's balance sheet leverage ratios, income statement coverage ratios, short-term liquidity ratios, profitability ratios, and return on investment. The relative importance of the various ratios may vary with the type of debt security being valued. For example, the short-term liquidity ratios are far more important in the valuation of short-term debt securities than in the valuation of long-term debt securities, since short-term liquidity ratios demonstrate the debt issuer's ability to meet its current obligations, one of which is the short-term debt.

The closely held debt issuer's operating performance and financial condition can be compared with those of a broad population of issuers of publicly traded debt securities. For example, Standard & Poor's Corporation calculates key financial ratios for industrial long-term debt issuers for which it provides debt ratings. These ratios are presented in Exhibit 23–1. Current values for these ratios can be found at www.corporatecriteria.standardandpoors.com. By calculating these same ratios for the issuer of the closely held debt security over the same time period, the analyst can estimate into which rating classification the closely held debt might fall if it were rated by Standard & Poor's.

Exhibit 23–1

Key Ratios Formulas

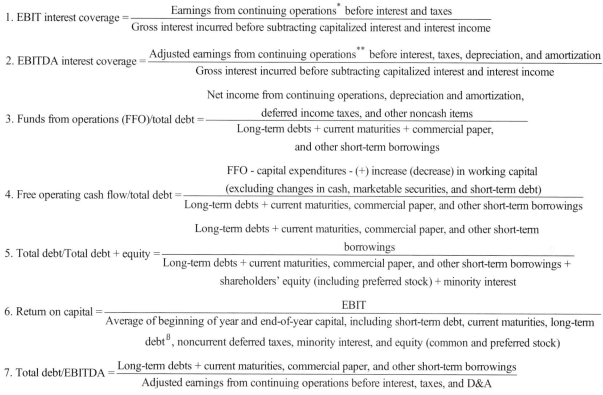

1. $\text{EBIT interest coverage} = \dfrac{\text{Earnings from continuing operations}^* \text{ before interest and taxes}}{\text{Gross interest incurred before subtracting capitalized interest and interest income}}$

2. $\text{EBITDA interest coverage} = \dfrac{\text{Adjusted earnings from continuing operations}^{**} \text{ before interest, taxes, depreciation, and amortization}}{\text{Gross interest incurred before subtracting capitalized interest and interest income}}$

3. $\text{Funds from operations (FFO)/total debt} = \dfrac{\substack{\text{Net income from continuing operations, depreciation and amortization,} \\ \text{deferred income taxes, and other noncash items}}}{\substack{\text{Long-term debts + current maturities + commercial paper,} \\ \text{and other short-term borrowings}}}$

4. $\text{Free operating cash flow/total debt} = \dfrac{\substack{\text{FFO - capital expenditures - (+) increase (decrease) in working capital} \\ \text{(excluding changes in cash, marketable securities, and short-term debt)}}}{\text{Long-term debts + current maturities, commercial paper, and other short-term borrowings}}$

5. $\text{Total debt/Total debt + equity} = \dfrac{\substack{\text{Long-term debts + current maturities, commercial paper, and other short-term} \\ \text{borrowings}}}{\substack{\text{Long-term debts + current maturities, commercial paper, and other short-term borrowings +} \\ \text{shareholders' equity (including preferred stock) + minority interest}}}$

6. $\text{Return on capital} = \dfrac{\text{EBIT}}{\substack{\text{Average of beginning of year and end-of-year capital, including short-term debt, current maturities, long-term} \\ \text{debt}^{\beta}, \text{ noncurrent deferred taxes, minority interest, and equity (common and preferred stock)}}}$

7. $\text{Total debt/EBITDA} = \dfrac{\text{Long-term debts + current maturities, commercial paper, and other short-term borrowings}}{\text{Adjusted earnings from continuing operations before interest, taxes, and D\&A}}$

*Including interest income and equity earnings; excluding nonrecurring items.

**Excludes interest income, equity earnings, and nonrecurring items; also excludes rental expense that exceeds the interest component of capitalized operating leases.

βIncluding amounts for operating lease debt equivalent, and debt associated with accounts receivable sales/securitization programs.

SOURCE: Standard & Poor's Corporate Ratings Criteria 2006 (New York: Standard & Poor's, a Division of The McGraw-Hill Companies, 2006), p.43. Reprinted with permission. For up-to-date ratings criteria, visit Standard & Poor's Web site at www.corporate criteria.standardandpoors.com.

After gaining an idea of the general rating classification into which the closely held debt security might fall, the analyst can select specific publicly traded debt securities similar in debt rating and nature to the subject security. Several rating agencies, including Moody's Investors Service[4] and Standard & Poor's Corporation[5] provide listings of publicly traded debt securities, along with credit ratings for nearly all of the securities. As would be expected, the lower-rated indexes have higher yields to maturity than the higher-rated indexes at any point in time.

The list of prospective guideline publicly traded debt securities compiled from one of these two debt listings should then be narrowed to those with characteristics or provisions similar to the privately held debt security. Thus the selection will help eliminate securities whose yields to maturity differ because of varying contract provisions. If unable to eliminate any publicly traded debt securities whose provisions differ from those of the closely held debt security from the guideline

[4] Mergent (formerly *Moody's*) *Bond Record* (New York: Moody's Investors Service, monthly).
[5] *Standard & Poor's Bond Guide* (New York: Standard & Poor's Corporation, monthly).

list, the analyst should carefully consider the differences in the securities' provisions and the associated risk characteristics when determining the appropriate yield to maturity to apply to the closely held debt security.

As stated previously, one of the factors impacting the yield to maturity of debt securities is the term or the maturity of the debt. When choosing guideline securities, the analyst should attempt to focus on securities of maturity close to the subject closely held debt security.

Standard & Poor's attaches one of approximately 200 industry codes or subcodes to nearly all the corporate bonds included in its listing. The analyst may want to consider including only publicly traded debt securities within the same general industry as that of the closely held debt security issuer, if enough publicly traded debt securities within that industry are available to provide meaningful insight into yields to maturity within that industry. Standard & Poor's description of the impact of industry analysis on its debt rating methodology is shown in Exhibit 23–2.

Exhibit 23–2

Standard & Poor's Rating Methodology

Industry Risk

Each rating analysis begins with an assessment of the company's environment. The degree of operating risk facing a participant in a given business depends on the dynamics of that business. This analysis focuses on the strength of industry prospects, as well as the competitive factors affecting that industry.

The many factors assessed include industry prospects for growth, stability, or decline, and the pattern of business cycles (see "Cyclicality"). It is critical, for example, to determine vulnerability to technological change, labor unrest, or regulatory interference. Industries that have long lead times or that require fixed plant of a specialized nature face heightened risk. The implications of increasing competition obviously are crucial. Standard & Poor's knowledge of investment plans of the major players in any industry offers a unique vantage point from which to assess competitive prospects.

While any particular profile category can be the overriding rating consideration, the industry risk assessment can be a key factor in determining the rating to which any participant in the industry can aspire. It would be hard to imagine assigning "AA" and "AAA" debt ratings to companies with extensive participation in industries of above-average risk, regardless of how conservative their financial posture. Examples of these industries are integrated steel makers, tire and rubber companies, homebuilders, and most of the mining sector.

Conversely, some industries are regarded favorably. They are distinguished by such traits as steady demand growth, ability to maintain margins without impairing future prospects, flexibility in the timing of capital outlays, and moderate capital intensity. Industries possessing one or more of these attributes include manufacturers of branded consumer products, drug companies, and publishing and broadcasting. High marks in this category do not translate into high ratings for all industry participants, but the cushion of strong industry fundamentals provides helpful support.

Again, the industry risk assessment sets the stage for analyzing specific company risk factors and establishing the priority of these factors in the overall evaluation. For example, if technology is a critical competitive factor, R&D prowess is stressed. If the industry produces a commodity, cost of production assumes major importance.

Keys to Success

As part of the industry analysis, key rating factors are identified: the keys to success and areas of vulnerability. A company's rating is, of course, crucially affected by its ability to achieve success and avoid pitfalls in its business.

The nature of competition is, obviously, different for different industries. Competition can be based on price, quality of product, distribution capabilities, image, product differentiation, service, or some other factor. Competition may be on a national basis, as is the case with major appliances. In other industries, such as chemicals, competition is global, and in still others, such as cement, competition is strictly regional. The basis for competition determines which factors are analyzed for a given company.

For any particular company, one or more factors can hold special significance, even if that factor is not common to the industry. For example, the fact that a company has only one major production facility normally is regarded as an area of vulnerability. Similarly, reliance on one product creates risk, even if the product is highly successful. For example, a pharmaceutical company has reaped a financial bonanza from just two medications. The company's debt is reasonably highly rated, given its exceptional profits and cash flow, but it would be viewed still more favorably were it not for the dependence on only two drugs (which are, after all, subject to competition and patent expiration).

SOURCE: Standard & Poor's Corporate Ratings Criteria 2006 (New York: Standard & Poor's, a Division of The McGraw-Hill Companies, 2006), pp. 20-21. Reprinted with permission. For up-to-date ratings criteria, visit Standard & Poor's Web site at www.corporatecriteria.standardandpoors.com.

After gathering an appropriate set of publicly traded equivalent securities, the analyst should examine several quantitative and qualitative factors of the privately held debt security issuer and compare them with those of the publicly traded debt security issuers. This analysis is similar to that for valuing common stock in a closely held business.

The analyst should quantitatively analyze and compare the operating performance and financial position of the debt security issuer with those of the guideline publicly traded debt security issuers. This analysis is similar to that described above in comparing the operating performance and financial condition of the closely held debt security issuer with the broad population of its publicly traded counterparts. This comparison will offer the analyst insight into the appropriate yield to maturity for the closely held debt security relative to those of the guideline publicly traded debt securities.

If the valuation is to be done in considerable depth, the appraiser may wish to analyze relevant economic and industry data, as well as the company's fundamental position, in some detail, as discussed elsewhere in the book.

After completing the quantitative and qualitative analysis discussed above, the analyst must develop an opinion of the risk associated with the payments from the closely held debt security in relation to the risk associated with the payments of the publicly traded debt securities. Based on the closely held security's risk and the publicly traded debt securities' yields to maturity, the analyst estimates the appropriate yield to maturity to apply to the closely held debt security payments.

An alternative approach for determining an interest rate is to first determine a bond rating appropriate for the subject company, and then determine the average interest rate for debt of companies with that bond rating. The company's bond rating can be benchmarked using the financial ratios discussed above. The ratings agencies publish tables that document the average of various financial ratios for companies in each ratings category.[6]

By comparing several of these ratios for the subject company with these benchmarks, one can conclude a likely bond rating for the debt of the subject company. Standard & Poor's publishes average interest rates on long-term debt of various ratings categories (S&P Bond Guide), and Bloomberg reports average interest rates for various ratings categories stratified by the term of the bonds in years.

Valuation Conclusion. Having estimated the appropriate yield to maturity to apply to the future payments associated with a closely held debt security, the analyst may value the debt security simply by computing the present value of its payments, using the formula presented earlier in the chapter.

Marketability Aspects of Closely Held Debt Securities

Chapter 17, "Lack of Marketability Discounts," presents a great deal of evidence in support of a discount for lack of marketability for the common stock of closely held businesses. The volume of trading in corporate bonds is lower than the volume in common stocks. Bonds are less liquid than stocks and have higher trading costs. On the surface, it appears that such a discount for lack of marketability might also be appropriate for closely held debt securities. However, such a discount often is

---

[6] S&P Rating Criteria 2006 has tables of average ratios for various bond ratings.

not required or, if required, would be much less than such a discount for a common stock.

Unlike investment returns on common stock, which are generated primarily by appreciation in the price of the common stock and contingent on the ability to sell the stock to realize the price appreciation, investment returns on most debt securities are generated predominantly by cash flows in the form of interest payments over the securities' lives. These payments are anticipated to be received by the debt security holder regardless of the security's marketability, and the repayment of principal is a contractual obligation for a given amount at a fixed point in time. Therefore, if the marketability of a debt security is to be considered at all, the discount associated with the security's lack of marketability should be much less than that associated with closely held common stock.

There are a few differences between publicly traded debt securities and privately placed debt securities. Private placements of debt are less standardized and usually have more strings attached. Privately issued debt can be as simple as an IOU, whereas publicly traded debt securities are more complicated contracts that include additional conditions such as procedures for the payment of interest and principal and who is to represent the holders in subsequent negotiations. Private placements of debt can be more simply arranged and can be more customized to match the concerns of the issuer and the holder. Private placements tend to have lower issuance costs but might have a higher rate of interest.

There may be a discount for lack of marketability for bonds, but it is hidden. Private bonds are tailored to the needs of both buyers and sellers and their yields reflect this. The marketability discount associated with a bond is a function of its risk class which is a function of the creditworthiness of the company and the size of the issue. Illiquid junk bonds sell at significantly higher yields than liquid junk bonds.

If the analyst thinks that marketability is a valid consideration in the valuation of a particular closely held debt security, the adjustment can be handled by either increasing the appropriate yield to maturity to apply to the debt security payments to compensate for the additional risk associated with lack of marketability or taking a discount from the value estimated by applying a yield to maturity unadjusted for marketability considerations.

An academic study by Hays, Joehnk, and Melicher conducted in the 1970s compared interest rates on privately-placed debt with interest rates on publicly-floated debt over the period from 1970 to 1975. They found that the yield to maturity on privately placed debt was, on average, issued with an interest rate approximately 50 basis points (0.46 percent) above public debt with similar terms.[7]

Special Characteristics of Various Debt Securities

In estimating the value of a debt security, it is extremely important to analyze the security's various characteristics or provisions that may impact on its value. In addition, if guideline publicly traded debt securities are used in the valuation, any differences between the provisions of the security being valued and those of the

---

[7] P.A. Hayes, M.D. Joenk, and R.W. Melicher, "Differential Determinants of Risk Premiums in the Public and Private Corporate Bond Markets," *Journal of Financial Research* (Fall 1979) Vol. II, No. 2.

guideline securities should be considered. The following discussion focuses on some of the most common provisions of various debt securities that should be analyzed in the valuation process.

Call Provisions

A feature associated with some debt securities, including most public debt, is a *call* provision. This allows the debtor to repay the debt prior to its maturity. Usually, the debt may not be called for some period early in its life, often the first five years. Furthermore, the debtor usually must pay a premium in addition to the amount of debt outstanding to the debtholder when the debt is called. A call provision benefits the debtor, since it allows the debtor to repay the debt early in a period of declining interest rates. A debt security with a call provision usually will require a higher yield to maturity than an identical security without such a provision. This is due to the fact that if the debt security is called, the investor usually will be unable to find a comparable alternative investment vehicle with a yield to maturity as high as that of the original debt issue that was called. If the stated interest rate on the debt is above market rates, making exercise of the call provision likely, the analyst usually will focus on the yield to call rather than on the yield to maturity.

Whether a call provision requires a yield premium is a function of the likelihood of the call being exercised. There is no significant call premium associated with deep discount bonds. A callable bond can be modelled as the value of straight debt minus the value of a call option at the call price.

Sinking Fund Provisions

A debt security also may have a *sinking fund* provision. This provision requires the debt issuer to call or retire a contractually determined portion of the entire debt issue periodically over time prior to the issue's maturity date. When a portion of a debt issue is retired under sinking fund provisions, the actual debt security to be retired is usually determined by lottery and the holder of the security typically is paid the security's face or par value. Although sinking fund provisions increase the uncertainty of the timing of future payments associated with a particular debt security, they also are thought to reduce the risk associated with the security. The sinking fund provisions ensure that a portion of the debt is retired periodically, thus reducing the amount of debt that will have to be paid off at maturity and lowering the risk of default on the debt.

Collateral Provisions

A debt security that has no pledge of specific property or assets as collateral for the debt is called a *debenture*. Although a debenture clearly will require a higher yield to maturity than an identical security secured by a specific asset, indenture provisions designed to protect the debtholder will reduce the relative risk associated with the debenture. Such indenture provisions might include restrictions on the amount of additional debentures the debtor can issue before paying off the original debentures; restrictions on the payment of cash dividends to equity owners of the debt issuer while the debentures are outstanding; and provisions that require the issuer to meet minimum liquidity (such as working capital) requirements while the debentures are outstanding. Despite the protection of such provisions, however, debentures generally are considered more risky than similar secured debt. Usually, the floor price for secured debt is the net liquidation value of the underlying collateral.

Income Tax Status

Interest earned on debt is subject to federal and state income taxation, with several exceptions. Interest earned on U.S. Treasury obligations and on many U.S. government agency obligations generally is exempt from income tax at the state level. Interest earned on most municipal obligations is exempt from federal income taxation and also may be exempt from state income taxation if the obligation originated in the state assessing the income tax. In addition, the purchaser must reside in the same state. As a result of this preferential tax status, debt securities not subject to some form of income taxation will require a lower yield to maturity than an identical security subject to income taxation. Conversely, a debt security subject to income taxation will require a higher yield to maturity than an identical security exempt from income taxation to compensate for the income tax liability associated with the interest on the debt security.

Zero Coupon Debt

An interesting form of debt security, known as a zero coupon debt security, allows the issuer to avoid paying cash to the debt holder for interest prior to the debt's maturity. The only cash payment from the debt issuer comes at maturity, when the debt's face value is repaid to the security holder. However, when the debt is originally issued, the debtor will receive proceeds substantially discounted from the debt's face amount. The difference between the amount of the proceeds the debtor receives at issue and the amount of debt the debtor repays at the maturity date is the investor's compensation in lieu of interest. The yield to maturity is simply the compound rate of return that equates the present value with the face value.

Because there are no annual interest payments and the holder is subject to tax on the amortization of the original issue discount, the taxable holder has negative cash flow. Therefore, zero coupon bonds sell at higher yields to maturity than bonds paying cash interest.

Another explanation is that coupon bonds provide for nearer-term payments that are discounted at a lower rate than longer-term par value payments. Shorter-term interest rates are typically lower than long-term rates due to extra risks of holding longer-term bonds. A long-term coupon bond can be viewed as a bundle of zero-coupon instruments, with each coupon payment, plus the terminal par value payment, being discounted at a rate of interest appropriate for the term of the payment. Since the value of the coupon bond is to a major extent comprised of the value of nearer-term coupon payments that are discounted at lower (short-term) interest rates than the longer-term coupon and par value payments, the overall

---

[8] Implied in discussion in Bodie, Kane, and Marcus, *Investments*, Irwin, 1989, pp. 418–419.

interest rate on the coupon bond will be lower than the interest rate on the zero-coupon bond of the same term, which is discounted only at the longest-term rate.[8]

Convertible Debt

Corporations periodically issue bonds with conversion privileges, known as convertible bonds. These conversion privileges give the holder the right to convert the bond into a given number of shares of the issuing corporation's common stock at some future point. The bondholder has no obligation to convert the bond to stock if the conversion is not to the holder's advantage. The terms of the conversion privilege are usually set such that at the time the convertible debt is issued, there is no economic benefit in immediately converting the debt to stock. For example, if a $1,000-par-value convertible bond is issued for $1,000 and is convertible into 20 shares of the issuer's common stock that pays no dividend, there will be no economic benefit in converting the debt to stock as long as the common stock is selling for less than $50 per share.

A convertible bond is unique in that its value depends, to a certain extent, on the value of the common stock into which it can be converted. The convertible bond has a minimum value equal to its value as straight debt with no conversion privilege. However, as the value of the common stock into which the bond is convertible rises, the bond's value also will begin to depend on the common stock's value. Finally, as the common stock price continues to rise, there will be a point at which the incremental increase in the bond's value is nearly equal to the increase in the aggregate value of the number of common shares into which the bond can be converted. Once this relationship begins, the bond value has entered what is known as the *equity-equivalent region*. Continuing with the above example, if the bond value is indeed in the equity-equivalent region, as the value of a single share of common stock increases $1, the bond's value will increase $20 ($1 increase × 20 common shares per bond).

The valuation of closely held convertible debt securities presents a problem not associated with publicly traded convertible debt securities. Closely held debt securities are usually convertible into closely held stock with no readily determinable market price. Although it is theoretically correct to value closely held convertible debt by direct comparison with publicly traded convertible debt with comparable conversion privileges and other provisions, it is extremely difficult to find publicly traded convertible debt that meets these criteria. As a consequence, it is difficult to estimate the value of the closely held convertible debt by comparison with publicly traded convertible debt other than when determining the minimum value of the convertible debt as a straight, nonconvertible issue.

One reasonable alternative approach to this dilemma is to segregate the convertible debt security into two parts: a straight, nonconvertible debt security and a derivative security in the form of an option or warrant to purchase the common stock at a given price. The nonconvertible debt portion of the security would then be valued in the manner for valuing nonconvertible debt securities described above. The option portion of the security would be valued in a manner described in Chapter 25, "Valuing Stock Options." These two values would then be added together to estimate the value of the convertible debt security. This may result in a slight overvaluation of the convertible bond, however, because the warrant and the bond cannot be separated. There is no empirical basis to measure the difference and it is relatively minor.

Summary

Debt security valuations are required for a wide range of purposes. Some of the more common reasons include the possible purchase or sale of a debt security, an exchange of equity securities for debt securities, gift and estate taxes on debt securities, allocation of the enterprise value of a business entity among debt and other classes of securities, and the adjustment of the balance sheet for debt securities owned or owed.

The debt security valuation process includes an analysis of the debt security contract provisions to determine the amount and timing of payments associated with the security's ownership. Various contract provisions or characteristics that affect the amount, timing, and riskiness of payments include call provisions, sinking fund provisions, collateral provisions, income tax status, and whether the debt is a zero coupon issue or has conversion privileges.

The risk or uncertainty associated with the payments is further assessed through the use of guideline quantitative and qualitative analysis. This involves comparing the closely held debt security with a broad population of debt securities in order to estimate the general ratings classification into which the security would fall if it were publicly traded. Then the closely held debt security is compared with specific guideline publicly traded debt securities similar in debt rating and nature in order to estimate an appropriate yield to maturity to apply to the subject security. The present value of the debt security payments is estimated by discounting the future payments at the appropriate yield to maturity. The analyst should consider the marketability of the debt security and determine whether a discount for lack of marketability or an increase in the debt security's yield to maturity is appropriate. However, such discounts, if any, are minor compared with discounts for lack of marketability for common stocks.

Finally, if a convertible debt security is being valued, the valuation process is further complicated by the security's "optionlike" features.

Bibliography

Budgyk, Marko A. "Valuation of Fixed-Income Securities: Bonds and Preferred Stock" (Chapter 7). In *Financial Valuation: Businesses and Business Interests*, James H. Zukin, ed. New York: Warren, Gorham & Lamont, 1990.

Dennis, Steve A., Travis Upton, and David W. Wiley. *Debt Securities*. New York: Kaplan Business, September 2005.

Fabozzi, Frank J. *Bond Markets, Analysis and Strategies*. 5th ed. New York: Prentice-Hall, October 2003.

_____. *Fixed Income Analysis for the Chartered Financial Analyst Program,* 2nd ed. New Hope, PA: Frank J. Fabozzi Associates, 2004. Available at www.frankfabozzi.com.

_____. *The Handbook of Fixed Income Securities*. 7th ed. New York: McGraw-Hill, April, 2005.

_____. *Security Finance: Securities Lending and Repurchase Agreements*. Hoboken, NJ: John Wiley & Sons, August 2005.

Fabozzi, Frank J., and Laurie S. Goodman. *Investing in Collateralized Debt Obligations*. Hoboken, NJ: John Wiley & Sons, May 2001.

Goodman, Laurie S., and Frank J. Fabozzi. *Collateralized Debt Obligations: Structure and Analysis*. Hoboken, NJ: John Wiley & Sons, September 2002.

Graham, Benjamin. *Security Analysis,* 3rd ed. New York: McGraw-Hill, December 2004.

Graham, Benjamin, and David Dodd. *Security Analysis: The Classic 1940 Edition*, 2nd ed. New York: McGraw-Hill, October 2002.

Gray, Gary, Patrick J. Cusatis, and J. Randall Woolridge. *Streetsmart Guide to Valuing a Stock: The Savvy Investor's Key to Beating the Market*. New York: McGraw-Hill, May 1999.

Julius, J. Michael. "The Skinny on Convertible Securities." *CPA Litigation Service Counselor*, October 1999, pp. 9–10.

Mercer Capital. Convertible Securities. *Mercer's Capital's Transaction Advisor*, vol. 2, no. 2, 1999.

Moore, M. Read, and D. Alan Hungate. "Valuation Discounts for Private Debt in Estate Administration." *Estate Planning*, June 1998, pp. 195–203.

Moyer, Stephen G. *Distressed Debt Analysis: Strategies for Speculative Investors*. Boca Raton, FL: J. Ross Publishing, November 2004.

Reilly, Frank K., and Keith C. Brown. "Parts 5: Analysis and Management of Bonds" and "Part 6: Derivative Security Analysis." In *Investment Analysis and Portfolio Management*, 7th ed. Mason, Ohio: South-Western, 2003.

Rini, William. *Fundamentals of the Securities Industry*. 1st ed. New York: McGraw-Hill, July 2002.

Tavakoli, Janet M. *Collateralized Debt Obligations and Structured Finance: New Developments in Cash and Synthetic Securitization*. Hoboken, NJ: John Wiley & Sons, August 2003.

_____. *Credit Derivatives & Synthetic Structures: A Guide to Investments and Applications*. 2nd ed. Hoboken, NJ: John Wiley & Sons, June 2001.

Tuckman, Bruce. *Fixed Income Securities: Tools for Today's Markets*. 2nd ed. Hoboken, NJ: John Wiley & Sons, August 2002.

Chapter 24

Valuing Preferred Stock

There are two basic types of equity ownership of companies and both (common stock and preferred stock) are frequently used in closely held companies. The main characteristic of preferred stock is that the holder is contractually promised a fixed dividend every period until its expiration. This dividend is typically required to be paid before any dividend can be paid to the common stockholders, hence the term *preferred*. The preferred distribution to a particular class of ownership also can exist in partnerships and limited liability companies.

In addition to the stated dividend, preferred stock can have many other characteristics that make it unique from the common stock. For example, preferred stock usually has a preference over common stock in the event that the corporation liquidates. Preferred stock need not have voting rights. Hence, preferred stock falls between debt and common stock in legal priority, privilege, and in the risk of ownership.

A good case can be made that preferred stock is really debt in disguise, a kind of equity bond. Unlike debt, however, preferred stock dividends cannot be deducted as interest expense when calculating the taxable income of the corporation. To the individual holder of preferred stock, the dividends received are taxable income. To the corporate owner, 70 percent of the dividends received are excluded from taxation.[1] It is no surprise to find that corporations hold most publicly traded preferred shares.

In this chapter, we consider the common situations that require the valuation of preferred stock, the special characteristics of closely held preferred stock, and the methods of valuing preferred stock.

Common Situations Requiring Valuation of Preferred Stock

There are many reasons for valuing preferred stock; these reasons are very similar to those for valuing debt securities, as discussed in Chapter 23. The most frequently encountered reasons are:

1. Purchase or sale of preferred stock for cash
2. Exchange of common equity or debt for preferred stock, or vice versa
3. Gift and estate taxes
4. Allocating total enterprise value among classes of securities in a leveraged buyout recapitalization, or bankruptcy reorganization
5. Adjusting a balance sheet for preferred securities owned or outstanding
6. Income Taxes—Code Section 409A

Purchase or Sale for Cash

As is the case with debt securities, a company may have occasion to purchase or sell preferred stock for cash. If the preferred stock is existing stock, it is necessary to determine the cash-equivalent value. If it is to be newly issued, it will be necessary to structure the provisions so that the value will be equal to the price paid or received. Transactions that have reached a stalemate can often be successfully

---

[1] According to Internal Revenue Code Section 243(a)(1). This 70 percent "dividends received deduction" applies as long as the corporation owns less than 20 percent of the distributing corporation. According to Section 243(c), the "dividends received deduction" is increased to 80 percent where the receiving corporation owns 20 percent or more of the distributing corporation. There is a 100% deduction if the company is in the same affiliated group.

structured by taking advantage of the financial and legal flexibility available from preferred stock.

Exchange of Common Equity or Debt for Preferred Stock

If preferred stock is to be exchanged for some consideration other than cash, such as common stock, debt securities, or other property, it usually is most expedient to determine the cash-equivalent values of both the preferred stock and the other consideration.

The most typical situation encountered is one in which a company, or some or all of its stock, is to be sold and a preferred stock received as all or part of the consideration. In this case, it is important that the seller know the cash-equivalent value of the consideration being received for the company or stock being sold.

Gift and Estate Taxes

Preferred stock may be gifted or may be an asset in an estate. In either situation, a determination of the preferred stock's fair market value is needed for tax purposes. It is not at all uncommon to find that the fair market value of a preferred stock is considerably less than its par value.

Allocating Total Enterprise Value among Classes of Securities

In many acquisitions, attracting capital requires creativity. For example, a leveraged buyout, by its very nature, results in the creation of new classes of securities, almost always including at least one class of debt. In addition, preferred stock may be issued in a transaction. Therefore, it is usually necessary not only to value the total enterprise but also to allocate the total value among the various classes of securities.

The issuance of preferred stocks as part of an acquisition is becoming increasingly popular, especially in situations involving ESOPs. Typically, the preferred stock is issued to the ESOP with other shareholders taking common stock. Issuing the preferred stock to the ESOP gives the ESOP a claim that is senior to the common shareholders' and at the same time allows a form of equity participation, thereby reducing the risk to the employees in a leveraged situation. One of the attractions of preferred stocks for ESOPs is the fact that, under the current tax law, dividends paid on preferred ESOP stock can be a tax-deductible expense to the corporation in most circumstances (see Chapter 32 on Employee Stock Ownership Plans).

Recapitalizations very often involve preferred stock, thereby requiring a valuation of the security. In recapitalizations involving preferred stock, a new class of preferred is issued, which the current owners of the business typically retain, while the common stock is passed along to other shareholders.

As noted in Chapter 23, bankruptcy reorganizations, by their nature, involve debt securities. Preferred stock often is issued along with the debt securities. As Chapter 23 notes, creative structuring of debt and preferred stock can be an essential tool in achieving a successful bankruptcy reorganization.

Adjusting a Balance Sheet for Preferred Stock Owned or Outstanding

The most common situation requiring a balance-sheet adjustment for preferred stock outstanding occurs when the analyst is using invested capital valuation methods to value common stock. In this situation, the market value of any preferred stock must be estimated as well as the market value of any debt outstanding. As discussed in Chapters 9 through 12, when the market value of debt and preferred stock is deducted from the value of the company's total invested capital, what remains is the value of the company's common equity.

Also, the company may own some preferred stock that may need valuing if the analyst is adjusting the various line items on the balance sheet to fair market value.

Income Taxes—Code Section 409A

Code Section 409A of the Internal Revenue Code was recently enacted and significantly impacts the need for private companies to support their determination of fair market value in setting exercise prices for nonqualified deferred compensation plans, such as stock options for the purchase of common shares. The strike price needs to be set at least equal to the fair market value of the common stock on the date of the grant in order to avoid taxability and penalties. Oftentimes the company being valued for 409A purposes has both common and preferred shares outstanding. In order to value the common stock, the preferred stock must be valued.

Special Characteristics of Closely Held Preferred Stocks

Preferred stock is often used to recognize that certain potential investors will have unique characteristics that call for special allocations of the proceeds of ownership. While the investor in preferred stock may be surrendering some of the "upside" potential that common shareholders have, the preferred stockholder will expect to be protected from some of the "downside" potential by demanding special characteristics and contingencies.

The special characteristics of the preferred stock that we typically[2] encounter include:

- Dividend rate
- Liquidation preference
- Cumulative versus noncumulative dividends
- Redeemable (e.g., call options) versus nonredeemable rights (i.e., expected life)
- Put options
- Voting versus nonvoting rights
- Participating versus nonparticipating rights in any future earnings
- Convertible versus nonconvertible rights into common equity

---

[2] In order to meet unique corporate governance situations, more complex preferred stock issues are often used, as in ESOP transactions. Beyond standard convertible preferred securities, complex ESOP securities include floor put convertible preferred stock, high-yield convertible preferred stock, super common stock, tracking stock, and performance stock. See Chester A. Gougis, "Use of Alternative Equity Securities in the Capital Structure of ESOP Companies," (Chapter 12) in *The Handbook of Advanced Business Valuation*, Robert F. Reilly and Robert P. Schweihs, eds. (New York: McGraw-Hill, 2000).

The difficulties encountered in valuing closely held preferred stock result primarily from estimating the required yield rate given the stock's myriad characteristics and evaluating the company's ability to pay the dividends. Because of the flexibility in characteristics, the ability to estimate the value of preferred stock of a closely held business depends on the analyst's experience and subjective judgment. The following discussion focuses on some of the most common special characteristics found in closely held preferred stock.

Dividend Rate

The dividend rate in and of itself is not special, but the type of dividend can be unique.

Fixed Dividend Rate. The most common form of dividend is one that is fixed at an amount usually stated as a percentage of the preferred stock's par value. For example, a $100-par-value, 10 percent preferred stock would pay an annual dividend of $10 per share. The value attributable to the stated dividend rate of the preferred stock depends on the issuing company's current and expected ability to pay the stated dividend rate and the current market yields of preferred stocks with similar dividend payment risk.

Adjustable Dividend Rate. A somewhat less common form of dividend is an adjustable-rate dividend. This form of dividend typically is adjustable within a stated range and is pegged to the general level of interest rates. However, the adjustable rate can be pegged to just about anything. The dividend rate could be adjustable based on a given time period—for example, 10 percent from 1997 to 2000, 11 percent from 2000 to 2003, and so forth. There are situations in which the dividend rate is adjusted based on the corporation's profits (in effect, a specialized form of participating preferred stock). In this case, the dividend might equal some percentage of the average of the corporation's last three fiscal years' earnings or some other measure of profits.

In order to estimate the appropriate yield, or discount rate, to apply to the subject company's adjustable-rate preferred stock, publicly traded adjustable-rate preferred stocks may be used as a benchmark, although the number of these in the public market has dwindled in recent years. The analyst must be careful to note the differences between the basis for the adjustability of the subject company's preferred stock dividend and that of the publicly traded guideline company's preferred stock dividends. The adjustability differences in the subject preferred stock compared to its publicly traded adjustable counterparts will require either an increase or a decrease in the adjustable dividend yield evidenced in the market. Just as the case with a "straight" or fixed-dividend preferred stock, the subject company's ability to pay the adjustable dividend and its liquidation preference must also be analyzed, making appropriate adjustments to the publicly traded adjustable dividend yields as necessary.

In general, all other things being equal, adjustable-rate preferred stocks require a lower dividend yield, thereby increasing the preferred stock's value. As presented in Exhibit 24–1, in March 2006, market evidence indicated that adjustable-rate preferred stocks generally required yields in the range of 42 to 445 basis points[3] below the yields required on similar fixed-rate preferred stocks.

---

[3] 100 basis points = 1 percentage point.

Exhibit 24–1

Preferred Stock Yield Comparison

| S&P Rating | Average Yield as of March 2006 | | | | |
	Adjustable %	Number of Observations	Fixed Rate %	Number of Observations	Yield Differential in Basis Points
BB+	6.45	2	6.87	52	42
NR	3.45	2	7.90	145	445

SOURCE: *Standard & Poor's Stock Guide*, March 2006, and the author's calculations.

However, at any given time, the reduction in required yield will depend on the level of interest rates prevailing in the market at the valuation date and the stated range of the adjustable dividend rate of the subject company's closely held preferred stock. For example, if market interest rates are at historically high levels at the valuation date, the likelihood of their going much higher is smaller. In this situation, the potential for a higher dividend rate in the future is diminished, thereby reducing the necessary adjustment to the yield. If the adjustable-rate range (or *collar*) on the closely held preferred stock is very small, there is less potential for an increase in the dividend, thereby reducing the required yield adjustment relative to an issue with a wider adjustable-dividend-rate range.

Liquidation Preference

Another important characteristic of a preferred stock is its liquidation preference and the subject company's ability to pay it in full at liquidation. In almost all cases, preferred stock carries a contractual right to preference (advantage) in the distribution of the issuing corporation's assets upon liquidation. The preferred stock's liquidation preference usually is stated as a certain dollar amount per share, such as $100 per share.

Revenue Ruling 83-120 requires that the issuing corporation's ability to pay the full liquidation preference at liquidation be taken into account in estimating the preferred stock's fair market value. According to the ruling, this risk can be measured by the protection afforded by the corporation's net assets. The ruling sets out the method of measuring this protection as follows:

Formula 24–1

$$\text{Liquidation coverage} = \frac{\text{Market value of assets} - \text{Market value of liabilities}}{\text{Aggregate liquidation preference of preferred stock}}$$

This ratio should be high enough that any unforeseen business downturns would not jeopardize the issuing corporation's ability to pay the liquidation preference. This ratio should be compared with ratios of publicly traded preferred stocks. All other things being equal, if the subject company's preferred stock liquidation coverage ratio is higher than the publicly traded preferred stock ratios, a lower yield (or, conversely, a higher value) will be required on the subject company preferred stock due to the lower risk of nonpayment of the liquidation preference upon liquidation. However, it should be noted that since most investors look at investments in preferred stock on a going-concern basis, the liquidation coverage ratio generally is a less important factor in the valuation than the dividend coverage ratio.

It should be noted that it is extremely difficult, if not impossible, to obtain adequate data about the guideline publicly traded preferred stocks to compute the market value of assets called for in the above liquidation coverage ratio. Therefore, as a practical matter, analysts will often use the book value of the issuing corporation's assets and liabilities in calculating the liquidation coverage ratios.

Cumulative versus Noncumulative Dividends

The term *cumulative*, when applied to preferred stock dividends, means that if the dividends are not paid for one or more periods, the corporation has a contractual obligation to make up the lapsed payments before declaring and paying any dividends on the common stock or on other junior issues. Furthermore, many cumulative issues also give preferred stockholders voting rights and/or the right to elect one or more members to the board of directors following the nonpayment of one or more dividends.

Cumulative dividends imply that the risk of nonpayment of dividends becomes secondary, because the cumulative feature requires that the shareholder not suffer a loss in income in the long run unless the company is never able to pay. In addition, when dividends are cumulative, liquidation coverage tends to become more important than dividend coverage, because in the event of liquidation, cumulative dividends in arrears must be paid in addition to the stated liquidation preference before making any assets available for distribution to common shareholders.

However, cumulative dividends on convertible preferred stock may be illusory, as the cumulated dividends are normally lost when the preferred is converted. Many venture deals offer cumulative convertible preferred stock where investors know in advance that they will never get the dividends except as a preference in liquidation.

Noncumulative preferred stocks are rare in the public market, and those few that do exist typically have special characteristics, making them unlikely to be useful as comparative securities. In general, all other things being equal, the value of a noncumulative preferred stock would be significantly less than an otherwise comparable cumulative preferred stock, because dividends not paid on a noncumulative issue are lost permanently. Revenue Ruling 83-120 addresses the cumulative-versus-noncumulative feature as follows:

> The absence of a provision that preferred dividends are cumulative raises substantial questions concerning whether the stated dividend rate will, in fact, be paid. Accordingly, preferred stock with noncumulative dividend features will normally have a value substantially lower than a cumulative preferred stock with the same yield, liquidation preference and dividend coverage.[4]

According to Graham, Dodd, and Cottle:

> One of the chief objections to the noncumulative provision is that it permits the directors to withhold dividends even in good years, when they are amply earned, the money thus saved inuring to the benefit of the common stockholders. Experience shows that noncumulative dividends are seldom paid

---

[4] Rev. Rul. 83-120, 1983-2 C.B. 170.

unless they are necessitated by the desire to declare dividends on the common; and if the common dividend is later discontinued, the preferred dividend is almost invariably suspended soon afterward.[5]

However, the analyst also must look at the subject company's history of dividend payments on noncumulative preferred stock and evidence of the company's intention to pay or not to pay preferred stock dividends. If the company has a solid history of paying dividends on its noncumulative preferred stock and a stated intention to do so in the future, and the company has the financial capability to pay dividends in the future, the diminution in value resulting from the noncumulative feature will be minimal. In addition, if the holder of a noncumulative preferred stock has full voting control of the corporation, the noncumulative feature becomes moot, since the shareholder controls the votes to pay or withhold dividends. With all these factors to consider, the impact of the noncumulative feature on value requires a considerable amount of experienced subjective judgment.

Redeemable versus Nonredeemable

Most privately held preferred stock is nonredeemable—that is, the issue has an infinite life. However, in many instances, a preferred stock has a contractual redemption provision. The type of redemption provision can vary significantly. The most common forms of redemption provisions found in privately held companies are as follows:

1. The entire issue is redeemable at the option of the issuing corporation at a specified price (typically par value) over a designated time period. These types of issues are commonly referred to as *callable*.
2. The entire issue is redeemable at the option of the issuing corporation at a specified price contingent upon a certain event, such as the death of a major shareholder, a change in ownership control, or issuance of other securities.
3. Future redemption by the issuing company is mandatory and based on a specific redemption schedule. These types of issues have sinking fund provisions similar to the vehicle by which bonds are retired at intervals up to their maturity dates and are referred to as *sinking fund preferreds*.

The impact on value of the redemption privilege varies depending on the specific redemption provisions. Therefore, it is extremely important that the analyst be aware of all the contractual provisions and contingencies of the redemption.

In general, the most important factors of the redemption provisions that affect value are:

1. Call (or redemption) price
2. Length of time the issuing company is *not* permitted to call the preferred
3. Likelihood that the contingent event triggering redemption will occur
4. Redemption schedule
5. Whether or not a sinking fund or some other means of financing the redemption is established
6. Issuing company's financial ability to cash out the preferred shares without some sort of redemption financing fund

---

[5] Benjamin Graham, David L. Dodd, and Sidney Cottle, *Security Analysis—Principles and Technique* (New York: McGraw-Hill, 1962), p. 391.

For a preferred issue that is redeemable at the issuing corporation's option at a specified price, the most important provisions affecting value are the call price and the length of time the issuing company is not permitted to call the preferred stock (the call protection period). All other things being equal, the shorter the call protection period, the lower the preferred stock's value. This is because redemption of the entire issue of preferred stock eliminates the shareholder's right to a future stream of income and forces the shareholder to accept a price (equal to the call price) for the stock that may be substantially lower than the fair market value the preferred stock might have in the absence of the redemption feature. A lower redemption, or call, price also reduces value to the shareholder, both by increasing probability that the preferred will be called (assuming that redemption is not contingent upon some future event) and by reducing the proceeds to shareholders upon redemption.

Fortunately, the public market for preferred stocks makes the task of estimating the appropriate yield rate to apply to a callable preferred stock, such as that described above, relatively straightforward. To value this type of issue, the analyst uses the same procedure discussed in the section "Method of Valuation," with one important distinction: The guideline publicly traded preferred stocks will be callable preferred stocks with similar call protection periods. As discussed in that section, the analyst chooses the appropriate yield based on a comparison of the dividend and liquidation payment risk of the subject preferred stock and the publicly traded callable preferred stock. An additional risk factor to consider in valuing callable preferred stock is the subject company's ability to fund redemptions.

When the preferred stock is redeemable contingent upon a future event, it is extremely difficult to ascertain the impact on value. This stems from the fact that the analyst is forced to make an educated guess as to the likelihood that the event triggering redemption will or will not occur. In addition, "contingent" redemption privileges are extremely rare, if not nonexistent, in the public market. Because the redemption of this type of issue is contingent upon some certain event, the importance of the likelihood of its occurring may outweigh the importance of the issuing corporation's financial ability to redeem the preferred shares should the contingent event occur when determining the appropriate yield to apply to the stock's future income stream.

One way to approach the valuation of a "contingently" redeemable preferred stock is to estimate the appropriate yield to apply to the future income stream absent the contingent redemption privilege and then adjust the yield based on an analysis of the likelihood of the contingent event occurring. Alternatively, the matter of the contingency can be handled as a separate adjustment. It should be noted that if the redemption is contingent upon the death of a major stockholder, the ability to use life insurance proceeds to redeem the preferred stock and the adequacy of those proceeds, or other evidence of the company's ability to pay, are important factors to consider in determining the appropriate yield adjustment.

Sinking fund preferred stocks differ from the types of redeemable preferred stocks discussed above in that it is known with certainty that the preferred stock will be redeemed at a specified price over a given time period. Both the redemption price and the redemption schedule are specified in the preferred stock contract. Sinking fund preferred stocks provide two advantages to their holders that are worth noting. First, the continuous reduction in the issue's size increases the likelihood that dividends will be paid. Second, the specified redemption guarantees a market, albeit limited, for the preferred stock.

The primary impact on the value of a sinking fund preferred stock results from the fact that redemption creates a finite stream of income to the investor plus a terminal value versus a theoretically infinite stream of income available to the nonsinking fund preferred stockholder. This can be illustrated with a simplified example. Assume that issue A is $100-par-value, nonredeemable, fixed-rate, voting, cumulative preferred stock that requires a market-derived yield of 10 percent. Issue A's fixed-dividend rate is 7 percent, or $7 per share. The value of issue A before consideration of lack of marketability is calculated as follows:

Formula 24–2

$$\text{Value} = \frac{\text{Dividend}}{\text{Required yield}} = \frac{\$7.00}{0.10} = \$70 \text{ per share}$$

Now assume that issue B is identical to issue A in all respects except that it is a sinking fund preferred stock that is redeemable at par value beginning in Year 5, with 10 percent of the entire issue redeemable each year. There are 100 shares of issue B outstanding. In order to determine the appropriate required yield for issue B, the procedure outlined in the "Method of Valuation" section is followed using guideline publicly traded, redeemable, fixed-rate, voting, cumulative, sinking fund preferred stock *with similar redemption schedules*. It is important to note that the appropriate yield measure for sinking fund preferred stock is yield to maturity (YTM) as opposed to the stated yield implied by the dividend rate alone.

For simplicity, we will assume that the appropriate yield to maturity given an analysis of issue B's dividend and liquidation payment risk is 10 percent. The value of issue B before consideration of lack of marketability, if applicable, is calculated as shown in Exhibit 24–2. In these examples, the value of issue B (the sinking fund preferred) is greater than the value of issue A (nonsinking fund preferred) because issue B is redeemed at par value, which, because the required yield is higher than the stated yield, is higher than its value absent the sinking fund provision. Therefore, a portion of issue B's return is derived from capital gains from the time of purchase to the time of redemption. If the stated yield and required yield in both issue A and issue B were equal, their values would be equal to par in both instances.

Put Option

A common characteristic of closely held preferred stock is a *put* option on the preferred shareholder's behalf. This option allows the shareholder to require the issuing corporation to buy back the stock at some fixed price, usually par value. When a preferred stock can be put back to the company at par value, its value usually is, at a minimum, its par value assuming the company has the financial ability to honor the put. This is true because if the preferred stock's value is determined to be less than par value based on the stock's other characteristics, the holder always has the right to put the stock back to the company at par value.

Voting versus Nonvoting

In general, voting rights increase the value of preferred stock, for obvious reasons. Numerous studies of publicly traded preferred stocks have been conducted in an attempt to isolate the reduction in yield (and thus increase in value) investors

Exhibit 24–2

Value of Sinking Fund Preferred

Year End	Income Stream			Present Value Factor @ 10.0% YTM	Value
	Dividends	Redemption	Total		
1	$700	$0	$700	0.909	$636.30
2	700	0	700	0.826	578.20
3	700	0	700	0.751	525.70
4	700	0	700	0.683	478.10
5	700	1,000	1,700	0.621	1,055.70
6	630	1,000	1,630	0.564	919.32
7	560	1,000	1,560	0.513	800.28
8	490	1,000	1,490	0.467	695.83
9	420	1,000	1,420	0.424	602.08
10	350	1,000	1.350	0.386	521.10
11	280	1,000	1,280	0.350	448.00
12	210	1,000	1,210	0.319	385.99
13	140	1,000	1,140	0.290	330.60
14	70	1,000	1,070	0.263	281.41
					8,258.61
				Shares outstanding	÷ 100
				Value per share	$82.59

YTM = Yield to maturity

accord to voting preferred stock. Unfortunately, these studies have yet to produce any meaningful results. Significant patterns of yield differentials due to voting versus nonvoting preferred stocks in the public market have not been developed on any consistent basis. Generally, this is because voting rights in publicly traded preferred stocks are incidental relative to the total outstanding voting power. Therefore, they have no significant impact on yield.

Lacking any concrete public market evidence, it is thus necessary for the analyst to subjectively adjust the required yield downward in valuing voting preferred stock. Industry practice dictates a discount in yield for voting stock ranging from 5 percent to 10 percent of the yield otherwise indicated.

In closely held companies, it is common for the preferred stock as a class to have voting control of the corporation. If the voting preferred stock being valued represents a controlling interest, the value increases considerably more (or the yield decreases even more). Perhaps the easiest way to approach the valuation of preferred stock in this situation is to value the stock absent the control feature and then add a premium for control.

Participating versus Nonparticipating

A participating preferred stock gives the preferred stockholder the right to share in additional earnings beyond the amount described in the preferred stock contract (beyond the stated dividend rate). On the other hand, a nonparticipating preferred stockholder can receive dividends only in the amount specified in the contract. A fully participating preferred stock allows the stockholder to share with the common stockholder in any earnings disbursements after the common stockholders have received a certain specified annual payment. The incremental amount to the preferred shareholders in such a case normally is equal to that paid to the common stockholders.

Another form of participating preferred stock, which is something less than fully participating, allows the preferred stockholder to share earnings disbursements with the common stockholder up to a certain dividend rate, and after this dividend has been paid in any one year, the right of the preferred stock to participate in the earnings ceases. The degree of participation allowed in any preferred stock can vary significantly from one issue to another, limited only by the creativity of financial advisers, legal counsel, and controlling stockholders' imaginations in designing the features of the issue. This is especially true of privately held participating preferred stock. Therefore, it is critical that the analyst review the preferred stock provisions to determine the level of participation.

The value of the participating feature in a preferred stock is derived from the stockholder's right to *potentially* higher dividends and depends on the likelihood that these potentially higher dividends will in fact be paid. Thus, the increment to value attributable to the participating feature is higher the greater the likelihood that dividends exceeding the stated dividend rate will be paid and the greater the participation (the higher the potential dividend).

When valuing a participating preferred stock, the analyst will need to analyze projected income statements, if available, and look at the common stock dividend payment history in order to estimate a level of future dividends to capitalize that can reasonably be expected given the preferred stock's contractual participation features.

A variation of a participating stock is a hybrid cumulative preferred stock. For example a company might issue a preferred stock that has a stated cumulative dividend and also participates in common stock dividends. Theoretically, one might logically approach a valuation of this type of preferred stock by valuing the fixed dividend and participating dividends separately and then adding these values together to get the preferred's total value. This approach requires that the required yield to be applied to the participating dividends be higher than the yield applied to the cumulative fixed dividends, because the risk of nonpayment of the participating dividends is much higher. Whether or not the preferred shareholder will receive additional dividends as a result of the participating feature depends upon whether or not dividends are declared on the common. The analyst must look at the subject company's history of paying dividends on common stock and assess the likelihood that its payment history will continue in order to assess the additional risk inherent in the preferred shareholder's receipt of participating dividends. In addition, the analyst should not view the appropriate required yield on the participating dividend portion of the preferred stock in isolation from the fact that the stock does, in fact, carry a stated cumulative dividend right. This fact, combined with the participation, reduces the overall risk of the participating portion of the issue compared with an issue that has only participating dividend rights. Thus, determining the appropriate required yield for the participating dividend requires a great deal of experienced subjective judgment.

Given these factors, perhaps a more appropriate approach to the valuation of such a hybrid preferred stock is to value both the cumulative stated dividends and the participating dividends together, adjusting the required yield to compensate for the added risk of nonpayment of the participating dividends. This process somewhat lessens the subjectivity required in estimating the appropriate required yield. Using this approach, the analyst can estimate the appropriate required yield to apply to the issue assuming that it lacked the participation feature by using public market evidence. Then the required yield is adjusted to reflect the added dividend payment risk attributable to the participating feature. If the valuation is approached by separating the cumulative stated dividend and the participating dividend, the analyst will be forced to determine the required yield on the participating dividend portion with no empirical market evidence base from which to start.

Convertible versus Nonconvertible

Convertible preferred stock is similar to a convertible bond in that it is a combination of a preferred stock issue and an option on a common equity issue. The conversion feature gives the preferred stock a speculative quality in addition to its investment value as a fixed-income security, which is derived through future dividend payments. Because of the speculative quality that the equity conversion feature imparts to the preferred stock, the stock's value depends not only on its conversion rights and expected future income stream, but on the value of the common stock as well.

Method of Valuation

Simply stated, the value of a preferred stock lacking any common equity kicker, such as convertibility or other special features, is equal to the present value of its future income stream discounted at its required rate of return, or yield. The higher the risk inherent in the investment, the higher the required yield.

Assessing Dividend and Liquidation Payment Risk

The single most important factor in the value of most preferred stock is the stock's dividend rate. Interest rates, especially subordinate debt rates, are a good benchmark for preferred rates. Another factor would be redemption in the case of a preferred stock that has a prospect of being redeemed. In most instances, the primary source of value to the preferred stockholder is the right to future levels of income through the receipt of dividends. Therefore, in estimating the appropriate required yield for the subject company preferred, the risk that the dividends on the preferred stock will not be paid is critical.

The most prevalent measure for assessing the likelihood of receiving future preferred dividends is the company's fixed-charge coverage ratio, commonly defined as the sum of pretax income plus interest expense divided by the sum of interest expense plus preferred dividends adjusted for taxes. The higher this ratio, the greater the subject company's capacity to pay its preferred dividends (or, conversely, the lower the risk that the company will miss dividend payments) and, therefore, the lower the required yield. Rating agencies use the fixed-charge coverage ratio as part of the analysis conducted to determine the appropriate rating to assign a particular preferred stock issue. Moreover, Revenue Ruling 83-120 (to be discussed later) specifically requires analysis of the fixed-charge coverage ratio for preferred stock valuations involving federal gift, estate, or income taxes.

Other ratios than the fixed-charge coverage ratio are used to assess the subject company's dividend payment risk. One example is the return on total capital, defined as the sum of pretax income plus interest expense divided by the sum of long-term debt and shareholders' preferred and common equity. Several variations of this ratio also can be used, such as pretax cash flow, return on total capital, or pretax earnings before interest and depreciation charges return on total capital. A higher ratio indicates superior profitability and, thus, a greater ability to meet preferred dividend obligations.

Another often-calculated ratio is the liquidation coverage ratio, defined as the sum of the market value of total assets less the market value of total liabilities divided by the aggregate liquidation value of the preferred stock. This ratio helps the analyst identify the risk that the preferred shareholder will not receive the full liquidation payment in the event of the corporation's liquidation. Analysis of this ratio also is specifically required in Revenue Ruling 83-120. A higher ratio implies greater protection of the shareholder's investment in the event of liquidation of company assets.

The problem with the above ratios is that they address the subject company's dividend payment risk only as of a certain point in time. Because many companies exhibit cyclical, earnings fluctuations, recent operating results may not accurately reflect a company's long-term dividend payment risk. A company subject to large swings in profits is more likely to suspend preferred dividends in down years, even though its average earnings may far exceed the annual preferred stock dividend requirements. Depending on the situation, the analyst may want to compute the above ratios using historical average financial statement figures.

The subject company's capitalization ratio is another measure of long-term dividend payment risk. The capitalization ratio is defined as the sum of long-term debt and the aggregate liquidation value of preferred stock divided by the sum of the long-term debt and total equity. This ratio measures the company's leverage and indicates how vulnerable the company will be in cyclical downturns. The higher the capitalization ratio, the greater the company's vulnerability to cyclical downturns; therefore, the risk of losing out on preferred dividend payments over the long term is higher.

The methods of calculating these ratios are shown in Exhibit 24–3. If the analyst is valuing a preferred stock that has not yet been issued, a situation that often occurs in recapitalizations, the subject company ratios must be calculated on a pro forma basis, assuming that the subject preferred issue is outstanding.

Comparison with Publicly Traded Preferred Stocks

None of the ratios discussed above indicate, in and of themselves, the appropriate required yield to apply to the subject preferred stock's income stream. In order to estimate the appropriate required yield, and thus the value of the preferred stock, the ratios determined for the subject company must be compared with similarly calculated ratios for a group of publicly traded preferred stocks having the *same rights and privileges as the subject company preferred stock*. Once these ratios are

Exhibit 24–3

Preferred Stock Dividend and Liquidation Payment Risk Ratios

$$\text{Fixed charge coverage} = \frac{EBIT}{1 + (\text{Preferred dividends}) \div (1 - t)}$$

$$\text{Liquidation coverage} = \frac{(\text{Market value of assets} - \text{Market value of liabilities})^a}{\text{Aggregate liquidation value of preferred stock}}$$

$$\text{Capitalization ratio} = \frac{\text{Total debt} + \text{Liquidation value of all preferred stock}}{\text{Total debt} + \text{Total equity}}$$

$$\text{Pretax return on total capital} = \frac{\text{Pretax income} + \text{Interest expense}}{\text{Long} - \text{term debt} + \text{Total equity}}$$

a. From a practical standpoint, total book value of equity is often used.

NOTE: All net income and cash flow figures are before preferred stock dividends, discontinued operations, nonrecurring items, and extraordinary items.

EBIT = Earnings before interest expense and taxes
t = Effective tax rate

---

calculated, the comparable publicly traded preferred stocks must be grouped by rating category.

Quantitative Comparison. Both Mergent (previously Moody's) and Standard & Poor's rate publicly traded preferred stock issues. Exhibit 24–4 shows Standard & Poor's ratings and its explanation of the nature of the risk of the preferred stocks contained in each category. Exhibit 24–5 shows the yields of nonconvertible publicly traded preferred stocks as they existed at the end of March 2006.

It is extremely important that the guideline publicly traded preferred stocks used to estimate appropriate yields for the subject stock be as similar as possible to the subject stock in rights, privileges, and all relevant characteristics. Differences among these factors can have a significant impact on the required yield. In addition, the analyst will probably want to exclude preferred stocks issued by utilities, banks, insurance companies, and other financial institutions when selecting guideline publicly traded preferred stocks (unless the preferred stock to be valued is issued by a utility, bank, or insurance company). The criteria the rating agencies use differ somewhat for these types of issues due to their unique financial statement presentation and the fact that they are regulated. Because preferred stock ratings affect the investor's perception of risk, they also impact the required yield.

Once the ratios are calculated for both the subject company and the guideline publicly traded companies and the publicly traded issues are categorized by rating, the yields of each issue must be calculated and averaged for each rating category. The ratios for each issue also need to be averaged in each rating category. Exhibit 24–6 shows an example of the end result of this process. Generally, the more favorable the ratios, the higher the rating and the lower the yield. In addition, once financial institutions and utilities are excluded, the number of guideline preferred stocks drops significantly. In most circumstances, it is not necessary to compute dividend yields and ratios for each rating category. This is because once

Exhibit 24–4

Standard & Poor's Preferred Stock Rating Definitions

"AAA" This is the highest rating that may be assigned by Standard & Poor's to a preferred stock issue and indicates an extremely strong capacity to pay the preferred stock obligations.

"AA" A preferred stock issue rated "AA" also qualifies as a high-quality fixed income security. The capacity to pay preferred stock obligations is very strong, although not as overwhelming as for issues rated "AAA."

"A" An issue rated "A" is backed by a sound capacity to pay the preferred stock obligations, although it is somewhat more susceptible to the adverse effects of changes in circumstances and economic conditions.

"BBB" An issue rated "BBB" is regarded as backed by an adequate capacity to pay the preferred stock obligations. Whereas it normally exhibits adequate protection parameters, adverse economic conditions or changing circumstances are more likely to lead to a weakened capacity to make payments for a preferred stock in this category than for issues in the "A" category.

"BB," "B," "CCC" Preferred stock rated "BB", "B", and "CCC" are regarded, on balance, as predominantly speculative with respect to the issuer's capacity to pay preferred stock obligations. "BB" indicates the lowest degree of speculation and "CCC" the highest degree of speculation. While such issues will likely have some quality and protective characteristics, these are outweighed by large uncertainties or major risk exposures to adverse conditions.

"CC" The rating "CC" is reserved for a preferred stock issue in arrears on dividends or sinking fund payments but that is currently paying.

"C" A preferred stock rated "C" is a non-paying issue.

"D" A preferred stock rated "D" is a non-paying issue with the issuer in default on debt instruments.

"r" The "r" is attached to highlight derivative, hybrid, and certain other obligations that S&P believes may experience high volatility or high variability in expected returns due to non-credit risks. Examples of such obligations are: securities whose principal or interest return is indexed to equities, commodities, or currencies; certain swaps and options; and interest only and principal only mortgage securities.

The absence of an "r" symbol should not be taken as an indication that an obligation will exhibit no volatility or variability in total return.

NR This indicates that no rating has been requested, that there is insufficient information on which to base a rating, or that S&P does not rate a particular type of obligation as a matter of policy.

Plus (+) or Minus (-) To provide more detailed indications of preferred stock quality, the ratings from "AA" to "CCC" may be modified by the addition of a plus or minus sign to show relative standing within the major rating categories.

SOURCE: *Standard & Poor's Stock Guide*, March 2006 (New York: Standard & Poor's Corporation, 2006). Reprinted with permission of Standard & Poor's, a Division of The McGraw-Hill Companies, Inc.

the dividend and liquidation payment risk ratios for the subject company have been calculated, it often becomes clear to the analyst into which rating category the subject preferred generally would fit.

Once all the necessary guideline data are available, the next step is to determine the rating category into which the subject preferred stock would fall given the subject company's dividend and liquidation payment risk. The appropriate yield is selected for the subject company based on the yields in the appropriate rating category.

Qualitative Factors. At this point, the analyst must consider any unique qualitative factors that might cause the required yield to be higher or lower than that based solely on the quantitative ratio analysis. These include many of the nonquantitative factors generally considered in valuing common stock that would increase or decrease the issuing company's risk. However, when assessing risk, the preferred shareholder will be most concerned with qualitative factors that may change the company's ability to meet its preferred stock obligations. These qualitative factors might include the following:

1. The competitive environment in the industry
2. Depth and competence of management

Exhibit 24–5

Nonconvertible Preferred Stock Yields as of March 2006

S&P Rating	Number of Companies	Number of Issues	Dividend Yield Range		Dividend Yield	
			Low %	High %	Mean %	Median %
AAA	1	1	5.9	5.9	5.9	5.9
AA–	3	18	3.5	7.2	5.3	5.6
A+	1	1	7.5	7.5	7.5	7.5
A	8	34	5.8	7.8	6.6	6.4
A–	19	40	2.9	7.7	6.6	6.8
BBB+	21	52	4.8	9.3	6.4	6.6
BBB	24	35	5.1	8.5	6.8	6.7
BBB–	33	54	4.5	9.3	7.1	7.2
BB+	30	54	4.9	9.0	6.9	7.3
BB	6	9	6.4	8.6	7.5	7.5
B+	3	9	7.3	9.9	8.3	7.8
B	8	9	4.9	9.3	8.1	8.4
B–	1	2	8.3	9.8	9.1	9.1
CCC+	2	3	7.6	8.4	8.0	8.0
CCC	3	3	6.4	8.6	7.7	8.0
NR	113	147	1.6	10.6	7.8	8.0

SOURCE: *Standard & Poor's Stock Guide*, March 2006, and author's calculations.

Exhibit 24–6

Nonconvertible, Nonsinking Fund, Fixed Rate Cummulative Preferred Stock
Excluding Utilities and Financial Institutions (Banks, Investment Companies, and REITS)

S&P Rating	Number of Issues	Yield Range		Average Yield %
		Low %	High %	
BBB+	17	5.2	7.8	6.7
BBB	7	5.1	8.5	6.7
BBB–	10	6.7	8.7	7.4
BB+	1	8.0	8.0	8.0
B–	2	8.3	9.8	9.1
NR	10	6.5	10.3	7.6

SOURCE: *Standard & Poor's Stock Guide*, March 2006, and author's calculations.

3. Federal and state regulatory climate
4. Rights of lenders and other stockholders to influence dividend policy
5. Trends in and diversification of supply sources
6. Trends in and diversification of revenue sources[6]

---

[6] Gerald R. Martin and E. Halsey Sandford, "Valuation of Preferred Stock," *Business Valuation Review*, March 1991, p. 35.

Standard & Poor's performs an extensive analysis of a company's qualitative factors in determining a security's appropriate rating. In addition, the outlook for the industry and economy also play an important role in assessing the subject company's preferred stock income stream risk.

Capitalizing the Income Stream

Once the appropriate required yield is estimated, the next step is to capitalize the preferred stock's future income stream by its required yield. Mechanically, this is a simple present value calculation. For a noncallable, non-sinking-fund preferred stock with no maturity and lacking a conversion feature, the formula for determining the value is as follows:

Formula 24–3

$$\text{Present value} = \frac{\text{Dividend}}{\text{Required yield}}$$

If the issue is nonconvertible and callable or subject to a sinking fund, its value is calculated as follows:

Formula 24–4

$$\text{Present value} = \sum_{i=1}^{n} \frac{E_i}{(1 + k_p)^i}$$

where:

E_i = Cash flow (including redemption price and dividends) in the ith period in the future

i = Period when cash flows are generated

k_p = Required yield at which preferred stock cash flows are to be discounted back to the present

n = Number of periods until redemption

It is important to note that even if a preferred stock is callable at the company's option, it usually is appropriate to value the issue as if it were noncallable if the stated dividend rate is below the rate currently required by the market for comparable issues. For example, if a $100-par-value preferred stock, callable at $100 per share and with a stated dividend of 6 percent, requires a yield of 10 percent under current market conditions, the call feature has little or no effect as a practical matter. If the required yield is above the stated yield, the company will not exercise its option to call the issue, which renders the call feature irrelevant for the preferred stockholder.

Marketability Aspects of Closely Held Preferred Stock

Chapter 17, "Lack of Marketability Discounts," presented a great deal of evidence in support of a discount for lack of marketability on common stock of closely held businesses. On the surface, it appears that such a discount might also be appropriate for closely held preferred stocks. However, such a discount for preferred stocks, if required, would be different from such a discount for common stocks. Unlike investment returns on closely held common stock, which are predominantly generated by appreciation in the common stock's price and contingent upon the ability to sell the stock to realize the price appreciation, investment returns on most preferred stocks, as on debt securities, are predominantly generated by cash flows in the form of dividend payments over the life of the security. These cash flows are anticipated to be received by the holder of the preferred stock regardless of how marketable the preferred stock happens to be. Therefore, the discount associated with the lack of marketability of a preferred stock is different from that associated with closely held common stock.

If the analyst thinks that marketability is a valid consideration in the valuation of a particular closely held preferred stock, the adjustment can be handled by either increasing the appropriate yield to apply to the preferred stock's dividends or by taking a discount from the value determined by applying a yield unadjusted for marketability considerations.

Revenue Ruling 83-120

At this writing, the only regulatory guidelines established for the valuation of closely held preferred stock are those issued by the Internal Revenue Service in Revenue Ruling 83-120 (see Exhibit 24–7). Although applicable to any valuation of preferred stock in a closely held corporation, the ruling was specifically designed to prevent the relative overvaluation of preferred stock and concurrent undervaluation of common stock in "estate freezing recapitalizations" in closely held corporations.

In the section entitled "Approach to Valuation—Preferred Stock," Revenue Ruling 83-120 invokes the standard tools of security analysis for the valuation of the closely held preferred stock based on the issuing company's ability to pay its dividend yield and its liquidation preference. Revenue Ruling 83-120 specifically addresses the following factors affecting the value of preferred stock:

1. Stated dividend rate and the risk associated with payment of it
2. Cumulative versus noncumulative dividends
3. Ability to pay the preferred stock's liquidation preference at liquidation
4. Voting rights
5. Redemption privileges

Specifically, the ruling calls on the valuation analyst to compute "coverage ratios" for the subject company's preferred stock dividend and liquidation value and to compare these ratios with those found for guideline publicly traded preferred stocks. The ruling indicates that if the ratios for the subject stock are substandard, the value of the subject preferred should be discounted from its par value on the basis of these criteria. Although the ruling is very specific with respect to these two factors, it leaves a wide area of uncertainty as to the value of features such as voting control and redemption rights, two extremely valuable features often found in closely held preferred stocks.

Exhibit 24–7

Revenue Ruling 83–120

Rev. Rul. 83-120

Section 1. Purpose

The purpose of this Revenue Ruling is to amplify Rev. Rul. 59-60, 1959-1 C.B. 237, by specifying additional factors to be considered in valuing common and preferred stock of a closely held corporation for gift + tax and other purposes in a recapitalization of closely held businesses. This type of valuation problem frequently arises with respect to estate planning transactions wherein an individual receives preferred stock with a stated par value equal to all or a large portion of the fair market value of the individual's former stock interest in a corporation. The individual also receives common stock which is then transferred, usually as a gift, to a relative.

Sec. 2. Background

.01 One of the frequent objectives of the type of transaction mentioned above is the transfer of the potential appreciation of an individual's stock interest in a corporation to relatives at a nominal or small gift tax cost. Achievement of this objective requires preferred stock having a fair market value equal to a large part of the fair market value of the individual's former stock interest and common stock having a nominal or small fair market value. The approach and factors described in this Revenue Ruling are directed toward ascertaining the true fair market value of the common and preferred stock and will usually result in the determination of a substantial fair market value for the common stock and a fair market value for the preferred stock which is substantially less than its par value.

.02 The type of transaction referred to above can arise in many different contexts. Some examples are:

(a) A owns 100% of the common stock (the only outstanding stock) of Z Corporation which has a fair market value of 10,500x. In a recapitalization described in section 368(a)(1)(E), A receives preferred stock with a par value of 10,000x and new common stock, which A then transfers to A's son B.

(b) A owns some of the common stock of Z Corporation (or the stock of several corporations) the fair market value of which stock is 10,500x. A transfers this stock to a new corporation X in exchange for preferred stock of X corporation with a par value of 10,000x and common stock of corporation, which A then transfers to A's son B.

(c) A owns 80 shares and his son B owns 20 shares of the common stock (the only stock outstanding) of Z Corporation. In a recapitalization described in section 368(a)(1)(E), A exchanges his 80 shares of common stock for 80 shares of new preferred stock of Z Corporation with a par value of 10,000x. A's common stock had a fair market value of 10,000x.

Sec. 3. General Approach to Valuation

Under section 25.2512-2(f)(2) of the Gift Tax Regulations, the fair market value of stock in a closely held corporation depends upon numerous factors, including the corporation's net worth, its prospective earning power, and its capacity to pay dividends. In addition, other relevant factors must be taken into account. *See* Rev. Rul. 59-60. The weight to be accorded any evidentiary factor depends on the circumstances of each case. *See* section 25.2512-2(f) of the Gift Tax Regulations.

Sec. 4. Approach to Valuation— Preferred Stock

.01 In general the most important factors to be considered in determining the value of preferred stock are its yield, dividend coverage and protection of its liquidation preference.

.02 Whether the yield of the preferred stock supports a valuation of the stock at par value depends in part on the adequacy of the dividend rate. The adequacy of the dividend rate should be determined by comparing its dividend rate with the dividend rate of high-grade publicly traded stock. A lower yield than that of high-grade preferred stock indicates a preferred stock value of less than par. If the rate of interest charged by independent creditors to the corporation on loans is higher than the rate such independent creditors charge their most credit worthy borrowers, then the yield on the preferred stock should be correspondingly higher than the yield on high quality preferred stock. A yield which is not correspondingly higher reduces the value of the preferred stock. In addition, whether the preferred stock has a fixed dividend rate and is nonparticipating influences the value of the preferred stock. A publicly traded preferred stock for a company having a similar business and similar assets with similar liquidation preferences, voting rights and other similar terms would be the ideal comparable for determining yield required in arms length transactions for closely held stock. Such ideal comparables will frequently not exist. In such circumstances, the most comparable publicly traded issues should be selected for comparison and appropriate adjustments made for differing factors.

.03 The actual dividend rate on a preferred stock can be assumed to be its stated rate if the issuing corporation will be able to pay its stated dividends in a timely manner and will, in fact, pay such dividends. The risk that the corporation may be unable to timely pay the stated dividends on the preferred stock can be measured by the coverage of such stated dividends by the corporation's earnings. Coverage of the dividend is measured by the ratio of the sum of pre-tax and pre-interest earnings to the sum of the total interest to be paid and the pre-tax earnings needed to pay the after-tax dividends. *Standard & Poor's Ratings Guide,* 58 (1979). Inadequate coverage exists where a decline in corporate profits would be likely to jeopardize the corporation's ability to pay dividends on the preferred stock. The ratio for the preferred stock in question should be compared with the ratios for high quality preferred stock to determine whether the preferred stock has adequate coverage. Prior earnings history is important in this determination. Inadequate coverage indicates that the value of preferred stock is lower than its par value. Moreover, the absence of a provision that preferred dividends are cumulative raises substantial questions concerning whether the stated dividend rate will, in fact, be paid. Accordingly, preferred stock with noncumulative dividend features will normally have a value substantially lower than a cumulative preferred stock with the same yield, liquidation preference and dividend coverage.

.04 Whether the issuing corporation will be able to pay the full liquidation preference at liquidation must be taken into account in determining fair market value. This risk can be measured by the protection afforded by the corporation's net assets. Such protection can be measured by the ratio of the excess of the current market value of the corporation's assets over its liabilities to the aggregate liquidation preference. The protection ratio should be compared with the ratios for high quality preferred stock to determine adequacy of coverage. Inadequate asset protection exists where any unforeseen business reverses would be likely to jeopardize the corporation's ability to pay the full liquidation preference to the holders of the preferred stock.

continued on next page

Exhibit 24–7

Revenue Ruling 83–120 (*continued*)

.05 Another factor to be considered in valuing the preferred stock is whether it has voting rights and, if so, whether the preferred stock has voting control. See, however, Section 5.02 below.

.06 Peculiar covenants or provisions of the preferred stock of a type not ordinarily found in publicly traded preferred stock should be carefully evaluated to determine the effects of such covenants on the value of the preferred stock. In general, if covenants would inhibit the marketability of the stock or the power of the holder to enforce dividend or liquidation rights, such provisions will reduce the value of the preferred stock by comparison to the value of preferred stock not containing such covenants or provisions

.07 Whether the preferred stock contains a redemption privilege is another factor to be considered in determining the value of the preferred stock. The value of a redemption privilege triggered by death of the preferred shareholder will not exceed the present value of the redemption premium payable at the preferred shareholder's death (i.e., the present value of the excess of the redemption price over the fair market value of the preferred stock upon its issuance). The value

of the redemption privilege should be reduced to reflect any risk that the corporation may not possess sufficient assets to redeem its preferred stock at the stated redemption price. *See* Section .03 above.

SEC. 5. APPROACH TO VALUATION— COMMON STOCK

.01 If the preferred stock has a fixed rate of dividend and is nonparticipating, the common stock has the exclusive right to the benefits of future appreciation of the value of the corporation. This right is valuable and usually warrants a determination that the common stock has substantial value. The actual value of this right depends upon the corporation's past growth experience, the economic condition of the industry in which the corporation operates, and general economic conditions. The factor to be used in capitalizing the corporation's prospective earnings must be determined after an analysis of numerous factors concerning the corporation and the economy as a whole. *See* Rev. Rul. 59-60, at page 243. In addition, after-tax earnings of the corporation at the time the preferred stock is issued in excess of the stated dividends on the preferred stock will increase the value of the common stock. Furthermore, a corporate

policy of reinvesting earnings will also increase the value of the common stock.

.02 A factor to be considered in determining the value of the common stock is whether the preferred stock also has voting rights. Voting rights of the preferred stock, especially if the preferred stock has voting control, could under certain circumstances increase the value of the preferred stock and reduce the value of common stock. This factor may be reduced in significance where the rights of common stockholders as a class are protected under state law from actions by another class of shareholders, *see Singer v. Magnavox Co.*, 380 A. 2d 969 (Del. 1977), particularly where the common shareholders, as a class, are given the power to disapprove a proposal to allow preferred stock to be converted into common stock. See ABA-ALI Model Bus. Corp. Act, Section 60 (1969).

SEC. 6. EFFECT ON OTHER REVENUE RULINGS

Rev. Rul. 59-60, as modified by Rev. Rul. 65-193, 1965-2 C.B. 370 and as amplified by Rev. Rul. 77-287,1977-2 C.B. 319, and Rev. Rul. 80-213, 1980-2 C.B. 101, is further amplified.

SOURCE: Rev. Rul. 83-120, 1983-2 C.B. 170.

Summary

The combination of rights and privileges found in closely held preferred stock are limited only by the imaginations of the issuer, the financial adviser, and the legal counsel. It is the flexibility of the myriad of characteristics of closely held preferred stock that makes the estimation of value so difficult. Some guidance is found in Revenue Ruling 83-120, but the ruling fails to address the specific value implications of several of the most important features often found in closely held preferred stocks but not in publicly traded preferreds.

A judge's opinion in a 1981 estate tax case, in which the fair market value of closely field preferred stock was at issue, sums up the difficulties in valuing closely held preferred stock with many features not found in publicly traded preferred stocks:

> Since these consummate negotiators, who invariably achieve an agreeable bargain, are mythical persons endowed with characteristics prescribed in authoritative writings, the undertaking of determining what they would decide on given evidence not exactly like any recounted in precedents, might better be discharged with the benefit of interpretive insights and skills associated more often with the theater than with the court. Like the actor or actress who recreates the character from the guidelines the playwright has

given, I must try first to understand the characters created in the authoritative statute regulations and precedents, and then, departing from the custom of the stage, occupy not one but two roles simultaneously—those of the willing buyer and the willing seller–coming finally to an agreement with myself— or more precisely between the two whom I am simultaneously impersonating—on the value of the stock at issue. A judge might be daunted by such an undertaking were it not for the reassuring thought that as surely as one who...

> ...never saw a moor,
> [And] never saw the sea;
> Yet [may] know ...how the heather looks,
> And what a wave must be.[7]

Bibliography

Barenbaum, Lester, and Walter Schubert. "Determining the Required Rate of Return for Preferred Stock of a Closely Held Firm." *Valuation*, June 1997, pp. 111–18.

Bloom, Gilbert D. "Certain Preferred Stock Gets the 'Boot'—But Does It Fit?" *Journal of Taxation*, February 1998, pp. 69–73.

Cortese, Christopher D. "The Subtraction Method of Valuing Preferred Stock: Chapter 14 Rules vs. Economic Reality." *Business Valuation Review*, June 1994, pp. 71–73.

Cowan, Arnold R. "Tax Options, Clienteles, and Adverse Selection: The Case of Convertible Exchangeable Preferred Stock—Statistical Data Included." *Financial Management*, June 1999.

Equity Valuations, Inc. "Guide to Valuation of Preferred Stock. Revenue Ruling 83-120." Available at www.equityvaluations.com/pubs/revenueruling83-120.html.

Freeman, Neal L. "Cost of Capital Establishes a Benchmark for Evaluation of Investments: Common Equity, Debt, and Preferred Stock All Play Important Roles." *Ophthalmology Times*, April 2004.

Goodwin Procter. "FASB Statement 149 and Redeemable Preferred Stock." *Private Equity Update*, March 2003. Available at www.goodwinprocter.com/ publications/peu_fasb149_3_03.pdf

Julius, J. Michael. "The Skinny on Convertible Securities." *CPA Litigation Service Counselor*, October 1999, pp. 9–10.

Mercer Capital. "Convertible Securities." *Mercer's Capital's Transaction Advisor*, vol. 2, no. 2, 1999.

Murphy, Austin. "An Analysis of Preferred Stock." *Financial Engineering News,* no. 35, January/February 2004.

Schneider, Willys H., and Sydney E. Unger. "TRA '97 Curtails Tax-Free Spinoffs and Use of Preferred Stock in Tax-Free Acquisitions." *Journal of Taxation*, December 1997, pp. 334–40.

Sherman, Lawrence F. "Valuation of Preferred Capital Stock for Business Enterprises." *ASA Valuation*, March 1994, pp. 72–83.

Thompson, James. "Letter Ruling 9420001: A Taxable Gift on Conversion of Preferred Stock to Common Stock." *Tax Adviser*, October 1994, p. 611.

Wise, Richard. "Closely Held Preferred Stock. A Review of the Common Value Drivers." *Business Valuation Review*, vol. 22, no. 3, September 2003, pp. 149-154.

---

[7] *Wallace v. United States*, 82-1 U.S.T.C. paragraph 13,442 (D. Mass. 1981). Verse from "Time and Eternity," in *Poems by Emily Dickinson*, vol. IV, George Monteiro, ed. (Delmar, NY: Scholars' Facsimiles & Reprints, 1967), p. XVII.

Chapter 25

Introduction to Valuing Stock Options

This chapter was revised from the previous edition by M. Mark Lee.

Stock options are derivative securities whose values are contingent upon the value of publicly traded or privately held common stock. There are many kinds of publicly traded derivative securities that depend on stock indices, currencies, futures contracts, and interest rates. Derivatives can be contingent on almost any variable, from the price of beans to the amount of snow falling at a ski resort. There are even options on options, called compound options. Some stock options are created specifically by a corporate acquirer to meet the particular needs of the holder of a corporate seller's equity. Others are made available to corporate clients by financial institutions or added to new issues of securities by underwriters. Derivative securities are being used more frequently by closely held businesses when their owners plan their estates, create an employee stock-ownership plan, provide employee incentives, and make corporate acquisitions and divestitures.

The derivative securities this chapter addresses are call options to purchase the common stock of either a publicly traded or a closely held company. This chapter explores the components of stock option values, including employee incentive stock options, for both income tax and financial reporting purposes. It discusses the factors relevant to the value of stock options, and explains the most widely recognized models in current use for the valuation of stock options. Finally, so-called "real options" are introduced.

Some of the stock options discussed in this chapter are called warrants in the public markets rather than options. Publicly traded options usually are issued by third parties and are settled with already outstanding common shares or cash. Warrants are issued by the company and (like employee stock options) are settled in additional outstanding common shares of the company. The initial time allowed to exercise a publicly traded warrant usually is much longer than for a publicly traded option.

Common Situations Requiring the Valuation of Options

The situations commonly requiring valuation of such securities are the following:

1. When the option is designed, granted, exchanged, or terminated
2. When the option value is disclosed in a company proxy statement disclosure
3. When financial statement disclosure requires that the option value is recognized
4. When the option value is required for determination of compensation of an executive for income tax purposes
5. When the option is transferred to a third party
6. When the option value is at issue in a damage suit, such as a breach of contract suit between an existing or former executive and the issuing company
7. When the option is a repurchased option by the issuing company
8. When the option value is required in the divorce of an executive who holds the option

Terminology

The most common form of stock option is the *call* option. In its simplest form, it is the right to buy a specific number of a company's common shares at a specific price for specific period of time. The opposite of a call option is a *put* option which is the right to sell a specific number of common shares for a specific price and period of time.

The financial analysis of stock options has become a specialty area in its own right, complete with its own jargon. Here is an explanation of some of the more common terms:

- The *option premium* is the market price of the option.
- The *strike, or exercise, price* is the fixed price at which the option is exercisable.
- The *expiration date* is the last date on which the holder may exercise his or her right.
- The *term* or *remaining life* of the option is the time between the valuation date and the option's expiration date.
- *Perpetual* options and warrants have no expiration date.
- A *European* option may only be exercised on the expiration date.
- An *American* option may be exercised at any time through the expiration date.
- The *early exercise premium* is the difference in value between an American option and a European option due solely to the ability to exercise an American option before the expiration date.
- The *underlying stock* is the common stock received when the option is exercised.
- The *intrinsic value* of an option is the difference between the price of its underlying stock and its strike price. It is never less than zero.
- *Time value* of a stock option is the difference between its price and its intrinsic value. Often it is better for the holder of an option to delay paying the exercise price to take advantage of the time value of money rather than exercising the option immediately.
- An option is *in-the-money* if the value of its underlying stock exceeds the exercise price.
- An option is *at-the-money* if the value of its underlying stock equals the exercise price.
- An option is *out-of the-money* if the value of its underlying stock is less than the exercise price.

While options that are at-the-money or out-of-the-money have no intrinsic value, they still can have time value.

The Basic Call Option Equation

A call option allows an investor to share in the potential capital appreciation of the common stock of a company with less risk of a major loss than from owning the stock directly. Imagine that an investor in the common stock of a company has two choices, either to (1) buy 100 shares of a company's common stock at $10 per share or (2) to purchase a call for $125 to purchase 100 shares at the same $10 price at the end of nine months. If the investor chooses to buy the stock, the investor must pay $1,000 immediately and is at risk for the entire $1,000 investment. If the investor chooses to purchase the call option, the investor will pay only $125 immediately and can wait until the option's expiration date to decide whether or not to buy the stock for an additional $1,000. The investor's risk is limited to $125. If the option is in-the-money (the price of the stock is above the strike price), the option will be exercised. If it is out-of-the money (the stock price is below the strike price) or at-the-money, the option will simply lapse. The investor's total risk is reduced. However, in exchange for this flexibility, the investor must pay the option premium and forego all of the underlying stock's voting and dividend rights until the option is exercised.

The relationship of the value of a simple call option to the value of its underlying common stock is shown in the following equation:

$$\text{Minimum Call Value} = \text{Stock Price} - \text{PV (Strike Price)}$$
$$- \text{PV (Dividends)} + \text{Put Value}$$

The minimum value of a simple call option is the value of its underlying common stock minus (1) the present value of its exercise price, assuming it is paid on the expiration date, and (2) the present value of the dividends paid on the underlying stock during the term of the option, plus the value of a put option having the same terms as the call option.

The exercise price and dividends are discounted to present value at the risk-free rate for the length of time until expiration. A greater discount rate would decrease the present value of the exercise price and dividends and thus increase the value of the call option. The put option captures the value of the investor's ability to avoid purchasing the stock if its price at expiration is below the option's exercise price. The equation assumes that the underlying common stock's voting rights do not have any value during the life of the option.

The components of the call option's value are:

1. The *price of the underlying stock*. As the stock price increases, call options become more valuable and put options become less valuable.
2. The *strike price*. As the strike price decreases, call options become more valuable and put options become less valuable.
3. The *time to expiration*. The owner of a longer-lived option can wait longer to exercise the option and further take advantage of the time value of money. Both call options and put options become more valuable as the time to expiration increases.
4. The *risk-free interest rate*. When the risk-free interest rate increases, the present values of both the strike price and the dividends decrease, and the value of the call option increases.
5. The *dividends expected during the life of the option*. As the dividends on the underlying stock increase, the value of the call option decreases.
6. The *value of the put option*. A put option has value if the market price of the underlying stock on the expiration date is *lower than* the strike price. As the strike price increases, the value of the put option increases.
7. The *volatility of the price of the underlying stock*. The wider the range of the stock price, the greater the chance that it will be more than the strike price on the expiration date. Both call options and put options are more valuable as volatility increases.

Options can be very complicated. For example, some options have strike prices that vary over time or under different market conditions. Other options have lives that vary depending on stock prices and market conditions. There are even *compound options*, which are options on options, and *barrier options*, which set price boundaries.

Almost all option valuation models incorporate the exercise price, the time to expiration date, the risk-free interest rate during the period, dividends, the underlying value of the stock, and stock price volatility. The most widely recognized stock option valuation models are the Black-Scholes model and the Binomial model.

The Black-Scholes Option Model

European Options on Non-dividend-Paying Stocks

In 1973, Fisher Black and Myron Scholes published a landmark paper entitled "The Pricing of Options and Corporate Liabilities[1]," which showed the derivation of the Black-Scholes model for the valuation of marketable options on non-dividend-paying stocks. The model is based on two critical assumptions: no arbitrage (or perfect hedge) and near-perfect markets.

The No Arbitrage or Perfect Hedge Assumption. The model assumes that it is possible to value a call option by setting up a perfectly hedged position consisting of buying the option and selling the underlying stock or a portfolio of securities in an arbitrage transaction short. The value of the call option is equal to the present value, discounted at the risk-free rate, of the net proceeds received after closing the hedge at the option's expiration date. The discount rate must be the risk-free rate because any movement in the price of the underlying stock will be offset by an equal but opposite movement in the option's value, resulting in no risk to the investor. If the option price results in a return greater than the riskless rate, profit-seeking arbitrageurs will buy the option, increasing its price, and sell the stock until the hedge yields the riskless rate. Similarly, if the option price is too high, resulting in too low a return, arbitrageurs will short the option, decreasing its price, and buy the stock until the hedge yields the risk-free rate of return. This crucial action of the arbitrageurs is called the *no arbitrage* or *arbitrage-free* assumption, meaning that when an option is correctly priced, no arbitrage hedge profit can be made in excess of the risk-free rate of return.

The no arbitrage assumption also means that an investor is not concerned with the growth or rate of return of the price of the underlying stock. The investor simply hedges each price movement of the underlying common stock, and the option is valued using the risk-free rate.

Near-Perfect Market Assumption. The Black-Scholes model assumes near-perfect markets for both the options and the underlying stock. Among other conditions, the model assumes the following:

1. There are no commissions or other transaction costs in buying or selling the stock or the option.
2. The short-term risk-free interest rate is known and is constant through time.
3. Trading never stops. It is continuous through time following a geometric Brownian motion.
4. The underlying stock pays no dividends and makes no other shareholder distributions.

---

[1] F. Black and M. Scholes, "The Pricing of Options and Corporate Liabilities," *Journal of Political Economy,* May 1973, pp. 637–59.

5. There is unrestricted access to credit, and the securities are perfectly divisible. It is possible to borrow any fraction of the price of a security to buy or to hold it, at the short-term risk-free rate.
6. The stock price follows a random walk with a log normal distribution.
7. The volatility of the stock is constant over the life of the option.
8. The option can be exercised only at maturity.
9. A seller who does not own a security (a short seller) will simply accept the price of the security from the buyer and agree to settle with the buyer on some future date by paying him an amount equal to the price of the security on that date. While this short sale is outstanding, the short seller will have the use of, or interest on, the proceeds of the sale.
10. The tax rate, if any, is identical for all transactions and all market participants.

The Formula. The formula for the call option version of the Black-Scholes model is expressed as follows:

$$\text{Call Value} = S \times N(d_1) - Ee^{-rt} \times N(d_2)$$

where:

$$S = \text{Stock price}$$
$$E = \text{Exercise (strike) price}$$
$$N(\cdot) = \text{Value of cumulative normal distribution at the point ()}$$

$$d_1 = \frac{\ln(S/E) + (r + 0.5\alpha^2)t}{\alpha\sqrt{t}}$$

$$d_2 = d_1 - \alpha\sqrt{t}$$
$$ln = \text{Natural logarithm}$$
$$r = \text{Short-term riskless rate (continuously compounded)}$$
$$t = \text{Time to expiration, in years}$$
$$e = \text{Base of natural logarithms}$$
$$\sigma = \text{Annual standard deviation of return (usually referred to as } \textit{volatility})$$

Many of the assumptions of this theoretical model, including the absence of transaction costs, are unrealistic in the marketplace. However, in 1973, not only were its concepts revolutionary, its predicted option values were reasonably close to the market prices of publicly quoted options on the newly created Chicago Board of Options Exchange. Despite its limitations, which are discussed below, it is still the basis of some of the most widely used models to value common stock options today.

This formula makes it possible to value marketable call options and warrants on non-dividend-paying marketable common stocks with only five variables: (1) the exercise price of the option, (2) the remaining term of the option in years, (3) the price of the underlying common stock, (4) the annual volatility of the underlying common stock, and (5) the annual risk-free rate for the remaining term of the option.

There are many handheld calculators, computers, and internet websites that have Black-Scholes programs to value put and call options.

Estimating the Variables. The exercise price of the option and the remaining term of the option are readily observed or calculated.

The *risk-free rate* is the yield to maturity on United States Treasury securities having the same maturity as the remaining term of the option. Many valuators use the yield on United States Treasury strips for this purpose.

Black Scholes uses a continuously compounded rate of return, that is, the natural log of $1 + i$, where i is the annual rate of interest.

The *stock price* is the price of the underlying common stock in the marketplace if exercising the option does not result in the issuance of additional shares or if the terms of the option are public knowledge. In both cases, the stock price incorporates any potential dilution of the interests of existing shareholders. Otherwise, the price of the option should be adjusted for dilution and equal to the following calculation[2]:

$$\frac{\text{Call Value}}{1 + q/n}$$

Where:

q = the number of shares into which the class of warrants are convertible

n = the number of outstanding shares of the issuer

The price of the closely held common stock should reflect the appropriate discounts for lack of control and lack of marketability.

Calculating the volatility of the underlying stock is more complicated. Volatility is the standard deviation in the price of the underlying stock. The volatility used in the model is the total volatility of the underlying stock's price. It is not its beta, which measures the relative movement of the stock's price to the market. Volatility can be calculated using historical stock price data, which assumes that the stock's price changes are relatively constant, or using *implied volatility*.

Historical price volatility for an option on a publicly traded common stock is computed by annualizing the standard deviation of the logarithm of daily stock price changes. Daily volatility is computed by: (1) for a representative period of time dividing each day's closing price by the previous day's closing price; (2) computing the logarithm of these daily changes; and (3) computing the standard deviation of these logarithms. The result is then multiplied by the square root of the number of trading days in a year, typically 250.[3] Exhibit 25–1 shows a sample of these calculations:

The natural logarithm is easily calculated using the *ln* function of spreadsheet programs like Microsoft's Excel. The computation in this table uses prices for only 15 trading days. Using more trading days in the calculation generally increases the accuracy of the computation of the variance, provided that nothing occurred during the sample period that changed the volatility of the stock.

Implied price volatility is computed by reverse-engineering the price of a publicly traded option on the same underlying stock. The implied volatility is the one which when used in the Black-Scholes model along with the other four known variables results in a calculated value that matches the market price of the publicly traded option.

Volatility for Closely Held Companies. Estimating the volatility of the stock of a closely held company is more difficult and subject to error. Many valuation practitioners use the volatilities of the common stocks of selected guideline companies as the basis for choosing the volatility to use for the common stock of the closely held company.

---

[2] See R. W. Kolb, *Futures, Options and Swaps*, 4th ed. Oxford: Blackwell Publishing, 2003, p. 572.
[3] See R. W. Kolb, *Futures, Options and Swaps*, 4th ed. Oxford: Blackwell Publishing, 2003, p. 441–442.

Exhibit 25–1

Calculation of Stock Price Volatility

Date	Stock Price	Change in Stock Price	Natural Logarithm of Change in Stock Price	Natural Logarithm of Change Less Mean	Square of Natural Log. of Change Less Mean
6/1/xx	50.00				
6/2/xx	51.50	1.0300	0.0296	0.0261	0.0007
6/3/xx	51.00	0.9903	−0.0098	−0.0132	0.0002
6/4/xx	51.50	1.0098	0.0098	0.0063	0.0000
6/5/xx	52.00	1.0097	0.0097	0.0062	0.0000
6/8/xx	52.50	1.0096	0.0096	0.0061	0.0000
6/9/xx	51.50	0.9810	−0.0192	−0.0227	0.0005
6/10/xx	50.25	0.9757	−0.0246	−0.0281	0.0008
6/11/xx	50.00	0.9950	−0.0050	−0.0085	0.0001
6/12/xx	49.50	0.9900	−0.0101	−0.0135	0.0002
6/15/xx	51.00	1.0303	0.0299	0.0264	0.0007
6/16/xx	52.00	1.0196	0.0194	0.0159	0.0003
6/17/xx	51.50	0.9904	−0.0097	−0.0131	0.0002
6/18/xx	50.75	0.9854	−0.0147	−0.0182	0.0003
6/19/xx	52.50	1.0345	0.0339	0.0304	0.0009
Total			0.0488		0.0049
Number of trading day changes in sample			14		
Mean			0.0035		
Number of trading day changes in sample					14
Daily variance (.0049/14)					0.00035
Daily standard deviation (the square root of the variance)					0.0187
Number of trading days in 1 year				250	
Square root of number of trading days in 1 year					15.8114
Annual volatility (0.0187 times 15.8114)					0.2959

European Options on Dividend-Paying Stocks— The Merton Model

A simple approach to valuing short-term options on dividend-paying common stocks with the Black-Scholes model is to deduct from the stock price the present value, using the risk-free rate, of the dividends expected to be paid during the remaining term of the option.

Robert Merton showed how to use the model to value longer-term options on dividend-paying common stocks.[4] In the Black-Scholes-Merton model, dividends are assumed to be paid continuously over the life of the option as a percentage of the underlying common stock's market price. The additional variable in the model is the assumed continuous dividend rate on the common stock as a percentage of the stock price. This model also is available on many Web sites.

---

[4] R. Merton, "Theory of Rational Option Pricing," *Bell Journal of Economics and Management Science*, 4, Spring 1973, pp. 141–183.

American Call Options—The Pseudo-American Call Option Model

American Call Options. Unlike European options, which only can be exercised on the expiration date, American options can be exercised anytime during the life of the option. This right may have added value for dividend-paying stocks, depending on its potential economic benefit. Assuming an efficient market, there is no economic benefit from exercising an American option on non-dividend-paying common stock before the expiration date. Its value is the same as a European option with the same terms.

The size of the early exercise premium of an American option on dividend-paying stocks depends on the size and timing of the dividends, the remaining term of the option, and the risk-free interest rate. The early exercise right may have significant value if an expected dividend is quite large in relation to a stock's price. For instance, assume that ABC Company has a five-month American common stock option outstanding, with an exercise price of $48 per share. Its current common stock price is $50 per share, and the stock has volatility as shown in Exhibit 25–1, of approximately 30 percent. The risk-free rate for the term of the option is 3.0 percent per annum. The company declared a special dividend of $10 per share, which goes ex-dividend in four weeks. If the American option is exercised immediately, the holder will have a profit of approximately $200 (the $50 stock price less the $48 exercise price for 100 shares). However, if, like a European option, the option is exercised on the expiration date and the stock price is reduced by $9.88, the present value of the dividend, the Black-Scholes model's indicated value of the option, is only $0.86. In this case, the early exercise premium for exercising immediately is $1.14 dollars per share or a total of $114.

However, the early exercise premium may have no value. If the option's life in the above example is increased to 2.5 years and the associated risk-free rate is increased to 3.75 percent, the Black-Scholes model's indicated value for the option is approximately $6.04 per share. Now, an investor who exercises the option early forgoes a profit of approximately $404 on the contract ($604 - $200).

If the early exercise right of American option has value, it is normally better to wait to exercise the option until just before the underlying stock goes ex-dividend than to exercise it immediately. The delay reduces the present value of the option's exercise price and increases the call option's value.

The Pseudo-American Call Option Model. Fisher Black developed a technique to value American stock options using the Black-Scholes model called the pseudo-American call option model. The technique views each American option as a combination of a European option with the same term as the American option, and a series of pseudo-European options with a remaining term beginning at the valuation date and ending sequentially just before each ex-dividend date. Dividends are treated as an adjustment both to the exercise price and the stock price. The value of the American option is equal to the European option with the greatest value. The steps in the method are as follows:

1. Compute the adjusted market price of the stock by deducting the present value, using the risk-free rate, of the future dividends payable during the remaining life of the option.
2. For each pseudo-option assumed to expire on a dividend date, deduct from the exercise price of the option the dividend payable on the dividend date and the

present value, using the risk-free rate, of all the remaining dividends to be paid after the dividend date during the term of the option.

3. Using the Black-Scholes model, compute the value of each of the pseudo-options using the adjusted market price and the adjusted exercise price. Compute the value of the actual option as well, using the adjusted market price and the unadjusted exercise price.

4. Select the European option with the highest value as the value of the American option.

There are newer, more accurate models for pricing American call options. However, no single model has gained universal acceptance in all situations. Some investors use the pseudo-American call option model to determine if the early exercise right of an American option has value, and then, if it does, use a more complex model to determine the American call option's price.

Empirical Tests of Black-Scholes Options Models

While the Black-Scholes model and its variations are widely used, a number of observers identify some problems when they compare the model's predicted values to the reported prices of publicly traded options. Robert W. Kolb, in his book, *Futures, Options and Swaps*[5], discusses the 1972 Black and Scholes study[6], the 1977 and 1978 Galai studies[7], the 1983 Bhattacharya study[8], the 1979 MacBeth-Merville Study[9], and the 1985 Rubenstein Study.[10]

The first three studies found that while there were statistically significant differences between the model's results and market prices, the differences were too small to be economically important due to trading costs. The results of the MacBeth-Merville study were different. The authors studied options that had remaining lives of at least 90 days and found significant discrepancies for long-term options which were significantly in or out of the money. The model's predicted results tended to be low for in-the-money options and high for out-of-the-money options. These differences tended to increase with longer option lives and greater differences between the stock and exercise price. The Rubenstein Study tested the model against other option pricing models that attempted to correct for some of the deficiencies. While the study confirmed some of the biases of the previous study, it concluded that no single model was superior to the Black-Scholes model.

A number of authors including N. Gassel and J. Legras in 1999[11] have commented on the change in the implied volatility of the underlying stock as the relationship between stock price and exercise price changes. This should not be

[5] Kolb, pp. 453–55.

[6] F. Black and M. Scholes, "The Valuation of Option Contracts and a Test of Market Efficiency," *Journal of Finance*, 27:2, 1972, pp. 399–417.

[7] D. Galai, "Tests of Market Efficiency of the Chicago Board Option Exchange," *Journal of Business*, 50:2, April 1977, pp. 167-97 and "Empirical Tests of Boundary Conditions for CBOE Options," *Journal of Financial Economics*, 6:2/3, June-September 1978, pp. 182–211.

[8] M. Bhattacharya, "Transaction Data Tests on the Efficiency of the Chicago Board Options Exchange," *Journal of Financial Economics*, 12:2, 1983, pp. 161–85.

[9] J. D. Macbeth and L. J. Merville, "An Empirical Examination of the Black-Scholes Call Option Pricing Model," *Journal of Finance*, 34:5 1979, pp. 1173–86.

[10] M. Rubenstein, "Nonparametric Tests of Alternative Option Pricing Models Using All Reported Trades and Quotes on the 30 Most Active CBOE Option Classes from August 23, 1976 Through August 31, 1978," *Journal of Finance*, 40:2, 1985, pp. 455–80.

[11] N. Gassel and J. Legras, "Black-Scholes … What's Next?" *Quants*, No. 35, September 1999, p. 4.

Exhibit 25–2

Average Pricing Errors by Time to Expiration
and the Degree of In or Out of the Money

Time to Expiration	Number of Observations	Black-Scholes Model	Dilution Adjusted Black Scholes	CEV
Out-of-the-money warrants (stock price 80% or less of exercise price)				
Less than two years	2,122	7.63%	7.23%	5.67%
More than two years	12,033	5.41%	4.98%	3.77%
At-the-money warrants (stock price more than 80% but no more than 110% of exercise price)				
Less than two years	1,334	5.20%	4.88%	4.52%
More than two years	3,551	3.68%	3.11%	2.77%
In-the-money warrants (stock price more than 110% of exercise price)				
Less than two years	687	2.78%	2.48%	2.27%
More than two years	2,163	2.37%	2.08%	1.89%

Note: Stock price is reported stock price less discounted future dividends until warrant expires.

SOURCE: "The Relative Performance of Five Warrant Pricing Models," Table 4, by Shmuel Hauser and Beni Lauterbach, *Financial Analysts Journal*, Jan/Feb 1997:60. Copyright 1997, CFA Institute. Reproduced and republished from *Financial Analysts Journal* with permission from CFA Institute. All rights reserved.

possible under the constant volatility assumption of the model. These authors point out additional pricing errors in the Black-Scholes model due to its assumptions of no transaction costs, Brownian motion, the lognormal distribution of stock prices, and continuous trading.

In 1997, Shmuel Hauser and Beni Lauterbach published a paper which tested five warrant pricing models based on over 20,000 warrant price observations. They concluded that although another model (CEV) based on the constant elasticity of variance generated the lowest average pricing observation, a dilution-adjusted Black-Scholes model remained a reasonable, economical alternative in many cases.[12] Exhibit 25–2 compares the authors' results for three of the models in the study:

The authors stated that part of the pricing error for the basic Black-Scholes model was due to the relatively large spread between the bid and asked prices for the warrants and the fact that the closing prices of the warrants and the underlying stock used in the study may have been based on trades that did not occur at the same time. The remainder of the pricing error was mainly due to the Black-Scholes model's constant volatility assumption.

The dilution-adjusted Black-Scholes model can have noticeable errors in pricing warrants and options that are out-of-the-money and have a remaining life of less than two years. However, the CEV model is not significantly better, and the degree of error is within normal valuation tolerances.

---

[12] S. Hauser and B. Lauterbach, "The Relative Performance of Five Alternative Warrant Pricing Models." *Financial Analysts Journal*, January/February 1997, pp. 55–61.

Valuing Options on the Stock of Closely Held Companies

There are significant additional problems in applying the dilution-adjusted Black-Scholes model to options and warrants for the common stock of closely held corporations. Not only are estimates of the volatility of the call option subject to greater error than in the case of options for publicly traded stock, the combination of two assumptions—the no arbitrage (or perfect hedge) assumption and the assumed absence of commissions and other trading costs—may cause significant liquidity-related errors.

In practice, valuators assign a discount for lack of marketability to the indicated values from these models to options for privately held common stock. Two studies provide support for this practice. In the article, "The Price of Options Illiquidity,"[13] Brenner, Eldor, and Hauser examined the effect of illiquidity on the value of Israeli currency options. They analyzed 566 observations of three-to six-month call options issued from April 1994 through June 1997 by the central bank, but not traded prior to maturity. The values of these options were compared to similar options traded on the exchange. However, as the liquid options did not have the same characteristics (they differed by strike price and expiration dates) replicating the illiquid options with liquid options would generate transactions costs. They found that the illiquid options were priced about 21 percent less than the exchange traded options. This gap could not be arbitraged away because of transaction costs and the risk that the exchange rate would change during the bidding process.

In the article entitled, "Quantifying Lack of Marketability Discounts of Employee Stock Options,"[14] Levine and Luft describe the results of their comparison of Black-Scholes option values to prices published in *The Wall Street Journal* from March 1965 to March 1973 by members of the Put and Call Brokers and Dealers Association (PCBDA). Prior to the establishment of the Chicago Board of Options Exchange in 1973, approximately 25 PCBDA dealers arranged transactions between those wanting to buy and those wanting to sell options. The members advertised their option prices in a wide variety of financial newspapers. In this study approximately 5,700 PCBDA option "asked" prices were compared to their corresponding Black-Scholes values. Dividends were part of the analysis. The authors concluded that the illiquidity discount from the Black-Scholes values for in-the-money call options was 22 percent, and the illiquidity discount for out-of-the money options was approximately 45 percent.

It should be noted that for employee stock option valuations for purposes of financial reporting (i.e., implementing SFAS), the lack of transferability of the option is handled by using the expected (early) exercise term of the option rather than the contractual life of the option, rather than a discount from the option's value (as explained later in this chapter).

---

[13] M. Brenner, R. Eldor, and S. Hauser, "The Price of Options Illiquidity," *Journal of Finance*, 56:2, April 2001, pp. 789–805.

[14] L. Levine and C. Luft, "Quantifying Lack of Marketability Discounts of Employee Stock Options," *Mergers & Acquisitions*, 38:1, January 2003, pp. 10–11.

The Binomial Model for American Call Options

Introduction

The Black-Scholes model can be viewed as a special case of the more versatile binomial model (also known as the Cox-Ross-Rubenstein Binomial Tree[15]). Both models are equally good for valuing European and American options on common stocks that do not pay a dividend. The binomial model is considered better for valuing American options on dividend-paying common stocks and special cases of American Options, such as employee stock options.

The binomial model divides the price movement of the underlying stock into a series of individual time periods or "steps" and assumes that the share price of common stock in a step can move only to one of two possible prices in the following time period. The probabilities of moving to each of these prices, or "nodes", must total 100 percent. Exhibit 25–3 shows a simple binomial "tree" or "lattice" for the common stock ABC Company, assuming the $10 dividend. Given the stock price lattice, the method then calculates an option price lattice by calculating the individual option value at each node of the stock price lattice. Exhibit 25–4 shows the binomial lattice for the ABC option, assuming it has a five-month term.

Like the option on ABC's common stock the value of an option is the present value of all the individual option values at each node of the lattice, weighted by its probability of occurrence.

The binomial model uses *risk-neutral probabilities* and *risk-free discount* rates to calculate present values. Normally, a valuator uses a *risk-adjusted* discount

Exhibit 25–3

Stock Price Lattice

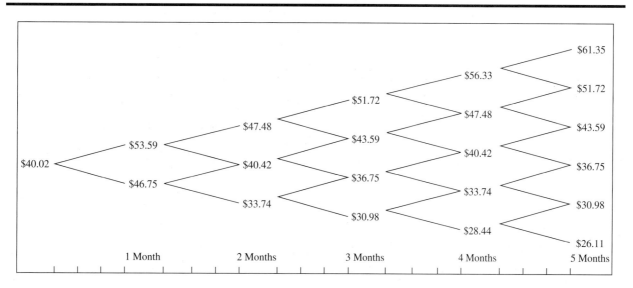

[15] J. Cox, S. Ross, and M. Rubenstein, "Option Pricing: A Simplified Approach," *Journal of Economics*, September 1979, 229–263.

rate, which includes a premium over the risk-free rate, for calculating the present value of a common stock's cash flows. This discount rate takes into consideration that the projected cash flows are not certain but are based on probabilities or risk. The actual cash flows may differ significantly from the expected cash flows. In contrast, risk-neutral probabilities are the result of a mathematical adjustment to the probabilities of the expected cash flows, which allows them to be discounted at the risk-free rate. Risk-neutral probabilities are a mathematical convenience for evaluating binomial trees and stem from the no arbitrage assumption.[16]

When the steps in the binomial model are infinitesimally small, and the other conditions of the Black-Scholes model are met, the results of the binomial model and the Black-Scholes model are identical. Using the binomial model is much more complicated than using the Black-Scholes model and its variations. However, it can be customized for specific applications using some algebra and a computer.[17]

Methodology

The first task in the process is to construct the lattice of the underlying common stock's future prices. After deciding on the number of steps to use for the life of the option, the valuator estimates the upward and downward movements at each step using the formula:

$$U = e^{\alpha \sqrt{t/\text{step}}}$$

$$D = 1 / U$$

where:

U	=	Upward movement during a step
e	=	Base of natural logarithms
σ	=	Annual standard deviation of returns (usually referred to as volatility)
t	=	Time to expiration, in years
Step	=	Number of steps or time periods the valuator has chosen to use during the time to expiration
D	=	Downward movement during a step

The value for U can be evaluated in Microsoft Excel and similar programs using the EXP function.

Assuming that the underlying stock pays no dividends or that it is reasonable to express the dividend as a percentage of the price of the underlying stock, the valuator starts with the initial stock price on the valuation date and projects two

---

[16] Risk-neutral probabilities are not the same as risk-adjusted or objective probabilities, that is, the actual risk of the expected cash flows. Forecasted cash flows should never be discounted at the risk-free rate unless the cash flows are risk free. Risk neutral probabilities reflect the assumption that as a *risk-neutral* investor always can hedge the individual outcomes of an investment at little or no cost, the investor is indifferent between an investment that always pays $10 and an investment that has an equal chance of paying nothing or $20. The investor considers only the expected payoffs of an investment, not its risk. For general discussion of the comparison risk-adjusted and risk-free probabilities and discount rates see Chapter 4 of *Real Options: A Practitioner's Guide*, by Tom Copland and Vladimir Antikarov, Texere LLC (2001).

[17] This discussion is based in part on A.R. Banks, "The Binomial Option-Pricing Model for Valuing American-type Employee Stock Options Parts; 1 and 2," *Shannon Pratt's Business Valuation Update*, 11:8-9, August and September 2005, and Kolb, Chapters 13 and 15.

possible prices for each succeeding step using the up U and down D movements calculated above.

If projected dollar dividends are known, the following procedure often is used to construct the stock price lattice:[18]

1.   Subtract the present value of the dividends payable on the underlying common stock during the life of the option from the stock price on the valuation date.
2.   Complete the lattice as for a non-dividend-paying common stock.
3.   At each step, add back to each calculated stock price the present value of all future dividends payable during the term of the option.

Exhibit 25–3 shows the lattice for the stock prices of ABC Company. The nodes on the lattice were calculated using the following information from the ABC Company example above:

1.   The initial stock price is $50 per share.
2.   A special dividend of $10.00 per share is expected to be paid in one month.
3.   The volatility of the stock is 0.2959.
4.   The maturity in years is 5/12, or 0.4167.
5.   The number of steps is 5.
6.   With Microsoft Excel formulas, U equals EXP (0.2959*(.4167/5)^(1/2)),[19] or 1.089.
7.   D equals 1/1.069, or 0.918.[20]

The initial stock price in the table is $40.02 (reflecting the deduction of the present value of the $10 dividend) instead of $50.00 to show the base for the increase or decrease in value in subsequent periods. Each price in each subsequent period was calculated by multiplying the prior period's price by the U or D movements. The $10.00 dividend per share was then added to the calculated value for the first month.

The second task is to calculate the risk-neutral probability of a price increase. The formula is:

$$P = \frac{e^{(i-div)(t/step)} - D}{U - D}$$

Where P is the risk-neutral probability of the stock price increase U, i is the annualized and continuously compounded risk-free interest rate for the same time as the remaining life of the option, div is the dividend yield and the other terms are the same as previously described. The probability of the stock price decrease D is 100 percent minus the probability of a stock price increase. The dividend yield is set at 0 percent if dollar dividends have been deducted from the projected stock prices.

In our example, assuming that the risk-free interest rate is 3 percent and the dividend yield is zero, the calculation of P is:

$$P = \frac{E^{(3\%-0)(.4167/5)} - 0.918}{1.089 - 0.918}$$

or 0.4933

---

[18] Kolb, p. 552.

[19] The formula often is written as EXP(σ)^(SQRT(t/Step)) or EXP(0.2959)^(SQRT(.4167/5))

[20] The values in Exhibits 25-1 and 25-2 and in Exhibits 25-3 through 25-5 are based on unrounded amounts.

The third task is to complete the call option price lattice using *backward induction*, which means that the last step in the table is filled out first, followed sequentially, by each prior step. Each of the indicated values of the option for the fifth month is simply calculated as the maximum of the stock price lattice less the exercise price or zero. The price for the fourth month and each of the prior months is given by the following formula:

$$C = \text{Max} \left((P \times C_u + (1 - P) \times C_d) \times e^{(-r(t/\text{step}))}, S - E \right)$$

Where:

C	=	Call price at current step
P	=	Probability of upward movement in the succeeding step
$(1 - P)$	=	Probability of downward movement in the succeeding step
C_u	=	Value of call after upward movement in the succeeding step
C_d	=	Value of call after downward movement in the succeeding step
e	=	Base of natural logarithms
r	=	Risk-free rate (continuously compounded)
t	=	Time to expiration in years
Step	=	number of steps or time periods
S	=	Stock price at the same step
E	=	Exercise price at same step

While the formula may look intimidating, it is not. It computes the higher value between exercising the option (the stock price S minus the exercise price E) and holding the option to the next step. The value of the next step is the probability P of an upward movement times the higher call value C_u plus the probability $1 - P$ of a downward movement times the lower call value C_d present valued for one step at the risk free rate for the time period $e^{(-r(t/\text{step}))}$. If at any step the value of exercising the option $S - E$ is greater than the expected value of the succeeding step, the option is exercised; otherwise, the option is held to the next step.

The call option price lattice is shown in Exhibit 25–4.

Exhibit 25–4

Call Option Price Lattice

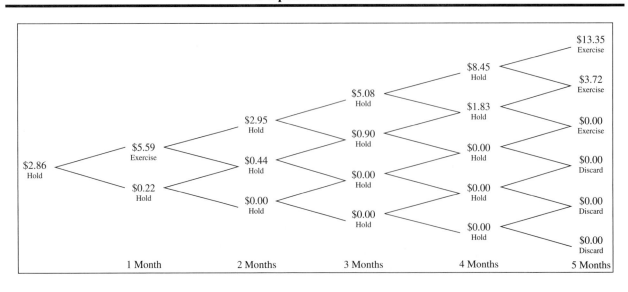

Working backward, the top right-hand number in the table of $13.35 in the fifth month is simply the greater of $61.35 projected stock price less the $48.00 exercise price or $0. The $8.45 value in the fourth month is the weighted present value of moving either up to $13.55 or down to $3.72 in the fifth month. This weighted value is greater than the option's intrinsic value of $8.33 (the $56.33 stock price in Exhibit 25-3 minus the $48 exercise price). Similarly, the $5.08 in the third month is the weighted present value of moving either up to $8.45 or down to $1.83 in the fourth month. The $5.08 value is greater than the option's intrinsic value of $3.72 (the $51.72 stock price in Exhibit 25-3 minus the $48 exercise price). If a step is labeled "Hold," the option's expected value of moving to the succeeding step is greater than its intrinsic value. If the step is labeled "Exercise," the option's intrinsic value is worth more than its expected value.

The value of the option before any discounts is the first value in the lattice. In this case, the value of the American call option is $2.86 per underlying share, and should be exercised in one month. The value of $50.00 stock price less the $48.00 exercise price is less than the weighted present value of holding the option for one more month.

Notice that after the second month, the option becomes more valuable with the passage of each succeeding month. If the option's term is sufficiently extended, the option's terminal values will be large enough to require holding the option to maturity despite the payment of the $10 dividend.

Using the Binomial Model in Microsoft *Excel*. While Exhibits 25–3 and 25–4 are good illustrations of how the binomial lattices for stock prices and the resulting option values work, a more practical method of calculating the values in Microsoft Excel is shown in Exhibit 25–5.

The model's variables are entered in cells E2 through E9. The model calculates the additional required values in cells E12 through E17 using the formulas shown next to the cells.

The value of each stock price in the stock price lattice is calculated using the formula:

$$\text{For the X row and Y Column } S_{xy} = S_{adj} * U^{y-x} * D^{x} + PV\_Dividend$$

The x and y subscripts are the cell's coordinates in the stock price matrix. The x and y superscripts are used to calculate the appropriate number of times the upward movements U and downward movements D are multiplied against each other to calculate the appropriate stock value. S_{adj} is the initial stock price minus the present value of the dividend in month 1. $PV\_Dividend$ is the present value of the $10 dividend. Its value is $9.98 initially, $10.00 in month 1, and $0 thereafter. Notice that only the upper triangle of the table is completed.

The price of each call option in the call option price lattice is calculated using the following formula:

$$C_{xy} = \text{Max } (S_{xy} - E, (P*C_{xy+1} + (1 - P) * C_{x+1+y+1}) * \text{EXP } (-i*(t/\text{step})))$$

The matrix is completed by first calculating the option price for the last column as simply S_{xy}-E, that is, the stock price in the equivalent cell in the stock price matrix minus the exercise price. Each preceding cell is completed using the above formula. The subscript $_{x+1}$ means the next row down; similarly the subscript $_{y+1}$ means the next column to the right. Again, only the upper triangle of the table is completed.

The Black-Scholes Model versus the Binomial Model. The advantages of the binomial model over the Black-Scholes model and its variations include the

Exhibit 25–5

Calculating Binomial Model Stock Values in Microsoft Excel

	A	B	C	D	E	F	G	H
1	**Input Values**				**Value**	**Name**		
2	Current Stock Price				$ 50.00	S		
3	Exercise Price				$ 48.00	E		
4	Dividend Rate				0%	Div_Rate		
5	Extra Dividend				$ 10.00	Dividend		
6	Present Value of $5 Dividend in Month 1				$ 9.98	PV_Dividend		
7	Option Life in Years (5/12)				0.4167	t		
8	Annual Risk-Free Rate				3.00%	i		
9	Standard Deviation of Returns				29.59%	Std_dev		
10	Number of Steps				5	Step		
11								
12	**Calculated Values**				**Value**	**Formula**		
13	Current Stock Price less Dividend S$_{adj}$				$ 40.02	= S – PV_Dividend		
14	Up Movement U				1.089	= Exp(Std_dev)^(SQRT(t/Step))		
15	Down Movement D				0.918	=1/U		
16	Risk Neutral Up Movement Probability P				0.4933	= (Exp((i-Div_Rate)*(t/Step))–D)/(U–D)		
17	Risk Neutral Down Movement Probability (1-P)				0.5067	=1 – P		
18								
19	**Stock Price Lattice**			For the X row and Y Column $S_{xy} = S_{adj}*U^{y-x}*D^{x}$ + PV_Dividend				
20								
21		X\Y	**0**	**1**	**2**	**3**	**4**	**5**
22		0	$ 50.00	$ 53.59	$ 47.48	$ 51.72	$ 56.33	$ 61.35
23		1		$ 46.75	$ 40.02	$ 43.59	$ 47.48	$ 51.72
24		2			$ 33.74	$ 36.75	$ 40.02	$ 43.59
25		3				$ 30.98	$ 33.74	$ 36.75
26		4					$ 28.44	$ 30.98
27		5						$ 26.11
28								
29	**Call Option Price Lattice**			C_{xy} = Max (S_{xy} – E, ($P*C_{xy+1}$+ (1 – P)*C_{x+1y+1})*EXP (–i*(t/step))				
30								
31		X\Y	**0**	**1**	**2**	**3**	**4**	**5**
32		0	$ 2.86	$ 5.59	$ 2.95	$ 5.08	$ 8.45	$ 13.35
33		1		$ 0.22	$ 0.44	$ 0.90	$ 1.83	$ 3.72
34		2			-	-	-	-
35		3				-	-	-
36		4					-	-
37		5						-

binomial model's ability to incorporate a variety of conditions which can increase accuracy, including variations in expected volatility, dividend rates and risk-free discount rates as well as transaction costs. The Black-Scholes model's assumption of constant volatility is not suitable for start-up or relatively young companies whose common stock volatilities are likely to change as the companies mature. The binomial model can be quite useful for valuing employee stock options as it is possible to include potential dilution, blackout periods, delayed vesting provisions, early exercise patterns and employee turnover in the model by increasing the number of periods and adjusting the option values at each node.

Nevertheless, the binomial model requires many more computations and is much more difficult to explain to uninformed clients and third parties. The Black-Scholes model is more commonplace. It can be very useful if the option's terms and environment are relatively straightforward. Furthermore, the binomial model has the same liquidity problem as the Black-Scholes model, when used to value restricted options on the closely held stock. A valuator should apply a discount for lack of marketability to the indicated value calculated by the binomial model for a restricted option on closely held stock, unless (1) the option's value is based on its immediate exercise or (2) the valuation is for financial reporting under SFAS 123 (revised).

Employee Incentive Stock Options

Federal Income Taxes. In creating employee stock options, the issuing company usually endeavors to set the option's strike price at the fair market value of the underlying shares. When the strike price is set at fair market value, the intrinsic value is zero, and the only value of the option is its time value. Under these circumstances, the Internal Revenue Service has determined that the recipient has no income to report during the year of issuance. The typical assignment for the business valuation professional is to estimate the fair market value of the underlying common stock so that management can establish the price of the employee incentive stock options (ISOs) to eliminate (or at least minimize) the income tax expense of issuing the options.

Income that is eventually derived from the qualified stock option (QSO) is determined to be ordinary income if the recipient exercises the option to buy the underlying securities and subsequently sells the securities within 12 months. To get a tax break, (1) the owner must hold the shares for at least one year and (2) the ISO must have been granted at least two years before the stock is sold. Any gain from the time of the exercise to the time of the sale is taxed at capital gains rates, which are lower than ordinary income rates.

For nonqualified stock options (NSOs), it is usually tax advantageous to consider exercising the options early on, especially if the company's stock has great upside potential. Any appreciation above the option-grant price is taxed as ordinary income, payable at the time of exercise. When the stock is sold, any appreciation subsequent to exercise is taxed as capital gains as long as the shares are held for more than one year. Exercising an NSO early in order to minimize the ordinary income tax hit and make the most of the capital gain income reduces taxes. Of course, whether the owner comes out ahead by exercising early depends on how the underlying stock performs during the holding period, on dividends, on voting rights, and so on. (The reader should consult a tax advisor regarding any possible tax consequences.)

Financial Reporting. In December 2004, the Financial Accounting Standards Board (FASB) adopted SFAS 123 (revised) for share-based payment. The statement specifies in detail the acceptable procedure for valuing employee stock options which do not have an independent market value. While the permitted methodology under SFAS 123 (revised) includes the Black-Scholes-Merton model as well as the binomial model and other lattice models, SFAS 123's (revised) procedure is quite controversial both from the point of view of the managements of public and private corporations and business valuation professionals.

SFAS 123's (revised) fair value of an option issued by a closely held corporation that does not have an immediate prospect of going public is *not* the same as the option's fair market value. In fact, the valuation of stock options under this pronouncement does not reflect the requirements of fair reporting for U.S. GAAP.[21] The statement does not permit explicit discounts for lack of marketability, lack of transferability, or inability to reasonably hedge. These three conditions are taken into consideration by shortening the option's time to expiration. In essence, the statement assumes that illiquid options on illiquid, privately held, common stock will be exercised early in order to gain liquidity. Furthermore, while the statement requires the use of a suitable stock market index for estimating the volatility for the common stock of most closely held companies, it does not permit a discount for the model risk of using an inaccurate standard deviation based on these sources.

As a result, most valuation practitioners believe the fair value methodology of SFAS 123 (revised) is not appropriate for valuing illiquid options on closely held common stock for tax, divorce, or corporate litigation valuations.

A Binomial Example of Valuing a Public Company ISO. Suppose you are faced with the following valuation problem. An executive is an employee of XYZ Company, Inc., a public corporation, has been awarded a restricted employee incentive stock option to purchase 1,000 common shares at a price of $50 per share. The option has a life of 2.5 years. There are no vesting or performance conditions. XYZ Company, Inc.'s common stock has a market price of $50, a dividend yield of 1 percent, and a stock price volatility equal to the amount calculated in Exhibit 25-1, 29.59 percent.[22] The company has announced that there will be an extraordinary dividend of the Company's excess cash of $10 per share in six months. However, the employee has been barred from exercising the option until after the special dividend. Employees of the executive's company generally exercise their restricted options when the common stock price exceeds 1.5 times the exercise price rather than hold the options until maturity because of the potential of a decline in the price of the common stock. Before any special discounts, what is the value of the executive's option?

While it is possible to value the option if it is exercised at expiration using the Black-Scholes-Merton model by deducting the present value of the $10 dividend from the stock price, the model does not include an early exercise parameter. However, the binomial model can handle this problem. Exhibit 25–6 shows the input tables and stock price forecast for XZY Company's common stock. The stock price forecast is divided into 5 six-month periods.

The inputs into the model are similar to those in Exhibit 25–5, except that the following values have changed:

1. The exercise price is $50.00.
2. The dividend rate is 1.0 percent.
3. The option life is 2.5 years.
4. The annual risk free rate is 3.75 percent.

---

[21] Paragraph 2.a of the FASB Statement of Financial Accounting Standards No. 157, *Fair Value Measurements*, issued in September 2006, specifically excludes SFAS 123 (Revised), *Share Based Payment*, from the requirements of fair value reporting.

[22] In practice, volatility for financial reporting under SFAS 123 (Revised) usually is measured by (1) calculating historical volatility for the same period as the option's expected life if the Black-Scholes-Merton model is used, or its contractual life if a lattice model is used, (2) calculating the implied volatility of the issuer's publicly traded options, warrants, and convertible securities, if any, and (3) weighting the results.

Exhibit 25–6

Calculating Binomial Model Stock Values—Example Using 6-Month Periods

Input Values	Value	Name
Current Stock Price	$ 50.00	S
Exercise Price	$ 50.00	E
Dividend Rate	1.0%	Div_Rate
Present Value of $10 Dividend in Period 1	$ 9.82	PV_Dividend
Option Life in Years	2.5	t
Annual Risk-Free Rate	3.75%	i
Standard Deviation of Returns	29.59%	Std_dev
Number of Steps	5	Step
Early-Exercise Ratio S_{xy}/E	1.50x	Ex_Ratio
Blackout Period	1	B_Period

Calculated Values	Value	Formula
Current Stock Price less Dividend S_{adj}	$ 40.18	= S – PV_Dividend
Up Movement U	1.233	=Exp(Std_dev)^(SQRT(t/Step))
Down Movement D	0.811	=1/U
Risk-Neutral Up Movement Probability P	0.4807	= (Exp((i – Div_Rate)*(t/Step))–D)/(U-D)
Risk-Neutral Down Movement Probability (1-P)	0.5193	=1-P

Stock Price Lattice   For the X row and Y Column $S_{xy} = S_{adj}*U^{y-x}*D^{x} + PV\_Dividend$

X\Y	0	1	2	3	4	5
0	$ 50.00	$ 59.53	$ 61.06	$ 75.27	$ 92.79	$ 114.39
1		$ 42.60	$ 40.18	$ 49.53	$ 61.06	$ 75.27
2			$ 26.44	$ 32.60	$ 40.18	$ 49.53
3				$ 21.45	$ 26.44	$ 32.60
4					$ 17.40	$ 21.45
5						$ 14.12

In addition, there are two new inputs, the early exercise ratio of stock price to exercise price and the blackout period. There values are 1.5 times and 1 respectively.

The formula for the stock value of each cell in the stock price lattice is the same as in Exhibit 25-5. The stock price lattice is similar, except that each period covers six months instead of one month.

Exhibit 25–7 shows three call option lattices and their formulas.

The first call option lattice uses the same formulas as in Exhibit 25-5. The bold numbers in the lattice show when the value of exercising the option exceeds holding it for one more period. If there were no restrictions on the exercise or transferability of the call option, its value per share would be $5.14.[23]

The blackout period is included in the formulas in the second call option lattice. With the blackout period, the value of the option per share drops to $4.70.

The impact of early exercise on the value of option is shown in the lattice. In the formulas, when the market price of the common stock exceeds 1.5 times the

---

[23] The Black-Scholes-Merton option value after deduction of the present value of the extra dividend is approximately $5.06. The difference from the $5.14 value in the table is due to the continuous compounding used in the Black-Scholes model and the six-month compounding, used for illustrative purposes, in this example. As the periods in the binomial model are shorter the results move closer to those of the Black-Scholes model.

Exhibit 25–7

Call Option Price Lattices

Call Option Price Lattice $C_{xy} = \text{Max} (S_{xy} - E, (P*C_{xy+1} + (1 - P)*C_{x+1y+1})*\text{EXP} (-i*(t/step)))$

X\Y	0	1	2	3	4	5
0	$ 5.14	$ **9.53**	$ 15.36	$ 26.49	$ 43.26	$ **64.39**
1		$ 1.25	$ 2.65	$ 5.63	$ 11.92	$ **25.27**
2			$ -	$ -	$ -	$ -
3				$ -	$ -	$ -
4					$ -	$ -
5						$ -

Call Option Price Lattice With Blackout Period

$C_{xy} = \text{If} (y <> \text{B\_Period}, \text{Max} (S_{xy} - E, (P*C_{xy+1} + (1 - P)*C_{x+1y+1})*\text{EXP} (-i*(t/step)))$
$C_{xy} = \text{If} (y = \text{B\_Period}, \text{Max} (P*C_{xy+1} + (1 - P)*C_{x+1y+1})*\text{EXP} (-i*(t/step)))$

X\Y	0	1	2	3	4	5
0	$ 4.70	$ 8.60	$ 15.36	$ 26.49	$ 4.26	$ **64.39**
1		$ 1.25	$ 2.65	$ 5.63	$ 11.92	$ **25.27**
2			$ -	$ -	$ -	$ -
3				$ -	$ -	$ -
4					$ -	$ -
5						$ -

Call Option Price Lattice With Blackout Period and Early Exercise

If y <> B_Period,
$C_{xy} = \text{if} (S_{xy}/E > 1.5, S_{xy} - E, \text{Max} (S_{xy} - E, (P*C_{xy+1} + (1 - P)*C_{x+1y+1})*\text{EXP} (-i*(t/step)))$
If y = B_Period,
$C_{xy} = \text{Max} ((P*C_{xy+1} + (1 - P)*C_{x+1y+1})*\text{EXP} (-i*(t/step)))$

X\Y	0	1	2	3	4	5
0	$ 4.57	$ 8.33	$ 14.79	$ 25.27	$ 42.79	$ 64.39
1		$ 1.25	$ 2.65	$ 5.63	$ 11.92	$ **25.27**
2			$ -	$ -	$ -	$ -
3				$ -	$ -	$ -
4					$ -	$ -
5						$ -

$50 per share exercise price, the option is exercised immediately, cutting off the future branches of the binomial tree. The shaded cells show the effect of the early exercise requirement. For example, C_{13} in the top two lattices have a value of $26.49, the value of holding the option for one more period, while C_{13} value in the bottom lattice is $25.27, the value of exercising the option. As a result, the value of the call option drops to $4.57.

Thus, the value of the executive's options is $4,570 before consideration of any special discounts.[24]

---

[24] For a more detailed discussion of the valuation of stock options for financial reporting purposes read *Share-Based Payment: An Analysis of Statement No. 123R*, by KPMG LLP's Department of Professional Practice dated November 2006.

Using Option Pricing to Value the Built-in Gains (BiG) Tax Liability

The Built-in Capital Gains Tax Controversy. "C" corporations are individual tax-paying entities under the United States Internal Revenue Code. When a "C" corporation sells its interest in the common stock of an unrelated corporation, it must pay a tax on the excess of the stock's net sales price over its cost. Under the asset approach, the value of the corporation's investment in common stock is the common stock's fair market value on the valuation date less the potential income taxes payable on the sale of this stock. This potential tax liability is known as the built-in capital gains tax liability (the "BiG").

There is considerable controversy as to how the BiG should be calculated. Most valuation experts agree that the BiG is a real liability of a "C" corporation. However, there is sharp disagreement as to how the tax should be calculated. One camp believes that the tax should be calculated as 100% of the capital gains tax payable, assuming the common stock is sold on the valuation date. The other camp agrees that the capital gains tax should be calculated as if the asset is sold on the valuation date, but believes that the amount of the tax should be present valued over the expected holding period of the asset.

Each side can claim legal authority for its position. The first camp can point to Estate of Dunn (T.C. Memo 2002-12 and U.S. Court of Appeals, Fifth Circuit, No. 00-60614), which stated that, using the asset approach, deduction of 100% of the capital gains tax as of the valuation date is correct as a matter of law. The second camp can point to the Estate of Frazier Jelke III (T.C. Memo. 2005-131), which stated that for minority interests that did not have the power to liquidate the "C" corporation, the BiG in the asset approach should be computed by present valuing the tax based on the portfolio's expected turnover.[25]

How a Common Stock Investment Affects a "C" Corporation's Taxes. A common stock investment can affect a "C" corporation's income taxes in two ways. First, if a "C" corporation owns less than 20 percent (by vote and value) of the stock of another American corporation, 30 percent of the annual dividends are taxable at ordinary income tax rates. The remaining 70 percent of the dividends are deducted from taxable income and excluded from tax pursuant to Section 243(e) of United States Internal Revenue Code.[26] Second, to the extent that the stock's appreciation exceeds its basis at the time of sale, the gain also is taxable at ordinary income tax rates.[27] The BiG is the sum of the present value of the tax on the dividends and the present value of the tax on appreciation.

Calculating the tax on the present value of the dividends during the holding period is straightforward given that the holding period can be estimated based on portfolio turnover. The problem is how to calculate the tax on potential appreciation given the wide possibilities of future stock prices. This dilemma has resulted in both valuation experts and the courts focusing on taxes payable as if the investment was sold on the valuation date (and whether or not these taxes should be present valued) rather than estimating the taxes that would likely be incurred both

---

[25] For example, if the historical turnover of the portfolio is 20 percent per year, one-fifth of the portfolio is projected to be sold at the end of each of the five years after the valuation date.

[26] The exclusion is increased to 80 percent for ownership of 20 percent or more (by vote or value) of the equity of the corporation but less than 100 percent.

[27] It is possible, if a stock pays significant dividends during the holding period, that the projected terminal value of the stock could be less than the value of the stock on the valuation date, in which case the projected appreciation would be negative and could result in a tax refund.

on the expected dividends paid during the holding period and on the expected appreciation at the end of the holding period.

The Tax on Appreciation Is a European Call Option Payable to the Government. The solution to the problem of estimating future stock prices is to view the tax on future appreciation as a European call option on the common stock investment. This "tax option" has a strike price equal to the investment's basis and a term equal to the expected holding period of the investment. The probability of future stock prices for this tax option is identical to the probability of future stock prices for a normal European call option on the same investment with the same life.

If at the end of the option's term, the stock price exceeds the basis, the government will receive an amount equal to the tax rate times the gain. However, if the basis exceeds the stock price, the government may lose an amount equal to the tax rate times the loss. Whether or not the government sustains the loss is a function of whether or not the "C" corporation can use the loss to shield taxable income.

If the Tax Loss *Cannot* be Used. If the "C" corporation cannot benefit from using the tax loss, perhaps because the investment is the bulk of the "C" Corporation's assets, then the tax option is no different than any other European call option. If the option is in-the-money at expiration, then the government will receive the tax rate times the gain. If the option is out-of-the money at expiration, the tax option will be worthless.

This tax option can be evaluated using the Black-Scholes model. In this case: (1) the market price of the underlying asset is the market value of the stock portfolio on the valuation date; (2) the term of the option is the expected holding period for the stock investment; (3) the exercise price is the basis of the stock investment; (4) the risk-free interest rate is the United States Treasury rate for the expected term; and (5) the volatility is the volatility of the stock investment. If the stock investment pays dividends, then the present value of the dividends is calculated at the risk-free rate and subtracted from the market value of the stock investment on the valuation date. The BiG is equal to the tax rate times the Black-Scholes option value and the present value of the tax on the dividends.[28] If the common stock investment is projected to be sold in a series of transactions based on portfolio turnover, then a Black-Scholes calculation can be made for each transaction.

If the Tax Loss *Can* Be Used. If the "C" corporation can use the tax loss used, then the binomial model can be used to compute the present value of the tax on expected appreciation. The stock price lattice should be calculated exactly the same way as for a normal call option. However, the call option lattice is different. The call values in the final step of the call option lattice should be revised to equal the tax payment or refund on the disposal of the investment using the following formula:

$$\text{Tax Rate} \times (S_{xy} - \text{Basis}),$$

where S_{xy} is the stock price in the last step and any tax refund is limited by the extent to which the loss can be used by the corporation.

The prior steps in the call option lattice are calculated using the same formula as in the normal call lattice without the option of early exercise. The revised formula is:

$$C = (P \times C_u + (1 - P) \times C_d) \times e^{(-r(t/\text{step}))},$$

---

[28] The tax on the dividends is computed using the expected tax rate times the dividend present valued at the appropriate equity rate, not the risk-free rate.

Where:

C	=	Call price at current step
P	=	Probability of upward movement in the succeeding step
$(1 - P)$	=	Probability of downward movement in the succeeding step
C_u	=	Value of call after upward movement in the succeeding step
C_d	=	Value of call after downward movement in the succeeding step
e	=	Base of natural logarithms
r	=	Risk-free rate (continuously compounded)
t	=	Time to expiration in years
Step	=	number of steps or time periods

After completing the call option lattice using backward induction, the first step in the lattice is the present value of the tax on the stock's appreciation during the holding period. The BiG is the sum of this option value and the present value of tax on the dividends during the holding period.

The Confusing Question of the Holding Period. One of most confusing questions asked regarding the BiG in court is: "How can you compute the tax liability for an investment if you don't know when the investment will be sold?" The implicit assumptions in the question are the longer a corporation holds an investment in common stock, the more uncertain is the amount of the future tax liability and the less will be the tax liability's present value. In fact, the opposite is true. The BiG, (like any other option on an asset that has the potential for appreciation) *increases* in value as the holding period increases.

The present value of the tax liability is greater because the extra time increases the probability that the investment will be sold at a higher price, which in turn increases the likelihood that a tax will be paid (that is, the sales price will exceed the basis) and increases the amount of the tax. While the extra time also increases the probability of a tax loss, the amount of the loss is limited by the investment's basis and the fact that the stock's price can never be less than zero. A tax option, which has almost a perpetual life, has an almost unlimited upside potential and a downside risk limited to the tax rate times the basis.

Real Options

Definition. Real option valuation (ROV) applies option pricing methods to value economic projects, companies, and financial securities. Just as option pricing models incorporate the flexibility of option holders' decisions as to whether and when to exercise an option by paying the exercise price, ROV incorporates the flexibility of the option holders as to whether or not to take certain actions that might increase the value of the investment.

ROV has provided significant insights into such business decisions as investment start-up operations, research and development projects, capital investment, abandonment decisions, and abandonment options. ROV and the Black-Scholes model have also provided significant insights in to the valuation of common stock of publicly held corporations. In essence, a corporation's common stock can be viewed as a perpetual option on its value, with the exercise price of the option being equal to the debt and preferred stock of the firm. A corollary of this view is the greater the volatility of the value of the firm short of bankruptcy, the greater will be the value of its publicly traded common stock.

ROV versus DCF. ROV challenges the validity of net present value methodology. DCF is one of the most widely accepted valuation techniques in finance. However, it is well known that the basic DCF model fails to incorporate flexibility; it does not incorporate the ability of the asset holder to make changes to the investment cash flows, such as making an additional investment, deferring an individual investment or abandoning all or part of the investment. To some extent, incorporating different scenarios for sensitivity analysis, decision trees, and statistical techniques, such as Monte Carlo simulations, in the DCF analysis reduces this problem. However, advocates of ROV believe that these adjustments are insufficient to capture the value of flexibility.

Evaluation of ROV for Business Valuation. The Research Foundation of AIMR (now the CFA Institute) published an analysis of real options in July of 2002, entitled *Real Options and Investment Valuation*, by Don M. Chance, CFA, and Pamela P. Peterson, CFA. The authors observed that real options, indeed all options, are highly sensitive to model risk, which is the use of a wrong model, the use of wrong inputs in the right model, or the incorrect use of a model. They also noted that ROV models often do not meet the assumptions inherent in option models in that the prices of the underlying assets rarely adhere to a lognormal distribution and are often not even random, and volatility is seldom known and constant—all violations of the model assumptions. In addition, they wrote that the estimation of inputs in real options models is particularly challenging because typically no active market exists for the underlying asset and rarely is it possible to find a set of data from which to estimate the historical volatility or implied volatility. Furthermore, empirical research has provided some, but very limited, support for the real-world applicability of real option models. Some studies have shown that real options in the real world are valued in a manner consistent with real option models, but other studies have not been very supportive of real options valuation.

However, the authors observed that while real options have not been well recognized, eventually, real options may become widely understood and properly incorporated into corporate investment decisions and valuations. ROV is a new technique which currently can be useful in specialized valuations and eventually may become quite common in general valuation practice.

Summary

Stock options permit their holders the flexibility to delay investment decisions or otherwise alter return distributions to satisfy particular investment objectives. The stock options addressed in this chapter are those issued by the company on whose stock the option or warrant constitutes a call, either as an employee incentive stock option or in conjunction with raising capital for the company.

The most famous stock option valuation formulas are the Black-Scholes Model and its variations and the binomial model. The former is relatively easy to use to value European options for both non-dividend-paying and dividend-paying marketable common stocks and American options on non-dividend-paying marketable common stocks. However, while the pseudo-American call option model can be used to determine if an American option on marketable dividend-paying common stock has an early exercise premium, other models, including the binomial model, may provide a more accurate estimate of the option's value.

Determining the fair market value of options for the stock of closely held corporations is more problematic due to the greater degree of difficulty in estimating the variance of the underlying stock and liquidity costs. Most valuation practitioners include a discount for lack of marketability to compensate for these problems.

SFAS 123 (revised) requires a specific methodology for the valuation of employee stock options for financial reporting purposes. As this methodology makes little sense when applied to illiquid options for the common stock of closely held corporations, most valuation practitioners believe the method is not appropriate for the valuation of these options for tax, divorce, or corporate litigation valuations.

Option pricing methodology is a useful technique for valuing the BiG tax associated with common stock held by a "C" corporation. The problem of estimating the tax on stock's future appreciation can be solved by viewing this tax liability as a European call option with a strike price equal to the basis and a life equal to the expected holding period of the investment. The problem of the uncertain as to the date of sale of the common stock by the corporation can be addressed by first recognizing that, like any other option on an appreciating asset, the tax liability increases the longer the investment is held.

Real option valuation theory applies financial option pricing theory more broadly than just to valuing options. It has provided significant insights to the valuation process and can be useful in specific situations. ROV is a developing technique that eventually may become quite useful in general valuation practice.

Bibliography

Articles

Ammann, Manuel, and Ralf Seiz. "Valuing Employee Stock Options: Does the Model Matter?" *Financial Analysts Journal*, September/October 2004, pp. 21–37.

Banks, Anthony R. "The Binomial Option-Pricing Model for Valuing American-Type Employee Stock Options, Parts, 1 and 2." *Shannon Pratt's Business Valuation Update*, August and September 2005.

Barenbaum, Les, Walt Schubert, and Bonnie O'Rourke. "Valuing Employee Stock Options Using A Lattice Model." *The CPA Journal*, December 2004, pp. 16–20.

Bhattacharya, M. "Transaction Data Tests on the Efficiency of the Chicago Board Options Exchange." *Journal of Financial Economics*, vol. 12, no. 2, 1983, pp. 161–85.

Black, Fisher, and Myron Scholes. "The Pricing of Options and Corporate Liabilities." *Journal of Political Economy,* May 1973, pp. 637–59.

_____. "The Valuation of Option Contracts and a Test of Market Efficiency." *Journal of Finance,* vol. 27, no. 2, 1972.

Brenner, Menachem, Rafi Eldor, and Shmuel Hauser. "The Price of Options Illiquidity." *Journal of Finance*, April 2001, pp. 789–805.

Cox, John, Stephen Ross, and Mark Rubenstein. "Option Pricing: A Simplified Approach," *Journal of Economics*, September 1979, 229–263.

One of the most controversial and unsettled issues in business valuation today is the valuation of S corporations and interests in them. And there are now more S corporations than C corporations in the United States.

Until mid-1999, most analysts relied on the advice of the Internal Revenue Service:

> S corporations lend themselves readily to valuation approaches comparable to those used in valuing closely held corporations (C corporations). You need only adjust the earnings from the business to reflect estimated corporate income taxes that would have been payable had the Subchapter S election not been made.[1]

Also, the IRS *Examination Technique Handbook for Estate Tax Examiners* states:

> If you are comparing a Subchapter S Corporation to the stock of similar firms that are publicly traded, the net income of the former must be adjusted for income taxes using the corporate tax rates applicable for each year in question...[2]

However, in 1999, the Service repudiated its own advice and won, in the now-famous *Gross*[3] case. One business valuation professional characterized it as "the most significant business valuation case in the last 20 years."[4] Since then, there have been three more cases that, in effect, rejected the tax-affecting of earnings. There is consensus in the business valuation community that the decisions generally do not comport to good economic theory. These cases sent the business valuation community into a frenzy to develop new theory for the valuation of S corporations and interests in them.

Case Law History

Four opinions, involving valuation of S corporations (three minority and one control) interests were issued by the U.S. Tax Court in the years 1999-2002. They all rejected, in effect, tax affecting earnings to put the S corporations on a comparable basis with C corporations. Each is a "T.C. Memo." Such opinions are case-fact specific and do not reflect the opinion of the Tax Court as a whole on a particular topic. No opinions involving S corporation valuation have been issued between 2002 and the time this book went to press.

Gross v. Commissioner[5]

The *Gross* case involved valuation of small minority interest in a family-owned Pepsi Cola bottler organized as an S corporation. The company was very profitable

---

[1] *IRS Valuation Training for Appeals Officers* (Chicago: CCH Incorporated, 1998), pp. 7–12. Also available at www.BVLibrary.com.

[2] *Examination Technique Handbook for Estate Tax Examiners* (IRM), MT 4350-31.

[3] T.C. Memo. 1999-254 No. 4460-97 (July 29, 1999), *aff'd.* 272 F.3d 333 (6th Cir. 2001).

[4] George W. Hawkins, "A gross result in the *Gross* case calls into question circumstances in which tax-affecting is valid," *Shannon Pratt's Business Valuation Update*, January 2002, p. 1.

[5] T.C. Memo. 1999-254 No. 4460-97 (July 29, 1999), *aff'd.* 272 F.3d 333 (6th Cir. 2001).

and had a history of distributing virtually all of its income to shareholders. Management said that the company would remain an S corporation and would continue to distribute virtually all of its income to shareholders.

The estate's expert applied a 40 percent corporate income tax rate to "tax affect" the company's projected earnings in connection with his valuation by the discounted cash flow method. The IRS's expert applied a 0 percent corporate income tax rate in conducting his discounted cash flow analysis.

After other issues of the discount for lack of marketability and the cost of capital by which to discount the future returns, the estate's expert concluded a value of $5,680 per share, and the IRS's expert concluded the value to be $10,910 per share. The Tax Court concluded the value to be $10,910 per share.

The estate's expert opined that the adjustment was necessary to address the following concerns:

- "The possibility that, if an S corporation distributes less than all of its income, the actual distributions might be insufficient to cover the shareholders' tax obligations.
- The risk that an S corporation might lose its favorable S corporation status, and
- The great disadvantage in raising capital due to the restrictions of ownership necessary to qualify for the S corporation election."

The court rejected each of these concerns:

- Tax affecting G&J's earnings is not an appropriate means of offsetting this possibility. Also, there is no basis for the assumption that insufficient distributions would be made because G&J had always distributed almost all of its income to shareholders.
- Tax affecting G&J's earnings is not appropriate "without facts or circumstances sufficient to establish the likelihood that the election would be lost."
- "This concern is more appropriately addressed in determining an appropriate cost of capital" and does not justify tax affecting G&J's earnings.[6]

The case was appealed to the 6th Circuit Court of Appeals and the Tax Court's conclusion was upheld.[7] None of the following three cases was appealed.

Wall v. Commissioner[8]

This case involved several small gifts of stock in an S corporation. The taxpayer filed gift tax returns at $221.75 per share, and the IRS Notice of Deficiency valued the stock at $260.13 per share. For various reasons, the Court concluded a value of $260.13.

In this case, *both* experts tax-affected earnings in their income approaches, the taxpayer's expert at 34 percent and the IRS's expert at 40 percent. Citing Gross, part of the Court's conclusion stated, "both experts' income-based analyses probably understated Demco's value, because they determined Demco's future cash flows on a hypothetical after-tax basis, and then used market rate of return on taxable investments to determine the present value of those cash flows."[9]

---

[6] *Shannon Pratt's Business Valuation Update*, September 1999, p. 9.
[7] Ibid.
[8] *Wall v. Commissioner*, T.C. Memo 2001-75, March 27, 2001.
[9] Ibid.

Estate of Heck v. Commissioner[10]

In *Estate of Heck* the issue was the value of shares equaling a 39.82 percent interest in F. Korbel & Bros., Inc., a California S corporation that is primarily a producer of premium champagne. Neither the estate's expert nor the IRS's expert tax affected earnings for the income approach, which was the approach accepted by the Court. The Court accepted a 10 percent discount for the risk the minority shareholder takes on due to S corporation status.

Estate of Adams v. Commissioner[11]

The issue in Adams was the value of shares equaling 61.59 percent of an insurance agency that operated as an S corporation. This was the only one of the four S corporation cases that involved a controlling interest.

In the expert for the estate adjusted his discount rate to reflect before-tax cash flow, while the IRS's expert made no such adjustment. The Court rejected the adjustment of the discount rate to before-tax cash flows (tantamount to tax-affecting the cash flows). The court stated:

> We disagree that Shriner's estimates for WSA's prospective net cash flows are before corporate tax because it is appropriate to use a zero corporate tax rate to estimate net cash flow when the stock being valued is stock of an S corporation. [citation omitted] WSA is an S corporation, and its cash flows are subject to a zero corporate tax rate. Thus, Shriner's estimates of WSA's prospective net cash flows are after corporate tax (zero corporate tax rate) and not before corporate tax as the estate contends.
>
> We disagree that Shriner properly converted the capitalization rate because there was no need to do so. The parties agree that Shriner's estimated capitalization rate (before he converted it to before corporate tax, is an after corporate tax rate. Thus, as in Gross, the tax character of Shriner's estimate of WSA's prospective net cash flows matches that of the unconverted capitalization rate because both are after corporate tax. It follows that Shriner should not have converted the capitalization rate from after corporate tax to before corporate tax because the tax character of both his estimated net cash flows for WSA and unconverted capitalization rates is after corporate tax[12]

The Court did not address the implication that not tax-affecting the earnings would limit the pool of potential buyers (at the concluded value) to those that could take advantage of S corporation status, thus eliminating C corporations from the pool of likely buyers, at least at the Court's concluded value.

Empirical Research on Sales of Controlling Interests

Two empirical research studies reach conflicting conclusions about whether controlling interests in S corporations sell at a premium over otherwise comparable C corporations. One study concludes that S corporations sell at a premium of

---

[10] *Estate of Heck v. Commissioner*, T.C. Memo 2002-34, January 30, 2002.
[11] *Estate of Adams v. Commissioner*, T.C. Memo 2002-80, March 28, 2002.
[12] *Shannon Pratt's Business Valuation Update*, May 2002, p. 5.

12 to 17 percent over otherwise comparable C corporations. The other study concludes that there generally is no difference in the prices at which controlling interests in S corporations sell compared to their C corporation counterparts.

In any case, the empirical research indicates that sales of controlling interests in S corporations would sell at nowhere near the 67 percent premium implied by doing nothing to tax affect the earnings (based on a 40 percent corporate tax rate). This research indicates that the lack of adjusting the discount rate to effectively tax affect the earnings resulted in a substantial overvaluation in the *Estate of Adams* (a controlling interest in the Korbel company), which was the only Tax Court case involving a controlling interest in an S corporation.

Erickson-Wang Study[13]

In September 2002, Merle Erickson and Shiing-wu Wang published a study that concluded that the average S corporation sold for 12 to 17 percent more than a comparable C corporation.

Erickson and Wang used 77 matched pairs of S corporation and C corporation stock sales. In a critique of the study, Alerding, Karam, and Chamberlain pointed out that the implication of the study was that *all* sales of S corporations are stock sales, because the acquiring company can use the Section 338(h)(10) election to achieve a "stepped up" tax basis on the acquired assets. They say that, "In fact, most acquirers do not want to purchase stock of another corporation because of the potential for liability assumption."[14] They also had other criticisms of the study, and Erickson and Wang offered explanations for their research methodology the following month.[15]

The purpose of the Erickson and Wang study was to empirically quantify the increase in selling price realized by sellers of entire companies in cases where the buyer realizes a step-up in tax basis of the underlying assets when acquiring a "seasoned" S corporation (i.e., one that has been an S corporation since inception or for at least 10 years) compared with price paid for the stock of (a nearly identical) C corporation and the buyer only realizes carry-over tax basis. That step-up in tax basis of the assets results in an increase in proceeds because the buyer will realize increased depreciation and amortization and lower income taxes in future years.[16]

Mattson, Shannon, and Upton Study

In November of 2002, Michael Mattson, Donald Shannon, and David Upton completed a comparative study of prices of sales of S corporations versus C corporations using the *Pratt's Stats* database. Even then, there were over 1,200 each of S and C corporations in the database, making it a fertile ground for the largest study to date on comparative prices.

Their first analysis was on the entire data set which included both stock and asset sales. They broke the transactions into 17 size categories based on face value of the transaction. They concluded that, "On an unadjusted basis, controlling only

---

[13] *Shannon Pratt's Business Valuation Update*, March 2002, p. 4.

[14] R. James Alerding, Yassir Karam, and Travis Chamberlain, "S Corporation Premiums Revisited: The Erickson-Wang Myth," *Shannon Pratt's Business Valuation Update*, January 2003, p. 2.

[15] Merle Erickson and Shiing-wu Wang, "Response to the Erickson Wang Myth," *Shannon Pratt's Business Valuation Update*, February 2003, pp. 1–5.

[16] Roger Grabowski and William McFadden, "Applying the Income Approach to S Corporation and Other Pass-Through Entity Valuations," *The Handbook of Business Valuation and Intellectual Property Analysis* (McGraw-Hill, 2004), pp. 114–115.

for size, the C corporations, on average, sold for more than the S corporations. After making some adjustments, however, the authors concluded that there is no discernible difference in the values of C corporations versus S corporations."[17]

Their second analysis focused only on stock sales, in an effort to test the Erickson-Wang findings. That subset of the database involved 721 C corporation stock sales and 506 S corporation stock sales. They used the same size breakdowns as they did for the entire database. Their conclusions for the stock-only sales remained the same as the conclusions for the entire database.

However, they also said that the results did not conflict with Erickson-Wang because the Erickson-Wang study was conducted on the largest of Mattson-Shannon-Upton's size categories, average transaction prices of $50.31 million for the S corporations and $46.24 million for the C corporations. The Mattson-Shannon-Upton study shows higher pricing ratios for S corporations in two of their top four size categories. The authors conclude that "when considering all 17 size categories, in our opinion no such statement can be made."[18]

Summary of Empirical Research

In summary, the empirical research to date shows slightly higher prices for stock sales of S corporations in the higher price ranges, but for stock sales of medium to small companies and asset sales of all sizes, there is no discernable difference between prices of S corporations and prices of C corporations.

Models for Valuation of S Corporation Minority Interests

There is general consensus among appraisers that there is little or no difference in controlling interest market values between S corporations and C corporations under most circumstances, and that any difference depends on finding a buyer that can take advantage of certain potential tax savings. There is also consensus that there may be differences in value at the shareholder level for noncontrolling interests. This recognition set off a flurry of attempts to design models to quantify values of S corporation interest at the noncontrolling interest level.

The result was the emergence of models by four leading business appraisers for valuing noncontrolling interests in S corporations. The specific models promulgated by Roger Grabowski, Chris Mercer, Chris Treharne, and Dan Van Vleet, are far too lengthy to be presented here. For the first time ever the *Business Valuation Review* dedicated an entire issue to a single topic: the September 2004 issue of that publication presented articles containing the models of all four practitioners.[19] Also, a lengthy chapter in the book *Business Valuation and Taxes* presented all four of the models.[20]

It is important to recognize that both C corps and S corps pay taxes on corporate income. Whether that tax is actually paid by the corporation or the individual

---

[17] *Shannon Pratt's Business Valuation Update*, November 2002, p. 1.

[18] *Shannon Pratt's Business Valuation Update*, December 2002, p. 3.

[19] Roger J. Grabowski, "S Corporation Valuations in the Post-*Gross* World—Updated;" Z. Christopher Mercer, "Are S Corporations Worth More Than C Corporations?;" Chris D. Treharne, "Valuation of Minority Interests in Pass-Through Entities;" Daniel R. Van Vleet, "The S Corporation Economic Adjustment Model;" *Business Valuation Review,* September 2004, pp. 105–180.

[20] *Business Valuation and Taxes: Procedure, Law, and Perspective*, by David Laro and Shannon P. Pratt (Hoboken, New Jersey: John Wiley and Sons, Inc. 2005), Chapter 8, "Valuation of S Corporations and Other Pass-Through Tax Entities: Minority and Controlling Interests," pp. 79–136.

is absolutely irrelevant. What is relevant is the difference between the value of a company valued as a C corporation, valued using publicly traded C corporation data (because it is by reference to publicly traded C corporations that we value the S corporation), and an S corporation. It is for this reason that most S corporation models begin by valuing the company "as if" a C corporation, using the rates of return derived from publicly traded C corporations, and then go on to recognize the benefits of the Subchapter S election. From the investor's perspective, there are two primary benefits: (1) the avoidance of dividend tax on the receipt of distributions, and (2) the ability to build up their basis in their stock. Many analysts have confused the S corporation tax issue by focusing on the deductibility of corporate taxes. However, this is not the tax that an investor avoids, and is not the tax that is forgone when a corporation elects subchapter S. Ibbotson rates of return inherently include an investor's expectation that when he or she receives his or her dividend from the publicly traded stock, the investor will have to pay a dividend tax on it. In the case of an S corporation, this tax is avoided; and since most S corporation models value the S corporations using Ibbotson rates of return, the benefit of the avoided dividend tax must be taken into consideration.

However, rates of return on the public markets are determined not only by an investor's expectation of dividends, but also by their expectation of capital. To the extent funds are not distributed, they are retained and contribute to the investor's basis in their stock. The analyst should consider whether it is appropriate to accumulate this benefit, and at what period it is appropriate to recognize it (e.g., an assumed exit 5, 10, or some other number of years hence).

The analyst may want to consider weighing these benefits by the likelihood that the buyer will realize them. For example, if the only possible buyers are other qualified holders of Subchapter S stock, then all of the benefit should be included; if the market also includes C corporation buyers, then a probability weighing of the added benefit may be more appropriate.

Summary

Four decisions in the U.S. Tax Court rejected the previously accepted practice of tax affecting the earnings when valuing interests in S corporations. There have been no recent decisions regarding pass-through entities other than S corporations. The S corporation decisions sent business valuation practitioners scurrying to do research on the valuation of S corporations and interest in them.

Two empirical research projects described in this chapter compared sales of controlling interests in C corporations with sales of controlling interests in S corporations. One study was limited to stock sales of corporations with an average value of about $50 million, which is on the high end of the range of companies that are commonly the subjects of business appraisals. This study concluded that S corporations tended to sell at a 12 to 17 percent premium over otherwise comparable C corporations.

A second, much broader, study examined both stock and asset sales. It concluded that there was no discernable difference between S corporation and C corporation prices in asset sales and that any differential in prices of stock sales was only significant at the top end of the range of values.

Four appraisers developed theoretical models for the valuation of minority interests in S corporations. While each of the models has merit, none has yet been used in court.

Bibliography

We are indebted to Mercer Capital for supplying most of the following bibliography.

Articles

Alerding, R. James, Travis Chamberlain, and Yassir Karam. "S Corporation Premiums Revisited: The Erickson-Wang Myth." *Shannon Pratt's Business Valuation Update*, January 2003.

Avener, Leslie. "An Appraiser Looks at *Davis v. Commissioner.*" *Business Valuation Review*, September 1998, pp. 72–78.

Barad, Michael W. "S Corporation Discount Rate Adjustment." *AICPA ABV E-Valuation Alert*, Volume 4, Issue 6, June 3, 2002.

Barber, Gregory A. "Valuation of Pass-Through Entities." *Valuation Strategies*, March/April 2001, pp. 4–11, 44–45.

Bowles, Tyler J., and W. Cris Lewis. "Tax Considerations in Valuing Nontaxable Entities." *Business Valuation Review*, December 2000, pp. 175–185.

Buckley, Allen, Crouse, Lynda M., and Kniesel, Greg. "S Corporation ESOPs in Dispositive Sales and Reorganization Transactions." *Valuation Strategies*, January/February 2001, pp. 20–29, 46–48.

Burke, Brian H. "The Impact of S Corporation Status on Fair Market Value." *Business Valuation Review*, June 2001, pp. 15–24.

———. "Letter to the Editor." *Business Valuation Review*, March 2002, p. 44.

Cassiere, George G. "The Value of S-Corp Election—The C-Corp Equivalency Model." *Business Valuation Review*, June 1994, pp. 84–95.

Condren, Gary. "S Corporations and Corporate Taxes." *Business Valuation Review*, December 1993, pp. 168–171.

Crow, Matthew R., and Brent A. McDade. "The Hypothetical Willing Seller: Maybe C Corporations Worth More Than S Corporations." *Mercer Capital's Value Matters*, November 26, 2003.

Dufendach, David C. "Valuation of Closely Held Corporations: 'C' vs. 'S' Differentials." *Business Valuation Review*, December 1996, pp. 176–179.

Duffy, Robert E., and George L. Johnson. "Valuation of 'S' Corporations Revisited: The Impact of the Life of an 'S' Election Under Varying Growth and Discount Rates." *Business Valuation Review*, December 1993, pp. 155–167.

Elam, Thomas E. "Quantifying the S Value Premium." *Business Appraisal Practice*, Summer 2004, pp. 6–34.

Erickson, Merle. "Tax Benefits in Acquisitions of Privately Held Corporations: The Way Companies Are Organized for Tax Purposes Affects Their Selling Price in an Acquisition." *Capital Ideas*, Vol. 3, No. 3, Winter 2002, Chicago GSB.

———. "To Elect or Not to Elect, That Is the Tax Question." Capital Ideas, Volume 2, No. 4, Winter 2001.

Erickson, Merle, and Shiing-wu Wang. "Response to the 'Erickson-Wang Myth.'" *Shannon Pratt's Business Valuation Update*, February 2003, pp. 1–5.

Finkel, Sidney R. "Is There an S Corporation Premium?" *Valuation Strategies*, July/August 2001, pp. 14–27.

Finnerty, John D. "Adjusting the Comparable-Company Method for Tax Differences When Valuing Privately Held 'S' Corporations and LLCs." *Journal of Applied Finance*, Fall/Winter 2002, pp. 15–30.

Fowler, Bradley A. "How Do You Handle It?" *Business Valuation Review*, March 1992, p. 39.

Gasiorowski, John R. "Tax Basis Does Matter in the Valuation of Asset Holding Companies." *Business Valuation Review*, September 1998, pp. 79–84.

Giardina, Edward. "The Gross Decision Revisited." *Business Valuation Review*, December 2000, pp. 213–218.

Gilbert, Gregory. "Letter to the Editor." *Business Valuation Review*, June 1989, pp. 92–93.

Graber, Adrian. "Business Valuations for S Corporation Elections." *Business Valuation Review*, December 1996, pp. 174–175.

Grabowski, Roger J. "S Corporation Valuations in the Post-*Gross* World." *Business Valuation Review*, September 2002, pp. 128–141.

Grabowski, Roger J. "S Corporation Valuations in a Post-*Gross* World." *Business Valuation Review*, September 2004.

Hawkins, George B., and Michael A. Paschall. "A Gross Result in the Gross Case: All Your Prior S Corporation Valuations Are Invalid." *Business Valuation Review*, March 2002, pp. 10–15.

Hempstead, John E. "Letter to the Editor." *Business Valuation Review*, March 1989, p. 42.

Jalbert, Terrance. "Pass-Through Taxation and the Value of the Firm." *American Business Review*, June 2002.

Johnson, Bruce A. "Tax Treatment When Valuing S-Corporations Using the Income Approach." *Business Valuation Review*, June 1995, pp. 83–85.

Johnson, Owen T. "Letter to the Editor." *Business Valuation Review*, December 2001, p. 56.

———. "Letter to the Editor." *Business Valuation Review*, March 2002, pp. 44–45.

Julius, J. Michael. "Converting Distributions from S Corporations and Partnerships to C Corporation Dividend Equivalent Basis." *Business Valuation Review*, June 1997, pp. 65–67.

Kato, Kelly. "Valuation of 'S' Corporations Discounted Cash Flow Method." *Business Valuation Review*, December 1990, pp. 117–122.

Kramer, Yale. "Letter to the Editor." *Business Valuation Review*, December 1994, p. 177.

Leung, T.S. Tony. "Letter to the Editor." *Business Valuation Review*, March 1991, p. 41–42.

———. "Tax Reform Act of 1986: Considerations for Business Valuators." *Business Valuation Review*, June 1987, pp. 60–61.

Light, David C. and Richard C. May, "Stock Valuation Issues for S Corporation ESOPS." *Shannon Pratt's Business Valuation Update*, August 1999.

Luttrell, Mark S., and Jeff W. Freeman. "Taxes and the Undervaluation of 'S' Corporations." *American Journal of Family Law*, Winter 2001, pp. 301–306.

Massey, Susan G. "How Do Unrealized Capital Gains Affect Valuation of S Corporation Stock?" *The Valuation Examiner*, May/June 2002, pp. 26–29.

Mattson, Michael, and Donald Shannon. "Part 1: Empirical Research Concludes S Corporation Values Same as C Corporations." *Shannon Pratt's Business Valuation Update*, November 2002.

Mattson, Michael, Donald Shannon, and Upton, David. "Part 2: Empirical Research Concludes S Corporation Values Same as C Corporations." *Shannon Pratt's Business Valuation Update*, December 2002.

Mercer, Z. Christopher. "Are S Corporations Worth More Than C Corporations?" *Business Valuation Review*, September 2004.

Mercer, Z. Christopher. "S Corporation Versus C Corporation Values." *Shannon Pratt's Business Valuation Update*, June 2002.

Mercer, Z. Christopher, and Travis W. Harms. "S Corporation Valuation in Perspective: A Response to the Article 'S Corporation Discount Rate Adjustment.'" *AICPA ABV E-Valuation Alert*, Volume 4, Issue 7, July 2, 2002.

Miller, Scott D. "New Opportunities for ESOP's—Subchapter S Corporations." *Valuation Examiner*, February/March 1999.

Phillips, John R. "S Corp. or C Corp.? M&A Deal Prices Look Alike." *Business Valuation Resources, Shannon Pratt's Business Valuation Update*, March 2004.

Pratt, Shannon. "Editor Attempts to Make Sense of S versus C Debate." *Business Valuation Resources, Shannon Pratt's Business Valuation Update*, March 2003.

Reilly, Robert F. "S Corporation Commercial Bank Valuation Methods and Issues." *Valuation Strategies*, May/June 2002, pp. 28–33, 48.

Reto, James J. "Are S Corporations Entitled to Valuation Discounts for Embedded Capital Gains?" *Valuation Strategies*, January/February 2000, pp. 6–9, 48.

———. "A Simplified Method to Value an S Corp Minority Interest." *Shannon Pratt's Business Valuation Update*, July 2004.

Serro, James A. "Valuing C-Corporations versus S-Corporations." *Valuation Examiner*, June/July 1998.

Shackelford, Aaron L. "Valuation of 'S' Corporations." *Business Valuation Review*, December 1988, pp. 159–162.

Sliwoski, Leonard J. "Capitalization Rates Developed Using the Ibbotson Associates Data: Should They Be Applied to Pre-tax or Aftertax Earnings?" *Business Valuation Review*, March 1994, pp. 8–10.

———. "Reflections on Valuing S Corporations." *Business Valuation Review*, December 1998, pp. 141–146.

Sonneman, Donald. "Business Valuation Controversies and Choices: Understanding Them and Their Impact (Controversy No. 7)." *Business Valuation Review*, June 2000, p. 85.

Treharne, Chris D. "Comparing Three Payout Assumptions' Impact on Values of S versus C Corps." *Shannon Pratt's Business Valuation Update*, September 2002.

———. "Valuation of Minority Interests in Subchapter S Corporations." *Business Valuation Review*, September 2004.

Treharne, Chris D., and Nancy J. Fannon. "Valuation of Pass-Through Tax Entities: Minority and Controlling Interests." S-Corp. Association, *www.S-Corp.org*, February 2004.

Van Vleet, Daniel. "A New Way to Value S Corporation Securities." *Trusts & Estates*, March 2003.

———. "The S Corp Economic Adjustment Model." *Business Valuation Review*, September 2004.

———. "The S Corporation Economic Adjustment Model Revisited." *Willamette's Insight*, Winter 2004.

———. "The Valuation of S Corporation Stock: The Equity Adjustment Multiple." *Pennsylvania Family Lawyer*, May–June 2003.

———. "The Valuation of S Corporation Stock: The Equity Adjustment Multiple." *Willamette's Insight*, Winter 2003.

Vinso, Joseph. "Distributions and Entity Form: Do They Make a Difference in Value?" *Valuation Strategies*, September/October 2003.

Wiggins, C. Donald, S. Mark Hand, and Laura L. Coogan. "The Economic Impact of Taxes on S corporation Valuations." *Business Valuation Review*, June 2000, pp. 88–94.

Books

Grabowski, Roger J., and William McFadden. Chapter 5: "Applying the Income Approach to S Corporation and Other Pass-Through Entity Valuations" *The Handbook of Business Valuation and Intellectual Property Analysis*. New York: Reilly/Schweihs, McGraw-Hill, 2004.

Hitchner, James R. *Financial Valuation: Application and Models*. New York: John Wiley & Sons, 2003.

Laro, David, and Shannon P. Pratt. Chapter 8: "Valuation of S Corporations and Other Pass-Through Entities: Minority and Controlling Interests." *Business Valuation and Taxes: Procedure, Law, and Perspective*. New York: John Wiley & Sons, 2005.

Mercer, Z. Christopher. *Quantifying Marketability Discounts*. Memphis, TN: Peabody Publishing, LP, 1997, pp. 233–239.

———. *Valuing Enterprise and Shareholder Cash Flows: The Integrated Theory of Business Valuation*. Memphis, TN: Peabody Publishing, LP, 2004.

Pratt, Shannon P., Reilly, Robert F., and Schweihs, Robert P. *Valuing a Business*, 3rd ed. New York: Irwin 1996, pp. 518–520.

———. *Valuing a Business*, 4th ed. New York: McGraw-Hill, 2000, pp. 568–569.

Reilly, Robert F., and Robert P. Schweihs. Chapter 6: "S Corporations—Premium or Discount," *The Handbook of Advanced Business Valuation*. New York: Reilly/Schweihs, McGraw-Hill, 1999, pp. 119–138.

Trugman, Gary R. *Understanding Business Valuation*. New York: AICPA, 1998, pp. 197–199.

Van Vleet, Daniel. Chapter 4: "The S Corporation Economic Adjustment," *The Handbook of Business Valuation and Intellectual Property Analysis*. New York: Reilly/Schweihs, McGraw-Hill, 2004.

Walker, Donna J. Chapter 24: "S Corporations," *Valuing Small Businesses and Professional Practices*, 2nd ed. Pratt/Reilly/Schweihs, Business One Irwin, New York, 1993, pp. 345–356.

Presentations

Bajaj, Mukesh, Z. Christopher Mercer, and George Hawkins. "Tax-Affecting S Corporation Earnings for the Purpose of Valuing Stock." Business Valuation Resources Audio Conference, August 13, 2002.

Crow, Matthew R. "Are S Corporations Worth More?" Presented to the New York City Chapter of the ASA's Current Topics in Business Valuations—2000 Conference, New York, NY, May 5, 2000.

Crow, Matthew R., and Daniel Van Vleet. "S Corporation Valuation Issues." Presented to the Business Valuation Association of Chicago, September 22, 2004.

Danyluk, Anne. "Valuing S Corporations: A Look at Adjustments." Presented to the 1991 International Appraisal Conference of the American Society of Appraisers, Philadelphia, PA, June 18, 1991.

S Corporation Bibliography

Grabowski, Roger, Z. Christopher Mercer, and Daniel Van Vleet. "S Corporation Valuation Issues." Presented to the American Society of Appraisers' Advanced Business Valuation Conference, October 17, 2003.

Griswald, Terrence, Z. Christopher Mercer, and Richard Schleuter. "Are S Corporations Worth More Than C Corporations." Presented to the New York City Chapter of the ASA's Current Topics in Business Valuations—2002 Conference, New York, NY, May 9, 2002.

Johnson, Bruce A. "S Corporation Tax Treatment." Presented to the 2001 International Appraisal Conference of the American Society of Appraisers, Pittsburgh, PA, July 25, 2001.

Mercer, Z. Christopher. "S Corporation Valuation." Presented to the Business Valuation Association of Chicago, September 19, 2002.

———. "S Corporation Valuation Issues." Presented to the American Bar Association S Corporation Committee Mid-Year Meeting, January 24, 2003.

Mercer, Z. Christopher, Daniel Van Vleet, Chris D. Treharne, and Nancy J. Fannon. "Valuation of Pass-Through Entities." Presented to the American Institute of Certified Public Accountants, November, 2004.

Mercer, Z. Christopher, and Joseph D. Vinso. "S Corporation Valuation." Presented to the American Society of Appraisers' 2002 International Appraisal Conference, August 27, 2002.

Pratt, Shannon, "Audio Conference Held on Tax-Affecting S Corp Earnings" (Summary of audio conference panelists' positions of Mukesh Bajaj, Chris Mercer, and George Hawkins). *Shannon Pratt's Business Valuation Update*, September, 2002, pp. 1–5. CD's and transcripts of the panel are available from *BVResources.com*

Smith, Philip M. "The Continuing Subchapter S Controversy." Presented to the 1998 International Appraisal Conference of the American Society of Appraisers, Maui, HI, June 24, 1998.

Treharne, Chris D., James Hitchner, and Nancy J. Fannon. "Valuation of Pass-Through Entities." Presented to the Institute of Business Appraisers Conference, Las Vegas, NV, June 10, 2004.

———. "Valuation of Pass-Through Entities." Presented to the American Society of Appraisers' Advanced Business Valuation Conference, October 8, 2004.

———. "Valuation of Pass-Through Entities: What's All the Fuss?" Presented to the American Institute of Certified Public Accountants, November 2003.

Van Vleet, Daniel. "The S Corporation Economic Adjustment Model." Presented to the Institute of Business Appraisers Conference, Las Vegas, NV, June 10, 2004.

Van Vleet, Daniel, Chris D. Treharne, and James Hitchner. "S Corporation Valuation Issues." Shannon Pratt's Business Valuation Update Audio Conference, June 29, 2004.

Walker, Donna J. "S Corporation Valuation for ESOPS." Presented to the 2001 International Appraisal Conference of the American Society of Appraisers, Pittsburgh, PA, July 24, 2001.

Wilusz, Edward A. "Does the S Corporation Election Create Value?" Presented to the 15th Annual Advanced Business Valuation Conference of the American Society of Appraisers, Memphis, TN, October 10, 1996.

Part VII

Valuations for Specific Purposes

Chapter 27*

Valuations for Gift and Estate Tax Purposes

---

* This chapter was revised and updated by Curtis R. Kimball, Willamette Management Associates, Atlanta, Georgia.

Say not that you know another entirely until you have shared an inheritance with him.

—Johann Kaspar Lavater,
Swiss theologian, 1788

Introduction

The four most important objectives of estate planning for owners of closely held businesses, or interests in businesses, are:

1. Providing for sufficient liquidity for the estate to pay taxes and expenses
2. Minimizing federal gift and estate taxes and state inheritance taxes
3. Providing for the continuity of the business and thus avoid the unplanned, forced sale of the business or business interest
4. Providing a way to allow the ownership of the business to end up in the hands of the appropriate heirs, while treating each beneficiary in a manner the owner desires (which may not always be viewed as "fair" treatment by each beneficiary)

Liquidity during the owner's lifetime can be achieved by going public, selling the company, selling shares to an employee stock ownership plan (ESOP), or selling an interest in the company by other means. Liquidity at the owner's death can be provided by any of the same means or through a buy-sell agreement funded by life insurance or some other predeath or postdeath funding method. The need for liquidity relates to the business owner's desires not only to cash in on the company's successful growth, but also to have funds available to allow the estate planning strategy to be carried out. This chapter discusses the valuation issues that arise in connection with gift and estate planning based on these key objectives.

Other chapters in this part of the book carry this topic further. Chapter 29 focuses on buy-sell agreements. Additional estate planning–related information is contained in Chapter 32 on ESOPs.

The first section of this chapter sets forth the nature of estate and gift taxes and the current rates, exemptions, special provisions, and penalties under the current Internal Revenue Code (IRC) and Regulations to the IRC. The next section discusses the valuation guidelines for valuation for gift and estate tax purposes (which can also be applied to income tax matters) and includes the text of the most relevant IRS Revenue Rulings. The last section deals with valuation issues arising from specific gift and estate tax planning techniques, including the special valuation rules under Chapter 14 of the IRC. No doubt, over time, new estate planning techniques will be developed in response to the constantly changing economic and tax environment.

The material in this book generally is limited to discussion of valuation issues. Anyone involved in appraisal work with tax planning or tax litigation implications should consult a competent attorney and/or certified public accountant (CPA) for guidance with regard to legal and/or tax issues.

Current Tax Rates and Penalties

Estate and gift taxes are a unified system of excise taxes levied on the transfer of wealth during life and at death. In other words, in calculating an individual's final estate taxes, the amount of all post-1976 taxable gifts that were made during his or her lifetime are added to the estate's gross value and all gift taxes that were paid on post-1976 gifts are subtracted from the estate tax payable.

Since the year 2000, the estate, gift, and generation-skipping tax system (collectively referred to as transfer taxes) has been undergoing a generally downward reduction designed to lead to a period in the year 2010 when transfer taxes, except for gift taxes, will be temporarily suspended. In 2011, for various political reasons beyond the scope of this book, the transfer tax rates and provisions return in full force to a level similar to those in existence in 2001–2002. The evolution of transfer tax rates, exemptions, and taxable amounts for the first decade of the 21st century are set forth in Exhibit 27–1.

The law provides for several basic exemptions and exclusions from the amount of net assets that otherwise would be taxable. These adjustments can include:

- A lifetime exemption for the first $2 million of the fair market value of the estate or previously gifted assets. In 2009 the estate tax exemption will be $3.5 million. In 2010 the estate taxes are repealed and no estate taxes will be due. In 2011 the estate tax exemption will return to $1 million. It is anticipated that the exemptions will be changed by Congress in 2009 or 2010.
- Any amounts given to one's spouse, either by gift or by will.[1]
- An annual exclusion of up to $12,000 gifted annually from any one donor to each of any number of donees.

Other special provisions affect:

- The value of farm or small-business, special-use real estate (IRC Section 2032A)
- The time over which estate tax payments can be made and the interest rate charged on such payments on the portion of the estate consisting of interests in a privately owned company engaged in an active trade or business (IRC Section 6166)
- A special deduction for Qualified Family-Owned Business Interests (QFOBIs); however, this is no longer in effect for tax years 2004 through 2010. Unless the law is changed, it will again become effective on January 1, 2011.
- The income tax treatment of redemptions of corporate stock owned by the estate, the proceeds of which are used to pay estate expenses and taxes (IRC Section 303)
- The choice of the estate asset valuation date (either as of date of death or the alternative valuation date six months after death)

---

[1] The transfers to the spouse must be "qualified," that is, they must be in a form that would cause the property to be taxed in the spouse's estate if retained until death.

Exhibit 27–1

Year-by-Year Changes in Federal Transfer Taxes
(Assuming No Further Changes in the Law)

	2001	2002	2003	2004	2005	2006	2007	2008	2009	2010	2011 on
Estate Tax											
Exclusion	$675,000	$1 million		$1.5 million		$2 million			$3.5m		$1 million
Lowest rate	37%	41%		45%		46%	45%				41%
Top rate	55%	50%	49%	48%	47%						55%
5% bubble [a]	Yes	No									Yes
QFOBI [b]	Yes			No							Yes
State tax credit	100%	75%	50%	25%	None. State taxes are deductible.						100%
GST Tax [c]											
Exemption	$1 million indexed (from 1998)			$1.5 million		$2 million			$3.5m		$1 million indexed
Rate	55%	50%	49%	48%	47%	46%	45%				55%
Gift Tax											
Exclusion	$675,000	$1 million									
Lowest rate	37%	41%								35%	41%
Top rate	55%	50%	49%	48%	47%	46%	45%			35%	55%
5% bubble	Yes	No									Yes

2010 column (Estate Tax and GST Tax): Repealed. Replaced with carryover basis.

[a] A 5 percent higher tax rate over the top tax rate is applicable to certain large estates between $10.00 and $21.04 million. This essentially recaptures the benefits of the lower tax brackets and the unified credit reductions for large estates.

[b] QFOBI—Qualified Family-Owned Business Interest: a special set of rules allowing an estate tax reduction for interests in family-owned companies in an active trade or business.

[c] GST = Generation Skipping Tax.

An additional tax can be levied on certain generation-skipping asset transfers (i.e., transfers designed to move assets down two or more generations, such as transfers from grandparents to grandchildren).

There are also penalties for undervaluation of estate and gift assets (IRC Section 6660); these are set forth in Exhibit 27–2. The Section 6660 penalties shown in Exhibit 27–2 are triggered by asset undervaluation and computed as a percentage of the tax underpayment. The IRS may decide not to apply these penalties if the returned value was made in good faith and had a reasonable basis,

Exhibit 27–2

Undervaluation Penalties

For Estate and Gift Taxes over $1,000:

Value Claimed on the Tax Return as a Percentage of the Value Finally Determined	Additional Penalty
over 65%	0%
between 40–65%	20%
below 40%	40%

modified by certain special considerations for schemes designed to be tax shelters.[2] A qualified appraisal prepared by a competent appraiser may constitute part of the establishment of a "reasonable basis."

Appraisers may be subject to a civil penalty of $10,000 for corporate tax matters and $1,000 for other tax matters for aiding and abetting an understatement of tax liability (IRC Section 6701). Appraisers may be subject to an additional penalty of the greater of $1,000 or 10 percent of the amount of the tax underpaid (but in no event more than 125 percent of the gross income received by the appraiser for preparing the appraisal) based on IRC Section 6695A in the recently enacted Pension Protection Act. Even more serious, the IRS may blacklist an appraiser pursuant to Circular 230 section 10.5(b).

Appraiser Penalty and Potential for Blacklisting[3]

According to new IRC Section 6695A from the Pension Protection Act of 2006, the appraisal penalty applies if the valuation misstatement is contained in an appraisal that the appraiser knows or has reason to know will be used "in connection with a tax return or claim for tax refund."

Section 6695A applies to any appraisal that supports a tax position with respect to a return or submissions after August 17, 2006, even if the appraisal was completed before that date.

The Section 6695A penalty may be imposed upon anyone who prepares an appraisal for tax purposes, whether or not the person who prepares the appraisal is a professional appraiser. The new appraisal penalty is applied only against appraisers hired by the taxpayer, not the appraisers hired by the IRS.

As a defense, the appraiser would have to prove that the appraised value was "more likely than not" the correct value. The determination of whether "the appraised value was more likely than not the correct value" is to be made by the Treasury Department, not by a court.

---

[2] See Circular 230 (31 C.F.R. pt. 10), final regulations effective June 2005.

[3] This discussion has been adapted from Steve Leimberg's Estate Planning Newsletter #1031 (October 9, 2006) at http://www.leimbergservices.com. Copyright 2006 Leimberg Information Services, Inc. (LISI).

Circular 230, Section 10.50(b) permits the IRS to "blacklist" appraisers — that is, to impose an administrative sanction barring the appraiser from submitting probative evidence in future IRS tax proceedings. The effective date of the new blacklisting rules is also August 17, 2006 (they apply to returns and submissions after that date). For a more detailed discussion of the Section 6695A penalty, see Chapter 30.

Guidelines for Federal Gift and Estate Tax Valuations

The basic guidelines for the appraisal of closely held business equity are set forth in the IRC, the Treasury Regulations to the Code, and various revenue rulings, technical advice memoranda, and private letter rulings.

The IRC addresses the valuation of closely held securities in Section 2031(b). The standard of value applied to all gift, estate, and income tax matters concerning the IRS is fair market value. Fair market value is defined as the price at which the property would change hands between a willing buyer and a willing seller when neither is under any compulsion to buy or to sell, both parties having reasonable knowledge of the facts.

The next most important source of guidance for valuation are the Treasury Regulations, which set forth the IRS's interpretation of the laws in the IRC. Each regulation is numbered in the same fashion as the Code section to which it relates. Regulation Section 20.2031-2(f) covers corporate stock and Section 20.2301-3 covers unincorporated interests in businesses. Parallel regulations cover gift taxes in Sections 25.2512-2(f) and 25.2512-3.

Revenue Rulings do not have as high a level of authority as regulations. Revenue Rulings are drafted to provide guidance for general types of situations not requiring a specific change in the regulations. The basic guidelines for the valuation of closely held common stock are contained in Revenue Ruling 59-60, which is presented in its entirety in Exhibit 27–3.

Other forms of IRS opinions are issued in the form of Technical Advice Memorandums (TAMs) and Private Letter Rulings (PLRs), which refer to specific situations in which a taxpayer has sought advice on a specific matter from the IRS. PLRs arise when the taxpayer seeks guidance on a valuation issue for a specific case. TAMs arise when a position on a specific issue on a case is initiated by the IRS. Although these TAMs and PLRs cannot be cited as precedent for anyone but the individual taxpayer, they do provide good evidence of the direction of the IRS's thinking on a topic.

Of course, the courts have final jurisdiction over tax matters. IRS regulations and positions taken in Revenue Rulings, TAMs, and PLRs can be overturned by a single or series of adverse rulings. The U.S. Tax Court, Federal District Court, and Court of Federal Claims systems all hear cases involving valuation issues for gift and estate taxes. Like any other federal law issue, these cases can be appealed to the appropriate Federal District Court of Appeals and ultimately the Supreme Court.

Revenue Ruling 59-60 has also been modified and amplified by other subsequent revenue rulings.

Revenue Ruling 77-287, presented as Exhibit 17–7 in Chapter 17, amplifies Revenue Ruling 59-60 by specifically recognizing criteria for determining

Exhibit 27–3

Revenue Ruling 59–60

SECTION 2031.—DEFINITION OF GROSS ESTATE

26 CFR 20.2031-2: Valuation of stocks and bonds. Rev. Rul. 59-60 (Also Section 2512.)

(Also Part II, Sections 811(k), 1005, Regulations 105, Section 81.10)

In valuing the stock of closely held corporations, or the stock of corporations where market quotations are not available, all other available financial data, as well as all relevant factors affecting the fair market value must be considered for estate tax and gift tax purposes. No general formula may be given that is applicable to the many different valuation situations arising in the valuation of such stock. However, the general approach, methods, and factors which must be considered in valuing such securities are outlined. Revenue Ruling 54-77, C.B. 1954-1, 187, superseded.

SECTION 1. PURPOSE.

The purpose of this Revenue Ruling is to outline and review in general the approach, methods and factors to be considered in valuing shares of the capital stock of closely held corporations for estate tax and gift tax purposes. The methods discussed herein will apply likewise to the valuation of corporate stocks on which market quotations are either unavailable or are of such scarcity that they do not reflect the fair market value.

SEC. 2. BACKGROUND AND DEFINITIONS.

.01 All valuations must be made in accordance with the applicable provisions of the Internal Revenue Code of 1954 and the Federal Estate Tax and Gift Tax Regulations. Sections 2031(a), 2032 and 2512(a) of the 1954 Code (sections 811 and 1005 of the 1939 Code) require that the property to be included in the gross estate, or made the subject of a gif, shall be taxed on the basis of the value of the property at the time of death of the decedent, the alternate date if so elected, or the date of gift.

.02 Section 20.2031-1(b) of the Estate Tax Regulations (section 81.10 of the Estate Tax Regulations 105) and section 25.2512-1 of the Gift Tax Regulations (section 86.19 of Gift Tax Regulations 108) define fair market value, in effect, as the price at which the property would change hands between a willing buyer and a willing seller when the former is not under any compulsion to buy and the latter is not under any compulsion to sell, both parties having reasonable knowledge of relevant facts. Court decisions frequently state in addition that the hypothetical buyer and seller are assumed to be able, as well as willing, to trade and to be well informed about the property and concerning the market for such property.

.03 Closely held corporations are those corporations the shares of which are owned by a relatively limited number of stockholders. Often the entire stock issue is held by one family. The result of this situation is that little, if any, trading in the shares takes place. There is, therefore, no established market for the stock and such sales as occur at irregular intervals seldom reflect all of the elements of a representative transaction as defined by the term "fair market value."

SEC. 3. APPROACH TO VALUATION.

.01 A determination of fair market value, being a question of fact, will depend upon the circumstances in each case. No formula can be devised that will be generally applicable to the multitude of different valuation issues arising in estate and gift tax cases. Often, an appraiser will find wide differences of opinion as to the fair market value of a particular stock. In resolving such differences, he should maintain a reasonable attitude in recognition of the fact that valuation is not an exact science. A sound valuation will be based upon all the relevant facts, but the elements of common sense, informed judgment and reasonableness must enter into the process of weighing those facts and determining their aggregate significance.

.02 The fair market value of specific shares of stock will vary as general economic conditions change from "normal" to "boom" or "depression," that is, according to the degree of optimism or pessimism with which the investing public regards the future at the required date of appraisal. Uncertainty as to the stability or continuity of the future income from a property decreases its value by increasing the risk of loss of earnings and value in the future. The value of shares of stock of a company with very uncertain future prospects is highly speculative. The appraiser must exercise his judgment as to the degree of risk attaching to the business of the corporation which issued the stock, but that judgment must be related to all of the other factors affecting value.

.03 Valuation of securities is, in essence, a prophesy as to the future and must be based on facts available at the required date of appraisal. As a generalization, the prices of stocks which are traded in volume in a free and active market by informed persons best reflect the consensus of the investing public as to what the future holds for the corporations and industries represented. When a stock is closely held, is traded infrequently, or is traded in an erratic market, some other measure of value must be used. In many instances, the next best measure may be found in the prices at which the stocks of companies engaged in the same or a similar line of business are selling in a free and open market.

Sec 4. Factors to Consider.

.01 It is advisable to emphasize that in the valuation of the stock of closely held corporations or the stock of corporations where market quotations are either lacking or too scarce to be recognized, all available financial data, as well as all relevant factors affecting the fair market value, should be considered. The following factors, although not all-inclusive are fundamental and require careful analysis in each case:

(a) The nature of the business and the history of the enterprise from its inception.

(b) The economic outlook in general and the condition and outlook of the specific industry in particular.

(c) The book value of the stock and the financial condition of the business.

(d) The earnings capacity of the company.

(e) The dividend-paying capacity.

(f) Whether or not the enterprise has goodwill or other intangible value.

continued on next page

Exhibit 27–3

Revenue Ruling 59–60 (*continued*)

(g) Sales of the stock and the size of the block of stock to be valued.

(h) The market price of stocks of corporations engaged in the same or a similar line of business having their stocks actively traded in a free and open market, either on an exchange or over-the-counter.

.02 The following is a brief discussion of each of the foregoing factors:

(a) The history of a corporate enterprise will show its past stability or instability, its growth or lack of growth, the diversity or lack of diversity of its operations, and other facts needed to form an opinion of the degree of risk involved in the business. For an enterprise which changed its form of organization but carried on the same or closely similar operations of its predecessor, the history of the former enterprise should be considered. The detail to be considered should increase with approach to the required date of appraisal, since recent events are of greatest help in predicting the future; but a study of gross and net income, and of dividends covering a long prior period, is highly desirable. The history to be studied should include, but need not be limited to, the nature of the business, its products or services, its operating and investment assets, capital structure, plant facilities, sales records and management, all of which should be considered as of the date of the appraisal, with due regard for recent significant changes. Events of the past that are unlikely to recur in the future should be discounted, since value has a close relation to future expectancy.

(b) A sound appraisal of a closely held stock must consider current and prospective economic conditions as of the date of appraisal, both in the national economy and in the industry or industries with which the corporation is allied. It is important to know that the company is more or less successful than its competitors in the same industry, or that it is maintaining a stable position with respect to competitors. Equal or even greater significance may attach to the ability of the industry with which the company is allied to compete with other industries. Prospective competition which has not been a factor in prior years should be given careful attention. For example, high profits due to the novelty of its product and the lack of competition often lead to increasing competition. The public's appraisal of the future prospects of competitive industries or of competitors within an industry may be indicated by price trends in the markets for commodities and for securities. The loss of the manager of a so-called "one-man" business may have a depressing effect upon the value of the stock of such business, particularly if there is a lack of trained personnel capable of succeeding to the management of the enterprise. In valuing the stock of this type of business, therefore, the effect of the loss of the manager on the future expectancy of the business, and the absence of management succession potentialities are pertinent factors to be taken into consideration. On the other hand, there may be factors which offset, in whole or in part, the loss of the manager's services. For instance, the nature of the business and of its assets may be such that they will not be impaired by the loss of the manager. Furthermore, the loss may be adequately covered by life insurance, or competent management might be employed on the basis of the consideration paid for the former manager's services. These, or other offsetting factors, if found to exist, should be carefully weighed against the loss of the manager's services in valuing the stock of the enterprise.

(c) Balance sheets should be obtained, preferably in the form of comparative annual statements for two or more years immediately preceding the date of appraisal, together with a balance sheet at the end of the month preceding that date, if corporate accounting will permit. Any balance sheet descriptions that are not self-explanatory, and balance sheet items comprehending diverse assets or liabilities, should be clarified in essential detail by supporting supplemental schedules. These statements usually will disclose to the appraiser (1) liquid position (ratio of current assets to current liabilities); (2) gross and net book value of principal classes of fixed assets; (3) working capital; (4) long-term indebtedness; (5) capital structure; and (6) net worth. Consideration also should be given to any assets not essential to the operation of the business, such as investments in securities, real estate, etc. In general, such nonoperating assets will command a lower rate of return than do the operating assets, although in exceptional cases the reverse may be true. In computing the book value per share of stock, assets of the investment type should be revalued on the basis of their market price and the book value adjusted accordingly. Comparison of the company's balance sheets over several years may reveal, among other facts, such developments as the acquisition of additional production facilities or subsidiary companies, improvement in financial position, and details as to recapitalizations and other changes in the capital structure of the corporation. If the corporation has more than one class of stock outstanding, the charter or certificate of incorporation should be examined to ascertain the explicit rights and privileges of the various stock issues including: (1) voting powers, (2) preference as to dividends; and (3) preference as to assets in the event of liquidation.

(d) Detailed profit-and-loss statements should be obtained and considered for a representative period immediately prior to the required date of appraisal, preferably five or more years. Such statements should show (1) gross income by principal items; (2) principal deductions from gross income including major prior items of operating expenses, interest and other expense on each item of long-term debt, depreciation and depletion if such deductions are made, officers' salaries, in total if they appear to be reasonable or in detail if they seem to be excessive, contributions (whether or not deductible for tax purposes) that the nature of its business and its community position require the corporation to make, and taxes by principal items, including income and excess profits taxes; (3) net income available for dividends; (4) rates and amount of dividends paid on each class of stock; (5) remaining amount carried to surplus; and (6) adjustment to, and reconciliation with, surplus as stated on the balance sheet. With profit and loss statements of this character available, the appraiser should be able to separate recurrent from nonrecurrent items of income and expense, to distinguish between operating income and investment income, and to ascertain whether or not any line of business in which the company is engaged is operated consistently at a loss and might be abandoned with benefit to the company. The percentage of earnings retained for business expansion should be noted when dividend-paying capacity is considered. Potential future income is a major factor in many valuations of closely held stocks, and all information concerning past income which will be helpful in predicting the future should be secured. Prior earnings

continued on next page

Exhibit 27–3

Revenue Ruling 59–60 (*continued*)

records usually are the most reliable guide as to the future expectancy, but resort to arbitrary five-or ten-year averages without regard to current trends or future prospects will not produce a realistic valuation. If, for instance, a record of progressively increasing or decreasing net income is found, then greater weight may be accorded the most recent years' profits in estimating earning power. It will be helpful, in judging risk and the extent to which a business is a marginal operator, to consider deductions from income and net income in terms of percentage of sales. Major categories of cost and expense to be so analyzed include the consumption of raw materials and supplies in the case of manufacturers, processors and fabricators; the cost of purchased merchandise in the case of merchants; utility services; insurance; taxes; depletion or depreciation; and interest.

(e) Primary consideration should be given to the dividend-paying capacity of the company rather than to dividends actually paid in the past. Recognition must be given to the necessity of retaining a reasonable portion of profits in a company to meet competition. Dividend-paying capacity is a factor that must be considered in an appraisal, but dividends actually paid in the past may not have any relation to dividend-paying capacity. Specifically, the dividends paid by a closely held family company may be measured by the income needs of the stockholders or by their desire to avoid taxes on dividend receipts, instead of by the ability of the company to pay dividends. Where an actual or effective controlling interest in a corporation is to be valued, the dividend factor is not a material element, since the payment of such dividends is discretionary with the controlling stockholders. The individual or group in control can substitute salaries and bonuses for dividends, thus reducing net income and understating the dividend-pay capacity of the company. It follows, therefore, that dividends are less reliable criteria of fair market value than other applicable factors.

(f) In the final analysis, goodwill is based upon earning capacity. The presence of goodwill and its value, therefore, rests upon the excess of net earnings over and above a fair return on the net tangible assets. While the element of goodwill may be based primarily on earnings, such factors as the prestige and renown of the business, the ownership of a trade or brand name, and a record of successful operation over a prolonged period in a particular locality, also may furnish support for the inclusion of intangible value. In some instances it may not be possible to make a separate appraisal of the tangible and intangible assets of the business. The enterprise has a value as an entity. Whatever intangible value there is, which is supportable by the facts, may be measured by the amount by which the appraised value of the tangible assets exceeds the net book value of such assets.

(g) Sales of stock of a closely held corporation should be carefully investigated to determine whether they represent transactions at arm's length. Forced or distress sales do not ordinarily reflect fair market value nor do isolated sales in small amounts necessarily control as the measure of value. This is especially true in the valuation of a controlling interest in a corporation. Since, in the case of closely held stocks, no prevailing market prices are available, there is no basis for making an adjustment for blockage. It follows, therefore, that such stocks should be valued upon a consideration of all the evidence affecting the fair market value.

The size of the block of stock itself is a relevant factor to be considered. Although it is true that a minority interest in an unlisted corporation's stock is more difficult to sell than a similar block of listed stock, it is equally true that control of a corporation, either actual or in effect, representing as it does an added element of value, may justify a higher value for a specific block of stock.

(h) Section 2031(b) of the Code states, in effect, that in valuing unlisted securities the value of stock or securities of corporations engaged in the same or a similar line of business which are listed on an exchange should be taken into consideration along with all other factors. An important consideration is that the corporations to be used for comparisons have capital stocks which are actively traded by the public. In accordance with section 2031(b) of the Code, stocks listed on an exchange are to be considered first. However, if sufficient comparable companies whose stocks are listed on an exchange cannot be found, other comparable companies which have stocks actively traded in on the over-the-counter market also may be used. The essential factor is that whether the stocks are sold on an exchange or over-the-counter there is evidence of an active, free public market for the stock as of the valuation date. In selecting corporations for comparative purposes, care should be taken to use only comparable companies. Although the only restrictive requirement as to comparable corporations specified in the statute is that their lines of business be the same or similar, yet it is obvious that consideration must be given to other relevant factors in order that the most valid comparison possible will be obtained. For illustration, a corporation having one or more issues of preferred stock, bonds or debentures in addition to its common stock should not be considered to be directly comparable to one having only common stock outstanding. In like manner, a company with a declining business and decreasing markets is not comparable to one with a record of current progress and market expansion.

SEC. 5. WEIGHT TO BE ACCORDED VARIOUS FACTORS.

The valuation of closely held corporate stock entails the consideration of all relevant factors as stated in section 4. Depending upon the circumstances in each case, certain factors may carry more weight than others because of the nature of the company's business. To illustrate: (a) Earnings may be the most important criterion of value in some cases whereas asset value will receive primary consideration in others. In general, the appraiser will accord primary consideration to earnings when valuing stocks of companies which sell products or services to the public; conversely, in the investment or holding type of company, the appraiser may accord the greatest weight to the assets underlying the security to be valued.

(b) The value of the stock of a closely held investment or real estate holding company, whether or not family owned, is closely related to the value of the assets underlying the stock. For companies of this type the appraiser should determine the fair market values of the assets of the company. Operating expenses of such a company and the cost of liquidating it, if any, merit consideration when appraising the relative values of the stock and the underlying assets. The market values of the underlying assets give due weight to potential earnings and dividends of the particular items of property underlying the stock, capitalized at rates deemed

continued on next page

Exhibit 27–3

Revenue Ruling 59–60 (*continued*)

proper by the investing public at the date of appraisal. A current appraisal by the investing public should be superior to the retrospective opinion of an individual. For these reasons, adjusted net worth should be accorded greater weight in valuing the stock of a closely held investment or real estate holding company, whether or not family owned, than any of the other customary yardsticks of appraisal, such as earnings and dividend paying capacity.

SEC. 6. CAPITALIZATION RATES.

In the application of certain fundamental valuation factors, such as earnings and dividends, it is necessary to capitalize the average or current results at some appropriate rate. A determination of the proper capitalization rate presents one of the most difficult problems in valuation. That there is no ready or simple solution will become apparent by a cursory check of the rates of return and dividend yields in terms of the selling prices of corporate shares listed on the major exchanges of the country. Wide variations will be found even for companies in the same industry. Moreover, the ratio will fluctuate from year to year depending upon economic conditions. Thus, no standard tables of capitalization rates applicable to closely held corporations can be formulated. Among the more important factors to be taken into consideration in deciding upon a capitalization rate in a particular case are: (1) the nature of the business; (2) the risk involved; and (3) the stability or irregularity of earnings.

SEC. 7. AVERAGE OF FACTORS.

Because valuations cannot be made on the basis of a prescribed formula, there is no means whereby the various applicable factors in a particular case can be assigned mathematical weights in deriving the fair market value. For this reason, no useful purpose is served by taking an average of several factors (for example, book value, capitalized earnings and capitalized dividends) and basing the valuation on the result. Such a process

excludes active consideration of other pertinent factors, and the end result cannot be supported by a realistic application of the significant facts in the case except by mere chance.

SEC. 8. RESTRICTIVE AGREEMENTS.

Frequently, in the valuation of closely held stock for estate and gift tax purposes, it will be found that the stock is subject to an agreement restricting its sale or transfer. Where shares of stocks were acquired by a decedent subject to an option reserved by the issuing corporation to repurchase at a certain price, the option price is usually accepted as the fair market value for estate tax purposes. See Rev. Rul. 54-76, C.B. 1954-1, 194. However, in such case the option price is not determinative of fair market value for gif tax purposes. Where the option, or buy and sell agreement, is the result of voluntary action by the stockholders and is binding during the life as well as at the death of the stockholders, such agreement may or may not, depending upon the circumstances of each case, fix the value for estate tax purposes. However, such agreement is a factor to be considered, with other relevant factors, in determining fair market value. Where the stockholder is free to dispose of his shares during life and the option is to become effective only upon his death, the fair market value is not limited to the option price. It is always necessary to consider the relationship of the parties, the relative number of shares held by the decedent, and other material facts to determine whether the agreement represents a bona fide business arrangement or is a device to pass the decedent's shares to the natural objects of his bounty for less than an adequate and full consideration in money or money's worth. In this connection see Rev. Rul. 157 C.B. 1953-2, 255, and Rev. Rul. 189, C.B. 1953-2, 294.

SEC. 9. EFFECT ON OTHER DOCUMENTS.

Revenue Ruling 54-77, C.B. 1954-1, 187, is hereby superseded.

SOURCE: Rev. Rul. 59-60, 1959-1 C.B. 237.

---

an appropriate discount for lack of marketability. It also provides guidance for discounts to be applied to publicly traded securities restricted under federal securities laws (see Chapter 17). Revenue Ruling 83-120, discussed in Chapter 24, contains guidelines for valuing preferred stock. Revenue Ruling 93-12, presented in Exhibit 27–4, acknowledges that stock interest transfers among family members, who in the aggregate own a controlling interest in the company, would not be valued as controlling interests solely due to the family relationship among the shareholders. This acknowledgement that minority interest transfers among relatives would normally be treated as minority interests for valuation purposes follows a long series of IRS losses in court on this issue, as referred to by Revenue Ruling 93-12 itself.

If the analyst follows the valuation procedures presented in this book with reasonable thoroughness, under the standard of value defined as "fair market value," the requirements of these rulings should be satisfied. However, when valuing interests for gift and estate tax purposes, the analyst must be aware of the special

Exhibit 27–4

Revenue Ruling 93–12

REVENUE RULING 93-12

ISSUE

If a donor transfers shares in a corporation to each of the donor's children, is the factor of corporate control in the family to be considered in valuing each transferred interest, for purposes of section 2512 of the Internal Revenue Code?

FACTS

P owned all of the single outstanding class of stock of *X* corporation. *P* transferred all of *P*s shares by making simultaneous gifts of 20 percent of the shares to each of *P*s five children, *A*, *B*, *C*, *D*, and *E*.

LAW AND ANALYSIS

Section 2512(a) of the Code provides that the value of the property at the date of the gif shall be considered the amount of the gift.

Section 25.2512-1 of the Gif Tax Regulations provides that, if a gift is made in property, its value at the date of the gif shall be considered the amount of the gif. The value of the property is the price at which the property would change hands between a willing buyer and a willing seller, neither being under any compulsion to buy or to sell, and both having reasonable knowledge of relevant facts.

Section 25.2512-2(a) of the regulations provides that the value of stocks and bonds is the fair market value per share or bond on the date of the gif. Section 25.2512-2(f) provides that the degree of control of the business represented by the block of stock to be valued is among the factors to be considered in valuing stock where there are no sales prices or bona fide bid or asked prices.

Rev. Rul. 81-253, 1981-1 C.B. 187, holds that, ordinarily, no minority shareholder discount is allowed with respect to transfers of shares of stock between family members if, based upon a composite of the family members' interest at the time of the transfer, control (either majority voting control or de facto control through family relationships) of the corporation exists in the family unit. The ruling also states that the Service will not follow the decision of the Fifth Circuit in *Estate of Bright v. United States*, 658 F.2d 999 (5th Cir. 1981).

In *Bright*, the decedent's undivided community property interest in shares of stock, together with the corresponding undivided community property interest of the decedent's surviving spouse, constituted a control block of 55 percent of the shares of a corporation. The court held that, because the community-held shares were subject to a right of partition, the decedent's own interest was equivalent to 27.5 percent of the outstanding shares and, therefore, should be valued as a minority interest, even though the shares were to be held by the decedent's surviving spouse as trustee of a testamentary trust. *See also, Propstra v United States, 680* F2d 1248 (9th Cir. 1982). In addition, *Estate of Andrews v Commissioner*, 79 T.C. 938 (1982), and *Estate of Lee v Commissioner*, 69 T.C. 860 (1978), *nonacq.*, 1980-2 C.B. 2, held that the corporation shares owned by other family members cannot be attributed to an individual family member for determining whether the individual family member's share should be valued as the controlling interest of the corporation.

After further consideration of the position taken in Rev. Rul. 81-253, and in light of the cases noted above, the Service has concluded that, in the case of a corporation with a single class of stock, notwithstanding the family relationship of the donor, the donee, and other shareholders, the shares of other family members will not be aggregated with the transferred shares to determine whether the transferred shares should be valued as part of a controlling interest.

In the present case, the minority interests transferred to *A*, *B*, *C*, *D*, and *E* should be valued for gift tax purposes without regard to the family relationship of the parties.

HOLDING

If a donor transfers shares in a corporation to each of the donor's children, the factor of corporate control in the family is not considered in valuing each transferred interest for purposes of section 2512 of the Code. For estate and gift tax valuation purposes, the Service will follow *Bright, Propstra, Andrews*, and *Lee* in not assuming that all voting power held by family members may be aggregated for purposes of determining whether the transferred shares should be valued as part of a controlling interest. Consequently, a minority discount will not be disallowed solely because a transferred interest, when aggregated with interest held by family members, would be a part of a controlling interest. This would be the case whether the donor held 100 percent or some lesser percentage of the stock immediately before the gift.

EFFECT ON OTHER DOCUMENTS

Rev. Rul. 81-253 is revoked. Acquiescence in issue one of Lee, 1980 2 C.B. 2.

SOURCE: Rev. Rul. 93-12, 1993-1, C.B. 202.

valuation rules of IRC Sections 2703 and 2704, which do not always follow the "typical" fair market value convention. Failure to be knowledgeable of these key code sections and recent significant case law in these areas can result in significant undervaluation. This section will call attention to a few points in Revenue Ruling 59-60 as well as relevant rulings. The following chapter discusses a variety of key factors in the context of various positions taken and decisions reached in court cases.

Revenue Ruling 59-60, Section 3, "Approach to Valuation," makes the general point that the public marketplace best reflects the consensus of the investing public, and it concludes by suggesting as a measure of value "the prices at which the stocks of companies engaged in the same or similar line of business are selling in a free and open market." The section also recognizes that the value can change as a result of factors internal to the company as well as external economic factors. The section emphasizes the complexity of the factors affecting valuation and the degree of uncertainty involved. Fair market value is a question of fact and depends on the circumstances. No formula is generally applicable and appraisers often find wide differences in opinion. It is not an exact science, and common sense, informed judgment, and reasonableness must enter the process.

Revenue Ruling 59-60, Section 4, "Factors to Consider," lists the eight key factors to consider with regard to the valuation of closely held corporations and elaborates on each. In any appraisal involving gift and estate taxes, the appraiser should review Section 4 to ensure that each of the eight points has been addressed in the valuation process.

Revenue Ruling 59-60, Section 4.02(c) notes, "In computing the book value per share of stock, assets *of the investment type* should be revalued on the basis of their market price and the book value adjusted accordingly" (emphasis supplied). It is important to recognize that this requirement to adjust asset values specifically applies to assets "of the investment type," not necessarily operating assets.

Section 4.02(d) notes that the profit and loss statements considered should be for a "representative period." The section states that the appraiser should separate recurrent from nonrecurrent items and operating income from investment income. It suggests placing more weight on recent years if there appears to be a trend in the earnings pattern.

Section 4.02(h) reemphasizes that the prices of stocks of publicly traded companies in the same or similar lines of business should be considered and the greatest care possible should be taken in analyzing the companies to select the ones that are most comparative to the subject securities. Chapter 11 discusses the identification and selection of guideline public companies.

Weight to Be Accorded Various Factors

Section 5, "Weight to Be Accorded Various Factors," essentially makes the point that earnings should be accorded the most weight in valuing operating companies, and asset values the most weight in valuing holding companies. The analyst obviously needs to weigh this in light of the appropriate values as determined for the subject company.

The section also notes that assets should be adjusted to market values if they are a factor in valuing an operating company. For family-held investment companies, comparisons of per share value to underlying asset value can then be made on the basis of the ratios of market value to net asset value for closed-end funds and other investment companies, since such companies report the values of their assets at market on a regular basis. For closely held real estate holding companies, for example, deriving a per share value by reference to publicly traded real estate holding companies may not be quite as easy, since many real estate companies do not report their underlying assets' market values. However, there are now enough companies reporting such market values of underlying assets (and outside analysts who provide reasonable estimates of net asset values) that a table of companies, with the ratios of market prices to adjusted asset values, can be constructed to provide guidance in valuing closely held investment company shares.

Capitalization Rates

Section 6, "Capitalization Rates," makes further reference to publicly traded shares and notes that appropriate capitalization rates vary considerably both among companies and over time due to economic conditions.

Average of Factors

Section 7, "Average of Factors," is the section referred to in Chapter 19 that discourages the use of a universal mathematical weighting system of various factors that, by implication, should be applied in every situation. The reason is that "such a process excludes active consideration of other pertinent factors" that might apply in the specific set of facts and circumstances of each case. However, as noted in this book and in the examples presented in the chapter on writing valuation reports, mathematical weighting frequently is used and relied on by analysts and in court decisions.

Restrictive Agreements

Section 8, "Restrictive Agreements," makes the point that to be binding for estate tax valuation purposes, a price fixed under a buy-sell agreement must be binding during the life as well as at the death of the stockholder and not "a device to pass the decedent's shares to the natural objects of his bounty for less than adequate and full consideration in money or money's worth." See Chapter 29, "Buy-Sell Agreements," for further discussion.

Summary of Guidelines

Although Revenue Ruling 59-60 was written over 45 years ago, it still offers considerable insight into the basic criteria and processes for valuing closely held common stocks. With minor modifications and amplification, it has stood the test of time.

Nevertheless, the nature of the process necessarily leaves much room for subjectivity and disagreement. Interpretations by analysts, the IRS, and courts have been somewhat less than consistent.[4] It is not a subject that lends itself to such sharp definition of criteria that gray areas can be eliminated.

---

[4] Mathew N. McErlean, "IRS Appraisal Practices 'Violate ... taxpayers' right to uniformity,'" *Shannon Pratt's Business Valuation Update*, June 1999, pp. 1, 3.

Chapter 14 Special Valuation Guidelines

Aside from the basic guidelines that have evolved over the years for valuing close-ly held securities for federal estate and gift taxes, in 1990 Congress passed a series of special valuation rules listed under a newly created Chapter 14 of the IRS to stem what the IRS convinced Congress to be certain abusive practices that involved valuation issues. Each of the four sections of Chapter 14, Sections 2701 through 2704, addresses a different series of issues and is discussed below. Three of the sections, 2701, 2703, and 2704 relate *only* to transfers of ownership between family members. Because of the limitations imposed on the length of this book, we can only address the major topics with which a business appraiser is likely to deal under Chapter 14.

These special valuation rules potentially apply to all transactions involving entities that are family-controlled (or involve valuations pursuant to modifications to prior existing arrangements) that occur after October 8, 1990, the effective date of the Chapter 14 statute.

It is very important to note that, if Chapter 14 special valuation rules do not apply, the basic guidelines discussed in the previous section of this chapter, and other generally accepted techniques used to determine fair market value, will apply. The special valuation rules of Chapter 14 themselves are designed to mod-ify the generally accepted appraisal guidelines for gift and estate tax valuation involving entities in which related parties have control. Consequently, the structure of the special valuation rules clearly shows that Congress did not intend to elimi-nate consideration of discounts for lack of ownership control for minority interest transfers or discounts for lack of marketability for estate and gift tax issues, even when family members as a group own control of an enterprise.[5]

Valuing Recapitalizations and Senior Equity Interests under Section 2701

Section 2701 of Chapter 14 sets forth special valuation rules utilized for lifetime gifts when a junior equity interest (corporate, partnership, or limited liability com-pany) is transferred from one family member to another and the transferor retains a senior equity interest in the company. In other words, Section 2701 deals with an attempt to "freeze" estate tax values by having the senior generation owners hold only equity securities with a fixed redemption value (e.g., preferred stock) that will not appreciate.

Triggering the Special Valuation Rules. To fall under the rules of 2701, the following characteristics must be present in a transaction:

- The retained security must be of a class senior to the transferred junior security.
- The subject securities (both the retained senior preferred and transferred junior securities) must be nonpublicly traded.

---

[5] However, in 2005, at the request of Senate Finance Committee Chairman Charles Grassley and Senator Max Baucus, a report was prepared by the staff of the Joint Committee on Taxation on proposals for closing the tax gap titled, "Options to Improve Tax Compliance and Reform Tax Expenditures" (Jan. 27, 2005). One of the report's numerous recommendations was to limit the availability of minority and marketability, as well as other discounts, through the use of aggregation and look-through rules—primarily in response to perceived abuses of FLPs and LLCs. See report pp. 396–404.

- The transaction must result in a transfer (directly or indirectly) between members of the family.[6]
- Immediately before the transfer, the transferor and applicable family members[7] in the aggregate have 50 percent or more (by vote or value) control of the corporate stock, or of the capital or profits interests in a partnership or limited liability company. Or, the transferor and the applicable family members must own any general partnership interest in a limited partnership.
- The transfer is not a proportionate transfer of all senior and junior equity interests and, as mentioned, the transferor must retain a senior equity interest.

If the transfer has these characteristics, then certain retained rights of the "applicable retained interest" (as the preferred senior security is called in Section 2701) must be ignored, and a special subtraction method of valuation must be followed in determining fair market value for federal gift tax purposes.

Section 2701 basically requires that all rights and features of the preferred senior security that have any optional features in terms of payment amounts or timing that can potentially be manipulated by the controlling family be ignored or valued in a manner that results in the lowest possible value for the preferred senior interest, making a large portion or the entire gift taxable.

As a result, all noncumulative distribution rights (such as dividends) are valued at zero. Similarly, any extraordinary payment right, such as a put, call, conversion, liquidation right, or option to acquire equity interests, is valued at zero—with certain exceptions described below.

The practical effect of these rules, from an appraisal standpoint, is that only a few features will provide a basis for attributing value to the applicable retained senior securities. These include:

- *Cumulative dividends or distribution rights.* These can be either fixed in amount or variable if linked by a fixed ratio to a public market interest rate. These are called "qualified distribution rights." The taxpayer may make a permanent election to treat any noncumulative distribution right as a cumulative, qualified distribution right.[8] Therefore, the appraiser should check with the client or the client's tax advisors to see if such an election has been made or will be made. If such qualified distributions are not actually made within four years of their scheduled payment date, then these unpaid distributions are treated as gifts and compounded forward for ultimate payment when the holder dies or transfers his or her interest.
- *Voting rights.* In valuing voting rights, however, any of the extraordinary payment rights discussed above are assumed either not to exist, or are exercised under the "lower of" rule, discussed below.

---

[6] *Member of the family* is defined as the transferor's spouse, the transferor's (or spouse's) lineal descendants (and their spouses), i.e., any natural or adopted children or offspring of the children of the transferor, and all associated spouses. Notice that such transfers do not apply to transfers from uncles and aunts to nieces and nephews.

[7] *Applicable family member* is defined differently from "member of the family." An applicable family member includes: (1) the transferor and spouse, (2) the transferor's (or spouse's) ancestors (or their ancestors' spouses). For purposes of measuring *control*, the transferor's brothers, sisters, or other lineal descendants of the parents of the transferor (or spouse) are also included as part of the measuring group of interest holders. Indirect applicable family member holdings through corporations, partnerships, and trusts are also included. Some background in genealogy is thus required as part of the due diligence for estate and gift tax valuation under Chapter 14.

[8] The taxpayer can also elect not to treat a cumulative dividend right as a qualified distribution right. This would be rather unusual, as the distribution right is then valued at zero for gift tax purposes. This may make sense when the subject company cannot be certain that distributions can be made consistently within the four-year grace period for payment under Section 2701(d).

- *Mandatory redemption rights.* This category of redemption rights must require the retained preferred senior interest to receive a specific amount at a specific date. Optional extraordinary payment redemption rights that can be voluntarily exercised by either the holder or the company do not count.
- *Nonlapsing conversion rights.* Conversion rights that add value under Section 2701 must require that the senior interests be convertible into a stated number of shares or percentage of the same class as the transferred interest. Obviously, this will tend to make the preferred interest increase in value with the underlying junior equity securities, and thus frustrate a freeze of the senior preferred interest. The timing of conversion can be optional.

There is also an additional "lower of" valuation rule, which requires that the appraiser determine whether any of the extraordinary payment rights, if exercised in conjunction with any qualified distribution right, would lower the total value of the preferred security. If so, then the lower of the values must be used as the value of the applicable retained interest in the preferred securities.

As an example of this "lower of" rule, if a preferred stock had a high fixed, cumulative dividend yield that would cause it to be valued in excess of par value, but the preferred stock also had a put right or right to compel liquidation at par value, then the value utilized for the preferred interest would be par value—the lower of the two values.

Applying the Subtraction Method. Once it is established that the transaction falls under the special valuation rules of Section 2701, and that certain rights and features of the applicable retained interest in the senior preferred securities either do or do not add value under Section 2701, then the value of the transferred junior equity interest is determined under the Section 2701 subtraction method. The value is determined by following a four-step process:

Step 1   Estimate the fair market value of all of the capital securities of the subject company held by the transferor (or spouse), any applicable family members, and any lineal descendants of the parents of the transferor (or spouse) utilizing standard business interest valuation procedures. Under Section 2701, the appraiser must assume that all of these family-held interests are owned by one person, using a consistent set of assumptions. At this point it is also appropriate to determine what percentage of each class of the senior and junior equity interests the transferor and his applicable family members own in the aggregate, as this information will be used in step 2. In many cases, step 1 may require the valuation of the entire company on a control basis as either a going concern or under a liquidation premise, when the family owns 100 percent of the securities.

Step 2   From this value subtract:
1.   The fair market value of all family-held senior equity interests, other than those of the transferor and applicable family members. Also, as discussed immediately below in number 2, any percentage of the retained senior equity interests owned by the transferor and applicable family members, in excess of the maximum percentage of junior equity interest classes held by the same transferor and the applicable family member group, is added back at this point in step 2. These senior equity interests are valued utilizing standard business interest valuation procedures (see Revenue Ruling 83-120 and Chapter 24 on valuing preferred stock). In most family-owned businesses this

calculation will not come into play, as all family member interest holders will be included in number 2 below.

2. The value determined under the Section 2701 special valuation rules of the transferor's and his applicable family members' retained senior equity interests. As noted above, this amount is further adjusted by reducing this amount so that it does not exceed the largest percentage interest owned by the transferor and his applicable family members of any of the junior classes of equity interests.

As an example, if the transferor and applicable family members owned 100 percent of the preferred stock in a recapitalized company, but only owned 90 percent of the common class of stock (the rest being held by non–family member employees), then the number of preferred shares valued under the special valuation rules of Section 2701 would be 90 percent of the preferred share class. The remaining preferred shares would be valued utilizing standard business interest valuation procedures, as noted above in number 1.

This procedure recognizes that any advantage in not exercising the nonqualified distribution and extraordinary payment rights of the senior securities may benefit all junior equity holders, not just the immediate members of the family.

Step 3   Allocate the remaining value to the family-held junior equity securities. If there is more than one class of junior equity securities, then the allocation must start with the class of junior equity securities with the greatest preference over the other junior equity classes. The allocation of the remaining value is made by continuing with the same set of assumptions utilized for valuing the entire family-held equity in step 1 and the senior equity in step 2 (i.e., using the "lower of" rule and zero value rules).

A final special "minimum value" rule under Section 2701 provides that the total allocated value to the junior equity interests can never be less than 10 percent of the sum of: (1) the total value of *all* of the enterprise's equity interests, plus (2) the total amount of any indebtedness owed to the transferor and any applicable family members.

Step 4   Determine the amount of the gift. The allocated values of the transferred junior equity interests are typically adjusted for discounts for minority interest (lack of ownership control) and lack of marketability. As noted in Revenue Ruling 93-12, the application of such discounts is considered without regard to a family's overall unity of ownership in the enterprise.

The final regulations also suggest that the total reduction to the allocated value, for lack of ownership control and lack of marketability discounts, should not cause the value of the transferred junior equity interests to be less than their fair market value utilizing standard business interest valuation procedures.

Also, any consideration paid to the transferor by the transferee would also require a reduction adjustment to the allocated value at this point in the process before determining the value of the gift under Section 2701. If this consideration is additional preferred stock, for example, swapped by the transferee to the transferor for common stock, the value of the preferred stock consideration is the value determined under the special valuation rules of Section 2701 (and not fair market value).

Lastly, any value determined under Section 2702 (regarding retained life, annuity, or unitrust interests in trust) is also subtracted during this step.

The remaining adjusted value allocated to the transferred junior equity shares is the deemed amount of the gift.

The discussion in the final regulations regarding the "minimum value" rule in step 3 and the maximum reduction for discounts in step 4 suggests that an additional iteration is also part of the subtraction process under Section 2701. We believe that the appraiser also needs to estimate the fair market value of the applicable retained senior equity interests and the junior transferred equity interests, without regard to the Section 2701 special valuation rules, in order to check these results against the results of the special valuation calculations.

Because value is assigned under Section 2701 only to payment of cumulative dividends on preferred stock, much of the current recapitalization activity is focused on partnerships and limited liability companies. Such entities do not have the income tax problem of having to pay taxes at the entity level before preferred interest payments are distributed.

However, the convoluted nature of the special valuation rules under Section 2701 has encouraged most estate planners to avoid transactions requiring its use. Consequently, the use of the traditional preferred stock estate freeze has greatly declined in popularity. However, there are still a number of private businesses with old pre–Chapter 14 preferred stock estate freezes outstanding that may require additional gifting of common stock after October 8, 1990. These subsequent transactions will fall under the rules of Section 2701. We urge all appraisers who may become involved with an appraisal under the special valuation rules of Section 2701 to read the statute language, final regulations, technical corrections, subsequent clarifying revenue rulings and private letter rulings, and court cases on this subject carefully.

Valuation Issues under Section 2702

Because Section 2702 deals with retained life, annuity, and unitrust interests transferred via trusts for lifetime gift tax purposes, there are no special valuation rules included in this section that directly relate to closely held business interests.

Closely held business interests are often placed into various grantor retained annuity trusts (GRATs) and grantor retained unitrusts (GRUTs), or charitable remainder annuity (CRATs), or charitable lead trusts (CLTs). But the primary valuation issue in these cases is the application of the IRS annuity and life expectancy tables.

Buy-Sell Agreements and Leases (Including Operating Agreements of LLCs) or Sale of Options under Section 2703

Chapter 29 discusses buy-sell agreements in detail. For now, let us note that there are four factors that determine whether the buy-sell agreement is conclusively binding for estate tax purposes:

1. The agreement must restrict the transfer of the securities to the buy-sell price during the owner's life as well as at death.

2. There must be a valid business purpose for establishing the agreement.
3. The value established in the agreement must have been an adequate and fair price at the time the agreement was executed.
4. The value must reflect those typical of arm's-length transactions in the subject company's industry.

Thus, a properly drawn, "grandfathered" buy-sell agreement (i.e., one that predates Chapter 14) with a fixed transfer price may, over time, have provided a way to freeze the value of family members' shares at a value perhaps less than fair market value as of a subsequent date of death. Since October 9, 1990, this technique is unworkable from an estate tax standpoint for newly created or substantially modified buy-sell agreements due to the enactment of Section 2703 of Chapter 14.

Section 2703 governs buy-sell agreements and leases between family members. It provides that "the value of any property shall be determined without regard to ... any restriction on the right to sell or use property ... unless ... the terms [of the restriction] are comparable to similar arrangements entered into by persons in an arm's length transaction."[9]

The major issue that an appraiser has to establish under Section 2703 is that any restriction is:

1. A bona fide business arrangement
2. Not a device to transfer the property to family members for less than fair market value
3. Comparable to similar arrangements entered into by persons in an arm's-length transaction

Valuation Rules for Lapsing Rights and Other Restrictions under Section 2704

This section of Chapter 14 addresses two basic areas of valuation issues. Subsection (a) of 2704 treats certain lapsed voting or liquidation rights in a family controlled corporation, partnership, or limited liability company as a deemed transfer subject to gift or estate tax. Subsection (b) requires the appraiser to ignore certain restrictions on liquidation rights of business interests when valuing a transfer of an interest in a family-controlled enterprise.

Lapse of Certain Rights. Section 2704(a) will come into play under the following set of circumstances:

- The holder of the lapsed voting or liquidation power and any applicable family members own, in the aggregate, a controlling interest in the subject company. The definitions of "applicable family member" and "control" are defined in the same manner as in Section 2701, discussed earlier.[10]
- Whenever a lapse of a voting right or liquidation right occurs.[11] If it occurs during life, it is treated as a gift; at death it is considered an estate tax issue.

---

[9] Stan miller, Carl R. Waldman, and D. Scott Schrader. "Estate Planning with Family Limited Partnerships and Limited Liability Companies." *WealthCounsel*, October 16-17, 2003.

[10] The IRS's use of a 50 percent ownership level as the threshold for control in this context is curious and not supported by financial valuation theory or legal rights theory, as a 50 percent voting interest cannot unilaterally vote to compel a liquidation.

[11] The Treasury is also given the right under this statute to determine if other lapsing rights should be added to this list.

A lapse is deemed to occur at the time a presently exercisable right is restricted or eliminated. The sale or transfer of a voting or liquidation right is not included under this section, as these types of transactions are valued under the existing gift and income tax statutes.

Section 2704(a) does not apply if the transfer was already valued under the special valuation rules of Section 2701, in order to prevent double taxation. Also, if there is a change in a state law that causes the lapse, then Section 2704(a) does not apply. Of course, if the family does not have control over the unilateral capacity to liquidate, then Section 2704(a) does not apply. As an example, for a company requiring the unanimous consent of all interest holders in order to liquidate, the presence of non–family member interest holders causes Section 2704(a) to not apply.

The practical effect of Section 2704(a) is to create the potential for additional gift or estate tax value only when the holder's interest has its highest fair market value under a premise of liquidation on a controlling ownership interest basis. This most often tends to affect companies in asset-intensive industries like heavy manufacturing, farming and ranching, and real estate development, in addition to holding companies.

Disregarding Applicable Restrictions. Under subsection 2704(b), an appraiser must disregard an applicable restriction on the ability to liquidate a company (in whole or in part) if the following conditions apply:

- If an interest is transferred to or for the benefit of a member of the transferor's family (either directly or indirectly).
- If the transferor and members of the transferor's family control the company immediately before the transfer. *Control* is defined in the same manner as in Section 2701, discussed earlier. However, the definition of *member of the family* is slightly different from that contained in Section 2701 and echoes the more inclusive definition utilized in Section 2702 and for determining family control under Section 2701. Under Section 2704, a member of the family for any individual includes: (1) the individual's spouse, (2) any ascendant of the individual and spouse, (3) any lineal descendant of the individual and spouse, (4) any brother or sister (and their spouses) of the individual.
- The applicable restriction is more restrictive than the limitations that would apply under the state law generally applicable to the entity in the absence of the restriction.
- The restriction either lapses after such a transfer, or the transferor and member of the transferor's family have the right, either individually or as a group, to remove (in whole or in part) such a restriction.

Section 2704(b) does not apply in the case of a restriction on liquidation that is imposed under federal or state law. Thus, the basic default statutes of the state laws under which a company was formed can have a significant impact on the degree to which an appraiser must consider the liquidation values of the company in valuing an individual interest.

In addition, Section 2704(b) does not apply if a restriction on liquidation arises as part of the company's financing and is a commercially reasonable restriction imposed by an unrelated arm's-length third party. A typical example of this is the restriction on distributing asset sale proceeds to shareholders while a loan is outstanding, contained in standard bank loan covenants.

An option or other agreement that is subject to Section 2703 regarding buy-sell agreements is not regarded as an applicable restriction. This provision avoids double coverage of the same issue under Chapter 14.

Section 2704(b) primarily concerns itself with restrictions that are more oner-ous than the basic rights contained in state statutes that could be conveniently applied and then removed by the controlling family at appropriate times. As with 2704(a), the practical effect of Section 2704(b) is to create the potential for addi-tional gift or estate tax value only when the holder's interest has its highest fair market value under a premise of liquidation on a controlling interest basis. Also like section 2704(a), this most often tends to affect companies in asset-intensive industries such as heavy manufacturing, farming and ranching, and real estate development, in addition to holding companies.

Locking in the Three-Year Gift Tax Statute of Limitations

The Taxpayer Relief Act of 1997 amended IRC Section 6501(c)(9) to provide that the three-year statute of limitations starts with the filing of a gift tax return, whether or not any tax is paid, *provided that the gift is adequately disclosed on the gift tax return*.

According to Ronald Aucutt, a leading estate tax attorney, "While most rou-tine gifts, particularly gifts of cash or marketable securities, are not affected, more complicated gifts (e.g., closely held business interests) will require greater care in the preparation of gift tax returns and are likely to require more use of formal appraisals."[12] The IRS regulations on this matter (published December 3, 1999) apply to all gifts made after August 5, 1997. The following requirements apply:

With Respect to the Person Who Prepares the Report:

1. The person must be an individual who holds himself or herself out to the pub-lic as an appraiser, or performs appraisals on a regular basis.
2. The appraiser is qualified to prepare appraisals of the type of property being valued.
3. The appraiser is not the donor, donee, or an employee of or a member of the family of any of the parties.

With Respect to the Contents, the Appraisal Report Must Include:

1. The date of the appraisal
2. The date of the transfer
3. The purpose of the appraisal
4. A description of the property
5. A description of the appraisal process employed, including the valuation method(s) utilized
6. A description of the assumptions utilized
7. A description of any hypothetical conditions considered
8. Descriptions of any restrictions or other limiting conditions present

---

[12] Ronald D. Aucutt, "IRS Proposes New Rules for Reporting Gifts," *Shannon Pratt's Business Valuation Update*, February 1999, pp. 6–7.

9. The information considered in determining the value, including all financial information, in sufficient detail to allow the reader to replicate the appraisal analysis and valuation
10. The reasoning that supports the analysis, opinions, and conclusions
11. Any specific comparative transactions utilized in the valuation analysis
12. The fair market value of 100 percent of the entity, determined without regard to any discounts in valuing the entity or the assets owned by the entity, unless this information is not relevant or material in determining the value of the interest

Shifting the Burden of Proof from the Taxpayer to the IRS

The IRS Restructuring and Reform Act of 1998, signed by President Clinton on July 22, 1998, includes IRC Section 7491, a provision shifting the burden of proof from the taxpayer to the IRS *if the taxpayer provides "credible evidence" supporting its position.*

In Tax Court, the taxpayer is the petitioner, or the "plaintiff." Thus, as to the valuation issue, to the extent valuation is a factual issue, the taxpayer has the burden of proof (burden of production), absent achieving benefit from IRC Section 7491. If both the petitioner and the respondent IRS were to sustain or meet their respective burdens of proof, then the burden of persuasion comes into play which is at the time the Tax Court reaches its own decision on valuation based upon all relevant evidence. Therefore, we must understand that the Tax Court ultimately will make its own valuation decision in each case.

Absent successful use of Section 7491, there exists a rebuttable presumption of the correctness of any IRS-proposed tax deficiencies.[13]

The taxpayer should cooperate with IRS requests for documents, meetings, interviews, information, and witnesses. In establishing fair market value taxpayers should obtain timely and reasonably complete appraisals of any nonpublic equity interests involved in a gift or estate transfer of ownership.

Valuation Issues in Estate and Gift Tax Planning

Placing Family Assets in Corporate, Limited Liability Company, or Partnership Form

It may be worthwhile to consider incorporating various family assets into a family-controlled holding company before transferring interests to heirs. Aside from the business purposes of such transfers, such as centralization of supervision, reduction of potential personal exposure to creditors, assurance of smoother

---

[13] Tax Court Rule 142, *Danville Plywood Corp. v. U.S.*, 16 Cl. Ct. 584 (1989).

management succession, and prevention of the assets' waste by inexperienced heirs, there may also be estate planning advantages. The assets could be almost anything, such as marketable securities, real estate, art, coins, or any kind of collectibles. Since publicly traded securities of companies holding such assets (such as closed-end investment companies and real estate investment trusts [REITs]) tend to sell at a discount from underlying net asset value, so should shares of family-controlled corporations. Interests in this type of closely held company are also valued at a further discount for lack of marketability.

Of course, in making the decision to incorporate a family holding company to execute a portion of the family estate plan in this manner, one must realize that the justification for the discounted values is real, not contrived, that is, the heir who receives a gift of a minority interest of a family holding company or limited partnership representing an undivided interest in a portfolio of assets will not have control over those assets. Owning 15 percent of the assets and owning 15 percent of the stock of the company that owns them are two different things. The power to liquidate, transfer assets, declare dividends, and exercise all the other various elements of control will not go to the donee. There may also be income tax considerations, so such a move should not be undertaken without the aid of competent tax counsel. If the donor understands and is satisfied with the various implications, the creation of a family-owned holding company could be a tax saving feature of the total estate plan.

An extension of this technique has seen the concentration of family assets in S corporations, limited liability companies, and limited partnerships, each of which allows pass-through of most types of income generated by the underlying assets without subjecting such income to income tax at the corporate or entity level (see Chapter 26, "Valuing S Corporation Stock"). Family assets have also been placed in partnerships or limited liability companies to facilitate the estate planning techniques described in the next two sections on minority ownership interest transfers and recapitalizations.

Minimizing Taxes through a Series of Timely Minority Ownership Interest Transfers

In general, estate planning techniques for minimizing transfer taxes revolve around timing transfers when the value of the stock is relatively low and structuring them such that they have the least possible value.

The more rapidly a company is growing in value, the more important it is to effect stock transfers to heirs early rather than later, after the value has increased. However, if the business is cyclical in nature, it may be possible to time transfers at a cyclical trough in the company's value.

For structure, the best technique usually is to plan transfers as a series of small minority ownership interests. To begin, a married couple can give up to $24,000 ($12,000 per donor) in value to each of as many persons as they wish each year without paying federal gift tax. More important for transfers of substantial size, however, is that, at least under the law and court rulings at this writing, minority ownership interests are subject to substantial discounts in value per share compared with the per share value of a controlling ownership interest. Minority ownership interests and discounts for lack of control are further discussed in Chapter 16. Discounts for lack of marketability are discussed in Chapter 17. Minority shares in closely held companies can be valued for tax purposes by estimating their potential market value as publicly traded stock and then discounting them for lack of marketability. In general, the smaller the minority ownership interest, the greater the extent to which this method can be applied. The net result may be that transfers of shares of closely held companies can be made at quite large discounts below the undiscounted control value of the entire company depending on the facts and circumstances.

Although the IRS has conceded in Revenue Ruling 93-12 that family relationships will not be the sole reason to challenge minority ownership interest transfers when a family owns control of an enterprise, the IRS remains sensitive to this issue. Appraisers should review all the facts and circumstances of each gift in a series of gifts for companies in which a single family owns control, as, sometimes, some minority interests deserve lesser discounts for relative lack of ownership control and lack of marketability. This could be due to some factor relating to the relative distribution of ownership (a so-called "swing vote" issue)[14] or the ability to unilaterally elect one or more directors to the board, and thereby influence the policies of the company.

Loss of Key Person

Often the appraiser faces the valuation of closely held stock in the estate of the president, founder, or other key executive of a business. In this circumstance, it is reasonable to investigate the possibility that the value of the company—and, thus, of its securities—has been impaired due to the loss of the services of a *key person* in the business's management.

Whether such decline in value actually has occurred depends on the facts of the case. Following are the elements to be investigated in establishing any discount or diminution from the loss of a key person.

First, the appraiser determines the deceased executive's actual duties and areas of active involvement. A key person may contribute value to a company in both day-to-day management duties and from strategic judgment responsibilities based on long-standing contacts and reputation within an industry.

Second, the appraiser assesses the ability of existing successor management to move up the organizational ladder and take over the duties of the vacated position. Ideally, a strong and stable corporate organization will provide this capability. This assumes that a succession plan actually exists. All too often, however, private business owners create "spider web" organization structures with themselves at the center—that is, all management decisions are made by the key executive-owner. The extent of organizational damage may also be related to the suddenness of the key manager's death.

Third, the appraiser calculates the amount of compensation necessary for replacing the key executive or filling the positions vacated or created when successors move up.

---

[14] The IRS addressed the swing vote issue in a National Office Technical Advice Memorandum (Letter Ruling 9436005, May 26, 1994). We find swing vote issues a relative rarity as real-world willing buyers, even those already owning shares in a company, are rarely willing to bid much in excess of the amount a potential investor without existing ownership would pay for an interest. There is also an issue of whether a swing vote assumption is improperly based on the notion that the willing buyer possesses a special relationship with the seller that is not typical of the hypothetical willing seller/ willing buyer standard of fair market value for estate and gift tax matters.

Fourth, to this quantitative calculation the appraiser adds the increase in potential costs arising from risks to the company in bringing in replacement executives who may be unfamiliar with the company's operations. These risks can be compounded by the appraiser's assessment of the complexity or precariousness of the company's competitive or financial position. This is especially true if the deceased was personal guarantor of the company's debts, as is often the case with closely held business loans. Sometimes these risks can be quantified as estimates of sales losses or declines in profit margins in future periods, or increases in borrowing costs due to loss of personal guarantee.

There are at least two offsets to these potential losses. One is the compensation, net of any continuing obligations, that the company ceases to pay to the deceased executive. The other is any insurance on the key person's life that is payable to the company and not earmarked for other purposes, such as repurchase of the deceased's stock in the company.[15]

The estimates of key person losses can be directly incorporated into the valuation methods appropriate for the particular case. This may be accomplished by adjusting normalized earnings or price to earnings multiples, or as reductions in estimated future cash flows to be discounted. Otherwise, the loss can be subtracted from the company's indicated value as a separate item, much like the discount for lack of marketability.

Evidence for the amount of the loss from the key person's death from securities' values in the public market shows that the magnitude of the decline varies with the particular circumstances. Generally, public companies have larger and more flexible professional management teams and thus can better absorb the shock of the loss of any one key person.

Trapped-In Capital Gains Discounts

One of the most important changes in the Tax Court's position was the recognition, starting in 1998, of a discount for trapped-in capital gains taxes on appreciated property in a C corporation. The important cases establishing this precedent up to the time of this writing are discussed in the following chapter. Also, there is discussion of trapped-in capital gains discounts in Chapter 18, "Other Valuation Discounts."

Other Estate Planning Situations Requiring Valuations

Strictly speaking, the two techniques reviewed below do not require consideration of any valuation factors different from those mandated under Revenue Ruling 59-60. But, an appraiser ought to be aware of these techniques, as he or she may be called upon to prepare a valuation of a closely held business that will be used in this fashion.

Sale of Remainder Interest. Applying this technique, the owner of a closely held business security sells to an heir a remainder interest in the security and retains a life interest in the current enjoyment of income and the security's voting

---

[15] See *Estate of Blount*, 428 F.3d 1338 (11th Cir. 2005).

rights. The *remainder interest* is valued by taking the security's appraised fair market value and discounting it to a present value under the IRS actuarial tables based on the seller's projected remaining life. Assuming a present value interest factor of 10 percent, the present value of the remainder interest could be a small fraction of the security's current fair market value if the seller is relatively young. Upon the seller's death, the life interest terminates, leaving the security, including any appreciation after the sale, to pass, untaxed, to the heir outside the seller's gross estate.

Valuation is crucial to this technique, because if the sale transaction is not for full and adequate consideration, the asset's entire value will be brought back into the seller's estate at fair market value as of the date of death.

Sale for a Private Annuity or a Self-Canceling Note. The business owner utilizes this technique to sell the entire business to an heir in exchange for a *private annuity*—a fixed periodic payment made to the seller for the rest of his or her life.

A *self-canceling installment note* (SCIN) is similar to an annuity but has the additional advantage that part of the periodic payment of principal and interest due from the heir can be forgiven (waived) by the seller under the annual gift tax exclusion. One of the key issues in the structure of this technique is the correct valuation of the closely held business interest sold and the terms of the annuity or note received so as to avoid gift taxes on the initial sale and estate taxes at the seller's death.

Other Gift and Estate Valuation Issues

There are three other issues regarding valuation for estate and gift taxes that an appraiser should be aware of.

In Revenue Ruling 85-75,[16] the IRS stated that it will not necessarily be bound by values that it accepted for estate tax purposes as the correct cost basis for determining depreciation deductions or income taxes on capital gains from an asset's subsequent sale.

On the other hand, it may be possible to use one value for calculating the gross estate value of a block of closely held stock and a different value for calculating the value of a portion of the block of stock that will be exempted from estate taxes as a marital deduction (i.e., the portion of the estate transferred to a spouse) or charitable deduction.[17]

Another valuation issue is the lower value for closely held business stock that may result if real estate used in a family-owned trade or business is valued for estate tax purposes for actively involved family members under the provisions of Section 2032A, "Special-Use Valuation." A detailed discussion of this section is beyond the scope of this book. Here, simply note that closely held company valuation methods based on net asset values may be lower if an appraisal of the underlying operating real property follows the guidelines of this section. This issue is particularly relevant for family-owned farming or other agricultural business securities.

---

[16] Rev. Rul. 85–75, 1985-1 C.B. 376.
[17] See *Estate of Chenoweth*, 88 T.C. No. 90 (1987).

Another issue that appraisers should be aware of involves Section 2036 of the IRC. The application of Section 2036 may cause the inclusion of the assets previously contributed to a Family Limited Partnership (FLP) or a Limited Liability Company (LLC) in the taxable estate. The IRS has been successful at challenging partnerships in which the transferor has retained either the right to the income from the property transferred or the right to designate the persons with the rights to the income. Some of the facts that lead to a successful challenge include:

- Commingling personal funds with FLP funds
- Receiving income directly from the property that was transferred to the FLP (for instance, receiving rent from a transferred property)
- Paying for personal expenses from partnership funds
- Using assets that were previously transferred to the partnership (for example, continuing to live in a house that was transferred to the partnership without paying rent)
- Retaining the right to select a general partner, in other words, retaining the right to distribute income

Chapter 28 includes a discussion of the application of Section 2036 in gift and estate tax court cases.

Still another issue is the estate or gift tax understatement penalty that the taxpayer is subject to under IRC Section 6662 if the value of the property that is reported on the return is 65 percent or less of the correct value. Ordinarily, the penalty is 20 percent of the tax, and no penalty is imposed unless the underpayment attributable to the understatement exceeds $5,000. However, if the understatement is considered a "gross misstatement," the penalty is doubled to 40 percent if the claimed valuation is 40 percent or less of actual value reported for estate and gift tax valuation purposes. (IRC Sections 6662(g),(h).) See Chapter 30 for a discussion of related Section 6662 penalties in the income tax context.

Summary

The entire area of estate and gift tax valuation can be a constantly shifting minefield of laws, regulations, and court decisions. Because of this, it is important that the appraiser is able to function as a knowledgeable contributor to the client's team of estate planning professionals.

With federal transfer tax rates routinely in excess of 40 percent, the tax implications of estate planning and gift and estate tax valuations can be huge. Inclusion into an estate of additional values that were originally thought to be gifted or transferred away via estate planning transactions can also create tremendous problems. The tax implications are exacerbated by the penalties that may be imposed on taxpayers for undervaluation for gift and estate tax purposes and overvaluation for charitable contribution purposes. Appraisers are also subject to significant penalties.

It is essential that valuations involving federal tax implications be performed in accordance with guidelines discussed in this chapter, as clarified and modified by ever-evolving tax and case law.

Bibliography

Articles

Aucutt, Ronald D. "Fourteen Tips and Traps in Dealing with Chapter 14." *Estate Planning,* September/October 1993, pp. 259–266.

_____. "IRS Proposes New Rules for Reporting Gifts." *Judges & Lawyers Business Valuation Update*, February 1999, pp. 6–7.

_____ "Valuation Developments Highlight the Importance of Appraisals." *Estate Planning*, July 2001.

August, Jerald David, and Guy B. Maxfield. "Valuation of Interests 'In Transit' in Family Limited Partnerships" (Parts 1 and 2). *Business Entities*, September/October 2003 and November/December 2003.

August, Jerald David, James Dawson, and Guy B. Maxfield. "IRS Section 2036 Assault Continues on Family Limited Partnerships." *Business Entities*, September/October 2005.

Bishop, David M. "Trapped-in Capital Gains: Where Do We Go from Here?" *Business Valuation Review*, June 1999, pp. 64–68.

Bogdanski, John A. "Bye Bye Byrum, Bonjour Bongard." *Estate Planning*, June 2005.

_____. "Maximizing Discounts for 'Built-in' Corporate Taxes." *Estate Planning*, December 2002.

_____. "Must a Family Limited Partnership Run a Business in Order to Achieve Transfer Tax Discounts?" *Estate Planning*, December 2005.

_____. "Section 2036 and Family Limited Partnerships: How Much Is Etched in Stone?" *Estate Planning*, February 2004.

_____. "Valuation and Hindsight." *Estate Planning*, July 2004.

_____. "Valuing Indirect Gifts Through Entities: *Shepherd.*" *Estate Planning*, June 2002.

Bradley, Wray E. "Tax Court Valuation Standards Go Beyond 'Relevant and Reliable.'" *Valuation Strategies*, November/December 1999, pp. 34–39.

Bronza, Timothy K., Gerald P. Valentine, and Roy H. Meyers. "Business Valuation in a Federal Tax Environment—Techniques to Enhance Appraisal Effectiveness." *Valuation Strategies*, May/June 2003.

Budyak, James T. "Estate Freeze Rules Affect Partnership Valuation Discounts." *Taxation for Lawyers,* January/February 1997, pp. 228–234.

Buettner, Jeffrey S., and Robert F. Reilly. "Estate/Gift Tax Valuation—Professional Guidance from IRS Publications." *Pennsylvania Family Lawyer* (May/June 2003).

Cammarono, Terry. "Valuation Remains the Toughest Issue When Donating Patents." *Valuation Strategies*, November/December 2003, pp. 18–27, 47–48.

"Clause Limiting Value of FLP Interest Not Valid for Gift Tax Purposes." *Estate Planning*, January 2004.

Collier, Robert Don, and Michael A. Denham. "*Kimbell* & Section 2036." *Business Entities*, September/October 2004.

DeFrancesco, Roccy. "The 75% Trap: A Strategy Using FLPs and Irrevocable Trusts Helps Heirs Avoid Losing up to 75% of an Inherited IRA's Value to Taxes." *Financial Planning*, October 2004.

"Discounts in Transfers of FLP Interests Limited by Tax Court." *Estate Planning*, January 2004.

Dondershine, Scott A. "Planning for the Transfer of a Successful Closely Held Business." *Estate Planning*, July 2002.

Dudley, B. Dane, Steven M. Fast, and Darren M. Wallace. "Get Real or Get Out." *Trusts & Estates*, July 2003.

Eastland, S. Stacy (interview). "Family Limited Partnership Interests Enjoy 40 to 85% Discounts from NAV." *Shannon Pratt's Business Valuation Update*, January 1997, pp. 1–3.

Easton, Reed W. "Court Again Considers Estate Tax Implications of an FLP." *Valuation Strategies*, November/December 2005, pp. 20–29.

_____. "Courts Affirm Family Limited Partnership Technique: Service Vows to Fight On." *Valuation Strategies*, May/June 2002, pp. 10–17, 45.

_____. "Section 2036: Hurdle Raised for Family Limited Partnerships." *Valuation Strategies*, January/February 2004, pp. 4–11.

_____. "Service Fails Again to Stop Use of Family Limited Partnerships." *Valuation Strategies*, November/December 2002, pp. 4–11, 44–45.

Eyberg, Terry, and Barbara J. Raasch. "FLP Planning After *Strangi*, *Kimbell* and *Thompson*." *The Tax Adviser*, December 2004.

"Final Regulations Update Special Valuation Rules." *Valuation Strategies*, May/June 2005, pp. 44–48.

Fiore, Owen G. "Entity-Driven Valuation Discounts: Reality and Fantasy Combined." *Business Valuation Alert*, March 2002.

Fishman, Jay, Bruce Bingham, and Peter Barash. "The Internal Revenue Service and Treasury Turn up the Enforcement Heat on Abusive Tax-Related Appraisals and Those Who Prepare Them." *Business Valuation Review*, Fall 2005, pp. 104–114.

Forsberg, William S., and Randall Schostag. "Valuing Loan Guarantees in a Sale to an Intentionally Defective Grantor Trust." *Valuation Strategies*, September/October 2003, pp. 20–25, 46–48.

Fox, Glenn G. "FLPs and FLLCs: Are They Still Viable Estate Planning Tools?" *Estate Planning*, February 2006.

Frazier, William H. "Quantitative Analysis of the Fair Market Value of an Interest in a Family Limited Partnership." *Valuation Strategies*, January/February 2005, pp. 4–17.

Gibbs, Larry W. "What You Can Do if the Government Uses Rambo Tactics (Estate Valuation Audit)." Parts I and II. *Trusts & Estates,* June/July 1994, pp. 60–65 and pp. 57–61.

Goldsbury, John. "Important Considerations When Making Gifts of Stock Options." *Estate Planning*, April 2005.

Graber, Adrian. "IRS Proposes Regs to Start Gift Tax Statute of Limitations." *Shannon Pratt's Business Valuation Update*, March 1999, pp. 8–9.

Gregory, Michael A., and Robin P. Ruegg. "Comparison of IRS and Taxpayer Experts as Stated by the Courts." *Business Valuation Review*, December 2004, pp. 205–209.

Haas, Brett D. "Valuation of Nonqualified Stock Options for Estate and Gift Tax Purposes." *Valuation Strategies*, July/August 2003, pp. 4–17.

Hader, Cheryl E. "Making the Intangible Tangible: Planning for Intellectual Property." *Estate Planning*, November 2002.

Hall, Lance. "Corporate Structure Discount and Valuation of Asset-Holding C Corps." *Trusts & Estates,* September 1996, pp. 45–48.

_____. "The Current State of FLP Valuation Discounts." *Trusts & Estates*, December 2001.

_____ "Section 2036—The Saga Continues." *Valuation Strategies*, July/August 2005.

_____. "Valuation Industry Breathes Sigh of Relief with Fifth Circuit's *Kimbell* Decision—FLPs Still in Vogue." *Valuation Strategies*, September/October 2004, pp. 36–39.

_____. "What You Don't Know about Fair Market Value Will Hurt You!" (Parts 1–3). *Valuation Strategies*, September/October to January/February 2006.

Hatcher, Milford B. Jr., and Gregory E. Kniesel. "Preferred Limited Partnerships: The FLPs of Choice?" *Valuation Strategies*, July/August 1999, pp. 12–33.

Hoffmann, Carsten. "Understanding the Fundamentals of Discounting Using Family Limited Partnerships and Family Limited Liability Companies." *Business Valuation Alert*, July 2004.

Hood, L. Paul Jr. "Defined Value Gifts: Does IRS Have It All Wrong?" *Estate Planning*, December 2001.

Horowitz, Steven A. "Family Limited Partnerships in *Strangi II*, *Kimbell* and *McCord*: An Idea Whose Time Has Come and Gone?" *Taxes*, August 2003.

_____. "Is There Rhyme or Reason to Business Valuation Cases in the Tax Court?" *Taxes*, June 2002.

Howitt, Idelle A. "Estate of Bailey." *Valuation Strategies*, May/June 2003, pp. 38–41.

_____. "Estate of Blount." *Valuation Strategies*, March/April 2005, pp. 40–42.

_____. "Estate of Dailey." *Valuation Strategies*, May/June 2003, pp. 37–38.

_____. "Estate of Deputy." *Valuation Strategies*, November/December 2003, pp. 35–39.

_____. "Estate of Dunn." *Valuation Strategies*, January/February 2003, pp. 40–44.

_____. "Estate of Frank M. Disanto." *Valuation Strategies*, March/April 2001, pp. 41–43.

_____. "Estate of Halder." *Valuation Strategies*, January/February 2004, pp. 43–44.

_____. "Estate of Heck." *Valuation Strategies*, May/June 2002, pp. 39–42.

_____. "Estate of Leichter." *Valuation Strategies*, July/August 2003, pp. 44–46.

_____. "Estate of Schneider." *Valuation Strategies*, May/June 2005, pp. 39–42.

_____. "Estate of Thompson." *Valuation Strategies*, May/June 2003, pp. 33–37.

_____. "Gow." *Valuation Strategies*, March/April 2002, pp. 41–43.

_____. "Hess." *Valuation Strategies*, January/February 2004, pp. 40–42.

_____. "Knight." *Valuation Strategies*, July/August 2001, pp. 41–44.

IRS Valuation Training for Appeals Officers. Chicago: Commerce Clearing House Inc., 1998.

Israel, Ted. "A Trio of FLP Valuation Cases." *Valuation Strategies*, January/February 2004, pp. 12–17, 47.

Johnson, Bruce A., and James R. Park. "Family Limited Partnerships—Tax Court Demands More from Valuation Experts." *Business Valuation Alert*, September 2001.

Jones, George G., and Mark A. Luscombe. "A Victory for Family Limited Partnerships, But Be Wary—Tax Strategy." *Accounting Today*, June 21, 2004.

Jurinski, James John. "Special Use Valuation Can Reduce Estate Tax for Timber Owners." *Valuation Strategies*, January/February 2002, pp. 34–41.

Kalinka, Susan. "FLPs and Code Sec. 2036(a)(1): What Makes Abraham Different from Stone?" *Taxes*, July 2004.

_____. "FSA 200143004: Must a Family-Owned Entity Have a Business Purpose to Be Respected for Estate and Gift Tax Purposes?" *Taxes*, January 2002.

_____. "Kimbell: FLPs Are Alive and Well in the Fifth Circuit." *Taxes*, August 2004.

Kasner, Jerry A. "Valuation of Family Partnership Interests." *Tax Analysts—Special Reports*, 97 TNT 50-47, March 14, 1997.

Katzenstein, Andrew M., and David P. Schwartz. "Tax Court Limits Annual Gift Tax Exclusion for Gratuitous Transfers of LLC Interests." *Journal of Taxation*, May 2002.

Korn, Donald Jay. "All in the Family: The Strangi Case Put a Troublesome Cloud over Using Family Limited Partnerships to Transfer Assets." *Financial Planning*, July 2004.

Korpics, J. Joseph. "The Practical Implications of *Strangi II* for FLPs—A Detailed Look." *Journal of Taxation*, November 2003.

_____. "Qualifying New FLPs for the Bona Fide Sales Exception: Managing Thompson, Kimbell, Harper, and Stone." *Journal of Taxation*, February 2005.

Leimberg, Stephan R., and Roland G. Thon. "The Advantages and Uses of ESOPs in Estate and Business Planning." *Estate Planning*, February 2003.

Loud, Adrian. "Appeals Court Remands *Estate of Mitchell* and Proof to the Service." *Willamette Management Associates Insights*, Autumn 2001.

Luscombe, Mark A. "The Latest Flip on FLPs." *Taxes*, July 2004.

Madden, Robert E., and Lisa H. R. Hayes. "CA-5 in *Kimbell* Rules That FLP Assets Escaped Estate Tax Inclusion under Section 2036(a)." *Estate Planning*, September 2004.

_____. "Discount Was Allowed in Valuing Transferred Partnership Interests." *Estate Planning*, November 2002.

_____. "Late Alternate Valuation Election Forced Estate to Value Property at the Date of Death." *Estate Planning*, January 2001.

_____. "Ninth Circuit Reverses Tax Court and Rules No Premium for Minority Voting Stock." *Estate Planning*, September 2001.

_____. "TC Allows Significant Discount for FLP with Marketable Securities." *Estate Planning*, March 2004.

_____. "Value of Underlying Assets in Family Limited Partnership Was Included in Decedent's Estate." *Estate Planning*, September 2002.

Meinhart, Timothy J. "*Church* Decision Affirmed: FLP Formed Two Days Prior to Death is Valid." *Willamette Management Associates Insights*, Autumn 2001.

Mellen, Chris M. "IRS Challenges to FLPs and Family LLCs." *Shannon Pratt's Business Valuation Update*, October 2003, pp. 24–27.

Mercer, Z. Christopher. "When Is Fair Market Value Determined?: Estate of Noble." *Valuation Strategies*, May/June 2005, pp. 4–13.

Mezzullo, Louis A. "Fifth Circuit's Remand in Kimbell Does Not Provide Carte Blanche for All FLPs." *Journal of Taxation*, July 2004.

_____. "IRS Finally Wins a FLOP Case on Appeal Where the Taxpayer Failed to Establish Business Purpose." *Journal of Taxation*, October 2004.

_____. "Is *Strangi* a Strange Result or a Blueprint for Future IRS Successes Against FLPs." *Journal of Taxation*, July 2003.

_____. "*Strangi* Question Remains." *Trusts & Estates*, November 2005.

Miller, Stan, and D. Scott Schrader. "*W.E. Kelley Est.*—Are We Headed into Calmer Waters in Partnership Valuation?" *Business Valuation Alert*, January 2006.

_____. "Current Issues Involving FLPs and LLCs." *Miller Schrader*, 2007.

Miller, Stan, Carl R. Waldman, and D. Scott Schrader. "Estate Planning with Family Limited Partnerships and Limited Liability Companies." *WealthCounsel*, October 16–17, 2003.

Nath, Eric, and Curtis R. Kimball. "Estate and Gift Tax, Valuation Issues and Wealth Planning Under the New Tax Law." *Willamette Management Associates Insights*, Autumn 2001.

O'Driscoll, David. "Tax Court Determines Valuation Discounts" (*Estate of Kelley*). *The Tax Adviser*, January 2006.

O'Hara, Gregory A., and Mark R. Fournier. "Carried Interests: Value from a Tax Planning Perspective." *Valuation Strategies*, January/February 2006.

Painter, Andrew D., and Jonathan G. Blattmachr. "How the Final Chapter 14 Anti-Freeze Regulations Affect Estate Planning Strategies." *Journal of Taxation of Estates and Trusts,* Spring 1992, pp. 5–14.

Palmer, David L., and Joseph D. Brophy. "Adequate Disclosure of Gifts and Charitable Contributions for Tax Valuations." *The Value Examiner*, July/August 2005.

Porter, John W. "FLP Wars Update." *Trusts & Estates*, July 2005.

_____. "*Strangi* and *Schutt*—The Code Sec. 2036 Battles Continue." *Business Valuation Alert*, January 2006.

Robinson, Debra A., and Edward J. Rappaport. "Impact of Valuation Discounts on Estate and Income Tax Basis." *Estate Planning*, June 1997, pp. 223–30.

Ryan, Daniel E., and Lucy Hoekema. "Bona Fide Sales in the Estate Environment." *The Tax Adviser*, November 2004.

Satchit, Vinu. "Bongard: Tax Court Incorrectly Expands Sec. 2036(a)'s Application." *The Tax Adviser*, August 2005.

Schlenger, Jacques T., Robert E. Madden, and Lisa H. R. Hayes. "Blocks of Stock Are Aggregated when Determining Estate Tax Values." *Estate Planning,* May/June 1994, pp. 176–178.

Schlueter, Joseph F. "Discounting FLP Interests." *The Tax Adviser*, February 2004.

"Section 6695A: Some Very Unpleasant Realities." *Steve Leimberg's Estate Planning Newsletter*, October 9, 2006.

Sederbaum, Arthur D. "Financial and Estate Planning Trends: Family Limited Partnerships." *Taxes*, January 2001.

Shorthouse, Mark. "Appeals Court Rejects Consideration of Post-Death Occurrences." *Willamette Management Associates Insights*, 2001 Autumn.

_____. "Estate and Gift Tax, Gifting Strategies in a Post-ESOP Transaction." *Willamette Management Associates Insights*, Autumn 2003.

Siwicki, Robert. "The Gifting of Stock Options as an Estate Planning Strategy." *Trusts & Estates*, November 1999, pp. 49–60.

Soled, Jay A. "Gifts of Partnership Interests: An Income Tax Perspective." *Business Entities*, May/June 1999, pp. 30–35.

"Third Circuit Gets Tough with FLPs." *Valuation Strategies*, November/December 2004, pp. 43–44.

Tiernan, Peter B. "How 50% Ownership Affects Estate Planning for Closely Held Stock." *Journal of Taxation*, October 1999, pp. 232–240.

_____ "Seventh Circuit Upholds *Hackl* on Annual Exclusions—How Far Will the Ripples Spread?" *Journal of Taxation*, February 2004.

Tiesi, Angelo F. "Why Section 2036(a)(2) Shouldn't Apply to FLPs." *Trusts & Estates*, January 2005.

Weinberg, Neil H. "Valuation Adjustments Applicable to Transfers of Family Business Interests." *Estate Planning*, June 2001.

Wise, Richard M. "Practice Standards, Tax Valuations and Valuation Methodologies—CICBV vs. ASA." *Proceedings of the 12th Biennial Conference of the CICBV.* Toronto: Canadian Institute of Chartered Business Valuators, 1997, pp. 235–58.

Yuhas, Michael A., and Richard W. Harris. "*D.A. Kimbell Est.*: The Courts Finally Get It Right Regarding FLPs and the Bona Fide Sales Exception." *Taxes*, October 2004.

Reference Books

Bogdanski, John A. *Federal Tax Valuation*. Valhalla, NY: Warren, Gorham & Lamont, 2003, supplemented through 2005.

Johnson, Bruce A., Spencer J. Jefferies, and James R. Park. *Comprehensive Guide for the Valuation of Family Limited Partnerships*, 2nd ed. Dallas: Partnership Profiles, 2003.

Laro, David, and Shannon P. Pratt. *Business Valuation and Taxes*. Hoboken, NJ: John Wiley & Sons, 2005.

Chapter 28

Estate and Gift Tax Court Cases

Always read the opinions on valuation that were written by the judge handling the case.[1]

This chapter summarizes federal courts' positions on many frequently encountered valuation issues. Out of the many hundreds of reported opinions, we have referenced a sampling that is generally representative of the federal courts' positions.

The published decisions cited are mostly from the period 1995–1999, although important earlier precedential cases are included as well. It is not possible to be comprehensive in a single chapter on federal courts' various positions on the myriad of valuation issues addressed. However, the full text of each decision cited usually includes reference to earlier precedent on point for the issues discussed.

The chapter is generally organized by type of primary valuation issue. In some cases, the federal court's position on issues other than the main issue is also mentioned. Other precedent may be referenced under more than one primary valuation issue section if the court's opinion was particularly important on more than a single issue.

Standard of Value

The federal Tax Court applies a fair market value standard of value in estate and gift tax cases, and this standard is accepted by the IRS. Section 20.2031-1(b) of the Estate Tax Regulations and Section 25.2512-1 of the Gift Tax Regulations define fair market value as:

> …the price at which the property would change hands between a willing buyer and a willing seller when the former is not under any compulsion to buy and the latter is not under any compulsion to sell, both parties having reasonable knowledge of relevant facts.[2]

Almost all states follow suit, but, occasionally, the courts confront the issue of which standard to apply. For example, in *In re the Estate of Patricia D. King*,[3] the Minnesota Court of Appeals had to decide whether to apply fair market value or investment value to determine the value of a minority block of stock that would be equally distributed to two recipients through a trust, giving one of the two recipients control of a closely held corporation. The trustee valued the shares using fair market value. However, one of the recipients challenged the valuation, arguing that the block should have been valued using investment value to give effect to the decedent's intent of equal distribution. The challenger pointed out that since the other recipient would gain control of the company, this would command a substantial value under the fair market approach and defeat the intent of equal distribution.

The state court rejected this argument, finding no indication that the decedent intended that the trust assets be of equal value to those of the beneficiaries, and also reasoning that applying an investment value standard of value would result in

---

[1] David Laro, "Judge Laro's Views on Discounts & Valuation Reports" (Part two), *Judges & Lawyers Business Valuation Update*, June 1999, p. 4.

[2] See Chapter 2, above, for a detailed discussion of the standard of value.

[3] *In re the Estate of Patricia D. King*, 668 N.W.2d 6 (Minn. App. 2003).

the beneficiaries having a different per share value attached to the same stock. At least hypothetically, the one share needed to achieve control would have tremendous value to the controlling recipient compared to other shares. The court thus concluded that, carried to a logical extreme, the investment value method might present formidable complications for those attempting to reasonably and impartially distribute assets to beneficiaries who own an interest in the same business or neighboring property, and ruled that the trustees had the discretion to avoid such a valuation trap.

Approaches to Value

The court's acceptance, rejection, or relative weight accorded to various valuation approaches and methods generally revolves around three factors:

1. The type of company.
2. The quality of available evidence relevant to the respective methods.
3. The prospects for liquidation or continued operation.

As suggested in Revenue Ruling 59-60, the Tax Court tends to rely more on an asset-based approach in valuing holding companies and on an earnings-related method (either an income approach or a market approach emphasizing economic income variables) for operating companies. For hybrid companies, the Tax Court often accords partial weight to methods related to assets and partial weight to approaches related to earnings. Thus, the relative characterization of a company as a holding company or an operating company often is a major issue.

Sometimes the relative qualifying evidence available to support the respective approaches becomes the driving force as to which are accepted.

For example, in *Estate of Jung*, the Tax Court accepted the discounted cash flow (DCF) method over the guideline publicly traded company method.

> In the instant case, we believe the DCF approach to valuing Jung Corp. is more reliable than the market comparable approach. The market comparable approach does not work well in the instant case because the comparable corporations do not have the same product mix (health and elastic textile) as Jung Corp.[4]

In *Rakow v. Commissioner*, the Tax Court accepted the IRS expert's DCF method over the taxpayer's market approach, and then applied a 31 percent discount for lack of control.[5]

In *Hess v. Commissioner*,[6] a gift tax case, the Tax Court split the difference between values returned by the taxpayer's DCF and guideline publicly traded company approach and the IRS's DCF, net asset value, prior transaction, and guideline publicly traded company approaches. The Tax Court concluded that less weight should be assigned to the DCF method when a company's future income is relatively unpredictable, or when the valuation conclusions are highly sensitive to

---

[4] *Estate of Mildred Herschede Jung v. Commissioner*, 101 T.C. 412 (1993).
[5] *Rakow v. Commissioner*, T.C. Memo 1999-177 (May 27, 1999).
[6] *Hess v. Commissioner*, T.C. Memo 2003-251 (August 20, 2003).

small changes in assumptions. However, the court stated that the method should still be considered in the valuation process.

In *Dockery v. Commissioner*, the Tax Court accepted a valuation derived by the discounted dividend method. It also accepted the 40 percent combined lack of control and lack of marketability discount applied by the analyst to the undiscounted value derived by the discounted dividend method.[7]

Estate of Jameson involved a controlling ownership interest in a holding company with timber as its principal asset. The Tax Court decided that the asset-based approach is "most reasonable in a case like this one, where the corporation functions as a holding, rather than an operating, company and earnings are relatively low in comparison to the fair market value of the underlying assets."[8]

The matter of the prospects for liquidation versus continued operation are especially important for companies like family limited partnerships that may own very valuable underlying assets. The relevant state laws and the partnership agreements may have a major bearing on this determination. In *Estate of Leichter v. Commissioner*,[9] for example, the appraiser opined that the company was worth less on a going-concern basis than on a liquidation basis. The Tax Court criticized the appraiser for not explaining why a hypothetical seller would choose not to liquidate under these circumstances. A classic case in point is *Estate of Watts*,[10] which involved a noncontrolling ownership interest in a partnership that owned extensive and very valuable timber and operated a sawmill and a plywood mill. The IRS used a liquidation basis and the taxpayer used a going-concern basis. Because of the binding partnership agreement, the Court concluded, "There was no reasonable prospect of liquidation. Therefore, we accept petitioner's going-concern valuation approach." The Court then accepted the taxpayer's expert's guideline publicly traded company valuation method and 35 percent discount for lack of marketability.

In *Estate of McFarland* on the other hand, the Tax Court denied a motion to value the partnership interest only on a going-concern basis. Distinguishing from *Watts*, the Tax Court noted that the trustee for the interest in the decedent's estate had the right, but not the obligation, to continue the partnership in the event of decedent's death.[11]

In *Furman v. Commissioner*, the Tax Court rejected *in toto* the valuation offered by the analyst retained by the IRS, and relied primarily on the taxpayer's expert's valuation, which used both (1) a capitalized economic income method using Ibbotson data and (2) an earnings before interest, taxes, depreciation, and amortization (EBITDA) pricing multiple method. The Court used the EBITDA pricing multiple method, modifying the expert's pricing multiple from 5.0 to 6.0. The expert had applied a 30 percent discount for lack of control and a 35 percent discount for lack of marketability. The Court allowed a combined 40 percent discount, plus a 10 percent key person discount preferred by the taxpayer's expert.[12] These cases demonstrate the importance of considering liquidation value when valuing a business.

---

[7] *Dockery v. Commissioner*, T.C. Memo 1998-114 (Mar. 19, 1998).

[8] *Estate of Helen Bolton Jameson v. Commissioner*, T.C. Memo 1999-43 (Feb. 9, 1999), *vacated and remanded by* 267 F.3d 366 (5th Cir. 2001).

[9] *Estate of Natalie M Leichter v. Commissioner*, T.C. Memo 2003-66 (March 6, 2003).

[10] *Watts v. Commissioner*, 51 T.C.M. 60 (1985), *aff'd* No. 86-8504 U.S. App. (11th Cir. Aug. 4, 1987).

[11] *Estate of Vera M. McFarland v. Commissioner*, T.C. Memo 1996-424 (Sept. 19, 1996).

[12] *Furman v. Commissioner*, T.C. Memo 1998-157 (Apr. 30, 1998).

Burden of Proof

Ordinarily in tax cases, the burden of proof is on the taxpayer, and the general rebuttable presumption is that the Commissioner is correct. This burden can shift to the Commissioner in limited circumstances, where the taxpayer can establish that all items required by law to be substantiated are substantiated; the taxpayer has maintained all records required by law to be maintained; and the taxpayer has fully cooperated with the IRS's reasonable requests.

A case involving the well-known Kohler Company required a determination of the fair market value of stock of the company owned by the estate of Frederic C. Kohler (the estate) on the alternate valuation date.[13] The estate elected the alternate valuation date and filed its return with a $47.01 million appraisal. The IRS determined the fair market value of the Kohler holdings on the alternate valuation date was $144.5 million. The parties stipulated that the value of the Kohler stock at issue in related gift tax cases would be calculated by reference to the value of the Kohler stock determined in the estate tax case. The parties also agreed that the per share value for the different classes of Kohler stock in each case would be determined by reference to an agreed formula that would take into account the value of the Kohler stock determined in the estate tax case.

Here, the court found that all the requirements for shifting the burden of proof were satisfied. Although the Commissioner argued that the estate did not cooperate fully because it filed a motion to quash certain discovery requests, the court determined that the estate had legitimate concerns about providing confidential and proprietary business information that was possibly irrelevant absent a court order. Once the Tax Court denied the estate's motion to quash the summons, the estate provided the documents respondent requested—in great quantity. Thus, the court found that the voluminous exhibits that were part of the record belied the IRS argument. Accordingly, the burden shifted to the IRS.

Selection of Guideline Companies

The Tax Code, revenue rulings, IRS practice, and the Tax Court all appear to favor the market approach. However, dozens of analysts' market approach conclusions have been rejected because of the selection of the guideline companies used in their analysis.

There is no set number of guideline companies to use. However, the more data there are about each company and the greater the similarity between the subject company and the companies chosen as guideline companies, the fewer guideline companies will pass muster. In *Estate of Heck v. Commissioner*,[14] the Tax Court rejected the use of a single comparable, saying "As similarity to the company to be valued decreases, the number of required comparables increases...." In *Heck*, although the appraiser discussed two comparables, he used only one, and the court

---

[13] *Herbert Kohler et al. v. Commissioner*, T.C. Memo 2006-152; 2006 Tax Ct. Memo LEXIS 156 (July 25, 2006).
[14] *Estate of Richie C. Heck v. Commissioner*, T.C. Memo 2002-34 (February 5, 2002).

found both to be too dissimilar to the subject company. The court thus rejected the use of the market approach in the case.[15]

In *Estate of Leichter v. Commissioner*,[16] both parties used comparables for an importer and wholesale distributor. The court criticized the IRS's approach to the extent that the guideline companies used were not similar to the subject company.

At issue in *Hess v. Commissioner*[17] was the value of the stock of a closely held corporation. In his guideline companies analysis, the IRS expert relied solely on price/earnings ratios (P/E ratios) to compare the subject company to the guideline companies. The taxpayers argued that use of P/E ratios was erroneous, claiming that P/E ratios are a "crude measure" for calculating value and do not consider important differences in interest levels, tax levels, and depreciation levels between the subject company and the guideline companies. The court agreed that the IRS expert's guideline companies method would have been more complete and more persuasive if it had employed additional measures of comparison. However, the court also noted that it is clear that P/E ratios bear a well-recognized relationship in the valuation of companies, and that reliance on P/E ratios was not inherently flawed. The P/E ratios of publicly traded companies do not compare to the P/E ratios of a closely held company if the companies themselves are not comparable.

Whether the stock price of one company with a given earnings stream will be similar to that of another company with the same earnings depends upon a wide variety of factors, including management policy, management ability, past performance, and dividend policy. Although taxpayers suggested that the guideline companies did not compare to the subject company, the court pointed out that two of the four guideline companies used by the IRS expert in his analysis were companies used by the subject to "benchmark" its performance, and three of the four guideline companies were also used by the taxpayers' expert in his market comparable analysis. Accordingly, the court found that the guideline companies, when properly adjusted, were comparable to the subject company.

In *Estate of Hendrickson*, the Tax Court accepted the guideline bank stocks selected by the taxpayer's expert and rejected those selected by the IRS expert. The IRS expert used geography as his primary selection criterion. In addition, all the selected companies were significantly larger than the subject, offered more services, and were multi-branch operations. The Tax Court characterized the taxpayer's expert's selection as "significantly more exacting" based on size and operating characteristics that more closely resembled the subject.[18]

Revenue Ruling 59-60 says that guideline companies should be in lines of business that are "the same or similar" relative to the subject company. In *Estate of Gallo*,[19] there were no sufficiently comparative guideline publicly traded wineries, so the experts on both sides used distilleries, breweries, soft drink companies, and even high brand recognition food companies. In *Estate of Hall*,[20] there was only one publicly traded greeting card company similar to Hallmark, so the Tax Court accepted a group of high market share consumer disposable products companies, such as Parker Pens.

---

[15] For a good discussion of the use of the guideline company method in the Tax Court, see David Laro and Shannon P. Pratt, *Business Valuation and Taxes: Procedure, Law and Perspective* (Hoboken, NJ: John Wiley & Sons, 2005), pp. 211-219.

[16] *Estate of Natalie M. Leichter v. Commissioner*, T.C. memo 2003-66 (March 6, 2003).

[17] *Johann Hess v. Commissioner*, T.C. Memo 2003-251 (August 20, 2003).

[18] *Estate of James Waldo Hendrickson v. Commissioner*, T.C. Memo 1999-278 (Aug. 23, 1999).

[19] *Estate of Mark S. Gallo v. Commissioner*, 50 T.C.M. 470 (1985).

[20] *Estate of Hall v. Commissioner*, 92 T.C. 312 (1989).

Buy-Sell Agreements

The extent to which a buy-sell agreement may be determinative of value for gift or estate tax purposes—or a factor to consider—is a frequently disputed issue. If the buy-sell price is very low and not concluded to be determinative of value for estate tax purposes, even though legally binding on the estate, the estate may have to sell the stock or interest at a price that does not even cover the estate taxes.

For buy-sell agreements entered into after October 8, 1990, a buy-sell price is binding for federal estate tax purposes if it meets all of the following criteria:[21]

- The price must be fixed or determinable as of a determinable date.
- The agreement must be binding on the parties both during life and after death.
- The agreement must have been entered into for a *bona fide* business reason.
- It must not be a substitute for testamentary disposition.
- The agreement must result in a fair market value for the subject business interest at the time the agreement is executed.
- Its terms must be comparable to similar arrangements entered into by persons in arm's-length transactions.

The Tax Court, in *Estate of Lauder v. Commissioner* (*Lauder II*),[22] adopted this test and ruled that the test's elements are conjunctive, meaning that all of them must be independently satisfied to give the buy-sell price dispositive effect. In *Lauder II*, the court, found that no formal appraisal of the shares of Estee Lauder, Inc., had been performed, that the buy-sell agreement used a formula based on the shares' book value, and that the parties to the agreement had neither considered trading prices of comparable companies nor negotiated using the formula. Thus, the court ruled that the agreement was intended as a testamentary device, and, accordingly, declined to give dispositive effect to the agreement price.

Regulations Section 20.2031-2(h) provides:

> Such price will be disregarded in determining the value of the securities unless it is determined under the circumstances of the particular case that the agreement represents a *bona fide* business arrangement and not a device to pass the decedent's shares to the natural objects of his bounty for less than full and adequate consideration in money or money's worth.

In *Estate of Blount v. Commissioner*,[23] the Tax Court disregarded a buy-sell agreement in determining decedent's interest in a closely held company on the date of his death. The agreement restricted the transfer of stock at death, and set a fixed, lump-sum purchase price. The only other shareholder was the company's employee stock ownership plan (ESOP). The estate's expert concluded that the buy-sell agreement was similar to other such agreements negotiated at arm's length.

The Tax Court ignored the agreement's set value because decedent had the unilateral ability to modify it, thus failing to satisfy the requirement that it be binding during life. The court also disregarded the agreement under IRC Section 2703, which requires that to be included in a valuation, a buy-sell agreement's terms

---

[21] This requirement is part of IRC Section 2703, Chapter 14. For a thorough discussion of the valuation considerations related to buy-sell agreements, see Chapter 29, below.

[22] *Estate of Joseph H. Lauder v. Commissioner*, T.C. Memo 1992-736 (December 30, 1992).

[23] *Estate of George C. Blount v. Commissioner*, T.C. Memo 2004-116 (May 12, 2004).

must be "comparable to similar arrangements entered into by persons in an arm's length transaction." Here, the court concluded that the parties were "related" and had not engaged in arm's-length bargaining.

The Eleventh Circuit affirmed the Tax Court's decision that the buy-sell agreement could not set the value of BCC for estate tax purposes.[24] The appellate court determined that the exception to the rule that the value of the taxable estate generally is the fair market value of the decedent's property at the date of death, codified by the Omnibus Budget Reconciliation Act of 1990, Pub. L. 101-508, 104 Stat. 1388 (OBRA), was inapplicable because the stock-purchase agreement in this case was unilaterally changeable during decedent's lifetime, and thus violated the exception's requirement that the buy-sell agreement must be binding during the life of the decedent.

The court came to the same conclusion under the different theory that the agreement did not satisfy the exception's requirement that the buy-sell agreement must be comparable to similar arrangements entered into at arm's length, because it found that the Tax Court had not erred in its determination that the agreement had not been made at arm's length. Additionally, there was a life insurance policy owned by the company that provided about $3.1 million to pay off the mandated buy-out of the shares. The Tax Court included the full amount of the insurance proceeds as nonoperating assets, and also concluded that because the buy-sell agreement had been disregarded, the issue of whether the company's obligation under that agreement to redeem decedent's stock should offset the proceeds was not before the court.

As to the insurance proceeds, the appellate court ruled that the Tax Court had erred because those proceeds had already been taken into account in the determination of net worth. The court noted that even when a buy-sell agreement is inoperative for purposes of establishing the value of the company for tax purposes, the agreement remains an enforceable liability against the valued company, if state law fixes such an obligation—which it had in this case. Here, the insurance proceeds were offset dollar-for-dollar by the company's obligation to satisfy its contract with the decedent's estate. The court thus concluded that such nonoperating "assets" should not be included in the fair market valuation of a company where, as here, there was an enforceable contractual obligation that offset such assets.

In *Estate of True v. Commissioner*,[25] one issue was whether the book value price specified in the buy-sell agreements controlled estate and gift tax values of the subject interests in several family companies gifted and deeded to children. The analysis focused on the *Lauder II* factors. The court found that the fact that the children did not have independent legal or accounting advice, while not dispositive, reasonably suggested less than arm's-length dealings. The court was critical that the companies' buy-sell agreements did not provide a mechanism for periodic review or adjustment to the tax book value formula. The court also considered an analysis under the adequacy of consideration test. This test requires that the formula price (1) be comparable to what persons with adverse interests dealing at arm's length would accept and (2) bear a reasonable relationship to fair market value. As the court said, "[T]hese standards must be applied with the heightened scrutiny imposed on intrafamily agreements restricting transfers of closely held businesses." The court concluded that, "[t]he True family buy-sell agreements do not satisfy the *Lauder II*

---

[24] *Estate of George C. Blount v. Commissioner*, 428 F.3d 1338, 2005 U.S. App. LEXIS 23502 (11th Cir. 2005).

[25] *Estate of H. A. True v. Commissioner*, T.C. Memo 2001-167 (July 6, 2001).

test, because they are substitutes for testamentary dispositions. As a result, under Section 2031 and the related regulations, the tax book value buy-sell agreement price does not control estate tax values of interests in the True companies at issue in the estate tax case." The court also determined that the buy-sell agreements were not controlling for the gift tax case. The Tenth Circuit affirmed on appeal.[26]

In contradistinction to those cases that have disregarded the buy-sell price, the Tax Court in *Hutchens Non-Marital Trust v. Commissioner*,[27] upheld the redemption price in the buy-sell agreement because it found that the negotiations had been at arm's length and in the ordinary course of business. In arriving at this decision, the court noted that a formal appraisal had been conducted, and that each of the parties to the agreement had been individually represented by attorneys during negotiations.

Failure to have a professional valuation at the time of entering into a buy-sell agreement or a transaction is a red flag to both the IRS and the courts. Cases like this should help make attorneys more aware of the need for independent, professional valuations for buy-sell agreements and transactions, especially those involving insider control owners.

Covenants Not to Compete

A common controversy is the value of covenants not to compete. The controversy can arise in both estate tax cases and income tax cases. For a discussion of this type of controversy, see Chapter 31.

Reliance on Subsequent Sales

There have been several instances in which the Tax Court relied primarily on sales of the business or an interest in it months or even years after the valuation date. The theory in support of this procedure is that the sale did not affect the value, but provided evidence of value that existed as of the valuation date. Many attorneys and analysts believe that the Tax Court has taken this procedure to unwarranted extremes in some cases. However, if a subsequent sale has occurred, most analysts now agree that it would be prudent to reconcile the valuation date value concluded by other approaches with the subsequent event transaction price.

In *Estate of Scanlan*, the date of death was July 16, 1991, and the stock at issue was a noncontrolling ownership block. The Tax Court ultimately relied on an offer to buy the entire company in March of 1993, resulting in a sale consummated in January 1994. The Tax Court rejected the taxpayer's expert's valuation of $35.20 per share for various aspects of inadequacy of the valuation discussed elsewhere in this chapter. The IRS offered no expert testimony. However, the IRS claimed a value of $72.15 per share—the January 1994 sale price of $75.15 per share less 4 percent "to account for minority interest in the company, a minor increase in earnings … and the deflation of the dollar."[28]

---

[26] *Estate of H. A. True v. Commissioner*, 390 F.3d 1210, 2004 U.S. App. LEXIS 24844 (10th Cir. 2004).
[27] *Lewis G. Hutchens Non-Marital Trust v. Commissioner*, T.C. Memo 1993-600 (Dec. 16, 1993).
[28] *Estate of Arthur G. Scanlan v. Commissioner*, T.C. Memo 1996-331 (July 25, 1996).

The Tax Court said: "We find it incredible that the 4 percent discount ... adequately accounts for both a marketability and minority discount, as well as the change in the setting from the ... date of the Decedent's death." The Court then decided to discount the $75.15 sale price by 30 percent, to conclude a value of $50.51 per share on the date of death. It is likely that the estate tax value filed may well have held up in court had it been adequately supported.

In *Estate of Cidulka*, the Tax Court relied primarily on a sale of the company, structured as an asset sale, to the company's arch competitor, four years following the valuation date. Not only was the sale four years removed in time, but it obviously involved a high level of *investment value*, as opposed to *fair market value*. Furthermore, the price certainly could have been influenced by the structure of the transaction as an asset sale, while the estate owned stock.[29]

In *Estate of Jung*, while the Court emphasized that the valuation should be based on what was known or knowable at the valuation date, and that the subsequent sale of the company was not forseeable, the opinion nevertheless made a major point of being able to reconcile the analyst's date of death estimate of value with the subsequent sale price (about two years later).[30]

Subsequent Events and Data

Related to the issue of using subsequent sales to determine value is the use of other subsequent events or data that were not available on the valuation date. The courts disfavor this practice.

In *Polack v. Commissioner*,[31] the taxpayer had gifted over 1 million shares of nonvoting stock of a closely held corporation to his children. The taxpayer valued the shares at about 60% of the IRS's valuation. The Tax Court[32] favored the IRS's appraisal and held for the IRS. On appeal, the taxpayer used unaudited financials for years subsequent to the valuation date to argue that the company's actual operating results were substantially less than the projections made by the IRS for those years. The Eighth Circuit affirmed, finding that these "post-transaction earnings would not have been known to a prospective purchaser" on the valuation date.

In *Okerlund v. United States*,[33] the Federal Circuit ruled that valuation must always be made as of the donative date relying primarily on ex ante information, and that ex post information should be used sparingly. However, the court emphasized that as with any other evidentiary concern, the critical issue is whether the evidence is relevant. The court said, "The closer the profile of the later-date company to that of the valuation-date company, the more likely ex post data are to be relevant (though even in some cases, they may not be). The Federal Circuit affirmed the Court of Federal Claims' ruling that estate plan provisions requiring the purchase of stock upon decedent's death should not have been included in valuing the stock when decedent's death was untimely and unexpected.

---

[29] *Estate of Joseph Cidulka v. Commissioner*, T.C. Memo 1996-149 (Mar. 26, 1996).

[30] *Estate of Jung*.

[31] *Leo J. Polack v. Commissioner*, 366 F.3d 608, 2004 U.S. App. LEXIS 8612 (8th Cir. 2004).

[32] *Leo J. Polack v. Commissioner*, T.C. Memo 2002-145 (June 10, 2002).

[33] *Okerlund v. United States*, 365 F.3d 1044 (Fed. Cir. 2004).

One of the issues in *Estate of Noble v. Commissioner*[34] was whether events subsequent to the valuation date could be used to value stock in a bank. At the date of death, the decedent owned an 11.6 percent interest in a bank, owning 116 shares out of 1000 shares outstanding. Prior to the valuation date, the bank bought two blocks of stock, paying $1,000 per share for ten shares and $1,500 per share for seven shares. After the decedent's death and after the valuation date, the controlling members offered to buy the decedent's shares for $878,004. The estate declined the offer. About ten months later, the estate sold the shares to the bank for $1.1 million.

The controlling member based its initial offer on a third-party appraisal that reduced the value of the shares by a 29 percent minority interest discount and a 35 percent discount for lack of marketability to arrive at the offered price of $878,004. That report was presented by the estate as evidence of value, but the court rejected it. The court, after an extensive review of the law and different methods of valuation, valued the interest at its post-death sale price, minus inflation. The court noted that there had not been any material change in circumstances between the sale date and the date of death. The court reasoned that, "An event occurring after a valuation date, even if unforeseeable as of the valuation date, also may be probative of the earlier valuation to the extent that it is relevant to establishing the amount that a hypothetical willing buyer would have paid a hypothetical willing seller for the subject property as of the valuation date....Unforeseeable subsequent events which fall within this latter category include evidence, such as we have here."

A list of notable subsequent events court cases is presented in Exhibit 28–1.

Discount for Lack of Marketability (DLOM)

Discounts for lack of marketability (DLOM) have been rising over the years. At this writing, the highest discount purely for lack of marketability (i.e., not combined with any other factors) recognized by the Tax Court has been 50 percent.[35] The DLOM is often the biggest and most controversial issue in a business valuation performed for gift and estate tax purposes.[36]

In *Estate of Mandelbaum*, the only issue before the Tax Court was the discount for lack of marketability. The Court stated that it used both the restricted stock studies and the pre-IPO studies as a starting point, and then considered several factors to adjust up or down from the average. Concluding that the balance of the adjustments was downward, the allowed lack of marketability discount was 30 percent.[37]

In *Huber v. Commissioner*,[38] the court allowed a 50 percent discount for lack of marketability. (This is the *first* case that allowed more than a 45 percent discount strictly for lack of marketability—previous higher total discounts included other factors.) The court permitted such a high discount on its finding that sales of

---

[34] *Estate of Helen M. Noble v. Commissioner*, T.C. Memo 2005-2 (January 6, 2005).

[35] See *Huber v. Commissioner*, T.C. Memo 2006-96; 2006 Tax Ct. Memo LEXIS 97 (May 9, 2006).

[36] For a general discussion of the discount for lack of marketability in the Tax Court, see David Laro and Shannon P. Pratt, *Business Valuation and Taxes: Procedure, Law and Perspective* (Hoboken, NJ: John Wiley and Sons, 2005), ch. 18.

[37] *Mandelbaum v. Commissioner*, T.C. Memo 1995-255 (June 12, 1995).

[38] *Huber v. Commissioner*, T.C. Memo 2006-96; 2006 Tax Ct. Memo LEXIS 97 (May 9, 2006).

Exhibit 28–1

Subsequent Event Court Cases (as of January 25, 2007)

United States Supreme Court

Ithaca Trust Co. v. United States, 279 U.S. 151; 49 S. Ct. 291; 73 L. Ed. 647; 1929 U.S. LEXIS 42; 1 U.S. Tax Cas. (CCH) P386; 7 A.F.T.R. (P-H) 8856; 1929-1 C.B. 313; 1929 P.H. P708 (April 8, 1929).

United States Courts of Appeals

Froelich v. Senior Campus Living, LLC, 355 F.3d 802; 2004 U.S. App. LEXIS (4th Cir. January 22, 2004).

McCord v. Commissioner, 461 F.3d 614; 2006 U.S. App. LEXIS 21473; 2006-2 U.S. Tax Cas. (CCH) P60, 530 (5th Cir. August 22, 2006).

Ebben v. Commissioner, 783 F.2d 906, 1986 U.S. App. LEXIS 22479; 86-1 U.S. Tax Cas. (CCH) P9250; 57 A.F.T.R.2d (RIA) 901 (9th Cir. February 25, 1986).

Estate of McMorris v. Commissioner, 243 F.3d 1254; 2001 U.S. App. LEXIS 4143; 2001-1 U.S. Tax Cas. (CCH) P60, 396; 87 A.F.T.R.2d (RIA) 1310; 2001 Colo. J. C.A.R. 1550 (10th Cir. March 20, 2001).

Okerlund v. United States, 365 F.3d 1044; 2004 U.S. App. LEXIS 6970; 2004-1 U.S. Tax Cas. (CCH) P60, 481; 93 A.F.T.R.2d (RIA) 1715 (Fed. Cir. April 9, 2004).

United States Court of Claims

Central Trust Co. v. United States, 305 F.2d 393, 158 Ct. Cl. 504; 1962 U.S. Ct. Cl. LEXIS 16; 62-2 U.S. Tax Cas. (CCH) P12, 092; 10 A.F.T.R.2d (RIA) 6203 (Ct. Cl. July 18, 1962).

Grill v. United States, 157 Ct. Cl. 804; 303 F.2d 922; 1962 U.S. Ct. Cl. LEXIS 17; 62-2 U.S. Tax Cas. (CCH) P9537; 9 A.F.T.R.2d (RIA) 1728 (Ct. Cl. June 6, 1962).

United States District Courts

Hartmann v. United States, 1999 U.S. Dist. LEXIS 10263; 99-2 U.S. Tax Cas. (CCH) P60, 349; 84 A.F.T.R.2d (RIA) 5154 (C.D. Ill. June 24, 1999).

United States Tax Court

Estate of Kaufman v. Commissioner, T.C. Memo 1999-119; 1999 Tax Ct. Memo LEXIS 134; 77 T.C.M. (CCH) 1779; T.C.M. (RIA) 99119 (April 16, 1999), *rev'd by Morrisey v. Commissioner*, 243 F.3d 1145; 2001 U.S. App. LEXIS 3913; 2001-1 U.S. Tax Cas. (CCH) P60, 395; 87 A.F.T.R.2d (RIA) 1250; 2001 Daily Journal DAR 2707 (9th Cir. March 15, 2001).

Estate of Busch v. Commissioner, T.C. Memo 2000-3; 2000 Tax Ct. Memo LEXIS 3; 79 T.C.M. (CCH) 1276 (January 5, 2000).

Estate of Foote v. Commissioner, T.C. Memo 1999-37; 1999 Tax Ct. Memo LEXIS 37; 77 T.C.M. (CCH) 1356; T.C.M. (RIA) 99037 (February 5, 1999).

Estate of Trompeter v. Commissioner, T.C. Memo 1998-35; 1998 Tax Ct. Memo LEXIS 36; 75 T.C.M. (CCH) 1653 (January 27, 1998).

Morton v. Commissioner, T.C. Memo 1997-166; 1997 Tax Ct. Memo LEXIS 184; 73 T.C.M. (CCH) 2520; T.C.M. (RIA) 97166 (April 1, 1997).

Estate of Scanlan v. Commissioner, T.C. Memo 1996-331; 1996 Tax Ct. Memo LEXIS 353; 72 T.C.M. (CCH) 160 (July 24, 1996).

Estate of Ford v. Commissioner, T.C. Memo 1993-580; 1993 Tax Ct. Memo LEXIS 595; 66 T.C.M. (CCH) 1507 (December 8, 1993).

Estate of Jung v. Commissioner, T.C. Memo 1990-5; 1990 Tax Ct. Memo LEXIS 5; 58 T.C.M. (CCH) 1127; T.C.M. (RIA) 90005 (January 11, 1990) and 101 T.C. 412; 1993 U.S. Tax Ct. LEXIS 69; 101 T.C. No. 28 (November 10, 1993).

Estate of Bennett v. Commissioner, T.C. Memo 1993-34; 1993 Tax Ct. Memo LEXIS 47; 65 T.C.M. (CCH) 1816 (February 1, 1993).

Estate of Gilford v. Commissioner, 88 T.C. 38; 1987 U.S. Tax Ct. LEXIS 4; 88 T.C. No. 4 (January 12, 1987).

Estate of Hillebrandt v. Commissioner, T.C. Memo 1986-560; 1986 Tax Ct. Memo LEXIS 43; 52 T.C.M. (CCH) 1059; T.C.M. (RIA) 86560 (November 24, 1986).

Estate of Gillet v. Commissioner, T.C. Memo 1985-394; 1985 Tax Ct. Memo LEXIS 227; 50 T.C.M. (CCH) 636; T.C.M. (RIA) 85394 (August 7, 1985).

Estate of Jepheson v. Commissioner, 81 T.C. 999; 1983 U.S. Tax Ct. LEXIS 1; 81 T.C. No. 64 (December 28, 1983).

Estate of Smith v Commissioner, T.C. Memo 1969-28; 1969 Tax Ct. Memo LEXIS 266; 28 T.C.M. (CCH) 127; T.C.M. (RIA) 69028 (February 12, 1969).

Estate of Prentice v. Commissioner, T.C. Memo 1956-3; 1956 Tax Ct. Memo LEXIS 295; 15 T.C.M. (CCH) 14; T.C.M. (RIA) 56003 (January 10, 1956).

United States Board of Tax Appeals

Couzen v. Commissioner, 11 B.T.A. 1040; 1928 BTA LEXIS 3663 (May 5, 1928).

State Cases

Skokos v. Skokos, 344 Ark. 420; 40 S.W.3d 768; 2001 Ark. LEXIS 244 (Ark. April 19, 2001).

Source: Adapted from a compilation by Stephen J. Bravo, ASA, CBA, CPA/ABV/PFS, CFP, MST, Apogee Business Valuations, Inc., 904 Concord Street, Framingham, MA 01701. Reprinted with permission.

shares between around 250 family members (many distantly related) and trusts who were shareholders in JM Huber Corporation—one of the largest family-held businesses in the country, reporting over $500 million in annual sales—were arm's-length transactions and supported the prices used for gift tax returns.

The prices used in the 90 stock transactions at issue, which occurred over several years for various purposes, were based on appraised values, including a 50 percent discount for lack of marketability that had been consistently applied by an independent third-party appraiser. The variety of the shareholder relationships was, according to the court, "a positive indicator of the existence of arm's length sales." The court said, "We reject [the IRS's] suggestion that almost 250 shareholders would harmoniously accept an artificially low valuation of the Huber stock so that a few people who may or may not be related to them can pay less estate tax."

The court also rejected the "hypothetical" notion that offering the stock for public sale would have obtained an optimum price. The court indicated that "[c]ourts have long recognized the rights of shareholders in closely held companies to remain private." Because there was "no basis to suggest" an available market where a potential buyer would purchase Huber shares at higher than the independently appraised values, these values—including the discounts—were the "best reference" available. Accordingly, the court affirmed the estate's valuation.

In *Estate of Jelke v. Commissioner*,[39] the court rejected the estate's expert's use of restricted stock studies, determining they were not sufficiently similar to the subject company. The IRS expert relied on the *Mandelbaum* factors to arrive at a 10 percent discount for lack of marketability. Although the court favored such an approach, the court disagreed with some of the IRS expert's analysis. Performing its own *Mandelbaum* analysis, the court concluded a 15 percent marketability discount, reasoning that a lower than average discount was justified.

In *McCord v. Commissioner*,[40] a gift tax case involving interests in a limited liability partnership holding company, the taxpayers' expert determined a 35 percent discount for lack of marketability based on pre-IPO restricted stock studies, whereas the IRS expert determined a 7 percent discount based on the expert's own study of 88 private placements (the "Bajaj study"). The Tax Court found that of the 88 private placements, only the 29 middle placements were useful. Using these, the court concluded a 20 percent DLOM. There was no rebuttal to the IRS DLOM evidence in this case.

On appeal, the Fifth Circuit reversed on legal, rather than valuation, grounds.[41] The appellate court found fault with the Tax Court majority's novel methodology:

> The Majority's key legal error was its confecting sua sponte its own methodology for determining the taxable or deductible values of each donee's gift valuing for tax purposes here. This core flaw in the Majority's inventive methodology was its violation of the long-prohibited practice of relying on post-gift events....[T]he Majority violated the firmly-established maxim that a gift is valued as of the date that it is complete; the flip side of that maxim is that subsequent occurrences are off limits.

---

[39] *Estate of Frazier Jelke III v. Commissioner*, T.C. Memo 2005-131 (May 31, 2005).
[40] *Charles T. McCord v. Commissioner*, 120 T.C. 358 (May 14, 2003).
[41] *McCord v. Commissioner*, 461 F.3d 614, 2006 U.S. App. LEXIS 21473 (5th Cir. Aug. 22, 2006).

Instead, the court relied on the Tax Court dissenters:

> …we cannot improve on the opening sentence of Judge Foley's dissent: Undaunted by the facts, well-established legal precedent, and respondent's failure to present sufficient evidence to establish his determinations, the majority allow their olfaction to displace sound legal reasoning and adherence to the rule of law.

Thus, the taxpayer' values were upheld, including the 35 percent DLOM based on restricted stock and pre-IPO studies (as opposed to Bajaj's lower discounts based on his own studies). However, practitioners should note that because the Court of Appeals did not address the DLOM issue per se, this case should not be read as favoring or disfavoring the approach used by the taxpayers' expert.

In *Lappo v. Commissioner*,[42] the Tax Court found that a 21 percent initial discount was appropriate for an interest in a family limited partnership consisting of marketable securities and real estate subject to a long-term lease. The court then made a further upward adjustment of 3 percent to the marketability discount, accounting for characteristics specific to the partnership, including: the partnership was closely held with no real prospect of becoming publicly held; the partnership was relatively small and not well known; there did not exist a present market for the partnership interests; and the partnership had a right of first refusal to purchase the interests. The result was a DLOM of 24 percent. Again, the taxpayer presented no strong evidence regarding the DLOM.

In *Estate of Kelley v. Commissioner*,[43] the Tax Court agreed that a discount for lack of marketability was appropriate in valuing the interests in an investment family limited partnership (FLP), finding that there is not a ready market for partnership interests in a closely held partnership. In determining the marketability discount, the taxpayer's expert used the restricted stock approach and concluded a 38 percent marketability discount. The IRS expert determined a 15 percent discount for lack of marketability on the basis of the Bajaj study (discussed above in the *McCord* case). The court was not persuaded by the taxpayer's approach, finding that the restricted stock studies examined mostly operating companies, and that "there are fundamental differences between an investment company holding easily valued and liquid assets (cash and certificates of deposit), such as [the limited partnership], and operating companies." However, it was also not persuaded by the IRS discount.

Because it declined to use either party's DLOM, the court conducted its own DLOM analysis, finding that a 20 percent initial marketability discount was appropriate. The court based this discount on the private placement approach found in the Bajaj study and found that a 20 percent marketability discount was appropriate for interests in an FLP classified as an investment company. It further found that an upward adjustment of 3 percent was proper, based on the approach used in *Lappo*, to incorporate characteristics specific to the partnership, thus concluding that a total DLOM of 23 percent applied.

In *Estate of Deputy v. Commissioner*,[44] involving the valuation of interests in a company held by a family limited partnership (FLP), the IRS concluded a 25 percent lack of marketability discount based on restrict stock studies. The taxpayer's

---

[42] *Clarissa W. Lappo v. Commissioner*, T.C. Memo 2003-258 (Sep. 3, 2003).

[43] *Estate of Webster E. Kelly v. Commissioner*, T.C. Memo 2005-235 (Oct. 11, 2005).

[44] *Estate of Helen A. Deputy v. Commissioner*, T.C. Memo 2003-176 (June 13, 2003).

expert applied a matrix his company created to replicate an investor's decision process and determined a combined 44 percent lack of marketability and minority interest discount. The Tax Court preferred the taxpayer's approach because it focused on the company's unique attributes, but questioned the matrix's weighting scheme. After independently analyzing each category in the matrix, the court concluded a 30 percent combined DLOM and minority discount.

In *Estate of Green v. Commissioner*,[45] the experts disagreed widely on the appropriate DLOM. The estate's expert relied on restricted stock studies indicating discounts ranging from 31 to 45 percent, and also relied on pre-IPO studies that indicated a range between 43 and 45.7 percent, as well as several transactions involving the stock of the subject company. Based on all these, the taxpayer's expert concluded a 40 percent DLOM. The IRS expert used one restricted stock study (MPI study) that included only two transactions with revenues that were comparable to those of the subject company. Those transactions had an average discount of 43 percent. Citing this book's 4th edition, the court noted that the MPI study indicates a "clear correlation between the size of a company's gross income and the size of the lack of marketability discount." Rejecting the IRS expert's 25 percent discount, the court concluded a 35 percent discount, which was at the higher end of the IRS expert's range, and was "consistent with the average discount that [taxpayer's expert] derived from the restricted stock studies." On a final note, the court said that although it believed the pre-IPO studies used by taxpayer's expert were "entitled to some consideration," it did not find that they justified a discount greater than 35 percent.

In *Estate of Thompson v. Commissioner*,[46] the issue was the value of a 20 percent interest in a publishing company. The estate's experts used a capitalization of income method and applied a 45 percent DLOM. The IRS's expert used two methods—the discounted cash-flow method and the comparable public company method—and found a 30 percent DLOM. Although the court criticized both experts for their lack of experience and for the general credibility of their valuations, the court seemed to adopt the IRS's position and concluded a 30 percent DLOM.

In *Peracchio v. Commissioner*,[47] the court rejected the methodology of the taxpayer's experts, who relied on the *Mandelbaum* factors to arrive at a DLOM of at least 35 percent. The court stated that nothing in *Mandelbaum* suggested that the range of discounts used in that case served any purpose other than to resolve the issues in that particular case. The court also criticized the taxpayer's experts for failing to analyze and apply data from restricted stock studies to the particular (partnership) interests being valued. The court was also dissatisfied with the IRS expert, who had determined that the DLOM range was between 5 and 25 percent and then, without justification, arbitrarily picked the midpoint of the range, 15 percent, as his conclusion of the appropriate DLOM. The court, treating the upper end of the IRS expert's range as a concession that 25 percent would be appropriate, ruled that 25 percent was the correct DLOM.

In *Okerlund v. United States*,[48] a Court of Federal Claims case, to support discounts for lack of marketability on two valuation dates, both parties' experts used

---

[45] *Estate of Mildred Green v. Commissioner*, T.C. Memo 2003-348 (Dec. 29, 2003).

[46] *Estate of Josephine T. Thompson v. Commissioner*, T.C. Memo 2004-174 (July 26, 2004).

[47] *Peter S. Peracchio v. Commissioner*, T.C. Memo 2003-280 (Sep. 25, 2003).

[48] *Okerlund v. United States*, 53 Fed. Cl. 341 (Fed. Ct. 2002), *motion for new trial denied*, 2003 U.S. Claims LEXIS 42 (Fed Cl. 2003), *aff'd*, 365 F.3D 1044 (Fed. Cir. 2004).

data that relied on restricted stock studies and pre-IPO studies. Although the data were similar, there was a 15 percentage point gap between the respective experts' DLOM conclusions for both dates—30 percent for the IRS, 45 percent for the taxpayer. The court found, however, that the taxpayer expert's analysis was far more detailed and persuasive than the IRS expert's, and commended the taxpayer's expert for emphasizing the pre-IPO studies, which, the court determined, were more comparable to the subject company. The court thus concluded a 40 percent DLOM for one date and 45 percent for the other.

The Tax Court in *Hess v. Commissioner*[49] accepted a 25 percent DLOM concluded by the IRS over a 30 percent discount used by the taxpayer because the court found that the taxpayer's expert commingled control issues with the marketability discount.

In *Estate of Davis*,[50] the taxpayer's experts testified to a 35 percent discount (exclusive of the capital gains issue), and the IRS expert opined to a 23 percent discount. The Tax Court ultimately concluded an approximate 32 percent discount. The significant point, noted in the published decision, in coming closer to the taxpayer's experts' opinion, was:

> … [the expert for the IRS] should have considered the … data reflected in those pre-IPO [initial public offering] studies because they, together with the restricted stock studies, would have provided a more accurate base range and starting point for determining the appropriate lack of marketability discount.…

In *Estate of Brookshire*, the Tax Court concluded a 40 percent discount for lack of marketability. Importantly, the taxpayer's expert utilized the pre-IPO as well as the restricted stock studies in quantifying the lack of marketability discount.[51]

In *Estate of Mellinger*, the decedent held stock—both outright and through two trusts—in Frederick's of Hollywood, a publicly held company. Based on the very large size of the blocks relative to very limited trading volume, the Tax Court allowed a 25 percent blockage discount. (This is very high for a blockage discount, although the Tax Court also referred to it as a "marketability discount" at one point in the published decision.)[52]

Estate of Branson[53] demonstrates the fact that every case depends on its own unique facts and circumstances. The Tax Court rejected the testimony of *both* the expert for the taxpayer and the expert for the IRS as to the proffered discount for lack of marketability, which ranged from 20 percent to 55 percent, and allowed only a 10 percent discount for blockage. The Tax Court explained:

> The fact that Savings maintained a waiting list of willing buyers is evidence that the stock's history of low trading volume is due to the shareholder's preference to hold Savings shares for investment, rather than sale.

In *Estate of Fleming*,[54] valuing a 50 percent ownership interest, the Court said, "We conclude that, in addition to a minority discount, some amount of marketability

[49] *Johann T. Hess v. Commissioner*, T.C. Memo 2003-251 (Aug. 20, 2003).

[50] *Estate of Artemus D. Davis v. Commissioner*, 110 T.C. 530 (1998).

[51] *Estate of Anne H. Brookshire v. Commissioner*, T.C. Memo 1998-365 (Oct. 8, 1998).

[52] *Estate of Harriett R. Mellinger v. Commissioner*, 112 T.C. 26 (1999).

[53] *Estate of Frank A. Branson v. Commissioner*, T.C. Memo 1999-231 (July 13, 1999), *aff'd*, 264 F.3d 904 (9th Cir. 2001).

[54] *Estate of Thomas A. Fleming v. Commissioner*, T.C. Memo 1997-484 (Oct. 27, 1997).

discount should be applied...." While the Court didn't specify the amounts of the respective discounts, the judicial conclusion was almost exactly a 27 percent discount from the value arrived at by the guideline merged and acquired company method. The wording suggests that this may imply a 19 percent lack of marketability discount applied in chain on top of a 10 percent lack of control discount opined on by one of the analysts.

Discounts for Lack of Marketability— Controlling Ownership Interests

Discounts for lack of marketability for controlling interests (otherwise known as *illiquidity discounts*, as discussed in Chapter 17) have ranged all the way from zero to 30 percent.

In *Estate of Hendrickson*,[55] the IRS expert applied a 10 percent discount for lack of marketability to a controlling ownership interest, and the taxpayer's expert used a 30 percent discount. The Tax Court concluded that a 30 percent lack of marketability discount was reasonable, citing the following factors:

1. Peoples had few opportunities for growth.
2. Peoples earnings were subject to significant interest rate risk.
3. Peoples had no employee stock ownership plan or history of repurchasing shares.
4. There was no readily available public or private market for Peoples shares.

The Tax Court then went on to explain its decision as follows:

> While we recognize that elements of control may enhance marketability, we do not think that the estate shares were rendered marketable by virtue of their affective [sic] control ... A buyer of the estate shares would either have to sell the block privately, cause Peoples to make a public offering, or seek an acquiror. Any of these three options could take a number of months, and require significant transaction costs for the services of accountants, lawyers, and investment bankers.

In addition to transaction costs, other factors, such as the risk that the price will change during the time it takes to sell, also support the DLOM. See Chapter 17.

In *Estate of Dunn v. Commissioner*,[56] the decedent owned 63 percent of a company that had been marginally profitable. The court permitted a 7.5 percent discount for lack of complete, supermajority control, and a 15 percent DLOM, even though decedent had owned over 50 percent of the company. (The state required a two-thirds supermajority vote for liquidation and other major corporate actions.)

In *Estate of Maggos v. Commissioner*,[57] the company repurchased the decedent's controlling block of stock of a small Pepsi Cola bottler. The court accepted a 25 percent discount because the sale of the shares would require Pepsi Cola Inc.'s

---

[55] *Estate of Hendrickson*. The 31-page opinion in this case explains the Court's position on many valuation issues and is particularly instructive reading for those interested in valuations for tax purposes.

[56] *Estate of Beatrice Ellen Jones Dunn v. Commissioner*, T.C. Memo 2000-12 (Jan. 12, 2000), *rev'd on other grounds*, 301 F.3d 339 (5th Cir. 2002).

[57] *Estate of Mary D. Maggos v. Commissioner*, T.C. Memo 2000-129 (April 11, 2000), *aff'd in part and remanded in part on other grounds*, 32 Fed. Appx. 305, 2002 U.S. App. LEXIS 3629 (9th Cir. 2002).

approval as well as that of the minority shareholder. However, in that case, the court also applied a 25 percent control premium based on average premiums paid in the industry at the time of the purchase.

In the gift tax case *Temple v. United States*,[58] in arriving at a DLOM for limited partnerships holding publicly held marketable securities, the taxpayer's expert had relied solely on restricted stock studies. Although the IRS expert also used these studies, he also used academic research; costs of going public; secondary market transactions; asset liquidity; partnership interest transferability; and historic distributions. This "fuller" analysis persuaded the federal district court to adopt the IRS's 12.5 percent DLOM.

Other cases that have allowed a discount for lack of marketability for a controlling interest include *Estate of Jameson v. Commissioner*[59] (3 percent) and *Estate of Dougherty v. Commissioner*[60] (25 percent).

An example of a case that did not permit a discount for lack of marketability for a 100 percent controlling interest is *Estate of Cloutier*,[61] where the court rejected in its entirety a proposed 25 percent discount because it was based on interests related to noncontrolling interests.

Discount for Lack of Control (DLOC)

As indicated in Chapter 16, discounts are applied to noncontrolling ownership interests, also referred to as minority interests or minority ownership interests. The discount is sometimes referred to as a discount for lack of control (DLOC) or minority discount. Although this discount is related to the DLOM, it is important to segregate these discounts.

In *Estate of Jelke v. Commissioner*,[62] the estate's expert discounted decedent's minority interest in a corporation by 25 percent for lack of control, whereas the IRS's expert applied a 5 percent discount. The taxpayer's expert based his discount on the assumption that the company was most like a closed-end and not widely traded investment fund holding publicly traded securities. Comparing the subject company to such funds, the expert arrived at a 20 percent discount base, and added an additional 5 percent discount because the subject company had fewer assets, paid fewer dividends, and posted lower short-term returns than the comparable funds. In contrast, the IRS expert's analysis began with an average discount (8.61 percent) for closed-end funds, and reduced this because he claimed that the company outperformed the comparables used by the estate. The court adopted a 10 percent lack of control discount, finding that the subject was smaller than some of the comparables presented, but that the subject was well diversified, which reduced investment risk, and that investors in the company would base their investments on the company's history of good performance.

In *Estate of Green v. Commissioner*,[63] the experts for each party disagreed only slightly on their discounts for lack of control for shares in a bank, with

[58] *Temple v. United States*, 2006 U.S. Dist. LEXIS 16171 (E.D. Tex. March 10, 2006).
[59] *Estate of Helen Bolton Jameson v. Commissioner*, T.C. Memo 1999-43 (Feb. 9, 1999).
[60] *Estate of Albert L. Dougherty v. Commissioner*, T.C. Memo 1990-274 (May 31, 1990).
[61] *Estate of Joseph R. Cloutier v. Commissioner*, T.C. Memo 1996-49 (Feb. 13, 1996).
[62] *Estate of Frazier Jelke III v. Commissioner*, T.C. Memo 2005-131 (May 31, 2005).
[63] *Estate of Mildred Green v. Commissioner*, T.C. Memo 2003-348 (Dec. 29, 2003).

the estate calculating a control premium of 20 percent and an implied lack of control discount of 20 percent, "but with little explanation." The IRS concluded an average discount range of 18.4 to 19.6 percent but reduced that to 15 percent for several factors: (1) decedent's "substantially larger interest" than typical minority interests in banks; (2) lack of concentration of ownership in the bank's stock; (3) the highly regulated and "transparent" banking industry; and (4) the bank's solid capitalization, high returns on equity and assets, high rating compared with other banks, and favorable dividend payout. The Tax Court did not adopt either side's analysis. It rejected the estate's control premium and found the IRS's discount reductions were not well supported. The court concluded a 17 percent DLOC.

In *Estate of Thompson v. Commissioner*,[64] the issue was the value of a 20 percent interest in a publishing company. The estate's experts used a capitalization of income method and applied a 40 percent minority discount. The IRS's expert used two methods, the DCF method and the comparable public company method, but did not apply a discount for lack of control, claiming such a discount is inherent in the DCF method. The court criticized both experts for their lack of experience and for the general lack of credibility of their valuations. The court also adjusted the estate's expert's capitalization rate, and applied a 15 percent minority discount.

The experts for both sides in *Hess v. Commissioner*[65] agreed that a 15 percent DLOC applied, but the court criticized the taxpayer's expert for using a discount under the guideline public company method, concluding that such a discount is already included and inherent in that method.

The court in *Adams v. United States*[66], after remand from the Fifth Circuit, which required the Tax Court to apply discounts to a partnership interest because the co-executors' receipt of a partner's share of the dissolved partnership's surplus was not a legal certainty, applied a 20 percent DLOC to a 25 percent interest in the estate partnership because the taxpayer's expert provided "the lone specific analysis of the issues."

In the gift tax case *Temple v. United States*,[67] the court determined the DLOC for limited partnerships holding publicly held marketable securities by using closed-end funds data. Although both parties had used this data, the taxpayer's expert limited the universe of funds and computed the discount using the 75th percentile of the limited universe. The IRS's expert used all reporting closed-end funds and calculated the discount based on the mean of the reported discounts and premiums from net asset value. The court preferred what it deemed the more comprehensive approach used by the IRS expert, and applying the IRS's analysis to three valuation dates, the court applied minority discounts in a range of 3.3 percent to 10.1 percent.

Blockage Discounts

Blockage discounts may apply to publicly traded stock where the size of the block is large enough relative to normal trading volume that it could not be sold in a short time without depressing the market price. The discount is also applied for

---

[64] *Estate of Josephine T. Thompson v. Commissioner*, T.C. Memo 2004-174 (July 26, 2004).

[65] *Johann T. Hess v. Commissioner*, T.C. Memo 2003-251 (Aug. 20, 2003).

[66] *Adams v. United States*, 2001 U.S. Dist. LEXIS 13092 (N.D. Tex., Aug. 27, 2001).

[67] *Temple v. United States*, 2006 U.S. Dist. LEXIS 16171 (E.D. Tex. March 10, 2006).

blocks of property, such as real estate or art. Blockage discounts concluded in most Tax Court cases are relatively modest—generally in the range of 3 percent to 10 percent—but have been as high as 25 percent. Also, there have been a number of cases in which the court has denied a blockage discount.

A typical case is a 3.3 percent blockage discount in *Estate of Foote*, where the block constituted 2.2 percent of the stock outstanding and was equal to 29 days of average trading volume.[68]

The *Estate of Wright* involved a large block of thinly traded stock, with a valuation date market price of $50 per share. The IRS expert said there should be no blockage discount, and the taxpayer's expert claimed a $12 discount for a net value of $38, reflecting various factors including blockages. The Tax Court used the $38 as a starting point, but concluded a value of $45 per share due to the company's "excellent financial condition," thus resulting in a final discount of 10 percent from the $50 market price.[69]

One of the largest blockage discounts was found in *Estate of Mellinger*, which involved significant blocks of the thinly traded public stock of Frederick's of Hollywood. After thoroughly reviewing the testimony and qualifications of the experts, the Tax Court concluded that the appropriate blockage discount was 25 percent, as testified to by the taxpayer's expert.[70]

In *Estate of Adams v. Commissioner*,[71] the court allowed both a restricted stock DLOM and an additional blockage discount on the same block of stock.

In *Estate of Gimbel v. Commissioner*,[72] decedent owned more than 3.6 million shares of Reliance Steel and Aluminum Company, a publicly traded company. The decedent's block of shares represented nearly 13 percent of the company's outstanding stock—enough that the estate was considered an affiliate; and nearly all of its holdings were subject to restrictions under applicable federal securities laws.

The corporation's board later repurchased 2.27 million shares of the estate's stock at $19.35 per share. The IRS experts asserted that the shares should be discounted from the valuation date trading price by only 8 or 9 percent, whereas an initial appraisal for the estate opined that 20 percent was a proper discount. At trial, the estate lowered this to 17 percent. The court found that a corporate repurchase of 20 percent of the estate's stock was foreseeable at the date of death. The court accepted a 13.9 percent repurchase discount that was appropriate to utilize in the valuation of the 20 percent of the shares. The court adopted the estate expert's dribble-out methodology for the sale of the remaining restricted stock over time, reflecting a 14.4 percent discount from the valuation date trading value. The net rate of discount thus amounted to 14.2 percent for all the shares, both restricted and nonrestricted.

In *Estate of Auker v. Comissioner*,[73] blockage discounts were sought for real property (three apartment building complexes) that constituted more than 20 percent of the apartment units in a city. The estate claimed a 15 percent blockage discount, and the IRS claimed no discount should be allowed. The court, using a weighted average of the capitalization rates used in the appraisal of the three apartment complexes, concluded a 6.189 percent blockage discount for each complex.

---

[68] *Estate of Dorothy B. Foote v. Commissioner*, T.C. Memo 1999-37 (Feb. 5, 1999).
[69] *Estate of W. Clyde Wright v. Commissioner*, T.C. Memo 1997-53 (Jan. 29, 1997).
[70] *Estate of Mellinger.*
[71] *Estate of William G. Adams v. Commissioner*, T.C. Memo 2002-80 (March 28, 2002).
[72] *Estate of Gimbel v. Commissioner*, 2006 Tax Ct. Memo LEXIS 274 (December 19, 2006).
[73] *Estate of Eldon L. Auker v. Commissioner*, T.C. Memo 1998-185 (May 19, 1998).

In another case involving real estate, *Estate of Brocato v. Commissioner*,[74] the estate asserted a 12.5 percent blockage discount for eight real properties, whereas the IRS argued that a 1.92 percent discount should apply to only seven of the eight properties. The court concluded an 11 percent discount on seven of the properties.

Key Person Discount

The Tax Court often allows a discount for the loss or potential loss of a key person.

In *Estate of Paul Mitchell*, the Tax Court applied a $15 million discount (10 percent) to the $150 million enterprise value for the death of Paul Mitchell, the company's principal key person. The Tax Court then dealt with other discounts (lack of control, lack of marketability, lawsuit contingency) at the 40 percent non-controlling ownership interest level.[75]

Estate of Renier v. Commissioner[76] serves as a reminder that discounts must be supported by evidence. In that case, the Tax Court rejected a key person discount because it found that factual reasons supporting such a discount were not included in the valuation report.

Contingent Liability Discounts

Discounts for contingent liabilities can cover a wide spectrum, such as environmental liabilities and pending lawsuits.

In *Estate of Paul Mitchell*, after taking a 10 percent key person discount at the enterprise level (as discussed above), the Tax Court then took a $1.5 million discount for a pending compensation lawsuit *after* computing the estate's 40 percent pro rata interest in the enterprise value and *after* deduction of a 35 percent combined lack of control/lack of marketability discount.[77]

In *Estate of Desmond*, the primary issue was a discount for potential environmental liability for a controlling ownership interest in a closely held paint and coating manufacturing company. The expert for the IRS claimed 0 to 5 percent. The taxpayer's expert, using equally weighted asset-based, income, and market valuation approaches, claimed 25 percent. The Tax Court decided that the values using asset-based and income approaches should be discounted 25 percent. However, the Tax Court concluded that this discount should not be applied to the result of the unadjusted guideline publicly traded company valuation method. This was because the market prices of the guideline public companies had already taken the potential environmental liability into account.[78]

In *Estate of Klauss v. Commissioner*,[79] the taxpayer asserted a 8.15 percent discount (amounting to $921,000) for product liability and environmental claims.

---

[74] *Estate of Eileen K. Brocato v. Commissioner*, T.C. Memo 1999-424 (December 29, 1999).

[75] *Estate of Paul Mitchell v. Commissioner*, T.C. Memo 1997-461 (Oct. 9, 1997), *vacated*, 250 F.3d 696 (9th Cir. 2001).

[76] *Estate of James J. Renier v. Commissioner*, T.C. Memo 2000-298 (Sept. 25, 2000).

[77] Id.

[78] *Estate of William J. Desmond v. Commissioner*, T.C. Memo 1999-76 (Mar. 10, 1999) *reaff'd*, T.C. Memo 2002-98 (April 9, 2002).

[79] *Estate of Emily F. Klauss v. Commissioner*, T.C. Memo 2000-191 (June 27, 2000).

The taxpayer's analysis was detailed and enumerated specific items. The IRS's expert applied a 10 percent discount for the contingent liabilities (amounting to $1,130,000). The court agreed with the taxpayer's analysis.

Combined Discounts

There are cases where the experts and/or the court will combine the various discounts. Most typically, the discount for lack of marketability is combined with the discount for lack of control, but other combinations of discounts are encountered.

In *Estate of Desmond v. Commissioner*,[80] where a discount was permitted for environmental liabilities, the court ruled that, of a 30 percent DLOM, 10 percent was attributable to the contingent liabilities. The court therefore applied the full 30 percent DLOM to the value derived under the income method, but only 20 percent derived under the market approach, since the contingent liabilities were already included in the value under the market approach.

In *Janda v. Commissioner*,[81] the taxpayer's expert used the Quantitative Marketability Discount Model (QMDM) to testify to a 65.77 percent DLOM. The IRS expert used restricted stock studies, and concluded a 20 percent DLOM. The court rejected the stock studies as being too general, and concluded that the IRS's analysis was too subjective. The court also criticized the QMDM approach because it determined that slight variations in the assumptions used in the model produce dramatic differences in the results. Accordingly, it stated that it had "grave doubts about the reliability of the QMDM model to produce reasonable discounts…." However, without supplying any justifications for its conclusions, the court applied a combined 40 percent discount for both lack of control and lack of marketability, without specifying the percentage attributable to each.

The taxpayer's expert in *Estate of Magnin v. Commissioner*[82] applied a combined DLOM and DLOC of 60 percent. The Tax Court found that these discounts were incorrectly combined, stating that "discounts for marketability and minority interest are separate and distinct" and should be separated to avoid distorting a valuation. The court held that the DLOC should be applied first, and the DLOM should be applied next. The court concluded that the discounts would have yielded a combined discount of 51.25 percent if they had been calculated independently.

In *Estate of Mitchell v. Commissioner*,[83] the Tax Court found a combined 35 percent DLOM and DLOC. This combined discount was derived, in part, from the testimony of the experts, who testified to discounts that ranged between 30 and 45 percent. On appeal, the Ninth Circuit held that the Tax Court had not explained how it had reached the combined discount, as required by *Leonard Pipeline Contractors, Ltd. v. Commissioner*[84]. On remand, the Tax Court applied the same combined discount, but explained the basis for its holding.

---

[80] *Estate of William J. Desmond v. Commissioner*, T.C. Memo 1999-76 (Mar. 10, 1999).

[81] *Donald J. Janda v. Commissioner*, T.C. Memo 2001-24 (Feb. 2, 2004).

[82] *Estate of Cyril I. Magnin v. Commissioner*, T.C. Memo 2001-31 (Feb. 12, 2001).

[83] *Estate of Paul Mitchell v. Commissioner*, T.C. Memo 1997-461 (Oct. 9, 1997), *vacated by* 250 F.3d 696 (9th Cir. 2001), *reaff'd on remand by* T.C. Memo 2002-98 (April 9, 2002).

[84] *Leonard Pipeline Contractors Ltd. v. Commissioner*, 142 F.3d 1133 (9th Cir. 1998).

In *Estate of Deputy v. Commissioner*,[85] the taxpayer's expert applied a matrix that his company created to replicate an investor's decision process, and determined a combined 44 percent lack of marketability and minority interest discount. The Tax Court preferred the taxpayer's approach because it focused on the company's unique attributes, but questioned the matrix's weighting scheme. After independently analyzing each category in the matrix, the court concluded a 30 percent combined DLOM and DLOC.

In the gift tax case *Temple v. United States*,[86] the federal district court determined a 33 percent combined discount for lack of control and marketability, plus an additional 7.5 percent incremental lack of marketability discount, for a total discount of 38 percent for a real estate (ranch) limited partnership. In arriving at its determination, the court rejected the taxpayer's expert's use of "the inverse of the premium for control" from a Mergerstat study to arrive at the lack of control discount, since that study related to sales of publicly held companies. The court also questioned that expert's holding period assumptions that supported her QMDM analysis in arriving at a DLOM. The court relied instead on the IRS expert's use of average discounts for limited partnerships holding primarily real estate that were similar to the entity under examination and used this data for arriving at both the DLOC and DLOM.

Premiums

The flip side of discounts is premiums, which can be added for a variety of factors, such as control, industry risk, or a swing vote.

In *Estate of Deputy v. Commissioner*,[87] the Tax Court ruled on the applicability of a negative industry risk premium. In determining the capitalization rate to apply, the industry risk premium represents the difference between the general industry risk premium for the market and the risk premium for the particular industry. The taxpayer's expert concluded a 17.5 percent capitalization rate, including a 3 percent industry adjustment. The IRS concluded a negative 5.2 percent industry risk premium, which resulted in a lower capitalization rate of around 10 percent. The court adopted the IRS's position, finding that its negative industry risk premium was supported by the fact that the company tended to outperform the industry and the economy.

In *Estate of Simplot v. Commissioner*,[88] the decedent owned a minority interest in a small control block of stock. The Tax Court, adopting the IRS's position, attributed a 3 percent premium to the swing vote block, and then took a 35 percent DLOC from the decedent's pro rata share in that block. This resulted in a multi-million-dollar control premium on the noncontrolling interest in the control block. On appeal, the Ninth Circuit reversed, finding that a buyer of the block could never recover the premium, and accepting the taxpayer's application of a zero premium. The appellate court decided that a controlling block of stock is not to be valued at a premium for estate tax purposes unless it can be shown that a purchaser of the block would be able to use it "in such a way to assure an increased economic advantage worth paying a premium for."

---

[85] *Estate of Helen A. Deputy v. Commissioner*, T.C. Memo 2003-176 (June 13, 2003).
[86] *Temple v. United States*, 2006 U.S. Dist. LEXIS 16171 (E.D. Tex. March 10, 2006).
[87] Ibid.
[88] *Estate of Richard R. Simplot v. Commissioner*, 112 T.C. 13 (1999), *rev'd*, 249 F.3d 1191 (9th Cir. 2001).

In *Estate of Maggos v. Commissioner*,[89] the decedent's controlling block of stock in a company was repurchased by the company without the benefit of a formal valuation. After applying a 25 percent DLOM, the court applied a 25 percent control premium based on average premiums paid in the industry at the time of purchase.

In *Estate of Wright v. Commissioner*,[90] the court refused to apply a control premium asserted by the IRS's expert that was based on a hypothetical scenario in which other investors might purchase decedent's block of stock.

Trapped-In Capital Gains Taxes

One of the most dramatic shifts in Tax Court decisions, starting in 1998, was explicit recognition of liability for capital gains taxes on significantly appreciated property.

Until 1986, a corporation could liquidate, distribute all proceeds to stockholders within a year, and avoid paying any capital gains tax at the corporate level under the so-called *General Utilities Doctrine*. The Tax Reform Act of 1986 repealed the General Utilities Doctrine, leaving no practical means for C corporations to avoid paying capital gains tax on the sale of appreciated assets. Nevertheless, the IRS steadfastly held to the position that, when valuing a corporation with appreciated assets, a discount to reflect the liability for the capital gains tax was illegal as a matter of law.

In *Estate of Davis*,[91] a family holding company's primary asset was stock in Winn-Dixie Stores, with close to a zero cost basis. The Tax Court concluded:

> We reject respondent's position that, as a matter of law, no discount or adjustment attributable to ADDI&C's built-in capital gains tax is allowable in the instant case.

> We are convinced on the record in this case, and we find, that, even though no liquidation of ADDI&C or sale of its assets was planned or contemplated on the valuation date, a hypothetical willing seller and a hypothetical willing buyer would not have agreed on that date on a price for each of the blocks of stock in question that took no account of ADDI&C's built-in capital gains tax.

Shortly before the *Davis* case, the Tax Court had rejected a discount for trapped-in capital gains, and the case was on appeal at the time of the *Davis* case. Soon after the *Davis* decision, the Second Circuit Court of Appeals, citing favorably the *Estate of Davis*, reversed *Estate of Eisenberg*:

> In the past, the denial of a reduction for potential capital gains tax liability was based, in part, on the possibility that the taxes could be avoided by liquidating the corporation.... These tax-favorable options ended with the Tax Reform Act of 1986 (TRA)....

---

[89] *Estate of Mary D. Maggos v. Commissioner*, T.C. Memo 2000-129 (April 11, 2000), *aff'd in part and remanded in part on other grounds*, 32 Fed. Appx. 305, 2002 U.S. App. LEXIS 3629 (9th Cir. 2002).

[90] *Estate of W. Clyde Wright v. Commissioner*, T.C. Memo 1997-53 (Jan. 29, 1997).

[91] *Estate of Davis*.

Now that the TRA has effectively closed the option to avoid capital gains tax at the corporate level, reliance on these cases in the post-TRA environment should, in our view, no longer continue.[92]

In a March 1999 decision, *Estate of Simplot*,[93] the Tax Court allowed deduction of the full amount of the trapped-in gains tax liability on the appreciated value of a large block of stock in a publicly traded company in its valuation of the company holding the block of stock.

This result was applauded by many in the professional business valuation community. Typical is the comment of a well-known valuation analyst who reviewed the case:

> The Court's finding is consistent with the position I have long advocated. This is an exciting result. Good economic evidence is the basis for sound decisions by the courts.[94]

Although the Ninth Circuit reversed on other grounds, the holding on the trapped-in capital gains tax was left intact.

One more 1999 case, *Estate of Jameson*,[95] also made clear the recognition of the trapped-in capital gains tax discount, in this case for a timber company. The Tax Court found:

> Where a timber company must recognize built-in capital gains under IRC § 1231, because of its IRC § 631(a) election, each time it cuts and sells timber, valuation of the company must take this built-in capital gains into account.

The IRS finally posted a notice on its Web site (www.irs.gov), acquiescing that there is no legal prohibition against a discount for trapped-in capital gains. Referring to the *Eisenberg* case, the notice stated:

> The Second Circuit reversed the Tax Court and held that, in valuing closely held stock, a discount for the built-in capital gains tax liabilities could apply depending on the facts presented. The court noted that the Tax Court itself had recently reached a similar conclusion in *Estate of Davis v. Commissioner.*...

We acquiesce in this opinion to the extent that it holds that there is no legal prohibition against such a discount. The applicability of such a discount, as well as its amount, will hereafter be treated as factual matters to be determined by competent expert testimony based upon the circumstances of each case and generally applicable valuation principles.

The Tax Court in *Jameson*, however, denied the discount, because it refused to believe that the property would be sold immediately, and, instead, assumed the sale of 10 percent of the property every year. On appeal, the Fifth Circuit vacated and remanded the case. It determined that the Tax Court had erred in assuming that a buyer would continue to operate the company for timber production. Instead, the appellate court stated that a potential buyer would have to account for "the consequences of the unavoidable, substantial built-in tax liability on the property."

---

[92] *Eisenberg v. Commissioner*, No. 97-4331 U.S. App. (2d Cir. Aug. 18, 1998), *rev'g* T.C. Memo 1997-483 (Oct. 27, 1997).

[93] *Estate of Richard R. Simplot v. Commissioner.*

[94] Z. Christopher Mercer, "Tax Court Accords Superpremium to Small Voting Block: Allows Deduction of 100% of Trapped-in Capital Gains Tax," *Judges & Lawyers Business Valuation Update*, April 1999, pp. 1, 6–7.

[95] *Estate of Jameson v. Commissioner.*

The court instructed the Tax Court to use an appropriate discount for trapped-in capital gains tax on remand.

Since these cases were decided, all but one—dealing with a partnership—have recognized the discount for trapped-in capital gains tax.

The Tax Court in *Estate of Welch v. Commissioner*,[96] denied a discount for trapped-in capital gains taxes, because the appreciated property at issue was subject to condemnation and because the company was eligible to defer the tax under IRC Section 1033—an option that it exercised. The Sixth Circuit reversed, stating that the availability of a Section 1033 election to roll over the sales proceeds and defer the capital gains tax does not automatically preclude application of the discount. According to the appellate court, "the value of that election and its effect on the value of the stock depends upon all the circumstances a hypothetical buyer of the stock would consider."

In *Estate of Borgatello v. Commissioner*,[97] the Tax Court allowed a 24 percent discount for trapped-in capital gains on a controlling interest in a real estate holding company, based on a holding period between 10 years and an immediate sale.

In *Estate of Dunn v. Commissioner*,[98] the decedent owned 63 percent of a company that had been marginally profitable. The Tax Court allowed only a 5 percent discount for trapped-in capital gains tax because it determined that a hypothetical buyer would have the option of avoiding the tax through various business strategies. The Fifth Circuit reversed, holding as a matter of law that the built-in gains tax liability of the company's assets had to be considered as a dollar-for-dollar reduction (34 percent in this case) when calculating its asset-based value, but not in calculating an earnings-based value.

In *Estate of Jelke v. Commissioner*,[99] an important issue was whether built-in capital gains tax liability should be discounted (indexed) to account for time value. The decedent's estate included a 6.44 percent interest in a well managed, closely held corporation, the assets of which consisted primarily of marketable securities. The company had a relatively high rate of return in the form of annual dividends coupled with capital appreciation of approximately 23 percent annually for the 5-year period before the decedent's death. Also during this 5-year period, there was no intent to completely liquidate the company, and its securities turnover (sales) averaged approximately 6 percent annually.

At the time of decedent's death, the securities had a market value of approximately $178 million and a built-in capital gain tax liability of approximately $51 million if all of the securities were to be sold on the valuation date. The net asset value of the company, without consideration of the effect of the built-in capital gain tax liability, was approximately $188 million.

The estate contended that the $188 million value should be reduced by the entire $51 million before considering discounts for lack of control and marketability. The IRS contended that the built-in capital gain tax liability should be discounted (indexed) to account for time value because it would be incurred in the future rather than immediately. The IRS's expert calculated an average asset turnover rate to predict a 16-year period over which the company's assets would be sold and the trapped-in capital gains tax liability would likely be incurred. Under

[96] *Estate of Pauline Welch v. Commissioner*, T.C. Memo 1998-167 (May 6, 1998), *rev'd* 208 F.3d 213 (6th Cir. 2000).

[97] *Estate of Charles A. Borgatello v. Commissioner*, T.C. Memo 2000-264 (Aug. 18, 2000).

[98] *Estate of Beatrice Ellen Jones Dunn v. Commissioner*, T.C. Memo 2000-12 (Jan. 12, 2000), *rev'd and remanded*, 301 F.3d 339 (5th Cir. 2002).

[99] *Estate of Frazier Jelke III v. Commissioner*, T.C. Memo 2005-131 (May 31, 2005).

the IRS approach, the reduction for built-in capital gain tax liability would be approximately $21 million.

The court agreed with the IRS. After a comprehensive review of case law on this issue, the Tax Court found that a hypothetical buyer of the company would, in most respects, be analogous to an investor/buyer of a mutual fund, especially given that the investor here would be a 6.44 percent investor who, inherently, would be unable to cause liquidation. The court held that an assumption of complete liquidation on the valuation date was inappropriate.

The court found that the IRS's asset turnover rate reasonably predicted the period over which the company's assets would be disposed of and, thus, built-in capital gain tax liability would likely be incurred. Based on this turnover rate, the court found it appropriate to use a 16-year period of recognition for the tax liability attributable to the built-in capital gain, and concluded that a 13.2 percent discount rate was reasonable. This holding resulted in an 11.2 percent reduction in value for built-in capital gain tax liability.

One case that has denied the trapped-in capital gains tax since *Davis*, was *Estate of Jones v. Commissioner*.[100] In that case, the estate owned an 83.08 percent partnership interest. Capital gains taxes could be avoided by an IRC § 754 election at the time of selling the partnership assets. The court reasoned that a hypothetical buyer and seller of the partnership interest would negotiate with the understanding that an election would be made and the price agreed upon would not reflect a discount for built-in gains. The court took pains to distinguish these circumstances from those in *Davis*.

Similarly, in the gift tax case *Temple v. United States*,[101] the federal district court agreed with the IRS position that no discount for trapped-in gains should be permitted with respect to limited partnerships holding publicly held marketable securities to reflect appreciation on the securities because a § 754 election was available. The court disagreed with the taxpayer's expert's conclusion that there was only a 75 to 80 percent chance that a buyer would make the election, and found that a willing buyer and willing seller would account for the built-in gains using a § 754 election.

S Corporations

There is a continuing trend to not tax affect S corporation earnings for valuation purposes.[102] The cases in this section are discussed in greater detail in Chapter 26.

The IRS chose *Gross v. Commissioner*,[103] to argue that S corporation earnings should not be tax affected. At issue were five separate gifts of less than a 1 percent interest each in a large soft-drink bottler. The shareholders had historically received distributions approximating taxable net income. A restrictive stock agreement permitted only intrafamily transfers, and required that the corporation continue as an S corporation. Moreover, none of the shareholders had expressed

---

[100] *Estate of W.W. Jones II v. Commissioner*, 116 T.C. 121 (Mar. 6, 2001).

[101] *Temple v. United States*, 2006 U.S. Dist. LEXIS 16171 (E.D. Tex. March 10, 2006).

[102] For a discussion of the recent debate surrounding whether S corporation earnings should, or should not, be tax affected, see Chapter 26. See also *Delaware Open MRI Radiology Associates, P.A. v. Kessler*, 2006 Del. Ch. LEXIS 84 (April 26, 2006), where the Delaware Chancery Court embraced the current thinking and economic substance of the issues in the context of an appraisal action. This case is discussed in Chapter 36.

[103] *Walter L. Gross, Jr. v. Commissioner*, T.C. Memo 1999-254 (July 29, 1999), *aff'd* 272 F.3d 333 (6th Cir. 2001).

an interest in selling their shares, and there was no evidence that the company would be sold or that distributions would not continue as they had.

The value of the shares arrived at by the IRS was almost double that reported by the taxpayers, with the difference being attributable to tax affecting. The IRS did not tax affect as if it were a C corporation because, it reasoned, the company was stable and profitable, net income was regularly paid out, the benefit of the company's tax-exempt tax status should not be ignored, and, since the company did not pay corporate taxes at the entity level, a discount rate should not have been applied to the company's tax-affected earnings. The Tax Court agreed with the IRS, finding that the taxpayer's expert introduced a "fictitious tax burden" that reduced earnings by 40 percent. The Sixth Circuit affirmed, finding that tax affecting was not appropriate. The court rejected taxpayers' arguments that tax affecting had been an accepted practice, that the IRS had accepted that practice, that tax affecting reflects the S corporation's forfeit of growth and capital appreciation in exchange for current income, and that tax affecting compensates shareholders for the contingency that income distributions may not cover the shareholders' liabilities and that the corporation may lose its tax-exempt status.

In *Estate of Wall v. Commissioner*,[104] the Tax Court took an approach similar to that in *Gross*, saying that tax affecting would result in an undervaluation of the S corporation stock. The court also noted that it believed value would be understated by determining cash flows on an after-tax basis, and then using market rates of return on taxable (C corporation) investments to determine the present value of those cash flows.

In *Estate of Adams v. Commissioner*,[105] the court had to decide the fair market value of decedent's common stock in an S corporation insurance agency. The taxpayer's expert attempted to match S corporation tax characteristics in discounting by converting his after-corporate-tax rate or return to a before-corporate-tax rate or return. Citing *Gross*, the court found that such an increase was inappropriate since an S corporation should be valued on an after-tax basis.

In *Estate of Heck v. Commissioner*,[106] although there was a discrepancy of almost $22,000 per share between the taxpayer's valuation and the IRS's valuation, neither side's expert tax affected the S corporation earnings, nor did the Tax Court. However, the court approved a 10 percent discount for additional risk assumed by a minority investor in an S corporation.

In *Robert Dallas v. Commissioner*,[107] the court, relying heavily on the Gross case, denied tax affecting. The taxpayer had contended that the company's practice of distributing only enough to cover individual income tax liability distinguished this case from *Gross*, in which the corporation distributed substantially all of its income, and that, because of this difference, tax-affecting was appropriate. However, the court rejected this contention, finding instead that:

> Our analysis [in *Gross*] did not depend on the proportion of corporate income distributed. We said that, in determining the present value of an expected stream of earnings, any tax-affecting to reflect the shareholder-level tax burden should be done equally (or not at all) to both the discount rate and the expected cashflows, with the result that, in either case,

---

[104] *Estate of John E. Wall v. Commissioner*, T.C. Memo 2001-75 (Mar. 27, 2001).

[105] *Estate of William G. Adams, Jr. v. Commissioner*, T.C. Memo 2002-80 (Mar. 28, 2002).

[106] *Estate of Richie C. Heck v. Commissioner*, T.C. Memo 2002-34 (Jan. 30, 2002).

[107] *Robert Dallas v. Commissioner*, T.C. Memo 2006-212; 2006 Tax Ct. Memo LEXIS 216 (Sept. 28, 2006).

the present value determined would be the same. That analysis is independent of the proportion of earnings distributed.

The court also rejected the taxpayer's 40 percent discount for lack of marketability and instead agreed with the IRS's 20 percent DLOM.

The Delaware Chancery Court, in *Delaware Open MRI Radiology Associates, P.A. v. Kessler*,[108] captured the current thinking about the legal and economic issues of the tax-affecting debate in the context of a combined appraisal and entire fairness action. This case is discussed in greater detail in Chapter 36.

Family Limited Partnerships

Family limited partnerships (FLPs) have been used successfully by business owners for business, gifting, and tax planning purposes. FLPs may help an owner maintain control of assets; may protect assets from creditors; may avoid fractionalization of title; may enable an owner to take advantage of economies and diversification opportunities; and may be used to maintain family control of a business. The IRS, however, has increasingly targeted FLPs for audit and has had increasing success in challenging FLPs.

To challenge an FLP—and the valuation discounts it can provide—the IRS must show that the FLP does not have a valid business, investment, or income-producing purpose. The IRS has also been successful in challenging FLPs under IRC Section 2036, which provides that assets transferred during a decedent's life will be included in the decedent's gross estate unless the assets have been transferred pursuant to a bona fide sale for full and adequate consideration, or have been transferred other than by sale and the decedent does not retain either possession, enjoyment, or rights in the transferred property, or the right to designate a person who would possess or enjoy the transferred property. A challenge under Section 2036 challenges the validity of the partnership itself, rather than the value of the partnership.

The following cases relate to FLP valuation issues, as well as to FLP validity issues, that arise in the estate and gift tax area.

FLP Valuation Issues

At issue in *Smith v. U.S.*[109] was the recognition of certain restrictions set out in the FLP partnership agreement. If the restrictions were recognized and declared valid, the partnership interest would be subject to a significant discount for lack of marketability that would result in a dramatic lowering of the estate's tax burden. The only asset of the FLP was the entire stock of an operating company.

In the partnership agreement, the parties agreed to limit the price and terms in which the partnership would be required to pay a partner for his or her limited partnership interest if the partnership exercised its right of first refusal. The taxpayer's valuation report reflected a DLOM discount based on the limitations in the partnership agreement. However, the IRS disregarded the limitations in the

---

[108] *Delaware Open MRI Radiology Associates, P.A. v. Kessler*, 2006 Del. Ch. LEXIS 84 (2006).
[109] *Smith v. U.S.*, 2004 U.S. Dist. LEXIS 14839 (W.D. Pa. June 30, 2004).

agreement, based on its reading of IRC Section 2703(a). The estate argued that § 2703(a) applied only to independent buy-sell agreements, not to "entity-creating partnership agreements." The court concluded that the restrictions set out in the partnership agreement were subject to § 2703(a) but that it had complied with the safe harbor exception that was required by § 2703(b)(1) (*bona fide* business arrangement test). However, the court left the issue of whether the restrictive provision satisfied § 2703(b)(2) (testamentary device test) for trial.

In *Kerr v. Commissioner*,[110] a key issue was whether liquidation restrictions in an FLP partnership agreement violated IRC Section 2704(b) because they were more restrictive than allowed under state (Texas) law. The agreement provided that the partnership would be liquidated at the earlier of a defined date or upon all the partners' consent. Because state law permitted such restrictions, the tax Court ruled that the FLP agreement was not more restrictive than permitted under state law. Accordingly, the court permitted a 17.5 percent discount for lack of control and a 35 percent discount for lack of marketability. The Fifth Circuit affirmed.[111]

Similarly, in *Estate of Harper v. Commissioner*,[112] the Tax Court held as a matter of law that the FLP agreement restrictions were not more restrictive than state (California) law. Thus, the court did not disregard those restrictions in determining the fair market value of the FLP.

Another issue in *Kerr* was whether the interests transferred to some partners were assignee interests or full limited partnership interests. Assignee interests are created when a partner transfers his or her interest to someone other than another partner, and the partnership agreement provides that the transferee acquires only the right to the transferor partner's share of distributions. Because assignee interests carry fewer rights than full partnership interests, they are usually worth less. The court ruled that the interests were not assignee interests because the partnership did not consistently follow the assignee interest provisions in the partnership agreement, and because the court found that the only significant difference between the rights of limited partners and assignees is that limited partners have the right to vote on major decisions. Because major decisions were rare, the court concluded there was no meaningful difference between assignee interests and limited partnership interests.

However, in *McCord v. Commissioner*,[113] the Tax Court concluded that gifted FLP interests were assignees interests. In that case, the taxpayers argued that because the partnership agreement required written consent of all partners before full partnership interests could be transferred, and because such consent had not been obtained, the gifted interests should be characterized as assignee interests. The Tax Court agreed, distinguishing this case from *Kerr*, because in this case, unlike in *Kerr*, the parties had previously adhered to the partnership agreement's transfer restrictions requiring written consent. Also, the agreement did not refer to transferred interests as full partnership interests. Moreover, the court found that the taxpayers had not intended to transfer all of their rights, but only their economic rights. On appeal, this issue was not reached by the Fifth Circuit in its reversal of the Tax Court's ultimate holding in the case.[114]

---

[110] *Baine P. Kerr v. Commissioner*, 113 T.C. 449 (Dec. 23, 1999).

[111] *Baine P. Kerr v. Commissioner*, 292 F.3d 490 (5th Cir. 2000).

[112] *Estate of Morton B. Harper v. Commissioner*, T.C. Memo 2002-121 (May 15, 2002).

[113] *Charles T. McCord v. Commissioner*, 120 T.C. 358 (May 14, 2003).

[114] See *McCord v. Commissioner*, 461 F.3d 614 (5th Cir. Aug. 22, 2006).

In *Jones v. Commissioner*,[115] the decedent formed two FLPs, one with his son and one with his four daughters, and received limited partnership interests of about 96 percent and 88 percent, respectively, in the two FLPs. The decedent then gifted an 83 percent limited partnership interest in the first FLP to his son, who was the only other limited partner, and simultaneously gifted a 17 percent interest in the second FLP to each of the other limited partners in that FLP (his four daughters). Again, the IRS raised the issue of whether the interests were assignee interests or limited partnership interests.

The Tax Court found that no gifts had been made upon formation of the FLPs, and that the interests to be valued were limited partnership interests because the decedent, his children, and their valuation expert each characterized the subsequent gifts as transfers of partnership interests. This was significant, because the gift to the son, if a limited partnership interest, would enable the son to control the first FLP, and eliminate lack of control discounts. The court concluded that no secondary market discount was appropriate since the son would not part with his interest for less than his pro rata share of the FLP. Accordingly, the court disallowed a 55 percent discount for lack of control. It also reduced a lack of marketability discount from 20 percent to 8 percent. As to the interests transferred in the second FLP, the court granted those interests a 40 percent discount for lack of control and an 8 percent discount for lack of marketability.

Another case in which the court found that interests were limited partnership interests because the transferor, transferees, transfer documents, and valuation professional characterized those interests as such was *Estate of Dailey v. Commissioner*.[116] In that case, the transferor received a 1 percent general partnership interest and her son received a 98 percent limited partnership interest. Soon after forming the FLP, the transferor gifted her entire limited partnership interest, as follows: 45 percent to her son; 15 percent to her son's wife; and 38 percent to a trust. Eventually, the son became the general partners, and the transferor's general partnership interest converted to a limited partnership interest.

Anther valuation issue that is raised by FLPs is whether the FLP has a valid business purpose. In *Church v. United States*,[117] the decedent died unexpectedly only two days after the FLP was formed. The IRS argued that the FLP was established for tax avoidance purposes. However, the estate presented evidence that decedent's death was unexpected and that there was a valid purpose for the FLP. The federal district court upheld the taxpayer's valuation, which represented a 57.6 percent discount from the partnership's net asset value. (On another issue in the case, the court ruled that the partnership agreement should not be disregarded because the restrictions in the agreement were similar to arm's-length transactions.) The Fifth Circuit upheld the district court's decision.

Still another valuation topic that arises in the FLP context—as in other valuation contexts—is whether the appropriate valuation methodology has been used. In *Knight v. Commissioner*,[118] the Tax Court rejected the IRS's valuation because it valued the FLP on a fair value, rather than a fair market value, basis. In *Estate of Weinberg v. Commissioner*,[119] the court made its own determination as to

---

[115] *Estate of W.W. Jones II v. Commissioner*, 116 T.C. 121 (Mar. 6, 2001).

[116] *Estate of Elma M. Dailey v. Commissioner*, T.C. Memo 2001-263 (Dec. 9, 2001).

[117] *Church v. United States*, 1999 U.S. Dist. LEXIS 19899 (W.D. Tex, Jan. 14, 1999), *aff'd w/o pub. op.*, 268 F.3d 1063 (5th Cir. 2001).

[118] *Ina F. Knight v. Commissioner*, 115 T.C. 506 (Nov. 30, 2000).

[119] *Estate of Etta H. Weinberg v. Commissioner*, T.C. Memo 2000-51 (Feb. 15, 2000).

the proper discounts for lack of marketability and lack of control. The court rejected the IRS's use of the QMDM and the taxpayer's reliance on averages from restricted stock studies to determine DLOM. In determining the DLOC, the court preferred the taxpayer's use of both the income and asset approach to the IRS's use of only the income approach, but favored the IRS's use of 16 guideline partnerships versus the taxpayer's use of only one. Ultimately, the court used its own preferred methods to conclude discounts.

Validity Issues

In *Estate of Bigelow v. Commissioner*,[120] the issue was whether the value of real property transferred to a FLP was included in the decedent's gross estate. Prior to her death, the decedent established a trust, which transferred real property—but not liabilities totaling $450,000 secured by the property—to an FLP that the decedent formed with her children right after she had a stroke. The trust was the FLP's sole general partner. After the transfer, the decedent was left with an insufficient amount of income to meet her living expenses or to satisfy her liability for the indebtedness. Her sole purposes in establishing the FLP were to facilitate gift giving and to reduce estate tax.

The Tax Court held that the value of the property should be included in the decedent's gross estate under IRC Section 2036. The court found that the decedent's use of partnership income to replace the income lost as a result of the transfer of the property to the FLP showed that there was an implied agreement between the decedent and her children that she would retain the right to the income from the property.

In determining that the FLP transaction did not constitute a bona fide sale for adequate and full consideration, the court determined that the transfer of the property was not made in good faith, because it left the decedent unable to meet her financial obligations or to pay expenses. Additionally, the FLP's failure to respect partnership formalities evidenced a lack of good faith.

Finally, the transfer did not provide and had no potential to provide any non-tax benefit to the decedent, because management of the assets did not change as a result of the transfer, there was no pooling of assets, and, as the FLP's sole general partner, the trust did not get any additional protection from creditors. The court found that the fact that the transfer facilitated the decedent's ability to make gifts to her children and grandchildren was not a bona fide purpose under § 2036 for establishing the FLP.

In *Estate of Korby v. Commissioner*,[121] the issue was whether the value of assets contributed to an FLP was includable in the decedent's gross estate. The decedent and one of his four sons were the trustees of decedent's living trust. The trust gave the decedent and his wife the authority to control and direct payments from the living trust, add or remove living trust property, and amend or revoke the living trust. Most of the decedent's and his wife's assets were transferred to the trust.

After the living trust was formed and funded, an FLP was established. All of the decedent's family members signed the partnership agreement, along with the living trust, which served as the general partner. The agreement provided for

---

[120] *Estate of Virginia A. Bigelow v. Commissioner*, T.C. Memo 2005-65 (Dec. 30, 2005).
[121] *Estate of Austin Korby v. Commissioner*, T.C. Memo 2005-103 (May 10, 2005).

management fees to be paid to the general partner, which also had the power to determine the amount of such fees. The agreement also required the FLP to reimburse the general partner for "all reasonable and necessary business expenses incurred in managing and administering the partnership."

The decedent contributed 58.46 percent of the FLP's assets, the wife contributed 38.26 percent, and the sons and trust contributed less than four percent. After the transfers to the living trust and FLP, the decedent and his wife, who had serious medical ailments, did not have any bank accounts open in their own names, but they incurred significant medical expenses. The trust used payments it received from the FLP and Social Security to pay for the decedent's and his wife's medical, household, and living expenses.

The IRS claimed that the full values of the assets held by the FLP and the living trust were includable in the gross estate under IRC Sections 2036 and 2038. The Tax Court agreed, concluding that an implied agreement existed between the decedent, on his own behalf and on behalf of his wife and the sons, that after the assets were transferred to the FLP, income from the assets would continue to be available to the couple for as long as they needed income. The court based this opinion on the fact that the decedent and his wife could have been expected to incur significant medical expenses in the future, but only retained relatively insignificant assets to provide for such expenses, as well as regular living expenses. Also a factor in the court's opinion was that the FLP distributed significant percentages of its income to the living trust, which totaled at least 52.6 percent of the couple's income.

The court rejected the argument that these were management fees because: they were not used by the son as co-trustee; no management contract had been executed; the fees were disproportionately large to the services rendered; and no self-employment income was reported for the fees. The court also used many of these factors, as well as the decedent's unilateral decisions surrounding the establishment and operation of the FLP, to arrive at its conclusion that the bona fide sale exception to Section 2036 was not met. The court held that 58.46 percent of the FLP's value was includable in the gross estate.

In *Strangi v. Commissioner*,[122] the Fifth Circuit affirmed the Tax Court's decision on remand[123] that the decedent had retained enjoyment of the assets he had transferred to an FLP through an implied agreement, and, thus, that the transferred assets were properly included in his estate under IRC Section 2036(a) for estate tax purposes. The Fifth Circuit also upheld the Tax Court's determination that the bona fide sale exception to § 2036(a) was inapplicable. The court agreed that the FLP's distribution of over $100,000 to pay for funeral expenses, estate administration expenses, specific bequests, and various personal debts that the decedent had incurred provided strong circumstantial evidence of an understanding between the decedent and his children that "partnership" assets would be used to meet the decedent's expenses. The court remarked that the "possession or enjoyment" of one's assets is the assurance that they will be available to pay various debts and expenses upon one's death, which is what the decedent received. Other "highly probative" factors supporting an implied relationship was the decedent's continued physical possession of his residence after its transfer to the FLP, and that the decedent's liquid assets were lower than his monthly living expenses.

---

[122] *Albert Strangi v. Commissioner*, 417 F.3d 468 (5th Cir. 2005).
[123] *Estate of Albert Strangi v. Commissioner*, T.C. Memo 2003-145 (May 20, 2003).

The court also agreed that the decedent's transfer of assets to the FLP lacked a substantial non-tax purpose, and that, therefore, the bona fide sale exception found in Section 2036(a) did not apply. The court found that none of the five non-tax rationales proffered by the estate were supported by the evidence. These rationales were: (1) deterring potential tort litigation by decedent's former house-keeper; (2) deterring a potential will contest; (3) persuading a corporate executor to decline to serve; (4) creating a joint investment vehicle for the partners; and (5) permitting centralized, active management of working interests owned by decedent. The result was that 98 percent of decedent's assets were included in his gross estate. Thus, this case raises concerns for estate planning about invalidation of FLP agreements where the estate holds virtually all of the outstanding partnership interest.

In *Estate of Disbrow v. Commissioner*,[124] the decedent gave her residence to a newly formed, assetless general partnership whose partners were the decedent, her children, and her children-in-law. Shortly thereafter, the decedent gave all of her interest in the partnership to the other partners for no consideration. The decedent continued to live at the residence until she died, paying the partnership less than fair rental value (FRV). The IRS determined that the fair market value of the residence was includable in the decedent's gross estate because the decedent, until her death, retained the possession and enjoyment of the residence within the meaning of Section 2036(a)(1).

The Tax Court agreed with the IRS, but expressed no opinion on the validity of the partnership, which the court concluded conducted no business and was not operated with an intent to make a profit, notwithstanding the partnership agreement's statement that the partnership had been "created to establish and conduct the business of real estate ownership and management." The court found that written lease agreements entered into between the partnership and the decedent were not adhered to as arm's-length leases would have been. Instead, the court found that the decedent's rights under the lease agreements to the exclusive possession and enjoyment of the residence were expressions of her retained interest in the residence that triggered the application of Section 2036(a)(1) to the residence in that the decedent did not pay FRV for that possession and enjoyment. The court also determined from the conduct of the parties to the lease agreements, as well as the lease agreements themselves, that there was an implied understanding and agreement between the decedent and the partnership as to her continued possession and enjoyment of the residence following its transfer to the partnership. The court further found that the annual lease agreements were subterfuge to disguise the testamentary nature of the transfer. According to the court, the partnership was not a business operated for profit but was a testamentary device whose goal was to remove the residence from the decedent's gross estate.

In *Estate of Bongard v. Commissioner*,[125] there were two issues: whether pursuant to IRC Sections 2035(a) and 2036(a), (b) the gross estate should have included: (1) shares the decedent transferred to a holding company and (2) the holding company's membership units the decedent then transferred to a FLP in exchange for a 99 percent limited partnership interest therein. The decedent had created the holding company to increase the chances of attracting outside investors to purchase his successful business.

---

[124] *Estate of Lorraine C. Disbrow v. Commissioner*, T.C. Memo 2006-34 (Feb. 28, 2006).
[125] *Estate of Wayne C. Bongard v. Commissioner*, 124 T.C. 95 (Mar. 15, 2005).

From its inception until the decedent's death, the FLP did not perform any activities, never acted to diversify its assets, or make any distributions. The holding company membership units in the FLP were nonvoting, and the decedent determined whether the shares held by the holding company would be redeemed. However, the holding company did not redeem any of its membership units held by the FLP before his death.

The IRS claimed a deficiency of over $50 million, determining, among other things, that the shares of stock decedent transferred to the holding company were includable in the decedent's gross estate because he had retained sections 2035(a) and 2036(a) and/or (b) rights and interests in the transferred property. The Tax Court disagreed, finding that the decedent received an interest that represented adequate and full consideration reducible to money value, and that the transaction was motivated by a legitimate and significant nontax purpose—positioning the company so that it could obtain additional capital through either a public or private offering ("corporate liquidity event"). Therefore, the court ruled that this transfer had satisfied the bona fide sale exception of Section 2036(a).

The court also rejected the IRS's argument that an arm's-length transaction cannot occur between related parties, noting that the bona fide sale exception has not been limited to transactions involving unrelated parties. The court also rejected the argument that the formation of the holding company was not a bona fide sale because there was not a true pooling of assets. Instead, the court concluded that, when the holding company was capitalized, the members' capital accounts were properly credited and maintained, the holding company's funds were not commingled with decedent's, and all distributions during his life were pro rata. For these reasons, the court determined that the transaction resulted in a true pooling of assets.

However, because the court found that estate tax savings did play an important role in motivating the second transfer—the transfer of the decedent's membership units in the holding company to the FLP—and because it found that an implied agreement existed that allowed the decedent to retain the enjoyment of the property held by BFLP, the court held that under Section 2036(a)(1), the decedent's gross estate included the value of the membership units.

The court rejected the estate's contention that the FLP had been established to provide another layer of credit protection for the decedent (the holding company provided this already) and to facilitate gift-giving. The court focused on the fact that the partnership made only one gift, never diversified its assets during the decedent's life, never had an investment plan, and never functioned as a business enterprise or otherwise engaged in any meaningful economic activity. Thus, the second transfer did not satisfy the bona fide sale exception, but did come within Section 2036(a)'s test relating to an implied agreement for the retention of benefits of the transferred property. Accordingly, the value of the holding company units transferred to the FLP were included in the decedent's gross estate.

The issue in *Estate of Abraham v. Commissioner*[126] was whether three family limited partnerships (FLPs) satisfied IRC Section 2036, so their value could be excluded from the decedent's gross estate. The decedent had numerous properties that were placed in three FLPs for purposes of estate planning. Her children purchased interests in the FLPs, but the partnership agreement provided that the decedent would benefit, to the exclusion of her children-partners, from the income generated by the FLPs to maintain her lifestyle.

---

[126] *Estate of Ida Abraham v. Commissioner*, T.C: Memo 2004-39 (Feb. 18, 2004), *aff'd*, 408 F.3d 26 (1st Cir. 2005).

The Tax Court noted that the decedent by definition violated Section 2036 by continuing to enjoy the property held by the FLPs. "Possession or enjoyment of the property transferred is retained where there is an express or implied understanding among the parties at the time of the transfer, even if the retained interest is not enforceable." The Tax Court concluded that the FLPs were "merely a testamentary vehicle employed to shift her assets to future generations while maintaining her continued right to benefit from the FLP interests transferred. This is precisely the type of situation for which Section 2036 was created." The Tax Court disregarded the FLPs and valued the property held in the FLPs at full fair market value. The First Circuit affirmed this decision.

In *Estate of Hillgren v. Commissioner*,[127] the decedent suffered from depression, and following her failed first attempt at suicide, she formed an FLP with her brother, and transferred all of her income-producing real estate to the FLP. The brother did not contribute any property to the FLP, but rather contributed his services. He was to receive 25 percent of the profits of the FLP under the partnership agreement. The decedent committed suicide several months later.

After formation of the FLP, the decedent's relationship to the real property that had been transferred to the FLP did not change. The same management company continued management of the properties in the same manner. The brother continued to deal with the properties in the same manner he had before, pursuant to a business loan agreement that the decedent and the brother had previously entered into. All of the FLP's income was distributed to the decedent and used for her personal living expenses. Thus, the partnership form was completely disregarded by the decedent and her brother. Therefore, the IRS argued that the FLP should be disregarded under IRC Section 2036(a), and its value, as well as the fair market value of the assets of the partnership, should be included in her gross estate.

The Tax Court ruled that, because the decedent and her brother did not respect the FLP entity, and the decedent's relationship to the property did not change after formation of the FLP, the entity would be disregarded for estate tax purposes. Therefore, the real estate held by the FLP was included in the decedent's gross estate. Nonetheless, the court ruled that several parcels of the real estate were still subject to the loan arrangement, and that, therefore, in determining the value of the real estate, the court accepted the discounts offered by the estate, and allowed lack of control and marketability discounts aggregating 50 percent as to one property, and as to the three others, from 35 percent to 40 percent, plus an additional 5 percent for each property due to lack of voting rights.

The Fifth Circuit in *Kimbell v. United States*[128] vacated and remanded the district court's decision that the transfer to the FLP was not a bona fide sale for full and adequate consideration under IRC Section 2036. The court ruled that the lower court had erroneously equated bona fide sale with an arm's-length transaction, and further erroneously found that a transfer could not be a bona fide sale if the decedent and family members were present on both sides of the transfer.

The court stated:

> [t]he government's inconsistency argument … is a classic mixing of apples and oranges: The government is attempting to equate the venerable "willing buyer-willing seller" test of fair market value (which applies

[127] *Estate of Lea K. Hillgren v. Commissioner*, T.C. Memo 2004-46 (Mar. 3, 2004).
[128] *Kimbell v. United States*, 371 F.3d 257 (5th Cir. 2004).

when calculating gift or estate tax) with the proper test for adequate and full consideration under § 2036(a). This conflation misses the mark: The business decision to exchange cash or other assets for a transfer-restricted, non-managerial interest in a limited partnership involves financial considerations other than the purchaser's ability to turn right around and sell the newly acquired limited partnership interest for 100 cents on the dollar. Investors who acquire such interests do so with the expectation of realizing benefits such as management expertise, security and preservation of assets, capital appreciation and avoidance of personal liability. Thus there is nothing inconsistent in acknowledging, on the one hand, that the investor's dollars have acquired a limited partnership interest at arm's length for adequate and full consideration and, on the other hand, that the asset thus acquired has a present fair market value, i.e., immediate sale potential, of substantially less than the dollars just paid—a classic informed trade-off.

The appellate court concluded that the facts of the case supported the contention that the transaction was bona fide, including that: (1) the decedent retained sufficient assets outside the FLP for her own support and there was no commingling of FLP and her personal assets; (2) FLP formalities were satisfied and the assets contributed to the FLP were actually assigned to the FLP; (3) the assets contributed to the FLP included working interests in oil and gas properties, which require active management; and (4) several credible and unchallenged non-tax business reasons for the formation of the FLP were advanced. Accordingly, the appellate court concluded that the transaction was bona fide for full and adequate consideration as a matter of law and remanded to the district court the issue of whether decedent's interest in the FLP was an assignee interest or limited partnership interest.

In another defeat for the taxpayer, the Third Circuit in *Estate of Thompson v. Commissioner*[129] affirmed the Tax Court's ruling that § 2036(a)(1) applied to FLPs, and, thus, that no discount from Net Asset Value (NAV) was permissible. The Tax Court had found that the 95-year-old decedent did not retain sufficient assets to support himself, that his children obtained assurances that decedent would be able to (and in fact did) withdraw assets from the FLPs to continue cash gift programs to his family, and that, if decedent ran short of funds to take care of himself, the FLPs would provide the "infusion" of money to cover his expenses, and indeed this occurred. The court of appeals, finding this arrangement to be a testamentary plan, refused to apply the "bona fide sale" exception to 2036(a).

Other cases where the IRS prevailed under Section 2036 are *Estate of Harper v. Commissioner*[130] (substantially, all of the decedent's assets were transferred to the FLP, income from FLP's assets were commingled with the decedent's other income, and FLP distributions were disproportionately favorable to the decedent), *Reichardt v. Commissioner*[131] (the decedent failed to maintain an arm's-length relationship with the FLP, and commingled FLP funds with personal assets, leading the Tax Court to conclude that the "decedent's relationship to the partnership assets did not change when he conveyed them....") and Estate of *Schauerhamer v. Commissioner*[132] (decedent commingled personal and FLP funds, depositing them in her personal checking account).

---

[129] *Estate of Theodore R. Thompson v. Commissioner*, T.C. Memo 2002-246, *aff'd* 382 F.3d 367, (3rd Cir. 2004).

[130] *Estate of Morton B. Harper v. Commissioner*, T.C. Memo 2002-121 (May 15, 2002).

[131] *Estate of Charles E. Reichardt v. Commissioner*, 114 T.C. 144 (Mar. 1, 2000).

[132] *Estate of Dorothy Morganson Schauerhamer v. Commissioner*, T.C. Memo 1997-242 (May 28, 1997).

The following are cases where the taxpayer prevailed against a Section 2036 challenge.

In *Estate of Stone v. Commissioner*,[133] the decedents, a married couple, formed five FLPs along with their children to avoid litigation amongst the children over the assets and operation of the couple's successful company. A different child (and/or spouse) was named general partner of each FLP. The couple had valuations performed for all of their assets, and contributed most of their assets, including their stock in their company, to the FLPs. They retained sufficient assets, however, to maintain their current standard of living. Within two years of the FLP formations, both decedents had died.

The IRS challenged the transfers under IRC Section 2036(a), claiming that they were not bona fide sales for adequate and full consideration. The IRS relied primarily on the *Estate of Harper, Estate of Reichardt, and Estate of Thompson*, arguing that there was no evidence in the record indicating that the decedents intended to conduct a "joint enterprise for the mutual profit of their children and themselves." The estates, on the other hand, claimed that the decedents' transfers of property to the FLPs were bona fide sales for full and adequate consideration. In support of their position, the estates pointed out that the decedents received pro rata ownership in the FLPs in return for their contributions.

The Tax Court agreed with the estates, distinguishing the instant case factually from *Harper* and the others. It rejected the IRS's argument that because the decedents did not actively participate in the children's negotiations regarding the various assets; the transfers were not bona fide, arm's-length transfers. The court noted that, although each member of the family was represented by legal counsel and had decision-making input, the decedents made the final decisions regarding the transfers of assets. The court also observed that the decedents did not unquestioningly accept their childrens' recommendations.

The court found that, unlike in *Harper* and other cases, the decedents did substantially more than just change the form of the contributed property. The court found that the FLPs had economic substance and "operated as joint enterprises for profit through which the children actively participated in the management and development of the respective assets of such partnerships during their parents' lives (and thereafter)." The court concluded by saying that the transfers in this case did not constitute a "recycling of value" as found in some previous Tax Court cases. Therefore, the value of the FLPs was not included in the estates.

In another case where the taxpayer prevailed against a Section 2036 challenge (but which involved business trusts rather than FLPs) was *Estate of Schutt v. Commissioner*.[134] There, decedent capitalized two business trusts through contributions of his stock by a revocable trust and by the trustee of various trusts created for the benefit of the decedent's children and grandchildren. At his death, the decedent held interests of less than 50 percent in each trust.

The IRS issued a notice of deficiency, determining that discounts amounting to about $20 million applied in valuing the interests in the trusts were excessive. The IRS also asserted that the full market value of the underlying assets contributed by the revocable trust to the business trusts should be included in the decedent's gross estate under IRC Sections 2036(a) and 2038. Finding that the decedent's transfer

---

[133] *Estate of Eugene E. Stone, III v. Commissioner*, T.C. Memo 2003-309 (Nov. 7, 2003).
[134] *Estate of Charles Porter Schutt v. Commissioner*, T.C. Memo 2005-126 (May 26, 2005).

was made for other than estate tax advantage, namely, to ensure the perpetuation of the decedent's "buy and hold" investment philosophy for the purpose of protecting his family's wealth, the Tax Court held that the transfers of stock to the business trusts were bona fide sales for adequate and full consideration within the meaning of Sections 2036(a) and 2038, such that the value of the transferred assets did not have to be included in the decedent's gross estate under these statutes. The court also found significant that by using the business trusts, the decedent was able to apply this philosophy to the stock of non-business trusts he had established. The decedent's motives were well-documented by his estate planning advisers. The court rejected the IRS's assertions that tax savings through valuation discounts constituted the dominant reason for formation of the business trusts, finding that although it was clear that estate tax implications were recognized and considered in the initial stages of the planning process, the record failed to reflect that such issues predominated in the decedent's thinking and desires. The court concluded that what may have originally been approached as a relatively routine estate planning transaction, rapidly developed into an opportunity and vehicle for addressing the decedent's more fundamental concerns.

Other indicia of a bona fide sale were that the contributed property was actually transferred to the business trusts in a timely manner; that entity and personal assets were not commingled; that the decedent was not financially dependent on distributions from the trusts, retaining sufficient assets outside of the business trusts amply to support his needs and lifestyle; and that the decedent did not effectively stand on both sides of the transactions.

Finally, the court also held that the discounted value attributable to entity interest valuation principles was not per se to be equated with inadequate consideration, and rejected the IRS's contention that the transactions featured prohibited value recycling. The key here, the court reasoned, was that others contributed more than half of the property funding the entities, and that, therefore, the decedent was not merely recycling his shareholdings. This case demonstrates the need for good documentation that estate tax reduction through discounts is not the primary motive for the transaction.

Focus on Willing Seller as Well as on Willing Buyer

Some judicial precedents have emphasized the point that the expert should consider the hypothetical willing seller as well as the hypothetical willing buyer.

In *Estate of Lehmann*, the Tax Court stated:

> [The taxpayer's expert] focuses exclusively on the hypothetical willing buyer. [He] failed to consider whether a hypothetical seller would sell his or her interest in the partnership for $399,000.... Ignoring the views of the willing seller is contrary to this well-established rule.[135]

In *Estate of Kaufman*, the Court observed:

> [The taxpayer's expert] seems to have focused too much on the willing buyer portion of the fair market value definition. He failed to consider

---

[135] *Estate of George A. Lehmann v. Commissioner*, T.C. Memo 1997-392 (Aug. 26, 1997).

whether a seller, under no compulsion to sell, would discount the pro rata value of his interest by 40 or 50 percent in order to consummate the sale.[136]

On appeal, however, the Ninth Circuit, in *Morrissey v. Commissioner*,[137] reversed, finding that, contrary to the Tax Court's finding, actual sales were arm's-length transactions that offered the best evidence of fair market value.

In *Estate of Simplot*,[138] the Ninth Circuit again reversed the Tax Court, which in giving a premium to a minority voting stock had created and relied on a scenario in which a buyer would purchase a minority share of voting stock, but over time could "play a role in the company." The appellate court found that the Tax Court's scenario constituted speculation and identified specific purchasers, rather than hypothetical purchasers.

Inadequacy of the Valuation

The instances and factors contributing to inadequate valuations for tax purposes by both taxpayer and IRS experts could easily fill an entire book of this size. Some of the most common inadequacies are the following:

- The valuation is out of date.
- Lack of site visits and/or management interviews.
- Inadequate selection and/or analysis/explanation of selected guideline company comparability.
- Inadequate empirical support for the valuation variables selected (e.g., pricing multiples, discount/capitalization rates, discounts/premiums).
- Successful *Daubert* challenges.

The Court rejected the taxpayer's expert's report in *Estate of Scanlan*[139] for several reasons, including:

- He was unable to explain certain parts of the analysis contained in the reports.
- He arbitrarily applied a 35 percent lack of marketability discount.
- He made no mention of a hypothetical seller.
- Whereas the report prepared by the expert two years prior to the date of death states that he toured the facilities, there was nothing in his testimony or in his report as of the date of death to suggest that he did likewise before preparing the report for estate tax purposes.
- The report did not adequately account for the fact that the company's earnings in the year of the estate tax report increased dramatically over the years covered by the earlier report.
- The report did not adequately take into account that the company began paying dividends after the time covered by the earlier report.
- The report referred to the financial data of publicly traded companies, yet never explains how those companies were selected, or in what respects their lines of business were similar to the subject company.

---

[136] *Estate of Alice Friedlander Kaufman v. Commissioner*, T.C. Memo 1999-119 (Apr. 6, 1999), *rev'd, Morrissey v. Commissioner*, 243 F.3d 1145 (9th Cir. 2001).

[137] *Morrissey v. Commissioner*, 243 F.3d 1145 (9th Cir. 2001).

[138] *Estate of Richard R. Simplot v. Commissioner*, 249 F.3d 1191 (9th Cir. 2001).

[139] *Estate of Scanlan*.

Another case where the Tax Court rejected the taxpayer's expert's valuation was in *Estate of Kaufman*.[140] The opinion of the Tax Court discusses, among others, the following flaws:

- Did not sufficiently explain why the guideline publicly traded companies he selected for his analysis were comparative, and why other publicly traded companies that appeared more comparable were not used. "A proper valuation report must contain enough data on each similar corporation to allow the Court to make an informed, independent decision as to whether the corporations are sufficiently similar to the subject corporation to perform a proper valuation analysis."
- Did not analyze all three valuation approaches. "Valuation experts must thoroughly analyze all applicable methods of valuation, and they may not simply assert without sufficient explanation that they have concluded that a particular method is irrelevant." (The valuation approach that was not used in this case was the asset-based approach.)
- Relied upon faulty assumptions regarding the equivalent value of different share blocks (of different sizes).
- Assumed that there was no market for the estate's stock, when several factors cited by the Tax Court indicated that there was a market for the stock.
- Did not address the nature of the two classes of stock issued by the corporation, whether they had cumulative voting rights or what differences existed between the two classes of stock.

In *Estate of Freeman*, the Tax Court accorded the taxpayer's expert's value no weight. Among other faults the Tax Court noted:

> [The taxpayer's expert] analyzed financial statements for the four fiscal years ended March 31, 1986 through 1989, but no interim statements between March 31, 1989 and the valuation date.
>
> He capitalized 1989 earnings at a rate he considered "appropriate" after discussing the "price/earnings ratio of Dow Jones Industrial Average at October 20, 1989, and the range of that average for 5 years." He capitalized 1989 revenues, but did not explain the capitalization rate that he used. He used a price/book value ratio, again referring to the DJIA but not to any specific comparable companies.[141]

The Tax Court ultimately made "corrections" to the IRS expert's valuation to arrive at a conclusion. The Court has to work with the evidence available to it, but it is likely that more complete evidentiary testimony on behalf of the taxpayer would have led to a lower value conclusion.[142]

In *Estate of Green v. Commissioner*,[143] the court criticized both experts. It found that the taxpayer's expert overstated a marketability discount by relying heavily on the subject company's prior transactions. The court also questioned the low range produced by restricted stock studies used by IRS's expert, and remarked that the discount he used was at the "rock bottom" of the range, rather than at the "slightly lower end" as he had inferred.

---

[140] *Estate of Kaufman*, T.C. Memo 1999-119, 1999 Tax Ct. Memo LEXIS 134 (April 6, 1999). The expert in this case wrote a very interesting rebuttal to Judge Laro's criticisms. See *Judges & Lawyers Business Valuation Update*, January 1999, pp. 11–13.

[141] *Estate of Ross H. Freeman v. Commissioner*, T.C. Memo 1996-372 (Aug. 13, 1996).

[142] See case summary and commentary in *Shannon Pratt's Business Valuation Update*, October 1996, pp. 14–15.

[143] *Estate of Mildred Green v. Commissioner*, T.C. Memo 2003-348 (December 29, 2003).

In *Polack v. Commissioner*,[144] the Tax Court found the IRS's expert's appraisal to be more credible, in part because the expert conducted a site visit and interviewed the company's president in charge of operations for substantiating evidence. In that case the court also rejected the taxpayer's uncorroborated testimony of an offsetting debt "in the face of evidence" that the asset was listed on the balance sheet.

In *Estate of Thompson v. Commissioner*,[145] the court criticized the experts for both sides for their lack of experience and for the general credibility of their valuations.

Similarly, in *Herbert Kohler et al. v. Commissioner*,[146] the court determined that it would give no weight to the valuation provided by the Commissioner's expert. First, the court noted that although he had a doctorate and a CFA, this expert was neither a member of the ASA nor the Appraisal Foundation. The court also noted that his report had omitted "the customary USPAP certification" regarding the appraiser's compliance with standards and independence.

The court then found that this expert did not understand Kohler's business since his background research on Kohler had been limited. He met with Kohler management just once, for about 2½ hours. He did obtain financial information from the company, including both the operations plan and management plan, however, and he also considered industry information. He decided the expense structure in the company's projections was wrong and invented his own for his discounted cash flow analysis, but he did not discuss his fabricated expense structure with management to test whether it was realistic. The court also held it against him that he admitted that his original report submitted to the court before trial overvalued the estate's Kohler stock by $11 million, or more than 7 percent of the value he finally decided was correct. The court said, "This is not a minor mistake. When we doubt the judgment of an expert witness on one point, we become reluctant to accept the expert's conclusions on other points." The court also concluded that his decision not to use a dividend-based method was not reasonable given that the company had periodically and historically paid large dividends.

In contrast to its conclusions about the Commissioner's expert, the court found that the taxpayers' experts were thoughtful and credible, and emphasized their sound credentials as experienced business appraisers as well as the fact that they spent a great deal of time interviewing Kohler personnel.

Because the Commissioner had the burden of proof, and because the court gave no weight to the opinion of the Commissioner's expert, the court found that the value of the estate's stock was the amount the estate reported on its return.

Two valuation dates were involved in *Okerlund v. United States*.[147] Although both experts used similar empirical data (restricted stock studies and pre-IPO studies), the experts' opinions of an appropriate discount for lack of marketability differed by 15 percentage points for each valuation date. The court found, however, that the taxpayer expert's analysis was far more detailed and persuasive than the IRS expert's, and commended the taxpayer's expert for emphasizing the pre-IPO studies, which, the court determined, were more comparable to the subject company.

---

[144] *Leo J. Polack v. Commissioner*, T.C. Memo 2002-145 (June 10, 2002), *aff'd*, 366 F.3d 608 (8th Cir. 2004).

[145] *Estate of Josephine T. Thompson v. Commissioner*, T.C. Memo 2004-174 (July 26, 2004).

[146] *Herbert Kohler et al. v. Commissioner*, T.C. Memo 2006-152; 2006 Tax Ct. Memo LEXIS 156 (July 25, 2006).

[147] *Okerlund v. United States*, 53 Fed. Cl. 341 (Fed. Ct. 2002), *motion for new trial denied*, 2003 U.S. Claims LEXIS 42 (Fed Cl. 2003), *aff'd*, 365 F.3d 1044 (Fed. Cir. 2004).

All these cases illustrate just how important it is for a valuation professional to be prepared and knowledgeable before undertaking a valuation, regardless by which party he or she has been retained.

Must Use Empirical Data to Quantify Variables

While it is appropriate to use judicial precedent in support of valuation *positions*, the analyst should use relevant market data to quantify valuation variables. Such variables would include, for example, market-derived pricing multiples, discount and capitalization rates, and magnitudes of discounts or premiums.

In *Estate of Berg*,[148] the taxpayer's expert relied on judicial precedent to quantify discounts for lack of control and lack of marketability, while the IRS experts used market-derived data. The Tax Court rejected the taxpayer's expert's reliance on judicial precedent, and found in favor of the IRS expert's position. The case was appealed to the Eighth Circuit Court of Appeals,[149] and the Tax Court's decision on the valuation was upheld.

In *Estate of Foote*, the taxpayer's expert reviewed 18 reported Tax Court cases that involved a blockage discount. Using the discounts awarded in those cases, he calculated a blockage discount of 22.5 percent. The IRS expert analyzed 16 factors relevant to the decedent's block and concluded a blockage discount of 3.3 percent, which the Court accepted because it "properly considered all the relevant factors."[150]

Sufficiency of Data

Not only do the courts prefer the use of relevant data to quantify valuation variables, they also prefer that the data be as reliable and objective as possible.

In *Estate of Deputy v. Commissioner*,[151] the taxpayer's expert applied a matrix his company created to replicate an investor's decision process, and determined a combined 44 percent lack of marketability and minority interest discount. The Tax Court preferred the taxpayer's approach because it focused on the company's unique attributes, but questioned the matrix's weighting scheme because no foundation or background had been provided to support the weighting scheme. Because the expert's company had created the matrix, the court found that it was "obviously subjective." The court then independently analyzed each category in the matrix.

In *Janda v. Commissioner*,[152] the court noted that business appraisers usually rely on "generalized" studies, such as restricted stock studies and pre-IPO studies in determining an appropriate marketability discount, and stated that the court would prefer to have more specific data for each appraisal engagement.

---

[148] *Estate of Edgar A. Berg v. Commissioner*, T.C. Memo 1991-279 (June 20, 1991).
[149] *Berg v. Commissioner*, No. 91-3198 U.S. App. (8th Cir. Oct. 5, 1992).
[150] *Estate of Foote.*
[151] *Estate of Helen A. Deputy v. Commissioner*, T.C. Memo 2003-176 (June 13, 2003).
[152] *Donald J. Janda v. Commissioner*, T.C. Memo 2001-24 (Feb. 2, 2004).

The taxpayer's expert in *Janda* used the Quantitative Marketability Discount Model (QMDM) to testify to a 65.77 percent DLOM. The court criticized the QMDM approach because it determined that slight variations in the assumptions used in the model produce dramatic differences in the results. Accordingly, it indicated that it had "grave doubts about the reliability of the QMDM model to produce reasonable discounts...."

In *Renier v. Commissioner*,[153] the court denied a proposed compensation adjustment because it was "unsupported by any objective criteria.... Some of the data were no more than a conclusory guess." The court also rejected the use of the multiple of discretionary earnings method plus certain assets because the expert "used his own judgment rather than providing adequate supporting data." The expert attempting to use this method had called it the "business broker method."[154] The court concluded that "on this record the reliability of the business broker method has not been established."

In *Knight v. Commissioner*,[155] the court noted that for each discount claimed by the taxpayer's expert, the expert did not show a relationship between the supporting data and the subject company when using average discount studies or comparable company information. The court stated that the expert's testimony was based on "erroneous factual assumptions" and that he was "acting as an advocate and that his testimony was not objective."

Robertson v. U.S.[156] demonstrates that discounts must be justified by solid data. This case involved the valuation of limited partnership interests in determining a Generation Skipping Tax (GST). The taxpayer's expert arrived at a 22 percent minority discount based on 8 percent median discounts in closed-end funds, plus 11 percent based on "structural differences" between closed-end funds and the subject limited partnership, plus 3 percent for other factors. The court rejected the 3 percent discount for other factors, finding it was unwarranted, since this was based on six factors unique to the partnership, none of which was empirically quantifiable—and many of which had already been factored into the closed-end fund analysis.

The IRS expert arrived at a 6 percent minority discount, based on an average discount for closed-end funds. The court not only found that the taxpayer's expert's analysis was more thorough, but also commented that use of the median was more appropriate than the average, which could be unduly influenced by outliers.

As to a discount for lack of marketability, the taxpayer's expert started with restricted stocks, but used "subjective factors, not supported by any empirical data," to reach 25 percent. "When questioned by the Court, [he] failed to adequately explain how he arrived at that percentage and admitted it was subject to some upward or downward adjustment."

The IRS's expert arrived at a 12.5 percent DLOM, starting with restricted stocks and supplementing that with "academic research." The court credited this expert's testimony over that of the taxpayer's expert and, therefore, concluded that a 12.5 percent DLOM was appropriate.

---

[153] *Estate of James J. Renier v. Commissioner*, T.C. Memo 2000-298 (Sept. 25, 2000).

[154] What the expert called the "business broker method" is referred to in this book as a "multiple of discretionary earnings." (See Chapter 17). The court did not reject the method; it merely rejected the lack of empirical data to support the chosen multiple.

[155] *Ina F. Knight v. Commissioner*, 115 T.C. 506 (Nov. 30, 2000).

[156] *Robertson v. U.S.*, 2006 U.S. Dist. LEXIS 1167 (N.D. Tex. Jan. 13, 2006).

Summary

Perhaps what comes through loudest and clearest in this chapter is that the courts demand strong, relevant evidence in support of each valuation position taken and each valuation variable used. Clearly, in selecting and weighting valuation approaches, the quality of relevant evidence is an important consideration.

It is also clear that the Tax Court exercises considerable discretion regarding what valuation factors are relevant under what circumstances and what constitutes adequate evidence for the quantification of the myriad of variables affecting the valuation conclusion. Both valuation analysts and lawyers should heed Judge David Laro's advice to read the relevant judicial precedent, especially the opinions of the judge who will hear their cases.

In summary, attorneys should not only retain competent valuation analysts for their clients, but they also should critically evaluate the analyst's work product in light of the anticipated judicial reaction.

References

Electronic Sources

Business Valuation Update Library, www.BVLibrary.com. Includes full text of tax case opinions involving valuation from 1990 forward and frequently referenced cases from earlier years. Searchable by keyword, name of the judge, and name of expert.

CCH Incorporated, http://tax.cchgroup.com. CCH has various on-line and CD-ROM services that provide full-text of Tax Court decisions, revenue rulings, letter rulings, and other tax-related information.

Kleinrock's Tax Library (CD-ROM). A Comprehensive tax library of tax cases (from Tax Court and other relevant courts) dating back to 1918, revenue rulings, letter rulings, technical advice memorandums, complete IRS Code and Regulations, IRS publications and other relevant information. Fully searchable by keyword or citation. Available monthly or quarterly from Kleinrock Publishing, 11300 Rockville Pike, Suite 1100, Rockville, MD 20852-3030 (877) 728-9776, www.kleinrock.com/taxsuite.

U.S. Tax Court, www.ustaxcourt.gov. Opinion section includes all applicable Tax Court opinions since 09/25/1995, posted the day they are released. Searchable by release date, petitioner's name, and judge's name.

Print Sources

Business Valuation Update. Monthly newsletter that summarizes tax cases with valuation Issues, with commentary by Shannon Pratt and other leading business appraisers. Published by Business Valuation Resources, 7412 S.W. Beaverton-Hillsdale Highway, Suite 106, Portland, OR 97215, 888 BUS-VALU, www.BVLibrary.com.

CPA Expert. Quarterly newsletter that frequently contains commentary on significant Court cases of all types by leading valuation practitioners, as well as articles on Valuation and litigation issues. Published by the American Institute of Certified Public Accountants, Harborside Financial Center, 201 Plaza Three,

3rd floor, Jersey City, New Jersey 07311-3881, (888) 777-7077, https://www.cpa2biz.com/CS2000/Products/CPA2BIZ/Publications/Sub+2/CPA+Expert.htm.

Howitt, Idelle A., ed. Federal Tax Valuation Digest. Published annually, this cumulative Digest contains summaries of all tax cases dealing with valuation issues from 1946 through the year prior to publication. Contains various indexes by keyword, Judge, court, case name, and valuation issue. Published by Warren, Gorham & Lamont, 31 St. James Avenue, Boston, Massachusetts, (800) 431-9025, www.ria.thomson.com.

Laro, David, and Shannon P. Pratt, *Business Valuation and Taxes: Procedure, Law, and Practice* (Hoboken, N.J.: John Wiley and Sons, 2005).

Valuation Case Digest. Quarterly newsletter summarizing court cases relating to valuation cases. The last page of each issue provides information on how to find the complete decision of each case (mostly from free, on-line sources). Published by Valuation Information, Inc. 8898 Commerce Rd., Ste 3C, Commerce, MI 48382, www.valuationinformation.com/otherservices.

Articles

Abraham, Mel. Kerr V. Commissioner: "A Christmas Gift for Taxpayers and Family Limited Partnerships." *Business Valuation Review*, June 2000, Vol. 19, No. 2.

Fiore, Owen, G. "Lappo and Peracchio—New Tax Court FLP Gift Tax Victories for Taxpayers." *CCH Business Valuation Alert*, January 2004, pp. 3, 7–9.

Gibbs, Larry and Mark Schwartzman. "Audit and Litigation Issues Pertaining to the Formation of Family Owned & Controlled Partnerships & Limited Liability Companies." Presentation and Reviewed Articles, *BV Papers*, January 2000.

Greene, Martin, and Douglas Schnapp. "Oppressed Shareholders' Rights Can Affect Estate and Gift Tax Valuation." *The CPA Journal*, February 2001.

Hall, Lance. "What You Don't Know About Fair Market Value Will Hurt You." Estate And Gift Tax Valuation. *Valuation Strategies*, March/April 2006, Vol. 9, No. 4.

Chapter 29

Buy-Sell Agreements

One of the most critical planning tasks facing a business owner is providing for the continuity of the enterprise. A buy-sell agreement can effectively prevent many potential problems regarding disposition of stock or a partnership interest of a departing or deceased stockholder or partner. The buy-sell agreement can accomplish the following objectives:

1. Smooth ownership transition while continuing the operation of the business
2. Provide a mechanism with which an owner can liquidate the ownership interest in the event of death, disability, termination, divorce, or retirement
3. Reduce uncertainty for noncontrolling shareholders
4. Document a framework to quantify the efforts of management's stewardship and the success of business operations
5. Prevent the ownership interest from being sold or otherwise transferred to any party not acceptable to the other owners
6. Provide litigation support or dispute resolution procedures regarding equity valuation matters, such as shareholder marital dissolution issues, shareholder disputes, or business interruption and insurance issues
7. Provide a payment scheme that is affordable in the least disruptive manner to the subject company
8. Provide a benchmark for valuation of the entire business or partial interest for sale, initial public offering, or collateralization purposes

It is important to recognize that the makeup of the ownership of closely held businesses is quite varied. Some closely held businesses are owned by members of a family, all of whom work at the company. Some businesses (for instance, some medical practices) are owned by professionals who are in essence owner/managers. Some closely held businesses are primarily owned by one individual who exercises the prerogatives of control. And, some businesses are owned by passive owners (outsiders who do not work at the company). As a result of these various ownership situations, there are many types of buy-sell agreements.

In addition, the analyst should be aware that provisions affecting the sale of stock may be found not only in these separate agreements, but also in company bylaws, Articles of Incorporation, Actions of Shareholders, LLC Operating Agreements, and other Corporate Regulation. Therefore it is important that the analyst ask and be familiar with the terms of any agreements that restrict the transfer of stock.

Types of Buy-Sell Agreements

Buy-sell agreements used in closely held corporations or partnerships to place restrictions on transfer and to provide for liquidation of the interest of a withdrawing or deceased shareholder or partner or for a variety of other reasons fall into one of three categories:

1. *Repurchase agreements* (also called *entity purchase agreements* or *redemption agreements*), in which the issuing corporation or partnership buys the interest from the transferring party or from the estate of the deceased party.

2. *Cross-purchase agreements*, in which one or more other individuals or entities buy the interest from the transferring party or from the estate of the deceased party.

3. *Hybrid agreements* (also called *wait-and-see agreements*), which usually allow the issuer first priority to buy the interest and other stockholders or partners the second-place option to buy. Such agreements can be drafted to allow both the company and the other shareholders the opportunity of waiting until after the date of death to determine which is in the better tax and liquidity condition to purchase the shares.

4. *Tag along rights* often call for the sale of interest on the same terms if the controlling owner sells. These have become more common in recent years.

Each type of agreement may be either mandatory—that is, binding on both parties—or optional on the part of one of the parties, usually the purchaser. Sometimes agreements are written with one set of buy-out options during an owner's lifetime and with another set of options for a decedent's estate.

It is not necessary that the same agreement apply to all the owners of a particular entity. One or a few owners may be subject to an agreement while others are not, or different owners may be subject to different agreements. For example, it is common to find noncontrolling owners of an enterprise subject to a buy-sell agreement while the controlling owner is not. In limited partnerships, provisions applicable to limited partners normally differ from those applicable to general partners.

It is not necessary for the price to apply in all events. The valuation provisions of the buy-sell agreement may be affected by the event that triggered them. For example, some buy-sell agreements price the subject shares differently if the shareholder's employment is terminated voluntarily rather than involuntarily, or if the employee leaves to go to work for a competitor.

The provisions of any buy-sell agreement should, of course, be designed to best carry out the objectives of all the parties. From a seller's viewpoint, an important objective is to provide liquidity in the event of withdrawal from the business or death. From a purchaser's viewpoint, important objectives include continuity of ownership, management without possible interference from outside parties and affordability. From the viewpoints of both seller and purchaser, an additional purpose is to establish the circumstances under which the agreement will become effective and a means of determining the price and terms of the transaction.

One consideration in the choice between the cross-purchase versus redemption form of buy-sell agreement is the number of shareholders or partners involved. The more there are, the more complicated the cross-purchase plan becomes relative to the redemption. In the cross-purchase arrangement, the number of party-to-party relationships, life insurance policies required, and so on rises exponentially with the number of parties involved. One solution to these problems is to create an insurance trust agreement, but this requires drafting another complicated agreement. In the redemption type of agreement, the corporation owns the life insurance policies, so there are no administrative or tax problems arising from the necessity to transfer policies at the death of one party (except for the possible alternative minimum tax, discussed later).

Naturally, the tax implications will be a major consideration in deciding which type of agreement to use. The tax implications, which are complicated and often subject to change, are beyond the scope of this book. Several references on tax implications appear in the bibliography at the end of this chapter.

Valuation Provisions of the Buy-Sell Agreement

The provision for valuation is a critical element of the buy-sell agreement. The parties have a great deal of flexibility in structuring this provision, but often it is neglected or done hastily and thus eventually turns out to be unfair to one or the other party.

Need for Clear Direction

The importance of having the valuation provisions of the buy-sell agreement thought through thoroughly by someone who understands valuation and is understood by all parties before the agreement is signed cannot be overemphasized. Attitudes and relationships change, and one cannot assume that any ambiguity in the buy-sell agreement will be resolved amicably when the time comes to consummate a transaction pursuant to the agreement. Most disputes relating to buy-sell agreements arise because one or several of the details of the agreement either were inadequately defined or were misunderstood by one or more of the parties.

For example, in one arbitration case over the value of a business interest under a buy-sell agreement, the document was so ambiguous about the applicable valuation date that the valuation of the interest as of four different dates was required so that the arbitration panel could select the most applicable one. The value differences on the various dates were considerable, because the business was undergoing a series of significant and somewhat unpredictable changes during the relevant time period. The ambiguity as to the applicable valuation date substantially increased the time and cost involved for the analysis, as well as the uncertainty of the outcome of the arbitration.

Even when the valuation criterion for the buy-sell agreement is simply book value, there can be disagreements over the definition of terms. Book value could be that determined for tax purposes or for business purposes, or financial reporting under GAAP; on a cash basis or on an accrual basis. It could be computed as of the date of death, as of the end of the month preceding death, as of the end of the last regular accounting period of the entity, as of the end of the fiscal year of the entity nearest the date of death, or as of some other date.

Chapters 3 and 16 discussed the fact that the fair market value of a minority ownership interest usually is less than a pro rata share of the value of the entire enterprise. Many parties to buy-sell agreements have been unpleasantly surprised to learn that the fair market value of their interest (the standard of value specified in the agreement that they hastily read and signed) was less than a proportionate share of the total enterprise value.

Buy-sell agreements may specify that the shares be valued strictly at their fair market value as noncontrolling ownership interests, at a proportionate share of the enterprise value with no discount for lack of control and/or no discount for lack of marketability, or at a specified percentage discount from a proportionate share of total enterprise value.

We suggest that the reader contemplating a buy-sell agreement read Chapter 2, "Defining the Assignment," carefully and be sure that the agreement covers all the relevant points. In addition, the terms of payment should be specified. The payment terms may differ under various circumstances, and the agreement may allow the company some flexibility, making allowance for the company's ability to pay. *The key point to keep in mind is that the buy-sell agreement is a legal document that will have to stand on its own at the time a triggering event occurs.*

One unique aspect of the valuation provision in a buy-sell agreement, as opposed to other valuation problems, is the extreme uncertainty concerning when a future event that triggers a transaction under the agreement will occur. This is one of the key reasons why there is no single approach to the problem of establishing the price, or even the method for a buy-sell agreement that one can recommend as completely satisfactory for all situations.

Most of the mechanisms for setting prices in buy-sell agreements generally fall into one or a combination of three categories:

1. Some type of formula based on the financial statements, such as book value, some type of adjusted book value, capitalization of earnings, or some combination of such variables
2. Negotiation among the parties
3. Independent outside appraisal

Formula Approaches

Formula approaches for setting the price in a buy-sell agreement can easily turn out to be unfair to one party or the other when the transaction eventually occurs. As this book indicates, the valuation process should reflect a complex set of factors—usually too complex to be adequately embodied in a formula. A formula that might produce an appropriate value in one year might not do so in another year when circumstances in the company and the economy differ. For example, in the case of *St. Louis County Bank v. United States*, the court refused to honor for estate tax purposes an agreement that gave a corporation the right to purchase the decedent's stock under a formula that produced a zero value, even though the formula may have originally produced an acceptable value.[1]

It is highly unlikely that the price established by a formula at the time of signing will be even close to the value of the interest at the time of the triggering event, which could be many years later. For this reason, I highly discourage the use of formulas in high-sell agreements.

Negotiation Among the Parties

Many practitioners believe that negotiation among the owners—usually annually—is the best approach to setting the buy-sell agreement price. The parties themselves usually have the most intimate knowledge of their own estate objectives as well as of their attitudes toward one another. They may also have a better idea than anyone else about the future operations of the business; in most cases, however, owners would benefit from professional outside guidance on its worth.

The problems with this approach arise when the annual valuation is neglected or when the parties cannot agree. In our experience, the annual valuations seem to be neglected more often than not. The buy-sell agreement must provide for dealing with both of these eventualities.

---

[1] *St. Louis County Bank v. United States*, 674 F.2d 1207 (8th Cir. 1982).

The most common method of handling potential neglect of the annual valuation is to stipulate that if the price is not set annually on a timely basis, after some period (typically 12 to 24 months following the last price agreement), the price-fixing mechanism automatically reverts to an independent appraisal. In that, it is necessary to either name a qualified appraisal firm or specify the method by which the appraiser will be selected. If a firm or person is named, provision must be made for an alternative selection procedure if the named appraiser is unable to serve.

O'Neal and Thompson offer the following guidance regarding provision for selecting appraisers in the buy-sell agreement. This guidance would apply whether appraisers are to be used in any case or to be used only in the event of inability to agree through negotiation:

> If the price of shares is to be fixed by appraisal, the names of the appraisers or a method of choosing them must be specified; and a statement should be made that the decision of a majority of the appraisers will be binding.... A typical appraisal provision states that the optionee or purchaser, as the case may be, shall select one appraiser, the offeror or vendor a second, and that the two appraisers shall choose a third.... Occasionally an independent third party, such as a corporate fiduciary, is given the power to appoint the third appraiser; or the third appraiser is designated by office... Sometimes the appraisers are selected in advance and designated by name.... If that is done, provision must be made for a method of appointing substitutes should the designated appraisers die, become incapacitated, or refuse to serve.[2]

Some buy-sell agreements provide for two or three appraisers to submit reports to an arbitration panel, which will make the final determination in case of a dispute, but this can get quite expensive.

One suggestion for avoiding the problem of neglecting the annual valuation is to ask one of the company's professional advisers, such as the attorney, accountant, insurance agent, or appraiser, to put a memo in his or her "tickler" file to remind the company to make its annual valuation.

Reversion to outside appraisal approaches is also the most common type of provision for dealing with circumstances in which the parties cannot agree on a value through negotiation.

Exhibit 29–1 is a sample valuation article for a buy-sell agreement, providing for negotiation and for the price to be determined by an arbitration panel if negotiation fails.

Buy-sell agreements with negotiation-based pricing for enterprises in which a family group holds 50 percent or greater controlling ownership interests are not likely to be regarded by the IRS as binding for estate and gift tax filings, because of the presumption that the family members have a donative intent toward each other that prevents impartial arm's-length transactions.

Independent Outside Appraisal

The advantages of having a formal, independent outside appraisal, kept current with periodic updates, are many. From a business planning perspective, the typical

---

[2] F. Hodge O'Neal (deceased) and Robert B. Thompson, *O'Neal and Thompson's Close Corporations and LLCs: Law and Practice*, revised 3rd ed. (Eagan, MN: Thomson West, 2004, supplemented 2005), pp. 7-147–7-148.

Exhibit 29–1

Sample Valuation Provision for Buy-Sell Agreement (Corporation Stock Redemption Example)

As soon as practical after the end of each fiscal year, the stockholders shall agree on the value per share of the stock that is applicable to this agreement. Such value will be set forth in Schedule A, which shall be dated, signed by each stockholder, and attached hereto. Such value shall be binding on both the corporation and the estate of any deceased stockholder whose date of death is within one year of the last dated and signed Schedule A.

If more than a year has elapsed between the date when Schedule A was last signed and the date of death of a deceased stockholder, then the value per share shall be determined, as of the date of death of the stockholder, by mutual agreement between the surviving stockholders and the personal representative or administrator of the deceased stockholder's estate.

If the surviving stockholders and the personal representative of the deceased stockholder's estate are unable to agree upon such a value within 90 days after such personal representative or administrator has qualified to administer the estate of the deceased stockholder, then such value shall be determined by binding arbitration. Either party may give written notice of such binding arbitration pursuant to this agreement to the other party. Within 30 days of such notice of arbitration, each party shall appoint one arbitrator. Within 30 days of the appointment of the two arbitrators, the arbitrators so appointed will select a third arbitrator. The first two arbitrators will have sole discretion in the selection of the third arbitrator, except that he must be an individual or qualified representative of a firm that regularly engages, as a primary occupation, in the professional appraisal of businesses or business interests. In the event that the first two arbitrators are unable to agree on a third arbitrator within 30 days of their appointment, the Executive Director of the ABC Trade Association shall appoint the third arbitrator.

The standard of value to be used by the arbitrators shall be fair market value of the shares being valued as of the date of death, under the assumption that the stockholder is deceased and the corporation has collected the proceeds, if any, of insurance on the life of the deceased stockholder payable to the corporation.

Each arbitrator shall use his sole discretion in determining the amount of investigation he considers necessary in arriving at a determination of the value of the shares. The corporation shall make available on a timely basis all books and records requested by any arbitrator, and all material made available to any one arbitrator shall be made available to all arbitrators.

Concurrence by at least two of the three arbitrators shall constitute a binding determination of value. The value concluded by the arbitrators shall be reported to the corporation and to the personal representative or administrator of the estate of the deceased in writing, signed by the arbitrators concurring as to the concluded value, within 90 days of the appointment of the third arbitrator unless an extension of time has been agreed upon between the corporation and the personal representatives of the estate.

The corporation and the estate shall each be responsible for the fees and expenses of the arbitrators they appoint. The fees and expenses of the third arbitrator shall be divided equally between the corporation and the estate.

---

strong management/ownership relationship in a closely held business often requires a valuation study in order to support various ownership strategies, business directions, and investment alternatives. A formal, professionally prepared appraisal incorporates current economic conditions and is more likely to assure fair treatment to all concerned. When an independent valuation program is implemented in a consistent manner during cordial points in time, the parties have an opportunity to challenge and discuss the results with less bias and an acceptable valuation philosophy is developed. A common compliment given to professional appraisers is that their annual investigation provides not only an opinion as to the value of a closely held business, but also an analysis of that business from a management consultant's point of view.

The obvious disadvantage of the formal appraisal with regular updates is the cost. However, the appraisal does not necessarily have to result in quite as lengthy and detailed a report as an employee stock ownership plan (ESOP) valuation, since there usually are fewer beneficiaries to be satisfied and the appraiser and the directors need not be concerned with meeting Employee Retirement Income Security Act (ERISA) requirements.

Whether or not a full, written appraisal report is prepared when pricing the buy-sell agreement, some degree of guidance from an independent professional business appraiser usually is helpful in arriving at a value that will be equitable to all parties and will forestall subsequent disputes.

Understanding an Agreement's Pricing Philosophy

Since business valuations rarely can be made with undisputable precision, there usually will be some relevant range of reasonable prices that will be acceptable to all the parties. Some flexibility in setting the price is possible.

Appraisers of real estate, equipment, or other physical property informally assert that their appraisals are accurate to within plus or minus 10 percent. However, few business interests can be appraised within such tolerances. Just look at how widely the prices of many publicly traded stocks fluctuate over relatively short periods. For many closely held businesses, it is not unreasonable for the high end of a value range to be 50 percent above the low end. For highly dynamic or speculative businesses, the reasonable range may be much wider.

Considering this flexibility, if the buy-sell agreement price is to be determined by an independent outside appraiser for unrelated parties, the appraiser can present the parties with a relevant price range, and the parties can make a decision based on their wishes. Of course, it is not uncommon for the various parties to the agreement to have differing circumstances and objectives that motivate them toward opposite pricing philosophies. In general, in arm's-length bargaining one would expect parties who anticipate withdrawing earlier to opt for a higher value and parties who expect to survive in the business the longest to choose a lower value. For tax valuations, or other valuations subject to the fair market value standard, that standard requires the appraiser to consider only those motives typical of hypothetical, arm's-length willing buyers and willing sellers.

The consensus among the many articles that address this subject leans from the middle of the range to a somewhat conservative valuation when setting up a buy-sell agreement, whether the value standard is one of fair market value or some other standard. There are several valid arguments for inclining toward a conservative value. One is that, recognizing that valuation is an imprecise matter, the parties tend to feel that they will enhance their favorable working relationship by leaning over backwards (a little) to be fair to one another. We have encountered some feeling that if some benefit is to be gained in the pricing by one party or another, it most properly should accrue to those who will remain with the business. This attitude is based on a recognition that none of the parties knows exactly when or for which owner a buy-sell agreement transaction may first be necessary, but that the surviving parties will bear the dual burden of carrying off the financing and payment of the transaction and of carrying on the management of the company during this process.

In a very close family situation, it is common to find the desire to minimize the price so as to lessen tax consequences. In these instances, it is especially important to have thoroughly documented justification of the price or basis selected, since the combination of a low price and a non-arm's-length family situation certainly will invite the scrutiny of the IRS and the state taxing authorities, not to mention the minority shareholder.

Terms and Funding

Two decisions that necessarily are integrally related in creating the buy-sell agreement are the provisions for payment terms and for funding.

Terms can run anywhere from immediate cash to payments spread out over several years, usually with interest. Funding can come from life insurance, from corporate funds in the case of a redemption, or from personal assets in the case of a cross-purchase. In some cases, borrowings may be used to fund either a redemption or a cross-purchase. In order for a buy-sell agreement to work, it is essential that funding adequate for carrying out its terms be available one way or another. Thus, provision for funding is an essential ingredient for a viable buy-sell agreement.

Term Payment Provisions

From the purchaser's viewpoint, the typical reason for preferring a term payment program to cash is to ease the funding burden. From the seller's viewpoint, the attraction of an installment payment program is the spreading out of the tax on the seller's gain over several of the seller's tax years. The seller, however, becomes a creditor subject to credit risk.

If a term payment plan is used, careful consideration must be given to establishing the interest rate, because this is an integral part of the pricing decision. Attention also should be given to the matter of collateral or other protection to ensure that the seller will receive the contractual payments in the full amount and on a timely basis.

As discussed elsewhere in this book, if the interest rate on a term contract is below the market interest rate for similar instruments at the time of the event that triggers the transaction, the cash equivalent value the seller receives will be less than the contract's face value. Similarly, if the interest rate is above the relevant market rate, the cash equivalent value will be greater than the face value. The arithmetic for computing the present value of a contract bearing interest above or below a comparable market rate is shown in Chapter 9 (see Exhibit 9–1).

However, in setting the interest rate in the buy-sell agreement, we face the problem that market interest rates fluctuate considerably over time, and we have no way of knowing at what time in the future the buy-sell transaction will be triggered nor what the market level of interest rates will be at that time. There are several possible approaches to dealing with this dilemma.

One approach is simply to agree on an interest rate despite these uncertainties and hope that it does not prove grossly off the mark in the future. If the price under the buy-sell agreement is set by annual negotiation or appraisal, the interest rate could be reviewed and adjusted annually at the same time. Another alternative is to set the interest rate by tying it to some index of interest rates at the time of the transaction. The interest rate index used should represent intermediate- to long-term rates, since such rates fluctuate less than short-term rates and would be more appropriate for a term payment contract. The yield on *Barron's* intermediate grade bonds or *Moody's* BBB bonds could provide benchmarks for setting the interest rate. The agreement could specify that the index rate or some specified amount above or below it be used depending on the credit of the company involved, the degree of security provided, and the desires of the parties to the agreement.

It might be appropriate to use an interest rate index that represents securities whose maturities coincide with the payout terms of the buy-sell agreement. For example, an index representing five-year maturities can be used if the payout term is five years. The *Federal Reserve Bulletin* gives indexes of interest rates on U.S. Treasury bonds maturing in 1, 2, 3, 5, 7, 10, 20, and 30 years.

Income tax considerations could suggest the desirability of some trade-of between the price and the interest rate. The portion of the contract payments designated as interest will be a deductible expense to the buyer and income to the seller. The portion of the contract payments designated as principal will not be deductible to the buyer (unless there is an ESOP involved) and will be taxed as capital gains to the seller to the extent that they exceed the seller's basis. Thus, if the seller is in a low tax bracket and the buyer in a high one, it may be advantageous to structure the program to increase the interest rate and lower the price. Conversely, if the seller is in a high tax bracket and the buyer in a low one, it may be advantageous to lower the interest rate and increase the price.

Minimum interest rates based on U.S. Treasury rates are required for transactions among family members, and such applicable federal rates are published regularly.

The buy-sell agreement should also provide for adequate collateral or security for the seller in a term payment agreement. Security could take the form of a mortgage or lien on physical assets, such as real estate or equipment. It is also common to require that certain financial criteria, such as some minimum level of working capital, specified minimum current ratio, and specified maximum debt-to-equity ratio, be met. A typical sanction for enforcing such protective standards would be to provide that the entire amount become due and payable immediately if any of the standards are violated. These are the types of protections that a bank would require in making a loan, and many people feel that a seller of a business interest should be no less protected.

Funding the Buy-Sell Agreement with Life Insurance

Life insurance can serve as an important source of funding for stock purchase agreements pertaining to deceased shareholders. The advantages of using life insurance for this purpose are several. First, deceased shareholders' estates get paid in cash, eliminating their need to rely on the corporation's continuing prosperity. Second, the corporation's investment in the cash value of an ordinary life policy is a business asset. Third, any excess insurance the corporation carries over and above the value of the stock purchase agreement can be retained as earned surplus.

In general, the use of life insurance can fulfill three basic needs:

1. Liquidation of the stock of a departed or disabled stockholder, either by the corporation or by other stockholders
2. Payment of estate taxes
3. Provision for continuity of the business after loss of a key person

The owner should constantly monitor the value of the business in order to know how much life insurance is needed to fulfill these needs and update the coverage accordingly. The owner should seek out and periodically consult with a professional who knows how to apply life insurance to businesses, especially the tax implications of the many types of policies and the various configurations of ownership and beneficiaries.

For example, under current tax laws, the receipt of life insurance proceeds from a policy owned by a corporation can give rise to additional corporate taxable income under the Alternative Minimum Tax calculations and may need to be included in the value of the corporation.

Liquidation of Departed or Disabled Owner's Stock. The beneficiary of life insurance purchased for the purpose of acquiring a deceased owner's stock is logically determined by the buy-sell agreement: the corporation is the beneficiary in connection with a repurchase agreement, and the various stockholders are the beneficiaries in connection with a cross-purchase agreement. The repurchase agreement, with the corporation as the beneficiary of the life insurance policies, usually is simpler administratively if there are three or more stockholders involved, but tax and other considerations may outweigh this advantage.

Funding of the purchase of a stockholder's interest if the stockholder is terminated but not deceased can be accomplished through an annuity or through life insurance with a cash value feature. The matter of insurance for covering needs in the event of the stockholder's permanent disability often is overlooked, but such needs are a common occurrence.

Payment of Estate Taxes. Estate taxes become a problem only to the extent that the estate's value exceeds the amounts exempted from estate taxes, under the unified credit, as discussed in Chapter 27. If the value exceeds the amount eligible for the unified credit exemption, the estate tax liability can be estimated from the estate and gift tax table in Chapter 27 (Exhibit 27–1). Provision for payment of the estimated amount of estate tax can be made with life insurance in that amount, as long as the insurance proceeds are structured so that they are not taxable as part of the estate.

Providing for Business Continuity. Life insurance payable to the corporation can also provide funding to ensure continuity of the business following the loss of a key person. It is common to find a key person contributing far more to the business's annual cash flow than he or she is taking out in salary and benefits. The company can be protected against the financial impact of the loss of such a valuable person by estimating the potential earnings or cash flow shortfall to be compensated for until the key person can be replaced and the replacement brought up to speed. The company can then cover the estimated amount of that risk with life insurance on the key person.

Review of Prior Life Insurance Funding. If funding of the foregoing requirements has been provided for through life insurance taken out in prior years, that insurance should be reviewed as to both amount and type.

The necessary amounts of insurance can change for several reasons. One, of course, is general inflation. Another likely reason is the increased value of the business due to its success. Still another could be changes in the makeup of the business's ownership. Finally, the value of a particular person in the role of a key person can change over time due to a variety of circumstances.

There is a wide variety of life insurance products available and important changes continue to occur at this writing. A review of the life insurance funding may very well reveal new products that are better suited to the owner's objectives and/or are more cost efficient.

Restrictions on Transfer

Most buy-sell agreements contain restrictions on the transfer of the ownership interest.

This is of particular importance for corporations who have elected to be taxed as an S corporation. These agreements should prohibit shareholders from transferring stock to anyone in such a way as would terminate the S election.

Generally, restrictions on transfer require that, before transferring shares to any outside party, they first be offered to the corporation and/or to other stockholders/members. The price at which the shares must be offered to the company and/or other stockholders may be the price offered by the outside party. More often, however, the price is the one that would be determined by the buy-sell agreement. Such restrictions often are determinative of, or at least useful evidence of, value for other purposes since they limit both the shares' marketability and the potential amount received for them.

In a case where there is more than one class of stock, the buy-sell agreement may provide that the shares automatically be converted from one class to another if transferred, such as from voting to nonvoting.

If the parties to a buy-sell agreement desire to have restrictive transfer provisions apply to involuntary transfers, such as in the cases of divorces or foreclosures when the securities have been hypothecated and a loan defaulted, such extensions of the restrictions should be spelled out in the agreement. Otherwise, courts may rule that the restrictions do not apply to such involuntary transfers.

Buy-Sell Agreement Values for Estate and Gift Tax Valuation under Chapter 14

Generally speaking, in valuations involving family controlled entities the price as determined by a buy-sell agreement will be binding on the IRS for estate tax purposes if the value falls within the range of what would be determined under Revenue Ruling 59-60 at the time of death. Of course, that value would be binding even in the absence of a buy-sell agreement, but it usually is easier to substantiate—or at least usually more readily acceptable to the IRS—in the presence of a buy-sell agreement, especially to the extent that the value in the agreement was established by arm's-length negotiation.

A review of the law, the literature, and the court cases indicates that the most important criterion is the extent to which the price was established on an arm's-length basis. Following is the complete text of Section 8 of Revenue Ruling 59-60, which addresses the effect of stockholder agreements on gift and estate tax values:

> Frequently in the valuation of closely held stock for estate and gift tax purposes, it will be found that the stock is subject to an agreement restricting its sale or transfer. Where shares of stock were acquired by a decedent subject to an option reserved by the issuing corporation to repurchase at a certain price, the option price is usually accepted as the fair market value for estate tax purposes. See Rev. Rul. 54-76, C.B. 1954-1, 194. However, in such cases the option price is not determinative of fair market value for gift tax purposes. Where the option, or buy and sell agreement, is the result of voluntary action by the stockholders and is binding during the life as well as at the death of the stockholders, such agreement may or may not, depending upon the circumstances of each case, fix the value for estate tax purposes. However, such agreement is a factor to be considered, with other relevant factors, in determining fair market value. Where the stockholder is free to dispose of his [or her] shares during life and the option is to become effective only upon his [or her] death, the fair market value is not limited

to the option price. It is always necessary to consider the relationship of the parties, the relative number of shares held by the decedent, and other material facts, to determine whether the agreement represents a bona fide business arrangement or is a device to pass the decedent's shares to the natural objects of his [or her] bounty for less than an adequate and full consideration in money or money's worth. In this connection, see Rev. Rul. 157 C.B. 1953-2, 255, and Rev. Rul. 189, C.B. 1953-2, 29.[3]

It should also be pointed out that a value fixed by a buy-sell agreement may be legally binding on the estate for transaction purposes even if it is not binding on the IRS for estate tax purposes. This could result in a situation where the estate ends up paying taxes on a value substantially higher than the price the estate actually receives.

Valuation Requirements under Section 2703

The Chapter 14 special valuation rules are applied to all applicable transfers after October 8, 1990. Section 2703 of Chapter 14 deals with buy-sell agreements, options, and other similar influences on value for estate or gift tax transfers.

Section 2703 applies to any family-owned business in which the family members (defined in the regulations) control 50 percent or more of the vote or value of the company.[4] Any buy-sell agreement, restriction, or other similar factor relating to the right to use or sell the property will be ignored for estate, gift, and generation-skipping tax purposes unless the agreement meets all three of the following tests:

1. It is a bona fide business arrangement.
2. It must not be a device to transfer the property to the natural objects of the transferor's bounty (such as family members) for less than adequate and full consideration in money or money's worth.
3. Its terms must be comparable to similar arrangements entered into by persons in an arm's-length transaction.

Because of the effective date of the statute, many old buy-sell agreements will be "grandfathered" under the law, and transactions under these agreements need only follow the requirements in Revenue Ruling 59-60 and any court decisions involving similar fact patterns. The regulations for Section 2703 make it plain that any grandfathered agreement that is substantially modified after October 8, 1990, will thereafter be required to follow the rules under Section 2703. The IRS defines "substantial modification" as any change in the buy-sell agreement or other restriction that would alter (beyond a *de minimis* amount) the quality, timing, or amount of the rights of the parties to the agreement. Also, if any parties of a generation younger than those originally participating in the agreement as of October 8, 1990, are added by voluntary modification of the agreement (i.e., added as parties to the agreement by some discretionary method other than by a mandatory action such as inheritance), this will be considered a substantial modification.

---

[3] Rev. Rul. 59-60, 1959-1 C.B. 237, Section 8.

[4] We find the use of 50 percent as a threshold for control an odd choice. A 50 percent interest in a company is not per se a controlling interest, but merely a right to deadlock the company's decision-making process.

Changes that are necessary to update the value of an agreement or restriction to make the value or terms of the agreement more nearly approximate fair market value are not to be considered material changes. An example of this would be a formula-based change in the earnings multiple utilized to calculate a value under the agreement. Failure to update an agreement requiring, say, an annual determination of value, constitutes a substantial modification.

What kind of formula-based value will work with buy-sell agreements under Section 2703? Under the pre-Chapter 14 rules, all that was basically necessary to make a buy-sell agreement (or other restriction) binding for estate and gift taxes was:

1. The agreement be binding during life as well as at death.
2. The agreement create a determinable value as of a specifically determinable date.
3. The agreement have at least some bona fide business purpose (this could include the promotion of orderly family ownership and management succession, so this was a reasonably easy test to meet).
4. The agreement resulted in a fair market value for the subject business interest when it was originally executed. Often, the buy-sell agreement value would generate future date of death or gift date values substantially below what the fair market value otherwise would have been for the subject interest—even though the value was reasonable when the agreement was made.

In the regulations on this fourth test, it was noted that this standard is not met by showing a few isolated comparables, but rather the general business practice in the industry. If several different valuation formulas are in general use, it is permissible to utilize only one of these.[5]

If more than one right or restriction is set forth in the buy-sell agreement, each is tested separately under the rules of Section 2703.

Bibliography

Abatemarco, Michael J., and Alfred Cavallaro. "The Importance of Buy-Sell Agreements for Closely Held Corporations." *CPA Journal*, February 1992, pp. 57–59.

Adams, Roy M., David A. Herpe, and James R. Carey. "Buy-Sell Agreements after Chapter 14." *Trusts & Estates*, May 1993, pp. 22–32.

Bell, Lawrence L. "Valuation of Buy-Sell Agreements under Chapter 14 of the Internal Revenue Code." *Journal of the American Society of CLU & ChFC*, September 1992, pp. 48–53.

Bogdanski, John A. "Buy-Sell Agreements and Marketability Discounts." *Estate Planning*, December 2004.

_____ "Hard Times for Buy-Sell Agreements." *Estate Planning*, June 1998, pp. 235–239.

"Buy-Sell Agreement Ignored in Valuing Decedent's Stock." *Estate Planning*, January 1998, pp. 32–35.

---

[5] Regulations, Section 25.2702-1(b)(4).

Drake, Dwight J., Kent Whiteley, and Timothy J. McDevitt. "The Ten Most Common Mistakes of Buy-Sell Agreements." *Journal of Financial Planning*, July 1992, pp. 104–12.

Ellentuck, Albert B. "Establishing the Estate Value of Stock by Using a Buy-Sell Agreement." *The Tax Adviser*, September 1998, pp. 637–38.

_____. "Reviewing a Buy/Sell Agreement." *The Tax Adviser*, November 1999, pp. 809–12.

Gamble, E. James. "How Do We Handle Buy-Sell Agreements under Chapter 14?" *Trusts & Estates*, March 1991, pp. 38–46.

_____."Tax Law Notes: Buy-Sell Agreements, Section 2703, and the Final Regulations." *Michigan Bar Journal*, July 1992, pp. 664–66.

Hall, Lance S. "Lack of Outside Appraisal Dooms Buy-Sell Formula Value Fix for Estate Tax Purposes." *Valuation Strategies*, March/April 2005.

Howitt, Idelle A. "Estate of Cameron W. Bommer." *Valuation Strategies*, September/October 1998, pp. 38–39, 42.

Kasner, Jerry A. "The IRS Loses One in the Buy-Sell Valuation Battle." *Tax Notes*, April 12, 1993, pp. 231–32.

Kelly, James P. III. "Waiving Rights under Buy-Sell Agreement Affects Stock Value." *Estate Planning*, September/October 1991, pp. 284–91.

Kimball, Curtis R. "Buy-Sell Agreements Rejected in *True* Case." *Willamette Management Associates Insights*, Autumn 2001.

Mezzullo, Louis A. "Buy-Sell Agreements after Chapter 14." *Trusts & Estates*, June 1994, pp. 49–59.

Porter, John W. "Buy-Sell Agreements: *True* Provision Does Not Control Value for Estate Tax Purposes." *Business Valuation Alert*, April 2005.

Strouse, Jonathan E. "Redemption and Cross-Purchase Buy-Sell Agreements: A Comparison." *Practical Accountant*, October 1991, pp. 44–53.

Wise, Richard M. "Buy-Sell Valuation." *Canadian Tax Highlights*, June 22, 1993, pp. 44–45.

Zuckerman, Michael H., and John G. Grall. "Corporate Buy-Sell Agreements as Estate and Business Planning Tools." *Estate Planning*, December 2001.

Chapter 30

Valuation for Income Tax Purposes

Introduction

First, this chapter discusses many of the reasons to value business entities and business interests for federal income tax purposes. These income taxation–related valuation purposes may be grouped into two general categories: (1) tax planning opportunities and (2) compliance requirements. Tax planning opportunities include valuations that may cause the deferral of income tax liability or that may reduce a current or future income tax liability. Tax compliance requirements typically involve transactions that trigger an immediate taxable event that must be quantified or otherwise measured in terms of value.

As part of this discussion, we list several income taxation transactions where a valuation is relevant. We describe the taxation–related reason for the valuation requirement—often in terms of a reference to the appropriate statutory authority, administrative rulings, or judicial precedent. And, we discuss any unusual or particular valuation considerations that relate directly to that particular taxation-related valuation requirement.

Second, we briefly discuss several of the valuation-related federal income tax penalties. Valuation practitioners, tax practitioners, and taxpayers should all be mindful of these penalties when accounting for a taxable transaction were valuation is relevant.

Third, we briefly discuss a common state income taxation–related reason to conduct a valuation analysis. This common reason relates to the state income tax consequences of an intercompany (and interstate) transfer of corporate intellectual properties—and the resulting intercompany (and interstate) royalty payments related to the intellectual property transfer.

This chapter excludes consideration of federal gift and estate tax–related valuation issues, which were addressed in Chapter 27. This chapter also excludes a discussion of state and local ad valorem property tax valuation issues. These issues will be addressed in Chapter 34.

As with all chapters in this book, this chapter is written from a valuation and economic analysis perspective. It is not intended to offer legal, accounting, or taxation advice. Appropriate professional advisers should be consulted for such advice.

Federal Income Tax Reasons to Conduct an Appraisal

Exhibit 30–1 lists several federal income tax transactions where valuation is relevant. This list is not intended to be exhaustive. It is intended to illustrate many of the more common income taxation–related reasons to conduct a valuation. Several of the most common income taxation–related reasons to conduct a valuation are described in greater detail in the following sections.

While Exhibit 30–1 lists numerous taxable transactions that may require a valuation, most of these transactions may be grouped into a fewer number of more general categories of taxable "events." For example, the first general category of taxable events that may require a valuation is when a taxpayer (whether individual, partnership, or corporation) claims a deduction for property that the taxpayer abandons or donates. Such a deduction is available in the case of abandonment losses, casualty losses, charitable contributions, and so forth.

The second general category of taxable events involves a valuation that is needed when a business owner and/or employee receives noncash distributions from a business (whether the business is a proprietorship, corporation, or partnership). This type of transaction occurs in the case of property distributed to employees as compensation, property distributed to shareholders as dividends, property distributed to shareholders as part of a partial or complete liquidation, employee stock options or other stock rights distributed to employees, and so on. In these instances, the valuation may affect the amount of the tax deduction available (if any) to the business. And, the valuation may affect the amount of income (as compensation or otherwise) recognized by the employee or shareholder.

A third general category of taxable events relates to the amount of recognition of income (if any) associated with economic benefits received by a business. Examples of this category of taxable events include: (1) the valuation of property received, such as rents, and (2) the valuation (or the solvency/insolvency test) related to the recognition (or nonrecognition) of cancellation of indebtedness income by a business involved in a debt restructuring.

Exhibit 30–1

Taxable Transactions Requiring Valuations

Abandonment losses	Foreclosure of mortgaged property
Bargain purchases	Incorporation of a business
Basis of property (for depreciation and amortization)	Insolvent corporation recapitalization
"Boot" in tax-free transfer	Intercompany transfer of goods or services
Cancellation of indebtedness income	Liquidation, when property is received by a shareholder
Casualty losses	Lump sum acquisition of various assets or properties
Charitable contributions of property	(purchase price allocation)
Compensation received in the form of property	"Reasonableness" of compensation (determination of)
Conversion of C corporation to S corporation	Rents received in the form of property
Dividends received in the form of property	Recapitalization
Employee stock options	Residence converted to a rental property
Excess accumulated earnings (quantification of)	Stock rights
Exchange of properties	Tax shelters

A fourth general category of taxable events involves the conversion of one property (or form of property) to another. Examples of this category of taxable events, which may require valuations, are the conversion of C corporations to S corporations (and the estimation of the associated built-in gains associated with the assets subject to the conversion of corporate form) and the general taxable or tax-free exchange of properties.

A fifth category of taxation-related events that may involve valuations are tests of reasonableness. These tests of reasonableness include, for example, the reasonableness of the amount of compensation paid to the owner of a business, the reasonableness of the amount of undistributed "excess" accumulated earnings retained in a corporation, or the reasonableness of the transfer price (or royalty payment) related to the intercompany transfer of goods, services, or properties between controlled or otherwise related taxpayers.

A sixth (and very common) category of taxable events that typically requires a valuation involves establishing the value-related tax basis for assets transferred into, purchased by, or transferred out of a business (whether a proprietorship, partnership, or corporation). Examples of this category of valuation opportunities include the incorporation of a business (i.e., when assets other than cash are transferred into the corporation in exchange for securities) and the allocation of a lump-sum purchase price paid for an assemblage of assets, properties, or business interests (i.e., for purposes of establishing a basis in each asset purchased).

The following sections describe several of these income taxation–related valuation opportunities in greater detail.

Valuation of Property Received in a Transaction

When any type of property (other than cash) is received on a sale, exchange, or other disposition, the amount recognized upon receipt of that property is its fair market value. This basic rule of income taxation valuation in property transactions is presented in Internal Revenue Code (IRC) Section 1001(b). The definition of fair market value used for property transaction and property basis purposes is the familiar: the most probable price that, at a particular time, will induce a willing buyer to buy and a willing seller to sell, neither being under undue pressure to buy or to sell, and both being informed as to all relevant facts.[1]

This familiar definition of value has been slightly expanded with regard to the income taxation valuation of transactional property so as to include consideration of: (1) the availability of a buyer at the particular time and place and (2) the assumption that the buyer is not only willing but also able to pay for the particular quantity involved.[2]

Determining Basis in a Property

When there is a sale or exchange of property, the taxpayer must determine the amount of the property transaction gain or loss, and whether it is taxable or

---

[1] See *H.H. Marshman*, 279 F.2d 27 (6th Cir. 1960), *cert. denied*, 364 U.S. 918 (1960).
[2] See *Helvering v. Walbridge*, 70 F.2d 683 (2d Cir. 1934), *cert. denied*, 293 U.S. 594 (1934).

deductible. For income tax purposes, the following factors are considered in calculating the amount of the property transaction gain or loss:

$$Basis + Additions - Reductions = Adjusted\ basis$$

$$Amount\ realized - Adjusted\ basis = Gain$$

$$Adjusted\ basis - Amount\ realized = Loss$$

Basis is the measurement of the taxpayer's investment in the property for income tax purposes. A taxpayer must know the property's basis in order to determine such taxation-related elements as depreciation, casualty losses, and gain or loss on the property's sale or exchange. Basis is ordinarily the property's original cost or purchase price (including transaction costs such as sales taxes and delivery costs, for instance). Basis normally includes cash, debt assumed, and the fair market value of any other property given up. However, if a taxpayer receives property by some other form, such as by gift or inheritance, the taxpayer must normally use the property's basis rather than its cost.

Various transactional and taxation events may occur that change the taxpayer's original basis in the property. These events increase or decrease the original basis. The result is called the adjusted basis.

In certain situations, the fair market value of property on a particular date is the key factor in determining its basis. When using value to determine basis, actual sales prices of similar property on the open market are typically reliable evidence of value. For example, for this purpose, various courts have concluded that stock exchange quotations represent good evidence of a stock's fair market value.

A taxable exchange involves an exchange of property in which the gain is taxable or the loss is deductible. If a taxpayer acquires one property in return for another property in a taxable exchange, then the basis of the property received is generally its fair market value at the time of the exchange.

There are two allowable methods for determining the basis of property received in exchange for other property:

1. The basis is the fair market value of the property when it is received
2. The basis is the fair market value of the property exchanged for it, increased by any payments made or decreased by any payments received, when the two properties are of unequal value

Occasionally, it may be impractical to estimate the fair market value of the property given up (in order to measure the cost of the property received). In these situations, taxpayers may presume the values of the exchanged properties are equal, if the exchange took place at arm's length.

If a taxpayer receives property for services, then the original basis of the property to that taxpayer is its fair market value. According to Treasury Regulation Section 1.61-2(d), the taxpayer will include this amount in his or her taxable income. The basis of any restricted property received as payment for services is the sum of any amount paid for the property, plus any amount the taxpayer includes in gross income when the property is no longer subject to a substantial risk of forfeiture. The results related to restricted property received as payment for services are presented in Regulation Section 1.83-4.

Joint Ownership of Property

The death of a joint tenant or a tenant by the entirety may create a problem in determining a property's basis for the survivor. The portion of the property included in the decedent's estate is considered to be acquired from the decedent by the survivor. The survivor's basis in this inherited portion of the property is its fair market value on the date of death (or on the alternate valuation date). The basis of that part of the joint property not included in the decedent's estate is its cost or other basis, per IRC Section 2040. These rules apply to *all* joint interests in property *except* for those involving a husband and wife, as discussed below.

Only half of the joint ownership interest's fair market value is included in the gross estate regardless of who paid for the property. For married decedents, qualified joint interests include *any* interest in property held by the decedent and by the spouse as tenants by the entirety, or as joint tenants with right of survivorship (but only if decedent and spouse are the only joint tenants).

Property Acquired from a Decedent

Generally, if a taxpayer inherits property from a decedent, then the property's basis will be its fair market value when the decedent died. This property valuation rule is pursuant to IRC Section 1015. However, if the executor of the estate elects the alternate valuation date for estate tax purposes, then the property's basis will be its fair market value on that alternate valuation date.

Valuation Requirements for Charitable Contribution Deductions

Individuals may deduct contributions they make to—or for the use of—qualified charitable organizations. A qualified charitable organization may be a public, private, or a governmental unit.

A list of qualified charitable organizations, to which contributions are tax-deductible, is contained in U.S. Treasury Department Publication 78.

Individual taxpayers are subject to a percentage limitation as to the amount of charitable contributions allowed for any one tax year; this annual deduction limitation is based on their "contribution base." According to IRC Section 170(b)(1), this percentage limitation is based on two factors:

1. The type of the organization to which the charitable contribution is made
2. The type of the property donated

An individual taxpayer's "contribution base" is his or her adjusted gross income, computed without regard to any net operating loss carryback.[3]

The 1993 Omnibus Budget Reconciliation Act added considerable documentation and substantiation requirements with regard to the charitable contribution of property. This section summarizes these appraisal-related documentation and substantiation requirements.

---

[3] According to Code Section 170(b)(1)(F).

Documentation Requirements—Contributions of Property

A corporate or individual taxpayer making a charitable contribution of property—other than money—must have a receipt from the donee charitable organization and a reliable written record of specified information with respect to the donated property, per Regulation Section 1.170A-13(b)(2).

The receipt must include the name of the donee, the date and location of the contribution, and a description of the property in detail reasonable under the circumstances, including the value of the property.

A reliable written record should include the following information:

1. Name and address of the donee organization
2. Date and location of the contribution
3. A description of the property in reasonable detail, including the value of the property (including, in the case of securities, the name of the issuer, the type of security, and whether such security is regularly traded on a stock exchange or over-the-counter)
4. In the case of ordinary income property (including capital gain property held for less than 12 months), the cost or basis of the property
5. If less than a 100 percent interest in the property is contributed, the total amount claimed as a deduction for the tax year and for prior years and the name of any person other than the donee organization that has actual possession of the property
6. The terms of any agreement entered into by the taxpayer relating to the use, sale, or other disposition of the contributed property
7. If an election is made to treat contributions and carryovers of 30 percent capital gain property as ordinary income property, the years for which the election is made and the contributions to which the election is made

Noncash Property Contributions

No deduction is allowed for any charitable contribution of $250 or more unless the taxpayer substantiates the contribution by a contemporaneous written acknowledgment from the donee organization of the contribution.

However, substantiation is not required if the donee organization files a return with the IRS reporting the information that is required to be included in the written acknowledgment to substantiate the amount of the deductible contribution.

An acknowledgment must include the following information:

1. The amount of cash and a description, but not the value, of any property other than cash contributed
2. Whether the donee organization provided any goods or services in consideration, in whole or in part, for any property contributed
3. A description and good-faith estimate of the value of any goods or services provided to the donor, or, if the goods and services consist solely of intangible religious benefits, a statement to that effect

Appraisals for Noncash Contributions

Most donors, including individuals, partnerships, S corporations, closely held corporations, and personal service corporations, must attach Form 8283, Noncash Charitable Contributions, to their federal income tax return when claiming charitable contributions deductions that include noncash gifts of more than $500.

However, C corporations, other than personal service corporations and closely held corporations, need to attach Form 8283 to their income tax returns only when the amount of the noncash contribution deduction is more than $5,000.

Form 8283 must be completed by all donors if the aggregate claimed or reported value of such property—and all similar items of property for which charitable deductions are claimed or reported by the same donor for the same tax year (whether or not donated to the same donee)—is more than $5,000. The phrase *similar types of property* means property of the same generic category or type, such as stamps, books, land, buildings, or non-publicly-traded stock.

In cases where the noncash charitable contributions deduction includes items with a value in excess of $5,000, Form 8283 must include an acknowledgment of receipt signed by the donee charity and a signed appraiser's certification of appraisal, per Regulation Section 1.170A-13(c)(3).

Publicly Traded Stock. Neither a qualified appraisal nor an appraisal summary is required for securities that are publicly listed and regularly traded on a national, regional, or over-the-counter established securities exchange or for mutual funds for which quotations are published daily in general circulation newspapers.

Closely Held Stock. Qualified appraisals are not required for deductions of $10,000 or less of non-publicly-traded stock. However, a partially completed appraisal summary signed by the donee must be attached to his or her tax return for charitable contributions of closely held stock valued between $5,000 and $10,000.

Qualified Appraisals. Pursuant to Regulation Section 1.170A-13(c)(3), a qualified appraisal is an appraisal document that:

1. Relates to an appraisal that is made not earlier than 60 days before the date of contribution of the appraised property and that must be updated if made earlier
2. Is prepared, signed, and dated by a qualified appraiser
3. Does not involve a prohibited type of appraisal fee, such as that in which a part or all of the fee arrangement is based on a percentage (or set of percentages) of the appraised value of the property
4. Includes the following information:
   a. A description of the donated property
   b. In the case of tangible property, the physical condition of the property
   c. The date of contribution
   d. The terms of any agreement entered into by the donor that relates to the use, sale, or other disposition of the contributed property
   e. The name, address, and taxpayer identification number of the qualified appraiser and the appraiser's employer or partnership
   f. The qualifications of the qualified appraiser
   g. A statement that the appraisal was prepared for income tax purposes
   h. The date on which the property was valued
   i. The appraised fair market value of the property on the date of contribution
   j. The method of valuation used

k. The specific basis for valuation, if any, such as any specific comparable sales transactions

l. A description of the fee arrangement between the donor and the appraiser

The appraisal summary, which is included on Form 8283, must be signed and dated by both the donee and the qualified appraiser, and it must be attached to the donor's return on which a deduction of the appraised property is first claimed or reported.

The person who signs the appraisal summary for the donee must be an official authorized either to sign the tax or information returns of the donee or to sign appraisal summaries. The signature of the donee does not indicate concurrence with the appraised value of the contributed property.

No part of the fee paid for a charitable contribution appraisal can be based on a percentage of the appraised value of the property—that is, the appraiser's fee cannot be a contingent fee (or other similar arrangement).

Also, the appraisal fees may not be deducted as part of the charitable contribution.

Qualified Appraisers. According to Regulation Section 1.170A-13(c)(5), a qualified appraiser is an individual who:

1. Holds himself or herself out to the public as an appraiser or who regularly performs appraisals
2. Is qualified to appraise property because of his or her qualifications
3. Is aware of the appraiser penalties associated with the overvaluation of charitable contributions

Certain individuals, however, may not act as qualified appraisers, including:

1. The property's donor (or the taxpayer who claims the deduction)
2. The property's donee
3. A party to the property transfer transaction (with certain very specific exceptions)
4. Any person employed by, married to, or related to any of the above persons
5. An appraiser who regularly appraises for the donor, donee, or party to the transaction and does not perform a majority of his or her appraisals for other persons

Year-End Charitable Gifting Considerations

Year-end personal tax planning is an important process for high income and high net worth individuals—especially owners of closely held businesses. The use of charitable contributions (e.g., the contribution of appreciated stock to a charitable organization) is one year-end personal tax planning technique that may be used to (1) reduce current year taxable income and (2) reduce the individual taxpayer's gross estate.

This tax planning technique is particularly relevant to high income or high net worth individuals who would otherwise not be inclined to financially support religious, academic, or other charitable organizations. This section presents some of the common taxpayer planning strategies—and some of the federal taxation considerations—with regard to year-end charitable contributions.

The following paragraphs summarize year-end charitable gifting techniques that are intended to reduce current year taxable income.

1. **Prepay Contribution Pledges.** The taxpayer may prepay any outstanding charitable contribution pledges. Accelerating tax deductions allows taxpayers to reduce income taxes now—rather than in the future. Another alternative is to make a larger charitable contribution this year, above the amount otherwise due on the pledge. Charitable pledge payments (and other cash gifts) are deductible in the year in which they are paid to the charity and not in the year in which the pledge is made.

2. **Contribute Appreciated Assets.** The taxpayer may contribute appreciated assets. Writing a contribution check to a charitable organization is a simple procedure. However, when the taxpayer contributes appreciated property (i.e., property held for more than a year), the taxpayer can claim a deduction for the property's full fair market value. Thus, the taxpayer avoids tax on the appreciation of the contributed assets.

   Generally, the fair market value of marketable securities is the mean between their high and low trading prices on the date of delivery of the securities to the charity. For mutual fund shares (e.g., open-end investment companies), their fair market value is the redemption price of these shares on the date of their delivery to the charity.

   Exhibit 30–2 illustrates the added federal income tax benefit that a donor can realize by a gift of appreciated securities to a charity. Let's assume that the appreciated stock is now worth $40,000 and that the stock originally cost only $10,000. Therefore, this stock has a built-in gain of $30,000.

   The indicated income tax savings are even greater for a taxpayer in a higher income tax bracket. State income taxes can also increase the tax savings associated with this illustrative charitable gift.

3. **Select Appropriate Delivery Date.** The taxpayer should be careful about the date of delivery of the gift to the charity. This date determines the year in which the income tax deduction is available. If you mail a check to the charity, the date of mailing is the delivery date. For securities, the date of delivery determines both (1) the date of valuation and (2) the year of the charitable contribution deduction.

   A stock certificate properly endorsed or a separate stock power should also be provided to the charity. If the securities are handed to the charity or

Exhibit 30–2

Comparison of the "Cost" of a Charitable Gift of Appreciated Stock versus a Charitable Gift of Cash

	Charitable Gift of Cash	Charitable Gift of Appreciated Stock
Fair market value of gift	$40,000	$40,000
Income tax savings in the 28% bracket	11,200	11,200
Capital gains tax avoided (20% × $30,000)		6,000
Net (of taxes) cost of $40,000 charitable gift	**$28,800**	**$22,800**

to the charity's agent, that determines the delivery date. If securities are mailed to the charity, then the date of mailing is the date of delivery. If the taxpayer arranges for stock certificates to be reissued in the charity's name, then delivery is effective on the date when the security is transferred to the charity on the corporation's books—that is, the date on the new stock certificate.

4. **Trigger a Capital Loss.** The taxpayer may trigger a capital loss on the sale of depreciated securities. If the taxpayer owns securities worth less now than when they were bought, the taxpayer (1) may sell them and (2) may then contribute the proceeds to the charity.

   The result is that the taxpayer can claim a capital loss on his or her federal income tax return. The taxpayer cannot take a capital loss if the depreciated securities were donated directly to the charity.

5. **Contribute Nonmarketable Assets.** The taxpayer may contribute real estate or other closely held property to a charity. Such assets are not actively traded on a public stock exchange (such as the over-the-counter market). Therefore, the fair market value of the contributed property is the price at which such property would change hands between a willing buyer and a willing seller. The fair market value of the contributed property should be substantiated by an independent professional appraiser.

   For such a contribution, the date of delivery is the date that the contributed property is received by the charity. For real estate, the date of the charitable contribution deduction is the date that the charity receives a properly executed deed (or its recording date in some states).

Limitations on Charitable Contribution Deductions

The IRC limits an individual taxpayer's charitable deduction each year to a percentage of adjusted gross income, depending on the type of gift. However, for each type of charitable gift described below, the individual taxpayer is allowed a five-year "carryover" of any amount that falls outside the deduction limit in the current year. These carryover amounts can be used as tax deductions in succeeding years.

Subsequent to the 1993 Omnibus Budget Reconciliation Act, the substantiation and documentation requirements have increased with regard to the appraisal of noncash property claimed for charitable contribution deductions.

Taxpayers, and their valuation advisers, should be familiar with these appraisal substantiation and documentation requirements when planning a noncash charitable contribution.

Valuation of Compensation

The reasonableness of compensation in the form of salaries, wages, and bonuses is at issue in several situations. One is where the IRS is challenging the reasonableness of an executive compensation deduction. Another is where compensation is challenged as disguised dividends or earnings used to avoid paying tax.

Multifactor Tests

Some judicial circuits use a multifactor test to determine whether compensation is reasonable or excessive. For example, the Ninth Circuit has used a five-factor test[4] where the factors are:

1. The employee's role in the company
2. Compensation paid to similarly situated employees in similar companies
3. The character and condition of the company
4. The relationship between the employee and company
5. Whether the compensation was paid pursuant to a structured, formal, and consistently applied program

Other circuits, such as the Tenth Circuit, have used up to as many as 10 factors.[5]

Independent Investor Test

The Seventh Circuit, in *Exacto Spring Corp v. Comm'r*,[6] rejected the multifactor test approach for reasonable compensation—finding it unreliable and setting up the Tax Court as a "personnel department" for companies—and instead adopted a test known as the independent investor test. Under this test, whatever factors the Tax Court uses are reviewed from the vantage of an independent investor in the company, and the rate of return such an investor would expect. The court in *Exacto Spring* said, "When, notwithstanding the [employee's] 'exorbitant' salary (as it might appear to a judge or other modestly paid official), the investors in his company are obtaining a far higher return than they had any reason to expect, his salary is presumptively reasonable."

For in-depth analyses of the cases that arise in the reasonable compensation context, see Chapter 31.

Valuation of Worthless and Abandoned Property

When misfortune strikes, leaving a taxpayer with worthless property, the taxpayer normally has a deductible loss equal to the adjusted basis of the worthless property. It is noteworthy, however, that the loss in these situations does not technically arise from a sale or exchange. The following discussion summarizes how the taxpayer is to justify and to quantify this deductible loss.

---

[4]*LabelGraphics, Inc. v. Commissioner,* T.C. Memo 1998-343 (Sept. 28, 1998), *aff'd,* 221 F.3d 1091 (9th Cir. 2000).

[5]*B&D Foundations, Inc. v. Commissioner,* T.C. Memo 2001-262, 2001 Tax Ct. Memo LEXIS 298, 82 T.C.M. (CCH) 692 (October 3, 2001). Factors included: (1) the employee's qualifications; (2) the nature, extent, and scope of the employee's work; (3) the size and complexities of the business; (4) a comparison of salaries paid with the gross income and the net income; (5) the prevailing economic conditions; (6) a comparison of salaries with distributions to shareholders; (7) the prevailing rates of compensation for comparable positions in comparable concerns; (8) the salary policy of the taxpayer as to all employees; (9) in the case of small corporations with a limited number of officers, the amount of compensation paid to the particular employee in previous years; and (10) the taxpayer's performance.

[6]*Exacto Spring Corp. v. Comm'r* (aka *Heitz v. Commissioner*), T.C. Memo 1998-220 (June 24, 1998), rev'd, 196 F.3d 833 (7th Cir. 1999).

Worthless Securities

In the event that a qualifying security[7] becomes worthless at any time during the taxable year, the resulting loss is treated as having arisen from the sale or exchange of a capital asset on the last day of the taxable year. Losses from worthless securities are then treated as either short-term or long-term capital losses, depending on the taxpayer's holding period with regard to the subject securities.

Whether a security actually becomes worthless during a given year is a question of fact. And, the burden of proof is on the taxpayer to show that the security became worthless during the tax year in question.

Worthless Securities in Affiliated Corporations. The basic rule for worthless securities is modified for a corporate taxpayer's investment in the securities of an affiliated corporation. If securities of an affiliated corporation become worthless, then the loss is treated as an ordinary loss and the limitations that normally apply if the loss were a capital loss are avoided.[8]

A corporation is considered affiliated with a parent corporation if the parent owns at least 80 percent of the voting power of all classes of stock and at least 80 percent of each class of nonvoting stock of the affiliated corporation. In addition, to be treated as an affiliated corporation for purposes of the worthless security provisions, the defunct corporation must have been truly an operating company. This test is met if the corporation has less than 10 percent of the aggregate of its gross receipts from passive sources such as rents, royalties, dividends, annuities, and gains from sales or exchanges of stock and securities. This condition prohibits ordinary loss treatment for what are really investments.

Abandoned Property. While the tax law creates a fictional sale or exchange for worthless securities, it takes a different approach for abandoned property. When worthless property (other than stocks and securities) is abandoned, the abandonment is not considered a sale or exchange. Consequently, any loss arising from an abandonment is treated as an ordinary loss rather than a capital loss—a much more favorable taxation result. However, the loss is deductible only if the taxpayer can demonstrate that the property has been truly abandoned and not simply taken out of service temporarily.

Valuation Aspects of Section 165

Businesses that own worthless assets or worthless security interests should consider the possibility of taking an abandoned asset or worthless security loss deduction under IRC Section 165. Particularly as businesses generate taxable income, this deduction would give rise to either current or future income tax benefits.

The federal income tax rules for taking the loss deduction vary greatly, depending on the type of nondepreciable business asset or security interest involved and the taxpayer's actions.

---

[7] For purposes of the worthlessness deduction, a *security* is defined (in Code Section 165 [g] [2]) as (1) bonds, debentures, notes, or certificates, or other evidence of indebtedness issued by a corporation (including those issued by a government or its political subdivision), with interest coupons or in registered form; (2) a share of stock in a corporation; or (3) a right to subscribe for, or to receive, a share of stock in a corporation.

[8] Internal Revenue Code section 165(g)(3).

The taxpayer "shall be allowed as a deduction any loss sustained during the taxable year and not compensated for by insurance or otherwise."[9] The amount of the loss equals the adjusted basis of the property calculated under Code Section 1011, as if the asset had been sold or exchanged at a loss.

However, the amount of the loss must be adjusted for any salvage value or for compensation received. If the loss arises from a capital asset, Code Sections 1211 and 1212 (relating to the capital loss limitation and carryover) restrict the deductibility of the loss.

A deduction is not permitted if the loss results from an actual sale or exchange of the worthless or abandoned property. In addition, if the abandonment or worthless net loss was incurred by an individual, it must have been incurred in a trade or business, in a transaction entered into for profit, or from an event classified as a casualty or theft.

The worthlessness or abandonment loss is deductible in the year sustained. However, it cannot be deducted if there is a reasonable prospect of recovery. The possibility of recovery is a question of fact that must be determined by the particular circumstances involved.

Abandonment Loss for Nondepreciable Business Assets

The loss is deductible when "evidenced by closed and completed transactions and as fixed by identifiable events occurring in such taxable year."[10]

The deduction of a loss is permitted for "the sudden termination of the usefulness in such business or transaction of any nondepreciable property, in a case where such business or transaction is discontinued or when such property is permanently discarded from use therein...."[11]

Accordingly, an abandonment loss on nondepreciable business assets (other than securities) is deductible, even though the assets may not be totally worthless. The criteria for establishing an abandonment loss for nondepreciable business assets—in cases other than worthlessness—are:

1. The occurrence of a closed and completed transaction coupled with the termination of the asset's usefulness
2. The discontinuance of the use of the asset
3. The discontinuation of the business

An event that meets either of the last two conditions qualifies as the abandonment of the asset. For a taxpayer to claim an abandonment loss for a business asset, there must be both the intent to abandon plus an actual act designed to accomplish that intent. The actual proof of an asset abandonment will be determined based on the facts and circumstances of the event.

The deductibility of an abandonment is effective when the taxpayer discontinues the use of the asset or the business in which the asset is used.[12]

[9] Code Section 165(a).
[10] Regulation Section 1.165-1(b) and (d).
[11] Regulation Section 1.165-2(a).
[12] Ibid.

Worthless Stock Deduction

In addition to allowing a deduction for the abandonment of nondepreciable business asset, IRC Section 165 (g) allows a deduction for the loss sustained by a taxpayer resulting from the worthlessness of a security.

For there to be a deduction without a sale, the security must be totally worthless and, therefore, unsalable. The loss deduction must be taken only for the year in which the security becomes completely worthless. A partial worthlessness of a security caused simply by a drop in value in the market price is not deductible until the taxpayer has sold the security. If the security is a capital asset, the loss is a capital loss. To determine if the capital loss is treated as long-term or short-term, the taxpayer is considered to have held the worthless stock or security until the last day of the year in which it became worthless.

The loss from a worthless security is treated as resulting from a sale or exchange on the last day of the tax year in which the security becomes worthless. In most cases, this worthlessness event will result in a long-term capital loss for the taxpayer.

As mentioned above, the worthless security loss will be treated as an ordinary deduction if it involves the security of an affiliated corporation (e.g., the stock of a subsidiary). To qualify as an affiliated corporation, the taxpayer must own stock possessing at least 80 percent of the voting power and at least 80 percent of each class of nonvoting stock. In addition, the "worthless" subsidiary must obtain over 90 percent of its gross receipts from active sources.

The determination of worthlessness is a question of fact. In a case in which the IRS had urged a finding that stock did not become worthless in the year chosen by the taxpayer, for want of an "identifiable event," such as appointment of a receiver, cessation of normal business operation, bankruptcy, or liquidation, the Tax Court held that exceptional circumstances—that is, the lack of liquidating value and potential operating value—justified the taxpayer's choice.[13]

A taxpayer's deduction for a loss sustained on a worthless security is based on his or her adjusted basis in the security. A cash-method taxpayer may deduct, for worthless stock purchased on the installment basis and not entirely paid for, only the amount paid up to the close of the tax year.

Summary of Worthless and Abandoned Property Valuation

From time to time, many business taxpayers suffer economic losses. In addition to operating losses, many businesses abandon nondepreciable business assets or experience the worthlessness of owned securities (in particular, the stock of corporate subsidiaries). This section briefly summarized the rules relating to substantiating a deduction for the abandonment of nondepreciable business assets or the worthlessness of owned securities.

---

[13] See *Steadman v. Commissioner*, 424 F.2d 1 (6th Cir. 1970), *cert. denied*, 400 U.S. 869 (1970).

Valuation Aspects of Cancellation of Indebtedness Income

When creditors cancel all or part of a business's debt, its tax consequences are determined by whether the business is in bankruptcy proceedings or is insolvent.[14] When debt is canceled under bankruptcy proceedings, there is no taxable income currently. The taxpayer has a choice as to how the reduction is recorded. First, the recognition of any income associated with the cancellation of debt may be offset by the following seven items.

1. Net operating losses (NOLs) and NOL carryovers
2. The general business credit
3. The minimum tax credit
4. Capital loss carryovers
5. The basis of the taxpayer's property
6. Passive activity loss and credit carryovers
7. Foreign tax credit carryovers

Although not involved in a bankruptcy proceeding, a business may still be financially insolvent—that is, the value of its liabilities exceed the value of its assets. And the question of business insolvency (and the relative values of assets and liabilities) is answered by a business valuation.

If a business remains insolvent after debt cancellation, the decrease in debt is offset by the seven tax items listed above. If, however, the business is insolvent before, but solvent after, the debt cancellation, then the debt cancellation—to the extent of solvency—is subject to the rules governing solvent businesses. In contrast, when the debt of a solvent business not in bankruptcy is canceled, then the taxpayer must report the debt reduction as taxable income.

Unfavorable Tax Consequences of Debt Restructuring

In almost every debt restructuring, some amount of debt is forgiven by the lender. As introduced above, there are usually unfavorable income tax consequences associated with such debt restructurings. Without adequate tax planning, and without a thorough and rigorous valuation analysis, these unfavorable tax consequences may surprise the unwary taxpayer.

These negative tax consequences typically occur when the taxpayer can least afford them. Income recognition may occur without the taxpayer enjoying any cash receipts. When this happens, a tax liability becomes due even though the taxpayer may not have any cash to pay the liability. And, this tax liability is triggered when the borrower is trying to restructure debt. Presumably, the debt restructuring is due to the severe economic condition of the borrower and attempts to avoid the stigma and costs associated with bankruptcy. In any event, the tax liability is created when the borrower is least able to pay it.

The two most common negative tax consequences of debt restructuring are (1) the recognition of gain or loss on the direct transfer of property to a creditor in exchange for debt discharge and (2) the recognition of discharge of indebtedness income when debt is partially or totally forgiven. Both of these common negative

---

[14] Code Section 198(1).

income tax consequences are directly affected by the valuation of the borrower's property.

Insolvency Provisions of Code Section 108

IRC Section 61(a)(12) includes as gross income the "discharge of indebtedness" associated with the reduction or forgiveness of debt. Code Section 108 provides for an exclusion of "discharge of indebtedness" income from gross income if the debt discharge occurs when the taxpayer is insolvent. The Code Section 108 income exclusion is limited to the amount by which the taxpayer is insolvent at the time of the discharge.

A taxpayer will not recognize income from the discharge of indebtedness if the discharge occurs when the taxpayer is insolvent, even if the taxpayer is not in Chapter 11 bankruptcy proceedings.[15] An insolvent taxpayer is permitted to exclude from gross income any amount of indebtedness forgiven by a creditor—subject only to the limitation that the amount excluded cannot exceed the amount of insolvency.

Code Section 108(d)(3) defines *insolvency* as the amount by which a taxpayer's liabilities exceed the fair market value of the taxpayer's assets immediately before the discharge of indebtedness. Accordingly, the determination of insolvency is entirely a valuation matter. This determination requires the fair market value appraisal of all the assets owned by the borrower immediately before the debt forgiveness.

The statutory authority and judicial precedent related to Code Section 108 make it clear that all of the taxpayer s assets are subject to appraisal in the determination of insolvency. These assets include: tangible personal property (e.g., machinery and equipment), tangible real estate (e.g., land and buildings), intangible real property (e.g., leasehold interests and easements), and intangible personal property (e.g., trademarks and goodwill). And the statutory and judicial guidance is clear that traditional valuation approaches (i.e., cost approach, market approach, and income approach) are appropriate for the appraisal of the fair market value of the taxpayer's assets.

Unquestionably, a rigorously prepared and thoroughly documented independent appraisal is required to support a claim of insolvency under Code Section 108.

The IRC does not provide a definition of *liabilities* in the determination of insolvency. Accordingly, the determination of what liabilities are included in the solvency test has become a matter of judicial and administrative interpretation. The rationale for Code Section 108 has been to provide the economically distressed taxpayer with a fresh start, not hampered by the imposition of an income tax liability that the taxpayer is not able to pay.

Insolvency Test Illustrative Example

The following simple example illustrates the application of the Code Section 108 insolvency test.

Real Estate Development Corporation is in financial distress. It has successfully negotiated with its bank for a partial reduction of the loan associated with its

---

[15] Ibid.

Exhibit 30–3

Real Estate Development Corporation
Analysis of Assets and Liabilities
as of Date of Debt Discharge

	Tax Basis	Fair Market Value Basis
Assets		
Cash and other assets	$ 100,000	$ 100,000
Office building	10,000,000	7,000,000
Goodwill and other intangibles	0	400,000
Total Assets	$10,100,000	$7,500,000
Liabilities		
Current liabilities	$ 100,000	$ 100,000
Construction project debt	9,000,000	9,000,000
Total Liabilities	$ 9,100,000	$9,100,000

current office building construction project. The analysis of insolvency for Real Estate Development Corporation is presented in Exhibit 30–3.

Real Estate Development Corporation is "insolvent" in the amount of $1,600,000 (i.e., the $9,100,000 of total liabilities less the fair market value of $7,500,000 in total assets).

Accordingly, Real Estate Development Corporation could exclude up to $1,600,000 of discharge of indebtedness income from its gross income. In other words, its bank could discharge, or forgive, up to $1,600,000 in debt without the recognition of discharge of indebtedness income to Real Estate Development Corporation.

The "Costs" of Code Section 108

Of course, this Code Section 108 exclusion from discharge of indebtedness in income is not without any negative income tax consequences. Taxpayers will not recognize income from the discharge of indebtedness if they are in bankruptcy, to extent they are insolvent (as illustrated above). However, in exchange for this income exclusion, taxpayers are required to reduce certain favorable tax attributes. These tax attributes are reduced by the amount of the discharge of indebtedness income that is excluded from gross income by the taxpayer. General business credits and foreign tax credits are reduced at the rate of 33.3 cents for every dollar of excluded discharge of indebtedness income.

Unless the taxpayer elects to reduce the basis in his or her depreciable assets e.g., real estate) before reducing other tax attributes, the taxpayer must reduce tax attributes in the following sequence:

1. Net operating losses or carryovers
2. Carryovers of the general business tax credit
3. Capital losses and carryovers
4. Basis in depreciable and nondepreciable assets
5. Foreign tax credit carryovers

As an alternative to the reduction of tax benefits, the borrower may elect to reduce the basis of any depreciable assets, but not below his or her basis in the assets.

In summary, the Code Section 108 insolvency discharge of indebtedness income exclusion is designed to provide a borrower with greater flexibility in arranging his or her financial affairs. It is not intended to allow taxpayers to avoid future taxes. Therefore, depending on the beneficial tax attributes otherwise available to the borrower, the Code Section 108 discharge of indebtedness income exclusion may provide some taxpayers with a permanent income exclusion and some taxpayers with only a temporary income exclusion.

Valuation-Related Income Tax Penalties

There are several taxation-related penalties that may be assessed as a result of adjustments made to valuation issues. These valuation issues may affect income tax returns (e.g., charitable contributions) as well as gift and estate tax returns. Most of these penalties are assessed against the taxpayer. However, certain penalties may also be assessed against the tax return preparer.

In this section, we discuss not only those penalties that deal exclusively with valuation issues, but also those general accuracy-related penalties that may be applicable to valuation issues. We discuss the current penalties related to valuation issues—that is, on those changes to the tax law that occurred since the passage of the Omnibus Budget Reconciliation Act of 1989 (OBRA).

Analysts who prepare valuations for taxation-related purposes should be familiar with these penalties. In addition, analysts who prepare tax returns that include valuation issues (even if the valuations were prepared by other consultants) should be familiar with these penalties.

The Section 6695A Appraiser Penalties

The Pension Protection Act of 2006 added Internal Revenue Code Section 6695A, which provides penalties that are aimed directly at appraisers who provide appraisals for income (as well as transfer) tax purposes. This is the first time that appraisers are subject to penalties; taxpayers have been subject to valuation misstatements for a while in IRC Section 6662, discussed below. The new penalties apply to appraisals provided in connection with returns or submissions, e.g., claims for refunds, filed after August 17, 2006 (date of enactment).

Several requirements must be met for the penalties to be triggered. First, an appraisal must have been prepared in connection with a return or a claim for a refund. Second, the person preparing the appraisal, i.e., the appraiser, needs to know or have reason to know that the appraisal will be used for such purpose. Finally, the appraisal must result in a "substantial valuation misstatement under Chapter 1" of the Code (within the meaning of Code Section 6662[e]) or a "gross valuation misstatement" (within the meaning of Code Section 6662[h]). IRC Chapter 1 covers normal taxes and surtaxes, whereas Section 6662(h) adds valuations of pension liabilities and estate and gift taxes.

A "substantial valuation misstatement under Chapter 1" arises where the value of property claimed on a return of tax imposed by Chapter 1 is 150 percent or more of the amount determined to be the correct value. A "gross valuation misstatement" under Section 6662(h) generally occurs where the value of property reflected on an estate or gift tax return is determined to be 40 percent or less of the correct value.

The amount of the penalty imposed is the lesser of:

1. the greater of:
   a. 10 percent of the amount of the underpayment (as defined in Section 6664[a]) attributable to the misstatement or
   b. $1,000, or
2. 125 percent of the gross income received by the appraiser from the preparation of the appraisal.

Under Section 6695A, no penalty is imposed where an appraiser can establish to the satisfaction of the IRS that the value reflected in the appraisal was "more likely than not" the proper value. However, this exception is likely to provide little relief, since once a court has determined that the appraisal produced a "substantial valuation misstatement" or a "gross valuation misstatement," an appraiser is likely to have difficulty persuading the IRS that his appraisal was more likely than not the proper value. Appraisers may appeal the Section 6695A penalty by first exhausting administrative appeals with the IRS Appeals Office, then by filing a claim for a credit or refund of the assessed penalty, and if that is refused, by filing with the appropriate federal district court or claims court.

The new penalties do not apply to appraisers engaged by the IRS. Taxpayer appraisers must face the possibility of penalties if their appraisals are later rejected; IRS appraisers face no similar penalties no matter how far their appraisals are from the values finally determined for tax purposes. This creates an inequitable situation that arguably should be redressed by corrective legislation.

In the meantime, taxpayer appraisers should consider revising their engagement agreements to explain, and seek reimbursement for, such penalties from their clients. This is especially true given that valuation opinions are arrived at, in part, on the basis of the appraiser's judgment and experience, and that courts have discretion to disagree with an appraiser's judgment calls, methodology, and ultimate value opinions.

The Section 6662 Accuracy-Related Penalties

OBRA consolidated into one IRC section (Section 6662) several different accuracy-related taxation penalties:

1. The negligence penalty
2. The substantial understatement of income tax penalty
3. The substantial valuation overstatement penalty
4. The substantial estate or gift tax valuation understatement penalty
5. The substantial overstatement of pension liabilities penalty

The accuracy-related penalty is applied to the portion of any underpayment of tax that is attributable to one or more of the above five issues.

The penalties under Section 6662 have a penalty rate of 20 percent of the tax underpayment. This is true except with respect to underpayment attributable to one or more "gross valuation misstatements."[16] The penalty rate increases to 40 percent of the tax underpayment when there is a "gross valuation misstatement."

Only the substantial valuation overstatement penalty[17] and the substantial estate or gift tax valuation understatement penalty[18] are limited exclusively to valuation issues. However, the other accuracy-related penalties may be applicable to valuation issues, as well. For example, there is nothing to prevent a negligence penalty[19] from being applied to a valuation issue, assuming the facts of the position support the assertion of taxpayer negligence. This is noteworthy because the negligence penalty does not have a minimum threshold of a $5,000 tax understatement, as do the penalties related exclusively to valuation.

The accuracy-related penalties are assessed on an issue-by-issue basis. And, each of the accuracy-related penalties is applied only to that part of the tax underpayment that is caused by the allegedly proscribed conduct.[20]

Negligence Penalty

The negligence penalty is applied only to the portion of the tax underpayment attributable to negligence. This represents a change from prior tax law, when the negligence penalty was applied to the entire amount of the tax underpayment. The definition of negligence remains the same as under the prior law.

The negligence-related penalty will be imposed (1) for negligence in the case of any careless, reckless, or intentional disregard of rules or regulations, and (2) for any failure to make a reasonable attempt to comply with the provisions of the tax law. No penalty is imposed if it can be shown that (1) there was reasonable cause for the tax underpayment and (2) the taxpayer acted in good faith with respect to the tax underpayment.

Substantial Valuation Overstatement Penalty

The substantial valuation overstatement penalty:

1. Can apply to all taxpayers.
2. May exist if the value or adjusted basis of any property claimed on a return is 200 percent (up from the previous 150 percent) or more of the correct value or adjusted basis.
3. Applies only if the amount of the tax underpayment attributable to a valuation overstatement exceeds $5,000 ($10,000 for a corporation other than an S corporation or personal holding company). This is a major increase in the threshold, as the previous penalty required an understatement of only $1,000 (under old Section 6659[d]).
4. Is 20 percent of the tax underpayment if the value or adjusted basis is 200 percent or more—but less than 400 percent—of the correct value or adjusted basis. The penalty is doubled to 40 percent if the value or adjusted basis is 400 percent or more of the correct value or adjusted basis.[21]

---

[16] Defined under Section 6662(h)(2).
[17] Section 6662(e).
[18] Section 6662(g).
[19] Section 6662(b)(12).
[20] Sections 6662(b) and (c).
[21] This penalty is codified in Sections 6662(b)(3), 6662(f), and 6662(h).

Substantial Overstatement of Pension Liabilities Penalty

The substantial overvaluation of pension liabilities was changed so as to be assessable only if the valuation difference is 200 percent or more. The minimum tax underpayment for the pension overvaluation penalty to apply remains at $1,000. The rate of the tax penalty is doubled to 40 percent if pension liabilities are overstated by 400 percent.[22]

Definitions and Special Rules under Section 6664

The penalties under Sections 6662 and 6663 apply only if a tax return is actually filed. For this purpose, a tax return does not include a return filed under Section 6020(b), where the IRS filed the return based on information available. The fraudulent failure to file a tax return is covered by Section 6651(f).

No accuracy-related penalties will be imposed (1) if there was reasonable cause of the tax underpayment and (2) if the taxpayer acted in good faith.[23] The valuation overstatement penalty will not apply to charitable contribution property if:

1. The claimed value was based on a "qualified appraisal" by a "qualified appraiser" as defined in the regulations under Section 170(a)(1), and
2. In addition to the appraisal, the taxpayer made a good faith investigation of the value of the property.[24]

Tax Return Preparer Penalties

Tax return preparers are subject to a different set of tax penalties than are taxpayers. First, preparers may be assessed a $250 penalty[25] for any tax return that understates a taxpayer's tax liability due to an undisclosed position for which there was not a realistic possibility of being sustained on the merits. Second, preparers may be subject to a $1,000 penalty[26] for any willful, reckless, or intentional understatement of tax liability. This penalty could relate to a valuation-related tax understatement.

Summary of Valuation-Related Income Tax Penalties

The accuracy-related penalty encompasses the entire spectrum of income tax, gift tax, and estate tax–related valuation matters (including, for example, the valuation aspects of transfer pricing under Section 482). The negligence penalty may be assessed on valuation-related tax disputes if the taxpayer acted in a careless or reckless manner.

In addition, the person who prepared the tax return could be assessed a penalty[27] related to a willful understatement of tax liability associated with an insupportable valuation position.

---

[22] This penalty is codified in Sections 6662(b)(4), 6662(f), and 6662(h).
[23] Section 6664(c).
[24] Section 6664(c)(2).
[25] Section 6694(a).
[26] Section 6694(b).
[27] Ibid.

Valuation Aspects of Intercompany Transfer Pricing

As part of an intercompany transfer, an explicit or implicit price is used to value the goods, services, or resources exchanged in the transaction. Since this transfer price is agreed upon by two related parties, the influence of market forces may be less prevalent than what unrelated parties would experience. Therefore, the actual intercompany transfer price may differ from that which would be established by two independent parties engaged in an arm's-length exchange.

As a result of the intercompany transaction, the revenue or expenses and, therefore, the taxable income of each related party is affected by the magnitude of the transfer price. To the extent that the related parties have some discretion in establishing their "internal" transfer price, this price may be set so as to minimize the combined companies' global tax liability by shifting taxable income between companies according to differences in national tax rates.

IRS Section 482 authorizes the Secretary of the Treasury to allocate income, deductions, and other tax items among related taxpayers to prevent the evasion of taxes or to clearly reflect income. The Tax Reform Act of 1986 amended Section 482 by providing that the income from a transfer or license of intangible property must be "commensurate with the income" attributable to the intangible.

In July 1994, the IRS issued the final regulations on the intercompany pricing of both tangible and intangible property under Section 482. This section briefly outlines the key features of the final Section 482 regulations, discusses the purposes and roles of the intercompany transfer pricing consultants and experts, presents the prescribed methods for analyzing transfer prices involving both tangible and intangible assets, and finally outlines the current penalty and safe harbor provisions with regard to valuation misstatements.

Key Features of the Final Section 482 Regulations

The final 1994 transfer pricing regulations elaborate on the issue that may arise when a company transacts with an affiliate on terms that are not at "arm's length." The issue is whether the company is required to report the "true taxable income" rather than the results of the actual transactions.

The 1994 regulations provide that, "if necessary to reflect an arm's-length result, a controlled taxpayer may report ... the results of its controlled transactions based upon prices different from those actually charged."[28]

Taxpayers wishing to use Section 482 must affirmatively report the results on a timely filed tax return and may not do so on an amended return

The construction of "true taxable income" remains the fundamental remedy of Section 482. According to the final regulations, true taxable income is a condition that exists when a controlled taxpayer reports financial results that are consistent with the results that an uncontrolled taxpayer would have attained under comparable circumstances.

This formulation contains two core components: "consistency" with uncontrolled results and "comparable circumstances." Consistency tests a controlled taxpayer's financial results against the "arm's-length results" of a comparable uncontrolled

----

[28] Reg. Section 1.482-1(a)(3).

taxpayer. The arm's-length results are established by using methods determined under the "best method rule." Rather than being the most accurate measure, the best method under the final regulations provides the most reliable measure of an arm's-length result.

The series of factors to be considered in searching for the most reliable result under the arm's-length standard of transfer pricing are: (1) the particular facts and circumstances of the transaction, (2) the completeness and accuracy of available data, and (3) the degree of comparability between controlled and uncontrolled transactions.

Consistency with an arm's-length result is determined by creating an arm's-length range based on comparable information. The arm's-length range is established by a group of comparables in the case where all the information of both the controlled transaction and the uncontrolled comparables is sufficiently complete, and any material differences that have an ascertainable effect on the prices or profits of the comparables can be adequately reconciled by adjustments. If the data on the comparables are not sufficiently complete, then all comparables with a similar level of comparability and reliability are considered with their reliability enhanced using appropriate statistical techniques.

The most useful portions of the regulations are the factors to determine comparability. All factors that could affect a financial result are to be taken into account.

The factors to be considered in determining comparability include:

1. *Functional Analysis*—An analysis of the economically significant activities of the controlled and uncontrolled taxpayers including research and development, manufacturing, marketing, distribution, and managerial functions. In order for the two transactions (i.e., the controlled and the uncontrolled) to be comparable, the entities should perform similar economic functions with respect to those transactions.
2. *Contractual Terms*—To be considered comparable, an uncontrolled transaction must have similar significant contractual terms that could affect the prices that would be earned.
3. *Risk Analysis*—The risks borne by each party in the controlled and uncontrolled transactions must be analyzed, including market risks, research and development, financial risks, product liability risks, and general business risks. The economic substance of transactions will be reviewed by the IRS to determine risks borne. Taxpayers must be certain not to mismatch the allocation of risks and potential rewards for bearing those risks.
4. *Economic Conditions*—The economic conditions surrounding the transactions must be similar and must consider factors such as: (1) alternatives realistically available to the buyer and seller (e.g., make versus buy); (2) the similarity of the geographic markets; (3) the relative size of each market and the extent of economic development; and (4) the level of the market, market share for items transferred, location specific costs, and competition in the market.

Special Circumstances

There are three special circumstances that may affect comparability: (1) market share strategies, (2) differences in geographic markets, and (3) extraordinary or tax-motivated transactions.

Multiple Year Data

The results of a controlled transaction ordinarily will be compared with the results of uncontrolled comparables occurring in the taxable year under review. It is appropriate to consider earlier or later year data to examine circumstances—such as the assumption of risk and market share strategies—that are perceived as involving longer time periods.

Multiple year averages are acceptable to establish a range. If the taxpayer's results for a particular year fall outside of the multiple year range, however, a new provision states that the requisite adjustment should ordinarily be based on the range of the uncontrolled comparable results for the single year and not the multiple year average. This requirement appears to be unfavorable to taxpayers and undermines the more economically relevant use of the multiple year averages.

Purposes and Roles of Valuation and Economic Analysis Experts

The critical element in evaluating, developing, and presenting transfer pricing issues from the standpoint of the taxpayer or tax administrator is the development and interpretation of the facts relevant to the matter at hand. The importance of the development of pricing positions has been highlighted by the Section 482 penalty provisions under Section 6662 and the reasonable cause exception thereto in Section 6662(e).

There are typically three steps that need to be followed in developing and presenting transfer pricing positions: (1) identify the pertinent facts and circumstances, (2) evaluate the facts and circumstances to determine the appropriate pricing methodology and result, and (3) present the position.

These steps are critical regardless of the purpose of the evaluation: development of a tax return position, identification of positions by the IRS in an examination, response to an examination by the IRS, formulation of a transfer pricing mechanism in an Advance Pricing Agreement context, or presentation of the position in a court of law.

The potential range of purposes that may necessitate an intercompany transfer pricing study is quite broad and may include the following:

1. An evaluation of existing or new intercompany pricing policies
2. Required documentation
3. Assessment of exposure in the event of an IRS—or a foreign taxing authority—examination
4. IRS examination positions
5. An Advance Pricing Agreement submission
6. Due diligence for a "reasonable documentation" opinion for Section 6662(e) purposes
7. State tax planning matters
8. Other purposes unique to particular situations

Types of Experts

The development and presentation of an intercompany transfer pricing position often requires the use of experts for the purpose of developing certain data, evaluating proper pricing methods, and determining the result of specific issues.

A frequent issue in transfer pricing cases is the appropriate financial accounting treatment of the respective elements of a multinational taxpayer's business. This is often critical to an appropriate determination of the situation, especially when the selected pricing method involves the use of financial margin analyses, such as the comparable profits method. In order to apply this method properly, the financial data of the entities or the product lines in question must be accurately determined. In these cases, it may prove useful to engage the services of a financial expert to prepare and present this type of product line segmentation.

A financial expert can assist the taxpayer in making a redetermination of the pertinent financial information on a profit center basis. This redetermination may include the partitioning of the taxpayer's sales revenue into major product categories. Net profits for each category can then be estimated by tracing all of the direct costs to each type of product revenue and by allocating the common costs (such as the fixed costs of production or research, engineering, selling, advertising, and general and administrative expenses) to each profit center using an appropriate allocation method.

Financial expertise can thereby be effectively used to present ambiguous or unreliable data in a manner appropriate for the pricing issues that develop in taxation disputes or with respect to intercompany transactions occurring in later periods. The need for financial expertise can also arise in a variety of circumstances, including the comparability of guideline transactions, the application of foreign accounting principles, and various other related matters.

Taxpayers can also draw upon the expertise of valuation consultants and experts to assess their exposure to potential IRS transfer pricing adjustments before the fact and to develop a defense of existing pricing practices once the IRS has begun a transfer pricing examination. Valuation consultants and experts can also develop planning strategies that minimize tax burdens and audit-associated risks. Among their virtues, both defense and planning have the salutary effect of reducing the likelihood of double taxation. Equally important, a well-conceived and economically defensible transfer pricing policy significantly reduces the likelihood of valuation misstatement penalties.

Summary of Transfer Pricing Valuation Issues

The principles and mechanics of the final Section 482 regulations set the stage for elaborate routines of investigation, analysis, comparison, and documentation. The final regulations also require careful analysis of the facts and circumstances surrounding each intercompany transaction—including comparable transactions—and impose a substantial factual burden of proof on the taxpayer—including detailed documentation of his or her intercompany transfer pricing policy and analysis in support of his or her prices at arm's-length.

As a result, multinational taxpayers will have to devote significant resources in order to comply with these regulations. Taxpayers need to increasingly rely on their advisers to assist in choosing and documenting the method(s) that best determines the most appropriate intercompany price—given the economic business circumstances of a controlled transaction.

Valuation of Intellectual Properties for State Income Taxation Purposes

In recent years, many national corporations have formed intellectual property holding companies and then transferred legal title to various intellectual properties to them. In the most common structure for this program, the entity transfers intellectual properties such as trademarks and trade names to the newly organized intellectual property holding company. As part of its normal business operations, the holding company licenses the use of the trademarks and trade names to the related business interests in other states. The business pays a license fee or royalty payment to the holding company for the use of the trademarks and trade names now owned by the holding company.

There is no tax liability in many states on the income derived from the licensing or leasing of intellectual properties, such as royalties received for the use of trademarks. The intercompany payments from outside the holding company state—the royalty payments for the use of the trademarks—represent deductible expenses for determining taxable income in other states in which the entity generates business income. The net result, therefore, can be a reduction in the total state income tax obligation of the consolidated entity. The taxpayer's consolidated federal income tax expense, however, is obviously not affected by this intercompany intellectual property transfer program.

This section presents the valuation, economic, and corporate management aspects related to the design and implementation of an intellectual property transfer program. Some of the issues include identification of specific intellectual properties to transfer, creation of the holding company, methods of quantifying arm's-length transfer prices for the intangible assets, and the most significant economic pros and cons of implementing an intellectual property transfer program.

Trademarks and Trade Names

Corporate trademarks and trade names are the most common intangible assets found in intellectual property transfer programs. Because of the critical importance of corporate trademarks and trade names combined with the need to protect, manage, and control their use, corporations in the retail industry frequently avail themselves of this intellectual property transfer strategy. Corporations in wholesale distribution, manufacturing, service, and other industries may also have the same needs, making the use of an interstate intellectual property transfer program a viable strategic option for many industries.

Transfer of Intellectual Properties

In determining which intellectual properties to include in an interstate transfer program, a taxpayer should consider which corporate intellectual properties:

- Have legal existence
- Have economic substance
- Can be legally transferred to a holding company

- Have a practical business reason for being transferred to the holding company
- Are actually used, or used up, in normal business operations in other states
- Can be associated with a determinable royalty rate or other transfer price, in order to effectively quantify the intellectual property transfer program
- Have a reasonably long-term and determinable remaining useful life
- Will not have to be sold, abandoned, or otherwise transferred back out of the holding company in the foreseeable future

In the case of trademarks and trade names, a number of additional issues should be considered including:

- Should all trademarks and trade names be transferred?
- Should only the overall corporation trademark be transferred?
- Should all individual brand, product, and service marks be transferred?
- Should future trademarks and trade names be transferred as they are developed?
- Should the trademarks be transferred in perpetuity or for a specific limited term?

These questions cannot be answered in a vacuum. They can be answered only after careful consideration of the above selection criteria and after thorough consideration of the business purpose and objectives of the intellectual property transfer program.

Creation of the Intellectual Property Holding Company

Besides advising in the creation of an intellectual property holding company, qualified legal counsel is also necessary before the taxpayer implements any intellectual property transfer program. Title to the trademarks, trade names, and/or other intellectual properties should be effectively transferred to the newly created holding company, using legal counsel familiar with intellectual property law.

The newly created holding company should have both form and substance. There should be a legitimate business purpose other than the exclusive goal of minimizing consolidated state tax liability. One traditional corporate purpose for the intellectual property transfer program is to allow the business entity to better control its intellectual properties. This means internal, as well as external, control, and this would include accounting, legal, administrative, and operational controls.

Another common corporate purpose for the intellectual property transfer program is to allow the corporation to explore the possibility of licensing its trademarks, trade names, technology, copyrights, and other intellectual properties. The holding company would be the vehicle to license various intellectual properties to independent, third-party licensees in arm's-length transactions. As with all stated corporate goals and objectives, these purposes do not ultimately have to be achieved.

To accomplish its business purpose, and to achieve substance as well as form, it is not unusual for the corporate parent to transfer assets, other than intangibles, to the newly created holding company. Often, the parent will transfer cash balances and certain banking relationships to the state of the holding company incorporation. Also, employees are frequently placed on the payroll of the holding company. These employees may be responsible for the management and control of the company's intellectual properties. They may also be accountable for developing and implementing the company's intellectual property licensing program.

As with any functioning business enterprise, the newly created holding company should prepare financial statements on a periodic basis. These statements should report the results of operations and the financial position of the corporation. The results of operations will include any licensing and investment income less the payroll, rent, utilities, and administrative costs of the business operations. Administrative, accounting, or other services provided to the holding company business operations should be charged through intercompany accounts to the holding company. The holding company's balance sheet will include among its assets the transferred intellectual properties.

Valuation of the Transferred Intellectual Properties

Intellectual properties included in an intercompany intellectual property transfer program are valued using the traditional cost approach, market approach, and income approach valuation methods.[29]

A valuation analyst experienced with intercompany transfer pricing analysis should be able to reasonably estimate a fair transfer price formula and an expected remaining life of the transfer agreement on a preliminary basis. These preliminary estimates should be adequate for planning, evaluation, and decision-making purposes. A more rigorous and thorough valuation and analysis of the remaining economic life of the intellectual property would be required in the actual pricing and structuring phase of implementing the intellectual property transfer program.

Summary

This chapter discussed some of the many reasons to value business entities and business interests for federal (and state) income tax purposes. In this chapter, we also explored several specific reasons to conduct federal income taxation–related valuations, including setting basis after a property transfer transaction, substantiating charitable contribution deductions, substantiating property abandonment and worthless security deductions, assessing corporate insolvency with regard to the nonrecognition of cancellation of indebtedness income, and intercompany transfer pricing. In addition, we presented the accuracy-related federal income tax penalties associated with the undervaluation or overvaluation of assets, properties, or business interests. Last, we discussed the valuation aspects of the interstate transfer of intellectual properties for state income taxation–related purposes.

Each of these topics was presented from a valuation and economic analysis perspective. This chapter was not intended to provide legal, accounting, or taxation advice. Appropriate professional advisers should be consulted for such advice.

Bibliography

Burke, Brian. "The Impact of S Corporation Status on Fair Market Value." *Business Valuation Review*, vol. 20, no. 2, June 2001, pp. 13–24.

Casinelli, Elio J., Kevin M. Hennessey, and Richard F. Yates. "Final Intercompany Transaction Regs. Focus on Broad Concepts Rather Than Mechanics." *The Journal of Taxation*, December 1995, pp. 325–32.

[29] For more information regarding the valuation and analysis of intangible assets and intellectual properties, see Robert F. Reilly and Robert P. Schweihs, *Valuing Intangible Assets* (New York: McGraw-Hill, 1999).

Eason, Pat, Raymond A. Zimmerman, and Tim Krumwiede. "A Changing Environment in the Substantiation and Valuation of Charitable Contributions." *Taxes*, April 1996, pp. 251–59.

"Failure to obtain Qualified Appraisals of Nonpublicly Traded Stock Limits Charitable Deductions to Basis, Not FMV." *The Tax Adviser*, January 1998, pp. 64–68.

Levey, Marc M., and Casey J. Schoen. "Better Comparable Analysis Persuades Tax Court in Westreco." *The Journal of International Taxation*, January 1993, pp. 39–42.

Lowell, Cym H. "Relationship of Section 482 to International Corporate Tax Planning." *The Journal of Corporate Taxation*, Spring 1996, pp. 36–56.

_____. "Strategies for Transfer Pricing Disputes." *Valuation Strategies*, May/June 1999, pp. 10–19, 46.

Mercer, Z. Christopher. "Fair Market Value vs. The Real World." *Business Valuation Review*, vol. 18, no. 1, March 1999, pp. 16–25.

Millon, Thomas J., and Robert F. Reilly. "Valuation of Tangible and Intangible Assets as Part of a Transfer Pricing Analysis." *ASA Valuation*, June 1997, pp. 46–54.

Pratt, Shannon P., and Dan Van Vleet. "Valuation Reports for Income Tax Purposes." *BV Q&A Newsletter,* May 2005. Available at www.BVLibrary.com.

Reilly, Robert F. "Tax Penalties Related to Valuation Issues." *CPA Expert*, Spring/Summer 1998, pp. 9–11.

_____. "Valuation Requirements for Charitable Contribution Deductions." *CPA Expert*, Winter 1997, pp. 7–10.

Rich, Jeffrey A. "Valuation of Intangible Property Transactions under the Final Transfer Pricing Regulations." *Valuation Strategies*, November/December 1999, pp. 26–33.

Robinson, Debra A., and Edward J. Rappaport. "Impact of Valuation Discounts on Estate and Income Tax Basis." *Estate Planning*, June 1997, pp. 223–30.

Robinson, Richard B. "Getting Money Out of the Family Business—Avoiding Conflicts Between the Income Tax and the Transfer Tax." *ALI-ABA Course of Study Materials: Estate Planning for the Family Business Owner*, vol. I, March 2001.

Sliwoski, Leonard. "Imbedded Income Taxes—Built-In Gains Taxes: Business Valuation Considerations." *BVPapers*, February 2005. Available at www.BVLibrary.com.

Sliwoski, Leonard J., Mary B. Bader and Thomas G. Pearce. "Reasonable Compensation: How Exact Is Exacto Spring." *Valuation Strategies*, vol. 5, no. 5, May/June 2002, pp. 18–27, 47.

Smith, Gordon V., and Russell L. Parr. "Valuation Issues in Transfer Pricing." (Chapter 2A). In *Valuation of Intellectual Property and Intangible Assets*, 2nd ed., 1996 Cumulative Supplement. New York: John Wiley & Sons, 1996.

Soled, Jay A. "Gifts of Partnership Interests: An Income Tax Perspective." *Business Entities*, May/June 1999, pp. 30–35.

Stockdale, John Jr. "Business Valuation Cases in Brief." *Business Valuation Review*, vol. 22, no. 2, June 2003, pp. 105–110.

Stockdale, John Jr. "Business Valuation Cases in Brief." *Business Valuation Review*, vol. 20, no. 4, December 2001, pp. 49–53.

Wrappe, Steven C., Ken Milani, and Julie Joy. "The Transfer Price Is Right." *Strategic Finance*, July 1999, pp. 39–43.

Chapter 31

Income Tax Court Cases

Stock Warrant Valuation
Kimberlin v. Commissioner
Valuation as Accounting Method
In re Heilig Meyers Company
Summary

Introduction

This chapter presents summaries of numerous federal income taxation-related court cases. The case summaries presented represent only a small fraction of the federal income tax valuation cases decided in the last several years. The cases selected are not necessarily the "best" judicial decisions—from either a judicial or a valuation perspective. However, they are intended to be a representative sample of federal judges' current thinking with regard to: valuation principles and standards, valuation methodology, selection of the appropriate market, and examples of minimum qualifications for valuation analysts and valuation expert reports.

The income tax case summaries are presented in the following categories:

1. General valuation methodology issues.
2. Charitable contribution issues.
3. Reasonable compensation issues.
4. Intangible asset valuation issues.

Obviously, these four categories do not encompass all valuation and economic analysis aspects of federal income taxation. Again, these categories are intended to represent the areas of federal income taxation that are affected by valuation and related economic analyses.

General Valuation Methodology Issues

Pabst Brewing Company v. Commissioner

In *Pabst Brewing Company v. Commissioner*,[1] the tax issue was the fair market value of certain assets. After stipulating to values of several assets, the remaining disputed values were of two breweries and brands of beer. The IRS claimed that these assets were transferred at less than their fair market values.

This case is particularly instructive to valuation analysts because the Tax Court articulates a number of principles regarding the estimation of fair market value. In addition, the Tax Court decision specifically comments on (1) the specific weaknesses of the respective experts' credentials for estimating fair market value and (2) the specific weaknesses in their methodology.

The Tax Court's Valuation Principles. The following are several quotes from the Tax Court's decision in this case. These quotes are illustrative of fundamental valuation principles:

---

[1] *Pabst Brewing Company v. Commissioner*, T.C. Memo 1996-506 (Nov. 12, 1996).

1. "The willing buyer and the willing seller are hypothetical persons, rather than specific individuals or entities, and the characteristics of these hypothetical persons are not necessarily the same as the personal characteristics of the actual seller or a particular buyer."

2. "Fair market value is determined as of the valuation date, and no knowledge of unforeseeable future events which may have affected the value is given to the hypothetical persons."

3. "Fair market value equals the highest and best use to which the property could be put on the valuation date, and fair market value takes into account special uses that are realistically available due to the property's adaptability to a particular business. Fair market value is not affected by whether the owner has actually put the property to its highest and best use. The reasonable, realistic, and objective possible uses for the property in the near future control the valuation thereof. Elements affecting value that depend upon events or a combination of occurrences which, while within the realm of possibility, are not reasonably probable, are excluded from this consideration."

4. "As typically occurs in a case of valuation, the parties rely primarily on their experts' testimony and reports. . . . Expert testimony sometimes aids the Court in determining valuation. Other times, it does not. For example, expert testimony is not useful to the Court when the expert is merely an advocate for the position argued by the party."

In this case, the Tax Court concluded: "We do not accept the conclusion of any of the experts in toto, but we find parts of each of their opinions to be helpful in understanding the operation of the beer industry."

Tax Court Review of Expert Credentials. The expert for the IRS was with a consulting firm that assists management in developing corporate strategy. With respect to his credentials and expertise, the Tax Court said, "That fact that [he] is knowledgeable about this industry does not compel us to credit the testimony on the Transferred Assets' fair market value. . . . We do not find that he has expertise in valuing assets for federal income tax purposes. The thrust of [his] expertise centers on marketing, economics, and the like, rather than on the ascertainment of fair market value."

The Tax Court also specifically commented that they were also "disturbed by [the expert's] lack of regard for comparable sales."

The experts for Pabst were (1) an investment banker with many years of valuation experience and (2) an individual with 40 years' experience as a brewing industry executive.

Tax Court Review of Valuation Methodology. With respect to the first taxpayer expert, the Court was complimentary about his valuation credentials. However, the Court rejected his methodology with limited discussion of the details.

With respect to the second Pabst expert, the Court concluded: "We find his testimony on the valuation issue to be unpersuasive." In the decision, the Court listed the following specific factors:

1. The dates of many of the purported comparable sales were too far removed from the valuation date.

2. The report did not set forth enough data on the comparable breweries to allow the Court to make a meaningful comparison. A proferred comparable sale without enough identifying data in order to explain the components of the sale was unhelpful to the Court.

3. The Court was troubled by the fact that his methodology focused on the views of the buyer, to the exclusion of the seller. Ignoring the views of the willing seller is contrary to the well-established criteria of a hypothetical willing buyer and hypothetical willing seller.

The Court's Decision. Ultimately, the Tax Court concluded the following:

> Although the values ascribed in the Allocation Agreement are not necessarily determinative of the actual fair market values of the underlying assets, these values are very persuasive as to the assets' true fair market value, given the fact that the parties to the agreement were dealing at arm's length and the agreement had independent economic significance. . . . We hold that the value of the Transferred Assets equals the $190,287,375 of consideration. . . . remitted to petitioner in connection with the transfer.

Summary and Conclusion. This case is informative to valuation analysts because the Tax Court comments specifically with regard to (1) expert professional credentials and (2) valuation principles and methodologies. Other cases have cited *Pabst* for the proposition that focusing too much on the view of one hypothetical person, neglecting the view of the other, is contrary to a determination of fair market value;[2] that the Court may reject an expert's opinion to the extent that it is contrary to the judgment the Court forms on the basis of its understanding of the record as a whole;[3] and that the Court may embrace or reject an expert's opinion *in toto*, or may pick and choose the portions of the opinion to adopt.[4]

Nathan and Geraldine Morton v. Commissioner

Introduction. In *Nathan and Geraldine Morton v. Commissioner*,[5] the Tax Court provides a critical review of the discounted cash flow valuation method.

The tax issue in this case was the fair market value of Soft Warehouse, Inc. (SWI) stock purchased by a key employee. Nathan Morton left Home Depot to join SWI (later CompUSA), which had three large computer stores at the time. Mr. Morton agreed to purchase 500 shares of SWI, at $60.98 per share pursuant to a recently adopted stock plan.

The share purchase was on a five-year vesting schedule. Income tax on any gains between purchase price and fair market value normally would be spread over the transaction consummation period. However, Section 83(b) allows an exception to realize gross income from any gain at the time of the agreement to purchase. Mr. Morton made the Section 83(b) election. And, he reported the fair market value of the stock to be $60.98 per share, resulting in no gross income.

The Facts of the Case. The stock plan did not require the stock to be sold at fair market value. No valuation of the SWI stock was made at the time the stock plan was adopted nor at the time of the purchase agreement.

The IRS concluded that the fair market value of the SWI stock was $1,739.82 per share, resulting in taxable income to Mr. Morton of $839,420.

---

[2] *Bank One Corporation v. Commissioner*, 120 T.C. 174, 2003 U.S. Tax Ct. LEXIS 13, 120 T.C. No. 11 (May 2, 2003).
[3] *Estate of Blount v. Commissioner*, T.C. Memo 2004-116 (May 12, 2004), *aff'd in part* and *rev'd in part*, 2005 U.S. App. LEXIS 23502 (11th Cir. 2005).
[4] *Caracci v. Commissioner*, 118 T.C. 379 (May 22, 2002).
[5] *Morton v. Commissioner*, T.C. Memo 1997-166 (Apr. 1, 1997).

In addition, the IRS asserted that taxpayer was liable for the penalty prescribed under Section 6662—for negligence in underreporting the value.

The Issues at Trial. A legal issue common to many Tax Court cases was the admissibility of documents prepared after the valuation date. In this case, the following post-transaction data documents proved controversial at the trial.

1. A valuation of a noncontrolling equity interest in SWI one year later prepared by a major accounting firm.
2. A confidential private placement memorandum 14 months after the purchase, prepared by two well-known investment banking firms.
3. A prospectus for CompUSA (the successor company to SWI) almost two and a half years after the purchase, prepared by two other well-known investment banking firms.

Regarding these document admissibility issues, the Tax Court stated the following:

This court has drawn a distinction between subsequent events which affect the value of the property and those which merely provide evidence of such value on the valuation date.

Subsequent events or conditions which affect the value of the property can be taken into account only if they are reasonably foreseeable on the valuation date.

Conversely, subsequent events which merely provide evidence of the value of the property on the valuation date can be taken into account regardless of whether they are foreseeable on the valuation date.

The valuation prepared by [the accounting firm] and the confidential private placement memorandum . . . both contain information regarding the value of SWI stock within a reasonable time after that date, and neither describes subsequent events which affected the value of SWI stock. Both documents also represent valuations of SWI stock by third parties who were not influenced by the biases of litigation. The fact that they were prepared after the valuation date is a factor that we must consider in determining the probative value of the evidence, but does not automatically make the documents irrelevant.

The CompUSA prospectus, on the other hand, is not relevant to our determination of the value of the stock at issue. This document describes a public offering of SWI stock almost 2½ years after the valuation date. Based upon the record of this case, we cannot find that the public offering was sufficiently foreseeable by the parties on the valuation date. Accordingly, we will sustain petitioners' objection insofar as the CompUSA prospectus is concerned.

In valuation reports prepared for trial, the taxpayer's expert valued the SWI stock at $55 per share. The expert hired by the IRS valued the SWI stock at $1,798 per share.

The IRS's Position. The Tax Court noted that the taxpayer had the burden of proof. And the Tax Court's written opinion offered no discussion whatsoever of the government expert's valuation methodology. The government expert used a guideline publicly traded company valuation method. He selected Home Depot, Toys R Us, and Staples as his guideline companies, based on the theory that SWI, in becoming CompUSA, was a "category killer retailer," in spite of the fact that SWI only had three stores at the time of the valuation date.

The Taxpayer's Position. The taxpayer's expert relied solely on the income approach to valuation—and particularly the discounted cash flow method. He justified this decision (1) because in his opinion, there were no sufficiently comparable companies in existence as of the valuation date, and (2) because the cost approach, in his opinion, tended to minimize the value of assets and failed to consider intangible assets such as goodwill. He used a standard discounted net cash flow model.

The taxpayer's expert assumed that increments to working capital would equal 7 percent of the increase in sales over the previous year. He used a present value discount rate of 35 percent, which he described as necessary to justify the high degree of risk involved. He described SWI as a venture capital situation. And, he wanted to account for that risk in his discount rate. Finally, the taxpayer's expert reduced his value estimate with a combined lack of control and lack of marketability discount of 50 percent.

The Tax Court's Opinion. The Tax Court noted wild fluctuations of the income approach value estimates when minor valuation assumptions were changed. One reason for this was that the company was extremely highly leveraged at the valuation date.

The Tax Court pointed out that just a 1 percentage point change in incremental working capital, from 7 percent to 6 percent of incremental sales, caused the income approach value per share to increase substantially. The Tax Court found this "troubling in light of the fact that [the taxpayer's expert] agreed on cross-examination that six percent was a reasonable figure for incremental working capital."

The Tax Court also found the 35 percent present value discount rate "bothersome." The Court noted that the expert did not provide any objective support, either at trial or in his expert valuation report, for selecting a discount rate in this range.

The Court calculated that changing the present discount rate to 33 percent produced a value of $1,161 per share and changing the discount rate to 30 percent produced a value of $3,551 per share.

Summary and Conclusion. In this case, the Tax Court was critical of the taxpayer expert's use of the discounted cash flow valuation method. In particular, the Court was critical of the fact that the taxpayer's analyst had never fully explained nor fully documented key and sensitive valuation variables in his valuation opinion report. This criticism should be noteworthy to valuation practitioners.

Caracci v. Commissioner

Introduction. The issue in *Caracci v. Commissioner,*[6] a consolidated case involving the Caracci family, was whether the value of the Sta-Home Health Agency, Inc. (SHHA) and related entities transferred into S corporations exceeded the consideration paid.

The Facts of the Case. The Caracci family started SHHA on May 3, 1976. SHHA was a tax-exempt entity. On July 11, 1995, SHHA's board of directors

---

[6] *Caracci v. Commissioner,* 118 T.C. 379, 118 T.C. No. 25, 2002 U.S. Tax Ct. LEXIS 25 (May 22, 2002).

authorized its election of S corporation status. The total consideration paid was the assumption of the liabilities.

The Issues of the Case. The IRS contended that the value of the entities exceeded the value of the liabilities, and that the transferring entities were therefore liable for excise taxes under IRC section 4958.

The Taxpayer's Position. The taxpayer's expert used an adjusted balance sheet method—a form of the cost approach—which involves the identification and valuation of tangible and intangible assets and liabilities. He concluded that the fair market value of SHHA's total tangible and intangible assets was between $10.5 million and $11.5 million. He also concluded that SHHA's total liabilities were between $12 million and $12.5 million. The taxpayer's expert's conclusion was that SHHA's liabilities exceeded the value of its assets by $.5 million to $2 million.

The expert also used a market approach and concluded that SHHAs liabilities exceeded its total tangible and intangible assets by $.6 million to $2.35 million under that approach.

The IRS's Position. The IRS's expert rejected the cost approach, noting that SHHA was a "service-based business with relatively low investment in tangible assets." He pointed out that the value of SHHAs intangible assets was especially important, including such assets as "operating licenses, Medicare certifications, patient lists, referral relationships, a trained and assembled workforce, proprietary policies and procedures and trade name, and a going concern value."

He opined that a better valuation method was the market approach. He considered two types of transfers: valuation of comparable publicly traded home health care agencies and valuation of merged or acquired companies. As a basis for valuations under the market approach, he estimated SHHAs market value of invested capital (MVIC), using a price/revenue multiple. He then concluded that MVIC for SHHA was $13,563,000 by using a multiple of 0.3 (based on the guideline public companies) with SHHAs 1995 revenues of $45,209,000. He also considered the merged and acquired company method, by which he arrived at an MVIC of $11,302,000 by using a 0.25 multiple.

The Tax Court's Opinion. The Tax Court rejected the taxpayer's valuation results. The court reasoned that a company's "negative book value does not require a finding that the company had a fair market value of less than a zero." The court also did not accept the IRS expert's valuations because he did not consider some sophisticated home health care techniques, such as "infusion and respiratory therapies."

The Tax Court concluded that the fair market value of the net assets was $5,164,000. The court reached its conclusion by first arriving at the SHHA fair market value:

Indicated MVIC	$11,300,000
Plus current liabilities	$11,475,000
Less withheld payroll	$(4,100,000)
Indicated asset value	$18,675,000

Then, the court took into account SHHAs liabilities as of September 30, 1995:

Fair market value	$18,675,000
Assumed liabilities	$13,511,000
Excess	$5,164,000

The court said:

> We believe that the best evidence of the value of [SHHA] arises from the use of the comparable value method employed by both experts. We also are persuaded that the fair market value is best determined by relying upon the rationale of [IRS expert]. His use of the MVIC approach to compare the privately held [SHHA] entities to similar publicly traded businesses is especially appropriate here . . . . We...believe [however] that the price-to-revenue multiple for publicly traded companies should be no higher than the .25 that he applied to the merged and acquired comparable companies . . . . On balance, we believe that the most weight is properly given to [IRS expert's] estimate of the MVIC for the [SHHA] entities, using a price-to-revenue multiple of .25. This results in an MVIC of $11.3 million.

The court concluded that taxpayers were subject to "excess benefit" taxes under Section 4958.

Tax Court Review of Expert Credentials. The IRS's expert, a certified public accountant, was a principal of a major business valuation firm who had performed a number of assignments involving the analysis and appraisal of professional practices, with a heavy concentration in the health care field. He had been involved with assignments requiring the valuation of intangible assets, including certificates of need (CONs), customer relationships, goodwill, and workforces. The taxpayer challenged the IRS's expert's qualifications as an expert, claiming that his qualification as an expert and his methodology were insufficient. The court said, "These contentions are nonsensical and border on the frivolous."

Summary and Conclusion. In this case, the Tax Court rejected the taxpayer's use of the cost approach, instead favoring a market approach based on the market value of invested capital. The court also rejected the notion that a seasoned business appraiser should not qualify as a valuation expert.

Gow v. Commissioner

One of the issues in *Gow v. Commissioner*,[7] was whether stock in a closely held corporation that is subject to voting trust restrictions has no value to a hypothetical buyer.

The Facts of the Case. Williamsburg Vacations, Inc. (WVI) was incorporated in July 1983 to develop a time-share resort. Dr. Gow was one of the initial shareholders, holding 650 shares. In September of 1983, Dr. Gow sold 200 of her shares to E. Corbell Jones and that same day entered into a voting trust agreement with Jones concerning all of their WVI shares. Dr. Gow's husband served as trustee of the voting trust.

In February 1989, WVI issued 800 shares to Dr. Gow as bonus compensation (the 1989 stock). In February 1990, WVI issued an additional 400 shares to Dr. Gow as bonus compensation (the 1990 stock). On their jointly filed 1989 and 1990 income tax returns, the Gows reported the value of these two bonus compensation stock awards as $40,000 and $20,000, respectively. The IRS claimed a deficiency, arguing that the fair market value of the stock was much greater than reported by the Gows.

---

[7] *Gow v. Commissioner*, 2001 U.S. App. LEXIS 20882 (4th Cir. 2001).

Expert Testimony at the Tax Court. At trial, the IRS's experts testified that the fair market value of the 1989 stock was $2,142,313 and that the fair market value of the 1990 stock was $597,353. The Gows' expert witness, on the other hand, valued the 1989 stock at only $685,000 and the 1990 stock at only $299,000.

The Tax Court's Decision. The Tax Court adopted the values proposed by the IRS but reduced them by applying the higher discounts for lack of control and lack of marketability presented by the Gows. The court considered and rejected the Gows' contention that the stock had no value whatsoever because it was subject to a voting trust.[8]

The Appeals Court Decision. On appeal, the Gows argued that the Tax Court should have valued all the stock at zero. They also contended that the court's methodology for determining the fair market values of the stock was clearly erroneous. The Gows reasserted on appeal their argument that, in valuing the bonus compensation stock, the Tax Court should have considered the restrictions imposed on the stock by the voting trust and therefore should have concluded that all of the stock was valueless.

The Fourth Circuit Court of Appeals disagreed. It observed that restrictions imposed by voting trusts only bind the parties to the voting trusts; they have no impact on a hypothetical purchaser who is not a party to the voting trust agreement. Thus, the court found, any hypothetical purchaser would have purchased the 1989 and 1990 stock free of the voting trust and therefore would have paid fair market value for the shares. The court concluded, therefore, that the Tax Court's holding was not clearly erroneous, and the court affirmed.

Summary and Conclusion. This case illustrates valuation methodology for determining fair market value using a hypothetical buyer and seller approach.

BTR Dunlop Holdings, Inc. v. Commissioner

Tax Issue. A key issue in *BTR Dunlop Holdings, Inc. v. Commissioner*[9], involving a corporate income tax dispute, was the fair market value, for purposes of determining capital gains taxes under IRC § 311(b) and 482, of Schlegel UK Holdings Ltd. and Schlegel GmbH, which were transferred from the taxpayer, BTR Dunlop Holding, Inc., to the taxpayer's parent corporation, BTR, Plc.

The Facts of the Case. All of the stock of Schlegel UK was transferred for $21,846,000, and Schlegel GmbH was transferred for $9,400,000, including $5,116,136 attributable to a silent partnership agreement. In determining the fair market value of the two subsidiaries for tax purposes, the court had before it six valuations.

The first valuation was performed prior to the sale of the corporations. This valuation relied on management-prepared sales forecasts, expense forecasts, and historical financial data in its calculations. In addition to determining the fair market value of the corporations, the valuation report opined that a bargain purchase price for Schlegel UK was $21,845,000.

---

[8] *Gow v. Commissioner*, T.C. Memo 2000-93, 2000 Tax Ct. Memo LEXIS 108, 79 T.C.M. (CCH) 1680 (T.C. March 20, 2000).
[9] *BTR Dunlop Holdings, Inc. v. Commissioner,* T.C. Memo 1999-377, 1999 Tax Ct. Memo LEXIS 432 (Nov. 15, 1999).

The taxpayer's return was audited by the IRS, which determined that the fair market value of Schlegel UK was $48,838,000, and that the fair market value of Schlegel GmbH was $13,246,000, including the silent partnership agreement. The disparity between the taxpayer's and IRS's values resulted in a significant tax deficiency.

The Taxpayer's Position. The taxpayer argued that the corporations should be valued on a net asset value basis, but the court rejected this argument for two reasons:

1. The expert witnesses all relied most heavily on the earnings potential of the corporations and used the discounted cash flow method, and
2. Operating companies are generally valued based on earnings because an asset valuation tends to undervalue such companies.

Key Valuation Issue—Should Synergies Be Considered? One of the primary issues was whether Schlegel UK should be valued on a stand-alone basis or with consideration of synergies with a potential buyer. The court noted that there were six potential synergistic buyers for Schlegel UK at the time of the sale. However, while bids were solicited from all potential synergistic buyers, only the actual buyer submitted a bid.

The Tax Court's Decision. In reviewing the expert valuations, the court determined that the taxpayer's experts did not give enough weight to the synergistic potential. The court indicated that in determining fair market value, the hypothetical buyer and hypothetical seller must be disposed to maximum economic gain, and since there were six potential synergistic buyers for the subject business, synergy should be considered. The court found that application of a small-company risk premium and a company-specific risk premium in building up the discount rate used in the discounted cash flow approach equated to a stand-alone valuation, which the court rejected. The court ruled, therefore, that these premiums were not justified by the evidence presented.

The court also ruled that the IRS's expert, on the other hand, relied too heavily on potential synergies, and applied a beta that was too low. The court stated the following:

> Just as determination of fair market value requires assumption of a willing seller, it does not assume hypothetical transactions that are "unlikely and plainly contrary to the economic interests" of a hypothetical buyer. See *Estate of Hall v. Commissioner*, 92 T.C. 312, 337 (1989) (quoting *Estate of Curry v. United States*, 706 F.2d 1424, 1429 (7th Cir. 1983)); see also *Estate of Newhouse v. Commissioner*, 94 T.C. 193, 232 (1990).

In fact, one of the taxpayer's experts had performed both a stand-alone and a synergistic-scenario discounted cash flow analysis and gave the results equal weight because there was not a clear indication that a synergistic buyer could be found other than the actual buyer. The IRS expert was able to find only one acquisition over a period of three years in the subject industry. The court found that there was not a large enough difference between the two scenarios (even though the actual difference was 28.6 percent—about the average size of observed acquisition premiums).

Conclusions of Value. Ultimately, the court did not rely completely on the opinion of any one of the experts, and using the cash-flow estimates of some of the experts, concluded that the fair market value of Schlegel UK was $31 million on the valuation date. The court also held that the fair market value of Schlegel GmbH was $3.77 million. In reaching this value, the court refused to considered the taxpayer's proposition that the company was worth less on the valuation date than it reported on its tax return. It noted, "Reported values in petitioner's return are admissions by petitioner." The value of the silent partnership agreement was stipulated to be $5.116 million. Accordingly, the court found no tax deficiency.

Charitable Contribution Issues

John T. and Linda L. Hewitt v. Commissioner

Introduction. In the case of *John T. and Linda L. Hewitt v. Commissioner,*[10] the U.S. Tax Court held that the taxpayers did not substantially comply with Section 1.170A-13 of the Income Tax Regulations and, therefore, were not entitled to charitable contribution deductions in excess of that allowed by the Internal Revenue Service.

The Facts of the Case. The petitioners, John and Linda Hewitt, were part of an investor group that acquired Mel Jackson's Tax Service. At the time of the acquisition, Mel Jackson's Tax Service, Inc., which was headquartered in Tidewater, Virginia, operated multiple offices and generated over $1 million in revenue. Later, the name of the company was changed to Jackson Hewitt Tax Services, Inc. ("the Company" or "Jackson Hewitt").

During the taxable year of 1990, the petitioners made gifts of the Company stock to the Hewitt Foundation and to the Foundry United Methodist Church. At the time of the gifts, there were approximately 700,000 shares of Jackson Hewitt stock outstanding and in the hands of around 400 individuals and organizations. These stockholders included employees, franchisees, and others related to the company. Also, at the time the gifts were made, the Company stock was not traded on an organized exchange or market.

Rather, the market for the Company stock operated primarily through individuals or organizations contacting the Company. These contacts took the form of offers to buy or sell shares in the stock of the Company at a given price. In making these offers, the potential market participants only had access to information regarding trades and offers to sell made by other shareholders.

In addition to transactions funneled through the Company, a separate market operated through Wheat First Securities, Inc., in which hundreds to thousands of shares of Jackson Hewitt common stock were traded between 1990 and 1992. During the period between May 1, 1990, and December 31, 1991, the Company recorded 317 stock transfers involving approximately 100,000 shares. The petitioners filed timely joint federal tax returns for the 1990 and 1991 taxable years.

In their 1990 federal tax return, the petitioners included Form 8283 (noncash contributions), on which they reported the donation of two blocks of Jackson Hewitt stock valued at $26,000 and $7,000. As part of petitioners' 1991 tax return, they reported two contributions of stock valued at $48,000 (with a basis of $2,832) and $40,000 (with basis of $3,057).

---

[10] *Hewitt v. Commissioner*, 109 T.C. 258 (1997), *aff'd* 166 F.3d 332, 1998 U.S. App. LEXIS 37216. (4th Cir. Nov. 19, 1998).

Petitioners did not obtain a qualified appraisal to support the values of the Jackson Hewitt common stock they donated in 1990 and 1991. The fair market values claimed by the petitioners were based upon the average per share price of Company stock traded in arm's-length transactions at approximately the same time as the petitioners' donations of stock.

In their notice of deficiency, the IRS only allowed the petitioners' deductions for their gifts in the stock of the Company in the amounts of their original tax bases.

The Issues of the Case. The provisions relevant to this case state that the Secretary of the Treasury shall prescribe regulations which require any individual, closely held corporation, or personal service corporation claiming a charitable contribution deduction to:

1   Obtain a qualified appraisal for the contributed property.
2.   Attach an appraisal summary to the tax return.
3.   Include on the tax return such additional information (including the cost basis and acquisition date of the contributed party).[11]

Contributions to which these requirements apply include those of property (other than publicly traded securities) with a value greater than $5,000.

The IRS did not dispute that the Hewitts made charitable contributions to qualified organizations within the respective tax years or that the claimed values represented the fair market values of these contributions. The IRS disallowed the charitable contribution deductions claimed by the Hewitts for the stock in Jackson Hewitt in excess of the basis due to the lack of qualified appraisals.

It is quite clear that the Hewitts did not obtain any qualified appraisals to support their claimed deductions. However, they maintained that they should be allowed the value of the claimed deductions because their use of the average per share price of Jackson Hewitt stock traded in bona fide arm's-length transactions constituted substantial compliance with the requirements of Regulation Section 1.170A-13.

The Hewitts' tax returns, which did not even include an appraisal summary, only reflected the gifts of stock without identifying the gifts as Jackson Hewitt stock, without any indication of the number of shares. These returns only set forth the cost basis and the claimed values.

To sustain their position that a qualified appraisal is not a requirement under their circumstances, the Hewitts cited *Bond v. Commissioner*,[12] which held that the taxpayer had substantially complied with the requirements of the statute and regulations even though a separate appraisal had not been obtained and the qualifications of the appraiser were omitted from the appraisal summary attached to the tax return.

The Court's Decision. In the *Hewitt v. Commissioner* matter, the Court found nothing in *Bond v. Commissioner* that relieves the Hewitts of the requirements of obtaining a qualified appraisal. No deduction is allowed for a contribution of property for which an appraisal is required unless the appraisal requirements are satisfied. The donor must obtain and retain a qualified written appraisal by a qualified appraiser for the property contributed and must attach a signed appraisal summary to the return on which the deduction is first claimed.

---

[11] Section 170(a)(1).
[12] *Bond v. Commissioner*, 100 T.C. 32 (1993).

The Court ruled that the Hewitts furnished practically none of the information required. The IRS must be provided with enough information to alert taxpayers to potential overvaluations. The Hewitts were found not to fall within the permissible boundaries of *Bond v. Commissioner*. In *Bond* an appraisal summary was completed by a qualified appraiser, and it contained most of the required information. The summary could therefore be treated as a written appraisal and be attached to the return.

The taxpayers also tried to support their position claiming that there was a market which provided support for their use of the average per share price of the Jackson Hewitt stock. This position was found to be without merit. Given the amounts of the gifts in this case, the exemption from the qualified appraisal requirements is statutorily limited to publicly traded securities.

The principal objective of the appraisal report requirement is to enable the IRS to deal more effectively with the prevalent use of overvaluations. Such need exists even though in a particular case, such as this, it turns out that the taxpayers' deduction was in fact based on the fair market value of the property. This happenstance is insufficient to constitute substantial compliance with a statutory condition to obtain the claimed deduction. In the Court's opinion, what the petitioners were seeking was not the application of the substantial compliance principle but an exemption from the clear requirement of the statute and regulations in a situation where there is no overvaluation of the charitable contribution.

The Court held that the taxpayers were not entitled to deduct amounts in excess of those allowed by the IRS for the contributions of Jackson Hewitt stock.

Appeals Court Decision. The taxpayers appealed the decision to the U.S. Court of Appeals for the fourth circuit. The Appeals Court affirmed the decision of the Tax Court, noting that the legislative history indicates that Congress intended the qualified appraisal requirement to be mandatory. The Appeals Court concluded deductions are a matter of "legislative grace," and a taxpayer seeking the benefits of a deduction must show that every condition Congress imposes has been "fully satisfied."

Summary and Conclusion. This case offers important lessons to taxpayers claiming charitable contribution deductions for gifts of shares of closely held, non-publicly traded common stock. Even though the fair market value of closely held stock involved in a gift or transfer is known with almost absolute certainty, the taxpayer is still required to provide the IRS with supporting evidence, in the form of an appraisal summary.

John C. Todd v. Commissioner

In *Todd v. Commissioner*,[13] the court noted that, in the context of charitable contributions, there is a common denominator for determining whether shares are qualified appreciated stock on the transfer date and whether taxpayers are subject to the substantiation requirements. That common denominator is whether, on the transfer date, market quotations with respect to the shares are readily available on an established securities market.

---

[13] *Todd v. Commissioner*, 118 T.C. 354, 118 T.C. No. 19, 2002 U.S. Tax Ct. LEXIS 19 (April 19, 2002).

The only issue in *Todd* was whether the taxpayer, who formed the Todd Family Foundation ("Foundation"), a nonprofit corporation, was entitled to charitable deductions.

The Facts of the Case. The taxpayer formed the Foundation on December 24, 1994. On December 27, 1994, he transferred 6,350 shares of stock of Union Colony Bancorp (UCB), a Colorado corporation, to the Foundation. On the date of transfer, the UCB shares were not listed on any state, regional, or city stock exchange. The taxpayer claimed the following charitable contribution deductions on his income tax returns from 1994–1997: $33,338 on 1994 return; $152,692 on 1995 return; $221,066 on 1996 return; and $56,906 on 1997 return. As the court noted:

> Attached to the Form 1040 is a Form 8283, Noncash Charitable Contributions (the Form 8283), on which petitioners provided information concerning the transfer, including petitioners' "cost or adjusted basis" in the shares, $33,338, the fair market value of the shares, $553,847, and a statement of the method used to determine the fair market value: "Sales of other shares at same time." The portion of the Form 8283 that provides for the certification of an appraiser is without entries. No appraisal summary with respect to the shares is attached to the Form 8283 or otherwise included with the Form 1040.

The "sale of shares" upon which the petitioner based the fair market value was the subsequent sale of the shares by the Foundation to First National of Nebraska, Inc., in January of 1995.

Tax Court Holding. The Court held that the deductions were not allowed because the shares were not qualified appreciated stock at the date of transfer. The Court reasoned that the common characteristic for determining whether the shares were qualified appreciated stock was whether, on the transfer date, the shares' market quotations were readily available on security markets. The petitioners failed to prove that market quotations were readily available for the UCB stock. Finding that such market quotations were unavailable, the Court held that "(1) the shares were not qualified appreciated stock, (2) petitioners are subject to the substantiation requirements (which they failed to satisfy), and (3) as a result of either (1) or (2), or both, they are not entitled to the disallowed deductions."

Summary and Conclusion. The Tax Court denied charitable deductions for shares of stock that were not qualified appreciated stock and the value of which was not substantiated. The case thus illustrates the importance of obtaining a formal appraisal where there is no readily available market quotation for the stock.

Gerald D. and Catherine Leibowitz v. Commissioner

Introduction. In *Leibowitz v. Commissioner*,[14] the U.S. Tax Court provided guidance with regard to the appropriate market from which to extract valuation pricing data for movie memorabilia.

The tax issues in this case were (1) the fair market value of the movie memorabilia ("the collection") donated by taxpayer Gerald Leibowitz to the American

---

[14] *Leibowitz v. Commissioner*, T.C. Memo 1997-243 (May 29, 1997).

Museum of the Moving Image (AMMI) for purposes of determining the charitable contribution deductions to which petitioners were entitled for the year of the gift, and for the later years by way of carryovers and (2) whether the taxpayers were liable for a valuation overstatement.

The Tax Court found the value of the collection to be less than the taxpayers claimed, but more than the IRS allowed. The Tax Court held that the taxpayers were not liable for a valuation overstatement.

The Collection. The collection donated to AMMI consisted of 7,378 items of movie memorabilia including 546 duplicates, from 659 different films. The exact number of items in each category was based on an inventory conducted by AMMI. Most of the titles in the collection were of films from the 1950s through the 1970s. The overall physical condition of the collection was mint, with many items having never been handled.

The duplicate items were physically separated from the rest of the collection and held for subsequent sale or trade. However, none of the duplicates had been disposed of at the time of trial.

The Taxpayer's Valuation. Leibowitz obtained two appraisals of the collection. The second appraisal, for $188,085, was used as the basis for a charitable contribution reported in the taxpayer's tax return. A copy of the report of that appraisal was attached to the return.

The Taxpayer's Trial Expert. The appraisers had performed approximately 1,500 appraisals of "reproduction masters" of works of art in connection with questionnable tax shelters.[15] Both appraisers, by reason of the inflated values in those appraisals, were also named as defendants in numerous lawsuits by investors in those tax shelters.

The Tax Court rejected both the appraisals, which exceed by more than 20 percent the values asserted by the taxpayer's expert at the trial. "The record fails to support either of these appraisals," the Tax Court concluded.

Leibowitz retained a different appraiser to appraise the collection and to prepare an expert valuation report for trial. At the time of trial, this appraiser had been a collector and dealer of movie memorabilia.

The taxpayer's trial expert based his valuation of the collection on prices in the retail store and catalog sales market as of the valuation date. In preparation for assigning values to the collection, the appraiser consulted dealers whom he knew or had dealings with who had owned or operated retail stores as of the valuation date. He also consulted various trade publications.

The taxpayer's expert included all 7,378 items in the inventory in his valuation, including the 546 duplicates. He assigned one or more premium units to the more desirable of the 659 titles, valued as a multiple of the "average value" assigned to items in that category. For example, each three-sheet poster was assigned an "average value" of $30. If the appraiser assigned three premium units to a title, the three-sheet would be valued at $90, or three times the "average value."

He took into account the overall mint condition of the collection and the development of the market. He believed that the market was developing slowly throughout the relevant time period. He took into account in his valuation report events

---

[15] See *Rose v. Commissioner* 88 T.C. 386, 398-399 (1987), *aff'd* 868 F.2d 851 (6th Cir. 1989).

that occurred both prior to and shortly after the donation when he valued the collection.

The IRS's Experts. The IRS retained an appraiser to estimate the fair market value of the collection and prepare an expert valuation report for trial. This expert was the author of a price guide, an editor of magazines devoted to movie memorabilia, a member of the International Appraiser's Society, and a senior price editor for a major comic book pricing guide.

The IRS expert began collecting memorabilia prior to the valuation date and became a dealer in movie memorabilia after the valuation date. Eventually, the IRS expert became a major dealer in movie memorabilia. At the time of trial, he maintained a database of prices of over 100,000 items of movie memorabilia.

He assumed that the relevant market was the movie memorabilia convention. He asserted that the single key element in pricing movie memorabilia is demand by collectors who conduct an appropriate amount of research prior to entering the convention market.

The IRS appraiser heavily discounted the value of foreign posters because he maintained that there was little or no demand for them as of the valuation date. In his view, collectors viewed foreign posters of American films as inauthentic novelties, and that only when domestic posters began to rise dramatically in price after the valuation date did collectors begin to show interest in foreign posters of American films.

The IRS expert considered the collection as a whole to have little intrinsic value because it consisted of "minor or unknown films." He evaluated the collection as little more than a hoard, virtually unsalable within a short period of time, even at distress sale prices in the convention market.

Based upon these foregoing considerations, the IRS expert assigned values as low as 25 cents to individual items. He appraised the collection at the time of its donation to AMMI in 1985 at $5,733.49.

Tax Court's Conclusion of the Relevant Market. The Tax Court noted that: "Selection of the proper market for valuation purposes is a question of fact." In determining the appropriate market to use in valuing most types of property, a sale "to the public" normally refers to a sale to the retail customer who is the ultimate consumer. A sale to an ultimate consumer is any sale to those persons who do not hold the item for subsequent resale. However, when used in this context, the term "retail" does not mean that the most expensive source is the only source for determining fair market value. Fair market value is determined in the market most commonly used by the ultimate consumer, which may or may not be the most expensive, since ultimate consumers may simultaneously participate in multiple markets with different price structures.

Stores specializing in movie memorabilia were located in such major metropolitan areas as New York, Los Angeles, and San Francisco. These stores also competed in nationwide markets through catalog sales along with dealers who specialized in catalog sales. Despite the lack of specific comparative sales data in the record concerning the different markets, the Tax Court concluded that it is more likely than not, based upon the testimony of both experts, that retail stores were the most common form of sale to "ultimate consumers" of movie memorabilia at the time.

The mint condition of the collection particularly suited it to sale on consignment in the retail store setting or in the catalog sales market. The absence of "high-end" titles would have precluded sale of most of the collection on an item-by-item basis in the auction market. These factors supported the Tax Court's finding that retail stores were the relevant market for the Leibowitz collection. In the written decision, the Tax Court reported: "We therefore reject [the IRS expert's] overall valuation of the collection."

The taxpayer's expert chose the correct market in which to value the collection. However, for other reasons, the Tax Court also rejected his valuation. The IRS expert conceded in testimony that the taxpayer's expert's valuation was accurate for the New York retail store market because retail store prices were markedly higher than those found at conventions. However, the Court's analysis of the record indicated that the taxpayer's valuation was too high.

The appraiser's use of flawed methodology in determining base prices inflated the entire valuation. In determining a base price for each category of item, the taxpayer's expert used an "average price" for that category. As the IRS correctly pointed out on brief, this meant that the taxpayer's appraiser assumed that each item in the collection was worth at least the average value in the marketplace of all such items for sale. Even when taking into account the mint condition of the collection, this approach improperly inflates the valuation.

The Tax Court rejected the expert for the taxpayer's valuation, even though he chose the correct market and his overall methodology of assigning premium values to more desirable titles relative to all the items in a category would have been a reasonable approach if he had used a valid base price.

The Tax Court's Valuation of the Collection. The parties' experts differed on the amount of time that it would take to sell the collection. The IRS expert postulated a period of no less than one to two years because of the difficulties attendant in gaining access to the market. However, this expert did not consider how long it would take a skilled dealer in movie memorabilia already present in the retail store market to sell the collection. The taxpayer's expert estimated that the collection could be sold on consignment in a retail store within a year without affecting the prices obtained for each individual item. The collection was relatively small in relation to the inventory carried by a movie memorabilia store or chain of stores.

A year to liquidate the collection at full retail store prices would not be unreasonable under the circumstances. The minimal physical storage requirements and comparatively stable prices in the movie memorabilia markets over the course of a year support such a finding.

Based upon the foregoing considerations, the Tax Court did not apply a blockage discount to the fair market value of petitioner's collection.

The Tax Court considered a number of factors in arriving at a fair market value of the collection. The agreed mint condition of the collection played a major role, both in determining the relevant market, as discussed above, and in valuing each item for sale on an individual basis. The taxpayer's testimony that the collection's mint condition would tend to increase the prices commanded in a retail store was strongly supported by commentary in all of the movie memorabilia pricing guides in evidence.

The level of collector demand for the titles in the collection was also very important. The taxpayer's appraiser characterized the collection as "middle-of-the-road." The pricing guides, the IRS expert's concession that at least some of the titles were marketable, and the evidence in the record that the collection as a whole could be sold support this characterization.

For several categories, the Tax Court found that the petitioners failed to carry their burden of proof in establishing a fair market value. Therefore, the IRS's valuation was used for those categories.

Summary and Conclusion. Ultimately, the Tax Court concluded that the total fair market value of the collection was $50,412. This case is instructive to both taxpayers and valuation practitioners. It illustrates how the Tax Court can select the relevant market and pick and choose the various components of each expert's valuation analysis and report. It also illustrates how the Tax Court can conclude its own value for property when it is not satisfied with either party's valuation experts.

Koblick v. Commissioner

The Facts of the Case. In *Koblick v. Commissioner*,[16] taxpayers owned a 45 percent share in Sealodge International, Inc. (Sealodge), which had two other shareholders owning 45 percent and 10 percent respectively, and which owned a "submersible" five-room hotel, which they donated to a charitable organization by transferring their interest simultaneously with those of Sealodge's two other minority shareholders.

The taxpayers claimed a $720,000 deduction for their interest, based in part on a valuation by a consulting engineer familiar with the vessel's original construction and on a valuation conducted by a marine surveyor.

In a subsequent audit, the IRS cut the deduction by half to $360,000. Taxpayers challenged the deficiency, submitting the marine surveyor's report, which estimated the entire vessel's replacement cost at $4.25 million, reduced by depreciation to $1.8 million.

Valuation Evidence. The replacement cost was supported by a letter from an oceanographic foundation, which claimed that the vessel was certified by the American Board of Shipping (ABS). The submersible sealodge was not ABS-certified, however; and the report by the taxpayer's original consulting engineer had taken this into account, estimating replacement cost at $1.97 million. An IRS expert had arrived at an even lower replacement cost of $1.1 million, which he reduced by depreciation and inflation to a final value between $368,000 and $464,000.

The Tax Court's Analysis. At the hearing, the Tax Court found the engineer's replacement cost to be the "best starting point." It then depreciated the value according to the surveyor's analysis, arriving at a fair market value of $1.06 million.

Discount for Lack of Control. The IRS had proposed a 22 percent minority interest (lack of control) discount, but taxpayers argued that because they had donated their 45 percent interest as part of a prearranged plan in "lockstep" with the other shareholders to transfer 100 percent control, the court should allow an even lower minority interest discount. The Tax Court agreed, citing *N. Trust Co. v. Commissioner*, 87 T.C. 349 (1986), and applied a 10 percent discount, but without further explanation of how it arrived at that percentage. The court also failed to explain how the "lockstep principle" justified *any* minority discount, given the simultaneous, collective transfer of a 100 percent controlling interest.

---

[16] Koblick v. Commissioner, 2006 Tax Ct. Memo LEXIS 63 (April 3, 2006).

Although taxpayers had won the discount battle, they lost the case. After applying a minority-position discount of 10 percent, the court found that the 45 percent interest in Sealodge had a value of $429,300 at the time of the gift of stock, and that, therefore, the deduction value was $429,300 less $90,000, or $339,300. Because the notice of deficiency determined a higher value, the court sustained that determination of deficiency.

Reasonable Compensation Issues

Multifactor Tests

LabelGraphics, Inc. v. Commissioner—9th Circuit

Introduction. In *LabelGraphics, Inc. v. Commissioner*,[17] the Tax Court provides practitioners with a five factor test for assessing the reasonableness of the executive compensation income tax deduction related to employee/owners of closely held corporations.

The main issue in this case was the amount that LabelGraphics, Inc., was entitled to deduct as reasonable compensation to its president, Lon Martin. Mr. Martin was the president and sole shareholder of this corporation during the year in question.

The IRS claimed Mr. Martin's compensation of $878,913 was overstated by $633,313. This amount, therefore, represented taxable income to the company.

The Tax Court's Five Factor Test. The Tax Court's Five Factor Test comprises the following factors.

Factor Number One. The first factor that the Tax Court considered was the employee's role in the company. The Tax Court determined that Mr. Martin was the primary reason for the company's success over the years from its inception. The Tax Court made note of the substantial contributions that he provided to the company over his years of service. However, the Tax Court questioned why his bonus was almost three times the amount of any other bonus that Mr. Martin had ever received. The taxpayer's first expert argued that the unusually high compensation was justified because Mr. Martin had been undercompensated in prior years. This expert offered no analysis or explanation in support of his claim. Because of this, however, the Tax Court gave his opinion little weight. The Tax Court found no other evidence to support the abnormal jump in Mr. Martin's bonus for the year in question.

Factor Number Two. The second factor that the Tax Court considered was a comparison of the compensation paid to similarly situated employees in similar companies. Both taxpayer experts believed that the bonus was reasonable based on their comparisons with other executives in high-tech companies.

Both taxpayer experts failed to offer any details concerning which companies they used to base their opinions on. Both experts failed to provide specifics on the particular executives involved, pertinent information on their particular qualifications and skills, and the exact compensation that was received.

---

[17] *LabelGraphics, Inc. v. Commissioner*, T.C. Memo 1998-343 (Sept. 28, 1998), *aff'd* 221 F.3d 1091 (9th Cir. 2000).

Accordingly, the Tax Court was unable to determine: (1) how similar these other unidentified companies and their businesses were to the petitioner and (2) how similar the services their executives rendered were to the services that Mr. Martin performed.

The taxpayer's second expert argued that Mr. Martin was entitled to even more compensation because he was performing the tasks of four different executives. However, the Tax Court gave little weight to this argument, just as it has in prior cases. This is due to the Court's opinion that it simply is not possible for one person to perform work equal to four full-time executives.

The taxpayer's second expert also contended that Mr. Martin should be receiving royalties for a new process that he developed, just as chief technical officers of high-tech companies receive royalties for products that they help develop. The Tax Court found that the expert did not elaborate enough to give this argument weight.

The IRS expert (1) used three comparable publicly traded companies in the printing industry and (2) considered two surveys of executive compensation in the printing industry to determine that reasonable compensation for Mr. Martin should have totaled $230,000. The Tax Court rejected the IRS expert's opinion for several reasons. First, two of the comparable companies that he used were exceedingly large and the third company was not nearly as profitable as LabelGraphics. Second, the surveys that he used were, admittedly, of limited use in determining what may be reasonable compensation. Third, he failed to take into consideration the substantial stock options that the executives of these companies received.

Factor Number Three. The third factor considered by the Tax Court was the character and condition of the company. The company had, over the years, been run well and profitably. The management had been able to build an excellent reputation in the label and printing industry.

Factor Number Four. The fourth factor examined whether a relationship existed between the company and employee that may permit the company to disguise nondeductible corporate distributions as deductible compensation. LabelGraphics suffered a loss of $98,639 that resulted in a -6.19 percent return on equity for the year in question.

The Tax Court did not agree that an independent investor would be satisfied with these results in light of the high salary payout.

Factor Number Five. The fifth factor focused on whether the compensation was paid pursuant to a (1) structured, (2) formal, and (3) consistently applied program. Mr. Martin's bonuses in prior years had been tied to the performance of the company.

The Tax Court concluded that there were no substantial changes in performance that would provide a reasonable explanation for paying Mr. Martin such an unusually high bonus.

Summary and Conclusion. The Tax Court determined that Mr. Marin deserved a larger than normal bonus for his development of a new process. However, the Court concluded that the bonus that he received was abnormally high.

The Tax Court determined that a total compensation of $406,000 was reasonable compensation, as it provided for a 10.20 percent return on stockholders' equity.

B & D Foundations, Inc. v. Commissioner—10th Circuit

In *B & D Foundations, Inc. v. Commissioner*,[18] the Tax Court applied a multifactor test adopted by the Tenth Circuit in *Pepsi-Cola Bottling Co. of Salina, Inc. v. Commissioner*[19] to determine reasonable compensation in a closely held corporation. *Pepsi-Cola* had listed nine factors; the court in this case reviewed 10.

The Facts of the Case. The IRS disallowed as unreasonable compensation under section 162(a)(1) $353,911 of salaries out of $1,113,800 paid and claimed by the taxpayer as salaries and bonuses to its only officer director-shareholders (Mr. and Mrs. Myers) for its fiscal year ended July 31, 1996. The taxpayer was a closely held C corporation whose shareholders had never elected pass-through treatment under subchapter S.

The taxpayer had no fixed formula for determining the annual salaries and bonuses paid to Mr. and Mrs. Myers. Until the fiscal year ended July 31, 1996, Mr. and Mrs. Myers, as the taxpayer's directors, generally around the beginning of the fiscal year, would set the respective salaries they were to receive for that year. Also, no dividends were paid.

Tax Court's Analysis. In determining whether the compensation to the Myers was reasonable, the Court looked to the following factors used by the Tenth Circuit: (1) the employee's qualifications; (2) the nature, extent, and scope of the employee's work; (3) the size and complexities of the business; (4) a comparison of salaries paid with the gross income and the net income; (5) the prevailing economic conditions; (6) a comparison of salaries with distributions to shareholders; (7) the prevailing rates of compensation for comparable positions in comparable concerns; (8) the salary policy of the taxpayer as to all employees; and (9) in the case of small corporations with a limited number of officers, the amount of compensation paid to the particular employee in previous years. The court also used the independent investor test and the taxpayer's financial performance.

1. **Qualifications.** Regarding the first factor, the Court found that Mr. Myers was quite knowledgeable about the industry the taxpayer was in, but that Mrs. Myers only had general business knowledge. This factor favored the taxpayer with respect to Mr. Myers but was neutral with respect to Mrs. Myers.

2. **Nature, Extent, and Scope of Work.** Here, the Court found that Mr. Myers put in very long hours and was the taxpayer's key employee, whereas Mrs. Myers handled the taxpayer's accounting, administrative, and support functions. The court concluded that this factor favored the taxpayer with respect to Mr. Myers but was neutral with respect to Mrs. Myers.

3. **Size and Complexity of Business.** For the 1996 fiscal year in issue, the taxpayer grossed more than $4.5 million. It employed up to as many as 35 to 40 construction workers during a year. Its jobs, however, did not require substantial scientific or highly technical knowledge. Nonetheless, the Myers were the company's only managers. The court accordingly concluded that this factor favored the IRS, but that the advantage to the IRS was offset by the leanness

---

[18] *B&D Foundations, Inc. v. Commissioner*, T.C. Memo 2001-262, 2001 Tax Ct. Memo LEXIS 298, 82 T.C.M. (CCH) 692 (October 3, 2001).
[19] *Pepsi-Cola Bottling Co. of Salina, Inc. v. Commissioner*, 528 F.2d 176 (10th Cir. 1975).

of the taxpayer's management team and the multiple functions Mr. and Mrs. Myers performed in managing the taxpayer's operations.

4. **Comparison of Compensation with Gross Receipt and Net, After-Tax Results.** For the 1996 fiscal year in issue, the taxpayer had a net loss after taxes of $61,904 as a result of the $586,500 salary and $163,000 bonus paid to Mr. Myers and the $288,500 salary and $75,800 bonus paid to Mrs. Myers. These payments equaled 105.88 percent of the taxpayer's net income for that year (before taxes and officer compensation). The taxpayer that year also experienced a $155,901 reduction in its equity ($534,443 net assets and equity at the beginning of the year, less $378,542 net assets and equity at year end, without regard to the obligation the taxpayer took on in that year to pay an additional $488,000 of "deferred compensation" to Mr. and Mrs. Myers). The Court ruled that this factor favored the IRS.

5. **Economic Conditions.** Although there was a boom in the taxpayer's business that contributed to the taxpayer's profitability during these years, the record also reflected that the taxpayer was a well-managed company whose work enjoyed an excellent reputation. The Court concluded that this factor was neutral because the taxpayer's financial success was not due merely to fortuitous economic conditions.

6. **Comparison of Compensation with Formal Dividend Distributions.** The failure to declare and pay dividends suggests that purported compensation payments may be disguised dividends. Although Mr. and Mrs. Myers were extremely well compensated, commencing with the taxpayer's fiscal year ended July 31, 1993, the taxpayer made no formal dividend distributions from the time of its incorporation in late 1986 through July 31, 1996. This factor favored the IRS.

7. **Compensation for Comparable Positions in Comparable Concerns.** The taxpayer's valuation expert opined that the $1,113,800 in compensation paid to Mr. and Mrs. Myers that year was reasonable. However, the Court observed that he failed to determine how similar the comparable companies he used were to the taxpayer and how similar the services their officers performed were to the services performed by Mr. and Mrs. Myers. The taxpayer's expert also failed to address the contribution for their benefit to the taxpayer's qualified retirement plan. The Court also rejected the suggestion of the taxpayer's expert that Mr. and Mrs. Myers were entitled to the compensation that would be provided to six full-time executives/employees serving as the taxpayer's chief executive officer, chief financial officer, chief operating officer, bookkeeper, personnel manager, and office manager.

Based on various compensation surveys, including his own, the IRS's expert opined that reasonable compensation would be $300,000 for Mr. Myers, and $200,000 for Mrs. Myers. The Court determined that the surveys used by the IRS did not cover companies comparable to the taxpayer. The Court faulted the expert's survey because he provided few specifics regarding the companies he selected, omitting, among other things, their number of employees, the business conditions in the area in which they operated, and how similar their businesses were to the taxpayer's business.

Thus, the Court gave little weight to either expert's opinion, and concluded that this factor was neutral because neither the taxpayer's expert nor the IRS's expert offered persuasive comparable pay data.

8. **Taxpayer's Salary Policy for All Employees.** All of the taxpayer's employees other than the Myers were paid on an hourly basis; all were given a Christmas

bonus; and certain key employees were paid additional bonuses. In contrast, Mr. and Mrs. Myers annually set their own compensation. Because none of the other employees performed services similar to those of Mr. and Mrs. Myers, the Court ruled that this factor was neutral.

9. **Compensation Paid in Previous Years.** While acknowledging that the Myers were undercompensated in earlier years, the IRS claimed—and the Court agreed—that they were extremely well compensated since the taxpayer's 1993 fiscal year, and that any past undercompensation was recovered by the 1996 fiscal year. The Court also concluded that the taxpayer failed to establish that any part of the salary payments the IRS disallowed for its 1996 fiscal year in issue qualified as reasonable compensation to Mr. and Mrs. Myers for past services in prior years. This factor, therefore, favored the IRS.

10. **Independent Investor Test and Taxpayer's Financial Performance.** Under the independent investor test, all the other factors are examined from the perspective of an independent investor. This requires an analysis of the return on equity (ROE) of the taxpayer-corporation (where the employee-shareholder receiving the compensation in issue also controls that taxpayer) from the perspective of a hypothetical independent investor. The taxpayer's expert contended that an independent investor would be satisfied with the 43.82 percent compounded annual rate of return he calculated was enjoyed through the year ended July 31, 1996, on that investor's initial $10,000 investment in the corporation. The Court noted that under the independent investor test, a company's annual ROE usually examines that company's net income after taxes for that year. More importantly, the shareholders' equity in the company, upon which an annual return is calculated, includes not just the shareholders' initial invested capital but the company's prior accumulated earnings. The Court found that, regardless of which approach was used to calculate the taxpayer's return on equity, for the 1996 fiscal year in issue, the taxpayer suffered a negative ROE even before consideration of the taxpayer's "deferred compensation" obligation to Mr. and Mrs. Myers.

For that year, even before consideration of its future deferred payment obligation to Mr. and Mrs. Myers, the taxpayer had a $61,904 net loss after taxes, suffered a negative ROE (ranging from a negative 11.58 percent return to a negative 16.35 percent return), and experienced a $155,901 reduction in its equity or net asset value (i.e., its $534,443 of equity at the beginning of the 1996 fiscal year, less its $378,542 year-end equity). Therefore, the Court concluded that an independent investor would not be happy with the taxpayer's financial performance for its 1996 fiscal year, especially where the total officer compensation paid to Mr. and Mrs. Myers for that year was almost three times the investor's year-end equity in the company ($1,113,800, divided by $378,542). This factor favored the IRS.

Weighing all these factors, the Court held that taxpayer had failed to show he was entitled to a larger deduction under §162 than the IRS had allowed in its statutory notice. Thus, $353,911 was disallowed as a deduction.

Summary and Conclusion. This case lays out the multiple factors that courts in some jurisdictions will consider in determining whether the compensation of a closely held business's owner is reasonable. Factors where the appraiser's opinion may be sought relate to whether compensation is comparable to compensation in similar companies for similar jobs, and whether an independent investor would consider that the company's ROE supports the compensation. For a case taking a similar approach, see, e.g., *Miller & Sons Drywall, Inc. v. Commissioner.*[20]

Brewer Quality Homes, Inc. v. Commissioner

Another case that weighed multiple factors in determining whether compensation was reasonable, and therefore deductible, is *Brewer Quality Homes, Inc. v. Commissioner.*[21]

The Facts of the Case. Brewer Quality Homes (BQH) was a closely-held corporation. Brewer, BQH's founder and principal officer and his wife each owned 50 percent. Brewer exercised complete control over the business at all times and performed virtually all of the company's job functions, although the company had 16 employees. He worked six to seven days a week, putting in about 70 hours per week in the early years of the business and about 60 hours per week in 1995 and 1996, the years at issue in the case.

In 1995, BQH paid Brewer $62,186 in salary over the course of the year and $700,000 as a bonus at the end of the year. In 1996 BQH paid him $63,559 in annual salary and $800,000 as an end-of-year bonus. Brewer's compensation in 1995 represented 82 percent of BQH's taxable income for that year, while his 1996 compensation accounted for 85 percent of BQH's total taxable income for 1996. During 1995 and 1996, the company paid no dividends and never had a retirement or profit-sharing plan for Brewer. The IRS determined that BQH could deduct only $604,117 for 1995 and $485,966 for 1996.

The Parties' Respective Positions. Both parties presented expert witnesses. BQH's experts opined that Brewer's compensation was reasonable, and the IRS's expert that it was not.

Only Brewer's expert used statistical data, based on the financial ratios found in Robert Morris Associates (RMA) surveys, including a ratio for executive compensation to company sales, as a measure of reasonable compensation. The expert determined that Brewer "achieved exceptional financial performance" at BQH, justifying compensation above the 75th percentile and as high as the 90th percentile. The IRS's expert criticized this use of the ratios, claiming, among other things, that the RMA data might not be "consistent with arm's length practices." However, the IRS expert did not provide anything to back up his suspicion, nor did he offer any other data focusing more directly on the retail mobile home industry.

Tax Court's Nine-Factor Analysis. The Tax Court's reasonableness inquiry was governed by the nine-factor test set forth in *Owensby & Kritikos, Inc. v. Cmm'r,* 819 F.2d 1315 (5th Cir. 1987).

1. Brewer's Qualifications

The Tax Court observed that Brewer was highly qualified and determined that this factor weighed in favor of a relatively high compensation for Mr. Brewer.

2. Nature, Extent, and Scope of Mr. Brewer's Work

The Tax Court found that Mr. Brewer worked long hours and that his hard work was the driving force behind BQH's success, noting Mr. Brewer's ability to fulfill numerous roles, including serving as BQH's president, chief financial officer,

[20] *Miller & Sons Drywall, Inc. v. Commissioner,* T.C. Memo 2005-114 (May 19, 2005).
[21] *Brewer Quality Homes, Inc. v. Commissioner,* T.C. Memo 2003-200 (July 10, 2003).

chief executive officer, general manager, sales manager, loan officer, credit manager, purchasing officer, personnel manager, advertising manager, insurance agent, and real estate manager. The Tax Court also determined that through Mr. Brewer's "enthusiasm, hard work, and dedication, he built [BQH] into a successful enterprise." As such, the Tax Court concluded that this factor weighed in favor of a high compensation for Mr. Brewer. Tempering this finding, however, this Court has observed that "nonetheless, limits to reasonable compensation exist even for the most valuable employees."

3. Size and Complexity of BQH

The Tax Court recognized the growth BQH made over the years, especially noting the substantial success it enjoyed beginning in the early 1990s. The Tax Court cited BQH's rise in the national rankings among retailers for BQH's products as evidence of this fact. The Tax Court also noted the different aspects of BQH's operations, specifically observing BQH's foray into the financing and insurance aspects of sales. In sum, the Tax Court made a determination that this factor favored a higher compensation for Brewer.

4. Comparison of Brewer's Salary with Gross and Net Income

The Tax Court found that the claimed compensation BQH paid to Mr. Brewer in 1995 and 1996 constituted 8.5 percent and 8.7 percent, respectively, of BQH's gross sales and 82 percent and 85 percent, respectively, of BQH's taxable income. The court employed financial ratios in its various computations from the RMA report. The court determined that the RMA study of comparable companies revealed a median value of compensation as a percentage of gross sales as 2.3 percent for 1995 and 1.8 percent for 1996. Nevertheless, the Tax Court did not rely on the median value in reaching its decision, relying instead on the values accorded to the 90th percentile of officer compensation payments, a reflection of the court's earlier finding regarding BQH's financial successes during the years in question. The Tax Court even accepted BQH's expert witness's suggestion that the percentage of gross sales for 1995 and 1996 were 6.0 percent and 6.3 percent, respectively. Nonetheless, the Tax Court determined that Brewer's compensation percentages were substantially higher than the figures urged by BQH's expert, thus leading the court to conclude that reasonable compensation would have been significantly less than BQH's actual payments to Brewer.

After making this determination, the Tax Court multiplied BQH's sales by the corresponding RMA ratio for each year in question to arrive at the appropriate compensation amounts for the services Brewer performed for BQH: $520,000 in 1995 and $600,000 in 1996. The court thereafter added $5,000 to the 1995 amount to account for Brewer's guarantee of a bank loan to BQH that year, and added 5 percent of Brewer's newly-calculated compensation to make up for the absence of retirement benefits. The total amount of reasonable compensation for Mr. Brewer as determined by the Tax Court was ultimately $610,000 for 1995 and $630,000 for 1996.

5. Prevailing General Economic Conditions

The Tax Court noted in its findings of fact that BQH had survived several economic downturns, evidencing BQH's resilience. The court specifically recognized Brewer's efforts in ensuring BQH's ability to survive those conditions, and as such found this factor favored a relatively high compensation.

6. Comparison of Salaries with Distributions to Stockholders

In 1993, BQH distributed $116,100 to its only two shareholders (Mr. and Mrs. Brewer). In 1994, BQH distributed $320,949 to the Brewers. Up to the end of the

1996 fiscal year, the 1993 and 1994 distributions were the only ones made by BQH. The Tax Court was troubled by the fact that the profitability of BQH was considerably higher in 1995 and 1996 than in previous years, yet BQH did not make any distributions whatsoever. By paying compensation to Brewer in the amounts BQH did in 1995 and 1996, the court concluded that this factor weighed heavily in favor of a low compensation for Brewer.

7. *Compensation for Comparable Positions in Comparable Concerns*

The Tax Court determined that Brewer received compensation higher than those executives in comparable companies. The court relied upon the RMA data, which systematically draws from numerous companies across the industry and permits objective comparisons between executive compensation and company performance.

8. *Salary Policy of BQH As to All Employees*

BQH did not maintain an official salary policy for any of its employees, including Brewer. The Tax Court expressed concern that because Brewer essentially controlled BQH, he was able to set his own compensation. While the IRS conceded that BQH paid its employees salaries equal to or greater than those paid by its competitors, it argued that the wide disparity between the salary paid Brewer and the next highest-paid employee supported a low compensation amount.

9. *Amount of Compensation Paid to Brewer in Previous Years*

BQH argued before the Tax Court that it underpaid Mr. Brewer in previous years, particularly in 1992 and 1993. The Tax Court rejected this argument, finding persuasive the absence of any corporate minutes reflecting any mention of BQH's intention to compensate Mr. Brewer for past years of undercompensation. Moreover, the Tax Court noted that neither of BQH's experts could provide any credible testimony regarding the alleged underpayments or the specific years in which they occurred, stating that BQH's "theory of compensation for prior services [appeared to be] only an afterthought developed at a time when the reasonableness of the compensation was already under attack."

RMA Ratios. Ultimately, the court used the RMA ratios to determine reasonable compensation. The court acknowledged that the RMA ratios left "much to be desired" but used them nonetheless because they were the only statistical information presented (the "only game in town," in the court's own words). Using these ratios, the Tax Court disallowed $152,186 of BQH's 1995 deduction and $233,559 of its 1996 deduction. On appeal, the Fifth Circuit affirmed the Tax Court's decision as not clearly erroneous.[22]

Summary and Conclusion. This case shows the importance of using well-supported statistical data. It is also a guide to the factors the Tax Court will weigh in determining whether compensation is reasonable and deductible.

O.S.C. & Associates, Inc. v. Commissioner

Introduction. In *O.S. C. & Associates, Inc. v. Commissioner*,[23] the U.S. Court of Appeals for the Ninth Circuit presented a hidden danger in a strategy used by some owners of closely held corporations—that is, those who pay themselves excessive deductible compensation to avoid paying nondeductible dividends.

---

[22] *Brewer Quality Homes, Inc. v. Commissioner,* 122 Fed. Appx. 88; 2004 U.S. App. LEXIS 25273; 94 A.F.T.R.2d (RIA) 7141 (5th Cir. Dec. 9, 2004).
[23] *O.S.C. & Associates, Inc. v. Commissioner,* 187 F.3d 1116 (9th Cir. 1999), *aff'g* T.C. Memo 1997-300 (June 30, 1997).

In this case, the usual taxpayer fallback position in reasonableness of compensation cases—in which the stockholder-employees expected to be able to at least deduct the reasonable compensation portion, if challenged—backfired. This occurred when, as a result of the disguised dividend taint, the Appeals Court denied a sizable portion of what the IRS had already admitted was reasonable compensation.

The Facts of the Case. As a result of their hard work and unique skills, the two stockholder-employees owned a successful silk-screening business. The taxpayer business, originally purchased for $180, grew from a kitchen table to a 65,000 square-foot plant, with over 200 employees. The taxpayer corporation grossed over $13 million a year.

During this increasingly successful 20-year journey, the owners incorporated, with (1) one becoming president and chief executive officer having 90 percent of the company's stock and (2) the other becoming vice president with the remaining 10 percent of the company's stock.

The taxpayer corporation formally adopted an incentive compensation plan. This compensation plan had the purpose of recognizing the two shareholders for their contributions to the business. The employee/shareholders were the plan's only participants. Payments were made "according to stock ownership." As a practical matter, this stock ownership-based allocation resulted in the corporation distributing nearly all of its net income as incentive payouts to the two owners in the years in question.

The Court's Two-Part Test. The Appeals Court, citing an earlier case,[24] applied a two-prong test to determine the deductibility of payments to the stockholder-employees. The two-part test included: (1) reasonableness of amount and (2) compensatory intent.

In the earlier case, the Ninth Circuit Court of Appeals acknowledged that most courts concentrate on the first prong—that is, reasonable amount—using that result to infer compensatory purpose. The Appeals Court, however, held that, "In the rare case where there is evidence that an otherwise reasonable compensation payment contains a disguised dividend, the inquiry may expand into compensatory intent apart from reasonableness."

In this case, however, the Appeals Court observed that this was just such a case where reasonableness alone was not sufficient to satisfy the compensatory intent prong.

Was the Compensation Disguised Dividends? As evidence that the corporation's compensation plan allocations were not intended as compensation but, rather, as disguised dividends, the Appeals Court noted that the percentages of the corporation's net income paid to its two stockholder-employees ranged from 81 percent to 94 percent. The Court concluded that this was a strong indication that profits were being siphoned out of the taxpayer corporation disguised as compensation.

In addition, the Appeals Court noted that the taxpayer corporation had never paid or declared a dividend. This was relevant in light of the taxpayer corporation's history of high profitability. Also, the 90 percent employee/owner had rejected professional advice to pay dividends.

---

[24] *Elliots, Inc. v. Commissioner*, 716 F.2d 1241. (9th Cir. 1983).

Furthermore, the taxpayer corporation's accountant manipulated the actual implementation of the compensation plan in order to increase the allocations above what the plan would have authorized.

Finally, the Appeals Court determined that the design of the compensation plan was inconsistent with compensatory intent because: (1) the plan applied only to the corporation's shareholders and no other employees; (2) the payments were calculated with reference to their proportionate stock ownership; and (3) the method of calculation was not based on the value of services rendered to the corporation, but was structured to distribute every dollar of net profit.

Summary and Conclusion. This case provides a very effective road map as to what a closely held business owner should not do in order to protect the "reasonable" component of an excessive compensation deduction.

Law Offices—Richard Ashare, P.C. v. Commissioner

Introduction. In *Law Offices—Richard Ashare*,[25] the U.S. Tax Court provides guidance to professional corporations involved in conflicts with the IRS regarding whether substantial amounts of compensation paid to their professional employees (e.g., doctors, lawyers, consultants, etc.) can be deducted by the corporation as reasonable compensation expense.

In this case, the Tax Court gave significant latitude to the professional corporation in allowing it to prove that a $1.75 million payment made to an attorney in a single year was intended solely as compensation. And, as reasonable compensation, the entire $1.75 million payment was totally deductible by the corporation.

The Tax Court's reasonable compensation finding is particularly noteworthy to professional firm owners. This is because the taxpayer corporation reported a taxable loss in the amount of $1,857,933 for the year of the $1.75 million compensation payment.

The Facts of the Case. Richard Ashare was the taxpayer corporation's sole shareholder attorney. He was also the taxpayer corporation's only professional employee. His compensation related exclusively to one class-action case.

The taxpayer corporation achieved a $70 million settlement after 15 years of litigation. The settlement included $12,567,000 in legal fees paid to the corporation over four years.

The taxpayer corporation paid the shareholder attorney $12,242,000 in salary over five years. This included the $1.75 million salary that was the subject of the IRS challenge.

The Court's Decision. In a surprising taxpayer victory, the Tax Court found that the $1.75 million payment to the attorney/employee met the first test for deductibility (i.e., reasonableness of amount). This was because the amount was reasonable for compensation paid by a personal service corporation, such as the law firm in the present case, to its key employee for his services. The employee's qualifications for his position with the employer firm justified high compensation.

In addition, the Tax Court noted the fact that the attorney was vital and indispensable in the operation of the employer's business. The nature of the employer's business was complex and highly specialized, requiring this employee's expertise.

---

[25] *Law Offices—Richard Ashare, P.C. v. Commissioner*, T.C. Memo 1999-282 (Aug. 24, 1999).

The Tax Court warned, however, that the fact that the $1.75 million was reasonable did not necessarily mean that it was fully deductible to the employer. Under the second test for deductibility, a deduction for compensation is allowed only to the extent that the compensation is paid for services actually rendered by the employee—in or before the year of payment.

The Tax Court concluded that the $1.75 million met this second test for deductibility. This was because it was paid to the attorney to compensate him for his work on the class litigation for which the employer received over $12 million in court-ordered legal fees.

The Tax Court also noted that the employer's board of directors determined that the employee was entitled to receive the $1.75 million in compensation for his past and present services on one case. That one case constituted the firm's work during the years of the employee's tenure. The taxpayer corporation's board, through the exercise of sound business judgment, resolved that the employee was entitled to the $1.75 notwithstanding the IRS's conclusions to the contrary.

The Tax Court was aware of the fact that the corporation's board of directors was made up of the practitioner himself, his wife, and his longtime tax adviser. Nonetheless, the Court refused to second-guess the taxpayer corporation board's determination.

Summary and Conclusion. In its decision, the Tax Court noted that careful scrutiny of the facts is appropriate in a case such as this one—that is, where the employer payer is controlled by the payee/employee. Nevertheless, the Court's published opinion did not include any of the usual analysis of whether the $1.75 million paid to the corporation's sole shareholder employee should have been characterized as a nondeductible dividend rather than as deductible compensation.

Alpha Medical, Inc. v. Commissioner

Introduction. In *Alpha Medical, Inc. v. Commissioner*,[26] the Sixth Circuit U.S. Court of Appeals reversed the judgment of the Tax Court.

The Tax Court held that $2.3 million (of the $4.4 million actual compensation) paid to the president and sole shareholder of a company could be claimed as a business expense deduction.

Reasonableness of Owner/Employee Compensation. Although the Appeals Court essentially agreed with the Tax Court's conclusions with respect to the individual factors examined to determine the reasonableness of the compensation, the Appeals Court concluded that the compensation was reasonable because it did not exceed the amount needed to remedy undercompensation in prior years.

The Facts of the Case. Mr. William Rogers incorporated Alpha Medical Management, Inc., in Tennessee with an initial capital contribution of $1,000. The company provided management services to home health care agencies and hospitals with home health care departments.

Mr. Rogers was the president, sole director, and sole shareholder of the company through the year in question. Mr. Rogers, who earned a doctorate degree in pharmacology, founded a durable medical equipment business and a drugstore chain, which he had previously sold.

---

[26] *Alpha Medical, Inc. v. Commissioner*, 172 F.3d 942. (6th Cir. Apr. 19, 1999), *rev'g* T.C. Memo 1997-464 (Oct. 14, 1997).

After selling the medical equipment business, Mr. Rogers turned down a management position in California with an annual salary of over $1 million so that he could stay in Tennessee and concentrate on developing Alpha Medical Management, Inc., as a successful business concern.

The shareholders' equity of Alpha Medical increased to $3.4 million for the year in question, from $97,000 four years earlier.

The salary of Mr. Rogers increased to $4,439,180 as deductible compensation and $1,500 as nondeductible dividends for the year in question, from $67,000 four years earlier.

The compensation of Mr. Rogers was equal to 64.6 percent of the taxpayer's net taxable income before the deduction of Mr. Rogers's compensation ($6,871,433) and 44.9 percent of gross receipts ($9,880,760).

The Internal Revenue Service allowed only $400,000 as a deduction for reasonable compensation of Mr. Rogers.

The Tax Court's Decision. The Tax Court examined nine relevant factors in order to determine the reasonableness of Mr. Rogers' compensation and concluded for each factor whether it favored the taxpayer, favored the Commissioner, or was neutral.

The factors considered by the Tax Court are listed below.

1. Employee's qualifications—favored taxpayer.
2. The nature, extent, and scope of the employee's work—favored taxpayer.
3. The size and complexities of business—favored taxpayer.
4. A comparison of salaries paid with gross income and net income—favored Commissioner.
5. The prevailing general economic conditions—favored Commissioner.
6. Comparison of salaries with distributions to stockholders—favored taxpayer.
7. The prevailing rates of compensation for comparable positions in comparable concerns—neutral.
8. The salary policy of the taxpayer as to all employees—favored Commissioner.
9. The amount of compensation paid to the employee in previous years—favored taxpayer.

The Tax Court concluded that the compensation paid to Mr. Rogers was in part unreasonable, agreeing with neither the taxpayer nor the Commissioner. The Tax Court held that $2.3 million constituted reasonable compensation for Mr. Rogers for services rendered the year in question and prior years.

The Appeals Court Decision. The Appeals Court decision noted that the Tax Court did not explain how it reached the $2.3 million figure and that it appeared to split the difference between the Internal Revenue Service's original position and the taxpayer's position.

The Appeals Court reviewed the nine factors considered by the Tax Court and agreed with the conclusions with respect to all but one. Regarding the salary policy of the taxpayer as to all employees, the Tax Court stated that this factor pointed to the conclusion that Mr. Rogers' compensation was in part unreasonable.

This conclusion was based on the great disparity between the compensation of the sole shareholder, Mr. Rogers, and the nonshareholders and the fact that his compensation plan was not the result of a longstanding arm's-length agreement.

The Appeals Court disagreed "in light of the fact that Rogers was grossly underpaid for several consecutive years." Furthermore, the Appeals Court noted that, in five years, Mr. Rogers had taken the company from nothing to a net profit of nearly $7 million, stating: "In this situation, the factual record and some notion of parity with other highly successful executives requires a different result from that reached by the Tax Court."

The Appeals Court reversed the judgment of the Tax Court, acknowledging Mr. Rogers' qualifications, responsibility for the success of the company, long hours, risks assumed in founding and developing the company, and opportunity cost in turning down the $1 million-plus position in California.

The Appeals Court concluded that Mr. Rogers' "compensation ... did not exceed the amount needed to remedy prior years of undercompensation, and was therefore reasonable."

Summary and Conclusion. *Alpha Medical, Inc. v. Commissioner* demonstrates that a level of compensation to a sole shareholder that may seem unreasonable at first glance may, in fact, be reasonable when all factors are considered, most notably undercompensation in prior years.

Beiner, Inc. v. Commissioner

The issue in *Beiner, Inc. v. Commissioner*[27] was whether the taxpayer could deduct compensation of $1,087,000 and $1,350,000 that it claimed for years 1999 and 2000 paid to its sole shareholder and corporate officer who served as chief executive officer (CEO), chief financial officer, president, secretary, and treasurer.

The Facts of the Case. The taxpayer was a wholesale distributor of motor controls (parts) manufactured by Allen-Bradley. During the relevant years, Allen-Bradley sold its parts only to its authorized distributors and to original equipment manufacturers (OEMs). The authorized distributors sold the parts that they purchased from Allen-Bradley directly to end users. Allen-Bradley sold its parts to OEMs, not for resale, but to incorporate the parts into equipment that they manufactured and sold as finished products.

The taxpayer was neither an OEM nor an authorized distributor of Allen-Bradley parts. The taxpayer bought and sold Allen-Bradley parts in a bootleg market for those parts. During the subject years, the taxpayer purchased Allen-Bradley parts primarily from three OEMs. These OEMs intentionally purchased more parts than needed for their manufacturing process and resold the extra (surplus) parts to the taxpayer at prices far less than the prices that the authorized distributors paid Allen-Bradley for the same parts. During the relevant years, the taxpayer also purchased Allen-Bradley parts at fire sale prices from distressed companies that had either overbought the parts for their own needs or gone out of business.

The three OEMs sold their surplus parts to the taxpayer in violation of an understanding that they had with Allen-Bradley to not sell those parts other than as part of their finished products or, in some cases, as replacement parts for those products. Over the years, The CEO had developed a relationship with the three OEMs such that they sold their surplus parts to the taxpayer at the risk of Allen-Bradley's declaring that it would no longer sell parts to them or that it would do so only at inflated prices. The three OEMs benefited from purchasing surplus parts and selling them to the taxpayer in that they paid less per unit when they purchased a greater quantity of parts that, in turn, increased their profit margins on their sale

[27] *Beiner, Inc. v. Commissioner*, T.C. Memo 2004-219, 2004 Tax Ct. Memo LEXIS 229 (September 28, 2004).

of the finished products. The taxpayer also improved the OEMs' cash flows because it paid very quickly. The three OEMs would have stopped selling their surplus parts to the taxpayer had the CEO become disaffiliated with it.

The Tax Court's Decision. Applying the five-part test used in the Ninth Circuit (because the case would be appealable there),[28] the court found that the CEO was primarily responsible for the taxpayer's business success. Although the CEO did not work exceptionally long hours for the company, nor did he devote 100 percent of his time to the taxpayer's business, the CEO arranged what the court felt was the most important element of the taxpayer's business—the purchase of Allen-Bradley motor parts at prices less than those paid by the authorized distributors. But for the CEO, the taxpayer would not have been able to obtain its inventory at the discount prices that allowed it to function as profitably as it did. In fact, the special relationships that the CEO developed with the three OEMs allowed the taxpayer to report greater gross profit margins and returns on sales and investment than virtually any other similar public company for which data was available for 1999 and 2000.

A compensation expert opined that the taxpayer was substantially more profitable than virtually all of the 34 companies he sampled in terms of the ratio of gross profit to sales. The taxpayer's ROE during the subject years was 28.1 percent and 50.1 percent, respectively. The Court determined that, although the CEO had compensation that was much greater than the separate or collective compensation of other employees, such compensation was justified because the taxpayer's profits were derived almost exclusively through the CEO's efforts. The Court also determined that a hypothetical inactive independent investor would consider each factor favorably to require the payment of the disputed compensation to the CEO in order to retain his services during each of the subject years.

Based on the compensation expert's data, however, the Court determined that the CEO's compensation for 1999 was unreasonable by $180,260. Nonetheless, the Court declined to impose a penalty because enough of the taxpayer's profits remained in equity for that year to have constituted a meaningful return to a hypothetical inactive independent investor.

Summary and Conclusion. As in some of the other reasonable compensation cases covered in this section, this case shows that it is critical to analyze the facts of each case carefully. In this case, the CEO's worth to the company was so great that it justified paying him, during the respective subject years, 31.3 and 38.7 percent of its gross receipts and 88.3 and 69.9 percent of its net income (adding back compensation).

E.J. Harrison and Sons, Inc. v. Commissioner

The issue in *E.J. Harrison and Sons, Inc. v. Commissioner*[29] was whether the amounts paid by the company to an officer-shareholder were deductible as reasonable compensation during the tax years at issue.

The Facts of the Case. Mr. and Mrs. Harrison entered into the waste pickup and disposal business in 1932. In 1967, they incorporated the business as

---

[28] For a detailed discussion of the Ninth Circuit's five-part test, see, e.g., *LabelGraphics, Inc. v. Commissioner*, T.C. Memo 1998-343 (Sept. 28, 1998), discussed above.

[29] *E.J. Harrison and Sons, Inc. v. Commissioner*, T.C. Memo 2003-239, 2003 Tax Ct. Memo LEXIS 239 (August 13, 2003).

E.J. Harrison and Sons, Inc. Mr. Harrison died in 1991, and Mrs. Harrison was elected president and chairman of the board, titles she held throughout the audit years of 1995 to 1997. During these years, she worked 40 or more hours per week.

Mrs. Harrison's work consisted primarily of: (1) attending board meetings and reviewing and voting on major proposals put forward by her sons, who, together, were responsible for the company's financing and operations; (2) community public relations activities on the company's behalf; and (3) acting as a coguarantor on company bank loans.

The amounts of Mrs. Harrison's compensation disallowed by the IRS as "unreasonable and excessive compensation" were $806,467, $762,019, and $541,325, for 1995, 1996, and 1997, respectively. The company never paid dividends.

Although both parties offered expert testimony to support their positions, the Court excluded the report of the taxpayer's expert, because it was not "based upon sufficient facts or data" and because he did not apply "principles and methods [for determining the reasonableness of Mrs. Harrison's compensation] reliably to the facts of the case." One-third of the report consisted of legal analysis and arguments, including citations and discussion of case law, and virtually all of his factual conclusions on which he based his opinion were either unsupported or incorrect.

The IRS's expert, James F. Carey, a certified management consultant specializing in compensation planning, likened Mrs. Harrison's services to those of an outside board chair and opined that her appropriate compensation should be "the median compensation paid to board chairs during the audit years by other companies with comparable sales revenues as derived from surveys conducted by [the] Economic Research Institute [ERI]." Carey described the ERI surveys as "broadly based" and said that he used a "large-sample survey." He declined to rely on the results of a narrower survey involving only five board chairs.

The Tax Court's Decision. The Tax Court analyzed Carey's opinion in conjunction with the five-factor test set out by the Ninth Circuit[30]: (1) the employee's role in the company; (2) a comparison of the compensation paid to the employee with the compensation paid to similarly situated employees in similar companies (external comparison); (3) the character and condition of the company; (4) whether a conflict of interest exists that might permit the company to disguise dividend payments as deductible compensation; and (5) whether the compensation was paid pursuant to a structured, formal, and consistently applied program.

Regarding Mrs. Harrison's role in the company, the Court noted that "[w]hatever lingering effect Mrs. Harrison's conservative business philosophy may have had on the decision-making process, it appears that her responsibility for and influence over the actual decisions of the board were sharply limited in practice. . . . The overall picture that emerges is of a company run during the audit years (and for many prior years) by Mrs. Harrison's sons. . . ." The court found that her titles did not reflect her actual status within the company and that her role as an "essentially compliant [board] member" justified only a small fraction of her compensation.

Similarly, the Court found that, although Mrs. Harrison projected a positive corporate image in the community, her public relations activities did not contribute

---

[30] For a discussion of these five factors, see, e.g., *LabelGraphics v. Commissioner*, T.C. Memo 1998-343 (1998), *aff'd* 221 F.3d 1091 (9th Cir. 2000), discussed above.

directly to the company's sales and profits. The court also dismissed Mrs. Harrison's guaranties as providing any support for her compensation, stating that the evidence did not establish any significant financial risk to her or what amount, if any, would constitute reasonable compensation. The Court was persuaded that the guarantees were given to protect the shareholders' ownership interests in the company.

Despite the favorable character and condition of the company, the Court said that Mrs. Harrison's limited management role during the audit years rendered this factor "of little or no relevance." Although the taxpayer fought the implication that Mrs. Harrison's compensation was disguised dividends, the Court said that the evidence strongly suggested such a conclusion, largely because the company's profits for the audit years were primarily attributable to the efforts of her sons. The Court concluded that an independent investor in the company would object to the size of the payments, even assuming, as the taxpayer argued, that the company's retained earnings for the audit years were a reasonable return on shareholder equity compared with that of comparable companies.

Finally, the Tax Court observed the large discrepancy between Mrs. Harrison's compensation and that of the highest-paid nonshareholder employee, $79,639, which was less than 10 percent of the amount paid to Mrs. Harrison that same year. Nothing in the evidence explained this difference.

For external comparisons, the Tax Court liked Carey's analogy of Mrs. Harrison as an outside board chair. It concluded, however, that her position in the company afforded her "additional benefits...(whether tangible or intangible)" that were not available to the average board chair. Accordingly, the Court added an 80 percent premium over the median compensation paid to an outside board chair to reflect Mrs. Harrison's reasonable compensation. Thus, the Tax Court agreed with the IRS that she was overcompensated for her services and disallowed part of the deduction.

Summary and Conclusion. This case shows that the Tax Court will, in appropriate cases, be persuaded by analogies, supported by factual analysis, to determine reasonable compensation.

Independent Investor Test

Exacto Spring Corporation v. Commissioner— 7th Circuit

Introduction. The CEO was the cofounder, chief executive officer, and principal owner of the Exacto Spring Corporation. For the two years in question, Exacto paid the CEO $1.3 million and $1 million in salary. Upon audit, the Internal Revenue Service concluded that these amounts were excessive. The IRS assessed a deficiency based on the disallowance of the excess compensation.

The Tax Court's Decision. In *Exacto Spring Corporation*,[31] the Tax Court concluded the amount of deductible reasonable compensation for the CEO. Based on a traditional seven-factor test, the Tax Court concluded that the amount of reasonable compensation for the CEO was approximately midway between his actual compensation and the IRS determination.

---

[31] *Exacto Spring Corporation v. Commissioner* (aka *Heitz v. Commissioner*), T.C. Memo 1998-220 (June 24, 1998).

In *Exacto Spring Corporation*,[32] the Court of Appeals reversed the Tax Court's decision. The seven-factor test applied by the Tax Court was "unclear and incomplete," according to the Appeals Court.

The Seven Factor Reasonable Compensation Case. The Tax Court applied a reasonableness of compensation test that involves the consideration of the following seven factors. However, none of these seven factors is entitled to any specified weight relative to another:

1. Type and extent of the services rendered.
2. Scarcity of qualified employees.
3. Qualifications and prior earning capacity of the employee.
4. Contributions of the employee to the business venture.
5. Net earnings of the employer.
6. Prevailing compensation paid to employees with comparable jobs.
7. Peculiar characteristics of the employer's business.

The Appeals Court Reaction to the Seven Factor Test. The Appeals Court concluded that this seven factor test leaves much to be desired. To begin with, the test is nondirective. No indication is given of how the seven factors are to be weighted in the likely event they do not all line up on one side. And, many of the seven factors (such as the type and extent of services rendered, the scarcity of qualified employees, and the peculiar characteristics of the employer's business) are vague, the Appeals Court concluded.

Second, the seven factors do not bear a clear relationship either (1) to each other or (2) to the primary purpose of Section 162(a)(1). The purpose of Section 162(a)(1) is to prevent dividends (or in some cases gifts) that are not deductible from corporate income from being disguised as salary, which is deductible.

Suppose that an employee like the CEO, the founder and the chief executive officer and principal owner of Exacto, rendered no services to the company at all—but received a huge salary. It would be absurd to allow the whole (or, for that matter any part) of his salary to be deducted as an ordinary and necessary business expense, even if he were well qualified to be the company's chief executive officer, the company had substantial net earnings, chief executive officers of similar companies were paid a lot, and it was a business in which high salaries were common.

The Appeals Court noted that the seven factor test would not prevent the Tax Court from allowing a deduction in such a case, even though Exacto obviously was seeking to reduce its taxable income by disguising earnings as salary. In that case, the Tax Court would not allow the deduction. But, this disallowance would have nothing to do with the seven factor test.

Third, the Appeals Court concluded that the seven factor test sets up the Tax Court as the ultimate personnel department for closely held corporations. The Appeals Court concluded that this is a role unsuitable for courts.

The test invites the Tax Court to decide what seven factors should be considered when deciding the amount that the Exacto employees should be paid on the basis of the judges' own ideas of what jobs are comparable, what relation an employee's salary should bear to the corporation's net earnings, what types of business should pay abnormally high (or low) salaries, and so forth. The Appeals Court

---

[32] *Exacto Spring Corporation*, 196 F.3d 833 (7th Circ. Nov. 16, 1999).

noted that the judges of the Tax Court are not equipped by training or experience to determine the salaries of corporate officers.

Fourth, since the seven factor test cannot itself determine the outcome of a dispute because of its nondirective character, it invites the making of arbitrary decisions based on discretion or unprincipled rules of thumb. The Tax Court in this case essentially added the IRS's conclusion of the maximum that the CEO should have been paid to what he was actually paid, and divided the sum by two.

Fifth, the Appeals Court noted that the reaction of the Tax Court to a challenge to the deduction of executive compensation is unpredictable under the seven factor test. Accordingly, corporations run unavoidable legal risks in determining a level of compensation that may be indispensable to the success of their business.

The Facts of the Case. The drawbacks of the seven factor test are well illustrated in this case. The Tax Court found that the CEO was indispensable to the Exacto business and essential to its success. The CEO was not only its chief executive officer. He was also the company's chief salesman and marketing man, plus the head of its research and development (R&D) efforts and its principal inventor. The company's entire success appears to have been due (1) on the one hand to the R&D conducted by him and, (2) on the other hand, to his marketing of these innovations. (The CEO did receive some additional compensation for his marketing efforts from a subsidiary of Exacto Spring Corporation.)

Likewise, the design of precision springs (which is the Exacto Spring Corporation specialty) is an extremely specialized branch of mechanical engineering. The Tax Court recognized that there are very few engineers who have made careers specializing in this area, let alone engineers like the CEO who have the ability (1) to identify and attract clients and, (2) to develop springs to perform a specific function for that client.

The Tax Court noted that the CEO was highly qualified to run Exacto as a result of his education, training, experience, and motivation. He had over 30 years of highly successful experience in the field of spring design. And, the Tax Court concluded that his efforts were of great value to Exacto.

With regard to Exacto net earnings, the Tax Court was noncommittal. Exacto had reported a loss in the first year in question and very little taxable income in the second year. But it conceded having taken some improper deductions in those years unrelated to the CEO's salary. After adjusting the Exacto Spring Corporation income to remove these deductions, the Tax Court concluded that Exacto had earned more than $1 million in each of the years at issue, net of CEO's supposedly inflated salary.

The Tax Court was noncommittal with regard to earnings of comparable employees as well. Expert witnesses had presented evidence, and the Tax Court was critical of both.

Exacto Spring Corporation's witness had arrived at his estimate of the CEOs maximum reasonable compensation in part by aggregating the salaries that Exacto would have had to pay to hire four people. The more roles or functions an employee performs, the more valuable his or her services are likely to be. However, the Tax Court concluded that an employee who performs four jobs, each on a part-time basis, is not necessarily worth as much to a company as four employees each working full time at one of those jobs. The Tax Court ruled that it is arbitrary to multiply the normal full-time salary for one of the jobs by four to compute the reasonable compensation of the employee who fills all four of them.

The expert witness for the IRS considered whether the CEO's compensation was consistent with Exacto investors' earning a reasonable return (adjusted for the risk of its business), which he calculated to be 13 percent. However, he neglected to consider the concessions of improper deductions, which led to adjustments to taxable income. The Tax Court determined that, with those adjustments, the investor's annual return was more than 20 percent, despite the CEO's large salary.

Finally, the Tax Court dismissed the IRS's argument that the Exacto low level of dividends (zero in the two years at issue, but never very high) was evidence that the corporation was paying the CEO dividends in the form of salary.

The Tax Court pointed out that shareholders might not want dividends. The Exacto shareholders may prefer that the corporation retain its earnings. That would cause the value of the corporation to increase and, therefore, allow the shareholders to obtain corporate earnings in the form of capital gains taxed at a lower rate than ordinary income.

The Tax Court also noted that, while the CEO, as the owner of 55 percent of Exacto common stock, obviously was in a position to influence his salary, the corporation's two other major shareholders (each with 20 percent of the stock) had approved it. These other shareholders had not themselves been paid a salary or other compensation and are not relatives of the CEO. Also, they had no financial or other incentive to allow the CEO to siphon off dividends in the form of salary.

Summary and Conclusion. It is noteworthy that the Appeals Court did not hold that a chief executive officer's salary is always reasonable. It did note that there could be situations in which a high rate of return was not due to the chief executive officer's exertions. In such situations, the presumption of reasonableness would be rebutted.

In addition, the IRS could still have prevailed if it could show that, while the CEO's salary was reasonable, Exacto did not in fact intend to pay him that amount as salary, and that this amount really did include a concealed dividend (even though it need not have). In such a case, because any deductible business expense must be bona fide (as well as reasonable), the deduction could be disallowed.

Other circuits have criticized the approach taken in this case. For example, in *Eberl's Claim Service, Inc. v. Commissioner*,[33] the Tenth Circuit refused to set aside the multifactor approach in favor of solely an independent investor approach espoused by *Exacto Spring*. That circuit seems to have adopted a hybrid approach, where the multifactor approach is applied and then assessed through an independent investor lens.[34] Further, of those circuits that have embraced an independent investor test, only the Seventh has gone so far as to jettison the multifactor approach entirely. Others have merely committed to viewing the totality of the circumstances through the "lens" of, or "from the perspective of," a hypothetical outside investor.

Menard, Inc. v. Commissioner

Another case to address the reasonableness of compensation under IRC § 162 and to use the independent investor test developed in Exacto Spring Corp. (see above),

---

[33] *Eberl's Claim Services v. Commissioner*, 249 F.3d 994 (10th Cir. 2001).

[34] For a detailed discussion of a case that applies such an approach, see *B&D Foundations, Inc. v. Commissioner*, T.C. Memo 2001-262, 2001 Tax Ct. Memo LEXIS 298, 82 T.C.M. (CCH) 692 (October 3, 2001), discussed above.

rather than a multifactor test, is *Menard, Inc. v. Commissioner*.[35] In this case, the IRS disallowed $19 million of a compensation deduction taken by Menard, Inc. in 1998 for compensation it paid to John Menard, its founder, president, CEO, and holder of all its voting stock and a majority of its nonvoting stock.

Menard, Inc. (the "company") operated a chain of home improvement stores throughout the Midwest. Since 1988, the company had a history of increasing total sales and return on investment. In 1998, Menard, Inc. had total revenue of $3.42 billion and an 18.8 percent return on equity. It has never declared dividends. That year, it paid Mr. Menard $20.6 million in compensation, which, following the same pattern of compensation the company had always followed, was comprised of a small salary and 5 percent of the company's net income before taxes.

Applicable Test of Reasonableness. The Tax Court initially noted that reasonable compensation would be determined under the independent investor test (see analysis of *Exacto Spring Corp. v. Commissioner*, 196 F.3d 833 [7th Cir. 1999], which introduced this test, above), which states "if a hypothetical independent investor would consider the rate of return on his investment in the taxpayer corporation 'a far higher return than . . . [he] had any reason to except,' the compensation paid to the corporation's CEO is presumptively reasonable." The IRS agreed that Menard's return on equity exceeded that of the comparable public company and, thus, met the independent investor test. However, it argued that the compensation was nonetheless excessive because the compensation paid to the CEO in those same comparable companies was substantially less than the amount paid to Mr. Menard.

The Tax Court noted that *Exacto Spring* did not address the situation before it, i.e., "Where the investors' rate of return on their investment generated by the taxpayer corporation, a closely held corporation, is sufficient to create a rebuttable presumption that the compensation paid to the corporation's CEO is reasonable, but the compensation paid by the taxpayer corporation to its CEO substantially exceeded the compensation paid by comparable publicly traded corporations to their CEOs," so it looked to § 162 for guidance. It concluded, "As we read section 1.162-7, Income Tax Regs., we are required to consider evidence of compensation paid to CEOs in comparable companies when such evidence is introduced to show the reasonableness or unreasonableness of a CEO's compensation." Accordingly, both parties introduced expert testimony regarding comparable companies.

The Taxpayer's Evidence. Menard, Inc.'s expert selected 12 comparable companies (Barnes & Noble, Best Buy, Borders, Circuit City, CVS, Home Depot, Kohl's, Lowe's, Staples, Target, Wal-Mart, and Walgreen) that sold hard goods, had growth in sales and profitability between 1988 and 1998, and had annual revenue greater than $1 billion. Using proxy statements from 1998, he determined the CEO's base compensation plus benefits. Using the 1999 proxy statement he determined the 1998 long-term incentives (LTI), such as stock options, because he believed that the comparables determined executive LTI after the close of the previous fiscal year. In his analysis of the comparison group's proxy statements, the expert used a formula for valuing LTI compensation that he referred to as the "Growth Model." According to him, the Growth Model projects the actual, as opposed to the theoretical, value of LTI compensation that a CEO will receive. Under that model, he assumed that the stock would grow at 10 percent annually, a

---

[35] *Menard, Inc. v. Commissioner*, T.C. Memo 2004-207, 2004 Tax Ct. Memo LEXIS 215, 88 T.C.M. (CCH) 229 (Sept. 16, 2004).

rate he derived from an SEC proxy statement instruction found in *17 C.F.R. sec. 229.402(c)(2)(vi)(A) (2004)*. He also assumed that the stock would be held for 10 years. He then discounted the LTI compensation to present value using the applicable treasury rate. After determining the CEO compensation for 1998 of the comparables, he determined that Mr. Menard's compensation would be in the 90th percentile or higher because Menard, Inc. was "… in the 90th percentile with respect to return on equity, return on assets, and return on capital and below the 10th percentile with respect to its average debt." The 90th percentile indicated a CEO salary of $19.272 million; thus, he concluded that Mr. Menard's salary was reasonable.

The IRS's Evidence. The IRS's expert considered two sets of comparables: The first set of directly comparable companies included Home Depot and Lowe's; the second set included seven major retail chains (Dollar General, Kohl's, May Department Stores, Office Depot, Staples, Target, and TJX). The expert utilized data regarding compensation from those companies' 1998 proxy statements, which he believed reflected the entire compensation of the executive earned in that fiscal year. He then valued the reported LTI using the Black-Scholes option-pricing model. To the results of that model, he applied a 50 percent discount to arrive at market value; this discount reflected the expert's belief that CEOs are risk-averse (while the Black-Scholes model assumes the investor is risk-neutral) and would exercise their options early or forfeit them, as well as accounted for restrictions on transferability. He further used a three-year moving average to "smooth out the volatility between varying magnitudes of options awarded in different years." He supported the use of three-year moving averages with SFAS No. 123, which "requires proration of stock option values over the vesting period and, as a result, reflects stock option values over a continued period of performance." He concluded that Mr. Menard was significantly overcompensated since his compensation was seven times higher than the compensation of the directly comparable companies' CEOs, and even higher for the other companies.

The Tax Court's Analysis. The Tax Court began its analysis by weeding out the comparables used by the experts to just those on both expert's lists—Home Depot, Kohl's, Lowe's, Staples, and Target. It rejected Menard, Inc.'s expert's position that LTI was reflected on the 1999 proxy statements. In doing so, it noted that under the SEC's instruction, all compensation earned for one year is to be reported on that year's proxy statement. Therefore, the court accepted the IRS's expert's compensation figures taken from the 1998 proxy statements.

The Tax Court then rejected Menard, Inc.'s expert's Growth Model. It reasoned, "Though the articles [in the American Compensation Association Journal] lend support to the existence of . . . [the] Growth Model, we are not persuaded that the model is generally accepted by valuation experts or that it provides a reasonably accurate value for the LTI compensation." It rejected the expert's unsupported position that CEOs hold their stock for 10 years. It also rejected the use of a 10 percent growth rate when that rate was derived from an SEC reporting instruction "intended to illustrate amounts that executives can earn on stock options at a 10 percent growth rate and is not a rule for valuing stock options." Therefore, adopting the IRS position, the court utilized the Black-Scholes model to calculate the stock's value.

Although the court agreed with the IRS's expert's application of the model, it rejected the 50 percent discount he applied as well as his use of three-year moving averages. With regard to the discount, the court found that the IRS's expert did not substantiate the discount with anything further than his personal observations. The Tax Court found the use of the three-year averages unsupportable because it "combines potentially less successful previous years with the TYE 1998 options' values" and because "the three-year moving average does not treat the options as only partially vested in the first year." Finally, the court found that SFAS No. 123 called for the proration of options over the vesting period, which it found was "quite different" than the application of three-year moving averages.

Using the valuation tools it had selected, the court then determined the amount of compensation reasonably deductible by Menard, Inc. for Mr. Menard. It noted that the compensation for comparable CEOs ranged from $2.8 million to $10.5 million. The court noted that while Menard, Inc. had a higher return on equity and return on assets than the direct comparables, it had lower gross revenue, lower revenue growth, and lower net income. The court then reasoned, "We conclude, therefore, that as the home improvement retailer with the highest return on equity, Menards's CEO's compensation should be the highest value within the range of its direct competitors' CEOs' compensation." Because there existed no correlation between rate of return and CEO compensation among the competitors, the court calculated the value by reference to a fraction of the rate of return divided by CEO compensation multiplied by 2.13 (the number of times Lowe's CEO's compensation exceeded Home Depot's CEO's compensation). Thus, the court determined that reasonable compensation was $7,066,912 in 1998, and disallowed the rest as a disguised dividend.

Intangible Asset Valuation Issues

Nestle Holdings, Inc. v. Commissioner

Introduction. In *Nestle Holdings, Inc. v. Commissioner*,[36] the corporate taxpayer appealed a decision of the Tax Court.[37]

In its decision, the Appeals Court reached two important conclusions. First, it ruled that the taxpayer realized a capital gain when it sold intangible assets to its parent company. Second, the Appeals Court ruled that the Tax Court erred in relying solely upon the relief-from-royalty method in its valuation of the taxpayer's trademarks.

Of these two conclusions, the second is much more important (1) to corporate owners of marketing-related intangibles such as trademarks and trade names and (2) to intangible asset and intellectual property valuation analysts.

This Appeals Court decision discusses the conceptual pros and cons of the use of (and of the sole reliance upon) the relief-from-royalty valuation method.

Fact Set Summary. Nestle Holdings, Inc. (Nestle) is a first-tier subsidiary of Nestle S.A. ("NSA").

The IRS concluded income tax deficiencies regarding the Nestle sale to NSA of various intangible assets, including patents, trademarks and trade names, and

---

[36] *Nestle Holdings, Inc. v. Commissioner*, Nos. 152 F.3d 83 (2d Cir. July 31, 1998).
[37] *Nestle Holdings, Inc. v. Commissioner*, T.C. Memo 1995-441 (Sept. 14, 1995).

proprietary technology. Nestle claimed that it had realized a capital loss on the sale. The IRS concluded that Nestle had overstated the fair market value of (and, in turn, its tax basis in) the transferred intangible assets. Accordingly, the IRS concluded that Nestle had realized a capital gain on the sale of the subject intangible assets.

Nestle appealed to the Tax Court regarding the matter. The Tax Court, in good measure, adopted the IRS's intangible asset valuations. And, the Tax Court concluded that Nestle had realized a capital gain.

The Appeals Court agreed with the Tax Court that Nestle realized a capital gain on the intangible asset sale transaction. However, the Appeals Court rejected the Tax Court's exclusive reliance on the relief-from-royalty method of estimating the fair market value of the Nestle trademarks.

The Facts of the Case. Nestle purchased the stock of Carnation Company (Carnation). Nestle intended to finance the acquisition with a capital contribution of $525 million from NSA and a $2.5 billion loan from third-party financing sources. Ultimately, this acquisition financing plan was revised.

Actually, the Carnation acquisition was financed by commercial loans of $1.6 billion and related-party loans of $1.325 billion. NSA provided some of the related-party loans, but it made no capital contributions to Nestle.

After the acquisition, Nestle made the required principal and interest payments to the related parties, and Nestle deducted the interest expense for federal income tax purposes.

As a result of the acquisition, Nestle became the owner of the Carnation intangible assets. It was an NSA policy to own all of the trademarks and trade names used by Nestle companies. Accordingly, Nestle sold the acquired Carnation intangibles to NSA. These intangible assets included trademarks and trade names, patents, and proprietary technology. Nestle and NSA agreed (1) that NSA would pay fair market value for the intangibles, and (2) that NSA would cancel a portion of the Nestle debt in exchange for the subject intangibles.

To estimate the fair market value of the Carnation intangible assets, Nestle commissioned an appraisal. The appraiser valued the Carnation trademarks and trade names at $315,000,000, the proprietary technology at $106,018,700, and the patents at $4,612,000—for an aggregate fair market value of $425,630,700. Accordingly, NSA cancelled $425,630,700 of the Nestle debt in exchange for the Carnation intangible assets.

Nestle accounted for the purchase of the Carnation stock as a purchase of the Carnation assets. Accordingly, Nestle adjusted the basis of the acquired assets to their fair market values.

Nestle also allocated to these intangible assets a small portion of the total price paid to acquire Carnation over and above the fair market value of the tangible and intangible assets Nestle had received.

As a result, the basis of the Nestle intangible assets was "stepped up" to $435,837,000, an amount that was in excess of the assets' fair market value. Consequently, Nestle claimed a capital loss on the subsequent sale of the acquired Carnation intangible assets to NSA.

The IRS challenged the claimed capital loss. In particular, the IRS challenged the Nestle valuation of the acquired intangible assets. The IRS ultimately valued the Carnation trademarks and trade names at $150,300,000 and its proprietary technology at $21,204,000.

The IRS agreed to the valuation of the Carnation patents at $4,612,000. It assigned the Nestle acquired intangible assets an aggregate basis of $163,556,000.

The IRS then alleged that since Nestle had received $425,630,700 from its parent for intangible assets that had a basis of $163,556,000, Nestle had realized a short-term capital gain of $262,074,700 on the sale of these intangibles. Since Nestle failed to report this "gain," the IRS determined a tax deficiency.

The Tax Court's Decision. Nestle argued that when a related party pays more or less than fair market value for an asset, the excess or shortfall should be attributable to the parties' relationship and should be reclassified accordingly. In this case, the relationship between the parties was that of a shareholder to a corporation. Therefore, the excess over the assets' fair market value that NSA paid to Nestle was a capital contribution.

The Tax Court rejected this argument. It concluded that allowing the excess purchase price to be treated as a capital contribution would impermissibly "allow petitioner retroactively to convert debt into equity, without any adverse tax consequences."

Nestle argued that even if there were a capital gain, the IRS had overestimated the tax deficiency by underestimating the fair market value of the trademarks and trade names that Nestle sold to NSA.

Nestle provided expert testimony that the fair market value of the Carnation trademarks and trade names was $346,000,000. The IRS provided expert testimony that the fair market value of the Carnation trademarks and trade names was only $146,100,000.

The Tax Court concluded that Nestle was not entitled to claim a "second-tier step-up" in the basis of the acquired assets. Accordingly, Nestle could only adjust the basis of the intangible assets to their fair market value.

The Tax Court also disagreed with the Nestle valuation expert and his estimate of the fair market value of the Carnation intangibles. The Tax Court concluded that the only trademark valuation method used by the IRS's expert—the relief-from-royalty method—was reasonable. And, the Tax Court concluded that Nestle had not "demonstrated that the Carnation trademarks and trade names are worth more than the value determined by [the IRS expert]."

Accordingly, the Tax Court concluded that the trademarks and trade names Nestle sold to NSA had a value of $146,100,000. The Tax Court concluded that the aggregate basis in all of the Carnation intangibles—including patents and proprietary technology—was $219,482,000. Therefore, the Tax Court ruled that Nestle realized a capital gain of $206,148,700 on the sale on the Carnation intangible assets to NSA.

Nestle appealed two aspects of the Tax Court's opinion.

The Appeals Court Decision—Tax Treatment of Sale. Nestle claimed that the excess of price over fair market value paid by NSA for the Carnation intangibles should be treated as a capital contribution. The Appeals Court concluded that such treatment would constitute a retroactive change in the form of the transaction with NSA.

Nestle already had selected the form of the transaction between Nestle and NSA, the Appeals Court concluded. Therefore, because the NSA transaction was structured as a sale of assets, any gain realized by Nestle must be treated as a capital gain.

The Appeals Court Decision—Valuation of Carnation Intangibles. The Tax Court had ruled that the evidence that Nestle presented regarding the fair market value of its trademarks was flawed. The Tax Court adopted the valuation provided by the IRS's expert.

That expert estimated the fair market value of the Nestle acquired trademarks using the relief-from-royalty method as his only valuation method. Underlying this valuation method is the premise that the only value that a purchaser of a trademark receives is the "relief" from paying a royalty for its use.

Using this method, the fair market value of a trademark is estimated by quantifying the present value of the stream of market-derived royalty payments that the owner of a trademark is "relieved" of paying. This royalty stream is estimated by the following steps:

1. Conclude whether the trademarks are profitable or capable of being commercialized.
2. Select a market-derived royalty rate for each trademark.
3. Multiply this market-derived royalty rate by the estimated revenue stream of the product associated with the trademark.

The IRS expert concluded that most of the Carnation trademarks were profitable and that the range of royalty rates in the food industry was from 0 to 5 percent. He then assigned royalty rates to the subject trademarks and quantified the present value of the estimated royalty payments. The Tax Court found this valuation method to be reasonable and adopted the conclusion of the IRS expert.

On the other hand, the Appeals Court disagreed with the sole reliance upon the relief-from-royalty method. The Appeals Court concluded that the relief-from-royalty method necessarily undervalues trademarks.

The Appeals Court concluded that the sole use of a relief-from-royalty method in the case of a sale is not appropriate. This is because it is the fair market value of a trademark, and not the cost of its use, that is at issue. It concluded that the relief-from-royalty method fails to capture the value of all of the rights of intangible asset ownership, such as: (1) the power to determine when and where the trademark may be used and (2) the ability to move the trademark into or out of product lines.

The Appeals Court concluded that the Tax Court's exclusive reliance on this valuation method fundamentally misunderstands the nature in trademarks and the reasons why the law provides for exclusive rights of ownership in a trademark.

Summary and Conclusion. This case illustrates how creative tax planning depends upon credible, independent valuation opinions. Given the inherent shortcomings of the relief-from-royalty valuation methodology, the Appeals Court concluded that the Tax Court erred when it adopted the Service's trademark valuations. The Appeals Court instructed the Tax Court to examine alternate methods for estimating the fair market value of the transferred Carnation trademark.

This case provides useful guidance with regard to the valuation of trademarks and trade names for federal income taxation purposes. In particular, the Appeals Court decision describes: (1) the analytical limitations of the relief-from-royalty valuation method, and (2) the potential problems associated with the exclusive reliance on the relief-from-royalty method to value trademarks and trade names.

Bemidji Distribution Company v. Commissioner

In *Bemidji Distribution Company v. Commissioner*[38] the Tax Court valued a noncompete agreement in the context of a sale where both the seller and the buyer had an interest in maximizing the value of the agreement.

---

[38] *Bemidji Distribution Company v. Commissioner*, T.C. Memo 2001-260; T.C. Memo 2001-260, 2001 Tax Ct. Memo LEXIS 295; T.C. Memo 2001-260, 82 T.C.M. (CCH) 677 (October 1, 2001).

The Facts of the Case. Langdon owned and operated Bemidji Distributing Company, Inc. (BDC), which was a wholesale beer distributorship. In an effort to sell BDC, Langdon retained Pohle Partners, a consulting firm that specializes in the sale of beer distributorships, to value BDC and help broker the sale. Pohle Partners valued BDC's tangible assets at $765,000 and its intangible assets, such as goodwill, franchise rights, and customer lists, at $1.2 million. Later, Langdon sold BDC to Bravo Beverage, Ltd. for $2,017,461. The parties allocated the purchase price as follows: $200,000 for a two-year consulting agreement; $1 million for a five-year covenant not to compete; and $817,461 for BDC's operating assets and accounts receivable. They did not allocate any value of the purchase price to BDC's intangible assets. The IRS found an income tax deficiency for the transaction, determining, among other things, that BDC failed to report $1.2 million of income received from Bravo.

The Tax Court's Decision. The Tax Court first noted that Langdon's and Bravo's tax interests were not adverse. The amount allocated to the covenant would be taxed to Langdon, as the shareholder, as ordinary income, but such amount would escape tax at the corporate level. Thus, it would be only taxed once, not twice. Bravo could also ratably deduct the cost of the covenant over the life of the covenant. Thus, the more that was allocated to the covenant, the greater the tax benefit to the seller and buyer. Because the parties' interests were not adverse, the Court applied strict scrutiny to the allocation (the rationale for this being that parties having adverse tax interests deter allocations that lack economic reality).

The Court considered the following nine factors in assessing the value of the noncompete agreement: (a) the seller's (i.e., covenantor's) ability to compete; (b) the seller's intent to compete; (c) the seller's economic resources; (d) the potential damage to the buyer posed by the seller's competition; (e) the seller's business expertise in the industry; (f) the seller's contacts and relationships with customers, suppliers, and others in the business; (g) the buyer's interest in eliminating competition; (h) the duration and geographic scope of the covenant; and (i) the seller's intention to remain in the same geographic area.[39]

The taxpayer did not put forward an expert witness, and the IRS's expert did not discuss these factors. Neither party offered any evidence as to the value of the other intangibles. The IRS's expert opined that the fair market value of the covenant was $121,000 based on a number of assumptions that the Tax Court characterized as being of "dubious validity." He assumed, for instance, a growth in the business of 2.7 percent per year, whereas there was evidence that, in recent years, the rate was closer to 9.19 percent. The court also rejected the expert's numerous discounts. For example, he applied a 24.2 percent discount on the basis of various cumulative "risk" factors. The Court, however, could not discern a risk factor in a covenant not to compete, other than that the covenant will be violated, and ruled that such a discount for risk is inappropriate in regard to a noncompete covenant.

On the other hand, the Court agreed with the IRS that the allocation of $1 million by the purchase agreement to the covenant was not the result of arm's length bargaining. The Court also determined that it was unreasonable to have allocated nothing to goodwill and going-concern value.

Applying all these factors, the Tax Court concluded that the noncompete agreement had a fair market value of $334,000, and that the remaining $666,000

---

[39] Compare the 11-factor test used by the Tax Court in *Thompson v. Commissioner*, T.C. Memo 1997-287 (June 24, 1997), discussed above.

of the $1 million in issue represented the other intangibles. This meant that BDC and Langdon needed to pay additional income taxes, and Langdon and BDC appealed.

The Appeals Court Decision. In *Langdon v. Commissioner*,[40] the Eighth Circuit affirmed the Tax Court's reduction of the value of the covenant not to compete. The Court ruled that the Tax Court correctly applied strict scrutiny to the transaction because the parties did not have competing tax interests, and that the Tax Court also correctly found that it was unreasonable for the parties not to allocate money for BDC's intangible assets.

BDC was an established and profitable wholesale beer distribution business. Bravo stepped into BDC's shoes at the time of the sale and acquired BDC's customer lists and exclusive brand and distribution rights. In fact, Pohle Partners listed these intangible assets in the sales materials for BDC. The Court ruled that it was thus reasonable for the Tax Court to conclude that Langdon and BDC transferred goodwill and going concern to Bravo, and that the parties appeared to have disguised these intangible assets in the price of the covenant to avoid paying additional taxes. The appellate court also agreed with the Tax Court's nine-factor analysis.

Summary and Conclusion. This case demonstrates the importance of substantiating the economic reality behind a transaction. In this case, not only did the Court look to a nine-factor test to determine economic reality, it also looked to what the parties failed to do—namely to allocate value to intangible assets such as goodwill and going-concern value.

Frontier Chevrolet Co. v. Commissioner

In *Frontier Chevrolet Co. v. Commissioner*,[41] the issue was whether a noncompete agreement entered into in connection with a company's stock redemption should be amortized over the life of the agreement or over its useful life.

The Facts of the Case. Frontier Chevrolet Company was in the business of selling and servicing new and used vehicles. Roundtree Automotive Group, Inc. was engaged in buying and operating automobile dealerships and providing them with consulting services. Frank Stinson was Roundtree's president and part of Frontier's management.

In 1987, Roundtree bought all of Frontier's stock. Frontier hired as executive manager one of Stinson's long-term employees, Dennis Menholt. From 1987 to 1994, Roundtree allowed Menholt to buy up to 25 percent of Frontier's stock as part of his employment by Frontier. Before August 1, 1994, Menholt owned 25 percent of Frontier, and Roundtree owned the other 75 percent.

Effective August 1, 1994, Frontier entered into a Stock Sale Agreement with Roundtree, under which Frontier redeemed its stock from Roundtree. As a result, Menholt became the sole shareholder of Frontier. In connection with the redemption, Roundtree, Stinson, and Frontier entered into a noncompete agreement that prohibited Roundtree and Stinson from competing with Frontier for five years.

[40] *Langdon v. Commissioner*, 59 Fed. Appx. 168, 2003 U.S. App. LEXIS 2714, 2003-1 U.S. Tax Cas. (CCH) P50,244, 91 A.F.T.R.2d (RIA) 912 (8th Cir. 2003).
[41] *Frontier Chevrolet Co. v. Commissioner*, 329 F.3d 1131, 2003 U.S. App. LEXIS 10590 (9th Cir. 2003).

Frontier amortized the covenant payments on its 1994 through 1996 income tax returns. In 1999, Frontier sought a refund for 1995 and 1996, claiming that the covenant should be amortized over the life of the agreement.

The Tax Court Decision. In a case of first impression, the Tax Court determined that Frontier's redemption was an "acquisition" within the meaning of IRC Section 197, because Frontier regained possession and control over 75 percent of its stock. Because Section 197 applied, the covenant not to compete was an intangible required to be amortized over 15 years rather than the life of the agreement.[42]

The Appeals Court Decision. Frontier appealed, arguing that its redemption was not an acquisition because it acquired no new assets and was engaged in the same line of business before and after the transaction. The Ninth Circuit Court of Appeals rejected this argument, holding that Section 197 does not require that the taxpayer acquire an interest in a new business, only that it acquire an interest in a trade or business. So, "[a]lthough Frontier continued its same business, acquired no new assets, and redeemed its own stock, Frontier acquired an interest in a trade or business because it acquired possession and control over 75 percent of its own stock." The Ninth Circuit affirmed the Tax Court.

Summary and Conclusion. This case demonstrates that in certain situations, such as where a stock redemption is treated as an acquisition, a noncompete agreement that ordinarily would be amortized over the life of the agreement is amortized for a different statutorily prescribed period.

DHL Corporation and Subsidiaries v. Commissioner

Introduction. In *DHL Corporation and Subsidiaries v. Commissioner*,[43] the Tax Court quantified the fair market value of the DHL Corporation trademark. This case is instructive to analysts who perform valuations, demographic analyses, or transfer price analyses with regard to intellectual properties.

The Facts of the Case. DHL and its subsidiaries provide services related to the pickup and delivery of time sensitive documents (and other materials) to domestic and international markets. During the 1970s and 1980s, DHL expanded rapidly and became the third largest courier service, operating in 195 countries.

The DHL subsidiaries served the international market, while DHL operated domestically. DHL and its subsidiaries had common ownership. Its subsidiaries did quite well, while the domestic operations lost money in an unsuccessful attempt to compete with the domestic leaders such as Federal Express. The international operations accounted for two-thirds of the DHL business.

Domestic DHL and its subsidiaries all used the same trademark. Under a license agreement with its subsidiaries, domestic DHL owned the trademark. However, the trademark title was besmirched because in some countries, the DHL subsidiaries had registered the trademark in their own name.

In the late 1980s, three foreign airline companies became interested in integrating their airlines with the DHL delivery network. The airlines offered to purchase (1) a 57.5 percent interest in the foreign subsidiaries for $450 million and (2) the DHL trademark for $50 million. After the transaction was negotiated, the total purchase price remained unchanged, but the amount of the purchase price

---

[42] *Frontier Chevrolet Co. v. Commissioner*, 116 T.C. 289, 2001 U.S. Tax Ct. LEXIS 22, 116 T.C. No. 23 (2001).

[43] *DHL Corporation and Subsidiaries v. Commissioner*, T.C. Memo. 1998-461 (Dec. 30, 1998).

allocated to the trademark was reduced to $20 million. Later, an appraisal confirmed that value.

The IRS's Position. The Internal Revenue Service concluded that the value of the DHL trademark was $300 million. The IRS presented two expert witnesses, who testified as to the value of the trademark. Both experts assumed that the entire DHL revenue stream was attributable to the trademark and not to any other existing intangible asset(s).

The first government expert valued the trademark using the relief-from-royalty method. After surveying a variety of businesses regarding royalty rates, he concluded that a 1 percent royalty rate was appropriate. In estimating the value under this method, he used a discounted cash flow analysis. In this analysis, he assumed that the income tax rate would be 30 percent and the expected long-term growth rate would be 6 percent. Using a present value discount rate of 12.5 percent, he estimated the trademark's fair market value to be $287 million.

The government's second expert valued the trademark using the relief-from-royalty method (and the discounted cash flow technique) coupled with the "other anticipated value" method. The secondary method "quantifies economic benefits accruing to an asset that may not be reflected in other income approaches, including marketing cost savings, operating synergies, lower costs of funds, etc. This benefit is supposedly measured in the form of incremental cash-flows that the expert believes are 'not necessarily the result of excess earnings or avoided royalties.'" Using slightly different valuation variables including a 3.6 percent expected long-term growth rate and a 1.15 percent royalty rate, he estimated that the value of the trademark was $327.5 million.

The Taxpayer's Position. At trial, the taxpayer also presented expert testimony regarding the value of the trademark. DHL initially argued that the $20 million allocated to the trademark was the fair market value of that asset. It claimed that the amount was arrived at through arm's-length negotiations. DHL attributed considerable value to other off-balance sheet assets, especially the DHL network which "enjoyed an intangible benefit from its existing infrastructure and operating know how that created a 'barrier to entry' of others into the same marketplace."

The taxpayer's expert calculated the value of the trademark at $55.2 million, based on a 0.31 percent royalty rate and a 7.6 percent expected long-term growth rate. The taxpayer's analyst discounted that amount by a 14.1 percent present value discount rate to arrive at fair market value.

The Tax Court's Decision. The Tax Court concluded that the amount allocated to the trademark in the purchase agreement was not arrived at through arm's length negotiations. It found that the initial $50 million offer was an attempt to bolster the DHL financial condition in the wake of its attempted expansion. However, the Court concluded that the purchase price was negotiated down because the buyers refused to negotiate the overall transaction price of $500 million.

The Tax Court also disregarded the taxpayer's expert valuation. It stated:

> We find it peculiar that petitioners' expert could expect to derive an independent fair market value by accepting the parties' values and rates, because his objective was to reach a fair market value. However, petitioner's expert accepted rates used in the transaction under consideration and then reduced their effect by discounting them to a present value. That approach does not serve to assist the Court in measuring . . . whether the value they used was a "fair market value."

The Tax Court also declined to accept the Internal Revenue Service claimed position. The Court reasoned that the entire value is not attributed solely to the DHL name recognition. The Court concluded that the DHL existing network had significant intangible value.

The Court concluded its own valuation by accepting the IRS $300 million figure as the value of all of the DHL intangible assets. The Court then reduced that amount by one-half. The Tax Court reasoned that the DHL in-place operating infrastructure had significant value at least equal to the DHL name recognition.

After concluding that the trademark had a $150 million value worldwide, the Tax Court separated the amount of value attributable to the DHL international business and then applied a lack of marketability discount to that amount. "A marketability discount is generally thought to be necessary where the buyer may incur out-of-pocket expenses or other costs due to some aspect or defect in the asset being purchased."

In this case, the Tax Court concluded that a 50 percent discount was appropriate because "The potential for delay, expense, inconvenience, etc. could be immense and would present a huge potential for out-of-pocket expenses or other costs [in securing the DHL's trademark rights in the foreign countries] to a potential willing buyer."

Based on this analysis, the Tax Court concluded that the fair market value of the DHL trademark and trade name was $100 million.

The Appeals Court Decision. On appeal, as to the value of the DHL trademark, the Ninth Circuit did not find that the Tax Court's valuation was clearly erroneous, and, thus, the appellate court upheld the $100 million value ($50 million for the U.S. rights, $50 million for the foreign rights).[44] The court rejected DHL's assertion that the Tax Court's valuation was arbitrary and unreasonable and that the Tax Court failed to articulate its reasoning. Instead, the Court found that the Tax Court gave a step-by-step account of its reasoning:

> First, following the IRS's approach, the Tax Court reached a $300 million value for all unbooked intangibles, measuring the equity value of DHL and DHL's intangibles based on what the Consortium paid for the company in excess of its book value. Although not without problems, this is a systematic, defensible approach. Second, the Tax Court determined that one-half of the total intangibles, or $150 million, was attributable specifically to the DHL trademark. The Tax Court, at several points, explained its belief that the trademark was worth at least as much as the other intangibles. Third, the Tax Court determined that two-thirds of the value of the trademark, or $100 million, was attributable to the non-U.S. rights to the trademark. Fourth, the Tax Court discounted the non-U.S. rights by 50% to reflect a marketability discount, based on potential problems with DHL's ownership of the foreign trademarks. The Tax Court therefore concluded that the foreign and domestic trademarks were each worth $50 million, for a combined value of $100 million.

DHL pointed out two problems with the Tax Court's approach. First, the approach was not used by any of the experts, all of whom measured the value of the trademark based on an "income" approach, where the value of the trademark

---

[44] *DHL Corporation and Subsidiaries v. Commissioner*, 285 F.3d 1210, 2002 U.S. App. LEXIS 6687 (9th Cir. 2002).

is based on the present value of the trademark's future stream of income. Second, the book value of a company is often understated, so it may have been misleading to assume that the value of the company in excess of its book value consisted entirely of intangibles. The appellate court found that these shortcomings were, in any event, debatable and did not warrant reversal on the valuation issue. The Court, however, reversed the Tax Court on other issues in the case.

Summary and Conclusion. In *DHL Corporation and Subsidiaries v. Commissioner*, the Tax Court had to conclude the fair market value of a service company's trademark with the contexts of (1) a purchase price allocation and (2) Section 482. In this case, the Tax Court rejected the analyses and conclusions of both the IRS experts and the taxpayer's experts.

In a classic compromise, the Tax Court concluded its own value for the DHL trademark, and the Ninth Circuit upheld that value as not "clearly erroneous"—the standard used to review factual determinations.

Other Income Tax Issues

Purchase Price Allocation

Indeck Energy Services, Inc. v. Commissioner

One of the issues for the Tax Court in *Indeck Energy Services, Inc. v. Commissioner*,[45] was whether $4,856,922 of a $19,886,922 settlement made by Indeck Energy Services, Inc. to Michael P. Polsky was interest deductible by Indeck and recognizable as ordinary income to Polsky, or whether it was part of the purchase price for shares of Indeck stock held by Polsky.

The Facts of the Case. Polsky was hired as the president of the Indeck Energy Services Division of Indeck Power Equipment Co. The division was subsequently incorporated as Indeck Energy Services, Inc.

Polsky and Indeck executed an employment agreement and a shareholder agreement. Indeck later terminated Polsky's employment, at which time he held 30 of Indeck's 100 issued and outstanding common stock.

Polsky began soliciting offers for his Indeck stock. A company called PowerLink Corp. offered to buy all the Indeck stock for $501,000 per share, but the offer did not receive the approval of a majority of Indeck's shareholders.

Arbitration Proceeding and Settlement Agreement. Polsky commenced an arbitration proceeding against Indeck for breach of his employment agreement. The arbitrator issued an award, concluding that Polsky's termination violated his employment agreement, awarding him $21,668,800 plus interest. The award stated that it was for damages plus Polsky's 30 Indeck shares. Although the award did not allocate the amount between the damages and the shares, it determined the value of the shares as $501,000 per share—the same as the offer from PowerLink.

Indeck sought to have the award vacated on the grounds that the arbitrator lacked jurisdiction over the issue of Polsky's Indeck stock. The Circuit Court vacated the award to the extent of the $15,030,000 for Polsky's stock. The Court

---

[45] *Indeck Energy Services, Inc. v. Commissioner*, T.C. Memo 2003-101 (April 11, 2003).

confirmed the damages based on the employment agreement and entered judgment against Indeck for $6,638,800 plus interest.

Both parties appealed. While the appeals were pending, the parties reached a settlement for $19,886,921.85. The settlement agreement allocated the entire amount to the "purchase price" for the Indeck shares held by Polsky.

The Tax Court's Decision. Indeck argued that the settlement payment consisted of a $15,030,000 purchase price for the shares and $4,856,922 in deductible interest. Polsky, on the other hand, claimed that the entire amount constituted the purchase price for the shares. The Tax Court agreed with Polsky.

The Court found that both the written terms of the agreement and the extrinsic evidence indicated that the parties intended to allocate the entire payment to the purchase price. Further, the Court noted that the parties entered into the agreement at arm's length.

Indeck contended that the agreement was modeled after the arbitrator's award for the shares plus interest and therefore demonstrated the parties' intent to allocate a portion of the settlement toward interest. The Court disagreed, stating that it did not "necessarily follow from the parties' use of the arbitrator's award to arrive at a settlement figure that they agreed to pay interest."

The Court was persuaded that, in the settlement, Polsky was "well positioned" to obtain a $19,886,922 purchase price for his shares "and in substance did so," and that the arbitrator's award "served merely as a formula for arriving at that purchase price. The parties' use of that formula was not tantamount to an agreement to pay $15,030,000 for the shares and the remainder as interest."

The Court concluded that the facts and circumstances suggested that the parties' allocation in fact reflected the economic reality of their agreement.

Summary and Conclusion. This case demonstrates that the Tax Court generally will not rewrite the terms of an agreement where that agreement has been entered into at arm's length.

Present Value as Indicator of "For Profit" Status

Walford v. Commissioner

In *Walford v. Commissioner*,[46] the issue was whether the taxpayer was entitled to an $18,956 deduction related to his limited partnership interest for 1981 and whether he was liable for a valuation overstatement.

The Facts of the Case. The taxpayer invested in Sav-Fuel Associates, a limited partnership whose stated sole purpose was to acquire an energy management system (EMS) to be installed in a manufacturing plant. A private placement memorandum (PPM) was distributed to all potential investors. Taxpayer held a 2.152174 percent interest in the company. The EMS was sold to an entity controlled by Sav-Fuel's promoter for $337,500. By the time the equipment was subsequently purchased by Sav-Fuel, the purchase price had escalated to $10,350,000. The bulk of that sum was to be paid by a nonrecourse note of $9,004,500, payable solely from 80 percent of the gross income actually received by Sav-Fuel from the use of the EMS.

The PPM made assumptions and projections of economic consequences for a 25-year period, yielding a net cash flow of $2,453,398. This figure was not

---

[46] *Walford v. Commissioner,* T.C. Memo 2003-296, 2003 Tax Ct. Memo LEXIS 299 (October 23, 2003).

discounted to present value. According to the PPM, depreciation on the EMS for the tax year at issue was expected to be \$1,478,571. The taxpayer's deduction of \$18,956—his distributive share of the partnership's losses—was based on the EMS's depreciation.

Valuation Evidence. Both parties presented expert testimony on the appropriate discount rate. The PPM assumed a useful life of 25 years. The taxpayer's expert presented evidence that the EMS had a useful life exceeding 30 years. The PPM assumed inflation in energy costs of about 20 percent per year. Based on his review of energy price projections, the IRS's expert concluded that an 18.5 percent inflation rate was "generous" by assuming a real price increase of 5 percent per year and adding 13.5 percent after reviewing the consumer price index.

Regarding the discount rate, the taxpayer claimed that 15 percent was appropriate, whereas the IRS, using the build-up method, arrived at a discount rate of 18.96 percent. As the risk-free rate, the IRS's expert used the rate of return of 11.36 percent on a 20-year government bond in the tax year and then added an equity risk premium of 7.6 percent, using data from Ibbotson Associates' SBBI.

Tax Court Findings and Conclusions. To determine whether the taxpayer was entitled to his deduction, the Tax Court undertook to determine whether Sav-Fuel was engaged in business for profit, but found numerous indicators that it was not. One of the factors was that net present value was negative. The court indicated that, "If net present value is positive, the investment is profitable, and a profit-seeking investor would pursue it. If net present value is zero, the investment is neither profitable nor unprofitable, and profit-seeking investor would be indifferent to it. If net present value is negative, the investment is unprofitable, and a profit-seeking investor would avoid it." The court found that the assumptions and projections from the PPM resulted in a negative present value, after discounting future cash flows and disregarding tax considerations.

The taxpayer challenged the court's underlying conclusions relating to useful life, inflation rate, and discount rate. The court dismissed his arguments regarding useful life, finding that taxpayer's expert cited no authority, facts, or data, other than his personal belief, to establish the useful life of the EMS. On the issue of inflation, the court found the IRS's expert "persuasive" but applied the 20 percent rate from the PPM anyway. Even after applying the higher rate, the court said, the net cash flow was still negative.

Finally, the Tax Court applied an 11.5 percent rate, "despite the fact that a more realistic rate is 15 percent." It used the lower rate because "if the investments did not show profit at those interest rates, then they would not show profit at the higher rates it could be assumed a profit-seeking investor would demand."

In sum, the court's net present value calculations showed Sav-Fuel's net cash flow to be negative \$178,656, demonstrating that "Sav-Fuel could not reasonably have hoped to recoup its investment in the EMS, much less earn an economic profit independent of tax considerations." Accordingly, the court denied the taxpayer's depreciation deduction and found him liable for a valuation overstatement under IRC § 6659 of EMS in the amount of 30 percent of the underpayment.

Decision on Appeal. The Tenth Circuit affirmed, concluding that the Tax Court had not committed clear error in determining that Sav-Fuel was created only for the purpose of providing a tax shelter, not as a profit-making business.[47]

---

[47] *Walford v. Commissioner,* 123 Fed. Appx. 952; 2005 U.S. App. LEXIS 3365; 95 A.F.T.R.2d (RIA) 1240 (10th Cir. Feb. 24, 2005).

Stock Warrant Valuation

Kimberlin v. Commissioner

In *Kimberlin v. Commissioner*,[48] a key issue was whether stock warrants received by the taxpayer should have been valued at the time of receipt or upon exercise.

The Facts of the Case. One of the taxpayers, an investment firm, had entered into an agreement to provide private placement financing. A dispute arose, and the entity that sought financing settled the dispute by providing the investment firm warrants for 45,000 shares of Class B stock at $2.00 per share, exercisable for a period of four years or sale of the company, whichever came first.

The settlement agreement entitled the investment firm's owner to receive 250,000 shares under the same terms, which he caused to be reissued to another of his firms, to exercise at his behest as a distribution. The warrants were issued in 1995, and that year, the corporate taxpayer distributed the warrants to its majority shareholder, the individual taxpayer. The warrants were exercised in 1997, at which time the mean selling price for the company's shares was about $29; two days later, the company went public and the stock rose to nearly $36 per share.

The investment banker and his two firms did not report the income on their 1997 tax returns, but filed amended returns for 1995, reporting receipt of the warrants pursuant to the settlement agreement. The IRS issued notices of deficiency to all the taxpayers, claiming that the exercise (not the receipt) of the warrants triggered liability. The difference between receipt and exercise values were substantial: The individual taxpayer had claimed $76,500 of income related to receiving the 1995 warrants, whereas the IRS claimed $36.6 million for the 1997 dividend relating to their exercise.

The Tax Court's Decision. The court held that the distribution of the warrants to the individual taxpayer was a dividend, and not compensation for services pursuant to IRC § 83. Based on the testimony of the taxpayers' financial expert, the court held that the warrants had an ascertainable fair market value on the date of grant. Thus, the value of the warrants was includable in 1995, and the Commissioner erred in determining a deficiency when the warrants were exercised in 1997. Accordingly, the warrants that the individual taxpayer received should have been valued at the time of receipt (i.e., 1995).

The court accepted the taxpayer's expert's valuation of the fair market value of the warrants in 1995. For his analysis, the expert considered the 7.3 million shares of Series B preferred stock placed with private investors for $1.50 per share in 1994 and 1995 and then applied "prudent" techniques (e.g., focusing on venture capitalist benchmark rates of return) to arrive at a fair market value, on the 1995 grant date, of $0.90 per share.

---

[48] *Kimberlin v. Commissioner*, 2007 U.S. Tax Ct. LEXIS 13, 128 T.C. No. 13 (May 8, 2007).

Valuation as Accounting Method

In re Heilig Meyers Co.

In re Heilig Meyers Co.[49] presents a situation where the court determined that a valuation must meet the "clear reflection of income" requirements of IRC § 446(b) because "where . . . the accounting method at issue essentially consists of a determination of market value, § 446(b) applies to that determination."

The Facts of the Case. Under pre-1998 law, companies that made installment loans could account for their accounts at year's end by using the mark-to-market accounting method under IRC § 475. This method is generally used to account for noninventory securities held by securities dealers. Under the mark-to-market method, any security that is held by a securities dealer at the end of the year and is not inventory must be "marked to market," that is, treated as though it had been sold for its fair market value on the last business day of the taxpayer's taxable year. The taxpayer recognizes a gain or loss equal to the difference between the fair market value so calculated and the security's basis. Heilig Meyers Companies (taxpayer), a group of retailers, elected to use the § 475's mark-to-market accounting method for tax year 1997, most of the assets for which year were accounts receivable.

Taxpayer's valuation used the discounted cash flow (DCF) method to determine the fair market value of the 1997 accounts receivable. In estimating the future cash flows, the analyst reduced their face value by: (1) a 3 percent servicing cost; (2) anticipated customer defaults; and (3) projected taxes on the income stream. In addition, the expert estimated the weighted investment returns related to seven consumer credit card companies to arrive at a weighted average cost of capital (WACC) of 11 percent.

From that rate, the expert derived discount rates of 8 percent for current receivables, 15 percent for those 61–120 days old, and 22 percent for those aged 121–180 days. Applying these, the fair market value of the accounts receivable came to $1,027 million. Because the stipulated book value of the accounts was $1,073 million, taxpayer recognized a loss (and a tax deduction) of approximately $46 million, which it used as a loss carryback to a prior year.

The IRS Position. The IRS questioned several aspects of the valuation methodology, including the estimated servicing costs and the reduction for taxes. It also found the taxpayer's discount rates "excessive and unfounded," allowing too much risk for potential customer defaults. The IRS applied a risk-free discount rate of 6.5 percent (the rate of 18-month Treasury securities in 1997), and recomputed the fair market value of the accounts receivable to $1,049 million, resulting in a loss/deduction of nearly $24.3 million—and a disallowance of over $21.6 million. At trial (in bankruptcy court), the IRS presented a new valuation of the receivables based on a DCF using a range of discount rates from 6.2 percent to 7.3 percent, applying the lower rate to accounts maturing earlier and the higher rates to those maturing later. The IRS also asserted that the taxpayer's valuation method failed to clearly reflect income under IRC § 446(b). Although the bankruptcy court found problems with both appraisers' methods and specific assumption, it

---

[49] *In re Heilig Meyers Co.,* 2007 U.S. App. LEXIS 11052 (May 9, 2007).

nonetheless accepted the IRS calculations of the 1997 tax loss. The federal district court affirmed, and the taxpayer appealed.

The Court of Appeals Decision. On appeal to the Fourth Circuit, the taxpayer argued that the dispute was really a "valuation" case as opposed to a "method of accounting case," and urged the court to sustain its valuations because the underlying methodology was sound. The court disagreed, citing the rule that "the reporting of income under Section 475, *inclusive of the valuation requirement subsumed therein*, is a method of accounting" (Court's emphasis), and that method of accounting must "clearly reflect income" under Section 446(b). The court said:

> [T]he accounting method at issue essentially consisted of the determination of the market value of the asset . . . The mark-to-market method of § 475 requires nothing other than that the taxpayer peg the asset's value to its fair market value on the last business day of the taxable year. In such instances, for the taxpayer to fail to assess market value appropriately is in essence for it to have failed to execute the accounting method. In contrast, a valuation that does not constitute the core of an accounting method will not implicate § 446(b).

In essence, the Court ruled that a taxpayer may not avail itself of an accounting method, the entire substance of which consists of accurately determining market value, only to implement it in a way that does no such thing.

Dissenting Opinion. The dissent asserted that the majority permitted the IRS simply to characterize the dispute in the case as one involving the taxpayer's method of accounting and thereby avoid a trial and decision by a factfinder on the fair market value of the taxpayer's accounts receivable. The problem with this approach, according to the dissent, was that the IRS and the taxpayer did not dispute a method of accounting, but only the valuation of the taxpayer's asset, that is, its accounts receivable. According to the dissent, all of the taxpayer's practices properly regarded as methods of accounting were never in dispute, and the methods the taxpayer used clearly reflected income (or loss) to the very last detail. In fact, the taxpayer and IRS valuations were apart by only 2 percent.

After pointing out that the taxpayer and IRS agreed on almost every aspect of the methodology to be used, the dissent noted that in essence "the narrow disagreement between the IRS and the taxpayer was over the proper risk premium to add to the risk-free rate of return to get a discount rate to apply to the book value, ultimately to reach the market value. That narrow issue is a factual question that must be resolved by a factfinder." The dissent summarized the result of the opinion, as well as the counterpoint to it:

> Under the majority's view, the taxpayer never receives a trial on the fact of the appropriate risk premium by which to discount the book value of its accounts receivable. Rather, the majority upholds the IRS's post-trial declaration that the selection of a particular risk premium is a method of accounting within the IRS's regulatory purview. Under the majority's view, at no point is the taxpayer entitled to a finding of fact on the disputed issue by a neutral adjudicator. Thus, the IRS may always decree that the taxpayer's position on [valuation] fails to clearly reflect income and therefore is subject to recomputation by the IRS under *26 U.S.C. § 446(b)* without a trial. The IRS's authority to regulate the tax accounting system, however, does not reach down to this level of detail, and it should not.

Although this is essentially a legal issue to be decided by the courts or Congress, it does indicate to valuation professionals and attorneys practicing in this area the need to be able to justify their valuation methodologies as much as possible, lest they be challenged as inappropriate accounting methods.

Summary

This chapter presented summary reviews of the valuation aspects of numerous federal income tax court cases. The cases that were reviewed were not selected based on their judicial precedent or noteworthy legal merits. Rather, they were selected because they were informative to taxpayers, their legal counsel, and to valuation practitioners with regard to issues of valuation principles and practices.

However, analysts should not naively rely upon the judicial decisions in these cases in their valuation practices for several reasons. First, all of the cases reviewed are very specific with regard to facts and circumstances. It is very unlikely that the facts and circumstances of another assignment would be sufficiently similar to the cases reviewed to allow for the naive application of a judicial guideline. Second, federal judges apply a specific set of legal and (sometimes) valuation principles in their decisions. These same valuation principles may not apply in valuations performed for purposes other than federal income taxation. Third, federal judges are not trained valuation analysts. A judicial decision that makes good legal sense may not be based on sound valuation principles or economic theory. And, fourth, decisions of federal judges (particularly in the U.S. Tax Court) seem to have a tendency to pick a point between the two valuation positions. Court decisions (particularly decisions that compromise between the taxpayer's and the IRS's position) may be judicially fair. But, they may not always be technically correct from a more academic valuation and economic analysis perspective.

One thing that is notable from a reading of the cases (both presented in this chapter, as well as a general comment) is that precise attention to detail does matter in the eyes of the factfinder. More cases are won on good, solid, substantial evidence, and it is the job of the valuation expert to provide it.

Chapter 32

Valuations for Employee Stock Ownership Plans

This is a descriptive chapter on the basics of ESOP valuation. For court decisions on aspects of ESOP valuation, see the next chapter.

An employee stock ownership plan (ESOP) is a qualified retirement plan under the Internal Revenue Code of 1986, as amended (the Code). The plan is designed to invest primarily in employer stock. The Code and the Employee Retirement Income Security Act of 1974, as amended (ERISA), impose a number of requirements for the ESOP to gain qualified status. The ESOP must comply with most of the requirements of other qualified retirement plans. There are additional requirements specific to ESOPs. Additionally, ESOPs are "exempt" from other qualified plan requirements due to prohibited transaction exemptions. For example, the ESOP may use borrowed funds from the sponsoring company to purchase employer stock.

As of this writing, there are approximately 11,000 to 12,000 ESOPs in the United States. In addition, the ESOP concept is currently expanding globally. During 1997, legislation was passed that allows S corporations to sponsor ESOPs.

ESOP transactions are complex because they encompass the incorporation of knowledge from various disciplines. The following is a summary of these disciplines:

- Valuation
- Legal and regulatory
- Qualified plan administration
- Finance
- Fiduciary concerns

There is also a great deal of crossover among disciplines on some issues. This chapter generally covers the major aspects of each of these disciplines and how each affects the ESOP transaction. To reduce one of the complexities and for ease in understanding, the S corporation ESOP issues are addressed in a separate section. Thus, all the other sections of this chapter assume the company sponsoring the ESOP is a C corporation.

General ESOP Framework

The starting point for understanding the complexities involved in ESOPs is the general ESOP framework. ESOPs serve the dual purpose of meeting corporate finance and compensation objectives. The following is a summary of various purposes for the use of an ESOP:

- Liquidity for shareholders
- Estate planning
- Management succession planning
- Capital for expansion
- Acquisitions
- Leveraged buyout (LBO) by management
- Divestiture
- Recapitalization
- Takeover defense
- Motivating employees
- Employee benefit
- Charitable giving
- Going private

Types of ESOPs

Nonleveraged ESOPs

The nonleveraged ESOP does not use debt to purchase employer securities. The nonleveraged ESOP acquires employer securities through tax-deductible stock contributions or tax-deductible cash contributions that are used to purchase employer securities. Stock is purchased gradually each year based on the company's annual contribution amount. The ESOP percentage ownership increases with each contribution. Thus, debt financing is not necessary.

Leveraged ESOPs

The typical leveraged ESOP transaction is accomplished through a series of steps that are best illustrated by the diagram presented in Exhibit 32–1.

ABC Company borrows money from the bank (the "Bank Loan"). The Company then loans the proceeds from the Bank Loan to a newly created ESOP, evidenced by the "ESOP Loan." The ESOP purchases stock from existing shareholders in return for the cash from the proceeds of the ESOP Loan.

Exhibit 32–2 illustrates the effects of the leveraged ESOP transaction on an annual basis. Annually, ABC Company makes tax-deductible employer contributions to the ESOP (or pays dividends on the ESOP stock). The ESOP uses its cash from these employer contributions to make payments on the ESOP Loan. ABC Company now actually has the cash it used for employer contributions and the ESOP has merely been a conduit for the cash. Therefore, ABC Company can now use the cash to make payments on the Bank Loan. As the ESOP Loan is paid back, employer securities are allocated to ESOP participant accounts.

Exhibit 32–1

Leveraged ESOP Transaction

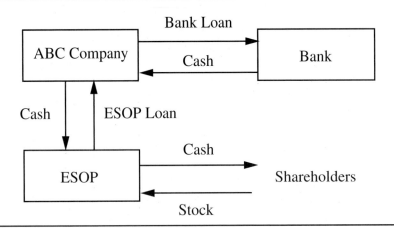

Exhibit 32–2

Annual ESOP Cash Flows

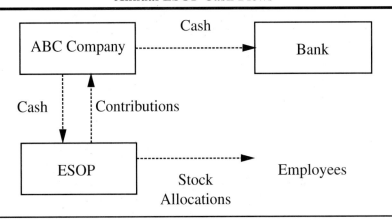

All Parties to a Leveraged ESOP Transaction Benefit

The tax and economic advantages of a leveraged ESOP transaction benefit all parties to the transaction, including the company, the shareholders, the employees, and the lenders.

The Company. The most significant benefit for the company is the ability to effectively deduct the principal payments on the ESOP acquisition loan for income tax purposes. This is a substantial tax savings for the company and increases after-tax cash flow as compared to conventional financing. These tax benefits also increase the company's debt-carrying capacity and thus enhance the ability to obtain financing.

The company may also experience productivity gains due to employee ownership. In addition, the ESOP should be helpful in attracting and retaining employees.

The Shareholders. The most significant benefit for the selling shareholder is the availability of the 1042 election. Under Code Section 1042, the selling shareholder can defer the capital gains tax on the sale to the ESOP. The specific requirements of

Section 1042 are discussed in detail later in this chapter. Therefore, the shareholder would realize greater net after-tax proceeds when selling to an ESOP.

The ESOP transaction is also a liquidity event for the selling shareholder. Many owners of privately held businesses have a significant portion of their net worth invested in the business. The sale to an ESOP can provide needed liquidity—and yet the selling shareholder can maintain ownership control. These events can also be beneficial to the individual shareholder's estate plan.

Additional equity incentives for management are still available in the ESOP company. In fact, equity-based incentive plans are common in ESOP companies because the ESOP is considered a passive financial investor—that is, the ESOP does not participate in daily management decisions.

The Employees. The major benefit for employees is the ability to share in the equity growth of the company. Since the value of the company is dependent on its performance, employees may be more motivated to act in ways that maximize shareholder value.

Generally, ESOP contributions are larger than typical profit-sharing contributions. ESOP contributions can even exceed 25 percent of annual compensation in some transactions.

And, just as in other qualified retirement plans, the employee does not recognize taxable income in the year the shares are allocated to the accounts. Rather, taxable income is recognized when the participant receives a distribution from the ESOP. During the period the stock is held by the ESOP, the appreciation in value is also not currently taxed.

The Lenders. The major benefit for the lenders in ESOP transactions is the reduced credit risk associated with the effective ability to deduct principal. The tax savings increase after-tax flow and provide a greater chance that the company can meet its debt obligations.

Most lenders prefer to be sure that the company can handle the debt obligations based on current cash flow. But the lender also looks to the balance sheet for collateral protection. The ESOP transaction can also enhance credit through a pledge of the qualified replacement property (QRP) purchased by the selling shareholder in a Section 1042 rollover transaction as collateral for the Bank Loan.

Valuation of a Company for ESOP Purposes

The first step in assessing the feasibility of an ESOP is estimating the value of the business. In estimating the value of a business for ESOP purposes, most of the valuation concepts discussed in prior chapters are applicable. However, ESOPs bring added complexities to the valuation process. This chapter assumes the reader has a basic knowledge of general valuation theories and expands upon the specific valuation issues related to ESOPs.

Adequate Consideration

ERISA requires that ESOPs pay no more than "adequate consideration" when investing in employer securities. Adequate consideration generally follows the specific guidelines for the definition of fair market value under Revenue Ruling 59-60.

For purposes of ERISA and the adequate consideration regulations, fair market value is defined as:

> The price at which an asset would change hands between a willing buyer and a willing seller when the former is not under any compulsion to buy and the latter is not under any compulsion to sell, and both parties are able, as well as willing, to trade and are well informed about the asset and the market for such asset.[1]

An ESOP appraisal is required to be performed (1) when the ESOP makes an acquisition of employer securities, (2) at least annually thereafter (although some companies routinely have their stock appraisals updated semiannually or quarterly), (3) whenever there is a transaction between the plan and a party in interest, and (4) if the ESOP sells out of its stock position.

The Department of Labor's (DOL's) proposed adequate consideration regulations provide that the written document include an assessment of all "relevant factors" including:

(A) The nature of the business and the history of the enterprise from its inception;

(B) The economic outlook in general, and the condition and outlook of the specific industry in particular;

(C) The book value of the securities and the financial condition of the business;

(D) The earning capacity of the company;

(E) The dividend-paying capacity of the company;

(F) Whether or not the enterprise has goodwill or other intangible value;

(G) The market price of securities of corporations engaged in the same or a similar line of business, which are actively traded in a free and open market, either on an exchange or over-the-counter;

(H) The marketability, or lack thereof, of the securities. Where the plan is the purchaser of securities that are subject to "put" rights and such rights are taken into account in reducing the discount for lack of marketability, such assessment shall include consideration of the extent to which such rights are enforceable, as well as the company's ability to meet its obligations with respect to the "put rights" (taking into account the company's financial strength and liquidity);

(I) Whether or not the seller would be able to obtain a control premium from an unrelated third party with regard to the block of securities being valued, provided that in cases where a control premium is taken into account:

(1) Actual control (both in form and substance) passes to the purchaser with the sale, or will pass to the purchaser within a reasonable time pursuant to a binding agreement in effect at the time of the sale, and

(2) It is reasonable to assume that the purchaser's control will not be dissipated within a short period of time subsequent to acquisition.[2]

---

[1] Proposed Regulation Relating to the Definition of Adequate Consideration, 53 Fed. Reg. 17,632 (1988), pp. 17,634.

[2] Ibid., pp. 17,637–38.

The requirement to assess factors (A) through (G) as well as all "relevant factors" is consistent with Revenue Ruling 59-60. Factors (H) and (I) are additional factors specific to ESOP valuations.

Independence of the Appraiser and the Appraiser's Role

The DOL's proposed adequate consideration regulations require that someone that is independent of all parties to the ESOP transaction conduct ESOP appraisals. The DOL notes that under Code Section 401(a)(28)(C), ESOP fiduciaries must employ an independent appraiser meeting requirements similar to Regulation 1.170A-13(c)(5) of the Code which relates to independent appraisals of donations to charitable organizations.

A qualified independent appraiser under these regulations is a person who, among other qualifications:

1. Is not a party to the transaction, is not related to any party to the transaction, is not married to any person with relationship to the transaction, and is not regularly used by any of the parties to the transaction and does not perform a majority of appraisals for these persons
2. Holds himself or herself out to the public as an appraiser or performs appraisals on a regular basis
3. Is qualified to make appraisals of the type of property being valued including, by background, experience, education, and memberships, if any, in professional associations
4. Understands that an intentionally false or fraudulent overstatement of value may subject the valuation practitioner to a civil penalty
5. Receives an appraisal fee that is not based on a percentage of the appraised value of the property

The role of the independent appraiser is to provide the fiduciary with the financial data and the documents that are required by law in order for the fiduciary to make its decisions on behalf of the ESOP participants. The fiduciary is actually the party responsible for the value and fairness decision—not the appraiser.

Providing investment advice to the plan on such matters as investment policies or strategies, overall portfolio composition, or diversification of plan investments could imply that the appraiser is a fiduciary. The law indicates that the fiduciary is determined not by label but by function. The appraiser does not make the decision to close the transaction. The fiduciary does.

Reporting Requirements

The DOL's proposed adequate consideration regulations also address the ESOP valuation reporting requirements. In order to comply with the regulations the ESOP valuation report must contain the following information:

(A) A summary of the qualifications to evaluate assets of the type being valued of the person making the valuation;

(B)   A statement of the asset's value, a statement of the methods used in estimating that value, and the reasons for the valuation in light of those methods;

(C)   A full description of the asset being valued;

(D)   The factors taken into account in making the valuation, including any restrictions, understandings, agreements, or obligations limiting the use or disposition of the property;

(E)   The purpose for which that valuation was made;

(F)   The relevance or significance accorded to the valuation methods taken into account;

(G)   The effective date of the valuation; and

(H)   In cases where a valuation report has been prepared, the signature of the person or firm making the valuation and the date the report was signed.[3]

Valuation Approaches and Methods

The three generally accepted approaches to valuation are the income approach (Chapters 9 and 10), the market approach (Chapters 11 and 12), and the asset-based approach (Chapters 13 and 14). In addition, the ESOP appraisal also includes a detailed qualitative and quantitative analysis of the subject ESOP company. While all of the three approaches may be used to value shares of company stock held by an ESOP, the asset-based approach is used less often than the other two approaches (and mainly for holding or investment companies).

ESOP-Specific Adjustments

ESOP Contributions

A normalized benefit expense should be determined taking into consideration any other existing retirement plan expenses. One practice is to add back the employer corporation ESOP contributions in estimating the normalized earnings of the business, if the contributions are in excess of normal retirement plan benefits. However, if ESOP contributions represent compensation in lieu of wages or benefits, or are expected to remain in place over an indefinite period of time, contribution expenses should not be added back in arriving at normalized earnings. If the ESOP is replacing another plan but at a higher level, the analyst also should make the adjustment for normalized employee benefit costs discussed below.

Normalized Employee Benefit Costs

If the company did not have an ESOP, the sponsoring company would probably consider another employee benefit plan. Or, the ESOP may be replacing another employee benefit plan for a period of time. Thus, the appraiser needs to assess the

---

[3] Ibid.

normalized level of employee benefit costs and subtract this as an expense from normalized earnings. Historical practices in the subject ESOP company are good indications of the market level of benefits expected by the employees.

This adjustment in combination with the ESOP contribution adjustment discussed previously basically adjusts the ESOP company's normalized earnings as the willing buyer would if they did not intend to continue the ESOP. Since ESOPs are specific buyers, the willing buyer test would require that the analyst make this assumption.

Compensation Adjustments

Analysts sometimes consider an adjustment for excess compensation if some members of management are earning amounts in excess of the market level of compensation. In an ESOP valuation, these adjustments are only appropriate if the compensation policies will be changed to reflect the reduced level of compensation. Even if excess compensation is being paid, if the higher level of compensation is expected to continue, the ESOP valuation should reflect the ongoing compensation practices.

ESOP Compensation Adjustment

Under American Institute of Certified Public Accountants Statement of Position (SOP) 93-6, defined and discussed in the section of this chapter on ESOP Accounting Standards, the audited income statement contains a recording of compensation expense associated with the ESOP at fair market value. This compensation expense is not cash compensation and should not be reflected as such. The true economics of the cash transactions indicate that the appreciation in the value of the shares held by the ESOP trust is actually earnings of the plan. Thus, when valuing ESOP stock, most analysts adjust for the fair market value component of the ESOP compensation expense in determining the normalized earnings of the company.

Control Premiums

Valuation practitioners generally agree that the basis for the ESOP valuation will differ depending on whether or not the block of stock subject to the valuation carries elements of control. Generally, a buyer of a controlling ownership interest will pay more for the stock, as discussed in Chapter 15.

In some control ESOP transactions, no changes are expected to enhance cash flows. Although, technically, a control premium may be applied to these transactions, the application of a control premium may not be prudent. Even though interim cash flows may not reflect enhanced cash flows, the ESOP, as a control shareholder, could sell the company and receive a control price. Most analysts take the position that the ESOP should be able to pay whatever a hypothetical third-party buyer would pay for the block of stock being purchased, including control.

The following are some factors, among others, to consider when estimating the appropriate control premium, if any, to apply in ESOP valuations:

1. The elements of control inherent in the particular block of stock
2. The degree of control—effective, operating, and absolute

3. The aggregate interest purchased or held by the ESOP regardless of whether the sellers constituted minority or controlling interests

4. The potential for control, such as binding agreements with other shareholders that result in the passing of control to the ESOP

5. The effects related to the distribution of stock ownership

6. Any empirical evidence of control premiums actually paid in similar transactions

7. Any value enhancements that may result from the passing of control (e.g., effective use of leverage, elimination of excess compensation paid to selling shareholders, sale of undervalued assets)

8. Any value enhancement due to a put right

9. The rights and obligations under the employer corporation's articles of incorporation and state law

10. Whether the company's articles of incorporation or state law provides for cumulative voting

11. Contractual restrictions under the company's debt agreements or employment contracts

12. Effects of regulations, including state statutes (i.e., what constitutes majority for voting purposes)

13. The current financial condition and policies of the company

If the ESOP purchases control over a period of time instead of in one transaction, the issue of whether a control premium applies becomes more complex. Evidence in the public marketplace generally suggests that control premiums are paid along the entire spectrum of creeping control, although at different levels. Consistency among ESOP valuations from year to year is essential for the fair treatment and nondiscrimination of employee participants. Thus, if a control premium has been applied in past ESOP valuations, there is a tendency among analysts to continue this practice.

Discount for Lack of Marketability

There is still continuing controversy surrounding the extent to which a lack of marketability discount should be applied in ESOP valuations. Marketability is the ability of the stock to be sold and turned into cash quickly. On the one end of the marketability spectrum, there are relatively few potential buyers for shares in most closely held companies (especially of noncontrolling ownership interests). On the other end of the spectrum, shares in publicly traded corporations have almost instant marketability on an organized exchange and high liquidity, since the seller can receive cash within three business days.

Put Option and Repurchase Liability

The economic factor that generally distinguishes ESOP shares in closely held corporations is that a "put option" is required to be attached to the ESOP shares. Without this put option, employees could be forced to hold employer securities for extended periods of time. The put option requires the employer to provide the needed liquidity by repurchasing the distributed employer securities. This employer obligation to purchase shares is referred to generally as the repurchase obligation.

Under Code Section 409(h)(1)(B), employer securities that are acquired by an ESOP after December 31, 1979, must be subject to a put option if the securities are not readily tradable on an organized market at the time of the distributions to employee participants.

Employer corporation securities acquired with the proceeds of an ESOP loan after September 30, 1976, must also be subject to a put option, if the shares are not readily tradable on distribution. For employer securities not subject to these mandatory put option requirements, the company may provide a voluntary put option.

The DOL's proposed regulations guide the analyst to consider (1) the extent to which the put rights are enforceable and (2) the company's ability to meet its obligation. Most ESOP valuation practitioners "interpret the ESOP put right as substantially mitigating, if not eliminating, any marketability discount that would otherwise apply."[4]

The principal economic factors that influence the discount for lack of marketability with regard to ESOP employer securities are as follows:

1. The provisions of the ESOP plan documents, including the put rights
2. The financial strength and solvency of the employer corporation
3. The size of the share block owned by the ESOP
4. The degree of liquidity in the ESOP trust and the company
5. The extra borrowing capacity of the employer corporation
6. The repurchase liability and the expected funding requirements
7. The extent to which the company has planned and managed the repurchase liability
8. Past practices in repurchases by the company
9. The form and timing of payments to selling shareholders and ESOP lenders
10. The overall priority of acknowledged and contingent claims that may conflict with achieving liquidity for plan participants over time

The ESOP company can best plan for the repurchase liability by setting corporation policies regarding how repurchases will be handled. These policies will aid the analyst in assessing the lack of marketability discount. The repurchase liability is discussed in greater detail later in this chapter.

Current Controversies

The *Eyler* case (discussed in Chapter 33) and others have created a resurgence of the lack of marketability discount issue in ESOPs. The general trend is an attempt by the IRS to significantly increase the lack of marketability discount applied in ESOP transactions to reduce deductions from taxable income available to the ESOP company. The bases for these opinions are not entirely justified. First of all, *Eyler* was a fact pattern that included violations of ESOP valuation and fiduciary guidelines. The marketability issue was a minor issue that was not even technically debated. The judge merely commented on marketability as an issue in the opinion.

In addition, in order to justify such a position, the analyst has to assume that the DOL misunderstood the definition of fair market value when drafting the language relating to lack of marketability discounts in the adequate consideration regulations. The other erroneous assumption needed is that the true economics of the

---

[4] J. Michael Julius, "ESOP Appraisals and Non-ESOP Shareholders," *CPA Litigation Service Counselor*, July 1998, p. 9.

put option should not be considered because it is not a right that is attached to the security. The put right is, however, a statutory right under the Code. The ESOP does not sell this right but most noncontrolling investors negotiate some buyout provision when the investment decision is made.

Despite all the debate over substantial lack of marketability discounts for ESOP transactions, the typical practice remains that these discounts should be between 0 and 20 percent. However, due to the recent controversies, many ESOP fiduciaries are taking the position that some discount should be applied to protect from protracted litigation.

Posttransaction Value in Leveraged ESOPs

After the ESOP purchases employer securities, the company has a significant demand on cash flow for debt repayments. Unless the sponsoring company receives substantial future cost or tax savings, the fair market value of the ESOP shares immediately after the transaction is reduced. This reduction in value is directly attributable to the reduction in cash flow available to the common equity as a result of the company's obligation to amortize the ESOP debt.

The tax shield created by the ESOP debt mitigates the reduction in value. This ESOP tax shield can be quantified by computing the present value of the tax savings over the period of the ESOP Loan. The present value of the ESOP tax shield would then be added back to equity value. It is important to note that, if the ESOP Loan and Bank Loan payments are not congruous, the present value of the tax shield is coincident with payments made on the ESOP Loan—not the Bank Loan. Payments on the ESOP Loan trigger the deductibility of principal payments.

If the value of the company does not change over the period the ESOP Loan is amortized, this reduction in value is recovered. However, it is important to note that the valuation impact is tied to the Bank Loan—not the ESOP Loan. It is the company's obligation to outside lenders that triggers the effect on common equity value.

Legislative and Regulatory Issues in ESOPs

The valuation practitioner conducting ESOP valuations needs to have a general understanding of the legislative and regulatory issues that impact ESOPs. The following is a general discussion of some of the legislated rules regarding ESOPs. These legal aspects of ESOPs are complex and further discussions with qualified ERISA counsel are necessary before implementing an ESOP.

Section 1042 Rollover

Code Section 1042 generally provides that, if certain requirements are met, no gain will be recognized by the selling shareholder upon the sale to an ESOP. The requirements of this tax deferral include:

- Immediately after the sale to the ESOP, the ESOP must own at least 30 percent of the voting stock of the business or 30 percent of the value of the business.

- QRP must be purchased with the proceeds within a 15-month period beginning three months prior to the sale to the ESOP. QRP is generally defined as stocks and bonds of domestic operating corporations.
- The selling shareholder must have owned the securities sold to the ESOP for at least three years prior to the sale.

The gain is deferred until the sale of the QRP. And, if the selling shareholder holds the QRP in his estate, the gain is never taxed, due to the step up in basis allowed upon death.

409(1) Employer Securities

The ESOP must purchase an employer security that meets the requirements of Code Section 409(1). This Code section generally provides that the security purchased by the ESOP be (1) the highest voting common stock, or (2) convertible into the highest voting common stock.

Principal Deductibility and Code Section 415

The company may deduct dividends paid on employer securities held by a leveraged ESOP, provided that the dividends paid are reasonable and are either (1) paid in cash directly to the participants after receipt by the ESOP trust, or (2) used to make payments on the ESOP Loan. At times, the ESOP valuation analyst may be asked to opine on the reasonableness of the ESOP dividend.

Dividends used to make payments on the ESOP Loan are not included in ESOP participants' annual additions for purposes of the Code Section 415 contribution limitations. This provision allows an ESOP design that provides for a dividend-paying security to enhance the debt payment abilities under the ESOP Loan without the constraints of the 25 percent of compensation limitations under Code Section 415.

Code Section 133 Interest Exclusion

There are still some Code Section 133 loans in existence, so this provision does bear mentioning—although briefly. Code Section 133 provided for an exclusion from taxable income of 50 percent of the interest earned on the ESOP debt by the ESOP lender. Certain conditions had to be met. Code Section 133 was repealed in August of 1996.

The IRS Audit Guidelines

The IRS has audited ESOPs from time to time. IRS Announcement 95-33 contains finalized examination guidelines for (among other things) audits of ESOPs. Familiarity with these guidelines will assist the valuation practitioner when analyzing the ESOP transaction structure and valuation issues so as to protect the transaction and valuations from attack by the IRS. These guidelines address the issues of (1) how much is "primarily invested," (2) the ESOP exempt loan, (3) the Code

Section 1042 rollover, (4) the Code Section 415 limitations, (5) dividends paid on ESOP stock, (6) the ESOP put option, (7) voting rights, (8) the date of the appraisal, (9) adequate consideration, (10) the independence of the appraiser, (11) appraisal conclusions, (12) subsequent events, and (13) proceeds from the sale of unallocated shares.

ESOP Specific Plan Administration Issues

The ESOP Association has published an administration handbook that was designed to assist its members on ESOP administration, record keeping, compliance, and technical issues. The following is a general discussion of some of the plan administration issues in ESOPs. These plan administration aspects of ESOPs are complex, and further discussions with a qualified, experienced ESOP plan administrator is necessary before implementing an ESOP.

An ESOP is a qualified plan and must therefore meet the minimum coverage, distribution, vesting, and participation requirements under ERISA. This section focuses on the issues specific to ESOP plan administration. Knowledge of the general requirements of qualified plans is assumed.

A general understanding of ESOP plan administration issues is an important concept for the ESOP valuation practitioner because it impacts the size and timing of the company's repurchase obligation.

Allocations to Participant Accounts

The ESOP plan document governs the operation of the ESOP. Therefore, the starting point in determining the allocations to participant accounts is the plan documents. The company then completes an employee census that consists of gathering certain demographic data on employees. The plan administrator then determines who among the employees is eligible to participate in the ESOP allocations.

The number of shares that are released from the plan is determined based on a choice between two methods. The first method is an allocation based on the ratio of principal paid in the current year over the total principal obligation. The second method is similar except that principal and interest are considered. Since interest payments are greater in the first years of an ESOP, participant allocations will be faster under the principal and interest method.

This ratio is then applied to the number of shares in the suspense account. Immediately after the leveraged ESOP transactions, all the shares are in suspense or "encumbered by debt." As the debt is paid, the shares are no longer encumbered and are thus released from suspense and allocated to eligible participant accounts.

Exhibit 32–3 is a graphical depiction of the allocation of ESOP shares over a seven-year ESOP loan. The participant account is further subject to vesting provisions on allocated shares.

Dividends are allocated in a different manner. Dividends on allocated shares that are not used to make payments on the ESOP debt are allocated to respective accounts of the participants to whom the shares are allocated. When dividend payments on allocated shares are used to repay an ESOP loan, shares will be released from the suspense account due to such payments.

Exhibit 32–3

Illustrative Example of the Allocation of ESOP Shares

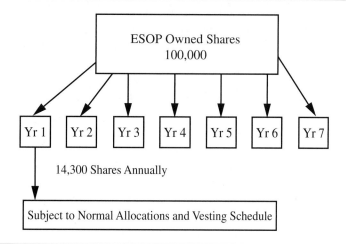

Distribution Policy

Distribution of benefits from an ESOP must commence no later than one year after the close of the plan year (1) in which the participant terminates employment due to reaching normal retirement age, disability, or death; or (2) that is the fifth plan year following the plan year in which the participant separates from service with the employer.

Distributions of securities acquired with the proceeds of an ESOP loan may be delayed until the loan is repaid. Benefits to ESOP participants may be distributed in installments over five years (up to 10 years where the benefits exceed $710,000). The ESOP participant has the right to demand a distribution of employer securities unless the articles of incorporation or bylaws restrict ownership of employer securities to employees.

Diversification

Qualified ESOP participants may elect to diversify their accounts. A qualified participant includes one who has attained age 55 and has at least 10 years participation in the ESOP. The election period is a six-year period that begins with or in the plan year during which the participant becomes qualified. The first five elections are limited to 25 percent of the participant's account balance. The final year, the qualified participant may diversify up to 50 percent of the account balance attributable to such participant.

Since the company must also provide the liquidity necessary for these diversification requirements, the company must consider these obligations in estimating the cash flow requirements of the ESOP.

Finance Issues in Leveraged ESOPs

Other qualified retirement plans are prohibited from borrowing funds under the prohibited transaction rules. ERISA Section 408(b)(3) and Code Section 4975(d)(3) contain the provisions that exempt the ESOP from this prohibited transaction rule. The following is a *general discussion* of some of the finance issues in ESOPs. These finance aspects of ESOPs are complex, and further discussion with an experienced ESOP lender is necessary before implementing an ESOP.

At times the ESOP valuation practitioner may also render a fairness opinion that includes a statement that the leveraged ESOP transaction is fair from a financial point of view. This fairness opinion requires an understanding of the typical terms and conditions offered by lenders in this type of transaction.

The leveraged ESOP transaction is significantly different from conventional financing. The inexperienced ESOP lender typically is concerned with the accounting provisions that can result in negative equity on the ESOP company's balance sheet. The ESOP lender must also consider the enhanced cash flow associated with the deductibility of principal payments in order to be competitive. Generally, the debt service coverage analysis is performed on a pretax basis. In addition, the pledge of Code Section 1042 securities is a typical structure in the ESOP financing that can make up for collateral shortfalls.

ESOP lenders also need to have an understanding of the leveraged ESOP to complete these transactions. For example, the ESOP lender may be concerned if the ESOP valuation is extremely aggressive. Benefit allocation issues can affect cash flows and thus the ability of the ESOP lender to be repaid. The repayment terms of an ESOP loan may be tied to Code Section 415/404 limitations. Certainly these constraints are important in the financing structure of the leveraged ESOP transaction. Other issues considered by the ESOP lender include environmental issues, product liability or other contingent liability issues, change of control issues, management continuity issues, and trustee issues.

If the ESOP valuation practitioner is issuing a fairness opinion, a review of the credit agreement is necessary to understand all the terms of the financing. A clear understanding of the constraints and benefits of the ESOP transaction is essential to the review of this document and the fairness of a transaction.

Repurchase Liability

Does repurchase liability affect the fair market value of ESOP stock? This has been a long debated and still unanswered question. However, today there is a better understanding of the repurchase liability and its impact on the economics of the ESOP company.

The repurchase liability is created by the employer's obligation to purchase shares from the ESOP trust at the time the participant receives a distribution. There are two methods that can be used by the company to satisfy the obligation. The general effect of each of these transactions on fair market value is discussed below.

Repurchase or Recycling

The first method is called a repurchase or recycling transaction. In a "repurchase," the ESOP trust purchases the shares of withdrawing participants and recycles them to other ESOP participants in the plan. The trust's cash for the purchase comes from the company in the form of a deductible employer contribution. *If the amount of this employer contribution is in excess of a market level of employee benefits, the recycling transaction can be dilutive.* The recycling transaction is a transfer of ownership between former and current ESOP participants. Exhibit 32–4 illustrates this repurchase transaction.

Redemption

The second method is called a redemption transaction. In a "redemption," the shares are purchased directly by the company and then canceled. *Redemptions by design are nondilutive.* Exhibit 32–5 illustrates this method.

Exhibit 32–4

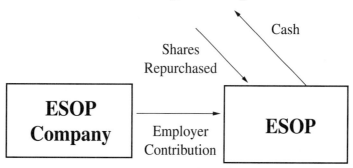

Repurchase of Shares from Participants

Exhibit 32–5

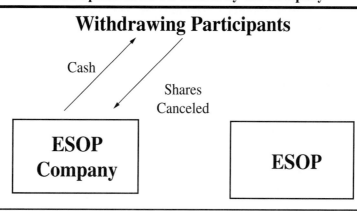

Redemption of ESOP Shares by the Company

Although redemptions do not use tax-deductible contributions, since the shares are no longer considered outstanding, the net effect on fair market value should be negligible if the transaction occurs at fair market value. The transfer of ownership in the redemption transaction is between former participants and all remaining shareholders. Since the shares are canceled in the redemption, the percentage ownership of all the remaining shareholders, including ESOP participants, increases. However, the amount of the ESOP trust's ownership percentage declines.

Managing the Repurchase Liability

When the ESOP company decides to recycle shares, a compensation event occurs. The redemption more closely resembles a capital transaction. The complexities of the ESOP contain the concept that the same dollar compensates employees as well as creates an equity obligation.

In order to manage the repurchase liability, management must decide on a compensation policy separate from the decision on who should be the shareholders of the company over the long term. Then, the decisions regarding repurchases of shares are clear. The following three choices indicate what actions would be necessary to comply with both objectives.

1. If the contributions (net of tax and dividends) necessary to fund the repurchase liability are within the amount agreed upon in the compensation policy, then recycling makes sense.
2. If the contributions (net of tax and dividends) necessary to fund the repurchase liability are below the amount agreed upon in the compensation policy, then an additional cash contribution may be necessary.
3. *If the contributions (net of tax and dividends) necessary to fund the repurchase liability are greater than the agreed upon compensatory amount, then the company should redeem the shares above the set limit and recycle for the compensatory amount.*

The employer can use any combination of redemption and recycling transactions. And, just as the ESOP solves an ownership transition problem, it creates one. *However, the ESOP operates like a perpetual redemption program for ESOP participants if recycling is always chosen.* And, the timing of the obligation is determined through the operation of the plan provisions. Planning for and managing this obligation should be completed annually both on a short-term and on a long-term basis. Repurchase liability studies that consider actuarial assumptions are helpful tools in this process.

Methods of Funding

There are a number of alternative strategies for funding the repurchase obligation. The following listing contains some options.

*   Current cash flow
*   Additional cash contributions
*   Company debt

- Company sinking fund
- Life insurance
- Sale to a third party
- Initial public offering
- Employee purchases
- Use of 401(k) balances
- Liquidation

Management must consider the effect of these decisions on both compensation and share ownership.

Fiduciary Issues in ESOPs

The following is a *general discussion* of some of the fiduciary issues in ESOPs. These fiduciary aspects of ESOPs are complex, and further discussion with an independent fiduciary or ERISA counsel are necessary before implementing an ESOP. Valuation practitioners are not fiduciaries and should be sure that their actions would not make them a fiduciary.

The independent valuation adviser is hired directly by the ESOP fiduciary or trustee even though the valuation fees are paid by the company. Thus, the ESOP's independent financial adviser needs an understanding of the role of the ESOP trustee and how the valuation assignment interfaces with that role. Valuation analysts should pay particular attention to voting rights as they affect the fairness of the leveraged ESOP transaction.

General fiduciary duties that apply to ESOP fiduciaries are outlined in ERISA (the Overriding ERISA Fiduciary Standards). These duties apply to all trustee actions. ERISA requires the fiduciary to manage and administer the ESOP trust (1) solely in the interests of plan participants and beneficiaries; (2) for the exclusive purpose of providing benefits to plan participants and their beneficiaries and defraying reasonable expenses of administering the ESOP trust; (3) with the care, skill, prudence, and diligence that, under the circumstances then prevailing, a prudent man or woman acting in like capacity and familiar with such matters would use in the conduct of an enterprise of a like character and with like aims; (4) in accordance with the plan and trust agreement in most circumstances; and (5) in accordance with applicable requirements of the law.

Voting Issues

When the ESOP holds unregistered securities (privately held stock not traded on an exchange), the participants in the plan must be given the right to vote allocated shares with respect to any corporate matter that involves the voting of such shares with respect to any corporate merger or consolidation, recapitalization, reclassification, liquidation, dissolution, or sale of substantially all assets of a trade or business, or such similar transaction as may be prescribed by regulation (Code Section 409[e][3]).

Trustee's Voting Rights

The ESOP trustee votes the unallocated shares. However, voting of both allocated and unallocated shares is subject to the Overriding ERISA Fiduciary Standards discussed in the previous section. The ESOP plan's provisions for voting unallocated shares can include any of the following three options:

1. The fiduciary can vote the stock as directed by an ESOP committee.
2. The fiduciary can vote the unallocated stock in the same proportions as the employees vote allocated stock.
3. The fiduciary can always vote the stock in its discretion.

Although one of the Overriding ERISA Fiduciary Standards is to follow the provisions of the plan document, the fiduciary has the final responsibility and fiduciary duty with respect to voting of the stock. This is true regardless of the provisions in the plan document. In his or her discretion, a fiduciary can override the participant's direction if the fiduciary believes the directions are not in the best interests of the plan.

Circularity of Control

The Board of Directors of a company selects the ESOP trustee. The shareholders of the company vote on the members of the Board of Directors. If the ESOP trustee owns a controlling interest in the company, then the ESOP selects the Board of Directors. For obvious reasons, this is sometimes referred to as the circularity of control.

Independent, Directed, or Internal Trustee

It is not required that companies retain an independent trustee. In practical terms, the trustee of the ESOP can be an officer or group of employees from the sponsoring company or members of the administration committee. However, due to the extent of fiduciary liability, it is prudent for the ESOP company to hire an independent bank or trust company. The ESOP plan document clearly defines the duties and responsibilities of the trustee and other fiduciaries. A directed trustee is typically an independent bank or trust company that is directed by the ESOP committee selected by the Board of Directors.

Each type of trustee is still required to meet the Overriding ERISA Fiduciary Standards previously discussed. Thus, it is important for ESOP trustees to have a complete understanding of their fiduciary duties and the resulting fiduciary liability. A complete discussion of these items is beyond the scope of this chapter.

Various actions can be taken against a fiduciary for breach of the fiduciary duties. Generally, any person who is a fiduciary with respect to a plan who breaches any of the responsibilities or duties imposed upon fiduciaries by ERISA, shall be *personally* liable to make good to such plan any losses to the plan resulting from each such breach. Therefore, this liability extends beyond the liability protection provided by incorporating a business. There are also civil penalties. It is entirely possible that an uneducated ESOP trustee could unknowingly breach a fiduciary duty.

Accounting for ESOPs

Most of the accounting rules that govern the accounting for ESOP related transactions are contained in the American Institute of Certified Public Accountants SOP 93-6. The following is a summary of its provisions excerpted from The ESOP Association's booklet on ESOP accounting standards.

> **Liabilities**—All ESOP debt will be recorded on balance sheet of plan sponsor, no exceptions. Issue of push down of obligation to subsidiary is still present, but not discussed in SOP 93-6.
>
> **Equity**—Contra equity account will still be the offsetting entry. Contra account will change as compensation is recognized. Mezzanine capital issue is still present, but not discussed in SOP 93-6. Equity recorded may be adjusted for immediate posttransaction valuation changes.
>
> **Income**—Compensation cost will be based upon the *fair market value* of the shares released or deemed to be released for the period.
>
> **Dividends**—Any compensation cost obligation will not be reduced to the extent satisfied with dividends on allocated shares. Dividends on allocated shares retain character of true dividends.
>
> **Earnings per share**—Unreleased shares will not be considered to be outstanding. All convertible preferred shares will be considered to be common stock equivalents.
>
> **Disclosures**—Repurchase liability as reflected by the current value of allocated shares must be disclosed, the use of an actuarial estimate of this future obligation is not authorized.
>
> **Effective date**—The SOP 93-6 is effective for ESOP stock acquisitions after December 31, 1992. Sponsors of ESOPs that were formed prior to the effective date can elect the SOP 93-6. The reporting in the standard is required for financial periods beginning after December 15, 1992.[5]

Since the ESOP company's auditor needs the fair market value of the ESOP shares to complete the income statement, there is a timing issue. The ESOP valuation practitioner needs the audit in order to complete the valuation. The typical procedure is for the ESOP valuation analyst to work with a preliminary audit that is only preliminary due to the ESOP compensation adjustment. The valuation is then conducted and the conclusion is communicated to the auditor. Then the audited financial statements can be finalized. The valuation is actually further finalized to reflect the fair market value entry made by the auditors. However, since the compensation expense entry is adjusted in the determination of normalized earnings, there is no valuation impact after the final audit report is issued.

There are no regulations that specifically say that the auditor cannot also be the ESOP valuation adviser. However, since the valuation is an input to the audit, it seems difficult to say that the auditor is independent with respect to the valuation. Leading ESOP attorneys strongly advise against an ESOP using the company's auditor as its valuation adviser. As of this writing, the Independence Standards Board is considering this issue.

---

[5] *ESOP Accounting Standards* (Washington, DC: The ESOP Association, 1999), p. 3.

Nuances of S Corporation ESOPs

The Small Business Job Protection Act of 1996 (the 1996 Act) amended the Code to allow ESOPs to hold shares of an S corporation, effective for tax years beginning after December 31, 1997; and the Taxpayer Relief Act of 1997 (the 1997 Act) added an exemption for S corporation ESOPs to the unrelated business income tax (UBIT Exemption). The following is a general summary of the specific aspects of S corporation ESOPs as they differ from C corporation ESOPs.

Although some of the issues have been settled, there is still significant uncertainty regarding some important technical issues. In addition, legislative changes are still expected.

The combination of S corporation tax law, ERISA, qualified plan requirements, and ESOPs adds even more complexities to the leveraged ESOP transaction.

Limitations on S Corporation Tax Benefits

Code Section 1042. The Section 1042 election is not available to shareholders in S corporations. However, in many cases, shareholders of S corporations have built up significant tax bases in the shares of their S corporations. S corporation shareholders realize an increase in tax basis equivalent to their pro rata share of the corporation's earnings annually. Shareholder basis in S corporations is reduced by distributions. The benefits of Section 1042 become less important the higher the shareholder's basis in the stock.

Dividend Deductibility. Dividend deductibility provisions of Code Section 404(k) do not apply in the S corporation context. In situations in which the annual ESOP loan payments exceed the maximum amount that can be contributed to an ESOP under Code Section 415, it is possible in C corporations to cover this shortfall with tax deductible dividends. The S corporation does not have this structuring option.

Limitations on Contributions to the Plan. The increased limit for tax deductions for contributions to a leveraged ESOP, when used to pay principal and interest, is not available to the S corporation. These limitations are 25 percent of compensation for C corporations and 15 percent of compensation for S corporations. However, an S corporation can increase the limits by implementing a combined ESOP/Money Purchase Pension Plan.

In addition, interest expense may be excluded from the Code Section 415 limitations if certain tests are met with respect to highly compensated employees. This exclusion is not available to S corporation ESOPs.

Voting Issues

Since the S corporation ESOP is not publicly traded, the voting issues reflect that circumstance. Thus, the voting rights of the participants in an S corporation ESOP may be limited to certain matters as discussed in the previous section on voting rights.

Form of Distribution

Not all possible shareholders are eligible S corporation shareholders (i.e., nonresident aliens, individual retirement accounts [IRAs], certain trusts, etc.). In addition, if individual shareholder participants are allowed to maintain share ownership upon a distribution, the S corporation could reach a point in which it violated the 75 shareholder limit. The ESOP trust is considered one shareholder for purposes of this S corporation rule, but departing participants would not be included. Thus, inadvertent terminations of S corporation status could occur. The S corporation ESOP company may, therefore, require employees to take their benefits in the form of cash.

S Corporation Distributions

Distributions on Allocated Shares. As of this writing, the IRS has taken the position that distributions by S corporations on stock that is not pledged as collateral to secure the ESOP loan cannot be used to make payments on that loan, even though this is not so in the C corporation context, although the technical arguments for this position are not coincident with legislative history and the intent of the S corporation ESOP laws.

Distributions Paid in Cash to Participants. In the C corporation context, dividends paid on ESOP shares that are distributed directly to participants are not subject to the excise tax on premature distributions. The ability to have participants receive company dividends without incurring an excise tax does not extend to S corporations.

Steps to Implementing an ESOP

The following is a summary of the steps to implementing a leveraged ESOP. These steps are intended to follow a logical sequence.

1. Retain qualified advisers with areas of expertise described in this chapter.
2. Conduct a feasibility study that addresses all of the constraints in ESOP transactions to see if an ESOP makes sense from a financial point of view.
3. Design and structure a transaction that addresses those constraints.
4. Estimate the value of the company.
5. Consider the design of the plan and trust provisions.
6. Obtain financing for the transaction.
7. Estimate the repurchase liability.
8. Begin the process of plan administration.
9. Use an effective communication program to inform employees.

Summary

The reader should now be equipped with an understanding of the ESOP valuation issues as they differ from typical valuation techniques. The other professional disciplines involved in the ESOP transaction interface with the valuation professional.

Therefore, it is important that the valuation professional also have a general knowledge of the other areas of expertise.

In a typical leveraged ESOP transaction, the valuation adviser may rely on other professionals in their areas of expertise to assist in resolving the issues that surface. The sections of this chapter addressing the expertise of other professionals involved in the ESOP transaction are intended to assist the appraiser in "surfacing issues" and addressing "fairness" concerns.

Bibliography

Articles

Abello, Kim S., and Robert S. Socol. "The Leveraged ESOP Transaction" (Chapter 8A). In *Financial Valuation: Business and Business Interests, 1997 Update*, Robert F. Reilly and Robert P. Schweihs, eds. New York: Warren Gorham & Lamont, 1997.

Ackerman, David. "Technical Issues under the New S Corporation ESOP Laws." *Journal of Employee Ownership Law and Finance*, Winter 1999, pp. 3–19.

Austin, Douglas V. "Beware of Your ESOP." *Hoosier Banker*, vol. 84, no. 4, April 30, 2000, pp. 9–10.

Berka, Jack W. "An ESOP Update Review of Current Issues." Presentation to the International Conference of the American Society of Appraisers, June 1997. Available on www.BVLibrary.com.

Best, Christopher. "ESOPs: Valuation Issues and Results of IBA Survey of ESOP Appraisers." *Institute of Business Appraisers, 2003 Annual Conference*, Orlando, Florida. Also available at www.BVLibrary.com.

Bonn, Karen. "Feasibility Studies Help Avoid ESOP Foibles." *The Tax Adviser*, February 1999, pp. 82–83.

Brown, Gregory K. "A Legal Perspective on Using Control Premiums in ESOP Transactions." *Insights*, Spring 2001, pp. 28–30.

Brown, Karen W. "Payment of Control Premiums by ESOPs." *ESOP Report*, November/December 1993, pp. 6–8.

Buckley, Allen, Lynda M. Crouse, and Greg Kniesel. "S Corporation ESOPs in Dispositive Sales and Reorganization Transactions." *Valuation Strategies*, January/February 2001, pp. 20–29, 46–48.

Cooley, Megan. "ESOP Being Formed to Buy WhiteRunkle." *Journal of Business*, vol. 18, no. 24, November 26, 2003, p. A3.

Etkind, Steven M., and Joseph E. Godfrey III. "ESOPs Rediscovered: Tax Advantages and Recyclable Refunding." *The CPA Journal*, vol. 72, no. 4, April 30, 2002, pp. 60–61.

Girard, Bryan. "Tax Reform Alters ESOP Landscape." *Journal of Accountancy*, online issue, June 2002.

Hall, C. Wells III. "The S Corporation ESOP: Incentivised Employee Stock Ownership or Tax Gimmickry?" *Business Entities*, January/February 1999, pp. 14–19, 62.

Hartman, Michael. "Update on Valuing ESOP Shares." *BV Papers*, November, 2003. Available at www.BVLibrary.com.

Hirschfeld, Christopher. "ESOPs as an Estate Planning Vehicle for Business Owners." *Journal of Financial Planning*, vol. 15, no. 11, November 30, 2002, pp. 92–97.

Julius, J. Michael. "ESOP Appraisals and Non-ESOP Shareholders." *CPA Litigation Service Counselor*, July 1998, pp. 9–10.

Kober, John A. "A Tool for Shareholder Liquidity, Estate Planning and Management Succession Planning." White paper (1999) available at www.BVLibrary.com.

Korschot, John. "Valuation Issues." *BV Papers*, December 2001. Available at www.BVLibrary.com.

Kubersky, Andrew S. "Marketability Discounts and ESOP Acquisitions of Minority Share Interests." *Journal of Employee Ownership Law and Finance*, Fall 1998, pp. 97–103.

Lippert-Gray, Carol. "An ESOP's Tale." *Financial Executive*, vol. 16, no. 1, February 28, 2000, pp. 40–42.

Long, Dennis J. "Creating an ESOP Distribution Policy." *The Journal of Employee Ownership Law and Finance*, Summer 1997, pp. 85–92.

Long, Dennis J., Peter J. Prodoehl, and John P. Prodoehl. "Tracking ESOP Shares." *The Journal of Employee Ownership Law and Finance*, Summer 1995.

Miller, Karren L. "Using an ESOP to Let Go." *Central Penn Business Journal*, vol. 16, no. 23, June 9, 2000, p. 3.

Mueller, Susan L., and Judith C. Gehr. "Valuation Issues in Multi-Investor ESOP LBOs" (Chapter 2). In *ESOP Valuation*, Scott S. Rodrick, ed. Oakland, CA: The National Center for Employee Ownership, 1999.

Nash, Claire. "Tax Matters." *Journal of Accountancy*, online issue, October, 2004.

Overman, Carl D. "The ESOP Solution." *Hoosier Banker*, vol. 88, no. 1, January 31, 2004, pp. 14–16.

Powell, David W., Thomas D. Terry, and Ian Lanoff. "Reinvigorating Aging ESOPs." *Journal of Accountancy*, online issue, March 2000.

Regnitz, Timothy J. "Understanding the ESOP Repurchase Obligation." *The Journal of Employee Ownership Law and Finance*, Winter 1999, pp. 21–34.

Reilly, Robert F. "Current Issues in the Valuations of ESOP-Owned Securities" *Journal of Pension Planning & Compliance*, Winter 1996, pp. 47–60.

"Repurchase Liability: What ESOP Companies Should Know About It." *The ESOP Newsletter of McBride Baker and Coles*, Winter 2000.

Sandquist, Andrew, and John J. Cresto. "Anticipating and Avoiding ESOP Financing Obstacles," *The Journal of Employee Ownership Law and Finance*, Summer 1999, pp. 63–72.

Suhre, Karen K. "Should the ESOP-Owned Company Elect to Become an S Corporation?" *Benefits Law Journal*, Spring 1998.

"To ESOP or Not to ESOP?" *The Tax Adviser*, May 2004.

Torolopoulos, Sam G. "Valuation of ESOP Shares: Opportunities and Challenges," *CPA Expert*, Fall 2005, pp. 9–12.

Books

Ash, Merri E., Virginia J. Bartlett, et al. *The ESOP Association Administration Handbook*. Washington, DC: The ESOP Association, 1996.

Bernstein, Ron, David Binns, Marshal Hyman, and Martin Staubus. *Transitioning Ownership in the Private Company: The ESOP Solution*. La Jolla, CA: Foundation for Enterprise Development, 2001.

Cook, Larry R. *Financial Valuation of Employee Stock Ownership Plan Shares*. Hoboken, NJ: John Wiley & Sons, 2005.

An Employer's Guide to Employee Stock Ownership Plans. St. Paul, MN: Minnesota Small Business Assistance Office, Minnesota Department of Trade and Economic Development, 1994.

ESOP Accounting Standards. Washington, DC: The ESOP Association, 2005.

ESOP Repurchase Obligations. Washington, DC: The ESOP Association, 2004.

Frisch, Robert A. *ESOP: The Ultimate Instrument in Succession Planning*, 2nd ed., Hoboken, NJ: John Wiley & Sons, 2001.

_____. *The ESOP Handbook: Practical Strategies for Achieving Corporate Financing Goals*. New York: John Wiley & Sons, 1994, supplemented 1998.

_____. *ESOP Workbook: The Ultimate Instrument in Succession Planning*. Hoboken, NJ: John Wiley & Sons, 2002.

How the ESOP Really Works. Washington, DC: The ESOP Association, 1997.

An Introduction to ESOP Valuations. Washington, DC: The ESOP Association, 2005.

Kaplan, Jared, John E. Curtis Jr., and Gregory K. Brown. *ESOPs* (Tax Management Portfolio). Washington, DC: Tax Management Inc., 1991.

The Ownership Advantage. Washington, DC: The ESOP Association, 2005.

Phillips, Perry. *Employee Share Ownership Plans: How to Design and Implement an ESOP in Canada*. Mississauga, Ontario: John Wiley & Sons Canada, 2001.

Reilly, Robert F., and Robert P. Schweihs. *Guide to ESOP Valuation and Financial Advisory Services*, Portland, OR: Willamette Management Associates, 2005.

Report on Valuation Considerations for Leveraged ESOPs. Washington, DC: The ESOP Association, 1998.

Rodrick, Scott S., ed. *Leveraged ESOPs and Employee Buyouts*. Oakland, CA: The National Center for Employee Ownership, 2005.

_____. *ESOP Valuation*. Oakland, CA: The National Center for Employee Ownership, 1999.

Rosen, Corey. *Understanding ESOP Valuation*. Oakland, CA: The National Center for Employee Ownership, 2000.

Rosen, Corey, John Case, and Martin Staubus. *Equity: Why Employee Ownership Is Good for Business*, Cambridge, MA: Harvard Business School Press, 2005.

Smiley, Robert W. Jr., and Ronald J. Gilbert, eds. *Employee Stock Ownership Plans: Business Planning, Implementation, and Law and Taxation*. New York: Warren, Gorham & Lamont, 1991, supplemented annually.

Staubus, Martin, David Binns, and Ron Bernstein. *Transitioning Ownership in the Private Company: The ESOP Solution*, 2nd ed. La Jolla, CA: The Beyster Institute, 2005.

Structuring Leveraged ESOP Transactions. Washington, DC: The ESOP Association, 1999.

Valuing ESOP Shares. Washington, DC: The ESOP Association, 2005.

ESOP Association Briefs

"The Benefits of Employee Stock Ownership" (2004).

"Employee Ownership & Corporate Performance" (2004).

"ESOP Accounting" (2004).

"The ESOP as an Employee Benefit" (2004).

"ESOP Distributions" (2004).

"ESOP Diversification" (2004).

"ESOP Dividends" (2004).

"ESOP Facts & Figures" (2004).

"ESOP Fiduciary Issues" (2004).

"ESOP Financing" (2004).

"ESOP/401(k) Plans" (2004).

"ESOP Repurchase Obligation" (2004).

"The ESOP Tax-Free Rollover" (2004).

"ESOPs and Subchapter C Corporations" (2004).

"How to Establish an ESOP" (2004).

"The Policy of Broadened Ownership" (2004).

"Tax Advantages for Business Planning" (2004).

"Using Convertible Preferred Stock in ESOPs" (2004).

"The Valuation of ESOP Stock" (2004).

"Voting Rights of ESOP Stock" (2004).

"What Is an ESOP?" (2004).

Associations

The ESOP Association

1726 M Street N.W., Suite 501

Washington, DC 20036

 (202) 293-2971 or (866) 366-3832

www.esopassociation.org

The National Center for Employee Ownership

1736 Franklin Street, 8th Floor

Oakland, California 94612

 (510) 208-1300

www.nceo.org

Web Resources

Gilbert J. Roland, "The ESOP Decision," ESOP Services, Inc., Employee Stock Ownership Plans, www.esopservices.com/decision.htm (June 2004).

Marshall Stevens Valuation Consulting. "What an ESOP Can Do for Your Clients," www.marshall-stevens.com/esop_can_do.htm.

Chapter 33

ESOP Court Cases

Introduction

The judicial decisions selected for review in this chapter should be of particular interest to ESOP valuation practitioners and ESOP financial advisers. Many of these decisions indicate what the courts are looking for with regard to (1) the content of valuation analyses and (2) the quality of valuation reports.

In addition, many of these decisions should be of interest to ESOP trustees, ESOP attorneys, and other ESOP practitioners. In addition to employer corporation stock valuation issues, many of these cases involve the fiduciary responsibilities of ESOP trustees—particularly with regard to reliance upon independent financial advisers during an ESOP stock purchase or sale transaction.

Because of the mix of fiduciary and valuation issues, unlike the other court case chapters, we have organized this chapter by case, rather than by valuation issue. As is true with the other court case chapters in this book, the full texts of cases are available to online library subscribers at www.BVLibrary.com.

Sommers Drug Stores

Introduction

In *Sommers Drug Stores Co. v. Corrigan Enterprises, Inc.*,[1] the U.S. Court of Appeals provided useful guidance with regard to what factors a valuation analyst should consider with regard to the valuation of close corporation stock for ERISA compliance purposes. Valuation practitioners should note the guidance provided by the Appeals Court in this case.

The Facts of the District Court Case

In December 1997, the trustee of the Sommers Drug Stores Company ("Sommers") employee profit sharing trust accepted an offer to sell the trust's holdings of stock in the company back to the company for $10,000 per share.

---

[1] *Sommers Drug Stores Co. v. Corrigan Enterprises, Inc.*, 793 F.2d 1456 (5th Cir. 1986).

Before the time of the stock sale, the company had sold its drug store operations. At the time of the sale from the profit sharing trust, Sommers was primarily a holding company owning cash and real estate. At that time, the trust owned approximately 20 percent of the Sommers outstanding stock.

In December 1980, the trust sued the company and its principal stockholder for breach of fiduciary duty under ERISA and under common law in connection with the stock sale. At the trial court level, the trust's expert witness testified that the stock was worth $27,171 per share. The defendants' expert testified at the trial level that the stock was worth only $8,500 per share.

At the trial, the jury found that both the principal stockholder and the company had breached their fiduciary duty under ERISA. It found that the stock was worth $27,171 per share. After granting the defendants' motion for a remittitur (i.e., a petition to reduce the damages that the jury had assessed), the District Court entered a judgment in favor of the trust for $552,612 in actual damages and $1,250,000 for punitive damages. The punitive damages were assessed $500,000 against the principal stockholder and $750,000 against the company.

The Facts of the Appeal

The principal stockholder and the company appealed. The U.S. Court of Appeals for the Fifth Circuit remanded the case for further proceedings. The Appeals Court held that "there is insufficient evidence in the record to support the jury's finding of fair market value, upon which the district court's judgment of actual damages was based." The Appeals Court also held that the trust could not recover punitive damages under the applicable section of ERISA.

The Plaintiff's Position

The method used by the plaintiff's expert for estimating fair market value per share was (1) to sum all the Sommers net assets—including the discounted present value of a 10-year employment contract received by the principal stockholder in connection with the sale of the drug store operations—and (2) to then divide by the number of shares outstanding.

The Defendants' Position

The defendants' principal contention was that the testimony of the plaintiff's expert lacked probative value. This is because his valuation conclusion was based on an asset liquidation value rather than on fair market value of the business.

The Appeals Court agreed with the defendants' position, stating:

> On cross-examination [the witness] acknowledged that market value and asset value were different measures, but he asserted that in this case they were the same. We conclude that [the witness's] testimony was so conclusory and lacking in analysis that no jury could reasonably have relied on it in determining the fair market value of the Trust's stock.

A particularly informative part of this decision from the perspective of the valuation practitioner is what the Appeals Court said the expert *should have* considered in estimating the fair market value of the trust's shares of stock for purposes of ERISA. The Court's comments are presented in the following excerpts from the published opinion:

> Although ERISA does not define the term "fair market value," it is defined in other contexts as the price that a willing buyer would pay a willing seller, both having reasonable knowledge of the pertinent facts.... We conclude that this definition is appropriate for purposes of ERISA.
>
> Determining fair market value for the stock of a closely held company can be difficult; typically no readily available market exists in which to determine what willing buyers are prepared to pay. This problem has arisen most frequently in the estate tax context, and it is to that area of law that we turn for guidance. The Internal Revenue Service's estate tax regulations provide that closely held stock for which there is no available market price should be valued according to "the company's net worth, prospective earning power and dividend-paying capacity, and other relevant factors."

The Appeals Court noted that the "other relevant factors" that should have been considered by the expert include the following:

> The goodwill of the business; the economic outlook in the particular industry; the company's position in the industry and its management; the degree of control of the business represented by the block of stock to be valued; and the values of securities of corporations engaged in the same or similar lines of business which are listed on a stock exchange.

Particularly noteworthy to ESOP valuation practitioners is the Court's critique of the analysis of the plaintiff's appraiser:

> [The witness's] valuation ignored most of these factors. Of particular significance, he failed to consider that the Trust's stock represented a minority position in [the company]. He also neglected to consider the prices at which shares of comparable companies were traded on the national exchanges. He did not take account of the prices at which Sommers stock had changed hands in a series of tender offers between 1970 and 1977, one of the factors mentioned in Rev. Rul. 59-60. See Rev. Rul. 59-60 & 4.02(g), 1959-1 C.G. 237, 241-42; see also *Fitts' Estate v. Commissioner*, 237 F.2d 729, 731 (8th Cir. 1956). ("In determining the value of unlisted stocks, actual sales made in reasonable amount at arm's length, in the normal course of business, within a reasonable time before or after the basic date, are the best criterion of market value."); (*Duncan Industries, Inc. v. Commissioner*, 73 T.C. 266 91979) (same). Nor did [the witness] consider whether a discount for lack of marketability should be applied to the Trust's stock. See *Estate of Andrews v. Commissioner*, 79 T.C. 938, 953, 957 (1982).
>
> We do not suggest that consideration of these factors would necessarily have changed [the witness's] valuation of the Trust's shares. Indeed in support of his apparent approach, we note that under Rev. Rul. 59-60, "[t]he value of the stock of a closely held investment or real estate holding company [which (the company) arguably was] ... is closely related to the value of the assets underlying the stock." Rev. Rul. 59-60, & 5(b),

1959 1 C.B. 237, 243. But [the witness's] utter failure to consider other relevant factors, or to explain his reasons for disregarding them, renders his testimony unworthy of credit.

Commentary and Conclusion

The Appeals Court was blunt in its disapproval of the valuation analysis performed by the plaintiff's appraiser. In this case, the analyst applied the wrong standard of value (i.e., asset liquidation value versus fair market value), and the analyst effectively disregarded each and every one of the valuation factors delineated in Revenue Ruling 59-60. This classic decision still provides useful guidance to ESOP valuation analysts as to what factors should be considered in the ESOP valuation.

U.S. News & World Report

Introduction

This case actually involves two related decisions: (1) *Charles S. Foltz, et al., v. U.S. News & World Report, Inc., et al.*, and (2) *David B. Richardson, et al., v. U.S. News & World Report, Inc., et al.*[2] The Foltz case, a class action case, dealt with the years 1973 through 1980; the Richardson case, not a class action case, covered 1981.

Although *U.S. News & World Report* cases concerned a profit sharing plan and a stock bonus plan, the issues were similar to those that would have been involved in an ESOP. The case was, therefore, followed with great interest by ESOP valuation practitioners.

The Facts of the Case

Suits were brought by retirees who claimed that they were underpaid at retirement because the closely held stock of U.S. News & World Report, Inc. (U.S. News), was undervalued by independent appraisers in the years 1973 through 1981. The defendants included: (1) U.S. News, (2) certain U.S. News directors, (3) the U.S. News Profit-Sharing Plan (the plan), and (4) the independent appraisal company.

During their employment, the plaintiffs had participated in the profit sharing plan. The retired employees were also beneficial owners of stock in the company under its stock bonus plan. Upon retirement or separation, U.S. News employees liquidated their plan accounts and redeemed their stock interests.

The plaintiffs sought recovery of benefits they claimed were owed to them by virtue of an alleged undervaluation of the company's stock during the class period.

In 1962, the U.S. News stock was sold to various parties associated with the company, including the profit sharing plan, for a total consideration of $15 million. That transaction price was based on an independent appraisal.

---

[2] *Charles S. Foltz, et al., v. U.S. News & World Report, Inc., et al.*, 663 F. Supp. 1494, 1987 U.S. Dist. LEXIS 5592 (D.D.C. June 22, 1987) and *David B. Richardson, et al., v. U.S. News & World Report, Inc., et al.*, 663 F. Supp. 1494, 1987 U.S. Dist. LEXIS 5592 (D.D.C. June 22, 1987).

In 1975, the U.S. News stock was appraised at $69 per share. By 1980, the appraised stock price had risen to $152 per share. And, in 1981, the U.S. News stock was appraised at $470 per share.

From 1962 until the company was sold in 1984 at $2,842 a share, the same independent appraisal firm appraised the company stock each year.

The amount of profit-sharing plan benefits distributed to retirees was based on the annual appraisal. In addition, the company exercised its option to purchase stock from certain stockholders who left the firm, at a price based on the annual appraisal.

Early in the 1970s, the profit-sharing plan ownership interest increased to the point of constituting a majority of the outstanding stock. The profit-sharing plan stock, as well as most of the nonplan stock, was voted by a voting trust.

After 1977, the voting trust could have been dissolved by a vote of the stock held by the profit sharing plan. However, there was never any movement to do so.

The company owned real estate at its headquarters located in Washington, D.C. During the 1970s, real estate values in the area increased significantly. There were discussions about developing the real estate for alternative uses, but no definite plans were implemented until 1981. At that time, an agreement was reached with Boston Properties for development of the property.

The Valuation Issues

In a 106-page memorandum opinion, the U.S. District Court judge stated that "the central issue requiring resolution in this litigation has always been the propriety of the methodology employed in appraising the U.S. News stock." The primary valuation issues in the case were as follows:

1. **Controlling versus Noncontrolling Ownership Interest Level of Value.** The annual appraisals valued the stock on a noncontrolling ownership interest basis. The plaintiffs contended that the stock should have been valued on a controlling ownership interest level of value.
2. **Discount for Lack of Marketability.** Most of the annual appraisals applied a 10 percent discount for lack of marketability. The plaintiffs contended that no discount for lack of marketability should have been taken. It is noteworthy that the stock had no put option. The company had a call option at the appraised price. The company exercised its call option consistently to retire stock from the stock bonus plan when employees left. Most such calls were for cash. However, on certain occasions, the company exercised its option to purchase the stock on extended terms and at a low interest rate. This payment scheme was allowed under the call option.
3. **Importance of Real Estate and Other Assets.** The annual appraisals placed various weights on the real estate values in different years, depending on the circumstances at the time. In all years, however, the primary emphasis of the valuation was on the company's earning power. The plaintiffs argued that considerably more weight should have been accorded to the analysis and values of the real estate and certain other assets.
4. **Subsequent Events.** The annual appraisals valued the stock on a going-concern basis, taking into consideration only facts and circumstances as they were known or knowable as of the valuation date. The plaintiffs argued that prospects for future changes, such as those that would be instituted by a strategic buyer

of the company (and thus impounded into the price that a buyer would be willing to pay for the company), should have been considered and reflected in the annual appraisals. As noted above, U.S. News was sold in 1984 at a price of $2,842 per share.

5. **Other Issues.** There were a variety of other allegations as to adjustments that the valuation analysts should have or should not have made to the company's income statements and balance sheets during the course of the annual appraisals.

The District Court's Decision

The Court's decision is particularly noteworthy for ESOP valuation practitioners. This abstract will highlight the most salient points. The Court concluded:

> After consideration of the expert testimony presented, the Court is not persuaded that the per share price arrived at each year by [the appraisal company] did not fall within a reasonable range of acceptable values.

Controlling versus Noncontrolling Ownership Interest Issue. Regarding the stock held by the plan, the District Court stated:

> [S]ince the terms of the U.S. News plan did not contemplate anything other than a series of minority-interest transactions… the valuation of its stock on a minority basis does not offend ERISA….
>
> [V]arious individuals concurrently held undivided, minority interests in a control block of stock…. The mere fact that Plan members' interest, if added together, amounted to a majority of the outstanding shares in the company does not, standing alone, entitle them to pro rata control value.

The following language from the published decision addresses the control-versus-noncontrol ownership issue. In addition, this narrative strongly supports the acceptance of the analyst's judgment when reasonable valuation alternatives exist:

> Clearly, in the absence of any statutory, administrative or judicial authority for the proposition that a control value might have been indicated, defendants cannot be faulted for employing a minority valuation…. ERISA does not require plan fiduciaries to maximize the benefits of departing employees …; it only requires them to make a reasonable choice from among possible alternatives.

The District Court also noted that the noncontrolling ownership interest level of value was consistent with the level of value used when the plan purchased the U.S. News stock in 1962 and in 1966.

Discount for Lack of Marketability Issue. The District Court concluded that:

> [T]he company was under no obligation to repurchase the stock. It has, rather, an option to call the stock…. Moreover, … the company could—and from time to time did—exercise its option … to pay for the stock on terms that would not have been accepted gladly by an outside investor…. [T]he modest 10 percent marketability discount that [the appraisal company] applied generally to the U.S. News stock in the aggregate was perfectly appropriate.

Real Estate and Other Assets Issue. With regard to the valuation implications of the various U.S. News nonoperating assets, the Court concluded:

> In a minority valuation ... assets may or may not play an important part in arriving at a per share figure, because a minority shareholder cannot reach those assets.... Generally speaking, if the valuation being undertaken is of a business, such as U.S. News, that produces goods or services, primary consideration will be given to the earnings of the company and the resultant return on a shareholder's investment.

Subsequent Events Issue. With regard to the consideration of subsequent events in the stock valuation, the Court noted:

> [T]he approach to be used is not retrospective, but prospective. One must look at the situation as of the time that each employee separated from the company. Therefore, the appropriate inquiry is whether the company was properly valued during the class period, not whether former employees become eligible for a greater share of benefits upon the contingency of a subsequent sale.

With respect to the possible future development of the real estate holdings, the Court cited testimony that:

> Any realizable value should be attributed to the real estate only if it was evident that the controlling interest had a firm and clear intent to dispose of the real estate within a very short or reasonable period of time [, that is,] absolute evidence ... not mere development plans.

The Appeals Court's Decision

On January 13, 1989, the U.S. Court of Appeals for the District of Columbia Circuit issued an opinion affirming on all counts the decision of the U.S. District Court involving the value of stock of U.S. News & World Report.[3]

Of considerable interest to ESOP valuation practitioners are several of the Appeals Court's statements rejecting the plaintiffs' contention that the plan fiduciaries had a duty to maximize pecuniary benefits to individual plan participants:

> Where the controlling instruments contemplate employee ownership, all participants are on notice that maximization of the firm's pecuniary value is not to serve as an exclusive goal....

Also of interest to ESOP valuation practitioners are statements of the Appeals Court supporting the proposition that, when valuing noncontrolling ownership interests, little weight should be accorded to potential liquidation value of assets. That is particularly true with regard to nonoperating assets (1) that are currently producing little or no income and (2) to which no firm decision has been made regarding development of those assets' income-producing capability in the near term.

Regarding the nonoperating assets, the Appeals Court concluded:

> After reviewing the testimony of the expert witnesses, the District Court found that [the] decision to give some, but very limited, weight to the

---

[3] *Foltz v. U.S. News & World Report, Inc.*, 865 F.2d 364, 1989 U.S. App. LEXIS 282 (D.C. Cir. Jan. 13, 1989).

value of the real estate "adequately took account of the Company's underlying assets." 663 F.Supp. at 1531. We find no error here.

Commentary and Conclusion

The Appeals Court decision concluded with the note that the filings in the U.S. News case (the trial of which lasted four months) are reported to be the largest in any civil case in the history of the District Court for the District of Columbia, and that "the district court threaded its way through the maze with patience and skill."

While not specifically an ESOP case, the various U.S. News decisions provide valuable professional guidance to ESOP valuation practitioners. The Court's detailed opinion in this case is very instructive regarding a multitude of valuation issues.

Andrade v. Parsons

Introduction

The Ralph M. Parsons Company employee stock ownership plan participated in a leveraged buyout (LBO) of the Parsons Corporation (Parsons) in September of 1984. After the LBO, the ESOP became the 100 percent owner of Parsons stock. This case is informative to all ESOP practitioners as to what constitutes prudent behavior on the part of the ESOP fiduciary.

The Facts of the Case

The case was brought as a class action by participants in the ESOP alleging that the LBO transaction violated ERISA.[4]

Counts I, II, and IV of the complaint were dismissed by the District Court prior to trial. The remaining counts III, V, and VI were tried by the Court and dismissed following the presentation of the plaintiffs' case. Count III alleged (1) that the members of the Parsons board of directors, certain senior executives of Parsons, and the members of the retirement committee were fiduciaries of the ESOP under ERISA and (2) that they breached their fiduciary duties in carrying out the LBO. Counts V and VI related exclusively to the "crossover election." This election allowed the ESOP participants who had been participants in predecessor plans the opportunity to invest up to 100 percent of their account balances in Parsons stock.

The District Court's Decision

The Court ruled that although the members of the Parsons board of directors were fiduciaries of the ESOP by virtue of their exclusive authority to appoint the members of the retirement committee, the members' fiduciary responsibility could not extend beyond the appointment of the retirement committee.

---

[4] *Andrade v. Parsons Corp.*, 1990 U.S. Dist. LEXIS 14932, 12 Employee Benefits Cas. (BNA) 1954 (C.D. Cal. June 21, 1990), *aff'd* 972 F.2d 1336 (9th Cir. July 31, 1992).

The Court determined that the three members of the retirement committee were "competent and trustworthy individuals." Therefore, the Parsons board had not breached its duty in appointing those members.

The Court then considered whether certain senior executives of Parsons should be deemed fiduciaries of the ESOP. The Court concluded that the plaintiffs failed to carry what it characterized as the "extraordinary light burden" of showing that the senior executives exercised any control or authority over the retirement committee or plan assets.

The plaintiffs' claim was based on the fact that the Parsons chief financial officer (1) resigned as chairman of the retirement committee immediately prior to the LBO, (2) helped select the financial adviser and legal adviser ultimately hired by the retirement committee, and (3) met separately with the members of the special committee to negotiate the tender offer price without the presence of any member of the retirement committee.

The Court ruled that based solely on the testimony of the members of the retirement committee, they understood their fiduciary obligations and acted independently and exclusively for the benefit of the ESOP participants. Accordingly, the Court determined that the senior executives were not fiduciaries under ERISA and could not be held liable for a breach of fiduciary duty.

Finally, the Court ruled that the members of the retirement committee had complied with their obligations to act exclusively in the interests of the plan participants and prudently in the performance of their duties. With respect to the first standard, the Court relied on each member's testimony (1) that there was awareness of and understanding of obligations under ERISA and (2) that an independent determination was made that the LBO was in the best interest of the participants.

The Court stated that in order to prove a breach of the prudent standard, the plaintiffs had an obligation to show that the retirement committee did not conduct a careful and impartial investigation prior to entering into the LBO. The Court concluded that the retirement committee (1) properly retained independent and competent legal and financial advisers, (2) considered the potential disadvantages of the LBO and implemented mechanisms such as the "prop price" to counteract any negative impact of the transaction, and (3) determined that the ESOP participants would receive substantial long-term benefits from the transaction. All of these factors demonstrated that the retirement committee acted prudently under ERISA.

The Appeals Court's Decision

On July 31, 1992, the U.S. Court of Appeals for the Ninth Circuit issued a memorandum opinion affirming the decision of the District Court in *Andrade v. Parsons Corporation* in favor of the defendants.

Commentary and Conclusion

The case involved the conduct of the individual ESOP fiduciaries in approving the 1984 leveraged buyout of Parsons Corporation by its ESOP. The District Court's 1990 opinion provides valuable guidance to individual fiduciaries for demonstrating that they have complied with ERISA by acting independently and with advice of independent legal and financial advisers in arranging and approving ESOP transactions.

This case is also noteworthy to all ESOP practitioners with regard to the District Court's assessment of what constitutes prudent behavior for an ESOP fiduciary.

Reich v. Valley National Bank of Arizona

Introduction

Reich v. Valley National Bank of Arizona[5] is also commonly referred to as the "Kroy" case. In this case, the U.S. District Court for the Southern District of New York provided an important precedent (1) for financial advisers and (2) for fiduciaries to ESOP-owned companies with regard to assessing the fairness of mergers and acquisitions transactions.

The Kroy case involved an action brought by the Department of Labor (DOL) against Valley National Bank of Arizona (Valley National) in its capacity as trustee of the Kroy, Inc., Employee Stock Ownership Plan (Kroy ESOP).

ESOP practitioners had anticipated that the resolution of this case would establish long-awaited guidelines for the equity allocation within multi-investor ESOP leveraged buyouts. Unfortunately, the District Court's decision only tangentially addressed the issue of multiple investor equity allocation.

The District Court's Findings

The District Court held that Valley National breached its fiduciary duty by causing the Kroy ESOP to purchase Kroy stock without obtaining "adequate consideration." Specifically, Valley National failed to conduct a good faith investigation in connection with the management-led leveraged buyout in which Kroy, Inc., was taken private (the "Transaction").

The District Court concluded Valley National failed to perform the proper due diligence in order to determine the following:

1. Whether the price to be paid by the ESOP for the Kroy stock was in excess of the fair market value of the underlying stock.
2. Whether the Transaction was fair to the ESOP from a financial point of view.

This resulted in the Court concluding that Valley National caused the ESOP to engage in various nonexempt prohibited transactions under ERISA.

The facts of this case and the Court's decision provide numerous insights for ESOP fiduciaries and for ESOP financial advisers. Among the more significant fiduciary issues are those pertaining to the fact that a fiduciary must:

1. Be an active participant in negotiating the price and terms of the transaction.
2. Retain its own financial advisers.
3. Conduct a thorough and diligent investigation of the company and of the security that it is purchasing.

---

[5] *Reich v. Valley National Bank of Arizona*, 837 F. Supp. 1259, 1993 U.S. Dist. LEXIS 11837 (S.D.N.Y. Aug. 19, 1993).

Commentary and Conclusion

The District Court defined fair market value as the price at which an asset would exchange hands between a willing buyer and a willing seller when the former is not under any compulsion to buy and the latter is not under any compulsion to sell, and both parties are able, as well as willing, to trade and are well informed about the asset and the market for that asset. The published decision provides valuable insights to ESOP practitioners with regard to the responsibilities (1) of ESOP fiduciaries and (2) ESOP financial advisers with regard to their assessment of an ESOP stock sale or purchase transaction.

Howard v. Shay

Introduction

Howard v. Shay[6] is also commonly called the "PAE" case. In this case, the U.S. District Court for the Central District of California found that the ESOP committee did not breach its fiduciary duties in selling ESOP stock to an entity created by the majority shareholder of the ESOP sponsor.

In *Howard v. Shay*, the District Court held that the administrative committee (the "Committee") of the ESOP of Pacific Architects and Engineers, Inc. (the "PAE ESOP") did not breach its fiduciary duties under ERISA by selling all of the Pacific Architects and Engineers, Inc. (PAE) stock held by the PAE ESOP to the E. & A. Shay Irrevocable Trust (the "Shay Trust"). The Shay Trust was an entity created by the majority shareholder of PAE.

The Facts of the Case

The plaintiffs were participants in an ESOP created for the benefit of employees of PAE, a California corporation. PAE was primarily a real estate holding company, but it also had engineering and architecture operations. The real estate owned by PAE was both foreign and domestic. The company also held a 50 percent ownership interest in K.K. Halifax, a Japanese real estate corporation.

The PAE ESOP was originally created in 1972 as an employee benefit plan. In 1974, the ESOP purchased approximately 40 percent of the PAE stock from Edward Shay, the president and chairman of PAE (and an ESOP fiduciary) for $10.67 per share. There was no put option in connection with the ESOP stock, and no put option was ever created. Prior to the sale, Edward Shay owned 100 percent of the outstanding stock of PAE.

In 1987, Richard Smith, a PAE senior executive and co-fiduciary, consulted with a financial adviser regarding the possibility of terminating the ESOP. The financial adviser informed Richard Smith about potential problems associated

---

[6] *Newman Howard, et al., v. Edward A. Shay, et al.*, 1993 U.S. Dist. LEXIS 20153 (C.D. Cal. Sept. 15, 1993), *rev'd and rem'd* 100 F.3d 1484 (9th Cir. 1996), *retried* 1998 U.S. Dist LEXIS 23146 (C.D. Cal. June 12, 1998).

with the valuation methodology used by the appraisal firm that had conducted the valuation of the PAE stock for ESOP annual update purposes.

On November 9, 1988, the Committee voted to sell all of the shares of PAE stock (38.05 percent of PAE) held by the PAE ESOP to the Shay Trust for $14.40 per share, for a total sum of $5,479,241.21. This stock sale was in connection with the termination of the PAE ESOP.

The stock sale occurred and was based on an independent stock valuation performed by an accounting firm. The independent valuation estimated a fair market value of $14.40 per share, the highest value ever assigned to the PAE stock held by the PAE ESOP. The stock valuation was accompanied and supported by a fairness opinion.

The accounting firm separated the PAE value into three components: (1) the PAE 50 percent interest in K.K. Halifax, which held Japanese real estate; (2) the PAE interests in other real estate; and (3) the PAE engineering and architecture operations.

The valuation was based on the standard of fair market value on a going-concern basis, based in part on PAE's attorney's assertion that California Corporations Code Section 1800 did not give the ESOP the right to trigger an involuntary dissolution of PAE.

The values for (1) and (2) above were based on independent appraisals of the domestic and Japanese real estate provided by the defendants. The Japanese real estate held by K.K. Halifax was valued at $120.2 million, or approximately $60 million for PAE's 50 percent interest, before consideration of any discounts or built-in capital gains taxes. The PAE interest in other real estate had been appraised at $18.2 million. The accounting firm valued the PAE engineering and architecture operations at $5.3 million, based on the market approach.

The accounting firm next considered the amount of valuation discounts to apply to the above values. First, a 60 percent discount was applied to the PAE ownership interest in K.K. Halifax. The valuation report justified this valuation discount in part by explaining that (1) the Japanese real estate market was overvalued and volatile, (2) PAE did not have a controlling ownership interest in K.K. Halifax, (3) the other 50 percent owner was more powerful than PAE, and (4) there would be very substantial taxes on any sale.

Second, a 40 percent to 50 percent discount for lack of control was applied on all real estate–related interests, including K.K. Halifax, to reflect the fact that the ESOP only owned approximately 40 percent of the PAE stock.

Third, a 50 percent discount for lack of marketability was applied, resulting in a fair market value of the ESOP stock of $14.40 per share. The discount for lack of marketability reflected the facts that (1) the PAE stock was not publicly traded and (2) the ESOP plan participants did not have the right to "put" the stock to the company.

The complaint was filed in the District Court on January 10, 1991. The complaint sought equitable and monetary relief from the Committee and PAE. The complaint alleged that the Committee breached its fiduciary duties under ERISA (1) by engaging in prohibited self-dealing and (2) by improperly selling the PAE stock to the Shay Trust for less than its fair market value.

The District Court's Decision

In reviewing the independent valuation and fairness opinion, the District Court found nothing wrong with either (1) the Committee's selection of the accounting firm or (2) the valuation procedures performed by that firm. The Court also found that (1) the lack of control discount and (2) the lack of marketability discount were neither improper nor excessive under the circumstances. Details of transactions involving 25 percent to 49.9 percent of a company's stock (from the Willamette Management Associates proprietary database), presented through expert testimony, were instrumental in supporting the 50 percent lack of marketability discount.

The District Court's Decision— Commentary and Conclusion

The District Court's comment regarding whether independent or neutral fiduciaries should have been retained for purposes of the PAE ESOP's sale of the PAE stock to the Shay Trust is noteworthy to ESOP practitioners. The District Court concluded that it was not "fatal" that an independent or neutral fiduciary was not involved.

In this case, the possible appointment of an independent or neutral fiduciary was considered and rejected because an international public accounting firm had been retained to render (1) an independent valuation of the PAE stock and (2) a fairness opinion with respect to the transaction.

The Appeals Court's Decision

The Ninth Circuit Court of Appeals reversed the District Court's decision, finding for the plaintiffs on breach of fiduciary duties of care and loyalty to the ESOP plan participants in engaging in a self-dealing transaction.

The Ninth Circuit Court decision focused in particular on the lack of thoroughness of the investigation by the fiduciaries. The Court stated:

> To justifiably rely on an independent appraisal, a conflicted fiduciary need not become an expert in the valuation of closely held corporations. But the fiduciary is required to make an honest, objective effort to read the valuation, understand it, and question the methods and assumptions that do not make sense. If after a careful review of the valuation and discussion with the expert there are still uncertainties, the fiduciary should have a second firm review the valuation. Adopting the alternative rule—that an independent appraisal is a complete defense to a charge of imprudence— should be foolish, especially in cases in which there is a strong possibility of self-dealing.... A fiduciary determined to self-deal has ample opportunity to sway the final valuation that will set the transaction.... This case illustrates the danger. Not only did Smith discuss liquidity and minority interest discounts with prospective valuators, but also, at least one firm ... balked at his conditions of retention. Conflicted fiduciaries do not fulfill ERISA's investigative requirements by merely hiring an expert. Shay, Smith, and Lehrer did nothing else. A day after they got [the] valuation, they completed the transaction. They did not meaningfully review, discuss, or question the valuation.

The District Court Retrial

On remand in 1998, the U.S. District Court reaffirmed its 1993 decision that the "price of $14.40 per share is found by the Court to be fair and adequate consideration for the self-dealing transaction."

However, based on the Ninth Circuit 1996 decision for the plaintiff regarding the breach of fiduciary duty, the District Court granted the PAE ESOP and/or any of its participants the election to buy back their PAE shares owned previously by tendering $14.40 per share to the trustee of the E. & A. Shay Irrevocable Trust. Additionally, the plaintiffs were allowed to recover their attorney's fees and costs.

The District Court Retrial—Commentary and Conclusion

This case offers important lessons both (1) to ESOP financial advisers and (2) to ESOP fiduciaries. For ESOP financial advisers, the case illustrates in particular the importance of providing ample case-specific support when selecting the discounts for lack of control and for lack of marketability used in the valuation report.

With regard to the fiduciary issues, the District Court provided an overview of requirements for fiduciaries in ESOP transactions. In particular, the District Court stated that a conflicted fiduciary "is required to make an honest, objective effort to read the valuation, understand it, and question the methods and assumptions that do not make sense."

Eyler v. Commissioner

Introduction

In *Gary L. Eyler v. Commissioner*, the petitioner appealed the earlier decision of the U.S. Tax Court.[7]

The Issues of the Case

Gary L. Eyler, the former CEO and majority shareholder of Continental Training Services, Inc. (CTS), disputed the Internal Revenue Service Commissioner's determination that he had engaged in a prohibited transaction with CTS's ESOP when he sold $10 million worth of CTS stock to the ESOP in December 1986. Eyler appealed the Commissioner's determination to the Tax Court.

In 1995, the Tax Court concluded that Eyler was not exempt from liability for the excise taxes imposed in connection with his sale of CTS stock to the ESOP because he failed to establish (1) that the fair market value per share of CTS stock on the transaction date was at least $14.50 per share or (2) that any fiduciary named in the ESOP made a good-faith determination that the fair market value per share of CTS stock on the transaction date was at least $14.50.

---

[7] *Gary L. Eyler v. Commissioner*, 88 F.3d 445, 1996 U.S. App. LEXIS 15831 (7th Cir. July 2, 1996), *aff'g* T.C. Memo 1995-123 (Mar. 23, 1995).

Internal Revenue Code Sections 4975(a) and (b) impose a two-tier excise tax on prohibited transactions between an ESOP and disqualified persons. A prohibited transaction includes any sale of stock between a plan and a disqualified person, with a disqualified person being an owner of 50 percent or more of the stock of a corporation whose employees are covered by the plan.

Internal Revenue Code Section 4975(a) imposes a yearly 5 percent tax on the amount involved. Internal Revenue Code Section 4975(b) imposes a second tier of tax equal to 100 percent of the amount involved if the prohibited transaction is not corrected (i.e., reversed) within the taxable period. Eyler was assessed on both tiers.

The Facts of the Case

From 1973 (when he started CTS) until 1986 (when he sold CTS), Eyler was its sole or majority shareholder as well as its chairman of the board and chief executive officer. CTS operated a series of vocational schools to train truck drivers and heavy equipment operators.

Government deregulation of the industry resulted in enormous growth for CTS. Enrollment at CTS schools increased from about 2,000 students in 1980 to more than 37,000 students in 1986. By 1986, it was the largest proprietary vocational training system in the United States.

In 1985, Eyler began exploring either selling CTS or taking it public. CTS had received inquiries and solicitations from a number of investment banking firms.

In early 1986, Eyler and CTS decided to take the company public through an initial public offering (IPO). During 1986, the underwriters conducted a due diligence investigation, which consisted of reviewing the financial records and history of CTS, visiting the company's facilities, interviewing the management, and evaluating financial and economic forecasts.

As a result of the due diligence, an estimated IPO price range of $13 to $16 per share was established.

The underwriters attempted to determine whether there was interest in purchasing CTS stock in the price range of $13 to $16 per share. Marketing the proposed IPO during October and the first week of November 1986, the underwriters determined that the "circled interest" for CTS stock at $13 to $16 was only around $1 million. ("Circled interest" is an investment banking term meaning specifically identified, likely syndicate participation in an offering.)

In November 1986, Eyler decided to look into establishing an ESOP for CTS and thereafter selling a substantial portion of his shares to the ESOP. On November 24, 1986, CTS approached a bank to negotiate a $10 million loan to be secured by the shares to be sold by Eyler to the ESOP.

At a meeting on December 12, 1986, the CTS board considered the proposed ESOP. Under the terms of the ESOP, CTS was designated plan administrator and named fiduciary. CTS's duties under the plan included appointing and overseeing the plan committee. The board approved the establishment of the plan under the terms proposed by the CTS chief financial officer during the meeting.

As a related aside, sometime in late 1986 or early 1987, seven of the CTS board members each purchased 1,882 shares of CTS stock from a minority shareholder of CTS at $14.50 per share, for a total purchase price of just over $27,000. One of the directors paid cash for his stock. The remaining six directors received funds for the purchase from Eyler by way of informal, unsecured "bridge loans," the terms of which were not reduced to writing. Eventually, the stock certificates evidencing the directors' purchases were prepared in March 1987, when loans from the bank for the purchase were formally approved.

In addition, in September 1986, two investigations of CTS were pending. The first investigation, by the attorney general of California, concerned allegations that CTS engaged in certain fraudulent practices and used untrue or misleading advertising with respect to its courses. The second, by the U.S. Department of Education, focused on the same areas. In 1988, the United States, on behalf of the Department of Education, filed a $366 million lawsuit against CTS.

The federal government also withdrew CTS's eligibility to participate in various government student loan programs. This withdrawal was later judicially determined to be a violation of CTS's constitutional right to due process, but by the time this news arrived, CTS was financially ruined.

The Issues before the Court

In 1991, the Internal Revenue Service began investigating the ESOP transaction. In April 1992, the Commissioner of the IRS determined that Eyler was a disqualified person who engaged in a nonexempt prohibited transaction within the meaning of Internal Revenue Code Section 4975. Eyler was said to be liable for the excise tax penalty, and a notice of deficiency was issued to him for assessments covering the years 1986 to 1990.

Eyler filed a petition in Tax Court seeking a redetermination of the deficiency. Eyler argued first that the $14.50 price paid by the ESOP for his stock was fair market value. Eyler's alternative argument was that even if $14.50 was not fair market value, the CTS board of directors acted in good faith in determining that it was, and thus "adequate consideration" was still received by the ESOP.

The Tax Court rejected both arguments.

First, it held that Eyler failed to meet his burden of establishing $14.50 as the fair market value on the date of the prohibited transaction. The underwriters' range of $13 to $16 per share did not, in the Tax Court's view, represent a final price determination, and it was also based on a number of assumptions that had not come to pass.

Second, the Tax Court found that because the board members knew that many of the assumptions underlying the underwriters' price range had changed and yet they did nothing further to investigate the suggested price, their actions did not rise to the level of prudence imposed on ERISA fiduciaries. Since "adequate consideration" was not received by the ESOP when it purchased Eyler's stock, the Tax Court sustained the deficiencies determined by the Commissioner.

The Petitioner's Position

Eyler argued that the fair market value of CTS stock was at least $14.50 based on the valuation set by the underwriters. Eyler also argued that the Tax Court erred when it adopted the Commissioner's argument regarding a lack of marketability discount. He also argued that the purchases of CTS stock by several directors for $14.50 per share shortly after the ESOP transaction was the basis for establishing fair market value.

Eyler argued that the ESOP still received adequate consideration when it purchased his stock because the CTS fiduciaries acted in good faith in determining that the fair market value of CTS stock was $14.50 per share.

The Appeals Court Decision—The Valuation Issues

The Appeals Court agreed with the Tax Court that there are several reasons why the underwriters' estimated price range of $13 to $16 per share did not establish the fair market value to be at least $14.50 on the date of the sale.

First, that price range was established after the underwriters conducted a due diligence investigation and as a part of CTS's anticipated IPO. That price range did not purport to determine the fair market value of CTS stock at any specific point in time, nor did it in any way purport to be a final determination. The purpose of selecting that price was to see how investors might respond.

Second, that price range was not binding and did not represent a firm commitment by the underwriters.

The Appeals Court concluded that the lack of public interest in CTS stock also weighed against Eyler's reliance on the underwriters' valuation. When the stock was offered nationally to individual and institutional investors, the "circled interest" was small, no more than $1 million. Clearly, the public showed little interest in buying CTS stock within the underwriters' price range.

The Appeals Court noted that many significant factors changed from the time the prospectus was filed by the underwriters in September to the date of completion of the ESOP sale on December 22, 1986. The $13 to $16 estimated price range was based on certain assumptions that did not come to fruition at the time of the ESOP transaction.

First, the underwriters assumed that as a result of the IPO, CTS would be a publicly traded corporation.

A second important assumption was that the IPO would result in a positive cash flow for CTS. When the IPO was shelved and the ESOP established, the CTS cash flow actually worsened because CTS committed itself to making contributions to the ESOP in amounts large enough for the plan to repay the $10 million loan.

In particular, the Appeals Court noted a significant factor not assumed, let alone considered, by the underwriters in preparing the preliminary prospectus was the establishment of the ESOP itself. Upon formation of the ESOP, CTS undertook two obligations that affected its balance sheet and future-operating income.

First, CTS guaranteed the $10 million loan to the ESOP, which was required to be classified as debt on CTS's balance sheet and a charge to shareholders' equity.

Second, CTS obligated itself to make contributions to the ESOP in an amount sufficient to cover the loan payments, or at least $2 million per year, resulting in a significant cash drain on the company.

The Appeals Court firmly stated that significant changes in these underlying assumptions, together with the limited nature of the underwriters' estimated price range and minimal circled interest, demonstrated that the valuation did not provide a basis for establishing fair market value.

With regard to the marketability discount, the Appeals Court concluded that Eyler's argument failed for the fundamental reason that, as of the date of the ESOP transaction, CTS had no history of paying ESOP distributions in cash. Whatever effect the CTS history of payouts might have had on the fair market value of CTS stock at the time of the ESOP transaction was pure speculation.

Similarly, the Appeals Court rejected Eyler's assertion that the marketability discount was inappropriate because the ESOP put option had no fixed price and could be paid out over five years under the terms of the ESOP.

The Appeals Court stated: "Nothing in the record convinces us that the Tax Court clearly erred when it concluded that the marketability discount should apply to the [underwriters'] valuation."

Regarding the allegedly arm's-length pre-ESOP sales at $14.50 per share, the Appeals Court stated that it was not unreasonable for the Tax Court to conclude that the sale of stock from the minority shareholder to the directors was not at arm's length. The purchases involved directors of CTS and a noncontrolling shareholder, not the corporation. Eyler, who benefited from the sale in his effort to establish the $14.50 value, provided unsecured bridge loans to six of the seven directors who purchased stock from the noncontrolling shareholder.

Concluding the valuation issue, the Appeals Court stated:

> For all of these reasons, we are unable to say that the Tax Court committed clear error when it found that Eyler failed to meet his burden of establishing that the fair market value of CTS stock on December 22, 1986, was at least $14.50.

The Appeals Court Decision—The Fiduciary Issues

The trustee and plan administrator of the ESOP was the vice president of human resources at CTS. Under the terms of the ESOP, the trustee was not responsible for day-to-day operations of the plan, but rather served in an administrative capacity, carrying out the discretionary decisions of the plan committee.

The Appeals Court concluded that the trustee played no role in pricing the CTS stock for the ESOP, made no good-faith determination of its fair market value, and, therefore, his actions failed to support Eyler's argument.

The Appeals Court also concluded that the actions of the members of the plan committee, who were appointed at the December 12, 1986 board meeting, were not helpful. There was no evidence that the committee even met in the 10 days between the board meeting and the ESOP purchase. There was also no evidence that any of the committee members conducted any investigation to determine the fair market value of the stock.

The Appeals Court stated: "Thus, as the Tax Court properly found, Eyler is not relieved of excise tax liability on the basis of the committee's alleged good-faith determination of fair market value of the stock."

Eyler argued that CTS, acting through its board of directors, qualified as a fiduciary of the ESOP. Eyler argued that in light of the opinion letter prepared by CTS's attorneys, and the board's knowledge of earlier takeover valuation opinions, the board acted in good faith in determining the price of the stock.

The Tax Court had rejected Eyler's contention, finding that the board's actions did not rise to the exacting level of prudence imposed on ERISA fiduciaries. The Appeals Court affirmed the Tax Court's conclusion.

With regard to the fiduciary issues, the Appeals Court concluded:

> In sum, the law requires a fiduciary of an ESOP to act with the care, skill, and diligence that a prudent person would undertake in acting on behalf

of ESOP beneficiaries. The degree to which a fiduciary makes an independent inquiry is critical. We find no merit to Eyler's contention that the board of directors was well-informed and, therefore, made a good-faith determination of the fair market value of the stock. The record does not show that even one director, let alone a majority, sought independent information on the fair market value of the stock. Rather, on the same day the project was presented, the board voted to guarantee a $10 million loan, the proceeds of which would be used to buy the majority shareholder's stock. A prudent person would not have relied upon the dated [underwriters'] estimated price range for the ESOP stock purchase in light of the failed IPO and changing financial conditions at the corporation. Moreover, there is not evidence that the board was knowledgeable about the effects of these changing conditions on the fair market value of CTS stock. Thus, it was not clear error for the Tax Court to conclude that Eyler did not meet his burden of showing that the directors acted in good faith in determining fair market value.

Commentary and Conclusion

This case, particularly due to the strong affirmation of the Tax Court decision by the Appeals Court, is instructive both (1) to ESOP financial advisers and other ESOP practitioners and (2) to any individuals who assume the responsibility of an ESOP fiduciary.

This case provides useful guidance with respect to (1) ESOP share purchase valuation issues (i.e., how much analysis is required to determine fair market value) and to (2) ESOP fiduciary issues (i.e., how much due diligence is required to assess adequate consideration).

The virtual unanimity of the Tax Court and the Appeals Court on these issues makes this judicial precedent particularly important and informative.

Davis v. Torvick

Introduction

In the case of *Davis v. Torvick, Inc.*,[8] the U.S. District Court decided a case involving both (1) ESOP valuation issues and (2) ESOP fiduciary duty issues. Accordingly, this case has relevance to both ESOP valuation analysts and ESOP trustees.

The Facts of the Case

The plaintiffs were employees of Torvick, Inc., a Mercedes-Benz dealership in Santa Rosa, California. One defendant was Torvick, Inc., the Mercedes-Benz dealership, and a California corporation. Torvick, Inc., was the employer of the plaintiffs and the corporate custodian of the Amended Profit Sharing Plan and Trust

---

[8] *William R. Davis, et al.v. Torvick, Inc., et al.*, C-93-1343 CW, 1996 WL 266217 (N.D.Cal. May 2, 1996).

Agreement of Torvick, Inc. ("Profit Sharing Plan"). Another defendant was Robert C. Torvick, a member of the board of directors of Torvick, Inc., and a trustee for the Profit Sharing Plan and the Torvick, Inc., Employee Stock Ownership Plan (ESOP).

Defendants Roy F. Bracket and Blain R. Torvick were members of the board of directors for Torvick, Inc., and trustees of the Profit Sharing Plan.

The lawsuit also named the company's accounting firm and law firm as defendants. The accounting firm settled with the plaintiffs for an undisclosed amount. Accordingly, the charges against them were dismissed by the time of the trial.

The Profit Sharing Plan was a trust fund to which the plaintiffs contributed a percentage of their salary. Torvick, Inc., was to make matching contributions in an amount depending on its profitability. The plaintiffs received periodic statements detailing the amount that they were supposed to have in their respective accounts.

The ESOP was a trust fund created after the Profit Sharing Plan. The only asset of the ESOP was Torvick, Inc., stock. The plaintiffs exchanged their assets in the Profit Sharing Plan in return for Torvick, Inc., stock. The amount of stock allotted to each plaintiff was proportional to each plaintiff's account balance in the Profit Sharing Plan.

The Issues of the Case

The plaintiffs alleged that Robert Torvick utilized the Employees' Profit Sharing Plan funds for his own use, the use of Torvick, Inc., or the use of other entities controlled by Robert Torvick. The total amount of money that should have been in the Profit Sharing Plan on March 31, 1990, was $870,152.75.

By Robert Torvick's own estimate, the maximum amount that was actually funded was $30,000 to $40,000. Over $800,000 was either never placed into the plan or was borrowed from the plan by Robert Torvick or by entities controlled by Torvick.

By Robert Torvick's own estimate, he—or entities controlled by him—owed over $200,000 to the Profit Sharing Plan in notes. The rest of the missing money was never contributed.

The plaintiffs alleged that Robert Torvick and Torvick, Inc., caused periodic statements to be distributed to the plaintiffs that misrepresented that the Profit Sharing Plan assets were safely invested.

The plaintiffs alleged that Torvick, Inc., employees, at the direction of Robert Torvick, negligently prepared inflation projections that were used by Torvick, Inc.'s CPA firm, in the valuation of Torvick, Inc. (the "Valuation Report"). The Torvick, Inc., employees prepared the projections within the span of a few days, and they based them only on past performance extrapolated into the future. The projections did not take into account any other factors, such as the outlook of the specific business. Robert Torvick ordered at least one of the projections to be made more "optimistic."

In addition to including the negligent projections, the Valuation Report did not include any clear reference to the large debt owed the Profit Sharing Plan.

Robert Torvick, in or about late 1989 and early 1990, met with the plaintiffs and presented the Valuation Report. The purpose of the meeting was to promote the ESOP and assure the plaintiffs that it was a good investment to transfer funds from the Profit Sharing Plan into the ESOP.

Allegedly, the defendants intentionally misled the employees by concealing the state of the Profit Sharing Plan. The employees relied on the representations to their detriment when they voted to transfer their Profit Sharing Plan assets to the ESOP in or about late 1989 or early 1990.

Torvick, Inc., subsequently went bankrupt. The value of the employees' shares in the corporation went to zero. The gross amount of the employees' loss was approximately $450,000 as of March 31, 1990.

The Plaintiffs' Position

Robert Torvick and Torvick, Inc., were acting as fiduciaries when they had the Valuation Report prepared by their accounting firm. They also were acting as fiduciaries when they met with the plaintiffs to encourage the employees to switch to the ESOP plan.

Valuations and representations concerning the future of a business are normally standard business practices, and are not connected with plan administration. When the valuation is created and used to make representations about the future of an alternative plan, and to convince participants to leave the current plan, however, it is an act of plan administration.

The Defendants' Position

Robert Torvick proposed two related defense arguments. The first argument is that the plaintiffs would have opted for the transfer even had they known of his misconduct. The second argument is that the plaintiffs had not been damaged because they received full value for their unfunded Profit Sharing Plan in the form of Torvick, Inc., stock when the ESOP plan was formed.

Robert Torvick argued that the Valuation Report was accurate and that Torvick, Inc., simply failed in the marketplace, a risk that all stockholders take.

The Valuation Report represented that Torvick, Inc. was worth approximately $1 million at the time of the employees' transfer to the ESOP. Robert Torvick argued that the employees were not damaged because if Torvick, Inc., had done well, as all parties hoped, the plaintiffs would have assets in the amount owed them in the form of Torvick, Inc., stock.

The fact that Torvick, Inc., went bankrupt does not change the value of what the employees received in 1990. According to this argument, the employees took the risk of failure in the marketplace.

The District Court's Decision

The District Court concluded that Robert Torvick violated ERISA and damaged the fund. The loans that Robert Torvick caused to be made from the Profit Sharing Plan to himself, and to entities controlled by him, were transactions between the plan and a party in interest, and were a violation of ERISA. The loans that Robert Torvick caused to be made from the Profit Sharing Plan to himself were transactions between the plan and a fiduciary and were a violation of ERISA.

The periodic statements provided to the plaintiffs clearly stated the amounts that were supposed to be in the Profit Sharing Plan. The plaintiffs were entitled to rely on these representations unless they were given timely notice that the information was incorrect.

By causing the Profit Sharing Plan to remain unfunded, and then lying about the state of the plan in these periodic statements, Robert Torvick engaged in a serious breach of duty to discharge his responsibilities as a trustee solely in the interest of the participants.

The District Court concluded that, as a result of these ERISA violations, Robert Torvick committed at least one more violation. In convincing the employees to switch to the ESOP by concealing his past ERISA violations, representing to the employees that all of the Profit Sharing Plan assets were being held in cash and that Torvick, Inc., would receive those assets, and causing the Valuation Report to be based, at least in part, on negligent projections, Robert Torvick did not operate in the interest of anyone other than himself.

Materially misleading the employees to erase his own debt and conceal his violations of ERISA is entirely inconsistent with Robert Torvick's fiduciary duties, the District Court concluded.

Commentary and Conclusion

This case offers important lessons both to ESOP valuation analysts and to ESOP fiduciaries. With regard to the valuation issues, the District Court specifically noted: "The Court has grave doubts about the accuracy of the Valuation Report based not only on the negligent projections used to formulate it, but also on the lack of any concrete reference to the large debt owed the Profit Sharing Plan."

With regard to the fiduciary issues, the District Court concluded: "A fiduciary that breaches any of the responsibilities imposed by ERISA is personally liable to make good to such plan any losses to the plan from such a breach, and shall be subject to such other equitable or remedial relief as the court may deem appropriate."

Henry v. Champlain Enterprises

Introduction

The court in *Henry v. Champlain Enterprises*[9] rejected the valuation by a nationally recognized appraisal firm of convertible preferred stock contributed to an ESOP on grounds that the valuation was biased. In addition, because the trustee failed to document that it had challenged some aspects of the valuation, the Court found the trustee failed to prove it had not breached its fiduciary duties.

The Facts of the Case

In 1994 the three owners of CommutAir, a closely held regional airline, wanted to establish an ESOP with a contribution of 30 percent of CommutAir's stock. In

---

[9] *Henry v. Champlain Enterprises*, 334 F. Supp. 2d 252, 2004 U.S. Dist. LEXIS 18140 (N.D.N.Y. Sept. 3, 2004).

1993, CommutAir had been approached by two investment banking firms, Prudential Securities and Alex Brown & Sons, interested in an IPO or strategic alliance. Those firms provided CommutAir with written materials indicating CommutAir had an equity value of between $140 million and $225 million. These offers were not pursued, but the CommutAir owners came to the conclusion, based on the offers, that their equity was worth $200 million. Accordingly, they wanted to sell their 30 percent stake for $60 million in a seller-financed transaction.

When they were ready to establish the ESOP, the owners hired U.S. Trust Co. (U.S. Trust), which routinely served as an ESOP trustee. Norman Goldberg, a senior fiduciary officer of U.S. Trust oversaw the formation of the ESOP. Although Goldberg had never prepared a valuation of a closely held corporation, he indicated that he generally understood valuation reports. Goldberg left the technical aspects to an in-house financial analyst. Goldberg stressed the need for due diligence and an appraisal of the company, and Houlihan, Lokey, Howard, & Zukin (Houlihan) was retained for this purpose.

Based on a comparable company analysis and a discounted cash flow analysis, Houlihan initially determined that CommutAir was worth $180 million. Subsequently, after Goldberg allegedly noted that Houlihan's selection of above-the-median multiples in the comparable company method would have to be justified and allegedly questioned the 9.5 percent terminal growth rate used in the discounted cash flow (DCF), Houlihan reduced CommutAir's equity value to $174 million. The financial measure containing the highest selected multiples was removed from the draft and the terminal growth rate was changed to 9.0 percent from 9.5 percent.

After negotiations with U.S. Trust, the cumulative dividend rate was changed from 7 percent to 9 percent, and the performance dividend was changed from the 10–50 percent range up to 6 percent of the face amount, to 20 percent up to 3 percent of the face amount. However, notwithstanding these changes, Houlihan did not alter its value opinion because it still concluded the ESOP was receiving "value in excess" as a result of the features of the convertible preferred stock. Ultimately, the stock sold for $60 million.

The Issues of the Case

ESOP participants brought suit against CommutAir and U.S. Trust over the issue of whether the sale constituted a prohibited transaction under ERISA Section 406 and, if so, whether it qualified under the adequate consideration exception set forth by ERISA.

Both sides agreed that the primary component of the valuation would be to determine CommutAir's total equity value by employing the DCF method and the comparable guideline public company method. The plaintiff's expert concluded a total equity value of just under $106 million and opined that the convertible preferred stock should have been valued at $41.5 million. The expert criticized Houlihan's terminal growth rate, the use of certain financial measures, and the selection of above-the-median multiples used in the comparable company method (finding CommutAir to be at or below the comparable companies while Houlihan found them to be at or above the comparable companies).

The District Court's Decision

The Court found that while correct and in agreement on many issues, there was serious doubt about the overall credibility of both Houlihan and the plaintiff's expert. The Court determined that Houlihan was not independent because it did not start with an open mind or independent approach to valuation. The Court determined that the plaintiff's expert was hired to provide the lowest valuation conclusion possible to maximize the potential damages sustained by the ESOP. Based on their testimony, however, the Trial Court determined that the equity value of CommutAir in 1994 was $145 million, and that, therefore, the fair market value of the stock purchased by the ESOP was $52.5 million.

As to the adequate consideration exception, the Court found that U.S. Trust failed to prove that it had made a good faith, independent determination of fair market value. Specifically, the Court questioned the reliability of management projections and the terminal value calculation, and, with respect to the comparable companies method, questioned the propriety of the selection of the comparable companies, the financial measures, and the multiples, and whether the most current information was used. The Court concluded that U.S. Trust failed to address these areas of concern, noting that U.S. Trust "barely produced a shred of evidence that shows what Goldberg and Shea did." Accordingly, the Court awarded the plaintiffs $7.75 million.

Commentary and Conclusion

This case should serve as a warning to ESOP trustees to document their conduct and decision-making process. In this case, the trustee's failure to create such documentation seems to have given the Court no choice but to find that the trustee failed to prove that it engaged in a good faith investigation of the merits of the transaction at issue. The Court also found the appraisals in this case suspect, again serving as a reminder of how crucial it is for valuation experts to remain independent throughout the appraisal. In quoting from *Eckelkamp v. Beste* (see summary of that case, below), the Court emphasized that "Little case law exists on valuation, so often a court's conclusion is determined by its evaluation of the credibility and background of the witnesses who performed the valuation."

Eckelkamp v. Beste

Introduction

In *Eckelkamp v. Beste*,[10] the court rejected a valuation where it found that it was fundamentally unsupported.

The Facts of the Case

Employees and former employees of Melton Machine and Control Company (Melton) brought suit against Melton, its employee stock ownership plan (ESOP),

---

[10] *Eckelkamp v. Beste*, 201 F. Supp. 2d 1012, 2002 U.S. Dist. LEXIS 9407 (E.D. Mo. Mar. 12, 2002), *aff'd*, 315 F. 3d 863 (8th Cir. Dec. 31, 2002).

and four officers of the company, alleging that the officers, who managed both Melton and the ESOP, breached their fiduciary duties "by overcompensating themselves and by failing to obtain accurate annual appraisals of Melton stock." In 2000, the company's appraiser valued the stock at $109,000 per share. The employees' expert asserted that the company's officers were overcompensated, that the company's appraiser had consistently undervalued the company, and that in 2000 the actual value per share was over $200,000.

The District Court's Decision

The District Court rejected the plaintiffs' expert's methodology with respect to both the overcompensation and improper appraisal theories. With respect to the expert's overcompensation analysis, the District Court found several methodological flaws. First, the Court found the expert failed to take into account the fact that all employees at Melton were paid considerably more than market rates, and that the compensation for production employees compared more favorably to the relevant market than that of the individual defendants. The Court also rejected the analysis on comparisons to executive compensation at companies that in many ways were not comparable to Melton. Many of the companies used for comparison were publicly held, none had achieved Melton's 20 percent annual rate of growth, and some were not even profitable. The expert also did not visit the Melton facility, interview its employees, research the job duties of executives at the comparison companies to ensure that their jobs were actually comparable to those of the individual defendants, or consider the fact that much of their compensation was paid in the form of bonuses contingent on Melton's performance.

The Court also found multiple flaws in the appraisal methodology. It criticized use of a 10 percent "control premium" in the appraisal. That premium was what the expert calculated a hypothetical buyer might pay to obtain control of the company, but there was no evidence that the company appeared likely to be sold. The expert also increased the valuation by $450,000 to reflect an amount previously paid in dividends. The District Court concluded this was a form of double counting by the expert, because already distributed dividends were being used to increase the value of the employee ESOP accounts. The expert also increased the valuation to account for savings that would accrue if the compensation of the individual defendants were reduced. The Court questioned this methodology because there was no indication that Melton's compensation policies would change and value added as a result, citing the Fourth Edition of this book.

For these reasons, the Court granted summary judgment to the defendants.

The Appeals Court's Decision

The Eight Circuit affirmed, noting that that the District Court thoroughly examined the expert's methodology and determined that it was unreliable. After carefully examining the record, the Court of Appeals concluded that the District Court did not abuse its discretion in rejecting the expert's report and opinion.[11]

---

[11] *Eckelkamp v. Beste*, 315 F.3d 863, 2002 U.S. App. LEXIS 27175 (8th Cir. Dec. 31, 2002).

Commentary and Conclusion

This case can serve as a mini-primer on mistakes and missteps a business valuator should avoid—whether in the ESOP context or in any other context. It serves as a reminder that comparables should be truly comparable, that an appraiser should get to know the subject company thoroughly through site visits and employee and officer interviews, and that the valuation should reflect a company's operational reality on the valuation date to the greatest extent possible.

Horn v. McQueen

Introduction

In *Horn v. McQueen*,[12] the Court determined that the trustees breached their fiduciary duties where the evidence indicated that the valuation of the company was backed into by the appraiser, who had advised the trustees about the creation of the ESOP and whose valuation seemed to comport with the trustees' desired value for the company, rather than being an independent appraisal.

The Facts of the Case

Plaintiffs were ESOP participants of the U.S. Corrections Corporation (USCC) ESOP. USCC was founded by Milton Thompson and Clifford Todd. Robert McQueen was later hired and given a nonvoting interest in the corporation. Todd and Thompson owned 50 percent voting interest in USCC, and they each owned 46.875 percent of the total stock of USCC. Todd was interested in selling his shares in USCC, and Thompson and McQueen wanted to maintain control of the company. Therefore, they created the ESOP, which entered into two separate stock purchase agreements (SPAs). The first SPA committed the ESOP to purchase all of Todd's shares for $15,624,990, while in the second SPA, the trustees committed the ESOP to purchase newly issued shares from USCC itself at the same per-share price, for an additional $15,277,768.

The trustees ultimately concluded that USCC was worth in excess of $52 million, or a per-share price of $132,472, based upon the valuation report of Steven Kerrick. Kerrick had initially advised Thompson and McQueen on the structure of any proposed ESOP; Kerrick proposed several scenarios for structuring a potential ESOP for USCC, and he explained to Thompson and McQueen how each scenario would operate. In preparing these scenarios, Kerrick assumed that the value of USCC was $50 million and derived certain calculations from that hypothetical value. Kerrick then used the results from his hypothetical to illustrate the options available to USCC. Later, he performed a valuation that the evidence showed was designed to yield a value of about $50 million. The ESOP borrowed a total of $34,427,353 and used the proceeds to acquire approximately 66 percent of the outstanding shares of USCC.

The plaintiffs' breach of fiduciary duty theory was that the trustees did not conduct a reasonably prudent investigation regarding the value of USCC and so caused the ESOP to pay too much for Todd's stock.

---

[12] *Horn v. McQueen*, 215 F. Supp. 2d 867, 2002 U.S. Dist. LEXIS 14064 (W.D. Ky. July 29, 2002).

The District Court's Decision

The Court ruled that Thompson and McQueen had breached their fiduciary duty to the ESOP participants. It reached its decision because: (1) the defendants created the ESOP for the primary purpose of retaining management control of the company; (2) the defendants did not negotiate the price the ESOP was to pay USCC for the newly issued shares; (3) the defendants became trustees for the ESOP while remaining corporate officers and did not act independently on behalf of the ESOP participants; (4) the valuation of the corporation's stock was subjected to a compressed timetable because of the closing deadline imposed by Todd, and was apparently based upon the price Todd was asking for his stock; and (5) Thompson and McQueen's only inquiry as trustees regarding a preliminary valuation prepared by Kerrick was to question why the company was valued at less than they thought it was worth. The final valuation was considerably higher.

The Court held that damages should be measured by the difference between the fair market value of Todd's stock at the time of the transaction and what the ESOP paid for it. Because of the complexity and technical nature of the valuation testimony necessary to determine damages, the Court referred the case to a special magistrate to determine the fair market value of Todd's stock and recommend damages.

Commentary and Conclusion

This case sends the message to valuation professionals that if they are going to serve as an adviser on setting up an ESOP as well as the appraiser, then they must conduct a thorough, independent valuation, and not back into the valuation from a predetermined value.

Chao v. Hall Holding Co., Inc.

Introduction

In *Chao v. Hall Holding Co., Inc.*,[13] the U.S. Department of Labor brought suit against Hall Holding Co. and others on the grounds, among others, that they breached their fiduciary duty by purchasing Hall Holding stock for the employee stock ownership plan (ESOP) without conducting a prudent and independent investigation to determine the stock's fair market value.

The Facts of the Case

Goldman Financial Group, Inc. (GFGI), purchased Hall Chemical Co., through Hall Holding Co. (Hall Holding). Hall Chemical was Hall Holding's primary asset, with Hall Holding owning 95 percent of Hall Chemical. The decision was made to create Hall Chemical ESOP, and a valuation expert was hired to value Hall Chemical. However, the expert was not informed and never knew that the purpose

---

[13] *Chao v. Hall Holding Co., Inc.*, 285 F.3d 415, 2002 U.S. App. LEXIS 5929 (6th Cir. Apr. 3, 2002).

of the valuation was to determine how much an ESOP should pay for Hall Chemical stock. The expert concluded that Hall Chemical was worth between $32.4 and $37.4 million, exclusive of debt.

Based on this valuation, Hall Chemical's president and vice president, who were also trustees of the ESOP, offered to and did purchase for Hall Chemical ESOP 110 shares, or 9.9 percent, of Hall Holding stock for $3.5 million (the appraiser had not valued Hall Holding, however).

The District Court's Decision

The District Court, finding that Hall Holding stock should have been valued, conducted its own valuation. The Court concluded that the fair market value of Hall Holding stock was $2,450,451. It arrived at this value by using the valuation expert's range of value for the Hall Chemical stock, subtracting a $13.6 million debt of Hall Holding, and applying a 13 percent minority discount to account for the fact that the ESOP purchased only a minority interest (9.96 percent) in Hall Holding. The Court also took into account the negative accounts receivable and liabilities of Hall Holding, applied a 5 percent marketability discount, and applied a 5 percent discount to reflect the president's 5 percent interest in Hall Chemical stock.

The Court concluded that the trustees did not conduct a prudent and independent investigation to determine the fair market value of Hall Holding stock purchased by the Hall Chemical ESOP. The court also held that the ESOP was entitled to an award of $1,049,549, which represented the difference between the amount originally paid for the stock and the fair market value of the stock as determined by the Court.

The Appeals Court's Decision

The Sixth Circuit affirmed, concluding that the plan trustees had failed to prove that they had made a good faith inquiry into fair market value when: (1) the trustees relied on a valuation by an individual who had valued the wrong company and who testified that, if had he been told that the valuation would be used for an employee stock ownership plan transaction, he would have done a different valuation; (2) the trustees generally were "unaware of what was going on"; (3) the trustees were not consulted on major decisions, such as the price to pay for the stock; (4) the trustees did not engage in any negotiation as to the price of the stock; (5) the trustees were more concerned with the return on the investment for the trust that had financed the stock purchase than for the plan; and (6) the trustees caused the plan to be charged several thousands of dollars simply to enable the trustees to communicate using round numbers.

Commentary and Conclusion

This case serves as a valuable reminder that valuation professionals should make a detailed inquiry into the purpose of their valuation. Such inquiry in this case might have led the appraiser to discover that the valuation was for the purpose of establishing an ESOP, and might have led the appraiser to value the correct company for that purpose.

Keach v. U.S. Trust Co.

Introduction

Keach v. U.S. Trust Co. has spawned over 20 reported decisions. Those of primary concern to valuators are a U.S. District Court case that decided whether a valuation firm hired by a company's board of directors has fiduciary liability to the company's ESOP, and a U.S. Court of Appeals case that decided the liability of an ESOP's trustee in relying on a valuator's due diligence.

The Facts of the Case

Foster & Gallagher, Inc. (F&G), was a direct mail marketing company. The F&G ESOP began in 1988, when it purchased about 30 percent of F&G's stock from the company's founders. F&G's largest subsidiary conducted direct mail sweepstakes promotions to its customers. In 1995, a leveraged purchase of a large number of F&G shares by the ESOP was proposed. At that time, F&G had been enjoying record profitability for several years and was forecasted to continue this trend into the future.

On December 20, 1995, the ESOP, with U.S. Trust Company (U.S. Trust) acting as its trustee, purchased 3,589,743 shares of F&G stock from several F&G officers and directors at a price of $19.50 per share (the "ESOP II transaction"). F&G had retained Valuemetrics, Inc. (Valuemetrics) as its financial adviser to help structure the proposed ESOP II transaction. On September 30, 1995, Valuemetrics issued its first transaction memorandum to the F&G board of directors describing a proposed offer to sell 2,916,667 shares to the ESOP at $24 per share. U.S. Trust served as an independent trustee for the ESOP to consider the merits of the proposed transaction.

U.S. Trust, in turn, engaged Houlihan, Lokey, Howard, & Zukin (Houlihan) to assist in valuing the transaction and to render a written opinion to U.S. Trust as to whether the transaction was fair to the ESOP from a financial perspective. At the time of the ESOP II transaction, the risk of government regulation of sweepstakes was not considered significant. In preparing its opinion, Houlihan did not know what percentage of the company's sales were generated by sweepstakes (between 80 and 85 percent), or what the sweepstakes practices were, and did not learn of any regulatory or other risks associated with the practices. However, both U.S. Trust and Houlihan had visited the company's facilities, interviewed management, reviewed business plans, and examined documents.

After its inquiries into F&G and its subsidiaries, Houlihan prepared an analysis for U.S. Trust of F&G financials with respect to the offer price of $24 per share. Based on Houlihan's analysis, U.S. Trust determined that Valuemetrics' analysis was too optimistic in some respects. Houlihan prepared a new analysis reflecting a lower valuation range for the price of the F&G shares. U.S. Trust suggested a share price of $18.50; the final price of the transaction was $19.50.

For the next two years, F&G did enjoy record business; however, in 1998, in the wake of significantly increased sweepstakes regulation, its profits began to decline steadily until F&G declared bankruptcy in 2001. ESOP participants sued after the value of F&G shares had reached less than 50 percent of their original purchase price.

The Issues before the District Court

In the District Court case,[14] the plaintiffs asserted that Valuemetrics was a fiduciary to the ESOP plan because it (1) exercised control over plan assets and (2) rendered investment advice with respect to the property of the plan. Valumetrics moved for summary judgment, countering that it was not a fiduciary to the ESOP plan.

The District Court's Decision

The District Court agreed with Valumetrics. The Court first observed that a showing of authority or control requires actual decision-making power, rather than the type of influence a professional adviser may have with respect to decisions made by trustees. The court also noted that Valuemetrics was not hired by the ESOP plan to manage the plan assets or make investment decisions, nor was it retained by U.S. Trust, the ESOP's trustee, to serve in any capacity with the ESOP stock purchase transaction.

To the contrary, it was U.S. Trust, not Valuemetrics, that made the final decision and caused the ESOP to purchase the shares of stock, and that had hired Houlihan as its own independent financial adviser for the transaction. The transaction memoranda issued by Valuemetrics explicitly stated that while the memoranda were being submitted to the ESOP trustee and the trustee's legal advisers, Valuemetrics was acting as an adviser to the F&G board of directors, that the memoranda were being furnished solely to assist the board of directors in determining a proposed offering price, and that the ESOP trustee should perform its own independent investigation of the transaction.

Thus, the Court concluded that there was simply no evidence in the record indicating that U.S. Trust was a mere puppet acting out Valuemetrics' directives in carrying out its duties as trustee. The Court also found that there was no evidence indicating that Houlihan and the U.S. Trust simply rubber-stamped Valuemetrics' opinion. In fact, the evidence indicated precisely the opposite—Houlihan and Valuemetrics were on opposite sides of the negotiating table and Valuemetrics' position did not ultimately prevail.

With regard to investment advice, the Court stated that the record did not support a finding that Valuemetrics gave any investment advice to the ESOP regarding the ESOP II transaction. In light of a Department of Labor advisory opinion indicating that appraising the value of closely held stock for an ESOP does not constitute the rendering of investment advice, the Court held that Valuemetrics should not be a party to the action.

The Issues before the Appeals Court

In the Court of Appeals case,[15] one of the issues was whether Houlihan should have foreseen that within two years of its due diligence, the government would crack down on the company's sweepstakes promotions, and within three years, F&G would be bankrupt. The plaintiffs alleged that U.S. Trust had breached its fiduciary duty in relying on Houlihan's report. The District Court had found that,

---

[14] *Keach v. U.S. Trust Co.*, 239 F. Supp. 2d 820, 2002 U.S. Dist. LEXIS 24829 (C.D. Ill. Dec. 30, 2002).
[15] *Keach v. U.S. Trust Co.*, 419 F.3d 626, 2005 U.S. App. LEXIS 17355 (7th Cir. Aug. 17, 2005).

rather than blindly accept the forecasts of F&G officers as to F&G's financial future, "U.S. Trust and Houlihan probed and challenged a number of assumptions in Valuemetrics' evaluation before developing their own independent evaluation that formed the basis for a price per share at closing that was almost 20% less than the selling shareholders' offering price."

The Appeals Court's Decision

The Seventh Circuit Court of Appeals agreed, saying that "When the record establishes that the overlooked matter was one that no one perceived to be a material concern at the time or to be outcome determinative, it cannot be said that the overall investigation was imprudent or in bad faith. ERISA's fiduciary duty of care 'requires prudence, not prescience.'" The Court distinguished this case from that in *Chao v. Hall Holding Co.* (see the summary of the *Chao* case, above), saying that in the *Chao* case, the trustees failed to show they made a good faith inquiry into fair market value because, in part, they relied on a clearly inadequate valuation.

Commentary and Conclusion

This case demonstrates that a thorough, independent valuation, conducted in light of all known facts at the time, will withstand ERISA's bad faith or breach of the duty of care claims. The case is also consistent with the principle that valuation professionals do not need to be "fortune tellers" to provide defensible valuations.

Armstrong v. LaSalle Bank National Ass'n.

Introduction

In *Armstrong v. LaSalle Bank National Ass'n.*,[16] a key issue was whether an ESOP trustee breached its fiduciary duty by failing to apply a discount for lack of marketability (DLOM) to a redemption.

The Facts of the Case

Under the company's ESOP, Amsted Industries employees received company stock from the date of hire until the date of separation, when they could redeem all their shares for cash. Historically, employee departures fell within a 9 to 11 percent range. In 1999, Amsted obtained $1 billion unsecured credit to purchase a trucking operation for $800 million, leaving a $200 million reserve. Valuation professionals from Duff and Phelps, LLC valued the company at $184 per share—about 32 percent higher than the prior year's valuation. The trustee accepted the valuation, but the 2000 redemptions turned out to be 32 percent—around three times higher than the historic range. Given the excessive demands on cash flow, the trustee amended the ESOP to permit deferred eligibility and redemption. A class of

---

[16] *Armstrong v. LaSalle Bank National Ass'n.*, 2006 U.S. App. LEXIS 11077 (7th Cir. May 4, 2006).

participants then brought suit for breach of fiduciary duty, charging the trustee with an imprudent valuation for failing to apply a discount for lack of marketability to the redemption price.

The District Court's Decision

The Court, applying a due deference standard, found that the trustee had acted within its discretion by accepting the valuation without a DLOM, based on Amsted's history of redeeming employees' stock in full and in cash, as though sold on the open market.

The Appeals Court's Decision

On appeal, although the Seventh Circuit upheld the due deference standard as correct, it added that "a discretionary judgment cannot be upheld when discretion has not been exercised." The appellate court observed that there was no indication in the record that the trustee had considered how best to balance the interests of the various participants in the ESOP in the novel circumstances created by the company's acquisition or how that affected the risks borne by ESOP participants. Accordingly, the court remanded for a determination as to whether, under the circumstances, the trustee had exercised discretion and, if so, if it acted unreasonably by failing to apply a DLOM.

The Court explained that the less marketable a property is, the lower its market value; shares in closed-end mutual funds typically trade at prices lower than the prices of the stocks held by the funds because the mutual fund investor cannot sell his share of the stocks in the mutual fund's portfolio other than by selling shares of the fund. A participant in an ESOP is in a parallel position: he can sell his shares of his employer's stock only by quitting his job. And the ESOP could always be changed by Amsted—ultimately it was—to limit redemptions in the event of a run, thus further reducing the liquidity of the participant's investment. The average person would therefore prefer to own shares in a publicly traded company than in Amsted (if they were priced the same), even if the two companies had identical cash flows and risk profiles. And so they wouldn't be priced the same. By increasing the probability of a run, the trucking company acquisition increased the probability that rights of redemption by Amsted's employee-shareholders would be further restricted, and so the acquisition created a further threat to liquidity. Thus, given this scenario, the trustee most likely should have applied a discount for lack of marketability to account for reduced liquidity.

The Court, however, was not willing to speculate on what the magnitude of such a discount should have been if appropriate valuation techniques were applied to Amsted, or on how far a trustee can deviate from such techniques before he can be adjudged imprudent. The Court left these issues for exploration on remand if it was determined that the trustee had not failed to exercise discretion.

Commentary and Conclusion

A critical stage in the administration of an ESOP of a company whose shares are not traded is establishing the price at which an employee who leaves the company can redeem his shares. If the price is set too low, employees who leave will feel shortchanged. If it is set too high, it may precipitate so many departures—a run—that it endangers the firm's solvency. Setting a price for redemptions is difficult because by definition there is no market valuation of stock that isn't traded. An appraisal conducted by an independent valuation professional can thus be critical in establishing this price and helping the trustee avoid breach of fiduciary claims.

Kennedy v. Trustmark National Bank

Introduction

A case that supports the principle that neither trustees nor appraisers need to know the future is *Kennedy v. Trustmark National Bank*,[17] in which an ESOP appraisal furnished the fair market value of stock under a buy-sell agreement.

The Facts of the Case

After Kennedy was terminated, he wanted to redeem 300 shares of company stock, which under a buy-sell agreement could be valued at either (1) the ESOP valuation date coinciding with or immediately preceding his termination; or (2) the date on which he was terminated. The company picked the first option, using an annual ESOP valuation of $1,516 per share that occurred just prior to Kennedy's termination. However, because 10 months later the company sold for about $4,000 per share, Kennedy brought suit claiming that the sale to him had amounted to a "fraudulent scheme" and that, among other things, the company failed to inform the appraiser of its "imminent" sale.

The District Court's Decision

The Court noted that although the appraiser did not factor in any potential sale of the company—despite being aware that management had entered into "conversations" with a potential buyer—there had been no letter of intent, no final terms, and no settled transaction as of the valuation date. In fact, not even the majority shareholders (whose approval would have been required for a sale) knew about the discussions. Accordingly, the Court ruled that "[I]t would have been inappropriate and pointless to utilize, reference, or give credence to such uncertain, imprecise information and unsettled activities…for determining the controlling interest value of the company for ESOP purposes." In other words, the Court held, the appraised fair market value of the stock did not need to consider a sale which was, on the date of valuation, purely "speculative and uncertain."

Commentary and Conclusion

This case demonstrates that a thorough, independent valuation, conducted in light of all known facts at the time, will withstand ERISA's bad faith or breach of the

---

[17] *Kennedy v. Trustmark National Bank*, 2006 U.S. Dist. LEXIS 59079 (N.D. Fla. Aug. 22, 2006).

duty of care claims. The case also espouses the principle that valuation professionals do not need to be "fortune-tellers" to provide defensible valuations.

Summary

This chapter has reviewed numerous court cases that are noteworthy to ESOP valuation practitioners. The cases subject to review have been informative with regard
to (1) the acceptable (and unacceptable) employer corporation stock methodology
and (2) the preferred content of ESOP valuation opinion reports.

In addition to ESOP valuation analysts, many of these cases are instructive to
ESOP trustees and other ESOP practitioners. These cases discuss the responsibilities of ESOP fiduciaries—particularly with regard to employer corporation stock
purchase or sale transactions. ESOP practitioners should be familiar with the professional guidance provided by these court cases.

Chapter 34

Valuations for Ad Valorem Taxation

Introduction

This chapter will present many business valuation analyses that are conducted for purposes of ad valorem property taxation. These purposes include: (1) compliance (i.e., the annual administrative filing of property tax renditions), (2) assessment appeal, and (3) valuation and equalization litigation (including expert witness testimony).

First, we will define certain terminology that is specific to the ad valorem taxation assessment and appeal process. Second, we will introduce the basic principles of the property tax valuation process. Third, we will introduce the basic principles of the property tax equalization process. Fourth, we will introduce the basic principles of the property tax appeal process. Fifth, we will discuss the general functions that appraisers perform in the ad valorem taxation planning and compliance process. Sixth, we will present several special topics related to specific analyses that valuation analysts typically perform to assist taxpayers in the property taxation assessment, appeal, and litigation process. These special topics include the identification and quantification of functional obsolescence, the identification and quantification of external (or economic) obsolescence, the identification and valuation of intangible assets for taxpayers assessed under the unitary method of valuation, and the identification and application of appropriate income approach methods for ad valorem unitary valuation.

Definitions of Ad Valorem Taxation Terminology

The following brief definitions will acquaint the reader with some general terms that are used regularly in the ad valorem taxation planning and compliance process.

These definitions are consistent with, but not necessarily identical to, those presented in *Property Taxation*, published by the Institute of Professionals in Taxation, a prominent organization of professionals involved in the ad valorem taxation process.[1]

- **Assess**—to make an appraisal of the property in connection with a listing of the property liable to ad valorem taxation. It implies the exercise of discretion on the part of the public officials charged with the duty of property assessment, including the listing—or inventory—of the property involved and the conclusion of an appropriate, defined value on that property. The word assess is sometimes used interchangeably with the word *levy*.
- **Assessor**—a public official elected or appointed to discover, list, and appraise privately owned property for ad valorem property tax purposes.
- **Assessed valuation**—the value placed on each taxable unit by the assessor, which provides the basis to which the applicable property tax rate is applied to determine the amount to be paid by the property owner as property taxes.
- **Assessment roll**—a list, or roll, of all privately owned taxable property within a taxing authority jurisdiction completed, verified, and deposited by the local assessor.

---

[1] *Property Taxation*, 3rd ed. (Washington, DC: Institute of Professionals in Taxation, 2004).

- **Tax rate**—typically developed by dividing the total cost of the local government's annual budget by the total assessed value on the tax roll (i.e., all privately owned property within the local taxing jurisdiction). An example of the way taxing authorities set the property tax rate in their jurisdiction follows:

$$\frac{\text{Annual municipal budget}}{\substack{\text{Total assessed value of} \\ \text{private property per the tax role}}} = \frac{\$2,000,000}{\$100,000,000} = \substack{\text{A tax rate of 20 mills} \\ \text{(\$2 per \$100 or \$20} \\ \text{per \$1,000 of assessed} \\ \text{property valuation)}}$$

- **Equal and uniform taxation**—ad valorem taxes are considered to be equal and uniform when no taxpayer or class of taxpayers in the taxing district—whether it be a state, county, city, town, or village—is taxed at a rate different from other taxpayers in the same taxing district upon the same value or the same type of property. The concept of equal and uniform taxation is a basic statutory and judicial goal of ad valorem property taxation. The departure of this standard by a taxing authority is one of the principal justifications for a taxpayer's assessment appeal.
- **Equalization ratio**—the percentage of market value at which a property is assessed. The equalization ratio is often simply called the ratio.
- **Ratio study**—generally the comprehensive comparison of actual property sales or of appraised values of selected parcels to the taxing jurisdiction's assessments in order to determine the effective equalization rate or ratio.
- **Ad valorem**—literally, this phrase means "according to value." The term ad valorem tax means a tax or duty on the value of the property subject to taxation. Such property could include tangible personal property, a parcel of tangible real estate, or a mass collection of income-producing assets (as in the case of a business subject to the unitary property assessment method).
- **Certiorari**—the name of a writ of review or inquiry. In ad valorem property tax practice, it brings the taxpayer's assessment appeal into a superior court, based on the record of the administrative tribunal (e.g., a board of tax review) or of an inferior judicial tribunal.

Market Value as the General Basis of Property Assessment

The most common basis for assessing real estate and personal property in the United States is market value. This market-derived property assessment basis is often referred to in state statutes, in judicial opinions, and in the property tax literature by such terms as fair cash value, fair value, cash value, true value, true cost value, economic value, and other similar terminology.

Notwithstanding these local statutory phrases, all these definitions have generally come to mean the most likely price at which a property will sell from a willing seller to a willing buyer, both cognizant of all pertinent facts and neither being under duress.

However, this classic "willing buyer–willing seller" definition should sometimes be tempered when there are no comparable sales transactions in the appropriate competitive market. This is often the situation in the case of special purpose properties such as mining operations, certain chemical processing operations, timber or other special agricultural businesses, or any other properties that are special purpose or unique properties. In these instances, a form of the cost approach to property valuation is often the most appropriate valuation approach when recent market data regarding property sale transactions are not available.

Nonetheless, when either a cost approach or an income approach is used to value special purpose assessable property—because a lack of recent transactional data regarding such special purpose properties does not allow the effective use of the market approach—the objective of the analysis is still to estimate the market value of the subject property.

The Property Tax Valuation Process

As with the valuation of tangible and intangible properties for any purpose, there are three basic approaches to the valuation of property for ad valorem taxation purposes: the cost approach, the income approach, and the sales comparison (or market) approach.

In the cost approach to property valuation, four basic steps are involved:

1. The subject land (if any) is valued as if vacant and unimproved.
2. The reproduction or replacement cost of the building, site improvements, or personal property is estimated at current prices.
3. Allowances for physical depreciation, functional obsolescence, technological obsolescence, and external (including location and economic) obsolescence are subtracted.
4. The land value (if any) is added to this estimate of the depreciated replacement cost of the improvements and the personal property.

In the income approach to property valuation, the value of the property is based on its ability to produce either a net operating income or a net rental income. A capitalization rate is then divided into this economic income stream to convert it into an estimate of the taxable property's current value.

In the sales comparison or market approach, actual sales of similar properties are analyzed and a value is estimated for the subject property by a process of comparison.

The Property Tax Equalization Process

In determining the equalized valuations required by state statutes, local property tax assessment authorities often make and issue comprehensive assessment ratio studies. These assessment ratio studies analyze the average level of assessment, the degrees of assessment, uniformity, and the overall compliance with the assessment and classification requirements for each major class of property in each jurisdiction. These assessment ratio studies are performed to indicate (1) the degree of compliance with the law and rules and regulations of the assessment jurisdiction and (2) the proper classification of property in each assessment jurisdiction.

To ensure the equalization of the assessment process, assessment authorities typically collect and tabulate information relative to the sales of properties within their jurisdiction. They also cause valuations to be made of properties of various classes in their jurisdiction (selected on a basis of random sampling or otherwise) to (1) confirm the assessment ratio derived from property sale prices, (2) assist in determining the appropriate assessment ratio when the number of actual property sales is insufficient to represent a specific class of properties in the jurisdiction, (3) provide a substitute for the actual sale prices of properties of a unique character or that are sold at infrequent intervals, and (4) establish an assessment ratio for the tangible personal property (as opposed to the real estate) assessed in their jurisdiction.

Assessment Ratio Studies

Assessment ratio studies, designed to compare the assessed value with the market value of property, are performed principally for evaluating the accuracy of the assessment process and for ensuring valuation equalization in the assessment process. Property tax assessment authorities often use assessment ratio studies: (1) to establish the necessity for general revaluations, (2) to identify any problems with their appraisal procedures, (3) to "trend" property valuations between general reappraisal dates, (4) to adjust actual property sale prices for time, and (5) to develop property depreciation factors. Tax equalization officials also use assessment ratio studies to estimate the total market value of taxable property in their jurisdiction. This estimation is made, in part, to bring centrally assessed properties in line with locally assessed properties, from an assessment fairness perspective.

Use of Assessment Ratio Studies in Administrative Appeals and Litigation

An assessment ratio study is a means of testing the fairness of the property assessment procedure in a given jurisdiction. Property tax assessment authorities are generally required by law to assess all property in an assessing district uniformly. Only through an assessment ratio study can one determine whether the assessor meets this statutory requirement.

After reviewing some basic tax equalization concepts, the following section will discuss how to determine whether an assessment ratio study is justified, how to conduct one, and how to use it in property tax assessment negotiations.

To understand how to use an assessment ratio study, taxpayers and their valuation advisers should understand the following basic concepts in ad valorem taxation: uniformity, changing values and their impact on uniformity, market values, and the assessment ratio.

Uniformity. The concept of uniformity in property tax assessment equalization is related to the most basic principle of ad valorem taxes. As mentioned above, ad valorem means "according to value." In very practical terms, this means that each dollar of property value is to be assessed so it will contribute the same amount of tax revenue to operate the local government. A $1 million personal residence should be assessed so the owner's tax burden will equal exactly the owner's tax burden that will result from a $1 million assessment on a retail commercial property, or a $1 million multifamily apartment house, or a $1 million parcel of vacant land, or a $1 million industrial building, or any other type of property in the assessment jurisdiction having a $1 million value on the same date.

A logical extension of this concept is that, as of a given date, the value of each separate property on an assessment roll in the taxing jurisdiction will be established for assessment purposes. This value will presumably relate to market value. The assessor then assesses each property in proportion to its market value. The assessment may be at 100 percent of market value (i.e., full value assessment), or, if the statute permits, the assessment may be at some fraction of market value (i.e., uniform assessment). So long as each property is treated equally, the assessment process has been equalized, and the ad valorem tax burden has been equalized.

Changing Values. Changing property values may create the need for an assessment ratio study. Even if the assessment roll was properly assembled and represented an equalized distribution of assessments at a given date, over time, the values of the various properties will typically change at different rates. Some types of property (for example, retail commercial property) may increase in value at a greater rate than other types of property.

Within a comparatively short time period, therefore, the assessment roll (which may have been uniform when it was assembled) is no longer equalized. The longer this situation continues without correction, the more inequitable the assessment roll becomes. If the assessments on these properties are not adjusted—that is, equalized—to reflect the varying rates of change in property value that occur over time, then the assessments no longer represent either (1) a full value assessment or (2) a uniform assessment.

Market Value. The definition of market value in the assessment process is no different from the definition of market value generally. In estimating market value, the valuation analyst considers all the usual marketplace factors involved in and affecting the value of property. Among other criteria, appraisers consider income potential, typical financing patterns, zoning, development capacity, street frontage, land area and/or plottage, neighborhood characteristics and influences, availability and sufficiency of municipal utilities and services, functional utility of the structural and site improvements, convenience of and proximity to transportation facilities, marketability, and all other factors usual and necessary to the formulation of an opinion of value.

The Assessment Ratio. The assessor begins with market value in assessing property for ad valorem tax purposes. Market value is generally the basis on which any assessment equalization is made. When an assessment roll is no longer uniform or equalized, one of the two items necessary to prove an inequitable or discriminatory property tax assessment is the market value of the subject property. The other item is the assessment ratio—that is, the ratio of the property's assessment to the property's market value—and whether the assessment ratio for the individual property exceeds the assessment ratio applicable to all other property on the same assessment roll as of the same date.

The Property Tax Unitary Valuation Process

Estimating the fair market value of an individual property such as an office building or an apartment complex is relatively straightforward. The taxable location of the property is readily ascertainable, and its value can be directly obtained by analyzing comparable sales, market-derived rental rates, and replacement or reproduction cost.

Many properties, however, are components of interrelated and interdependent operating business systems that span numerous taxing jurisdictions. Examples of such operating business systems include: traditional utilities, such as electric power generating companies; partially regulated but highly competitive businesses, such as long-distance telecommunications companies, railroads and airlines; and businesses in transition, such as telephone companies.

The reason for the unitary valuation concept is the recognition that it is not possible to accurately value, for property tax purposes, the property of (for example) a railroad in one taxing jurisdiction simply by analyzing that property in isolation. Rather, it is more practical to value the entire operating system and then apportion some of that value to each taxing jurisdiction. This is the basic concept of unit value, sometimes referred to as *unitary value* or *system value*.

This approach to valuing an integrated bundle of operating assets has been extended to value business enterprise types other than railroads. This extension logically covers other interstate, capital-intensive businesses that employ operating systems of interdependent interrelated assets in multiple taxing jurisdictions. Historically (although much less so today), these companies were almost always publicly regulated utilities.

One issue that is implicitly present in the unit valuation process is that the going-concern value of the entire operating business is being estimated rather than the market value of the taxpayer's tangible property only. In other words, a fundamental question of the unitary valuation process is: Does this process value the overall business enterprise or does it value only the assessable assets of a taxpayer (albeit on a collective basis)?

The Property Tax Appeal Process

When assessment and millage rate formulas are consistently applied, the ad valorem assessment and taxation process is inherently fair and equitable. Disputes regarding valuation and/or equalization are inevitable, however.

Such disagreements usually arise when property owners believe that the market value placed on their property is excessive or overstated (either in absolute terms or in comparison with other properties in the same taxing jurisdiction).

For this reason, ad valorem assessments of property values are often vigorously contested and appealed. Such disputes are often resolved (at varying points in the administrative or judicial appeal process) through soundly reasoned, rigorously prepared, and comprehensively documented independent appraisals.

The ad valorem property tax assessment appeal process encompasses systematic procedures employed to answer specific questions regarding the value of real estate and tangible personal property. This process starts with the identification of the valuation problem and ends with a reporting on the valuation results.

For each ad valorem assessment appeal valuation, the analytical and quantitative procedures depend on the nature of the assignment, the type of properties appraised, the purpose and objective of the valuation, and the quantity and quality of available data.

Steps in the Ad Valorem Taxation Valuation Process

All ad valorem assessment appeal valuations generally follow the process below:

1. Definition of the scope, objective, and purpose of the valuation.
2. Identification, inspection, and inventory of the assets subject to valuation.
3. Market research and analysis of all available valuation data.
4. Contemplation of the three generally accepted approaches to property valuation.
5. Selection of the quantitative and qualitative valuation methods and procedures to be used in the subject valuation.
6. Performance of the selected valuation approaches, methods, and procedures.
7. Integration and synthesis of the results of the various valuation approaches, methods, and procedures.
8. Reporting of the final conclusion of property value.

The Assessing Authority's Objective

The objective of the property tax assessing authorities in setting ad valorem taxes is to estimate the value of all taxable properties within a given jurisdiction fairly and equitably—yet also efficiently and economically. Assessing authorities are supposed to treat owners of similar properties fairly and equally.

The Property Owner's Objective

The objective of a property owner is to ascertain the correct market value of his or her property and to file a property tax return reflecting that value. If an initial assessment is overstated or if the assessing authority does not accept a property owner's value for the property, extensive administrative and judicial appeal processes are available.

The Independent Valuation Analyst's Objective

The objective of the independent valuation analyst is to prepare the most soundly reasoned and thoroughly documented valuation possible. The analyst should also remain independent and objective during the ad valorem assessment appeal process. While valuation analysts can perform certain advisory and consultative services—and act as intermediaries on behalf of their taxpayer clients—independent valuation analysts cannot become advocates or perform advocacy functions with regard to valuation or equalization appeals.

Special Topics

Many ad valorem taxation valuation issues are best addressed in textbooks related to real estate appraisal or personal property appraisal. However, financial valuation analysts often become involved in the economic analysis aspects of property taxation valuation. These "special topics" are appropriately covered in this book.

In the next few sections of this chapter, we will explore several "special topics" in which financial valuation analysts may be particularly helpful to property owners in the ad valorem tax property valuation and equalization process—and in the ad valorem tax assessment appeal process.

Identification and Quantification of Functional Obsolescence

While functional obsolescence is most closely associated with the cost approach to property valuation, it is a consideration in the sales comparison and the income approaches to property valuation as well. In the sales comparison approach, the analyst attempts to select and analyze comparable properties with similar levels of functional obsolescence. In the income approach, the analyst attempts to ensure that the subject property's economic income stream is properly adjusted for the economic detriments associated with the subject property's functional obsolescence.

Definition of Functional Obsolescence. Functional obsolescence is an impairment of the functional utility of a property according to current market tastes and standards. To apply the concept properly—and it applies to all types of property—one needs to be aware that functional obsolescence can be curable or incurable. In addition, functional obsolescence represents more than practical usefulness—that is, it can take the form of superadequacies, as well as inadequacies.

A superadequacy is an excess in the capacity or quality of a property as compared with market standards. One example of a superadequacy is a warehouse with a ceiling height far greater than that required by the existing operations of the tenant or of the marketplace at large. An inadequacy is a characteristic of the subject property that is of a lower standard as compared with the marketplace. A three-bedroom apartment with only one bathroom is an example of an inadequacy.

Sample Situations. It is possible to construct an endless list of examples of functional obsolescence. The following examples are intended only to be illustrative in nature:

- Commercial office buildings may have public spaces such as corridors that are abnormally wide or oversized.
- Some commercial amenities are considered standard in office complexes (e.g., express elevators, telecommunication hookups, inside parking, and retail space); the lack of these amenities may indicate the existence of functional obsolescence.
- Shopping centers that are nonenclosed or have an inappropriate floor plan (e.g., one with an unsuccessful skating rink in the center).
- Instances of inadequate lighting, heating, or air conditioning typically represent functional obsolescence. These instances occur mostly in older buildings. They also may occur in cases in which facilities are currently being used for a purpose other than that for which they were constructed. Instances of excessive (and therefore partially unused) lighting, heating, or air conditioning also can represent functional obsolescence.
- A manufacturing or processing plant that is too large to accommodate the current or planned levels of business operations. In other words, there is significant excess capacity. Or a manufacturing or processing plant may be too small to accommodate the current level of business operations, so there are operating inefficiencies and a paucity of capacity.

- For the particular type of production or processing operation in the facility, the plant ceilings may be too low—or too high. Likewise, for the particular type of production or processing operating in the facility, the plant floors may be too thin—or too thick.
- There may be excess construction costs in an older plant because the walls are too thick (as compared with modern construction techniques and materials). Likewise, in older plants, the walls may be too thin to allow for the current production or processing operations to occur on higher floors. In addition, in many older plants, concrete or other types of load-bearing columns consume excessive plant floor area or disrupt an otherwise efficient materials or production flow.
- Other than the load-bearing columns mentioned previously, there may be numerous examples of structural or physical impediments to material-processing flow or product-manufacturing flow. Inefficient layout or design, related both to real estate and to tangible personal property, are among the most common examples of functional obsolescence.

Identification of Functional Obsolescence. Many property owners realize that their existing properties are experiencing functional obsolescence only after they have purchased or constructed new properties. When the input, output, or operations of the older properties are compared with those of the newer properties, instances of functional obsolescence become clearly evident.

In some cases, the property owner may identify functional obsolescence not by comparison of the subject properties with new properties, but rather by comparison of the subject properties with competitors' properties. When competitors have purchased new assets or constructed new facilities, these new properties provide a basis for comparison with the subject properties. Such a comparison can indicate instances of functional obsolescence.

Proper Applications. Functional obsolescence enters the property valuation process in each of the three traditional approaches to property value.

Income Approach. Property tax assessors often estimate a fair market value indication using the income approach by projecting a prospective economic income stream and then capitalizing it. This simple approach may ignore the future costs to be incurred to make necessary corrections of design deficiencies (e.g., the costs involved in eliminating excess office space in an office/warehouse). Because of this design deficiency, the prospective economic income may not be stable. Furthermore, the comparable properties used to estimate the appropriate capitalization rate may not be suffering from the same amount of functional obsolescence as the subject property is subject to.

Sales Comparison Approach. Any sales comparison approach to analysis depends on the degree of comparability of the "comparable" property sales considered. Adjustments to comparable properties are made to account for, among other things, the functional deficiencies of the subject property—as compared with the functional deficiencies experienced by the comparable properties.

Cost Approach. Property tax assessors often use some version of the cost approach, particularly with regard to the valuation of special purpose properties. Original costs are often increased based on indexing factors that adjust for property inflation factors and are then adjusted downward in an attempt to adjust for all forms of depreciation and obsolescence, including functional obsolescence. When used properly, the cost approach considers the various functional obsolescence factors impacting the subject property. To be curable, the cost of correcting the functional obsolescence must be the same or less than the anticipated increase in the subject property value. Functional obsolescence is curable if correcting it on the date of the appraisal is economically feasible—otherwise, it is incurable. Curable functional obsolescence is typically measured by the cost to correct the deficiency.

Quantification of Functional Obsolescence. Clearly, after identifying and documenting significant instances of functional obsolescence, the next step in the property tax valuation process is the quantification of functional obsolescence. Although many individual methods and procedures are available to quantify specific instances of functional obsolescence, all these procedures and techniques are often categorized into one or two methods.

The first method of quantifying functional obsolescence involves calculating the difference between the reproduction cost new and the replacement cost new of the subject property. The second method of quantifying functional obsolescence involves the capitalization of excess operating expenses (i.e., the costs of materials, labor and overhead) associated with the operation of the subject property.

Reproduction versus Replacement Cost New. This method is particularly useful when estimating incurable functional obsolescence associated with special purpose real estate and tangible personal property. In fact, the principal difference between the reproduction cost and the replacement cost of the subject property is the amount of incurable functional obsolescence. Those elements of functional obsolescence that are incurable should be eliminated before the estimation of replacement cost new (i.e., the cost to purchase or construct a new, state-of-the-art productive asset or property).

Although it is a complex engineering and appraisal process to estimate both the reproduction cost new and the replacement cost new for the subject property, it is relatively easy to estimate the associated functional obsolescence. Once both the reproduction cost and the replacement cost have been estimated, the amount of incurable functional obsolescence is typically the mathematical difference between the two cost estimations.

Capitalization of Excess Operating Expenses. This method typically quantifies the amount of curable functional obsolescence associated with the subject property. The approach quantifies the economic penalty associated with operating the subject property (given all its elements of functional obsolescence) instead of curing the subject property (and thereby eliminating the excess operating costs).

As mentioned previously, excess operating expenses include the material, labor, and overhead expenses associated with operating the subject property. In the appraisal of tangible personal property, for example, excess material expenses should include the expense of carrying excess raw material and work-in-process inventory, as well as the excess expense of waste and scrappage due to a functionally obsolete machine or process. Excess labor expenses should include the costs of employee fringe benefits and employment taxes, as well as the direct expenses of excess machine operators, material handlers, and so on. Excess overhead expenses should include the costs of excess electricity, gas, water, property and casualty insurance, rent, security, and property tax expense associated with operating the functionally obsolete property.

It is somewhat more difficult to quantify the amount of curable functional obsolescence associated with the capitalized excess operating expense method than with the replacement cost versus reproduction cost method. First, the excess expenses have to be identified and documented. This requires an estimation of what a normal level of operating expenses would be. Normal operating expenses may mean industry norms, expense data from specific competitors, expense data from other facilities operated by the same property owner, or historical operating expense data related to the subject property. Next, these excess operating expenses must be projected over the remaining useful life of the subject property. For the purposes of this projection, the remaining useful life typically means the lowest of the subject property's physical life or economic life.

The projection of excess operating expenses should be quantified as a present value, using an appropriate present value discount rate. This discount rate should reflect the property owner's cost of capital, the time value of money, and the risk associated with property ownership. Accordingly, the quantification of functional obsolescence using the capitalized excess operating expense method requires the appraiser to perform several detailed analyses.

Summary of Functional Obsolescence Issues. Functional obsolescence is an impairment (inadequate or superadequate) of the functional utility of a property according to current market tastes and standards. It can be curable or incurable. The cost to correct incurable functional obsolescence exceeds the resulting increase in value.

Using the income approach to property valuation, functional obsolescence is quantified indirectly. That is because a property with functional obsolescence will generate less economic income to be capitalized in the income approach analysis. In the sales comparison approach to property valuation, functional obsolescence also will be quantified indirectly. That is because the analyst will be required to make a number of adjustments to allow for the noncomparability of less functionally obsolete properties in the market data comparison base. In the cost approach to property valuation, functional obsolescence is specifically identified and quantified. This direct approach to the quantification of functional obsolescence requires the application of appraisal procedures to the financial and operational results caused by the elements of functional obsolescence.

In many ad valorem property assessments, functional obsolescence is not adequately identified or quantified by either the property owner or the assessing authority. However, a competent and comprehensive ad valorem property tax valuation will both identify and quantify all elements of functional obsolescence—and thus properly estimate the fair market value of the subject property.

Identification and Quantification of the Economic Component of External Obsolescence

There are two components to external obsolescence: (1) locational obsolescence and (2) economic obsolescence. Both of these components can directly impact the valuation of properties for ad valorem assessment purposes.

Locational obsolescence is a decrement in the value of a property due to changes in the physical environment in which the property operates. An example of locational obsolescence would be the construction of a nuclear power plant next to a luxury hotel—presumably the value of the hotel would decrease. Another example would be the construction of a high-rise office building between the subject office building and the lakefront—without its current lakefront views, the rental rates of the subject office building will decline and the value of the subject office property will decrease.

Economic obsolescence is the decrement in the value of a property due to changes in the economic condition of the industry in which that property operates. For example, as the trucking industry proves to be a cost-effective substitute to the railroad industry (and railroad industry profit margins decline due to the effect of the competition), then the value of special purpose properties used in the railroad industry will decrease.

Locational obsolescence is a topic that may more fully be explored in a text related to real estate appraisal. In this section, we will further discuss economic obsolescence and its effect on the value of properties for ad valorem assessment purposes.

Definition of Economic Obsolescence. Economic obsolescence is a reduction in the value of real estate and of tangible personal property due to the impact of events or conditions that are external to and not controlled by the physical nature or the structural or mechanical operation of the property.

Due to the dual characteristics of being (1) beyond the control of the property owners and (2) physically separate from the property, economic obsolescence is considered to be a form of external obsolescence. Although economic obsolescence manifests itself externally to the subject property, its valuation impact is as real and quantifiable as any other form of obsolescence.

Identification of Economic Obsolescence. Of all the forms of obsolescence, economic obsolescence is, arguably, the most difficult to identify and quantify. In fact, economic obsolescence is often best evidenced by a reduction in the value of property that cannot be explained by any of the other forms of obsolescence.

With respect to special purpose properties, the following conditions may indicate the existence of economic obsolescence:

- Changes in zoning or zoning requirements.
- A significant increase in the number of comparable properties on the market.
- Changes in pedestrian or other traffic flow patterns around the subject property.
- The plan for or the erection of unsightly or incongruous-use properties near the subject property.
- A sudden or gradual decrease in the maintenance of properties in the subject locale (e.g., the deterioration of an older residential neighborhood).
- Otherwise unexplained decreases in occupancy or rental rates and increases in tenant turnover.
- Increases in local or regional unemployment, local or regional interest rates, or local or regional utility rates.
- Changes in local or regional government policies regarding economic development and local or regional industry mix.

Forms of Economic Obsolescence. There are two significant categories or forms of economic obsolescence. The first category deals with curability; the second deals with universality. Curability relates to whether the economic obsolescence is curable or incurable. Universality relates to whether the economic obsolescence is local, regional, or national.

Curable economic obsolescence means the events or conditions that caused the obsolescence can be cured (i.e., fixed, repaired, or terminated) as the result of some expenditure of time, effort, or money. Incurable economic obsolescence means the events or conditions that caused the obsolescence cannot be changed, at least not by the owner of the property, regardless of the amount of expenditure of time, effort, or money.

Because economic obsolescence is caused by factors external to the physical structure of the property, most economic obsolescence is considered to be incurable. That is, the owner of the property cannot change the events or conditions that are causing the decrease in the value of the subject property. However, as there are no absolutes in valuation science, it is erroneous to assume all economic obsolescence is incurable.

For example, a real estate developer may construct a luxury hotel. Shortly after the hotel's construction, the neighborhood zoning is changed to allow a garbage dump to be operated next to the new hotel. Clearly, as occupancy rates dwindle, the otherwise luxurious hotel will experience substantial economic obsolescence. However, such economic obsolescence may be curable. It is conceivable, and perhaps economically astute, for the real estate developer to purchase the garbage dump site and turn it into an appealing, verdant park. In this example, the curative expenditure was not made on the subject property, yet the substantial economic obsolescence was cured.

However, it is true that most economic obsolescence is incurable. For example, suppose the same real estate developer constructed his luxury hotel at what was to be a major exit of a planned limited-access interstate highway. After the hotel is built, federal funds are canceled and the highway is never constructed. Clearly, this luxury hotel will experience prodigious economic obsolescence. Without the powers of eminent domain, it would be impossible, if not otherwise impractical and uneconomical, for the real estate developer to complete the highway. Thus, this hypothetical situation illustrates incurable economic obsolescence.

Universality. The universality of economic obsolescence relates to its geographic impact. The degree of the impact of universality on the value of a property is a function of two factors. First, the special purpose versus general purpose nature of the property determines the impact of universality. Second, the breadth and scope of the secondary market for that property type determine the level of influence on universality.

Local economic obsolescence affects the value of properties located only within a locally defined geographic vicinity. For example, changes in zoning affect only those properties within a certain business district. Regional economic obsolescence affects the value of properties on a regional, statewide, or multistate basis. For example, when the semiconductor industry becomes depressed, real estate up and down the Silicon Valley will experience some economic obsolescence. Of course, national economic obsolescence affects all properties used in a certain industry, or in some other global category, on a nationwide basis. For example, when spot oil prices drop below $10 per barrel, the secondary market values for oil well drilling equipment decrease materially, due to economic obsolescence, on a nationwide basis.

Typically, properties that are very general purpose in nature are affected more by local economic obsolescence. Properties that are very special purpose in nature are affected more by national economic obsolescence. For example, the value of a general purpose commercial office building would be affected by local zoning requirements, local economic conditions, local interest rates, and local supply and demand for leased office space. A special purpose sulfuric acid processing plant would be affected by national economic trends, national and international trends in the sulfuric acid industry, and the supply and demand from both plant inputs and outputs on a global basis.

Properties that sell in specialized local secondary markets are affected more by local economic obsolescence. Properties that sell in broad general secondary markets are affected more by national economic obsolescence.

Quantification of Economic Obsolescence. On a local level, economic obsolescence affects real estate to a greater extent than tangible personal property. Each of the three real estate valuation approaches encompasses procedures to quantify economic obsolescence.

Multiple regression analyses—or other quantitative procedures—are often used in the sales comparison approach. These procedures allow for the identification and quantification of the impact of several independent variables on the value of the dependent variable (i.e., the value of the subject property). The actual independent variable elements that are used in the analysis will vary, based on the quality and quantity of available data, the kind of property valued, and the judgment and experience of the analyst. However, independent variables such as interest rates, time adjustments (i.e., elapsed time while the property was listed on the market before sale), and rental rates, or changes in rental rates, are not uncommon. Such independent variables encompass measures of local economic obsolescence.

The income approach to property valuation requires both current analyses of—and prospective projections of—rental income, vacancy and collection losses, tenant renewal rates, operating expenses, and capitalization rates. Clearly, projections that encompass lower rental rates, higher vacancy and collection losses, lower renewal rates, higher operating expenses, and higher capitalization rates have included implicitly, if not explicitly, a quantification of local economic obsolescence.

The specific identification and quantification of economic obsolescence are most closely associated with the cost approach to property valuation. The cost approach requires an estimate of either the replacement cost or the reproduction cost of the subject real property. From this estimate, allowances are subtracted for all forms of accrued depreciation and obsolescence—including economic obsolescence.

Using the cost approach, there are several commonly used methods for quantifying local economic obsolescence. One method involves estimating the reduction in annual net operating income associated with the specific economic obsolescence factors. This reduction in annual net operating income is capitalized to estimate the total amount of local economic obsolescence.

As with local economic obsolescence, there are several methods for quantifying national or industrywide economic obsolescence. For the most part, these methods all involve factors that are relatively macroeconomic and affect an industry on a global basis. Also, these methods typically involve an analysis of the relative change in these factors—for example, a specific macroeconomic factor today compared with the five-year average value for that factor.

One element frequently associated with industrywide economic obsolescence is the change in product selling prices. Typically, if average product selling prices across the industry decline materially, and with some anticipated level of permanence, then economic obsolescence occurs with respect to the special purpose real property and tangible personal property used in that industry. For example, a general and prolonged reduction in the price of a barrel of crude oil will cause economic obsolescence to occur in the assets used in the oil and gas exploration industry.

A current and sustained reduction in the level of investor returns, compared with historical industry averages, also indicates economic obsolescence on an industrywide basis. Appropriate measures of investor returns would include return on net assets, return on total assets, return on investment, return on equity, and return on tangible assets.

When rates of investor return are reduced industrywide, property owners cannot afford to replace worn-out productive properties with either new or used properties. If the property owners are earning an inadequate rate of return on their investments in the productive properties, they will not expect to earn an adequate rate of return on investment in new or replacement properties. Since the "return" portion of the formula is controlled by macroeconomic events, the "investment" portion of the formula will be affected by the property owners. That is, the property owners will continue to bid down or reduce the value of the subject properties until their level of investment in the subject properties is low enough to allow them to earn a fair return on investment. For example, as across-the-board rates of investor return declined in the steel industry a few years ago, the value of properties employed in the steel industry correspondingly declined, due to industrywide economic obsolescence.

Associated with rates of investor return, current and sustained reductions in the levels of profit margins also may be indicative of industrywide economic obsolescence. For example, in an industry that has historically earned a 10 percent net profit margin (e.g., return on sales) and now earns only 6 percent, industrywide economic obsolescence associated with the special purpose real estate and tangible personal property will become evident.

One method that may be used to quantify both company-specific (nonsystematic) economic obsolescence and industrywide (systematic) economic obsolescence involves the estimation of a company's business enterprise value. The business enterprise valuation encompasses the going-concern value of all the company's assets, including financial assets, real estate, tangible personal property, and intangible personal property. To determine the existence of economic obsolescence, the business enterprise value is compared with the depreciated replacement cost of the company's productive assets. If the business enterprise value is less than the depreciated replacement cost of the company's assets, then economic obsolescence typically exists.

Issues in Unit Valuation for Ad Valorem Purposes

Under the summation concept, each real property and personal property asset of the taxpayer is appraised individually. The respective values for all of the individual real property and personal property assets are summed (hence, the name "summation concept"). The sum of the individual asset values represents the collective valuation of all of the industrial or commercial taxpayer assets subject to property taxation.

Under the unitary concept, first, the entire business enterprise of the industrial or commercial taxpayer is valued as a "unit"—or as a single mass assemblage of operating assets. Second, the value of any individual asset or property type not assessable as part of the taxable unit is removed from the overall unit valuation. The residual, or remainder, is the taxable unit—that is, the value of the industrial or commercial taxpayer's assets subject to assessment. Third, for businesses that operate in several different taxing jurisdictions, an allocation of the taxpayer's total unit value to a particular jurisdiction is made. Last, the value of any assets exempt from unitary assessment in the local jurisdiction (e.g., locally assessed assets or over-the-road vehicles) is removed from the allocated taxable unit.

As we will explore in our discussion of "what is the unit subject to ad valorem taxation?" the objective of the taxpayer's unit valuation is not always the same as the objective of the taxpayer's business enterprise valuation. Nonetheless, the approaches, methods, and procedures generally used in both valuations are essentially the same.

In this section, we will summarize the generally accepted unit valuation approaches. We will compare and contrast these unit valuation approaches with the generally accepted business enterprise valuation approaches. Next, we will consider the related questions of:

1. What is the "unit" subject to ad valorem taxation?
2. Do the generally accepted unit valuation approaches actually value that appraisal subject?

Then, we will explore some of the current controversial issues related to the application of the individual unit valuation approaches. Lastly, we will consider some of the valuation differences between an assemblage of operating assets and a capitalization structure of negotiable securities—from an investment risk and expected return perspective.

Unit Valuation. First, we will describe the types of industrial and commercial companies that are typically subject to unit valuation for ad valorem taxation purposes. Second, we will introduce the standard unit valuation approaches. And, third, we will compare the standard unit valuation approaches with the standard business valuation approaches.

The Background of Unit Valuation. Traditionally, the unit valuation concept was applied to transportation, communication, and utility companies. These categories of industries include railroads and airlines; local exchange, long-distance, and cellular telephone companies; gas, water, and electric utilities; and oil and gas pipeline companies. The rationale for applying the unit valuation concepts to these types of taxpayers includes the following arguments:

1. The taxpayer assets are located in numerous taxing jurisdictions; in fact, they often cross numerous state lines.
2. The taxpayer assets are fully integrated from a physical, functional, and an economic perspective; it does not make sense to analyze any one set of assets separately from the overall operating unit.
3. The individual taxpayer assets are physically, functionally, technologically, and economically part of one system; most of the systematic and nonsystematic risk factors that affect the system also affect the individual assets.
4. The value of any of the taxpayer assets is a function of the assets being part of an income-producing mass assemblage of assets; the independent values of the individual assets are not reflective of the contributory value of the assets to the overall unit.
5. For some of these taxpayers (e.g., railroads and airlines), the taxpayer assets physically move; it may be difficult—and unfair—to independently value the

individual assets based upon their physical location on any one particular assessment (i.e., valuation) date.

Many of these arguments for the use of the unit valuation concept are factual and logical. However, there is an additional factor that distinguishes companies in most (if not all) of the above-mentioned industries: Historically, they were all regulated. And, many of these industries were rate regulated—that is, subject to the mechanism of an allowed maximum rate of return on investment times an allowed "rate base" (i.e., the level of investment of assets placed in service).

The unit valuation concept essentially equates the value of the taxpayer's debt and equity instruments (sometimes called the market value of invested capital) to the value of the taxpayer's assessable assets in place as of a particular valuation date. For many reasons that are not relevant to this discussion, the concept of unit valuation may have been much more appropriate when these taxpayers were regulated (and, particularly, when they were subject to a "rate base" related regulatory environment).

However, most of the taxpayers that are currently subject to unit valuation are no longer regulated companies. In fact, most transportation, communications, and (to some extent) utilities now operate in an unregulated, competitive economic structure. In a free market, competitive economic structure, prices, rates of return, and profits are much less predictable. Therefore, the basic premise of unit valuation (i.e., that the value of negotiable securities equals the value of assessable assets) may not be as applicable as it once was.

Some local assessment taxing jurisdictions have expanded the category of companies that are subject to unit valuation to include physically local (i.e., located within one taxing jurisdiction) but still functionally integrated business operations. Examples of such companies include: cable television operators; mining operations; racetracks and sporting facilities; hotels and resort properties; and complex, process-type manufacturing facilities.

Unit Valuation Approaches. The three standard and generally accepted unit valuation approaches are the cost approach, the income approach, and the market approach. Assuming that the taxpayer is subject to the unit valuation concept, these three approaches are used to provide independent indications of value for the taxpayer's overall operating unit. The value indications of the three approaches are synthesized and correlated into a final value reconciliation.

Jurisdictional Differences

In some jurisdictions, there is uncertainty on the parts of—and controversy between—taxpayers and assessing authorities as to what exactly is included in (or excluded from) the taxable unit. The following paragraphs will outline some of the issues with regard to assets that may be either included in—or excluded from—the taxable unit.

In some jurisdictions, current assets are excluded from the taxable unit. These current assets (e.g., cash, receivables, inventory, etc.) may be excluded from property taxation altogether. Or, they may be subject to a different level of property taxation than that applied to the overall unit.

In some jurisdictions, over-the-road vehicles are excluded from the taxable unit. This is because the vehicles are subject to a different type of taxation—through the vehicle licensing procedures.

In some jurisdictions, construction work-in-process is excluded from the unit subject to taxation. This is because those assets are not yet fully functional as of the assessment date.

In most jurisdictions, locally assessed properties (e.g., buildings, plants, etc.) are excluded from the taxable unit. This exclusion is to avoid double taxation of the same property. That is, if a facility is locally assessed as real property (for example, at the county level), it should not also be included in the overall unit subject to centrally assessed property taxation.

In many jurisdictions, identified intangible assets are excluded from the unit subject to ad valorem taxation. Depending upon the jurisdiction, all identified intangible assets may be excluded from property taxation—or only certain statutorily specified intangible assets (e.g., software, trademarks, patents, copyrights) may be excluded from property taxation.

In virtually all jurisdictions, only assets in place as of the assessment date are subject to taxation. However, this concept has not been fully developed—either in practice, in the literature, or in judicial deliberations. This point relates to the fact that the asset structure appraised in the unit valuation includes the goodwill of the taxpayer business enterprise. And, the goodwill of the taxpayer business enterprise includes the economic value of both tangible and intangible assets not yet in existence as of the valuation date.

Value Excluded from the Taxable Unit

Accordingly, it is important for both taxpayers and assessing authorities to understand the total composition of the asset structure that is the result of the unit valuation (and the business valuation) process. Those assets that are statutorily excluded from the taxable unit should be removed from the overall unit value conclusion—prior to the property tax assessment procedure.

Some of the assets to be excluded are easy to identify. Obvious examples include cash account balances, over-the-road vehicles, and construction work-in-progress. Some of the other assets to be excluded are not as easy to identify. Less obvious examples include identifiable intangible assets (e.g., customer relationships, a trained and assembled workforce, proprietary technology, etc.). And, perhaps the least obvious example—but arguably the most universal example—would be unidentifiable intangible value in the nature of goodwill. This unidentifiable intangible goodwill (or the present value of the future income from tangible and intangible assets not in existence on the assessment date) may be an important element in the reconciliation of:

1. The taxpayer's overall business enterprise value (as estimated by the standard unit valuation methods).
2. The value of the portion of the taxpayer's unit subject to ad valorem property taxation.

Identification and Valuation of Intangible Assets in the Unit Method of Assessment

Using the unit method of property tax assessment, the indicated values derived from the income approach (using either the direct capitalization method or the yield capitalization method) and from the market approach (using the stock and debt method) represent the total value of the assets of the subject taxpayer business enterprise, including all tangible and all intangible assets. However, in many taxing jurisdictions, intangible personal property assets are not subject to ad valorem taxation. Therefore, in jurisdictions in which they are not subject to property taxation, the value of the intangible personal property assets should be identified and deducted from the indicated total asset value of the unit (derived from either the income approach or the market approach) to arrive at the residual value of the taxpayer's assessable tangible assets.

Numerous examples of intangible personal property assets are commonly found in the business enterprise unit. Intangible personal property assets are identifiable, separable, and capable of systematic valuation and may include, for example, the following: trademarks and trade names, a trained and assembled workforce, computer software and systems, customer relationships, patents, supplier contracts, and royalty agreements.

Alternatives to Use of Stock Market Data

There are several alternatives to the use of stock market data for estimating the cost of equity capital in either a direct capitalization or a yield capitalization valuation analysis. For purposes of identifying these alternatives only, the following methods can be used for estimating the cost of equity capital:

1. The cost of debt of the subject company plus an equity risk premium.
2. The sum of the dividend yield plus the capital gain yield for selected guideline companies.
3. The arbitrage pricing theory.

All of these alternative methods have strengths and weaknesses. However, none of these methods corrects for all of the problems encountered when using the Capital Asset Pricing Model (CAPM).

The conceptual and practical problems with CAPM are even greater in the valuation of operating properties subject to ad valorem taxation when using a standard yield capitalization method on a net cash flow basis. However, problems are not as severe when using the model in the valuation of operating properties subject to ad valorem taxation, if the following valuation methods are utilized:

1. An asset accumulation method, including the aggregate appraisal of all real and tangible personal property (typically using a cost approach), and including going-concern and goodwill value (but based on the capitalization of historical and not prospective economic income).
2. A yield capitalization method that assumes no future growth in economic earnings. The implicit assumption in the use of this method is either:
   a. Capital expenditures equal annual depreciation expense (so that there is only direct asset replacement in the valuation model), or
   b. Incremental (new) capital expenditures yield exactly the subject firm's weighted average cost of capital (so that there is no increase in unit value due to these incremental capital expenditures).
3. A direct capitalization method that assumes no growth in economic earnings. The implicit assumption in the use of this method is that annual depreciation expense exactly equals prospective capital expenditures, so that there is a stable asset base in the valuation model.

Problems with the Use of Stock Market Data in Property Tax Valuations

Introduction

In this section, we will summarize the conceptual and the practical problems with the use of stock market data sources in the property tax valuation of any unit of real estate. This will include the use of stock market data to extract direct capitalization rates, present value (yield capitalization) discount rates, and pricing multiples. As part of this discussion, we will focus on the valuation differences between an investment in operating real estate (i.e., the property tax valuation subject) and an investment in negotiable securities (i.e., often the property tax valuation data source). We will consider these differences from an investment risk and expected return perspective.

There are general comparability problems regarding the use of capital market data (i.e., pricing multiples, capitalization rates, and security prices) in all unit valuation methods—including both income and market approach methods. These general comparability problems include: (1) the potential lack of comparability of the selected guideline companies and the taxpayer unit of operating property and (2) the lack of comparability of the selected guideline securities (i.e., marketable, noncontrolling securities traded on efficient stock exchanges) and the taxpayer unit (i.e., nonmarketable, controlling ownership interests in operating property for which there is no ready secondary market).

In addition to these general comparability problems, there may be several other analytical problems associated with the use of capital market–derived data in unit valuation methods:

1. Security prices are substantially variable (and sometimes erratic) in the short term.
2. Security prices are often affected by macroeconomic events not related to the subject company.
3. Security prices can be quickly and substantially distorted based upon short-term industry-specific or company-specific phenomena.
4. Security prices are always forward looking—accordingly they reflect investors' expectations of income that has not yet been (and may never be) earned.
5. Capital market pricing multiples tend to artificially inflate the value indications of the more successful companies in an industry—particularly if the multiples include consideration of companies that have poor financial performances.

Security prices change quickly and substantially. Daily changes of 10 percent, 20 percent, or more in the stock prices of public companies are not uncommon. Daily changes of 100 points, 200 points, or more in broad market indices such as the Dow Jones Industrial Average are also not uncommon. While these rapid and significant price changes clearly reflect investors' perceptions of security values, they do not necessarily reflect investors' perceptions of underlying operating property values. If the price of a guideline company security was to change (increase or decrease) 20 percent in one day, no rational investor—or informed analyst—would expect that the market value of that guideline company's operating property also would change 20 percent in one day. Nonetheless, the use of capital market data in unit valuation methods can lead to that conclusion.

Exhibit 34–1 presents some of the more salient differences between the typically efficient and organized markets in which investment securities are transacted and the typically inefficient unorganized markets in which real estate/personal property operating assets transact. Thus, although the use of stock market data works well for estimating nondiversified risk and required rate of return in the securities market, it may not work well for estimating those same variables in the real estate/personal property markets.

Exhibit 34–2 summarizes some of the intrinsic differences between securities (whether debt or equity instruments) and operating real estate/personal property (either individual assets or going-concern assemblages of assets) as investment alternatives.

As Exhibit 34–2 indicates, there are fundamental investment risk and return differences between marketable minority interests in debt and equity securities and nonmarketable controlling interests in operating real estate and tangible personal property. Because of these differences, it is unlikely that a model that effectively correlates nondiversified risk and expected return for securities will be able to serve the same function for such real estate or personal property.

Income Approach Valuation Issues

This section will explore several of the current issues with regard to the application of the income approach to property valuation. This discussion will address the relative weighting of the yield capitalization method versus the direct capitalization method.

Exhibit 34–1

**Differences between Securities Exchange Markets and
Real Estate/Personal Property Exchange Markets**

Securities Transactions Market	Operating Real Estate/Personal Property Transactions Market
1. Generally homogeneous properties competing for investment funds.	1. Substantially heterogeneous properties competing for investment funds.
2. Large number of buyers and sellers.	2. Few buyers and sellers in any one price range at any one location (particularly for special purpose assets).
3. Relatively uniform, stable, and low transaction prices.	3. Relatively high and fluctuating transaction prices.
4. Low cost of individual transactions (including brokerage, information, and title-transfer fees).	4. High cost of individual transactions (including brokerage, information, and title-transfer fees).
5. Relatively few government restrictions on secondary market transactions.	5. Secondary market transactions subject to regulations, registration, and legislation at all levels.
6. Supply and demand of properties never far out of balance.	6. Volatile demand for and sluggish supply of properties.
7. Reasonably knowledgeable and generally informed buyers and sellers.	7. Potentially uninformed buyers and sellers who interact infrequently.
8. Public disclosure of substantial financial and operational information regarding properties.	8. Restricted disclosure of limited information (if any disclosure at all) regarding properties.
9. Organized market mechanism, allowing for rapid consummation and confirmation of transaction.	9. Small, fragmented, overlapping market segments causing delayed consummation of transaction.
10. Readily "consumed," quickly supplied, and easily transported properties.	10. Durable, relatively immobile, and illiquid properties.

Exhibit 34–2

Intrinsic Differences between Securities and Operating Real Estate/Personal Property

Securities (Debt or Equity Instrument)	Real Estate/Personal Property (Individual or as a Mass Assemblage)
1. Liquid, marketable investments.	1. Illiquid investments.
2. Noncontrolling interest income production and distribution.	2. Controlling interest in income production and distribution.
3. Small absolute dollar investment required.	3. Large absolute dollar investment required.
4. Small percentage of overall wealth committed to investment.	4. Large percentage of overall wealth committed to investment.
5. Diversified portfolio of investments.	5. Nondiversified portfolio of investments.
6. Short-term investment time horizon.	6. Long-term investment time horizon.
7. Does not require investment to maintain investment base.	7. Requires replenishment investment to maintain investment base.
8. Investments expected to appreciate over time.	8. Investments expected to depreciate over time.
9. Income typically subject to only individual tax (from investor's perspective).	9. Income typically subject to both corporate and individual tax (from investor's perspective).
10. Portfolios can be created in limitless combinations of risky securities and risk-free securities.	10. Portfolio limited to the particular combination of real estate and personal property that operates the business.

Many analysts assign a greater weighting to the yield capitalization method than to the direct capitalization method in the valuation synthesis and conclusion. This section describes some of the reasons for this relative weighting.

In the application of the yield capitalization method, both the measurement of economic income and the yield capitalization rate are intended to be specific to the subject property. The discrete income projection is the best estimate of the prospective income generation of the subject property. And, the yield capitalization rate (or present value discount rate) is typically estimated based on a risk analysis of the subject property compared with all other classes of investment opportunities.

The yield capitalization method is specific to the subject property. It can accommodate projected cyclical changes in economic income. It can accommodate uneven expected rates of changes in prospective economic income, and it can accommodate expected fundamental changes in the economic income—or in the investment risk—of the subject property.

In the direct capitalization method, the economic income subject to capitalization is intended to relate directly to the subject property. However, the guideline publicly traded companies from which direct capitalization rates are often estimated are, at best, indirectly related to the subject property. For several reasons, as will be discussed below, these guidelines companies often do not provide useful valuation guidance with regard to direct capitalization rates.

First, with regard to the income subject to capitalization, the direct capitalization method requires the estimation of a single period stabilized income projection. Since this estimation is for a single period, it cannot vary over time. In other words, the direct capitalization method does not allow for (1) any expected cyclical changes in income or (2) any changes in income not represented by a constant growth rate.

Second, while the estimation of the single period stabilized income is very important to direct capitalization, it is difficult to project this stabilized income.

Careful analysis is required in order to determine if the stabilized income should be based on (1) last year's actual income, (2) an average of the last three years, (3) an average of the last five years, or (4) some other base period. The projection of stabilized income is intended to be an estimate of the most likely level of income, on average, in the future. However, many analysts simply inflate a prior period's actual income in order to estimate the prospective stabilized income.

Third, with regard to the typical direct capitalization rate estimation process, there are two serious comparability problems:

1. The guideline companies selected for analysis are often not comparable enough to the taxpayer business to provide meaningful valuation guidance.
2. The guideline company data subject to analysis relate to marketable, noncontrolling securities that trade in efficient capital markets; the taxpayer property unit relates to nonmarketable, controlling ownership interests in operating properties that have no organized secondary market.

Accordingly, there may be a fundamental lack of comparability between the capital market data used to estimate the direct capitalization rate and the operating property included in the taxpayer unit.

Fourth, there are well defined comparability criteria for the application of the direct capitalization method to the valuation of real estate. There are also well defined criteria of the identification and quantification of adjustments (to increase the comparability of the comparable properties with the subject property) in the application of the direct capitalization method to the valuation of real estate. However, many analysts do not follow these same well defined criteria for comparability and adjustments in the application of the direct capitalization method for unit valuation purposes. If these well defined criteria are not followed, then the results of the direct capitalization analysis may be unreliable.

Many analysts prefer to weight the yield capitalization method more heavily than the direct capitalization method in the overall valuation synthesis and conclusion. This section has summarized some of the reasons for this preference of the yield capitalization valuation method as compared with the direct capitalization valuation method. The yield capitalization method uses income and yield capitalization rate (i.e., risk and expected return) factors that are more directly associated with the subject taxpayer. The direct capitalization method often uses capital market data that are indirectly associated with the subject taxpayer.

Within the unit valuation context, the direct capitalization method may lead to unreasonable valuation conclusions for several reasons. The analyst may attempt to identify and quantify adjustments to the capital market-derived data in order to mitigate the problems with the direct capitalization method. However, if the quantity and magnitude of these adjustments are significant, then it is logical to assign a weighting preference to the yield capitalization method in the value reconciliation and correlation procedure.

Resolving Circularity Due to Property Tax Expenses

A problem with applying the income approach in a disputed ad valorem case is that the property tax is often a material expense for the property in question (impacting value), while the tax expense itself is a function of the disputed value (e.g., the higher the estimated value, the higher the tax expense). It is common practice to resolve this circularity by discounting or capitalizing cash flows on a pre-property-tax basis. That is, the cash flows are adjusted (upwards) by excluding the property tax expense. This approach requires an upward adjustment to the discount rate to compensate for the adjustment to the cash flows. One can show mathematically that the pre-property-tax discount rate is equal to:

$$k + p(1 - t)$$

where k equals the post-property-tax rate (e.g., the Weighted Average Cost of Capital), t equals the corporate income tax rate applicable to the property's earnings, and p equals the typical annual property tax expense as a percent of the *market* value of the property (not the assessed value, if this typically differs from market value in the given jurisdiction). For analyses performed on a pre-income-tax basis, one can show that the adjusted discount rate is:

$$r + p$$

where r is the pre-income-tax discount rate, and p is as defined above.

Differences in the Risk and Expected Return Investment Characteristics between Operating Property and Negotiable Securities

This section explores the use of capital market–derived data (e.g., price/earnings multiples, earnings/price capitalization rates, and security prices) in the income approach and the market approach to unit valuation. This discussion focuses on the differences between the risk and expected return investment characteristics of capital market–derived data (i.e., data derived from negotiable securities) and the appraisal subject (i.e., the unit of taxpayer operating property).

Typically, there are 12 differences in the risk and expected return investment characteristics identified between operating property and negotiable securities. These differences are listed below:

1. Lack of marketability.
2. Lack of absolute control.
3. Investment time horizon.
4. Regulatory risk.
5. Litigation risk (a form of unlimited liability risk).
6. Bankruptcy risk (a form of unlimited liability risk).
7. Environmental risk (a form of unlimited liability risk).
8. Lack of diversification (with regard to the subject investment).
9. Concentration of wealth (with regard to the subject investor).
10. Transaction cost.
11. Market inefficiency.
12. Investment depreciation.

Each of these 12 investment characteristics is summarized below.

Lack of Marketability. Negotiable securities are eminently liquid. They trade easily and quickly on organized stock market exchanges (e.g., the New York Stock Exchange). Investors know that their securities trade will occur on the day of their market order, and that they will receive the proceeds from their transaction (in the case of a sale) within three trading days.

Operating property, on the other hand, is eminently illiquid. It is difficult and expensive to sell special purpose operating property—such as most industrial and commercial real estate. Operating property owners have no organized exchange market to go to; they are not sure what price their transaction will result in; they do not know when the transaction will occur; and, they do not know when they will receive the proceeds from a sale transaction.

Lack of Absolute Control. Controlling owners of many types of businesses can unilaterally decide most important business management decisions. For example, they can decide which customers to service—and which not to serve; they can decide which product lines to offer—and which not to offer; they can decide which assets to buy and which assets to sell; and, they can decide which services and territories to discontinue—in order to quickly change strategic direction and to maximize their profits.

Controlling owners in regulated (or partially regulated) industries need to obtain regulatory approval in order to implement certain critical management decisions—such as a merger, acquisition, liquidation, or divestiture. Therefore, control is not as substantial a value increment in regulated industries as it is in non-regulated industries, because management does not enjoy "absolute control."

Investment Time Horizon. Typically, investors in capital market negotiable securities, on average, turn over their investments every two to three years. In other words, they only expect to hold the investment for a two- to three-year horizon. They can then remain liquid—or they can invest in other negotiable securities.

Capital-intensive businesses (such as most industrial and commercial companies), on average, turn over their investments in operating assets every 20 to 30 years. In other words, they expect to hold their investments in operating assets for long periods of time.

The longer the expected investment time horizon, the greater the risk to the investor (due to missed alternative investment opportunities, inflation risk, and other factors).

Regulatory Risk. Transactions involving negotiable securities are, for the most part, unregulated. And, once the securities are owned by the investor, the securities themselves are almost totally unregulated.

Transactions involving operating property in a regulated industry are, for the most part, highly regulated. And, once the operating property is owned by the business, the operating property itself is subject to considerable regulation.

The greater the restrictions placed on any property type—whether negotiable securities or operating property—the lower the value of the property.

Litigation Risk. Securities owners are not subject to any risk greater than the cost of their original investment. If the business they invest in loses a substantial lawsuit (of any type), the most the investor can lose is his or her original investment in the subject stocks or bonds.

Operating property owners are subject to the direct risk of litigation claims. There is no limit to the amount of their liability. If a taxpayer corporation has a $100 million net worth investment in operating property, and the taxpayer loses a $500 million lawsuit, then the taxpayer is responsible to pay the judgment (out of other resources or out of future profits, if necessary). The taxpayer owner can lose much more than the original cost investment in the operating property.

Bankruptcy Risk. Securities owners are not subject to any risk greater than the cost of their original investment. If the business they invest in becomes bankrupt, the most the investor can lose is his or her original investment in the subject stocks or bonds.

Operating property owners are subject to the direct risk of bankruptcy. There is no limit to the amount of their liability. If a taxpayer corporation suffers a bankruptcy action, the operating property owner is responsible to pay creditors (out of other resources or out of future profits, if necessary). The taxpayer is at risk for much more than the original cost of investment in the operating property.

Environmental Risk. Securities owners are not subject to any risk greater than the cost of their original investment. If the business they invest in has an environmental problem, the most the investor can lose is his or her original investment in the subject stocks or bonds.

Operating property owners are subject to direct environmental risk—including the cost of environmental cleanup. If a taxpayer corporation must clean up an environmental problem, the operating property owner is responsible to pay the costs (out of other resources or out of future profits, if necessary). The taxpayer is at risk for much more than the original cost of investment in the operating property.

Transaction Cost. Transaction costs to capital market securities investors are low—and predictable. This predictability (and competitiveness) of securities brokerage fees is one of the hallmarks of trading on organized securities exchanges.

Transaction costs to capital intensive industrial and commercial operating property owners are high—and unpredictable. For example, if an industrial or commercial company decides to sell some excess operating property, brokerage fees (as a percent of the final sale price) are relatively high and relatively noncompetitive.

Market Inefficiency. The organized stock exchange markets (e.g., the New York Stock Exchange) are the very paradigm of an efficient trading market. Market participants (i.e., investors) essentially know when, where, and how their trade will take place. They are confident that a buyer will be found (if they are a seller) and that a seller will be found (if they are a buyer). They know that there is a system of brokers, dealers, and market specialists that will make the transaction quick, inexpensive, and painless.

The secondary market in which capital-intensive industrial and commercial operating property trades is the antonym of market efficiency. There are few market participants. There are few brokers and dealers. There are not market specialists (at least as they exist in the stock exchanges). Operating property buyers and sellers are uncertain as to when—or if—their transaction will take place and at what price the transaction will take place.

Investment Depreciation. Capital market investors expect their investments to appreciate. And, over time, negotiable security investments generally do appreciate. Therefore, capital market investors do not need to replenish their investment portfolio (i.e., continue to invest in their portfolio) just to maintain their investment base. Rather, even without replenishment, capital market investment portfolios tend to appreciate over time.

Operating property investors expect their investments to depreciate. And, over time, capital intensive industrial and commercial operating property generally does depreciate. Therefore, capital intensive businesses need to constantly replenish their operating property portfolios (i.e., continue to make investments in replacement operating property) just to maintain their investment base. Accordingly, without constant replenishment, operating property investment portfolios tend to depreciate over time.

Capitalization of Leased Equipment Rental Expense

Introduction

Some taxing authorities add back the rental expense associated with operating leased equipment to the level of the taxpayer's economic income subject to capitalization. This add-back is made by some taxing authorities in the application of both income approach and market approach valuation methods, including the direct capitalization method, the yield capitalization method, and the stock and debt method.

These taxing authorities perform this add-back procedure because they believe that the value of the operating leased equipment (1) would otherwise not be included in the unit value of the taxpayer and, therefore, (2) would otherwise escape property taxation during the term of the lease. This conclusion is based upon the premises that (1) the lessee is responsible for paying the property tax on the leased equipment during the lease term, and (2) the lessor is responsible for paying the property tax on the leased equipment after the conclusion of the lease term. These property tax payment responsibilities are typically assigned in the actual equipment operating lease contract.

These taxing authorities justify this add-back adjustment with the following arguments: (1) All the income derived from the use of the operating leased equipment is not being included in the taxpayer's unit valuation (because the rental expense of the equipment is subtracted before arriving at the level of economic income subject to capitalization), and (2) because the taxpayer uses the leased equipment in its business operations, the leased equipment should be valued as if it were an owned asset, but this is not occurring because the rental expense is greater than the corresponding ownership expense (i.e., depreciation expense).

Operating Lease Rental Expense

Corporate taxpayers typically assert that there are several reasons not to capitalize operating lease rental expense in the application of either income approach or market approach methods of unit valuation. These reasons are both conceptual and practical in nature. Several of these reasons are discussed here.

Consistency. As a basic methodological axiom, any adjustment that is made to the operating results of the subject taxpayer also should be made to the operating results of the selected guideline companies. For purposes of this argument, guideline companies are the publicly traded securities from which direct capitalization rates, capital market multiples, or stock and debt security pricing data are derived.

If the rental expense add-back is made to subject taxpayer data, it should also be made to the guideline companies' data. For example, this is required to be reported in 10-K footnotes.

It is noteworthy that this argument does not address whether the rental expense adjustment is methodologically correct. Rather, this argument indicates that unless this adjustment (or any other adjustment) is not made consistently both to the subject taxpayer and to the guideline companies, it is procedurally incorrect, and it will result in distorted valuation conclusions.

Ownership Interest Subject to Appraisal. Some taxing authorities assert that taxpayers should be taxed on the fee simple ownership interest in operating leased property. Whether it correctly does so or not, add-back of the associated rental expense is intended to tax the fee simple interest in the leased property. However, many taxpayers assert that this basic position is fundamentally flawed. Taxpayers do not own a fee simple interest in operating leased equipment. Therefore, this add-back attempts to value a bundle of legal rights that the taxpayer does not own.

Regarding operating leased equipment, the taxpayer owns the lessee's rights to the property only, and the lessor continues to own the lessor's rights on the property. For example, the taxpayer lessee typically cannot sell or otherwise transfer, borrow against, hypothecate or otherwise pledge, enjoy, and value appreciation in, and so on, the operating leased equipment. At most, the taxpayer owns a term interest in the equipment. The lessor retains the reversionary interest in the equipment.

If the taxpayer is taxed on the fee simple interest in the leased equipment (by effectively capitalizing the add-back as annuity in perpetuity), then (1) the taxpayer is taxed on a bundle of legal rights that it does not enjoy, and (2) the fee simple interest in the property will be subject to double taxation, once to the taxpayer (during the lease term) and once to the lessor (at the conclusion of the lease term).

Instances of Operating Lease Capitalization. Operating leases are capitalized, for example, by ratings agencies such as Moody's and Standard & Poor's in determining debt for credit ratings. Standard & Poor's uses a financial model that capitalizes off-balance sheet operating lease commitments and allocates minimum lease payments to interest and depreciation expenses. Not only are debt-to-capital ratios affected; so are interest coverage, funds from operations to debt, total debt to EBITDA, operating margins, and return on capital. Standard & Poor's believes this technique is superior to the alternative "factor method," which multiplies annual lease expense by a factor reflecting the average life of leased assets.[2]

Summary

This chapter presented many of the reasons to conduct a valuation analysis for ad valorem property tax assessment purposes. These purposes include: initial assessments for newly constructed properties, re-assessments for properties that have transferred ownership, periodic property tax compliance (i.e., filing) purposes, and ad valorem property tax assessment appeal purposes. The basis of such an appeal could be either on grounds of property valuation (i.e., an overassessment) or on grounds of assessment equalization (i.e., an unfair assessment). In either case, a valuation analysis is required.

In addition to general topics related to ad valorem property tax terminology and procedural methodology, we discussed several special topics of particular interest to financial valuation analysts, including: the identification and quantification of functional obsolescence, the identification and quantification of economic obsolescence, the identification and valuation of intangible assets under the unit assessment method, and the identification and application of appropriate income approach methods for ad valorem unit valuation purposes. Issues such as

---

[2] For a detailed explanation of this model and considerations underlying the methodology, see www.corporatecriteria.standardandpoors.com.

the use of the capital asset pricing model in property tax valuation, the use of stock market data in property tax valuation, and capitalization of leased equipment rental expense were also discussed.

Bibliography

Ancel, Mark G. "Should Intangibles Be Used as a Basis for Determining Market Value?" *Journal of Multistate Taxation*, September/October 1993, pp. 166–73.

Barad, Michael. "Ibbotson Clarifies Controversies on How to Estimate Size Premium; Prefers Return in Excess of CAPM for Both Build-Up and CAPM Models." *Shannon Pratt's Business Valuation Update*, July 2002, pp. 1–4.

Booth, Lawrence. "The CAPM + Equity Risk Premiums and the Privately-Held Business." *BV Papers*, Presentation and Reviewed Articles, September 1998. Available at www.BVLibrary.com.

Chen, Yueyun, Iskandar S. Hamwi, and Tim Hudson. "Capital Asset Pricing Model with Default Risk: Theory and Application in Insurance." Atlantic Economic Society: *International Advances in Economic Research*, vol. 9, no. 1, February 1, 2003, p. 20.

Chiugn-Min, Tsai. "Alternative Dynamic Capital Asset Pricing Models: Theories and Empirical Results." (Dissertation) (New Brunswick, NJ: Rutgers, the State University of New Jersey, November 2005).

Cook, Cline G. "The Appraiser's Role in the Tax Appeal Process." *Real Estate Appraiser*, August 1991, pp. 17–20.

Davis, Joseph M., and John R. Cesta. "The Valuation of Operating Leased Property in the Unitary Method." *ASA Valuation*, August 1994, pp. 42–56.

Donias, Claire H. "Valuation for Ad Valorem Taxation" (Chapter 13). In Robert F. Reilly and Robert P. Schweihs, eds. *The Handbook of Advanced Business Valuation*. New York: McGraw-Hill, 2000.

Fletcher, Gregory G. "Significant Court Cases Concerning Ad Valorem Taxation of Public Utility and Railroad Property." *Assessment Journal*, January/February 1994, pp. 43–55.

Fowler, Bruce A. "Unit Valuation: Oklahoma's Illegal Tax on Intangible Property." *Tulsa Law Journal*, Winter 1995, pp. 367–93.

Hanke, Steve H., and Stephen J.K. Walters. "Tax Appraisal in Evolving Industries: An Econometric Approach." *Journal of Legal Economics*, Fall 1995, pp. 43–54.

Hellerstein, Walter. "State and Local Taxation of Intangibles Generates Increasing Controversy." *Journal of Taxation*, May 1994, pp. 296–302.

Hess, Alan C. "Do Regulated Utilities Have Growth Opportunities?" *Assessment Journal*, July/August 1995, pp. 45–53.

Hoffert, Myles. "ABA Annual Meeting: Property Tax Treatment of Intangibles and Business Value." *BV Papers*. Available at www.BVLibrary.com.

Ibbotson Associates. *Stocks, Bonds, Bills & Inflation 2000 Yearbook* (Valuation Edition). Chicago: Ibbotson Associates, 2000.

James-Earles, Melanie, and Edwin H. Duett. "Use of the Capital Asset Pricing Model for Valuing Closely Held Busines." *Valuation Strategies*, July/August 2002, pp. 12–17.

King, David. "Do Data Biases Cause the Small Stock Premiums?" *Business Valuation Review*, vol. 22., no. 2, June 2003, pp. 56–61.

Kletke, Darrel D. "Supplementary Report to the Oklahoma Tax Commission Concerning Recommendations on Oklahoma Rural Land Valuation for Ad Valorem Tax Purposes." Dept. of Agricultural Economics, Oklahoma State University, January 1, 2002.

Laro, David, and Shannon Pratt. *Business Valuation and Taxes: Procedure, Law and Perspective.* New York: John Wiley and Sons, 2005.

Lo, Andrew W. "Trading Volume: Implications of an Intertemporal Capital Asset Pricing Model." *National Bureau of Economic Research*, January 1, 2001.

Matonis, Stephen J., and Daniel R. DeRango. "The Determination of Hotel Value Components for Ad Valorem Tax Assessment." *Appraisal Journal*, July 1993, pp. 342–47.

McNulty, James M., Tony D. Yeh, William S. Schulze, and Michael H. Lubatkin. "What's Your Real Cost of Capital?" *Harvard Business Review*, October 2002, p. 114.

Mo, Douglas. "Ad Valorem Taxation of Cable Television Intangibles: The Search for the Holy Grail." *Assessment Journal*, May/June 1996, pp. 33–36.

Pratt, Shannon P. "Discount Rates Based on CAPM Don't Always Lead to Minority Value." *Shannon Pratt's Business Valuation Update*, March 2001, pp. 1–3.

Rabe, James G., and Robert F. Reilly. Valuation of Intangible Assets for Property Tax Purposes." *National Public Accountant*, April 1994, pp. 26–28+.

_____. "Valuing Intangible Assets as Part of a Unitary Assessment." *Journal of Property Tax Management*, Winter 1994, pp. 12–20.

Reilly, Robert F. "Assessing Your Assessment: Valuation Techniques for Finding out What Your Property's Really Worth." *Commercial Investment Real Estate Journal*, Summer 1995, pp. 30–33.

_____. "Valuation of Trademarks for Property Tax Purposes." *Journal of Property Tax Management*, Fall 1999, pp. 36–50.

Rife, Knute. "Appealing Property Tax Assessments." *Practical Real Estate Lawyer*, January 1991, pp. 69–88.

Schilt, James. "CAPM and Business Valuation." *Business Valuation Review*, vol. 23, no. 2, June 2004, pp. 60–62.

Shank, David W. "How Regulation Affects the Valuation of Public Utility Property." *Valuation*, July 1993, pp. 46–52.

Shreve, Steven E. *Stochastic Calculus for Finance I: The Binomial Asset Pricing Model.* New York: Springer Science + Business Media, Inc., 2005.

Stanton, Thomas C. "The Market Model: An Alternative to the CAPM." Business *Valuation Review*, March 1999, pp. 12–15.

Sun, Changyou, and Daowei Zhang. "Assessing the Financial Performance of Forestry-Related Investment Vehicles: Capital Asset Pricing Model vs. Arbitrage Pricing Theory." American Agricultural Economics Association: *American Journal of Agricultural Economics*, vol. 83, no. 3, August 1, 2001, p. 617.

Ukren, Perry. "Estimating Discount Rates — An Alternative to CAPM." *Valuation Strategies,* vol. 8, no. 10, March/April 2005, pp. 10–15.

Walters, Lawrence C., et al. "Measuring Obsolescence in Regulated Firms: Enhancements to the Cost Approach." *Assessment Journal*, May/June 1994, pp. 47–58.

Wiley, Richard N. "The Unit Valuation Method: Not a License to Commit Unit Taxation." *Journal of Property Tax Management*, Spring 1996, pp. 49–61.

Chapter 35

Dissenting Stockholder and Minority Oppression Actions

The incidence of adjudicated actions brought by minority stockholders increased dramatically from 1995 through 2005. All indications are that this trend will continue.

These actions brought by minority shareholders generally fall into one of two categories:

1. Dissenting stockholder actions.
2. Minority oppression actions.
  Either may be accompanied by claims of breach of fiduciary duty.

Dissenting Stockholder Actions

All states and the District of Columbia have dissenting stockholder statutes. These statutes essentially provide that if a company effects an extraordinary corporate action—typically identified in the statutes—stockholders may dissent from the action and be paid the *fair value* of their shares.

The "triggering events" allowing a dissent action vary somewhat from state to state. They apply in all states if a stockholder is forced to give up his or her stock, such as a cash-out merger (sometimes called a "squeeze-out") or a merger where the stockholders would receive stock in the acquiring corporation. In many states, dissenters' rights are triggered by the sale of major corporate assets, as defined in the respective states' statutes.

Most states require that if a minority stockholder wishes to dissent from a corporate action, the decision must be registered in writing at or within a few days following the stockholder meeting at which the action is approved by the majority of stockholders. This process often is referred to as *perfecting dissenters' appraisal rights*. The courts are virtually unanimous in prohibiting dissenters' appraisal rights unless they have been perfected within the time specified in the statute and pursuant to the procedures specified therein. In addition, there typically are other procedural "hoops" that a stockholder must jump through.

In virtually all states, the statutory standard of value is *fair value*. The Revised Model Business Corporation Act (RMBCA), which many of the states have adopted, defines fair value as:

> The value of the shares immediately before the effectuation of the corporate action to which the dissenter objects, excluding any appreciation or depreciation in anticipation of the corporate action unless exclusion would be inequitable.[1]

None of the state statutes gives any further definition to the standard of fair value. According to the official comment of the Model Business Corporation Act, the definition of fair value leaves to the parties (and, ultimately, to the courts) the details by which fair value is to be determined within the broad outlines of the definition. Thus, case law precedent provides guidance as to how each state interprets the standard of fair value. The interpretations vary greatly, as discussed in the next chapter, but virtually no state specifically equates *fair value* with *fair market value*. In some cases, the ultimate value standard that is applied is fair market

---

[1] Model Business Corporation Act, Section 13.01(3) (1998).

value but this is a consequence of following the fair value guidance rather than the other way around. Many states have no precedential case law on fair value, in which case they look at decisions from other states for guidance.

In 1999, following the development of substantial case law on dissent and oppression cases, the RMBCA was revised so that the definition of fair value reads:

> "The value of the shares immediately before the effectuation of the corporate action to which the shareholder objects using customary and current valuation concepts and techniques generally employed for similar businesses in the context of the transaction requiring appraisal, and without discounting for lack of marketability or minority status except, if appropriate, for amendments to the certificate of incorporation pursuant to section 13.02(a)(5)."[2]

Although still not outlining a specific method of calculating value, the 1999 RMBCA definition adds two important concepts to the framework: (1) the use of customary and current valuation techniques, and (2) the rejection of the use of marketability and minority discounts except, "if appropriate, for amendments to the certificate of incorporation pursuant to section 13.02(a)(5)."

Very few states have incorporated this revision into their statues. However, some judicial decisions, even in states that have not incorporated the revision in their statutes, reference the revised version in rejecting minority and marketability discounts.

Interpretation of the Fair Value Standard in Dissent Cases

"That Which Has Been Taken"

A typical interpretation of the philosophy of fair value in a dissenting stockholder situation is the following:

> Fair value, in an appraisal context measures "that which has been taken from [the shareholder], viz., his proportionate interest in a going concern." *Tri-Continental Corp. v. Battze*, Del. Supr. 74 A.2d 71, 72 (1950).[3]

The Delaware Block Method

Prior to 1983, dissenting stockholder cases primarily utilized the "Delaware block method." This method develops values in each of three categories:

1. Investment value.
2. Market value.
3. Asset value.

Mathematical weightings are then assigned to the indications of value from each of the three categories (although the weight to one, or even two in extreme cases, could be zero), and the resulting weighted average is the concluded value.

---

[2] Model Business Corporation Act, 1999 revision.
[3] *In Matter of Shell Oil Co.*, 607 A.2d 12B (Del. Supr. 1992).

Exhibit 35–1

Delaware Block Method
Sample Valuation Conclusion

	Indicated Value per Share	Weight	Weighted Value
Investment value			
Capitalization of earnings	$10.00	0.40	$4.00
Capitalization of dividends	6.00	0.10	0.60
Market value	12.00	0.25	3.00
Asset value	15.00	0.25	3.75
Weighted value per share			$11.35

The definitions of *investment value* and *market value* in the context of the Delaware block method are different from those discussed in the three basic approaches to value (see Part III of this book).

Investment value in the context of the Delaware block method means value based on expected earnings and/or dividends. It is akin to the value based on the income approach in the three basic approaches to value. It may be arrived at by discounted cash flow (DCF), capitalization of earnings, or capitalization of dividends. In this sense, it mixes the traditional income approach and market approach in that it may derive capitalization rates either by traditional income approach methods (see Chapters 9 and 10) or by traditional market approach methods (see Chapters 11 and 12).

Market value, on the other hand, has historically been based on prior transactions in the subject company's securities. This contrasts with the traditional appraisal concept of *market value*, as discussed in Chapters 11 and 12, where market value uses multiples of both income statement and balance sheet parameters based on comparable transactions.

A summary of a valuation conclusion under the Delaware block method would typically appear in the form presented in Exhibit 35–1.

Should Consider All Relevant Factors

A landmark case in 1983 decided that the traditional factors considered under the Delaware Block Rule alone were not necessarily sufficient; instead, "all relevant factors" should be considered. In that particular case, the court specifically made the point that projections of future earnings were available and should be considered. The court also made the point that a determination of *fair value* "must include proof of value by any techniques or methods which are generally considered acceptable in the financial community."[4]

The interpretation of fair value is a subject of continued debate and is difficult to generalize. Most states, however, have embraced the notion that "all relevant factors should be considered." Note that the Delaware block method factors are not abandoned by *Weinberger*; the case just states that all relevant factors must be

---

[4] *Weinzberger v. UOP, Inc.*, 457 A.2d 701 (Del. 1983).

considered. Both historically and currently, courts have treated *investment value* (defined in this context as value based on earning capacity) as the most important of the three categories of value.

Requirement for Entire Fairness

There are many subtleties to the application of fair value for corporate law purposes. For example, some states consider concepts of "entire fairness." There are two major aspects of entire fairness:

1. Fair consideration.
2. Procedural fairness.

Fair Consideration

The notion of fair consideration within the context of entire fairness also encompasses two criteria:

1. Absolute fairness.
2. Relative fairness.

Absolute fairness generally addresses whether the consideration received was adequate relative to the value of the interest that was given up.

Relative fairness means whether the consideration received was fair in comparison with what other stockholders received. For example, are the controlling stockholders receiving some consideration that actually should be shared with all stockholders (e.g., an "employment agreement" for which no services are required and which contributes nothing to the buying company)?

Procedural Fairness

Within the concept of procedural fairness, there generally are two broad criteria:

1. Independence.
2. Competence and thoroughness.

Independence refers both to parties affiliated with the company and also to outside legal and financial advisers.

If there are potentially conflicted board members, some companies appoint a committee of outside directors with authority to retain independent legal counsel and independent financial advisers, and to negotiate on an arm's-length basis. They have the fiduciary responsibility to protect the interests of all the stockholders, especially those not a part of the control group.

Independence with respect to outside advisers means retaining legal counsel and financial advisers who are independent of the control parties. Generally speaking, this means professional advisers who do not have a direct or indirect financial interest in the company or the parties to the dispute.

Competence and thoroughness similarly applies to parties affiliated with the company and also to their outside advisers.

It is not expected that board members themselves be expert in either legal matters or in financial valuation or deal structuring. It is, however, expected that they use prudent diligence and care in evaluating the qualifications of the expert that they choose to retain. It is also expected that they exert the time and effort necessary to understand and evaluate the recommendations of the outside experts in exercising their fiduciary responsibility to make recommendations in reliance on those experts. The experts merely provide advice. It is the directors who have the fiduciary responsibility to recommend action based on that advice.[5]

It obviously is beyond the scope of this book to address the issue of competence or thoroughness of legal counsel. With respect to competence of financial advisers, considerable guidance is provided in Chapter 1 on business valuation credentials. With respect to thoroughness of the financial adviser, the responsible fiduciary can find guidance in evaluating the financial adviser's work in Chapter 22, Reviewing a Business Valuation Report.

Consequences of Lack of Entire Fairness

Lack of entire fairness implies that the directors violated some duty owed to the shareholders. If the plaintiffs establish such liability, then the measure of damages may go beyond simply fair value as contemplated in the dissenters' rights statutes.

As explained by former Vice Chancellor Jack Jacobs of the Delaware Court of Chancery (currently a justice of the Delaware Supreme Court):

> The statutory appraisal case limits damages, on the upside, in that the value
> is fixed at one point in time, and is not supposed to include any synergies.

---

[5] In *Smith v. Van Gorkom,* 488 A.2d 858 (1985), the Delaware Supreme Court pierced the business judgment rule and imposed individual liability on independent (even eminent) outside directors of Trans Union Corporation because the court thought they had not been careful enough, and had not inquired enough, before deciding to accept and recommend to Trans Union's shareholders a cash-out merger at a per-share price that was less than the "intrinsic value" of the shares. At no time did the board engage either a formal valuation of the stock or a fairness opinion. The court also indicated that "[a] substantial premium may provide one reason to recommend a merger, but in the absence of other sound valuation information, the fact of a premium alone does not provide an adequate basis upon which to assess the fairness of an offering price. . . . Using market price as a basis for concluding that the premium adequately reflected the true value of the Company was a clearly faulty, indeed fallacious, premise."

The business judgment rule is a common law rule used by courts to minimize the number of shareholder complaints that undergo judicial review by protecting a corporate board decision from substantive review (e.g., under a "fairness" or "reasonableness" test) if four conditions are met. First, the board must make a decision. A decision not to act meets this requirement. Second, the board must have engaged in a process to become adequately informed of all material information reasonably available to make its decision. Third, the board must have made its decision in good faith. Fourth, disinterested directors of the board must have made the decision.

In *Van Gorkom,* the Delaware Supreme Court essentially indicated that it was serious about the "informed" element of the business judgment rule. At the time, the decision shocked the legal, corporate, and insurance communities by demonstrating that directors could be found liable for monetary damages if not sufficiently informed when making a board decision. The decision closely linked the duty of care with being sufficiently informed, and is credited with the practice of corporate boards of obtaining a fairness opinion before recommending a merger. Because the board and management are often familiar with the business and in a better position than outsiders to gather relevant information, there is no absolute requirement for a fairness opinion, but such an opinion will be given weight by a court assessing the fairness of a merger, as will the approval of the terms of the merger by disinterested directors.

Soon after *Van Gorkom* was decided, the Delaware legislature added Delaware General Corporation Law Code Section 102(b)(7), a statutory provision that largely protects directors from monetary liability for any actions arising from a breach of their duty of care if the corporation's shareholders incorporate into the certificate of incorporation a provision exculpating directors from such liability. Most Delaware corporations have incorporated such exculpatory provisions into their certificates of incorporation.

Notwithstanding the enactment of § 102(b)(7), directors still have a duty of care to be informed. Moreover, the exculpatory provision only relates to money damages against the director personally, and does not preclude injunctive relief. Also, by invoking the exculpatory clause, directors can place the burden of proof on themselves where breaches of fiduciary duties in addition to the duty of care are asserted, thus placing themselves at a procedural disadvantage in judicial proceedings. In the final analysis, it is very important for directors to be informed when making decisions, for legal as well as practical reasons.

There is no issue of burden of proof. If the court does not accept the valuation presented by one side or the other, it must perform independently its own valuation.

In a breach of fiduciary duty case, the traditional burden of proof rules apply, whereby if the evidence on both sides is even (we say "in equipoise") then the party that has the burden of proof loses.

Another bright line difference is that in a fiduciary duty action, other measures of damages may be available, including damages calculated as of a date after the transaction. "Rescissory" damages would be an example. Damages measured by that method would be available in a breach of fiduciary duty action, but not in a statutory appraisal case.[6]

Minority Interest Dissolution Actions

An increasing number of states have been enacting "judicial dissolution statutes." These generally allow minority shareholders to sue for dissolution of the corporation or partnership if they can demonstrate minority oppression or a deadlock on decision making. As can be seen in Exhibit 35–2, a majority of states now have such statutes.

The triggering events vary from state to state. In some states, the minority bringing suit must constitute some minimum percentage of the ownership, while other states have no minimum percentage requirement.

In California, the leading state in minority dissolution actions, if stockholders owning 33⅓ percent or more of a company's stock can demonstrate minority oppression, their remedy is a dissolution of the corporation. The majority stockholders can prevent such a dissolution by paying, in cash, the fair value pursuant to California Corporations Code Section 2000. The following is the process involved:

1. Minority stockholders sue for dissolution.
2. The court determines whether conditions warranting the dissolution have occurred.

Exhibit 35–2

Dissolution Statutes

Has Judicial Dissolution Statute

Alabama, Alaska, Arizona, Arkansas, California, Colorado, Connecticut, District of Columbia, Florida, Georgia, Hawaii, Idaho, Illinois, Indiana, Iowa, Kentucky, Louisiana, Maine, Maryland, Massachusetts, Michigan, Minnesota, Mississippi, Missouri, Montana, Nebraska, New Hampshire, New Jersey, New Mexico, New York, North Carolina, North Dakota, Ohio, Oregon, Pennsylvania, Rhode Island, South Carolina, South Dakota, Tennessee, Texas, Utah, Vermont, Virginia, Washington, West Virginia, Wisconsin, Wyoming, Indiana, Delaware, Kansas, Nevada, Oklahoma, Juan, Northern Mariana Islands, Puerto Rico, Virgin Islands

SOURCE: Jay Fishman, Shannon Pratt, and William Morrison. *Standards of Value: Theory and Applications.* Hoboken, N.J. John Wiley & Sons, 2006.

---

[6] Shannon P. Pratt, "Fair Value: A View from the Delaware Court of Chancery" (interview with Jack B. Jacobs), *Shannon Pratt's Business Valuation Update*, September 1999, p. 2.

3. If so, and parties cannot agree on a price to buy out the minority stockholders, majority stockholders move to stay the dissolution pending valuation to determine how much the minority stockholders would receive if liquidation proceeded.

4. Court appoints three appraisers. Parties can agree upon, and seek court confirmation in an appointee process, or can allow the court to select the appraisers. Unless otherwise agreed by the parties, the conclusion of the appraisers is advisory to the court rather than binding.

5. The court adopts a value.

6. The court enters a decree "which shall provide in the alternative for winding up and dissolution of the corporation unless payment is made for the shares within the time specified by the decree."

7. The majority stockholders may elect to pay the amount in cash prior to the deadline.

8. If the majority stockholders decline to pay, the company is liquidated and all shareholders receive a proportionate share of the resulting cash proceeds.[7]

Interpretation of the Fair Value Standard in Dissolution Cases

Courts in different states vary from one to another (and sometimes from one case to the next in the same state) in their interpretation of fair value for dissolution cases, and may not interpret this standard in the same manner as for dissenting stockholder cases.

California has what might seem at first reading an internally contradictory definition of fair value in the context of its dissolution statutes:

> The fair value shall be determined on the basis of the liquidation value as of the valuation date but taking into account the possibility, if any, of sale of the entire business as a going concern in a liquidation.

While the above may seem abstruse at first blush, the evolution of case law makes it clear. The value may be based on a liquidation of assets and/or selling all or parts of the operations as a going concern if that would produce higher net proceeds.

In any case, as with fair value in the context of dissent cases, the definition of fair value in dissolution cases is missing some of the elements of the traditional definition of fair market value. As California corporate attorney Art Shartsis points out, many of the assumptions underlying fair market value are not present:

- There is no willing seller. In the dissolution the seller is involuntarily disposing of the assets.
- The seller is under compulsion to sell.
- The involuntary seller under compulsion does not have the luxury of waiting for a top offer; the sale must be completed under the adverse conditions of a corporate dissolution conducted in accordance with California law.
- Implicitly, the buyer is aware of the seller's weakened position.[8]

---

[7] Arthur J. Shartsis, "Dissolution Actions Yield Less Than Fair Market Enterprise Value," *Judges & Lawyers Business Valuation Update*, January 1999, p. 5.
[8] Ibid., pp. 5–6.

Summary

Stockholder disputes that are resolved under the statutory standard of fair value typically fall clearly into one of two distinct categories:

1. Dissenting stockholder actions.
2. Minority owner dissolution actions.

Actions under both types of statutes have been on the increase in recent years.

All states have dissenting stockholder statutes. The standard of value is usually fair value.

A majority of states now have "judicial dissolution statutes" which allow minority shareholders demonstrating oppression to sue for dissolution of the entity. To prevent dissolution, the controlling owners can pay the oppressed minority owners the fair value of their shares.

For both types of actions, the respective states' court case precedents interpret the standard of fair value. Some states do not have precedential case law on fair value, in which instance they tend to look at case precedents from other states. In almost any case, the strict definition of fair value differs from the traditional definition of fair market value, although, in some cases, the outcome is the same.

The next chapter provides a sampling of cases showing the states' varying interpretations of the standard of fair value in various contexts.

Bibliography

Bauman, Jeffrey D., et al. *Corporations Law and Policy: Materials and Problems,* 4th ed., Supp. 2000.

Blair, Margaret M. "Locking in Capital: What Corporate Law Achieved for Business Owners in the Nineteenth Century." *51 UCLA Law Review*, 2003, p. 387.

Calio, Joseph Evan. "New Appraisals of Old Problems: Reflections on the Delaware Appraisal Proceeding." *American Business Law Journal*, May 1994.

Cory, Jacques. *Business Ethics: The Ethical Revolution of Minority Shareholders.* New York: Springer, 2004.

Dankoff, Timothy. "Shareholder Disputes." *The Litigation Newsletter*, Spring 2001, pp. 15–16.

Eggart, James. "Replacing the Sword with a Scalpel: The Case for a Bright-Line Rule Disallowing Application of Lack of Marketability Discounts in Shareholder Oppression Cases." *Arizona Law Review*, Vol. 44, No. 1, 2002, pp. 213–246.

Emory, John D. Jr. "The Role of Discounts in Determining 'Fair Value' under Wisconsin's Dissenters' Rights Statutes: The Case for Discounts." *Wisconsin Law Review*, March 1996, pp. 1155–75.

Fishman, Jay E., Shannon P. Pratt, et al. "Fair Value under Shareholder Dissent and Minority Oppression Actions" (Chapter 15). In *Guide to Business Valuations*, 16th ed. Fort Worth, TX: Practitioners Publishing Company, 2006.

Fishman, Jay E., and Anne C. Singer. "Fair Value for Oppressed and Dissenting Shareholders" (Chapter 15). In Robert F. Reilly and Robert P. Schweihs. *The Handbook of Advanced Business Valuation*. New York: McGraw-Hill, 2000.

Hempstead, John E. "Conduct of the Parties Now a Factor in New Jersey Fair Value Determinations." *Business Valuation Review*, September 1999, pp. 131–33.

Kruschke, Linda L. "Business Valuation Case Law Update." Presented at 2001 IBA National Conference, Orlando, Florida, May 11, 2001. Available at www.BVLibrary.com.

Lee, M. Mark, and Gilbert E. Matthews. "Fairness Opinions" (Chapter 16). In Robert F. Reilly and Robert P. Schweihs. *The Handbook of Advanced Business Valuation*. New York: McGraw-Hill, 2000.

Malick, S.A. "Oppression of and Relief for Minority Shareholders: Cases and Commentaries." Golden Books Centre, 2000.

Mantese, Gerard V. and Ian Williamson. "Minority Shareholder Oppression: From *Estes* to *Franchino*." *Michigan Bar Journal*, August 2005, pp. 16–20.

Miller, Sandra K. "What Buy-Out Rights, Fiduciary Duties and Dissolution Remedies Should Apply in the Case of Minority Owner of a Limited Liability Company." *38 Harvard Journal on Legislation,* 2001, pp. 413, 456.

Moll, Douglas K. "Minority Oppression and the Limited Liability Company: Learning (or Not) from Close Corporation History." *Wake Forest Law Review*, Vol. 40, 2005, p. 883.

_____. "Reasonable Expectations vs. Implied-In-Fact Contracts: Is the Shareholder Oppression Doctrine Needed?" *42 B.C. L. Rev.,* 2001, p. 989.

_____. "Shareholder Oppression and Dividend Policy in the Close Corporation." *Washington and Lee Law Review*, Vol. 60, No. 3, September 2003, pp. 841–924.

_____. "Shareholder Oppression and 'Fair Value': Of Discounts, Dates, and Dastardly Deeds in the Close Corporation." *54 Duke L.J,* 2004, p. 293.

_____. "Shareholder Oppression and Reasonable Expectations: Of Change, Gifts, and Inheritances in Close Corporation Disputes." *86 Minn. L. Rev*, 2002, p. 717.

_____. "Shareholder Oppression in Close Corporations: The Unanswered Questions of Perspective." *Vanderbilt Law Review*, Vol. 53, No. 3, April 2000, pp. 749–827.

O'Neal, F. Hodge, and Robert B. Thompson. *O'Neal's Oppression of Minority Shareholders*, 2nd ed. St. Paul MN: West Group, 1999.

Pratt, Shannon P. *The Market Approach to Valuing Businesses,* 2nd Ed. New York: John Wiley & Sons, 2005.

_____. "Marketability Discounts Frequently a Big Money Appraisal Controversy." *Shannon Pratt's Business Valuation Update*, April 2001.

_____. "Shareholder Suit Valuation Criteria Vary from State to State." *Valuation Strategies*, January/February 1999, pp. 12–15.

Quick, Daniel D. and Nakisha N. Chaney. "The Murkey Pit of Minority Shareholder Standing: A Moot Point?" *19 Mich. LW, 31*, 2004.

Shartsis, Arthur J. "Dissolution Actions Yield Less Than Fair Market Enterprise Value." *Judges & Lawyers Business Valuation Update*, January 1999, pp. 5–6.

Steinberg, Marc. "Short Form Mergers in Delaware." *Delaware Journal of Corporate Law,* Vol. 27, No. 2, 2002, pp. 489–504.

Utset, Manuel A. "Theory of Self-Control Problems and Incomplete Contracting: The Case of Shareholder Contracts." *Utah Law Review*, 2003, p. 1329.

Van Vleet, Daniel R., and Frederick W. Axley. "Fair Value in Dissenting Stockholder Disputes" (Chapter 9A). In Robert F. Reilly, Robert P. Schweihs et al., eds. *Financial Valuation: Businesses and Business Interests*, 1997 Update. New York: Warren, Gorham & Lamont, 1997, pp. U9A-1-26.

Chapter 36

Dissenting Stockholder and Minority Oppression Court Cases

Delaware has by far the most judicial precedent in the realm of dissenting stock-holder actions. Many states have none at all or none that may have addressed certain specific issues. When states lack their own precedent, they often look to other states' precedents.[1] Delaware tends to be the leader, but states also look particularly at decisions in other states that have statutes worded the same or similarly to their own.[2]

In the realm of stockholder oppression cases for judicial dissolution, California has by far the most precedential case law. As noted in the previous chapter, Delaware is one of the states that does not have a judicial dissolution statute.

A primary purpose of appraisal statutes is to protect minority shareholders and, to this end, courts generally give weight to the highest realistic price that a willing, able, and fully informed buyer would pay for the corporation as an entity.

Readers Must Interpret Cases Carefully

A study of the relevant case law is an essential prerequisite to estimation of fair value for either a dissenting stockholder action or a suit for dissolution in any jurisdiction. After having done one's best, however, rarely will the reader have clear-cut guidance as to the court's likely posture on every possible valuation issue.

The facts and circumstances of cases vary significantly from one to another. Thus, while prior cases should be studied for guidance, one must be very careful in interpreting them as a bright line of final authority.

Former Vice Chancellor Jack Jacobs of the Delaware Court of Chancery, now a Justice on the Delaware Supreme Court, clearly sounds this warning:

> Both my Court and the Delaware Supreme Court recognize that valuation cases are *extremely* fact-driven. Very few conclusions on valuation issues have universal applicability, though statements found in some opinions may have the appearance, and might be interpreted by some, as having sweeping generality.[3]

A case in point is a decision by the Supreme Court of Kansas on a dissenting stockholder suit arising out of a reverse stock split forcing a cash-out of minority stockholders. The Westlaw head-notes make the sweeping statement, without qualification, that "minority and marketability discounts are not appropriate when the purchaser of the stock is either the majority shareholder or the corporation itself." It would seem misleading to accept this broad interpretation, since the question put to the Kansas Supreme Court was limited to a forced cash-out, not to all events that could trigger a dissenting stockholder action.

The question put to the Kansas Supreme Court was:

> Is it proper for a corporation to determine the "fair value" of a fractional share pursuant to K.S.A. § 17-6405 by applying minority and marketability discounts when the fractional share resulted from a reverse stock split intended to eliminate the minority shareholder's interest in the corporation?[4]

---

[1] See, e.g., *Casey v. Amboy Bancorporation*, No. A-0715-04T3 (N.J. Supr. App. Div. Aug. 8, 2006).

[2] Because statutes of several states undergo revision every year, it is impractical to publish even summaries of all of them in a book such as this. Many state government web pages provide their state statutes on-line or they are available at law libraries.

[3] Shannon P. Pratt, "Fair Value: A View from the Delaware Court of Chancery" (interview with Jack B. Jacobs), *Shannon Pratt's Business Valuation Update*, September 1999, p. 2.

[4] *Katherine B. Arnaud, et al. v. Stockgrowers State Bank of Ashland, Kansas, et al.*, 992 P.2d 216, 1999 Kan. LEXIS 645 1999 WL 1000415 (Kan. Nov. 5, 1999).

The court concluded as follows:

> In answering the certified question before us, we hold that minority and marketability discounts should not be applied when the fractional share resulted from a reverse stock split intended to eliminate a minority shareholder's interest in the corporation.[5]

The sweeping generality of the Westlaw head-notes combined with the actual very specific applicability prompted the following comment:

> I think that it is important to recognize that this decision's applicability is limited to the narrow circumstances of the question put to the court.... There are many other actions where dissenters' rights are triggered even though the stockholders are not forced to be pushed out, a fact set which would seem to be very distinguishable from this case.[6]

Fair Value Is Not Fair Market Value

In most states, the standard of value for dissenting stockholder suits and for minority oppression suits is fair value.[7] Some states apply the fair value standard to withdrawing limited partners, comparing them to dissenting stockholders.[8] Several states statutes indicate that either "fair cash value" or simply "value" is the appropriate standard. The majority of states have adopted the fair value definition found in the Revised Model Business Corporation Act (RMBCA), promulgated by the American Bar Association. The RMBCA was revised in 1999.

Until 1999, the RMBCA definition was:

> The value of the shares immediately before the effectuation of the corporate action to which the shareholder objects, excluding any appreciation or depreciations in anticipation of the corporate action unless exclusion would be inequitable.

In 1999, the definition changed to:

> "Fair value" means the value of the corporation's shares determined:
>
> (i) immediately before the effectuation of the corporate action to which the shareholder objects;
> (ii) using customary and current valuation concepts and techniques generally employed for similar businesses in the context of the transaction requiring appraisal; and
> (iii) without discounting for lack of marketability or minority status except, if appropriate, for amendments to the articles....

The majority of states use the pre-1999 definition, and only a handful have adopted the 1999 version. A minority of states use the pre-1999 definition without the "unless exclusion would be inequitable" phrase, and some states omit this

---

[5] Ibid.

[6] Shannon P. Pratt, "Kansas Supreme Court Disallows Discounts in Reverse Split Forced Cashout," *Judges & Lawyers Business Valuation Update*, December 1999, p. 6.

[7] For a comprehensive discussion of fair value in shareholder dissent and oppression cases, see Jay E. Fishman, Shannon P. Pratt, and William J. Morrison, *Standards of Value: Theory and Applications* (Hoboken, NJ: John Wiley & Sons, 2007).

[8] See *East Park Ltd. Partnership v. Larkin*, 2006 Md. App. LEXIS 32 (Md. Ct. App. 2006).

phrase but, in addition, add a clause that states that all relevant factors should be considered in determining value. Florida uses a hybrid of the pre-1999 and 1999 definitions,[9] as does Illinois. Exhibit 36–1 groups the states by the definition they have adopted. However, even some states that have not adopted the 1999 revisions in their statutes have adopted the language in their case law by reference. While the various states interpret fair value quite differently from one another, and sometimes differently under differing facts and circumstances, they do *not* strictly equate fair value with fair market value.

This point is illustrated well by a New York court's rejection of an expert's valuation report based on fair market value in a dissenting stockholder case. The court stated:

> Because the petitioner's expert ... in its valuation report (on title page) and on 15 occasions refers to its valuation to be based on Fair Market Value, and the Business Corporation Law only uses the term Fair Value ... the Court considers it a threshold question as to whether Fair Value and Fair Market Value are synonymous.

> The Standard upon which [the company's expert's] valuation was based was Market Value.... the statutory standard is much broader.... The Court may give *no weight* [emphasis supplied] to market value if the facts of the case so require.[10]

The court ultimately did reject the report based on the standard of fair market value (concluding $52 per share) and awarded the dissenters $99 per share.

In *Le Beau v. M.G. Bancorporation, Inc.*, the investment banker had issued a fairness opinion on a squeeze-out merger based on fair market value rather than on fair value. The Delaware Court of Chancery stated that this was "legally flawed" as evidence regarding fair value.[11]

In *Pueblo Bancorporation v. Lindoe, Inc.*,[12] the Colorado Supreme Court, after an extensive review of the law in other jurisdictions, said, "We are convinced that 'fair value' does not mean 'fair market value.'" The New Jersey Supreme Court has expressed a similar sentiment,[13] as have the majority of other courts.[14]

In another Colorado case—but not a dissenters' rights case—involving a minority shareholder's challenge of a transaction as "unfair," in response to the shareholder's contention that no discounts should be allowed, the court admonished that "this case is not a dissenters' rights action....It involves the question of whether a transaction was fair, not the 'fair value' of dissenters' shares." Accordingly, the court held it was proper to discount the stock value by 15 to 20 percent for lack of marketability.[15] The case demonstrates the importance not only of being clear as to which standard of value is being applied, but also what kind of case is involved.

---

[9] In *Boettcher v. IMC Mortgage Co.*, 871 So. 2d 1047, 2004 Fla. App. LEXIS 6582; (Fla. App. May 12, 2004), the Florida Court of Appeals ruled that "'Fair value,' with respect to a dissenter's shares, means the value of the shares as of the close of business on the day prior to the shareholders' authorization date, excluding any appreciation or depreciation in anticipation of the corporate action unless exclusion would be inequitable."

[10] *Matter of Slant/Fin. Corp. v. The Chicago Corp.*, (N.Y. Sup. Ct. Oct. 5, 1995), *aff'd* 236 A.D.2d 547, 654 N.Y.S.2d 627 (N.Y. App. Div. Feb. 18, 1997).

[11] *Le Beau v. M.G. Bancorporation, Inc.*, 1998 Del. Ch. LEXIS 9, 1998 WL 44993 (Del. Ch. Jan. 29, 1998).

[12] *Pueblo Bancorporation v. Lindoe, Inc.*, 63 P.3d 353, 2003 Colo. LEXIS 53 (Colo. Jan. 21, 2003).

[13] In *Lawson Mardon Wheaton, Inc. v. Smith*, 160 N.J. 383, 734 A.2d 738 (N.J. 1999), the Court concurred with the intermediate appellate court, which said, "Fair Value carries with it the statutory purposes that shareholders be fairly compensated, which may or may not equate with the market's judgment about the stock's value. This is particularly appropriate in the close corporation setting where there is no ready market for the shares and consequently no Fair Market Value." 716 A.2d 550, 558 (N.J. Super. App. Div. Aug. 26, 1998).

[14] See, e.g., *Swope v. Seigel-Robert, Inc.*, 243 F.3d 486, 2001 U.S. App. LEXIS 2760 (8th Cir. 2001); *Wenzel v. Hopper & Galliher, P.C.*, 779 N.E.2d 30, (Ind. Ct. App. 2002); *First W. Bank Wall v. Olsen*, 2001 SD 16, 621 N.W.2d 611, (S.D. 2001); *Matthew G. Norton Co. v. Smyth*, 112 Wn. App. 865, 51 P.3d 159, (Wash. Ct. App. 2002); *HMO-W, Inc. v. SSM Health Care Sys.*, 2000 WI 46, 234 Wis. 2d 707, 611 N.W.2d 250 (Wis. 2000).

[15] *Kim v. The Grover C. Coors Trust*, 2007 Colo. App. LEXIS 394 (Colo. App. March 8, 2007).

Exhibit 36–1

States That Adopted the RMBCA Definition of Fair Value

State	Applicable State Statute
Pre-1999 Definition of Fair Value	
Alabama	Ala. Code §10-2B-13.01(4) (Michie 2006)
Arizona	Ariz. Rev. Stat. Ann §10-1301(4) (2006)
Arkansas	Ark. Code Ann. §4-27-1301(3) (2006)
Colorado	Colo. Rev. §7-113-101(4) (2006)
Hawaii	Haw. Rev. Stat. §414-341 (2006)
Indiana	Burns Ind. Code §23-1-44-3 (2006)
Kentucky	Ky. Rev. Stat. Ann. §271 B.13-010(3) (Michie 2006)
Massachusetts	Ann. Laws of Mass. GL Ch. 156D §13.01 (2006)
Michigan	Mich. Comp. Laws Serv. §450.1761(d) (2006)
Missouri	Mo. Ann. Stat. §351.870 (2006)
Montana	Mont. Code. Ann. §35-1-826(4) (2006)
Nebraska	Neb. Rev. Stat. §21-20,137(4) (2006)
Nevada	Nev. Rev. Stat. §92A.320 (2006)
New Hampshire	N.H. Rev. Stat. Ann. §293-A:13.01(3) (2006)
North Carolina	N.C. Gen. Stat. §55-13-01(3) (2006)
Oregon	Or. Rev. Stat. §60.551(4) (2006)
South Carolina	S.C. Code Ann. §33-13-101(3) (2005)
Vermont	Vt. Stat. Ann. Tit. 11A, §13.01(3) (2006)
Washington	Wash. Rev. Code §23B.13.010(3) (2006)
Wisconsin	Wis. Stat. §180.1301 (2006)
Wyoming	Wyo. Stat. § 17-16-1301 (a) (iv) (2006)
Pre-1999 Definition of Fair Value Without "Exclusion" Phrase	
Georgia	Ga. Stat. Ann. §14-2-1301(5) (2006)
New Mexico	N.M. Stat. Ann. §53-15-4(A) (Michie 2007)
Rhode Island	R.I. Gen. Laws §7-1.2-1202(a) (2006)
Tennessee	Tenn. Code Ann §48-23-101(4) (2006)
Utah	Utah Code Ann. §16-10a-1301(4) (2006)
Pre-1999 Definition of Fair Value With "Relevant Factors" Phrase and Without "Exclusion" Phrase	
Delaware	Del. Code Ann. Tit. 8, §262(h) (2006)
Oklahoma	Okla. Stat. Ann. Tit. 18, §1091(H) (2006)
Pennsylvania	15 Pa.C.S. §1572 (2006)
1999 Definition of Fair Value	
Connecticut	Conn. Gen. Stat. §33-855(4) (2006)
Idaho	Idaho Code §30-1-1301 (2006)
Iowa	Iowa Code §490.1301(4) (2005)
Maine	13-C Maine Rev. Stat. §1301(4) (2006)
Mississippi	Miss. Code Ann. §79-4-13.01(4) (2006)
South Dakota	S.D. Codified Laws §47-1A-1301 (2006)
Virginia	Va. Code Ann §13.1-729 (Michie 2006)
West Virginia	W. Va. Code §31D-13-1301 (4) (2006)
Hybrid Definition of Fair Value	
Florida[a]	Fla. Stat. §607.1301(4) (2006)
Illinois[b]	Ill. Compiled Statutes Ch. 805, §5/11.70(j) (i) (2006)

Notes

[a] The Florida Statute incorporates the first two clauses of the 1999 definition, but then adds the last clause of the pre-1999 definition and a clause limiting the definition to a corporation with 10 or fewer shareholders. Florida also uses this definition for appraisal rights of limited liability company members [Fla. Stat §608.4351 (2006)].

[b] Before the pre-1999 definition, the Illinois Statute adds the following: "the proportionate interest of the shareholder in the corporation, without discount for minority status or, absent extraordinary circumstance, lack of marketability."

SOURCE: Jay E. Fishman, Shannon P. Pratt, J. Clifford Griffith, *Guide to Business Valuations*, 17th ed. (Fort Worth, TX: Practitioner's Publishing Company, 2007), 15-1, copyright © 2007. All rights reserved. Reprinted with permission of Practitioner's Publishing Company. Copies of this *Guide* can be ordered by calling PPC at (800) 323-8724 or log onto *www.ppc.thomson.com*.

Premise of Value

In a dissenters' rights action, Delaware case law provides that a shareholder is entitled to a proportionate share of the corporation as a going concern based on the operative reality of the company at the time of merger, rather than on a liquidation basis.[16] In an oppressed shareholder context, Oregon courts have held that the minority shareholder is entitled to his proportionate share of the value of the corporation as a going concern.[17]

A related issue decided by the Delaware courts is that the value of change-of-control synergies must be excluded from a merger price in determining the value of a company on a going-concern basis. In *Union Illinois v. Union Financial Group, Ltd.*,[18] the Court applied a 13 percent deduction for synergies. Other items that are excluded in determining going-concern value are prospective tax benefits,[19] actions planned by a third-party acquirer before a change of control (but definite plans of an acquirer made after a change of control may be accounted for),[20] excessive compensation,[21] and improperly issued shares.[22]

In *Cede & Co., Inc. v. Medpointe Healthcare, Inc.*,[23] the Chancery Court ruled that where an asset sale and merger were contingent on each other, capital gains taxes and other expenses related to the asset sale should be deducted in determining the value of the merged company. The Court reasoned that the asset sale was a part of the merged company's operative reality on the valuation date.

Breach of Fiduciary Duty Expands Plaintiffs' Potential Damages

As noted in the previous chapter, the concept of "entire fairness" includes both procedural fairness and fair consideration paid. If the test of entire fairness is not met, then plaintiffs' damages may go well beyond the simple dissenting stockholder appraisal rights remedy. Conceptually, this is because the courts will treat the claims independently, as though there were an appraisal action and, in addition, a separate breach of fiduciary duty action.[24]

An example of lack of entire fairness is discussed in the Delaware case of *M.G. Bancorporation v. Le Beau*:

---

[16] See, e.g., *Rapid-American Corp. v. Harris*, 603 A.2d 796 (Del. Jan. 23, 1992); *Paskill Corp. v. Algoma Corp.*, 747 A.2d 549, 2000 Del. LEXIS 117 (Del. Mar. 7, 2000); *Montgomery Cellular Holding Co. v. Dobler*, 880 A.2d 206, 2005 Del. LEXIS 295 (Del. Aug. 1, 2005).

[17] *Hayes v. Olmstead & Assoc., Inc.*, 173 Ore. App. 259, 21 P.3d 178(Ore. Ct. App. Mar. 28, 2001)(rejecting majority shareholders' argument that awarding the oppressed shareholder his pro rata share of the company on a going-concern basis would unduly burden the company); *Cooke v. Fresh Express Foods Corp.*, 169 Ore. App. 101, 7 P.3d 717, 2000 Ore. App. LEXIS 1128 (Ore. Ct. App. July 12, 2000).

[18] *The Union Illinois 1995 Investment Limited Partnership v. Union Financial Group, Ltd.*, 847 A.2d 340 (Del. Ch. Dec. 19, 2003).

[19] *Ng v. Heng Sang Realty Corp.*, 2004 Del. Ch. LEXIS 62 (Del. Ch. May 20, 2004), *aff'd w/o op.*, 2005 Del. LEXIS 45 (Del. Jan. 27, 2005).

[20] *Cede & Co. v. Technicolor, Inc.*, 684 A.2d 289 (Del. Oct. 14, 1996).

[21] *Gonsalves v. Straight Arrow Publishers*, 701 A.2d 357 (Del. Oct. 21, 1997).

[22] *Gentile v. SinglePoint Financial*, 2003 Del. Ch. LEXIS 21, 2003 WL 1240504 (Del. Ch. Mar. 5, 2003).

[23] *Cede & Co., Inc. v. Medpointe Healthcare, Inc.*, 2004 Del. Ch. LEXIS 124 (Del. Ch. Aug. 16. 2004).

[24] See, e.g., *In re Emerging Communications, Inc. Shareholders Litigation*, 2004 Del. Ch. LEXIS 70 (May 3, 2004), where the court stated that in "(1) In the appraisal action, Innovative, as the surviving corporation, is liable to [plaintiff] in the amount of $38.05 per share for each of the 750,300 shares that are subject to the appraisal, plus interest at the rate of 6.27%, compounded monthly, from the date of the merger to the date of the judgment" and "(2) In the fiduciary duty action, defendants Innovative, ICC, Prosser, Raynor and Muoio are jointly and severally liable to the plaintiff class and to [plaintiff] … in an amount equal to $27.80 per share."

In assessing the validity of the substantive unfairness claims, at least two factors are pivotal. The first is the defendants' failure to establish an independent committee of directors to represent the minority stockholders' interests.... [I]n the [short-form merger] context the absence of a negotiating committee of independent directors, without more, does not constitute unfair dealing as a matter of law. Nonetheless, that circumstance is evidence of unfair dealing that, when combined with other pleaded facts, may state a cognizable unfair dealing claim that the fiduciaries will ultimately have the duty to negate.

The second critical factor, of which the Court takes judicial notice, is that the fair value of the plaintiffs' shares has now been adjudicated at $85 per share [in the judicial appraisal action]. The significant gap between the $41 merger price and the $85 appraisal value, combined with the other substantive unfairness allegations (including the improper manner in which the $41 merger price was arrived at), create an inference that the Merger was the product of unfair dealing.[25]

We noted in the previous chapter that the issue of independence went not only to the appointment of a committee of independent directors, but also to the requirement that the committee retain legal counsel and financial advisers that are independent of the control parties. Failure on the latter requirement is illustrated by a case in which the trial court was willing to accept that the procedure was fair based on appointment of an independent committee of the board. The decision, however, was reversed at the appellate level because neither the legal counsel nor the financial advisers retained were deemed independent of the control parties.

In *Kahn v. Tremont Corporation*,[26] the Delaware Court of Chancery found that Tremont's appointment of a special committee of disinterested directors adequately shifted the burden of proof to the plaintiffs on the issue of fairness. Plaintiffs appealed and the Supreme Court of Delaware noted that the committee chose as its financial adviser a bank that had lucrative past dealings with related companies controlled by the same stockholder as the subject company. Furthermore, the committee's legal adviser was previously retained by two of the controlling stockholders' related companies in connection with past transactions. The court concluded that the special committee did not act in an independent and informed manner. The case was reversed and remanded for a new fairness determination, with the burden of proof remaining with the defendants.

A classic case in which the directors' breach of fiduciary duty resulted in damages not being limited to fair value is *Ryan v. Tad's Enterprises, Inc..*[27] Certain salient facts of the transactions were as follows:

1. The Townsend brothers owned 72.6 percent of the stock.
2. Prior to the merger, Tad's sold its chain of six restaurants. In conjunction with the restaurant sale, the two Townsend brothers received $1 million each for noncompete and consulting agreements.
3. An attorney acted in the capacity of a board member, represented the corporation in the transactions, and represented the Townsend brothers personally in negotiating the consulting and noncompete agreements.

---

[25] *M.G. Bancorporation v. Le Beau*, 737. A.2d 513 (Del. Apr. 30, 1999). See also, for example, *Boyer v. Wilmington Materials, Inc.*, 754 A.2d 881, 1999 Del. Ch. LEXIS 4, 1999 WL 393549 (Del. Ch. Jan. 20, 1999).

[26] *Kahn v. Tremont Corporation*, 694 A.2d 422, 1997 Del. Ch. LEXIS 205, 1997 WL 332976 (Del. June 10, 1997).

[27] *Ryan v. Tad's Enterprises, Inc.*, 709 A.2d 682, 1996 Del. Ch. LEXIS 54 1996 WL 204502 (Del. Ch. Apr. 24, 1996), *aff'd w/o opp.*, 693 A.2d 1082 (Del. 1997).

4. Tad's board did not retain any unaffiliated law firm, financial adviser, or other independent representative to represent or negotiate the merger on behalf of Tad's minority shareholders.

5. Tad's board did hire an investment banking firm to furnish an opinion that the $13.25 merger price was fair to the minority stockholders. However:

   a. It was not asked to, nor did it, opine on the fairness of the Townsends' noncompete and consulting agreements.

   b. At the board meeting when the merger was approved, the firm did not discuss its valuation analysis or provide any written materials.

   c. The investment banking firm's subsequent written opinion listed information considered, but no projections or forecasts were provided by the board.

The court noted that it normally would defer to a board's judgment, on the presumption of due care and good faith.

> However, that presumption vanishes in cases where the minority shareholders are compelled to forfeit their shares in return for a value that is "determined as a result of a bargaining process in which the controlling shareholder is in a position to influence both bargaining parties." In such cases, the Court will carefully scrutinize the board's actions to ascertain:

> • whether the board instituted measures to ensure a fair process, and
> • whether the board achieved a fair price for the disinterested stockholder minority....

> The business judgment review standard will not apply where the decision under challenge is made by a board, a majority of whom have a material conflict of interest in the transaction.

The court concluded:

> Defendants are liable to the plaintiffs for breaching their fiduciary duty of loyalty. The question then becomes, what is the extent of that liability.... *the measure of damages for breach of fiduciary duty is not limited to the corporation's fair value as determined in an appraisal.* [emphasis supplied]

> Ultimately, the court ordered the noncompete proceeds to be distributed to all shareholders, and dissenters were awarded a total of $23.86 per share, compared with $13.26 originally offered.

Approaches to Value

Most courts embrace all three broad approaches to value (income, market, and asset-based approaches) in dissenting stockholder and judicial dissolution cases. The Chancery Court of Delaware has repeatedly expressed a preference for the discounted cash flow method (citations will be provided in sections to follow on the income approach). However, reliance on the DCF method is dependent on reasonable projections, which are not always available.

Should Consider Market Value, Asset Value, and Investment Value

In Utah's dissenters' case of first impression, *Oakridge Energy v. Clifton*,[28] the Supreme Court of Utah reviewed and cited case law from other states that had similar statutes, including Iowa, Maryland, Maine, Delaware, and Massachusetts. The company (which was public before the triggering event) paid dissenting stockholders $2.75 per share, based on a $2.50 market price plus a $0.25 dividend. Plaintiffs claimed $3.57 per share based on a pro forma balance sheet after taking the effect of the proceeds of the asset sale that triggered dissenters' rights.

The court noted that the consensus of the cases cited is that the component elements to be relied on in estimating fair value are market value, net asset value, and investment value, and "the courts have traditionally favored investment value,[29] rather than asset value, as the most important of the three elements." The court stated:

> We conclude that the trial court erred in using the stock market price … as the sole criterion for determining the fair value…. We agree with the courts cited above that a dissenting shareholder disclaims both the burden and the benefit of the disfavored corporate action … under the plain language of the statute, any effect of the Cometra sale must be excluded…. No informed expert even ventured to suggest the Oakridge assets could be valued at $21.5 million prior to Cometra's offer…. "fair value" is not measured by any unique benefits that will accrue to the acquiring corporation….the sale price here was not reinforced by several buyers bidding against each other.

The defendants had introduced testimony that net asset value before the events was $2.13 per share. Neither side had introduced evidence of investment value. Therefore, the Supreme Court concluded:

> The stock market price and a reasonable approximation of the asset value were before the trial court, each supported by substantial evidence of investment value….Absent evidence of investment value, the trial court should at least have considered the asset value as well as the market price of the stock.
>
> However, since the per share value based on asset value ($2.13) is less than the stock market price ($2.50), no choice of weighting would have resulted in a per share value greater than $2.50 for the Oakridge stock. Thus the trial court's error is harmless, indeed beneficial to the dissenters since Oakridge has not sought an adjustment of the $2.75 already paid.
>
> We affirm the judgment of the trial court.

Unfortunately, courts' interpretations of market value, investment value, and asset value vary. For example, asset value usually means the net assets adjusted to some premise of current value. However, one decision used the market price to the book value pricing multiple of a group of guideline companies as a proxy for asset value, resulting in asset value being measured as 1.29 times book value.[30]

---

[28] *Oakridge Energy, Inc. v. Clifton*, 937 P.2d 130, 1997 WL 191487 (Utah Apr. 18, 1997).

[29] Investment value, as used here, is as defined in the previous chapter (a value based on earnings), as opposed to the definition of investment value in contexts other than fair value determinations—that is, the value to a particular buyer or seller.

[30] *Berens v. Ludwig, Comptroller of the Currency*, 953 F. Supp. 249, 1997 WL 64073 (N.D. Ill. Feb. 13, 1997).

In *In the Matter of Markman*,[31] a judicial dissolution/oppression case, investment value based upon the capitalization of excess earnings via a cash flow analysis was accepted for a determination of fair market value. The court ruled that evidence of corporate wrongdoing was relevant to a valuation using investment value since, if proven, the alleged misappropriation of corporate funds would have had a detrimental effect on the corporation's earning power and value under that method. Specifically, net income would have to be adjusted by eliminating excess compensation and the unauthorized purchase of personal life insurance and rental of a luxury car.

Consideration of all these major elements, that is, market value, investment value, and asset value, does not necessarily mean that all three will be utilized in the final analysis. In some cases weight will be accorded to all three, in some cases, only two, and some cases will be decided entirely on the basis of one of the three major elements. Investment value typically is accorded the greatest weight, followed by market value, with asset value usually accorded the least weight. Some Delaware cases, for example, have ultimately been decided entirely on the basis of investment value measured by the discounted cash flow method and others based entirely on guideline companies.

Market Approach

As is true with tax cases, the acceptance of evidence and conclusions using the market approach is very sensitive to the comparability of the guideline companies chosen.

In *Doft & Co. v. Travelocity.com, Inc.*,[32] experts for both sides used both a discounted cash flow (DCF) method and a comparable guideline public company method to value Travelocity.com Inc. (Travelocity). In performing their comparable company analyses, both experts used Expedia—one of Travelocity's main competitors—as the single comparable company. The Delaware Chancery Court rejected the DCF method because it found that management projections were unreliable, but accepted the comparable company method, even though it was based on only one company, because it found that Expedia was clearly comparable to Travelocity. The Court also used a comparable companies approach in *Agranoff v. Miller*.[33]

In *Borruso v. Communications Telesystems International*,[34] both experts used only the guideline publicly traded company method, both relying primarily on multiples of revenue, because the financial history was insufficient to provide a basis for a DCF analysis or even multiples of economic income variables such as earnings before interest, taxes, depreciation, and amortization (EBITDA). Each expert used eight guideline companies. The court used the five that were in common between the two experts, plus one from the dissenters' expert's group. The court opinion provided a discussion worth reading about its reasons for acceptance and rejection of various guideline companies offered by the experts.

The dissenters' expert started with the median of the pricing multiples of his guideline companies, and adjusted from there for differences in general between

---

[31] *In the Matter of Markman*, 2006 N.Y. Misc. LEXIS 3810 (N.Y. Sup. Ct. December 18, 2006).

[32] *Doft & Co. v. Travelocity.com Inc.*, 2004 Del. Ch. LEXIS 75 (Del. Ch. May 20, 2004).

[33] *Agranoff v. Miller*, 2001 Del. Ch. LEXIS 71 (Del. Ch. May 15, 2001).

[34] *Carl Borruso and William Lee v. Communications Telesystems International*, 1999 Del. Ch. LEXIS 197 (Del. Ch. Sept. 24, 1999).

the guideline group and the subject company. The company's expert applied adjustments to the multiples of each individual company to reflect differences between each of them and the subject. The court adopted the latter procedure. The court rejected the upward adjustment made by the dissenters' expert to reflect superior growth in the most recent fiscal year, because there was no evidence in the record that this growth was sustainable.

The court's position on discounts and/or premiums applicable to the result of the guideline company analysis is discussed in the subsequent section on discounts and premiums.

Another case that accepted the market approach involved shares of a bank stock in a dissenting stockholder case. The court ultimately relied on a pricing multiple of total capital and a price/earnings multiple.[35]

An opinion in a dissenting stockholder case concluded that a multiple of EBITDA procedure was better than the DCF method in that particular case. It based its concluded multiple on that paid by the subject company in two prior acquisitions that it had made.[36]

In other instances, the Court has averaged the results of the guideline public company method with those returned by other methods, such as DCF,[37] or has accorded the comparable companies method significantly less weight than another method.[38]

Guideline Merged and Acquired Company (Transaction) Method

In contrast to most Delaware appraisal cases, the court in a bank holding company case, *Le Beau v. M.G. Bancorporation*[39] rejected both the discounted cash flow and the guideline publicly traded company analysis, both of which were presented by experts on both sides, because of perceived errors. Instead of adjusting the experts' valuations for the alleged errors, the court relied on an analysis of guideline merged and acquired companies (also known as the transaction method), which it normally rejects as unpermissably including a control premium. The Court justified the methodology in this case by reference to *Rapid American* (see section on control premiums):

> In *Harris v. Rapid American*, the Supreme Court ruled that a holding company's ownership of a controlling interest in its subsidiaries is an independent element of value that must be taken into account in determining a fair value for the parent company.
>
> Although the respondents argued that this decision should apply only to subsidiaries operating in different businesses, the Vice Chancellor disagreed.[40]

---

[35] *Mark H. Berens v. Eugene A. Ludwig*, 160 F.3d 1144, 1998 WL 797169 (7th Cir. Nov. 17, 1998), *aff'g Berens v. Ludwig, Comptroller of the Currency*, 953 F. Supp. 249, 1997 WL 64073 (N.D. Ill. Feb. 13, 1997).

[36] *Connector Service Corporation v. Jeffrey Briggs*, 1998 U.S. Dist. LEXIS 18864 (N.D. Ill. Oct. 30, 1998).

[37] *Taylor v. American Specialty Retailing Group, Inc.*, 2003 Del. Ch. LEXIS 75 (July 15, 2003); *Gray v. Cytokine Pharmasciences, Inc.*, 2002 Del. Ch. LEXIS 48 (Apr. 25, 2002).

[38] See, e.g., *Andaloro v. PFPC Worldwide, Inc.*, 2005 Del. Ch. LEXIS 125 (Del. Ch. Aug. 19, 2005) (the court gave the DCF method 75 percent weight, and the comparable companies method only 25 percent).

[39] *Le Beau v. M.G. Bancorporation, Inc.*

[40] Ibid.

The Court continues to accept this method, especially when it finds that other methods are unreliable in a particular case. For example, in *Prescott Group Small Cap, L.P. v. The Coleman Co.*,[41] the Court accepted a comparable transaction methodology, among others, but did not attribute a particular weight to each of the methods it relied on.

In reviewing the case, Gilbert Matthews criticized the decision:

> This reasoning leads to the absurd conclusion that a business conducted through a subsidiary is entitled to a control premium, but an identical business conducted through a division is not! The application of a control premium at a subsidiary level, when such premium is not permitted at the parent level, is an anomaly that is difficult to justify.[42]

Discounted Cash Flow Method

In *Gholl v. eMachines, Inc.*,[43] the Court said of the DCF method: "This method is widely accepted in the financial community and has frequently been relied upon by this Court in appraisal actions." In that case, the Court rejected the appraisers' valuations and conducted its own DCF analysis. In *Andaloro v. PFPC Worldwide, Inc.*,[44] the Court echoed this sentiment, saying "The DCF model of valuation is a standard one that gives life to the finance principle that firms should be valued based on the expected value of their future cash flows, discounted to present value in a manner that accounts for risk. The DCF method is frequently used in this court and, I, like many others, prefer to give it great, and sometimes even exclusive, weight when it may be used responsibly." In that case, the Court gave 75 percent weight to the DCF method. In *In re United States Cellular Operating Co.*,[45] the Court said, "While DCF analyses have become the dominant approach in appraisal proceedings … the ultimate selection of a valuation framework remains within the court's discretion."

In *Cede & Co. v. Technicolor, Inc.*,[46] the Court used a DCF method to value the company in a squeeze-out cash merger by using DCF to value each of the company's operating business segments separately. The Court valued businesses that were to be sold at the present value of expected proceeds, and then deducted debt and capitalized corporate expenses (excluding the parent's management fee).

In *In re PNB Holding Co.*,[47] involving appraisal as well as entire fairness claims relating to a cash-out merger that permitted the corporation—a bank holding company—to reclassify itself as an S corporation, the court rejected comparable company and comparable acquisitions approaches and focused exclusively on the experts' DCF analyses.

The court determined that the entire fairness standard of review applied, and determined that shareholders who had not sought appraisal, but who had accepted the merger consideration, would be entitled to the same compensation as those who had sought appraisal. The measure of compensation for these shareholders

[41] *Prescott Group Small Cap, L.P. v. The Coleman Co.*, 2004 Del. Ch. LEXIS 131 (Del. Ch. Sept. 8, 2004).
[42] Gilbert E. Matthews, "Delaware Court Relies on Comparable Acquisition Method," *Shannon Pratt's Business Valuation Update*, March 1998, p. 11.
[43] *Gholl v. eMachines, Inc.*, 2004 Del. Ch. LEXIS 171 (Del. Ch. Nov. 24, 2004).
[44] *Andaloro v. PFPC Worldwide, Inc.*, 2005 Del. Ch. LEXIS 125 (Del. Ch. Aug. 19, 2005).
[45] *In re United States Cellular Operating Co.*, 2005 Del. Ch. LEXIS 1 (Del. Ch. Jan. 6, 2005).
[46] *Cede & Co. v. Technicolor, Inc.*, 2003 Del. Ch. LEXIS 146, 2003 WL 23700218 (Del. Ch. Dec. 31, 2003), *aff'd in part, rev'd in part, and remanded by* 884 A.2d 26, 2005 Del. LEXIS 535 (Del. 2005).
[47] *In re PNB Holding Co.*, 2006 Del. Ch. LEXIS 158 (August 18, 2006).

would be the difference between the fair value of the shares, as determined by the court, and the consideration they had received. Because there was no useful market information about the company's value, the court looked to valuation metrics. In other words, to measure whether the merger price was unfair, the court indicated it would conduct the same essential inquiry as in an appraisal, albeit with more leeway to consider fairness as a range and to consider the remedial objectives of equity.

In *Gilbert v. M.P.M. Enterprises*,[48] both sides presented both a guideline publicly traded company method and a DCF method. The court decided to base its conclusion on the DCF method. The dissenters presented what they called a "buy side DCF" and a "sell side DCF." The court said that the sell side model was the only appropriate one to consider because the law requires valuation as a going concern without "any element of value arising from the accomplishment or expectation of a merger." After an argument over whether to use the build-up or capital asset pricing model (CAPM) procedure to develop a discount rate, the court decided in favor of CAPM.

In *Hintmann v. Fred Weber*, the Delaware Court of Chancery was presented with both the build-up method and the CAPM method for estimating the appropriate present value discount rate. The court rejected the build-up method, noting that, "This method differed from the CAPM in only one respect: It did not employ beta. The CAPM would seem to be more useful than the 'build-up' method because it offers more complete information. Specifically, the CAPM includes a measure of the stock's systematic risk."[49]

Reliability of Underlying Assumptions and Projections. The Court has emphasized that it will accept the DCF method only if it finds that the underlying projections and assumptions are reliable,[50] and has concluded that, generally, premerger projections are more reliable than postmerger projections.[51] It has also cautioned that if a method DCF appraisal is so heavily dependent on the determination of a company's terminal value that the entire exercise amounts to little more than a special case of the comparable companies approach to value, then the DCF value has little or no independent validity.[52]

Thus, in *The Union Illinois 1995 Investment Limited Partnership v. Union Financial Group, Ltd.*,[53] the Court rejected both sides' experts DCF valuations, and the DCF method altogether, because it was not comfortable with the adjustments the experts made to management projections and other inputs they used. In *Finkelstein v. Liberty Digital, Inc.*,[54] the Court found the appraiser's DCF analysis "incredible" because the appraiser eschewed any reliance on the real-world beliefs of the company's management team about the company's prospects and, in the absence of any management projections of cash flows, invented his own.

---

[48] *Gilbert v. M.P.M. Enterprises, Inc.*, 1998 Del. Ch. LEXIS 60 (Del. Ch. Apr. 24, 1998), *aff'd M.P.M. Enterprises, Inc. v. Jeffrey D. Gilbert*, 731 A.2d 790 (Del. June 25, 1999).

[49] *Hintmann v. Fred Weber, Inc.*, 1998 Del. Ch. LEXIS 26, 1998 WL 853052 (Del. Ch. Feb. 17, 1998).

[50] *In re United States Cellular Operating Co.*, 2005 Del. Ch. LEXIS 1 (Del. Ch. Jan. 6, 2005) ("This Court repeatedly has recognized that the reliability of a DCF analysis depends on the reliability of the inputs to the model."); *Andaloro v. PFPC Worldwide, Inc.*, 2005 Del. Ch. LEXIS 125 (Del. Ch. Aug. 19, 2005) ("a DCF valuation is the best technique for valuing an entity when the necessary information regarding the required inputs is available").

[51] *Cede & Co. v. Technicolor, Inc.*, 2003 Del. Ch. LEXIS 146, 2003 WL 23700218 (Del. Ch. Dec. 31, 2003) ("contemporary pre-merger management projections are particularly useful in the appraisal context because management projections, by definition, are not tainted by post-merger hindsight and are usually created by an impartial body.").

[52] *Prescott Group Small Cap, L.P. v. The Coleman Co.*, 2004 Del. Ch. LEXIS 131 (Del. Ch. Sept. 8, 2004).

[53] *The Union Illinois 1995 Investment Limited Partnership v. Union Financial Group, Ltd.*, 847 A.2d 340 (Del. Ch. Dec. 19, 2003).

[54] *Finkelstein v. Liberty Digital, Inc.*, 2005 Del Ch. LEXIS 53 (Del. Ch. April 25, 2005).

In *Lane v. Cancer Treatment Centers of America, Inc.*,[55] the Court encountered an appraisal action involving a short-lived, niche company. Although the Court said that "[o]ne can reasonably have doubts about the ability of a DCF analysis to capture accurately the fair value of an emerging company with an earnings history of less than two years," the Court essentially adopted a DCF method, because it found it to be the more reasonable of the two presented. The Court, however, revised the approach in the projection of costs, the estimate of long-term growth, and other assumptions.

In *Gesoff v. IIC Industries, Inc.*,[56] the Delaware Chancery Court rejected the values arrived at by both experts' DCF analyses. As to the minority shareholders' expert, the court found that he used concocted calculations, used country-specific risk premia that were too low, incorrectly applied control premia to DCF analysis, and incorrectly discounted the existence of a small stock risk premium in all circumstances. As for the company's expert, the court found that he used sound methodology, but would require adjustments to the specific company risk premium, size premia, and the international cost of capital. Making these adjustments, the court performed its own DCF.

Tax Affecting Pass-Through Entities. In *Delaware Open MRI Radiology Associates, P.A. v. Kessler*,[57] a group of practicing radiologists formed Delaware Open MRI Radiology Associates, P.A. (Delaware Radiology), an S corporation, to capture additional revenues by owning MRI centers—several of which were proposed by the time of litigation.

Eventually, various disputes among the doctors fractured them into two groups: a majority group with 62.5 percent ownership and a minority group with 37.5 percent. To "squeeze out" the minority in a forced merger, the majority formed an acquisition company and hired a valuation analyst to calculate a price for the minority shares. The appraiser opined that the value was $16,228.55 per share. The minority shareholders brought suit in a combined appraisal and entire fairness action in Delaware Chancery Court, claiming, among other things, that the price was unfair.

The court, agreeing with the minority, found that the majority's valuation did not represent a fair price. Instead, the court determined that the minority shareholders were entitled to their pro rata share of Delaware Radiology's appraisal value on the merger date, which it concluded was $33,232.26 per share. The court arrived at this value by examining the company as a going concern on the merger date, considering all relevant, non speculative data. Specifically, the court used the minority group's expert's DCF method, but applied an entity level tax rate of 29.4 percent to account for the advantages of the entity being an S corporation. This tax rate was determined from the minority group's members' marginal personal taxes.

The majority group's expert tax affected the company's earnings as if it were a C corporation rather than an S corporation. Applying "high" discount rates of 21.4 percent and 22.4 percent to two MRI centers, the expert came to a value of $6.8 million for the company, or $17,039 per share. The minority's expert did not tax affect the company's earnings at all. He also used a lower discount rate to arrive at a value of $26.4 million for the company, or $66,074 per share.

The court also found fault with the majority expert's treatment of the company as if it were a C corp, since there was absolutely no evidence that the small but

[55] *Lane v. Cancer Treatment Centers of America, Inc.*, 2004 Del. Ch. LEXIS 108 (Del. Ch. July 30, 2004).
[56] *Gesoff v. IIC Industries, Inc.* 902 A.2d 1130, 2006 Del. Ch. LEXIS 91 (Del. Ch. 2006).
[57] *Delaware Open MRI Radiology Associates, P.A. v. Kessler*, 2006 Del. Ch. LEXIS 84 (Del. Ch. 2006).

highly profitable company would ever convert to a C corporation. Its shareholders—all in premium tax brackets—placed a substantial value on the company's tax status as an S corp. The court found that the merger had deprived them of these benefits, and that, therefore, the majority expert's valuation approach "denied [them] the value they would have received as continuing S Corp stockholders," ensuring the merger price was lower than fair value.

The court also found fault with the minority expert's failure to tax affect the company's earnings as a going concern, since this would overstate the value of the company at the stockholder level. To capture the precise advantage of the S corp structure to the minority shareholders, the court considered the difference between the value that a minority member would receive if the company was a C corp, and the value received as an S corp. In its undertaking, the court "embraced" the leading Tax Court cases (*Gross, Heck,* and *Adams*—see Chapter 28 for a detailed discussion of these cases), which have "given life to the advantages of S corporation status by refusing to tax affect the… earnings at all." It also relied on the factual realities to depart from these cases' precedent:

> My difference with these prior decisions is at the level of implementation rather than at the level of principle. Certainly, in this context when minority stockholders have been forcibly denied the future benefits of S corporation status, they should receive compensation for those expected benefits and not an artificially discounted value that disregards the favorable tax treatment….But the minority should not receive more than a fair S corporation valuation. Refusing to tax affect at all produces such a windfall…The amount that should be the basis for an appraisal or entire fairness award is the amount that estimates the company's value to the [minority] as S corporation stockholders paying individual income taxes at the highest rates—an amount that is materially more…than if the [company] were a C corporation.

To accurately capture this value, the court estimated what an equivalent, hypothetical "predividend" S corporation tax rate would be, assuming annual earnings of $100 and highest marginal tax rates.

Although this was not a tax case, the Chancery Court comprehensively reviewed the key legal and economic issues surrounding the tax-affecting debate. See Chapter 28 for a discussion of tax affecting pass-through entities in the estate and gift tax area.

Net Asset Value

In *Paskill Corp. v. Algoma Corp.*,[58] the Delaware Supreme Court indicated that using net asset value as the *sole* criterion for determining fair value of stock in an appraisal action is erroneous because to do so is akin to determining the company's theoretical liquidation value; under Delaware law, the company's fair value must be determined on a going-concern basis, and a determination on a theoretical liquidation basis is prescribed (see the section above on "Fair Value Is Not Fair Market Value").

However, in *Ng v. Heng Sang Realty Corp.*,[59] the Chancery Court accepted net asset value where it was not the exclusive criterion for valuation, and where it

---

[58] *Paskill Corp. v. Algoma Corp.*, 747 A.2d 549, 2000 Del. LEXIS 117 (Del. Mar. 7, 2000).
[59] *Ng v. Heng Sang Realty Corp.*, 2004 Del. Ch. LEXIS 62 (Del. Ch. May 20, 2004), *aff'd w/o op.*, 2005 Del. LEXIS 45 (Del. Jan. 27, 2005).

found that the appraiser's determination of adjusted net asset value was not a theoretical liquidation value because it reflected a future income stream, taxes, and maintenance expenses.

In *Rainforest Café, Inc. v. State of Wisconsin Investment Board*,[60] the Minnesota trial court was confronted with vastly conflicting valuation evidence, including evidence on the subject company's net asset value, which was based on book value. The Court rejected this measure of value, indicating that book value is not a good indicator of fair value. On appeal, the Minnesota Court of Appeals affirmed, finding that the company's stock never traded anywhere near book value, and stating that Minnesota law is clear that "book value is not a reliable indicator of fair value."

Excess Earnings Method

Although it is not common in fair value cases, the excess earnings method has been accepted. The method was accepted over defendants' objections, and was upheld on appeal, in a New Jersey case, *Balsamides v. Protameen Chemicals, Inc.*[61] The Supreme Court explained:

> The court noted that although not preferred, "excess earnings" is an acceptable method, and [plaintiff's expert] chose it, in part, because defendants would not provide the information needed to employ any other method.

> This suggests to us that resisting providing information for valuation probably does not serve the company's best interests.

Weighting of Methods

Sometimes courts assign specific mathematical weights to the results of the analysis by each of two or more valuation methods. For example, in *In re United States Cellular Operating Co.*,[62] the Court gave a 70 percent weight to DCF and a 30 percent weight to comparable transactions. In *Andaloro v. PFPC Worldwide, Inc.*,[63] the Court gave 75 percent weight to the DCF method and 25 percent to the comparable companies method. An illustrative example of this is found in a Nevada case, *Steiner v. Benninghoff*.[64] In that case, the court weighted methods as presented in Exhibit 36–2.

While the above breakdown is unique to the particular case, there have been many cases that have reached conclusions by some form of mathematical weighting of results of two or more appraisal methods.

A South Carolina appellate court upheld a minority oppression case decision where one appraiser used only an asset approach, one used only an income approach, and the trial court's decision was an average of the two.[65]

---

[60] *Rainforest Café, Inc. v. State of Wisconsin Investment Board*, 677 N.W.2d 443, 2004 Minn. App. LEXIS 330 (Minn. App. Apr. 13, 2004).

[61] *Emanuel Balsamides, et al. v. Protameen Chemicals, Inc., et al.*, 160 N.J. 352, 734 A.2d 721, 1999 N.J. LEXIS 836, 1999 WL 492630 (N.J. July 14, 1999).

[62] *In re United States Cellular Operating Co.*, 2005 Del. Ch. LEXIS 1 (Del. Ch. Jan. 6, 2005).

[63] *Andaloro v. PFPC Worldwide, Inc.*, 2005 Del. Ch. LEXIS 125 (Del. Ch. Aug. 19, 2005).

[64] *Steiner v. Benninghoff*, 5 F. Supp. 2d 1117, 1998 U.S. Dist. LEXIS 8040, 1998 WL 276136 (D. Nev. May 26, 1998).

[65] *McDuffie v. O'Neal*, 324 S.C. 297, 476 S.E.2d 702, 1996 S.C. App. LEXIS 123, 1996 WL 452905 (S.C. App. Aug. 12, 1996).

Exhibit 36–2

Example of Mathematical Weighting

Enterprise Value:

	Per Share	Weight		Weight	Final Value
Discounted cash flow	$1,273.64	70% }	$1,479.22	75% }	
Mergers and acquisitions	1,958.95	30% }			$1,407.22
Market Value:					
Guideline public companies			$1,191.98*	25% }	

*After a 25% discount for lack of marketability

SOURCE: *Steiner v. Benninghoff*, No. 5 F. Supp. 2d 1117, 1998 U.S. Dist. LEXIS 8040, 1998 WL 276136 (D. Nev. May 26, 1998).

Discounts and Premiums

A major issue in many fair value cases is whether or not discounts and/or premiums are applicable. If so, there is always the issue of the magnitudes of such discounts and/or premiums.

The primary issues are lack of control (i.e., minority ownership interest) discounts, ownership control premiums, and discounts for lack of marketability. The published opinions that have addressed these issues vary considerably from state to state:

1. Some do not allow either lack of control or lack of marketability discounts.[66]
2. Some allow both lack of control and lack of marketability discounts.
3. Some allow discounts for lack of control but not for lack of marketability.
4. Some allow discounts for lack of marketability but not for lack of control.
5. Several states have taken the position that discounts for lack of control and lack of marketability must be decided in each case on the basis of the facts and circumstances of that case.
6. Some states have applied ownership control premiums under certain specific circumstances.

Lack of Control Discounts Rejected

In its case of first impression on the issue of a lack of control discount in a dissenting stockholder suit, the Wisconsin Court of Appeals rejected the 30 percent minority interest (i.e., lack of control) discount that had been applied by the trial court. The court reviewed cases from several states (including Delaware,

---

[66] In the Maryland case, *East Park Ltd. Partnership v. Larkin*, 2006 Md. App. LEXIS 32 (Md. Ct. App. 2006), the court, in determining whether discounts should be applied to determining fair value of withdrawing limited partner interests, noted that the majority of states that have considered the issue in the dissenting shareholder context have concluded that discounts do not apply to a fair value analysis. The court also ruled, however, that as with dissenting shareholder cases, the method used in determining the fair value of shares is specific to each case.

New York, and Oklahoma) and concluded that lack of control discounts should not be applied. The court agreed with the rationale that was stated in *Cavalier Oil Corp. v. Harnett*:

> Discounting individual shareholdings injects into the appraisal process speculation on the various factors which may dictate the marketability of minority shareholdings. More important, to fail to accord to a minority shareholder the full proportionate value of his shares imposes a penalty for lack of control, and unfairly enriches the majority shareholders who may reap a windfall from the appraisal process by cashing out a dissenting shareholder, a clearly undesirable result.[67]

Because of this "clearly undesirable result," the Wisconsin Court of Appeals held that lack of control discounts are inappropriate in dissenters' rights cases as a matter of law, and it remanded to the lower court to award SSM the pro rata share of HMO-W's net assets without a lack of control discount.[68] The Wisconsin Supreme Court affirmed.

In *Pueblo Bancorporation v. Lindoe, Inc.*,[69] the Colorado Court of Appeals rejected lack of control discounts, saying:

> [I]n determining the "fair value" of a dissenter's shares in a closely held corporation, the trial court must first determine the value of the corporation and the pro rata value of each outstanding share of common or equity participating stock. In the case of a going concern, no minority discount is to be applied...."[70]

Numerous other courts have come to the same conclusion,[71] and some federal Courts of Appeals have adopted this line of reasoning and have rejected lack of control discounts in determining fair value in appraisal actions.[72]

In *Brown v. Arp and Hammond Hardware Co.*,[73] the Wyoming Supreme Court, finding that the clear majority of courts have held that minority discounts do not apply when determining fair value in the appraisal context, ruled that it would join the majority and not permit such discounts.

A 1998 Montana Supreme Court decision demonstrates the need to always research the latest decisions. The Montana Supreme Court reversed itself! In a 1998 dissenting stockholder case,[74] the Supreme Court disallowed a lack of control discount, overruling its own decision to allow a lack of control discount in a 1996 shareholder oppression suit.[75]

---

[67] *Cavalier Oil Corp. v Harnett*, 564 A.2d 1137 (Del. 1989).

[68] *HMO-W v. SSM Health Care System*, 598 N.W.2d 577, 1999 WL 395650 (Wis. App. June 17, 1999), *aff'd*, 611 N.W.2d 250, 2000 Wisc. LEXIS 313 (W.SC. 2000).

[69] *Pueblo Bancorporation v. Lindoe, Inc.*, 37 P.3d 492, 2001 Colo. App. LEXSI 1330 (Colo. App. August 16, 2001).

[70] *Pueblo Bancorporation v. Lindoe, Inc.*, 63 P.3d 353, 2003 Colo. LEXIS 53 (Colo. 2003).

[71] *Blitch v. Peoples Bank*, 246 Ga. App. 453, 540 S.E.2d 667 (Ga. Ct. App. 2000); *Security State Bank v. Ziegeldorf*, 554 N.W.2d 884 (Iowa 1996); *Arnaud v. Stockgrowers State Bank*, 268 Kan. 163, 992 P.2d 216 (Kansas 1999); *In re Valuation of Common Stock of McLoon Oil Co.*, 565 A.2d 997 (Maine 1989); *Rigel Corp. v. Cutchall*, 245 Neb. 118, 511 N.W.2d 519 (Neb. 1994); *Cooke v. Fresh Express Foods Corp.*, 169 Ore. App. 101, 7 P.3d 717, 2000 Ore. App. LEXIS 1128 (Ore. Ct. App. July 12, 2000). *First Western Bank Wall v. Olsen*, 2001 SD 16, 621 N.W.2d 611 (South Dakota 2001); *In re Stock of Trapp Family Lodge, Inc.*, 169 Vt. 82, 725 A.2d 927 (Vt. 1999); see also Barry M. Wertheimer, "The Shareholders' Appraisal Remedy and How Courts Determine Fair Value," *47 Duke L.J. 613*, February 1998, p. 635 (noting the unavailability of minority discounts in the majority of courts).

[72] *Swope v. Seigel-Robert, Inc.*, 243 F.3d 486, 2001 U.S. App. LEXIS 2760 (8th Cir. 2001).

[73] *Brown v. Arp and Hammond Hardware Co.*, 141 p. 3d 673, 2006 Wyo. LEXIS 115 (Wyo. 2006).

[74] *Hansen v. 75 Ranch Company*, 957 P.2d 32, 1998 WL 180831 (Mont. Apr. 9, 1998).

[75] *McCann Ranch, Inc. v. Sharon Quigley-McCann*, 276 Mont. 205, 208, 915 P.2d 239, 241 (1996).

Lack of Control Discounts Accepted

Although the majority trend is to reject lack of control discounts, some courts have accepted such discounts. For example, in *Johnson v. Johnson*,[76] a stockholder oppression case, the Connecticut court, finding that the alleged conduct (failure to declare dividends) did not constitute oppression, assessed a 20 percent lack of control discount. The Court indicated that the decision was within its discretion, and that assessing the discount was in accord with "sound business judgment."

In *Hall v. Glenn's Ferry Grazing Assoc.*,[77] an oppression case, the court referenced a comment to the appraisal statute, which stated in pertinent part that "[i]n cases where there is dissension but no evidence of wrongful conduct, fair value should be determined with reference to what [the minority shareholder] would likely receive in a voluntary sale of shares to a third party, taking into account his minority status." The court found dissension but no wrongful conduct and, accordingly concluded that fair value should be determined by taking into account a minority discount.

Ownership Control Premium Accepted

The Delaware Court of Chancery has accepted the application of an ownership control premium under two specific circumstances:

1. When the base valued is a publicly traded equivalent value derived by the guideline publicly traded company method.
2. When valuing a controlling ownership position in a subsidiary company.

Otherwise, premiums may not be applied at the shareholder level. The Delaware cases permitting premiums for subsidiaries lead to the anomaly that, whereas a business conducted through a subsidiary is entitled to a premium, an identical business conducted through a division is not.[78]

The most common control premium applied is one that is essentially the inverse of the discount for lack of control, which some courts believe is inherent in a comparable company analysis because that method depends on comparisons to market multiples derived from trading information for minority blocks of comparable companies. For example, in *Doft & Co. v. Travelocity.com, Inc.*,[79] the Court, on its own, without prompting by the parties, added a 30 percent control premium, saying that "The equity valuation produced in a comparable company analysis does not accurately reflect the intrinsic worth of a corporation on a going-concern basis. Therefore, the Court, in appraising the fair value of the equity, 'must correct this minority trading discount by adding back a premium designed to correct it.'"

In *Agranoff v. Miller*,[80] the Delaware Chancery Court explained that the determination of such a control premium is necessarily imprecise because to determine what the implicit minority discount in a comparable companies analysis is, one is forced to look at the prices paid for control blocks. Such prices are frequently paid in connection with a merger or other fundamental transaction. The Court found that

---

[76] *Johnson v. Johnson*, 30 Conn. L. Rptr. 260, 2001 Conn. Super. LEXIS 2430 (Conn. Super. Ct. Aug. 15, 2001).

[77] *Hall v. Glenn's Ferry Grazing Assoc.*, 2006 U.S. Dist. LEXIS 68051 (D. Idaho 2006).

[78] Gilbert E. Matthews, "A Review of Valuations in Delaware Appraisal Cases, 2004-2005," *Business Valuation Review*, Vol. 25, No. 2 (Summer 2006).

[79] *Doft & Co. v. Travelocity.com, Inc*, 2004 Del. Ch. LEXIS 75 (Del. Ch. May 20, 2004).

[80] *Agranoff v. Miller*, 2001 Del. Ch. LEXIS 71 (Del. Ch. May 15, 2001).

this source of data is therefore problematic, because the premiums arguably reflect value that is not related to the value of the acquired companies as going concerns under their preexisting business plans, such as synergistic values attributable to transactionally specific factors. The Court acknowledged that it is impossible to make precise determinations about what motivated an acquirer to pay a control premium. In this case, the Court decided that the adjustment should be 30 percent.

In *In re Valuation of Common Stock of Penobscot Shoe Company*,[81] a dissenters' rights action involving a small, closely held business, the Court permitted a control premium adjustment, concluding that the control premium could properly be used as an upward adjustment of the value of the subject company's shares when compared to similar companies in the industry.

In *Bomarko, Inc. v. International Telecharge, Inc.*,[82] the Delaware Chancery Court permitted the addition of a control premium as part of a comparative public company analysis.

In *Borruso v. Communications Telesystems International*,[83] the Court relied on the guideline publicly traded company method. Both experts agreed that an ownership control premium should be applied, but disagreed as to the stage of the analysis at which it should be applied. The dissenters' expert applied a premium to the market value of invested capital (MVIC) to revenue pricing multiples to reflect the control issue. The company's expert applied the control premium to the guideline publicly traded company analysis result. The court accepted the latter procedure, noting that the dissenters' expert's procedure had the effect of altering the methodology itself.

Two cases in which the Delaware Court of Chancery placed an ownership control premium on the indicated values of wholly owned subsidiaries are *Rapid American Corporation v. Harris*[84] and *Hintmann v. Fred Weber, Inc.*[85] In *Rapid American*, the court valued the subsidiaries by the guideline publicly traded company method. The Delaware Supreme Court concluded that an ownership control premium was appropriate, explaining, "The exclusion of a control premium artificially and unrealistically treated Rapid as a minority shareholder."

In *Hintmann v. Fred Weber*, the Court valued the subsidiaries on the basis of a simple average of the guideline publicly traded company method and the DCF method. Saying that the case was analogous to *Rapid American*, the Court then added a 20 percent ownership control premium to the resulting indicated values of the subsidiaries. However, a commentator on the decision, investment banker Gil Matthews, criticized the decision as distinguishable from *Rapid American* in that the subsidiary values were based partly on the DCF method:

> DCF value should represent the full value of the future cash flows of the business. Excluding synergies, a company cannot be worth a premium over the value of its future cash flows. Thus, it is improper and illogical to add a control premium to a DCF valuation.[86]

In another case, the Delaware Court of Chancery implicitly allowed an ownership control premium by accepting the guideline merged and acquired company method (see *Le Beau v. M.G. Bancorporation* referenced earlier).

[81] *In re Valuation of Common Stock of Penobscot Shoe Company*, 2003 Me. Super. LEXIS 140 (Me. Super. May 30, 2003).

[82] *Bomarko, Inc. v. International Telecharge, Inc.*, 794 A.2d 1161, 1999 Del. Ch. LEXIS 211 (Del Ch. Nov. 4, 1999), *aff'd*, 766 A.2d 437 (Del. 2000).

[83] *Carl Borruso and William Lee v. Communications Telesystems International*.

[84] *Rapid American Corporation v. Harris*, 603 A.2d 796 (Del. 1992).

[85] *Hintmann v. Fred Weber, Inc.*, 1998 Del. Ch. LEXIS 26 (Del. Ch. 1998).

[86] Gilbert E. Matthews, "Delaware Court Adds Control Premiums to Subsidiary Value," *Shannon Pratt's Business Valuation Update*, May 1998, p. 10.

Lack of Marketability Discounts Rejected

The Delaware Court of Chancery is one venue that has regularly rejected discounts for lack of marketability. For example, in *Borruso v. Telesystems International*,[87] the Court rejected the company's expert's "discount for lack of liquidity," citing *Cavalier Oil*[88] and saying that it was essentially a discount for lack of marketability which is inappropriate in a fair value determination.

In *Ex parte Baron Services, Inc.*,[89] a shareholder oppression case, the Alabama Supreme Court rejected the application of an entity-level marketability discount because the company's expert did not rely on publicly traded companies and did not use the guideline public companies approach. The Court also rejected a shareholder-level marketability discount because it found that any "cost of capital" difference between the subject company and public companies was accounted for in the discount and capitalization rates used in the valuation.

In *Pro Finish USA Ltd. v. Johnson*,[90] in a case of first impression in Arizona, the Court denied the application of a lack of marketability discount, concluding that the focus should be upon the value of the company as a whole, and prorated equally, rather than discounting the dissenting shareholders' pro rata share of the sale price. Similarly, the Supreme Court of Colorado, in *Pueblo Bancorporation v. Lindoe, Inc.*,[91] rejected the application of lack of marketability discounts. In determining the proper interpretation of fair value in a dissenters' rights case, the Court held that it is the shareholders' proportionate ownership interest in the corporation's value, without discounting for lack of marketability. The Court stated that this (majority) view is consistent with the underlying purpose of appraisal rights statutes and the national trend against both lack of control and lack of marketability discounts in dissenters' rights cases.[92]

Iowa courts have not issued a definitive opinion on discounts for lack of marketability. In *Sieg v. Kelly*,[93] the trial court disallowed the lack of marketability discount and the case was appealed. The Supreme Court of Iowa noted: "Iowa was clear at the time Sieg made its valuation that a ... discount is not permitted." It noted, however, that some jurisdictions allow lack of marketability discounts and other do not. In the final analysis, it found no error in rejecting the lack of marketability discount, but did not issue a generalized pronouncement on the issue.

In the New Jersey dissenting stockholder case of *Wheaton v. Smith*,[94] the Supreme Court overturned the trial court's acceptance of a discount for lack of marketability, which had been affirmed by the New Jersey Appellate Division.

---

[87] *Carl Borruso and William Lee v. Communications Telesystems International.*

[88] *Cavalier Oil Corp. v. Harnett.*

[89] *Ex parte Baron Services, Inc.*, 874 So. 2d 545 (Ala. April 4, 2003).

[90] *Pro Finish USA Ltd. v. Johnson*, 63 P.3d 288, 204 Ariz. 257 (Ariz. App. Feb. 6, 2003).

[91] *Pueblo Bancorporation v. Lindoe, Inc.*, 63 P.3d 353, 2003 Colo. LEXIS 53 (Colo. 2003).

[92] See, e.g., James H. Eggart," Replacing the Sword with a Scalpel: The Case for a Bright-Line Rule Disallowing the Application of Lack of Marketability Discounts in Shareholder Oppression Cases," *44 Ariz. L. Rev. 213* (Spring 2002), urging the adoption of a bright-line rule denying discounts in all dissenters' rights cases. The article emphasizes the inappropriateness of allowing discretion in the application of discounts and explains why a bright-line rule disallowing the application of lack of marketability discounts in all cases would be superior to a discretionary approach, or even one that permits discounts in "extraordinary circumstances." Oregon is an example of a state that disallows both lack of marketability and lack of control discounts. See, e.g., *Cooke v. Fresh Express Foods Corp.*, 169 Ore. App. 101, 7 P.3d 717, 2000 Ore. App. LEXIS 1128 (Ore. Ct. App. July 12, 2000).

[93] *Sieg Company v. Kelly*, 568 N.W.2d 794, 1997 Iowa Sup. LEXIS 243, 1997 WL 575996 (Iowa Sept. 17, 1997).

[94] *Lawson Mardon Wheaton, Inc. v. Smith, et al.*, 160 N.J. 383, 734 A.2d 738, 1999 WL 492634 (N.J. July 14, 1999).

Relying on 2 ALI, *Principles of Corporate Governance: Analysis and Recommendations*, ∂7.22(a), the trial court concluded that the application of a lack of marketability discount was appropriate because of "extraordinary circumstances" that were present. The New Jersey Supreme Court explained as follows:

> Such circumstances require more than the absence of a trading market in shares; rather, the court should apply this exception only when it finds that the dissenting shareholder has held out in order to exploit the transaction giving rise to appraisal so as to divert value to itself that could not be made available proportionately to other shareholders.

On the same day, the New Jersey Supreme Court accepted a lack of marketability discount in the minority oppression case of *Balsamides v. Protameen Chemicals*, discussed in the next section.

Lack of Marketability Discounts Accepted

In *Matthew G. Norton Co v. Smyth*,[95] the Washington Court of Appeals ruled, in a case of first impression in that state, that a discount for lack of marketability was appropriate at the entity level, and rejected a "bright-line rule" that such a discount is never available at the shareholder level. However, the Court also held that the trial court's decision would be affirmed to the extent that the trial court's order was intended to declare that, absent extraordinary circumstances, no such discount can be applied at the shareholder level.

Similarly, in *Advanced Communication Design, Inc. v. Follett*,[96] an oppressed shareholder case, the Minnesota Supreme Court, noting that the value assigned by the trial court must be "fair and equitable to all parties," rejected a bright-line rule denying the application of a marketability discount in all cases. According to the Court, establishing a bright-line rule foreclosing consideration of discount would be inconsistent with the legislative policy of flexibility and fairness to all parties and could hamper the Courts' ability to take into account circumstances that might lead to an unfair wealth transfer. Such a transfer of wealth would constitute an example of "extraordinary circumstances," as where the exercise of a minority shareholder's appraisal rights in a financially strained corporation with illiquid assets would yield a price far greater than the price that would actually be paid for the shares in a market transaction. Finding such extraordinary circumstances in the case at bar, the Court directed that the discount should be somewhere between 35 and 55 percent.

In *Devivo v. Devivo*,[97] a Connecticut court relied on the decision in *Advanced Communication* when it found "extraordinary circumstances"—the fair value of the company was 1.6 times the company's net worth, more than 2.7 times its operating cash flow, and 7 times its net income for that year—that warranted application of a 35 percent lack of marketability discount.

In a New Jersey minority oppression case, *Balsamides v. Protameen Chemicals, Inc.*,[98] the trial court accepted a 35 percent discount for lack of marketability. The New Jersey Superior Court, Appellate Division, reversed, and, on appeal, the

---

[95] *Matthew G. Norton Co v. Smyth*, 51 P.3d 159, 112 Wash. App. 865 (Wash. App. Aug. 5, 2002).
[96] *Advanced Communication Design, Inc. v. Follett*, 615 N.W.2d 285 (Minn. Aug. 3, 2000).
[97] *Devivo v. Devivo*, 30 Conn. L. Rptr. 52, 2001 Conn. Super. LEXIS 1285 (Conn. Super. Ct. May 7, 2001).
[98] *Emanuel Balsamides, et al. v. Protameen Chemicals, Inc., et al.*

New Jersey Supreme Court upheld the lack of marketability discount. The New Jersey Supreme Court explained as follows:

> The position of the Appellate Division ignores the reality that Balsamides is buying a company that will remain illiquid because it is not publicly traded and public information about it is not widely disseminated. Protameen will continue to have a small base of available purchasers. If it is resold in the future, Balsamides will receive a lower purchase price because of the company's closely-held nature.
>
> If Perle and Balsamides sold Protameen together, the price they received would reflect Protameen's illiquidity. They would split the price and also share that determent. Similarly, if Balsamides pays Perle a discounted price, Perle suffers half of the lack-of-marketability markdown now; and Balsamides suffers the other half when he eventually sells his closely-held business. Conversely, if Perle is not required to sell his shares at a price that reflects Protameen's lack of marketability, Balsamides will suffer the full effect of Protameen's lack of marketability at the time he sells. Accordingly, we find that Balsamides should not bear the brunt of Protameen's illiquidity merely because he is the designated buyer.

On the same day, the New Jersey Supreme Court rejected a lack of marketability discount in the dissenting stockholder case of *Wheaton v. Smith*, discussed in the previous section.

It is not unheard of to apply some particular discount to the results of one or more valuation methods but not to the results of one or more other methods. For example, as seen in an earlier case reference, the court applied a 25 percent discount for lack of marketability to the results of the guideline publicly traded company method, but no discount to the results of the DCF method or the guideline merged and acquired company method.

Lack of Combinatorial Value Discount Rejected

In *Dobler v. Montgomery Cellular Holding Company, Inc.*,[99] the Court rejected a discount for lack of combinatorial value. The case involved a telecommunications holding company. The expert for the company argued that cellular companies are significantly more valuable in specific combinations, and, since the subject company was a stand alone cellular company, it had a lack of combinatorial value as part of a network. Accordingly, the expert proposed discounting the company's value by 48 percent. The Court disagreed with this argument, reasoning that the company was already in combination with other cellular companies owned by the company's parent. In addition, the Court found that the expert was intending to deprive the minority shareholders of existing value through the discount for lack of combinatorial value. The Delaware Supreme Court agreed,[100] indicating that the expert incorrectly attempted to value the company on a stand-alone basis, as if it were not a going concern that had contractual relationships with other cellular providers. However, those relationships represented value to which the minority shareholders were entitled.

---

[99] *Dobler v. Montgomery Cellular Holding Company, Inc.*, 2004 Del. Ch. LEXIS 139 (Del. Ch. Sept. 30, 2004).
[100] *Montgomery Cellular Holding Co. v. Dobler*, 880 A.2d 206, 2005 Del. LEXIS 295 (Del. Aug. 1, 2005).

Discounts for Trapped-In Capital Gains

In *Matthew G. Norton Co. v. Smyth*,[101] the valuation consultant for the company recognized built-in capital gains in its final valuation. The Washington trial court held that, as a matter of law, a corporation may not use trapped-in capital gains in determining the fair value of a dissenter's shares. The Washington Court of Appeals, however, rejected a bright-line rule in this regard. The Court ruled that, while discounts for built-in capital gains are not generally appropriate in dissenters' rights appraisal cases where no liquidation of the corporation is contemplated, such discounts might be appropriate, at the corporate level, if the business of the company is such that appreciated property is scheduled to be sold in the foreseeable future, in the normal course of business.

The Court, therefore, remanded, with instructions that if the company wished the trial court to consider the tax implications of built-in capital gains, it would need to provide the trial court with a reasonable explanation of why such built-in gains should be considered in light of the fact that it had converted to Subchapter S status, thereby avoiding the double taxation problems of C corporations, and would need to show the Court by substantial evidence and appropriate briefing that the dissenting shareholders were not already taxed for their fair share of the gain on any such appreciated assets by virtue of the corporation's redemption of their appreciated shares for "fair value." The Court discussed the 10-year rule, based on changes to the tax code in the Tax Reform Act of 1986 by which future taxation of appreciated assets became a virtual certainty unless a C corporation was to convert to an S corporation and hold the property for 10 years, by which means it could, indeed, avoid recognizing the gain on the property.[102]

In *Brown v. Arp and Hammond Hardware Co*,[103] the Wyoming Supreme Court ruled that under the state's appraisal statute, based on the pre-1999 version of the Model Business Corporation Act (MBCA), absent clear evidence that the company was undergoing liquidation, a discount for trapped-in capital gains would violate the purpose of the statute: to compensate dissenting shareholders for the "fair value" of their shares in a going concern.

Discounts Left to Court's Discretion

Opinions in a minority of states have rejected the notion that there should be a sweeping policy that lack of control discounts, ownership control premiums, and/or lack of marketability discounts should be either accepted or rejected in all fair value cases.

Instead they have taken the position that the issue of lack of control and lack of marketability discounts should be decided on a case-by-case basis depending on the facts and circumstances of the particular case.

Illinois, for example, is in the camp of leaving lack of control and lack of marketability discounts to the courts' discretion. In *Wigel Broadcasting v. Smith*,[104] a reverse split squeeze-out, the company's independent expert concluded $115 per

---

[101] *Matthew G. Norton Co. v. Smyth*, 112 Wn. App. 865, 51 P.3d 159, (Wash. Ct. App. 2002).

[102] See generally 26 U.S.C. §§ 1374, 1374(d)(7) (1988). If a corporation is eligible for a subchapter S election, therefore, a technique does exist for avoiding recognition of gain.

[103] *Brown v. Arp and Hammond Hardware Co.*, 2006 Wyo. LEXIS 115 (Wyo. 2006).

[104] *Weigel Broadcasting Company v. Smith, et al.*, 682 N.E.2d 745 (Ill. App. July 24, 1997).

share, reflecting a combination discount for lack of control and lack of marketability of 50 percent. The Dissenter's expert was at $78.14 per share. The Appellate Court of Illinois concluded $126 per share. The appellate court cited case law supporting discounts for lack of control and lack of marketability and concluded, "Applying such discounts is left to the trial court's discretion."

In *Jahn v. Kinderman*,[105] involving a freeze-out of minority members in a closely held corporation, the Illinois Court of Appeals reiterated that whether to apply such discounts is within the Court's discretion, but also noted the preponderant view that such discounts are not to be applied in determining fair value. The Court upheld the lower court's discretionary decision not to apply a discount for lack of marketability. This discretionary approach has come under increasing attack.[106]

Sufficiency of Valuation Evidence

A court may, and often will, reject valuation evidence presented by an appraiser if the court determines that the evidence is insufficient or irrelevant.

In *Rainforest Cafè, Inc. v. State of Wisconsin Investment Board*,[107] the Court was confronted with vastly conflicting valuation evidence. The trial court found that the experts' conflicting evidence did not help the Court to determine the fair value of the stock to be valued, and, therefore, determined that fair value was the market price tendered during the merger. The Minnesota Court of Appeals held that it was not a reversible error to reject the conflicting expert testimony of both parties and for the trial court to establish its own value based on market price.

In *Christians v. Stafford*,[108] a minority oppression case, the Texas Court of Appeals reversed a jury award favoring the minority shareholder. The Court found that there was insufficient evidence as a matter of law to support the fair value of assets that had been allegedly leased at less than fair value to insiders, and the lease of which was at the heart of the minority shareholder's claim.

The Delaware Chancery Court, in *In re United States Cellular Operating Co.*,[109] noted that, in appraisal actions, "both sides have the burden of providing their valuations by a preponderance of the evidence," but that, if neither side meets its burden, "the Court must use its own independent judgment to determine the fair value of the shares." The Court, concluding that neither side satisfied its burden, conducted its own valuation.

In *Dobler v. Montgomer Cellular Holding Co., Inc.*,[110] the Delaware Chancery Court was extremely critical of the company's expert's valuation. The Court said that the expert, "constructed his DCF analysis in a way that is meaningless as an analytical tool." The Court was also critical because the expert had created projections entirely on his own, without consulting with company management, without referencing valuable sources of information, and without analyzing the company's operations or strategy. Conversely, the Court was impressed with the shareholder's

---

[105] *Jahn v. Kinderman*, 351 Ill. App. 3d 15, 814 N.E.2d 116, 2004 Ill. App. LEXIS 865 (Ill. App. July 26, 2004).

[106] See, e.g., Charles W. Murdoch, "Squeeze-outs, Freeze-outs, and Discounts: Why Is Illinois in the Minority in Protecting Shareholder Interests?" *35 Loy. U. Chi. L.J. 737* (Spring, 2004).

[107] *Rainforest Cafè, Inc. v. State of Wisconsin Investment Board*, 677 N.W.2d 443, 2004 Minn. App. LEXIS 330 (Minn. App. Apr. 13, 2004).

[108] *Christians v. Stafford*, 2000 Tex. App. LEXIS 6423 (Sept. 21, 2000).

[109] *In re United States Cellular Operating Co.*, 2005 Del. Ch. LEXIS 1 (Del. Ch. Jan. 6, 2005).

[110] *Dobler v. Montgomery Cellular Holding Company, Inc.*, 2004 Del. Ch. LEXIS 139 (Del. Ch. Sept. 30, 2004), *aff'd*, 880 A.2d 206, 2005 Del. LEXIS 295 (Del. Aug. 1, 2005).

expert's thorough methodology. Accordingly, the Court adopted, with some modification, the shareholder's expert's valuation. The Delaware Supreme Court affirmed, concluding that the company's expert had used inputs that were legally and factually flawed and irrelevant to the company's valuation.

"Dr. Pangloss and Mr. Scrooge"

Former Vice Chancellor Steele, now Chief Justice of the Delaware Supreme Court, expressed a degree of cynicism toward the desired objectivity of experts in *Gilbert v. MPM Enterprises*.

> One might expect the experts' desire to convince the Court of the reasonableness and validity of their assumptions and financial models would produce a somewhat narrow range of values, clearly and concisely supported, despite the individual parties' obvious conflicting incentives. Unfortunately, as this case and other cases most decidedly illustrate, one should not put much faith in that expectation, at least when faced with appraisal experts in this Court....
>
> Reading petitioner's submissions, one might easily conclude that MPM was poised to become the Microsoft of the SMT industry. By contrast, respondent's submissions give the impression that a more likely comparison, given MPM's myriad management, technical, and legal problems, is Apple. In sum, one report is submitted by Dr. Pangloss, and the other by Mr. Scrooge."[111]

The Court's distrust of appraisers' independence has not abated. In *Lane v. Cancer Treatment Centers of America, Inc.*,[112] the Court said, "All too often in appraisal actions, the Court is presented with two competing experts espousing 'wildly divergent' interpretations of the circumstances confronting the corporation. This case is no exception." In *Henke v. Trilithic, Inc.*,[113] the Court said, "The parties' experts have presented remarkably divergent valuations. As is often the case in an appraisal action, the Court does not find either party to have fully satisfied its burden of persuasion regarding its valuation. The Court therefore must conduct its own independent valuation." And, in *Finkelstein v. Liberty Digital, Inc.*,[114] the Court said, "This appraisal case is unusual in one respect that is refreshing....what is less typical is that the parties were able to stipulate to the value of all but one of [the corporation's] assets." In that case, the Court added, "Men and women who purport to be applying sound, academically-validated valuation techniques come to this court and, through the neutral application of their expertise to the facts, come to widely disparate results, even when applying the same methodology. These starkly contrasting presentations have, given the duties required of this court, imposed upon trial judges the responsibility to forge a responsible valuation from what is often ridiculously biased 'expert' input."

---

[111] *Gilbert v. MPM Enterprises, Inc.*, 709 A.2d 663, 1997 Del. Ch. LEXIS 141, 1997 WL 633298 (Del. Ch. Sept. 29, 1997), *aff'd*, 731 A.2d 790, 1999 Del. LEXIS 205 (Del. June 25, 1999).

[112] *Lane v. Cancer Treatment Centers of America, Inc.*, 2004 Del. Ch. LEXIS 108 (Del. Ch. July 30, 2004).

[113] *Henke v. Trilithic, Inc.*, 2005 Del. Ch. LEXIS 170 (Del. Ch. Oct. 8, 2005).

[114] *Finkelstein v. Liberty Digital, Inc.*, 2005 Del Ch. LEXIS 53 (Del. Ch. April 25, 2005).

The courts seek a high degree of objectivity with regard to valuation expert witnesses. The courts place great weight on the credibility of the valuation analyst in deciding what evidence and testimony to accept or not accept. Typically, the courts will find an apparently neutral valuation expert to be much more credible than an apparently biased or goal-oriented valuation expert.

Summary

By selected examples, this chapter has demonstrated the great diversity of positions taken by courts in interpreting the standard of fair value in dissenting stockholder and minority oppression cases. One conclusion that is obvious is that virtually no court specifically equates "fair value" with "fair market value."

It also seems apparent that both the valuation analyst and/or the attorney need to read relevant judicial precedent with great care. In particular, analysts should be careful about attributing broad applicability to seemingly sweeping statements. Facts and circumstances vary greatly from one case to another, and courts will consider these variations in deciding whether a principle articulated in one case is applicable to the instant case at bar.

Another important point in estimating fair value is whether or not there was procedural fairness in the entire transaction. If controlling owners acted unfairly toward noncontrolling stockholders (or vice versa), there may, in some jurisdictions, be considerable elements of damages incurred beyond just the basic appraisal under dissenters' stockholder rights.

Generally speaking, the elements of market value, investment value, and asset value should all be considered, although the final conclusion may be based on only one or two of these elements. The most important element in most cases is *investment value*, followed by market value and asset value. Investment value in this context means value based on production of income, as opposed to value to a particular owner or investor, as the standard of investment value is defined in other appraisal contexts.

Accepted valuation methods vary greatly, depending on the type of company, the facts and circumstances of each case, the relative quality of evidence available for different valuation methods, and the preferences of the court. Courts sometimes weight two or more methods and other times ultimately depend on the results of a single method.

The courts' postures toward discounts and premiums is highly variable, both from jurisdiction to jurisdiction and, in many jurisdictions, depending on the distinguishable facts and circumstances from one case to another within a jurisdiction.

Many states have no precedential case law in the area of dissenting stockholder suits and/or minority oppression suits. Others have some case law, but most have not addressed all the various issues that may arise. In the face of the lack of their own precedential case law, courts usually look to precedential case law from other states. Thus, although dissent and oppression valuation cases are nominally state-specific, it is important for valuation analysts and attorneys working in this area to have a broad familiarity with the various precedents of many states. This chapter has not attempted to provide a comprehensive treatise, but has provided examples to illustrate variations of courts' positions on issues commonly encountered.

Chapter 37

Valuations for Marital Dissolution Purposes

Although marital dissolutions may be a small proportion of the typical business valuation practice, they account for a high proportion of the times that business valuation experts appear in court as expert witnesses. However, there are many business appraisers who do primarily divorce valuations, and often that is how appraisers are first exposed to business valuations. Often, the business or business interest is the largest asset in the marital estate. And, the resolution of the value of the subject business property often cannot be settled by logical negotiation between disputing spouses.

To make matters worse, guidelines for business valuations prepared for marital dissolution purposes are less well settled in most states than for business valuations prepared for virtually any other purpose. For example, no state marital dissolution statute specifies a definition of value. Even in states with an abundance of marital dissolution judicial precedent, family law trial courts have wide latitude in exercising their discretion. Published judicial precedent is often confusing and (sometimes) contradictory.

The Marital Estate

The marital estate comes into being upon filing for divorce. It represents the assets that must be divided according to the property laws of the state. Currently, each state adheres to either (1) the *community property* standard or (2) the *equitable distribution* standard with regard to the division of assets included within the marital estate.

The question as to what property is or is not included in the marital estate is often a major issue. The analyst sometimes must value property before the court has determined the extent to which it is or is not included in the marital estate.

Community Property

In states adhering to the community property standard, distributable property is referred to as community property. The community property standard is based on the premise of joint and equal ownership of the marital estate. In a community property standard state, all assets acquired during a marriage are assumed (1) to be acquired by the marital community and (2) to be owned jointly by the community. These states generally follow the practice of an equal division of the marital estate upon divorce.

Equitable Distribution

Most states follow the standard of equitable distribution. Under this concept, equitable distribution of the marital estate may mean equal distribution, or it may not. The court may make adjustments and decisions related to the allocation process based on the specific facts and circumstances.

Active or Passive Appreciation During Marriage

Many states take the position that appreciation in the value of property that was separate at the time of marriage is part of the marital estate. This would be the case if the appreciation was due to the active efforts of one spouse, but not if the appreciation was "passive"—that is, due to external factors such as the market. This distinction may require the analyst to value the property both as of the date of marriage and also at the marital dissolution valuation date. In some cases, the valuation analyst is asked to opine as to whether the appreciation was due to the spouse's efforts or not.

Active or Passive Post–Valuation Date Appreciation

Some states (e.g., North Carolina) have enacted legislation to include passive appreciation in the marital estate *after* the basic valuation date. For example, if the valuation date is the date of separation, but the trial to determine the property division is two years later, a portion of the passive appreciation after the date of separation in the property awarded to one spouse may have to be shared with the other spouse. This distinction creates yet another element of valuation. This increase in value is accounted for at the time of the actual property distribution, and it is called *divinable property*.

Standard of Value[1]

Since most state statutes are silent with respect to the standard of value for marital property valuation, it is necessary to look at each state's judicial precedent for guidance. In general, the standards of value adopted by the family law courts are *investment value*, *fair market value*, and *intrinsic value*. At least one state, New Jersey, has adopted *fair value*.

However, even when the courts call it one standard, in practice, the analyst may find it to be something else. Therefore, it is important to understand the precedent that has been set in your state before proceeding with a divorce valuation engagement.

Investment Value

Investment value, as defined in Chapter 2, is the value of a business (or business interest) to a specific owner. Unlike the fair market value standard, this standard considers (1) the specific owner's expectation of risks, (2) the potential synergy associated with ownership of the subject business, (3) the specific earnings expectations resulting from the subject ownership, and, in some cases, (4) the relationship of the spouse/owner to the other owners of the business.

Those practitioners espousing the investment value standard say that the marital property value should be "current value to the marital community in the hands of the present owner."[2]

---

[1] For a through discussion of standards of value for material dissolution by state, see Fishman, Pratt, and Morrison, *Standards of Value: Theory and Applications*, Chapter 4, "Standards of Value in Divorce," Hoboken, NJ: John Wiley & Sons, 2007.

[2] Alan S. Zipp, "Business Valuation Standard for Divorce Is Different from Fair Market Value," *American Journal of Family Law*, Fall 1997, pp. 167–72.

Fair Market Value

Many state courts have adopted fair market value as the relevant standard of value. Fair market value is based on the price that would be negotiated between an informed hypothetical buyer and an informed hypothetical seller, as discussed in Chapter 2. The fair market value concept is more thoroughly defined in Revenue Ruling 59-60.

Those practitioners espousing the fair market value standard say that it is unfair to value the property that one spouse will receive at more than that spouse could realize on a sale. Proponents of the fair market value standard explain, for example:

> The relevant point to the court should be the amount the business assets could bring in cash or cash equivalent at the appropriate date. The point of whether or not the business or any other asset will actually be sold is beside the point. In fact, there is a sale of sorts which occurs within the dissolution. The net effect of the separation of marital assets is that each spouse purchases a (let's assume) 50 percent interest in certain assets from their spouse and pays for the purchase by selling back their 50 percent interest in other assets. The transfers occur and the marital assets are separated. The end result is not substantially different than when both spouses agree jointly to each sell a marital asset and divide the funds received. The primary difference is they are the buyers and sellers, there are no outside parties involved, and the mode of payment is the exchange of interests in the marital assets.[3]

Bishop and Schroeder make the point that lack of marketability discounts should be recognized, just as they are in Tax Court, because one spouse usually gets liquid assets while the other spouse lacks the flexibility and safety of being able to "cash out" readily at the owner's option. They also make the point that "underlying principles are much more consistent and broadly accepted" under the fair market value standard than they are in marital dissolutions not using the fair market value standard. However, most analysts take the position that we are not there to make the law or set the standard; we just follow and interpret precedents the best we can.

Intrinsic Value

Intrinsic value, also discussed in Chapter 2, is a concept of value based on the fundamental, or real value of the asset. Intrinsic value assumes a higher level of insight and knowledge about the asset than a typical investor may possess. For example, for a publicly traded company, the intrinsic value would represent someone's estimate of the "true" value of the stock of the company versus the published stock price.

Fair Value

The Appellate Division of New Jersey said that the standard of value in a marital dissolution case should be fair value, as defined in dissenting stockholder cases.[4]

---

[3] David M. Bishop and Steven F. Schroeder. "Business Valuation Standard of Value for Divorce Should Be Fair Market Value." *American Journal of Family Law*, Spring 1999, pp. 48–52.

[4] *Brown v. Brown,* 348 N.J. Super. 466, 792 A.2d 463, 2002 N.J. Super. LEXIS 105 (N.J. App. Div. 2002). See also, *Piscopo v. Piscopo,* 232 N.J. Super. 559, 557 A.2d 1040 (N.J. Super. 1989).

A handful of other state also have applied the fair value standard in marital dissolution cases.[5]

Internal Contradictions in the Case Law

Most state courts claim to espouse the philosophy that the value of assets in the marital estate should *not* include any value attributable to either spouse's post marital efforts nor any value resulting from restrictions on post marital efforts. Having said that, the courts often go on to decide on values of companies or professional practices where post-marital efforts or restrictions thereon are clearly reflected in the valuation methods accepted. Some specific situations illustrating this are discussed in the next chapter.

For example, the "capitalized excess earnings method," often used in family law courts, includes a value that can only be realized if the operating spouse continues to work. Otherwise, the "excess earnings" that are capitalized will never be realized (unless it can be shown that they are tied completely to the entity, rather than to the individual).

When the courts use *market value*, they often rely on comparable business sales that include a covenant not to compete that restricts the activities of the sellers. Yet, the values of the covenants not to compete are not subtracted out of the total consideration received by the sellers in the allegedly comparable sale transactions unless the analyst specifically does so. *Pratt's Stats* provides a good source of data for determining amounts allocated to non-compete agreements in guideline transactions.

And, it is not at all uncommon for courts to use the term *market value* or *fair market value* and then to conclude a value that incorporates elements of investment value or some other standard.

The analyst should carefully study the case law in the relevant family law jurisdiction and discuss the interpretations with the client's attorney. In many situations, this will still leave room for a high level of confusion. It is incumbent upon the attorney to educate the analyst as to the valuation methods that are acceptable in the subject jurisdiction.

Valuation Date

Selecting the appropriate valuation date is an important step in the valuation process. In a marital dissolution valuation, relevant state-specific statutory authority and judicial precedent sometimes specifies the appropriate valuation date or dates. In many instances, however, the appropriate valuation date is unclear based on the state-specific judicial precedent. Accordingly, the appropriate valuation date for the ownership interest included in the marital estate is a question most appropriately answered by legal counsel, and not by the valuation analyst.

Based on judicial precedent in numerous states and jurisdictions throughout the country, and based on the specific circumstances of the particular marital dissolution, the valuation date is generally one or more of the following dates:

---

[5] These states include Indiana, North Dakota, Virginia, and Wyoming. For a discussion of the pertinent case law in these states, see the "Standards of Value" section in Chapter 38, below.

1. The date of marriage (in cases in which appreciation during the marriage is included in the marital estate).
2. The date of separation.
3. The date of filing.
4. The date of the trial.

Since the selection of the appropriate valuation date can affect the value of the subject business, it is important that the attorney instruct the analyst regarding the applicable valuation date (or dates) early in the valuation process. However, the analyst may have to go to court prepared to testify as to the value on several different dates if the court does not address that issue beforehand.[6]

Discovery

There are often obstacles in the discovery process for the analyst in a marital dissolution proceeding. In the case where the analyst is working for a nonowner spouse, information regarding the subject business or professional practice may be difficult to obtain. Also, the owner spouse may not readily share strategic and financial information with the analyst.

In these cases, it is advisable for the analyst to prepare a comprehensive data and document request to give to the client or to the client's attorney. Often, it is difficult to add to or amend an initial document request. Therefore, the analyst is advised to prepare as comprehensive a document request list as possible for submission. Exhibit 4–1 (in Chapter 4) presents a sample document request list. Some of these documents may be accessible from the subject company's accountants, attorneys, or bankers.

Most valuation experts consider it preferable to conduct discovery in the most informal (from a legal point of view) and most direct manner possible, with the greatest possible interaction. In this sense, most analysts prefer direct management interviews over depositions and depositions over interrogatories. The answers to each question may raise other questions. The management interview provides opportunity for dialogue. If forced to do discovery through depositions rather than interviews, the attorney rather than the analyst usually has to ask the questions. It is highly desirable to have the analyst present at any depositions in order to provide the attorney with follow-up questions.

Interrogatories are the most cumbersome and generally least satisfactory form of discovery, lacking virtually all interaction. If they are absolutely necessary, the attorney should try to leave the door open for follow-up sets of interrogatories to fill in unanswered questions, including those that may arise throughout the course of the valuation process.

The independent valuation analyst should be objective and not an advocate for the client's position. If this can be communicated to the operating spouse, that spouse may be more open to direct contact with the analyst. It is the operating spouse's opportunity to fully expose the analyst to his or her side of the story. A competent and objective analyst will take all factors presented into consideration.

---

[6] The date of valuation is a frequent issue. See, for example. *Else v. Else*, No. A-95-488, 1997 WL 22615 (Neb. App. Jan. 14, 1997), where the appellate court decided that the trial court erred by using the date of trial rather than the date of separation. See also *Quillen v. Quillen*, No. 29502-9608-CV-531, Sup. Ct. Ind. (Aug. 6, 1996), where the court decided the date should be before the husband lost financing capacity for his construction company because of sex offenses against his daughter since he brought it on himself.

In many cases, the analyst can get a more complete understanding directly from the operating party than through other means of discovery. This may narrow the differences between the analysts, and may sometimes facilitate a settlement.

Goodwill

In many divorce cases, the inclusion and/or measurement of goodwill as a marital asset is by far the largest issue in the valuation of the marital estate's business or professional practice.

The classic definition of goodwill is "the propensity of customers to return for repeat business." The criterion as to whether goodwill exists usually is the ability to earn a rate of return in excess of a normal rate of return on the net assets of the business, after reasonable compensation to operating personnel. The measurement of goodwill often is performed by capitalizing amounts of economic return in excess of a normal rate of return on the net other assets of the business (see Chapter 13 on the Capitalized Excess Earnings Method).

In marital dissolution cases, goodwill may require allocation between two types: (1) institutional (or practice) goodwill and (2) professional (or personal) goodwill. Professional or personal goodwill may be described as the intangible value attributable solely to the efforts of or reputation of an owner spouse of the subject business. Institutional or practice goodwill may be described as the intangible value that would continue to inure to the business without the presence of that specific owner spouse.

As with many matters related to marital dissolution valuations, the consideration of goodwill varies among states. In general, the various judicial precedents follow one of three positions regarding the consideration of goodwill:

1. Goodwill is never a distributable marital asset.
2. Business or practice goodwill *only* is a distributable marital asset.
3. All intangible value in the nature of goodwill (both personal and practice goodwill) related to the business or practice is distributable.

States that adhere strictly to the fair market value standard in marital property dissolution follow option number two above. That is, they recognize the fact that the value of personal goodwill can only be realized as a result of the continuing involvement of that person (post-marital efforts), and, therefore, only the business goodwill is a marital asset. (An exception could be genuine celebrity goodwill, where a person may receive a royalty from endorsing a product or service, with no actual future effort expended by that person.)[7]

The analyst should consult the attorney regarding the appropriate treatment of goodwill early in the assignment. This consultation procedure should be performed in order to determine what information should be requested and what valuation methods should be used. The analyst also should carefully study the relevant judicial precedent. There are literally hundreds of cases dealing with goodwill as a marital asset. A representative sampling of these is discussed in the next chapter.

---

[7] See especially Michael C. Wierwille and Neil J. Beaton. "Valuing of Celebrity or Professional Goodwill—A New Paradigm," *The Journal of Business Valuation* (Proceedings of the Fourth Joint Business Valuation Conference of The Canadian Institute of Chartered Business Valuators and the American Society of Appraisers, 1998), pp. 269–78. Also available at www.BVLibrary.com.

Valuation Methods

Family law courts generally recognize each of the three basic approaches to value:

1. Income approach (both direct capitalization and, increasingly, discounted cash flow).
2. Market approach.
3. Asset-based approach (including the capitalized excess earnings method).

Having said this, however, it should be noted that the courts often take considerable latitude in their applications of these valuation approaches. This situation makes it even more important for the analyst to consider any applicable state statutes and relevant judicial precedent when concluding which valuation approaches and methods are most appropriate.

Income Approach

The commonly used income approach valuation methods (especially for valuing operating companies) are (1) the discounted future economic income (often cash flow) method and (2) the direct capitalization of economic income (often earnings) method. The trend in many family law courts is to emphasize income approach methods more than asset-based approach and market approach methods of valuation.

The capitalized economic income method (discussed in Chapter 10) is one of the more frequently used methods in marital dissolution valuations.[8] However, recent family law court cases have indicated that the courts are turning more frequently to other valuation methods. This is because these other methods (such as the discounted cash flow method) have achieved wide acceptance in the valuation community at large.

In the direct capitalization of economic income method, the value of the company is estimated by dividing the expected economic income of a company by an appropriate direct capitalization rate. If the economic income measure is net cash flow, this direct capitalization rate is generally equal to the present value discount rate less the expected long-term growth rate for the cash flow stream.

In the discounted cash flow method (one version of the discounted economic income method, discussed in Chapter 9), the value of a company is based on the present value of the future economic income (measured as cash flow), at a yield capitalization rate (present value discount rate) appropriate the level of risk associated with an investment in the subject company. This valuation method is gaining more widespread acceptance by the family law courts.[9]

Market Approach

The market approach valuation methods rely on prices paid for (1) guideline publicly traded companies (discussed in Chapter 11) or (2) for guideline merged and acquired

---

[8] See, for example, *DeLucia v. DeLucia*, No. FA 950249319S, 1997 WL 16832. Conn. Super. Ct. (Jan. 10, 1997), and *Giuliani v. Giuliani*, No. CA 930526886S, 1996 WL 409324, Conn. Super. Ct. (June 19, 1996).

[9] See, for example, *Guiffre v. Baker*, No. 95-G-1904, 1996 WL 535254, Ohio Ct. App. 11th Dist. (Aug. 30, 1996), and *Sergi v. Sergi*, No. 17476, 1996 WL 425914, Ohio Ct. App. 9th Dist. (July 31, 19961). In both these cases, the courts rejected the excess earnings method and accepted the discounted cash flow method.

companies (discussed in Chapter 12) as the basis for estimating the value of a business. As discussed in these chapters, the market approach has become increasingly feasible in recent years because of the development and accessibility of both publicly traded guideline company data and also data on the sales of privately held companies.

Asset-Based Approach

Asset-based approach methods (discussed in Chapters 13 and 14) are often recognized by courts in marital dissolution valuations. These methods rely on the adjusted balance sheet of the subject company in order to estimate the value of the subject ownership interest in the subject company. This method, although widely used, is often incorrectly performed.

Often—and inappropriately—the net book value of the business assets less the book value of the liabilities is used to value the subject ownership interest. Rather, an asset accumulation method should be used to value the subject ownership interest by valuing all of the assets and all of the liabilities of the subject business. This valuation should include adjustments for off-balance sheet items as well. Such items may include unrecorded liabilities, unrecorded intangible assets, and unrecorded (or nonoperating) assets. The net difference in the value of all of the assets and all of the liabilities will indicate the value of the subject business equity. Adjustments to that business value in order to value the subject ownership interest will depend on the individual facts and circumstances.

The Capitalized Excess Earnings Method

An asset-based approach method that is used extensively in marital dissolution valuations is the *capitalized excess earnings method* (see Chapter 13). Although this method is sometimes disparaged in valuation texts, it remains a common valuation method in analyses performed for marital dissolution purposes.

Under this method, the value of the subject business is the sum of the value of the tangible assets and the intangible assets less the value of the outstanding liabilities. The method takes its name from the fact that the intangible asset value is estimated based on the direct capitalization of the economic income earned by the business in excess of a fair return on its tangible assets.

Usually Employ More Than One Method

Other valuation methods have been used in marital dissolution cases. However, the above paragraphs describe the most common valuation methods. The selection of the appropriate valuation method(s) will depend on the facts and circumstances of the particular case. However, the latitude afforded judges in the marital dissolution process should persuade the analyst to adopt more than one valuation method—in order to provide mutually supportive evidence as to the valuation conclusion.

In general, once the valuation method(s) has been selected, implementing it in the divorce context is similar to implementing it outside of the divorce context. However, certain issues are dealt with differently or assume unique significance in a divorce proceeding. Some of these nuances are addressed in the following chapter on Marital Dissolution Court Cases.

Compensation

Another area in which the analyst may perform procedures of particular significance to the marital dissolution assignment is in the area of adequate compensation. In certain cases, the court may want to establish whether or not the amount paid to an owner spouse in salary and benefits has adequately compensated the marital estate for the owner spouse's efforts. This issue usually arises in the case of a spouse who is the owner of a business that is arguably a nonmarital asset.

Using "marital income" that is not paid in the form of compensation may be considered an investment in the nonmarital asset. An attorney may want to discern whether the value of a nonmarital business has been enhanced because the owner spouse has not withdrawn adequate compensation from the company. This issue could trigger some argument as to the extent of the exclusion of the enterprise from the marital estate.[10] Thus, the analyst in a valuation for divorce purposes should be familiar with compensation issues and with sources of information regarding reasonable compensation (see Chapter 6 on Gathering Economic and Industry Data for useful sources of compensation information).

Many states also do not allow "double-dipping," which occurs when spousal support is awarded on the same dollars that generate value in the business. The analyst should be aware of this issue in his or her state, and the impact on the level of compensation used in the valuation.

Noncompete Covenants

Noncompete covenants and employment agreements require special attention in a marital dissolution proceeding. If the sale of the marital asset business occurs, a noncompete covenant and/or an employment agreement may be required of the owner spouse. This issue may trigger argument over whether the value of the proceeds attributable to the noncompete covenant and/or employment agreement are part of the marital estate.

In addition, in the case of a jointly owned business, one spouse may be required to buy out the other—and some form of a noncompete and/or employment agreement could be required. The value assigned to these agreements may have special significance in the divorce valuation.

Generally speaking, the value of the noncompete covenant would *not* be a marital asset because it restricts the postmarital activity of the spouse, and the employment agreement would not be a marital asset because it involves future efforts of the spouse. However, these agreements may need to be valued to ascertain whether the amount allocated to them is the fair market value of these agreements.[11]

---

[10] The issue of adequate compensation may be a factor in the court deciding whether (or the extent to which) appreciation in the value of a company was active or passive. To the extent that the operating spouse was adequately compensated, the appreciation may be attributed to other factors. To the extent that the spouse was undercompensated, the appreciation may be attributed to the spouse's efforts for which the marital estate was not adequately compensated during the marriage.

[11] See, for example, *In re Marriage of Monaghan*, 899 P2d 841 (Wash. App. Aug. 9, 1995) and *Sweere v. Gilbert-Sweere*, 534 NW2d 294 (Minn. App. July 18, 1995), discussed in the next chapter.

As noted earlier, family law courts often (perhaps even usually) ignore the implications of these elements of value in the market approach when using pricing multiples derived from private sales of guideline companies.

Buy-Sell Agreements

One of the very common controversies is whether a buy-sell agreement value should be controlling for marital dissolution purposes, or whether it should be accorded any weight at all. Family law court decisions on this issue vary greatly.

As a broad generality, in states where professional (personal) goodwill is considered a marital asset, the buy-sell agreement price (the amount that would be realized if the spouse withdrew from the enterprise) usually is not found to be controlling. In other states a buy-sell agreement may be controlling or the issues may be decided on the basis of individual facts and circumstances.

In some cases, the buy-sell agreement value may be given some weight even though it is not controlling. Examples of the treatment of buy-sell agreements for divorce valuations are presented in the next chapter.

Treatment of Trapped-In Capital Gains Taxes

Another issue that is often important in the marital dissolution analysis is the inclusion of the capital gains tax effect with regard to the value conclusion. This influence is often considered in the valuation of business ownership interests using asset-based methods. This influence is intended to reflect the contingent tax liability for the unrealized capital gains on appreciated business assets. In concluding whether this adjustment is appropriate, it is noteworthy that the repeal of the so-called General Utilities doctrine (by the Tax Reform Act of 1986) makes it virtually impossible for a corporation to sell or distribute appreciated assets without incurring a taxable gain.

In marital dissolution proceedings, however, courts have generally found that consideration of tax consequences is appropriate only (1) when the tax liability is imminent or (2) when the tax will arise directly from the court's property disposition. In situations where there is some speculation as to when (or if) the assets will be sold and the magnitude of the associated tax liability, family law courts have generally found that it is inappropriate to consider the tax consequences related to the sale.[12] However, it often falls to the analyst to determine—and to defend—an independent opinion regarding the appropriate consideration of capital gains taxes.

In 1998, the U.S. Tax Court and the Second Circuit Court of Appeals finally recognized that trapped-in capital gains were appropriate to recognize as a valuation factor and the IRS has acquiesced to this position (see Chapter 27 and 28 on gift and estate valuations and related court cases). Family law courts often quote IRS authority and Tax Court cases in support of positions taken. And, this movement on the part of the Tax Court and the IRS could be a catalyst in family law courts for increased recognition of trapped-in capital gains liability. Many practitioners believe that it is

---

[12] See, for example, *In re the Marriage of Hay*, No. 14368-6-111, 1995 WL 757772, Wash. Ct. App. (Dec. 26, 1995).

unfair to distribute free and clear liquid assets to one spouse and give the other spouse what would be an equal value except for assuming the liability for capital gains taxes when and if the spouse decides to sell.

Nevertheless, in some jurisdictions, the recognition of the trapped-in capital gains tax liability may result in the court using an equitable distribution technique—rather than an equal division of the marital property.

Valuation Discounts and Premiums

The applicability of valuation discounts and premiums offers further challenges in a marital dissolution valuation. The size of valuation discounts and premiums is often a matter of informed professional judgment on the part of the analyst. The situations in which discounts and premiums are applicable—and the reasonable range of these valuation adjustments—are fairly well addressed within most legal contexts, such as federal income, gift, and estate tax and employee stock ownership plan (ESOP) transactions. In a valuation for divorce, however, the state-specific nature of the statutes and judicial precedent encourages the analyst to become familiar with both (1) the types of valuation adjustments and (2) the circumstances under which each has been accepted within each state. The analyst should form an independent opinion regarding the appropriate application of discounts and premiums. This includes valuation adjustments that are fairly common, such as the discount for lack of marketability, the discount for lack of ownership control or the ownership control premium, and the discount for key person dependence.

One argument often made against discounts is that there should be none because there is no change of ownership. Many consider this argument to be fatally flawed because, as noted earlier in the chapter, one spouse is, in effect, buying out the other spouse's interest.

As seen in Chapters 15 through 18, differences of opinion about the discount and premium adjustments are often a much larger dollar issue than differences about the value of the company itself. Some examples of court opinions on discount and premium issues are given in the next chapter.

The Role of the Analyst

The valuation of businesses and business interests for marital dissolution purposes is a complex and challenging task due to the diverse jurisdictions and unique issues in these cases. In addition, the analyst in a marital dissolution engagement may often assume an expanded role. In addition to performing a valuation, the analyst may often assume a more forensic accounting or forensic economics role, by assisting attorneys in identifying distributable assets and tracing their origins. The valuation process may require the analysis of the flow of financial resources into and out of the subject business enterprise. However, in some instances, the analyst will defer such investigative analysis to a forensic accountant.

Since many divorce valuations are performed within a litigation environment, the analyst should function effectively and should offer several services to legal counsel. These services should begin with assisting counsel in the discovery process. In addition, the analyst may be asked to analyze and evaluate settlement offers that occur frequently during the marital dissolution process. In this capacity, the analyst would be called upon to evaluate the reasonableness of a settlement offer in light of the value or estimated value of the assets in the marital estate.

A consideration sometimes present in family law engagements that is not found in engagements for other purposes is a tradeoff between the value determined for property distribution and awards of ongoing spousal support or alimony. Frequently, the value of the business exceeds all other marital assets combined, so that it is not possible to achieve an equitable distribution if the operating spouse is awarded the business and the nonoperating spouse all the other assets. One way to handle this problem is to give the nonoperating spouse a note for a portion of the difference. Some courts, however, prefer to set a very conservative value on the business and offset that with more generous support or alimony payments. The analyst should be aware of these considerations if consulting with the attorney on settlement options.

As with most litigation support assignments, the analyst may be called upon to assist legal counsel in the deposition and subsequent trial examination of opposing valuation experts. This may involve assessing the strengths and weaknesses of the opposing expert's position in terms of both factual interpretation and valuation methodology.

Throughout all of the processes, the analyst should remain objective. More often in family law than in any other area of valuation, the courts justifiably accuse experts of bias and advocacy in favor of their clients. This does not help the client, the analyst, or the profession. The client is best served by having the court accept a reasonable value rather than having the court reject the expert's evidence as not credible.

"Jointly Retained" Assignments

I have heard some appraisers say that they encourage joint retention by the husband and wife, and other appraisers say that they resist joint retention like the plague, or even refuse joint retention cases. It can be done. If so, I would advise that the engagement letter contain language to the effect that both sides acknowledge their willingness and recognize that they could have engaged separate professionals.

With respect to protocol, I suggest transparency with all forms of communication and offer joint site visits so that each spouse or his or her advocate can attend the same discussion. Also, always insist on the fees up front, because one or both spouses are very likely to be unhappy with the results.[13]

Adequacy of Evidence

Our study of appellate opinions in the 1990s reveals that there is a larger incidence of remand for lack of adequate supporting evidence for business value conclusions in family law cases than in taxation, shareholder dispute, bankruptcy, or any other category of business valuation.

---

[13] Thanks to Steve Bravo of Apogee Business Valuations, Framingham,, Mass., for these suggestions.

On the one hand, trial courts have wide discretion in deciding factual matters, such as value, especially in family law courts. On the other hand, appellate courts do, quite consistently, require that the trial court must have an adequate evidentiary basis for reaching its conclusion of fact. Appellate courts have remanded many cases for new evidence and hearings on the value of the business because the evidence presented by the "experts" at the trial court was insufficient to support the court's conclusion of value. This usually results in money that has been spent on "experts" and the related attorney fees being wasted. Attorneys should be able to avoid such remands by hiring competent experts, critically reviewing their work product (see Chapter 22 on Reviewing a Business Valuation Report), and being sure to make a complete record at trial.

It is important for the analyst to present his or her opinions credibly and persuasively in deposition and in court testimony. The analyst should be able to effectively explain complicated financial issues to a judge or attorney whose expertise is not accounting or finance. The analyst should be experienced in the application of valuation procedures within a contrarian environment.

Summary

Many aspects of valuations for marital dissolution differ totally or in some respects from valuation assignments for other purposes.

For example, the analyst may become involved in an issue as to whether or not certain property should or should not be included in the marital estate. The most common debate that may involve the appraiser is whether or not appreciation in the value of a business during marriage is classified as active or passive.

The applicable standard of value is generally less clear in the context of marital dissolution than for practically any other valuation purpose. The expert needs to study the relevant case law and interpret it from a valuation point of view. Often, family law courts lean toward *investment value* (value to the particular spouse), even though they may use the phrase *fair market value*.

The date of valuation is important, and the analyst may have to prepare valuations for more than one effective date. However, sometimes the court will bifurcate the matter and rule on the valuation date ahead of the trial addressing the property settlement.

Discovery is often more of an issue in marital dissolution cases than in other types of valuation engagements, because the operating spouse may resist permitting access to records, premises, and/or management, or may even conceal relevant information. This problem may lead to engaging a forensic accountant.

The issue of goodwill tends to loom larger in family law valuations than in other areas of valuation. The problem is not just the measurement of the value of goodwill, but the issue as to who owns it—the individual or the marital estate. Sometimes an allocation must be made between personal and business (or professional) goodwill.

Valuation methodology varies greatly, with much discretion on the part of the court. Family law courts gradually are moving toward acceptance of the valuation methods typically used in the financial community, such as the discounted cash flow valuation method.

Owners' compensation adjustments are often a bigger issue in marital dissolutions than in other types of cases. Sometimes the question of whether an owner was adequately compensated during marriage bears on the issue of whether appreciation in the value of the business or business interest is or is not a marital asset.

The value of noncompete covenants and employment agreements is another major issue being accorded growing recognition (and deservedly so). The value of such agreements is usually (but not always) regarded as personal rather than marital property. Yet most courts so far have not adjusted comparable company sale prices for the inclusion of such agreements in the market approach to valuation, probably because valuation experts have presented little evidence on this important matter.

Deduction of liability for trapped-in capital gains on appreciated assets is often an issue. Family law courts have generally disallowed such a deduction unless a sale is imminent, but recent IRS and Tax Court acquiescences to such a deduction may lead family law courts to be more prone to consider it. One reviewer comments:

> Don't bet on it. My experience is that judges point out that the divorce court is a court of equity, not a tax court, and refuse to be bound by tax law.

But it seems to me that it is extremely inequitable to award one spouse with assets free and clear while awarding the other spouse assets saddled with a potential capital gains tax liability, and not taking that liability into consideration.

Few state family law courts treat valuation discounts and premiums the same way that they would be treated in a conventional fair market value context. The analyst should study the relevant case law when it comes to discount or premium issues.

The analyst should be objective and must avoid any inclination or pressure toward bias in favor of the client. Although this applies to all types of cases, a reading of the opinions suggests that lack of objectivity may be a more prevalent problem in family law than in other types of cases.

The role of the valuation analyst is critical. It is important to bring in a competent, experienced analyst at the outset and to have the analyst involved at every step. It is important for the analyst and the attorney working together to build an adequate evidentiary record at trial. On appeal, courts look to the question of whether or not the lower court had adequate evidence on which to base its decision. If so, the decision normally is upheld. If not, the decision often is remanded for further proceedings.

Bibliography

Articles

Barrett, John E., Jr. "Bifurcating Enterprise and Personal Goodwill." *American Journal of Family Law*, Vol. 16, No. 2, Summer 2002, pp. 129–132.

Berning, Richard C., and Michele G. Miles. "Surviving a Divorce Engagement." *Shannon Pratt's Business Valuation Update*, October 1999, pp. 1–4.

Bishop, David M. and Steven F. Schroeder. "Business Valuation Standard of Value for Divorce Should Be Fair Market Value," *American Journal of Family Law*, Spring 1999, pp. 48–52.

Brandes, Joel R., and Carole L. Weidman. "Valuation of a Professional License." *New York Law Journal*, December 24, 1996, pp. 3–5.

Chorney, Marc A. "Interests in Trusts as Property in Dissolution of Marriage: Identification and Valuation." *Real Property, Probate and Trust Journal,* Spring 2005.

Cohen, Robert S., and Arthur H. Rosenbloom. "The Whole May Be Worth Less Than the Sum of Its Parts." *New York Law Journal,* December 18, 1995, pp. 1–4.

Connell, John R., and William H. Vincent. "Valuing Pension Benefits in Divorce: Look before You Leap." *Journal of Accountancy,* January 1994, pp. 98–100.

Cowhey, Gregory J., Lester Barenbaum, and Sandra R. Klevan. "Putting a Price Tag on the Company." *Family Advocate,* Spring 1995, pp. 44–52.

Darrah, William C. "The Antolik Case and the Determination of Professional Goodwill." Presentation to the International Appraisal Conference of the American Society of Appraisers, June 1998. Available on www.BVLibrary.com.

Dietrich, Mark O. "Identifying and Measuring Personal Goodwill in a Professional Practice." *CPA Expert,* Spring 2005, pp. 6–11.

Feder, Robert D. "Direct Examination of a Business Appraiser in a Divorce Action." *American Journal of Family Law,* Spring 1993, pp. 1–11.

Felder, Myrna. "A Blueprint for a 'McSparron' Evaluation." *New York Law Journal,* October 29, 1996, pp. 3–5.

Fishman, Jay E., Shannon P. Pratt, et al. "Premiums and Discounts in Business Valuation." *Fair$hare: The Matrimonial Law Monthly,* June 1992, pp. 14–16.

Gitlin, Gunnar J. "Business Valuation in Divorce—What Is Double-Dipping and How Is it Quantified?" *American Journal of Family Law,* Summer 1997, pp. 109–18.

Goodman & Company. "Failure to account for Personal Goodwill Is Error." *Valuation Outlook,* Spring 2005.

Goodman, Stanley L. "The Three Big Issues in Business and Professional Practice Valuation." *Fair$hare: The Matrimonial Law Monthly,* April 1996, pp. 2–3.

Gross, Mark. "Buy-Sell Agreements and Divorce." *CPA Litigation Service Counselor,* Vol. 21, No. 2, February 2000, pp. 11–12.

Grossman, Andrew S. "Avoiding Legal Malpractice in Family Law Cases: The Dangers of Not Engaging in Financial Discovery." *Family Law Quarterly,* Vol. 33, No. 2, Summer 1999, p. 361.

Hitchner, James R. "Valuation Date Is Critical in Divorce Case." *CPA Expert,* Fall 1998, pp. 7–10.

Jimmerson, James J. "Celebrity Goodwill: Is it Real or Is it a Mirage?" *American Journal of Family Law,* Summer 1997, pp. 145–51.

Kendig, Robert E. "Discovery Issues in Valuation Cases." *American Journal of Family Law,* Spring 1992, pp. 55–74.

Kinser, Katherine A. "Practical Approaches to the Presentation of Business Values in Divorce." *Fair$hare: The Matrimonial Law Monthly,* August 1992, pp. 3–5.

Kramer, James F. "The Handbook for Divorce Valuations." *The National Public Accountant,* Vol. 45, No. 2, April 2000, p.31.

Luttrell, Mark S., and Jeff W. Freeman. "Taxes and the Undervaluation of 'S' Corporations." *American Journal of Family Law,* Winter 2001, pp. 301-306.

Mason, Miriam E., and Michael S. Cohen. "From a Matrimonial Lawyer's Perspective—The Ten (and a Few More) Most Frequent Errors Made by Business Appraisers." Presentation to the AICPA National Business Valuation Conference, 1999. Available on www.BVLibrary.com.

Mastracchio, James N., and Nicholas J. Mastracchio. "Professional License Value in a Divorce." *CPA Journal*, December 1996, pp. 34–39+.

Mastracchio, Nicholas J., Jr., and Victoria M. Zunitch. "Differences between Mergers and Acquisitions: A CPA Valuator Can Help Clients Decide Whether to Merge or Acquire-Business evaluation. *Journal of Accountancy*, November 2002.

Miod, Donald John. "The Double Dip in Valuing Goodwill in Divorce" (Parts I and II) *CPA Litigation Service Counselor*, April 1998, pp. 1–4, and May 1998, pp. 5–7.

Petig, Becky. "Marital Dissolution Case Summary by State." *BVPapers*, January 24, 2000. Available at www.BVLibrary.com.

_____. "Estimating Intangible Asset Remaining Useful Life for Marital Dissolution." *American Journal of Family Law,* Fall 2001, pp. 199-210.

_____. "Valuation of Customer/Client Relationships for Marital Dissolution Purposes." *American Journal of Family Law*, Winter 2002, pp. 273-288.

_____. "Willamette Management Associates' Discount for Lack of Marketability Study for Marital Dissolution Valuations." *American Journal of Family Law*, Spring 2005, pp. 44-51.

Pratt, Shannon P. "Coping with Business Valuation in Family Law." *American Journal of Family Law*, Winter 1998, pp. 212–17.

_____. "Lack of Clear Definition of Value Confounds Both Attorneys and Appraisers." *Valuation Strategies*, January/February 2000, pp. 35–37.

_____. "Separating Entity from Personal Intangible Assets." *Valuation Strategies*, May/June 1999, pp. 4–9.

_____. "What Is Value?" *Family Advocate*, Spring 1995, pp. 28–33.

Raymond, Richard. "A Biased Valuation: The Treatment of a Professional Degree in Divorce Actions." *American Journal of Economics and Sociology*, July 1995, pp. 268–87.

Reilly, Robert F. "The Differences in Valuing Big and Small Businesses for Divorce." *Fair$hare: The Matrimonial Law Monthly*, September 1995, pp. 3–8.

_____. "The Identification and Qualifications of Business Valuation Discounts and Premia." *Fair$hare: The Matrimonial Law Monthly*, July 1996, pp. 2–5.

Reilly, Robert F., and Robert P. Schweihs. "Valuation Testimony Guidelines in the Post *Daubert* Era." *Fair$hare: The Matrimonial Law Monthly*, March 2000, pp. 7–9.

Riggs, William. "Concepts of Valuations of Celebrity Goodwill as Property." American Bar Association Conference, San Francisco, May 3-5, 2001. Also available at www.BVLibrary.com.

Skoloff, Gary N., and Cary B. Cheifetz. "Direct Examination of Marital Property Valuation Experts." *The Practical Litigator*, May 1992, p. 25.

Steffan, Carl. " Divorce in Utah – Business Valuation Issues." Utah State Bar, Family Law Section, February 18, 2000. Also available at www.BVLibrary.com.

Utley, Chris. "Clients' Divorce Lands CA in Hot Water." *Beyond Numbers*, April 2004.

Weinstein, Jeffrey P. "The Use and Abuse of Economic Experts in Divorce Litigation." *Fair$hare: The Matrimonial Law Monthly*, February 1995, pp. 3–6.

Wierwille, Michael C. and Neil J. Beaton, "Valuing of Celebrity or Professional Goodwill—A New Paradigm," *The Journal of Business Valuation* (proceedings of the Fourth Joint Business Valuation Conference of The Canadian Institute of Chartered Business Valuators and the American Society of Appraisers, 1998), pp. 269–78.

Wietzke, Robert R. "Marital Dissolution and Divorce Valuations: Be Sure You Understand Your Commitment." *CPA Litigation Service Counselor,* Vol. 21 No. 6, June 2000.

Wise, Richard M. "Valuing Private Shares in Divorce Litigation: The Whole Seldom Equals the Sum of the Parts." *Canadian Family Law Quarterly,* August 1990, pp. 295–319.

Zipp, Alan S. "Business Valuation Standard for Divorce is Different from Fair Market Value," *American Journal of Family Law,* Fall 1997, pp. 167–72.

Zipp, Alan S. "Business Valuation Standards in Divorce." *Business Valuation Review,* Vol. 19, No. 3, September 2000.

Books

Barson, Kalaman A. *Investigative Accounting in Divorce.* 2nd ed., Hoboken, NJ: John Wiley & Sons, December 2001 (E-book, April 2002).

Brown, Ronald L. *Valuing Professional Practices and Licenses: A Guide for the Matrimonial Practitioner,* 3rd ed. New York: Aspen Law & Business, 1999 (cumulative supplement 2005).

Feder, Robert D. Valuing Specific Assets in Divorce, New York: Aspen Law & Business, 2000 (cumulative supplement 2005).

_____. *Valuation Strategies in Divorce,* 4th ed. New York: Aspen Law & Business, 1997 (cumulative supplement 2005).

Feigenbaum, Alan, and Heather Linton. *The Complete Guide to Protecting Your Financial Security When Getting a Divorce.* New York: McGraw-Hill, 2004.

Fishman, Jay E., Shannon P. Pratt, and J. Clifford Griffith. *Guide to Business Valuations,* 16th ed. Forth Worth, TX: Practitioners Publishing Company, 2006.

Fishman, Jay E., William Morrison, and Shannon P. Pratt. *Standards of Value: Theory and Applications.* Hoboken, NJ: John Wiley & Sons, 2006.

Freedman, Andrew J., and Stephen R. Cole. *Property Valuation and Income Tax Implications of Marital Dissolution.* Scarborough, Ontario: Carswell Legal Publications, 2000.

Goldberg, Barth H. *Valuation of Divorce Assets.* St Paul: West Publishing Company, 1984 (cumulative supplement 2005).

Hitchner, James R. *Financial Valuation: Applications and Models.* Hoboken, NJ: John Wiley & Sons, 2003.

Kleeman, Robert E., Jr., R. James Alerding, and Benjamin D. Miller. *The Handbook for Divorce Valuations.* Hoboken, NJ: John Wiley & Sons, 1999.

Meltzer, Stanton L., David A. Rooney, et al. *Guide to Divorce Engagements,* 14th ed. Fort Worth, TX: Practitioners Publishing Company, 2005.

Oldham, J. Thomas. *Divorce, Separation and the Distribution of Property.* New York: Law Journal Seminars-Press, 1987 (supplement annually).

Pratt, Shannon P. *The Lawyers Business Valuation Handbook.* Chicago: American Bar Association, 2000.

Richman, Bruce L. *J.K. Lesser Pro Guide to Tax and Financial Issues in Divorce.* Hoboken, NJ: John Wiley & Sons, 2002.

Trugman, Gary R. *Understanding Business Valuation: A Practical Guide to Valuing Small to Medium-Sized Businesses,* 2nd ed. New York: American Institute of Certified Public Accountants, 2002.

_____. *Valuation Issues in Divorce Settings,* 2nd ed. New York: American Institute of Certified Public Accountants, 1999.

Periodicals

American Journal of Family Law, quarterly, Aspen Publishers, 76 Ninth Avenue, New York, NY 10011, (800) 638-8437. www.aspenpublishers.com.

Fair$hare: The Matrimonial Law Monthly, monthly. Aspen Publishers, 76 Ninth Avenue, New York, NY 10011, (800) 638-8437. www.aspenpublishers.com.

Family Advocate, quarterly, American Bar Association, P.O. Box 10892, Chicago, IL 60610-0892, (312) 988-5522, www.abanet.org/family/advocate/home.html.

The Matrimonial Strategist, monthly. Law Journal Newsletters, 345 Park Avenue South, New York, NY 10010, (215) 557-2300, www.lawcatalog.com.

Shannon Pratt's Business Valuation Update, monthly. Business Valuation Resources, 7412 S.W. Beaverton-Hillsdale Highway, Suite 106, Portland, OR 97225, (888) 287-8258, www.bvresources.com.

Chapter 38

Marital Dissolution Court Cases

Treatment of various factors in business and professional practice valuation are more diverse from one jurisdiction to another in marital disolution cases than in any other context of business valuation. Furthermore, the statutes provide very limited guidance. Therefore, the analyst needs to be knowledgeable about the case law as it relates to divorce for each jurisdiction in which the analyst practices.

The purpose of this chapter is to provide a small but representative sampling of the often diverse positions that various state appellate courts have taken on some of the most important business valuation issues frequently encountered in the context of marital dissolution. When state courts address a particular issue for the first time, they often look to precedents in other states for guidance. Therefore, it is helpful to have a general knowledge of various states' positions on issues and to have the ability to research case precedent on controversial issues.[1]

Standards of Value

Most decisions give no explicit definition of the acceptable standard of value. It usually is necessary to infer the court's acceptable standard(s) of value from the language of decisions and valuation methods and procedures accepted. Thus, this section gives only a few examples of clearly articulated standards of value.

Fair Market Value

Several states adhere quite consistently to the standard of fair market value. These include, for example, Wisconsin,[2] Illinois,[3] Pennsylvania,[4] Florida,[5] Missouri,[6] Hawaii,[7] and South Carolina.[8] These states do not include any personal goodwill in the value of the business on the grounds that personal goodwill is the property of the individual and not marital property. A few states mandate by statute that fair market value be used.[9]

Fair Value

Although no state expressly uses the term "fair value" as the standard of value to be used in a divorce proceeding, a few states have essentially used that standard. These states typically reference shareholder dissent and oppression cases, which

---

[1] Full texts of virtually all precedential marital dissolution case opinions involving business or professional practice valuations are available at www.BVLibrary.com.

[2] See *In re Marriage of Herlitzke*, 2006 Wisc. App. LEXIS 972 (Wisc. Ct. App. 2006); *Siker v. Siker*, 1999 WL 74599 (Wis. Ct. App. Feb. 18, 1999); *Huebner v. Huebner*, No. 96-2397-F, 1997 WL 106572 (Wis. Ct. App. Mar. 12, 1997); and *Sommerfield v. Sommerfield*, 454 N.W.2d 55, 58 (Wis. Ct. App. 1990).

[3] See *Grunsten v. Grunsten*, 1999 WL 64479 (Ill. App. Ct. Feb. 11, 1999).

[4] See *Campbell v. Campbell*, 483 A.2d 363, 367 (Pa. Super. Ct. 1986).

[5] See *Christians v. Christians*, 732 So.2d 47 (Fla. Dist. Ct. App. 1999) and *Makowski v. Makowski*, 613 So.2d 924 (Fla. Dist. Ct. App. 1999).

[6] *Theilen v. Theilen*, 847 S.W.2d 116 (Mo. Ct. App. 1992).

[7] *Antolik v. Harvey*, 7 Haw. App. 313, 761 P.2d 305 (Haw. Ct. App. 1988).

[8] See *Hickum v. Hickum*, 463 S.E.2d 321, 325 (S.C. Ct. App. 1995); *RGM v. DEM*, 410 S.E.2d 564, 568 (S.C. 1991); and *Reid v. Reid*, 312 S.E.2d 724, 727 (S.C. Ct. App. 1984).

[9] Louisiana requires that parties to a divorce list their community assets at fair market value for distribution and prohibits the inclusion of personal goodwill in the determination of fair market value (La. R.S. §9:2801); Arkansas requires that securities in a divorce be appraised at fair market value (Ark. Code Ann. §9-12-315[a][4]).

overwhelmingly use a fair value standard. Under the fair value standard, the court exercises a great deal of discretion in delimiting the standard's parameters, and, ordinarily, discounts are disallowed. In addition, in shareholder cases, fair value is often regarded as the pro-rata share of an enterprise's value. Similarly, in the divorce setting, a court evaluating discounts may see the application of discounts as an unfair advantage to the party that will continue to enjoy the benefits of the asset. In this respect, divorce and shareholder oppression cases are similar in that they can both be viewed in terms of the reasonable expectations of those entering into a partnership or contract (business or marital).

For example, in *Brown v. Brown*,[10] a New Jersey trial court used the language of fair value and referred to New Jersey shareholder dissent and oppression cases to determine the standard of value to be used in the case. As another New Jersey court indicated in *Piscopo v. Piscopo*,[11] since both shareholder oppression and marital dissolution cases are actions brought in a court of equity, it would be unreasonable to treat value one way in one type of case, and another in another type of case; equity requires that the court find a value that is fair.

Bobrow v. Bobrow[12] concluded value as the pro-rata share of the enterprise value, despite a buy-sell agreement that specified that the husband's interest in the accounting firm Ernst & Young was only what was in his capital account. Such an approach is similar to the way value would be treated under a fair value standard in a dissenting or oppressed shareholders' case.

Occasionally, courts will use a hybrid standard that involves fair value and investment value, which is discussed in the next section. Although the Louisiana case of *Ellington v. Ellington*[13] referenced investment value concepts in the continuing benefits of ownership and employment, the predominant language of the case involved fair value constructs. In that case, the wife's expert used an excess earnings method and came to a value of $668,000, whereas the husband's expert determined that the fair market value of liabilities outweighed assets by approximately $55,000, and therefore the company had negative value. The court rejected both experts' testimonies, as they both used a fair market value standard, which the court ruled was inappropriate because neither party was a willing seller. Based on its own approach, the court came to a value of $293,000. The appellate court approved this decision on the fair value logic that the husband would retain ownership, current management would continue, and the husband would continue to benefit from his ownership.

In other instances, some cases are considered either as using an investment standard of value or a fair value standard of value. For example, in *Neuman v. Neuman*,[14] the dispute was over the value of the husband's mintority interest in a trucking business. The trial court accepted the wife's valuation, which applied no discounts on the argument that the husband had no plans to sell his stock. The Wyoming Supreme Court affirmed,[15] creating a difference between the value of a business to a willing buyer and the value of a business for divorce purposes. On one hand, this could be considered an investment value case because value was measured by the value to the husband of his retained interest. On the other hand,

---

[10] *Brown v. Brown*, 348 N.J. Super. 466, 792 A.2d 463, 2002 N.J. Super. LEXIS 105 (N.J. App. Div. 2002).
[11] *Piscopo v. Piscopo*, 232 N.J. Super. 559, 557 A.2d 1040 (N.J. Super. 1989).
[12] *Bobrow v. Bobrow*, No. 29D01-0003-DR-166 (Ind. Super. 2002).
[13] *Ellington v. Ellington*, 842 So. 2d 1160 (La. Ct. App. 2003).
[14] *Neuman v. Neuman*, 842 P.2d 575 (Wyo. 1992).
[15] *Neuman v. Neuman*, 842 P.2d 575 (Wyo. 1992).

this could be considered a fair value case because the husband was receiving his pro-rata share of the company's value.

In *Howell v. Howell*,[16] (also discussed in the next section on investment value) the court recognized personal goodwill and excluded discounts on the grounds that "intrinsic" value should be determined based on the husband's staying with his law firm. Thus, this can be categorized as an investment value case, where the value is measured by the value to the owner, or as a fair value case, because value is calculated as a percentage of the enterprise value.

Investment Value

Without specifically saying so, many family law courts utilize *investment value*— that is, value to a *particular* buyer or seller. They tend to zero in on value to the operating spouse.

A good example is a Colorado case that said that the accepted valuation of business goodwill is based on the value of the business to the operating spouse.[17]

In Virginia, business interests normally are valued at fair market value. For closely held companies, the goal is to arrive at a fair market value for a stock for which there is no market. However, in Virginia, interests in law practices cannot be bought or sold. So the court has adopted what it termed "intrinsic value," which comports to what we have called "investment value" in this book—that is, value to a *particular* owner, in this case, the operating spouse. The Court stated, "the highest and best use for defendant's share is to remain with Hunton & Williams." The Court thus accepted a valuation that included a goodwill component, even though the buy-sell agreement did not.[18]

The Court in the case above quoted from another case:

> Goodwill is an asset of a professional practice subject to valuation as marital property ... to hold otherwise would result in a windfall to the professional spouse. This would derive from the failure to consider part of the value of an asset already classified as marital property.[19]

California is one of the few states in which courts have clearly taken the position that the standard of value should be investment value rather than market value.[20]

> We hold section 4800, subdivision (a) of the Family Law Act (Civ. Code, SS 4800, subd. (a)) is satisfied when the investment value of closely held shares is determined rather than their market value.[21]

The *Hewitson* case notes three approaches that have been accepted to determine investment value:

> The three basic approaches, or their variations, which have been recognized in determining the investment value of closely held shares are commonly termed (1) capitalization of earnings approach #3 (see *Worthen v. United*

---

[16] *Howell v. Howell*, 46 Va. Cir. 339; 1998 Va. Cir. LEXIS 256 (Va. Cir. Sept. 4, 1998), *aff'd*, 31 Va. App. 332, 523 S.E.2d 514 (2000).

[17] *In re Marriage of Nichols*, 606 P.2d 1314 (Colo. Ct. App. 1979).

[18] *Howell v. Howell*, 46 Va. Cir. 339; 1998 Va. Cir. LEXIS 256 (Va. Cir. Sept. 4, 1998), *aff'd*, 31 Va. App. 332, 523 S.E.2d 514 (2000). See also *Lannes v. Lannes*, 2005 Va. App. LEXIS 176 (Va. Ct. App. 2005) (intrinsic value).

[19] *Russell v. Russell*, 11 Va. App. 411 (1990).

[20] *In re Marriage of Hewitson*, 142 Cal.App.3d 874, 191 Cal.Rptr. 392 (Part I) (Cal. Ct. App. 1983).

[21] Ibid.

States (D.Mass. 1961) 192 F.Supp. 727; Cohan, Valuation of Interests in Closely Held Businesses (1966) 44 Taxes 504, 508), (2) dividend paying capacity #4 (see *Estate of Goar v. Comm'r.* (1950) 9 T.C.M. 854; *Righter v. United States*, supra, 439 F.2d 1204, 1210), and (3) book value #5 or net asset value #6 (see *Estate of Rowell* (1955) 132 Cal.App.2d 421, 428). The application of these approaches, or their variations, will determine the investment value of the closely held shares, not their market value.[22]

Other states that use an investment or intrinsic value standard include Arizona,[23] California,[24] Colorado,[25] Kentucky,[26] Michigan,[27] Montana,[28] Nevada,[29] New Mexico,[30] North Carolina,[31] and Washington.[32] However, these states may adopt other standards of value, depending on the particular facts of the case.[33]

Premise of Value

Usually the issue presented in the determination of the correct premise of value is whether the business should be valued on a going-concern basis or on a liquidation basis.

For example, in *Sommers v. Sommers*,[34] the wife's expert valued the husband's orthodontic practice on a going-concern basis, whereas the husband's expert used a liquidation value. The trial court accepted the husband's valuation, but, on appeal, the North Dakota Supreme Court reversed, finding no evidence that the husband intended to sell the practice.

In *Bausano v. Bausano*,[35] the husband's expert claimed liquidation value was the appropriate premise of value because the company had operated at a loss in recent years. The court rejected this approach and found the valuation of the wife's expert more credible because it used replacement value and valued the business as a going concern. The court found that the business had potential, especially since the husband indicated he planned to focus his efforts on the business once the divorce was final. Similarly, in *Hoverson v. Hoverson*,[36] the court rejected liquidation value for valuing a farm that had losses of about $1 million, finding that the assets had value to the farm as long as it continued in business. The court indicated that the business had to be valued as a going concern despite its current financial condition.

---

[22] Ibid.

[23] *Mitchell v. Mitchell*, 152 Ariz. 317, 732 P.2d 208 (Ariz. 1987).

[24] *Golden v. Golden*, 75 Cal. Rptr. 735 (Cal. Ct. App. 1969).

[25] *In re Marriage of Huff*, 834 P.2d 244 (Colo. 1992).

[26] *Clark v. Clark*, 782 S.W.2d 56, 1990 Ky. App. LEXIS 3 (Ky. Ct. App. 1990).

[27] *Kowaleski v. Kowaleski*, 148 Mich. App. 151; 384 N.W.2d 112; 1986 Mich. App. LEXIS 2380 (Mich. App. Ct. 1986).

[28] *In re Marriage of Hull*, 219 Mont. 480, 712 P2d 1317, 43 St. Rep. 107 (Mont. 1986).

[29] *Ford v. Ford*, 782 P.2d 1304 (Nev. 1989).

[30] *Mitchell v. Mitchell*, 719 P.2d 432 (N.M. Ct. App. 1986).

[31] *Poore v. Poore*, 75 N.C. App. 414, 331 S.E.2d 266, *cert. denied*, 314 N.C. 543, 335 S.E.2d 316 (1985).

[32] *Matter of Marriage of Fleege*, 588 P.2d 1136 (Wash. 1979).

[33] See, e.g., in New Jersey, *Brown v. Brown*, 348 N.J. Super. 466, 792 A.2d 463, 2002 N.J. Super. LEXIS 105 (N.J. Super. 2002) (applying a fair value standard of value).

[34] *Sommers v. Sommers*, 660 N.W.2d 586, 2003 ND 77 (N.D. 2003).

[35] *Bausano v. Bausano*, 632 N.W.2d 123, 246 Wis.2d 987 (Wis. Ct. App. 2001).

[36] *Hoverson v. Hoverson*, 629 N.W.2d 573, 2001 N.D. 124 (N.D. 2001).

Active versus Passive Appreciation

States are divided on the issue of whether appreciation in a premarriage separate asset is a marital asset, or the conditions to determine that issue.

"Active" Appreciation as a Marital Asset

Many states consider the amount of appreciation in an asset that was separate property before marriage to be a marital asset. For example, an Arizona case said that classification of increase in community property depends on whether the increase resulted from natural growth of the business (separate property) or from an individual's management skills (community property).[37]

In Tennessee, if the separate property of one spouse appreciates in value during the marriage as a result of the efforts of either spouse, the appreciation becomes a marital asset.[38]

In New York, a separate account managed by the husband was deemed to be marital property on the grounds that the wife's management of household duties indirectly contributed to the account's appreciation by providing the husband with the time to manage the account.[39]

However, it is not always clear what constitutes "active" appreciation. In *Scottston v. Scottston*,[40] the stock of a bank holding company held separately by the husband appreciated. Although the husband was an executive and board member of the bank, and at the time of divorce was the bank's president, the court nevertheless held that it was "market forces" that contributed to the appreciation, so that the appreciation was nonmarital property.

"Active" Appreciation Must Be Proven

As of this writing, only New York has considered the value of a license to practice to be a marital asset.[41] However, the wife in a North Carolina case tried to have the *appreciation* in her husband's medical license during the marriage classified as a marital asset. The Court said that:

> Active appreciation of separate property is marital property, but appreciation must be proven ... to demonstrate active appreciation of separate property, there must be a showing of:
>
> - Value of the asset at time of acquisition.
> - Value of the asset at time of separation.
> - Difference between the two values.[42]

In this case, the court found that the evidence presented tended to show that marital efforts led to the acquisition of the medical license rather than to an active appreciation in its value.

---

[37] *Baum v. Baum*, 584 P.2d 604, 609 (Ariz. Ct. App. 1978).
[38] *Brown v. Brown*, 913 S.W.2d 163, 167 (Tenn. Ct. App. 1994).
[39] *Spencer v. Spencer*, 646 N.Y.S.2d 674, 230 A.D.2d 645 (N.Y. App. Div. 1996).
[40] *Scottston v. Scottston*, 1995 WL 550925 (Minn. Ct. App. 1995).
[41] *O'Brien v. O'Brien*, 66 N.Y.2d 576; 489 N.E.2d 712; 498 N.Y.S.2d 743 (N.Y. 1985).
[42] *Conway v. Conway*, 1998 WL 865157 (N.C. Ct. App. 1998).

In *Deffenbaugh v. Deffenbaugh*,[43] the Missouri court held that where the husband failed to prove that his acumen and effort contributed to the appreciation in the wife's separate mutual fund shares, the appreciation was nonmarital property. The court found that the increase in value was attributable not to the husband's efforts but to favorable market trends and the professional management of the fund.

In a case of first impression, a New York trial court held that the party that asserts that an asset is nonmarital has the burden of proving the proper valuation date. The court reasoned that the party who has the burden to prove the character of an asset should also bear the burden of proving its appropriate valuation date, as this maintains consistency with prior court decisions and efficiency with allocation of the parties' responsibilities.[44]

Valuation Date

It is difficult to generalize about courts' positions regarding valuation dates. Even states that have generally fixed policies on this issue often allow trial courts considerable discretion to make exceptions.

Many courts use date of trial (or as close to it as practical) as the valuation date.[45] In a similar vein, some accept a date as near as possible to the final divorce decree.[46]

The effective date in some cases is the date the complaint was filed.[47] Some use date of separation.[48] Trial courts may exercise discretion in determining valuation dates.[49] And, unlike estate tax valuations, the date does not always have to be the same for all assets.[50]

An interesting case involving a dispute as to the appropriate valuation date erupted because the husband was arrested and incarcerated for child molestation the day before the wife's expert's going-concern valuation date, jeopardizing the construction company's ability to obtain financing. The husband ultimately was convicted. The trial court accepted the wife's expert's valuation, which included

---

[43] *Deffenbaugh v. Deffenbaugh*, 877 S.W.2d 186 (Mo. Ct. App. 1994).

[44] *Mahoney-Buntzman v. Buntzman*, 2006 N.Y. Misc. LEXIS 533 (N.Y. Sup. Ct. 2006).

[45] See, for example, *Hargrave v. Hargrave*, 209 Cal. Rptr. 764, 769 (Cal. Ct. App. 1985); *Aufmuth v. Aufmuth*, 152 Cal Rptr. 668, 670 (Cal. Ct. App. 1979); *Moffitt v. Moffitt*, 813 P.2d 674, 678 (Alaska 1991), *Ogard v. Ogard*, 808 P.2d 815, 818–19 (Alaska 1991); *Taylor v. Taylor*, 736 P.2d 388, 391 (Mo. 1987); *Butler v. Butler*, No. 82077, 1998 WL 933354, at *2 (N.Y. App. Div. Dec. 30, 1998).

[46] For example, *In re Marriage of Olinger*, 707 P.2d 64, 68 (Or. Ct. App. 1985); *Koch v. Koch*, 874 S.W.2d 571, 576 (Tenn. Ct. App. 1993); *Wilson v. Wilson*, 741 S.W.2d 640, 643 (Ark. 1987); *In re Marriage of Talty*, 623 N.E.2d 1041, 1046 (Ill. App. Ct. 1993); *In re Marriage of Thomas*, 608 N.E.2d 585, 587 (Ill. App. Ct. 1993); *In re Marriage of Lopez*, 841 P.2d 1122, 1125 (Mont. 1992); *In re Marriage of Swanson*, 716 P.2d 219, 222 (Mont. 1986); *Vivian v. Vivian*, 583 P.2d 1072, 1074 (Mont. 1978); *In re Marriage of Wagner*, 679 P.2d 753, 758 (Mont. 1984); *Dunn v. Dunn*, 802 P.2d 1314, 1320 (Utah Ct. App. 1990); *Sommerfield* 454 N.W.2d at 60; *Skokos v. Skokos*, 40 S.W. 3d 768 (Ark. 2001).

[47] *Mallett v. Mallett*, 473 S.E.2d 804, 810 (S.C. Ct. App. 1996); *Hickum v. Hickum*, 463 S.E.2d 321, 323 (S.C. Ct. App. 1995); *Hillebrand v. Hillebrand*, 546 A.2d 1047, 1049 (N.H. 1988); *Rosenberg v. Rosenberg*, 510 N.Y.S.2d 659, 662 (N.Y. App. Div. 1987), *Muller v. Muller*, 456 N.Y.S.2d 918, 922 (Sup. Ct. 1982); *Siegel v. Siegel*, 523 N.Y.S.2d 517, 520 (N.Y. App. Div. 1987) (because possibility of dissipation of corporate assets existed). But see *Scharfman v. Scharfman*, 2005 N.Y. App. Div. LEXIS 6584 (N.Y. App. Div. 2005), where the trial court agreed with the husband that the valuation date for the parties' 85 operating entities, which, in turn, owned more than 100 residential rental real estate properties, should be the action's commencement date and rejected the wife's assertion that the valuation date should be the trial date. The appellate court ruled that the trial court had abused its discretion, finding that the husband failed to offer evidence in support of his assertion that any change in the value of the properties since the commencement of the action was due solely to his efforts rather than to other factors, including market forces.

[48] *Kilbourne v. Kilbourne*, 284 Cal. Rptr. 201, 204 (Cal. Ct. App. 1991); *Moffitt*, 813 P.2d at 678; *Ogard*, 808 P.2d at 818–19; *Richmond v. Richmond*, 779 P.2d 1211, 1214 (Alaska 1989); *Carlson v. Carlson*, 487 S.E.2d 784, 786 (N.C. Ct. App. 1997); *Bergeland v. Bergeland*, 2000 Minn. App. LEXIS 952, 2000 WL 1239754 (Minn. Ct. App. 2000), *Morton v. Morton*, 2005 Mich. App. LEXIS 1406 (Mich. Ct. App. 2005).

[49] *Scalero v. Scalero*, No. 71738, 1998 WL 23845, at *3 (Ohio Ct. App. Jan. 22, 1998); *Wallace v. Wallace*, 733 S.W.2d 102, 106 (Tenn. Ct. App. 1987); *Reese v. Reese*, 671 N.E.2d 187, 191 (Ind. Ct. App. 1996); *Favell v. Favell*, 957 P.2d 556, 462 (Okla. Ct. App. 1997).

[50] *Green v. Green*, No. 97CA2333, 1998 WL 363840, at *3 (Ohio Ct. App. June 30, 1998).

goodwill. The Court of Appeals reversed, opining that, as long as the husband was incarcerated or under threat of incarceration, financing was not available. Thus, the goodwill (defined as "the expectation of public patronage") was eliminated. However, the Indiana Supreme Court concluded:

> The selection of the valuation date for any particular marital asset has the effect of allocating the risk of change in the value of that asset between the date of valuation and the date of the hearing. We entrust this allocation to the discretion of the trial court.[51]

The Supreme Court thus upheld the $328,000 valuation of the trial court, which included the value of the goodwill.

In another case, the principal asset of the couples' business resided in its patent. The husband valued the business as of a date that did not take into account an approximately $500,000 patent infringement judgment (plus pre- and postjudgment interest) the business won against Wal-Mart, the nation's largest retailer, about a year later. The judgment was rendered before the divorce trial occurred, but was on appeal during the divorce trial. The wife's valuation, using a valuation date much closer to the date the judgment was rendered, did account for the judgment. The trial court, reasoning that the judgment was "all or nothing" and that the value of the patent would either be confirmed or denied, accepted the husband's valuation. The appellate court reversed, concluding that the husband's valuation was stale and did not bear a rational relationship to the value of the company.[52]

At issue in another case was the valuation date to use for the husband's neurology practice, which he was scaling back and planned to close in 2001. The husband's expert valued the practice at $223,214 at the end of 1999, approximately two months before the parties' separation. The wife's expert conducted two appraisals—one at the end of 1999 ($295,000) and another at the end of 2000 ($68,300). The trial court decided to use the wife's second appraisal at the approximate time of separation, since that took into account the decrease in the value of the practice by the time of trial. On appeal, the appellate court considered the fact that the practice had significant economic value during the marriage and the decrease in its value was due to the husband's own decision to close the business. Accordingly, the appellate court ruled that the trial court did not abuse its discretion in accepting the value of the practice at the time of separation.[53]

In *Washington v. Washington*,[54] the husband argued that the correct valuation date was the date of separation, rather than the date of the evidentiary hearing, which occurred over two years later. The husband had the burden of proving good cause for changing the date to the earlier date of separation.

The appellate court found that although the evidence established that the husband's business increased in value between the date of the parties' separation and the date of the evidentiary hearing, no evidence established that this increase occurred due to any extraordinary effort on the husband's part beyond the effort he was already expending before the separation to develop the business. The court also surmised that any increase could just as easily have been attributable to the husband's and the wife's preseparation efforts, or from postseparation factors not

---

[51] *Quillen v. Quillen*, 671 N.E.2d 98 (Indiana 1996).
[52] *Gohl v. Gohl*, 700 N.W.2d 625, 13 Neb. App. 685 (Neb. Ct. App. 2005).
[53] *In re Marriage of Rubens*, 2003 Wash. App. LEXIS 1544 (Wash. Ct. App. 2003).
[54] *Washington v. Washington*, 2005 Va. App. LEXIS 177 (Va. Ct. App. 2005).

directly within the husband's control. Absent evidence of extraordinary effort, the court held that the husband had not established that he was entitled to have the court use an alternate valuation date.

Goodwill

The "Market Value of Goodwill" Paradox

The paradox of many family law courts' conclusions as to the value of goodwill is well illustrated in the California case of *Fortier*.[55] The case states that goodwill value is separate and must be established without dependence upon the potential or continuing net income of the selling doctor. It then goes on to say that the community goodwill value is the market value at which the goodwill could be sold, assuming the expectancy of continuity of the practice.

But "continuity of the practice" would seem to somehow involve the future actions of the spouse. It is rare that a practice is sold without a noncompete agreement, which would limit the spouse's activities. Furthermore, practice sales usually involve transition services of the selling party for several months, and sometimes a year or even longer. Yet the cases don't mention that the "market value" usually includes a noncompete covenant and an agreement for services, which would seem to be assets personal to the spouse.

Similarly, in a subsequent case, the Court stated:

> Value must be established without dependence on the potential or continuing net income of the professional spouse. (*In re Marriage of Fortier*, supra, 34 Cal.App.3d 384, 388, 109 Cal. Rptr. 915.)
>
> In sum, we conclude the applicable rule in evaluating community goodwill to be that such goodwill may not be valued by any method that takes into account the post-marital efforts of either spouse....[56]

Having said this, the Court of Appeals accepted a goodwill value of $27,000, based on expert witness testimony described, in part, as follows:

> He explained that if appellant continued in his practice, his business had a value of $27,000 in excess of tangible items, but that it depended on how long appellant let the practice "sit," whether he abandoned it, or whether he passed away. He said he had no opinion as to whether appellant could obtain $27,000 for goodwill from a buyer, but stated he would receive an amount for goodwill if he sold the practice. Heller reiterated that the $27,000 valuation for goodwill did not mean that appellant could obtain that sum by selling the medical practice and that he had no opinion as to the amount of money that could be obtained for goodwill upon a sale.[57]

So, postmarital efforts do not count, but the goodwill value of $27,000 "if the appellant continued in his practice" is a marital asset. Is this a paradox or what?

---

[55] *In re Marriage of Fortier*, 34 Cal.App.3d 384, 109 Cal. Rptr. 915 (1973).
[56] *In re Marriage of Foster*, 42 Cal.App.3d 577, 117 Cal. Rptr. 49 (1974).
[57] Ibid.

North Carolina cases regularly reflect the same paradox. The case most often cited states:

> Any legitimate method of valuation that measures the present value of goodwill by taking into account past results *and not the postmarital efforts of the professional spouse*, is a proper method of valuing goodwill (emphasis supplied).[58]

The case then goes on to list methods to value the goodwill of a professional practice that have been accepted in various jurisdictions:

- The price a willing buyer would pay
- Capitalization of excess earnings
- One year's average gross income
- Evidence of sales of comparable practices

All of these valuation methods reflect, to some extent, implied continuing participation and/or a noncompete covenant.

The opinion notes "the execution of a covenant not to compete, in connection with the sale of a business, is essentially a sale of the goodwill of the business."[59] Many would consider this a very confused statement, because they would regard the covenant not to compete as a contract giving up the practitioner's *personal* goodwill rather than the goodwill of the business or practice.

In the same vein, a Maine case determined that goodwill of an insurance company is marital property, even though the Court assumed that the goodwill of the agency and its customer pool would be protected by a noncompetition agreement.[60]

A key issue in marital dissolution cases involving goodwill valuation is whether it is necessary to distinguish between personal (professional) goodwill and enterprise (practice) goodwill and, if such a distinction is necessary, which type of goodwill is a marital or distributable asset.

A number of courts, but not a majority, make no distinction between personal and enterprise goodwill. These jurisdictions have taken the position that both personal and enterprise goodwill in a professional practice constitute marital property. A minority of courts have taken the position that neither personal nor enterprise goodwill in a professional practice constitutes marital property. The majority of states differentiate between enterprise goodwill and personal goodwill. Courts in these states take the position that personal goodwill is not marital property, but that enterprise goodwill is marital property. In many states, professional goodwill is an element of marital property value even if it is not transferable. Some states have not issued a decision on whether types of goodwill must be distinguished. Exhibit 38–1 indicates the position each state has taken (if at all) on these issues.

Personal Goodwill Not a Marital Asset in Many States

Typical of those states that reject the inclusion of personal goodwill as a marital asset is Nebraska. A 1999 case citing *Taylor*[61] explained:

---

[58] *Poore v. Poore*, 75 N.C.App. 414, 331 S.E.2d 266 (July 2, 1985).
[59] *Jewel Box Stores v. Morrow*, 272 N.C. 659, 158 S.E. 2d 840 (1968).
[60] *Lord v. Lord*, 454 A.2d 830, 833 (Me. 1983).
[61] *Taylor v. Taylor*, 222 Neb. 721, 386 N.W. 2d 851 (1986).

Exhibit 38–1

Goodwill in Divorce

STATE	POSITION	CASE	TYPE OF PRACTICE
ALABAMA	No decision		
ALASKA	Enterprise goodwill is marital, personal goodwill is not.	*Richmond v. Richmond*, 779 P.2d 1211 (Alaska 1989)	Law practice
ARIZONA	No distinction; personal and enterprise goodwill are marital.	*Mitchell v. Mitchell*, 732 P.2d 208 (Ariz. 1987)	Accounting practice
ARKANSAS	Enterprise goodwill is marital, personal goodwill is not.	*Tortorich v. Tortorich*, 902 S.W. 2d 247 (Ark. App. 1995)	Dental practice (oral surgery)
CALIFORNIA	No distinction; personal and enterprise goodwill are marital.	*In re Foster*, 42 Cal. App. 3d 577 (1974)	Medical practice
COLORADO	No distinction; personal and enterprise goodwill are marital.	*In re Marriage of Huff*, 834 P.2d 244 (Colo. 1992)	Law practice
CONNECTICUT	Enterprise goodwill is marital, personal goodwill is not.	*Elsami v. Eslami*, 591 A.2d. 411 (Conn. 1991)	Medical practice
DELAWARE	Enterprise goodwill is marital, personal goodwill is not.	*E.E.C. v. E.J.C.*, 457 A.2d 688 (Del. 1983)	Law practice
DISTRICT OF COLUMBIA	Enterprise goodwill is marital, personal goodwill is not.	*McDiarmid v. McDiarmid*, 649 A. 2d 810 (D.C. App. 1994)	Law practice
FLORIDA	Enterprise goodwill is marital, personal goodwill is not.	*Thompson v. Thompson*, 576 So. 2d 267 (Fla. 1991)	Law practice
GEORGIA	No decision.		
HAWAII	Enterprise goodwill is marital, personal goodwill is not.	*Antolik v. Harvey*, 761 P. 2d 305(Haw. App. 1988)	Chiropractic business
IDAHO	Majority declines to distinguish personal and business goodwill; dissent strongly disagrees.	*Stewart v. Stewart, 2007 Ida. LEXIS 17 (Jan. 26, 2007)*	Dermatology practice
ILLINOIS	Enterprise goodwill is marital, personal is not.	*In re Marriage of Head*, 652 N.E. 2d 1246 (Ill. App. 1995)	Medical practice
INDIANA	Enterprise goodwill is marital; personal goodwill MAY BE (a party wishing to exclude personal goodwill must submit evidence of its value to the trial court).	*Balicki v. Balicki,837 N.E.2d 532, (Ind. App. 2005)*	Mechanical/ Construction
IOWA	Not clear; recognizes goodwill is dependent on the professional continuing in practice, and is a factor bearing on his/her future earning potential.	*In re Marriage of Hogeland*, 448 N.W.2d 678 (Iowa App. 1989)	Dental practice
KANSAS	Neither personal nor enterprise goodwill is marital.	*Powell v. Powell, 648 P. 2d 218 (Kan. 1982)*	Medical practice
KENTUCKY	No distinction; both personal and enterprise goodwill are marital.	*Heller v. Heller, 672 S.W.2d 945 (Ky. App. 1984)*	Accounting practice
LOUISANA	Enterprise goodwill is marital, personal goodwill is not.	*Statute: La. R.S. 9:2801.2 added by Acts 2003, No. 837 ß 1 and amended by Acts 2004, No. 177 ß 1*	
MAINE	No decision.		
MARYLAND	Enterprise goodwill is marital, personal is not.	*Hollander v. Hollander*, 597 A.2d 1012 (Md. App. 1991)	Dental practice
MASSACHU-SETTS	Enterprise goodwill is marital, personal goodwill is not.	*Goldman v. Goldman*, 554 N.E.2d 860 (Mass. App. 1990)	Medical practice
MICHIGAN	No distinction; personal and enterprise goodwill are marital.	*Kowalesky v. Kowalesky*, 384 N.W.2d 112 (Mich. App. 1986)	Dental practice
MINNESOTA	Enterprise goodwill is marital, personal goodwill is not.	*Roth v. Roth, 406 N.W.2d 77 (Minn. App. 1987)*	Chiropractic business
MISSISSIPPI	Neither personal nor enterprise goodwill is marital.	*Watson v. Watson, 882 So.2d 95 (Miss. 2004)*	Veterinary clinic

STATE	POSITION	CASE	TYPE OF PRACTICE
MISSOURI	Enterprise goodwill is marital, personal goodwill is not.	*Hanson v. Hanson, 738 S.W.2d 429 (Mo. 1987)*	Medical practice
MONTANA	No distinction; personal and enterprise goodwill are marital.	*In re Marriage of Stufft, 950 P. 2d 1373 (Mont. 1997)*	Law practice
NEBRASKA	Enterprise goodwill is marital, personal goodwill is not.	*Taylor v. Taylor, 386 N.W. 2d 851 (Neb. 1986)*	Medical practice
NEVADA	No distinction; personal and enterprise goodwill are marital.	*Ford v. Ford, 782 P.2d 1304 (Nev. 1989)*	Medical practice
NEW HAMPSHIRE	Enterprise goodwill is marital, personal goodwill is not.	*In re Watterworth, 821 A. 2d 1107 (N.H. 2003)*	Medical practice
NEW JERSEY	No distinction; personal and enterprise goodwill are marital.	*Dugan v. Dugan, 457 A.2d 1 (N.J. 1983)*	Law practice
NEW MEXICO	No distinction; personal and enterprise goodwill are marital.	*Mitchell v. Mitchell, 719 P.2d 432 (N.M. App. 1986)*	Accounting practice
NEW YORK	No distinction; personal and enterprise goodwill are marital.	*Moll v. Moll, 722 N.Y.S. 2d 732 (2001)*	Stockbroker
NORTH CAROLINA	No distinction; personal and enterprise goodwill are marital.	*Poore v. Poore, 7331 S.E.2d 266 (N.C. App. 1985)*	Dental practice
NORTH DAKOTA	No distinction; personal and enterprise goodwill are marital.	*Sommers v. Sommers, 660 N.W.2d 586 (N.D. 2003)*	Medical practice
OHIO	Personal and enterprise goodwill in professional practice is marital.	*Kahn v. Kahn, 536 N.E.2d 678 (Oh. 1987)*	Medical practice
OKLAHOMA	Enterprise goodwill is marital, personal is not.	*Traczyk v. Traczyk, 891 P.2d 1277 (Okla. 1995)*	Medical practice/ foot clinic
OREGON	Enterprise goodwill is marital, personal is not.	*Matter of Marriage of Maxwell, 876 P.2d 811 (Or. App. 1994)*	Self employed advertising copywriter
PENNSYLVANIA	Enterprise goodwill is marital, personal goodwill is not.	*Butler v Butler, 63 A.2d 148 (Pa. 1995)*	Accounting firm
RHODE ISLAND	Enterprise goodwill is marital, personal goodwill is not.	*Moretti v Moretti, 766 A.2d 925 (R.I. 2001)*	Professional landscaper
SOUTH CAROLINA	Neither personal nor enterprise goodwill is marital.	*Donahue v Donahue, 384 S.E.2d 741 (S.C. 1989)*	Dental practice
SOUTH DAKOTA	Enterprise goodwill in professional practice is marital; expressly declined to decide whether personal goodwill in professional practice is marital.	*Endres v. Endres, 532 N.W.2d 65 (S.D. 1995)*	Dairy and concrete business
TENNESSEE	Neither personal not enterprise goodwill is marital.	*Smith v. Smith, 709 S.W.2d 558 (Tenn. App. 1985)*	Law firm
TEXAS	Enterprise goodwill is marital, personal goodwill is not.	*Guzman v. Guzman, 827 S.W.2d 445 (Tex. App. 1992)*	Accounting firm
UTAH	Enterprise goodwill is marital, personal goodwill is not.	*Sorensen v. Sorensen, 839 P.2d 774 (Utah 1992)*	Law practice
VERMONT	Enterprise goodwill is marital, personal goodwill is not.	*Mills v. Mills, 167 Vt. 567 (1997)*	Law practice
VIRGINIA	Enterprise goodwill is marital, personal goodwill is not.	*Hoebelheinrich v. Hoebelheinrich, 43 Va App. 543 (2004)*	Medical practice
WASHINGTON	No distinction; personal and enterprise goodwill are marital.	*In re Marriage of Hall, 692 P.2d 175 (Wash. 1984)*	Medical practice
WEST VIRGINIA	Enterprise goodwill is marital, personal goodwill is not.	*May v. May, 214 W.Va 394 (2003)*	Dental practice
WISCONSIN	Enterprise goodwill is marital, personal goodwill is not.	*Moser v. Moser, 247 Wis.2d 496 (2001)*	Veterinary practice
WYOMING	Enterprise goodwill is marital, personal goodwill is not.	*Root v. Root, 65 P.3d 41 (Wyo. 2003)*	Medical practice

SOURCE: Adapted from "Goodwill Hunting in Divorce," by Business Valuation Resources. ©2007. Reprinted with permission of Business Valuation Resources, Portland, Oregon. www.buresources.com.

If goodwill depends on the continued presence of a particular individual, such goodwill, by definition, is not a marketable asset distinct from the individual. Any value which attaches to the entity solely as a result of the personal goodwill represents nothing more than probable future earning capacity, which, although relevant in determining alimony, is not a proper consideration in dividing marital property in a dissolution proceeding ... "There is a disturbing inequity in compelling a professional practitioner to pay a spouse a share of intangible assets at a judicially determined value that could not be realized by a sale or another method of liquidating value."[62]

Virginia defines goodwill and distinguishes business goodwill from personal goodwill with the following explanation:

Goodwill has been defined as "the increased value of the business, over and above the value of its assets, that results from the expectation of continued public patronage." The reputation of an individual, as well as his or her future earning capacity, are not considered to be components of goodwill. *Russell v. Russell*, 11 Va. App. 411, 415–16 (1990).[63]

In Mississippi, neither personal nor business enterprise goodwill should be used to determine the value of a solo professional practice in a divorce proceeding, since these two types of goodwill are inseparable in such a practice.[64]

Personal Goodwill Is a Marital Asset in Many States

Washington is one of the states that recognizes professional (personal) goodwill as an intangible asset subject to division in a divorce. Its value is determined by considering the *Fleege*[65] factors which include, but are not limited to the practitioner's:

- Age
- Health
- Past earning power
- Reputation in the community for judgment, skill, and knowledge
- Comparative professional success[66]

California courts also look at the nature and duration of the practice and whether the spouse was a sole practitioner or a contributing member.[67]

In Montana, the Court accepted the analysis of a wife's expert of the medical doctor husband's earnings compared with similar medical doctors to value goodwill as a marital asset.[68] Other courts value professional practice goodwill by estimating a similarly situated professional.[69]

---

[62] *Kriscfeld v. Kriscfeld*, No. A-97-720 Neb. App., 1999 WL 8819 (Jan. 5, 1999). See also *Utter v. Utter*, No. A-94-984 Neb. App. Ct., 1996 WL 169911 (Apr. 9, 1996); *Yoon v. Yoon*, 711 N.E.2d 1265 (Ind. 1999).

[63] *Howell v. Howell*, No. HH-1013-3 Va. Cir. Ct., 1998 WL 972312 (Sept. 4, 1998).

[64] *Watson v. Watson*, 882 So. 2d 95 (Miss. 2004). See also *Singley v. Singley*, 846 So. 2d 1004 (Miss. 2002).

[65] *In re Marriage of Fleege*, 91 Wash. 2d 324, 588 P.2d 1136 (1979).

[66] *Crosetto v. Crosetto*, No. 17911-3-11 Wash. App. Div. 2, 1996 WL 389337 (July 12, 1996), also citing *In re Marriage of Luckey*, 73 Wash. App. 201, 206, 868 P.2d 189 (1994).

[67] *Lopez v. Lopez*, 38 Cal. App. 3d 93, 113 Cal. Rptr. 58 (Cal. Ct. App. 1974).

[68] *In re Marriage of Hull*, 712 P.2d 1317, 1321 (Mont. 1985).

[69] *Iredale v. Cates*, 121 Cal. App. 4th 321, 16 Cal. Rptr. 3d 505 (Cal. App. 2 Dist. 2004). In *Ackerman v. Ackerman*, 2006 Cal. App. LEXIS 2056 (Cal. Ct. App. 2006), in arriving at a professional goodwill value, the court rejected national compensation surveys, even as honed by broad geographic regions (e.g., the Western states) as probative of the reasonable compensation of a plastic surgeon practicing in the highly affluent Newport Beach, California, community. Instead, the court determined reasonable compensation by determining what a similarly situated plastic surgeon would earn in that particular, relatively small, community.

In Alaska, the state's Supreme Court found that a medical practice had goodwill, but that because there was no market for medical practices, that goodwill had no value.[70]

However, in Louisiana, professional goodwill in a CPA firm is not included in community property (see the next section on other goodwill issues).[71] These courts essentially equate professional goodwill with personal goodwill.[72]

Other Goodwill Issues

Commercial and Enterprise Goodwill. Some states include a business's goodwill as a marital asset as long as the business is a commercial business and is not a sole proprietorship providing professional services, such as a legal, medical, or engineering services (essentially viewing professional goodwill as personal goodwill).[73] The fact that a professional business hires independent contractors and outside consultants does not change that nature of the business for the purpose of characterizing goodwill.[74]

Other states use the concept of enterprise goodwill. For example, in *Desalle v. Gentry*[75] the valuation issue focused on the classification of the goodwill in the business. The husband and wife operated multiple toy show venues under one business name. The husband contended that all the goodwill in the business should have been classified as personal goodwill because he was well known in the industry, as opposed to the wife, and thus should have been excluded from the marital estate and been immune from marital division.

The trial court determined that the goodwill was enterprise goodwill and divided the venues between the parties. The appellate court upheld the trial court's ruling, noting the distinction between the two types of goodwill:

> Enterprise goodwill is based on the intangible, but generally marketable, existence in a business of established relations with employees, customers and suppliers, and may include factors such as a business location, its name recognition and its business reputation, … On the other hand, personal goodwill is goodwill that is based on the personal attributes of the individual.

Distinguishing Personal from Enterprise Goodwill. In *Held v. Held*,[76] the issue was whether the trial court correctly included enterprise goodwill in valuing the husband's insurance agency. Although husband and wife agreed that book value was around $2.9 million, they hotly contested the existence and value of the company's enterprise goodwill above the adjusted book value. The trial court determined that such goodwill was around $7.6 million.

---

[70] *Manelick v. Manelick*, 59 P.3d 259 (Alaska 2002).

[71] *Gill v. Gill*, 895 So. 2d 807, 2005 La. App. LEXIS 587 (La. Ct. App. 2005).

[72] See, e.g., *In re Schneider*, 824 N.E.2d 177, 214 Ill. 2d 152 (Ill. 2005).

[73] *Ellington v. Ellington*, 842 So. 2d 1160 (La. Ct. App. 2003); *Schiro v. Schiro*, 839 So. 2d 304 (La. Ct. App. 2003).

[74] *Collier v. Collier*, 790 So. 2d 759 (La. Ct. App. 2001).

[75] *Desalle v. Gentry*, 2004 Ind. App. LEXIS 2297 (Ind. Ct. App. 2004).

[76] *Held v. Held*, 2005 Fla. App. LEXIS 14138 (Fla. Ct. App. 2005).

To arrive at its valuation, the court relied mostly upon the testimony of the wife's expert. Central to the court's determination of fair market value, which included enterprise goodwill, was the court's assumption that in any sale of the business, the husband would sign a nonsolicitation/nonpiracy agreement preventing him from doing business with the company's existing customers. The court reasoned that the nonsolicitation agreement had nothing to do with personal goodwill of the business, but was part of enterprise goodwill.

The appellate court found that, for the purpose of distinguishing enterprise goodwill from personal goodwill in the valuation of a business, there is no distinction between a "nonsolicitation/nonpiracy agreement" and a covenant not to compete, because both limit a putative seller's ability to do business with existing clients. The court also noted that a covenant not-to-compete is attributable to the personal reputation of the seller/spouse and not to the enterprise goodwill of the business. Accordingly, the court reversed and ruled that the trial court impermissibly inserted into enterprise goodwill an aspect of personal goodwill—the value of the husband's personal relationship with the company's 60 clients.

As can be seen from the discussion of personal versus practice goodwill, it is very important to clearly distinguish between the two. For example, in *Geaccone v. Geaccone*,[77] the wife's expert valued the husband's dental practice, asserting that he excluded personal goodwill. The husband's expert did not conduct an independent valuation, but disagreed with the wife's valuation, claiming that the wife's expert had included a significant amount of goodwill in the valuation. The trial court accepted the valuation of the wife's expert. On appeal, the court noted that the valuation of the wife's expert was admitted without objection and that the husband never requested the trial court to make amended or additional findings regarding the method of valuation. Thus, because the husband had not challenged the valuation and did not attempt to separate or distinguish personal and practice goodwill, the appellate court could not determine whether the trial court had erred; therefore, the appellate court affirmed.

The appellate court in *Ledwith v. Ledwith*,[78] noting that commercial goodwill in the marital estate is subject to equitable distribution, whereas personal goodwill is not, ruled that the trial court erred by not finding any personal goodwill and by failing to account for such personal goodwill before dividing the practice, in light of the testimony of the husband's expert that half of the goodwill in the husband's orthodontic practice was personal goodwill.

Separating Personal from Enterprise Goodwill. Indiana's *Yoon v. Yoon*[79] exemplifies a case where a court attempted to distinguish personal and enterprise goodwill in a professional corporation. The court said:

> Before including the goodwill of a self-employed business or professional practice in a marital estate, a court must determine that the goodwill is attributable to the business as opposed to the owner as an individual. If attributable to the individual, it is not a divisible asset and is properly

---

[77] *Geaccone v. Geaccone*, 2005 WL 1774964 (Tex. Ct. App. 2005).
[78] *Ledwith v. Ledwith*, 2004 Va. App. LEXIS 488 (Va. Ct. App. 2004).
[79] *Yoon v. Yoon*, 711 N.E.2d 1265 (Ind. 1999).

considered only as future earning capacity that may affect the relative property division. In this respect, the future earning capacity of a self-employed person (or an owner of a business primarily dependent on the owner's services) is to be treated the same as the future earning capability and reputation of an employee."

In cases following *Yoon*, Indiana courts remanded for reconsideration of business valuations in divorce proceedings where there was evidence presented regarding the possible existence of goodwill in the business that was personal to the one of the spouses, but the trial court's findings and conclusions made no mention of the issue of goodwill.[80] By contrast, courts in that state declined to remand for reconsideration on the issue of personal goodwill in a business where the parties failed to present competent evidence to the trial court regarding the value of any such goodwill.[81]

An Illinois case, *In re Marriage of Alexander*,[82] presented a novel method for calculating the enterprise and personal components of goodwill in the valuation of a professional practice, called the multiattribute utility theory (MUT), and also known as the multiattribute utility model (MUM). This particular methodology had not previously been used or presented in litigation.

MUM involves several steps. First, the valuator sets forth an objective. Next, the valuator establishes "alternatives." An alternative is a "range of percentages" that will define the choices "in which the method will result." Each alternative is then assigned a "range." After the objective and the alternatives are set, the valuator must then define the "attributes."

An attribute is an element of goodwill to which the valuator must assign a value. Examples of attributes are personal reputation and business location. Attributes are categorized as either personal or enterprise. There are no universal attributes that must be defined in every situation, and there is not a set number of attributes that must be defined. Instead, MUM leaves the creation and categorization of attributes to the discretion of the valuator, based on the valuator's experience and observations.

After defining the attributes, the valuator then assigns a value to each. This involves a two-step process. First, the valuator assigns a value known as an attribute's "utility of importance." The utility of importance is a value placed on an attribute based on how important the valuator feels the attribute is to the value of goodwill. The value assigned is taken from a range created by the valuator. Next, the valuator assigns a value known as an attribute's "utility of existence." The utility of existence is a value placed on an attribute based on the valuator's determination of the presence of that attribute in the business that the valuator is analyzing. The value is also taken from a range created by the valuator. After assigning each attribute two values (a utility-of-importance value and a utility-of-existence value), the valuator then "aggregates the results." Aggregating the results simply involves multiplying the values assigned to an attribute to come up with a final value for that attribute.

Once each attribute has a final value, the valuator then takes the sum of the final values for each attribute from its assigned category (personal or enterprise) and derives a "total multiplicative utility" for that category. Through the use of

---

[80] See *Frazier v. Frazier*, 737 N.E.2d 1220, 1225 (Ind. Ct. App. 2000); *Bertholet v. Bertholet*, 725 N.E.2d 487, 496-97 (Ind. App. 2000).

[81] See *Houchens v. Boschert*, 758 N.E.2d 585 (Ind. Ct. App. 2001).

[82] *In re Marriage of Alexander*, 2006 Ill. App. LEXIS 836 (Ill. Ct. App. 2006).

division, the valuator arrives at what percentage of the total goodwill is personal goodwill and what percentage is enterprise goodwill.

The court found MUM to be "thoughtful and persuasive," and had no problem in admitting it as evidence not subject to the test for the admissibility of novel scientific evidence developed under *Frye v. United States*.[83]

Goodwill vs. Going-Concern Value. *Gaydos v. Gaydos*,[84] 693 A.2d 1368 (Pa. Super. 1997) clarifies that personal goodwill and enterprise goodwill can be a part of going-concern value. The court said, "Goodwill is…one benefit among many of owning a fully-functional business rather than a collection of assets. It follows that goodwill value is a *component* of the going-concern value of a business; goodwill and going-concern are not 'separate methods' of valuing the same intangible thing."

Going-concern value, as indicated by the court in this case, thus cannot be the same as goodwill. The latter is subsumed within the former. Going-concern value is the intangible value attached to the physical assets of the business, including the business's fixtures, equipment, and its assemblage of personnel, as well as goodwill.

Definition of "Business" for Determining Goodwill. *In re Marriage of McTiernan*[85] raised the question of whether a superstar Hollywood director's career could constitute a "business" for the purpose of determining goodwill. The case involved the divorce of John McTiernan, who directed such movies as *Die Hard*, *The Hunt for Red October*, and *The Thomas Crown Affair*. The court held that there was no goodwill in McTiernan's career as a motion picture director. Since under California law the goodwill *of a business* is property, the question as framed by the court was: What is the meaning of "a business" in the definition of goodwill? According to the court, the trial court used the term "a business" to include "a person doing business." However, the court indicated that another definition is that "a business" refers to a professional, commercial, or industrial enterprise with assets, that is, an entity other than a natural person. According to the court, McTiernan's career as a director was not a "business." It reached this conclusion by looking at the historical understanding of goodwill, the plain meaning of "business," and the purpose of ensuring that the interest that is divided as goodwill is "property." The court went on to add that McTiernan's elite professional standing could not be sold or transferred, and that his high standing among other motion picture directors was entirely personal to him. The court said:

> He cannot confer on another director his standing…. He cannot sell this standing to another, because a buyer would not be John McTiernan, no matter how much the buyer was willing to pay. For the same reason, and unlike a law or medical practice, a husband cannot transfer his "elite professional standing." That standing is his, and his alone, and he cannot bestow it on someone else. Thus, an essential aspect of a property interest is absent.

---

[83] *Frye v. United States*, 54 App. D.C. 46, 293 F. 1013 (D.C. Cir. 1923).
[84] *Gaydos v. Gaydos*, 693 A.2d 1368 (Pa. Super. 1997).
[85] *In re Marriage of McTiernan*, 2005 Cal. App. LEXIS 1692 (Cal. Ct. App. 2005).

Goodwill as Earning Capacity. Several courts, in attempting to determine what constitutes goodwill, have ruled that goodwill is indistinguishable from earning capacity, which is not a distributable asset. These courts view goodwill in a professional practice as merely assuring the continuation of earnings in the future.[86] This view has been criticized on the grounds that, at least when it comes to equitable distribution in marital dissolutions, the contributions of each spouse to specific assets must be recognized. Others, however, take the opposite view, and argue that goodwill is just not a product of a marital partnership. Other courts have ruled that goodwill is separate from earning capacity where the professional's interest in a practice is transferable and separable from reputation.

In a case that involved the valuation of a dental practice, the court indicated that to the extent that the evidence shows that goodwill exists, is marketable, and that its value is something over and above the value of a business practice's assets and the professional's skills and services, it may be included as an asset in the marital estate and be subject to division. The court also warned, however, that double counting an asset is not permitted and that, therefore, care must be taken to ensure that the goodwill is indeed a separate asset, rather than the established employment or earning capacity of the professional. If it is not established as a separate asset, but merely a measure of earning capacity, its value would then improperly be taken into consideration more than once. It would be a factor in setting support and maintenance, as well as an asset to be divided in the property division.[87]

Still, other courts view goodwill as supplementing earning capacity, rather than merging with it.[88] This concept was well illustrated by *In re Hall*,[89] where both spouses had identical educations as doctors, but one owned a practice, and the other worked as a salaried professor. The court found that although both doctors had equal earning capacities, only the practicing doctor had goodwill, as the goodwill needed to adhere to an entity, not a person. The court said:

> Goodwill is a property or asset which usually supplements the earning capacity of another asset, a business or a profession. Goodwill is not the earning capacity itself. It is a distinct *asset* of a professional practice, not just a *factor* contributing to the value or earning capacity of the practice.... Discontinuance of the business or profession may greatly diminish the value of the goodwill but it does not destroy its existence. When a professional retires or dies, his earning capacity also either retires or dies. Nevertheless, the goodwill that once attached to his practice may continue in existence in the form of established patients or clients, referrals, trade name, location, and associations which now attach to former partners or buyers of the practice. *In re Hall*, 103 Wn.2d 236, 241.

Enhanced Earning Capacity. Normally, earning capacity is a consideration for the determination of spousal support or the division of assets rather than in the determination of marital property as equitable distribution or community property.

---

[86] See *Holbrook v. Holbrook*, 103 Wis. 2d 327, 309 N.W.2d 343, 1981 Wisc. App. LEXIS 3322 (Wisc. App. 1981) ("The concept of professional goodwill evanesces when one attempts to distinguish it from future earning capacity"); *Donahue v. Donahue*, 299 S.C. 353, 384 S.E.2d 741 (S.C. 1989); and *Hickum v. Hickum*, 463 S.E.2d 321 (S.C. Ct. App. 1995).

[87] *Peerenboom v. Peerenboom*, 433 N.W.2d 282 (Wisc. Ct. App. 1988).

[88] See, e.g., *In re Bookout*, 833 P.2d 800 (Colo. Ct. App. 1991), *cert. denied*, 846 P.2d 189 (Colo. 1993).

[89] *In re Hall*, 103 Wn.2d 236, 692 P.2d 175 (Wash. 1984).

Enhanced earning capacity is an individual's ability to earn over and above what would be earned following a "normal" career path resulting from joint efforts over the life of the marriage that results from an "enhancement" to earnings capacity. Typically, the enhancement is a degree, license, training, specialized knowledge, a unique talent, etc. The value of enhanced earning capacity is often measured by attempting to quantify the difference between the amounts an individual could earn without the enhancement to the amount that individual was earning at the end of the marriage with the enhancement.

Currently, only New York considers professional degrees, licenses, or career enhancement as martial property. The rationale for this seems to be that, based on his or her contributions, the nonprofessional spouse should share in the future benefits he or she helped to achieve. Without such a distribution, at least in theory, the dependent spouse who contributed to the enhancement may be left without any assets at all. This concept of distributing some portion of the enhancement of human capital also applies to the inclusion of personal goodwill in the marital estate in the states that recognize it as a distributable asset. This inclusion is basically the recognition of joint-spousal investments in the degree or license holder's career.[90]

Hougie v. Hougie[91] involved the inclusion of the enhanced earning capacity of an investment banker in the property distribution. The facts of the case ultimately revealed that the husband needed and had a license that allowed him to perform his job, but the court stated that the husband's enhanced earning capacity was a distributable asset regardless of whether a license was required.

Professional Licenses. The value of a professional license is generally interrelated with the value of professional goodwill. However, in some instances the professional license is considered to have value independent of professional goodwill.

In *Daniels v. Daniels*,[92] the husband's dental degree was considered a marital asset, a portion of which was to be awarded to his wife either as part of the property settlement or as alimony. The court reasoned that professional licenses or degrees, although not necessarily marital assets, should nevertheless be considered in awarding alimony. Because alimony was not awarded in this case, and the husband's degree was considered the main asset acquired during the marriage, the court concluded that the wife should be awarded a portion of the degree's value.

In the well-known New York case *O'Brien v. O'Brien*,[93] that state's highest court ruled that professional licenses or degrees must be valued in a divorce. In this case, when the couple married, they were both employed as teachers at a private school. The wife had a bachelor's degree and a teaching certificate, but required further education to obtain certification in New York. The court found that she relinquished the opportunity for that permanent certification to allow her husband to pursue his education. Two years into the marriage, the parties moved to Mexico, where the husband became a full-time medical student. Returning to New York three years later, the husband completed the last two semesters of medical school and the wife resumed her former teaching position. The husband

---

[90] See Jay E. Fishman, Shannon P. Pratt, and William J. Morrison, *Standards of Value: Theory and Applications* (Hoboken, NJ: John Wiley & Sons, 2007), pp. 232-233.

[91] *Hougie v. Hougie*, 261 A.D.2d 161, 689 N.Y.S.2d 490, 1999 N.Y. App. Div. LEXIS 4588 (N.Y. App. Div. 1999).

[92] *Daniels v. Daniels*, 418 N.W.2d 924, 163 Mich. App. 726 (Mich. Ct. App. 1988).

[93] *O'Brien v. O'Brien*, 489 N.E.2d 712, 66 N.Y.2d 576, 498 N.Y.S.2d 743 (N.Y. 1985).

received his license to practice four years later, and around two months thereafter, commenced the action for divorce.

During the marriage, both parties had contributed to the education and living expenses, receiving additional help from their families. The wife's expert presented the value of the medical license as $472,000 by comparing the average income of a general surgeon and a college graduate between the time when her husband's residency would end and the time he reached age 65. Factoring for inflation, taxes, and interest, that value was capitalized and reduced to present value. The expert also opined that the wife's contribution to the husband's education was $103,390.

The court made a distributive award of 40 percent of the value of the license to be paid in 11 annual installments. The appellate court overturned this, based on a prior case where the value of the license was not deemed to be marital property.

On further appeal to New York's highest court, the Court of Appeals, the husband claimed that his license should be excluded because it was not property, either marital or separate, but was representative of personal attainment of knowledge. The court reviewed the portion of the statute that stated "the court shall consider: ... (6) any equitable claim to, interest in, or direct or indirect contribution made to the acquisition of such marital property by the party not having title, including joint efforts or expenditures and contributions and services as a spouse, parent, wage earner and homemaker, and to the career or career potential of the other party [and] the impossibility or difficulty of evaluating any component asset or any interest in a business, corporation or profession."

The court interpreted these words to mean that an interest in a profession or professional career is marital property. The court interpreted the history of the statute as confirming this interpretation, as the traditional common law title system had caused inequity. The purpose of that statute, considering marriage as an economic partnership, was seen to be consistent with the inclusion of the value of the license.

The court stated that the lack of market value or alienability was irrelevant. Ultimately, the court decided that if the court receives evidence of the present value of the license and the working spouse's contribution toward its acquisition, it may make an appropriate distribution of that license as marital property. The outcome of this case was codified in New York statutory law, and New York is the only state where professional licenses or degrees must, as a matter of law, be valued in a divorce for equitable distribution. The view of O'Brien, that enhanced earnings capacity can appreciate during the marriage due, in part, to the efforts and/or sacrifices of the dependent spouse and that this creates marital property appears to result from a conscious decision to treat increased earning capacity developed during the marriage as an asset rather than as maintenance or support.

A few other states have dealt with this issue. Iowa may include increased earning capacity in distribution, but not the license. Alaska and Minnesota seem have left the door open to inclusion under compelling circumstances.

Merger Doctrine. After the *O'Brien* case was decided, a doctrine developed that held that where the licensed professional has maintained a professional practice over a long period of time, the license is deemed to have merged with the practice itself and has no value separate from the practice. This doctrine is called the "merger doctrine."

Some courts jettisoned this doctrine, finding that it generally favored a nonlicensed spouse in a shorter marriage over a nonlicensed spouse in a longer marriage.

These courts cautioned that care must be taken to ensure that the monetary value assigned to the license does not overlap with the value assigned to other marital assets that are derived from the license such as the licensed spouse's professional practice.[94]

Celebrity Goodwill. Some states, such as New York[95] and New Jersey,[96] also recognize celebrity status or celebrity goodwill as marital property. This concept of goodwill is based on the enhanced earnings capacity of a celebrity.

New Jersey considers celebrity goodwill as a part of marital property, recognizing that the development of celebrity, like that of personal goodwill in a business, is created by virtue of the noncelebrity spouse's contributions to the marital partnership.

New York has had several cases involving the goodwill of a celebrity, but these cases dealt with the enhanced earning capacity of a spouse over the course of a marriage and called this celebrity status. The *Golub* case,[97] for example, decided that a celebrity's status and concomitant enhanced earning capacity should be included because the noncelebrity spouse contributed to the earning capacity's formation and appreciation during the marriage.

The "Double Dipping" Issue

The issue of "double dipping," or double counting, arises when a court in a matrimonial dispute considers excess earnings (or other factors that assume continued involvement by the operating spouse) in determining the value of a business as well as in setting alimony.

In *Steneken v. Steneken*,[98] the trial court had determined that the husband's annual compensation was excessive and normalized the compensation in determining the value of his company using the excess earnings method. The court then determined alimony using the husband's actual annual compensation—which was $50,000 more. The husband argued that distributing his excess earnings as the goodwill portion of the value of his business, and also considering it for alimony purposes, was impermissible double counting.

The intermediate appellate court ruled that the value of the business was as of the date of dissolution and was based on past excess earnings, whereas the alimony determination was based on future income. The court also noted that even if this was double counting, it was not banned by New Jersey law, which bans only the double counting of pensions.

The New Jersey Supreme Court expressly rejected the premise that because alimony and equitable distribution are interrelated, a credit on one side of the ledger must perforce require a debit on the other side. Instead, the court focused on the "bedrock proposition" that all alimony awards and equitable distribution

---

[94] See, e.g., *McSparron v. McSparron*, 662 N.E.2d 745, 87 N.Y.2d 275, 639 N.Y.S.2d 265 (N.Y. App. Div. 1995). *McSparron* considered factors such as a change in circumstances and location of a practicing professional and decided that no matter how far along one's career is, the license has a value outside of one's career.

[95] *Golub v. Golub*, 139 Misc. 2d 440, 527 N.Y.S.2d 946 (N.Y. Sup. Ct. 1988); *Elkus v. Elkus*, 169 A.D.2d 134, 572 N.Y.S.2d 901 (N.Y. App. Div. 1991).

[96] *Piscopo v. Piscopo*, 232 N.J. Super. 559, 557 A.2d 1040 (N.J. Super. 1989).

[97] *Golub v. Golub*, 139 Misc. 2d 440, 527 N.Y.S.2d 946 (N.Y. Sup. Ct. 1988).

[98] *Steneken v Steneken*, 843 A.2d 344 (N.J. App. 2004), *aff'd*, 873 A.2d 501, 183 N.J. 290 (N.J. 2005).

determinations must satisfy basic concepts of fairness, and that, although clearly interrelated, the structural purposes of alimony and equitable distribution are different.

With these principles in mind, the court rejected the contention that permitting the different salary values would allow double dipping. The court said that the husband "mistakenly equates the statutory and decisional methodology applied in the calculation of alimony with a valuation methodology applied for equitable distribution purposes that requires that revenues and expenses, including salaries, be normalized so as to present a fair valuation of a going concern."

The court concluded that it is not inequitable to use a valuation method that normalizes salary in an ongoing closely held corporation for equitable distribution purposes, and to use actual salary received in calculating alimony—the valuation methodology chosen for equitable distribution purposes should not alter the alimony award. According to the court the "interplay of those two calculations does not constitute 'double counting.'" The ultimate judicial inquiry must be whether the ultimate result, both in its whole as well as in its constituent parts, is fair under the circumstances and congruent with the standards set forth in the alimony and equitable distribution statutes.

Although the high court embraced the intermediate appellate court's reasoning by declining to adopt an either-or notion inherent in the double counting rule, the court did modify the appellate court's approach to the extent that it expressly rejected the distinction made by the appellate court between the fact that "valuation of the corporate asset was based on [the husband's] past earnings, not his future earnings," whereas "[the husband's] actual current and future compensation may be treated as income for alimony purposes."

Justice Long, in a dissenting opinion, agreed with the husband that the majority's holding would allow the impermissible double counting of income (albeit not dollar-for-dollar). Justice Long's position was that the majority converted a certain amount of the husband's projected future income stream into an asset and then calculated the amount of alimony based on that asset. According to Justice Long, this was improper, as "[o]nce a court converts a specific stream of income into an asset, that income may no longer be calculated into the maintenance formula and payout."

Justice Long's solution would have been to adopt the appellate court's approach, which neither allows the unfettered dual use of a single income stream, nor requires the use of the same figure for both calculations. "Rather, judges should be able to use the 'real' income for alimony and the 'normalized' income for the corporate valuation so long as the ultimate outcome recognizes that a single income source (the difference between the real and normalized income) played a part in both."

It is arguable that, to the extent the court used excess compensation as the basis for alimony, the court used that money twice: once to value the distributed value of the business, and again to determine the amount of alimony—a classic case of double dipping.

One of the issues in *Sampson v. Sampson*[99] was double dipping that the wife claimed in connection with the valuation of the wife's insurance agency. The value of the insurance agency was offset in the husband's property distribution and then was counted as credit towards his alimony support obligations. The wife

---

[99] *Sampson v. Sampson*, 2004 Mass. App. LEXIS 1223 (Mass. App. Ct. 2004).

argued that this was double counting. The court noted that, "Courts and commentators have often disagreed, however, as to what constitutes double dipping, whether double dipping ought to be prohibited as a matter of law, and if not so prohibited, whether it is inequitable in the circumstances of the particular divorce settlement."

The court was unable to determine whether double counting occurred, given there were inconsistencies in the experts' reports concerning owner salary. The court remanded the case for further factual determinations on this point.

The court in *Champion v. Champion*,[100] noting that there is a split among jurisdictions on the issues of what constitutes double dipping and whether it ought to be prohibited as a matter of law, rejected a claim of double dipping and found the business to be both a marital asset and a source of income.

In *Keane v. Keane*,[101] New York's highest court, the Court of Appeals, decided that the prohibition against double counting applies only to intangible assets, such as professional licenses or goodwill, or the value of a service business, not income-producing tangible assets such as rental property. The court said:

> We do not see why an inquiry as to double counting should depend on the valuation method used. After all, any valuation of an income-producing property will necessarily take into account the income-producing capacity of that property. To prevent any income derived from any income-producing property from being "double counted" would, therefore, significantly limit the trial court's considerable discretion in equitably distributing marital property and awarding maintenance.

The court indicated that it is only where the asset is totally indistinguishable and has no existence separate from the income stream from which it is derived that double counting results. Here, the rental property was split between the parties for distributive purposes. The rental income from that property was then considered in determining maintenance. According to the court, the property would continue to exist, quite possibly in the husband's hands, long after the lease term expired, as a marketable asset separate and distinguishable from the lease payments. "The mortgage payments, in contrast, were properly distributed as an asset and not counted for maintenance purposes because the payments themselves *were* the marital asset."

In *Sander v. Sander*,[102] the court ruled that it is not double counting to assign a value to a business, as well as to attribute gross income from that business to the spouse, without adjusting either. Specifically, the court valued the husband's business at $340,000 while also attributing to him a gross income of $138,000 per year. The husband argued that if a buyer of the business were to pay someone other than him his salary, the value of the business would be reduced. This argument failed, according to the appellate court, because the trial court, in its discretion, was entitled to value the company at the value it would have to a buyer who would pay a manager's salary of $75,000 per year, a reasonable amount for the position. Thus, the court held that the trial court could use both of its findings together, and that its decision to do so was both logical and supported by the record.

---

[100] *Champion v. Champion*, 54 Mass. App. Ct. 215, 764 N.E.2d 898, 2002 Mass. App. LEXIS 363 (Mass. App. Ct. 2002).
[101] *Keane v. Keane*, 2006 N.Y. LEXIS 3751 (N.Y. 2006).
[102] *Sander v. Sander*, 2006 Conn. App. LEXIS 280 (Conn. Ct. App. 2006).

Valuation Methods in the Family Law Courts

A study of the valuation methods accepted in family law cases of the 50 states and other jurisdictions reveals a picture so convoluted it is hard to imagine and impossible to describe. Probably the most incisive summary statement is that "there is no uniform rule for fixing the value of a going business for equitable distribution."[103]

Similarly, one opinion explained that the choice of method used to value a company depends on the "unique status of each corporation."[104]

The worst that can be said is that courts have accepted many "methods" that have no definition in the literature of business valuation and are not described in the opinions that accepted them. The best that can be said is that the more enlightened courts seem to be moving toward trying to adopt methods that are actually favored in the financial community.

Typical of the latter is a gradual movement toward recognition of the discounted cash flow (DCF) method. An example is an Ohio case that accepted a value of $14 million based on the DCF method as opposed to a value of $24.6 million based on the capitalized excess earnings method.[105] An abstract of the case makes the following comment:

> The trial judge stated from the bench that the DCF method had never been used before within her family law jurisdiction. She was willing to consider it based on testimony that members of the professional financial community would be likely to use the method in valuing a company of this type. It goes to show that "we haven't used the method here before" isn't adequate cause for rejection, as long as it is a method generally accepted in the financial community.

Also, this case again demonstrates the importance of making a thorough record of evidence at trial, adequate to be persuasive to an appellate court that the trial court's decision was based on competent, credible, and sufficient evidence.[106]

Unlike practice in the U.S. Tax Court and most state courts dealing with shareholder disputes, valuation decisions in family law courts are not usually neatly classified into variations of the income, market, and asset-based approaches. In fact, the courts often mix standards of value with valuation methods. For example, one opinion recognized "fair acceptable methods" for valuing goodwill:

1. The price a willing buyer would pay
2. Capitalization of excess earnings method
3. One year's average gross income of the practice
4. Evidence of sale of comparable practice[107]

To most valuation analysts, the price a willing buyer would pay would be regarded as a standard of value (specifically fair market value), not a method of valuation.

---

[103] See *Amodio v. Amodio*, 509 N.E.2d 936 (N.Y. 1987).

[104] *Cheatham v. Cheatham*, No. 01A01-9508-CH-00380 Tenn. Ct. App., 1997 WL 731784 (Nov. 25, 1997).

[105] *Sergi v. Sergi*, No. 17476 Ohio Ct. App., 9th Dist., 1996 WL 425914 (July 31, 1996).

[106] *Shannon Pratt's Business Valuation Update*, September 1996, p. 9. Other cases that have accepted the DCF method include, for example, *Giuffre v. Baker*, No. 95-G-1904 Ohio Ct. App., 1996 WL 535254 at *4 (Aug. 30, 1996), and *Oatey v. Oatey*, No. 67809, 67973 Ohio Ct. App., 1996 WL 200273 at *7 (Apr. 25, 1996).

[107] *Conway v. Conway*, No. COA97-1439 N.C. Ct. App., 1998 WL 865157 (Dec. 15, 1998).

To most valuation analysts, something to be called a "method" would have to deal with the question of how one estimates what the willing buyer would pay, which might include numbers 2 and 4. But, number 3, "one year's average gross income," is a specific pricing multiple, but the "method" should imply an exercise in arriving at what the pricing multiple should be.

In one case, the court accepted the price at which stock actually sold as the value of the stock, rather than relying on a value stipulated to by the parties.[108]

In another case, the court agreed that use of an asset valuation method was inappropriate to value a minority interest that had no voting control—and thus, no access to the assets. Instead, the court valued the cash flow resulting from a stock transfer agreement combined with the value of a possible future liquidation.[109]

Pickard v. Pickard[110] held that the value of the spouses' interest in multiple properties was not too speculative where the properties' reversionary value was used to compute present value. The court said:

> [T]he properties' total reversionary value should not have been relied upon to cast doubt on the expert's assessment of the *present* value of this investment. The present value of this asset is no more speculative than that of any other asset with limited marketability; it may be properly determined by standard valuation techniques. Rather than rendering the asset's value too speculative to determine, the marketability limitation simply creates the need to apply discounting factors to the future value—exactly the procedure the expert here employed.

In *Kerce v. Kerce*,[111] the court rejected the husband's use of the Delaware block method, finding that the wife's use of the income method was better suited for a marital dissolution valuation than a method used primarily in shareholder appraisal actions.

The market approach,[112] income approach,[113] and asset approach[114], or a combination of these,[115] are all used to value marital property, but the courts seem to be leery of new approaches that have not gained wide acceptance in the valuation community (see also the later section on "Adequacy of Evidence").[116]

---

[108] *Lazarchic v. Lazarchic*, 2005 WL 1719054 (Va. Ct. App. 2005).

[109] *Gibbons v. Gibbons*, 94 P.3d 879, 194 Or. App. 257 (Or. Ct. App. 2004).

[110] *Pickard v. Pickard*, 2006 N.Y. App. Div. LEXIS 9961 (N.Y. App. Div. 2006)

[111] *Kerce v. Kerce*, 2003 WL 22037526 (Tenn. Ct. App. 2003).

[112] See, e.g., *In re Marriage of Helzer*, 2004 Mont. LEXIS 619 (Mont. 2004); *Ayers v. Ayers*, 2000 Tenn. App. LEXIS 376 (Tenn. Ct. App. June 6, 2000); *In re Marriage of Schleif*, 2002 Minn. App. LEXIS 1339 (Minn. Ct. App. 2002).

[113] See, e.g., *Washington v. Washington*, 2005 Va. App. LEXIS 177 (Va. Ct. App. 2005).

[114] See, e.g., *D.K.H v. L.R.G.*, 102 S.W.3d 93 (Mo. Ct. App. 2003); *Collier v. Collier*, 790 So. 2d 759 (La. Ct. App. 2001); *In re Marriage of Lowry*, 2001 WL 1043209 (Iowa Ct. App. 2001).

[115] See, e.g., *Richards v. Knuchel*, 2005 Mont. LEXIS 215 (Mont. 2005); *Bersin v. Golonka*, 2005 N.C. App. LEXIS 1032 (N.C. App. 2005) (market and income approaches); *Hanson v. Hanson*, 86 P.3d 94, 192 Or. App. 422 (Or. Ct. App. 2004) (market and income approaches); *Covert v. Covert*, 2004 Ohio App. LEXIS 3190 (Ohio Ct. App. 2004) (asset, income, and market approaches).

[116] In *Stageberg v. Stageberg*, 2005 Minn. App. LEXIS 484 (Minn. Ct. App. 2005), the court rejected what it called "The Historical Average Income Approach" to value a lawyer-husband's contingency-fee income. Not only did the court not find support for this method, it also found that by using an annual-income figure in its formula and applying the formula to only one year of the husband's practice of law, the approach implicitly assumed that all of the husband's contingent-fee cases that were in progress on the valuation date would be resolved within one year of that date. The court indicated that this assumption was supported neither by evidence in the record nor by general experience. In addition, because the judgment *currently* awarded the wife a share of the marital interest in fees the husband had yet to receive, the judgment overstated the wife's interest in those fees by not reducing her interest to its present value.

The capitalization of excess earnings method is encountered far more in family law cases than in any other type of cases.[117] Unfortunately, as discussed in Chapter 13, the details of its implementation are extremely varied.

With little truly definitive case law on proper methodology, it is incumbent on the analyst, through the written report and/or testimony, to educate the court on the details of the methodology used and why it is the proper methodology for the specific case at bar.

An area of contention in some cases is whether or not the guideline publicly traded company method should be used to value closely held companies or interests in them. The most frequently cited case rejecting the method is a California case, *In re Marriage of Lotz*, in which the appellate court reversed the trial court's value of $469,000, which was based on guideline publicly traded companies' price/earnings multiples. The Appellate Court explained as follows:

> We agree that the price earnings ratios of publicly traded corporations have little relevance in valuing a closely held corporation. There are enormous differences between the two types of corporations. The sales volume of publicly traded corporations is much higher than the volume of closely held corporations. The stock in a publicly traded corporation has liquidity value because its owners can sell stock and get money in a matter of days, whereas the stock in "Your Own Things" has no liquidity value. There is less risk in owning stock in public corporations because they can "miss on two or three lines" without being hurt too much. Finally, the cost "to go public" is between $150,000 and $200,000 for legal and accounting fees. Therefore, there is no substantial support for the use of the above formula in evaluating a closely held corporation, even considering the attempts to adjust the formula.[118]

A subsequent oft-cited California case, *Hewitson*, relied on *Lotz* and also rejected a valuation based on publicly traded company market-derived pricing multiples. The *Hewitson* case added another dimension in that multiples seen in *acquisitions* of publicly traded companies were also used, and were also rejected by the Court, even though the business interest being valued was 100 percent of the stock.

In justifying its rejection of acquisition prices paid for public companies, the Court explained:

> Cash is rarely paid for the acquired company. The company is usually acquired in exchange for stock in the acquiring company. The shares used

[117] See, e.g., *Ackerman v. Ackerman*, 2006 Cal. App. LEXIS 2056 (Cal. Ct. App. 2006) (the court accepted the capitalization of excess earnings method, used by both spouses, but rejected the experts' use of different national compensation surveys, finding they could not account for the reasonable compensation of an established plastic surgeon practicing in a highly affluent community); *In re Marriage of Alosio*, 2005 Cal. App. Unpub. LEXIS 4562 (Cal. Ct. App. 2005) (the court rejected the capitalization of excess earnings method as being too subjective); *Gohl v. Gohl*, 2005 Neb. App. LEXIS 143 (Neb. Ct. App. 2005) (trial court accepted a weighted average of the net asset value and a capitalization of excess earnings value); *Walker v. Walker*, 600 S.E.2d 900, 2004 WL 1609095 (N.C. Ct. App. 2004) (where tangible assets were insignificant, the capitalization of earnings method produced an estimate of intangible assets that represented the entire value of the business); *Buzanell v. Miller*, 590 S.E.2d 332, 162 N.C. App. 180, 2004 WL 26524 (N.C. Ct. App. 2004) (capitalization of earnings method should be used for a newly established professional practice); *Waddell v. Waddell*, 2003 WL 1996066 (Cal. Ct. App. 2003) (court accepted excess earnings method over a multiple of discretionary earnings method, rejecting the argument that the excess earnings method valued goodwill as if it were wholly community property, even though goodwill arose after the parties separated); *Washington v. Washington*, 2005 Va. App. LEXIS 177 (Va. Ct. App. 2005) (the court ruled that close to two years' worth of earnings were not too speculative to capitalize); *Sampson v. Sampson*, 2004 Mass. App. LEXIS 1223 (Mass. Ct. App. 2004) (both experts used capitalization of earnings method); *Clymer v. Clymer*, 2000 WL 1357911, 2000 Ohio App. LEXIS 4248 (Ohio Ct. App. 2000) (both experts used capitalization of earnings method); *Douglas v. Douglas*, 281 A.D.2d 709, 722 N.Y.S.2d 87 (N.Y. App. Div. 2001) (interest in a law firm).
[118] *In re Marriage of Lotz*, 120 Cal. App. 3d 379, 174 Cal.Rptr. 618 (1981).

to acquire the comparable company are normally issued without any substantial effect on the stock exchange price of the acquiring company. Hence, the acquiring company will pay a premium to acquire the company because (1) it is paying cheaper than cash consideration, and (2) such a controlling interest in the acquired company will insure the safety of its investment.[119]

The second point would seem to have no merit at all, since it would apply equally to acquisitions of public or private companies, and would affect the investment value as well as the market value. The first point should be able to be handled by adjusting to an estimate of cash equivalent value in those cases where there may be a disparity between face value and cash equivalent value.

The wife in *Hewitson* argued that the case should be distinguished from *Lotz* because the company was much bigger. The Court found that argument "without merit" because the "primary difference" between public and closely held corporations is the "lack of marketability, i.e., liquidity of close corporation stock."

It should be noted that, even if one accepts the courts' findings in light of conditions at the time (1981 and 1983), conditions have changed to the extent that the guideline publicly traded company method and the acquisition transaction method (acquisitions of *either* public or private companies) should not suffer, at least to the same extent, from the same criticisms today. Nonetheless, these methods are not yet entirely free from suspicion.[120]

The Size Argument

As of this writing, partly due to congressional encouragement and partly due to market reaction, there are thousands of public companies with equity values under $10 million, so the generalization about public companies always being much larger than private companies is no longer valid.

The Liquidity Argument

For controlling ownership interests, two significant factors have changed. First, as noted in the previous paragraph, it is much easier today than 15 or 20 years ago for smaller companies to gain liquidity through an initial public offering (IPO). Second, the business of business intermediaries (business brokers and small to midmarket company merger and acquisition specialists) has burgeoned in the late 1990s, making it much easier for private companies to find acquirers.

For noncontrolling ownership interests, the matter of lack of marketability is no less of a negative factor, but the issue of making an appropriate valuation adjustment has been greatly facilitated by the development of noncontrolling ownership interest lack of marketability discount databases over the last 15 years, as discussed in detail in Chapter 17. The restricted stock studies were in their infancy at the time of the *Lotz* and *Hewitson* cases, and the pre-IPO studies didn't even

---

[119] *In re Marriage of Hewitson.*

[120] See, e.g., *Duncan v. Duncan*, 90 Cal.App.4th 617, 108 Cal.Rptr.2d 833 (Cal. Ct. App. 2001) where the court rejected both the comparable public company sales method and the comparable sales of public and private companies method, saying that sales of publicly traded companies were not "comparable." The court, however, did accept a comparable sales of privately held companies method.

exist. Today there are substantial empirical data to help quantify an adjustment from an "as if publicly traded" level of value to a nonmarketable, noncontrolling level of value.

The Risk Argument

The notion that there is less risk in publicly traded companies because they can "miss on two or three lines" without being hurt too much certainly is not valid for many of today's smaller public companies that have only one or a few lines.

The Cost of Flotation Argument

While there certainly is a size below which it is not economical to go public, the lower limit is much lower today than in the early 1980s. This is largely because Congress passed legislation, implemented by the Securities and Exchange Commission (SEC) regulations, that allows smaller companies to go public with far lower accounting and legal requirements than are necessary for larger company registrations. These smaller company IPOs have been further facilitated by a substantial network of investment banking companies that specialize in such smaller offerings.

Noncompete Covenants

Most, but not all, states that have addressed the issue conclude that a noncompete covenant is separate property, *not* a marital asset, since it restricts the future activities of the spouse. For example, in its first case to address the issue, the Nebraska Court of Appeals looked to other jurisdictions and concluded that the covenant not to compete is *not* a marital asset.[121]

In a Washington case, a dentist sold his practice, including a noncompete covenant. Of the total proceeds of $180,000, $109,000 was allocated to the noncompete covenant, which the trial court found was separate property, not part of the marital estate. The appellate court agreed that the covenant not to compete was separate property. However, it found nothing in the record to substantiate the fairness of the portion of the total proceeds allocated to the covenant. Therefore, the appellate court stated, "On remand, the trial court is to segregate the value of the practice from the value of the covenant not to compete based on all of the evidence rather than one party's bold assertions."[122]

In South Carolina's case of first impression on the noncompete issue, the Court of Appeals found that the husband's contract receivable for a noncompete covenant was *not* a marital asset. Seeking precedent from other states, the Court concluded:

> Although we find no definitive majority view, we are persuaded by the reasoning of cases which find that a covenant not to compete is not marital property and, therefore, is not subject to equitable distribution ... We

---

[121] *Kriscfeld v. Kriscfeld.*

[122] *In re the Marriage of Delores A. Monaghan and Robert D. Monaghan*, 78 Wash. App. 918, 899 P.2d 841 (Aug. 9, 1995). Other cases cited regarding fairness of allocation to covenant included *Lucas v. Lucas*, 95 N.M. 283, 285, 621 P.2d 500, 502 (1980); *Carr v. Carr*, 108 Idaho 684, 701 P.2d 304 (1985); and *In re Marriage of Quay*, 18 Cal. App. 4th 961, Cal. Rptr. 2d 537, 541–42 (1993).

remand this issue for the family court to distribute the husband's share of the purchase price of the Insurance Centre assets as marital property. However, the court should exclude from the marital estate the value of the husband's share of the covenant not to compete.[123]

The Supreme Court of New Mexico concluded that the $10,000 per year proceeds of a covenant not to compete resulting from the sale of a funeral home company should be separate property.

Appellee successfully argued at the trial level that the payments to be received under the covenant constituted additional compensation for the sale of stock and as such, was community property within the meaning of Section 40-3-8(B), N.M.S.A. 1978. The trial court reached its decision by finding that the terms of the covenant were too extreme and invalidated the covenant thereby adding $100,000 to the sale price of the stock. Neither view is correct in light of the record.

Although the covenant was contemporaneously negotiated with the sale of the stock, a review of the record fails to indicate that the $100,000 due under the covenant was to be considered as part of the stock's purchase price. To the contrary, the record is replete with evidence that the price paid for the stock was both fair and reasonable. The price paid exceeded the total assets of the corporation after allowing for depreciation. Other evidence indicated that covenants not to compete are common in the mortuary business and there is nothing in the record which suggests that the terms of appellant's covenant were so extreme as to make it invalid.

Upon the lawful dissolution of marriage, the right to compete becomes a personal right and as such, the separate property of the owner, who may then relinquish or exercise that right to his or her own benefit.[124]

As with many issues, the positions do vary from state to state. The Court of Appeals of Indiana concluded that the proceeds of a covenant not to compete *are* a marital asset.

Theodore next contends that the trial court's determination that the proceeds he received from the covenant not to compete were marital property and subject to distribution was error. Theodore's argument fails. Theodore characterizes the proceeds of the covenant not to compete as future income. Future earnings of one spouse are not marital property subject to division in a dissolution proceeding. *Bressler v. Bressler*, 601 N.E.2d 392, 397 (Ind. Ct. App. 1992). However, a restrictive covenant not to compete which is signed in conjunction with the sale of a business represents the goodwill of that business absent evidence to the contrary. *Berger v. Berger*, 648 N.E.2d 378, 383 (Ind. Ct. App. 1995). The value of the goodwill of a business is included in the marital estate. *Cleary v. Cleary*, 582 N.E.2d 851, 853 (Ind. Ct. App. 1991).

---

[123] *Ellerbe v. Ellerbe*, 323 S.C. 283, 473 S.E.2d 881 (S.C. Ct. App. 1996). Citations referenced were *Cutsinger v. Cutsinger*, 917 S.W.2d 238 (Tenn. Ct. App. 1995) (court excluded monetary amounts for covenant not to compete from purchase price of chiropractic practice); *Hoeft v. Hoeft*, 74 Ohio App. 3d 809, 600 N.E.2d 746 (Ohio Ct. App. 1991) (court determined that while proceeds received for the sale of the husband's dental practice were marital property, monies received from a covenant not to compete were nonmarital); *Johnston v. Johnston*, 778 S.W.2d 674 (Mo. Ct. App. 1989) (covenant not to compete properly excluded in the valuation of dental practice); *Donahue v. Donahue*, 299 S.C. 353, 384 S.E.2d 741 (1989) (goodwill of a professional practice is not subject to equitable distribution).

[124] *Lucas v. Lucas*.

Here, Theodore signed the covenant not to compete in conjunction with the sale of his interest in Petro-Chem. The total proceeds were $11,450,000. There is evidence in the record that the value of his interest in the business was approximately $11 million. There is also evidence that Theodore's goal was to sell the business for between $10 million and $12 million. This evidence all supports the determination that the noncompete agreement was to protect the goodwill of the business. Absent evidence to the contrary, the noncompete agreement represents the goodwill of the company, which is includable in the marital estate.[125]

Minnesota's Court of Appeals concluded that consideration for a noncompete agreement was marital property to the extent that it was intended to interfere with the transfer of marital goodwill rather than govern postmarital labor.[126]

In *In re Marriage of Mally*,[127] the Iowa Court of Appeals accepted the husband's contention that selling his chiropractic practice would require a noncompete agreement, and accordingly reduced the practice's value from $569,000 to $240,000.

California distinguishes between a covenant actually executed and one that probably would have to be executed to sell the business. A California decision says:

> Consideration paid for a noncompetition agreement, or the value of that agreement, is the separate property of the covenanting spouse if such a covenant actually has been negotiated as part of the sale of the property. (*Carr v. Carr* [Idaho App. 1985] 701 P.2d 304; *Dillion v. Anderson* [Tex. App. 1962] 358 S.W.2d 694; *Lucas v. Lucas* [N.M. 1980] 621 P.2d 500.) However, it is inappropriate when awarding the property to one spouse to reduce the value of the business by the speculative value of a hypothetical noncompetition agreement. (*Mitchell v. Mitchell* [N.M. App. 1986] 719 P.2d 432; *McGehee v. McGehee* [La. App. 1 Cir. 1989] 543 So.2d 1126.)[128]

The appellate court thus reversed the trial court's decision to deduct from the estimated proceeds if a sale were to take place the portion of those proceeds estimated to be attributable to a covenant not to compete.

Consistent with the above decision, a subsequent California appellate opinion concluded that the entire $1,320,000 proceeds from a covenant not to compete executed in conjunction with the sale of a business was separate property.[129]

Other courts hold that adjustments for hypothetical employment contracts and noncompete covenants will not be permitted, even though comparable transactions include employment contracts of similar duration, where the appraiser does not present evidence on the nature of the contracts or their impact on value.[130]

Still other courts have ruled that noncompete agreements may not be used to calculate enterprise goodwill, but are a part of personal goodwill, since a covenant not-to-compete is attributable to the personal reputation of the seller/spouse and not to the enterprise goodwill of the business.[131] For more details on this issue, see the earlier section on goodwill.

---

[125] *Reese v. Reese.*

[126] *Sweere v. Gilbert-Sweere*, 534 N.W.2d 294 (Minn. Ct. App. 1995).

[127] *In re Marriage of Mally*, 2001 WL 539669 (Iowa Ct. App. 2001).

[128] *In re Marriage of Czapar*, 232 Cal. App. 3d 1308, 284 Cal. Rptr. 41 (1991).

[129] *In re Marriage of Quay.*

[130] *Duncan v. Duncan*, 90 Cal.App.4th 617, 108 Cal.Rptr.2d 833 (Cal. Ct. App. 2001) (rejecting adjustments for a hypothetical 5- to 10-year contract where guideline transactions included such contracts, but the appraiser did not present evidence as to the specific nature of the agreements in the comparable transactions, did not correlate the value of the agreements to the value of the comparable companies, and did not justify the percentage adjustment he used).

[131] *Held v. Held*, 2005 Fla. App. LEXIS 14138 (Fla. Ct. App. 2005).

Buy-Sell Agreements

It is uncommon but not unheard of for the valuation provisions of a buy-sell agreement to be controlling in a valuation for marital dissolution distribution purposes. The clear majority hold that the buy-sell price in a closely-held corporation can be manipulated and does not necessarily reflect true market value.

Cases Rejecting Buy-Sell Agreements

Virginia, for example, has rejected buy-sell agreement valuation provisions as being controlling for interests in professional practices.[132]

Other examples of rejecting buy-sell or restrictive agreements for valuation purposes include *Ullom v. Ullom*;[133] *Argyle v. Argyle*, in which the buy-sell agreement did not contemplate evaluation for such purposes;[134] *In re Marriage of Brooks*, where the buy-sell agreement was made in close proximity to the divorce;[135] *Berenberg v. Berenberg*;[136] *In re Marriage of Bowen*;[137] *Bersin v. Golonka*;[138] and others.[139]

Cases Finding Buy-Sell Price Controlling

A buy-sell agreement price was found determinate when the court concluded that if the husband were to sell his shares in an insurance company, he would do so according to the stipulations of the buy-sell agreement.[140]

A buy-sell agreement was found controlling for a block of unregistered stock of a public company, according other shareholders a right of first refusal. The Court said, "Any appraisal of the value of the stock based on a potential sale outside the terms of the agreement would have been purely speculative."[141]

A Supreme Court of New Mexico case found a law firm's buy-sell agreement to be controlling, partly because over 150 transactions had taken place, all in accordance with the agreement.[142]

Another case also affirmed a buy-sell agreement price because it was what had been paid in arm's-length transactions and was all the owner could receive under the buyout agreement.[143]

---

[132] *Howell v. Howell*, discussed further in the section on investment value earlier in this chapter.

[133] *Ullom v. Ullom*, 559 A.2d 555, 558 (Pa. Super. Ct. 1989).

[134] *Argyle v. Argyle*, 688 P.2d 468, 471 (Utah 1984).

[135] *In re Marriage of Brooks*, 756 P.2d 161, 163 (Wash. Ct. App. 1988).

[136] *Berenberg v. Berenberg*, 474 N.W.2d 843, 847 (Minn. Ct. App. 1991).

[137] *In re Marriage of Bowen*, 473 A.2d 73, 78 (N.J. 1984).

[138] *Bersin v. Golonka*, 2005 N.C. App. LEXIS 1032 (N.C. Ct. App. 2005).

[139] *Ballas v. Ballas*, 2004 Ohio 5128, 2004 WL 2334329 (Ohio App. 7 Dist. 2004); *D.K.H v. L.R.G.*, 102 S.W.3d 93 (Mo. Ct. App. 2003); *Cole v. Cole*, 110 S.W.3d 310, 82 Ark. App. 47 (Ark. Ct. App. 2003); *Barton v. Barton*, 2007 Ga. LEXIS 21 (Ga. 2007).

[140] *In re Marriage of Gillespie*, No. 19978-5-11 Wash. Ct. App., 1997 WL 795692 (Dec. 31, 1997).

[141] *Rosenberg v. Rosenberg*, 510 N.Y.S.2d 659, 662 (N.Y. App. Div. 1987).

[142] *Hertz v. Hertz*, 657 P.2d 1169, 1174–75 (N.M. 1983).

[143] *Johnson v. Johnson*, 771 P.2d 696, 698 (Utah Ct. App. 1989).

Buy-Sell Agreement May Be Considered

It is quite common for a buy-sell or similar agreement to be considered as one factor affecting the valuation, although it isn't necessarily determinative in valuing the stock.[144]

Discounts for Lack of Control and Lack of Marketability

Discount for Lack of Control

Many jurisdictions have recognized that a lack of control discount is frequently appropriate if the spouse does not own a controlling interest in the subject company. For example, an Alaska case, referencing other jurisdictions, rejected as a matter of law testimony to the effect that no discount for lack of control was appropriate.[145]

In a North Dakota case, the Court rejected the testimony of one expert who said that "there should be no minority discount in a family-owned business in divorce cases, where, as here, Lillian's family owns the corporation and the minority shares are not being sold to unrelated, unknown buyers." However, the Court concluded a discount for lack of control of only 11.3 percent rather than the 25 to 40 percent sought by the party being awarded the business interest in question.[146]

There have been many other cases in which discounts for lack of control have been accepted.[147] On the other hand, there have been many cases where experts' testimony in favor of a discount for lack of control has been rejected.[148]

Discount for Lack of Marketability

States vary in their treatment of discounts for lack of marketability. In one case, for example, one expert testified in favor of a discount and the other opined that

---

[144] See, for example, *Bosserman v. Bosserman*, 384 S.E.2d 104, 107–08 (Va. Ct. App. 1989) (spouse did not consent to buy-sell agreement or is not bound by its terms); *Naddeo v. Naddeo*, 626 A.2d 608, 610–11 (Pa. Super. Ct. 1993) (partner did not have the ability to sell interest); *Stearns v. Stearns*, 494 A.2d 595, 598 (Conn. App. Ct. 1985) (closely held, family-run business); *Mitchell v. Mitchell*, 732 P.2d 208, 212 (Ariz. 1987); *Lyon v. Lyon*, 439 N.W.2d 18, 20 (Minn. 1989); *Buckl v. Buckl*, 542 A.2d 65, 69 (Pa. Super. Ct. 1988); *Rogers v. Rogers* 296 N.W.2d 849; 852 (Minn. 1980); *Schecter v. Schecter*, No. FA 9703276678 Conn. Super. Ct., 1999 WL 34857 (Jan. 12, 1999); *Drake v. Drake*, 809 S.W.2d 710, 713 (Ky. Ct. App. 1991) (closely held corporation); *In re Marriage of Dieger*, No. 97-1493 Iowa Ct. App., 1998 WL 690075 (June 24, 1998); *In re Marriage of Herlitzke*, 2006 Wisc. App. LEXIS 972 (Wisc. App. 2006) (buy-sell agreement may establish fair market value of partnership or S corporation, but does not do so as a matter of law); *Herron v. Herron*, 2004 Ohio App. LEXIS 5209 (Ohio Ct. App. November 1, 2004) (court gave weight to the closely held company's buy-sell agreement because "[a]ny willing buyer would certainly take into account the buy/sell agreement before making any offer on the stock"); *R.V.K. v. L.L.K*, 2002 WL 31421572 (Tex. Ct. App. 2002); *Harmon v. Harmon*, 2000 WL 286718 (Tenn. Ct. App. 2000); *Howell v. Howell*, 46 Va. Cir. 339; 1998 Va. Cir. LEXIS 256 (Va. Cir. Sept. 4, 1998), *aff'd*, 31 Va. App. 332, 523 S.E.2d 514 (Va. Ct. App. 2000).

[145] *Hayes v. Hayes*, 756 P.2d 298 (Alaska 1988).

[146] *Kaiser v. Kaiser*, No. 960013 N.D. Sup. Ct., 1996 WL 663189 (Nov. 18, 1996).

[147] *Priebe v. Priebe*, 556 N.W.2d 78, 81 (S.D. 1996) (40 percent); *DeCosse v. DeCosse*, No. 96-118 Mont., 1997 WL 19374 (Apr. 15, 1997) (20 percent); *Arneson v. Arneson*, 355 N.W. 2d 16 (Wis. Ct. App. 1984) (25 percent); *Rattee v. Rattee*, 767 A. 2d 415, 146 N.H. 44 (N.H. 2001); *L.R.M. v. R.K.M.*, 46 S.W.3d 24 (Mo. Ct. App. 2001) (32 percent combined discount), *Anderson v. Anderson*, 2006 Tenn. App. LEXIS 592 (Tenn. App. 2006) (38.3 percent DLOC).

[148] For example, *Howell v. Howell*; *Oatey v. Oatey*, No. 67809, 67973 Ohio Ct. App., 1996 WL 200273 at *22 (Apr. 25, 1996); *Nardini v. Nardini*, 414 N.W. 2d 184, 189 (Minn. 1987); *Cross v. Cross*, 586 P.2d 547, 549 (Wyo. 1978); *Ferraro v. Ferraro*, 2000 WL 251678 (Va. Ct. App. 2000); *Brown v. Brown*, 348 N.J. Super. 466, 792 A.2d 463, 2002 N.J. Super. LEXIS 105 (N.J. Super. 2002) (discounts disallowed absent extraordinary circumstances); *Baltrusis v. Baltrusis*, 113 Wash. App. 1037 (Wash. Ct. App. 2002) (25 percent); *Hanson v. Hanson*, 2005 Alas. LEXIS 166 (Alaska 2005) (no discount where majority spouse acquires the minority spouse's interest).

marketability is not a factor in cases where a business is not being sold to a third party. The Court concluded:

> Where a sale of the business is not contemplated, the value of the stock should be determined without discounting for lack of marketability. Under these circumstances, the fact that H & H stock is not publicly traded does not warrant application of the discount to reduce the value of Linda's interest. See and compare *Mexic v. Mexic*, 577 So.2d 1046, 1050 (La. App. 4th Cir. 1991).[149]

Many other cases have rejected discounts for lack of marketability.[150] On the other hand, there are many cases in which discounts for lack of marketability have been accepted.[151]

Adequacy of Evidence

The Need for a Solid Record

As noted in the previous chapter, while trial courts have broad discretion regarding findings of fact, the record must indicate that there was adequate evidence to support those findings. The incidence of remand for lack of adequate evidence supporting business values is higher in family law case appeals than in any other business valuation litigation context.

Typical of court opinions to this effect is the following:

> In allocating property between the parties to a divorce and in making an award of sustenance alimony, the trial court must indicate the basis for its award in sufficient detail to enable a reviewing court to determine that the award is fair, equitable and in accordance with the law.[152]

Citing the above case, a subsequent appellate decision remanded a case on similar grounds:

> The trial court failed to indicate the basis of its award and valuation of Get Out of Town on a Rail, Inc. with sufficient detail to enable this court to conduct a meaningful review of the award.[153]

---

[149] *Head v. Head*, No. 30, 585-CA LA. App., 1998 WL 257217 (2d Cir. May 22, 1998).

[150] See, for example, *Howell v. Howell* (no amount specified); *Neuman v. Neuman*, 842 P.2d 575, 579 (Wyo. 1992) (35 percent); *Hanson v. Hanson*, 86 P.3d 94, 192 Or. App. 422 (Or. Ct. App. 2004) (25 percent); *Brown v. Brown*, 348 N.J. Super. 466, 792 A.2d 463, 2002 N.J. Super. LEXIS 105 (N.J. Super. 2002); *Baltrusis v. Baltrusis*, 113 Wash. App. 1037 (Wash. Ct. App. 2002) (25 percent); *Ferraro v. Ferraro*, 2000 WL 251678 (Va. Ct. App. 2000); *Anderson v. Anderson*, 2006 Tenn. App. LEXIS 592 (Tenn. Ct. App. 2006) (10 percent for marketing costs associated with only a hypothetical sale of minority interest); *Hanson v. Hanson*, 2005 Alas. LEXIS 166 (Alaska 2005) (no discount where majority spouse acquires the minority spouse's interest); *Kapp v. Kapp*, 2005 Ohio App. LEXIS 6144 (Ohio App. 2005) (no discount for contingent transaction costs—broker, legal, accounting fees— where no sale is being contemplated).

[151] For example, *In re Marriage of Tofte*, 895 P.2d 1387, 1392 (Or. Ct. App. 1995) (35 percent); *Ellis v. Ellis*, No. 77407 N.Y. App. Div., 1997 WL 35218 at *2 (Jan. 30, 1997) (25 percent); *Michael v. Michael*, 469 S.E.2d 14, 17 (W. Va. 1996) (25 percent); *Kapp v. Kapp*, 2005 Ohio App. LEXIS 6144 (Ohio App. 2005) (litigation contingency discount accepted where proof of a pending lawsuit was presented); *Rattee v. Rattee*, 767 A.2d 415, 146 N.H. 44 (N.H. 2001); *L.R.M. v. R.K.M.*, 46 S.W.3d 24 (Mo. Ct. App. 2001) (32 percent combined discount); *Collier v. Collier*, 790 So. 2d 759 (La. Ct. App. 2001) (25 percent combined discount for lack of marketability and contingent liabilities).

[152] *Kaechele v. Kaechele*, 35 Ohio St.3d 93, 97 (1988).

[153] *Giuffre v. Baker*.

Another typical example is a Louisiana case:

The evidence presented by both parties as to the valuation of the corporation is patently unsound…. We are unable to make a determination of the valuation of the husband's medical corporation based upon the record before us…. The matter should be remanded to the trial court for an evidentiary hearing.[154]

Similarly, in a North Carolina case:

The trial court … should clearly indicate the evidence on which its valuations are based, preferably noting the valuation method or methods on which it relied…. We vacate that portion of the equitable distribution order which determines the value of defendant's goodwill in his medical practice, and remand this case to the district court for a proper determination of such value….[155]

In one case, a certified public accountant (CPA) employed the income approach to place a value on the corporation, although he avowed that he had insufficient information to give an opinion on the value at the time of the marriage in 1989.

The trial court, using the figures the CPA considered insufficient, purported to find the corporation's value on that date. The Court of Appeals determined that if the information available to the CPA was insufficient for that purpose, it was inadequate to support a finding of value by the court. The Court of Appeals declared that the judgment decreeing a division of the community estate was to be reversed and remanded to the trial court.[156]

The Virginia Court of Appeals upheld the striking of the testimony of the wife's expert (using the discounted cash flow method for a start-up business) on the basis that it was speculative. The trial court concluded, "I don't think it's the law that you can get somebody to get on the stand and project earnings of a company that has done no business, has no record of income. That's pure speculation. Couldn't be more pure." The Court of Appeals concluded, "Based on the evidence presented to the court at trial, we find no error in this ruling."[157]

A Washington case emphasizes to both the expert and the attorney the necessity of making a good record at trial. Professional goodwill, defined as "the expectation of continued public patronage," is recognized as intangible property subject to division in a divorce. The Court must first determine whether goodwill exists, and, if so, determine its value considering several factors (discussed in the earlier section on goodwill). One expert testified that there was no goodwill, and the value of the business was $2,040 (assets minus liabilities). The other expert testified that the business was worth $125,582 (1.5 times the last four years' average gross income less operating expenses). The trial court determined that the value of the business was $50,000. The Court of Appeals explained:

The trial court must state on record which factors … were used …; failure to do so will deem the valuation to be unsupported by sufficient evidence, necessitating reversal and remand….

---

[154] *Fox v. Fox*, No. 97-1914 La. App. 1 Cir., 1998 WL 781651 (Nov. 6, 1998).

[155] *Conway v. Conway*.

[156] *In re Marriage of Cassel*, No. 07-96-0268-CV Tex. App., 1997 WL 260099 (May 19, 1997).

[157] *Shoolts v. Shoolts*, Nos. 2205-96-4 Vir. Ct. App., 1998 WL 201536 (Apr. 28, 1998).

We cannot determine from the record before us whether the trial court actually found "goodwill." Once the trial court finds goodwill, it must set forth on the record the factors and method used in reaching a finding of goodwill and its value…. Because the trial court here did not state how it reached the valuation figure, we remand and direct the trial court to set forth the factors and methods used in valuation if it indeed finds goodwill exists.[158]

Preserving the Record

Not only is it important to make a good record at trial, it is also important to preserve the record and present it on appeal. *Lannes v. Lannes*[159] demonstrates this principle. In that case, the husband's expert, using a fair market value standard, valued the business at $0. The wife's expert concluded the company's worth to be $313,048. The experts differed in three major areas: the husband's income, the business's profit, and the capitalization rate. Ultimately, the trial court issued a letter opinion accepting the wife's valuation. On appeal, as to the testimony of the husband's expert, the record filed with the Court did not contain his direct testimony. The record contained neither the direct nor the cross-examination testimony of the wife's expert. It contained only the rebuttal, the cross-examination rebuttal, and the redirect rebuttal testimony of the wife's expert. Thus, the Court was limited to the testimony adduced in the husband's expert's cross-examination and the wife's expert's rebuttal to resolve the issues before it. Because there was nothing in the record to assist the Court in determining whether the trial court's rejection of the husband's valuation was an error, the appellate court essentially felt it had no choice but to affirm.

The Court said that:

[W]ithout the full testimony of each expert, we are left with the futile task of having to interpret a portion of each expert's opinion without the context of the testimony in full. Thus, from the record before us it is impossible to determine how and why [the husband's expert] arrived at his ultimate opinion on valuation.

An appellant has the primary responsibility of ensuring that a complete record is furnished to an appellate court so that the errors assigned may be decided properly; here, the husband failed to carry out this responsibility and lost any chance of convincing the Court to reverse.

An appellate court reversed and remanded a trial court's conclusion of value for a hair transplant practice: "Because no evidence supports the valuation, we reverse and remand for new trial."[160]

In another case, the husband offered no expert testimony, and the appellate court found the wife's expert's testimony inadequate, which the trial court had accepted. The appellate court reversed and remanded.[161]

---

[158] *Crosetto v. Crosetto*, No. 17911-3-11 Wash. App. Div. 2, 1996 WL 389337 (July 12, 1996), also citing *Hall*, 103 Wash.2d at 247, 692 P.2d 175, and *Marriage of Monaghan*, 78 Wash. App. 918, 927–28, 899 P.2d 841 (1995).

[159] *Lannes v. Lannes*, 2005 Va. App. LEXIS 176 (Va. Ct. App. 2005).

[160] *Kelsey v. Kelsey*, 918 P.2d 1067 (Ariz. App. Div. 1 Jan. 1, 1996).

[161] *Simmons v. Simmons*, No. 95 T 5237 Ohio Ct. App., 1996 WL 297003 (May 10, 1996).

In another case example, the wife presented no expert testimony, and the trial court found the testimony and analysis of the husband's expert not to be credible. The appellate court stated:

> The burden of presenting … sufficient evidence … does not fall on the petitioning spouse alone, but … is an obligation existing with both parties … [and] neither party met this burden with respect to the valuation of the three corporations.…
>
> On review of a case such as this, where the record does not support any valuation of a very substantial marital asset, we conclude that the only reasonable course is for us to order further proceedings at which sufficient evidence on the question of valuation can be presented.… Accordingly, we reverse and remand the case so that the trial court can take additional evidence on the valuation.…[162]

What a waste! Another case with no credible evidence on either side, resulting in extended delay and costs on both sides to resolve the matter!

Inadequate Evidence

In *Snider v. Snider*,[163] the court rejected the wife's "best estimate" of the business's value because she was not personally involved in, and had no knowledge of, the business. In *Barnes v. Sherman*,[164] the court similarly rejected the wife's testimony as being "nonexpert."

In *Stribling v. Stribling*,[165] the wife's business records were incomplete and prevented a full valuation. Accordingly, the court failed to assign a value to this asset and relied exclusively on gross sales and net income. The wife argued that the court's failure to assign value to the business constituted error. The appellate court rejected her argument, finding that the record showed that the wife had failed to cooperate in the valuation of the business and provided improper financial information. The court concluded that, where "a party fails to provide accurate information, or cooperate in the valuation of assets," the trial court is "entitled to proceed on the best information available." Accordingly, the court affirmed the trial court on this issue.

Similarly, in *Weinstein v. Weinstein*,[166] Connecticut's highest court reversed lower court decisions valuing a software company at $200,000—after a $2.5 million post-trial offer for the business was revealed. The court found, among other things, that the husband knew that the company's intellectual property asset—its software—was worth much more than he disclosed. The court concluded that the husband's conduct in excluding from his valuation the worth of an asset that his company had spent more than $1 million developing and was the "lifeblood" of the company reasonably could be viewed only as a blatant and deliberate misrepresentation. The court ruled that the husband's duty to disclose fully and frankly required more than merely alluding to the fact that the company owned source codes; similarly, that duty was not met by his providing to the wife's expert reams of documents in which information was buried that *might* have alerted the expert as to the asset's worth.

---

[162] *Blackstone v. Blackstone*, No. 1-94-2780 Ill. App. (1st Dist. May 30, 1997).

[163] *Snider v. Snider*, 2001 WL 32670 (Va. Ct. App. 2001).

[164] *Barnes v. Sherman*, 758 A.2d 936 (D.C. Ct. App. 2000).

[165] *Stribling v. Stribling*, 2005 Miss. App. LEXIS 58 (Miss. Ct. App. 2005).

[166] *Weinstein v. Weinstein*, 2005 Conn. LEXIS 348 (Conn. 2005).

The husband's first valuation in *Clymer v. Clymer*[167] was rejected by the appellate court for lack of sufficient evidence. On second appeal, the court upheld the valuation, which was the same as the first valuation, because it was supported by adequate evidence.

In *Zerbe v. Zerbe*,[168] the wife's expert valued the husband's medical practice at about $63,000, excluding goodwill. The husband's expert valued it at around $16,000. The trial court valued the practice at $20,000, but gave no reasoning for that value, except to state that, "There being no testimony regarding the value of the medical practice and [husband's] testimony makes it clear there is no market for the sale of the practice, the Magistrate set an appropriate value." However, the Court of Appeals stated, "A finding of value must be supported by competent, credible evidence. The court cannot take the two extremes presented by the evidence and choose a value somewhere between those two extremes …. Consequently, we hold that the trial court erred in setting the medical practice's value at $20,000."

In *Augoshe v. Lehman*,[169] the wife's expert presented two valuations for a motel, one based on the comparable sales approach ($4.40 million) and another based on the income approach ($4.31 million). The only evidence of value offered by the husband was a $2,842,858 purchase price. The trial court concluded the motel was worth $3,576,429. On review, the appeals court was unable to find "any competent evidence to support this finding," other than that the value was the "exact midpoint" between the purchase price and the income approach valuation by the wife's expert. The court ruled that "simply splitting the difference" between two divergent appraisals was an "improper method of valuation."

In *In re Marriage of Keener*[170] inadequate evidence for a valuation of intangible assets resulted in reversal. At trial, the wife's expert had assigned a zero value to intangibles, but the husband's expert cited two prior sales of trademarks—one for $7.7 million, the other for nearly $500,000—which he used to value the company's intellectual property at between $20 and $30 million. The husband also put the company's trademark's value in this range. However, the expert had not received relevant financial records to review, and the valuation was a "haphazard guess" based on sales of other trademarks. Based on this evidence, the trial court valued the intangibles at $5 million, and the intermediate appeals court let this stand, finding sufficient support from the two prior sales. On further appeal, however, the state's highest court concluded that "the record lacks sufficient evidence concerning a specific dollar amount to attach to these assets." The court found that the expert's opinion related only to the assets' potential future value, not their present value, and that the husband's opinion was "conjecture." The court summed up its position by saying, "This anecdotal evidence is simply an insufficient basis upon which to determine fair market value."

The court in *Pickard v. Pickard*[171] rejected a discount rate of 18 percent where the court determined the rate had been arbitrarily selected and no support for the rate was given.

---

[167] *Clymer v. Clymer*, 2000 WL 1357911 (2000).

[168] *Zerbe v. Zerbe*, 2005 Ohio 1180 (Ohio Ct. App. 2005).

[169] *Augoshe v. Lehman.* 2007 Fla. App. LEXIS 6367 (Fla. Ct. App. 2007).

[170] *In re Marriage of Keener*, 2007 Iowa Sup. LEXIS 13 (Iowa 2007).

[171] *Pickard v. Pickard*, 2006 N.Y. App. Div. LEXIS 9961 (N.Y. App. Div. 2006).

Greater Weight Given to Valuation Professionals

In a related vein, the courts seem to give significantly greater weight to valuations of independent, qualified experts (as they should!). For example, in *In re Marriage of Bidwell*,[172] the wife's expert estimated that the husband's stock brokerage business was worth between $57 million and $86 million. The husband did not hire an independent appraiser, instead relying on the $15 million estimate provided by his vice president of operations. The court accepted the low end of the wife's expert's range of values. This case suggests that the husband's failure to hire a valuation professional was, potentially, a costly mistake.

Likewise, in *In re Marriage of Gabriel*,[173] the husband relied on his own testimony and the wife hired a valuation expert; the court based its valuation on the expert's opinion of value. The same was true in *Miller v. Miller.*[174]

The court in *Ballas v. Ballas*[175] accepted the opinion of the wife's expert over that of the husband's business manager, finding that the expert's testimony was very credible, whereas the business manager's opinion was insufficient.

In *Dunn v. Dunn*,[176] neither party hired an expert. When the husband and wife each appealed, claiming the trial court had erred, the appellate court concluded that the trial court had done the best it could with the evidence it had before it and that "the fault for the dearth of evidence rests solely on the shoulders of the parties."

In a case where neither side presented expert valuation opinions, the appellate court recommended that both parties provide expert valuation on remand.[177]

Rejection of Unqualified Experts and Unaccepted Methodologies

Although the courts prefer an expert's valuation opinion to that of a nonexpert, generally, they will reject the opinion of an unqualified expert, or an expert who uses unaccepted methodologies.

In *Schumann v. Schumann*,[178] the trial court struck the testimony of the wife's valuation expert, who only had prior experience in an advisory role to the company's employee stock ownership plan (ESOP) trustee. The expert testified that the ESOP valuations did not provide a fair market value and/or relate to the actual shares of the company. Therefore, the appellate court reasoned that even if his testimony had not been stricken by the trial court, it would have been irrelevant to establishing a value for the husband's interest. In addition, the expert's analysis set forth an increase in the company's value from year to year, when, in reality, its gross sales were decreasing each year.

Where the husband's expert attempted to value the husband's interest in a law partnership, the court rejected the expert's use of withdrawal and death analyses, followed by deductions for passive appreciation and taxes, because such a method

---

[172] *In re Marriage of Bidwell*, 12 P.3d 76, 170 Or. App. 239 (Or. Ct. App. 2000).
[173] *In re Marriage of Gabriel*, 2005 Cal. App. Unpub. LEXIS 8101 (Cal. Ct. App. 2005).
[174] *Miller v. Miller*, 14 S.W.3d 903, 70 Ark. App. 64 (Ark. Ct. App. 2000).
[175] *Ballas v. Ballas*, 2004 Ohio 5128, 2004 WL 2334329 (Ohio App. 7 Dist. 2004).
[176] *Dunn v. Dunn*, 2005 Miss. App. LEXIS 637 (Miss. Ct. App. 2005).
[177] *Mace v. Mace*, 818 So. 2d 1130 (Miss. 2002).
[178] *Schumann v. Schumann*, 2005 Ohio 91 (Ohio 2005).

was not generally accepted by any court. Instead, the court accepted the wife's expert's use of the capitalization of excess earnings method.[179]

Appraiser's Due Diligence Duties

In *Weinstein v. Weinstein*, 2005 Conn. LEXIS 348 (Conn. 2005), an important issue was whether an appraiser was responsible for discovering that an offer for the sale of the husband's business had been made during the pendency of the divorce proceedings, or the value of the company's intellectual property asset.

After the trial court had entered a divorce decree and ordered the division of marital property, the wife sought to open and vacate the judgment dissolving her marriage to the husband on the grounds that the stipulation on which the judgment was based was the result of a fraudulent misrepresentation by the husband. The alleged misrepresentation occurred because the husband failed to disclose a $2.5 million offer he and his business partners had received for the purchase of a software company that they owned during the pendency of the marriage dissolution proceedings and had also failed to disclose that he rejected the offer because he believed it was significantly less than the company was worth. The wife argued that his rejection of the original offer compelled the conclusion that the husband fraudulently had undervalued his ownership interest in the company in his financial affidavit submitted to the court in the marriage dissolution proceedings, which valued the husband's interest at $14,000 to $40,000, and the company at no more than $200,000.

Five months after the entry of the judgment of dissolution, the husband and his partners sold the company to the purchaser for $6 million. As a result of the sale, the husband received approximately $1.45 million for his interest in the company. Both the trial court and the appellate court rejected the wife's motion to open and vacate the dissolution judgment's financial orders because they concluded that there was insufficient evidence that the husband had committed fraud since they apparently concluded that the husband's duty to disclose ended at the conclusion of the evidence, not upon the date on which judgment was rendered.

Connecticut's highest court reversed, finding, among other things, that the husband knew that the company's intellectual property asset—its software—was worth much more than he disclosed. The court concluded that the husband's conduct in excluding from his valuation the worth of an asset that his company had spent more than $1 million developing and was the "lifeblood" of the company reasonably could be viewed only as a blatant and deliberate misrepresentation.

A dissenting opinion suggested that because the wife's expert was an expert in valuing businesses, he should have either independently assessed the worth of the intellectual property asset or asked more questions concerning its worth. The majority, however, found that the husband was best equipped to value that asset because he created it and knew its worth better than anyone else involved in the marriage dissolution proceedings. Additionally, the wife's expert's valuation necessarily was limited by the information disclosed by the husband. Therefore, the court ruled that the husband's duty to disclose fully and frankly required more than merely alluding to the fact that the company owned source codes; similarly, that duty was not met by his providing to the wife's expert reams of documents in which information was buried that *might* have alerted the wife's expert as to the asset's worth.

---

[179] *Douglas v. Douglas*, 281 A.D.2d 709, 722 N.Y.S.2d 87 (N.Y. App. Div. 2001).

Accordingly, the court rejected the argument that the wife and her expert had a due diligence duty to dig deeper than they had to uncover the true worth of something the husband had a duty to fully and frankly disclose in the first place. Finally, the court rejected the husband's argument that the $2.5 million offer reflected the purchaser's willingness to pay a premium to avoid a lawsuit over the intellectual property rights. The court said, "It defies reason…to think that anyone would spend $1.25 million just to avoid litigation over something worth only $200,000." The "huge disparity" led the court to find that the husband knew that the company was worth far more than he told the trial court—or the wife's appraiser.

The incidence of lack of credible evidence on one side or both in family law cases involving business valuation is amazing. There is a great need to educate the legal community that there is a professional community with thousands of qualified valuation analysts, and that clients are best served by engaging these qualified professionals at the onset of any actual or potential dispute regarding the value of a business or professional practice.

Treatment of Tax Liabilities

As noted in the previous chapter, family law courts rarely allow the deduction of a tax liability assumed in connection with a business or other property unless the payment of the liability is imminent.[180]

For example, "theoretical tax liabilities should not have been deducted in valuing Sun Well Service, Inc., and Marvin's retirement accounts."[181]

Similarly typical is the statement in a California case:

> It is improper to take into consideration the tax consequences of an order dividing a community asset unless the tax liability is immediate and specific and will arise in connection with the division of the community property. (See *In re Marriage of Fonstein* (1976) 17 Cal.3d 738, 749, fn. 5; *In re Marriage of Davies* (1983) 143 Cal.App.3d 851, 857; *In re Marriage of Sharp* (1983) 143 Cal.App.3d 714, 718; *In re Marriage of Slater* (1979) 100 Cal.App.3d 241, 249.[182]

In one case, an Appellate Court reversed a decision that valued stock options after a deduction of capital gains taxes. The Court of Appeals stated:

> A trial court must consider tax consequences related to the disposition of marital property. However, "the statute requires the trial court to consider only the direct or inherent and necessarily incurred tax consequences of the property disposition." Future tax consequences incident to the disposition of stock awarded one party is not a proper consideration before the trial court. Reversed.[183]

In Washington, the wife successfully appealed the trial court's decision that reduced the value of a real estate partnership by the capital gains tax that would

---

[180] See, e.g., *Buzanell v. Miller*, 590 S.E.2d 332, 162 N.C. App. 180, 2004 WL 26524 (N.C. Ct. App. 2004) (consideration of taxes too speculative); *In re Marriage of Black*, 2001 WL 57999 (Iowa Ct. App. 2001); *Guill v Guill*, 2001 WL 770942 (Neb. Ct. App. 2001); *Skokos v. Skokos*, 40 S.W.3d 768, 344 Ark. 420 (Ark. 2001).

[181] *Kaiser v. Kaiser.*

[182] *In re Marriage of Czapar.*

[183] *Knotts v. Knotts*, No. 32405-9710-CV-430 Ind. Ct. App., 1998 WL 159207 (Apr. 7, 1998).

have to be paid if the property were sold. Since it was the first Washington case addressing this issue, the Court looked to other states for precedent, citing cases in seven other states. In denying the deduction for the impounded capital gains tax liability, the Court explained:

> Courts have generally found that consideration of tax consequences is either required or at least appropriate where the consequences are immediate and specific and/or arise directly from the court's decree, but find they are not an appropriate consideration where speculation as to a party's future dealings with property awarded to him or her would be required...[184]
>
> We agree with the rule adopted by most jurisdictions.... Mr. Hay testified at trial that he had no plans to sell his partnership interest.... We remand to enable the trial court to consider the property division without regard to the capital gains tax consequences of a hypothetical sale of H & L Investments.[185]

In a case of first impression in Nebraska, the Court held that it was erroneous to consider future tax consequences to the husband in valuing his corporation, as there was no evidence that a sale of the company would be reasonably certain to occur in the near future. However, the Court acknowledged that such tax consequences may be considered if the court determines that the property division award will force a party to sell the business to generate the cash needed to pay the court-imposed obligations.[186]

In *Hamilton v. Hamilton*,[187] where the husband would effectively have been forced to purchase the wife's shares in a company, the Court permitted a credit for capital gains taxes, even though there was no evidence of an imminent sale.

In *DeBuff v. DeBuff*,[188] the Montana Supreme Court held that the trial court committed an error when it failed to consider the tax consequences and liquidation costs the wife would incur when selling the farm business assets that were distributed to her because, the Court determined, the sale of the assets was imminent given that the wife had left the farm and was working as a grocery clerk.

In *Seiler v. Seiler*,[189] reasoning that the exact nature and amount of any tax consequences to the husband were speculative, the trial court considered the potential tax consequences in setting the amount of the wife's equalizing judgment. The appeals court affirmed, saying that "[a] business has a fair market value separate and apart from the financial circumstances of those who own it," and that "value can and should be established independently of the owner's individual tax liabilities."

This and similar cases lead us to raise a question as to the appropriate valuation approach or approaches. If the sale of the assets is so remote a possibility as to eliminate consideration of the capital gains tax liability, that calls into question using asset value as the only primary valuation approach. Perhaps an income approach would be more appropriate, or maybe an income approach should be blended with an asset-based approach.[190]

---

[184] Tracy A. Bateman, *Annotation Divorce and Separation: Consideration of Tax Consequences in Distribution of Marital Property*, 9 A.L.R. 5th 568, 592, 52[a] (1993).

[185] *Hay v. Hay*, No. 14368-6-III Wash. Ct. App. (Div. 3 Dec. 26, 1995).

[186] *Schuman v. Schuman*, 658 N.W.2d 30, 265 Neb. 459 (Neb. 2003).

[187] *Hamilton v. Hamilton*, 2002 Ohio 2417 (Ohio Ct. App. 2002).

[188] *DeBuff v. DeBuff*, 1999 Mt. 278N (Mont. 1999).

[189] *Seiler v. Seiler*, 118 Wash. App. 1022, 2003 WL 22022087 (Wash. Ct. App. 2003).

[190] See Shannon P. Pratt, "Trapped-in Capital Gains Affects Real-World Value," *Shannon Pratt's Business Valuation Update*, February 1996, pp. 1, 3.

Summary

This chapter discussed various states' appellate decisions on a variety of business valuation issues in the context of a marital dissolution. About the only issue on which there is general agreement is that the trial court must have adequate, credible evidence on which to base its findings.

Decisions varied considerably on most other issues:

- Standard of value
- Active versus passive appreciation
- Effective date of valuation
- When goodwill is or isn't marital property and how to value it
- Valuation methods
- The marital or nonmarital status of the value of actual or potential noncompete covenants and/or employment agreements
- The weight accorded buy-sell agreements
- Discounts for lack of control and/or lack of marketability
- Treatment of trapped-in capital gains tax liabilities

It is a frequently encountered paradox that courts say that they will not accept valuations that are dependent on future efforts of a spouse, and then in the same case accept valuation methods that inherently impound future efforts of the spouse (or restrictions on the spouse's future activities). An important part of the analyst's job is to educate the courts as to what credible evidence is available and why certain valuation methods are and are not appropriate in the particular situation. There is no business valuation litigation context in which this need is greater than in the family law courts.

In any case, within the marital dissolution context, it is incumbent on the attorney to provide the valuation analyst with a thorough review of the relevant judicial precedent.

Chapter 39

Fair Value for Financial Reporting

Definition of Fair Value
Differences from Fair Market Value
Disclosures

SFAS 157, "Fair Value Measurements," is effective for financial statements issued for fiscal years beginning after November 15, 2007, and for interim periods within those fiscal years.

Definition of Fair Value

The definition of fair value in SFAS 157 applies to all prior FASB pronouncements that require or permit fair value measurements. The definition is as follows:

> The price that would be received to sell an asset or paid to transfer a liability in an orderly transaction between market participants at the measurement date.

The important feature of this definition is that it is an *exit* price, *not* the price that would be paid to acquire the asset or to assume the liability (an *entry* price). SFAS 157 emphasizes that assets should not be valued at cost (an *entry* price) unless they can be disposed of at cost. They also should not be valued at either a constant discount or a formula discount, but between the purchase date and the first test for goodwill impairment. Remember, most assets are not written down to fair value unless they fail the 144 test.

The "market" referred to in this definition is "the market in which the reporting entity would transact for the asset or liability, that is, the principal or most advantageous market for the asset or liability." Thus, the definition specifies an orderly transaction in the most advantageous market. Market participants are buyers and sellers in the principal (or the most advantageous) market for the asset or liability. These market participants are (1) unrelated, (2) knowledgeable about factors relevant to the asset or liability and the transaction, (3) able to transact (i.e., have the legal and financial ability to do so), and (4) willing to transact (i.e., motivated but not forced or otherwise compelled to transact).

SFAS 157 clarifies that the term *fair value* is intended to mean a market-based measure, not an entity-specific measure. The fair value premise for an asset is the asset's highest and best use from the perspective of market participants, which would maximize a company's future cash inflows. A company's intended use of an asset is not necessarily indicative of the highest and best use of that asset as determined by a market participant; the fair value measure is *not* an entity-specific measure that reflects only the company's expectations for the asset. SFAS 157 requires that fair value measures consider the perspectives of market participants and the assumptions that those participants would use to price an asset or a liability. Determining market participants' assumptions will require companies to use a significant amount of judgment.

The market price on the valuation date is fair value if there is an active market for the subject asset or liability, but not if the market is thin. The FASB identifies three levels in the hierarchy of measurements to quantify fair value, with the highest level available to be used:

Level 1 (highest-priority) inputs are quoted prices in active markets for identical assets or liabilities.

Level 2 inputs are those other than quoted prices included within Level 1 that are directly or indirectly observable.

Level 3 inputs are unobservable inputs that reflect assumptions about what market participants would use in their pricing analyses.

This would imply that, if there is an active market for the subject asset, the quoted price on the valuation date would apply. For those assets for which there is not an active market but for which there is an active market for close comparables, the prices for the comparables, with appropriate adjustments for differences, could be used as inputs. The standard clearly favors observable market data. For other subject assets (Level 3 assets), other valuation methods, including DCF, could be used as inputs. The company may use its own assumptions, but Level 3 inputs must be adjusted if information is available that indicates that market participants would use different assumptions.

The FASB says that, for "unobservable inputs," the valuation should include market participant assumptions about risk, even if this adjustment is difficult to determine. Interestingly, it breaks risk into two categories:

1. The risk inherent in a particular valuation technique
2. The risk inherent in the inputs to the valuation technique

Differences from Fair Market Value

However, although the FASB emphasizes "market participant assumptions at the measurement date," there are differences between "fair value" for financial reporting purposes and "fair market value." For example, SFAS 157 apparently makes a (perhaps unintended) distinction between legally imposed restrictions on sale (e.g., restricted stock, which normally *should* be discounted) and market-imposed restrictions (e.g., blocks of stock that are too large to be sold without depressing the market, which *should not* be discounted for what the market refers to as "blockage"). Blocks of stock are to be valued at price times quantity, with no discount applied for the size of the block. However, there is the contrary opinion that no discounts are applied for SFAS 123R.[1]

The FASB says that it did not adopt the definition of fair market value because it did not want the definition of fair value to be saddled with the nuances of court interpretations of fair market value.

The fair value of a liability reflects its nonperformance risk (the risk that the obligation will not be fulfilled). Because the nonperformance risk includes the reporting entity's credit risk, the reporting entity should consider the effect of its credit risk (credit standing) on the fair value of the liability in all periods in which the liability is measured at fair value under other accounting pronouncements.

Disclosures

SFAS 157 expands disclosures about the use of fair value to measure assets and liabilities in both interim and annual periods subsequent to the initial recognition.

---

[1] Scott Beauchene and Robert Duffy, "Getting Ready for 409A: Some Practical Considerations," *Business Valuation Update,* May 2007.

The disclosures must specify in which level in the hierarchy the measurement falls. The disclosures focus on the inputs used to measure fair value using "significant unobservable inputs" (within Level 3 of the fair value hierarchy) and the effect of the measurements on earnings (or changes in net assets) for the period. The disclosures need to specify the valuation techniques used and any changes to the valuation techniques used.

SFAS 157 applies to derivatives and other financial instruments. It supersedes and nullifies contrary guidance in earlier accounting pronouncements. As such, it is intended to increase the consistency and comparability of fair value requirements and to expand the disclosures about fair value measurements. With its emphasis on expanded disclosure, it probably will mean many more footnotes in financial statements where inputs of Levels 2 and 3 are used to measure fair value.

Adjustments should be made to valuations made in accordance with prior practices that conflict with SFAS 157, such as discounts for blockage. The differences should be booked as an adjustment to retained earnings on the opening balance sheet for the fiscal year in which the statement is applied.

Part VIII

Litigation and Dispute Resolution

Chapter 40

Litigation Support Services

Valuation-Related Controversy Matters
Types of Litigation
    Contract Disputes
    Commercial Torts
    Business Interruption Claims
    Antitrust Claims
    Shareholder Disputes and Securities Litigation
    Marital Dissolution
    Personal Injury or Wrongful Termination Cases
    Estate, Gift, and Income Taxes
    State and Local Property Taxes
    Bankruptcy/Insolvency/Reorganization
    Intellectual Property Rights Infringement
Engaging the Appraiser
    Qualifications
    Conflicts of Interest
    Engagement Agreement
Discovery
Assessing the Case
Business Appraisal Discovery
    Permanent Files
    Accountant's Files
    Bank Files
    Invoices
    Interrogatories
    Depositions
    Research
Calculating the Amount of Damages
    The Before-and-After Method
    The Yardstick (Comparable) Method
    Sales Projections ("But For") Method
    Mitigation
    Summary of Damages
Work Product
    Affidavits

Frequently, commercial, taxation, or family law litigation involves a controversy over the value of assets, properties, or business interests. Appraisals that are performed within a litigation environment require that the analyst understand the legal context within which the appraisal is being made. The analyst should tailor his or her valuation work to address the facts and circumstances of the case, while taking into consideration all relevant statutory authority, judicial precedent, and administrative rulings. Prevailing statutory, judicial, or administrative law often varies considerably from one valuation purpose to another, and even from one jurisdiction to another for valuations for the same purpose (e.g., dissenting stockholder actions or marital property distribution). This means that the very same business interest could have a different value depending on the legal context in which it applies.

This chapter precedes the chapter on expert witness testimony, deliberately separating the subject of general litigation support from the subject of expert testimony. In this chapter, we discuss several valuation consulting, economic analysis, and financial advisory services within the context of litigation support and dispute resolution.

Valuation-Related Controversy Matters

Many valuation-related disputes can be resolved before a trial is necessary. The odds of a favorable resolution are substantially increased when clients work closely from the very beginning with an appraiser who is experienced in litigation and dispute resolution matters. An experienced appraiser can be very helpful in assessing the merits of the case, both in estimating a reasonable range of values and in weighing the risks involved in going to court. If the case cannot be resolved outside the courtroom, then at least the decision to go to court will be based on a sound assessment of the situation from a valuation viewpoint. And, the preparation for the litigation may be more orderly, thorough, and cost-efficient.

When clients or their counsel assess valuation-related litigation issues without the assistance of an experienced appraiser, then the interests of the client are not best served. These situations usually arise when principals or their counsel attempt to minimize the expert's fees, when they do not know how to locate an appraiser experienced in controversy matters, or when they do not fully understand the best way to utilize the appraiser's experience and expertise. In any event, when contacted late, the appraiser's ability to provide the best advice may be constrained.

It is also important to integrate expert witness testimony with other litigation support services. In order to support or refute a plaintiff's claim of damages, expertise in several areas is often required in order to assess the significant factors affecting the plaintiff's likely activities (absent the alleged wrongful action) and in order to ascertain whether the defendant's actions were indeed the principal cause for the harm to the plaintiff. Damage cases in which significant dollar amounts are at stake may require that a number of experts—including industry, accounting, finance, and economics experts—be retained both by the plaintiff and by the defendant, in order to adequately address the specific questions relating to their areas of expertise.

An appraiser can sometimes help select and supervise other experts. Specialized experts may be needed to address certain elements that impact the value of an asset, property, or business interest, such as industry experts or experts in specific types of property. Appraisers often maintain relationships with such advisers because they need to call on them from time to time for informational or other purposes. For various reasons, the attorney may call in more than one appraisal expert: (1) in order to place more than one expert's opinion before the trier of fact; (2) in order to have an expert concentrate on certain especially controversial or critical aspects of the case, such as the appropriateness of a certain method or the quantification of some premium or discount; or (3) in order to have one expert for the case in chief and another for rebuttal.

One valuable litigation support service of an experienced appraiser is to review and critique materials and expert reports prepared by other experts on the same side of the case. In some situations, for a variety of reasons, such a review can be part of the input an attorney needs in order to decide whether to call in a particular expert to testify. In other cases, the review may help focus and buttress the testimony to be presented by a particular expert.

An independent appraiser is an advocate for his or her position only, and not an advocate for the client. The independent appraiser may assist both the client and the lawyer in preparing the best possible case. However, when it comes to the independent expert's opinion, the expert must present an unbiased, impartial position on all substantive issues on which he or she has been asked for an opinion. The independent expert must remain free from both actual bias and the appearance of bias. If the attorney believes that any litigation support functions that the independent expert otherwise might logically perform would create the perception of a bias, then the attorney might wish to have these services performed by other professionals.

The vast majority of valuation-related controversy matters never reaches the stage of requiring expert testimony before a trier of fact (judge, jury, arbitrator, or other tribunal). Accordingly, thoroughly documented appraisals can contribute significantly to successful settlements of valuation-related controversies. The same level of analytical rigor and appraisal documentation that leads to successful settlements can also provide the underpinnings for proper trial preparation. It is often said that the best way to facilitate a successful settlement is to begin preparing from the outset as if the case were going to court; the client's best position in negotiating is from a position of strength.

Types of Litigation

Commercial litigation claims typically involve the determination of the occurrence of an action, the cause of the action, and the amount of damages that are related to the action. Appraisers and economists are frequently called upon to

timberland and forestry operations, chemical processing plants, gas and electric utilities and power generation plants, data processing and telecommunications facilities, high-technology properties, railroads and regulated industries, farm land and agricultural properties, hotels and motels, strip and enclosed shopping malls, and mixed-use properties. In such valuation controversies, it is often important to separately identify and appraise nontaxable intangible personal property (or other nonassessable) assets. See Chapter 34 for further discussion on the topic of ad valorem taxation–related valuation matters.

Bankruptcy/Insolvency/Reorganization

The appraiser may be called upon to independently create or assess a reorganization plan, to analyze debt and equity capital restructuring proposals, to review financial forecasts and projections, to value various classes of collateral, to test the going-concern versus liquidation presumptions of plans of reorganization or liquidation, to identify spinoff opportunities, to prepare fraudulent conveyance analyses, or to express a solvency or insolvency opinion—to name a few typical financial advisory services.

Intellectual Property Rights Infringement

In what has become a common occurrence in the information age, claims of intellectual property rights infringement involve trademarks, trade names, copyrights, patents, proprietary technology and trade secrets, computer software, and many other intangible assets and intellectual properties.[1]

Engaging the Appraiser

An appraiser providing expertise in a litigated valuation case serves as a "forensic economist" in that the appraiser is using expertise in the microeconomic analysis of property valuation. It is important to retain appraisers who can not only use their education and experience to develop and support a sound position but also communicate that position intellengtly in terms that a judge and/or jury can understand. It is important to evaluate appraisers' abilities through the examination of their credentials and experience, their reputations, their references, and/or personal interviews. There have been three U.S. Supreme Court cases upholding the lower courts' exclusions of expert testimony. These cases are discussed further in the following chapter on expert testimony.

Qualifications

Although previous litigation experience is helpful, it is also important for the appraiser to have the benefit of "real-world" transactional experience along with the experience of testifying in a courtroom.

---

[1] For further information on this subject, see Robert F. Reilly and Robert P. Schweihs, *Valuing Intangible Assets* (New York: McGraw Hill, 1999).

Valuation issues are affected by a wide variety of legal mandates and precedents. Such mandates and precedents differ significantly in their application to various valuation purposes. Even for valuations for similar purposes, both statutory authority and judicial precedent are subject to considerable variation from one jurisdiction to another. Many statutes and court decisions contain vague or ambiguous wording, so that an understanding of different interpretations from one jurisdiction to another may require study of several cases. Ignorance of these variations can result in misdirection in litigation-related valuation work. Of course, the attorney must finally decide any legal matter; nevertheless, such decisions can be greatly enhanced by appraisers who have a good working knowledge of the valuation-related aspects of the law.

The research and other professional resources of the appraiser's firm are often an essential component of the appraiser's ability to successfully perform litigation support and dispute resolution services. Accordingly, the appraiser should have a collegial staff with appropriate qualifications, with the ability to meet the required deadlines, and of a size necessary to carry out the research and analytical requirements of the case. Library and other research resources are time-consuming and expensive to develop. Even in this age of online services, a crucial task in the controversy process is to index and organize documents, articles, statistical data, published court cases, and miscellaneous economic, industry, and corporate reports. Having the relevant research material is critical to the appraiser involved in a controversy matter, but so is having that material well organized, indexed, and easily accessible.

Active involvement in professional organizations and activities may increase an appraiser's ability to provide effective litigation support. These activities include attending seminars sponsored by leading professional appraisal organizations and by specific industry trade associations, speaking at such programs, and writing for well-recognized professional publications. These activities help to keep the appraiser current on the thinking and the developments in the mainstream of the profession and to expose the appraiser's own thinking to peer scrutiny.

To establish whether there is a concurrence of valuation philosophy, the attorney may wish to approach the prospective witness with a hypothetical scenario. In this way, the attorney can get some idea of the methods and parameters the witness would use in reaching the value conclusion without revealing the client's name or identifying the actual asset, property, or business interest to be valued. One of the nuances of this exercise is that the credibility of the potential witness is maintained if it can be established that he or she was hired to ascertain a value independently, and not to testify to some value predetermined by the interested party.

This comparison of valuation philosophies is as important to the appraiser as it is to the client, since no reputable appraiser wants to be under pressure to testify to a conclusion that cannot be professionally supported. Usually, a brief dialogue between an experienced attorney and an experienced appraiser is all that is necessary to determine whether the appraiser can be useful as a witness on the specific case.

Conflicts of Interest

The appraiser should be independent of the parties on both sides of the case. Very early in the proceedings, the attorney must disclose the names of all of the parties in the case to the prospective witness in order to ascertain that there is no conflict of interest. Apart from having already been retained by the opposing party, the most common conflict of interest would be having a financial or investment interest that would introduce a conflict of interest whether actual or perceived. Potential conflicts should be promptly disclosed to the client and/or the client's attorney, because the appearance of a conflict can discredit a witness (whether the witness considers it a conflict or not).

In general, it is not a disqualifying conflict for the appraiser to have performed services for the opposing party. It is never a disqualifying conflict that the appraiser has been retained on unrelated assignments by the opposing party's law firm. On the contrary, that may be viewed as a sign of professional integrity and independence. For example, the author has performed quite a number of taxation-related valuation and economic analysis assignments both for the Internal Revenue Service and for corporate and individual taxpayers.

One common problem that can arise is when the appraiser is interviewed by one side and not retained, and then is contacted by the other side. A potential problem can be avoided if the appraiser makes it clear to the attorney in initial interviews that no confidential information or analysis should be shared until after the appraiser has been formally retained.

Engagement Agreement

In many cases, engagement agreements for litigation support services give very little detail, often because the attorneys have not yet determined exactly what services they will need from the appraiser. It is not uncommon for the appraiser to assist the attorney at various points in the case with regard to focusing the issues, gathering the data, and developing the scope of the assignment. While it is important to include as many of the elements of the assignment as possible, the engagement agreement may become discoverable by the other side, along with drafts and modifications to the agreement. Since the legal strategy of the case may change after the engagement has commenced—and since attorneys don't want their legal strategies to be discovered—standardized, nondescriptive engagement letters are often used for litigation support projects. However, analysts will want to balance this with protecting their own self-interests, as an engagement letter that says too little will not afford analysts the very protection it is supposed to be designed to offer in the first place.

If the appraiser knows enough about the property to be analyzed to estimate the time required, the assignment itself may be performed for a fixed fee or within a narrow estimated fee range. Otherwise, a fee based upon hourly billing rates is usually adopted.

Often, litigation cases can be structured in advance around specific tasks and a specific work product. For example, the first phase, at a predetermined budgeted amount, could include an assessment of the case, some preliminary consultation with the attorney regarding the apparent merits of the case, and a brief critique of the opponent's work product. Subsequent phases might include a detailed valuation work plan, a review of material provided in response to a document request, a preliminary range of value conclusions, an analysis of the benefits and costs of pursuing litigation, a full narrative valuation opinion report, and so forth.

The amount of time to be spent in depositions, preparation with attorneys for court, observation and testifying in court, and other aspects of litigation support are normally beyond the appraiser's control. For that reason, the compensation for these services usually is made on an hourly basis, at a specific hourly rate. The attorney and the appraiser often cooperate in order to structure the compensation to be flexible enough to accommodate the many uncertainties involved in litigation but rigid enough that the expert will not become a party at interest to the outcome of the case.

> Make sure you receive the check for your airfare, estimated hotel expenses and three days of your time before you leave home for a trial.... If it comes out in court that you have not been paid lately, the jury may think the outcome of the case is very important to you. Your objectivity may be suspect....
>
> **Q:** *Does your client owe you any money?*
> **A:** *No. My bills have been paid to date and my expenses for this trip were paid in advance. My being paid does not depend on the outcome of this case.*[2]

Discovery

Within the area of litigation, one of the most important tasks that can be performed by the appraiser or economist is assisting the attorney with discovery. Unfortunately, many appraisers concentrate on selecting the correct valuation procedures, which are then applied to either meaningless or unreliable financial information. It is extremely important that the appraiser be brought in at the early stages of a case in order to assure that the necessary information is gathered before the actual valuation is started.

In most cases, the more cooperative and less formalized the discovery process, the better both parties are served. If all parties are willing to cooperate, it is often easiest for experts to gather sufficient information for a thorough understanding by directly contacting the information sources rather than by working through the attorneys. It is not unusual for an unconstrained discovery process to uncover previously misinterpreted facts, leading to a settlement of the case, especially in divorce cases and shareholder disputes.

When the parties are unwilling to cooperate, the experts must, of course, rely on the attorneys to enforce discovery of the necessary information. If the information is delayed or documents do not arrive on a timely basis, then the attorneys must follow up immediately and vigorously. Further, it is up to the experts to keep the attorneys informed about whether the requested information is arriving in a timely manner. Keeping the attorneys apprised in this way will facilitate their follow-up and make it possible for them to accurately report to the court about the receipt of information.

In virtually all valuation cases, there is a standard set of documents that are needed for the business valuation. For private companies, these documents will usually include historical and (if available) prospective operating statements, income tax returns, ownership lists, prior transaction information, important contracts, and documentation of the ownership of the subject assets, properties, and business interests (for an example of a document request list, see Exhibit 4–1).

---

[2] Daniel F. Poynter, *Expert Witness Handbook* (Santa Barbara, CA: Para Publishing, 1987).

Public companies may also have additional documents such as management or outside advisers' presentations to the board of directors.

The appraiser should compose a list tailored as specifically as possible to the particular situation, given what is known about it at the time, and provide for one or more follow-up requests. This is because it is usually impossible to know what every relevant document will be until the appraiser has reviewed the initial batch of data and knows more about the appraisal subject. It may be possible to fill in unknowns through questions at depositions.

If the appraiser can expect to receive the parties' cooperation, then the initial documents request need cover only the known essentials, and the expert can inspect additional documents during a field visit and/or include them in a supplementary request as necessary. If the parties refuse to cooperate, then the initial documents list must be as complete as possible. Even so, lists that demand voluminous material of little or no direct relevance serve no useful purpose and often delay discovery on the grounds that the demand is unreasonably burdensome. The appraiser's experience and judgment can help generate a reasonable and manageable documents list for the specific circumstances.

Assessing the Case

Matters such as the applicable standard of value and the relevant valuation date or dates are not always as obvious as they might appear on the surface. In many controversy cases, there is no statutorily defined standard of value or applicable valuation date. Sometimes the relative rights of various parties at interest are very complex and careful definition of the property and its relevant rights and restrictions is a crucial prerequisite to the assignment itself. Ultimately, the attorney must decide the question or questions to ask the appraiser to address. Often the appraiser's knowledge and experience can be very helpful in focusing the relevant questions, in defining the case, and to achieving a successful outcome.

Once the basic work plan is framed, the appraiser may be asked to do some preliminary work to suggest a reasonable range of value within which the final conclusion might be expected to fall. Often, it is possible to provide such information on a preliminary basis. The preliminary range of values can help the attorney decide on the litigation posture. Sometimes the most valuable service that an appraiser can perform for clients is to tell them what they don't want to hear—that the value is not what they suspected and, at least from a monetary standpoint, the case is not what it appeared to be. Heading off financially unproductive litigation can save the client tens of thousands of dollars. When each side is provided with an opinion as to a reasonable range of value from a genuinely competent appraiser, the groundwork for a settlement is often laid. On the other hand, if a settlement cannot be reached, the preliminary range of value the appraiser provides lends some confidence to a decision to proceed with litigation.

Often the appraiser can facilitate the identification and quantification of areas of financial uncertainty so that the attorney can better assess the risks of litigation. Sometimes reasonable people will reach different conclusions because of different assessments of the economic or other exogenous factors affecting the subject asset, property, or business interest. Sometimes there may be contingent assets or liabilities that may have a substantial impact on the appraiser's estimation of value.

It often helps to try to quantify the risk that arises from various uncertainties. For example, if the preliminary range of value is between $8 million and $12 million, the litigation posture could be significantly different than if the preliminary range of value is between $0 and $20 million.

After the valuation issues have been framed and a preliminary range of values has been estimated, the attorney is in a better position to assess the relationship between the litigation's potential benefits and costs. In making this analysis, the attorney may ask the appraiser to estimate some range of likely or possible costs to complete the case, including preparation for testimony, depositions, direct- and cross-examination at trial, and the preparation of post-trial briefs. Possibly the most important of all of these fees are those related to pretrial preparation between the appraiser and the attorney handling the case. Also, in the heat of litigation, costs tend to exceed expectations more often than be less. Appraisers, attorneys, and clients should fully consider the difficulty of controlling deposition and court time and, especially, the costs of responding to possible unknown material that the opposition may present.

Business Appraisal Discovery

A business valuation is heavily influenced by the company's financial condition and its operations, so it is important for the appraiser to have the necessary and meaningful financial and operational data regarding the subject company. Many times this data comes from outside the company and from atypical places.

Discovery can be very time-intensive. Engagements often require a high-level professional to be on site (someone who can think on his or her feet as information is discovered). In some cases, it may not be possible to delegate the assignment at all. Scheduling also becomes quite important in terms of properly managing the engagement.

Permanent Files

A set of documents that may provide meaningful information is the company's permanent files, such as the stock register, articles of incorporation, bylaws, shareholder and/or board of director meeting minutes, and other legal documents. The originals of these documents are sometimes maintained by the company's corporate counsel. Many times, these documents will contain financial projections, buy-sell agreements, references to contractual commitments, evidence of prior sales of interests in the company, and so on.

Accountant's Files

The company's independent accounting firm is often a source of information. These files contain working copies of the historical financial statements and tax returns, but will also contain supporting documents, legal documents, accountants' notes, correspondence with the company, and other data that are not necessarily part of the company's records. When reviewing these records, the appraiser should understand the accountant's materiality standard. The materiality standard adopted by the accountant for financial statement reporting purposes may not be consistent with the materiality standard required for the subject litigation. For example, the company's capital expenditure practices and fixed asset record keeping practices may be summarized by the accountant for financial statement reporting purposes, but may contain details that would be extremely relevant to the litigation. Another example is when employee stock option grants are not required to be reported on financial statements but would be critical to accurately report the per share valuation conclusion. An offer to buy or sell the company may be in the accountant's files too.

Many times, the accountant's working papers will resolve questions that the appraiser may have, thus saving the time and expense of the appraiser replicating the already completed work. As an example, the accountant's papers may explain why certain expense categories increased or decreased from normal levels during a single accounting period, or may disclose unusual or nonrecurring income or expenses of the business. The analyst should always realize, of course, that generally accepted accounting principles allow substantial flexibility, and accounting practices for many closely held businesses may be influenced by tax issues.

Bank Files

If the company has an operating line of credit, or has used bank financing to finance the purchase of business assets, then the bank that provides the financing will maintain a loan file on the company. This bank loan file may contain many documents that are relevant to the subject valuation, including the following:

1. The loan application and financial worth statement of the company and/or the company's owner
2. Prior financial statements of the company
3. Memorandums from the loan officer that disclose additional information on the company or the financial statements that may not be apparent from a review of those statements
4. Articles and other data on the company and on the industry in which the company participates

The analyst must always consider, of course, the extent to which information submitted to the bank may paint an especially optimistic picture to support the credit accommodation. It should also be noted that accountants' files legally belong to the accountant, and bank files are the property of the bank. Therefore, in some cases, these files may not be accessible, even by subpoena, in a litigation.

Invoices

Many times a review of selected company invoices may be necessary. As an example, if the company is being valued for purposes of a marital dissolution and if the appraiser notices that the legal and accounting expenses for the business have increased substantially in the most recent financial statements, a review of the paid invoices may be in order. A review may disclose that the fees were not for business purposes but were primarily related to the owner's own personal legal and accounting problems. Also, payments near year-end may be prepayments of future expenses even though they were classified as payments for goods or services already rendered.

Interrogatories

Interrogatories are far more cumbersome than interactive questions and answers. For one thing, the next logical question often depends upon the answer to the prior question. Moreover, in an interactive situation, the respondent has the opportunity to clarify and perhaps narrow the scope of a broad inquiry, which may save considerable time and expense in complying with the inquiry. As with the documents request list, the burden of the initial interrogatories can be eased for both parties if they provide for follow-up interrogatories. In developing suggested questions, the appraiser must keep in mind both the scope of the inquiry and the clarity of wording in order to elicit what is intended and relevant. Also, as with the document request list, the appraiser's experience and judgment can be invaluable in developing relevant and incisive interrogatories.

Depositions

Information can be gathered from depositions of fact witnesses and from other expert witnesses. The appraiser can help the attorney prepare for both categories of deposition. The appraiser can suggest areas of questioning that will enhance the information on which to base his or her expert opinion. The purpose of deposing the fact witness is to get information to supplement that obtained from documents and to ensure that the witness is as committed as far as possible to whatever the factual testimony will be.

The purpose of deposing opposing experts usually is to understand what they have done, what they have concluded, and the basis for their conclusions. In some cases, where settlement is the object, the deposition can be a powerful tool of persuasion by exposing the weaknesses in the expert's analysis. Attorneys can widen their perspective by calling on their own experts for some guidance in deposing opposing experts.

The attorney may have his or her own expert, or a member of the expert's staff, on hand when deposing the opponent's experts. The appraiser can thus point out lines of questioning that might elude the attorney but are perfectly logical to one with specific knowledge of information sources, various valuation techniques, and all the calculations and jargon current in the valuation profession. A meaningful deposition prevents experts from going into court still wondering exactly what the opposing experts did in developing their opinions. In many cases, information and insights gained through an incisive deposition can lead the parties to a settlement.

Research

Appraisers and their staffs can support litigation by providing research on such topics as economic and industry data, guideline company data, comparative transaction data, authority for positions on valuation issues, and many others. Specific research assignments may be tailored to the needs of a particular case.

The results of this research may eventually be incorporated into expert testimony or brought into evidence in other ways. Attorneys in cross-examination, arguments, and briefs may also use such information.

Calculating the Amount of Damages

Although the burden of proof regarding damages rests with the plaintiff, and at times may appear to represent a near monumental task, defendants assume significant risk when they rely upon a plaintiff's inability to calculate exact damages. This is because the court may merely require that the plaintiff's presentation be reasonable. It is essential that defendants provide expert evidence as to the actual amount of damages (or lack of damages). Otherwise, a defendant may end up facing a significant liability at the conclusion of the trial, regardless of how weak the plaintiff's presentation may have been, because that presentation was the only proof provided.

Economic damages often require or may benefit from the use of business valuation methods. Both disciplines rely heavily on the income approach method. Damages experts need not consider more than one approach or method and need not limit their examination to data that were available prior to the valuation date. Any business valuation analyst who is asked to express an opinion regarding economic damages should be careful to recognize the many differences between these two disciplines.[3]

Though the circumstances surrounding different damage claims will determine the specific type of claim filed (e.g., breach of contract, antitrust, lost business opportunity), the methods used to calculate claims are fairly standard. With the exception of breach of contract, which is often covered by liquidated damages and other provisions within the contract itself, most damage claims can be calculated by administering one or more of the following methods:

1. Before and after
2. Yardstick (comparable)
3. Sales projection ("but for")

However, no matter what measure of damages is used, the analysis of the amount of loss is always calculated as: [what the plaintiff would have made] minus [what the plaintiff did make] equals loss. If the losses are projected into the future, then they are subject to present value based on the certainty of their receipt. If damages are for historical periods, then the award will be subject to prejudgment interest. Such interest varies by jurisdiction.

The Before-and-After Method

Using the before-and-after method, economic income is estimated during the damage period based upon results (1) attained prior to the alleged damaging acts, and/or (2) after the effects of the alleged acts have subsided, and either or both of

---

[3] For more information on the differences between economic damages estimates and business valuation, see John R. Phillips and Michael Joseph Wagner, "Economic Damages: Use and Abuse of Business Valuation Concepts" (Chapter 14) in *The Handbook of Advanced Business Valuation*, Robert F. Reilly and Robert P. Schweihs, eds. (New York, McGraw-Hill, 2000).

these is compared with results during the period of the effect of the alleged acts. The success of this method depends, of course, on the ability of the expert to establish and support a proven historical financial record for the subject property so that operations preceding and succeeding the event are able to serve as "damage bookends," clearly illustrating the effects of the interruption or the violation period. Ideally, operations before and after the damage period will show similar trends, thereby enabling the expert to estimate the subject property's performance during the damage period using either pre- or postdamage operations as a performance standard with comparable damage amounts resulting. In many cases, only the "before" period or the "after" period is available for use to predict the "but for" performance during the damage period.

The Yardstick (Comparable) Method

The yardstick, or comparable, method requires the expert to identify companies or industries that are comparable to the plaintiff's company and plot the performance of the plaintiff's company along the lines of the comparable companies' or industry's performances. This method, of course, requires that the expert not only satisfy the often difficult task of identifying similar companies or industries, but also that the companies or industries selected by the expert be, themselves, unaffected by the alleged damaging acts of the defendant. Applying as a proxy the performance of another company or a particular industry to project the performance of the subject company, absent the alleged damaging actions of the defendant, is a straightforward, understandable method in estimating losses. Once again, the key lies in carefully identifying the most appropriate guideline companies or industry. In some instances, a comparable but unaffected branch or division of the subject company may provide the needed yardstick.

Sales Projections ("But For") Method

The sales projections, or "but for," method entails the creation of a performance model for the subject company, complete with growth and return estimates. Using the model, operations for the subject company are projected during the damage period absent (i.e., "but for") the alleged effects of the defendant's actions. The returns suggested by the model are then compared with the actual results realized by the company during the period.

Of these three methods, probably the most often applied method is some variation of the sales projection method. Typically, most business operators are in a position to provide sales projections for their businesses, and fit within one of a countless number of industries subject to annual, semiannual, or even quarterly projections by a variety of both public and private data sources. Such circumstances lend themselves quite nicely to the development of simulation models designed specifically for the subject business. However, a key factor to keep in mind when developing a sales projection and the resulting profits is that courts tend to prefer projections based on historical track records, even in light of numerous concurring industry forecasts and other published financial data regarding "normal" growth and returns for participants within the relevant industry.

Regardless of the method undertaken, the extent to which projected results exceed actual results represents the plaintiff's loss. This loss often not only represents profits lost during the damage period, but also can, and often does, represent a decrease in overall business value separate from lost profits. Whatever is represented by the total damage claim, all concerned parties should bear in mind that the sum total of combined lost profits and any decrease in overall business value is limited to the present value of total future profits anticipated by the business prior to the alleged damaging acts. The reason is that the value of any business is the present (discounted) value of all expected future profits. Intuitively, this should serve as a recurring reasonableness check throughout the calculation process.

Mitigation

The principle of mitigation suggests that even victims of contract breaches have a duty to mitigate damages—that is, to keep them as low as possible—and that damages are not recoverable for losses that the injured party could have avoided without undue risk, burden, or humiliation. Even in fraud situations, courts have long held that once a plaintiff learns of the fraud, alleged damages that accrue thereafter are not caused by the fraud, but rather by the plaintiff's decision to continue its relationship with the defendant irrespective of the plaintiff's knowledge of the fraud.

With regard to buyers and sellers of goods or services, the buyer is required by the principle of mitigation to "cover" by making reasonable efforts to find replacement goods or services to purchase, while a breached seller is obligated to make reasonable efforts to find an alternative purchaser for the breached goods or services. Excess costs incurred by the buyer in acquiring replacement goods, differences between the contract price and the resale price incurred by the seller, and incidental damages such as expenses incurred in stopping the manufacture of goods, and inspecting, transporting, receiving, or storing goods that resulted from the breach are normally recoverable. The burden of proof for mitigation of damages lies with the defendant, and if the defendant fails to raise it during the case in chief, the issue cannot be raised on appeal. Therefore, it should be a part of the defense where appropriate.

Summary of Damages

In general, damage cases require a creative, but realistic, approach to calculating "hypothetical" values absent the alleged effects of the damaging party's actions. A thorough understanding of the damaged party's industry is important in any damage calculation, and, if available, a historical record of the damaged party's operations should be beneficial. Knowledge of case law will provide the expert with important guidance regarding approaches and methods that the courts will or will not accept in the calculation of damages in the specific legal context in question.

Work Product

Reports that the expert may provide can range from an oral expression of the analysis and conclusions, a single letter addressing a single fact or conclusion, to a detailed narrative report.

Affidavits

The purpose of an affidavit is to put a sworn statement before the court without the author's physical presence. Affidavits are most commonly used in connection with pretrial matters, but sometimes they are introduced as evidence in a trial. The subject matter of an affidavit can be anything from scheduling information, such as the days on which an expert is and is not available for testimony, to a statement of an expert's opinion with a summary of the supporting reasons. Care must be given as to the information provided because it can be damaging to the credibility of the affiant if later his or her opinion changes during the course of the trial.

Written Reports

For valuation cases in some jurisdictions, it is mandatory for the opposing parties to exchange written reports no later than 30 days prior to the call of the trial docket. In U.S. Tax Court, for example, the expert report typically serves as the appraiser's direct testimony. In other jurisdictions, the manner in which expert opinion is expressed is a critical component of the litigation strategy and is left to the attorney's discretion. In such jurisdictions, some attorneys insist on a written report, others decide whether to have a written report on a case-by-case basis. Some attorneys believe that a written report or even knowledge that a written report is available detracts from the court's attention to the expert's testimony during the trial. If a written report is to be prepared for litigation purposes, then it normally will follow the guidelines discussed in Chapter 20, "Writing the Business Valuation Report."

Critique of the Opposition

In many litigated valuations, the process of critiquing the opposition's position is as important to reaching a satisfactory resolution as preparing the valuation case in chief—or even more so. After all, if the opposition's position is found to be unsound and indefensible, there probably would be no case.

The critique of an opposing expert's report or presentation may take place at any time from the outset of possible litigation throughout the trial itself. If an expert's report is available at the beginning stage of assessing the case, it is important to review it at that time. It may be an entirely sound piece of work, and an early review may result in a recommendation to accept it or possibly to negotiate some minor modifications, thus forestalling thousands of dollars of futile litigation costs.

If the opposition's expert is off base, it is good to know why as soon as possible. The more sophisticated the expert on the other side, the more likely it is that a settlement can be reached through narrowing and compromising on the valuation issues that are genuinely arguable. If the other side has used an inexperienced expert, then it is usually much more difficult to engage in a constructive exchange leading to a resolution short of the courtroom. However, settlement may be achieved on the basis of a rebuttal report which exposes the other side's weaknesses. In any case, the appraiser must provide the attorney with an understanding of the strengths and weaknesses of the opposing expert's position.

Expert Testimony

Obviously, one of the most important litigation support services available from appraisers and economists is expert witness testimony. Deposition and court testimony are the subjects of the next chapter.

Rebuttal

The type of rebuttal needed largely depends, of course, on what is wrong with the other expert's work. If the expert has made a mathematical error, that should be brought to the court's attention, along with its impact on the conclusion. If the expert has taken a position unsupported by the preponderance of authority on an issue, evidence as to the preponderance of authority must be researched and developed. For example, if the opposition takes the position that there should be no discount from enterprise value when estimating the fair market value of a noncontrolling stock interest, then the rebuttal should cite authoritative regulations, texts, articles, and other sources that make it clear that such a discount should be taken. If the expert's approaches are basically sound, but the expert has reached a poor conclusion because of inadequate and/or erroneous data, then the best rebuttal approach may be to recalculate the results with his or her own methodology, but using complete and accurate data.

Assistance in Preparing Briefs

Appraisers who have testified and either listened to or read the testimony of an opposing expert tend to have a sharp sense of the difference between their own and their opponents' positions on the important valuation issues. Briefs in a case are enriched by a good expert's insights; the appraiser can help bring these differences into sharp focus, particularly as they apply to issues that have the greatest monetary impact, and can express clear, concise reasons why his or her position is superior. The attorney may want to take advantage of the appraiser's insights by discussing the briefs before preparing them or by having the appraiser review the briefs in draft form.

Similarly, the appraiser often can provide a special understanding of the opponent's briefs. One thing to look for is any mischaracterization of the appraiser's own evidence or testimony; another is any unjustifiable conclusions or implications made on the basis of the opposing expert's testimony. Sometimes the appraiser reviewing the opposing briefs will notice a clearly erroneous factual statement on some valuation matter that the attorney reading the brief might not realize is an error. A review by the appraiser is a good safety check for ensuring that any unwarranted contentions do not go unnoticed but are treated with a firm and convincing reply.

Summary

This chapter has presented a brief discussion of many of the important litigation support services that an appraiser or economist can provide in addition to expert testimony. It is beneficial to engage the expert's assistance at an early point in the litigation proceedings so that such services, particularly as they relate to the discovery process, can be fully integrated with the anticipated expert testimony. Very often, the expert's services may facilitate a settlement rather than culminate in expert testimony in court.

Although the appraiser may be of great assistance in many ways in preparing and administrating the case, it is essential that the attorney and the client fully respect the appraiser's independence in arriving at any opinion. The appraiser should not only avoid bias in fact, the appraiser should also avoid the appearance of bias. For this reason, it may be preferable to have certain litigation support services performed by another appraiser. In any case, the effective use of the appraiser's expertise in providing litigation support services can facilitate an expeditious and satisfactory outcome in many controversy cases.

Chapter 41

Expert Testimony

"Give your evidence," said the King; "and don't be nervous, or I'll have you executed on the spot."[1]

Court testimony challenges an expert witness because it is part of an adversarial proceeding. If the opposite side were willing to accept the witness's valuation, there probably would be a settlement instead of a trial. Indeed, most valuation cases settle before they reach the courtroom, especially if the witness has prepared the case thoroughly and the attorney has drawn on the expert's research in negotiating with the opposition. Thus, if the case goes to court, it's because of sharp disagreement. Competent, thorough preparation must culminate in a clear and convincing presentation.

It is essential that an analyst be objective and unbiased when legal testimony is involved. One school of thought holds that, since courts in some situations tend to split the difference between opposing positions, an analyst must take an extreme position, because that is the only strategy that will lead to a fair court result. To be effective, the expert witness should arrive at a figure that he or she expects to present and defend without compromise on cross-examination. Usually, a rigorously prepared, convincingly presented, objective case will prevail over an extreme position, which a competent judge will tend to discredit. The only reasonable expectation is that courts will adopt the well-supported position of one side of a case without compromise.[2] Before preparing the presentation of the analysis, consider the typical areas of impeachment:

- Unsatisfactory credentials
- Advocacy or bias
- Contrary prior opinions
- Report inconsistencies
- Faulty facts or foundation
- Incompetent authority
- Insufficient or inaccurate data

This chapter follows the typical sequence of a business valuation expert witness engagement. As it relates to damage cases, this chapter focuses on the damages calculations and not on the "liability" or "causation" portions of such cases.

Background Preparation

When legal controversy is involved, there is no substitute for thorough homework and preparation. The expert witness virtually must prepare not only his or her own case, but the other side's as well. The expert valuation witness must attempt to anticipate any apparent weaknesses that the opposing attorney may seize upon in cross-examination and be prepared to defend against attacks on them. Also, the expert witness should be prepared to critique the case the opposing side presents.

Basic Preparation and Documentation

The basic research itself should follow the principles and procedures previously outlined in this book. In legal testimony, one must rely as much as possible on

---

[1] Lewis Carroll, *Alice's Adventures in Wonderland* (Middlesex, England: Puffin Books, Penguin Books, Ltd., 1946).

[2] See, for example, *Estate of Saul R. Gilford v. Commissioner*, 88 T.C. 38 (1987); *Estate of Albert L. Dougherty v. Commissioner*, 59 T.C.M. 772 (1990); and *Estate of Eric Stroben v. Commissioner*, T.C. Memo 1992-350 (June 22, 1992).

facts, not on conjecture. Documentation is the foundation of every step. It makes no difference how thoroughly the witness is personally convinced of the validity of the facts and conclusions if he or she is unable to convince the court. While complete documentation undoubtedly helps the opposition, omitting or obscuring helpful information deprives the judge and the jury of useful assistance.

If the witness were presenting the company in question to a prospective buyer, it might be valid to presume that the buyer knows something about the business or industry involved. However, an appraiser cannot presume that the court can have the prospective buyer's sophistication about every business brought before it. Every fact on which the witness intends to rely in reaching his or her conclusion must be presented, along with whatever supporting documentation is necessary for convincing the court that it should indeed rely upon that fact.

Moreover, unlike the situation of presenting the company to a prospective buyer, in which the analyst would have an opportunity, at the buyer's request, to research and provide supplementary information, the expert has no such chance in court. The analyst cannot take a couple of weeks to do additional homework and come back for another audience. The court, however concerned it may be with reaching an equitable decision, will make its determination based on the initial presentation, however inadequate. Thus, the research had better be thorough the first time around.

Federal Rules of Civil Procedure

Rule 26 of the *Federal Rules of Civil Procedure* took effect December 1, 1993. Particularly relevant for expert witnesses are the requirements for disclosure of expert testimony:

(2) Disclosure of Expert Testimony.

(A) In addition to the disclosures required by paragraph (1), a party shall disclose to other parties the identity of any person who may be used at trial to present evidence under rules 702, 703, or 705 of the federal rules of evidence.

(B) Except as otherwise stipulated or directed by the court. This disclosure shall, with respect to a witness, who is retained or specially employed to provide expert testimony in the case or whose duties as an employee of the party regularly involve giving expert testimony, be accompanied by a written report prepared and signed by the witness. The report shall contain a complete statement of all opinions to be expressed and the basis and reasons therefore; the data or other information considered by the witness in forming the opinions; any exhibits to be used as a summary of or support for the opinions; the qualifications of the witness, including a list of all publications authored by the witness within the preceding 10 years; the compensation to be paid for the study and testimony; and a listing of any other cases in which the witness has testified as an expert at trial or by deposition within the preceding four years.

(C) These disclosures shall be made at the times and in the sequence directed by the court. In the absence of other directions from the court or stipulation by the parties, the disclosures shall be made at least 90 days before the trial date or the date the case is to be

court a better understanding of what is being valued and, one would hope, making the financial analysis more meaningful. The pictures used in the courtroom usually can be prints that the judge can see and that can be entered as official exhibits. If the proceeding is a jury trial, the attorney and witness may wish to present the pictures as slides so that all parties in the courtroom can see the same thing while the witness is describing the company's operations. If a slide or computer presentation is used, copies should be prepared for possible submission as exhibits.

For exhibits of a size and format that can be readily copied, such as 8½-by-11-inch pages that would be included in a written report, it is convenient to prepare an extra set for the judge in addition to the set to be labeled by the clerk and entered as the official exhibit in the court record. Doing so will make it convenient for the judge to look at the tables and other exhibits while the witness is discussing them in direct testimony, as well as during cross-examination. It is also a courtesy, and in some cases a requirement, to provide a set of copies for the opposing attorney.

The exhibits the witness proposes to use should be reviewed with the attorney who will conduct the examination to ensure that all are appropriate and are legally admissible.

Preparation with the Attorney

Once the testimony outline and exhibits have been drafted, the attorney should review them thoroughly with the expert. The attorney should understand the significance of the major points in the expert's work in order to be able to phrase questions most meaningfully, spend the most time on the most salient points, and know what topics, if any, to revisit on redirect examination. The expert should be sure to understand any legal issues that bear on the testimony and how his or her testimony fits into the overall case. Even though the trial attorney is preoccupied and under pressure, both he or she and the appraiser must understand how important it is to work together to prepare a well-focused and persuasive presentation of the expert's work. All too often the attorney fails to gain the full impact of the expert's knowledge and research because of inadequate preparation.

In the Courtroom

The expert should appear in court as rested, alert, and neatly groomed as possible. In general, the witness should bring what he or she expects to have to refer to, a calculator, perhaps a note pad, and no more. If asked questions about any document, the witness is entitled to request a copy of it and examine it. Documents should be sufficiently organized so that the witness will have little trouble finding references.

The witness should not plan to read testimony except quotations from documents when it is important to have the record reflect the document's exact wording. An outline of testimony points might help ensure that the witness overlooks no important point. The expert should keep in mind, however, that opposing counsel may examine and copy all materials brought to or referred to while on the witness stand.

General Guidelines for Testimony

Perhaps the most critical thing for the witness to keep in mind in the courtroom is the need to be objective and unbiased—not an advocate. An advocate is defined as "one who pleads the cause of another" or "one who supports something as a cause." Pleading and supporting the client's cause is the attorney's role. The expert witness's role is to present the facts as they are and to use his or her professional expertise to interpret those facts to reach an objective conclusion.

Another key responsibility on the witness stand is to respond to the questions asked. The witness first must pay attention to the question and be sure of understanding it, and should pause long enough before answering to (1) allow any objections to be made by the attorneys, and (2) be *sure* that the answer will satisfy the question. If unsure whether the question is understood, the witness should ask for clarification.

Although answers should be concise but complete, how far to go is a matter of judgment. However, the witness definitely should avoid introducing material or ideas irrelevant to the question. Nevertheless, there is a fine line of judgment. A question may be worded such that a direct answer without clarification could leave a misleading impression. Naturally, in such cases the witness should volunteer the necessary clarification. (Of course, such questions are more likely to come from the opposing attorney during cross-examination, because he or she either doesn't understand the material or wishes to lead the witness into creating a false impression.)

The witness should speak distinctly and slowly enough for the judge and attorneys to understand the ideas and for the court reporter to type the words into the record. If it is necessary to use proper names or esoteric terminology, the appraiser should spell them so that the court reporter can enter them into the record correctly.

The witness should make enough eye contact with the judge and/or jury to ensure that they are following the testimony and understanding the ideas. If not sure whether the judge and/or jury understands, the witness should pause and rephrase the point more clearly. The key point is that the witness is trying to communicate to the trier of fact—either judge or jury—*not* to the client's counsel or opposing counsel.

In general, the expert witness should avoid technical language and jargon. Usually there is no reason to believe that the judge and/or jurors are trained in the very technical discipline of business valuation or in the specifics of the industry in which the subject business operates. If a technical term is necessary for making a point, it should be defined or explained in terms intelligible to a lay person.

In referring to an exhibit, the witness should say something like, "I direct your attention to Exhibit 10" and give the judge time to find Exhibit 10 before proceeding.

The witness should avoid distracting mannerisms and utterances such as "well," "ummm," and "uhhh." Unconscious habits, such as clicking a ballpoint pen or tapping a pencil, should be eliminated.

Otherwise, the witness should be his or her natural self, exuding competence and confidence but never arrogance.

Direct Examination

The expert witness must be careful not to omit any material facts, even (or especially) if their implications do not support the client's case. One should always assume that the opposing attorney and expert witness are properly prepared (even if one suspects they are not) and will not allow any facts that help their position to be overlooked. If the expert witness omits material facts, whether because of incompetence or advocacy, his or her credibility with the court will be in question. It is also essential that the expert witness not distort any facts or their interpretations. "Straightforward" is a good key word to go by.

Whether the expert enters all exhibits in one batch at the beginning of the testimony or one by one as they become relevant is a matter of preference. Many attorneys think the latter approach helps keep the court's attention focused on the subject at hand. After the oral qualification of the expert witness, his or her written credentials may be entered as an exhibit. From that point forward, each exhibit can be introduced immediately before the witness discusses it so that the judge can view it as the witness describes and interprets it.

Exhibits are numbered by the court as they are entered, and usually other exhibits have been entered earlier in the case; therefore, the witness's Table II may be the court's Exhibit 15, for example. As the exhibits are entered, the witness should write the court's exhibit number at the top of his or her own copy, since that usually is how the exhibit will be identified when the witness is called to discuss it on cross-examination.

The witness should not be surprised if the opposing attorney raises frequent objections. He or she may object to the form or substance of a question, an answer given by a witness, or the introduction of an exhibit. When an objection is raised, the witness must pause while the attorneys argue it out, then proceed when so instructed by the judge or by the attorney conducting the examination.

Cross-Examination

It is the opposing attorney's job to expose to the court any weaknesses in the expert witness's testimony. The witness should not take it personally. The attorney may attempt to discredit the witness in various ways, such as asking questions designed to attack the witness's competence to present expert testimony on the valuation issue at hand or to bring out possible conflicts of interest that would impugn the witness's independence. If the witness has testified in previous cases, he or she should assume that the opposing attorney has read the transcripts of such cases and will ask questions to bring out any apparent inconsistencies between previous and present testimony. The witness should also assume that the attorney has reviewed all the books and articles that he or she has written.

As discussed earlier, in preparing for direct testimony the witness must also prepare for cross-examination. If the witness did not use a particular approach that may seem reasonable on the surface, he or she should be prepared to explain why. If the witness did not use a company as a comparative, he or she should be prepared to explain why the company was disqualified. (This particular problem will be taken care of almost automatically if the procedures outlined in Chapter 11, "Market Approach: Guideline Publicly Traded Company Method," are followed and documented.)

Some attorneys use a cross-examination technique of asking questions in a manner designed to leave the court with an impression that they might like to convey but that may be misleading. A favorite ploy is to carefully frame a complicated question so as to leave a certain impression and then demand a yes or no answer. The witness should realize that he or she cannot be compelled to limit the answer to yes or no if it would not be completely appropriate. The witness has the right to clarify the answer and should demand to be allowed to do so if failure to clarify would leave a misimpression. The witness should first answer yes or no if it is possible to do so and then give the clarification. If it is a compound question and the answer is yes to one or more parts and no to others, the witness should make clear to which part or parts each response refers. If the question simply cannot be answered yes or no, the witness should explain why. The witness may also request the attorney to rephrase a question, either for clarification or to "unbundle" a compound question.

Another cross-examination ploy is to ask a question that contains a misleading presumption. In such a case, the witness must correct the false presumption in the answer; otherwise, he or she will risk leaving the impression of accepting the false premise.

It also is common for cross-examining attorneys to mischaracterize a witness's prior testimony, reading into it some impression that was never intended. In replying to such a misrepresentation, the witness may need to preface the answer with wording such as, "To put the answer to your question in proper context, I need to correct the misunderstanding of my prior testimony that was implied in your paraphrasing of it."

The hardest questions to deal with are those that are so abstruse that they are unintelligible. Usually the expert should not heroically attempt to interpret such questions but admit not understanding them and request clarification.

Through all of this, the witness should try to remain courteous. Nevertheless, he or she must also be firm and not feel intimidated by an overbearing attorney.

A witness must avoid attempting to bluff if he or she does not know an answer. Any suspicion of bluffing could cast doubt on the credibility of the witness's entire testimony. If the witness does not know the answer, he or she must say so. Also, if there is some error in the data, the witness should admit it and correct it, making whatever adjustment to the conclusion the correction would indicate.

If the expert witness has done his or her homework thoroughly, the cross-examination actually can help the case. With each answer explaining why a particular approach was rejected, for example, the opposing position may be discredited.

Redirect Examination

Even when the cross-examination has been completed, it is not time for the witness to breathe a sigh of relief. The attorney who conducted the original examination usually will want to keep the witness on the stand to ask redirect examination questions. The limited purpose of redirect is to expand any points brought out in the cross-examination that the attorney thinks need elaboration. It is the attorney's opportunity to counter possible misimpressions that might have been left with the court during the cross-examination and to reinforce any positions about which the cross-examination may have raised doubts.

If there is a recess between cross- and redirect examinations and the witness feels the need to clarify any points further, he or she should inform legal counsel so that counsel can ask the appropriate questions (provided, of course, that the court hasn't prohibited discussion of the case). If the witness feels strongly that something should be brought out on redirect examination and there is no scheduled recess, he or she usually can request a conference with the attorney. The redirect and recross-examinations can go back and forth indefinitely, limited only by the material presented in the immediately preceding testimony, the attorneys' restraint, and the judge's patience.

The judge may break in at any time during the direct examination, cross-examination, or any part of the proceedings to ask questions. Some judges are more apt to do so than others. Questions from the judge usually are a good sign—at least the judge is paying attention, and judges often ask penetrating and perceptive questions. Also, the witness should prefer that the judge ask for clarification of something the witness has left unclear or omitted rather than just leaving the issue alone.

Rebuttal Testimony

Attorneys often ask experts to present testimony for the purpose of rebutting testimony presented by the opposition's expert. Such testimony can take a wide variety of forms. Rebuttal testimony is most often presented to correct factual errors or errors in appraisal procedure committed by the opposing expert. Of course, if factual errors are to be corrected, it is important to present complete documentation for the correction. If procedural errors are to be corrected, the appraiser must present as strong authority as is possible for the correct procedures.

In many cases, rebuttal testimony is at least as important as the basic testimony and it should be presented as constructively as possible. Often, when the errors are corrected, the different approaches of the opposing experts ultimately lead to similar conclusions.

Exclusion of Witnesses

From time to time, the opposing attorney may move to have the expert witness excluded from the courtroom when testimony of the opposing expert is presented. As a generality, the purpose of the exclusion rule is to keep fact witnesses from being influenced in their testimony by the testimony of other fact witnesses. It is often *very* important to have the expert in the courtroom to hear opposing expert testimony, sometimes to give the attorney technical advice about the testimony, especially for cross-examination, and sometimes so the expert can rebut testimony of an opposing expert. A witness cannot be excluded when that person's presence is essential to the presentation of the party's cause.[15] Rarely, if ever, will a judge exclude an expert when this is called to the court's attention.

Courts' Expectations Regarding Expert Testimony

There are several common expectations that triers of fact have as to a valuation practitioner's expert testimony. This listing of expectations is not necessarily presented in order of relative significance.

1. Courts are increasingly expecting valuation analysts to comply with USPAP as the valuation industry professional standard, even in cases where compliance with USPAP is not required by statutory authority or by judicial precedent.

---

[15] FED. R. EVID. 615.

2. Judges expect expert valuation reports to be more comprehensive, more thorough, more rigorous—and more readable—than was the industry standard even a few years ago. The expectation is that the valuation report will stand on its own, and that it will tell the entire valuation "story."

3. Courts look for the presentation of market-derived, empirical data as the justification for a valuation analysis (e.g., transactional pricing multiples, direct and yield capitalization rates, valuation discounts and premiums). Courts are less persuaded by the analytical justification of "in my opinion ..." and more persuaded by the analytical justification, "based on the market-derived, empirical evidence presented in my appraisal report...."

4. Quantitative analysis and qualitative explanation for the selection of valuation variables (e.g., pricing multiples, capitalization rates, comparable sale pricing data, valuation adjustments—such as discount/premium percentages) are what judges want. Courts have come to realize that it is unusual that the naive selection of averages (means or medians) is appropriate with regard to the application of valuation variables to the subject property valuation analysis. The use of averages implies that everything about the facts and circumstances of the subject property in the instant case is average; in practice, this situation is very rarely the case.

5. Courts prefer expert witnesses to avoid the use of vague phrases such as "in my opinion ...," "based on my judgment ...," or "based on my experience...." When possible, triers of fact seem to prefer that valuation experts use positive phrases such as "my analysis indicates ...," "the data supports ...," or "the market tells us...." These positive phrases provide the triers of fact with explanations and justifications of their ultimate opinions.

6. In recent years, courts seem to be more willing to consider *Daubert*[16] motions. Based on the U.S. Supreme Court *Daubert* decision, these *Daubert* motions (usually made by motions in limine or after the voir dire phase of the examination) ask the judge to exclude the testimony of an expert witness that is based on "junk science"—or, in the case of a business valuation, on "junk economics."

7. In recent years, triers of fact more commonly seem to prefer that valuation experts avoid statements such as, "It is the State's position that ..." or "It is my firm's position that...." Analysts should be mindful of the fact that they are the experts—not their corporate or governmental employers. All valuation opinions should be an analyst's professional opinion, based on his or her personal professional training, experience, expertise, and reasoned judgment—and not based on the employer's or organization's dogma.

8. Courts seem to prefer for valuation experts to rely upon authoritative treatises, credentialling society courses, and promulgated professional standards—as opposed to the positions (published or otherwise) of single individuals (however well credentialled). What this implies is that valuation witnesses should generally endorse valuation industry practices. As a corollary, valuation witnesses should generally avoid relying upon a single individual's unproven position, such as "Dr. Jones says ..." or "Professor Smith says...."

9. The professional valuation practitioner should not let his or her expert testimony deteriorate into personal attacks on the opposing valuation experts. Courts don't seem to like "he said" versus "she said" expert valuation testimony.

---

[16] *Daubert v. Merrell Dow Pharmaceuticals, Inc.*

Courts appear to prefer to rely upon empirical and market-derived pricing evidence, authoritative literature, and informed professional judgment—and not upon juvenile comments between temperamental experts.

10. Courts appear to desire that the valuation experts bring all aspects of the valuation analysis back to the specific facts and circumstances of the instant case. Abstract formulas and conceptual theories are great—but triers of fact seem to want to understand how they apply to the specific set of facts and circumstances in front of them in the instant litigation.

Summary

Providing expert testimony in an adversarial proceeding is considered by most professional business analysts to be the most challenging aspect of the profession. By the time an adversarial proceeding reaches the courtroom, settlement efforts have been exhausted and the disagreements are razor sharp.

Many aspects of the courtroom drama are very much like theater in style, posturing, and pace. However, when legal controversy is involved, the expert witness has no substitute for thorough homework and preparation. The expert witness virtually prepares not only for his or her own case, but for the other side's as well.

Bibliography

Articles

Bingham, Dennis. "Making Persuasive Presentations in Court." *Business Appraisal Practice*, Fall 1999, pp. 13–23.

Bradley, Wray E. "Tax Court Valuation Standards Go Beyond 'Relevant and Reliable.'" *Valuation Strategies*, November/December 1999, pp. 34–39.

Bring, Brian. "Business Valuation Litigation." Presentation to the Advanced Business Valuation Conference of the American Society of Appraisers, October 1996. Available on www.BVLibrary.com.

_____. "Expert Testimony—The Appraiser as an Expert Witness." Presented at 22nd Annual Advanced Business Valuation Conference, Chicago, October 16–18, 2003. Also available at *BVPapers*, www.BVLibrary.com.

"Challenging Expert Witnesses." *Litigation Journal*, vol. 20, no. 1, April 2001.

Crain, Michael A., Dan L. Goldwasser, and Everett P. Harry. "Expert Witnesses—In Jeopardy?" *Journal of Accountancy*, December 1994, pp. 42–48.

Dennis, Stephen G. "Selecting and Using a Financial Expert in Dissolution Practice." *Family Law Quarterly*, Spring 1992, pp. 17–25.

Feder, Robert D. "Direct Examination of a Business Appraiser in a Divorce Action." *American Journal of Family Law*, Spring 1993, pp. 1–11.

Ford, David J. "Plan to Succeed: Prepare, Prepare, Prepare." *CPA Litigation Service Counselor*, August 1999, pp. 7–8.

Frank, Todd. "Common Errors Made by Appraisers in Valuing Businesses and Professional Practices in Arizona Divorce Cases." *BVPapers*. Available at www.BVLibrary.com.

Gregory, Michael, and Robin Ruegg. "Comparison of IRS and Taxpayer Experts as Stated by the Courts." *Business Valuation Review*, vol. 23, no. 4, December 2004.

Hansen, Mark. "Admission Tests." *ABA Journal*, vol. 87, February 2001.

Hawkins, George B. "Identifying and Excluding Faulty Valuation Report Content and Testimony." *Fair Value*, vol. 10, no. 2, Summer 2001.

Herber, William C., Robert J. Strachota, and G. Dennis Bingham. "The Appraiser as an Expert Witness: Courtroom Do's and Don'ts." *Business Appraisal Practice*, Winter 2000–2001, pp. 4–9.

Jackson, Daniel L. "The Next Hurdle: The Second Prong of the Daubert Test." *CPA Litigation Service Counselor*, November 1999, pp. 1–2, 4–5.

Kaplan, Michael J. "Effective Expert Testimony." 2001. *BVPapers*. Available at www.BVLibrary.com.

Kendig, Robert E. "Discovery Issues in Valuation Cases." *American Journal of Family Law*, Spring 1992, pp. 55–74.

Lewis, Elaine. "Effective Valuation Expert Testimony: Preparation and Practice Are the Keys." *Judges & Lawyers Business Valuation Update*, October 1999, pp. 1, 3–4.

_____. "Preparing for Trial: Packaging the Presentation." *Shannon Pratt's Business Valuation Update*, October 1998, pp. 1–3.

Lewis, Mark, and Mark Kitrich. "*Kumho Tire Co. v. Carmichael*: Blowout from the Overinflation of *Daubert v. Merrell Dow Pharmaceuticals*." *The University of Toledo Law Review*, vol. 31, no. 1, Fall 1999.

Locke, R. Christopher. "Expert Testimony in the Post-Daubert Era." *CPA Expert*, Spring 1996, pp. 3–7.

Markel, John R. "Experts Should Be Alert to New Trends in Deposition Questioning Tactics." *CPA Litigation Service Counselor*, June 1999, pp. 5–8.

McFarland, Matt. "Beyond Daubert: The Rules Have Changed." *CPA Litigation Service Counselor*, August 1999, pp. 1–5.

"New '*Daubert*' Database Tracks Challenges to Financial Expert Testimony." *Shannon Pratt's Business Valuation Update*, October 2003, Also available at www.BVLibrary.com.

Nissenbaum, Gerald. "The Expert Who Should Have Stayed Home in Bed under the Covers." Rhode Island CPA's Conference, November, 2003. Also available at *BVPapers*, www.BVLibrary.com.

Pratt, Shannon P. "Questions to Ask Expert Business Valuation Witnesses." *Fair$hare*, June 1999, pp. 9–11.

_____. "Recent Court Decisions Raise the Standards for Valuation Experts." *Valuation Strategies*, September/October 1999, pp. 35–39.

Real, Manuel L. Hon. "*Daubert*—A Judge's View." *The Practical Litigator*, vol. 11, no. 3, May 2000.

Reilly, Robert F. "Accountants' Considerations of *Daubert*-Related Decisions on Valuation Expert Testimony." *The National Public Accountant*, vol. 45, no. 8, October 2000, p. 12.

_____. "Expert Witness Procedures for Accountants: Dos and Don'ts for Success in the Courtroom." *The CPA Journal*, March 1999, pp. 25–28.

_____. "Guidelines for Guarding against Daubert Challenges to Expert Testimony." *CPA Expert*, Summer 1999, pp. 15–19.

Reilly, Robert F., and Robert P. Schweihs. "Expert Testimony: Lessons Learned from Sons of Daubert." *Valuation Strategies*, January/February 2000, pp. 26–31, 42.

Russell, Deirdre, and Steven F. Schroeder. "Kumho Tire—A View of Your Future as an Expert Witness." *Business Appraisal Practice*, Fall 1999, pp. 5–12.

Shirely, Mark W. "*Daubert*—The Evolution of a Profession." *The Valuation Examiner*, May/June 2001.

Taylor, Robin E. "Not Being an 'Expert' Expert: Four Ways to Falter Before Even Speaking a Word." *National Litigation Consultants' Review*, October 2002, pp. 1–4.

Weinstein, Jeffrey P. "The Use and Abuse of Economic Experts in Divorce Litigation." *Fair$hare: The Matrimonial Law Monthly*, February 1995, pp. 3–6.

Wise, Richard. "The Cross-Examiner's Tactics: What the Expert Witness Should Know." *Business Valuation Review*, vol. 23, no. 4, December 2004.

_____. "Objectivity and Credibility as a Valuation Expert." *Business Valuation Review*, vol. 24, no. 2, June 2005.

_____. "The Use and Abuse of Experts" (Chapter 40). In *Handbook of Business Valuation*, 2nd ed. Thomas L. West and Jeffrey D. Jones, eds. New York: John Wiley & Sons, 1999.

York, Timothy W. "Preparation Pays Off." *National Litigation Consultants' Review,* January 2005, pp. 9–10.

Books

Babitsky, Steven. *How to Become a Dangerous Expert Witness: Advanced Techniques and Strategies*. Falmouth, MA: Seak, 2005.

Babitsky, Steven, and James J. Mangraviti Jr. *How to Excel During Depositions: Techniques for Experts That Work*. Falmouth, MA: Seak, 2001.

_____. *Writing and Defending Your Expert Report*. Falmouth, MA: Seak, 2002.

Babitsky, Steven, James J. Mangraviti Jr., and Christopher J. Todd. *The Comprehensive Forensic Services Manual*. Falmouth, MA: Seak, 2000.

Brodsky, Stanley L. *The Expert Expert Witness: More Maxims and Guidelines for Testifying in Court*. Washington, DC: American Psychological Association, 1999.

Crawford, Robert J. *The Expert Witness: A Manuel for Experts*. Bloomington, IN: AuthorHouse, 2001.

Feder, Harold A. *Succeeding as an Expert Witness*. 3rd ed. Glenwood Springs, CO: Tageh Press, 2000.

Laro, David, and Shannon P. Pratt. *Business Valuation and Taxes: Procedure, Law, and Perspective*. New York: John Wiley & Sons, 2005.

Miles, Michael G. *A Guide to Better Business Appraisal Expert Testimony*. New York: John Wiley & Sons, 2001.

Poynter, Dan. *The Expert Witness Handbook: Tips and Techniques for the Litigation Consultant*, 3rd ed. Santa Barbara, CA: Para Publishing, 2004.

Pratt, Shannon P. *The Lawyer's Business Valuation Handbook: Understanding Financial Statements, Appraisal Reports, and Expert Testimony*. Chicago: American Bar Association, 2000.

Reilly, Robert F., and Robert P. Schweihs. *Guide to ESOP Valuation and Financial Advisory Services*. Portland, OR: Willamette Management Associates, 2005.

Tindall, Laura Jane. *Ethics Reference Guide for Expert Witnesses: A Tool to Assist in Identifying and Resolving Moral Dilemmas in Providing Expert Witness Testimony*. Loxahachee, FL: Dynamic Ingenuity, 2003.

Wise, Richard M. *Financial Litigation: Quantifying Business Damages and Values*. Toronto: The Canadian Institute of Chartered Accountants, 1990.

Chapter 42

Arbitration and Mediation

*Clogged courts and escalating litigation costs have made arbitration as a
solution for civil disputes and claims of conflict more necessary than ever
before. Arbitration is a process by which a dispute is settled by an impartial,
disinterested person or group who is authorized to render a decision that is
legal, final, and binding. Arbitration is used as an alternative to litigation
because it provides for an expeditious and inexpensive resolution of disputes
by arbitrators having expert knowledge within a particular field, who act in
an informal process that maintains the privacy of business transactions.[1]*

The process of "arbitration" usually results in a binding conclusion, as
opposed to "mediation," the product of which is advisory rather than binding.
Mediators do not decide disputes; their only role is to encourage the parties to
reach an equitable settlement of their differences.

Depending on the directive giving rise to the arbitration, the arbitrator(s)' conclusion may be contractually binding by itself, or it may be subject to limited
review and confirmation by a court. Whether or not the product is binding, these
services are categorized as "alternative dispute resolution" (ADR).

Business valuation disputes lend themselves exceedingly well to the arbitration
process, partly because there normally is a single, unambiguous conclusion—that
is, a value. The author has had extensive experience serving as an arbitrator, expert
witness before arbitrators, and consultant to attorneys contemplating or conducting an arbitration process. Whenever the arbitrators themselves are experts in the
field, as suggested in the above quote, my experiences have been very positive with
respect to the fairness of the conclusion and, in most cases, the expeditiousness of
the process.

Advantages of ADR over Court Trial

The primary advantages of ADR over a court trial are the following:

1. The hearings are private rather than public, and in many cases are not recorded
    by a court reporter, a compelling advantage in many circumstances. This often
    allows the parties a chance to maintain an ongoing business relationship.
2. There is less likelihood of an outlandish result in favor of one side over the
    other, provided the arbitrators are qualified, professional business appraisers.
    In cases where the issue is a dispute over the value of a business or a business
    interest, an appraiser, if properly chosen, is usually in a better position as a
    result of experience and knowledge to assess the testimony regarding the value
    of a business or business interest than either a judge or jury.
3. ADR usually takes less elapsed time from start to finish.
4. Scheduling normally can be made more convenient for all parties involved.
5. Arbitration usually costs less. Attorneys' time and experts' fees frequently are
    considerably reduced. The appraisal process itself may not be less expensive than
    a court trial, but the amount of time required for preparing for cross-examination
    and rebuttal to an opposing expert in court can be substantially less.
6. Arbitration usually is less acrimonious, less formal, and less taxing on all
    participants, especially the principals in the disputed issue.

---

[1] Jerome N. Block, "The Process of Arbitration," *The Appraisal Journal*, April 1993, pp. 234–38.

7. The award of the arbitrators in most situations is final and binding and can be confirmed in court on motion.

8. The parties can handpick the trained professional who will conduct the ADR process.

Situations Suitable for Arbitration

Almost any dispute over the value of a business or a partial interest in a business can lend itself to resolution by arbitration instead of trial. If the parties in divorce and corporate or partnership dissolutions decide ahead of time to resolve any valuation issues by arbitration, they may never reach the point of dispute.

In mediation, the counselor can sometimes uncover unrealistic expectations and identify hidden concerns or objectives. This process can overcome personality conflicts and prevent the parties from some of the more humbling or embarrassing aspects of litigation in open court. This process usually narrows the issues, at least, if it does not reach a satisfactory conclusion between the parties.

The following have been the major categories, in my experience, where arbitration has proven most effective:

- Corporate and partnership dissolutions and buyouts of minority interests
- Dissenting stockholder actions
- Damage cases
- Divorces

Corporate and Partnership Dissolutions and Buyouts of Minority Interests

As with marriages, many business ownership relationships that appeared to be made in heaven end up with an agreement to disagree. Often the best solution is to sever the ownership relationship, usually sooner rather than later.

Arbitrating the valuation issue usually is a far lesser distraction of management's focus on running the business than is going to court. Arbitration in this very common situation also has all the other advantages listed above. Often especially relevant is the issue of fairness of the outcome, avoiding the tendency of judges and juries to become biased by the "good guy, bad buy" epithets that often characterize such court proceedings. Besides the issue of fairness, the arbitration process generally results in a far less rancorous parting of the ways than a court trial.

Arbitration also works well in those few states where a corporate or partnership dissolution occurs pursuant to a state dissolution statute, such as California[2] and Rhode Island.[3] Such dissolutions are discussed further in Chapter 35.

Dissenting Stockholder Actions

As discussed in Chapter 35, a merger, sale, or other major corporate action can give rise to dissenting stockholders' appraisal rights. The expediency and lower cost make

---

[2] Cal. Corp. Code §§1300 and 2000.
[3] R.I. Bus. Corp. Code §7-1.1-90.1.

the arbitration process an attractive alternative to a trial for determination of the value under appraisal rights in such cases, especially smaller ones for which prolonged and expensive court proceedings can result in a no-win situation for everyone.

Damage Cases

Damage cases, in which the valuation of a business or practice often is the central issue in determining the amount of relief, include the following:

1. Breach of contract
2. Condemnation
3. Antitrust
4. Lost profits
5. Lost business opportunity
6. Amount of casualty insurance proceeds or allocation of proceeds among parties at interest
7. Infringement of intellectual property
8. Business torts
9. Violation of securities laws

We have observed that the risk of the court reaching an outlandish determination of value is greater in damage cases—especially those involving breach of contract and antitrust—than in any other major category of disputed valuation cases. One of the reasons for such extreme decisions is that some juries or courts allow their view that there should be liability for damages to affect their objectivity about the valuation issue; similarly, they may be swayed by some sentiment toward the parties involved. This risk can be significantly reduced through the use of an arbitration process using qualified appraisers as arbitrators.

Plaintiffs may resist arbitration by qualified valuers in favor of "rolling the dice" for a high award based on a jury's indignation over the defendants' egregious actions. However, witnesses testifying to extreme amounts may lack credibility (especially if faced with a strong rebuttal witness), and judges often have authority to vacate or substantially reduce jury awards. Furthermore, the costs of court trials often exceed the depths of plaintiffs' pockets when faced with the unlimited resources of some defendants.

Divorces

Of all situations involving disputed valuations of businesses or professional practices, those arising from divorces often are the most difficult for the parties to resolve by amicable negotiation. Although divorces are only a small part of my firm's valuation practice, they account for a large proportion of the occasions on which we prepare for, and appear on, the witness stand in court to present expert testimony.

Disputed valuation issues can become a major element in the already intense emotional strain accompanying divorce proceedings. Frequently, the valuation for the property settlement is the major, if not the only, disputed issue. Besides the time and cost advantages, arbitration spares the parties the tension and added antagonism of fighting it out in court.

I believe that the trend toward settling business valuation issues by arbitrating in marital property divisions will accelerate as more family law attorneys become familiar and comfortable with the arbitration process in this context.

The Arbitration Agreement

The arbitration agreement is critical, because it is a document governing the arbitration that is binding on both the parties and the arbitrators. The arbitration agreement usually originates in one of the following ways:

1. An arbitration clause is included as part of a corporate document or contract among the parties, such as a buy-sell agreement. When such an agreement is triggered, it generally is desirable for the attorneys to draw up—and for the parties to execute—a supplemental agreement addressing details discussed below that may not have been covered in the general arbitration clause.
2. An arbitration agreement is created specifically for the situation at hand, sometimes with direction or assistance from a court.

In any case, we highly recommend that a valuation consultant experienced in arbitration be engaged to assist the lawyer in drafting or reviewing the arbitration clause or agreement, so that the valuation clause will actually result in accomplishing the objective of the parties.

The arbitration document must be clear, complete, and unambiguous. We have seen incredible amounts of unnecessary frustration and wasted time and energy expended as a result of parties' and arbitrators' disagreements as to the interpretation of the arbitration agreement.

We also highly recommend that all parties to the arbitration agreement read and understand it before they agree to become bound by it. For example, many buy-sell agreements specify the standard of value as "the fair market value of the shares." Noncontrolling stockholders often are shocked when they learn that they have been forced to sell out under this clause at a price considerably lower than a pro rata portion of the enterprise as a whole.

Factors Specified in the Arbitration Agreement

Factors that should be mandated by the agreement include the following:

1. Procedure for selection of arbitrators
2. Definition of the property to be appraised
3. Date as of which the property is to be valued
4. Standard of value to be used (as discussed in Chapter 2 and elsewhere in the book)
5. What constitutes a conclusion by the arbitrators, such as:
   a. Agreement by at least two out of three
   b. Average of the two closest to each other
   c. Conclusion of the third (neutral) arbitrator, such as in a "special master" situation
6. Format and procedure or the arbitrators' rendering of their conclusion
7. Terms of payment of the amount determined by the arbitrators, including interest, if any
8. Time schedule for the various steps in the arbitration process, at least the selection of arbitrators and some outside time limit for the total process

Failure to specify any of the above factors may leave the door open for costly and extensive legal battles.

The agreement may specify a reporting deadline, or a schedule may be worked out in conjunction with the process of engaging the arbitrators. In our experience, reporting deadlines written into arbitration agreements often are too optimistic to allow for the time necessary to work out legal details, collection and transmission of all the information necessary for the arbitrators, and accommodation of the schedules of the arbitrators, attorneys, parties, and witnesses.

Factors Left to the Arbitrators' Discretion

Factors that can, and in most cases should, be left to the discretion of the arbitrators include the following:

1. Whether or not each arbitrator is expected or required to make a complete, independent appraisal, or the extent to which each arbitrator considers it necessary to do independent work, as opposed to relying on certain data or analyses furnished by other arbitrators and/or appraisers
2. The obligation of the arbitrators to communicate with each other (writing, telephone calls, personal meetings), and the rules for sharing information
3. Scheduling of the arbitrators' work and meetings, within the constraint of the agreed upon reporting schedule
4. The valuation approaches and criteria to be taken into consideration, within the constraints of any legally mandated criteria
5. The facts, documents, and other data on which to rely (although the principals may agree to stipulate certain facts or assumptions, which could make the arbitrators' job easier with respect to some matters of possible factual uncertainty)

Other Factors to Address

As a generality, the arbitration agreement may specify rules on various matters, or, in the absence of specific rules, it should contain some broad language giving the arbitrators authority to make rules on points not addressed in the agreement. An example would be rules regarding contacts between parties and the arbitrators. Often participants in arbitrations are given no rules as to whether ex parte contact is permitted, and arbitration statutes provide little or no guidance.

Another topic often not addressed is rules specifying whether the arbitrators are free to obtain property-specific information independent of that provided by the parties, or they should rely solely on information presented to them by the parties and their witnesses and made part of the arbitration record.

Selection of Arbitrators

Two factors need to be delineated regarding the selection of arbitrators: (1) the criteria for selection and (2) the procedure for selection.

Criteria for Selection

The arbitration process produces the most equitable results for all parties if all the arbitrators (or the arbitrator) are experienced, qualified, professional appraisers of businesses, professional practices, intangible property, or whatever the subject property may be. If there are three arbitrators, it is most desirable that all three should be full-time professional appraisers, but two out of three are far better than only one or none at all.

In some cases, if the business or profession is highly specialized, it may be desirable to seek as arbitrators one or more appraisers who have experience in appraising the specific line of business or professional practice. It is generally not desirable to gain the desired industry expertise by utilizing as an arbitrator someone who is an active or retired participant in the industry or profession involved, or who has done ancillary functions such as accounting or economic analysis work in the industry or profession, but who is not experienced in matters related directly to valuation. Many of these people lack the requisite training to deal professionally with the specific issue of valuation, and there is also the risk that such people's biases toward the industry or profession could prevent objective valuation. The expertise of industry experts can be gained through informal discussion with the arbitrator(s) or by formal testimony presented to the arbitrator(s). This is preferable to having them act as arbitrators themselves.

We have observed sound valuation conclusions reached by arbitration panels composed of industry people knowledgeable in finance, along with attorneys knowledgeable in both the industry and valuation matters. However, in these instances, costs were incurred not only for the three arbitrators, but also for expert testimony to be presented to the arbitration panel by at least two appraisers (one or more retained by each party) in each case. I also have seen nonprofessional panels reach conclusions that I do not believe a consensus of responsible professional appraisers would consider supportable within a reasonable range of value.

Obviously, one criterion for selection is the availability of the desired arbitrator(s) so that the arbitration can taken place reasonably promptly.

Procedure for Selection

The most typical procedure is that each party selects one arbitrator and the two arbitrators select the third. It is preferable for the two arbitrators appointed by the parties to have complete authority to select the third, rather than having the selection of the third arbitrator subject to the approval of the principals. This avoids delays and dealing with pressures arising from the principals' biases, which are almost sure to be injected.

It is important that there be an alternative procedure for the selection of a third arbitrator in case of a deadlock. This contingency procedure should be planned in advance or in conjunction with entering into the arbitration agreement. There should be a deadline, at which time the alternate selection process takes effect if the first two arbitrators have failed to reach agreement on a third arbitrator. In case of a deadlock, the procedure should call for the appointment of the third arbitrator, who is a qualified appraiser, by some predetermined entity, such as the American Society of Appraisers, the American Arbitration Association, a court, or some designated official in the industry or profession. This procedure will almost assure that at least two of the three arbitrators will be professional appraisers, if one side has already chosen one. If one side insists that the third arbitrator be a qualified professional appraiser, and presents a list of appraisers who are independent of the principals involved, it is not likely that anyone charged with making such an appointment would select someone not so qualified over someone who is qualified.[4]

Another possibility is to establish the procedure so that the two arbitrators attempt to reach agreement, bringing in the third arbitrator only if they are unable to do so. In that case, I recommend, based on my experiences, that the prospective third arbitrator be agreed upon between the first two at the outset, before they get involved in other aspects of interaction with each other in the arbitration process.

American Arbitration Association Procedure

The American Arbitration Association (AAA) procedure for appointing arbitrators is different from that described in the foregoing section. When parties agree to submit a disputed matter to arbitration through the AAA, the association sends the parties a list of suggested arbitrators from the association's panel of arbitrators. Each party may veto nominees and indicate its preferences, but the final decision is made by the AAA.

In many AAA arbitrations, each party will retain its own expert appraiser who will present testimony before the arbitration panel, rather than having the expert actually participate as an arbitrator. In this sense, the preparation and presentation of expert testimony is similar to a court trial, although it is slightly less formal.

The next few sections of this chapter discuss the type of situation where the appraiser is acting as a member of the arbitration panel rather than as a presenter of expert testimony.

Engagement and Compensation of Arbitrators

Once the arbitrators have been appointed, the engagement should be committed to writing. The description of the engagement may take the form of a standard professional services agreement initiated by an appraiser serving as arbitrator, an engagement letter drafted by one of the attorneys or parties, or both. All aspects of the engagement should be adequately covered. Sometimes, addenda to the initial engagement document(s) may be necessary, since decisions on some items, such as schedules and some expenses, may be made or changed as the engagement progresses.

The engagement document(s) should include by reference the statute and/or document(s) giving rise to the arbitration (e.g., a buy-sell agreement) and should cover compensation of the arbitrator and all necessary instructions not addressed or not made clear in the arbitration document(s).

All documents relating to the engagement of an arbitrator should be signed by the arbitrator and whoever is responsible for compensating the arbitrator for his or her services. The most common compensation arrangement is that each party assumes responsibility for the compensation and expenses of the arbitrator it has

---

[4] Accredited senior appraisers of the American Society of Appraisers who are certified in business valuation may be found on the Web site of the American Society of Appraisers, www.appraisers.org, or by calling (800) ASA-VALU.

nominated or appointed, with the parties equally sharing the compensation and expenses of the third arbitrator. Such arrangements vary, however, from case to case.

The amount of compensation is usually based on each arbitrator's normal professional hourly or daily billing rate (or some mutually agreed upon rate) plus out-of-pocket expenses. It is much less common for an arbitrator's compensation to be based on a fixed fee, because it is very difficult to determine in advance just how much time the total appraisal and arbitration process will require. However, it is reasonable to expect to discuss some estimate of probable fees and the daily rate or other basis for the fees. Under the procedures of the AAA, these arrangements are carried out by a representative of that organization. If the association is to be directed to appoint qualified business appraisers, it also should be directed to expect to pay the fees normally charged by such qualified appraisers.

The Arbitration Process

One of the major variables in the arbitration process is the extent to which each arbitrator is expected or required to carry out independent appraisal work. Some arbitration documents specify that each expert on the arbitration panel do a complete, independent appraisal. At the other extreme, some arbitration documents specify that the arbitrator(s) rely entirely on evidence presented by the parties or their witnesses. More commonly, however (and we think preferably in most cases), the extent of independent appraisal work to be done is left to the judgment of each individual arbitrator, or to the arbitration panel as a group. This subject should be discussed with the parties or their representatives before the arbitration commences. It would be useful to have this addressed in the arbitrators' engagement letter, preferably allowing them considerable discretion.

Review of Arbitration Document

Each arbitrator should begin with a careful review of the statute and/or document(s) giving rise to the arbitration. If there is any confusion or disagreement about any details of the assignment, such as the exact definition of the property, the effective date of the valuation, or the applicable standard of value, the arbitrators should seek clarification immediately. This should be done in writing to avoid any possible disputes later.

Initial Communication among Arbitrators

We recommend that the arbitrators establish communication among themselves at the earliest possible time after their appointment. A face-to-face meeting is ideal if geographic proximity to each other makes that feasible, but a conference call or a series of conference calls is usually sufficient, perhaps supplemented by correspondence. While each case is unique, the following is a generalized list of points to try to establish early:

1. Status of work already accomplished, if any (who has done what work up to that point).

2. An agreement as to sharing of information. (My preference is to agree that all information gathered or developed by one arbitrator will be shared with the other arbitrators as quickly as possible.)

3. An agreement, if possible, as to the relevant valuation approaches to consider. (Where this becomes an issue, it seems fair to allow the parties' representatives to be heard as to their preferences. However, in my experience, this often results in highly biased supplications by parties' representatives who have no technical knowledge of relevant valuation approaches.)

4. A list of documents and data needed, and assignment of responsibility for obtaining each and seeing that the necessary distribution to other arbitrators is made. (It should be agreed up front that any such documents in the possession of the parties will be provided as evidence to the arbitrators promptly and completely.)

5. Any other possible division of the research effort, such as searches for comparable transactions, development of economic and/or industry data, and routine financial statement analysis (spreadsheets, ratio analysis, comparison with industry averages, and so on). Division of research effort, of course, must depend on each arbitrator's willingness to accept certain efforts of another, which must be based on a judgment of professional ability and unbiased presentation of data and analysis.

6. Scheduling.

Field Visit

In most cases, arbitrators will want to visit the operating premises and interview relevant principals and/or management. It works out best if the arbitrators can conduct this field trip together, if possible, rather than separately. Together, the arbitrators will see the same things at the same time, and all can benefit from hearing each other's questions and answers firsthand. A joint field trip also gives the arbitrators an opportunity to address any items not fully covered in their previous communications. Also, this gives arbitrators who did not know each other previously an opportunity to get to know each other and form a basis for working together.

Hearings

The arbitrators should offer each party the opportunity to present oral and written information and opinions if they so desire. It is frequently convenient to hold a meeting to accommodate such input in conjunction with the field trip.

The Valuation Meeting

Usually, the arbitrators will meet in person to reach the valuation conclusion. In some instances, this meeting may be replaced by a conference call. In either case, all should be as prepared as possible, having exchanged and assimilated as much information as possible prior to the meeting.

In the meeting, it is usually most productive to come to agreements issue by issue, identifying and keeping track of each point of agreement and disagreement.

Good notes should be kept so that it is clear exactly what points have been agreed upon, and what the respective positions are on points that have been addressed but on which agreement has not been reached. Each arbitrator should be receptive to the others' information and viewpoints and attempt to reach compromises on points where reasonable judgments may differ.

It is most desirable to come to a conclusion that can be endorsed as fair by all members of the arbitration panel. This agreement can usually be achieved if all of the arbitrators are qualified professional business appraisers. If unanimous agreement cannot be reached, the arbitrator in the minority position may render a dissenting opinion for the record if he or she so desires.

Reporting the Results of the Arbitration

The formal report of the valuation conclusion reached by the arbitrators is usually contained in a very brief letter that does no more than reference the arbitration agreement, state that the arbitrators have completed their assignment in accordance with the agreement, and state the conclusion reached. The arbitrators concurring in the conclusion sign the letter. In the parlance of arbitration, this is called an *award*. In some cases, the letter must be notarized as well as signed.

In a significant proportion of cases, the principals on both sides would like to have a brief report explaining how the valuation conclusion was reached. In arbitration parlance, this is called an *opinion*. In such situations, we suggest that such an advisory report be the sole responsibility of the third appraiser. To make such a report a joint task of two or more arbitrators, each of whom probably judged various factors a little bit differently—though they were able to agree on a conclusion—would usually be an unnecessarily complicated and costly exercise.

If the valuation conclusion is reached unilaterally by a special master, normally he or she would be the only one to sign the report. An explanation of the procedures and criteria used is usually included.

Mediation

While an arbitrator's role is to reach a conclusion that is binding on the parties, the mediator's role is to reach closure by convincing the parties to come to a settlement.

> The ultimate goal of mediation is to assist the parties in designing a solution that specifically addresses their needs and interests. Mediation is much more flexible than either arbitration or litigation in that it allows the parties themselves to design a very particularized solution to their particular dispute that is as detailed or general as the parties desire. Additionally, at least in family mediation, attorneys are usually not present at most of the mediation sessions and therefore legal fees are reduced.[5]

---

[5] Deborah Iwanyshyn, "Mediation as a Form of Dispute Resolution," *Shannon Pratt's Business Valuation Update*, October 1998, p. 5.

How Mediation Differs from Arbitration and Litigation

Mediation is a voluntary process that involves the use of an impartial person or persons, by the parties to a dispute, to facilitate informed decision making so as to assist parties to work together to design a customized solution to their dispute. The parties can customize their solution to suit their needs in a far more detailed fashion than will generally occur if a decision is made for them by either a judge or an arbitrator.

No party is ever forced to continue to mediate if she or he decides that mediation is not working. No party ever gives away rights during a mediation session. All decisions are subject to review no matter how far along in the process the parties may be.

Arbitration involves the use of a third person, sometimes selected by the parties and sometimes appointed for them, to listen to their arguments and to examine their evidence and to make a decision for them. Private arbitration, if agreed to by both parties, can be customized to eliminate a lot of the formalities and requirements of litigation. However, the arbitrator still makes the final decision, and it generally is not as detailed as an agreement that the parties design themselves.[6]

Self-Determination Is the Fundamental Principle

The Standards of Conduct for Mediators published as joint standards for the American Bar Association (ABA) and the Society of Professionals in Dispute Resolution (SPIDR) states, "Self-determination is the fundamental principle of mediation. It requires that the mediation process rely upon the ability of the parties to reach a voluntary, uncoerced agreement."

Role of the Business Valuation Expert in Mediation

Experts can act as comediators as well as neutral experts, although the roles are significantly different. If acting as a comediator the expert must comply with the ethical constraints of impartiality and neutrality and the goal of self-determination by the parties. The expert comediator can't give an opinion as to value but can provide information to assist the parties in making informative decisions and in formulating their own settlement.

When consulted as a neutral expert, the appraiser's role requires him or her to utilize his or her expertise to give an opinion that the parties can choose to either use or ignore. The recommendation by a mediator to employ the services of a neutral expert is far more common than the use by the mediator of an expert to comediate. Peter Adler, former president of SPIDR, noted that he has utilized the services of appraisers as both experts and comediators. In larger cases, where the parties themselves have independently employed two experts, it is also acceptable to ask the experts to select a third expert if the parties do not feel that they can rely upon either of the experts selected by the other.[7]

---

[6] Ibid.
[7] Ibid., p. 6.

Mediation in Family Law

One of the fastest-growing applications of mediation in recent years has been in the area of divorce. A group called the Academy of Family Mediators has published a document titled *Standards of Practice for Family and Divorce Mediation.* It explains: "The role of the mediator includes reducing the obstacles to communication, maximizing the exploration of alternatives, and addressing the needs of those it is agreed are involved or affected."

Mediation in Federal Tax Disputes

The Internal Revenue Service authorized mediations to resolve gift and estate tax matters starting late in 1995, and several successful tax mediations have been concluded since then.

Summary

The two most critical elements for an expeditious and successful arbitration are:

1. *A definitive arbitration agreement that provides the arbitrators with unambiguous instructions on the key matters listed above and that all parties understand*
2. *The appointment of competent and independent arbitrators with a high degree of relevant valuation expertise who will be fair in reaching a conclusion about the value of the subject property*

If these two elements are properly addressed, the arbitration process can be a very efficient and fair way of resolving business or professional practice valuation matters.

Mediation is rapidly growing in popularity as a form of alternative dispute resolution. In order for mediation to succeed:

1. *The parties must desire to resolve the conflict.*
2. *There needs to be a well-qualified mediator.*
3. *If a business valuation is involved, the mediator, comediator, or neutral adviser to the mediator should be a well-qualified business valuation analyst.*

As of this writing, there are only a few valuation analysts qualified as mediators. Therefore, the valuation analyst's role usually would be as a comediator or neutral adviser to the mediator. In addition, valuation practitioners have an obvious role in providing expert testimony in mediation proceedings.

Bibliography

Berman, Peter J. "Resolving Business Disputes Through Mediation and Arbitration." *CPA Journal*, November 1994, pp. 74–77.

Brinig, Brian P., et al. "Alternative Dispute Resolution" (Chapter 12). In *Guide to Litigation Support Services*, 11th ed. Fort Worth, TX: Practitioners Publishing Company, 2006.

Demery, Paul. "Is Mediation in Your Future?" *Practical Accountant*, January 1996, pp. 48–55.

Diana, James C. "The New Mediation Procedure in Appeals: The Latest Development in the IRS' ADR Initiative." *Tax Management Memorandum*, November 13, 1995, pp. 331–39.

Fiore, Nicholas. "Pros and Cons of the New IRS Mediation Program." *Journal of Accountancy*, May 1996, p. 36.

Ford, David J. "CPAs and ADR: A Civilized Alternative to Litigation." *CPA Litigation Service Counselor*, February 2000, pp. 1–5.

Goldsheider, Robert. "Measuring the Damages: ADR and Intellectual Property Disputes." *Dispute Resolution Journal*, October–December 1995, pp. 55–63.

Iwanyshyn, Deborah. "Mediation as a Form of Dispute Resolution." *Shannon Pratt's Business Valuation Update*, October 1998, pp. 5–6.

Saltzman, Michael I. "Tax Court Mediation: A Case Study." *Tax Executive*, November/December 1996, pp. 449–53.

Professional Arbitration and Mediation Organizations

The Academy of Family Mediators
5 Militia Drive
Lexington, Massachusetts 02173
(781) 674-2663
www.mediators.org

American Arbitration Association
335 Madison Avenue, 10th Floor
New York, New York 10017
(212) 484-4000
www.adr.org

American Bar Association Dispute Resolution Section
740 15th Street, N.W.
Washington, DC 20005
(202) 662-1680
www.abanet.org/dispute

Association for Conflict Resolution
1015 18th Street, N.W., Suite 1150
Washington, DC 20036
(781) 674-2663
www.acrnet.org

Association for Family and Conciliation Courts
6525 Grand Teton Plaza
Madison, Wisconsin 53719
(608) 664-3750
www.afccnet.org

CDR Associates
100 Arapahoe Avenue, Suite 12
Boulder, Colorado 80302
(303) 442-7367
www.mediate.org

Center for Public Resources Institute for Dispute Resolution
575 Lexington Avenue, 21st Floor
New York, New York 10022
(212) 949-6490
www.cpradr.org

Mediation and Conflict Management Services
PO Box 51090
Eugene, Oregon 97405
(541) 345-1629
www.mediate.com

Appendix A

International Glossary of Business Valuation Terms

To enhance and sustain the quality of business valuations for the benefit of the profession and its clientele, the societies and organizations listed here have adopted these definitions for the terms included in this glossary:

American Institute of Certified Public Accountants
American Society of Appraisers
Canadian Institute of Chartered Business Valuators
National Association of Certified Valuation Analysts
The Institute of Business Appraisers

The performance of business valuation services requires a high degree of skill and imposes upon the valuation professional a duty to communicate the valuation process and its conclusions in a manner that is clear and not misleading. This duty is advanced through the use of terms whose meanings are clearly established and consistently applied throughout the profession.

If, in the opinion of the business valuation professional, one or more of these terms needs to be used in a manner that materially departs from the definitions given here, it is recommended that the way that term is used within that valuation engagement be defined.

This glossary has been developed to provide guidance to business valuation practitioners by further cataloging the body of knowledge that constitutes the competent and careful determination of value and, more particularly, the communication of how that value was determined.

Departure from this glossary is not intended to provide a basis for civil liability and should not be presumed to create evidence that any duty has been breached.

Definitions defined exclusively by the American Society of Appraisers are marked with an asterisk (*).

Adjusted Book Value*—the book value that results after asset or liability amounts are added to, deleted from, or changed from their respective book amounts.

Adjusted Book Value Method—a method within the asset approach whereby all assets and liabilities (including off-balance-sheet, intangible, and contingent items) are adjusted to their fair market values. [*Note:* In Canada, this is done on a going concern basis.]

Adjusted Net Asset Method—*see* Adjusted Book Value Method.

Appraisal—*see* Valuation.

Appraisal Approach—*see* Valuation Approach.

Appraisal Date—*see* Valuation Date.

Appraisal Method—*see* Valuation Method.

Appraisal Procedure—*see* Valuation Procedure.

Appraised Value*—the appraiser's opinion or conclusion of value.

Arbitrage Pricing Theory—a multivariate model for estimating the cost of equity capital that incorporates several systematic risk factors.

Asset (Asset-Based) Approach—a general way of determining a value indication for a business, business ownership interest, or security by using one or more methods based on the value of the assets net of liabilities.

Beta—a measure of the systematic risk of a stock; the tendency of a stock's price to be correlated with changes in a specific index.

Blockage Discount—an amount or percentage deducted from the current market price of a publicly traded stock to reflect the decrease in the per share value of a block of stock that is of a size such that it could not be sold at the market price in a reasonable period of time given normal trading volume.

Book value—*see* Net Book Value.

Business—*see* Business Enterprise.

Business Appraiser*—a person who, by education, training, and experience, is qualified to develop an appraisal of a business, business ownership interest, security, or intangible asset.

Business Enterprise—a commercial, industrial, service, or investment entity (or a combination thereof) pursuing an economic activity.

Business Risk—the degree of uncertainty of realizing the expected future returns of the business resulting from factors other than financial leverage. *See* Financial Risk.

Business Valuation—the act or process of determining the value of a business enterprise or ownership interest therein.

Capital Asset Pricing Model (CAPM)—a model in which the cost of capital for any stock or portfolio of stocks equals a risk-free rate plus a risk premium that is proportionate to the systematic risk of the stock or portfolio.

Capitalization—a conversion of a single period of economic benefits into value.

Capitalization Factor—any multiple or divisor used to convert the anticipated economic benefits of a single period into value.

Capitalization of Earnings Method—a method within the income approach whereby economic benefits for a representative single period are converted to value through division by a capitalization rate.

Capitalization Rate—any divisor (usually expressed as a percentage) used to convert the anticipated economic benefits of a single period into value.

Capital Structure—the composition of the invested capital of a business enterprise; the mix of debt and equity financing.

Cash Flow—cash that is generated over a period of time by an asset, group of assets, or business enterprise. This term may be used in a general sense to encompass various levels of specifically defined cash flows. When the term is used, it should be supplemented by a qualifier (for example, "discretionary" or "operating") and a specific definition in the given valuation context.

Common-Size Statements—financial statements in which each line is expressed as a percentage of the total. On the balance sheet, each line item is shown as a percentage of total assets, and on the income statement, each item is expressed as a percentage of sales.

Control—the power to direct the management and policies of a business enterprise.

Control Premium—an amount or a percentage by which the pro rata value of a controlling interest exceeds the pro rata value of a noncontrolling interest in a business enterprise, to reflect the power of control.

Cost Approach—a general way of determining a value indication of an individual asset by quantifying the amount of money required to replace the future service capability of that asset.

Cost of Capital—the expected rate of return that the market requires in order to attract funds to a particular investment.

Debt-Free—we discourage the use of this term. *See* Invested Capital.

Discount for Lack of Control—an amount or percentage deducted from the pro rata share of 100 percent of the value of an equity interest in a business to reflect the absence of some or all of the powers of control.

Discount for Lack of Liquidity*—an amount or percentage deducted from the value of an ownership interest to reflect the relative inability to quickly convert property to cash.

Discount for Lack of Marketability—an amount or percentage deducted from the value of an ownership interest to reflect the relative absence of marketability.

Discount for Lack of Voting Rights—an amount or percentage deducted from the per share value of a minority interest voting share to reflect the absence of voting rights.

Discount Rate—a rate of return used to convert a future monetary sum into present value.

Discounted Cash Flow Method—a method within the income approach whereby the present value of future expected net cash flows is calculated using a discount rate.

Discounted Future Earnings Method—a method within the income approach whereby the present value of future expected economic benefits is calculated using a discount rate.

Discretionary Earnings*—earnings that may be defined, in certain applications, to reflect the earnings of a business enterprise prior to the following items:

- Income taxes
- Nonoperating income and expenses
- Nonrecurring income and expenses

- Depreciation and amortization
- Interest expense or income
- Owner's total compensation for those services that could be provided by a sole owner/manager

Economic Benefits—inflows such as revenues, net income, net cash flows, and so on.

Economic Life—the period of time over which property may generate economic benefits.

Effective Date—*see* Valuation Date.

Enterprise—*see* Business Enterprise.

Equity—the owner's interest in property after deduction of all liabilities.

Equity Net Cash Flows—those cash flows available to pay out to equity holders (in the form of dividends) after funding the operations of the business enterprise, making necessary capital investments, and increasing or decreasing debt financing.

Equity Risk Premium—a rate of return added to a risk-free rate to reflect the additional risk of equity instruments over risk-free instruments (a component of the cost of equity capital or the equity discount rate).

Excess Earnings—the amount of anticipated economic benefits that exceeds an appropriate rate of return on the value of a selected asset base (often net tangible assets) used to generate those anticipated economic benefits.

Excess Earnings Method—a specific way of determining a value indication for a business, business ownership interest, or security; it is determined as the sum of (a) the value of the assets derived by capitalizing excess earnings and (b) the value of the selected asset base. Also frequently used to value intangible assets. *See* Excess Earnings.

Fair Market Value—the price, expressed in terms of cash equivalents, at which property would change hands between a hypothetical willing and able buyer and a hypothetical willing and able seller, acting at arm's length in an open and unrestricted market, when neither is under compulsion to buy or sell and when both have reasonable knowledge of the relevant facts. [*Note:* In Canada, the term *price* should be replaced with the term *highest price*.]

Fairness Opinion—an opinion as to whether or not the consideration in a transaction is fair from a financial point of view.

Financial Risk—the degree of uncertainty of realizing the expected future returns of the business resulting from financial leverage. *See* Business Risk.

Forced Liquidation Value—the liquidation value at which the asset or assets can be sold as quickly as possible, such as at an auction.

Free Cash Flow—we discourage the use of this term. *See* Net Cash Flow.

Going Concern—an ongoing operating business enterprise.

Going Concern Value—the value of a business enterprise that is expected to continue to operate into the future. The intangible elements of going concern value result from factors such as having a trained workforce, an operational plant, and the necessary licenses, systems, and procedures in place.

Goodwill—the intangible asset that arises as a result of name, reputation, customer loyalty, location, products, and similar factors not separately identified.

Goodwill Value—the value attributable to goodwill.

Goodwill Value*—the value attributable to the elements of intangible assets above the identifiable tangible and intangible assets employed in a business.

Guideline Public Company Method—a method within the market approach whereby market multiples are derived from the market prices of stocks of companies that are engaged in the same or similar lines of business, and that are actively traded on a free and open market.

Holding Company*—an entity that derives its return from investments rather than from the sale of products or services.

Hypothetical Condition*—something that is contrary to what exists but is supposed for the purpose of analysis.

Income (Income-Based) Approach—a general way of determining a value indication for a business, business ownership interest, security, or intangible asset by using one or more methods that convert anticipated economic benefits into a present single amount.

Intangible Assets—nonphysical assets such as franchises, trademarks, patents, copyrights, goodwill, equities, mineral rights, securities, and contracts (as distinguished from physical assets) that grant rights and privileges and have value for the owner.

Internal Rate of Return—a discount rate at which the present value of the future cash flows of the investment equals the cost of the investment.

Intrinsic Value—the value that an investor considers, on the basis of an evaluation or available facts, to be the "true" or "real" value that will become the market value when other investors reach the same conclusion. When the term is applied to options, it is the difference between the exercise price or strike price of an option and the market value of the underlying security.

Invested Capital—the sum of equity and debt in a business enterprise. Debt is typically either (a) all interest-bearing debt or (b) long-term interest-bearing debt. When the term is used, it should be supplemented by a specific definition in the given valuation context.

Invested Capital Net Cash Flows—those cash flows that are available to pay out to equity holders (in the form of dividends) and debt investors (in the form of principal and interest) after funding the operations of the business enterprise and making necessary capital investments.

Investment Risk—the degree of uncertainty as to the realization of expected returns.

Investment Value—the value to a particular investor based on individual investment requirements and expectations. [*Note:* In Canada, the term used is *Value to the Owner.*]

Key Person Discount—an amount or percentage deducted from the value of an ownership interest to reflect the reduction in value resulting from the actual or potential loss of a key person in a business enterprise.

Levered Beta—the beta reflecting a capital structure that includes debt.

Limited Appraisal—the act or process of determining the value of a business, business ownership interest, security, or intangible asset with limitations on the analyses, procedures, or scope.

Liquidity—the ability to quickly convert property to cash or pay a liability.

Liquidity*—the ability to readily convert an asset, business, business ownership interest, or security into cash without significant loss of principal.

Liquidation Value—the net amount that would be realized if the business were terminated and the assets were sold piecemeal. Liquidation can be either orderly or forced.

Majority Control—the degree of control provided by a majority position.

Majority Interest—an ownership interest greater than 50 percent of the voting interest in a business enterprise.

Market (Market-Based) Approach—a general way of determining a value indication for a business, business ownership interest, security, or intangible asset by using one or more methods that compare the subject to similar businesses, business ownership interests, securities, or intangible assets that have been sold.

Market Capitalization of Equity—the share price of a publicly traded stock multiplied by the number of shares outstanding.

Market Capitalization of Invested Capital—the market capitalization of equity plus the market value of the debt component of invested capital.

Market Multiple—the market value of a company's stock or invested capital divided by a company measure (such as economic benefits or number of customers).

Marketability—the ability to quickly convert property to cash at minimal cost.

Marketability*—the capability and ease of transfer or salability of an asset, business, business ownership interest, or security.

Marketability Discount—*see* Discount for Lack of Marketability.

Merger and Acquisition Method—a method within the market approach whereby pricing multiples are derived from transactions involving significant interests in companies engaged in the same or similar lines of business.

Midyear Discounting—a convention used in the Discounted Future Earnings Method that reflects economic benefits being generated at midyear, approximating the effect of economic benefits being generated evenly throughout the year.

Minority Discount—a discount for lack of control applicable to a minority interest.

Minority Interest—an ownership interest of less than 50 percent of the voting interest in a business enterprise.

Multiple—the inverse of the capitalization rate.

Net Assets*—total assets less total liabilities.

Net Book Value—with respect to a business enterprise, the difference between total assets (net of accumulated depreciation, depletion, and amortization) and total liabilities as they appear on the balance sheet (synonymous with Shareholders' Equity). With respect to a specific asset, the capitalized cost less accumulated amortization or depreciation as it appears on the books of account of the business enterprise.

Net Cash Flow—when the term is used, it should be supplemented by a qualifier. *See* Equity Net Cash Flows and Invested Capital Net Cash Flows.

Net Income*—revenue less expenses and taxes.

Net Present Value—the value, as of a specified date, of future cash inflows less all cash outflows (including the cost of investment), calculated using an appropriate discount rate.

Net Tangible Asset Value—the value of the business enterprise's tangible assets (excluding excess assets and nonoperating assets) minus the value of its liabilities.

Nonoperating Assets—assets that are not necessary to the ongoing operations of the business enterprise. [*Note:* In Canada, the term used is *Redundant Assets.*]

Normalized Earnings—economic benefits adjusted for nonrecurring, noneconomic, or other unusual items to eliminate anomalies and/or facilitate comparisons.

Normalized Financial Statements—financial statements adjusted for nonoperating assets and liabilities and/or for nonrecurring, noneconomic, or other unusual items to eliminate anomalies and/or facilitate comparisons.

Operating Company*—a business that conducts an economic activity by generating and selling or trading in a product or service.

Orderly Liquidation Value—the liquidation value at which the asset or assets can be sold over a reasonable period of time to maximize the proceeds received.

Premise of Value—an assumption regarding the most likely set of transactional circumstances that may be applicable to the subject valuation, e.g., going concern or liquidation.

Present Value—the value, as of a specified date, of future economic benefits and/or proceeds from sale, calculated using an appropriate discount rate.

Portfolio Discount—an amount or percentage deducted from the value of a business enterprise to reflect the fact that it owns dissimilar operations or assets that do not fit well together.

Price/Earnings Multiple—the price of a share of stock divided by the company's earnings per share.

Rate of Return—an amount of income (loss) and/or change in value realized or anticipated on an investment, expressed as a percentage of that investment.

Redundant Assets—*see* Nonoperating Assets.

Replacement Cost New—the current cost of a similar new property having the nearest equivalent utility to the property being valued.

Report Date—the date on which conclusions are transmitted to the client.

Reproduction Cost New—the current cost of an identical new property.

Required Rate of Return—the minimum rate of return acceptable by investors before they will commit money to an investment at a given level of risk.

Residual Value—the value as of the end of the discrete projection period in a discounted future earnings model.

Return on Equity—the amount, expressed as a percentage, earned on a company's common equity for a given period.

Return on Invested Capital—the amount, expressed as a percentage, earned on a company's total capital for a given period.

Return on Investment—*See* Return on Invested Capital and Return on Equity.

Risk-Free Rate—the rate of return available in the market on an investment that is free of default risk.

Risk Premium—a rate of return added to a risk-free rate to reflect risk.

Rule of Thumb—a mathematical formula developed from the relationship between price and certain variables based on experience, observation, hearsay, or a combination of these; usually industry-specific.

Special-Interest Purchasers—acquirers who believe that they can enjoy postacquisition economies of scale, synergies, or strategic advantages by combining the acquired business interest with their own.

Standard of Value—the identification of the type of value being utilized in a specific engagement, e.g., fair market value, fair value, or investment value.

Sustaining Capital Reinvestment—the periodic capital outlay required to maintain operations at existing levels, net of the tax shield available from such outlays.

Systematic Risk—the risk that is common to all risky securities and cannot be eliminated through diversification. The measure of systematic risk in stocks is the beta coefficient.

Tangible Assets—physical assets (such as cash, accounts receivable, inventory, property, plant and equipment, and so on).

Terminal Value—*See* Residual Value.

Transaction Method—*See* Merger and Acquisition Method.

Unlevered Beta—the beta reflecting a capital structure without debt.

Unsystematic Risk—the portion of total risk that is specific to an individual security and can be avoided through diversification.

Valuation—the act or process of determining the value of a business, business ownership interest, security, or intangible asset.

Valuation Approach—a general way of determining a value indication for a business, business ownership interest, security, or intangible asset by using one or more valuation methods.

Valuation Date—the specific point in time as of which the valuator's opinion of value applies (also referred to as the "Effective Date" or "Appraisal Date").

Valuation Method—within approaches, a specific way to determine value.

Valuation Procedure—the act, manner, and technique of performing the steps of an appraisal method.

Valuation Ratio—a fraction in which a value or price serves as the numerator and financial, operating, or physical data serve as the denominator.

Value to the Owner—[*Note:* A Canadian term; *see* Investment Value.]

Voting Control—*de jure* control of a business enterprise.

Weighted Average Cost of Capital (WACC)—the cost of capital (discount rate) determined by taking the weighted average, at market value, of the cost of all financing sources in the business enterprise's capital structure.

Working Capital*—the amount by which current assets exceed current liabilities.

Index